The PETA Celebrity Cookbook

Edited by Ingrid E. Newkirk

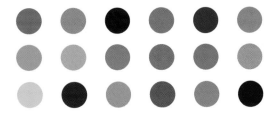

Grant Aleksander Fiona Apple Christina
Applegate **Bea Arthur** Jason Baker **Alec
Baldwin** Brigitte Bardot **Bob Barker** Carla
Bennet Amber Benson Candice Bergen
Elizabeth Berkley **Dr. Brian Black Stephanie
Boyles** Belinda Carlisle Dawn Carr Jackie
Chan James Cromwell John Paul Dejoria
Fabio Corey Feldman John Feldmann **Raquel
Fournier** Bruce Friedrich Bill Goldberg Robson
Greene Nina Hagen Chrissie Hynde T'Keyah
Crystal Keymáh Lisa Lange Twiggy Lawson
Kristine Lilly **Michael Madsen Wendie Malick**
Dan Mathews Sir Paul McCartney **Rue
McClanahan** Moby Martina Navratilova
Kevin Nealon **Ingrid E. Newkirk** Carré Otis
Tatjana Patitz Jannette Patterson Cassandra
Peterson Chef Ronald A. Pickarski **Kate
Pierson and Fred Schneider of the B-52's**
Sherry Ramsey Charlotte Ross **Peter
Schaffrath** Sir Ravi Shankar William Shatner
Kristie Sigmon Alicia Silverstone Russell
Simmons Amy Smart Joe E. Tata Tiffani
Thiessen Harald Ullman **Montel Williams**

2002
Lantern Books
One Union Square West, Suite 201
New York, NY 10003

Printed in the United States of America

Cover and book design by Erin K. MacLean

Index by Kim Nordberg-Fickas

Library of Congress Cataloging-in-Publication Data

The PETA celebrity cookbook : delicious vegetarian recipes from your favorite stars.
    p. cm.
   ISBN 1-59056-027-2 (alk. paper)
   1. Vegetarian cookery. I. People for the Ethical Treatment of Animals.
   TX837 .P513 2002
   641.5'636—dc21

                                                            2002151372

Acknowledgments

Thanks to all who donated their time and effort to create this book, especially Carrie Beckwith, whose patience and perseverance resulted in the recipe collection within; Laura Frisk, an extraordinary friend to animals and talented chef; Robyn Wesley and her baking brigade; Paula Moore, Heather Moore, Liz Welsh, and Karin Bennett for their writing skills; and Gabrielle Langholtz and Karen Porreca for their indispensable editing input.

Table of Contents

Introduction

by James Cromwell

In 1995, a little sleeper film called *Babe* caused a big stir when it hit the big screens—and woke many people up to vegetarianism. The movie was about a precocious, mischievous little pig who saves himself from becoming a Christmas ham by making the farmer who cared *for* him start to care *about* him.

When I was first approached to play Farmer Hoggett, the lead human role in *Babe*, I counted the lines— only 16! My anticipation wilted—I would be the pig's Ed McMahon. But when I read through the script, I quickly realized there was no way I *couldn't* take the role. Who could resist a story with such a positive message?

Although *Babe* largely featured amazingly realistic animatronics (its stunning visual effects won the film an Oscar that year), the time I spent on the set with the live pigs forever changed my life. I discovered how wonderfully playful, smart, and friendly pigs are. The sentiment conveyed so eloquently in *Babe,* that animals are so much more than meat, made me swear off not only bacon and sausage, but all meat and animal products. Two decades earlier, I had been a vegetarian, but I had strayed from my meat-free ways over the years. The whole experience of filming *Babe* caused me to come back to vegetarianism, for good.

Several years after making *Babe*, I got involved in another "pig project." This one wasn't a heart-warmer, it was a stomach-turner. I was asked by People for the Ethical Treatment of Animals (PETA) to narrate an undercover video exposé of Belcross Farm in North Carolina. This footage showed farm workers torturing vulnerable pigs, pigs just like those I had worked with so closely before. It was hard to watch, but I found strength and relief in knowing I no longer personally supported that dirty business.

For my role as Farmer Hoggett in *Babe*, I received an Oscar nomination—the farm workers featured in PETA's video received felony animal cruelty convictions. *Babe* reminded audiences that animals, like us, enjoy playing and companionship and cherish their lives. PETA's video inspired viewers to lay down their pork and pick up the fun, guilt-free habit of vegetarian eating.

Thank you for showing that you care about your health, the environment, and, of course, the animals, by exploring and enjoying the delicious recipes in this book. Congratulations—and bon appétit!

Foreword

by Ingrid E. Newkirk
President and Co-Founder
People for the Ethical Treatment of Animals

Dear Reader,

Vegetarianism has come a long way since the founding of PETA back in 1980. Twenty years ago, most people's idea of a vegetarian meal was bean sprouts and tofu. Today, veggie burgers appear on supermarket shelves and restaurant menus everywhere. In the U.S. alone, more than 17 million people are vegetarians and one million Americans—college students, Boy Scouts, "Meals on Wheels" recipients, parents, and their babies—are joining us every year. Just days after *Men's Health* named Arizona's Phoenix and Mesa among 2001's "ten fattest cities in the U.S," we received almost 500 requests for our Vegetarian Starter Kit from Arizona residents making the connection between pork chops and the plus-size department.

Even Hollywood is vegging out. Alicia Silverstone, Alec Baldwin, and Charlotte Ross are all eating their veggies, and they've contributed their most scrumptious vegan recipes to this cookbook. We've also included some recipes from vegan icons and activist "celebrities" of our own.

The PETA Celebrity Cookbook has something for everyone—from veteran vegans to budding vegetarians, from gourmet gurus to those for whom boiling water is a feat. We are confident that, whoever you are, you'll grow passionate about many of the recipes within these pages. We hope that you'll make them often, share them with friends, family, and co-workers, and savor every mouthful as you enrich your health and help fight animal cruelty one bite at a time.

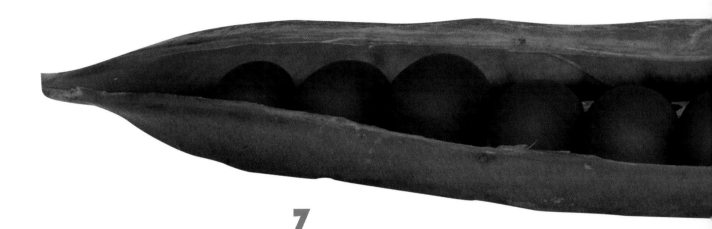

How This Book May Save Your Life

Dr. Neal Barnard
President
Physicians Committee for Responsible Medicine

As you probably know, adopting a vegetarian diet is one of the best decisions we can make for many reasons. To start with, vegetarians have healthier hearts, because our arteries are clear of the fat and cholesterol buildup that is found in people who eat meat. We're also leaner. The American Dietetic Association reports that "vegetarians, especially vegans, often have weights that are closer to desirable weights than do nonvegetarians."

In general, vegetarians have more stamina, energy, and endurance than meat-eaters. Not surprisingly, vegetarians and vegans live an average of six to ten years longer than the rest of the population!

In addition to being lower in fat, plant-based foods also have plenty of fiber and lots of complex carbohydrates, unlike animal products, which are devoid of fiber and have no complex carbs at all. A diet based on grains, vegetables, legumes (beans, peas, and lentils), and fruits is overflowing with all the nutrients you need to stay healthy and active.

By contrast, animal products wreak havoc on human health. Meats, eggs, and dairy products contain high amounts of cholesterol and saturated fat, which contribute to heart attacks, strokes, high blood pressure, obesity, diabetes, cancer, and many other diseases.

Heart disease is America's number one killer. Every day, 3,000 Americans suffer from heart attacks, and more than 1,200 of them die. Countless studies have linked animal products with heart disease and clogged arteries. Heart researchers Dr. Caldwell Esselstyn and Dr. Dean Ornish have each shown, working independently, that patients with blocked arteries can actually reverse their condition and avoid surgery. Both of them used a low-fat vegan diet as a part of their programs.

Dr. William Castelli, the director of the Framingham Heart Study, the longest-running epidemiological study in medical history, reports: "Vegetarians have the best diet. They have the lowest rates of coronary disease of any group in the country....They have a fraction of our heart attack rate and they have only 40 percent of our cancer rate."

According to the American Cancer Society (ACS), at least one-third of the annual cancer deaths in the United States are diet-related. The ACS's first two recommendations for cancer prevention are to choose foods from plant sources and to limit intake of high-fat foods, particularly from animal sources.

Animal products are also much more likely to harbor dangerous bacteria, such as E. coli, salmonella, listeria, and other potentially life-threatening contaminants. The Centers for Disease Control and Prevention estimates that 76 million people get sick, more than 300,000 are hospitalized, and 5,000 Americans die from foodborne illness each year.

Going vegetarian is an invaluable, progressive step that will promote long-lasting health benefits that you will enjoy for the rest of your life. This book will help you progress down the road to optimal health!

Animal-Friendly Grocery Shopping

When it comes to vegetarianism, the number one question on most meat-eaters' minds is, "What do you eat?" The answer: Anything we want! Most vegetarians find that they actually have *more* food choices—not fewer—than their meat-eating counterparts. For example, many add ethnic dishes like stir-fries and samosas, falafel and fajitas, and spicy curries to their repertoires. And thanks to mock meats and soy cheeses, vegetarians can still enjoy all their favorite tastes, too.

Practically all supermarkets now carry a wide variety of convenience foods for vegetarians, including veggie burgers, "not dogs," and soy milk, and health food stores everywhere stock even more—everything from soy "sausage" and tofu "turkey" to dairy-free "ice cream" and soy yogurt. The next time you're on a grocery run, try some of these fabulous fakes:

Instead of Milk:
When news show *20/20* conducted a taste test of cow's milk and soy milk, soy milk won. Said one first-time soy-milk sampler: "I've been buying the wrong thing!" Chocolate, vanilla, and plain soy milk (as well as rice milk, oat milk, and almond milk) can be used any way you would use cow's milk—in baked goods and sauces, on cereal, in coffee and hot chocolate, or drink it straight out of the carton!

Instead of Cheese:
Soy cheese shreds and slices are great on pizza, tacos, and grilled "cheese" sandwiches, and non-dairy cream cheese—which comes in a variety of flavors—is terrific spread on toasted bagels. Health food stores also sell grated parmesan-style soy cheese—perfect for pasta.

Instead of Ice Cream:
When asked her favorite flavor of ice cream, Madonna replied "Chocolate Tofutti." Try it and you'll know why! Tofutti and other dairy-free frozen desserts, such as Rice Dream, are so rich and creamy, they'll satisfy any sweet tooth. They are available in pints, "ice cream" sandwiches and cookies, and even "ice cream" cakes.

Instead of Eggs:
Commercial egg replacers, such as Ener-G Egg Replacer (Ener-G Foods, Inc., 800-331-5222, www.ener-g.com), are made mainly from potato starch and are available in health food shops. They can be used in cookies, cakes, and other baked goods. Baking substitutes equivalent to one egg are:

General
1½ tsp. Ener-G Egg Replacer mixed with 2 Tbsp. water

1 Tbsp. arrowroot, 1 Tbsp. soy flour mixed with 2 Tbsp. water

2 Tbsp. flour, ½ Tbsp. shortening, ½ tsp. baking powder mixed with 2 tsp. water

For cakes
½ large banana, mashed

½ cup applesauce or puréed fruit

For breakfast, scramble tofu with fresh vegetables and soy sauce, and try crumbled, lightly seasoned tofu for an eggless salad sandwich. Health food stores also carry egg-free mayonnaise, such as Nayonaise or Veganaise, and scrambled-tofu mixes.

Instead of Burgers and Hot Dogs:
Veggie burgers and "not dogs" can be found everywhere these days, from supermarkets to fast food restaurants like Burger King or chains like the Hard Rock Café. Whether you grill them or pop them in the microwave, they're guaranteed crowd-pleasers. Veggie burger crumbles, such as Morningstar Farms, are great in recipes that call for ground beef, such as chili, meatloaf, and spaghetti sauce, and are found in almost every grocery store.

Instead of Chicken:
For incredible "chicken" salads and fried "chicken," try one of the many faux poultry products sold in supermarkets and health food stores. Many varieties come pre-seasoned or smothered in sauces, so you can just toss them into stir-fries or on a sandwich. Poultry seasoning adds homestyle flavor to pot pies, casseroles, and soups.

Instead of ... Everything Else:
Fib ribs, Tuno, vegan jerky, phony baloney—these and other mock meats are as close as your local health food store. If you can't find mock meats in your town, try cyberspace! You can order everything from mock "lobster" to cheese-free "cheesecake" online. To get started, visit PETAMall.com, and let your fingers do the shopping.

benevolent

breakfasts

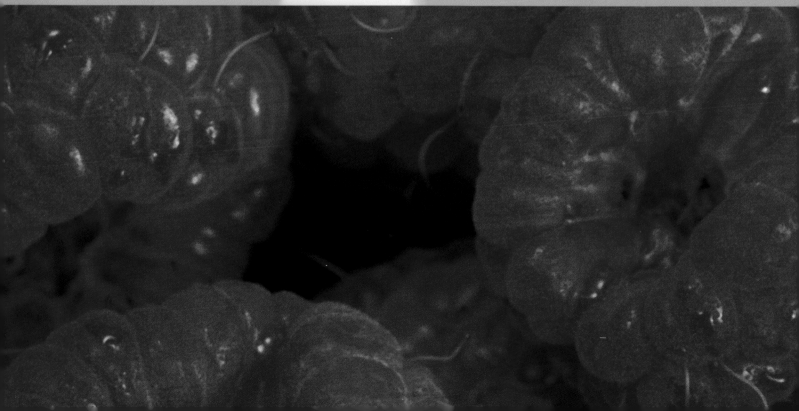

photo by David Goldner

"One of my favorite things in life is cooking, and vegetarian food offers such a rich, tantalizing array of possibilities. I frequently entertain in my home, and I love to serve delicious vegetarian meals to my guests."

Actor
Credits include: All in the Family, Maude, and The Golden Girls

Bea Arthur

Good Morning Mushroom-Tomato Toast

4 slices bread, toasted
1 Tbsp. margarine
2 medium tomatoes, sliced
¾ cup chopped fresh mushrooms
Salt and pepper, to taste
2 tsp. nutritional yeast (optional)

Preheat oven to 250°F. Melt the margarine in a small pan over medium heat, add the tomatoes and mushrooms, and sauté over high heat until soft, about 4 minutes. Add the salt and pepper. Put some tomato-mushroom mixture on each piece of toast and, if desired, sprinkle some nutritional yeast on top. Heat in the oven for 2 minutes, then serve immediately.

Makes 4 servings.

Also see Bea's Applesauce Cake, page 102.

John Feldmann

Musician: Goldfinger lead singer and guitarist

"I like vegan food because it involves no suffering."

"Foxy (shown) is my 'daughter,' and [my cat] Hissy is my 'son.' I treat them as if they were my own flesh and blood. They are the loves of my life—my sunshine."

Tofu French Toast

8 slices vegan French bread (a couple of days old is best)
1 cup whole wheat flour
2 cups soy or rice milk
4 Tbsp. tofu
2 tsp. cinnamon
1 tsp. vanilla
2 Tbsp. vegetable shortening

In a blender, blend all ingredients except the shortening and bread. Transfer the mixture into a bowl and dip the bread in it, covering both sides. Melt the shortening in a pan and place dipped bread in pan. Add extra cinnamon on top. Brown on both sides. Serve topped with fresh fruit or maple syrup.

Makes 2 servings.

Bruce Friedrich

PETA Director of Vegan Outreach

photo by Tal Ronnan

"I can survive without greasy chicken wings— but the chicken can't."

Breakfast Herb Croquettes

11 oz. (about 1¼ cups) prepared lima beans
(canned, frozen, or cooked)
⅔ cup vegetable broth
¼ tsp. ground dried sage
¼ tsp. ground dried rosemary
6 Tbsp. cornmeal
1–2 Tbsp. vegetable oil

In a blender, coarsely purée the lima beans. Add vegetable broth and blend in. In a medium pan, heat the lima bean mixture with the sage and rosemary. Slowly add 4 Tbsp. cornmeal, and continue cooking until the mixture thickens and begins to bubble. Cool to room temperature. Put the remaining cornmeal on a plate. Form small patties of lima bean mixture and roll in cornmeal. In a large frying pan over high heat, heat oil and fry the patties for about 5 minutes, until they are crisp on both sides.

Makes 6 servings.

"Some of my best friends have been animals."

Bill Goldberg *Professional wrestler*

Jackhammer Soy Slammer

1 cup soy or rice milk
1 banana, peeled, cut into chunks and frozen
½ cup frozen fruit (try strawberries, blueberries, or pitted cherries)
1 Tbsp. maple syrup
Dash of cinnamon
1 scoop vegan energy powder (Peaceful Planet or Nature's Life brand) for an added boost of protein and vitamins

Purée all the ingredients in a blender until smooth.

Makes 1 serving.

Did you know?

In 2002, a group of nutritionists, biochemists, pediatricians, and others with the Institute of Medicine, hired by the U.S. Food and Drug Administration to study the recommended dietary levels of trans-fatty acids, found that they raised cholesterol levels and clogged arteries. All meat, dairy, and egg products contain trans-fatty acids, which should be completely avoided "if at all possible," according to researchers.

Tiffani Thiessen

Actor
Credits include: Son-in-Law, Hollywood Ending
and TV's Beverly Hills, 90210

"One of the greatest privileges we have is to experience love and compassion for animals."

Mediterranean Muesli

1 cup rolled oats (Irish oatmeal is my favorite)
¼ cup oat bran
1 cup vanilla soy or rice milk
1 cup plain soy yogurt
½ cup chopped walnuts
3 Tbsp. chopped dried apricots
3 Tbsp. chopped dates

Mix ingredients together in a large bowl and refrigerate for 2 hours.
Top with berries or your favorite fruit.

Makes 4 servings.

luscious

lunches

Belinda Carlisle

Musician

Mad About Macaroni Salad

1¼ cups dried macaroni

1 Tbsp. margarine for the cooked macaroni

1 can chickpeas with 1–2 Tbsp. liquid from the can reserved

6–8 Tbsp. eggless mayonnaise

1 small onion, diced

1 stalk celery, chopped

Onion salt, to taste

Dash of dill

Boil the macaroni in salted water until done, drain, and toss with the margarine to coat. Pour the liquid off the chickpeas, saving 1 to 2 Tbsp. Mash the chickpeas and mix them with the remaining ingredients, then add to macaroni and gently mix. Serve the salad lukewarm.

Makes 4 to 6 servings.

photo by Victoria Pearson

Did you know?

Children raised as vegans are less likely to suffer from childhood illnesses such as asthma, diabetes, ear infections, and colic.

Tofu To Go-Go Sandwich

8 oz. tofu, mashed
1 onion, diced
1 Tbsp. roasted sunflower seeds
1 Tbsp. eggless mayonnaise
1 Tbsp. relish
2 tsp. mustard
2 tsp. soy sauce
¼ tsp. turmeric
¼ tsp. garlic powder or 1 tsp. minced fresh garlic
4 slices toast
4 leaves lettuce
2 small tomatoes, sliced

Mix all the ingredients except the toast, lettuce, and tomatoes together. Spread mixture on the toast. Serve with tomato slices and lettuce.

Makes 4 servings.

Jackie Chan

Actor
Credits include: Rumble in the Bronx, Shanghai Noon, Rush Hour, Rush Hour 2, and The Tuxedo

Chan's Corn Chowder

5 medium potatoes, peeled and chopped
3 cups water or vegetable broth
2 tsp. vegetable oil or water
1 medium onion, finely chopped
2 stalks celery, diced
Salt and pepper, to taste
1 cup plain soy milk
2½ cups corn kernels

In a medium saucepan, boil the potatoes in the water or broth for 20 minutes. While the potatoes are cooking, heat the oil or water in a medium frying pan over medium heat. Add the onion, celery, salt, and pepper. Cook until just tender, about 5 to 7 minutes.

When the potatoes are soft, remove them from the saucepan and reserve the stock. Blend the potatoes with the soy milk in a blender or food processor until smooth. Return the soup to the saucepan and stir in the corn, onion mixture, and enough of the reserved stock to achieve a creamy, thick consistency. Heat thoroughly before serving.

Makes 6 servings.

Did you know?

Soldiers no longer have to worry about combating the mystery meat in their field rations. In response to growing demand, vegetarian "Meals Ready-to-Eat" such as black-bean-and-rice burritos and pasta with vegetables in tomato sauce are now available.

Eggplant "Steaks"

2 small eggplants
1 tsp. salt
3 Tbsp. olive oil
¼ tsp. hot sauce
1 clove garlic, minced
1 Tbsp. balsamic vinegar
1 tsp. minced fresh parsley
⅓ tsp. dried rosemary, crumbled
Salt and pepper, to taste

Remove the stem ends from the eggplants and trim the skin to square the sides. Slice each eggplant lengthwise into two pieces, each approximately ¾ inch thick. Sprinkle 1 tsp. salt evenly over the slices and place in a bowl for about 20 minutes to draw out the bitterness. Rinse well and pat dry.

Heat the oven to 350°F. In a small bowl, stir together 2 Tbsp. of the oil and the hot sauce. Brush evenly over both sides of the eggplant slices. Place the "steaks" in a single layer on a rimmed sheet and bake for 15 minutes, turning once halfway through. Then broil for 1 minute per side or until the slices are well browned and tender. In a small bowl, stir together the remaining oil, garlic, vinegar, parsley, and rosemary. Brush on the cooked eggplant and season with salt and pepper. Let stand 5 minutes before serving.

Makes 4 servings.

James Cromwell

Actor
Credits include: Babe, L.A. Confidential, The Green Mile, and The Sum of All Fears

"If any kid realized what was involved in factory farming they would never touch meat again."

Did you know?

he famous 50-year Framingham Heart Study in
Massachusetts showed that total cholesterol levels
elow 150 milligrams make most people heart-attack-
roof. The average American has a cholesterol level of about
10. The average vegan has a cholesterol level of 133.

27

Ribollita Con Crostini Di Pane
(Thick Veggie Soup with Bread)

¼ cup olive oil plus extra for serving

¼ cup each chopped fennel, celery, onions, carrots

1 garlic clove, minced

¼ tsp. dried thyme

6 cups vegetable broth

1 28-oz. can plum tomatoes, chopped

2 cups peeled and diced russet potatoes

1⅓ cups rinsed and drained canned cannelini beans

1 cup finely shredded Swiss chard or Savory cabbage

1 cup diced zucchini

2 Tbsp. each chopped fresh parsley and basil

8 slices (1 per bowl) ½-inch-thick diagonally sliced Italian bread

Salt and freshly ground pepper, to taste

Combine the olive oil, fennel, celery, onions, carrots, garlic, and thyme in a large, heavy saucepan. Cover and cook over medium-low heat until the vegetables are very soft, about 15 minutes. Do not brown. Stir in the broth, tomato, potato, beans, and Swiss chard. Heat to boiling. Reduce heat to low and simmer 15 minutes. Add the zucchini, parsley, and basil. Cover and cook 2 minutes. Add salt and pepper. Remove from heat. Refrigerate for 24 hours. Just before serving, heat to boiling. Place a piece of bread in each of 8 soup plates. Drizzle with a little olive oil. Ladle soup over the bread and allow bread to soak up the soup.

Makes 8 servings.

"It is very healthy to be vegetarian and, as I love animals, it is the best option to respect their life."

Model: Winner of the Mrs. Venezuela beauty pageant

Raquel Fournier

Delectable Veg Calzones

For filling

1 medium carrot, sliced

Broccoli florets from 1 large head of broccoli

1¾ cups tofu cheese

½ cup chopped red bell pepper

½ tsp. olive oil

½ small yellow onion, chopped

1 garlic clove, minced

1 Tbsp. chopped fresh parsley

⅛ tsp. black pepper

For dough

3 cups all-purpose flour

1 package (or ¼ oz.) active dry yeast

2 Tbsp. vegetable oil

1 tsp. salt

1 tsp. sugar

1 cup boiling water

Preheat oven to 350°F and spray a baking sheet with vegetable cooking spray. Bring 2 quarts of water to a boil over medium heat, add the carrot and broccoli, and cook until crisp but tender, about 1 minute. Drain and rinse under cold water. In a large bowl, combine the carrot, broccoli, tofu cheese, and red pepper. Mix well. In a small saucepan, heat oil over medium heat. Add the onions and garlic and sauté until softened, about 3 minutes. Add to the vegetable mixture. Add parsley and pepper. Mix well.

For the dough, combine flour, salt, sugar, and yeast in a large bowl. Mix in oil and warm water. Divide the dough into 4 balls. Roll each ball into an 8-inch circle. Place the filling evenly over half of each circle, leaving a 1-inch border. Fold the dough over the filling and pinch the edges together to seal. Place on the prepared baking sheet. Prick the tops with a fork. Bake the calzones until golden brown, about 25 minutes. Serve hot.

Makes 4 servings.

Nina Hagen

Musician

"The more I learned about the cruel practices of the meat industry and how pigs, cows, and chickens have to suffer, the less I wanted to eat meat. I realized that my meat-eating was supporting this industry on a daily basis. That's why I became a vegetarian. This decision was one of the best and most important that I've ever made!"

Manic Panic Spinach Salad

1½ cups raw spinach, chopped
2 Tbsp. watercress
4 spring onions, chopped
2 tablespoons cashews
Your favorite salad dressing
½ cup croutons

In a serving bowl, mix the spinach, watercress, spring onions, and cashews. Pour the dressing over all and mix well. Garnish with croutons and serve.

Makes 4 servings.

Also see Nina's Legendary Chickpea Stew, page 74.

Chrissie Hynde

Musician

"When animals are killed for their meat or skin, they are being slaughtered for vanity and pleasure, and to me that's murder."

Easy "Cheezy" Veggie Melts

12 sundried tomato halves
1 15-oz. can chickpeas, rinsed and drained
4 Tbsp. finely chopped green bell pepper
4 Tbsp. finely chopped red onion
4 Tbsp. vegan mayonnaise
(try Nayonaise or Veganaise brand)
1 Tbsp. lemon juice
½ tsp. onion powder
¼ tsp. garlic powder or 1 tsp. minced fresh garlic
¼ tsp. paprika
3 whole wheat pita breads
6 slices mozzarella soy cheese

Preheat the oven to 375°F. Pour boiling water over the tomato halves, let sit for 10 minutes, then drain and chop. In a large bowl, mash the chickpeas with a potato masher. Add the green pepper, onion, mayonnaise, lemon juice, onion, garlic, and paprika and mix well.

Divide each piece of pita bread into 2 round halves and place on baking sheets. Spread ⅙ of the chickpea mixture on each piece of bread and top with the tomatoes. Bake for 7 minutes. Top each pita half with 1 slice of soy cheese and bake for 3 more minutes. Serve open-faced.

Makes 3 servings.

Also see Chrissie's Zesty Blueberry Poppyseed Cupcakes, page 108.

Kristine Lilly

Athlete: Member of the 2000 Olympic silver-medal-winning women's soccer team

"If you want to stay healthy and energetic on and off the playing field, use your head when deciding what to put on your plate!"

"Neatball" Subs

1 cup textured vegetable protein (TVP) granules
1 cup boiling water
½ cup bread crumbs
¼ cup flour
½ tsp. salt
¼ tsp. cayenne pepper
1 tsp. oregano
1 tsp. sage
½ tsp. thyme
½ tsp. fennel seed
1 clove garlic, minced
1 tsp. olive oil
4 submarine rolls
1 cup spaghetti sauce
2 green peppers, sliced into strips and lightly sautéed

Combine the TVP and boiling water in a bowl and leave until the water is absorbed, about 5 minutes. Add the bread crumbs, flour, salt, cayenne pepper, oregano, sage, thyme, fennel, and garlic, mix well, and shape into 12 balls. Oil your palms and roll each ball to lightly coat with oil. Place on a lightly oiled baking sheet and broil until browned, about 10 minutes. While the "neatballs" are broiling, heat the spaghetti sauce in a pan. Place 3 "neatballs" in each roll and top with warmed sauce and sautéed peppers.

Makes 4 servings.

Variation: Form the TVP mixture into smaller balls for a terrific spaghetti and "neatball" dinner.

Sir Paul McCartney

Musician

"If slaughterhouses had glass walls, everyone would be vegetarian."

"All You Need Is Avocado" Soup

2 ripe avocados
1½ cups plain soy milk, warmed to room temperature
1 jar or can green chilies (about 4 oz.)
1 medium onion, chopped
Salt and pepper, to taste
2 tsp. lemon juice
2 tsp. dry sherry
Chopped chilies or fresh parsley, to garnish

Cut the avocados in half and remove the pits. Spoon the avocado into a mixer and purée. Add the remaining ingredients (except the garnish) and purée until creamy. Garnish and serve immediately.

Makes 4 to 6 servings.

Also see Paul's "Ob-La-Di" Enchiladas and Tofu Sour Cream, pages 80 and 81.

Moby

Musician

"Each time you eat animals, you cause suffering. Since we have the choice between an action that causes suffering (eating an animal) and an action that causes no suffering (not eating an animal), doesn't it make sense to choose only actions that don't cause suffering?"

Benevolent Rice Cakes in a European Hotel

1 shabby hotel room
6 organic rice cakes
Organic peanut butter
Organic jam
Organic vegan pâté (Moby's favorite is carrot pâté; recipe on page 44)
Knife
Towel

Spread the towel on a level surface. Open the package of rice cakes and set out the various toppings. Begin with the carrot pâté and end with the peanut butter and jam as dessert. For something especially tasty, you can try ending the meal with an organic, soy-based, nondairy dessert.

Makes 2 servings.

Also see Moby's Big City Cashew-Chili, page 82.

"My ideal is to be able to avoid all animal products, in food as well as clothing."

photo by Robert Sebree

Athlete: Winner of the French Open, the Australian Open, the U.S. Open, and nineteen-time winner at Wimbledon

Martina Navratilova

Longline Leek Soup

4 leeks (white part only), sliced
6 medium potatoes, diced (Yukon Gold potatoes recommended)
3 vegetable bouillon cubes
2 spring onions, chopped, for garnish

Place the leeks and potatoes in a large pot. Add water to cover and bring to a boil. Add the bouillon cubes and simmer, covered, for 20 minutes. Remove from the heat. Transfer to a blender or food processor and process until thick and smooth. Divide the soup evenly among five bowls and garnish with onions.

Makes 5 servings.

Also see Martina's Ace Apple Sweet Potatoes Serving, page 54.

animal-friendly

appetizers

photo by Ebet Roberts

Grant Aleksander & Sherry Ramsey

"We have numerous dogs and cats—they are our family. If you wouldn't eat the family dog, you shouldn't eat the factory farmed cow."

Grant & Sherry's Great Guacamole

1 ripe tomato, finely chopped
2 Tbsp. of finely minced white onion
3 Jalapeno chilies, finely chopped
Sea salt, to taste
2 Tbsp. finely minced fresh cilantro
3 large avocados
Extra tomato for garnish

Combine tomato, onion, chilies, and salt in a small bowl or a *molcajete* (mortar and pestle). Mash with pestle or spoon into a coarse paste. Halve the avocados, remove the pits, and scoop flesh into the mix. Add the cilantro and mix it all together. Add salt and garnish with tomatoes. Serve at once.

If you want to keep any leftovers for a short time, cover with plastic wrap, pressing it directly onto the surface of the guacamole to keep it from turning brown.

Makes 10 servings.

For a variation, sprinkle dip with 2 tsp. lemon or lime juice.

Bob Barker

Entertainer
Credits include: Truth or Consequences
and The Price is Right

*"I became a vegetarian because of my
concern for animals, but I soon learned
to appreciate the many health benefits."*

Savory Italian Bruschetta

6 large ripe tomatoes (about 2½ lbs.),
peeled, seeded, and cut into ½-inch pieces*
Salt and pepper, to taste
½ cup tightly packed fresh basil leaves
8 garlic cloves, peeled and halved
1 cup extra virgin olive oil
4 1-inch-thick slices of sourdough or coarse
Italian bread

Place peeled tomatoes in a large bowl and
season with salt and pepper. Set aside 6
large basil leaves. Stack the remaining basil
leaves. Roll them up and thinly slice them with
a sharp knife. Sprinkle over the tomatoes.
Add the olive oil and all but 2 pieces of the
garlic and stir to combine. Set aside to marinate at room temperature for 1 to 2 hours.

Grill or toast the bread, and rub each slice
with the reserved garlic. Pick out the garlic
cloves from the tomatoes and discard.
Generously spoon the tomato mixture onto
the toast, being sure to include some olive
oil with each spoonful. Garnish each
bruschetta with one of the reserved basil
leaves and serve.

Makes 4 servings.

*To peel the tomatoes, remove stem, cut a small "X"
on the bottom of the tomato, place in boiling water
for 30 seconds, then place in iced water for 40 seconds. Peel.*

photo by Tal Ronnan

Lisa Lange

PETA Vice President of Communications

"Veggie food tastes vibrant, while meat is heavy and boring. I'm enjoying all the veggie food I would have missed if I'd stuck with eating meat."

Did you know?

No government laws or standards regulate the use of terms like "free-range" or "free-roaming" on egg cartons. And on both free-range and factory egg farms, male chicks are considered worthless and disposed of quickly.

Eat Your Heart Out Stuffed Mushrooms

1 lb. firm tofu, drained and mashed
2 tsp. dried basil or 2 Tbsp. fresh chopped basil
1 Tbsp. fresh lemon juice
¾ tsp. salt
½ tsp. minced fresh garlic (or ⅛ tsp. powdered garlic)
1 Tbsp. minced fresh parsley
2 lbs. regular-sized mushrooms

Preheat oven to 350°F. Combine all ingredients except mushrooms and mash together well. Remove stems and insides of mushrooms. Stuff mushroom caps with tofu mixture and place on baking sheet. Bake for 20 to 30 minutes. Let cool 10 minutes or so before serving.

Makes 9 servings.

"I like vegetarian food because it doesn't bleed."

PETA Vice President of Media Relations

Dan Mathews

Sinless Spring Rolls

package (3½ oz.) dried bean
ead vermicelli (woon sen)
cup finely diced onion
carrots, grated
scallions including tops,
ely sliced
garlic cloves, minced
cups chopped cilantro,
:luding stems
cup sliced bamboo shoots
Tbsp. soy sauce
Tbsp. sugar
½ tsp. pepper, preferably white
package (12 oz.) spring roll
rappers
il for frying
veet and spicy dipping sauce

Soak vermicelli in a large bowl of warm water until soft, about 15 minutes. Drain well in colander. Turn out onto cutting board and cut noodles into pieces about 2" long. Combine noodles, onions, carrots, scallions, garlic, cilantro, and bamboo shoots in a large mixing bowl. Add soy, sugar, and pepper. Mix well. Cook and stir the above mixture over medium-high heat until noodles and vegetables are tender, about 4 minutes. Set aside to cool.

Preheat oven to 375° F. Remove spring roll wrappers from the package and cover with a damp cloth. Rolls may be baked or deep-fried. For baked spring rolls, place one wrapper on work surface with a pointed edge toward you. Place about ¼ to ⅓ cup filling in center of wrapper, fold point up and over filling, tucking it under, roll sides in toward middle, then roll tightly to the opposite point. Moisten edges with water to seal. With pastry brush, brush all sides of rolls with vegetable oil. Bake preheated oven until golden brown, about 15 minutes.

For deep-fried rolls, use 2 wrappers for each one and make in the same manner. Fry in 2 inches of oil at 365° F until golden brown, about 3 minutes. Drain and serve with dipping sauce.

Makes 12 rolls.

Sweet and Spicy Dipping Sauce

½ cup white vinegar
1 cup sugar
½ tsp. salt
1 Tbsp. Chinese style chili garlic sauce (sambal)

Bring sugar and vinegar to boil in small saucepan and cook until sugar is dissolved. Add salt and simmer 5 minutes. Stir in chili sauce and remove from heat. Let cool.

Makes 1½ cups.

Also see Dan's Tom Kha Kai, page 79.

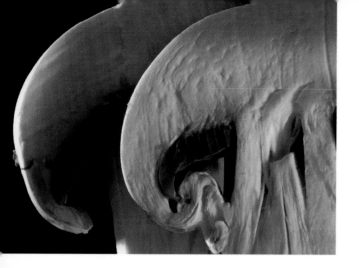

"Dead meat should be buried, not eaten. It's never too late to go vegetarian."

Actor
Credits include:
Pee-Wee's Big Adventure and Allan
Quartermain and the Lost City of Gold

AKA *"Elvira, Mistress of the Dark"*

Cassandra Peterson

Mushroom Pâté en Croute

1 package frozen puff pastry sheets, thawed

1 onion, minced

2 Tbsp. margarine

12 cups minced mushrooms

4 garlic cloves, minced

2 Tbsp. fresh minced parsley

2 Tbsp. fresh minced rosemary

2 Tbsp. lemon juice

2½ cups dried bread crumbs

In a large pot, over medium heat, sauté the onion in the margarine for a few minutes. Add the garlic and the mushrooms and sauté 20 to 30 minutes until the liquid has evaporated. The mixture should be somewhat dry. Add the parsley, bread crumbs, lemon juice, and rosemary and mix well, forming a sticky clump. Allow mixture to cool slightly or store in refrigerator overnight.

Thaw puff pastry sheets for 30 minutes. Preheat the oven to 400°F. Place one sheet of dough on a floured board and roll it out into a large square. Spread half of the mushroom mixture on ½ the dough, leaving a 1-inch space along edges. Fold other half of the dough over the half with the mushrooms, pressing the edges together with your fingers, then crimp with a fork to form a good seal.

Make three slit-shaped airholes on top, then place the pastry on an ungreased cookie sheet and put it in the refrigerator while you prepare the other sheet of dough in the same manner, using the remaining mushroom mixture. Put this on same or another cookie sheet and refrigerate for a few minutes. Then put tray(s) in oven and bake for 20 minutes until dough is puffed and golden. Cut into bite-sized pieces for serving.

Makes approximately 32 pieces.

Also see Cassandra's "Wake up the Dead"
Asparagus Risotto, page 89.

Chef Ronald A. Pickarski, CEC

The first professional vegetarian chef to be certified as an Executive Chef by the American Culinary Federation and the Founder/Director of the American Natural Foods Team, which competes at the International Culinary Olympics in Germany, where he has won seven medals with plant-based foods.

Carrot Pâté

From *Friendly Foods* by Ronald A. Pickarski (Ten Speed Press; Berkeley, Calif., available at www.Eco-Cuisine.com)

2 cups sliced carrots
¼ cup diced onion
1 garlic clove, slivered
¼ teaspoon dill
2 Tbsp. olive oil (or corn oil)
½ cup water
1 Tbsp. arrowroot dissolved in 1 tablespoon water
2 Tbsp. white miso
¼ tsp. sea salt
2 Tbsp. tahini (optional)

"What first drew me to vegetarian cuisine was my health. I observed a radical improvement, then I began to see the larger picture of the positive ecological, economic, and humane implications of the vegetarian diet. As a professional chef, what I love about vegetarian cuisine is that it's an entirely new world of cuisine that is yet to be discovered."

photo by Michael Pizzuto

Preparation Tips: For this recipe you may use a food processor instead of a blender to purée the carrots. Mash the carrots roughly before puréeing them. You might need to add a little extra water, in which case, simmer the puréed, flavored carrots for a while longer. The pâté should not feel wet. The addition of two tablespoons of tahini will make the pâté taste richer and help hold the ingredients together.

In a medium saucepan, sauté the carrots, onions, garlic, and dill in the oil for 2 to 3 minutes. Add the water, cover, and simmer until the carrots are tender, about 20 minutes. Purée to a smooth paste and return to the saucepan.

Combine the dissolved arrowroot, miso, salt, and tahini, if you wish. Add this mixture to the puréed carrots. Bring to a slow simmer, stirring constantly, and cook until the pâté detaches itself from the sides of the pan. Remove from heat, turn the pâté mixture out into a lightly oiled serving dish, and let cool. Serve pâté with crackers or toast, or serve it as a dip with crisp raw vegetables.

Makes 4 servings.

Also see Chef Ronald's Broccoli Seitan Delmonico, page 90.

William Shatner

Actor
Credits include: American Psycho II: All American Girl,
Star Trek, and Rescue 911

Layered Dip Mexicana de Frijoles

2 cans vegan refried beans

1 pack taco seasoning

⅔ cup vegan mayonnaise

1 cup vegan sour cream (such as Tofutti Sour Cream)

2 4-oz. cans chopped green chilies, drained

2 large, ripe avocados

2 tsp. lime juice

1 tsp. garlic powder or 4 tsp. fresh minced garlic

1 cup chopped green onions

2 cups diced tomatoes

2 4-oz. cans sliced black olives

William Shatner and wife Elizabeth.

Spread refried beans evenly on a large serving platter. Combine vgean mayonnaise, sour cream, and taco seasoning. Spread evenly on the beans. Spoon the green chilies as evenly as possible into the taco seasoning mixture. Peel the avocados, remove the pits, and scrape the fruit into a bowl. Add the lime juice and garlic. Mix well and spread evenly on the chilies. Finally, top with the green onions, the tomatoes, and the black olives.

Makes 9 to 12 servings.

"Other than our swimming pool, this is the best dip around!"

"If you want to say 'goodbye' to plus-size shops and thighs that have their own zoning laws, go veg! Studies have shown that most vegetarians are leaner than meat-eaters. Vegetarianism is the easiest method of 'girth control' around!"

PETA Senior Campaigns Coordinator

Kristie Sigmon

I adopted Mudd from the shelter as a puppy. His mother and siblings were abandoned at the shelter by a hunter. Mudd is the love of my life. He comes to work with me every day and wags his tail while he sleeps under my desk.

Cow-Friendly Creamy Cheezy Dip

¼ cup (or ½ stick) margarine

¼ cup flour

1¾ cups plain soy milk

1 tsp. salt

2 tsp. tamari or soy sauce

1 tsp. garlic powder or 4 tsp. minced fresh garlic

½ tsp. onion powder

½ cup nutritional yeast

4 Tbsp. salsa

⅓ cup diced jalapeño peppers (more or less, to taste)

Melt the margarine over medium heat. Whisk in the flour until smooth. Slowly whisk in the soy milk, then the salt, tamari or soy sauce, garlic, and onion powder. Cook for about 2 minutes, until thick. Whisk in the nutritional yeast and heat for an additional 2 minutes on low heat. Add the salsa and peppers, to taste. Serve with your favorite vegan chips.

Makes 2¼ cups.

Alicia Silverstone

Actor
Credits include: Clueless, The Crush,
Batman and Robin, TV's Braceface,
and Broadway's The Graduate

"Going vegan is the single best thing I've done in my life. I am so much happier and more confident. I made the decision based on my moral beliefs."

Steamy, Creamy Artichoke Dip

2 8½-oz. cans of quartered artichokes
1 cup vegan mayonnaise (such as Nayonaise)
1 cup soy parmesan "cheese"
1 tsp. paprika
Garlic powder to taste

Preheat oven to 350°F. Drain the liquid from the artichokes, mash, and combine with the other ingredients. Scoop into a casserole dish and bake for ½ hour. Sprinkle paprika on top before serving. Serve with chips, toasted and cut pita bread, or sliced fresh vegetables.

Makes 10 servings.

photo by Robert Sebree

sumptuous

side dishes

Brigitte Bardot

Model and actor
Credits include: Contempt, A Very Private Affair, and And God Created Woman.

Also the founder of The Brigitte Bardot Foundation, which works to establish and protect animal rights

"I'm vegetarian because animals are my friends and I don't eat my friends."

photo by F. Guillou

Saintly Orange Aromatic Sweet Potatoes

6 baked sweet potatoes
5 Tbsp. orange juice
½ tsp. grated orange rind
½ tsp. grated lemon rind
1 tsp. grated fresh ginger root
Pinch of ground nutmeg
2½ Tbsp. maple syrup
Salt, to taste
Lightly toasted chopped pecans for garnish

Preheat the oven to 350°F. Peel the sweet potatoes and put them into a food processor, along with the remaining ingredients. Process until smooth. Bake the purée in a casserole dish until heated through, about 15 minutes. Garnish with the pecans and serve hot.

For a more dramatic presentation, spoon the hot purée into halved, hollowed-out orange shells and garnish with the pecans.

Makes 6 servings.

(Recipe can be halved and made in a loaf pan or other smaller pan.)

"I like vegetarian food because I don't have to worry or feel bad about what I eat."

Actor
Credits include: Bye Bye, Love, The Crush, and TV's Buffy the Vampire Slayer

Amber Benson

Potent Potato Salad

6 medium potatoes with skin, boiled and cooled
½ cup vegan mayonnaise
4 Tbsp. mustard
2 Tbsp. distilled white vinegar
½ onion, chopped
½ cup chopped celery
Salt and pepper, to taste
Paprika

Cut the potatoes into cubes. Combine all the ingredients in a bowl and season to taste. Sprinkle paprika on top.

Makes 4 to 6 servings.

Did you know?

According to Cornell University's Dr. T. Colin Campbell, director of the renowned "China Project," a long-term epidemiological study of the relationship between diet and health, "The vast majority, perhaps 80 percent to 90 percent, of all cancers, cardiovascular diseases, and other forms of degenerative illness can be prevented, at least until very old age, simply by adopting a plant-based diet."

Martina Navratilova

Ace Apple Sweet Potatoes Serving

⅔ cup apple cider
5 large sweet potatoes or yams, scrubbed but unpeeled
4 Tbsp. margarine
2 Tbsp. light brown sugar
½ tsp. salt
Lightly toasted, chopped pecans or thinly sliced pineapple rings, for garnish.

Bring a large pot of lightly salted water to a boil. Add the sweet potatoes and cook until tender, 30 to 40 minutes. Meanwhile, boil the cider in a small saucepan over high heat until it is reduced by half, about 7 minutes. Set aside. When the sweet potatoes are done, drain well. Peel using a kitchen towel to protect your hands. Return to the warm pot, add the cider, margarine, brown sugar, and salt, and mash until well blended. Garnish and serve hot.

Makes 8 to 10 servings.

Also see Martina's Longline Leek Soup, page 35.

Kevin Nealon

Comedian
Credits include: Saturday Night Live,
Roxanne, The Wedding Singer, and
Happy Gilmore

"I became interested in animal rights after seeing the injustice involved in animal treatment and becoming educated and informed about the cruelty involved in circuses, zoos, and stockyards."

Mr. Subliminal's Sweet (No Meat) Roasted Rosemary Root Vegetables

1 ¼ lb. rutabagas
1 ¼ lb. yams
1 lb. carrots
1 lb. turnips
1 lb. yellow potatoes
8 garlic cloves, halved
3 cups apple juice
4 Tbsp. balsamic vinegar
3 Tbsp. olive oil
Salt and pepper, to taste

Preheat oven to 425°F. Cut the vegetables into ½-inch cubes. In a large saucepan, boil the apple juice and vinegar for 30 minutes until reduced to 1 cup. Stir in the olive oil. Toss the vegetables in the glaze and place in a single layer in 2 roasting pans. Season with salt and pepper. Bake 40 minutes.

Makes 8 servings.

photo by Robert Sebree

Peter Schaffrath is the former Executive Chef at the Willard Inter-Continental Washington Hotel and current Executive Chef at the historic Hay-Adams Hotel in Washington D.C.

Peter Schaffrath

Potato, Black Bean, and Corn Cakes

For the carrot purée

1 lb. carrots, peeled
1 small onion, peeled and quartered
1 bay leaf
Salt and pepper, to taste
4 stems dill weed, cut into small pieces

For the cake

3 large raw potatoes
1 cup corn kernels
1 large carrot, peeled and grated
1 cup sliced scallion greens
1 cup cooked black beans
2–3 Tbsp. olive oil
1 lb. spinach leaves, washed and stems removed

Place the whole carrots, onion, and bay leaf into a 2- to 3-quart pan, cover with cold water, and bring to a boil. Reduce the heat, cover, and simmer for 20 minutes, until the carrots are tender. Discard the bay leaf, strain the vegetables, and purée in a blender or food processor. Add salt, pepper, and dill. Keep the purée warm.

Peel and grate the potatoes. Combine with the corn, grated carrot, scallions, and black beans. Heat the oil in two large skillets. Form 8 patties by spooning the mixture into the pans and flattening into circles. Sauté over medium heat 3 minutes on each side until golden brown. The cakes can be kept warm in a 250°F oven for 10 minutes if necessary.

Arrange beds of spinach on 4 serving plates and top each with 2 potato cakes. Surround with the warm carrot purée and serve immediately.

Makes 4 servings.

"I like cooking vegetarian food because I want to help people stay healthy. Both my daughters are vegetarian, and can't stand the thought of hurting an animal."

Tomato Julienne and Savory Coriander Seed Soup

3 cucumbers, peeled and seeded
3 oz. (6 Tbsp.) fresh dill, chopped (keep 6 nice sprigs for decoration)
Salt and pepper, to taste
1 yellow tomato, julienned
1 red tomato, julienned
1 ripe green tomato, julienned
1 oz. (2 Tbsp.) crushed coriander seeds

Blend the cucumbers at high speed in a blender. Season with the chopped dill, salt, and pepper. Pour into soup cups and garnish with the julienned tomatoes, coriander seeds, and remaining dill sprigs.

Makes 6 servings.

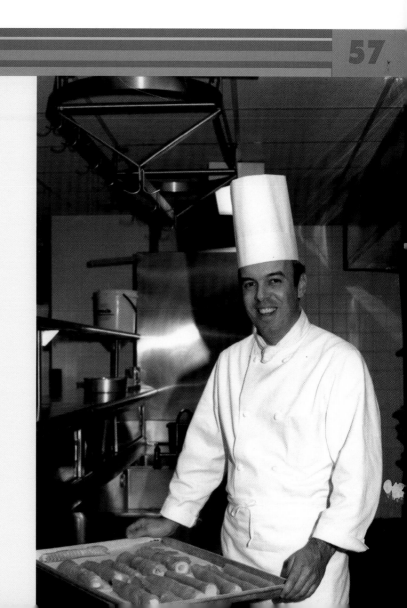

Sir Ravi Shankar

Musician

"Throughout the centuries, India has relied on vegetarian food. If you haven't tried the vegetarian fare at your local Indian restaurant, now is the time to indulge yourself."

Did you know?

It takes 5,200 gallons of water to produce a pound of beef, but only 25 gallons to produce a pound of wheat.

Masala Potatoes

4 medium-large potatoes, well boiled and peeled

1 Tbsp. sunflower oil or canola oil

1 tsp. water

½ tsp. mustard seed

Pinch of hing, an Indian spice (optional)

1 inch root ginger, peeled and grated

2 garlic cloves, minced

1 tsp. chopped cashew nuts

2 medium tomatoes

½ tsp. turmeric powder

1½ tsp. salt

1 large onion, chopped

2 or 3 curry leaves (optional)

½ tsp. sugar

1 tsp. lemon juice

1 Tbsp. chopped cilantro

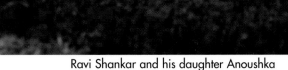

Ravi Shankar and his daughter Anoushka

Heat oil in a pan or wok over high heat. Add mustard seeds. When oil bubbles, add (one after another in the following order) cashew nuts, hing, curry leaves, onions, ginger, garlic, and turmeric. Add chopped tomatoes, sugar, and salt. Break up the potatoes with a fork, add water, and cook for about 10 minutes on low heat. Then add the lemon juice and chopped coriander.

Serve with breads such as puri, roti, naan, pita, or whole wheat flour tortillas. Tastes good with kachumbar (sliced onion, tomato, and green chili seasoned with salt and lemon juice).

Makes 6 servings.

enticing

entrées

Fiona Apple

Musician

photo by Dawn Carr

"Millions of people are learning that a vegetarian diet is the healthy choice for themselves, the earth, and animals."

Sweet-and-Sour Cheatmeatballs

1 14-oz. package beef-flavored Lightlife Gimme Lean (available in health food stores) or your favorite ground beef substitute (such as Morningstar Farms burger crumbles, available in the frozen vegetable section in most grocery stores)
½ green pepper, finely chopped
1 small onion, finely chopped
1–2 garlic cloves, minced
2 slices white bread, toasted and crushed into crumbs
Egg replacer, equivalent to 2 eggs (See egg replacement suggestions, page 10)
Dash each of salt and pepper
Oil, for frying
¾ cup (6 oz.) chili sauce
4½ Tbsp. (5 oz.) red currant jelly (or your favorite jelly)

Combine all the ingredients, except the oil, chili sauce, and jelly, in a bowl and stir until well mixed. Heat the oil in a skillet, using enough to coat the bottom of the pan. Form the mixture into 1-inch balls and fry in the oil until they are brown and thoroughly cooked. Meanwhile, place the chili sauce and jelly together in a saucepan. Heat and stir until smooth. When the mock meatballs are finished cooking, add them to the sauce and stir to coat well. Simmer over low heat for 10 to 15 minutes. Serve with noodles, rice, or a vegetable side dish.

Makes approximately 20 1-inch balls.

Jason Baker

PETA India's Campaign Coordinator

"Why ruin delectable spicy Indian curry or creamy coconut Thai stew by throwing a carcass in it?"

Tempting Asian Tahini Medley

¼ cup tahini

¼ cup soy sauce

2 Tbsp. rice vinegar

1 Tbsp. sesame chili oil or hot sauce

1 Tbsp. fresh grated ginger

2 garlic cloves, minced

2 Tbsp. sesame oil

1 lb. pasta, cooked

1 bunch scallions, chopped (optional)

Sundried tomatoes, julienned (optional)

Broccoli or asparagus, blanched (optional)

Shiitake mushrooms, sautéed (optional)

Mix together the first 7 ingredients, then pour the mixture over the pasta. Add any of the remaining 4 ingredients, if desired.

Makes 4 to 6 servings.

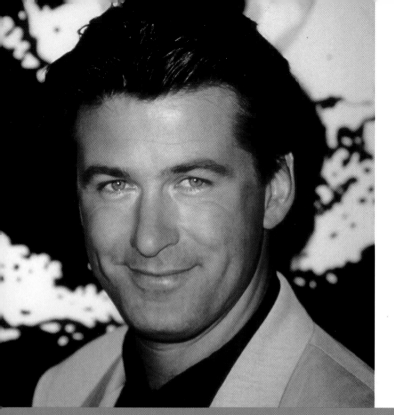

Alec Baldwin

Actor
Credits include: The Hunt for Red October, Miami Blues, Prelude to a Kiss, Malice, The Shadow, Ghosts of Mississippi, and The Edge

"You can improve your health, help the environment, and save animals by going vegetarian."

Miami Blues Red Beans with Garlic

18 oz. (about 2½ cups) dried kidney beans
3 Tbsp. vegetable oil
2 garlic cloves, minced
9 oz. (1½ cups) white rice
4 cups water
2 whole garlic cloves
Salt and pepper, to taste

Soak the dry beans in a big pot or a covered bowl for 8 hours. Drain the beans, cover with fresh water, and cook over low heat 1½ to 2 hours, until the beans are soft. Drain water into container and set it aside.

Put the oil in a pot and sauté the beans with the whole garlic for a few minutes. Don't stir so much that the beans fall apart. If necessary, add more oil.* Add 4 cups of the beans' cooking water to the pot and cook in it the beans and the minced garlic. Add the rice and stir. Cook covered over low heat, stirring occasionally, for 25 to 30 minutes, until rice is done.

Makes 6 servings.

Variation: For extra taste, add ½ tsp. paprika, dash of cayenne pepper, 1 chopped onion, and ¾ cup chopped sundried tomatoes.

"I adopted Bailey, a dear little tousled all-black mixed breed dog, from a rescue group. Bailey had been hit by a car, but now she's recovered and overflowing with life."

"I would kill for falafel, Boca Burgers, barbecued seitan, and chickpea stew. Fortunately, they're all vegan, so I don't have to."

PETA Senior Staff Writer and Author of Animal Times's "Ask Carla" Column

Carla Bennet

Heroic Shepherd's Pie

5 russet potatoes, chopped
4 Tbsp. margarine
1 tsp. salt (optional)
1 tsp. pepper
2 cups plain soy milk
2 cups chopped onion
2 garlic cloves, minced
2 carrots, diced
2 cups fresh sliced mushrooms
1½ Tbsp. all-purpose flour
3 cups ground beef substitute (such as Morningstar Farms burger crumbles, available in the frozen vegetable section in most grocery stores, or Gimme Lean ground "beef" by Lightlife, available in health food stores or by visiting www.lightlife.com)
1 cup corn kernels, blanched

Preheat oven to 350°F. Boil potatoes for 20 minutes, or until tender. Drain and mash with 2 Tbsp. margarine, salt, and ½ cup soy milk until fairly smooth. Set aside.

In a large saucepan, melt the remaining 2 Tbsp. margarine over medium heat. Add onions, garlic, and carrots, and sauté. Add mushrooms, and continue to cook and stir for 3 to 4 minutes. Sprinkle in flour and stir constantly for 2 or 3 minutes. Pour remaining 1½ cups soy milk over the vegetables, and increase heat to high. Whisk until smooth. Add ground beef substitute. Reduce heat and simmer for 5 minutes. Stir in corn and black pepper.

Spoon into a greased 10-inch pie pan and smooth with a spatula. Spread mashed potatoes over top. Bake for 30 minutes.

Makes 6 servings.

Candice Bergen

Actor
*Credits include: The Wind and the Lion,
Carnal Knowledge, Starting Over, and TV's
Murphy Brown*

*"I have my daughter to thank for the fact that I was able to
develop such a sensitivity to animals. She has always considered
animals to be wonderful beings. I would never wear fur and try
to help animals as much as possible."*

Bergen's News Breaking Burger

8 oz. firm tofu, pressed to drain excess water

1 small onion, chopped

¼ cup mushrooms, diced

1 Tbsp. chives, chopped

2 Tbsp. wheat germ

2 Tbsp. flour, plus extra to roll patties in

2 tsp. garlic, minced

2 Tbsp. soy sauce

2 tsp. nutritional yeast (optional)

Pepper, to taste

Mix the ingredients in a medium-sized bowl. Form 4 burgers and
roll them in flour. Place them on a lightly oiled cookie sheet and
broil them for 5 to 10 minutes on each side, until brown.

Makes 4 burgers.

Elizabeth Berkley

Actor
Credits include: Showgirls, The First Wives Club, Any Given Sunday, The Curse of the Jade Scorpion, and TV's Saved by the Bell

"I went vegetarian because I don't want to be the cause of any animal losing his or her life."

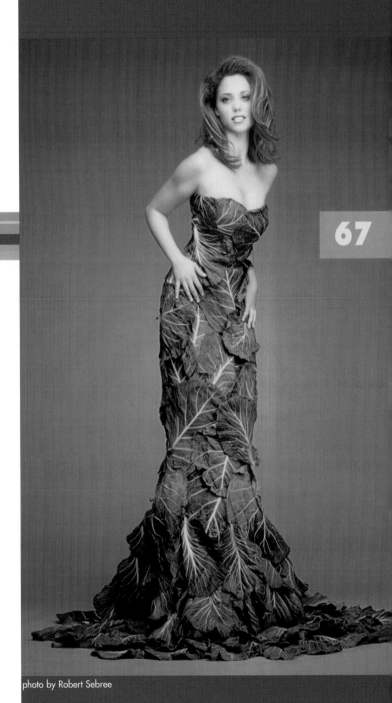

67

Berkley's EZ BBQ Chickpeas

2¼ cups uncooked chickpeas, or
6¼ cups canned chickpeas
1 cup tomato sauce
1½ cup molasses
1 onion, minced

If you are using uncooked chickpeas, soak them overnight. Drain and cook in a big pot with fresh water for about an hour, until soft. Let cool. If you are using canned chickpeas, drain.

Heat the oven to 350°F. Mix all the ingredients well in a big bowl and then put them into a baking dish. Cover and bake for about an hour, until the sauce is dark and thick. Serve with rice or noodles.

Makes 8 servings.

photo by Robert Sebree

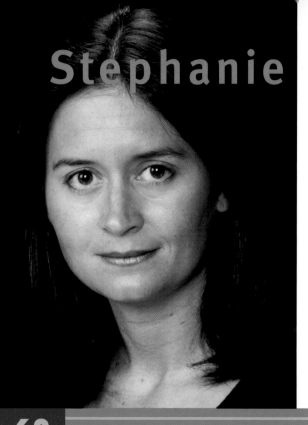

Stephanie Boyles

PETA Wildlife Specialist

"I'm from Louisville, Kentucky, home of the Corporate Headquarters of Kentucky Fried Chicken. When I went veg twelve years ago, I made it my mission to 'veganize' my favorite southern dishes, and the results have been outstanding! The most popular is my fried 'chicken.' Try it with a vegan gravy (Loma Linda makes great instant vegan gravy) but be prepared: after one bite, you won't want to share this."

Feel Good Kentucky Fried Chic-Kett

1 package of Chic-Ketts*
Several sheets of thawed yuba**
2–3 cups unbleached all-purpose flour
1–2 cups vegetable oil
1 tsp. salt
1 tsp. pepper
1 tsp. paprika

Cut dry yuba into 5-inch by 5-inch pieces and soak in hot water on a cookie sheet. Meanwhile, cut the Chic-Ketts roll into bite-sized pieces. When yuba has soaked up enough water to become white and pliable, firmly wrap each yuba piece around each "chicken" piece to make a "chicken" nugget with "skin."

Combine flour, salt, pepper, and paprika in a bowl. Cover each "chicken" nugget by pressing into flour mixture until water is soaked up and all sides are covered. Place each on a plate until you have covered all of the nuggets.

Fill a large, deep frying pan with ¼ to ½ inch of vegetable oil and place on medium heat. When the oil is hot, gently place nuggets in the frying pan with a spatula. Turn nuggets every few minutes. When the nuggets become golden brown, remove from the frying pan and place on a serving dish lined with paper towels. Allow excess oil to drain from nuggets before serving. You may need to add more oil between each batch.

Makes 6 servings.

*Made by Worthington Foods. Available in the freezer section in health food stores or at www.nomeat.com

**Yuba, also called "bean curd sheet" or "bean curd skin," can be purchased as fragile, dry sheets in the freezer section of most Asian food stores. It is a Japanese food made from soy milk.

Dawn Carr

Director of PETA Europe

"People know that going vegetarian is good for us, good for the animals, and good for the earth. It doesn't take long to learn it's good for our taste buds, too!"

Nutritious British Broccoli and Spinach Quiche

2–3 garlic cloves
1½ cups fresh broccoli florets
2 cups fresh spinach
1 lb. tofu, drained and cut into chunks
2–3 Tbsp. nutritional yeast
1 tsp. salt
¼ tsp. cayenne (optional)
1 vegan pie crust (see Joe Tata's Flaky Pie Crust recipe, page 118)
1 tsp. paprika

Preheat oven to 350°F. Mince garlic in a food processor. Add broccoli and spinach, and process till finely chopped. Add chunks of tofu and process. Add nutritional yeast, salt, and cayenne, and purée until mixture is smooth. Roll out pie crust and place in pie dish. Spoon mixture into unbaked pie crust. Sprinkle paprika on top. Bake for 1 hour. Let quiche sit for 15 minutes before serving

Makes 6 to 8 servings.

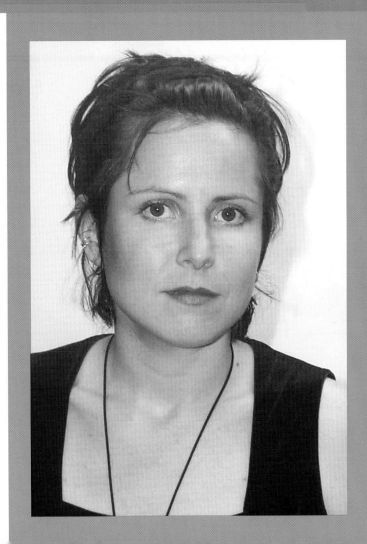

Fabio
Model and Actor

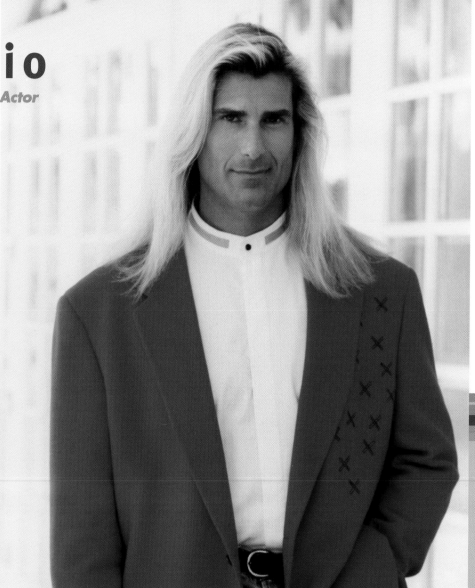

Portobello Passion

½ cup (8 Tbsp. or 1 stick) margarine

2 whole large portobello mushrooms

2 Tbsp. vegetarian Worcestershire sauce

4 garlic cloves, minced

¼ cup pine nuts

2 small red or yellow bell peppers, chopped

1 small zucchini, chopped

½ cup fresh peas

1 cup alfalfa or bean sprouts

1 Tbsp. finely chopped fresh basil, or 1 tsp. dried crushed basil

¼ tsp. salt

1 tsp. white pepper

Pinch of cayenne pepper

Did you know?

The latest edition of the Boy Scout handbook advises scouts to consider using tofu instead of meat in campfire stews.

For the sauce

⅓ cup chopped shallots or onions

1 cup plain soy or rice milk

½ cup dry white wine or vegetable broth

¼ cup orange juice

1 tsp. grated orange peel

Preheat the oven to 375°F. In a large skillet, melt 2 Tbsp. of the margarine over medium heat and cook the mushrooms with the Worcestershire sauce for 4 minutes, turning once. Remove the mushrooms and arrange them on a baking sheet. In the same skillet, melt 2 more Tbsp. margarine over medium-high heat and brown the garlic and pine nuts. Add the bell peppers and cook 4 minutes, stirring occasionally, until almost tender.

Stir in the remaining vegetables, basil, salt, white pepper, and cayenne pepper. Evenly spoon the vegetable mixture onto the mushrooms. Bake 10 minutes.

For the sauce, melt the remaining margarine over medium heat and cook the shallots for 4 minutes, stirring occasionally, until just golden. Stir in the soy or rice milk, wine, orange juice, and orange peel. Bring to a boil over high heat. Reduce heat to medium and continue boiling, stirring occasionally, until the mixture thickens, about 3 minutes. Strain. To serve, spoon the sauce over the mushrooms.

Makes 2 servings.

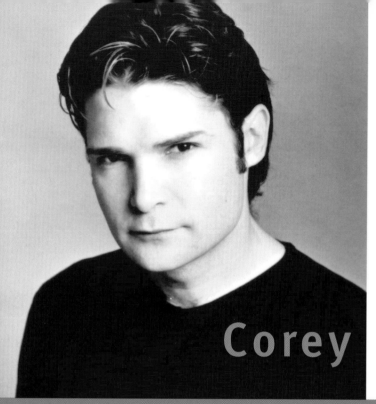

"As far as politics go, I endorse vegetarianism and human rights."

Actor and Musician
Credits include: Gremlins, The Goonies, Stand By Me, and The Lost Boys and member of Truth Movement

Corey Feldman

Feldman's Unforgettable Tangy Tacos

¼ cup diced onions
1 bag (3 cups) Morningstar Farms burger crumbles
(available in the frozen vegetable section in most grocery stores)
Chili powder, to taste
6 taco shells
2 cups lettuce
½ cup diced tomatoes
1 cup grated soy cheese

Sauté the onions in the margarine until brown. Add the burger crumbles and stir. Sprinkle the chili powder, then stir until the burger crumbles start browning. Combine with the other ingredients to make tacos.

Makes 3 servings.

For extra zest, top with sautéed mushrooms and onions, sliced avocado, vegan sour cream, salsa, chopped green onions, and/or chopped black olives.

> *"I love cooking vegetarian meals for friends and family."*

Actor
Credits include: TV dramas Soldier Soldier, Reckless, Touching Evil, and Take Me

Robson Greene

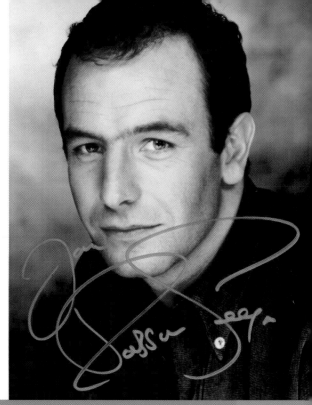

All Star Chili

1 medium zucchini
1 medium yellow squash
2 medium green peppers, chopped
1 medium onion, chopped
2 Tbsp. olive oil
2 Tbsp. chili powder
1 Tbsp. sugar
¾ tsp. salt
¼ tsp. cayenne pepper
2 15-oz. cans stewed tomatoes
2 15-oz. cans pinto beans, undrained
2 15-oz. cans kidney or black beans
(or one of each), undrained
1 4-oz. can chopped mild green chilies, undrained
2 cups fresh or frozen corn

Quarter the zucchini and squash lengthwise and cut into ½-inch-thick slices. Sauté peppers and onion in olive oil in a large pot over medium heat until tender. Add zucchini, squash, chili powder, sugar, salt, and cayenne. Cook 1 minute. Add tomatoes, beans, chilies, and corn. Bring to a boil. Reduce heat to medium-low and simmer uncovered for 20 minutes.

Makes 10 servings.

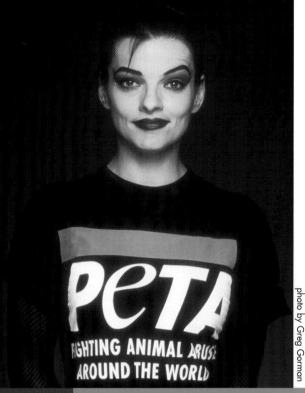

photo by Greg Gorman

Nina Hagen

Did you know?

According to the Environmental Protection Agency, meat and dairy consumers are taking in 22 times the acceptable level of dioxins in their food. Ninety-five percent of dioxin exposure comes from consuming meat, dairy, or egg products.

Legendary Chickpea Stew

2 Tbsp. vegetable oil or water

2 Tbsp. water

1 large onion, chopped

4 garlic cloves, minced

2 bay leaves

6½ cups cooked brown or white rice

2 cans corn (about 10 oz.)

2 cans chickpeas (about 16 oz)

4 tsp. curry powder

1 tsp. turmeric

1 tsp. ground cumin

½ tsp. cayenne pepper

Preheat oven to 300°F. Lightly grease an 8-inch square baking dish with oil. Heat the oil or water in a large pot over medium heat. Fry the onion, garlic, and bay leaves for about 5 minutes, until the onion becomes translucent. Remove the pot from the stove and remove the bay leaves.

Drain corn and put the corn, 1 Tbsp. water, and spices into the blender, purée, and add to the onion in the pot. Drain the chickpeas and add to the pot. Stir well and transfer into the soufflé pan. Bake uncovered for 30 minutes. Spoon over hot cooked rice and serve.

Also see Manic Panic Spinach Salad, page 30.

Makes 6 servings.

Twiggy Lawson

Actor

"I like vegetarian food because it's healthy and no animal has been harmed."

"Cheese-Impasta" Penne

6 oz. (about 1¾ cup) uncooked penne pasta

14-oz. can whole plum tomatoes, drained

2 Tbsp. olive oil

5 oz. (about 1½ cup) diced soy mozzarella cheese

4 oz. (about 1 cup) soy parmesan cheese

2 Tbsp. freshly chopped basil

Salt and freshly ground black pepper, to taste

Boil a pot of water and cook the pasta for 10 minutes until just tender, then drain. Preheat oven to 400°F. Meanwhile, heat the tomatoes and oil in a pan, breaking down the tomatoes gently with a wooden spoon. Add the soy mozzarella, half the soy parmesan, and all of the basil and seasoning to taste. Bring to a boil and remove from heat. Place pasta in a 1½ pint ovenproof dish. Pour the sauce over the pasta and mix well. Sprinkle with remaining soy parmesan and place in a pre-heated oven for 8 minutes until faux cheese is melted. Serve hot.

Makes 3 to 4 servings.

Michael Madsen

Actor
Credits include: Donnie Brasco, Reservoir Dogs, Thelma and Louise, and Free Willy

Exotic Orange Curry

2 raw potatoes

3 carrots

½ red bell pepper

2 Tbsp. curry powder or equal portions of cumin, coriander, dill weed, turmeric, and black mustard seed combined to make 2 Tbsp.

1 Tbsp. dried orange peel

Pinch of red pepper flakes

Pinch of sugar

Pinch of salt

2 garlic cloves

2 Tbsp. grated fresh ginger

Olive oil

2 cups uncooked couscous

2 cups boiling water

Mango chutney

Toasted pumpkin seeds

Dried pineapple

Olive oil for sautéing

Did you know?

NASA-funded researchers at Cornell University who are designing recipes for future lunar and Martian colonies are choosing only vegetarian foods. Astronauts will be trained to prepare dishes like bell-pepper-filled fajitas topped with soy sour cream and tofu cheesecake.

Slice the vegetables into bite-sized pieces. Sauté ⅔ of the spices with the garlic and ginger in a small amount of olive oil. Add sliced vegetables and enough water to cook in but not enough to cover them. Simmer until tender. Add more spices, to taste, if desired. In a separate pot, boil the water and soak the couscous in the boiling water, covered, until all the water is absorbed, about 10 minutes. Ladle the vegetable mixture over the couscous, then top with the chutney, pineapple, and pumpkin seeds.

Makes 4 servings.

Wendie Malick

Actor
Credits include: Dream On, Just Shoot Me

"I like vegetarian food because it's positive fuel: healthy, light, and no guilt."

"I have the privilege of sharing my life with my husband, three dogs, three horses, and a cat. They're my best friends."

Sizzling Cornucopia

2 Tbsp. extra virgin olive oil

6 garlic cloves, minced

1 large leek, white part only, sliced

1 lb. firm tofu, patted dry, cubed

1 cup French green beans, ends trimmed

1 cup cauliflower florets

1 cup broccoli or aspiration florets
 (a cross between cauliflower and broccoli)

1 large or 2 small portobello mushrooms, sliced

2 Tbsp. soy sauce

1 Tbsp. ginger, minced

1 cup cherry tomatoes, halved

In oil, sauté garlic with sliced leek. Add tofu, cauliflower, and beans. When nearly cooked, add mushrooms and broccoli or aspiration florets, soy sauce, and ginger. At the end, throw in fresh halved cherry tomatoes and serve over brown rice. Pepper to taste.

Makes 6 servings.

Dan Mathews

photo by Russell Maynor

Did you know?

The best way to help animals is to stop eating them! By avoiding meat, the average vegetarian saves more than 83 chickens, cows, and other animals every year.

Tom Kha Kai without the Kai (chicken)

(Dan's favorite meal, this Thai hot and sour soup, comes from PETA Campaign Coordinator Brandi Valladolid's fabulous chef mother, Cathy Valladolid.)

3 cups vegetable stock

8 large slices unpeeled ginger

1 large stalk lemon grass, outer leaves removed, cut into 2-inch pieces

12 fresh Kaffir lime leaves, or strips of peel from 1 lime

2 large russet potatoes

2 14-oz. cans unsweetened coconut milk

2 Tbsp. tamarind paste

¼ cup fresh lime juice

2 Tbsp. brown sugar

2 Tbsp. soy sauce

½ pound mushrooms, sliced

1 cup sugar snap pea pods, strings removed, cut in pieces

5 small Thai chilies, stemmed and lightly crushed.

Put stock, ginger, lemon grass, lime leaves or peel, and potatoes into a soup pot. Bring to boil over medium heat. Cover and cook until potatoes are almost tender. Stir in coconut milk and return to a boil. Add tamarind paste, lime juice, sugar, and soy sauce. Stir until the tamarind and sugar are dissolved. Add mushrooms and simmer 1 minute. Stir in chilies and pea pods. Turn off heat. Cover and set aside for 30 minutes.

Re-heat before serving. Remove ginger, lemon grass, lime leaves, and chilies before eating. Soup is better the second day.

Makes 6 servings.

Also see Dan's Sinless Spring Rolls and Sweet and Spicy Dipping Sauce, page 41.

Sir Paul McCartney

"When I see bacon, I see a pig, I see a little friend, and that's why I can't eat it. Simple as that."

"Ob-La-Di" Enchiladas

For the Sauce

1 cup tomato sauce

1 cup water

1 large onion, chopped

2 garlic cloves, minced

1 tsp. chili powder

½ tsp. ground cumin

½ tsp. oregano

2 Tbsp. cornstarch dissolved in 4 Tbsp. water

For the Filling

1 lb. firm tofu, drained and mashed

1 onion, chopped

½ tsp. chili powder

¼ tsp. cumin

¼ tsp. garlic powder, or 1 tsp. minced fresh garlic

¼ tsp. black pepper

1⅓ cups picante sauce

3 cups steamed spinach

12 tortillas

Pre-heat the oven to 350°F. Place all the sauce ingredients, except for the cornstarch, in a small pot and cook over low heat, covered, for 20 minutes. Stir in the cornstarch and cook until the sauce thickens.

In the meantime, prepare the filling: Mix the tofu, onion, chili powder, cumin, garlic, pepper, and picante sauce. Put some of the spinach in the middle of each tortilla, then add 3 to 4 heaping teaspoons of the tofu mixture, and roll up the tortillas. Top with vegan sour cream, such as Tofutti Sour Cream, or make your own with the recipe below. Lay the enchiladas in a baking dish, cover with sauce, and bake for 20 to 25 minutes.

Makes 12 enchiladas.

photo by Linda McCartney

Tofu Sour Cream

½ lb. tofu, patted dry

3 Tbsp. vegetable oil

1 tsp. maple syrup

Juice of 1 lemon

½ tsp. salt, or to taste

Mix all the ingredients in a blender or food processor until smooth.

Also see Paul's "All You Need is Avocado" Soup, page 33.

This recipe is from TeaNY, a tea house in New York City owned by Moby and friend Kelly Tisdale. TeaNY offers a variety of teas and delicious vegan fare, including the following scrumptious chili.

Moby

Big City Cashew-Chili

¾ cup olive oil

2 cups diced onions

¼ cup chopped garlic

¾ cup red peppers

¾ cup green peppers

1 Tbsp. ground cumin

⅛ cup chili pepper

½ Tbsp. crushed red chili peppers

⅛ cup cocoa powder

½ shot espresso or ¼ cup strong coffee

4 cups crushed red tomatoes with liquid

½ cup chopped cashews

¾ package beef-flavored Lightlife Gimme Lean (available in health food stores) or 11 oz. of your favorite ground beef substitute (such as Morningstar Farms burger crumbles, available in the frozen vegetable section in most grocery stores)

2 cups kidney beans

2 cups white beans

Salt and pepper, to taste

1 tub vegan sour cream (try Tofutti Sour Cream)

photo by Aimee Herring

In a large stockpot (1 gallon), heat ½ cup of olive oil. When hot, add onions. When onions are translucent (after about 3 or 4 minutes) add garlic. Sauté for 1 minute, then add red and green peppers. Cook for 2 minutes and then add cumin, chili pepper, crushed red chili peppers, cocoa powder, and espresso or coffee. Let spices cook for five minutes, stirring constantly. Then add crushed red tomatoes and cashews.

In a separate pan, pan fry beef substitute with rest of oil until all pieces are crispy and brown on the outside. Once the vegetable mixture in the big pot has come to a simmer, add beef substitute, kidney beans, and white beans. Add salt and pepper, then let chili simmer on medium-low heat until some of the liquid has evaporated and chili is nice and thick, approximately 1 hour. Serve topped with tofu sour cream.

Makes 5 servings.

Also see Moby's Benevolent Rice Cakes in a European Hotel, page 34.

photo by Tal Ronnan

Hearty Artichoke Steamy Stew

2 Tbsp. olive oil

1½ medium onions, diced

2 to 5 garlic cloves, thinly sliced

3 cups vegetable broth (or substitute up to 1½ cups water)

2 tsp. Italian seasonings

½ tsp. red pepper flakes

1 tsp. fresh ground black pepper

3 16-oz. cans great northern white beans, drained

1 16-oz. can of artichoke hearts in water, drained and quartered

1 bunch fresh kale, chopped (remove center vein first)

½ cup orzo

Salt to taste

Heat olive oil in a large saucepan. Sauté onions and garlic for a few minutes. Add all other ingredients except kale and orzo. Simmer covered for 20 minutes, stirring occasionally, adding more liquid if mixture becomes too thick. Add salt, chopped kale, and orzo. Simmer covered for another 10 minutes, stirring occasionally.

Makes 5 servings.

Ingrid E. Newkirk

PETA President and Co-Founder

*"Veggie food not only saves animals' lives,
 saves our lives. It's as easy as popping a
 cholesterol pill—but much tastier."*

Eggplant Zucchini Pizza

1 small eggplant, sliced

1 medium zucchini, sliced

1 red onion, cut into small wedges

1 red bell pepper, thinly sliced

1 yellow bell pepper, thinly sliced

1 Tbsp. olive oil

1 Tbsp. balsamic vinegar

½ tsp. dried thyme

¼ tsp. black pepper

4 individual pizza crusts, or 1 big pizza crust

½ cup tomato sauce

½ cup grated soy cheese (optional)

Preheat the oven to 425°F. Combine the eggplant, zucchini, onion, bell peppers, oil, vinegar, thyme, and pepper in a large baking dish, and toss to mix well. Bake, stirring occasionally, for 20 minutes, or until the vegetables are tender. Place the pizza shells on baking sheets. Spread tomato sauce on crust, then top with the roasted vegetables and soy cheese if desired. Bake for 10 to 12 minutes or until the pizza shells and vegetables are heated through.

Makes 4 servings.

Carré Otis

Model and Actor

"I have been a vegetarian most of my life. The suffering that animals endure for human consumption is appalling and has touched and affected me since I was a child."

Sumptuous Simple Spaghetti Squash Marinara

1 spaghetti squash
1 8-oz. box tofu
8 oz. jar spaghetti sauce
Seasonings to taste

Preheat oven to 350°F. Wash the squash and cut in half. Remove seeds. Place the halves facing down in baking dish. Cook squash for approximately 40 minutes or until flesh is tender.

Meanwhile, marinate tofu in tomato sauce and seasonings, and place on low to medium heat 10 minutes before squash is cooked.* When spaghetti squash is finished, let it sit until it is cool enough to handle. Scoop out the inside into a bowl. Cover thoroughly with the sauce.

Makes 2 servings

*Variation: Add sautéed onions, olives, mushrooms, and "neatballs" from Kristine Lilly's "Neatball" recipe (page 32) for extra flavor.

"I became a vegetarian as a teenager. At that time, I was frequently making the connection between animals and the food on my plate....Now that I share my home with so many living beings—dogs, cats, horses—it would never occur to me to eat animals! As a model, I am frequently questioned on beauty and health tips. I really only have one piece of advice: a vegetarian diet. I stay slim, my hair shines, and my skin is healthier and cleaner!"

Model

Tatjana Patitz

photo by Robert Sebree

Spicy and Lean Black Bean Chili

¾ cup dried black beans (equivalent to about 2 cups canned beans)

6⅔ cups water

1 Tbsp. oil

1 medium onion, chopped

4 garlic cloves, minced

1 tsp. chili powder

1 tsp. ground cumin

1 tsp. oregano

½ tsp. paprika

¼ tsp. salt

4¾ cups vegetable bouillon

18 oz. canned tomatoes, chopped and juice reserved

3 Tbsp. dry sherry or water

If using dried beans, wash and bring to a boil in a large pot. Reduce heat and let simmer for 2 minutes. Remove from heat, cover, and let stand for 1 hour. Drain and rinse.

In a large pot, sauté onion and garlic. Stir in the chili powder, cumin, oregano, paprika, salt, and cayenne, and cook for 1 minute, stirring. Add the beans, vegetable bouillon, tomatoes with their juice, and sherry or water and bring to a boil. Reduce the heat, cover, and simmer for 1½ hours until beans are soft.

Makes 4 servings.

Also see Tatjana's Coconut-Orange Ambrosia Bites, page 111.

Jannette Patterson

PETA Executive Director

"I stopped eating meat many years before I stopped eating dairy products. Then a friend told me that, in effect, there is a piece of veal in every glass of milk. After I learned that calves born on dairy farms are sold to the veal industry, I quickly learned the joy of soy!"

West Coast Soy Sausage Artichoke Lasagna

Tofu Ricotta filling

1 lb. firm tofu, drained
1 Tbsp. lemon juice
2 tsp. dried basil
¾ tsp. salt
½ tsp. minced fresh garlic
(or ¼ tsp. powdered garlic)

Other Ingredients

14-oz. vegetarian soy sausage
(such as Lightlife soy sausage, available at www.nomeat.com)
2 Tbsp. olive oil
1 or 2 16-oz. cans artichoke hearts packed in water
1 small bag frozen peas
1 box lasagna noodles
1 28-oz. jar prepared tomato sauce

Mash all ingredients for the tofu ricotta filling together and set aside. In a large pan, cook the soy sausage in olive oil, breaking it up into crumbles. Set aside. Drain the artichoke hearts, cut into quarters or smaller pieces, and set aside. Put frozen peas in a colander, run hot tap water over the peas to defrost. Set aside. Cook lasagna noodles according to package.

Cover the bottom of your lasagna pan with some of the tomato sauce. Put down a layer of pasta. Put half the tofu mixture over the noodles, followed by half the soy sausage, half the artichoke hearts, and half the peas. Repeat layering until all ingredients are used, ending with pasta and sauce. Cover with aluminum foil and bake for 1 hour at 350°F. Before cutting and serving, let sit for 15 minutes to allow pasta to settle.

Makes 6 to 9 servings.

Did you know?

No species naturally drinks milk beyond infancy, and no species would naturally drink the milk of a different species. Cow's milk is designed for baby cows, who have four stomachs, double their weight in 47 days, and weigh 800 pounds within a year.

Cassandra Peterson

"Wake Up the Dead" Asparagus Risotto

4⅓ cups water

1 lb. (approximately 16 stalks) fresh young asparagus, cut into 2-inch pieces and halved

4 Tbsp. vegetable bouillon concentrate

1 Tbsp. olive oil

2 Tbsp. margarine

1 small onion, minced

Salt and pepper, to taste

3 garlic cloves, minced

1⅓ cups Arborio rice

30 saffron threads softened in 1 Tbsp. hot water

⅓ cup dry white wine

½ cup soy parmesan

2 Tbsp. parsley, finely chopped

In a medium pot, bring the water to a boil. Add a teaspoon of salt. Add the asparagus to the boiling water and boil over high heat for 2 minutes. Be careful not to overcook it. Remove the asparagus with a large slotted spoon, drain, and set aside. Add the bouillon to the cooking water, cover, and keep warm over low heat.

Heat the olive oil and the margarine in a big pan, and add the onion, salt, and pepper. Over medium heat, sauté for 3 to 4 minutes, then add the garlic. Over low heat, sauté for 2 more minutes. Add the uncooked rice (use only Italian Arborio) and sauté for 2 to 3 minutes, stirring constantly. Add the water with saffron. Next, add the bouillon you prepared one cup at a time so that the rice has enough time to soak up the liquid before you add more. Stir constantly.

When the rice has soaked up 3 cups of bouillon, add the wine. Add more broth and continue stirring until about 4 to 4½ cups have been mixed in. While stirring in the last of the bouillon, add the asparagus and a dash of salt and pepper. Now the risotto should be tender but firm and creamy. Add the soy parmesan and the parsley, and serve hot. If desired, add additional soy parmesan.

Makes 4 servings.

Also see Cassandra's Mushroom Pâté en Croute page 42.

Did you know?

A survey conducted by the National Restaurant Association and the National Association of College and University Foodservice found that as many as 20 percent of college students are vegetarian—and that number is rising. Colleges from coast to coast now offer meatless entrées in their dining halls.

Chef Ronald A. Pickarski

Broccoli Seitan Delmonico

From *Friendly Foods* by Ronald A. Pickarski (Ten Speed Press; Berkeley, Calif., available at www.Eco-Cuisine.com)

3 Tbsp. corn oil

1 cup finely chopped onions

½ cup sliced mushrooms

¼ tsp. sea salt

¼ tsp. nutmeg

6 Tbsp. unbleached flour

2 tsp. nutritional yeast

½ cup chopped green olives, pimiento-stuffed

¼ cup cashew nuts

2 cups plain soy milk

2½ cups broccoli florets

1½ cups cooked and diced seitan

6 cups cooked pasta (spaghetti, linguine, soba, or other pasta)

Heat the oil in a medium saucepan. Sauté the onions and mushrooms with the salt and nutmeg until the onions are translucent. Stir in the flour and yeast and cook 3 to 5 minutes longer. Then add the chopped olives. Set aside.

Blend the cashews with 1 cup of soy milk until it makes a smooth paste. (You should be able to feel only a slight gritty texture if you rub the mixture between your fingers.) Add the remaining 1 cup of soy or rice milk and blend for a few seconds. Pour the cashew milk over the sautéed onion mixture and stir until well blended. Cook over medium heat, stirring occasionally, until the sauce thickens. (This would be a good time to begin cooking the pasta.) Steam the broccoli for about 5 minutes, or until tender but crisp. Add it to the sauce mixture. Finally, stir in the diced seitan. Spoon the broccoli seitan sauce over the pasta and serve hot.

Makes 5 servings.

Also see Chef Ronald's Carrot Pâté, page 44.

"Liberate your diet—go meat free!"

Did you know?

According to the U.S. Government Accounting Office, or GAO, inadequate regulations mean that unsafe, contaminated, and spoiled fish often end up on our nation's grocery shelves. In fact, 15 percent of all food-borne illnesses in the U.S. are caused by contaminated fish, even though fish represents only a small fraction of the total food consumed.

Kate Pierson & Fred Schneider of the B-52's

Mock Rock Lobster

For the lobster
4 medium fresh potatoes
1½ cups corn
½ cup green peas
12 oz. seitan, shredded or chopped
into small pieces
1 tsp. chopped parsley
½ tsp. salt
½ tsp. sugar
Pinch of pepper
1½ cup flour
1 Tbsp. soy sauce

For the breading
3½ cups flour
2½ cups water
Oil for frying

For dusting
¼ cup cornstarch

Peel the potatoes, slice thinly, and boil until soft. Mix the rest of the ingredients (except the ingredients for the breading) with the potatoes and purée. Divide into 10 portions. Form into lobster "sticks" and dust with a little cornstarch.

For the breading, mix the flour and water and coat each "lobster" with it. Heat the oil in a fryer to 300°F. Fry the "lobsters" until golden brown. Drain on paper towels.

Makes 10 servings.

Also see Kate's Cosmic Carrot Cake, page 112.

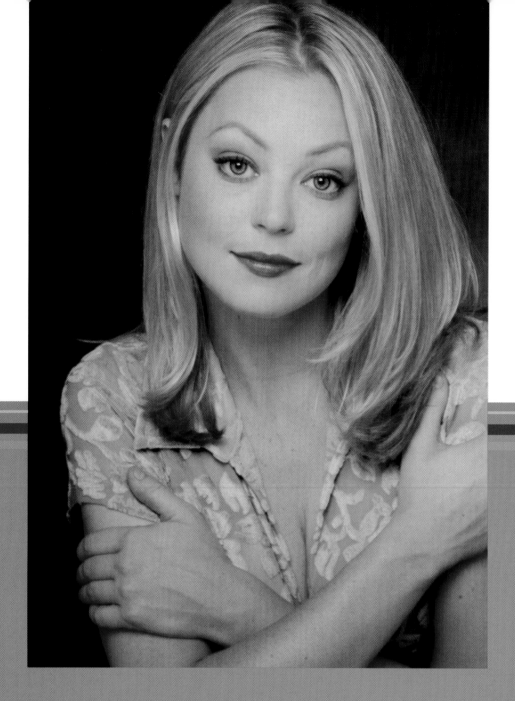

"I used to dream when I was a little girl that I could have notoriety to bring attention to animal rights and animal cruelty."

Charlotte Ross

Actor
Credits include: NYPD Blue and the daytime drama Days of Our Lives

Low-Fat Super Savory Asian Forest Curry

1½ tsp. olive oil

1 medium red onion, quartered and thinly sliced

6 garlic cloves, minced

1 green bell pepper, thinly sliced

2 cups sliced onion

1 medium zucchini, thinly sliced

2 cups green beans with ends removed
cut into 2-inch pieces

1½ cups shredded cabbage

15 large basil leaves

½ cup white wine

15-oz. can diced tomatoes

3 Tbsp. fresh lime juice

1 Tbsp. grated lemon zest

½ cup plus 1 Tbsp. lite silken tofu (firm), drained

½ cup low-fat soy milk

1 tsp. coconut extract

1 jalapeno pepper

1 Tbsp. tamari

Heat oil in a large saucepan over medium-high heat. Add the next 3 ingredients and sauté for 3 minutes. Add the next 4 ingredients and cook for 5 minutes. Add basil leaves, white wine, tomatoes, lime juice, and lemon zest.* Reduce heat to medium and cover, stirring occasionally.

Meanwhile, blend tofu in food processor. Add soy milk and coconut extract. Remove stem from jalapeno pepper and quarter. (Wash hands after handling jalapeno.) Add pepper to food processor (include seeds for extra heat). Pulse to blend. Fold tofu mixture into pot with vegetables and simmer for 25 minutes. Add tamari. Serve with jasmine rice.

Makes 6 servings.

*If you like spices, try adding ½ tsp. cumin, ½ tsp. coriander and/or ¼ tsp. cloves. For more bulk, add ¼ cup green peas.

photo by Ebet Roberts

Russell Simmons

Music Producer: Co-founder of Def Jam Records

Hip Hoppin' John

1 Tbsp. olive oil

1 medium onion, chopped

6 oz. smoked tofu, cut into small cubes

2 16-oz. cans black-eyed peas, rinsed and drained

3 cups cooked white rice

1½ cups cooked collard greens, chopped

½ tsp. salt

Hot sauce, to taste

Heat the oil in a large skillet over medium-high heat. Add the onion and sauté for 5 minutes, until the onion begins to soften. Add the smoked tofu, black-eyed peas, rice, and collards. Cook for 5 minutes or until heated through. Season with salt and hot sauce.

Makes 4 to 6 servings.

Baby-Get-Back "Ribs"

2 8-oz. packages bean curd stick (available at Asian markets; not to be confused with bean curd sheets)

2 Tbsp. warm melted margarine

¼ cup (or more) peanut butter

¼ cup nutritional yeast

2 Tbsp. miso paste

2 tsp. paprika

2 cups barbecue sauce

Soak the bean curd in warm water for 4 to 6 hours. When the bean curd has softened, drain, squeezing out the excess water, and cut into 4- to 6-inch lengths. In a large bowl, mix together the margarine, peanut butter, nutritional yeast, miso, and paprika to form a paste.

If the mixture is too thick, add 1 tsp. of water at a time to thin it. Preheat the oven to 370°F. Add the bean curd "ribs" to the paste and mix together, coating thoroughly. Place the "ribs" side by side on a large baking sheet and bake for 25 minutes, turning them so that they bake evenly, until the bottoms are crisp and brown.

Remove from the oven and, using a barbecue brush, apply the barbecue sauce. Return "ribs" to the oven and bake for 10 to 15 minutes.

Makes 4 to 6 servings.

"I became a vegetarian about four years ago, and I stopped eating milk, eggs, and all animal products about three years ago. A big part of it was health, at the beginning, and then the more I went to vegetarian restaurants and the more I talked to other vegetarians, the more I was reminded of the stuff I saw in John Robbins' video 'Diet for a New America.' First, you see how you're going to kill yourself by eating meat. You watch the tape again, and it reminds you about the animals, then it reminds you about the environment. You become less selfish. You start to see things in a different way."

Mama's Mock "Meatloaf"

Loaf ingredients

1 medium onion, diced

½ green pepper, diced

3 Tbsp. vegetable oil

28 oz. beef substitute (such as Morningstar Farms burger crumbles, available in the frozen vegetable section in most grocery stores, or Gimme Lean ground "beef" by Lightlife, available in health food stores or by visiting www.lightlife.com)

¼ cup uncooked oatmeal

2 slices white bread, crumbled

3 Tbsp. ketchup

2 tsp. garlic salt

1 tsp. pepper

Coating ingredients

¼ cup ketchup

¼ cup brown sugar

½ tsp. dry mustard

½ tsp. nutmeg

Preheat oven to 375°F. Sauté the onion and green pepper in the oil over medium heat until soft. Combine in a bowl with the "beef," oatmeal, bread, ketchup, garlic salt, and pepper. Thoroughly mix with a spoon or your hands. Press the mixture into an oiled loaf pan. Cover with foil and bake for 30 minutes. Meanwhile, mix together the ingredients for the coating and set aside. Remove the loaf from the oven and turn it out onto a baking sheet. Spread the coating over the entire loaf. Cook uncovered on the baking sheet for another 15 minutes.

Makes 6 servings.

"I agree with Albert Einstein, who said, 'Nothing will benefit human health and increase the chances for survival of life on Earth as much as the evolution to a vegetarian diet.' "

Director of PETA Germany

Harald Ullman

"Meaty" Stuffed Peppers

2 Tbsp. vegetable oil
1 large onion, chopped
3 cloves garlic, minced
4 Tbsp. uncooked white rice
1 cup vegetable broth
1 lb. beef substitute (such as Morningstar Farms burger crumbles, available in the frozen vegetable section in most grocery stores, or Gimme Lean ground "beef" by Lightlife, available in health food stores or by visiting www.lightlife.com)*
¼ cup chopped fresh parsley

1 cup chopped mushrooms
Egg replacer equivalent to 2 eggs (See egg replacement suggestions, page 10)
¼ cup dry bread crumbs
1 cup chopped walnuts
1 Tbsp. vegetarian Worcestershire sauce
½ tsp. black pepper
1 Tbsp. soy sauce
1 Tbsp. paprika
6 bell peppers
1 8-oz. can crushed tomatoes
¼ cup wine
1 Tbsp. tomato paste

Preheat oven to 350°F. Heat oil in a medium-sized pan over medi[um] heat. Sauté onions and ⅔ of garlic until onions are translucent. A[dd] rice and sauté 2 minutes. Stir in vegetable broth, cover, and cook u[ntil] rice is done, about 15 minutes. Meanwhile, in a large bowl comb[ine] meat substitute, parsley, mushrooms, egg replacement, bread crum[bs,] walnuts, Worcestershire sauce, black pepper, soy sauce, and papri[ka.] Add rice mixture when it has finished cooking.

In a shallow baking dish, combine tomatoes, wine, tomato paste, [and] remaining garlic. Slice the tops off the peppers and save. Remove [the] core and seeds, and stuff with meat substitute mixture. Replace to[ps.] Place peppers in dish and cover. Bake for 1 hour. Serve with tom[ato] and wine sauce spooned on top of peppers.

Makes 6 servin[gs]

Variation: The meat substitute can be replaced by 1 lb. tofu.

Montel Williams

Actor

*Credits include: The Montel Williams
Show, JAG, and Peacekeeper*

*"I like vegetarian food because it is
delicious, gives me energy, and allows
me to maintain a healthy lifestyle."*

Heart-Healthy Wild Rice With Walnuts and Raisins

1 cup defatted low-sodium vegetable broth

½ cup unsweetened apple juice

⅔ cup wild rice

1½ tsp. reduced-calorie margarine

4 oz. fresh mushrooms, sliced (about 1½ cups)

½ cup chopped onions

1 stalk celery, chopped

½ tsp. dried thyme

Pinch of dried sage

½ cup raisins

¼ cup chopped walnuts

In a medium saucepan bring the broth and juice to a boil. Meanwhile, rinse the rice with cold water. Stir the rice into the broth mixture and return to a boil. Reduce the heat, cover, and simmer for 45 to 50 minutes or until the rice is tender and the liquid is absorbed. Meanwhile, in a medium non-stick skillet, melt the margarine. Add the mushrooms, onions, celery, thyme, and sage. Cook and stir over medium heat about 4 minutes or until the vegetables are tender. Add the raisins and walnuts. Cook and stir for 2 minutes more. Remove from the heat and transfer to a large bowl. Add the rice and toss until well mixed. Spray a 1-quart casserole with no-stick spray. Transfer the mixture to the casserole. Cover and bake at 325°F about 30 minutes or until heated through.

Makes 3 servings.

decadent

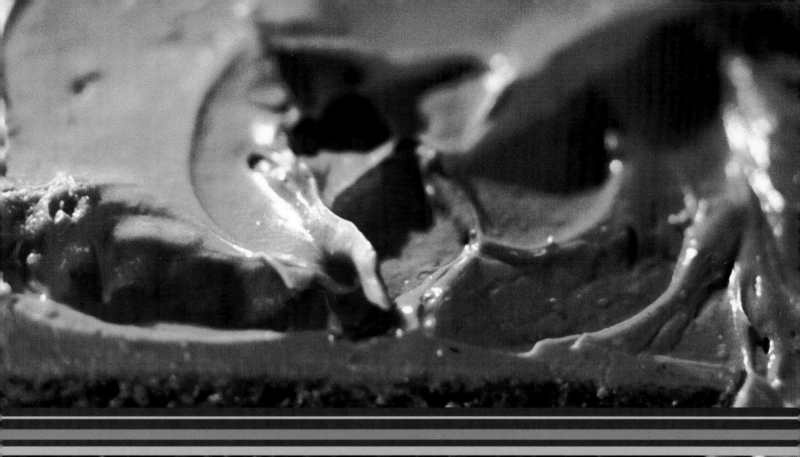

desserts

Christina Applegate

Actor
Credits include: Don't Tell Mom the Babysitter's Dead, The Sweetest Thing, and TV's 21 Jump Street, Family Ties, Married...With Children, and Jesse

"I like vegetarian food because it is lighter and healthier for me, but mainly because no animal has suffered and died for it."

The Sweetest Truffles

1 8-oz. package nondairy plain cream cheese (try Tofutti Better Than Cream Cheese) softened at room temperature
3 cups powdered sugar
12 oz. semi-sweet chocolate, melted in a double boiler or on lowest power in the microwave, stirred frequently
1½ tsp. vanilla
Ground nuts, unsweetened cocoa, or toasted flaked coconut

Beat the "cream cheese" until smooth. Gradually add the powdered sugar, beating until well blended. Add the melted chocolate and vanilla and mix well. Refrigerate for about 1 hour. Shape into 1-inch balls and roll in the nuts, cocoa, or coconut. Chill in the refrigerator.

Makes about 5 dozen truffles.

Did you know?

A report released by the Population Reference Bureau said that "if everyone adopted a vegetarian diet and no food were wasted, current [food] production would theoretically feed 10 billion people"—more than the entire human population.

Bea Arthur

Did you know?

A totally vegetarian diet requires 300 gallons of water per day, while a meat-eating diet requires more than 4,200 gallons of water per day.

Applesauce Cake

2 cups flour

¾ cup sugar

1 tsp. baking powder

1 tsp. cinnamon

½ tsp. nutmeg

¼ tsp. cloves

1 stick or ½ cup margarine, melted

2½ cups unsweetened applesauce (about 22 oz.)

½ cup raisins

¾ cup chopped walnuts

Powdered sugar to sprinkle on top

Preheat oven to 300°F. Grease a 10-inch round cake pan. In a large mixing bowl, mix flour, baking powder, sugar, and spices, then mix in applesauce and margarine until fully combined. Mix in the raisins and walnuts. Put the batter into the cake pan and bake for approximately 35 minutes. Cake is done when a knife inserted into the center comes out clean.

Makes 9 to 12 servings.

Also see Bea's Good Morning Mushroom-Tomato Toast, page 14.

Did you know?

Vegetarians are 30 percent likely to die of heart disease than meat-eaters, 40 percent less likely to die of cancer, and 20 percent less likely to die of other diseases.

Elizabeth Berkley

103

Opiate Temptation Fruit Salad

Fresh-squeezed juice of one orange (or 6 Tbsp. orange juice)
Fresh-squeezed juice of half a grapefruit (or 10 Tbsp. grapefruit juice)
1½ tsp. cornstarch
2 tsp. vegetable oil
2 tsp. sugar
1 tsp. poppy seeds
1 honeydew melon, cubed
1 cantaloupe, cubed
2 nectarines, chopped
2¼ cups strawberries, halved
¼ cup blueberries

Put the first five ingredients into a pot and stir until the sugar and cornstarch are dissolved. Cook over medium heat, stirring constantly, until thick. Remove from heat and add the poppy seeds. Stir well, cover, and chill. Mix the fruit in a large serving bowl and pour the sauce over all just before serving.

Makes 6 to 8 servings.

Also see Elizabeth's Berkley's EZ BBQ Chickpeas, page 67.

Melt in Your Mouth Yellow Cake

Egg replacer, equivalent to 4 eggs (See egg replacement suggestions, page 10)
2 cups sugar
½ cup margarine, warmed
2 cups flour
2 tsp. baking powder
½ tsp. salt
1 tsp. vanilla extract
1 cup heated soy or rice milk

Preheat the oven to 350°F and grease an 8-inch by 8-inch cake pan (or one of similar dimensions). Beat egg replacement, vanilla extract, and sugar together for 5 minutes. In a separate bowl, mix the flour, salt, and baking powder together. In a large bowl, cream the margarine with a mixer, then mix in the sugar/"egg" mixture. Then, add the flour mixture and soy or rice milk a little at a time, alternating between the two. Transfer the mixture to the cake pan and smooth. Bake 30 to 40 minutes. Let cool and, if desired, ice with vegan icing or cover with berries.

Makes 6 to 8 servings.

"At our spay/neuter clinic we work to save the lives of animals every day. Of course, you don't have to work in a veterinary clinic to help animals. This dessert is cruelty-free, and your friends and family will love you for sharing it."

PETA's Mobile Spay and Neuter Clinic Veterinarian

Dr. Brian Black

Tantalizing Trifle

1 yellow cake
1 cup + 2 Tbsp. vanilla soy pudding (available at health food shops or at www.healthy-eating.com)
¼ cup sherry
⅔ cup raspberry jam
1 small can cherries
2 medium bananas
Dairy-free whipped cream
Toasted sliced almonds to garnish

Cut the cake into 1-inch by 3-inch pieces. Line the bottom and sides of a 2½-liter (11-cup) glass bowl with the pieces of cake laid out side by side. Moisten the cake with the sherry and spread the raspberry jam over everything. Cut the cherries and bananas into pieces and add. Pour the pudding over the fruit, then place the bowl in the refrigerator. Before serving, garnish with the nondairy whipped cream and sliced almonds.

Makes 8 servings.

John Paul **Dejoria**

CEO and co-founder of Paul Mitchell Professional Salon Products, one of the world's largest manufacturers of hair and skin care products. All Paul Mitchell products are tested on humans, not animals.

Sublime Key Lime Pie

2 8-oz. containers plain nondairy cream cheese (try Toffuti Better Than Cream Cheese) at room temperature
1 cup sugar
1 tsp. vanilla
4 Tbsp. lime juice (about 2 limes)
2 tsp. lime zest (about 2 limes)
2 Tbsp. cornstarch
1 9-inch vegan graham cracker crust (see Rue McClanahan's recipe on page 110)
3 to 4 kiwis and/or strawberries, sliced

Preheat the oven to 350°F. Blend the cream cheese, sugar, vanilla, lime juice, zest, and cornstarch in a blender until smooth. Pour the mixture into the crust. Place the filled pie shell on a cookie sheet (to catch spills) and bake for 45 minutes. Let cool. Refrigerate overnight, then top with sliced fruit and serve.

Makes 8 servings.

"I like vegetarian food because it tastes good and lets us live longer!"

Cranberry-Pear To-Die-For Pie

For the filling
5 cups pears, peeled, cored, and cut into ¼-inch slices

1½ cups fresh (or frozen and thawed) cranberries

4 Tbsp. sugar

1 Tbsp. margarine, melted

1 tsp. ground cinnamon

1 deep-dish pie crust, unbaked (see Joe Tata's Flaky Pie Crust recipe on page 117; increase ingredients by ¼ so it will fit a deep-dish pan)

For the crumb topping
½ cup sugar

¾ cup flour

½ cup margarine, at room temperature

Preheat the oven to 375°F. Place pie crust dough in deep baking dish. Combine the filling ingredients in a large bowl and stir well, making sure the pears are evenly coated with the cinnamon. Transfer to the pie crust.

For the topping, crumble together the sugar, flour, and margarine. Add small amounts of additional flour, if necessary, until small crumbs form. Top the pie with crumbs, covering completely. Bake at 375°F for 10 minutes. Reduce the oven temperature to 325°F and bake for about 30 more minutes, or until the crumb topping is golden brown and the pears and cranberries are soft (test with a toothpick). Let cool for at least 1 hour before serving.

Makes 8 servings.

Chrissie Hynde

Did you know?

When TIME magazine asked a New York City chef to prepare a meat-free meal for the year 2025—one that would be good for the body and for the planet—they raved: "If the future can be made this appetizing, even a T-bone palate could learn to be happy in a tofu world."

Zesty Blueberry Poppyseed Cupcakes

1 cup flour
2½ Tbsp. sugar
2 tsp. baking powder
4 tsp. poppy seeds
¼ tsp. salt
½ cup plain soy or rice milk
4 Tbsp. creamed margarine
Egg replacer, equivalent to 1 egg (See egg replacement suggestions, page 10)
¼ tsp. grated lemon peel
1 tsp. lemon juice
¾ cup fresh or frozen blueberries, thawed and dried

Preheat oven to 325°F. Grease a cupcake pan. Combine the flour, sugar, baking powder, poppy seeds, and salt. Add the soy or rice milk, margarine, egg replacer, lemon peel, and lemon juice, and stir until moist, but don't overstir. Fold the blueberries into the mixture. Spoon the batter into the cupcake pan and bake for 20–25 minutes, or until a toothpick comes out clean.

Makes 8 servings.

Also see Chrissie's Easy "Cheezy" Veggie Melts, page 31.

T'Keyah Crystal Keymáh

Actor
Credits include: In Living Color, On Our Own, The Show, and Cosby

"I am vegetarian by nature."

109

Berry Delicious Tangy Sorbet

1 cup frozen organic blueberries
1 cup frozen organic cranberries
1 cup frozen organic raspberries
2 Tbsp. organic maple syrup
1 cup water
1 tsp. organic vanilla extract
¼ cup fresh organic strawberries
1 tsp. organic maple syrup
4 sprigs fresh organic mint

Pour frozen berries into a blender. Add syrup and vanilla. Frappé the mixture for a few seconds at a time. Stop to add water (½ cup at a time) and stir ingredients. Repeat until all of the water is in and the mixture seems even. Be careful not to over-mix, or you will have a liquid better suited for popsicles. Place in the freezer for at least 20 minutes for a more solid consistency. Scoop into dessert cups and garnish with mint leaves. (Don't forget to eat the mint.)

Makes 2 to 4 servings.

Rue McClanahan

Actor
Credits include: All In The Family,
Maude, and The Golden Girls

"If you carry the power of compassion
to the marketplace and the dinner table,
you can make your life really count."

Extreme Dream Cheesecake

For the filling

2 8-oz. containers plain nondairy cream cheese (try Tofutti Better Than Cream Cheese)
1 cup sugar
Juice of one whole lemon (or 2–3 Tbsp. pure lemon juice)
1 tsp. vanilla
Fresh raspberries or canned cherry pie filling

For the crust

2 cups vegan graham cracker or cookie crumbs
⅛ cup sugar
¼ cup margarine, softened

For the crust, combine the graham cracker crumbs, sugar, and margarine and mix well. Transfer to an 8-inch pie pan, and use a big spoon to press the dough firmly against the sides and bottom of the pan. Chill for 30 minutes in the refrigerator.

Preheat the oven to 350°F. Blend together the nondairy cream cheese, sugar, lemon juice, and vanilla, and pour into the graham cracker crust. Place the filled pie shell on a cookie sheet (to catch spills) and bake for 60 minutes. Allow to cool. Cover the top of the "cheese" cake with the fresh raspberries or cherry pie filling and chill several hours.

Makes 8 servings.

Tatjana Patitz

Did you know?

"Green" equals "lean." Vegetarian diets are typically 25 percent lower in fat than meat-based diets, and vegetarians tend to weigh 10 percent less than their carnivorous counterparts—without having to count calories.

Coconut-Orange Ambrosia Bites

oz. (3½ cups) vegan cake or ookie crumbs

½ cups powdered sugar

½ Tbsp. margarine

ice and pulp of a freshly queezed orange, without the eel (or 6 Tbsp. orange juice)

cup chopped nuts (optional)

oz. (about ⅓ cup) shredded oconut

ake crumbs can be made by mply crumbling vegan cake ee Brian Black's Melt in Your louth Yellow Cake, page 104).

Mix the cake crumbs and powdered sugar. Add the margarine, orange juice and pulp, and nuts. Mix well, then form balls about 1 inch across. Roll balls in the shredded coconut, place on a cookie sheet, and chill in the refrigerator for an hour, until firm.

Makes 3 to 4 dozen balls.

Also see Tatjana's Spicy and Lean Black Bean Chili, page 87.

Kate Pierson & Fred Schneider of the B-52's

Cosmic Carrot Cake

For the cake

2 cups grated carrots

1½ cups raisins

2 cups water

½ cup vegetable oil

1¼ cups maple syrup

1½ tsp. ground cinnamon

1½ tsp. allspice

½ tsp. ground cloves

1½ tsp. salt

3 cups whole wheat flour

1½ tsp. baking powder

¾ cup chopped walnuts

Did you know?

The director of pediatrics at Johns Hopkins University, Dr. Frank Oski, says, "There's no reason to drink cow's milk at any time. It was designed for calves, it was not designed for humans, and we should all stop drinking it today, this afternoon."

For the frosting

cups powdered sugar

8-oz containers plain nondairy cream cheese (try Tofutti Better than Cream Cheese), room temperature

cup (1 stick or 8 Tbsp.) unsalted margarine, room temperature

tsp. vanilla extract

Pre-heat the oven to 300°F. Grease a 10-inch cake pan. Cook the carrots and raisins in the water over medium heat in a big pot, until the raisins are soft, about 7 to 10 minutes, then remove from heat. Add the oil, maple syrup, cinnamon, allspice, cloves, and salt, stir, and let cool.

In a large bowl, combine flour, baking powder, and walnuts. Add the carrot mixture and stir until combined. Pour the batter into the cake pan and bake for 45 minutes to 1 hour. The cake is done when a knife inserted in the center comes out clean.

In a medium bowl, use an electric mixer to beat all ingredients for the frosting until smooth and creamy. Spread on cake.

Makes 9 to 12 servings.

Also see Kate's Mock Rock Lobster, page 91.

Amy Smart

Actor
Credits include: Varsity Blues, Outside
Providence, and TV's Felicity

"Vegetarianism is a way of living consciously on the planet."

Cherry Heart Smart Cookies

1 cup (2 sticks) margarine
1 cup dark brown sugar
½ cup sugar
Egg replacer equivalent to 2 eggs (See egg replacement suggestions, page 10)
1 tsp. vanilla extract
1½ cups all-purpose flour
½ tsp. salt
½ tsp. baking soda
½ tsp. baking powder
1 tsp. cinnamon
2 cups oatmeal, uncooked
1 cup dried cherries

Preheat the oven to 350°F. Cream the margarine with the sugars until well blended. Add the prepared egg replacer and vanilla, and beat for several minutes. In a separate bowl, combine the flour, salt, baking soda, baking powder, and cinnamon. Add to the margarine mixture and blend well. Stir in the oatmeal and dried cherries. Drop the batter by tablespoonfuls onto lightly greased cookie sheets and bake until the edges are just turning brown, about 12 minutes.

Makes about 4 dozen cookies.

photo by Christopher Ameruoso

Choco-Gingerbread Cookies

1½ cups plus 1 Tbsp. all-purpose flour

1¼ tsp. ground ginger

1 tsp. cinnamon

¼ tsp. cloves

¼ tsp. nutmeg

1 Tbsp. cocoa powder

8 Tbsp. (1 stick) margarine, softened

1 Tbsp. freshly grated ginger root

½ cup dark brown sugar, packed

¼ cup molasses

1 tsp. baking soda dissolved in 1½ tsp. boiling water

1 cup semisweet chocolate chips

¼ cup granulated sugar

In a medium bowl, whisk together the flour, ground ginger, cinnamon, cloves, nutmeg, and cocoa. Set aside. With an electric mixer, beat together the margarine and grated ginger root until well blended, about 4 minutes. Beat in the brown sugar and molasses until well combined. Beat half of the flour mixture into the margarine mixture. Beat in the baking soda mixture, then the rest of the flour mixture. Stir in the chocolate chips. Chill, covered, for about one hour.

Preheat the oven to 325°F. Roll the dough into 1½-inch balls, then roll each ball in the granulated sugar. Place on baking sheets lined with parchment paper. Bake until the surfaces crack slightly, about 13 to 15 minutes.

Makes about 2 dozen cookies.

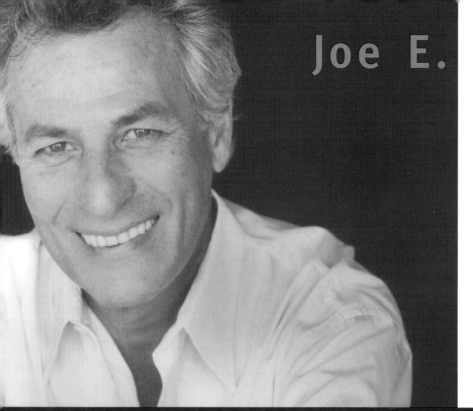

Joe E. Tata

Actor
Credits include: The Red Skelton Show, Gomer Pyle, Batman, and Beverly Hills 90210

Sunset Boulevard Peach Pie

6 cups fresh peaches, peeled and sliced (see directions below)
3 Tbsp. all-purpose flour
¼ cup firmly packed light brown sugar
¼ tsp. nutmeg
⅛ tsp. allspice
2 Tbsp. margarine, cut in small pieces
1 Tbsp. soy or rice milk (plain or vanilla)
1 tsp. sugar

Prepare one Flaky Pie Crust Dough (see recipe on next page) and refrigerate, or use store-bought vegan pastry dough.

Pre-heat the oven to 375°F. To peel peaches, drop them in boiling water for a few seconds each, remove, then slide off the skin. Place the peaches in an 8-inch square baking dish or 2-quart casse-role. Mix the flour, ¼ cup brown sugar, allspice, and nutmeg in a bowl. Combine this flour mixture with the peaches, mixing gently until coated. Sprinkle the pieces of margarine onto peaches.

On a lightly floured surface, roll out the pastry to be 1 inch larger than the casserole dish. Lay pastry on top of the peach-filled casserole dish and press the pastry around the top of the dish, crimping the edges with a fork. Cut off any excess pastry. Brush pastry with soy or rice milk and sprinkle with 1 tsp. sugar. With a sharp knife cut 4 slits in the pastry to allow steam to escape. Bake for 35 to 40 minutes or until the crust is golden. Serve warm along with a scoop of vanilla soy or rice ice cream.

Makes 9 servings.

Did you know?

Following your heart is good for your heart! The average American man has a fifty-percent chance of dying from a heart attack. Vegetarian men have a miniscule four-percent risk.

Flaky Pie Crust Dough

2 cups all-purpose flour
1½ Tbsp. sugar
½ tsp. salt
½ cup and 2 Tbsp. margarine
2 Tbsp. vegetable oil
3 Tbsp. cold water

Mix the flour, sugar, and salt in a large bowl. Cut the margarine into small pieces and mix into the flour. Quickly work in the margarine until clumps are reduced to the size of raisins. Mixture should be crumbly.

Thoroughly mix together the oil and water in a small bowl and combine with the flour/margarine mixture. Knead until it barely holds together. Don't over-work the dough. Flatten the dough into a disc, wrap in plastic, and chill in refrigerator for at least 30 minutes.

Makes 9 servings.

A

B

C

U

V

Contents in Brief

Contents

**Chapter 6   Entrepreneurship and Small-Business
                Ownership   166**

PART 3

**Guiding the Enterprise: Leadership,
Organization, and Operations   189**

**Chapter 7   Management Roles, Functions,
                and Skills   189**

PART 5
Satisfying the Customer: Marketing, Sales, and Customer Support   330

Chapter 13   The Art and Science of Marketing   330

Chapter 14   Product and Pricing Strategies   354

Appendixes (available online at www.mybizlab.com)

Preface

Are You Ready to Build Your Future?

If you like challenge and change, you've picked a good time to enter the field of business.

By the time you read this, the economy should be climbing out of the worst recession in decades. However, employment, consumer confidence, and the stock market could take years to recover. The U.S. economy is struggling with massive levels of debt and rising health care costs that will hobble growth if they can't be brought under control.

Against this backdrop of serious challenges, however, are exciting opportunities. The social media revolution is fundamentally changing the relationship between businesses and their customers, empowering customers and giving forward-thinking companies new ways to grow. Communication and collaboration tools are knocking down barriers of organization and geography, giving the best ideas a better chance of reaching the marketplace.

Your community, your country, and the global economy can all benefit from the fresh thinking and fresh energy of a new generation of business leaders.

Will you be ready?

Business in Action, fifth edition, is ready to help. Its key features include

- **An objective-driven structure** with easy-to-read chapters that eliminate frills, distractions, and wasted energy—through careful planning and writing, *Business in Action* is up to 20 percent shorter than some other textbooks that cover the same information
- **Information "chunking"** that helps you absorb new concepts in small, carefully metered segments and get confirmation before moving on to the next segment
- **Clear, concise writing** with a conversational style that conveys professional respect for both you and the material
- **No compromises in essential coverage**, including dedicated chapters on employee motivation, customer communication, accounting, financial management, financial markets, and banking

Major Changes and Improvements in This Edition

The fifth edition is the most significant revision in *Business in Action's* publication history. The following pages highlight the major changes and improvements.

Concise but Comprehensive 20-Chapter Treatment of Business Concepts

With the expansion from 14 to 20 chapters, this edition gives your instructor greater flexibility in structuring a course around specific learning goals. It also gives you a more valuable reference book to use after you complete the course. However, even at a full 20 chapters, the fifth edition's focused, objective-driven structure produced a text that is up to 20 percent shorter than the typical comprehensive business text.

Objective-Driven Structure

Every chapter in this edition is divided into six segments of equal importance, each with its own learning objective and comprehensive checkpoint (see pages 21–22). In addition to simplifying your reading and review efforts, this objective-driven structure forced a tight focus for every segment of every chapter. There are no rambling, poorly organized chapters, and there is no extraneous material.

Clear, Relevant Coverage of the Forces and Events Reshaping the Business World

This edition offers a thoroughly revised and up-to-date look at the contemporary business landscape. Here are just a few examples:

- The multiple causes and lasting effects of the subprime mortgage crisis
- The pervasive use and widespread impact of "exotic" financial products
- The high-stakes controversy over the Employee Free Choice Act
- The growing use of social media in customer communication and the way these technologies are fundamentally reshaping the relationships between companies and their stakeholders
- The spread of brand communities
- Innovative pricing strategies, including participative pricing and free pricing
- New research into the forces that drive employee motivation
- The increasing awareness of the risks and limitations of goal-setting theory
- The reevaluation of the costs and benefits of outsourcing and offshoring

Integration with mybizlab

Your instructor may opt to use **mybizlab** (www.mybizlab.com) to deliver all or a portion of the course online, including using its homework and test management tools. If **mybizlab** was selected for your course, you can use it to create your own learning plan and to access a variety of tools to help you study and gauge your learning progress. See page 22 for more.

"Learn More" Multimedia Resources

This book extends the learning experience with unique "Learn More" media elements that connect you with dozens of videos, podcasts, PowerPoint presentations, and other items personally selected by the authors to complement chapter content. This text has more media support that you can directly access to enhance and reinforce learning than any other introduction to business text in publishing history.

New *Behind the Scenes* Vignettes and Case Studies

More than half the Behind the Scenes narrative vignettes and case studies are new in this edition; see page 23 for a complete list.

New Exhibits

More than 40 all-new exhibits and numerous updated and revised exhibits help you quickly grasp essential concepts and business trends.

Significant Content Additions

In addition to being thoroughly revised, updated, and reorganized, the fifth edition includes a significant amount of new content. This sample helps convey the extent of this revision:

- Adding Value: The Business of Business (in Chapter 1)
- Accepting Risk (in Chapter 1)
- Appreciating the Role of Business in Society (in Chapter 1)
- Using This Course to Jump Start Your Career (in Chapter 1)
- Recognizing the Multiple Environments of Business (in Chapter 1)
- Identifying the Major Functional Areas in a Business Enterprise (in Chapter 1)
- Achieving Professionalism (in Chapter 1)
- What Is This Thing Called the Economy? (in Chapter 2)
- Unemployment (in Chapter 2)
- Organizational Strategies for International Expansion (in Chapter 3)
- Corporate Officers (in Chapter 5)
- The Entrepreneurial Spirit (in Chapter 6)
- Why People Start Their Own Companies (in Chapter 6)
- Innovating Without Leaving: Intrapreneurship (in Chapter 6)
- Define the Mission, Vision, and Values (in Chapter 7)
- Top Management (in Chapter 7)
- Middle Managers (in Chapter 7)
- First-Line Managers (in Chapter 7)
- Establishing Performance Standards (in Chapter 8)
- Crisis Management: Maintaining Control in Extraordinary Circumstances (in Chapter 8)
- The Offshoring Controversy (in Chapter 8)

- Scalability Challenges and Opportunities (in Chapter 8)
- Performance Variability and Perceptions of Quality (in Chapter 8)
- McClelland's Three Needs (in Chapter 10)
- Risks and Limitations of Goal-Setting Theory (in Chapter 10)
- The Job Characteristics Model (in Chapter 10)
- Approaches to Modifying Core Job Dimensions (in Chapter 10)
- Types of Reinforcement (in Chapter 10)
- Unintended Consequences of Reinforcement (in Chapter 10)
- Provide Timely and Frequent Feedback [motivational strategy] (in Chapter 10)
- Make It Personal [motivational strategy] (in Chapter 10)
- Adapt to Circumstances and Special Needs [motivational strategy] (in Chapter 10)
- Don't Let Problems Fester [motivational strategy] (in Chapter 10)
- Be an Inspiring Leader [motivational strategy] (in Chapter 10)
- Ability [as dimension of workforce diversity] (in Chapter 11)
- The Role of Labor Unions (in Chapter 12)
- Unionization: The Employee's Perspective (in Chapter 12)
- Unionization: Management's Perspective (in Chapter 12)
- Unionization in Historical Perspective (in Chapter 12)
- Power to the Unions: The Wagner Act of 1935 (in Chapter 12)

Extend the Value of Your Textbook with Free Multimedia Content

Business in Action's unique **Real-Time Updates** system automatically provides weekly content updates, including podcasts, PowerPoint presentations, online videos, PDFs, and articles. You can subscribe for updates chapter by chapter, so you get only the material that applies to the chapter you are studying. Access Real-Time Updates through **mybizlab** (www.mybizlab.com) or by visiting http://real-timeupdates.com/bia5.

1 See breaking news from CNBC, *BusinessWeek*, and CNN.

2 Read messages from the authors and access special assignment materials and "Learn More" media items.

3 Click on any chapter to see the updates and media items for that chapter.

4 Scan headlines and click on any item of interest to read the article or download the media item.

Every item is personally selected by the authors to complement the text and support in-class activities.

5 Subscribe via RSS to individual chapters to get updates automatically for the chapter you're currently studying.

6 Media items are categorized by type so you can quickly find podcasts, videos, PowerPoints, and more.

Take Each Chapter One Segment at a Time

Every chapter in *Business in Action* is divided into six segments of roughly equal length. Each segment corresponds to one of the six learning objectives listed at the beginning of the chapter and focuses on the most essential concepts and terminology to help you achieve that particular objective. After you read a segment, review and reinforce what you've just read using the Checkpoint feature (see the next page for an example).

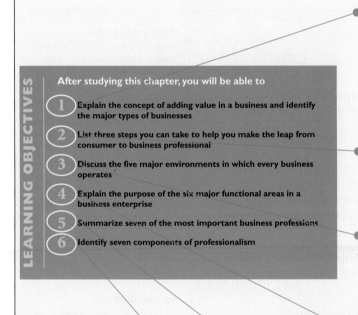

LEARNING OBJECTIVES

After studying this chapter, you will be able to

1. Explain the concept of adding value in a business and identify the major types of businesses

2. List three steps you can take to help you make the leap from consumer to business professional

3. Discuss the five major environments in which every business operates

4. Explain the purpose of the six major functional areas in a business enterprise

5. Summarize seven of the most important business professions

6. Identify seven components of professionalism

Understanding What Businesses Do

The term *business* is used in a number of ways:

- As a label for the overall field of business concepts, as in "I plan to major in business."
- As a collective label for the activities of many companies, as in "This legislation is viewed as harmful to American business."
- As a way to indicate specific activities or efforts, as in "Our furniture business earned record profits last year, but our housewares business has lost money for the third year in a row."

Making the Leap from Buyer to Seller

Even if this course is your first formal exposure to the business world, you already know a great deal about business, thanks to your experiences as a consumer. You understand the impact of poor customer service, for example— or great customer service. You have a sense for product value and why some products meet your needs but others don't. In fact, you're an expert in the entire experience of searching for, purchasing, and owning products.

Recognizing the Multiple Environments of Business

The potential effects of business, both positive and negative, highlight the fact that no business operates in a vacuum. Every company operates within a number of interrelated environments that affect and are affected by business.

Identifying the Major Functional Areas in a Business Enterprise

Throughout this course, you'll have the opportunity to learn more about the major functional areas within a business enterprise. In the meantime, the following sections offer a brief overview to help you see how all the pieces work together (see Exhibit 1.4).

Exploring Careers in Business

Whether you're getting ready to start your career or you've been in the workforce for a while, you can use this course as an opportunity to explore the many career track options in the world of business. To help stimulate your thinking, this section offers a quick overview of seven major business fields.[11] However, don't limit yourself to these seven by any means. For just about any professional interest you might have, you can probably find a business-related career to pursue, from entertainment and sports to health care and sciences and everything in between. Also, pay attention to employment trends; as the business environment evolves, employment opportunities in various fields grow and shrink at different rates (see Exhibit 1.5).

Achieving Professionalism

As you map out your career, think about what kind of businessperson you want to be. Will you be someone who just puts in the hours and collects a paycheck? Or will you be someone who performs on a higher plane, someone who wants to make a meaningful contribution and be viewed as a "real pro"? Professionalism is the quality of performing at a high level and conducting oneself with purpose and pride. True professionals exhibit seven distinct traits: striving to excel, being dependable and accountable, being a team player, communicating effectively, demonstrating a sense of etiquette, making ethical decisions, and maintaining a positive outlook.

Use the Checkpoints to Confirm and Review

Each of the six segments in a chapter has its own Checkpoint to help you review material in manageable doses, rather than being forced to take in an entire chapter at once. With this approach, each learning objective is addressed almost as a mini-chapter within the chapter. When you're reading a chapter, you might want to take a short break after each Checkpoint to let that segment "sink in" before moving on to the next segment.

These Checkpoints also provide a great way to study for tests—you can simply skim all six Checkpoints in a chapter for a quick refresher on important concepts and key terms.

CHECKPOINT

LEARNING OBJECTIVE 2: Define *corporate social responsibility (CSR),* **and explain the difference between philanthropy and strategic CSR.**

Summary: Corporate social responsibility (CSR) is the notion that business has obligations to society beyond the pursuit of profits. However, there is no general agreement over what those responsibilities are or which elements of society should determine those obligations or benefit from them. Philanthropy involves donating time, money, or other resources without regard for any direct business benefits. In contrast, strategic CSR involves contributions that are aligned with the company's business needs and strategies.

Critical thinking: (1) How can society decide what the responsibilities of business are in a CSR context? (2) Is philanthropy morally superior to strategic CSR? Why or why not?

It's your business: (1) Have a company's philanthropic or CSR efforts ever influenced your purchasing behavior? (2) Have you ever benefited personally from a company's philanthropic or CSR efforts?

Key terms to know: corporate social responsibility (CSR), philanthropy, strategic CSR

Learning Objective

Repeats the learning objective to remind you of the goal for this chapter segment

Summary

Offers a concise summary of the material you need to understand in order to achieve the learning objective

Critical Thinking

Hones your analytical skills by encouraging you to think through some important implications of the concepts learned in this segment

Its your Business

Personalizes the material by asking questions that relate the concepts learned in this segment to aspects of your own life

Key terms to know

Lists the most essential terminology to grasp from this segment

Create Your Own Learning Plan Using mybizlab

mybizlab (www.mybizlab.com) offers a personalized, interactive learning environment where you can learn at your own pace and measure your progress along the way:

- **Get unlimited opportunities for practice and mastery.** Homework and practice questions are correlated to the textbook. Helpful feedback coaches you whenever you enter incorrect answers.

- **Create a self-paced learning plan.** mybizlab generates a personalized study plan for you based on your test results, and the study plan links directly to interactive, tutorial exercises for topics you haven't yet mastered. You can monitor your own progress and see at a glance exactly which topics you need to practice.

See How Business Professionals Apply the Concepts You're Studying

Behind the Scenes

Enter the Haggis Enters the Music Business

www.enterthehaggis.com

Chances are Trevor Lewington, Brian Buchanan, Craig Downie, Mark Abraham, and James Campbell don't wake up every morning and head off to work thinking of themselves as businesspeople. They are musicians first and foremost, members of Enter the Haggis (ETH), a Toronto-based Celtic rock band that has been steadily building a fan base across North America since the lads met in college in the early 2000s.

The five members of Enter the Haggis need to treat their music as a business to ensure a long and healthy career in the music industry.

They're musicians, but they can't help being businesspeople as well. Being a musician can be a lifetime calling and a consuming passion, but earning a living as a professional musician requires much more than artistic inspiration and talent. Musicians who want to survive and thrive in today's fragmented media landscape are increasingly taking control and managing their careers as business operations.

Any music fan who has been purchasing music over the last decade or so knows that the music industry has been undergoing some profound changes. Sales of compact discs have dropped in half since their peak in 2000, as online sales through digital downloads and digital streaming services have grown rapidly. Legal sales of digital music are increasing, although the vast majority of downloads are illegal. However, not all musicians are dead set against unauthorized downloading, and many openly encourage it as a way to build audiences for their music and increase demand for concert ticket sales.

As revolutionary as it has been, the transition to digital song files is not the only seismic shake-up affecting the music industry. Behind the scenes, a battle is raging between a handful of large record labels (companies that produce and promote recorded music) and hundreds of smaller independent companies usually know as the "indies." Musicians who can't get signed by one of the majors—or who don't care for the terms of a major label contract—can try to find a home at an indie label instead.

If you were one of the lads in ETH, what path would you like the group to take? Would you try to sign with a major label or go with an indie? What stance would you take on unauthorized music downloads? How would you build a business to support your dreams of a successful career in music?[1] ■

Behind the Scenes chapter-opening vignette

Each chapter opens with a brief story featuring a business professional facing the sort of challenges that make or break companies and careers—and needing to use the same skills and knowledge that you will acquire in the chapter. Over half the vignettes are new in this edition.

Behind the Scenes chapter-closing case study

Each chapter ends with a case that expands on this vignette and shows how the professional role model used the skills and knowledge you have just learned. Three critical-thinking questions encourage you to apply the concepts covered in the text. Plus, you can find out more about the company featured in the case by completing the "Learn More Online" exercise.

All new in this edition

Chapter 1	How the Toronto-based Celtic rock band **Enter the Haggis** uses business concepts to turn a love of music into a sustainable business operation
Chapter 2	How the Chinese solar energy company **Suntech** is innovating to improve the economics of photovoltaic panels
Chapter 5	How **Sirius** and **XM Radio** engineered a merger to save two companies on the brink
Chapter 6	How two Native American sisters built **Sister Sky** using ancient remedies and tribal wisdom
Chapter 10	How **Deloitte** redefined the very notion of the corporate ladder to accommodate and motivate its highly skilled workforce
Chapter 12	How **American Axle** and the **United Auto Workers** struggle during the darkest days of the U.S. auto industry
Chapter 14	How professional golfer Annika Sorenstam is transforming herself from Annika the champion into **ANNIKA** the brand
Chapter 16	How SeaWorld San Antonio uses social media to foster relationships in the tight-knit community of roller-coaster enthusiasts
Chapter 17	How **Google** began implementing comprehensive cost controls after years of free-spending exuberance
Chapter 18	How **Visa** staged the largest IPO in U.S. history while the economy was tumbling into a recession
Chapter 19	How **Chesapeake Energy** uses hedging strategies to bring some semblance of financial stability to the wild world of energy trading
Chapter 20	How **JPMorgan Chase** avoided following its Wall Street competitors into the bottomless chasm of the subprime mortgage mess

---

Behind the Scenes

Build a Band, Then Build a Business

The beginnings of the Celtic rock band Enter the Haggis (ETH) coincided with the beginning of the revolution in the music industry. Millions of music listeners were fed up with the business model that had been in place for decades, in which record labels forced customers to purchase entire albums for $15 to $20, even when they might want only one or two songs on an album—and usually without the opportunity to listen to rest of the album first.

Within the music business, thousands of musicians were fed up with the mainstream business model as well. The industry was dominated by a small number of large record companies, also known as *record labels*. These labels made major investments in the careers of a small number of musicians, from paying for recording sessions to promoting the music to radio stations, which to a large degree dictated the music the public got to hear.

This business model worked out nicely for those musicians lucky enough to get signed by one of the major labels, lucky enough to get significant radio airplay, lucky enough to get significant album and concert sales as a result of that radio exposure, and lucky or smart enough to sign a contract that actually passed some of the resulting profits back to the musicians.

However, the dominant business model was far less satisfying for thousands of other musical acts. With a business model built around big investments made in the hope of big paybacks, the big labels focused on acts with the best chance of appealing to a wide audience. Musicians and groups without a mainstream sound usually needed to look elsewhere. And when the major labels did sign an act, they often exerted a lot of creative and financial control, influencing the sound, the public image, and the career track of the artists in which they invested. Moreover, they recouped their costs before the artist saw any money from album sales, meaning an artist usually had to sell a pile of albums to start seeing any money at all from a recording contract. In other words, for many artists, the chances of getting a major label contract were slim, and the chances of being satisfied with such a contract were even slimmer.

Against this backdrop of widespread dissatisfaction on the part of both consumers and creators, a number of forces in the technological environment were turning the industry upside down. The compact disc (CD) gradually replaced most sales of vinyl albums, but it triggered something much more disruptive than simply replacing one album format with another. CDs store music in digital format, which means the music can be transferred to and played on computers and other digital devices—and distributed over computer networks. The introduction of widely accepted standard file formats, most notably MP3, made it easy to copy and share song files from one device to another. The rapid spread of high-speed Internet connections, low-cost digital music players such as the iPod, and social media such as MySpace and Last.fm added the final pieces of the puzzle. The music industry would never be the same again.

ETH stepped right into this upheaval and embraced a new way of thinking. The group signed with United for Opportunity (UFO), which describes itself as "an organization of experienced, independent-thinking music activists that have come together to create a new model for a record label/music distribution company." Not only does UFO support the band's philosophy of giving musicians and their fans more control, but signing with an indie makes more financial sense, too. According to ETH's Brian Buchanan, "The average independent musician sees more real cash from 10,000 independent sales than many major artists see from a million sales."

Will the lads in ETH ever become filthy rich playing Celtic-influenced music? Probably not. However, as Buchanan puts it, "Success is making any kind of a living doing the thing you love." By meshing their business model with the changing business environment and working tirelessly to connect with their customers, ETH stands a good chance of making enough money to keep doing what they love for as long as they love doing it.

Critical Thinking Questions

1. Assume that ETH really was in it for the money and not the music. Would it still make sense to stick with an indie label, or should the band pursue a major label contract and all the potential marketing exposure that comes with it? Explain your answer.
2. Search online for "Enter the Haggis" and identify how many ways you can listen to the band's music for free. Why is it in the group's long-term interest to make its music available for free like this?
3. If the band had begun its professional existence 10 years earlier, how might its business strategy be different from the path it took?

LEARN MORE ONLINE

Explore the band's website at www.enterthehaggis.com and its presence on Facebook, YouTube, MySpace, Twitter, and Ustream. How does the band use its online presence to build a relationship with fans? ■

Build Skills, Awareness, and Insight

Test Your Knowledge

Questions for Review

1. What is a business model?
2. What are four ways that business can benefit society?
3. Do all companies have an R&D function? Explain your answer.
4. How does the role of a financial manager differ from the role of an accountant?
5. What is professionalism?

Questions for Analysis

6. Why is it often easier to start a service business than a goods-producing business?
7. Does a downturn in the economy hurt all companies equally? Provide several examples to support your answer.
8. Do laws and regulations always restrict or impede the efforts of business professionals, or can they actually help businesses? Explain you answer.
9. Why is it important for IT specialists and managers to understand business in addition to information technology?

10. **Ethical Considerations.** Is managing a business in ways that reflect society's core values always ethical? Explain your answer.

Questions for Application

11. How will you be able to apply your experience as a consumer of educational services to the challenges you'll face in your career after graduation?
12. What are some of the ways a company in the health-care industry could improve its long-term planning by studying population trends?
13. Identify at least five ways in which your life would be different without digital technology. Would it be more or less enjoyable? More or less productive?
14. Identify three ways in which the principles of professionalism described in this chapter can make you a more successful student.

> **Test Your Knowledge**
>
> Fourteen carefully selected questions help you review information, analyze implications, and apply concepts.

Practice Your Knowledge

Sharpening Your Communication Skills

Select a local service business where you have been a customer. How does that business try to gain a competitive advantage in the marketplace? Write a brief summary describing whether the company competes on speed, quality, price, innovation, service, or a combination of those attributes. Be prepared to present your analysis to your classmates.

Building Your Team Skills

In teams assigned by your instructor, each member will first identify one career path (such as marketing or accounting) that he or she might like to pursue after graduation and share that choice with the rest of the team. Each team member will then research the others' career options to find at least one significant factor, positive or negative, that could affect someone entering that career. For example, if there are four people on your team, you will research the three careers identified by your three teammates. After the research is complete, convene an in-person or online meeting to give each member of the team an informal career counseling session based on the research findings.

> **Practice Your Knowledge**
>
> - **Sharpening Your Communication Skills:** Communication skills are one of the top concerns among today's hiring managers; this exercise lets you practice listening, writing, and speaking in a variety of real-life scenarios.
> - **Building Your Team Skills:** Teaches important team skills, such as brainstorming, collaborative decision making, developing a consensus, debating, role playing, and resolving conflict.

Expand Your Knowledge

Discovering Career Opportunities

Your college's career center offers numerous resources to help you launch your career. Imagine that you write a blog for students at your college, and you want to introduce them to the center's services. Write a blog post of 300 to 400 words, summarizing what the center can do for students.

Developing Your Research Skills

Gaining a competitive advantage in today's marketplace is critical to a company's success. Research any company that sounds interesting to you and identify the steps it has taken to create competitive advantages for individual products or the company as a whole.

1. What goods or services does the company manufacture or sell?
2. How does the company set its goods or services apart from those of its competitors? Does the company compete on price, quality, service, innovation, or some other attribute?
3. How do the company's customer communication efforts convey those competitive advantages?

Improving Your Tech Insights: Digital Products

The category of digital products encompasses an extremely broad range of product types, from e-books to music and movie files to software and instruction sets for automated machinery. Digital products are commonplace these days, but the ability to remotely deliver product value is quite a staggering concept when you think about it. (As just one example, consider that a single iPod or other digital music player can carry the equivalent of two or three thousand tapes or CDs.)

Supplying music over the Internet is amazing enough, but nowadays even *tangible* products can be delivered electronically: The technology that deposits layers of ink in inkjet printers is being adapted to deposit layers of other liquefied materials, including plastics and metals. Called *3D printing*, *inkjet fabrication*, or *additive fabrication*, this technology is already being used to "print" product prototypes and simple electronic components. As the price of the technology continues to drop, it's not too far-fetched to imagine a day when you'll be able to download product description files from the Internet and fabricate physical items right on your own home "printer." For more about this technology, visit Dimension 3D Printing (www.dimensionprinting.com), Stratasys (www.stratasys.com), or Z Corporation (www.zcorp.com).

Choose a category of products that has been changed dramatically by the ability to deliver value digitally. In a brief e-mail message to your instructor, explain how digital technology revolutionized this market segment.[14]

Video Discussion

Access the Chapter 1 video discussion in the End of Chapter Assignments section at www.mybizlab.com.

> **Expand Your Knowledge**
>
> - **Discovering Career Opportunities:** Gives you the opportunity to explore career resources on campus, observe businesspeople on their jobs, interview businesspeople, and perform self-evaluations to assess your career skills and interests.
> - **Developing Your Research Skills:** Familiarizes you with a wide variety of business reference material and offers practice in developing research skills.
> - **Improving Your Tech Insights:** Introduces you to such revolutionary developments as nanotechnology, location and tracking technologies, and assistive technologies for people with disabilities.

Additional Learning Resources

Study Guide

The study guide includes a chapter outline, review questions, and study quizzes. Suggested answers to the review questions and quizzes are included.

CourseSmart eTextbook

CourseSmart Textbooks Online is an exciting new choice for students looking to save money. As an alternative to purchasing the print textbook, you can subscribe to the same content online and save up to 50% off the suggested list price of the print text. With a CourseSmart eTextbook, you can search the text, make notes online, print out reading assignments that incorporate lecture notes, and bookmark important passages for later review. For more information, or to subscribe to the CourseSmart eTextbook, visit www .coursesmart.com.

"Learn More" Multimedia Elements

The unique Real-Time Updates "Learn More" media elements connect you with dozens of handpicked videos, podcasts, and other items that complement chapter content. Simply follow the link to the "Learn More" webpage and click on the item of interest.

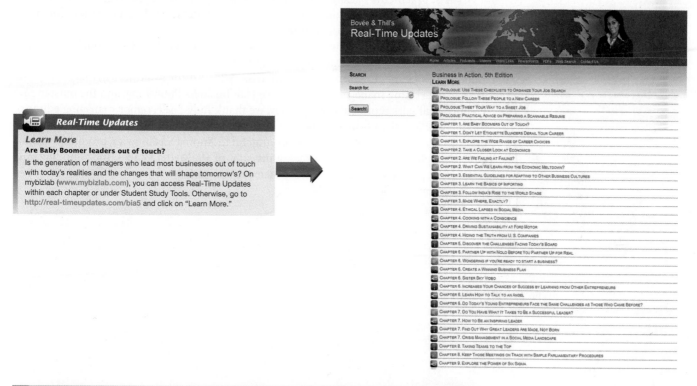

Feedback

The authors and the product team would appreciate hearing from you! Let us know what you think about this textbook by writing to college_marketing@prenhall.com. Please include "Feedback about Bovee/Thill BIA 5e" in the subject line.

If you have questions related to this product, please contact our customer service department online at www.247.prenhall.com.

About the Authors

Courtland L. Bovée and John V. Thill have been leading textbook authors for more than two decades, introducing millions of students to the fields of business and business communication. Their award-winning texts are distinguished by proven pedagogical features, extensive selections of contemporary case studies, hundreds of real-life examples, engaging writing, thorough research, and the unique integration of print and electronic resources. Each new edition reflects the authors' commitment to continuous refinement and improvement, particularly in terms of modeling the latest practices in business and the use of technology.

Professor Bovée has 22 years of teaching experience at Grossmont College in San Diego, where he has received teaching honors and was accorded that institution's C. Allen Paul Distinguished Chair. Mr. Thill is a prominent business consultant who has worked with organizations ranging from Fortune 500 multinationals to entrepreneurial start-ups. He formerly held positions with Pacific Bell and Texaco.

Acknowledgments

A very special acknowledgment goes to George Dovel, whose superb writing and editing skills, distinguished background, and wealth of business experience assured this project of clarity and completeness. Also, we recognize and thank Jackie Estrada for her outstanding skills and excellent attention to details. Jill Gardner's attention to detail improved the quality of the text throughout.

The supplements package for *Business in Action* has benefited from the able contributions of numerous individuals. We would like to express our thanks to them for creating a superb set of instructional supplements.

We want to extend our warmest appreciation to the devoted professionals at Prentice Hall. They include Jerome Grant, president; Sally Yagan, publisher; Eric Svendsen, editor-in-chief; James Heine, executive editor; Melissa Arlio, editorial project manager; Maggie Moylan, marketing manager; all of Prentice Hall Business Publishing; and the outstanding Prentice Hall sales representatives. Finally, we thank Judy Leale, senior managing editor of production; Jonathan Boylan, senior art director; and Lynne Breitfeller, production project manager, for their dedication; and we are grateful to Andrea Stefanowicz, production editor at GGS Higher Education Resources, a division of PreMedia Global, Inc.; and Suzanne DeWorken, permissions supervisor, for their superb work.

Courtland L. Bovée
John V. Thill

Real-Time Updates—Learn More

"Learn More" is a unique feature you will see strategically located throughout the text, connecting you with dozens of carefully screened online media. These elements, categorized by the icons shown below representing podcasts, PDFs, articles, videos, and PowerPoints, complement the text's coverage by providing contemporary examples and valuable insights from successful professionals.

Prologue

Your Future in Business Starts Right Now

You might not be thinking about your long-term career path as you dive into this business course, but this is actually the perfect time to start planning and preparing. Even though you may not have decided which area of business interests you the most, it's never too early to start accumulating the skills, experiences, and insights that will give you a competitive advantage when it's time to enter (or reenter) the business job market. By thinking ahead about the qualifications you'd like to have on your résumé when you graduate, you can select courses, seek out part-time employment and internship opportunities, and pursue extracurricular activities that will give you the professional profile that top employers look for.

This Prologue offers an overview of all the steps you'll need to take as you research, plan, and prepare for the job search process. First, you'll answer some questions that will help you figure out just what you'd like to do in the world of business. The two sections following that offer up-to-date advice on preparing your résumé and getting ready for job interviews. The final section offers some tips on keeping your career momentum going after you join the workforce.

Looking Ahead to Your Career

Finding the right job at every stage of your career is a lifelong process of seeking the best fit between what you want to do and what employers are willing to pay you to do. For instance, if money is more important to you than anything else, you can certainly pursue jobs that promise high pay; just be aware that most of these jobs require years of experience, and many produce a lot of stress, require frequent travel, or have other drawbacks you'll want to consider. In contrast, if location, lifestyle, intriguing work, or other factors are more important to you, you may well have to sacrifice some level of pay to achieve them. The important thing is to know what you want to do, what you have to offer, and how to make yourself more attractive to employers.

What Do You Want to Do?

Economic necessities and the vagaries of the marketplace will influence much of what happens in your career, of course; nevertheless, it's wise to start your employment search by examining your own values and interests. Identify what you want to do first, then see whether you can find a position that satisfies you at a personal level while also meeting your financial needs.

- **What would you like to do every day?** Research occupations that interest you. Find out what people really do every day. Ask friends, relatives, or alumni from your school. Read interviews with people in various professions to get a sense for what their careers are like.

- **How would you like to work?** Consider how much independence you want on the job, how much variety you like, and whether you prefer to work with products, machines, people, ideas, figures, or some combination thereof. Are you looking for constant change or a predictable role?

- **What specific compensation do you expect?** What do you hope to earn in your first year? What's your ultimate earnings goal? Are you willing to settle for less money in order to do something you really love?

- **Can you establish some general career goals?** Consider where you'd like to start, where you'd like to go from there, and the ultimate position you'd like to attain.

- **What size company would you prefer?** Do you like the idea of working for a small, entrepreneurial operation or a large corporation?

- **What sort of corporate culture are you most comfortable with?** Would you be happy in a formal hierarchy with clear reporting relationships? Or do you prefer less structure? Do you like a competitive environment or one that emphasizes teamwork?

- **What location would you like?** Would you like to work in a city, a suburb, a small town, an industrial area, or an uptown setting? Do you favor a particular part of the country? Another country?

Filling out the assessment in Exhibit 1 might help you get a clearer picture of the nature of work you would like to pursue in your career.

What Do You Have to Offer?

Knowing what you *want* to do is one thing. Knowing what you *can* do is another. You may already have a good idea of what you can offer employers. If not, some brainstorming can help you identify your skills, interests, and characteristics. Start by jotting down 10 achievements and contributions you're proud of, such as creating a website, tutoring a child, or editing your school paper. Think carefully about what specific skills these achievements demanded of you. For example, leadership skills, speaking ability, and artistic talent may have helped you coordinate a winning presentation to your school's administration. As you analyze your achievements, you'll begin to recognize a pattern of skills. Which of them might be valuable to potential employers?

Next, look at your educational preparation, work experience, and extracurricular activities. What do your knowledge and experience qualify you to do? What have you learned from volunteer work or class projects that could benefit you on the job? Have you held any offices, won any awards or scholarships, or mastered a second language?

Take stock of your personal characteristics. Are you aggressive, a born leader? Or would you rather follow? Are you outgoing, articulate, great with people? Or do you prefer working alone? Make a list of what you believe are your four or five most important qualities. Ask a relative or friend to rate your traits as well.

If you're having difficulty figuring out your interests, characteristics, or capabilities, consult your college placement office. Many campuses administer a variety of tests to help you identify interests, aptitudes, and personality traits. These tests won't reveal your "perfect" job, but they'll help you focus on the types of work best suited to your personality.

How Can You Make Yourself More Valuable?

While you're figuring out what you want from a job and what you can offer an employer, you can take positive steps toward actually building your career. You can do a lot before you graduate from college and even while you are seeking employment:

- **Keep an employment portfolio.** Collect anything that shows your ability to perform, whether it's in school, on the job, or in other venues. Your portfolio is a great resource

ACTIVITY OR SITUATION	STRONGLY AGREE	AGREE	DISAGREE	NO PREFERENCE
1. I want to work independently.				
2. I want variety in my work.				
3. I want to work with people.				
4. I want to work with technology.				
5. I want physical work.				
6. I want mental work.				
7. I want to work for a large organization.				
8. I want to work for a nonprofit organization.				
9. I want to work for a small family business.				
10. I want to work for a service business.				
11. I want to start or buy a business someday.				
12. I want regular, predictable work hours.				
13. I want to work in a city location.				
14. I want to work in a small town or suburb.				
15. I want to work in another country.				
16. I want to work outdoors.				
17. I want to work in a structured environment.				
18. I want to avoid risk as much as possible.				
19. I want to enjoy my work, even if that means making less money.				
20. I want to become a high-level corporate manager.				

EXHIBIT I

Career Self-Assessment

What work-related activities and situations do you prefer? Evaluate your preferences in each of these areas and use the results to help guide your job search.

for writing your résumé, and it gives employers tangible evidence of your professionalism. An *e-portfolio* is a multimedia presentation of your skills and experiences (see Exhibit 2).[1] Think of it as a website that contains your résumé, work samples, letters of recommendation, articles you may have written, and other information about you and your skills. Be creative. For example, a student who was pursuing a degree in meteorology added a video clip of himself delivering a weather forecast.[2] The portfolio can be burned on a CD-ROM for physical distribution or, more commonly, posted online—whether it's a personal website, your college's site (if student pages are available), or a networking site such as www.collegegrad.com or www.creativeshake.com.

EXHIBIT 2

Professional Portfolio

Erik Jonsson, a digital media designer, uses e-portfolio services such as Behance.net (www.behance .net/erikj) to display samples of his work. Potential clients or business partners can click on the images shown here to learn more about each project. No matter what your intended profession or level of experience, you can use an e-portfolio to help potential employers learn more about your skills and qualifications.

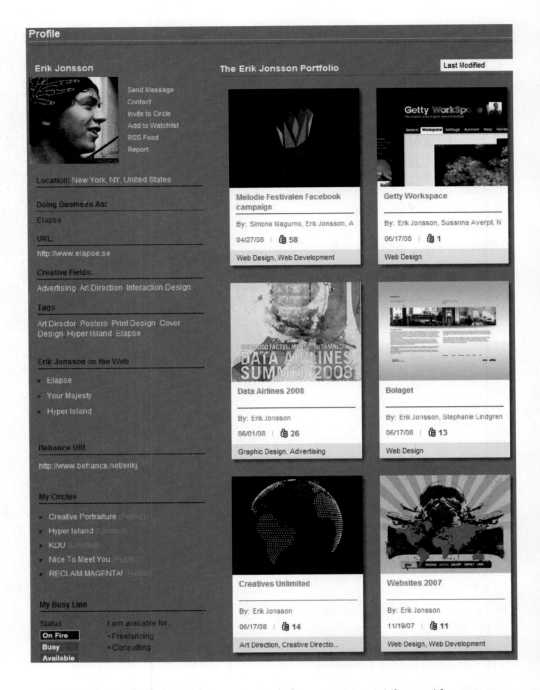

- **Take interim assignments.** As you search for a permanent job, consider temporary jobs, freelance work, or internships. These temporary assignments not only help you gain valuable experience and relevant contacts but also provide you with important references and with items for your portfolio.[3] Consider applying your talents to *crowdsourcing* projects, in which companies and nonprofit organizations invite the public to contribute solutions to various challenges. For example, Fellowforce (www.fellowforce.com) posts projects involving advertising, business writing, photography, graphic design, programming, strategy development, and other skills.[4] Even if your contributions aren't chosen, you still have solutions to real business problems that you can show to potential employers as examples of your work. You can also find freelance projects on Craigslist (www.craigslist.org) and numerous other websites; some of these pay only nominal fees but do provide the opportunity to display your skills.

- **Learn more about the industry or industries in which you want to work.** Join networks of professional colleagues and friends who can help you keep up with trends and events. Many professional societies have student chapters or offer students discounted memberships. Take courses and pursue other educational or life experiences that would be hard to get while working full-time. Identify insightful and influential bloggers who cover industries and professions that interest you.

- **Continue to polish and update your skills.** Join networks of professional colleagues and friends who can help you keep up with your occupation and industry. Many professional societies have student chapters or offer students discounted memberships. Take courses and pursue other educational or life experiences that would be hard to get while working full-time.

Seeking Employment Opportunities and Information

Whether your major is business, biology, or political science, once you know what you want and what you have to offer, you can start finding an employer to match. If you haven't already committed yourself to any particular career field, review the career overviews in the *Occupational Outlook Handbook*, a nationally recognized source of career information published by the U.S. Bureau of Labor Statistics. Revised every two years, the handbook (available in print and online at www.bls.gov/oco) describes what workers do on the job, working conditions, the training and education needed, earnings, and expected job prospects in a wide range of occupations.[5] "Exploring Careers in Business" in Chapter 1 offers a brief introduction to the major career areas in business (see page 64).

Staying Abreast of Business and Financial News

Thanks to the Internet, staying on top of business news is easy today. In fact, your biggest challenge will be selecting new material from the many available sources. To help you get started, here is a selection of periodical websites that offer business news (in some cases, you need to be a subscriber to access all of the material, including archives):

- *Wall Street Journal:* http://online.wsj.com/public/us
- *New York Times:* www.nyt.com
- *BusinessWeek:* www.businessweek.com
- *Business 2.0:* http://money.cnn.com/magazines/business2
- *Fast Company:* www.fastcompany.com
- *Fortune:* http://money.cnn.com/magazines/fortune
- *Forbes:* www.forbes.com

In addition, thousands of bloggers and podcasters offer news and commentary on the business world. To identify some that you might find helpful, start with directories such as Technorati (www.technorati.com/blogs/tag/business) for blogs or Podcast Alley (www.podcastalley.com; select the "Business" genre) for podcasts. AllTop (http://alltop.com) is another good resource for finding people who write about topics that interest you. For all these online resources, use a newsfeed aggregator to select the type of stories you're interested in and have them delivered to your screen automatically.

Twitter has also become a great resource for business news, job leads, and other employment-related information. Using services such as TweepSearch (http://tweepsearch.com) or Just Tweet It (http://justtweetit.com), you can find Twitter users who specialize in your industry or profession.

Of course, with all the business information available today, it's easy to get lost in the details. Try not to get too caught up in the daily particulars of business. Start by examining "big picture" topics—trends, issues, industry-wide challenges, and careers—before delving into specific companies that look attractive.

Most companies, even small firms, offer at least basic information about themselves on their websites. Look for the "About Us" or "Company" part of the site to find a company profile, executive biographies, press releases, financial information, and information on employment opportunities. Any company's website is going to present the firm in the most positive light possible, of course, so look for outside sources as well, including the business sections of local newspapers and trade publications that cover the company's industries and markets.

Don't limit your research to easily available sources, however. Companies are likely to be impressed by creative research, such as interviewing their customers to learn more about how the firm does business. "Detailed research, including talking to our customers, is so rare it will almost guarantee you get hired," explains the recruiting manager at Alcon Laboratories.[6]

Exhibit 3 lists some of the many websites where you can learn more about companies and find job openings. Start with The Riley Guide, www.rileyguide.com, which offers links to hundreds of specialized websites that post openings in specific industries and professions. Your college's career center placement office probably maintains an up-to-date list as well.

Networking

Networking is the process of making informal connections with mutually beneficial business contacts. Networking takes place wherever and whenever people talk: at industry functions, at social gatherings, at sports events and recreational activities, at alumni reunions, and so on. Social networks, including Facebook, www.facebook.com, and business-oriented websites such as www.linkedin.com, www.ryze.com, and www.spoke.com, have become powerful networking resources. Read news sites, blogs, and other online sources. Follow industry leaders on Twitter or on *lifestreaming* sites, which integrate a person's text, audio, and video content from multiple social networking tools. Participate in student business organizations, especially those with ties to professional organizations. Visit *trade shows* to learn about various industries and rub shoulders with people who work in those industries.[7] Don't overlook volunteering; you not only meet people but also demonstrate your ability to solve problems, plan projects, and so on. You can do some good while creating a network for yourself.

Remember that networking is about people helping each other, not just about other people helping you. Pay close attention to networking etiquette: Try to learn something about the people you want to connect with, don't overwhelm others with too many messages or requests, be succinct in all your communication efforts, don't give out other people's names and contact information without their permission to do so, never e-mail your résumé to complete strangers, and remember to say thank you every time someone helps you.[8]

To become a valued network member, you need to be able to help others in some way. You may not have any influential contacts yet, but because you're actively researching a number of industries and trends in your own job search, you probably have valuable information you can share. Or you might simply be able to connect one person with another who can help. The more you network, the more valuable you become in your network—and the more valuable your network becomes to you.

WEBSITE*	URL	HIGHLIGHTS
Riley Guide	www.rileyguide.com	Vast collection of links to both general and specialized job sites for every career imaginable; don't miss this one—it'll save you hours and hours of searching
College Recruiter.com	www.collegerecruiter.com	Focused on opportunities for graduates with less than three years of work experience
Monster	www.monster.com	One of the most popular job sites, with hundreds of thousands of openings, many from hard-to-find small companies; extensive collection of advice on the job search process
Monster Trak	www.monstertrak.com	Focused on job searches for new college grads; your school's career center site probably links here
Yahoo! Hotjobs	http://hotjobs.yahoo.com	Another leading job board; like Monster and CareerBuilder, offers extensive advice for job seekers
CareerBuilder	www.careerbuilder.com	One of the largest job boards; affiliated with more than 150 newspapers around the country
Jobster	www.jobster.com	Uses social networking to link employers with job seekers
USAJOBS	www.usajobs.opm.gov	The official job search site for the U.S. government, featuring everything from jobs for economists to astronauts to border patrol agents
IMDiversity	www.imdiversity.com	Good resource on diversity in the workplace, with job postings from companies that have made a special commitment to promoting diversity in their workforces
Dice.com	www.dice.com	One of the best sites for high-technology jobs
Net-Temps	www.nettemps.com	Popular site for contractors and freelancers looking for short-term assignments
WetFeet	www.wetfeet.com	Posts listings from companies looking for interns in a wide variety of professions
Simply Hired Indeed	www.simplyhired.com www.indeed.com	Specialized search engines that look for job postings on hundreds of websites worldwide; they find many postings that aren't listed on job board sites such as Monster

EXHIBIT 3

Job Search Resources
Use these helpful sites to gather information for your job search and find interesting career opportunities.

*Note: This list represents only a small fraction of the hundreds of job-posting sites and other resources available online; be sure to check with your college's career center for the latest information.

Real-Time Updates

Learn More
Tweet your way to a sweet job

This simple introduction to Twitter focuses on using the microblogging service for career networking. On mybizlab (www.mybizlab.com), you can access Real-Time Updates within each chapter or under Student Study Tools. Otherwise, go to http://real-timeupdates.com/bia5 and click on "Learn More."

Real-Time Updates

Learn More
Follow these people to a new career

Alison Doyle maintains a great list of career experts to follow on Twitter. On mybizlab (www.mybizlab.com), you can access Real-Time Updates within each chapter or under Student Study Tools. Otherwise, go to http://real-timeupdates.com/bia5 and click on "Learn More."

Seeking Career Counseling

Your college's career center probably offers a wide variety of services, including individual counseling, job fairs, on-campus interviews, and job listings. Counselors can give you advice on résumé-writing software and provide workshops in job search techniques, résumé preparation, job readiness training, interview techniques, self-marketing, and more.[9] You can also find career planning advice online. Many of the websites listed in Exhibit 3 offer articles and online tests to help you choose a career path, identify essential skills, and prepare to enter the job market.

Preparing Your Résumé

A **résumé** is a structured, written summary of a person's education, employment background, and job qualifications. Although many people have misconceptions about résumés (see Exhibit 4), the fact is that a résumé is a form of advertising. It is intended to stimulate an employer's interest in you—in meeting you and learning more about you. A successful résumé inspires a prospective employer to invite you to interview with the company. Thus, your purpose in writing your résumé is to create interest—*not* to tell readers every little detail.[10]

Your résumé is one of the most important documents you'll ever write. You can help ensure success by remembering four things: First, treat your résumé with the respect it deserves. A single mistake or oversight can cost you interview opportunities. Second, give yourself plenty of time. Don't put off preparing your résumé until the last second and then try to write it in one sitting. Try out different ideas and phrases until you hit on the right combination. Also, give yourself plenty of time to proofread the résumé when you're finished—and ask several other people to proofread it as well. Third, learn from

Career fairs give companies the chance to meet potential employees—and for you to learn more about career opportunities.

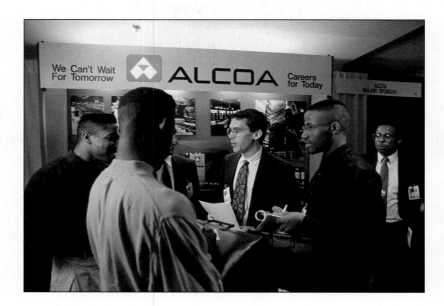

FALLACY	FACT
The purpose of a résumé is to list all your skills and abilities.	The purpose of a résumé is to kindle employer interest and generate an interview.
A good résumé will get you the job you want.	All a résumé can do is get you in the door.
Your résumé will always be read carefully and thoroughly.	In most cases, your résumé needs to make a positive impression within 30 or 45 seconds; only then will someone read it in detail. Moreover, it may be screened by a computer looking for keywords first—and if it doesn't contain the right keywords, a human being may never see it.
The more good information you present about yourself in your résumé, the better, so stuff your résumé with every positive detail you can think of.	Recruiters don't need that much information about you at the initial screening stage, and they probably won't read it.
If you want a really good résumé, have it prepared by a résumé service.	You have the skills needed to prepare an effective résumé, so prepare it yourself—unless the position is especially high level or specialized. Even then, you should check carefully before using a service.

EXHIBIT 4

Fallacies and Facts About Résumés

Some people incorrectly believe that a good résumé will get them the job they want; the real purpose of a résumé is to secure an invitation to a job interview.

good models. You can find thousands of sample résumés online at college websites and job sites such as Monster.com. Fourth, don't get frustrated by the conflicting advice you'll read about résumés; they are more art than science. Consider the alternatives and choose the approach that makes the most sense in your specific situation.

By the way, if anyone asks to see your "CV," they're referring to your *curriculum vitae*, the term used instead of *résumé* in some professions and in many countries outside the United States. Résumés and CVs are essentially the same, although CVs can be more detailed. If you need to adapt a U.S.-style résumé to CV format, or vice versa, Monster.com has helpful guidelines on the subject.

Gathering Pertinent Information

If you haven't been building an employment portfolio thus far, you may need to do some research on yourself at this point. Gather all the pertinent personal history you can think of, including all the specific dates, duties, and accomplishments of any previous jobs you've held. Collect every piece of relevant educational experience that adds to your qualifications—formal degrees, skills certificates, academic awards, or scholarships. Also, gather any relevant information about personal endeavors: dates of your membership in an association, offices you may have held in a club or professional organization, any presentations you might have given to a community group. You probably won't use every piece of information you come up with, but you'll want to have it at your fingertips before you begin composing your résumé.

Selecting the Best Medium

Selecting the medium for your résumé used to be a simple matter: it was typed on paper. These days, though, your job search might involve various forms, including an uploadable Word document, a plain-text document that you paste into an online form, or a multimedia résumé that is part of your online e-portfolio. Explore all your options and choose those that (a) meet the requirements of target employers and (b) allow you to present yourself in a compelling fashion. For instance, if you're applying for a sales position, in which your personal communication skills would be a strong point, a video podcast showing you making a sales presentation (even a mock presentation) could be a strong persuader.

No matter how many media you eventually use, it's always a good idea to prepare a basic paper résumé and keep copies on hand. You'll never know when someone might ask for it, and not all employers want to bother with electronic media when all they want to know is your basic profile. In addition, starting with a traditional paper résumé is a great way to organize your background information and identify your unique strengths.

Keeping Your Résumé Honest

Somehow, the idea that "everybody lies on their résumés" has crept into popular consciousness, and dishonesty in the job search process has reached epidemic proportions. Estimates vary about just how bad the problem is, but one comprehensive study uncovered lies about work history in more than 40 percent of the résumés tested.[11] And it's not just the simple fudging of facts here and there. Dishonest applicants are getting bolder all the time—going so far as to buy fake diplomas online, pay computer hackers to insert their names into prestigious universities' graduation records, and sign up for services that offer phony employment verification.[12]

Applicants with integrity know they don't need to stoop to lying to compete in the job market. If you are tempted to stretch the truth, bear in mind that professional recruiters have seen every trick in the book, and employers who are fed up with the dishonesty are getting more aggressive at uncovering the truth. Nearly all employers do some form of background checking, from contacting references to verifying employment to checking for criminal records. In addition to using their own resources, U.S. companies now spend more than $2 billion each year on outside services that specialize in verifying résumés and application information.[13] Employers are also beginning to craft certain interview questions specifically to uncover dishonest résumé entries.[14]

More than 90 percent of companies that find lies on résumés refuse to hire the offending applicants, even if that means withdrawing formal job offers.[15] And even if you do sneak past these filters and get hired, you'll probably be exposed on the job when you can't live up to your own résumé. Résumé fabrications have been known to catch up to people many years into their careers, with embarrassing consequences. Given the networked nature of today's job market, lying on a résumé could haunt you for years—and you could be forced to keep lying throughout your career to hide the original misrepresentations on your résumé.[16]

If you're not sure whether to include or exclude a particular point, ask yourself this: Would you be willing to say the same thing to an interviewer in person? If not, don't say it in your résumé. Keep your résumé honest so that it represents who you really are and leads you toward jobs that are truly right for you.

Organizing Your Résumé Around Your Strengths

Organize your résumé to highlight several qualities employers seek: that you (1) think in terms of results, (2) know how to get things done, (3) are well rounded, (4) show signs of career progress and professional development, (5) have personal standards of excellence, (6) are flexible and willing to try new things, and (7) communicate effectively.

In each category, align your career objectives with the needs of your target employers, without distorting or misrepresenting the facts.[17] If you have any significant weaknesses in your history, here are some common problems and quick suggestions for overcoming them:[18]

- **Frequent job changes or contracting assignments.** Group similar jobs and contracts under a single heading. If past job positions were eliminated as a result of layoffs or mergers, find a subtle way to convey that information (if not in your résumé, then in your cover letter).

- **Gaps in work history.** Mention relevant experience and education you gained during employment gaps, such as volunteer or community work. If gaps are due to personal circumstances such as injuries, illness, or caring for a relative, you can use a cover letter to offer honest but general explanations about your absences ("I had serious health concerns and had to take time off to fully recover").

- **Inexperience.** Mention related volunteer work. List relevant course work and internships. If appropriate, offer hiring incentives such as "willing to work nights and weekends."

- **Overqualification.** Tone down your résumé, focusing exclusively on the experience and skills that relate to the position.

- **Long-term employment with one company.** Itemize each position held at the firm to show career progress with increasing responsibilities.

- **Job termination for cause.** Be honest with interviewers. Show that you're a hard-working employee and counter their concerns with proof, such as recommendations and examples of completed projects.

- **Criminal record.** You don't necessarily need to disclose on your résumé a criminal record or time spent incarcerated, but you may be asked about it on a job application form. Laws regarding what employers may ask (and whether they can conduct a criminal background check) vary by state and profession, but if you are asked and the question applies to you, you must answer truthfully, or you risk being terminated later if the employer finds out. Use the interview process to explain any mitigating circumstances and to emphasize your rehabilitation and commitment to being a law-abiding, trustworthy employee.[19]

To focus attention on your strongest points, adopt the appropriate organizational approach for your résumé, based on your background and your goals.

The Chronological Résumé

In a **chronological résumé**, the work-experience section dominates and is placed in the most prominent slot, immediately after the name and address and optional objective. You develop this section by listing your jobs sequentially in reverse order, beginning with the most recent position and working backward toward earlier jobs. Under each listing, describe your responsibilities and accomplishments, giving the most space to the most recent positions. If you're just graduating from college with limited professional experience, you can vary this chronological approach by putting your educational qualifications before your experience, thereby focusing attention on your academic credentials.

The chronological approach is the most common way to organize a résumé, and many employers prefer it. This approach has three key advantages: (1) Employers are familiar with it and can easily find information, (2) it highlights growth and career progression, and (3) it highlights employment continuity and stability.[20] Korn/Ferry International's Robert Nesbit speaks for many recruiters: "Unless you have a really compelling reason, don't use any but the standard chronological format. Your résumé should not read like a treasure map, full of minute clues to the whereabouts of your jobs and experience. I want to be able to grasp quickly where a candidate has worked, how long, and in what capacities."[21]

The chronological approach is especially appropriate if you have a strong employment history and are aiming for a job that builds on your current career path (see Exhibit 5).

The Functional Résumé

A **functional résumé**, sometimes called a *skills résumé*, emphasizes your skills and capabilities, identifying employers and academic experience in subordinate sections. This pattern stresses individual areas of competence, so it's useful for people who are just entering the job market, want to redirect their careers, or have little continuous career-related

EXHIBIT 5 Chronological Résumé

Roberto Cortez calls attention to his most recent achievements by setting them off in list form with bullets. The section titled "Intercultural and Technical Skills" emphasizes his international background, fluency in Spanish and German, and extensive computer skills—all of which are important qualifications for his target position.

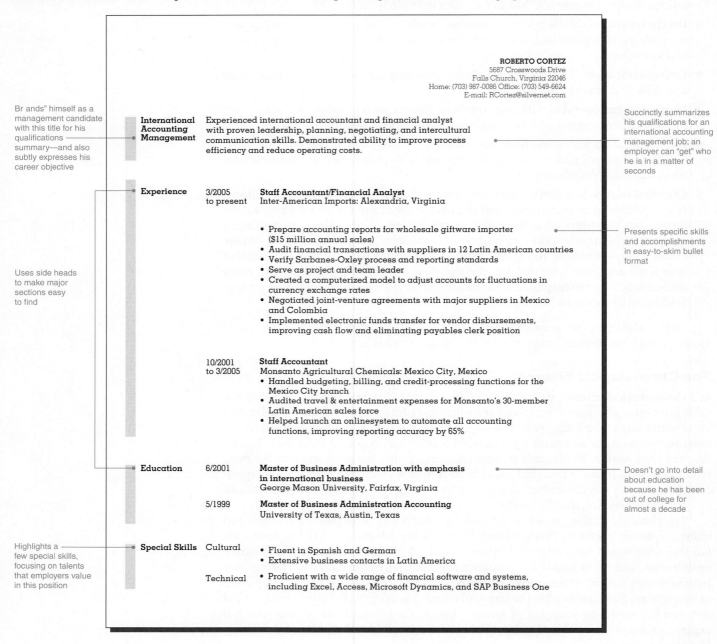

Br ands" himself as a management candidate with this title for his qualifications summary—and also subtly expresses his career objective

Uses side heads to make major sections easy to find

Highlights a few special skills, focusing on talents that employers value in this position

Succinctly summarizes his qualifications for an international accounting management job; an employer can "get" who he is in a matter of seconds

Presents specific skills and accomplishments in easy-to-skim bullet format

Doesn't go into detail about education because he has been out of college for almost a decade

ROBERTO CORTEZ
5687 Crosswoods Drive
Falls Church, Virginia 22046
Home: (703) 987-0086 Office: (703) 549-6624
E-mail: RCortez@silvernet.com

International Accounting Management

Experienced international accountant and financial analyst with proven leadership, planning, negotiating, and intercultural communication skills. Demonstrated ability to improve process efficiency and reduce operating costs.

Experience

3/2005 to present — **Staff Accountant/Financial Analyst**
Inter-American Imports: Alexandria, Virginia

- Prepare accounting reports for wholesale giftware importer ($15 million annual sales)
- Audit financial transactions with suppliers in 12 Latin American countries
- Verify Sarbanes-Oxley process and reporting standards
- Serve as project and team leader
- Created a computerized model to adjust accounts for fluctuations in currency exchange rates
- Negotiated joint-venture agreements with major suppliers in Mexico and Colombia
- Implemented electronic funds transfer for vendor disbursements, improving cash flow and eliminating payables clerk position

10/2001 to 3/2005 — **Staff Accountant**
Monsanto Agricultural Chemicals: Mexico City, Mexico
- Handled budgeting, billing, and credit-processing functions for the Mexico City branch
- Audited travel & entertainment expenses for Monsanto's 30-member Latin American sales force
- Helped launch an onlinesystem to automate all accounting functions, improving reporting accuracy by 65%

Education

6/2001 — **Master of Business Administration with emphasis in international business**
George Mason University, Fairfax, Virginia

5/1999 — **Master of Business Administration Accounting**
University of Texas, Austin, Texas

Special Skills

Cultural
- Fluent in Spanish and German
- Extensive business contacts in Latin America

Technical
- Proficient with a wide range of financial software and systems, including Excel, Access, Microsoft Dynamics, and SAP Business One

experience. The functional approach also has three advantages: (1) Without having to read through job descriptions, employers can see what you can do for them, (2) you can emphasize earlier job experience, and (3) you can deemphasize any lack of career progress or lengthy unemployment. However, you should be aware that not all employers like the functional résumé, perhaps partly because it can obscure your work history and partly because it's less common. In any event, many seasoned employment professionals are suspicious of this résumé style, and some assume that candidates who use it are trying to hide something. In fact, Monster.com lists the functional résumé as one of employers' "Top 10 Pet Peeves."[22] If you don't have a strong, uninterrupted history of relevant work, the combination résumé might be a better choice.

The Combination Résumé

A **combination résumé** includes the best features of the chronological and functional approaches. Nevertheless, it is not commonly used, and it has two major disadvantages: (1) It tends to be longer, and (2) it can be repetitious if you have to list your accomplishments and skills in both the functional section and the chronological job descriptions.[23]

Producing Your Résumé

With less than a minute to make a good impression, your résumé needs to look sharp and grab a recruiter's interest in the first few lines. A typical recruiter devotes 45 seconds to each résumé before tossing it into either the "maybe" or the "reject" pile. Few recruiters read every résumé from top to bottom; most give them a quick glance to look for key words and accomplishments. If yours doesn't stand out—or stands out in a negative way—chances are a recruiter won't look at it long enough to judge your qualifications.[24]

Good design is a must, and it's not hard to achieve. Good designs feature simplicity, order, plenty of white space, and straightforward typefaces such as Times Roman or Arial (keep in mind that many of the fonts on your computer are not appropriate for a résumé). Make your subheadings easy to find and easy to read, placing them either above each section or in the left margin. Use lists and leave plenty of white space. Color is not necessary by any means, but if you add color, make it subtle and sophisticated, such as in a thin horizontal line under your name and address. If any part of the design "jumps out at you," tone it down. An amateurish design could end your chances of getting an interview. As one experienced recruiter put it, "At our office, these résumés are rejected without even being read."[25]

Depending on the companies you apply to, you might want to produce your résumé in as many as six forms:

- **Printed traditional résumé.** Format your traditional résumé simply but elegantly to make the best impression on your employer. Naturally, printed versions must be delivered by hand or by mail.

- **Printed scannable résumé.** Prepare a printed version of your résumé that is unformatted and thus electronically scannable so that employers can store your information in their database.

- **Electronic plain-text file.** Create an electronic plain-text file to use when uploading your résumé information into web forms or inserting it into e-mail messages.

- **Microsoft Word file.** Keep a Microsoft Word file of your traditional résumé so that you can upload it on certain websites.

- **HTML format.** By creating an HTML version, you can post your résumé on your own website, on a page provided by your college, or on some of the many job board sites now available. (If you don't have HTML experience or other means to create an HTML version, you can save your résumé as a webpage from within Word. This method won't necessarily create the most spectacularly beautiful webpage, but it should be functional at least.)

- **PDF file.** This is an optional step, but a portable document format (PDF) file of your traditional résumé provides a simple, safe format to attach to e-mail messages. Creating a PDF version of your résumé is a simple procedure, but you need the right software. Adobe Acrobat (not the free Acrobat Reader) is the best known program, but many others are available, including some free versions. You can also use Adobe's online service at http://createpdf.adobe.com to create PDFs without buying software.

Some applicants also create PowerPoint presentations or videos to supplement a conventional résumé. Two key advantages of a PowerPoint supplement are flexibility and multimedia capabilities. For instance, you can present a menu of choices on the opening screen and allow viewers to click through to such items as a brief biography or images that document important accomplishments (such as screen shots of websites you designed).

A video résumé can be a compelling supplement as well, but videos are not without controversy. Some employment law experts advise employers not to view videos, at least not until after candidates have been evaluated solely on their credentials. The reason for this caution (which also applies to sending photographs with your résumé) is that seeing visual cues of the age, ethnicity, and gender of candidates early in the selection process exposes employers to complaints of discriminatory hiring practices. In addition, videos are more cumbersome to evaluate than paper or electronic résumés.[26]

Printing a Scannable Résumé

To cope with the flood of unsolicited paper résumés in recent years, many companies now optically scan incoming résumés into a database that hiring managers can search for attractive candidates. Whether they use simpler key word matching or sophisticated linguistic analysis, these system displays lists of possible candidates, each with a percentage score indicating how closely the résumé reflects a given position's requirements.[27] Nearly all large companies now use these systems, as do many midsized companies and even some smaller firms.[28]

The use of such scanning systems has important implications for your résumé. First, computers are interested only in matching information to search parameters, not in artistic attempts at résumé design. In fact, complex designs can cause errors in the scanning process. Second, *optical character recognition* (*OCR*) software doesn't technically "read" anything; it merely looks for shapes that match stored profiles of characters. If the OCR software can't make sense of your fancy fonts or creative page layout, it will enter gibberish into the database (for instance, your name might go in as "W>$..3r ?00!#" instead of "Walter Jones"). Third, even the most sophisticated databases cannot conduct a search with the nuance and intuition of an experienced human recruiter.

For job searchers, this situation creates two requirements for a successful scannable résumé: (1) Use a plain font and simplified design, and (2) compile a **key word summary** that lists all the terms that could help match your résumé to the right openings. Other than the key word summary, a scannable résumé contains the same information as your traditional résumé but is formatted to be OCR-friendly (see Exhibit 6):[29]

- Use a clean sans serif font such as Verdana or Arial and size it between 10 and 14 points.
- Make sure characters do not touch one another, including the slash (/).
- Don't use side-by-side columns.
- Don't use ampersands (&), percent signs (%), accented characters (such as é and ö), or bullet symbols (use a hyphen, not a lowercase *o*, in place of a bullet symbol).
- Put each phone number and e-mail address on its own line.
- Print on plain white paper.

Your scannable résumé will probably be longer than your traditional résumé because you can't compress text into columns and because you need plenty of white space between headings and sections. If your scannable résumé runs more than one page, make sure your name appears on every subsequent page (in case the pages become separated). Before sending a scannable résumé, check the company's website or call the human resources department to see whether it has any specific requirements other than those discussed here.

When adding a key word summary to your résumé, keep your audience in mind. Employers generally search for nouns (because verbs tend to be generic rather than

EXHIBIT 6 Scannable Résumé

This version of the chronological résumé from Exhibit 5 shows the changes necessary to ensure successful scanning. Notice that the résumé doesn't have any special characters, formatting, or design elements that are likely to confuse the scanning software.

Puts each contact element on its own line

ROBERTO CORTEZ
5687 Crosswoods Drive
Falls Church, Virginia 22046
Home: (703) 987-0086
Office: (703) 549-6624
E-mail: RCortez@silvernet.com

Adds a summary of keywords taken from job descriptions and industry publications

KEYWORDS

Financial executive, accounting management, international finance, financial analyst, accounting reports, financial audit, exchange rates, Sarbanes-Oxley, joint-venture agreements, budgets, billing, credit processing, MBA, fluent Spanish, fluent German, Microsoft Dynamics, SAP Business One, leadership, planning, negotiating, Latin America

Uses enough white space to ensure successful scanning, without worrying about a pleasing visual design

INTERNATIONAL ACCOUNTING MANAGEMENT

Experienced international accountant and financial analyst with proven leadership, planning, negotiating, and intercultural communication skills. Demonstrated ability to improve process efficiency and reduce operating costs.

EXPERIENCE

Staff Accountant Financial Analyst, Inter-American Imports, Alexandria, Virginia, March 2005 to present
- Prepare accounting reports for wholesale giftware importer ($15 million annual sales)
- Audit financial transactions with suppliers in 12 Latin American countries
- Verify Sarbanes-Oxley process and reporting standards
- Serve as project and team leader
- Created a computerized model to adjust accounts for fluctuations in currency exchange rates
- Negotiated joint-venture agreements with major suppliers in Mexico and Colombia
- Implemented electronic funds transfer for vendor disbursements, improving cash flow
   and eliminating payables clerk position

Uses a clean, scanner-friendly font

Removes slashes, bullet points, ampersands (&), and other characters that might confuse the OCR software

Staff Accountant, Monsanto Agricultural Chemicals, Mexico City, Mexico, October 2001 to March 2005
- Handled budgeting, billing, and credit-processing functions for the Mexico City branch
- Audited travel and entertainment expenses for Monsanto's 30-member Latin American sales force
- Helped launch an online system to automate all accounting functions, improving reporting accuracy by 65 percent

EDUCATION

Master of Business Administration with emphasis in international business, George Mason University, Fairfax, Virginia, June 2001
Bachelor of Business Administration, Accounting, University of Texas, Austin, Texas, May 1999

Simplifies layout by removing multiple-column format

CULTURAL SKILLS

- Fluent in Spanish and German
- Extensive business contacts in Latin America

TECHNICAL SKILLS

Proficient with a wide range of financial software and systems, including Excel, Access, Microsoft Dynamics, and SAP Business One

specific to a particular position or skill), so make your key words nouns as well. Use abbreviations sparingly and only when they are well-known and unambiguous, such as *MBA*. List 20 to 30 words and phrases that define your skills, experience, education, and professional affiliations as they relate to your target position (review job descriptions to find words most relevant to a given position.) Place this list right after your name and address. Note that you can also use your keywords as tags on your blog, social networking profile, or other elements of your online presence.[30]

One good way to identify which keywords to include in your summary is to find all the skills listed in ads for the types of jobs you're interested in. Another advantage of staying up to date with industry news and networking widely is that you'll develop a good ear for current terminology.

If you're tempted to toss in impressive keywords that don't really apply to you, don't. Increasingly sophisticated résumé analysis systems can now detect whether your keywords truly relate to the job descriptions and other information on your résumé. If a system suspects that you've padded your keyword list, it could move you to the bottom of the ranking or delete your résumé entirely.[31]

Creating a Plain-Text File of Your Résumé

Many employers now prefer to enter résumé information directly into their tracking systems through the use of electronic **plain-text versions** (sometimes referred to as *ASCII text versions*). If you have the option of mailing a scannable résumé or submitting plain text online, go with plain text because it is less prone to errors. Note that a plain-text version should include a keyword summary (see the previous section).

Plain text is just what it sounds like: no font formatting, no bullet symbols, no colors, no lines or boxes, and so on. A plain-text version is easy to create with your word processor. Start with the file you used to create your scannable résumé, use the "Save As" choice to save it as "plain text" or whichever similarly labeled option your software has, and verify the result by using a basic text editor (such as Microsoft Notepad). If necessary, reformat the page manually, moving text and inserting space as needed. For simplicity's sake, left-justify all your headings rather than try to center them manually.

Preparing Your Application Letter

Whenever you submit your résumé, accompany it with an *application letter* or *cover letter* to let readers know what you're sending, why you're sending it, and how they can benefit from reading it. (Application letters are sometimes called *cover letters*, and they can be either printed or e-mailed.) Start by researching the organization and then focus on your audience so that you can show you've done your homework. During your research, try to find out the name, title, and department of the person you're writing to. If you can't find a specific name, use something like "Dear Hiring Manager."[32]

Remember that your reader's in-box is probably overflowing with résumés and application letters, and respect his or her time. Avoid gimmicks and don't repeat information that already appears in your résumé. Keep your letter straightforward, fact based, short, upbeat, and professional (see Exhibit 7).

Following Up on Your Application

If your application letter and résumé fail to bring a response within a month or so, follow up with a second letter to keep your file active. This follow-up letter also gives you a chance to update your original application with any recent job-related information. Even if you've received a message acknowledging your application and saying that it will be kept on file, don't hesitate to send a follow-up letter three months later to show that you are still interested. Such a letter can demonstrate that you're sincerely interested in working for the organization, that you're persistent in pursuing your goals, and that you're upgrading your skills to make yourself a better employee. And it might just get you an interview.

Interviewing with Potential Employers

An **employment interview** is a formal meeting during which you and the prospective employer ask questions and exchange information. These meetings have a dual purpose: (1) The organization's main objective is to find the best person available for the job by

EXHIBIT 7 Application Letter

In this response to an online job posting, Dalton Smith highlights his qualifications while mirroring the requirements specified in the posting. Notice how he grabs attention immediately by letting the reader know that he is familiar with the company and the global transportation business.

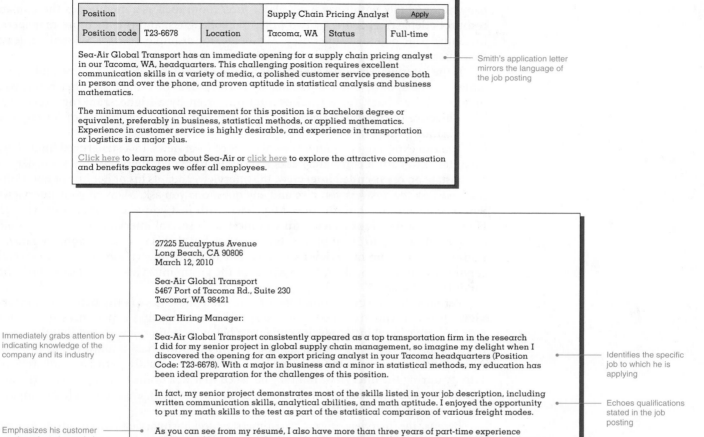

Position			Supply Chain Pricing Analyst		Apply
Position code	T23-6678	Location	Tacoma, WA	Status	Full-time

Sea-Air Global Transport has an immediate opening for a supply chain pricing analyst in our Tacoma, WA, headquarters. This challenging position requires excellent communication skills in a variety of media, a polished customer service presence both in person and over the phone, and proven aptitude in statistical analysis and business mathematics.

The minimum educational requirement for this position is a bachelors degree or equivalent, preferably in business, statistical methods, or applied mathematics. Experience in customer service is highly desirable, and experience in transportation or logistics is a major plus.

Click here to learn more about Sea-Air or click here to explore the attractive compensation and benefits packages we offer all employees.

Smith's application letter mirrors the language of the job posting

27225 Eucalyptus Avenue
Long Beach, CA 90806
March 12, 2010

Sea-Air Global Transport
5467 Port of Tacoma Rd., Suite 230
Tacoma, WA 98421

Dear Hiring Manager:

Sea-Air Global Transport consistently appeared as a top transportation firm in the research I did for my senior project in global supply chain management, so imagine my delight when I discovered the opening for an export pricing analyst in your Tacoma headquarters (Position Code: T23-6678). With a major in business and a minor in statistical methods, my education has been ideal preparation for the challenges of this position.

In fact, my senior project demonstrates most of the skills listed in your job description, including written communication skills, analytical abilities, and math aptitude. I enjoyed the opportunity to put my math skills to the test as part of the statistical comparison of various freight modes.

As you can see from my résumé, I also have more than three years of part-time experience working with customers in both retail and commercial settings. This experience taught me the importance of customer service, and I want to start my professional career with a company that truly values the customer. In reviewing your website and reading several articles on Lloyd's List and other trade websites, I am impressed by Sea-Air's constant attention to customer service in this highly competitive industry.

My verbal communication skills would be best demonstrated in an interview, of course. I would be happy to meet with a representative of your company at the earliest convenience. I can be reached at dalton.k.smith@gmail.com or by phone at (562) 555-3737.

Sincerely,

Dalton Smith

Immediately grabs attention by indicating knowledge of the company and its industry

Emphasizes his customer service orientation and also shows he has done his homework by researching the company

Doesn't include a handwritten signature because the letter was uploaded to a website along with his résumé

Identifies the specific job to which he is applying

Echoes qualifications stated in the job posting

Politely asks for an interview in a way that emphasizes yet another job-related skill

determining whether you and the organization are a good match, and (2) your main objective is to find the job best suited to your goals and capabilities.

Most employers interview an applicant multiple times before deciding to make a job offer. At the most selective companies, you might have a dozen or more individual interviews across several stages.[33] Depending on the company and the position, the process may stretch out over many weeks, or it may be completed in a matter of days.[34]

The interviewing process starts with a *screening stage*, in which an employer filters out applicants who are unqualified or otherwise not a good fit for the position. Screening can take place on campus, at company offices, or via telephone or computer. If your screening interview will take place by phone, try to schedule it for a time when you can be focused and free from interruptions.[35]

The next stage of interviews helps the organization narrow the field a little further. During this *selection stage*, show interest in the job, relate your skills and experience to the organization's needs, listen attentively, ask insightful questions that show you've done your research, and display enthusiasm. Typically, if you're invited to visit a company, you will talk with several people in succession, such as a member of the human resources department, one or two potential colleagues, and one or more managers, including your potential supervisor. At Google, for example, recruits talk with at least four interviewers, both managers and potential colleagues.[36]

If the interviewers agree that you're a good candidate, you may receive a job offer, either on the spot or a few days later by phone, mail, or e-mail. In other cases, you may be invited back for a final evaluation, often by a higher-ranking executive. The objective of this *final stage* is often to sell you on the advantages of joining the organization.

You can expect to encounter several types of interviews. In a **structured interview**, the interviewer (or a computer) asks a series of prepared questions in a set order. In contrast, in an **open-ended interview**, the interviewer adapts his or her line of questioning based on the answers you give and any questions you ask. Many of your interviews will be conventional one-on-one interviews, with just you and a single interviewer. However, in a **panel interview**, you will meet with several interviewers at once (some companies have up to 50 employees on the panel, but that is unusual).[37] Some organizations perform **group interviews**, in which one or more interviewers meet with several candidates simultaneously. A key purpose of the group interview is to observe how the candidates interact.[38]

Perhaps the most common type of interview these days is the **behavioral interview**, in which you are asked to relate specific incidents and experiences from your past.[39] A **situational interview** is similar to a behavioral interview except that the questions focus on how you would handle various hypothetical situations on the job. A **working interview** is the most realistic of all: You actually perform a job-related activity during the interview. You may be asked to lead a brainstorming session (sometimes with other job candidates), solve a business problem, engage in role playing, or even make a presentation.[40]

Because the interview process takes time, start seeking interviews well in advance of the date you want to start work. Some students start their job search as early as nine months before graduation. Early planning is even more crucial during downturns in the economy because many employers become more selective when times are tough. Whatever shape the economy is in, try to secure as many interviews as you can, both to improve the chances of receiving a job offer and to give yourself more options when you do get offers.

What Employers Look For in an Interview

Interviews give employers the chance to go beyond the basic data of your résumé to get to know you and to answer two essential questions. The first is whether you can handle the responsibilities of the position. You'll probably be asked to describe your education, previous job experiences, and skill set. You may also be asked how you would apply those skills to hypothetical situations on the job. By learning as much as you can about the company, the industry, and the specific job, you have a great opportunity to stand apart from the competition.

The second essential question is whether you will be a good fit with the organization and the target position. All good employers want people who are confident, dedicated, positive, curious, courteous, ethical, and willing to commit to something larger than their own individual goals. You could have superstar qualifications, but if an employer suspects that you might be a negative presence in the workplace, you probably won't get a job offer. Beyond these general qualities, interviewers judge whether you fit the specific culture of the organization. Some companies are more intense; others are more laid back. Some emphasize teamwork; others expect employees to forge their own way and even to compete with one another. Numerous candidates might have the technical qualifications for a particular job, but not all will have the right mix of personal attributes.

What You Should Look For in an Interview

What things should you find out about the prospective job and employer? By doing a little advance research and asking the right questions during the interview (see Exhibit 8), you can probably find answers to these questions and more:

- Are these my kind of people?
- Can I do this work?
- Will I enjoy the work?
- Is this job what I want?
- Does the job pay what I'm worth?
- What kind of person would I be working for?
- What sort of future can I look forward to with this organization?

QUESTION	REASON FOR ASKING
1. What are the job's major responsibilities?	A vague answer could mean that the responsibilities have not been clearly defined, which is almost guaranteed to cause frustration if you take the job.
2. What qualities do you want in the person who fills this position?	This will help you go beyond the job description to understand what the company really wants.
3. How do you measure success for someone in this position?	A vague or incomplete answer could mean that the expectations you will face are unrealistic or ill defined.
4. What is the first problem that needs the attention of the person you hire?	Not only will this help you prepare, but it can signal whether you're about to jump into a problematic situation.
5. Would relocation be required now or in the future?	If you're not willing to move often or at all, you need to know those expectations now.
6. Why is this job now vacant?	If the previous employee got promoted, that's a good sign. If the person quit, that might not be such a good sign.
7. What makes your organization different from others in the industry?	The answer will help you assess whether the company has a clear strategy to succeed in its industry and whether top managers communicate it to lower-level employees.
8. How would you define your organization's managerial philosophy?	You want to know whether the managerial philosophy is consistent with your own working values.
9. What is a typical workday like for you?	The interviewer's response can give you clues about daily life at the company.
10. What systems and policies are in place to help employees stay up to date in their professions and continue to expand their skills?	If the company doesn't have a strong commitment to employee development, chances are it isn't going to stay competitive very long.

EXHIBIT 8

Ten Questions to Ask the Interviewer

Use the interview to ask questions that will supplement the information you were able to gather in your research.

How to Prepare for a Job Interview

Thorough preparation is the key to success in interviewing. Here are some pointers to help you prepare:

- **Think ahead about questions.** Most job interviews are a combination of some fairly generic questions and some specific questions about your background and capabilities. Review the questions in Exhibit 9 and think about how you'll answer these common questions.

EXHIBIT 9

Twenty-Five Common Interview Questions

Prepare for an interview by thinking about your answers to these questions.

Questions About College

1. What courses in college did you like most? Least? Why?
2. Do you think your extracurricular activities in college were worth the time you spent on them? Why or why not?
3. When did you choose your college major? Did you ever change your major? If so, why?
4. Do you feel you did the best scholastic work you are capable of?
5. How has your college education prepared you for this position?

Questions About Employers and Jobs

5. What jobs have you held? Why did you leave?
7. What percentage of your college expenses did you earn? How?
8. Why did you choose your particular field of work?
9. What are the disadvantages of your chosen field?
10. Have you served in the military? What rank did you achieve? What jobs did you perform?
11. What do you think about how this industry operates today?
12. Why do you think you would like this particular type of job?

Questions About Personal Attitudes and Preferences

13. Do you prefer to work in any specific geographic location? If so, why?
14. How much money do you hope to be earning in 5 years? In 10 years?
15. What do you think determines a person's progress in a good organization?
16. What personal characteristics do you feel are necessary for success in your chosen field?
17. Tell me a story.
18. Do you like to travel?
19. Why should I hire you?

Questions About Work Habits

20. Do you prefer working with others or by yourself?
21. What type of boss do you prefer?
22. Have you ever had any difficulty getting along with colleagues or supervisors? With instructors? With other students?
23. What would you do if you were given an unrealistic deadline for a task or project?
24. How do you feel about overtime work?
25. What have you done that shows initiative and willingness to work?

- **Bolster your confidence.** By overcoming any tendencies to feel self-conscious or nervous during an interview, you can build your confidence and make a better impression. If some aspect of your background or appearance makes you uneasy, correct it or exercise positive traits to offset it, such as warmth, wit, intelligence, or charm. Instead of dwelling on your weaknesses, focus on your strengths so that you can emphasize them to an interviewer.

- **Polish your interview style.** Confidence helps you walk into an interview and give the interviewer an impression of poise, good manners, and good judgment. You're more likely to be invited back for a second interview or offered a job if you maintain natural eye contact, smile frequently, sit in an attentive position, and use frequent hand gestures. These nonverbal signals convince the interviewer that you're alert, assertive, dependable, confident, responsible, and energetic.[41] Work on eliminating speech mannerisms such as "you know," "like," and "um." Speak in your natural tone, and try to vary the pitch, rate, and volume of your voice to express enthusiasm and energy. Practice interviewing with friends or use an interview simulator if you have access to one.

Make a positive first impression with careful grooming and attire. You don't need to spend a fortune on new clothes, but you do need to look clean, prepared, and professional.

- **Dress the part.** Physical appearance is important because clothing and grooming reveal something about a candidate's personality, professionalism, and ability to sense the unspoken "rules" of a situation. When it comes to clothing, the best policy is to dress conservatively. Wear the best-quality businesslike clothing you can, preferably in a dark, solid color. Wearing clothes that are appropriate and clean is far more important than wearing clothes that are expensive.

- **Be ready when you arrive.** Be sure you know when and where the interview will be held. Take a small notebook, a pen, a list of your questions, a folder with two copies of your résumé, an outline of your research findings about the organization, and any correspondence about the position. You may also want to take a small calendar, a transcript of your college grades, a list of references, and, if appropriate, samples of your work. After you arrive, relax. You may have to wait, so bring something to read that is related to the company or industry.

At every step, even before you meet your interviewer, show respect for everyone you encounter. If the opportunity presents itself, ask a few questions about the organization or express enthusiasm for the job. Refrain from smoking before the interview (nonsmokers can smell smoke on the clothing of interviewees), and avoid chewing gum, eating, or drinking in the lobby. Anything you do or say while you wait may well get back to the interviewer, so make sure your best qualities show from the moment you enter the premises.

How to Follow Up After the Interview

Touching base with the prospective employer after the interview, either by phone or in writing, shows that you really want the job and are determined to get it. It also brings your name to the interviewer's attention again and reminds him or her that you're waiting to know the decision.

The two most common forms of follow-up, the thank-you note and the inquiry, are generally handled by letter or e-mail. But a phone call can be just as effective, particularly if the employer favors a casual, personal style. Express your thanks within two days after the interview, even if you feel you have little chance for the job. In a brief message, acknowledge the interviewer's time and courtesy, convey your continued interest, and ask politely for a decision. If you're not advised of the interviewer's decision by the promised date or within two weeks, you might make an inquiry, particularly if you don't want to accept a job offer from a second firm before you have an answer from the first. Assume that a simple oversight is the reason for the delay, not outright rejection.

Building Your Career

Having the right skills is vital to your success at every stage of your career. Employers seek people who are able and willing to adapt to diverse situations, who thrive in an ever-changing workplace, and who continue to learn throughout their careers. In addition, companies want team players with strong work records and leaders who are versatile. In some cases, your chances of being hired are better if you've studied abroad or learned another language. Many employers expect college graduates to have a sound understanding of international affairs, and they're looking for employees with intercultural sensitivity and an ability to adapt in other cultures.[42]

Even after an employer hires you, continue improving your skills to distinguish yourself from your peers and to make yourself more valuable to current and potential employers:[43]

- Acquire as much technical knowledge as you can, build broad-based life experience, and develop your social skills.
- Learn to respond to change in positive, constructive ways; this will help you adapt if your "perfect" career path eludes your grasp.
- Keep up with developments in your industry and the economy at large; read widely and use social media tools to find and follow experts in your chosen field.
- Learn to see each job, even so-called entry-level jobs, as an opportunity to learn more and to expand your knowledge, experience, and social skills.
- Take on as much responsibility as you can outside your job description.
- Share what you know with others instead of hoarding knowledge in the hope of becoming indispensable; helping others excel is a skill, too.
- Understand the big picture; knowing your own job inside and out isn't enough any more.

Best wishes for success in this course and in your career!

CHAPTER 1

Developing a Business Mindset

After studying this chapter, you will be able to

1 Explain the concept of adding value in a business and identify the major types of businesses

2 List three steps you can take to help you make the leap from consumer to business professional

3 Discuss the five major environments in which every business operates

4 Explain the purpose of the six major functional areas in a business enterprise

5 Summarize seven of the most important business professions

6 Identify seven components of professionalism

Behind the Scenes

Enter the Haggis Enters the Music Business

www.enterthehaggis.com

Chances are Trevor Lewington, Brian Buchanan, Craig Downie, Mark Abraham, and James Campbell don't wake up every morning and head off to work thinking of themselves as businesspeople. They are musicians first and foremost, members of Enter the Haggis (ETH), a Toronto-based Celtic rock band that has been steadily building a fan base across North America since the lads met in college in the early 2000s.

The five members of Enter the Haggis need to treat their music as a business to ensure a long and healthy career in the music industry.

They're musicians, but they can't help being businesspeople as well. Being a musician can be a lifetime calling and a consuming passion, but earning a living as a professional musician requires much more than artistic inspiration and talent. Musicians who want to survive and thrive in today's fragmented media landscape are increasingly taking control and managing their careers as business operations.

Any music fan who has been purchasing music over the last decade or so knows that the music industry has been undergoing some profound changes. Sales of compact discs have dropped in half since their peak in 2000, as online sales through digital downloads and digital streaming services have grown rapidly. Legal sales of digital music are increasing, although the vast majority of downloads are illegal. However, not all musicians are dead set against unauthorized downloading, and many openly encourage it as a way to build audiences for their music and increase demand for concert ticket sales.

As revolutionary as it has been, the transition to digital song files is not the only seismic shake-up affecting the music industry. Behind the scenes, a battle is raging between a handful of large record labels (companies that produce and promote recorded music) and hundreds of smaller independent companies usually know as the "indies." Musicians who can't get signed by one of the majors—or who don't care for the terms of a major label contract—can try to find a home at an indie label instead.

If you were one of the lads in ETH, what path would you like the group to take? Would you try to sign with a major label or go with an indie? What stance would you take on unauthorized music downloads? How would you build a business to support your dreams of a successful career in music?[1] ∎

Introduction

Like all professional bands, Enter the Haggis (profiled in the chapter-opening Behind the Scenes) is more than just an artistic endeavor. It is also a business with customers, suppliers, payroll, production costs, taxes, legal issues, and most everything else that comes with being in business. And like all businesses, it is affected by external forces, from population trends to new technologies. This chapter gets you ready for the whirlwind tour of the business world you'll get in this course, starting with a quick overview of what businesses do and then some advice on making the leap from consumer to business professional.

Understanding What Businesses Do

The term *business* is used in a number of ways:

- As a label for the overall field of business concepts, as in "I plan to major in business."

- As a collective label for the activities of many companies, as in "This legislation is viewed as harmful to American business."

- As a way to indicate specific activities or efforts, as in "Our furniture business earned record profits last year, but our housewares business has lost money for the third year in a row."

- As a synonym for *company*, as in "Apple is a successful business." Other common synonyms here are *firm* and *enterprise*.

In this last sense, a **business** is any profit-seeking organization that provides goods and services designed to satisfy customers' needs. Enter the Haggis, for example, satisfies an important aspect of consumers' entertainment needs. Although the band is not in it primarily for the money, generating positive financial outcomes is essential to the group's survival in the music industry.

business
Any profit-seeking organization that provides goods and services designed to satisfy customers' needs

Adding Value: The Business of Business

A good way to understand what any business does is to view it as a system for satisfying customers by transforming lower-value inputs into higher-value outputs (see Exhibit 1.1). If you want a loaf of bread, for instance, a silo full of wheat isn't of much value to you. After that wheat has been milled into flour, it gets one step closer but is valuable only if you want to bake your own bread. A bakery can take care of the baking, but that helps only if you're willing to travel to the bakery instead of going to the supermarket where you normally shop. At every stage, a company adds value to create the product in a way that makes it appealing to the next customer in the chain.

Each company in this chain has made certain choices about what it will do to generate **revenue**, money the company brings in through the sale of goods and services. The result of these decisions is a company's **business model**, a clear, simple outline of how the business intends to generate revenue. Of course, generating revenue isn't enough; the business model must also indicate how the company is going to realize **profit**, the amount of money left over after *expenses*—all the costs involved in doing business—have been deducted from revenue.

revenue
Money a company brings in through the sale of goods and services

business model
A concise description of how a business intends to generate revenue

profit
Money left over after all the costs involved in doing business have been deducted from revenue

Competing to Satisfy Customers

As businesses create their value-added products and offer them for sale to customers, they obviously don't do so in a vacuum. Other companies are also trying to sell their products to those same customers, and the result is competition. Competition not only

EXHIBIT 1.1 Adding Value to Satisfy Customers

Every company in this chain adds value for the next customer and for the ultimate consumer.

| Wheat farm | Converts soil, seed, and time to wheat | Flour mill | Converts wheat to flour | Bakery | Converts flour to bread | Grocery store | Makes bread easier to purchase | Consumer | Benefits from value added at every stage |

gives customers a wider range of options, but it also tends to increase quality, improve customer service, and lower prices as companies try to satisfy customers. In fact, this competition is considered so vital to the health of the economy that the U.S. government goes to great lengths to preserve competition in virtually all industries (you'll read about these *monopoly* exceptions in Chapter 2).

One of the beauties of a free-market economy is that companies generally have considerable freedom in deciding which customers they want to focus on and how they want to compete. For instance, one bakery might decide to compete on price and structure its business model in such a way as to mass-produce bread at the lowest possible cost. Another might decide to compete on quality or uniqueness and structure its business model around handcrafted "artisan" bread that costs two or three times as much as the mass-produced bread. Each company seeks a **competitive advantage** that makes its products or the company as a whole more appealing to its chosen customers.

competitive advantage
Some aspect of a product or company that makes it more appealing to target customers

Accepting Risk

Take another look at Exhibit 1.1. Notice how every company from the farmer to the grocery store must accept some level of risk in order to conduct its business. Bad weather or disease could destroy the wheat crop. A shift in consumer behavior (such as a shift to low-carb diets) could leave bakers, distributors, and retailers with bread nobody wants to buy. Businesses take these risks in anticipation of future rewards, and it's easy to imagine what will happen if any participant in this chain decides the risks are too high or the rewards are too uncertain. Without entrepreneurs and organizations willing to accept risk, very little would get done in the economy.

This linking of risk and reward is critical for two reasons. The first and most obvious is that without the promise of rewards, businesses would have little incentive to take on the risks. Second, the risk associated with business decisions needs to "stay attached" to those decisions to encourage smart decision making. For example, when mortgage companies and banks decide whether to lend money for home mortgages, they will be much more careful if they have to live with the consequences of those decisions. However, if they make loans knowing they will sell the loans to someone else as investments—thereby transferring the risk of borrower defaults to those investors—they might be tempted to abandon common sense and make unwise lending decisions. This is exactly what happened with the recent subprime mortgage mess, when thousands of borrowers could no longer make payments on loans they never should've received in the first place. The result was calamity in both the housing and credit markets, triggering a worldwide recession.

Identifying Major Types of Businesses

The driving forces behind most businesses are the prospects of earning profits and building *assets*, which are anything of meaningful value, from patents and brand names to real estate and company stock. In contrast, **not-for-profit organizations** (also known as *nonprofit organizations*) such as museums, most universities, and charities do not have a profit motive. However, they must operate efficiently and effectively to achieve their goals, and successful nonprofits apply many of the business-management principles you'll learn in this course.

Businesses can be classified into two broad categories. **Goods-producing businesses** create value by making "things," from Pop-Tarts to school furniture to spacecraft. Most goods are *tangible*, meaning they have a physical presence, although software, music downloads, and other digital products are intangible. **Service businesses** create value by performing activities that deliver some benefit to the customer, such as finance, insurance, transportation, construction, utilities, wholesale and retail

not-for-profit organizations
Organizations that provide goods and services without having a profit motive; also called nonprofit organizations

goods-producing businesses
Companies that create value by making "things," most of which are tangible (digital products such as software are a notable exception)

service businesses
Companies that create value by performing activities that deliver some benefit to the customer

trade, banking, entertainment, health care, maintenance and repair, and information. Twitter, Jiffy Lube, HBO, and Verizon Wireless are examples of service businesses.

Over the past few decades, the U.S. economy has undergone a profound transformation from being dominated by manufacturing to being dominated by services. The service sector now accounts for three-quarters of the nation's economic output.[2] Although the United States remains one of the world's manufacturing powerhouses, more than half of the 100 largest U.S. companies are now primarily service providers.[3] For example, IBM is well known as a manufacturer of computers and other technological goods, but 60 percent of the company's sales revenue now comes from services such as systems design, consulting, product support, and financing.[4]

Because they require large amounts of money, equipment, land, and other resources to get started and to operate, goods-producing businesses are often *capital-intensive businesses*. The capital needed to compete in these industries is a **barrier to entry**, a resource or capability a company must have before it can start competing in a given market. Other barriers to entry include government testing and approval, tightly controlled markets, strict licensing procedures, limited supplies of raw materials, and the need for highly skilled employees. Service businesses tend to be *labor-intensive businesses*, in that they rely more on human resources than buildings, machinery, and equipment to prosper. However, the Internet and other technologies have reduced the labor required to operate many types of service businesses.

Capital-intensive businesses often have high barriers to entry, given the amount of money needed to start operations.

barrier to entry
Any resource or capability a company must have before it can start competing in a given market

CHECKPOINT

LEARNING OBJECTIVE 1: Explain the concept of adding value in a business, and identify the major types of businesses.

Summary: Businesses add value by transforming lower-value inputs to higher-value outputs. In other words, they make goods and services more attractive from the buyer's perspective, whether it's creating products that are more useful or simply making them more convenient to purchase. Companies fall into two general categories: goods-producing businesses, which create tangible things (except in the case of digital goods), and service businesses, which perform various activities of value to customers. Many companies are both goods-producing and service businesses. Businesses can also be categorized as capital-intensive or labor-intensive.

Critical thinking: (1) What inputs does a musical group use to create its outputs? (2) Can not-for-profit organizations benefit from practices used by for-profit companies? Why or why not?

It's your business: (1) Think back to the last product you purchased; how did the companies involved in its manufacture and sale add value in a way that benefited you personally? (2) Can you see yourself working for a not-for-profit organization after you graduate? Why or why not?

Key terms to know: business, revenue, business model, profit, competitive advantage, not-for-profit organizations, goods-producing businesses, service businesses, barrier to entry

Making the Leap from Buyer to Seller

Even if this course is your first formal exposure to the business world, you already know a great deal about business, thanks to your experiences as a consumer. You understand the impact of poor customer service, for example—or great customer service. You have a sense for product value and why some products meet your needs but others don't. In fact, you're an expert in the entire experience of searching for, purchasing, and owning products.

Seeing Business from the Inside Out

As you progress through this course, you'll begin to look at things through the eyes of a business professional rather than those of a consumer. Instead of thinking about the cost of buying a particular product, you'll start to think about the cost of making it, promoting it, and distributing it. You'll think about what it takes to make a product stand out from the crowd. You'll recognize the importance of finding opportunities in the marketplace and meeting the challenges companies encounter as they pursue those opportunities. You'll begin to see business as an integrated system of inputs, processes, and outputs. You'll start to develop a **business mindset** as you gain an appreciation for the myriad decisions that must be made and the many problems that must be overcome before companies can deliver the products that satisfy customer needs (see Exhibit 1.2).

business mindset
A view of business that considers the myriad decisions that must be made and the many problems that must be overcome before companies can deliver the products that satisfy customer needs

Appreciating the Role of Business in Society

Your experiences as a consumer, an employee, and a taxpayer have also given you some insights into the complex relationship between business and society. Chapter 4's discussion of *corporate social responsibility* digs deeper into this important topic, but for now, just consider some of the major elements of this relationship. Business has the potential to contribute to society in many useful ways:

- *Offering valuable goods and services.* If you look around in your daily life, you'll probably realize that most of the goods and services you consider essential to your quality of life were made possible by someone with a profit motive.

- *Providing employment.* U.S. businesses pay out more than $2 trillion in salaries and wages every year, giving millions of employees the means to provide for themselves and their families.[5] In addition, many companies help their employees meet the costs of health care, child care, insurance, retirement, and other living expenses.

- *Paying taxes.* U.S. businesses pay roughly a half trillion dollars in taxes every year,[6] money that helps build highways, fund education, further scientific research, enhance public safety and national defense, and support other vital functions of government.

- *Contributing to national growth, stability, and security.* Beyond the mere dollars of taxes paid, a strong economy helps ensure a strong country. As one example, by providing job opportunities to the vast majority of people who want to work, businesses help the country avoid the social unrest and family disruptions that often result from high unemployment.

Unfortunately, businesses don't always operate in ways that benefit society. No episode in recent years illustrates this situation as dramatically as the meltdown in the global economy created in large part by the irresponsible risk taking of a relatively small group of companies in the financial sector. (Chapter 20 has more on this story.) Thousands of businesses and millions of employees and investors who had nothing to do with these risky practices suffered long-term financial harm.

The Consumer's Perspective

The Manager's Perspective

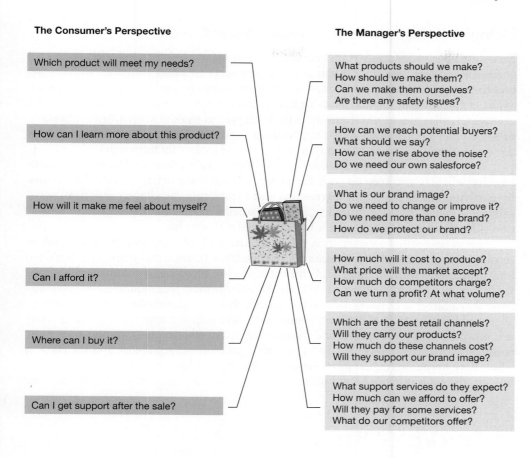

Which product will meet my needs?

How can I learn more about this product?

How will it make me feel about myself?

Can I afford it?

Where can I buy it?

Can I get support after the sale?

What products should we make?
How should we make them?
Can we make them ourselves?
Are there any safety issues?

How can we reach potential buyers?
What should we say?
How can we rise above the noise?
Do we need our own salesforce?

What is our brand image?
Do we need to change or improve it?
Do we need more than one brand?
How do we protect our brand?

How much will it cost to produce?
What price will the market accept?
How much do competitors charge?
Can we turn a profit? At what volume?

Which are the best retail channels?
Will they carry our products?
How much do these channels cost?
Will they support our brand image?

What support services do they expect?
How much can we afford to offer?
Will they pay for some services?
What do our competitors offer?

EXHIBIT 1.2

The Business Mindset

Your experiences as a consumer have taught you a great deal about business already; now the challenge is to turn those experiences around and view the world from a manager's perspective. Here is a small sample of how a business professional approaches some of the questions you've asked as a consumer.

As you progress into positions of increasing responsibility in your career, be aware of the potentially negative effects that business can have on society:

- *Generating pollution and creating waste.* Just like all individuals, all companies consume resources and produce waste and therefore have an impact on the natural environment and the soil, air, and water upon which all living creatures depend.

- *Creating health and safety risks.* Many business operations involve an element of risk to the health and safety of employees and surrounding communities. For instance, some of the products you use every day, from your digital music player to your laptop computer, are full of toxic materials. If these materials are not created, handled, and disposed of properly, they can cause serious illness or death.

- *Disrupting communities.* From occupying land to displacing existing businesses to overloading schools and roads with employees and their children, growing businesses can disrupt communities even as they provide employment and other benefits. And when businesses fall into decline, they can leave behind everything from abandoned buildings to laid-off workers.

- *Causing financial instability.* The recent credit market collapse demonstrates how a single industry can throw the entire global economy into chaos. In addition, poorly managed companies in any industry can become a liability to society if they are unable to meet their financial obligations and need assistance from the government.

The potential negative effects of business are serious matters, but the good news is that you have a say in how business operates. Even as an employee early in your career, you can conduct yourself in ways that balance the profit motive with society's shared interests. And as you climb the corporate ladder or perhaps launch your own business, you'll be in a position to make decisions that help your company prosper in an ethical and sustainable manner.

Using This Course to Jump-start Your Career

No matter where your career plans take you, the dynamics of business will affect your work and life in innumerable ways. If you aspire to be a manager or an entrepreneur, knowing how to run a business is vital, of course. If you plan a career in a professional specialty such as law, engineering, or finance, knowing how businesses operate will help you interact with clients and colleagues more effectively. Even if you plan to work in government, education, or some other noncommercial setting, business awareness can help you as well; many of these organizations look to business for new ideas and leadership techniques.

As you progress through this course, you'll develop a fundamental business vocabulary that will help you keep up with the latest news and make better-informed decisions. By participating in classroom discussions and completing the chapter exercises, you'll gain some valuable critical-thinking, problem-solving, team-building, and communication skills that you can use on the job and throughout your life.

This course will also introduce you to a variety of jobs in business fields such as accounting, economics, human resources, management, finance, and marketing. You'll see how people who work in these fields contribute to the success of a company as a whole. You'll gain insight into the types of skills and knowledge these jobs require—and you'll discover that a career in business today is fascinating, challenging, and often quite rewarding.

In addition, a study of business management will help you appreciate the larger context in which businesses operate and the many legal and ethical questions managers must consider as they make business decisions. Both government regulators and society as a whole have numerous expectations regarding the ways businesses treat employees, shareholders, the environment, other businesses, and the communities in which they operate.

√CHECKPOINT

LEARNING OBJECTIVE 2: List three steps you can take to help you make the leap from consumer to business professional.

Summary: To accelerate your transition from consumer to professional, develop a business mindset that views business from the inside out rather than the outside in, recognize the positive and negative effects that business can have on society, and use this course to develop a business vocabulary and explore the wide variety of jobs in the field of business.

Critical thinking: (1) How can consumer experiences help a business professional excel on the job? (2) If organized businesses didn't exist and the economy was composed of individual craftspeople, would the result be more or less pollution? Explain your answer.

It's your business: (1) Have you thought about how you might contribute to society as a business professional? (2) What is your view of business at this point in your life? Negative? Positive? A mixture of both?

Key terms to know: business mindset

Recognizing the Multiple Environments of Business

The potential effects of business, both positive and negative, highlight the fact that no business operates in a vacuum. Every company operates within a number of interrelated environments that affect and are affected by business.

The Economic Environment

Directly or indirectly, virtually every decision a company makes is influenced by the **economic environment**, the conditions and forces that (a) affect the cost and availability of goods, services, and labor and (b) thereby shape the behavior of buyers and sellers. Chapter 2 explores economic factors in more detail, but for now, it's important to recognize the profound impact that external economic forces can have on a company.

For example, a growing economy can help companies by increasing demand and supporting higher prices for their products, but it can also raise the costs of labor and the materials the companies need to do business. A strong economy can also prompt managers to make decisions that turn out to be unwise in the long term, such as adding costly facilities or employee benefits that the company can't afford when the economy slows down again. A shrinking economy, on the other hand, can damage even well-run, financially healthy companies by limiting demand for their products or the availability of loans or investments needed to expand operations.

economic environment
The conditions and forces that affect the cost and availability of goods, services, and labor and thereby shape the behavior of buyers and sellers

The Market Environment

Within the overall economic environment, every company operates within a **market environment** composed of three important groups: (1) its *target customers*, (2) *buying influences* that shape the behavior of those customers, and (3) *competitors*—other companies that market similar products to those customers. The nature and behavior of these groups and their effect on business strategy vary widely from industry to industry.

In commercial air travel, for instance, airlines have two choices for purchasing large passenger planes, the U.S. company Boeing and the European consortium Airbus. In this industry, purchase decisions aren't influenced by the latest fashion craze, so Boeing and Airbus can make reasonably informed decisions about buying trends years into the future, and neither company has to worry much about a new competitor popping up overnight. In sharp contrast, clothing fashions and fads can change in a matter of months or weeks, and the behavior of celebrities and other buying influences can have a major impact on consumer choices. Moreover, because it is much easier to launch a new line of clothing than a new airplane, competitors can appear almost literally overnight.

market environment
A company's target customers, the buying influences that shape the behavior of those customers, and competitors that market similar products to those customers

The Legal and Regulatory Environment

Every business is affected by the **legal and regulatory environment**, the sum of laws and regulations at the local, state, national, and even international level. Some businesses, such as electricity and other basic utilities, are heavily regulated, even to the point of government agencies determining how much such companies can charge for their services.

The policies and practices of government bodies also establish an overall level of support for businesses operating within their jurisdictions. Taxation, fees, efforts to coordinate multiple regulatory agencies, the speed of granting permits and licenses, labor rules, environmental restrictions, protection for assets such as patents and brand names, roads and other infrastructure, and the transparency and consistency of decision making all affect this level of support. Not surprisingly, businesses prefer to locate and do business in jurisdictions that offer lower costs, lower complexity, and greater stability and predictability (see Exhibit 1.3 on the next page).

legal and regulatory environment
Laws and regulations at the local, state, national, and even international level

The Social Environment

Beyond purely economic and legal factors, every business also operates within the broad **social environment**, the trends and forces in society at large. Every company is affected by population trends that change the composition of consumer markets and the workforce.

social environment
Trends and forces in society at large

EXHIBIT 1.3 State Regulatory Environments

According to *Forbes* magazine, Virginia's legal and regulatory environment is currently the most friendly to business.

RANK	STATE	RANK	STATE
1	Virginia	26	Maryland
2	North Carolina	27	Delaware
3	South Carolina	28	Illinois
4	Michigan	29	Idaho
5	Georgia	30	New Mexico
6	Washington	31	Pennsylvania
7	Missouri	32	Maine
8	Oklahoma	33	Vermont
9	Kansas	34	Nevada
10	Ohio	35	Kentucky
11	Tennessee	36	Hawaii
12	Nebraska	37	Wisconsin
13	Texas	38	Arizona
14	North Dakota	39	Alaska
15	Indiana	40	New Jersey
16	Mississippi	41	Oregon
17	Alabama	42	Connecticut
18	Florida	43	Louisiana
19	Utah	44	New Hampshire
20	Minnesota	45	California
21	New York	46	South Dakota
22	Colorado	47	Montana
23	Iowa	48	Wyoming
24	Massachusetts	49	Rhode Island
25	Arkansas	50	West Virginia

One great example of these trends is the so-called Baby Boom generation, a generational "bulge" in the population made up of people born between 1946 and 1964. This generation has affected business in numerous ways as it has moved through childhood, then into adulthood as consumers and workers, and finally back out of the workforce as the first wave of boomers reach retirement age. This generation of consumers has been in its peak buying years for a couple of decades, boosting demand for cars, houses, vacations, and other goods and services. Within businesses, this population bulge has occupied a large number of middle and upper management positions, frustrating younger professionals who would like to climb the company ladder and causing many to leave and start their own companies. This situation creates a double whammy for companies that fear a talent vacuum when boomers retire by the thousands and there aren't enough next-generation managers to take their places.[7]

In addition to aggregate numbers of consumers and employees, various segments of society also have expectations about the appropriate relationship of business and society.

The responsibility of a company to its **stakeholders**, all those groups affected by its activities, is a subject of ongoing controversy. You can read more about stakeholders in Chapter 4's discussion of corporate social responsibility.

The Technological Environment

The story of ETH—and virtually every other participant in the music business these days—highlights the influence of the **technological environment**, forces resulting from the practical application of science to innovations, products, and processes. The fact that music can even be recorded and played again in a different time and place is a profound advance made possible by technology. (Imagine how different your life would sound if the only way to hear music was for it to be played live.) In the 130 years or so that recorded music has been around, it has been available on numerous technological platforms, from wax cylinders and wire recorders to vinyl discs, a variety of tape formats, compact discs, and finally digital formats such as MP3. The last of these is arguably the most significant because it disconnects music from a physical medium, thereby making it much easier to copy and transmit.

Technological changes have the potential to change every facet of business, from altering internal processes to creating—or destroying—market opportunities. With recorded music, for instance, digital file technology has adversely affected every aspect of CD album sales, from the chemicals used in the manufacture of blank CDs to retail stores that sell CDs to all the products associated with CDs (such as CD players and storage cases). Conversely, if music weren't available as individual digital files, Apple might still be just a computer company and not the biggest music retailer in the United States (through its iTunes store).[8]

Real-Time Updates

Learn More

Are Baby Boomer leaders out of touch?

Is the generation of managers who lead most businesses out of touch with today's realities and the changes that will shape tomorrow's? On mybizlab (www.mybizlab.com), you can access Real-Time Updates within each chapter or under Student Study Tools. Otherwise, go to http://real-timeupdates.com/bia5 and click on "Learn More."

stakeholders
Internal and external groups affected by a company's decisions and activities

technological environment
Forces resulting from the practical application of science to innovations, products, and processes

CHECKPOINT

LEARNING OBJECTIVE 3: Discuss the five major environments in which every business operates.

Summary: Business influences and is influenced by (1) the economic environment, the conditions and forces that affect the cost and availability of goods, services, and labor and thereby shape the behavior of buyers and sellers; (2) the market environment, composed of target customers, buying influences, and competitors; (3) the legal and regulatory environment, comprising all the rules and regulations relating to business activities; (4) the social environment, trends and forces in society at large; and (5) the technological environment and its ability to create and destroy markets and alter business processes.

Critical thinking: (1) Is it wise for cities and states to compete with each other to be more business friendly, specifically with regard to lower tax rates on businesses? Why or why not? (2) Even though it never sells directly to consumers, does a company such as Boeing need to pay attention to population trends? Why or why not?

It's your business: (1) How has technology made your educational experience in college different from your experience in high school? (2) Have current economic conditions affected your career-planning decisions in any way?

Key terms to know: economic environment, market environment, legal and regulatory environment, social environment, stakeholders, technological environment

Identifying the Major Functional Areas in a Business Enterprise

Throughout this course, you'll have the opportunity to learn more about the major functional areas within a business enterprise. In the meantime, the following sections offer a brief overview to help you see how all the pieces work together (see Exhibit 1.4).

Research and Development

research and development (R&D)
Functional area responsible for conceiving and designing new products

Products are conceived and designed through **research and development (R&D)**, sometimes known as *product design* or *engineering*, depending on the company and the industry. Of course, not all companies have an R&D function; many companies simply resell products that other firms make or continue to make the same goods or perform the same services year after year, for example. However, for many companies, R&D is essential to their survival because it provides the ideas and designs that allow these firms to meet customer needs in competitive markets. Three industries in particular invest enormous sums in R&D: computers and other electronic products, automobiles, and health care.[9] For instance, U.S. pharmaceutical and biotechnology companies spend some $65 billion a year on R&D, and roughly a quarter of the employees in these firms are engaged in research and product development.[10]

information technology (IT)
Systems that promote communication and information usage through the company or allow companies to offer new services to their customers

Companies can also engage in *process* R&D to design new and better ways to run their operations. Much of this effort goes into **information technology (IT)** systems that promote communication and information usage through the company or allow companies to offer new services to their customers.

EXHIBIT 1.4

Major Functional Areas in a Business Enterprise

The functional areas in a business coordinate their efforts to understand and satisfy customer needs. Note that this is a vastly simplified model, and various companies organize their activity in different ways.

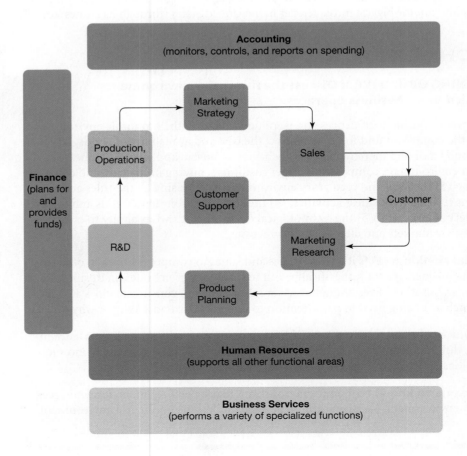

Manufacturing, Production, and Operations

Variously called *manufacturing*, *production*, or *operations*, this area is where the company makes whatever it makes or does whatever it does (for service companies). In addition to supervising the actual production activity, operations managers are responsible for a wide range of other strategies and decisions, including *purchasing* (arranging to buy the necessary materials for manufacturing), *logistics* (coordinating the incoming flow of materials and the outgoing flow of finished products), and *facilities management* (everything from planning new buildings to maintaining them). Chapter 9 explores operations management in more detail.

Marketing, Sales, Distribution, and Customer Support

Your experience as a consumer probably gives you more insight into marketing, sales, distribution, and customer support than any other functional area in business. Although the lines separating these three activities are often blurry, generally speaking, *marketing* is charged with identifying opportunities in the marketplace, working with R&D to develop the products to address those opportunities, creating branding and advertising strategies to communicate with potential customers, and setting prices. The *sales* function develops relationships with potential customers and persuades customers, transaction by transaction, to buy the company's goods and services. Depending on the type of product, a *distribution* function can be involved both before the sale (helping to promote products to retailers, for example) and after (to physically deliver products). After products are in buyers' hands, *customer service* then goes to work after the sale, making sure customers have the support and information they need.

Perhaps no aspect of business has been changed as dramatically by recent technological advances as these marketing, sales, distribution, and customer support activities. For example, the advent of *social media* such as blogs and user-generated-content sites has enabled customers to participate in a multidirectional conversation with companies and with each other. Numerous websites also let customers compare prices and read product reviews in a matter of minutes. The result is a profound power shift that puts buyers on much more equal footing with sellers, as you'll read about in Chapters 13 through 16.

Finance and Accounting

The finance and accounting functions are responsible for virtually every aspect of the firm's finances, including ensuring that the company has the funds it needs to operate, monitoring and controlling how those funds are spent, and drafting reports for company management and outside audiences such as investors and government regulators. Roughly speaking, *financial managers* are responsible for planning, while *accounting managers* are responsible for monitoring and reporting.

Accounting specialists work closely with other functional areas to ensure profitable decision making. For instance, accountants will coordinate with the R&D and production departments to estimate the manufacturing costs of a new product and then work with the marketing department to set the product's price at a level that allows the company to be competitive while meeting its financial goals. Chapters 17 through 20 address accounting, finance, and related concepts.

Human Resources

As you'll read in Chapter 11, the human resources (HR) function is responsible for recruiting, hiring, developing, and supporting employees. Like finance and accounting, HR supports all the other functional areas in the enterprise. Although managers in other functional areas are usually closely involved with hiring and training the employees in their respective departments, HR usually oversees these processes and supports the other departments as needed. The HR department is also charged with making sure the company is in compliance with laws concerning employee rights and workplace safety.

Business Services

In addition to these core functions, a wide variety of *business services* exist to help companies with specific needs in accounting, law, banking, real estate, and other areas. These services can be performed by in-house staff, external firms, or a combination of the two. For example, a company might have a small permanent legal staff to handle routine business matters such as writing contracts but then engage a specialist law firm to help with a major lawsuit or trial. Similarly, virtually all but the smallest companies have accounting professionals on staff, but companies that sell shares of stock to the public are required to have their financial records *audited* by an outside accounting firm.

✓CHECKPOINT

LEARNING OBJECTIVE 4: Explain the purpose of the six major functional areas in a business enterprise.

Summary: (1) Research and development (R&D) creates the goods and services that a company can manufacture or perform for its customers. (2) Manufacturing, production, or operations is that part of the company where the firm makes whatever it makes or performs whatever services it performs. (3) The related group of functions in marketing, sales, distribution, and customer support are responsible for identifying market opportunities, crafting the promotional strategies, and making sure customers are supplied and satisfied with their purchases. (4) Finance and accounting plan for the company's financial needs, control spending, and report on financial matters. (5) Human resources recruits, hires, develops, and supports employees. (6) A variety of business services provide expertise in law, real estate, and other areas.

Critical thinking: (1) Do service companies ever need to engage in research and development, since they're not creating tangible products? Why or why not? (2) Why is good customer support essential to the success of marketing and sales activities?

It's your business: (1) Think of a strongly positive or strongly negative experience you've had with a product or company. What feedback would you like to give the company, and to which functional area would you direct your feedback? (2) Have you already chosen the functional area where you want to work after graduation? If so, what led you to that choice?

Key terms to know: research and development (R&D), information technology (IT)

Exploring Careers in Business

Whether you're getting ready to start your career or you've been in the workforce for a while, you can use this course as an opportunity to explore the many career track options in the world of business. To help stimulate your thinking, this section offers a quick overview of seven major business fields.[11] However, don't limit yourself to these seven by any means. For just about any professional interest you might have, you can probably find a business-related career to pursue, from entertainment and sports to health care and sciences and everything in between. Also, pay attention to employment trends; as the business environment evolves, employment opportunities in various fields grow and shrink at different rates (see Exhibit 1.5).

EXHIBIT 1.5 Business Occupations: Growth and Decline

As conditions in the business environment change, employment outlook rises and falls in specific professions. Here are projected gains and losses among selected business occupations in the coming years. (Note that these government estimates were compiled before the recent upheavals in the housing and financial sectors, and contraction in those industries could affect long-term employment.)

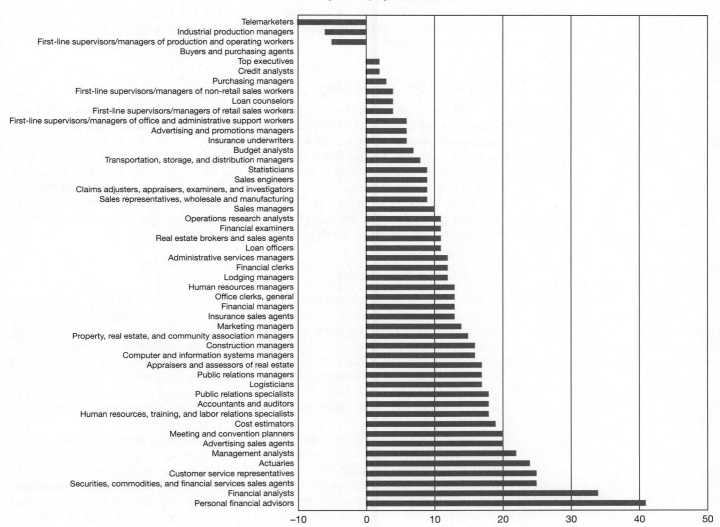

Career Opportunities
% Change in Employment, 2006–2016

Operations Manager

Operations management encompasses all the people and processes used to create the goods and services that a company sells. The work can involve a wide range of tasks and disciplines, including production engineering, assembly, testing, scheduling, quality assurance, information technology, forecasting, finance, logistics, and customer support. Some degree of technical acumen is always required, and many managers begin their careers in technical positions such as industrial engineering.

The work can be stressful as the organization deals with fluctuating demand levels and the inevitable process and supply problems. On the other hand, if you want to balance your business interests with the feel of being involved in creating a company's products, one of these management positions might be perfect for you.

operations management
Management of the people and processes involved in creating goods and services

Human Resources Specialist

HR specialists and managers plan and direct human resource activities that include recruiting, training and development, compensation and benefits, employee and labor relations, and health and safety. Additionally, HR managers develop and implement human resources systems and practices to accommodate a firm's strategy and to motivate and manage diverse workforces. In the past, HR was seen by many as a lower-level function concerned mostly with processing employee records and other tactical duties. However, in many companies, the HR function is becoming more strategic and focused on the global competition to find, attract, and keep the best talent on the market.[12]

Information Technology Manager

Like HR, information technology (IT) is evolving from a tactical support function to a critical strategic component. Reflecting IT's strategic importance, many midsize and large companies now have a *chief information officer* (CIO) position at the executive level to plot IT strategy. IT specialists design, implement, and maintain systems that help deliver the right information at the right time to the right people in the organization. Jobs in IT typically require a degree in a technical field, but an understanding of business processes, finance, and management is also important—particularly as you progress up through the ranks of IT management. Many IT managers and executives also have a business degree, although not all companies require one.[13]

Marketing Specialist

A wide range of career opportunities exist in the interrelated tasks of identifying and understanding market opportunities and shaping the product, pricing, and promotional strategies needed to pursue those opportunities. Whether your interests lie in branding strategy, electronic commerce, advertising, public relations, creative communication, or interpersonal relations, chances are you can find a good fit somewhere in the world of marketing, sales, and customer support. All but the very smallest companies in virtually every industry have marketing and sales staff, but many of these jobs are also found in advertising agencies, public relations (PR) firms, and other companies that offer specialized services to clients.

Some marketing jobs are highly specialized (advertising copywriter and e-commerce architect, for instance), whereas others encompass many different aspects of marketing (brand managers, for example, often deal with virtually every aspect of the marketing and sales functions). Communication skills are paramount for marketers, particularly those dealing with promotions. The ability to write and speak clearly and persuasively will serve you well throughout your career in marketing, even if you don't specialize in a job in which writing or speaking is the primary function. For example, marketing managers need to be able to communicate strategic plans to their teams, as well as to advertising agencies, public relations specialists, distribution channels, industry media, and other stakeholders.

Real-Time Updates

Learn More
Explore the wide range of career choices

Don't limit yourself to familiar career choices—explore the full range at this comprehensive website. On mybizlab (www.mybizlab.com), you can access Real-Time Updates within each chapter or under Student Study Tools. Otherwise, go to http://real-timeupdates.com/bia5 and click on "Learn More."

Sales Professional

If you thrive on competition, enjoy solving problems, and get energized by working with a wide range of people, you should definitely consider a career in sales, becoming one of those professionals responsible for building relationships with customers and helping them make purchase decisions. As a consumer, your exposure to sales might be limited to the retail sector of professional selling, but the field is much more diverse. Salespeople sell everything from design services to pharmaceuticals to airliners.

Many salespeople enjoy a degree of day-to-day freedom and flexibility not usually found in office-bound jobs. On the other hand, the pressure is usually intense—few jobs have the immediate indicators of success or failure that sales has, and most salespeople have specific targets or *quotas* they are expected to meet.

The qualifications for professional selling depend on the industry and the types of goods and services being sold. Personal characteristics are of utmost importance in the sales professional as well, including the ability to listen carefully to customers' needs and communicate information about solutions clearly and persuasively.

Accountant

If working at the intersection of mathematics and business sounds appealing, a career in accounting or finance could be just the place for you. Accounting tasks vary by job and industry, but in general, *management accountants* are responsible for collecting, analyzing, and reporting on financial matters—such as analyzing budgets, assessing the manufacturing costs of new products, and preparing state and federal tax returns. *Internal auditors* not only verify the work of the company's accounting effort but also look for opportunities for efficiency and cost-effectiveness. *Public accountants* offer accounting, tax preparation, and investment advice to individuals, companies, and other organizations. *External auditors* verify the financial reports of public companies as required by law, and *forensic accountants* investigate financial crimes.

Accounting professionals need to have an affinity for numbers, analytical minds, and attention to detail. Their work can have wide-ranging effects on investors, employees, and executives, so accuracy and timeliness are critical. Communication skills are important in virtually every accounting function. Computer skills are also increasingly important, particularly for accountants closely involved with the design or operation of accounting systems.

Financial Manager

Financial managers perform a variety of leadership and strategic functions. *Controllers* oversee the preparation of income statements, balance sheets, and other financial reports; they frequently manage accounting departments as well. *Treasurers* and *finance officers* have a more strategic role, establishing long-term financial goals and budgets, investing the firm's funds, and raising capital as needed. Other financial management positions include *credit managers*, who supervise credit accounts established for customers, and *cash managers*, who monitor and control cash flow. Financial managers can rise to the upper echelons of a corporation, and many CEOs reach their position by excelling in finance.

Unlike accounting tasks, for which there is a long tradition of outsourcing, the work of financial managers is generally kept "in house," particularly in midsize and large companies. The work of a financial manager touches every part of the company, so a broad understanding of the various functional areas in business is a key attribute for this position. The ability to communicate with people who aren't financial experts is also vital. Moreover, awareness of information technology developments is important for chief financial officers and other top financial managers, so that they can direct their companies' investments in new or improved accounting systems as needed.

CHECKPOINT

LEARNING OBJECTIVE 5: Summarize seven of the most important business professions.

Summary: (1) Operations managers oversee all the people and processes used to create the goods and services that a company sells. (2) HR specialists and managers plan and direct human resource activities that include recruiting, training and development, compensation and benefits, employee and labor relations, and health and safety. (3) IT managers oversee the design, implementation, and maintenance of systems that help deliver the right information at the right time to the right people in the organization. (4) Marketing specialists perform one or more tasks involved in identifying and understanding market opportunities and shaping the product, pricing, and promotional strategies needed to pursue those opportunities. (5) Sales professionals build relationships with customers and help them make purchase decisions. (6) Accountants collect, analyze, and report on financial matters; they also perform audits to verify financial reports or find ways to lower costs. (7) Financial managers plan for the company's financial needs, invest funds, and raise capital.

Critical thinking: (1) Why are communication skills essential in all seven of the functional areas discussed in this section? (2) Why would financial managers be in a good position to rise up the company ladder?

It's your business: (1) Which of these seven general career areas appeals to you the most? Why? (2) What is your view of the sales profession? If it is not entirely positive, what would you do as a sales professional to change that public image?

Key terms to know: operations management

Achieving Professionalism

As you map out your career, think about what kind of businessperson you want to be. Will you be someone who just puts in the hours and collects a paycheck? Or will you be someone who performs on a higher plane, someone who wants to make a meaningful contribution and be viewed as a "real pro"? **Professionalism** is the quality of performing at a high level and conducting oneself with purpose and pride. True professionals exhibit seven distinct traits: striving to excel, being dependable and accountable, being a team player, communicating effectively, demonstrating a sense of etiquette, making ethical decisions, and maintaining a positive outlook.

professionalism
The quality of performing at a high level and conducting oneself with purpose and pride

Striving to Excel

Pros are good at what they do, and they never stop getting better. No matter what your job might be at any given time—even if it is far from where you aspire to be—strive to perform at the highest possible level. Not only do you have an ethical obligation to give your employer and your customers your best effort, but excelling at each level in your career is the best way to keep climbing up to new positions of responsibility. Plus, being good at what you do delivers a sense of satisfaction that is hard to beat.

In many jobs and in many industries, performing at a high level requires a commitment to continuous learning and improvement. The nature of the work often changes as markets and technologies evolve, and expectations of quality tend to increase over time as well. View this constant change as a positive thing, as a way to avoid stagnation and boredom.

Being Dependable and Accountable

Developing a reputation as somebody people can count on is a vital step in demonstrating professionalism. That means meeting your commitments, including staying on schedule and staying within budgets. Even with the best intentions, this is a skill that takes some time to develop as you gain experience with how much time and money are required to accomplish various tasks and projects. With experience, you'll learn to be conservative with your commitments. The last thing you want to be known as is someone who overpromises and underdelivers.

Being accountable also means owning up to your mistakes and learning from failure so that you can continue to improve. Pros don't make excuses or blame others. When they make mistakes—and everybody does—they face the situation head on, make amends, and move on.

Being a Team Player

Professionals know that they are contributors to a larger cause, that it's not all about them. Just as in athletics and other team efforts, being a team player in business is something of a balancing act. On the one hand, you need to pay enough attention to your own efforts and skills to make sure you're pulling your own weight. On the other hand, you need to pay attention to the overall team effort to make sure the team succeeds. Remember that if the team fails, you fail, too.

Great team players know how to make those around them more effective, whether it's lending a hand during crunch time, sharing resources, removing obstacles, making introductions, or offering expertise. In fact, the ability to help others improve their performance is one of the key attributes many executives look for when they want to promote people into management.

Being a team player also means showing loyalty to your organization and protecting your employer's reputation. One of the most important assets any company has is its reputation. Pros don't trash their employers in front of customers or in their personal blogs. When they have a problem, they solve it; they don't share it.

Communicating Effectively

If you're looking for a surefire way to stand out from your competition and establish yourself as a competent professional, improving your communication skills may be the most important step you can take. Follow these guidelines to improve your effectiveness as a communicator (see Exhibit 1.6 on the next page):

- *Provide practical information.* Give people useful information, whether it's to help them perform a desired action or understand a new company policy.
- *Give facts rather than vague impressions.* Use concrete language, specific detail, and information that is clear, convincing, accurate, and ethical.
- *Don't present opinions as facts.* If you are offering an opinion, make sure the audience understands that.
- *Present information in a concise, efficient manner.* Audiences appreciate—and respond more positively to—high-efficiency messages.
- *Clarify expectations and responsibilities.* Clearly state what you expect from your readers or listeners and what you can do for them.
- *Offer compelling, persuasive arguments and recommendations.* Make it clear to people how they will benefit from responding to your messages the way you want them to.

Demonstrating Etiquette

A vital element of professionalism is **etiquette**, the expected norms of behavior in any particular situation. The way you conduct yourself, interact with others, and handle conflict can have a profound influence on your company's success and on

etiquette
The expected norms of behavior in any particular situation

EXHIBIT I.6 **Professional Communication**

Note how this e-mail message differs from the casual style most people are accustomed to in their personal communication. The ability to write and speak effectively in a professional context will help you reach your career goals.

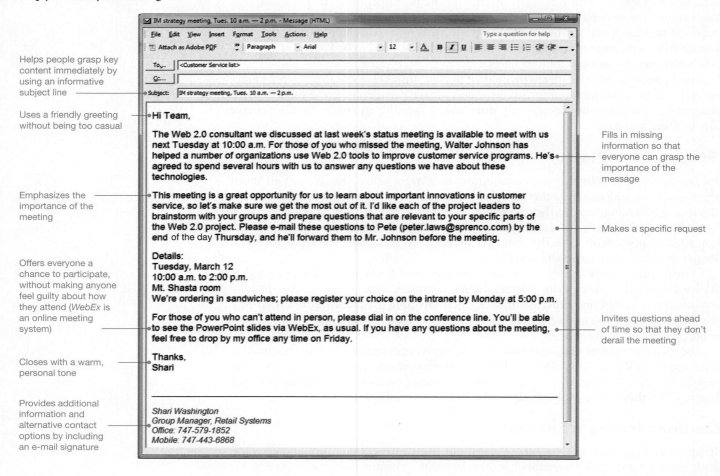

Helps people grasp key content immediately by using an informative subject line

Uses a friendly greeting without being too casual

Emphasizes the importance of the meeting

Offers everyone a chance to participate, without making anyone feel guilty about how they attend (WebEx is an online meeting system)

Closes with a warm, personal tone

Provides additional information and alternative contact options by including an e-mail signature

Fills in missing information so that everyone can grasp the importance of the message

Makes a specific request

Invites questions ahead of time so that they don't derail the meeting

your career. When executives hire and promote you, they expect your behavior to protect the company's reputation. The more you understand such expectations, the better chance you have of avoiding career-damaging mistakes. Moreover, etiquette is an important way to show respect for others and contribute to a smooth-running workplace.

Long lists of etiquette "rules" can be overwhelming, and you'll never be able to memorize all of them. Fortunately, you can count on three principles to get you through any situation: respect, courtesy, and common sense. Moreover, following these principles will encourage forgiveness if you do happen to make a mistake. As you prepare to encounter new situations, take some time to learn the expectations of the other people involved. Travel guidebooks are a great source of information about norms and customs in other countries. See if your library has online access to the CultureGrams database, or review the country profiles at **www.kwintessential .co.uk** or **www.culturecrossing.net**. Don't be afraid to ask questions, either.

Real-Time Updates

Learn More
Don't let etiquette blunders derail your career

Get great advice on developing professional telephone skills, making a positive impression while dining, and dressing for success in any career environment (including great tips on buying business suits). On mybizlab (**www.mybizlab.com**), you can access Real-Time Updates within each chapter or under Student Study Tools. Otherwise, go to **http://real-timeupdates.com/bia5** and click on "Learn More."

People will respect your concern and curiosity. You will gradually accumulate considerable knowledge, which will help you feel comfortable and be effective in a wide range of business situations.

Making Ethical Decisions

Day in, day out and in decisions great and small, professionals conduct themselves with a clear sense of right and wrong. They avoid committing *ethical lapses,* and they carefully weigh all the options when confronted with *ethical dilemmas.* Chapter 4 discusses these situations in more detail.

Maintaining a Confident, Positive Outlook

Spend a few minutes around successful people in any field and chances are you'll notice how optimistic they are. They believe in what they're doing, and they believe in themselves and their ability to solve problems and overcome obstacles.

Poor business etiquette (such as using your mobile phone during a meeting) shows disrespect for colleagues.

Being positive doesn't mean displaying mindless optimism or spewing happy talk all the time. It means acknowledging that things may be difficult but then buckling down and getting the job done anyway. It means no whining and no slacking off, even when the going gets tough. We live in an imperfect world, no question—jobs can be boring or difficult, customers can be unpleasant, and bosses can be unreasonable. But when you're a pro, you find a way to power through.

Your energy, positive or negative, is also contagious. If you work in a conventional office setting, you'll spend as much time with your officemates as you spend with family and friends. Personal demeanor is therefore a vital element of workplace harmony. No one expects (or wants) you to be artificially upbeat and bubbly every second of the day, but one negative personality can make an entire office miserable and unproductive. Every person in the company has a responsibility to contribute to a positive, energetic work environment.

For the latest information on developing a business mindset and becoming a successful professional, visit http://real-timeupdates.com/bia5 and click on Chapter 1.

✓CHECKPOINT

LEARNING OBJECTIVE 6: Identify seven components of professionalism.

Summary: Professionalism is the quality of performing at a high level and conducting yourself with purpose and pride. Seven key traits of professionalism are striving to excel, being dependable and accountable, being a team player, communicating effectively, demonstrating a sense of etiquette, making ethical decisions, and maintaining a positive outlook.

Critical thinking: (1) How much loyalty do employees owe to their employers? Explain your answer. (2) Would it be unethical to maintain a positive public persona if you have private doubts about the path your company is pursuing? Why or why not?

It's your business: (1) In what ways do you exhibit professionalism as a student? (2) You can see plenty of examples of unprofessional business behavior in the news media and in your own consumer and employee experiences. Why should you bother being professional yourself?

Key terms to know: professionalism, etiquette

Behind the Scenes

Build a Band, Then Build a Business

The beginnings of the Celtic rock band Enter the Haggis (ETH) coincided with the beginning of the revolution in the music industry. Millions of music listeners were fed up with the business model that had been in place for decades, in which record labels forced customers to purchase entire albums for $15 to $20, even when they might want only one or two songs on an album—and usually without the opportunity to listen to rest of the album first.

Within the music business, thousands of musicians were fed up with the mainstream business model as well. The industry was dominated by a small number of large record companies, also known as *record labels*. These labels made major investments in the careers of a small number of musicians, from paying for recording sessions to promoting the music to radio stations, which to a large degree dictated the music the public got to hear.

This business model worked out nicely for those musicians lucky enough to get signed by one of the major labels, lucky enough to get significant radio airplay, lucky enough to get significant album and concert sales as a result of that radio exposure, and lucky or smart enough to sign a contract that actually passed some of the resulting profits back to the musicians.

However, the dominant business model was far less satisfying for thousands of other musical acts. With a business model built around big investments made in the hope of big paybacks, the big labels focused on acts with the best chance of appealing to a wide audience. Musicians and groups without a mainstream sound usually needed to look elsewhere. And when the major labels did sign an act, they often exerted a lot of creative and financial control, influencing the sound, the public image, and the career track of the artists in which they invested. Moreover, they recouped their costs before the artist saw any money from album sales, meaning an artist usually had to sell a pile of albums to start seeing any money at all from a recording contract. In other words, for many artists, the chances of getting a major label contract were slim, and the chances of being satisfied with such a contract were even slimmer.

Against this backdrop of widespread dissatisfaction on the part of both consumers and creators, a number of forces in the technological environment were turning the industry upside down. The compact disc (CD) gradually replaced most sales of vinyl albums, but it triggered something much more disruptive than simply replacing one album format with another. CDs store music in digital format, which means the music can be transferred to and played on computers and other digital devices—and distributed over computer networks. The introduction of widely accepted standard file formats, most notably MP3, made it easy to copy and share song files from one device to another. The rapid spread of high-speed Internet connections, low-cost digital music players such as the iPod, and social media such as MySpace and Last.fm added the final pieces of the puzzle. The music industry would never be the same again.

ETH stepped right into this upheaval and embraced a new way of thinking. The group signed with United for Opportunity (UFO), which describes itself as "an organization of experienced, independent-thinking music industry activists that have come together to create a new model for a record label/music distribution company." Not only does UFO support the band's philosophy of giving musicians and their fans more control, but signing with an indie makes more financial sense, too. According to ETH's Brian Buchanan, "The average independent musician sees more real cash from 10,000 independent sales than many major artists see from a million sales."

Will the lads in ETH ever become filthy rich playing Celtic-influenced music? Probably not. However, as Buchanan puts it, "Success is making any kind of a living doing the thing you love." By meshing their business model with the changing business environment and working tirelessly to connect with their customers, ETH stands a good chance of making enough money to keep doing what they love for as long as they love doing it.

Critical Thinking Questions

1. Assume that ETH really was in it for the money and not the music. Would it still make sense to stick with an indie label, or should the band pursue a major label contract and all the potential marketing exposure that comes with it? Explain your answer.

2. Search online for "Enter the Haggis" and identify how many ways you can listen to the band's music for free. Why is it in the group's long-term interest to make its music available for free like this?

3. If the band had begun its professional existence 10 years earlier, how might its business strategy be different from the path it took?

LEARN MORE ONLINE

Explore the band's website at www.enterthehaggis.com and its presence on Facebook, YouTube, MySpace, Twitter, and Ustream. How does the band use its online presence to build a relationship with fans? ■

Key Terms

barrier to entry (55)	goods-producing businesses (54)	profit (53)
business (53)	information technology (IT) (62)	research and development (R&D) (62)
business mindset (56)	legal and regulatory environment (59)	revenue (53)
business model (53)	market environment (59)	service businesses (54)
competitive advantage (54)	not-for-profit organizations (54)	social environment (59)
economic environment (59)	operations management (65)	stakeholders (61)
etiquette (69)	professionalism (68)	technological environment (61)

Test Your Knowledge

Questions for Review

1. What are four ways that business can benefit society?
2. What is professionalism?
3. How does the role of a financial manager differ from the role of an accountant?
4. Do all companies have an R&D function? Explain your answer.
5. What is a business model?

Questions for Analysis

6. Do laws and regulations always restrict or impede the efforts of business professionals, or can they actually help businesses? Explain you answer.
7. Why is it important for IT specialists and managers to understand business in addition to information technology?
8. Why is it often easier to start a service business than a goods-producing business?
9. Does a downturn in the economy hurt all companies equally? Provide several examples to support your answer.

10. **Ethical Considerations.** Is managing a business in ways that reflect society's core values always ethical? Explain your answer.

Questions for Application

11. Identify at least five ways in which your life would be different without digital technology. Would it be more or less enjoyable? More or less productive?
12. What are some of the ways a company in the health-care industry could improve its long-term planning by studying population trends?
13. How will you be able to apply your experience as a consumer of educational services to the challenges you'll face in your career after graduation?
14. Identify three ways in which the principles of professionalism described in this chapter can make you a more successful student.

Practice Your Knowledge

Sharpening Your Communication Skills

Select a local service business where you have been a customer. How does that business try to gain a competitive advantage in the marketplace? Write a brief summary describing whether the company competes on speed, quality, price, innovation, service, or a combination of those attributes. Be prepared to present your analysis to your classmates.

Building Your Team Skills

In teams assigned by your instructor, each member will first identify one career path (such as marketing or accounting) that he or she might like to pursue after graduation and share that choice with the rest of the team. Each team member will then research the others' career options to find at least one significant factor, positive or negative, that could affect someone entering that career. For example, if there are four people on your team, you will research the three careers identified by your three teammates. After the research is complete, convene an in-person or online meeting to give each member of the team an informal career counseling session based on the research findings.

Expand Your Knowledge

Discovering Career Opportunities

Your college's career center offers numerous resources to help you launch your career. Imagine that you write a blog for students at your college, and you want to introduce them to the center's services. Write a blog post of 300 to 400 words, summarizing what the center can do for students.

Developing Your Research Skills

Gaining a competitive advantage in today's marketplace is critical to a company's success. Research any company that sounds interesting to you and identify the steps it has taken to create competitive advantages for individual products or the company as a whole.

1. What goods or services does the company manufacture or sell?
2. How does the company set its goods or services apart from those of its competitors? Does the company compete on price, quality, service, innovation, or some other attribute?
3. How do the company's customer communication efforts convey those competitive advantages?

Improving Your Tech Insights: Digital Products

The category of digital products encompasses an extremely broad range of product types, from e-books to music and movie files to software and instruction sets for automated machinery. Digital products are commonplace these days, but the ability to remotely deliver product value is quite a staggering concept when you think about it. (As just one example, consider that a single iPod or other digital music player can carry the equivalent of two or three thousand tapes or CDs.)

Supplying music over the Internet is amazing enough, but nowadays even *tangible* products can be delivered electronically: The technology that deposits layers of ink in inkjet printers is being adapted to deposit layers of other liquefied materials, including plastics and metals. Called *3D printing*, *inkjet fabrication*, or *additive fabrication*, this technology is already being used to "print" product prototypes and simple electronic components. As the price of the technology continues to drop, it's not too far-fetched to imagine a day when you'll be able to download product description files from the Internet and fabricate physical items right on your own home "printer." For more about this technology, visit Dimension 3D Printing (www.dimensionprinting.com), Stratasys (www.stratasys.com), or Z Corporation (www.zcorp.com).

Choose a category of products that has been changed dramatically by the ability to deliver value digitally. In a brief e-mail message to your instructor, explain how digital technology revolutionized this market segment.[14]

Video Discussion

Access the Chapter 1 video discussion in the End of Chapter Assignments section at www.mybizlab.com.

PEARSON mybizlab

Log on to www.mybizlab.com to access the following study and assessment aids associated with this chapter:

- Interactive exercises
- Pre/post test
- Real-Time Updates
- Video application
- Customized study plans
- Biz Skills Simulations
- Quick Learning Guide

If you are not using mybizlab, you can access Real-Time Updates and Quick Learning Guides through http://real-timeupdates.com/bia5. The Quick Learning Guide (located under "Learn More" on the website) provides all six Checkpoints in a handy two-page format to help you study for exams or review important concepts whenever you need a quick refresher.

Understanding Basic Economics

After studying this chapter, you will be able to

1 Define *economics* and explain why scarcity is central to economic decision making

2 Differentiate among the major types of economic systems

3 Explain the interaction between demand and supply

4 Identify four macroeconomic issues that are essential to understanding the behavior of the economy

5 Outline the debate over deregulation and identify four key roles that governments play in the economy

6 Identify the major ways of measuring economic activity

Behind the Scenes

Will the Sun Keep Shining on Suntech Power?

www.suntech-power.com

Strike up a conversation about solar power, and it probably won't take long for the discussion to turn to economics. Specifically, when will solar-generated electricity reach *grid parity* with coal, oil, natural gas, and nuclear, which now generate most of the world's electricity? Reaching grid parity means it would cost the same to generate electricity using the sun as it does using the energy sources that currently power the "grid," the electricity transmission network. In other words, when will solar become an economically viable alternative to conventional sources, all of which have significant disadvantages?

Shi Zhengrong's answer to that question is soon—very soon. Shi is founder and CEO of the Chinese company Suntech Power, one of the world's largest suppliers of photovoltaic (PV) solar modules. (PV is one of two main solar electricity methods; an alternative method uses mirrors to concentrate sunlight to boil water for steam generators.) Shi's ambitious goal is to achieve grid

As a worldwide leader in solar energy products, Suntech Power influences the economies of many countries.

parity by 2012 and eventually to make PV even cheaper than coal or gas.

Suntech became one of the world's fastest-growing companies after its founding in 2001, quickly shooting past a billion dollars in revenue and making China a major player in solar energy. The company has a strong presence in Europe—Germany and Spain are among the world's largest markets for PV power—and plans to begin production in the United States soon to pursue the vast U.S. energy market.

Shi is a brilliant engineer and an astute manager, but the challenges Suntech faces are formidable. Is grid parity a realistic goal? Can Shi oversee the necessary technical advances while guiding the company through a turbulent economy with costs, demand levels, and material supplies bouncing all over the place? If you were in Shi's place, how would you apply the principles of economics to achieve grid parity while maintaining Suntech's profitability?[1] ∎

Introduction

The experience of Suntech Power (profiled in the chapter-opening Behind the Scenes) is a clear reminder of how economic forces affect every aspect of business. This chapter offers a brief introduction to economics from a business professional's perspective, starting with a high-level look at the study of economics and the all-important concept of scarcity. Understanding basic economic principles is essential to successful business management, and this knowledge can make you a more satisfied consumer and a more successful investor, too.

What Is This Thing Called the Economy?

economy
The sum total of all the economic activity within a given region

The **economy** is the sum total of all the economic activity within a given region, from a single city to a whole country to the entire world. The economy can be a difficult thing to get your mind wrapped around because it is so complex, constantly in motion, and at times hard to see—even though it's everywhere around us. People who devote their lives to studying it can have a hard time agreeing on how the economy works or how to fix it when it's "broken," but business leaders need to understand and pay attention to some key principles. **Economics** is the study of how a society uses its scarce resources to produce and distribute goods and services.

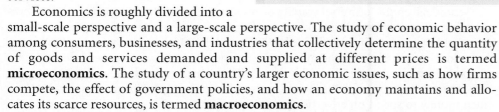

Real-Time Updates

Learn More

Take a closer look at economics

Dig a little deeper into essential economics with this handy tutorial from Investopedia.com. On mybizlab (www.mybizlab.com), you can access Real-Time Updates within each chapter or under Student Study Tools. Otherwise, go to http://real-timeupdates.com/bia5 and click on "Learn More."

Economics is roughly divided into a small-scale perspective and a large-scale perspective. The study of economic behavior among consumers, businesses, and industries that collectively determine the quantity of goods and services demanded and supplied at different prices is termed **microeconomics**. The study of a country's larger economic issues, such as how firms compete, the effect of government policies, and how an economy maintains and allocates its scarce resources, is termed **macroeconomics**.

While microeconomics looks at the small picture and macroeconomics looks at the big picture, understanding the economy at either scale requires an understanding of how the small and large forces interact. For instance, a number of macro forces and policies determine whether homeowners can afford to install solar energy systems. In turn, the aggregate behavior of all those homeowners at the micro level affects the vitality and direction of the overall economy.

Factors of Production

Each society must deal with how its finite resources, or *factors of production,* should be used to satisfy that society's needs. These factors have been defined in a number of ways, but one useful model is dividing them into natural resources, human resources, capital, entrepreneurship, and knowledge. **Natural resources** are things that are useful in their natural state, such as land, forests, minerals, and water. **Human resources** are people and their individual talents and capacities. **Capital** includes resources such as money, computers, machines, tools, and buildings that a business needs in order to produce goods and services. **Entrepreneurship** is the spirit of innovation, the initiative, and the willingness to take the risks involved in creating and operating businesses. **Knowledge** is the collective intelligence of an organization. *Knowledge workers* are employees whose primary contribution to their companies involves the acquisition, analysis, and application of information.

Traditionally, a business or a country was considered to have an advantage if its location offered plentiful supplies of natural resources, human resources, capital, and entrepreneurs. In today's global marketplace, however, intellectual assets are often the key. Companies can now obtain capital from one part of the world, purchase supplies from another, and locate production facilities in still another. They can relocate some of their operations to wherever they find a steady supply of affordable workers, or they can assemble virtual teams of knowledge workers from anywhere on the planet. Chapter 3 discusses this issue of economic globalization in more detail.

Scarcity and Trade-Offs

The notion of scarcity in economics is a crucial idea to remember. Note that "scarcity" doesn't mean a shortage of a particular resource; rather, it means that the resource has a finite supply.[2] Looking back over the factors of production, you can see that the supply of all these resources is limited. Even entrepreneurial energy and brainpower are limited in the sense that there are only so many entrepreneurs in the economy and that each entrepreneur can accomplish only so much during a given time span.

economics
The study of how society uses scarce resources to produce and distribute goods and services

microeconomics
The study of how consumers, businesses, and industries collectively determine the quantity of goods and services demanded and supplied at different prices

macroeconomics
The study of "big picture" issues in an economy, including competitive behavior among firms, the effect of government policies, and overall resource allocation issues

natural resources
Land, forests, minerals, water, and other tangible assets usable in their natural state

human resources
All the people who work for an organization

capital
The physical, human-made elements used to produce goods and services, such as factories and computers; can also refer to the funds that finance the operations of a business

entrepreneurship
The combination of innovation, initiative, and willingness to take the risks required to create and operate new businesses

knowledge
Expertise gained through experience or association

Scarcity is an important concept for two reasons: It creates competition for resources and forces trade-offs on the part of every participant in the economy. First, at every stage of economic activity, people and organizations compete for the resources they need. Businesses and industries compete with each other for the materials, employees, and customers. Suntech Power competes with other photovoltaic manufacturers for supplies of semiconductor-grade silicon, and the entire photovoltaic industry competes with the computer industry for silicon as well. As a consumer, you compete with other consumers. If you were the only person in town who needed a loaf of bread, you would have tremendous power over the bakeries and grocery stores because you're the only customer in town. However, because you compete with thousands of other consumers for a limited supply of bread, you have far less control over the situation.

Second, given this universal scarcity of resources, consumers, companies, and governments are constantly forced to make *trade-offs*, meaning they have to give up something to get something else. You have to decide how to spend the 24 hours you have every day; every choice involves a trade-off—the more time you spend on one activity means less time for every other activity you could possibly pursue. The same goes for whatever limited amount of money you have to spend. Businesses must make similar trade-offs, such as deciding how much money to spend on advertising a new product versus how much to spend on the materials used to make it, or deciding how many employees to have in sales versus customer support. Just like you, businesses never have enough time, money, and other resources to accomplish what they'd like to, so success is largely a matter of making smart trade-offs.

Economists have a name for the option you don't select when you make a trade-off. **Opportunity cost** refers to the value of the most appealing alternative from all those you didn't choose.[3] In other words, opportunity cost is a way to measure the value of what you gave up when you pursued a different opportunity.

opportunity cost
The value of the most appealing alternative not chosen

CHECKPOINT

LEARNING OBJECTIVE 1: Define *economics,* and explain why scarcity is central to economic decision making.

Summary: Economics is the study of how individuals, companies, and governments use scarce resources to produce the goods and services that meet the society's needs. Scarcity is a crucial concept in economics because it creates competition for resources and forces everyone to make trade-offs.

Critical thinking: (1) Why is entrepreneurship considered a factor of production? (2) If you had an unlimited amount of money, would you ever need to make trade-offs again? Why or why not?

It's your business: (1) Did you consider opportunity cost when you chose the college or university you are currently attending? (2) What trade-offs did you make in order to read this chapter at this exact moment in your life? (Think about the decisions you made to get to a point in your life where you're taking a business course.)

Key terms to know: economy, economics, microeconomics, macroeconomics, natural resources, human resources, capital, entrepreneurship, knowledge, opportunity cost

Economic Systems

The roles that individuals, businesses, and the government play in allocating a society's resources depend on the society's **economic system**, the basic set of rules for allocating resources to satisfy its citizens' needs. Economic systems are generally categorized as either *free-market systems* or *planned systems,* although these are really theoretical extremes; every economy exhibits aspects of both approaches.

economic system
Means by which a society distributes its resources to satisfy its people's needs

Free-Market Systems

In a **free-market system**, individuals and companies are largely free to decide what products to produce, how to produce them, whom to sell them to, and at what price to sell them. In other words, they have the chance to succeed—or to fail—by their own efforts. **Capitalism** and *private enterprise* are the terms most often used to describe the free-market system—one in which individuals own and operate the majority of businesses and where competition, supply, and demand determine which goods and services are produced.

In practice, however, no economy is truly "free" in the sense that anyone can do whatever he or she wants to do. Local, state, national, and even international governments such as the European Community intervene in the economy to accomplish goals that leaders deem socially or economically desirable. This practice of limited intervention is characteristic of a *mixed economy* or *mixed capitalism,* which is the economic system of the United States and most other countries. For example, government bodies intervene in the U.S. economy in a variety of ways, such as influencing particular allocations of resources through tax incentives, prohibiting or restricting the sale of certain goods and services, or setting *price controls.* Price controls can involve maximum allowable prices (such as limiting rent increases or capping the price on gasoline or other products during emergencies and shortages) and minimum allowable prices (such as supplementing the prices of agricultural goods to ensure producers a minimum level of income or establishing minimum wage levels).[4]

Mixed economies, particularly those with a strong capitalist emphasis, offer opportunities for wealth creation but usually attach an element of risk to the potential reward. For instance, it's relatively easy to start a company in a mixed economic system such as the United States, but you could lose all of your start-up money if the company isn't successful (and perhaps even your house and your car and everything else you own, depending on how the company is structured). Entrepreneurs and investors willing to face these risks are a vital force in capitalist economies, and they can be rewarded handsomely when they are successful.

free-market system
Economic system in which decisions about what to produce and in what quantities are decided by the market's buyers and sellers

capitalism
Economic system based on economic freedom and competition

Planned Systems

In a **planned system**, governments largely control the allocation of resources and limit freedom of choice in order to accomplish government goals. Because social equality is a major goal of planned systems, private enterprise and the pursuit of private gain are generally regarded as wasteful and exploitive. The planned system that allows individuals the least degree of economic freedom is *communism,* which still exists in a few countries, most notably North Korea and China. As an economic system, communism can't be regarded as anything but a dismal failure. In fact, as you'll read in Chapter 3, even as its government remains strongly communist from a political perspective, China has embraced many concepts of capitalism in recent years and has become one of the world's most powerful and important economies as a result.

Socialism lies somewhere between capitalism and communism. Like communism, socialism involves a relatively high degree of government planning and some government ownership of capital resources. However, government involvement is focused on industries considered vital to the common welfare, such as transportation, utilities, medicine, steel, and communications. Private ownership is permitted in industries that are not considered vital, and in these areas, both businesses and individuals are allowed to benefit from their own efforts.

Although "socialism" is sometimes used as a pejorative term in today's heated political and economic dialogues, and many people believe capitalism is inherently superior to socialism, that opinion is not universal. For example, many European countries, including economic heavyweights France and Germany, incorporate varying degrees of socialism. Norway is strongly socialist; while most of the world's economies sank into a deep recession after the collapse of the U.S. housing and credit markets in 2008, Norway's economy remained stable.[5]

planned system
Economic system in which the government controls most of the factors of production and regulates their allocation

socialism
Economic system characterized by public ownership and operation of key industries combined with private ownership and operation of less-vital industries

The potential rewards available in a free-market economy encourage innovators to create new and exciting products such as Apple's iPhone.

Moreover, while free-market capitalism remains the foundation of the U.S. economy, some important elements of the U.S. economy are socialized and have been for many years. Public schools, the postal service, much of the transportation infrastructure, various local and regional utilities, and several major health-care programs all fit the economic definition of socialism. Socialism and capitalism are competing philosophies in an important sense, but they are not mutually exclusive, and each approach has strengths and weaknesses, which is why most modern economies combine aspects of both.

Nationalization and Privatization

The line between socialism and capitalism isn't always easy to define, and it doesn't always stay in the same place, either. Governments can change the structure of the economy by **nationalizing**—assuming ownership of—selected companies or in extreme cases even entire industries. They can also move in the opposite direction, **privatizing** services once performed by the government by allowing private businesses to perform them instead.

In recent years, governments of various countries have done both, for different reasons and in different industries. In the United States, private companies now own or operate a number of highways, bridges, ports, prisons, and other infrastructure elements, providing services once provided by the government. The primary reason for this trend is the belief that private firms motivated by the profit incentive can do a more efficient job of running these facilities.[6] Nationalization is less common and more drastic, but it has happened in recent years, most notably during the recent global banking crisis. For example, the second-largest bank in Britain, the Royal Bank of Scotland, was effectively nationalized after the British government became the majority owner in an attempt to prevent the bank from collapsing.[7] The U.S. government also made enormous investments in banks during the crisis, and while it hasn't nationalized any of the major U.S. banks yet, some economists contend it will have to in order to restore the banking system to full health.[8] The U.S. government in effect temporarily nationalized General Motors when the giant automaker declared bankruptcy in 2009, taking an ownership share of 60 percent (the government of Canada took a 12.5 percent share as well). President Barack Obama made it clear, however, that the U.S. government has no intention of running the company but stepped in only to save it from collapse.[9]

nationalizing
Government takeover of selected companies or industries

privatizing
Turning over services once performed by the government by allowing private businesses to perform them instead

√CHECKPOINT

LEARNING OBJECTIVE 2: Differentiate among the major types of economic systems.

Summary: The two basic types of economic systems are free-market systems, in which individuals and companies are largely free to make economic decisions, and planned systems, in which government administrators make all major decisions. *Capitalism* and *private enterprise* are often used to describe free-market systems. Communism is the most extreme type of planned system; socialism lies somewhere between capitalism and communism and generally refers to government ownership of fundamental services. The U.S. economy, like virtually all economies, blends elements of free-market capitalism and government control.

Critical thinking: (1) Why are no economies truly free, in the sense of having no controls or restrictions? (2) What are some possible risks of privatizing basic services such as the transportation infrastructure?

It's your business: (1) What is your emotional reaction to the terms *capitalism* and *socialism*? Explain why you feel the way you do. (2) Would you rather pay lower taxes and accept the fact that you need to pay for many services such as health care and education or pay higher taxes with the assurance that the government would provide many basic services for you? Why?

Key terms to know: economic system, free-market system, capitalism, planned system, socialism, nationalizing, privatizing

The Forces of Demand and Supply

At the heart of every business transaction is an exchange between a buyer and a seller. The buyer wants or needs a particular service or good and is willing to pay the seller in order to obtain it. The seller is willing to participate in the transaction because of the anticipated financial gains. In a free-market system, the marketplace (composed of individuals, firms, and industries) and the forces of demand and supply determine the quantity of goods and services produced and the prices at which they are sold. **Demand** refers to the amount of a good or service that customers will buy at a given time at various prices. **Supply** refers to the quantities of a good or service that producers will provide on a particular date at various prices. Simply put, *demand* refers to the behavior of buyers, whereas *supply* refers to the behavior of sellers. Both work together to impose a kind of order on the free-market system.

demand
Buyers' willingness and ability to purchase products

supply
Specific quantity of a product that the seller is able and willing to provide

Understanding Demand

The airline industry offers a helpful demonstration of supply and demand. A **demand curve** is a graph showing the relationship between the amount of product that buyers will purchase at various prices, all other factors being equal. Demand curves typically slope downward, implying that as price drops, more people are willing to buy. The black line labeled "Initial demand" in Exhibit 2.1 shows a possible demand curve for the monthly number of economy tickets for an airline's Chicago to Denver route at different prices. You can see that as price decreases, demand increases and vice versa. If demand is strong, airlines can keep their prices consistent or perhaps even raise them. If demand weakens, they can lower prices to stimulate more purchases. (Airlines use sophisticated *yield management* software to constantly adjust prices in order to keep average ticket prices as high as possible while also keeping their planes as full as possible.)

This movement up and down the demand curve is only part of the story, however. Demand at all price points can also increase or decrease in response to a variety of factors. If demand for air travel decreases, the entire demand curve moves to the left (the red line in Exhibit 2.1). If overall demand increases, the curve moves to the right (the green line). The bullet lists in Exhibit 2.1 indicate the effects of some of the major factors that can cause overall demand to increase or decrease:

- customer income
- customer preferences toward the product (fears regarding airline safety, for example)

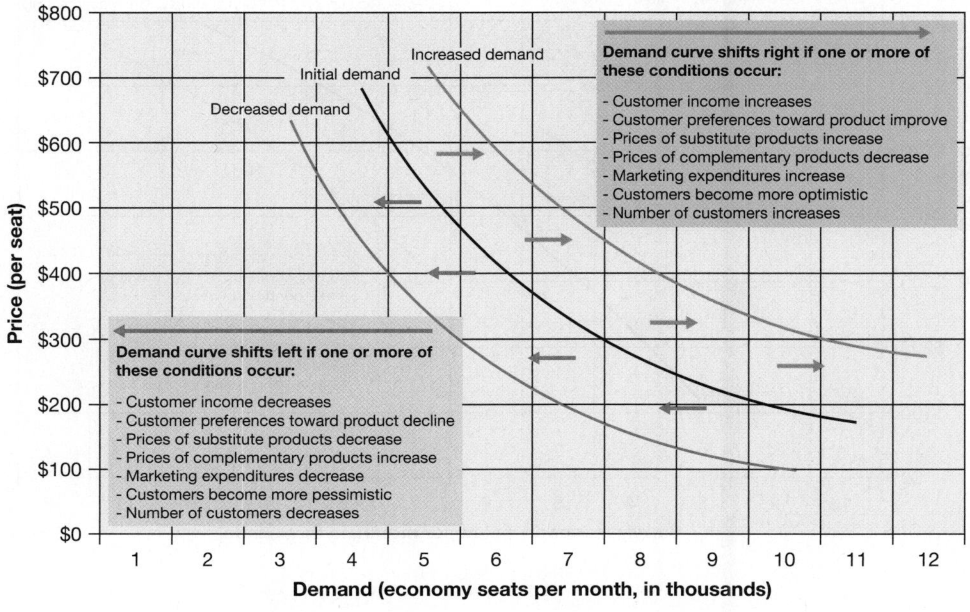

demand curve
Graph of the quantities of product that buyers will purchase at various prices

EXHIBIT 2.1

Demand Curve

The demand curve (black line) for economy seats on one airline's Chicago to Denver route shows that the higher the ticket price, the smaller the quantity demanded, and vice versa. Overall demand is rarely static, however; market conditions can shift the entire curve to the left (decreased demand at every price, red line) or to the right (increased demand at every price, green line).

- the price of *substitute products* (products that can be purchased instead of air travel, including rail tickets, automobile travel, or web conferencing)
- the price of *complementary products* (such as hotel accommodations or restaurant dining for the airline industry)
- marketing expenditures (for advertising and other promotional efforts)
- customer expectations about future prices and their own financial well-being

For example, if the economy is down and businesses and consumers have less money to spend, overall demand for air travel is likely to shrink. Conversely, if customers have more money to spend, more of them are likely to travel for business or leisure, thereby increasing overall demand. Similarly, if the price of substitute products increases, the demand for air tickets could increase as train travelers look for cheaper alternatives. The price of complementary products can affect air travel demand as well. If the hotels in Denver started a price war, Chicagoans looking for a vacation in the Mile High City might decide it's time to travel.

Understanding Supply

supply curve
Graph of the quantities that sellers will offer for sale, regardless of demand, at various prices

Demand alone is not enough to explain how a company operating in a free-market system sets its prices or production levels. In general, a firm's willingness to produce and sell a good or service increases as the price it can charge and its profit potential per item increase. In other words, as the price goes up, the quantity supplied generally goes up. The depiction of the relationship between prices and quantities that sellers will offer for sale, regardless of demand, is called a **supply curve**. Movement along the supply curve typically slopes upward. So as prices rise, the quantity that sellers are willing to supply also rises. Similarly, as prices decline, the quantity that sellers are willing to supply declines. Exhibit 2.2 shows a possible supply curve for the monthly number of economy tickets (seats) supplied on an airline's Chicago to Denver route at different prices. The graph shows that increasing prices for economy tickets on that route should increase the number of tickets (seats) an airline is willing to provide for that route, and vice versa.

EXHIBIT 2.2

Supply Curve

This supply curve, again in this case for economy seats on the Denver–Chicago route, shows that the higher the price, the more tickets (seats) the airline would be willing to supply, all else being equal. As with demand, however, the entire supply curve can shift to the left (decreased supply) or the right (increased supply) as producers respond to internal and external forces.

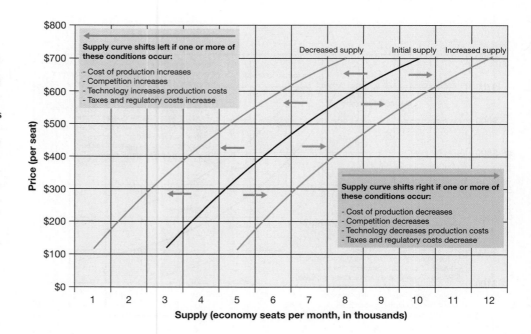

As with demand, supply is dynamic and is affected by a variety of internal and external factors. These include the cost of inputs (such as wages, fuel, and planes for the airlines), the number of competitors in the marketplace, and advancements in technology that allow companies to operate more efficiently. A change in any of these variables can shift the entire supply curve, either increasing or decreasing the amount offered at various prices, as Exhibit 2.2 suggests.

Understanding How Demand and Supply Interact

Customers and suppliers clearly have opposite goals: Customers want to buy at the lowest possible price, and suppliers want to sell at the highest possible price. Neither side can "win" this contest. Customers might want to pay $100 for a ticket from Chicago to Denver, but airlines aren't willing to sell many, if any, at that price. Conversely, the airlines might want to charge $1,000 for a ticket, but customers aren't willing to buy many, if any, at that price. So the market in effect arranges a compromise known as the **equilibrium point**, at which the demand and supply curves intersect (see Exhibit 2.3). At the equilibrium price point, customers are willing to buy as many tickets as the airline is willing to sell.

Because the supply and demand curves are dynamic, so is the equilibrium point. As variables affecting supply and demand change, so will the equilibrium price. For example, increased concerns about passenger safety or longer lines at airport security checkpoints could encourage travelers to make alternative economic choices such as automobile travel or web conferencing, thus reducing the demand for air travel at every price and moving the equilibrium point as well. Suppliers might respond to such a reduction in demand by either cutting the number of flights offered or lowering ticket prices in order to restore the equilibrium level.

Questions of supply, demand, and equilibrium pricing are among the toughest issues you'll face as a manager. Imagine that you're a concert promoter planning for next year's summer season. You have to balance the potential demand for each performer across a range of prices in the hope of matching the supply you can deliver (the seating capacity of each venue and the number of shows)—and you have to make these predictions months in advance. Predict well, and you'll make a tidy profit. Predict poorly, and you could lose a pile of money.

equilibrium point
Point at which quantity supplied equals quantity demanded

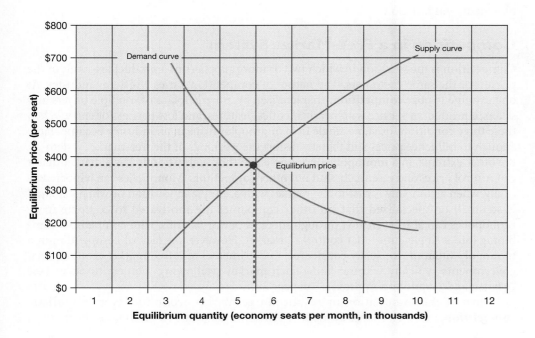

EXHIBIT 2.3

The Relationship Between Supply and Demand

The equilibrium price is established when the amount of a product that suppliers are willing to sell at a given price equals the amount that consumers are willing to buy at that price.

✓CHECKPOINT

LEARNING OBJECTIVE 3: Explain the interaction of demand and supply.

Summary: *Demand* is the amount of a good or service that customers will buy at a given time at various prices; it can be shown visually as a *demand curve*. The entire demand curve can shift as market conditions change. Similarly, *supply* is the amount of a good or service that producers will provide on a particular date at various prices; it can be shown with a *supply curve*, which can also shift in response to market forces. In the simplest sense, demand and supply affect price in the following manner: When the price goes up, the quantity demanded goes down, but the supplier's incentive to produce more goes up. When the price goes down, the quantity demanded increases, but the quantity supplied may (or may not) decline. The point at which the demand and supply curves intersect—the point at which demand and supply are equal—is the *equilibrium point*.

Critical thinking: (1) How does the interaction of demand and supply keep a market in balance, at least approximately and temporarily? (2) If the prices of complementary products for a given product go up, what effect is this increase likely to have on demand for that product?

It's your business: (1) Are there any products or brands you are so loyal to that you will purchase them at almost any price? Will you accept cheaper substitutes? (2) Have you ever purchased something simply because it was on sale? Why?

Key terms to know: demand, supply, demand curve, supply curve, equilibrium point

The Macro View: Understanding How an Economy Operates

All these individual instances of supply and demand, all the thousands and millions of transactions that take place over time, all add up to the economy. This section explores four "big picture" issues in the economy that are essential to understanding the overall behavior of the economy: competition in a free-market system, business cycles, unemployment, and inflation.

Competition in a Free-Market System

Competition is the situation in which two or more suppliers of a product are rivals in the pursuit of the same customers. The nature of competition varies widely by industry. At one extreme is **pure competition**, characterized by a marketplace of multiple buyers and sellers, a product or service with nearly identical features, and low barriers of entry. When these three conditions exist, no single firm or group of firms in an industry becomes large enough to influence prices and thereby distort the workings of the free-market system. At the other extreme, in a **monopoly**, one supplier so thoroughly dominates a market that it can control prices and essentially shut out other competitors. Monopolies can happen naturally, when a company is first to the market with a unique innovation or when a market is so small or specialized that no other companies are motivated to compete in it. Monopolies can also be created through mergers or acquisitions, with competitors combining into a single entity that controls a market. However, the lack of competition in a monopoly situation is usually considered so detrimental to a free-market economy that governments typically will not allow such market-swallowing mergers to occur (see "Merger and Acquisition Approvals" on page 89).

Most of the competition in advanced free-market economies is **monopolistic competition**, in which a large number of sellers (none of which dominates the market)

---

competition
Rivalry among businesses for the same customers

pure competition
Situation in which so many buyers and sellers exist that no single buyer or seller can individually influence market prices

monopoly
Situation in which one company dominates a market to the degree that it can control prices

monopolistic competition
Situation in which many sellers differentiate their products from those of competitors in at least some small way

offer products that can be distinguished from competing products in at least some small way. Toothpaste, cosmetics, soft drinks, Internet search engines, and restaurants are examples of products that can vary in the features each offers. The risk/reward nature of capitalism promotes constant innovation in pursuit of competitive advantage, rewarding companies that do the best job of creating appealing goods and services. For example, Suntech Power competes on cost-efficient products and responsiveness to customer needs.[10]

Real-Time Updates

Learn More

What can we learn from the economic meltdown?

Learn seven valuable lessons for investors from the recent meltdown in the economy. On mybizlab (www.mybizlab.com), you can access Real-Time Updates within each chapter or under Student Study Tools. Otherwise, go to http://real-timeupdates.com/bia5 and click on "Learn More."

Business Cycles

The economy is always in a state of change, expanding or contracting in response to the combined effects of such factors as technological breakthroughs, changes in investment patterns, shifts in consumer attitudes, world events, and basic economic forces. *Economic expansion* occurs when the economy is growing and people are spending more money. Consumer purchases stimulate businesses to produce more goods and services, which in turn stimulates employment and wages, which then stimulate more consumer purchases. *Economic contraction* occurs when such spending declines. Businesses cut back on production, employees are laid off, and the economy as a whole slows down.

If the period of downward swing is severe, the nation may enter into a **recession**, traditionally defined as two consecutive quarters of decline in the *gross domestic product* (see page 92), a basic measure of a country's economic output. The U.S. economy entered a severe recession in December 2007, and it promises to be one of the longest in history.[11] A deep and prolonged recession can be considered a *depression*, which doesn't have an official definition but is generally considered to involve a catastrophic collapse of financial markets. Debate continues as to whether this most recent recession might devolve into a depression—or perhaps already has.[12] When a downward swing or recession is over, the economy enters into a period of **recovery**: Companies buy more, factories produce more, employment is high, and consumers have more to spend. These up-and-down swings are commonly known as **business cycles**, although this term is somewhat misleading, because real economies do not expand and contract in regular and predictable "cycles." *Economic fluctuations* is a more accurate way to characterize the economy's real behavior (see Exhibit 2.4 on the next page).[13]

Unemployment

Unemployment is one of the most serious effects of economic contraction. It is traumatic at a personal level for idle workers and their families, and the decrease in the number of active workers affects the overall economy in terms of lost output.[14] Moreover, unemployed workers increase the financial burden on state governments when they require unemployment benefit payments.

The **unemployment rate** indicates the percentage of the *labor force* currently without employment. The labor force consists of people aged 16 and older who are either working or looking for jobs.[15] Not all cases of unemployment are the same, however. Economists identify several types of unemployment, each with unique implications for business and political leaders:[16]

- *Frictional unemployment* is the "natural" flow of workers into and out of jobs, such as when a person leaves one job without first lining up a new job. There is always some level of frictional unemployment in the economy.

- *Structural unemployment* results from a mismatch between workers' skills and current needs of employers. Structural unemployment is a never-ending concern as

recession
Period during which national income, employment, and production all fall; defined as at least six months of decline in the GDP

recovery
Period during which income, employment, production, and spending rise

business cycles
Fluctuations in the rate of growth that an economy experiences over a period of several years

unemployment rate
Portion of the labor force (everyone over 16 who has or is looking for a job) currently without a job

EXHIBIT 2.4

Fluctuations in the U.S. Economy

The U.S. economy has a long history of expansion and contraction.

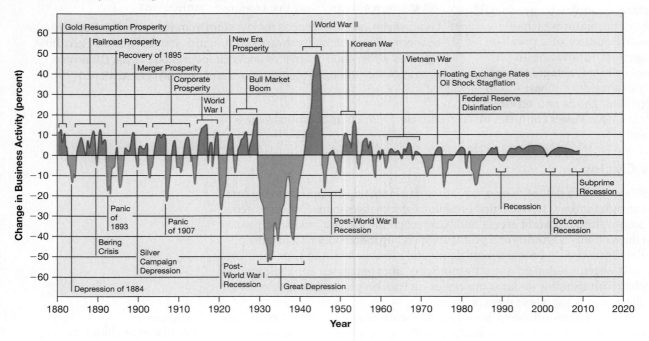

changes in the external environments of business (see page 58) make some skills obsolete and create demand for new skills.

- *Cyclical unemployment* is caused by economic fluctuations. During the Great Depression of the 1930s, the U.S. unemployment rate ran as high as 25 percent, but even in the worst recessions since then, it hasn't (yet) risen much above 10 percent.

- *Seasonal unemployment* reflects job subtractions and additions in industries that need different numbers of workers throughout the year. For instance, farms and orchards need more workers during harvest season, accounting firms need more employees during the April income tax season, and retailers need more sales clerks during holidays.

Inflation

inflation
Economic condition in which prices rise steadily throughout the economy

deflation
Economic condition in which prices fall steadily throughout the economy

Like most everything else in the economy, prices of goods and services rarely stay the same for very long. **Inflation** is a steady rise in the average prices of goods and services throughout the economy. **Deflation**, on the other hand, is a sustained fall in average prices. Inflation is a major concern for consumers, businesses, and government leaders because of its effect on *purchasing power*, or the amount of a good or service you can buy for a given amount of money. When prices go up, purchasing power goes down. If wages keep pace with prices, inflation is less worrisome, but if prices rise faster than wages, consumers definitely feel the pinch. The discussion of "Price Indexes" on page 91 discusses the measurement of inflation in more details and offers a graphical view of U.S. inflation rates over time.

In addition to the average rate of inflation or deflation across the entire economy, consumers and businesses can suffer from above-average increases for specific goods or services—and no one knows this pain more acutely than today's college students and their parents. Over the past two decades, average college tuition has increased four times faster than the overall inflation rate for the economy. (The reasons are complex, but it's safe to say that college tuition follows its own special logic, including the fact that raising tuition sometimes *increases* the number of applicants because it enhances the perceived quality of a school.[17])

✓CHECKPOINT

LEARNING OBJECTIVE 4: Identify four macroeconomic issues that are essential to understanding the behavior of the economy.

Summary: First, competition in a free-market system occurs on a spectrum from pure competition to monopolies; most competition in free-market economies is monopolistic competition, meaning that the number of sellers is large enough that none can dominate the market and products can be distinguished in at least some small way. Second, the economy expands and contracts, or fluctuates over time; this activity is commonly called the business cycle, although the fluctuations do not follow a regular cyclical pattern.

Critical thinking: (1) Are colleges and universities an example of pure competition or monopolistic competition? Why? (2) Are monopolies always harmful to consumers? Why or why not?

It's your business: (1) What state of the business cycle is the economy currently in? Is this influencing your career plans? (2) Have you ever been unemployed (at a time when you were actively looking for work)? Which of the four categories of unemployment would you have fallen under?

Key terms to know: competition, pure competition, monopoly, monopolistic competition, recession, recovery, business cycles, unemployment rate, inflation, deflation

Government's Role in a Free-Market System

The severe recession that began in December 2007, caused and amplified in large part by excesses in the U.S. housing and banking industries, rekindled a debate that has been going for many years: Just how free should the free market be? This most recent incarnation of the debate focuses on the banking system, but government decisions and policies affect business in every industry. Moreover, this debate will never end, for two reasons. First, different groups have different ideas about the role of government; even professional economists don't agree on what role the government should play in the economy. Second, the economy continually evolves, creating new opportunities and new dangers.

Much of this debate about the government's role can be framed as a question of **regulation** versus **deregulation**—having more rules in place to govern economic activity or having fewer rules in place and relying more on the market to prevent excesses and correct itself over time. Generally speaking, proponents of more regulation assert that companies can't always be counted on to act in ways that protect stakeholder interests and that the market can't be relied on as a mechanism to prevent or punish abuses and failures. Proponents of deregulation contend that government interference can stifle innovations that ultimately help everyone by boosting the entire economy and that some regulations burden individual companies and industries with unfair costs.

regulation
Compared to deregulation, relying on laws and policies to govern economic activity

deregulation
Relying on the market to prevent excesses and correct itself over time

Four major areas in which the government plays a role in the economy are protecting stakeholders, fostering competition, encouraging innovation and economic development, and stabilizing and stimulating the economy.

Protecting Stakeholders

Chapter 1 points out that businesses have many stakeholders, groups that are affected by (or that affect) a business's operations, including colleagues, employees, supervisors, investors, customers, suppliers, and society at large. In the course of serving one or more of these stakeholders, a business may sometimes neglect, or at least be accused of neglecting, the interests of other stakeholders in the process. For example, managers who are too narrowly focused on generating wealth for shareholders might not spend the funds necessary to create a safe work environment for employees or to minimize the business's impact on the community.

In an attempt to balance the interests of stakeholders and protect those who might be adversely affected by business, the U.S. federal government has established numerous regulatory agencies (see Exhibit 2.5), and state and local governments have many additional agencies as well. Many of these agencies have the power to pass and enforce rules and regulations within their specific area of authority. Chapter 4 takes a closer look at society's concerns for ethical and socially responsible behavior and the ongoing debate about business's role in society.

Fostering Competition

Based on the belief that fair competition benefits the economy and society in general, governments intervene in markets to preserve competition and ensure that no single enterprise becomes too powerful. For instance, if a company has a monopoly, it can potentially harm customers by raising prices, cutting output, or stifling innovation. Furthermore, because most monopolies have total control over certain products and prices and the market share for those products, it's extremely difficult for competitors to enter markets where monopolies exist. A number of laws and regulations have been established to help prevent individual companies or groups of companies from taking control of markets or acting in other ways that restrain competition or harm consumers.

EXHIBIT 2.5

Major Government Agencies and What They Do

Government agencies protect stakeholders by developing and promoting standards, regulating and overseeing industries, and enforcing laws and regulations.

GOVERNMENT AGENCY OR COMMISSION	MAJOR AREAS OF RESPONSIBILITY
Consumer Product Safety Commission (CPSC)	Regulates and protects public from unreasonable risks of injury from consumer products
Environmental Protection Agency (EPA)	Develops and enforces standards to protect the environment
Equal Employment Opportunity Commission (EEOC)	Protects employees from discriminatory employment practices
Federal Aviation Administration (FAA)	Sets rules for the commercial airline industry
Federal Communications Commission (FCC)	Oversees communication by telephone, telegraph, radio, and television
Federal Energy Regulatory Commission (FERC)	Regulates rates and sales of electric power and natural gas
Federal Highway Administration (FHA)	Regulates vehicle safety requirements
Federal Trade Commission (FTC)	Enforces laws and guidelines regarding unfair business practices and acts to stop false and deceptive advertising and labeling
Food and Drug Administration (FDA)	Enforces laws and regulations to prevent distribution of harmful foods, drugs, medical devices, and cosmetics
Interstate Commerce Commission (ICC)	Regulates and oversees carriers engaged in transportation between states: railroads, bus lines, trucking companies, oil pipelines, and waterways
Occupational Safety and Health Administration (OSHA)	Promotes worker safety and health
Securities and Exchange Commission (SEC)	Protects investors and maintains the integrity of the securities markets
Transportation Security Administration (TSA)	Protects the national transportation infrastructure

Antitrust Legislation

Antitrust laws limit what businesses can and cannot do to ensure that all competitors have an equal chance of producing a product, reaching the market, and making a profit. Some of the earliest government moves in this arena produced such landmark pieces of legislation as the Sherman Antitrust Act, the Clayton Antitrust Act, and the Federal Trade Commission Act, which generally sought to rein in the power of a few huge companies that had financial and management control of a significant number of other companies in the same industry. Usually referred to as *trusts* (hence the label *antitrust legislation*), these huge companies controlled enough of the supply and distribution in their respective industries, such as Standard Oil in the petroleum industry, to muscle smaller competitors out of the way.

In recent years, some of the highest-profile antitrust actions have been in high-technology industries. For example, after complaints that Microsoft was using the dominant market position of its Windows operating system to restrain competition, the federal government and 19 states sued the company. The court ordered that Microsoft be split into two separate companies, one with the operating system software and the other with the application software (such as Microsoft Word). Microsoft successfully appealed the ruling that would've forced it to break up, but it did agree to a variety of changes in its business practices.[18] U.S. companies also need to be aware of antitrust laws in international markets. The U.S. semiconductor giant Intel was recently fined $1.45 billion by the European Commission (EC) for activities the EC said harmed competitor AMD (also a U.S. company) and limited choices for European PC buyers.[19]

Merger and Acquisition Approvals

To preserve competition and customer choice, governments occasionally prohibit companies from combining through mergers or acquisitions (see Chapter 5). In other cases, they may approve a combination but only with conditions, such as *divesting* (selling) some parts of the company. For example, as the Behind the Scenes on page 93 explains, the U.S. Department of Justice allowed the merger of XM and Sirius, even though the combined firm now has a monopoly in the satellite radio market. Antitrust regulators concluded that satellite radio has so much competition from other technologies that consumer choice wasn't unduly limited; they also forced the company to make several major concessions, such as making more channels available for minority programming.

Companies don't have to be competitors, as XM and Sirius were, for mergers to come under close scrutiny. When Ticketmaster, the country's largest seller of concert tickets, proposed a merger with Live Nation, the country's largest owner and operator of concert venues, competitors complained that the combined company would have too much power in the live concert marketplace. Whether the Justice Department eventually approves the deal could signal a shift toward stronger antitrust enforcement under President Barak Obama.[20]

Encouraging Innovation and Economic Development

Governments can use their regulatory and policymaking powers to encourage specific types of economic activity. A good example is encouraging the development and adoption of specific innovations that government officials or bodies deem beneficial in some way, such as promoting the growth of solar power through economic incentives for customers (see page 94).Governments can also encourage businesses to locate or expand in specific geographic areas by establishing *economic development zones* that offer a variety of financial incentives. For instance, the Broome County Empire Zone in New York state offers tax credits, low-interest loans, reduced electricity rates, and other advantages to businesses that meet specific job creation and local investment criteria.[21]

Real-Time Updates

Learn More

Are we failing at failing?

Is the system for saving worthy companies and letting failed companies disappear broken? On mybizlab (www.mybizlab.com), you can access Real-Time Updates within each chapter or under Student Study Tools. Otherwise, go to http://real-timeupdates.com/bia5 and click on "Learn More."

Stabilizing and Stimulating the Economy

In addition to these specific areas of regulation and policy, governments have two sets of tools they can use to stabilize and stimulate the national economy. **Monetary policy** involves adjusting the nation's money supply, the amount of "spendable" money in the economy at any given time, by increasing or decreasing interest rates. In the United States, monetary policy is controlled primarily by the Federal Reserve Board (often called "the Fed"), a group of appointed government officials who oversee the country's central banking system. Chapter 20 discusses the objectives and activities of the Fed in more detail.

Fiscal policy involves changes in the government's revenues and expenditures to stimulate a slow economy or dampen a growing economy that is in danger of overheating. On the revenue side, governments can adjust the revenue they bring in by changing tax rates and various fees collected from individuals and businesses (see Exhibit 2.6). When the federal government lowers the income tax rate, for instance, it does so with the hope that consumers and businesses will spend and invest the money they save by paying lower taxes.

On the expenditure side, local, state, and federal government bodies constitute a huge market for goods and services, with billions of dollars of collective buying power. Governments can stimulate the economy by increasing their purchases, sometimes even to the point of creating new programs or projects with the specific purpose of expanding employment opportunities and increasing demand for goods and services.

No instance of government spending in recent years has generated more heated controversy than the "bailouts" made during the financial crisis of 2008 and 2009. The federal government made billions of dollars of investments in and loans to troubled banks to encourage lending after the credit markets dried up and to prevent several large financial companies, most notably the insurer American International Group (AIG), from collapsing. After the government also stepped in to help save General Motors and Chrysler, debate continued on whether it was wise to intervene by rescuing these ailing companies or whether it should've let market forces play out—allowing the corporations to fail as a consequence of their own actions and the state of the economy.

monetary policy
Government policy and actions taken by the Federal Reserve Board to regulate the nation's money supply

fiscal policy
Use of government revenue collection and spending to influence the business cycle

EXHIBIT 2.6

Major Types of Taxes

Running a government is an expensive affair. Here are the major types of taxes that national governments, states, counties, and cities collect to fund government operations and projects.

TYPE OF TAX	LEVIED ON
Income taxes	Income earned by individuals and businesses. Income taxes are the government's largest single source of revenue.
Real property taxes	Assessed value of the land and structures owned by businesses and individuals.
Sales taxes	Retail purchases made by customers. Sales taxes are collected by retail businesses at the time of the sale and then forwarded to the government.
Excise taxes	Selected items such as gasoline, tobacco, and liquor. Often referred to as "sin" taxes, excise taxes are implemented to help control potentially harmful practices.
Payroll taxes	Earnings of individuals to help fund Social Security, Medicare, and unemployment compensation. Corporations match employee contributions.

✓ CHECKPOINT

LEARNING OBJECTIVE 5: Outline the debate over deregulation, and identify four key roles that governments play in the economy.

Summary: Proponents of increased regulation assert that companies can't always be counted on to act in ways that protect stakeholder interests and the market can't be relied on to prevent or punish abuses and failures. Proponents of deregulation contend that government interference can stifle innovations that ultimately help everyone by boosting the entire economy and that some regulations burden individual companies and industries with unfair costs. Four key roles the government plays in the economy are protecting stakeholders, fostering competition, encouraging innovation and economic development, and stabilizing and stimulating the economy.

Critical thinking: (1) Would it be wise for the government to put price controls on college tuition? Why or why not? (2) Under what conditions, if any, should the federal government step in to rescue failing companies?

It's your business: (1) How do you benefit from competition among the companies that supply you with the goods and services you need? (2) Does this competition have any negative impact on your life?

Key terms to know: regulation, deregulation, monetary policy, fiscal policy

Economic Measures and Monitors

Economic indicators are statistics such as interest rates, unemployment rates, housing data, and industrial productivity that let business and political leaders measure and monitor economic performance. *Leading indicators* suggest changes that may happen to the economy in the future and are therefore valuable for planning. In contrast, *lagging indicators* provide confirmation that something has occurred in the past. Business and political leaders pay close attention to economic indicators in the hope of making better decisions on everything from production levels to shifts in government policy.

economic indicators
Statistics that measure the performance of the economy

Unemployment statistics, for example, signal future changes in consumer spending. When unemployment rises, people have less money to spend, so retail sales are likely to take a hit. Housing starts, another leading indicator, show where several industries are headed. When housing starts drop, construction employment shrinks. Orders for plumbing fixtures, carpet, and appliances also drop, so manufacturers of those items reduce production and workers' hours. Home-improvement and furniture retailers, real estate agents, and others dependent on housing-related transactions begin to feel the pinch as well. These cutbacks ripple through the economy and lead to slower income and job growth and weaker consumer spending.

Another key leading indicator is durable-goods orders, or orders for goods that typically last more than three years (which can mean everything from desk chairs to airplanes). A rise in durable-goods orders is a positive indicator that business spending is turning around. In addition to all these indicators, economists closely monitor several *price indexes* and the nation's economic output to get a sense of how well the economy is working.

Price Indexes

Price changes, especially price increases, are a significant economic indicator. Price indexes offer a way to monitor the inflation or deflation in various sectors of the economy. An index is simply a convenient way to compare numbers over time and is computed by dividing the current value of some quantity by a baseline historical value and

Food is one of the major elements of the consumer price index.

consumer price index (CPI)
Monthly statistic that measures changes in the prices of a representative collective of consumer goods and services

producer price index (PPI)
A statistical measure of price trends at the producer and wholesaler levels

gross domestic product (GDP)
Value of all the final goods and services produced by businesses located within a nation's borders; excludes outputs from overseas operations of domestic companies

gross national product (GNP)
Value of all the final goods and services produced by domestic businesses that includes receipts from overseas operations and excludes receipts from foreign-owned businesses within a nation's borders

then multiplying by 100. Rather than saying something has increased by 28 percent, for example, economists would say the index is at 128.

The best known price index, the **consumer price index (CPI)**, measures the rate of inflation by comparing the change in prices of a representative "basket" of consumer goods and services, such as clothing, food, housing, and utilities. The CPI has always been a hot topic because it is used by the government to index Social Security payments, by businesses in various contracts to calculate cost-of-living increases, and as a gauge of how well the government is keeping inflation under control. However, like most economic indicators, the CPI is not perfect. For example, although it is based on data from thousands of retail establishments across the country, the representative basket of goods and services may not reflect the prices and consumption patterns of the area in which you live or of your specific household. It also doesn't reflect such consumer behaviors as substituting lower-quality goods for higher-quality goods.[22] The U.S. Bureau of Labor Statistics (BLS) periodically adjusts the mix of products used in the CPI, but the CPI should always be viewed as a general indicator of price trends, not as a specific measurement. Note also that the widely quoted CPI is actually one of thousands of CPIs the BLS computes every month.[23]

In contrast to the CPI, the **producer price index (PPI)** measures price at the producer or wholesaler level. (Like the CPI, the PPI is usually referred to as a single index, but it is actually a family of more than 600 industry-specific indexes.) PPI calculations cover virtually the entire goods-producing segment of the U.S. economy and many service sectors as well. In recent years, economists have noticed an important change in the relationship between the PPI and the CPI. Historically, cost increases at the producer level were generally passed along to the consumer level. For instance, if automakers had to pay more for steel, they would work that increase into the price of new cars. As global competition heats up, however, producers find they can't always pass along price increases and remain competitive. The alternative is to accept lower profit levels or else find ways to improve productivity, such as by investing in more-efficient factories or clamping down on labor costs.[24]

National Economic Output

The broadest measure of an economy's health is the **gross domestic product (GDP)**. The GDP measures a country's output—its production, distribution, and use of goods and services—by computing the sum of all goods and services produced for *final* use in a country during a specified period (usually a year). The products may be produced by either domestic or foreign companies as long as the production takes place within a nation's boundaries. Sales from a Honda assembly plant in California, for instance, would be included in the U.S. GDP, even though Honda is a Japanese company. Although far from perfect, the GDP enables a nation to evaluate its economic policies and to compare its current performance with prior periods or with the performance of other nations.

GDP has largely replaced an earlier measure called the **gross national product (GNP)**, which excludes the value of production from foreign-owned businesses within a nation's boundaries and includes receipts from the overseas operations of domestic companies. GNP considers *who* is responsible for the production; GDP considers *where* the production occurs.

For the latest information on economic issues in business, visit http://real-timeupdates .com/bia5 and click on Chapter 2.

✔CHECKPOINT

LEARNING OBJECTIVE 6: Identify the major ways of measuring economic activity.

Summary: Economic activity is monitored and measured with statistics known as *economic indicators*; leading indicators help predict changes, and lagging indicators confirm changes that have already occurred. Two major indicators are *price indexes*, which track inflation or deflation over time for a fixed "basket" of goods and services, and *gross domestic product (GDP)*, the total value of the goods and services produced for final use in a country during a specified time period.

Critical thinking: (1) Why would anyone bother to monitor lagging indicators? (2) Why is GDP considered a more accurate measure of a country's economic health than GNP?

It's your business: (1) In your multiple economic roles as a consumer, employee, and investor, is inflation a good thing, a bad thing, or both? Explain your answer. (2) How is the federal budget deficit likely to affect you? What about your children as they grow up?

Key terms to know: economic indicators, consumer price index (CPI), producer price index (PPI), gross domestic product (GDP), gross national product (GNP)

Behind the Scenes

The Push for Grid Parity at Suntech Power

With energy costs trending upward and more people becoming attuned to the geopolitical complexities of petroleum-based energy, interest in solar, wind, and other alternative energy sources continues to grow. Alternatives can't replace all the energy generated from conventional sources, but they can become increasingly important elements of the world's energy mix. As one of the leading manufacturers of photovoltaic (PV) solar modules for generating electricity, China's Suntech Power is ideally positioned to take advantage of the worldwide opportunities in solar power.

Under the leadership of founder and CEO Shi Zhengrong, Suntech is lowering the cost and raising the energy-conversion efficiency of PV to become competitive with conventional energy sources such as coal and natural gas, a goal known in the industry as grid parity. Shi has set 2012 as the date at which Suntech's PV modules will reach grid parity—three years ahead of the date set as a goal by the Solar America Initiative launched by the U.S. Department of Energy.

Grid parity is a simple enough concept, but it is no small challenge to achieve—or even to calculate so you can tell when you've achieved it. Every form of energy has its own unique mix of direct costs, from initial construction and installation costs to ongoing fuel, maintenance, and operations expenses.

Every energy source also has a mix of indirect costs, including expenses that enable or mediate the effects of using a particular type of energy. Examples of such costs include health-care expenses linked to air pollution caused by burning fossil fuels and the need to secure nuclear power plants from terrorist attacks. Also, every energy source, even "clean" energies such as solar and wind power, has an *ecological footprint*, the sum total of its impact on the environment.

Furthermore, even with a single type of energy source, specific implementations can have different cost profiles for different customers. For instance, when PV panels are installed on the roof of a house, the individual homeowner has to bear the full cost of installation (unless financial incentives are involved—more on this shortly), but there are no transmission costs because the electricity is used right where it is generated. Conversely, when a utility company builds a large-scale solar facility, the cost can be shared by all its customers—but large facilities require a lot of land and abundant sunshine, which means they are often built out in the desert somewhere and often require new transmission lines and circuitry to connect to the electrical grid. Location also plays a major role in cost comparisons, even for identical methods. For example, solar has an advantage over coal in Hawaii, given that state's abundant sunshine and the high cost of shipping coal across the ocean. And as if this all weren't complicated enough, costs rarely stand still as supplies and demands fluctuate and technologies mature. Energy costs can be particularly volatile, making comparisons across energy formats even trickier.

Clearly, identifying all these costs accurately for each energy source is a complex task, and different assumptions in the calculations can lead to different conclusions. However, the numbers are starting to look appealing for solar. At least by some calculations and in some locations—such as Hawaii—PV has already reached parity with the grid. With prices for competing energies expected to keep rising, PV has another advantage in that it has become a big enough industry that it can start to put pressure on suppliers of silicon, a major component of PV modules, to lower their prices.

Now for those financial incentives mentioned a moment ago. In many locales, until the actual cost is driven down far enough by technical advances and production efficiencies, some governments are helping solar along with tax credits and other incentives. One particularly interesting governmental boost is the *feed-in tariff*. Homeowners and businesses whose solar installations generate more electricity than they need can sell it back to utilities, and to spur the growth of solar, some governments pay these individual suppliers above-market rates for their power. Germany, for instance, one of the pioneers of feed-in tariffs, pays homeowners as much as four times the rate paid for electricity from a nuclear plant. In 2009, Gainesville, Florida, became the first city in the United States to offer feed-in tariffs and within a few days signed up the maximum number of customers the program could support.

Things were definitely looking, well, sunny, for Suntech and other PV suppliers. And then the world economy fell off a cliff. As PV supplies were ramping up, demand began ramping down. Supply currently outpaces demand, putting pressure on the prices companies can charge and the resulting profit margins. Shi has responded by slowing down expansion plans and laying off 800 employees, but he is keeping prices high enough to maintain profitability. The recession is also likely to produce an industry "shakeout," in which smaller and financially troubled suppliers either disappear or are acquired by healthy companies such as Suntech. If there's an economic bright spot here for Suntech, the recession has also hammered the price of silicon, lowering the company's production costs.

Shi is confident Suntech will survive the recession and be in a strong position when the economy recovers. And he is still confident of reaching grid parity by 2012 and eventually reaching a point where PV is even cheaper than coal or gas. With its low-cost production, technical innovations, and global marketing presence, Suntech is well on its way to meeting this ambitious goal.

Critical Thinking Questions

1. What effect are feed-in tariffs likely to have on electricity users who don't adopt solar? Is this outcome fair? Why or why not?
2. If a particular government believes that solar is a more desirable energy source than nonrenewables such as coal and gas, why wouldn't it simply grant solar energy utilities monopoly rights?
3. Does it make sense for Suntech to acquire ailing competitors during a deep recession? Why or why not?

LEARN MORE ONLINE

Visit the Suntech website at www.suntech-power.com and explore the sections written for homeowners, commercial customers, architects and builders, dealers and distributors, investors, and the press. How does the company modify its message for each of these audiences? Next, explore "A Guide to Solar Energy," in the "Press" section. Does this information do a good job of helping website visitors understand solar energy technology? ∎

Key Terms

business cycles (85)
capital (77)
capitalism (79)
competition (84)
consumer price index (CPI) (92)
deflation (86)
demand (81)
demand curve (81)
deregulation (87)

economic indicators (91)
economic system (78)
economics (77)
economy (76)
entrepreneurship (77)
equilibrium point (83)
fiscal policy (90)
free-market system (79)
gross domestic product (GDP) (92)

gross national product (GNP) (92)
human resources (77)
inflation (36)
knowledge (77)
macroeconomics (77)
microeconomics (77)
monetary policy (90)
monopolistic competition (84)
monopoly (84)

nationalizing (80)
natural resources (77)
opportunity cost (78)
planned system (79)
privatizing (80)

producer price index (PPI) (92)
pure competition (84)
recession (85)
recovery (85)
regulation (87)

socialism (79)
supply (81)
supply curve (82)
unemployment rate (85)

Test Your Knowledge

Questions for Review

1. Does the United States have a purely free-market economy or a mixed economy?
2. Why is government spending an important factor in economic stability?
3. Why might a government agency seek to block a merger or acquisition?
4. Why is the economic concept of scarcity a crucial concept for businesspeople to understand?
5. Why are knowledge workers a key economic resource?

Questions for Analysis

6. Are the fluctuations in the business cycle predictable?
7. How do countries know if their economic systems are working?
8. Why is competition an important element of the free-market system?
9. Why do governments intervene in free-market systems?

10. **Ethical Considerations.** The risk of failure is an inherent part of free enterprise. Does society have an obligation to come to the aid of entrepreneurs who try but fail? Why or why not?

Questions for Application

11. If you wanted to increase demand for your restaurant but are unable to lower prices or increase advertising, what steps might you take?
12. How might government and education leaders work with business to minimize structural unemployment?
13. How would a decrease in Social Security benefits to retired persons affect the economy?
14. **Concept Integration.** What effect might the technological environment, discussed on page 61 in Chapter 1, have on the equilibrium point in a given market?

Practice Your Knowledge

Sharpening Your Communication Skills

The subprime mortgage crisis (see Chapter 20) that helped throw the economy into a recession in December 2007 bewildered a lot of people. In a brief paragraph (no more than 100 words), explain what a subprime mortgage is and why these loans helped trigger the recession.

Building Your Team Skills

Economic indicators help businesses and governments determine where the economy is headed. With a team assigned by your instructor, analyze these newspaper headlines for clues to the direction of the U.S. economy:

- Housing Starts Lowest in Months
- Fed Lowers Discount Rate and Interest Rates Tumble
- Retail Sales Up 4 Percent Over Last Month
- Business Debt Down from Last Year
- Businesses Are Buying More Electronic Equipment
- Local Economy Sinks as Area Unemployment Rate Climbs to 9.2 Percent
- Telephone Company Reports 30-Day Backlog in Installing Business Systems

Is each item good news or bad news for the economy? Why? What does each news item mean for large and small businesses? Report your team's findings to the class. Did all the teams come to the same conclusions about each headline? Why or why not? With your team, discuss how these different perspectives might influence the way you interpret economic news in the future.

Expand Your Knowledge

Discovering Career Opportunities

Thinking about a career in economics? Find out what economists do by reviewing the *Occupational Outlook Handbook* in your library or online at www.bls.gov/oco. This is an authoritative resource for information about all kinds of occupations. Search for "economists," then answer these questions:

1. Briefly describe what economists do and their typical working conditions.
2. What is the job outlook for economists? What is the average salary for starting economists?
3. What training and qualifications are required for a career as an economist? Are the qualifications different for jobs in the private sector as opposed to those in the government?

Developing Your Research Skills

Some career paths have higher unemployment risks during the ups and downs of economic fluctuations. Research three business careers that should be relatively "recession proof" in the coming years, meaning employment doesn't drop dramatically during a recession (or may even increase during a recession). Summarize your findings in a one-page report.

Improving Your Tech Insights: Data Mining

To find a few ounces of precious gold, you dig through a mountain of earth. To find a few ounces of precious information, you dig through mountains of data using *data mining*, a combination of technologies and techniques that extract important customer insights buried within thousands or millions of transaction records. (Data mining has many other uses as well, such as identifying which employees are most valuable to a firm.)

Data mining is an essential part of *business intelligence* because it helps extract trends and insights from millions of pieces of individual data (including demographics, purchase histories, customer service records, and research results). Data mining helps marketers identify who their most profitable customers are, which goods and services are in highest demand in specific markets, how to structure promotional campaigns, where to target upcoming sales efforts, and which customers are likely to be high credit risks, among many other benefits. You may hear the term *business analytics* used in this context as well, describing efforts to extract insights from databases.

Research one of the commercially available data mining or business analytics systems. You might start with *Intelligent Enterprise* magazine (www.intelligententerprise .com), or check out a company such as Angoss (www .angoss.com; click on "Sales & Marketing"). In a brief e-mail message to your instructor, describe how the system you've chosen can help companies market their goods and services more effectively.[25]

Video Discussion

Access the Chapter 2 video discussion in the End of Chapter Assignments section at www.mybizlab.com.

PEARSON mybizlab

Log on to www.mybizlab.com to access the following study and assessment aids associated with this chapter:

- Interactive exercises
- Pre/post test
- Real-Time Updates
- Video application
- Customized study plans
- Biz Skills Simulations
- Quick Learning Guide

If you are not using mybizlab, you can access Real-Time Updates and Quick Learning Guides through http://real-timeupdates.com/bia5. The Quick Learning Guide (located under "Learn More" on the website) provides all six Checkpoints in a handy two-page format to help you study for exams or review important concepts whenever you need a quick refresher.

🇨🇦 CANADA	CAD	0.9512	0.8883
🇨🇳 CHINA	CNY	7.3169	6.0910
🇪🇺 EURO	EUR	0.6644	0.6100
🇯🇵 JAPAN	JPY	109.00	102.00
🇸🇬 SINGAPORE	SGD	1.3712	1.2630
🇭🇰 HONG KONG	HKD	7.0043	6.4072

LEARNING OBJECTIVES

After studying this chapter, you will be able to

1 Explain why nations trade and describe how international trade is measured

2 Discuss the nature of conflicts in global business, including free trade, fair trade, and government interventions into international trade

3 Identify the major organizations that facilitate international trade and the major trading blocs around the world

4 Discuss the importance of understanding cultural and legal differences in the global business environment

5 Define the major forms of international business activity

6 Discuss the strategic choices that must be considered before entering international markets

Behind the Scenes

MTV Base Africa: Extending the Reach of One of the World's Biggest Media Brands

www.mtvbase.com

Children everywhere grow up fighting—fighting over toys, homework, bedtime, a turn at the videogame. But many, too many, of the young people in Alex Okosi's target audience grew up fighting, period. Of the estimated 300,000 child soldiers in the world, more than a third live in Africa, the region Okosi calls both home and his target market.

After years of colonialism, warfare, famine, widespread poverty, and rampant health problems ranging from malnutrition to the AIDS epidemic, Africa might not strike the average businessperson as a promising market. But Okosi saw reasons for hope, with economies showing signs of recovery in Angola, Uganda, Kenya, and elsewhere.

A native of Nigeria, Okosi immigrated to the United States as a boy and after college in Vermont wound up out West, working for Viacom, the parent company of MTV Networks. However, a trip home convinced him that his future was back in Africa, not selling Viacom channels to cable operators in Idaho, Nevada,

Alex Okosi combined his entrepreneurial spirit and his love of music to lead the successful launch of MTV Base Africa.

and Wyoming. And when he returned to Africa, he would bring MTV with him.

After some market research suggested that advertising, the lifeblood of any television business, was growing as local economies expanded, he knew the time was right. "If you had any entrepreneurial spirit at all," he explained, "You'd say, 'Okay, I can do this.'" After several years of making contacts throughout the company, he transferred to MTV International's headquarters in London, ready to put his plans into action.

By this time, MTV had already launched nearly 100 country-specific channels around the world, so it was no stranger to doing business in the global marketplace. But none of those markets presented the challenges that Africa did. If you were in Alex Okosi's shoes, what steps would you take to bring MTV to Africa? How would you build a consumer market in a region where many people were still learning to adjust to the notion of a modern consumer economy?[1] ∎

Introduction

The experience of MTV's Alex Okosi (profiled in the chapter-opening Behind the Scenes) in Africa is a great example of the opportunities and challenges of taking a business international. As you'll read in this chapter, international business has grown dramatically in recent years, and it's no stretch to say this growth affects virtually every company now, even those that never reach beyond their own borders. Studying international business is essential to your career, too. The future professionals and managers from Asia and Europe, people you'll be competing with for jobs in the global employment market, take international business very seriously.[2]

Fundamentals of International Trade

Wherever you're reading this, stop and look around for a minute. You might see cars that were made in Japan running on gasoline from Russia or Saudi Arabia, mobile phones made in South Korea, food produced in Canada or Mexico or Chile, a digital music player made in China, clothing from Vietnam or Italy, industrial equipment made in Germany—and dozens of other products from every corner of the globe. Conversely, if you or a family member works for a midsize or large company, chances are it gets a

EXHIBIT 3.1 The World's Most Competitive Countries

According to the World Economic Forum, these are the 10 most competitive countries in the world, based on their ability to sustain economic growth.

RANK	COUNTRY
1.	United States
2.	Switzerland
3.	Denmark
4.	Sweden
5.	Singapore
6.	Finland
7.	Germany
8.	Netherlands
9.	Japan
10.	Canada

significant slice of its revenue from sales to other countries. In short, we live and work in a global marketplace. Moreover, while the United States remains one of the world's most competitive countries, dozens of other countries now compete for the same employees, customers, and investments (see Exhibit 3.1).

Why Nations Trade

Commerce across borders has been going on for thousands of years, but the volume of international business has roughly tripled in the past 30 years.[3] One significant result is **economic globalization**, the increasing integration and interdependence of national economies around the world. Six reasons help explain why countries and companies trade internationally:

- **Focusing on relative strengths.** The classic theory of *comparative advantage* suggests that each country should specialize in those areas where it can produce more efficiently than other countries, and it should trade for goods and services that it can't produce as economically. The basic argument is that such specialization and exchange will increase a country's total output and allow both trading partners to enjoy a higher standard of living.

- **Expanding markets.** Many companies have ambitions too large for their own backyards. Well-known U.S. companies such as Microsoft and Boeing would be a fraction of their current size if they were limited to the U.S. marketplace. Similarly, companies based in other countries, from giants such as Toyota, Shell, and Nestlé to thousands of smaller but equally ambitious firms, view the U.S. consumer and business markets as a vast opportunity.

- **Pursuing economies of scale.** All this international activity involves more than just sales growth, of course. By expanding their markets, companies can benefit from **economies of scale**, enabling them to produce goods and services at lower costs by purchasing, manufacturing, and distributing higher quantities.[4]

- **Acquiring materials, goods, and services.** No country can produce

economic globalization
The increasing integration and interdependence of national economies around the world

economies of scale
Savings from buying parts and materials, manufacturing, or marketing in large quantities

Real-Time Updates

Learn More
Follow India's rise to the world stage

Find out how India has become one of the world's most important economies. On mybizlab (www.mybizlab.com), you can access Real-Time Updates within each chapter or under Student Study Tools. Otherwise, go to http://real-timeupdates.com/bia5 and click on "Learn More."

everything its citizens want or need at prices they're willing to pay. For instance, the United States doesn't produce enough oil to meet its needs, so the nation buys oil from Canada, Russia, Saudi Arabia, and other countries that produce more than they can use. Similarly, most countries lack the ability to make commercial aircraft, so most of them buy planes from Boeing, a U.S. company, or Airbus, a consortium of companies based in Europe.

■ **Keeping up with customers.** In some cases, companies have to expand in order to keep or attract multinational customers. For example, say a retailer with stores in 20 countries wants to hire a single advertising agency to manage all its ad campaigns. Any agency vying for the account might need to open offices in all 20 countries in order to be considered.

■ **Keeping up with competitors.** Companies are sometimes forced to engage on a global scale simply because their competitors are doing so. Failing to respond can allow a competitor to increase its financial resources and become a greater threat everywhere the companies compete, even on home turf.[5]

These motivations have provided the energy behind the rapid growth in global business, but the level of growth would not have been possible without two key enablers. First, the world's borders are much more open to trade than they were just a few decades ago, thanks to the advent of international trade organizations (see page 105) and a growing awareness by most governments that healthy trade can help their economies. Second, advances in communication and transportation technologies have made global trade safer, easier, and more profitable.[6]

How International Trade Is Measured

Chapter 2 discusses how economists monitor certain key economic indicators to evaluate how well a country's economic system is performing, and several of these indicators measure international trade. As Exhibit 3.2 illustrates, the United States imports more goods than it exports, but it exports more services than it imports.

Two key measurements of a nation's level of international trade are the *balance of trade* and the *balance of payments*. The total value of a country's exports *minus* the total value of its imports, over some period of time, determines its **balance of trade**. In years when the value of goods and services exported by a country exceeds the value of goods and services it imports, the country has a positive balance of trade, or a **trade surplus**. The opposite is a **trade deficit**, when a country imports more than it exports.

The **balance of payments** is the broadest indicator of international trade. It is the total flow of money into the country *minus* the total flow of money out of the country over some period of time. The balance of payments includes the balance of trade plus the net dollars received and spent on foreign investment, military expenditures, tourism, foreign aid, and other international transactions. For example, when a U.S. company buys all or part of a company based in another country, that investment is counted in the balance of payments but not in the balance of trade. Similarly, when a foreign company buys a U.S. company or purchases U.S. stocks, bonds, or real estate, those transactions are part of the balance of payments.

Foreign Exchange Rates and Currency Valuations

When companies buy and sell goods and services in the global marketplace, they complete the transaction by exchanging currencies. The process is called *foreign exchange,* the conversion of one currency into an equivalent amount of another currency. The number of units of one currency that must be exchanged for a unit of the second currency is known as the **exchange rate** between the currencies.

Most international currencies operate under a *floating exchange rate system*, meaning that a currency's value or price fluctuates in response to the forces of global supply and demand. The supply and demand of a country's currency are determined in part by what is happening in the country's own economy. Moreover, because supply and

---

balance of trade
Total value of the products a nation exports minus the total value of the products it imports, over some period of time

trade surplus
Favorable trade balance created when a country exports more than it imports

trade deficit
Unfavorable trade balance created when a country imports more than it exports

balance of payments
Sum of all payments one nation receives from other nations minus the sum of all payments it makes to other nations, over some specified period of time

exchange rate
Rate at which the money of one country is traded for the money of another

EXHIBIT 3.2 U.S. Exports and Imports Since 1990

The U.S. trade deficit has been growing dramatically in recent years. Although the United States maintains a trade surplus in services (middle graph), the international market for services isn't nearly as large as the market for goods. Consequently, the trade deficit in goods (top graph) far outweighs the trade surplus in services, resulting in an overall trade deficit (bottom graph).

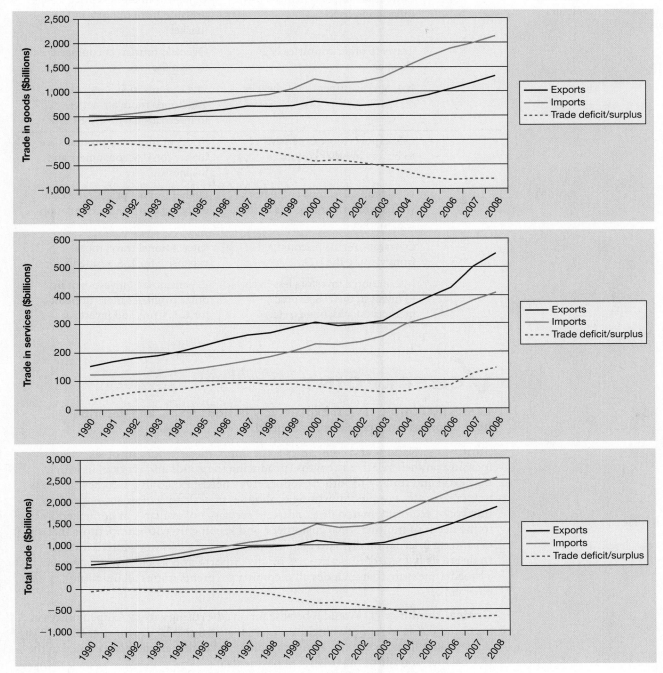

demand for a currency are always changing, the rate at which it is exchanged for other currencies may change a little each day.

A currency is called *strong* relative to another when its exchange rate is higher than what is considered normal and called *weak* when its rate is lower than normal ("normal" is a relative term here). Note that "strong" isn't necessarily good, and "weak" isn't necessarily bad when it comes to currencies, as Exhibit 3.3 on the next page illustrates. Exchange rates can dramatically affect a company's financial results by raising or lowering the cost of supplies it imports and raising or lowering the price of goods it exports.

EXHIBIT 3.3

Strong and Weak Currencies: Who Gains, Who Loses?

A strong dollar and a weak dollar aren't necessarily good or bad; each condition helps some people and hurts others.

		STRONG DOLLAR	WEAK DOLLAR
How it helps		U.S. buyers pay less for imported goods and services	U.S. products more price-competitive in foreign markets
		Lower-cost imports help keep inflation in check	U.S. firms under less price pressure from imports in U.S. market
		Travel to other countries is cheaper	Overseas tourists encouraged to visit the U.S.
		Foreign investments are cheaper	Investments in U.S. stocks and bonds more attractive to international investors
How it hurts		U.S. exports more expensive to buyers in other countries	Prices of imported products are higher for U.S. consumers and businesses
		U.S. companies must compete with lower-priced imports in the U.S. market	Higher import prices raise cost of living; contribute to inflation
		Overseas tourists discouraged from visiting the U.S.	International travel more expensive for U.S. residents
		International investors less likely to invest in the U.S. capital markets (stocks, bonds, etc.)	Expansion and investment in other countries more difficult for U.S. firms and investors

✓CHECKPOINT

LEARNING OBJECTIVE 1: Explain why nations trade, and describe how international trade is measured.

Summary: Nations and companies trade internationally for any of six reasons: focusing on their relative strengths (producing the goods and services in which they excel and trading for other products they need); expanding into new markets to increase sales revenues; pursuing economies of scale to achieve lower production costs; acquiring materials, goods, and services not available at home; tending to the needs of multinational customers; and keeping up with competitors that are expanding internationally. Two primary measures of a country's international trade are its *balance of trade*, exports minus imports, and its *balance of payments*, a broader measure that includes all incoming payments minus all outgoing payments.

Critical thinking: (1) Would it be wise for an advertising agency to open offices in Europe and Asia to service a single multinational client? Why or why not? (2) If IBM invests $40 million in a joint venture in China, would that amount be counted in the U.S. balance of trade or the balance of payments?

It's your business: (1) In the last major purchase you made, did you take into consideration whether the product was made in the United States or another country? (2) Does country of origin matter to you when you shop?

Key terms to know: economic globalization, economies of scale, balance of trade, trade surplus, trade deficit, balance of payments, exchange rate

Conflicts in International Trade

Just as employees compete with one another for jobs and companies compete for customers, countries compete with one another for both. The ability of firms such as Viacom, the company that owns MTV (profiled in the chapter-opening Behind the Scenes), to conduct business across national borders depends on the complex economic relationships the United States maintains with other countries. Naturally, the U.S. government promotes and protects the interests of U.S. companies, workers, and consumers. Other countries are trying to do the same thing for their stakeholders. As you might expect, the many players in world trade sometimes have conflicting goals, making international trade a never-ending tug of war.

Free Trade and Fair Trade

The benefits of the comparative advantage model are based on the assumption that nations don't take artificial steps to minimize their own weaknesses or to blunt the natural advantages of other countries. Trade that takes place without these interferences is known as **free trade**. (Like free-market capitalism, no trade is completely free in the sense that it takes place without regulations of any kind. Instead, international trade should be viewed along a continuum from "more free" to "less free.")

> **free trade**
> International trade unencumbered by restrictive measures

Free trade is not a universally welcomed concept, despite the positive connotation of the word *free*. Supporters claim it is the best way to ensure prosperity for everyone, but detractors call it unfair to too many people and a threat to the middle class.[7] In addition, some critics argue that free trade makes it too easy for companies to exploit workers around the world by pitting them against one another in a "race to the bottom," in which production moves to whichever country has the lowest wages and fewest restrictions regarding worker safety and environmental protection.[8] This complaint has been at the heart of recent protests over free trade and economic globalization in general. However, this criticism is rebutted by some researchers who say that companies prefer to do business in countries with stable, democratic governments. Consequently, says this camp, less-developed nations are motivated to improve their economic and social policies, which not only helps business but can raise the standard of living.[9] As one example, from 1981 to 2005, a period during which China became much more actively involved in free-market capitalism and global trade, the country's poverty rate dropped by 68 percent.[10]

One common example of the criticism of free trade involves the negotiating advantages that large international companies can have when buying from small farmers and other producers in multiple countries. The result, it is argued, is that prices get pushed so low that those producers struggle to earn enough money to survive because somebody, somewhere is always willing to work for less or sell for less. One response to this situation is the concept of **fair trade**, in which buyers voluntarily agree to pay more than the prevailing market price in order to help producers earn a *living wage*, enough money to satisfy their essential needs.[11] Organizations such as the Fair Trade Federation (www. fairtradefederation.org) and TransFair USA (www.transfairusa.org) work to raise awareness of fair trade issues.[12]

> **fair trade**
> A voluntary approach to trading with artisans and farmers in developing countries, guaranteeing them above-market prices as a way to protect them from exploitation by larger, more powerful trading partners

Methods of Government Intervention in International Trade

When a government believes that free trade is not in the best interests of its national security, domestic industries, workforce, or consumers, it can intervene in a number of ways. Some of these methods are collectively known as **protectionism** because they seek to protect a specific industry or groups of workers. While they can help in the short term, many protectionist measures actually end up hurting the groups they were intended to help. When an industry is isolated from real-life competition for too long, it can fail to develop and become strong enough to compete efficiently.[13]

> **protectionism**
> Government policies aimed at shielding a country's industries from foreign competition

The most commonly used ways to intervene in international trade are *tariffs*, *quotas*, *embargoes*, *sanctions*, and *export subsidies*.

- **Tariffs.** Taxes, surcharges, or duties levied against imported goods are known as **tariffs**. Sometimes tariffs are levied to generate revenue for the government, but

> **tariffs**
> Taxes levied on imports

import quotas
Limits placed on the quantity of imports a nation will allow for a specific product

embargo
Total ban on trade with a particular nation (a sanction) or of a particular product

dumping
Charging less than the actual cost or less than the home-country price for goods sold in other countries

export subsidies
A form of financial assistance in which producers receive enough money from the government to allow them to lower their prices in order to compete more effectively in the world market

more often they are imposed to restrict trade or to punish other countries for disobeying international trade laws.

- **Quotas. Import quotas** limit the amount of particular goods that countries allow to be imported during a given year.

- **Embargoes.** In its most extreme form, a quota becomes an **embargo**, a complete ban on the import or export of certain products or even all trade between certain countries.

- **Sanctions.** Sanctions are politically motivated embargoes that revoke a country's normal trade relations status; they are often used as forceful alternatives, short of war. Sanctions can include arms embargoes, foreign-assistance reductions and cutoffs, trade limitations, tariff increases, import-quota decreases, visa denials, air-link cancellations, and more.

- **Restrictive import standards.** Countries can assist their domestic producers by establishing restrictive import standards, such as requiring special licenses for doing certain kinds of business and then making it difficult for foreign companies to obtain such a license. Some countries restrict imports by requiring goods to pass special tests.

- **Dumping.** The practice of selling large quantities of a product at a price lower than the cost of production or below what the company would charge in its home market is called **dumping**. This tactic is most often used to try to win foreign customers or to reduce product surpluses. If a domestic producer can demonstrate that the low-cost imports are damaging its business, most governments will seek redress on their behalf through international trade organizations. Dumping is often a tricky situation to resolve, however; buyers of the product being dumped benefit from the lower prices, and proving what a fair price is in the country of origin can be difficult.[14]

- **Export subsidies.** In contrast to these interventions on imported goods, countries can also intervene to help domestic industries export their products to other countries. **Export subsidies** are a form of financial assistance in which producers receive enough money from the government to allow them to lower their prices in order to compete more effectively in the world market.

✓ CHECKPOINT

LEARNING OBJECTIVE 2: Discuss the nature of conflicts in global business, including free trade, fair trade, and government interventions into international trade.

Summary: The root cause of trade conflict is that every country has a natural interest in protecting its own security and supporting its industries, workers, and consumers. The result is that countries often deviate from the notion of free trade by intervening in various ways, including the use of tariffs, import quotas, embargoes, sanctions, restrictive import standards, dumping, or export subsidies. Fair trade is an effort to make sure producers in developing countries receive a sufficient level of income to support *living wages* for workers.

Critical thinking: (1) What would happen to U.S. workers if all trade intervention suddenly disappeared? (2) What would be the effect on U.S. consumers?

It's your business: (1) Would you be willing to pay more for your clothes in order to keep more apparel manufacturing in the United States? Why or why not? (2) Would you consider purchasing "fair trade" products, even if their prices are higher than comparable products without the fair trade designation?

Key terms to know: free trade, fair trade, protectionism, tariffs, import quotas, embargo, dumping, export subsidies

International Trade Organizations

With international trade becoming such a huge part of the world's economies, organizations that establish trading rules, resolve disputes, and promote trade now play an important role in global business.

Organizations Facilitating International Trade

Establishing rules and standards and solving business disputes within a country is relatively simple, since all parties are subject to the rules of the same government. However, disputes between countries are another matter entirely, often involving complicated negotiations that can take years to resolve. In an effort to ensure equitable trading practices and iron out the inevitable disagreements over what is fair and what isn't, governments around the world have established a number of important agreements and organizations that address trading issues, including WTO, IMF, and the World Bank.

The World Trade Organization (WTO)

The World Trade Organization (WTO), www.wto.org, is a permanent forum for negotiating, implementing, and monitoring international trade procedures and for mediating trade disputes among member countries (its membership includes more than 150 nations around the world). The organization's work is guided by five principles: preventing discriminatory policies that favor some trading partners over others or a country's own products over others'; reducing trade barriers between countries; making trade policies more predictable and less arbitrary; discouraging unfair practices such as dumping; and helping less-developed countries benefit from international trade.[15]

Critics of globalization often direct their ire at the WTO, but the organization says these criticisms are unjustified and based on misunderstandings of the WTO's missions and methods. For example, the WTO asserts that contrary to claims by some critics, it does not dictate policies to national governments, it does not ignore the special circumstances faced by the world's poorest countries, and it does not ignore health and environmental concerns when trying to mediate commercial disputes.[16] One point everyone seems to agree on is that the WTO's work is exceedingly complex and therefore excruciatingly slow. For example, reaching agreement to eventually eliminate agricultural export subsidies, in which government payments to farmers allow them to set artificially low prices on the world market, took several decades.[17]

The International Monetary Fund (IMF)

The International Monetary Fund (IMF), www.imf.org, was established in 1945 to foster international financial cooperation. Its primary functions are monitoring global financial developments, providing technical advice and training, and providing short-term loans to countries that are unable to meet their financial obligations.[18] The IMF's 185 member countries can borrow against the deposits they made to join the fund. However, to borrow more than 25 percent of its deposit amount, a country must agree to various conditions designed to ensure its ability to pay back the loan. These conditions can include significant changes to a country's economic policies, such as banking reforms and modifications to trade barriers.[19]

The World Bank

The World Bank (www.worldbank.org) is a United Nations agency owned by its 185 member nations. It was founded to finance reconstruction after World War II and is now involved in hundreds of projects around the world aimed at addressing poverty, health, education, and other concerns in developing countries.[20] While it is not as directly involved in international trade and finance as the WTO and IMF, the World Bank does indirectly contribute to trade by working to improve economic conditions throughout the developing world.

Trading Blocs

Trading blocs, or *common markets*, are regional organizations that promote trade among member nations. Although specific rules vary from group to group, their primary objective is to ensure the economic growth and benefit of members. As such, trading blocs generally promote trade inside the region while creating uniform barriers against goods and services entering the region from nonmember countries. Three of the largest trading blocs are the North American Free Trade Agreement (NAFTA), the European Union (EU), and the Asia-Pacific Economic Cooperation (APEC). Exhibit 3.4 shows the members of these three and several other blocs around the world.

North American Free Trade Agreement (NAFTA)

In 1994, the United States, Canada, and Mexico formed a massive trading bloc, the North American Free Trade Agreement (NAFTA). The agreement paved the way for the free flow of goods, services, and capital within the bloc through the phased elimination of tariffs and quotas.[21] NAFTA primarily affects trade between the United States and Mexico and between the United States and Canada; trade between Mexico and Canada is small in comparison.[22]

NAFTA was controversial when first implemented, and it has remained controversial ever since. Mexican exports are up dramatically, and U.S. and other foreign companies have invested billions of dollars in Mexico. Some Mexican companies are thriving, thanks to those export opportunities, while others, particularly in agriculture, have been hurt severely by low-cost imports from the United States. Many of the manufacturing jobs Mexico hoped to attract wound up in China instead. And outside the business sphere, hoped-for improvements in education and health care in Mexico haven't materialized to the extent NAFTA backers expected, although they place the blame on government inaction, not on the free-trade agreement. In the United States, critics of NAFTA claim that much of the promised benefits of lower consumer prices and steady export markets for small farmers didn't materialize, that benefits of NAFTA have gone mostly to huge agribusiness corporations, and that contrary to promises of job creation in the United States NAFTA has cost U.S. jobs.[23]

The Office of the United States Trade Representative, the U.S. government agency responsible for negotiating international trade agreements, disputes many of the criticisms of NAFTA. For example, the agency offers statistics to show that NAFTA has more than tripled trade among the three countries and that unemployment rates in the United States were lower after NAFTA than before.[24] Arriving at clear answers in such disputes is often difficult, given the complexity of the economic relationships between countries, the shifting economic and political landscapes within countries, and the effects of developments in other countries.

The euro eases price comparisons for products sold in the member countries of the European Union.

The European Union (EU)

One of the largest trading blocs is the European Union (EU), http://europa.eu, whose membership now encompasses more than two dozen countries and a half billion people. The EU constitutes the world's second-largest economy after the United States. EU nations have eliminated hundreds of local regulations, variations in product standards, and protectionist measures that once limited trade among member countries. Trade now flows among member countries in much the same way as it does among states in the United States. And the EU's reach extends far beyond the borders of Europe; to simplify design and manufacturing for world markets, many companies now create their products to meet EU specifications. If you've seen the "CE" marking on any products you may own, that stands for *Conformité Européene* and indicates that the product has met EU standards for safety, health, and environmental responsibility.[25]

EXHIBIT 3.4 Members of Major Trading Blocs

As the economies of the world become increasingly linked, many countries have formed powerful regional trading blocs that trade freely with one another but place restrictions on trade with other countries and blocs.

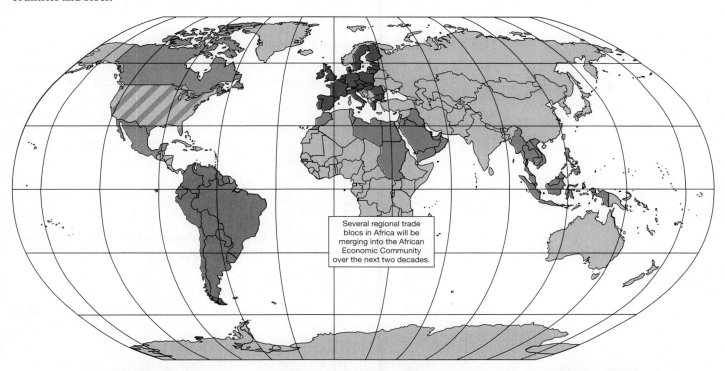

Several regional trade blocs in Africa will be merging into the African Economic Community over the next two decades.

European Union (EU)	North American Free Trade Agreement (NAFTA)	Association of Southeast Asian Nations (ASEAN)	Union of South American Nations	Asia-Pacific Economic Cooperation (APEC)	Greater Arab Free Trade Area (GAFTA)
Austria	Canada	Brunei Darussalam	Argentina	Australia	Algeria
Belgium	Mexico	Cambodia	Bolivia	Brunei Darussalam	Bahrain
Bulgaria	United States	Indonesia	Brazil	Canada	Egypt
Cyprus		Laos	Chile	Chile	Iraq
Czech Republic		Malaysia	Colombia	China	Jordan
Denmark		Myanmar	Ecuador	Hong Kong	Kuwait
Estonia		Philippines	Guyana	Indonesia	Lebanon
Finland		Singapore	Paraguay	Japan	Libya
France		Thailand	Peru	Republic of Korea	Morocco
Germany		Vietnam	Suriname	Malaysia	Oman
Greece			Uruguay	Mexico	Palestine
Hungary			Venezuela	New Zealand	Qatar
Ireland				Papua New Guinea	Saudi Arabia
Italy				Peru	Syria
Latvia				Philippines	Sudan
Lithuania				Russian Federation	Tunisia
Luxembourg				Singapore	United Arab Emirates
Malta				Chinese Taipei	Yemen
Netherlands				Thailand	
Poland				United States	
Portugal				Viet Nam	
Romania					
Slovakia					
Slovenia					
Spain					
Sweden					
United Kingdom					

The EU has taken a significant step beyond all other trading blocs in the area of money by creating its own currency, the *euro*, which has been adopted by roughly half the member states of the EU. By switching to a common currency, these countries have made financial transactions simpler and less expensive. According to EU leadership, the euro has lowered inflation and interest rates, improved transparency in pricing, and provided a more stable currency.[26]

The Asia-Pacific Economic Cooperation Council (APEC)

The Asia-Pacific Economic Cooperation Council (APEC), www.apec.org, is an organization of 21 countries that is making efforts to liberalize trade in the Pacific Rim (the land areas that surround the Pacific Ocean). Member nations, which include the United States, Japan, China, Mexico, Australia, South Korea, and Canada, represent 40 percent of the world's population and more than 50 percent of the world's gross domestic product (GDP). APEC's long-term goal is to reduce tariffs and trade barriers among industrialized countries of the Pacific Rim by 2010 and among developing countries by 2020.[27]

√CHECKPOINT

LEARNING OBJECTIVE 3: Identify the major organizations that facilitate international trade and the major trading blocs around the world.

Summary: Major organizations that facilitate trade include the World Trade Organization (WTO), the International Monetary Fund (IMF), and at least indirectly, the World Bank. Major regional trading blocs include NAFTA (Canada, Mexico, and the United States), the European Union (more than two dozen countries across Europe), and APEC (21 countries around the Pacific Rim).

Critical thinking: (1) Why do trade disputes sometimes take years to resolve? (2) If a country currently benefits from high tariffs on imports, why might it consider joining a trading bloc that requires it to lower or eliminate those tariffs?

It's your business: (1) Can you identify any ways in which your life as an employee or a consumer has been affected by U.S. membership in trading blocs such as NAFTA and APEC? (2) How can you confirm that the effect was caused by trading bloc membership?

Key terms to know: trading blocs

The Global Business Environment

Doing business internationally is neither easy nor simple, but it has become essential for thousands of U.S. companies. Venturing abroad can be a boon, but it also presents many challenges. Every country has unique laws, customs, consumer preferences, ethical standards, labor skills, and political and economic forces. All these factors can affect a firm's international prospects. Furthermore, volatile currencies, international trade relationships, and the threat of terrorism can make global expansion a risky proposition. Still, in most cases, the opportunities of the global marketplace greatly outweigh the risks.

Cultural Differences in the Global Business Environment

culture
A shared system of symbols, beliefs, attitudes, values, expectations, and norms for behavior

Culture is a shared system of symbols, beliefs, attitudes, values, expectations, and norms for behavior. Your cultural background influences the way you prioritize what is important in life, helps define your attitude toward what is appropriate in a situation, and establishes rules of behavior.[28] Successful global business leaders recognize and respect differences in language, social values, ideas of status, decision-making habits, attitudes toward time, use of space, body language, manners, religions, and ethical standards. Ignorance of or indifference to cultural differences is a common cause of communication breakdowns in international affairs. Above all else, businesspeople dealing with other cultures avoid the twin traps of **stereotyping**, assigning a wide range of generalized (and often superficial or even false) attributes to an individual on the basis of membership in a particular culture or social group, and **ethnocentrism**, the tendency to judge all other groups according to one's own group's standards, behaviors, and customs.

Real-Time Updates

Learn More

Essential guidelines for adapting to other business cultures

Learn great etiquette tips for doing business in France, Germany, Japan, Mexico, and Russia. On mybizlab (www.mybizlab.com), you can access Real-Time Updates within each chapter or under Student Study Tools. Otherwise, go to http://real-timeupdates.com/bia5 and click on "Learn More."

The best way to prepare yourself for doing business with people from another culture is to study that culture in advance. Numerous books and websites (such as www.culturecrossing.com) offer advice on traveling to and working in specific cultures. Also try to sample newspapers, magazines, and even the music and movies of another country. For instance, a movie can demonstrate nonverbal customs even if you don't grasp the language. Learn everything you can about the culture's history, religion, politics, and customs—especially its business customs. Who makes decisions? How are negotiations usually conducted? Is gift giving expected? What is the proper attire for a business meeting? In addition to the suggestion that you learn about the culture, seasoned international businesspeople offer the following tips for improving intercultural communication:

- **Be alert to the other person's customs.** Expect the other person to have values, beliefs, expectations, and mannerisms that may differ from yours.

- **Deal with the individual.** Don't stereotype the other person or react with preconceived ideas. Regard the person as an individual first, not as a representative of another culture.

- **Clarify your intent and meaning.** The other person's body language may not mean what you think, and the person may read unintentional meanings into your message. Clarify your true intent by repetition and examples. Ask questions and listen carefully.

- **Adapt your style to the other person's.** If the other person appears to be direct and straightforward, follow suit. If not, adjust your behavior to match.

- **Show respect.** Learn how respect is communicated in various cultures—through gestures, eye contact, social customs, and other actions.

These are just a few tips for doing business in the global marketplace. Successful international businesses learn as much as they can about political issues, cultural factors, and the economic environment before investing time and money in new markets. Exhibit 3.5 on the next page can guide you in your efforts to learn more about a country's culture before doing business in other countries.

stereotyping
Assigning a wide range of generalized attributes, which are often superficial or even false, to an individual based on his or her membership in a particular culture or social group

ethnocentrism
Judging all other groups according to the standards, behaviors, and customs of one's own group

Legal Differences in the Global Business Environment

Differences in national legal systems may not be as immediately obvious as cultural differences, but they can have a profound effect on international business efforts. For instance, the legal systems in the United States and the United Kingdom are based on *common law*, in which tradition, custom, and judicial interpretation play important roles. In contrast, the system in countries such as France and Germany is based on *civil law*, in which legal parameters are specified in detailed legal codes. One everyday consequence of this difference is that business contracts tend to be shorter and simpler in civil law systems, since the existing legal code outlines more aspects of the transaction or relationship. A third type of legal system, *theocratic law*, or law based on religious principles, predominates in such countries as Iran and Pakistan. Beyond the differences in legal philosophies, the business of contracts, copyrights, and other legal matters can vary considerably from one country to another.

Perhaps no issue in international business law generates as much confusion and consternation as bribery. In some countries, payments to government officials are so common

EXHIBIT 3.5 **Checklist for Doing Business Abroad**

Use this checklist as a starting point when investigating a foreign culture.

ACTION	DETAILS TO CONSIDER
Understand social customs	✓ How do people react to strangers? Are they friendly? Hostile? Reserved?
	✓ How do people greet each other? Should you bow? Nod? Shake hands?
	✓ How do you express appreciation for an invitation to lunch, dinner, or someone's home? Should you bring a gift? Send flowers? Write a thank-you note?
	✓ Are any phrases, facial expressions, or hand gestures considered rude?
	✓ How do you attract the attention of a waiter? Do you tip the waiter?
	✓ When is it rude to refuse an invitation? How do you refuse politely?
	✓ What topics may or may not be discussed in a social setting? In a business setting?
	✓ How do social customs dictate interaction between men and women? between younger people and older people?
Learn about clothing and food preferences	✓ What occasions require special clothing?
	✓ What colors are associated with mourning? Love? Joy?
	✓ Are some types of clothing considered taboo for one gender or the other?
	✓ How many times a day do people eat?
	✓ How are hands or utensils used when eating?
	✓ Where is the seat of honor at a table?
Assess political patterns	✓ How stable is the political situation?
	✓ Does the political situation affect businesses in and out of the country?
	✓ Is it appropriate to talk politics in social or business situations?
Understand religious and social beliefs	✓ To which religious groups do people belong?
	✓ Which places, objects, actions, and events are sacred?
	✓ Do religious beliefs affect communication between men and women or between any other groups?
	✓ Is there a tolerance for minority religions?
	✓ How do religious holidays affect business and government activities?
	✓ Does religion require or prohibit eating specific foods? At specific times?
Learn about economic and business institutions	✓ Is the society homogeneous or heterogeneous?
	✓ What languages are spoken?
	✓ What are the primary resources and principal products?
	✓ Are businesses generally large? Family controlled? Government controlled?
	✓ What are the generally accepted working hours?
	✓ How do people view scheduled appointments?
	✓ Are people expected to socialize before conducting business?
Appraise the nature of ethics, values, and laws	✓ Is money or a gift expected in exchange for arranging business transactions?
	✓ Do people value competitiveness or cooperation?
	✓ What are the attitudes toward work? Toward money?
	✓ Is politeness more important than factual honesty?

that they are considered by some businesspeople to be standard operating practice. These payments are used to facilitate a variety of actions, from winning contracts for public works projects (such as roads or power plants) to securing routine government services (such as customs inspections) to getting preferential treatment (such as the approval to raise prices).[29] In one of the most stunning examples of systematic, long-term bribery to surface in recent years, the German manufacturing firm Siemens paid out over a billion dollars in bribes to get contracts in more than 60 countries around the world.[30]

These payment systems discourage much-needed investment in developing countries, weaken trust in government, raise prices for consumers by inflating business costs, and can even present security risks by essentially putting officials' actions up for the highest bid. Some businesspeople have argued that critics of such payoffs are trying to impose U.S. values on other cultures, but Transparency International, a watchdog group that works to reduce business-government corruption around the world, discredits that argument by saying that all countries have laws against corruption, so it can hardly be considered a cultural issue.[31] (To learn more about Transparency International's work, visit **www.transparency.org**.)

All U.S. companies are bound by the Foreign Corrupt Practices Act (FCPA), which outlaws payments with the intent of getting government officials to break the laws of their own countries. The FCPA allows payments that expedite actions that are legal, such as clearing merchandise through customs, although critics such as Transparency International consider this behavior unethical as well because it permits private profits to be gained from public trust.[32] Other types of payments can also be considered forms of influence but aren't covered by the FCPA, such as foreign aid payments from one government to another, made with the intent of securing favorable decisions for business.

Significantly, the FCPA also gives the U.S. government authority to investigate and charge foreign companies that engage in bribery using subsidiaries, banks, or other resources based in the United States. For example, even though Siemens is a German company, it was charged by the U.S. Department of Justice with FCPA violations and fined hundreds of millions of dollars by the U.S. government. The number of FCPA investigations has been increasing in recent years, with some companies even contacting the government on their own to make sure they haven't been in violation.[33]

Following the FCPA, the Organisation for Economic Co-Operation and Development (OECD), an international body dedicated to fostering economic prosperity and combating poverty, established antibribery guidelines for its member nations as well.[34] The good news is that more laws and expectations are in place around the world; the bad news is that enforcement is still spotty.[35]

✓CHECKPOINT

LEARNING OBJECTIVE 4: Discuss the importance of understanding cultural and legal differences in the global business environment.

Summary: Elements of culture include language, social values, ideas of status, decision-making habits, attitudes toward time, use of space, body language, manners, religions, and ethical standards. Awareness of and respect for cultural differences is essential to avoiding communication breakdowns and fostering positive working relationships. Understanding differences in legal systems and specific laws and regulations in other countries is another vital aspect of successful international business. One of the most confusing and frustrating aspects of international trade law is the issue of bribery.

Critical thinking: (1) What steps could you take to help someone from another country adapt to U.S. business culture? (2) How can you convey respect for another person's culture even if you don't agree with it or even understand it?

It's your business: (1) Have you ever experienced a communication breakdown with someone from another country? (2) If so, how did you resolve it, and how could you apply this experience to your business career?

Key terms to know: culture, stereotyping, ethnocentrism

Forms of International Business Activity

Beyond cultural and legal concerns, companies that plan to go international also need to think carefully about the right organizational approach to support these activities. The five common forms of international business are *importing and exporting, licensing, franchising, strategic alliances and joint ventures,* and *foreign direct investment;* each has varying degrees of ownership, financial commitment, and risk.

Importing and Exporting

importing
Purchasing goods or services from another country and bringing them into one's own country

exporting
Selling and shipping goods or services to another country

Importing, the buying of goods or services from a supplier in another country, and **exporting**, the selling of products outside the country in which they are produced, have existed for centuries. In the last few decades, however, the increased level of these activities has caused the economies of the world to become tightly linked.

Exporting, one of the least risky forms of international business activity, permits a firm to enter a foreign market gradually, assess local conditions, and then fine-tune its product offerings to meet the needs of foreign consumers. In most cases, the firm's financial exposure is limited to the costs of researching the market, advertising, and either establishing a direct sales and distribution system or hiring intermediaries. Such intermediaries include *export management companies,* which are domestic firms that specialize in performing international marketing services on a commission basis, and *export trading companies,* which are general trading firms that will buy products for resale overseas as well as perform a variety of importing, exporting, and manufacturing functions.

Another alternative is to use foreign distributors. Working through a distributor with connections in the target country is often helpful to both large and small companies because such intermediaries can provide you with the connections, expertise, and market knowledge you will need to conduct business in a foreign country.[36] In addition, many countries now have foreign trade offices to help importers and exporters interested in doing business within their borders. Other helpful resources include professional agents, local businesspeople, and the International Trade Administration of the U.S. Department of Commerce (www.export.gov). This trade organization offers a variety of services, including political and credit-risk analysis, advice on entering foreign markets, and financing tips.[37]

International Licensing

licensing
Agreement to produce and market another company's product in exchange for a royalty or fee

Licensing is another popular approach to international business. License agreements entitle one company to use some or all of another firm's intellectual property (patents, trademarks, brand names, copyrights, or trade secrets) in return for a royalty payment.

Low up-front costs are an attractive aspect of international licensing. Pharmaceutical firms such as Germany's Boehringer Ingelheim, for instance, routinely use licensing to enter foreign markets.[38] After a pharmaceutical firm has developed and patented a new drug, it is often more efficient to grant existing local firms the right to manufacture and distribute the patented drug in return for royalty payments. (Licensing agreements are not restricted to international business, of course; a company can also license its products or technology to other companies in its domestic market.)

Real-Time Updates

Learn More

Learn the basics of importing

From initial research to finding foreign product sources, learn all you need to know to get started in importing. On mybizlab (www.mybizlab.com), you can access Real-Time Updates within each chapter or under Student Study Tools. Otherwise, go to http://real-timeupdates.com/bia5 and click on "Learn More."

International Franchising

Some companies choose to expand into foreign markets by *franchising* their operations. Chapter 6 discusses franchising in more detail, but briefly, franchising involves selling the right to use a *business system*, including brand names, business processes, trade secrets, and other assets. For instance, there are roughly 18,000 McDonald's restaurants in more than 100 countries outside the United States, and the vast majority are run by independent franchisees.[39] Franchising is an attractive option for many companies because it reduces the costs and risks of expanding internationally.

International Strategic Alliances and Joint Ventures

Strategic alliances (discussed in Chapter 5), long-term partnerships between two or more companies to jointly develop, produce, or sell products, are another way to reach the global marketplace. Alliance partners typically share ideas, expertise, resources, technologies, investment costs, risks, management, and profits. In some cases, a strategic alliance might be the only way to gain access to a market, which was the reason Viacom (which owns CBS, MTV, and other media) decided to form an alliance with Beijing Television to expand its presence in China.[40]

A *joint venture*, in which two or more firms join together to create a new business entity that is legally separate and distinct from its parents, is an alternative to a strategic alliance. In some countries, foreign companies are prohibited from owning facilities outright or from investing in local business. Thus, establishing a joint venture with a local partner may be the only way to do business in that country. In other cases, foreigners may be required to move some of their production facilities to the country to earn the right to sell their products there.

foreign direct investment (FDI)
Investment of money by foreign companies in domestic business enterprises

multinational corporations (MNCs)
Companies with operations in more than one country

Foreign Direct Investment

Many firms prefer to enter international markets through partial or whole ownership and control of assets in foreign countries, an approach known as **foreign direct investment (FDI)**. To enter the Chinese market, for instance, Amazon.com purchased Joyo, an established e-commerce company. The company is now known there as Joyo Amazon.cn (**www.amazon.cn**).[41] Some facilities are set up through FDI to exploit the availability of raw materials; others take advantage of low wage rates; others minimize transportation costs by choosing locations that give them direct access to markets in other countries. In almost all cases, at least part of the workforce is drawn from the local population. Companies that establish a physical presence in multiple countries through FDI are called **multinational corporations (MNCs)**. MNCs can approach international markets in a variety of ways; see "Organizational Strategies for International Expansion" on page 114.

The growth of FDI mirrors the rapid pace of economic globalization over the past several decades; annual FDI amounts now exceed $10 trillion worldwide.[42] FDI typically gives companies greater control, but it carries much greater economic and political risk and is more complex than any other form of entry in the global marketplace. Consequently, most FDI takes place between the industrialized nations (a group that includes such large, stable economies as the United States, Canada, Japan, and most countries in Europe), which

Amazon.com used foreign direct investment to enter the Chinese market, purchasing the established e-commerce company Joyo.

tend to offer greater protection for foreign investors. The top three countries in which U.S. companies own facilities through FDI are the United Kingdom, the Netherlands, and Canada; the top three countries that invest in the United States through FDI are the United Kingdom, Japan, and Canada.[43]

✓CHECKPOINT

LEARNING OBJECTIVE 5: Define the major forms of international business activity.

Summary: The major forms of international business activity are importing and exporting (buying and selling across national boundaries), licensing (conferring the rights to create a product), franchising (selling the rights to use an entire business system and brand identity), strategic alliances and joint ventures (forming partnerships with other companies), and foreign direct investment (buying companies or building facilities in another country).

Critical thinking: (1) Can a company successfully export to other countries without having staff and facilities in those countries? Why or why not? (2) Why does so much foreign direct investment take place between the industrialized nations?

It's your business: (1) What connotations does the word "imported" have for you? (2) On what do you base your reaction?

Key terms to know: importing, exporting, licensing, foreign direct investment (FDI), multinational corporations (MNCs)

Strategic Approaches to International Markets

Expanding internationally is obviously not a decision any business can take lightly. The rewards can be considerable, but the costs and risks must be analyzed carefully during the planning stage. This section offers a brief look at overall organizational strategies for international expansion, followed by strategic questions in the various functional areas of the business.

Organizational Strategies for International Expansion

When a firm decides to establish a presence in another country, it needs to consider its long-term objectives, the nature of its products, the characteristics of the markets into which it plans to expand, and the management team's ability to oversee a geographically dispersed operation. These considerations can lead to one of several high-level strategies:[44]

multidomestic strategy
Decentralized approach to international expansion in which a company creates highly independent operating units in each new country

global strategy
Highly centralized approach to international expansion, with headquarters in the home country making all major decisions

transnational strategy
Hybrid approach that attempts to reap the benefits of international scale while being responsive to local market dynamics

- In the **multidomestic strategy**, a company creates highly independent operating units in each new country, giving local managers a great deal of freedom to run their operations almost as though they are independent companies. While this strategy can help a company respond more quickly and effectively to local market needs, it doesn't deliver the economy of scale advantages that other strategies can bring.

- In the **global strategy**, a company embraces the notion of economic globalization by viewing the world as a single integrated market. This is essentially the opposite of the multidomestic strategy. Managerial control with the global strategy is highly centralized, with headquarters in the home country making all major decisions.

- In the **transnational strategy**, a company uses a hybrid approach as it attempts to reap the benefits of international scale while being responsive to local market dynamics. This is the essence of the often-heard advice to "think globally, act locally." With this approach, major strategic decisions and business systems such as accounting and purchasing are often centralized, but then local business units are given the freedom to make "on the ground" decisions that are most appropriate for local markets. For example, Canada's ICICI Bank uses a global branding strategy to ensure

Real-Time Updates

Learn More
Made where, exactly?

Not every product that appears to be "made in America" is really made in the United States. On mybizlab (**www.mybizlab.com**), you can access Real-Time Updates within each chapter or under Student Study Tools. Otherwise, go to **http://real-timeupdates.com/bia5** and click on "Learn More."

consistency in all countries where it does business, but within that framework, it allows country managers to adapt marketing efforts to local conditions.[45]

Functional Strategies for International Expansion

Choosing the right form of business to pursue is the first of many decisions that companies need to make when moving into other countries. Virtually everything you learn about in this course, from human resources to marketing to financial management, needs to be reconsidered carefully when going international. Some of the most important decisions involve products, customer support, pricing, promotion, and staffing:

- **Products.** You face two primary questions regarding products. First, which products should you try to sell in each market? Second, should you *standardize* your products, selling the same product everywhere in the world, or *customize* your products to accommodate the lifestyles and habits of local target markets? Customization seems like an obvious choice, but it can increase costs and operational complexity, so the decision to customize is not automatic. The degree of customization can also vary. A company may change only the product's name or packaging, or it can modify the product's components, size, and functions. Understanding a country's regulations, culture, and local competition plays into the decisions. For instance, LG Electronics, a South Korean appliance maker, markets refrigerators in India with extra-large vegetable compartments (catering to India's many vegetarians), a different version in Saudi Arabia that has a special cooler for dates (which are popular there), and yet another version in South Korea with a sealed compartment for *kimchi* (to keep the richly aromatic dish from interacting with other foods).[46]

- **Customer support.** Cars, computers, and other products that require some degree of customer support add another layer of complexity to international business. Many customers are reluctant to buy foreign products that don't offer some form of local support, whether it's a local dealer, a manufacturer's branch office, or a third-party organization that offers support under contract to the manufacturer.

- **Promotion.** Advertising, public relations, and other promotional efforts also present the dilemma of standardization versus customization. After years of trying to build global brands, many U.S. companies are putting new emphasis on crafting customized messages for each country. As one British advertising executive put it, "One size doesn't fit all. Consumers are more interesting for their differences rather than their similarities."[47] For example, Pepsi-Cola didn't catch on in India until the company started featuring Indian movie star Shahrukh Khan and cricket player Sachin Tendulka in its TV commercials.[48]

- **Pricing.** Even a standardized strategy adds costs, from transportation to communication, and customized strategies add even more costs. Before moving into other countries, businesses need to make sure they can cover all these costs and still be able to offer competitive prices.

- **Staffing.** Depending on the form of business a company decides to pursue in international markets, staffing questions can be major considerations. Many companies find that a combination of U.S. and local personnel works best, mixing company experience with local connections and lifelong knowledge of the working culture. Staffing strategies can evolve over time, too, as conditions change in various countries. In recent years, for example, U.S. and European countries with operations in China have begun filling more middle and upper management positions with local talent, rather than relocating managers from headquarters. The costs of hiring locally are often considerably lower, and there is less risk of a foreign manager failing to adapt to working and living in China.[49] When transferring managers to foreign posts, some U.S. companies have experienced failure rates as high as 50 percent.[50]

Given the number and complexity of the decisions to be made, you can see why successful companies plan international expansion with great care—and adapt quickly if their strategies and tactics aren't working. For the latest information on internal business, visit http://real-timeupdates.com/bia5 and click on Chapter 3.

✓CHECKPOINT

LEARNING OBJECTIVE 6: Discuss the strategic choices that must be considered before entering international markets.

Summary: The strategic choices to make include the basic organizational strategy that defines what kind of company the firm will be in each country and a variety of functional strategies involving such aspects as products, customer support, promotion, pricing, and staffing. Organizational strategic choices include *multidomestic* (a highly decentralized approach), *global* (a highly centralized approach), and *transnational* (a hybrid approach).

Critical thinking: (1) If a multidomestic approach gives local managers the most flexibility for responding to local market conditions, why wouldn't every international company use this strategy? (2) How might the choice of overall organizational strategy affect a company's staffing plans in each country?

It's your business: (1) Have you ever purchased an imported product that seemed poorly adapted to the U.S. market? (2) How would you advise the company in order to satisfy U.S. customers more effectively?

Key terms to know: multidomestic strategy, global strategy, transnational strategy

Behind the Scenes

Adapting an American Cultural Icon to the African Market

By the time Alex Okosi was ready to launch MTV in Africa, the company had already set up 99 other versions of the music and entertainment channel around the world. International experience was not a problem. However, no market could've presented the challenges that Africa presented. From low consumer income to limited availability of television, the hurdles to success would require a unique approach.

On the positive side, Africa did present a potentially huge opportunity as countries up and down the continent began to develop stronger consumer economies. Moreover, Okosi wasn't the only African émigré who wanted to return home; while working in the United States he had met a number of other people from African nations who wanted to return and help rebuild their respective countries.

Then there was the incredibly rich music culture and the millions of people who were passionate about their music. The musical connection between Africa and America goes back centuries, actually, when the ancient singer-songwriter tradition from countries such as Mali found its way to the United States as a consequence of the slave trade. The music eventually evolved into American blues and jazz, which then inspired rock, soul, R&B, hip-hop, and other styles. Meanwhile, today's African popular music is a vibrant blend of traditional local styles and contemporary imports. For instance, the *hip-life* style popular in Ghana combines hip-hop with *highlife*, a jazzy, guitar-driven dance sound that dates from the 1920s.

The musical tradition was rich, but music television needs quality videos, and those were few and far between. To increase the supply, Okosi nurtured local talent, even visiting some aspiring directors in their homes to help them learn how to create broadcast-quality videos.

After several years of work, Okosi and his colleagues were ready to launch, and MTV Base went live with "African Queen" by the popular Nigerian artist 2Face Idibia. Will Smith and Ludicris were among the American celebrities who helped launch the new channel at dance parties and other events around Africa.

MTV Base combines videos and shows produced in Africa with content imported from the United States. Locally produced videos now account for 40 percent of the channel's musical fare, and Osaki wants to raise that to at least 50 percent in the near future. He describes the channel's goal as showcasing "the creativity and diversity of contemporary music in Africa, giving an international platform to African genres such as Kwaito, Hip-Life, Mbalax, and Zouk and putting African artists in the spotlight alongside their international peers." MTV Base is also active in health and social causes, such as offering educational programming about HIV protection.

As a business venture, MTV Base looks to be a success, with over 50 million viewers in 48 countries across sub-Saharan Africa. The channel is profitable and attracts a variety of local and international advertisers. And it has already become an exporter: Videos produced in Africa are now shown in a special program on MTV in the United Kingdom, and rising African stars such as D'Banj have appeared on MTV in the United States.[51]

Critical Thinking Questions

1. Why would MTV use the MTV brand name for its launch in Africa, rather than coming up with a new name more closely identified with the target market, such as African Music Television?

2. What ethical responsibilities does MTV have relative to its expansion into Africa? Why?

3. Do global media such as MTV have the potential to improve international relations? Do they have the potential to harm international relations? Explain your answers.

LEARN MORE ONLINE

Visit the MTV Base Africa website at www.mtvbase.com. Compare the site with MTV's U.S. homepage at www.mtv.com. What differences and similarities do you see? How much American culture do you see reflected on the MTV Base website, as either content on the site itself or content on the cable channel that is described on the website? ■

Key Terms

balance of payments (100)
balance of trade (100)
culture (108)
dumping (104)
economic globalization (99)
economies of scale (99)
embargo (104)
ethnocentrism (109)
exchange rate (100)
export subsidies (104)

exporting (112)
fair trade (103)
foreign direct investment (FDI) (113)
free trade (103)
global strategy (114)
import quotas (104)
importing (112)
licensing (112)
multidomestic strategy (114)

multinational corporations (MNCs) (113)
protectionism (103)
stereotyping (109)
tariffs (103)
trade deficit (100)
trade surplus (100)
trading blocs (106)
transnational strategy (114)

Test Your Knowledge

Questions for Review

1. What is the balance of trade, and how is it related to the balance of payments?

2. What is dumping, and how does the United States respond to this practice?

3. What two fundamental product strategies do companies choose between when selling their products in the global marketplace?

4. How can a company use a licensing agreement to enter world markets?

5. What is a floating exchange rate?

Questions for Analysis

6. How do companies benefit from forming international joint ventures and strategic alliances?

7. What types of situations might cause the U.S. government to implement protectionist measures?

8. How do tariffs and quotas protect a country's own industries?

9. Why would a company choose to work through intermediaries when selling products in a foreign country?

10. **Ethical Considerations.** Is it unethical for a U.S. company to choose export markets specifically for their less-stringent consumer protection standards? Why or why not?

Questions for Application

11. How has your current employer or any previous employer been affected by globalization? For instance, does your company compete with lower-cost imports? (If you don't have any work experience, ask a friend or family member.)

12. Suppose you own a small company that manufactures baseball equipment. You are aware that Russia is a large market, and you are considering exporting your products there. What steps should you take? Who might be able to give you assistance?

13. Would a major shopping mall developer with experience all across Europe be a good strategic alliance partner for your fast-food chain's first overseas expansion effort? Why or why not?

14. **Concept Integration.** You just received notice that a large shipment of manufacturing supplies you have been waiting for has been held up in customs for two weeks. A local business associate tells you that you are expected to give customs agents some "incentive money" to see that everything clears easily. How will you handle this situation? Evaluate the ethical merits of your decision by answering the questions outlined in Exhibit 4.2 on page 125.

Practice Your Knowledge

Sharpening Your Communication Skills

Languages never translate on a word-for-word basis. When doing business in the global marketplace, choose words that convey only their most specific denotative meaning. Avoid using slang or idioms (words that can have meanings far different from their individual components when translated literally). For example, if a U.S. executive tells an Egyptian executive that a certain product "doesn't cut the mustard," chances are that communication will fail.

Team up with two other students and list 10 examples of slang (in your own language) that would probably be misinterpreted or misunderstood during a business conversation with someone from another culture. Next to each example, suggest other words you might use to convey the same message. Make sure the alternatives mean exactly the same as the original slang or idiom. Compare your list with those of your classmates.

Building Your Team Skills

In April 2009, eight U.S. steel companies and the United Steelworkers union accused Chinese pipe manufacturers of dumping $2.7 billion worth of a particular type of stainless steel pipe on the American market the previous year. (Specifically, the type of pipe is called "oil country tubular goods" and is used in oil and gas wells.) In a petition to the U.S. International Trade Commission (ITC) and the U.S. Department of Justice (DOJ), the group said 2,000 U.S. employees had lost their jobs as a result of the unfairly priced Chinese imports. The petition asked for tariffs of up to 99 percent on the Chinese steel.[52]

With your team, research the outcome of the steel industry's petition. Did the ITC and DOJ enact tariffs on Chinese steel? After you have discovered the outcome of the petition, analyze the potential effect of the government's position on the following stakeholders:

- U.S. businesses that buy this type of steel
- U.S. steel manufacturers
- Employees of U.S. steel manufacturers
- The United Steelworkers union
- Chinese steel manufacturers

Present your analysis to the class and compare your conclusions with those reached by other teams.

Expand Your Knowledge

Discovering Career Opportunities

If global business interests you, consider working for a U.S. government agency that supports or regulates international trade. For example, here are the duties of an international trade specialist working for the International Trade Administration of the U.S. Department of Commerce:[55]

The International Trade Specialist, at the full performance level, will carry out a wide range of economic and trade analysis as a regional desk officer (Office covers Central and Southeast Europe). Will advise the Director of the Office of European Country Affairs and other departmental officials on matters pertaining to bilateral and multilateral trade policy development and implementation, market access and trade agreements compliance. Performance of these duties will require familiarity with and monitoring of U.S. and assigned countries' trade policies, programs and procedures. Will be responsive to companies' requests for assistance and perform outreach to the private sector. Will maintain close liaison and coordination with other departmental offices, other U.S. Government agencies, business organizations and foreign government entities. Will attend and report on meetings both in the Department and at other U.S. agencies, including but not limited to the Office of the U.S. Trade Representative and the Department of State. These meetings will involve development and advancement of trade policies, negotiating positions, and economic/commercial initiatives in the European region. He or she will prepare reports, talking points, speech materials, statistical data and correspondence for use by senior Commerce officials, utilizing word processing and computer software programs. Will review Foreign Service and intelligence reports on economic trends and issues in the region.

1. On the basis of this description, what education and skills (personal and professional) would you need to succeed as an international trade specialist?
2. How well does this job description fit your qualifications and interests?
3. How important would interpersonal skills be in this position? Why?

Developing Your Research Skills

Companies involved in international trade have to watch the foreign exchange rates of the countries in which they do business. Use your research skills to locate and analyze information about the value of the Japanese yen relative to the U.S. dollar. As you complete this exercise, make a note of the sources and search strategies you used.

1. How many Japanese yen does one U.S. dollar buy right now? (You can find the foreign exchange rate for the yen at www.x-rates.com and many similar sites.)
2. Investigate the foreign exchange rate for the yen against the dollar over the past month. Is the dollar growing stronger (buying more yen) or growing weaker (buying fewer yen)?
3. If you were a U.S. exporter selling to Japan, how would a stronger dollar be likely to affect demand for your products? How would a weaker dollar be likely to affect demand?

Improving Your Tech Insights: Telepresence

Telepresence systems start with the basic idea of video-conferencing but go far beyond with imagery so real that colleagues thousands of miles apart virtually appear to be in the same room together. The interaction feels so lifelike that participants can forget that the person "sitting" on the other side of the table is actually in another city or even another country. The ability to convey nonverbal subtleties such as facial expressions and hand gestures makes these systems particularly good for negotiations, collaborative problem-solving, and other complex discussions.[53]

Conduct research to identify a company that has installed a telepresence system. What kinds of meetings does the firm use the telepresence system for? What advantages does the system give the company?[54]

Video Discussion

Access the Chapter 3 video discussion in the End of Chapter Assignments section at www.mybizlab.com.

PEARSON
mybizlab

Log on to www.mybizlab.com to access the following study and assessment aids associated with this chapter:

- Interactive exercises
- Pre/post test
- Real-Time Updates
- Video application
- Customized study plans
- Biz Skills Simulations
- Quick Learning Guide

If you are not using mybizlab, you can access Real-Time Updates and Quick Learning Guides through http://real-timeupdates.com/bia5. The Quick Learning Guide (located under "Learn More" on the website) provides all six Checkpoints in a handy two-page format to help you study for exams or review important concepts whenever you need a quick refresher.

CHAPTER 4
Business Ethics and Corporate Social Responsibility

Behind the
Scenes

Protestors Pour on the Trouble for PepsiCo in India

www.pepsiindia.co.in

Every business wants consumers to feel passionate about its products—but not the sort of passion where they set fire to cardboard replicas of the products during public demonstrations or issue press releases calling the company dishonest and its products dangerous.

Such is the situation that PepsiCo, the global beverage and snack food giant based in Purchase, New York, recently faced in India. For several years, the company has been the target of a publicity campaign organized and led by the small nonprofit Centre for Science and Environment (CSE) and its director, Sunita Narain, a well-known activist.

The protests focused on two issues, the use of water and the safety of Pepsi bottled waters and sodas. Water is in short supply in much of India. For millions of Indians, acquiring safe water to drink and enough water to serve a family's daily needs is a major challenge. Critics such as Narain accuse Pepsi and other businesses of overusing a scarce resource that belongs to the people. Pepsi acknowledged it could do better in this respect: To make 24 eight-ounce bottles of beverage—a gallon and a half—the company's production process used over nine gallons of water.

The issue of product contamination is less clear but no less volatile. Pesticides and industrial chemicals in

After a nonprofit organization accused Pepsi of selling tainted beverages in India, protesters burned Pepsi products in effigy.

the soil have been seeping into groundwater supplies for years, and after government studies showed those contaminants were moving into the food supply, CSE tested a variety of beverages made in India by Pepsi and Coke. Although the level of contaminants it found was far lower than those found previously in the milk supply, Narain announced in a press conference that pesticides in Pepsi's brands of bottled water were 36 times higher and Coke's were 30 times higher than European safety standards (which were used for comparison because the Indian government hadn't set its own safety standards).

Narain's awareness campaign had an immediate effect, with protesters taking to the streets and local governments banning or restricting sales of Pepsi products. As sales dropped and Pepsi's reputation eroded, one of the Pepsi executives responsible for responding to the situation was ironically also a prominent woman with roots in India. Indra Nooyi, Pepsi's president and chief financial officer at the time, had vivid memories of water shortages while growing up in India. She was deeply sensitive to the water and safety issues but was adamant that CSE's tests were flawed and that Pepsi's products were safe. If you were Nooyi, how would you respond to the critics?[1] ∎

Introduction

Like PepsiCo's Indra Nooyi (profiled in the chapter-opening Behind the Scenes), managers in every industry today must balance the demands of running a profitable business with running a socially responsible company. As a future business leader, you will face some of the challenges discussed in this chapter, and your choices won't always be easy. You may struggle to find ethical clarity in some situations, to even understand what your choices are and how each option might affect your company's various stakeholders. You may need to muster the courage to stand up to colleagues, bosses, or customers if you think ethical principles are being violated. Fortunately, by having a good understanding of what constitutes ethical behavior and what society expects from business today, you'll be better prepared to make these tough choices. This chapter explores the basic ideas of business ethics and corporate social responsibility and then takes a closer look at business's responsibility toward the natural environment, consumers, and employees.

Ethics in Contemporary Business

Every few years, it seems, some new crisis erupts in the business world and focuses attention on the complex and sometimes contentious relationship between business and society. Most recently, the financial meltdown that helped trigger the global recession had many people questioning the ethics of the entire banking industry (even though many banks avoided the risky decisions at the heart of the crisis). In a public opinion poll taken about a year into the recession, only 23 percent of the American public gave bankers "very high" or "high" marks for honesty and integrity, the lowest marks ever in the 20-year history of this particular survey. And even at 23 percent, bankers scored quite a bit better than top executives (12 percent), stockbrokers (12 percent), and advertising practitioners (10 percent).[2] Harvard Business School professor Rakesh Khurana probably speaks for many when he says, "One way of looking at the problem with American business today is that it has succeeded in assuming many of the appearances and privileges of professionalism, while evading the attendant constraints and responsibilities."[3]

The news is not all bad, of course. When you hear about illegal or unethical behavior on the part of a few managers, bear in mind that the vast majority of businesses are run by ethical managers and staffed by ethical employees whose positive contributions to their communities are unfortunately overshadowed at times by headline-grabbing scandals. Companies around the world help their communities in countless ways, from sponsoring youth sports teams to raising millions of dollars to build hospitals.

Moreover, even when companies are simply engaged in the normal course of business—and do so ethically—they contribute to society by making useful products, providing employment, and paying taxes. Business catches a lot of flak these days, some of it rightly deserved, but overall, its contributions to the health, happiness, and well-being of society are beyond measure.

What Is Ethical Behavior?

ethics
The rules or standards governing the conduct of a person or group

Ethics are the principles and standards of moral behavior that are accepted by society as right versus wrong. Practicing good business ethics involves, at a minimum, competing fairly and honestly, communicating truthfully, and not causing harm to others.

- **Competing fairly and honestly.** Businesses are expected to compete fairly and honestly and not knowingly deceive, intimidate, or misrepresent themselves to customers, competitors, clients, or employees.

- **Communicating truthfully.** Communicating truthfully is a simple enough concept: Tell the truth, the whole truth, and nothing but the truth. However, matters sometimes aren't so clear. For instance, if you plan to introduce an improved version of a product next year, do you have an obligation to tell customers who are buying the existing product this year? Suppose you do tell them, and so many decide to delay their purchases that you end up with a cash flow problem that forces you to lay off several employees. Would that be fair for customers but unfair for your employees? Business communication ethics often involve the question of **transparency**, which can be defined as "the degree to which information flows freely within an organization, among managers and employees, and outward to stakeholders."[4]

transparency
The degree to which affected parties can observe relevant aspects of transactions or decisions

- **Not causing harm to others.** All businesses have the capacity to cause harm to employees, customers, other companies, their communities, and investors. Problems can start when managers make decisions that put their personal interests above those of other stakeholders, underestimate the risks of failure, or neglect to consider potential effects on other people and organizations. For example, **insider trading**, in which company insiders use confidential information to gain an advantage in stock market trading, harms other investors. (Insider trading is illegal, in addition to being unethical.) Of course, harm can also result even when managers have acted ethically—but they're still responsible for these negative outcomes.

Factors Influencing Ethical Behavior

Of the many factors that influence ethical behavior, three warrant particular attention: cultural differences, knowledge, and organizational behavior.

Cultural Differences

Globalization exposes businesspeople to a variety of cultures and business practices. What does it mean for a business to do the right thing in Thailand? In Nigeria? In Norway? What may be considered unethical in one culture could be an accepted practice in another. Managers may need to consider a wide range of issues, including acceptable working conditions, minimum wage levels, product safety issues, and environmental protection.

Knowledge

As a general rule, the more you know and the better you understand a situation, the better your chances of making an ethical decision. In the often frantic churn of daily business, though, it's easy to shut your eyes and ears to potential problems. However, as a business leader, you have the responsibility not only to pay attention but to actively seek out information regarding potential ethical issues. Ignorance is never an acceptable defense in the eyes of the law, and it shouldn't be in questions of ethics, either.

For example, after MySpace received numerous complaints that adult pedophiles were posing as teenagers on the popular social networking site, the company hired a former federal prosecutor to establish systems and policies to protect underage users. As a result, every week, MySpace deletes thousands of profiles of people who lie about their ages, patrols the site with artificial intelligence software that looks for words and phrases child molesters tend to use, and recently agreed to make teens' profiles private by default.[5]

Organizational Behavior

Companies with strong ethical practices create cultures that reward good behavior—and don't intentionally or unintentionally reward bad behavior.[6] At United Technologies (www.utc.com), a diversified manufacturer based in Hartford, Connecticut, ethical behavior starts at the top, where executives are responsible for meeting a number of clearly defined ethical standards, and their annual compensation is tied to how well they perform.[7] The company's ethical policies have teeth, too; in 2008, 357 employees were fired for violating ethical standards.[8] To help avoid ethical breaches, many companies develop programs to improve ethical conduct, typically combine training, communication, and a **code of ethics** that defines the values and principles that should be used to guide decisions (see Exhibit 4.1 on the next page for an example).

Employees who observe unethical or illegal behavior within their companies and are unable to resolve the problems through normal channels may have no choice but to resort to **whistleblowing**—expressing their concerns through company ethics hotlines or even going to the news media if they perceive no other options. The decision to "blow the whistle" on one's own employer is rarely easy or without consequences; more than 80 percent of whistleblowers in a recent survey said they were punished in some way for coming forward with their concerns.[9] Although whistleblowing is sometimes characterized as "ratting on" colleagues or managers, it has an essential function. According to international business expert Alex MacBeath, "Often whistleblowing can be the only way

insider trading
The use of unpublicized information that an individual gains from the course of his or her job to benefit from fluctuations in the stock market

code of ethics
Written statement setting forth the principles that guide an organization's decisions

whistleblowing
The disclosure of information by a company insider that exposes illegal or unethical behavior by others within the organization

EXHIBIT 4.1 AT&T's Code of Ethics

AT&T's Code of Ethics addresses nine areas of conduct and decision making. You can read the Code at www.att.com (look in the "Investor Relations" section, under "Corporate Governance").

PRINCIPLE	EXAMPLES OF HOW THE CODE ADDRESSES EACH PRINCIPLE
Honest and Ethical Conduct	The Code explicitly states that corporate directors, corporate officers, and employees have a duty to the company to behave honestly and ethically.
Conflicts of Interest	When a director, officer, or employee encounters a conflict between what is best for the company and what is best for him or her personally, the company's interests take priority.
Disclosure	The Code requires that anyone who is involved with Securities and Exchange Commission requirements for disclosing financial information be familiar with the company's disclosure policies and avoid knowingly misrepresenting the company in any way.
Compliance	The company requires all directors, officers, and employees to follow all laws and regulations that pertain to the company's operations and to their individual roles within the company. For example, the Code has specific guidelines for the use of confidential information to avoid insider trading and other violations of federal law.
Reporting and Accountability	The Code also outlines procedures that directors, officers, and employees are required to follow if they discover any violation of the Code. A toll-free number is provided for voicing concerns or asking questions about ethical matters, and the Code outlines the procedures that will be taken whenever a potential violation is reported. Moreover, the Code prohibits retaliation against anyone who reports ethical concerns or violations.
Corporate Opportunities	The Code prohibits directors, officers, or employees who become aware of business opportunities during the course of their work for the company from pursuing those opportunities on their own unless the company has been informed of the opportunity first and has declined to pursue it.
Confidentiality	Recognizing that directors, officers, and employees often handle confidential information about the company, its customers, and its business partners, the Code provides guidelines for preventing the disclosure of this information.
Fair Dealing	The Code prohibits anyone working on the company's behalf from gaining unfair advantage through unethical business practices and requires everyone to treat customers, competitors, and other parties fairly.
Protection and Proper Use of Company Assets	Everyone in the company has a duty to protect corporate assets and to use those assets efficiently. The Code specifies that these assets are to be used "only for legitimate business purposes."

that information about issues such as rule breaking, criminal activity, cover-ups, and fraud can be brought to management's attention before serious damage is suffered."[10] Recognizing the value of this feedback, many companies have formal reporting mechanisms that give employees a way to voice ethical and legal concerns to management.

Ethical Decision Making

Roughly speaking, ethical decisions can be grouped into two categories of difficulty. When the question of what is right and what is wrong is clear, the decision is easy. You simply choose to do the right thing. Granted, actually *doing* the right thing might be incredibly difficult (or expensive or painful), but the ethical decision itself is easy because you can clearly identify a right course of action and a wrong course. If you choose the wrong course, such as cheating on your taxes or stealing from your employer, you commit what is known as an **ethical lapse**. The choices were clear, and you made the wrong one.

However, you will encounter situations in which choices are not so clear. In contrast to an ethical lapse, an **ethical dilemma** is a situation in which you must choose between conflicting but arguably valid options. These dilemmas can be much more difficult to resolve

ethical lapse
Situation in which an individual or group makes a decision that is morally wrong, illegal, or unethical

ethical dilemma
Situation in which more than one side of an issue can be supported with valid arguments

and often involve making painful compromises. Let's say you need to lay off one employee to cut costs. Employee A, who is competent but unspectacular, has a family to support and depends heavily on your company's health insurance. Employee B, a top performer, is single and healthy with no dependents. Getting laid off would be a greater blow to Employee A, but laying off Employee B would be a greater blow to the company. Which employee do you let go? Like most ethical dilemmas, the right answer is not easy to identify.

Exhibit 4.2 identifies six well-known approaches to resolving ethical dilemmas. Regardless of which approach you take, the following steps can help you find the right answer when faced with an ethical dilemma:

- Make sure you frame the situation accurately, taking into account all relevant issues and questions and identifying all parties who might be affected by your decision.

- Consider the rights of everyone involved. For instance, if you own the company, you could choose to keep Employee A in the previous example even though that decision is worse for the company. However, if you are a manager in a company owned by someone else, you also have a responsibility to protect the interests of the investors who have entrusted you with their money.

- Be as objective as possible. First, make sure you're not making a decision just to protect your own emotions. Second, don't automatically assume you're viewing a situation fairly and objectively. Psychological research suggests that many people are influenced by unconscious biases that may even run counter to their stated beliefs.[11]

- Don't assume that other people think the way you do. The time-honored "Golden Rule" of treating others the way you want to be treated can cause problems when others don't *want* to be treated the same way you do.

- Watch out for **conflicts of interest**, situations in which competing loyalties can lead to ethical lapses. For instance, if you are in charge of selecting an advertising agency to do your company's next campaign, you would have an obvious conflict of interest if your husband or wife worked for one of the agencies under consideration. Companies and government agencies have established numerous guidelines and regulations to prevent conflicts of interest in business.

conflicts of interest
Situations in which competing loyalties can lead to ethical lapses; in business, situations in which a business decision may be influenced by the potential for personal gain

Real-Time Updates

Learn More
Ethical lapses in social media

Social media make a lot of things easier—including committing ethical lapses. On mybizlab (www.mybizlab.com), you can access Real-Time Updates within each chapter or under Student Study Tools. Otherwise, go to http://real-timeupdates.com/bia5 and click on "Learn More."

EXHIBIT 4.2 Approaches to Resolving Ethical Dilemmas

These approaches can help you resolve ethical dilemmas you may face on the job. Be aware that in some situations, different approaches can lead to different ethical conclusions.

APPROACH	SUMMARY
Justice	Treat people equally or at least fairly in a way that makes rational and moral sense
Utilitarianism	Choose the option that delivers the most good for the most people (or protects the most people from a negative outcome)
Individual rights	To the greatest possible extent, respect the rights of all individuals, particularly their right to control their own destinies
Individual responsibilities	Focus on the ethical duties of the individuals involved in the situation
The common good	Emphasize qualities and conditions that benefit the community as a whole, such as peace and public safety
Virtue	Emphasize desirable character traits such as integrity and compassion

✓CHECKPOINT

LEARNING OBJECTIVE 1: Discuss what it means to practice good business ethics, and highlight three factors that influence ethical decision making.

Summary: Three essential components of good business ethics are competing fairly and honestly, communicating truthfully, and not causing harm to others. Three major influences on ethical decision making are culture, knowledge, and organizational culture. When facing an ethical dilemma, you can often find clarity by starting with universal standards of justice, considering the rights of everyone involved, being as objective as possible, not assuming that other people think the way you do, and avoiding conflicts of interest.

Critical thinking: (1) If you go to work tomorrow morning and your boss asks you to do something you consider unethical, what factors will you take into consideration before responding? (2) How can you balance the business need to inspire employees to compete aggressively with the moral need to avoid competing unethically?

It's your business: (1) In your current job (or any previous job you've held), in what ways does your employer contribute to society? (2) Have you ever encountered an ethical dilemma in your work? If so, how did you resolve it?

Key terms to know: ethics, transparency, insider trading, code of ethics, whistleblowing, ethical lapse, ethical dilemma, conflicts of interest

Corporate Social Responsibility

corporate social responsibility (CSR)
The idea that business has obligations to society beyond the pursuit of profits

Corporate social responsibility (CSR) is the notion that business has obligations to society beyond the pursuit of profits. There is a widespread assumption these days that CSR is both a moral imperative for business and a good thing for society, but the issues aren't quite as clear as they might seem at first glance.

The Relationship Between Business and Society

What is the nature of the relationship between business and society—what does business owe society, and what does society owe business?

Any attempt to understand and shape this relationship needs to consider four essential truths:

- Consumers in contemporary societies enjoy and expect a wide range of benefits, from education and health care to available credit and products that are safe to use. Most of these benefits share an important characteristic: They require money.
- Profit-seeking companies are the economic engine that powers modern society; they generate the vast majority of the money in a nation's economy, either directly or indirectly. When companies pay taxes or pay for the right to use a public asset (such as a mobile phone company buying the right to use part of the radio spectrum), they directly contribute to the nation's economic well-being. When companies pay employees, those employees spend money on goods and services and pay income taxes on what they earn as well as a variety of other taxes on what they buy and own. People who expect "the government" to pay for something need to remember that the government gets most of its income from taxpayers, both businesses and individuals.

- Aside from money, much of what we consider when assessing a society's standard of living, from medication to building materials to leisure and recreation opportunities, involves goods and services created by profit-seeking companies.

- Conversely, companies cannot hope to operate profitably without the many benefits provided by a safe and relatively predictable business environment: talented and healthy employees, a transportation infrastructure, opportunities to raise money, protection of assets, and customers with the ability to pay for goods and services, to name just a few.

Taking these four factors into account, it is clear that business and society need each other—and each needs the other to be healthy and successful. Generally speaking, when one suffers, the other suffers, and when one succeeds, the other succeeds. In the words of Professors Michael Porter and Mark Kramer, "The most important thing a corporation can do for society, and for any community, is contribute to a prosperous economy."[12]

Philanthropy Versus Strategic CSR

Companies that engage in CSR activities can choose between two courses of action, general philanthropy or strategic CSR. **Philanthropy** involves donating money, employee time, or other resources to various causes without regard for any direct business benefits for the company. For instance, a company might support the arts in its hometown in the interest of enhancing the city's cultural richness. In addition to free products, employee time, use of company facilities, and other noncash contributions, U.S. companies donate billions of dollars to charity every year.[13]

philanthropy
The donation of money, time, goods, or services to charitable, humanitarian, or educational institutions

In contrast to generic philanthropy, **strategic CSR** involves social contributions that are directly aligned with a company's overall business strategy. In other words, the company helps itself and society at the same time. This approach can be followed in a variety of ways. A company can help develop the workforce by supporting job training efforts, for example. A company can also help develop markets for its goods and services, as the British firm Thames Water did by assisting groups trying to improve water supplies in Africa.[14] And a company can make choices that position it favorably in the minds of target customers and give it a competitive advantage. Toyota's decision to invest in hybrid automotive technology helps reduce pollution (its hybrid engines consume half the fuel while reducing harmful emissions by up to 90 percent) and gave Toyota a commanding lead in a major new segment of the car market.[15]

strategic CSR
Social contributions that are directly aligned with a company's overall business strategy

Strategic CSR makes more sense than general philanthropy or an antagonistic business-versus-society mindset, for several reasons. First, because business and society are mutually dependent, choices that weaken one or the other will ultimately weaken both. Second, investments that benefit the company are more likely to be sustained over time. Third, making sizable investments in a few strategically focused areas, rather than spreading smaller amounts of money around through generic philanthropy, will yield greater benefits to society.[16] Thames Water CEO Bill Alexander emphasizes that "Philanthropy won't be enough. To achieve real scale we need a new business model."[17]

Exactly how much can or should businesses contribute to social concerns? This is a difficult decision because all companies have limited resources that must be allocated to a number of goals, such as upgrading facilities and equipment, developing new products, marketing existing products, and rewarding employee efforts, in addition to contributing to social causes. As Exhibit 4.3 on the next page suggests, stakeholders' needs sometimes conflict, requiring managers to make tough decisions about resource allocation.

EXHIBIT 4.3

Balancing Business and Stakeholders' Rights

Balancing the individual needs and interests of a company's stakeholders is one of management's most difficult tasks.

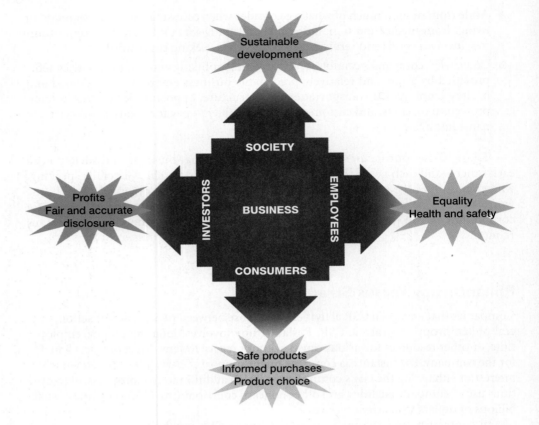

✓CHECKPOINT

LEARNING OBJECTIVE 2: Define *corporate social responsibility (CSR)*, **and explain the difference between philanthropy and strategic CSR.**

Summary: Corporate social responsibility (CSR) is the notion that business has obligations to society beyond the pursuit of profits. However, there is no general agreement over what those responsibilities are or which elements of society should determine those obligations or benefit from them. Philanthropy involves donating time, money, or other resources without regard for any direct business benefits. In contrast, strategic CSR involves contributions that are aligned with the company's business needs and strategies.

Critical thinking: (1) How can society decide what the responsibilities of business are in a CSR context? (2) Is philanthropy morally superior to strategic CSR? Why or why not?

It's your business: (1) Have a company's philanthropic or CSR efforts ever influenced your purchasing behavior? (2) Have you ever benefited personally from a company's philanthropic or CSR efforts?

Key terms to know: corporate social responsibility (CSR), philanthropy, strategic CSR

Perspectives on Corporate Social Responsibility

To encourage ethical behavior and promote a mutually beneficial relationship between business and society, it is clearly necessary to establish expectations about how businesses should conduct themselves. However, both business and society are still grappling with exactly what those expectations should be. "Social responsibility" certainly sounds admirable, but it's not always clear which segments of society this involves or what those responsibilities are.[18] Approaches to CSR can be roughly categorized into four perspectives (see Exhibit 4.4), from minimalist through proactive.

Minimalist CSR

According to what might be termed the *minimalist* view, the only social responsibility of business is to pay taxes and obey the law. In a 1970 article that is still widely discussed today, Nobel Prize–winning economist Milton Friedman articulated this view by saying, "There is only one social responsibility of business: to use its resources and engage in activities designed to increase its profits so long as it stays within the rules of the game, which is to say, engages in open and free competition without deception or fraud."[19] This view, which tends to reject the stakeholder concept described in Chapter 1, might seem selfish and even antisocial, but it raises a couple of important questions. First, any business that operates ethically and legally provides society with beneficial goods and services at fair prices. Isn't that meeting the business's primary social obligation?

Second—and this is a vital point to consider even if you reject the minimalist view—should businesses be in the business of making social policy and spending the public's money? Proponents of the minimalist view claim this is actually what happens when companies make tax-deductible contributions to social causes. For example, assume that in response to pressure from activists, a company makes a sizable contribution that nets it a $1 million tax break. That's $1 million taken out of the public treasury, where voters and their elected representatives can control how money is spent, and put

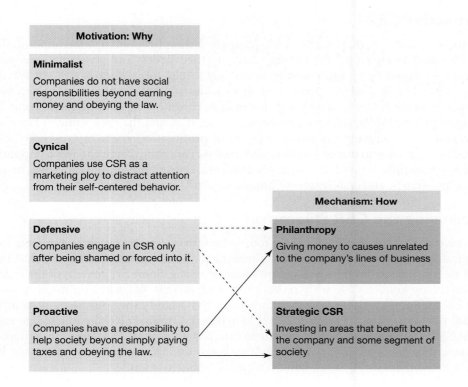

Motivation: Why

Minimalist
Companies do not have social responsibilities beyond earning money and obeying the law.

Cynical
Companies use CSR as a marketing ploy to distract attention from their self-centered behavior.

Mechanism: How

Defensive
Companies engage in CSR only after being shamed or forced into it.

Philanthropy
Giving money to causes unrelated to the company's lines of business

Proactive
Companies have a responsibility to help society beyond simply paying taxes and obeying the law.

Strategic CSR
Investing in areas that benefit both the company and some segment of society

EXHIBIT 4.4

Perspectives on Corporate Social Responsibility

The perspectives on CSR can be roughly divided into four categories, from minimalist to proactive. Companies that engage in CSR can pursue either generic *philanthropy* or *strategic CSR*.

nongovernmental organizations (NGOs)
Nonprofit groups that provide charitable services or promote social and environmental causes

into whatever social cause the company chooses to support. In effect, the corporation and the activists are spending the public's money, and the public has no control over how that money is spent. Would it be better for society if companies paid full taxes and let the people and their elected representatives decide how their tax money is spent?

Defensive CSR

Many companies today find themselves facing pressure from a variety of activists and **nongovernmental organizations (NGOs)**, nonprofit groups that provide charitable services or promote causes, from workers' rights to environmental protection. One possible response to this pressure is to engage in CSR activities as a way to avoid further criticism. In other words, the company takes positive steps to address a particular issue but only because it has been embarrassed into action by negative publicity.

Cynical CSR

Another possible response is purely cynical, in which a company accused of irresponsible behavior promotes itself as being socially responsible without making substantial improvements in its business practices. For example, environmental activists use the term *greenwash* (a combination of *green* and *whitewash*, a term that suggests covering something up) as a label for publicity efforts that present companies as being environmentally friendly when their actions speak otherwise. Ironically, some of the most ardent antibusiness activists and the staunchly probusiness advocates of the minimalist view tend to agree on one point: that many CSR efforts are disingenuous. Thirty-five years after his provocative article, Friedman said he believed that "most of the claims of social responsibility are pure public relations."[20]

Proactive CSR

In the fourth approach, proactive CSR, company leaders believe they have responsibilities beyond making a profit, and they back up their beliefs and proclamations with action—without being prompted to by outside forces. John Mackey, CEO of Whole Foods Market, is a strong proponent of this view: "I believe that the enlightened corporation should try to create value for all of its constituencies," which he identifies as customers, employees, vendors, investors, communities, and the environment. From its inception, the company has given 5 percent of profits to a variety of causes. "Whole Foods gives money to our communities because we care about them and feel a responsibility to help them flourish as well as possible." Mackey says the minimalist view is based on a "pessimistic and crabby view of human nature."

Resolving the CSR Dilemma

So what's the right answer? Of these four perspectives, we can instantly eliminate the cynical approach simply because it is dishonest and therefore unethical. Beyond that, the debate is less clear, but the opinions are certainly strong. Some proponents of the minimalist view equate CSR with *collectivism*, a term that suggests communism and socialism. Some consider CSR demands from NGOs and other outsiders to be little more than extortion.[21] Professor Alexei Marcoux of Loyola University in Chicago says that CSR is "fundamentally antagonistic to capitalist enterprise."[22] At the other extreme, some critics of contemporary business seem convinced that corporations can never be trusted and that every CSR initiative is a cynical publicity stunt.

A two-tiered approach to CSR can yield a practical, ethical answer to this complex dilemma. At the first tier, companies must take responsibility for the consequences of their actions and limit the negative impact of their operations. This can be summarized as "do no harm," and it is not a matter of choice. Just as it has a right to expect certain behavior from all citizens, society has a right to expect a basic level of responsible behavior from all businesses, including minimizing pollution and waste, minimizing the depletion of natural resources, being honest with all stakeholders, offering real value in exchange for prices asked, and avoiding exploitation of employees, customers, suppliers, communities, and investors. Some of these issues are covered by laws, but others aren't, thereby creating the responsibility of ethical decision making by all employees and managers in a firm.

At the second tier, moving beyond "do no harm" does become a matter of choice. Companies can choose to help in whatever way that investors, managers, and employees see fit, but the choices are a matter of free will. Even John Mackey of Whole Foods says that decisions to help the community should be voluntary and companies should not be coerced into them.[23] For the latest information on CSR, visit http://real-timeupdates .com/bia5 and click on Chapter 4.

√CHECKPOINT

LEARNING OBJECTIVE 3: Distinguish among the four perspectives on corporate social responsibility.

Summary: The spectrum of viewpoints on CSR can be roughly divided into minimalist (business's only obligation is to compete to the best of its abilities without deception or fraud), defensive (in which businesses engage in CSR efforts only in response to social pressure), cynical (in which businesses engage in CSR as a public relations ploy), and proactive (in which businesses contribute to society out of a belief that they have an obligation to do so).

Critical thinking: (1) Do you agree that giving companies tax breaks for charitable contributions distorts public spending by indirectly giving companies and activists control over how tax revenues are spent? Why or why not? (2) If Company A takes a cynical approach to CSR while Company B takes a proactive approach but they make identical contributions to society, is one company "better" than the other? Why or why not?

It's your business: (1) Have you ever suspected a company of engaging in greenwash or other disingenuous CSR activities? How would you prove or disprove such a suspicion? (2) If you were the head of a small company and wanted to give back to society in some way, how would you select which organizations or causes to support?

Key terms to know: nongovernmental organizations (NGOs)

CSR: The Natural Environment

In the past few decades, few issues in the public dialog have become as politicized and polarized as pollution and resource depletion. Environmentalists and their political allies sometimes portray business leaders as heartless profiteers who would strip the Earth bare for a few bucks. Corporate leaders and their political allies, on the other hand, sometimes cast environmentalists as "tree huggers" who care more about bunnies and butterflies than human progress. As is often the case, the shouting match between these extreme positions obscures real problems—and opportunities for real solutions.

To reach a clearer understanding of this situation, keep three important points in mind. First, the creation, delivery, use, and disposal of products that society values

EXHIBIT 4.5

Sources of Electricity in the United States

More than 70 percent of the electricity used in the United States produced by burning coal, petroleum, or natural gas. Nuclear and hydroelectric provide most of rest.

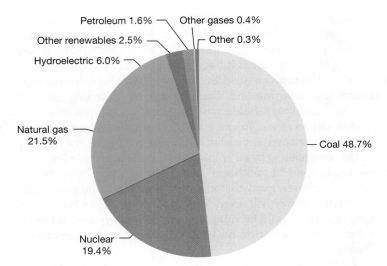

Petroleum 1.6%
Other gases 0.4%
Other renewables 2.5%
Other 0.3%
Hydroelectric 6.0%
Natural gas 21.5%
Coal 48.7%
Nuclear 19.4%

virtually always generate pollution and consume natural resources. For example, there's a temptation to assume that web-based businesses are "clean" because there is no visible pollution. However, the Internet and all the computers attached to it have a voracious appetite for electricity, and the generation of electricity seriously affects the environment—over 70 percent of the electricity used in the United States is generated by burning coal, oil, or natural gas (see Exhibit 4.5).[24] (Although it should be noted that Google, one of the largest users of electricity in the world, reportedly gets most of the power for its massive data centers from nuclear and renewable sources such as hydro, wind, and solar power.[25] See more about Google's energy conservation efforts under "Efforts to Conserve Resources and Reduce Pollution.")

Second, "environmental" causes are often as much about human health and safety as they are about forests, rivers, and wildlife. The availability of clean air, water, and soil affects everyone, not just people concerned with wild spaces.

Third, many of these issues are neither easy nor simple. They often require tough trade-offs, occasional sacrifice, disruptive change, and decision making in the face of uncertainty. Meeting these challenges will require people to be clear-headed, open-minded, adaptable, responsible, and courageous.

Efforts to Conserve Resources and Reduce Pollution

Concerns over pollution and resource depletion have been growing since the dawn of the Industrial Age in the 19th century. However, widespread concern for the environment really dates to the 1960s when *ecology*, the study of the relationship between organisms and the natural environment, entered mainstream public discussion. In 1963, federal, state, and local governments began enacting laws and regulations to reduce pollution (see Exhibit 4.6). In 1970, the federal government established the Environmental Protection Agency (EPA) to regulate air and water pollution by manufacturers and utilities, supervise the control of automobile pollution, license pesticides, control toxic substances, and safeguard the purity of drinking water. A landmark piece of legislation, the Clean Air Act, was also passed that year, and the Clean Water Act followed in 1972. Many states and cities have also passed their own tough clean-air laws.

You've no doubt heard the phrase "reduce, reuse, recycle" as advice for conserving resources and minimizing pollution. Businesses large and small are following that same advice, using both technological and political/economic solutions. Google offers a great example of what businesses can do. As mentioned earlier, the company is a major consumer of energy—but it is taking responsibility for that

Many of the electronic products thrown out in the United States are shipped to environmentally unsound reclamation centers such as this one near the Lianjiang River in China.

EXHIBIT 4.6 Major Federal Environmental Legislation

Since the early 1960s, major federal legislation aimed at the environment has focused on providing cleaner air and water and reducing toxic waste. (Many of these have been amended since their original passage dates.)

LEGISLATION	KEY PROVISIONS
Clean Air Act (1963)	Assists states and localities in formulating control programs; sets federal standards for auto-exhaust emissions; sets maximum permissible pollution levels; authorizes nationwide air-pollution standards and limitations to pollutant discharge; requires scrubbers in new coal-fired power plants; directs EPA to prevent deterioration of air quality in clean areas; sets schedule and standards for cutting smog, acid rain, hazardous factory fumes, and ozone-depleting chemicals
Solid Waste Disposal Act (1965)	Authorizes research and assistance to state and local control programs; regulates treatment, storage, transportation, and disposal of hazardous waste
National Environmental Policy Act (1969)	Establishes a structure for coordinating all federal environmental programs
Resource Recovery Act (1970)	Subsidizes pilot recycling plants; authorizes nationwide control programs
Clean Water Act (1972)	Authorizes grants to states for water-pollution control; gives federal government limited authority to correct pollution problems; authorizes EPA to set and enforce water-quality standards
Noise Control Act (1972)	Requires EPA to set standards for major sources of noise and to advise Federal Aviation Administration on standards for airplane noise
Endangered Species Act (1973)	Establishes protections for endangered and threatened plants and animals
Safe Drinking Water Act (1974)	Sets standards of drinking-water quality; requires municipal water systems to report on contaminant levels; establishes funding to upgrade water systems
Toxic Substances Control Act (1976)	Requires chemicals testing; authorizes EPA to restrict the use of harmful substances
Comprehensive Environmental Response, Compensation, and Liability Act (1980)	Establishes the "Superfund" program to oversee the identification and cleanup of uncontrolled or abandoned hazardous waste sites
Nuclear Waste Policy Act (1982)	Establishes procedures for creating geologic repositories of radioactive waste
Marine Protection, Research, and Sanctuaries Act (1988)	Prohibits ocean dumping that could threaten human health or the marine environment
Oil Pollution Act (1990)	Sets up liability trust fund; extends operations for preventing and containing oil pollution

consumption in several significant ways. First, through careful engineering, Google has reduced energy usage in its data centers (massive complexes that house the thousands of computers that make Google searches possible and that account for most of the company's energy use) by more than half.[26] Second, it takes numerous other steps to reduce consumption and shift to cleaner energy, from installing solar panels at company headquarters to recycling water. Third, it is a significant investor in energy-reduction and renewable-energy technologies, including eSolar (www.esolar.com), which makes solar-power energy plants.[27] Fourth, Google uses its position as a major corporation to help shape energy policy and public awareness in favor of renewables and reduced dependence on fossil fuels.[28] Fifth, it contributes to *carbon offset* projects (such as helping livestock operators in Mexico and Brazil reduce greenhouse gas emissions) to compensate for the portion of its *carbon footprint* it isn't yet able to neutralize through its own internal efforts.[29] Pepsi's efforts to conserve water (see Behind the Scenes on page 140) are another good example of positive steps companies can take.

In addition to technological solutions to reduce pollution and resource consumption, businesses, governments, and NGOs are pursuing a variety of political and economic solutions. **Cap and trade** is a good example of an approach that tries to balance free-market economics with government intervention. Lawmakers first establish a maximum allowable amount of a particular pollutant that a designated group of companies or industries is allowed to emit (the "cap") and then distributes individual emission allowances to all the companies in that group. If a company lowers its emissions enough to stay under its prescribed limit, it can sell, trade, or save leftover allowances (the "trade"). If a company exceeds its emission allowances, it must buy or trade for enough allowances to cover the excess emissions. In this way, companies can choose the lowest-cost means of taking responsibility for their emissions.[30] During the 1990s, a cap and trade program to reduce sulfur dioxide emissions from coal-burning power plants, a leading cause of acid rain, reduced emissions by 50 percent.[31] A newer program designed to reduce greenhouse gases will auction off emissions rights as a way to bring in revenue while battling pollution.[32]

cap and trade
Type of environmental policy that gives companies some degree of freedom in addressing the environmental impact of specified pollutants, either by reducing emissions to meet a designated allowance or buying allowances to offset any amount by which it is over its allowance

The Trend Toward Sustainability

Efforts to minimize resource depletion and pollution are part of a broader effort known as *sustainability* or **sustainable development**, which the United Nations has defined as development that "meets the needs of the present without compromising the ability of future generations to meet their own needs."[33] Notice how this idea expands the stakeholder concept from Chapter 1 by including stakeholders from the future, not just those with an immediate interest in what a company does.

Sustainable development can certainly require changes to the way companies conduct business, but paying attention to a broader scope of stakeholders and managing for the longer term doesn't automatically mean that companies have to take a financial hit to go "green." Many businesses are discovering that taking steps now to reduce consumption and pollution can end up saving money down the road by reducing everything from cleanup and litigation expenses to ongoing production costs. As Xerox CEO Ursula Burns puts it, "The greener we get, the more we can reduce costs and boost efficiency."[34]

In other words, in addition to better stewardship of shared natural resources, sustainable development is also a smart business strategy. By taking a broad and long-term view of their companies' impact on the environment and stakeholders throughout the world, managers can ensure the continued availability of the resources their organizations need and be better prepared for changes in government regulations and shifting social expectations. In fact, some experts believe sustainability is a good measure of the quality of management in a corporation. According to investment researcher Matthew J. Kiernan, companies that take a sustainable approach "tend to be more strategic, nimble, and better equipped to compete in the complex, high-velocity global environment."[35]

sustainable development
Operating business in a manner that minimizes pollution and resource depletion, ensuring that future generations will have vital resources

General Electric (GE) and Dow Chemical, two corporations long criticized for their environmental practices, now appear to be embracing sustainability as core business strategies. Both companies are investing heavily in wind and solar power, hybrid engines, water treatment, and other technologies aimed at sustainability. According to Dow CEO Andrew N. Liveris, "There is 100% overlap between our business drivers and social and environmental interests."[36]

 Real-Time Updates

Learn More
Driving sustainability at Ford Motor
Ford's Director of Sustainable Business Strategies discusses the challenges of translating sustainable concepts into customer-focused business practices. On mybizlab (**www.mybizlab.com**), you can access Real-Time Updates within each chapter or under Student Study Tools. Otherwise, go to **http://real-timeupdates.com/bia5** and click on "Learn More."

✓CHECKPOINT

LEARNING OBJECTIVE 4: Discuss business's role in protecting the natural environment, and define *sustainable development*.

Summary: As major users of natural resources and generators of waste products, businesses play a huge role in conservation and pollution-reduction efforts. Many businesses are making an effort to reduce, reuse, and recycle, and governments are trying market-based approaches such as *cap and trade* to encourage businesses to reduce emissions. All these efforts are part of a trend toward *sustainable development*, which can be defined as "meeting the needs of the present without compromising the ability of future generations to meet their own needs."

Critical thinking: (1) Should all industries be required to meet the same levels of pollution control? Why or why not? (2) How would you respond to critics who say that cap and trade programs allow polluters to buy their way out of the responsibility of cleaning up their operations?

It's your business: (1) In what ways could your employer (or your college, if you're not currently working) take steps to reduce resource depletion? (2) How did you dispose of the last electronic product you stopped using?

Key terms to know: cap and trade, sustainable development

CSR: Consumers

The 1960s activism that awakened business to its environmental responsibilities also gave rise to **consumerism**, a movement that put pressure on businesses to consider consumer needs and interests. (Note that some people use *consumerism* in a negative sense, as a synonym for *materialism*.) Consumerism prompted many businesses to create consumer affairs departments to handle customer complaints. It also prompted state and local agencies to set up bureaus to offer consumer information and assistance. At the federal level, President John F. Kennedy announced a "bill of rights" for consumers, laying the foundation for a wave of consumer-oriented legislation (see Exhibit 4.7 on the next page). These rights include the right to buy safe products, the right to be informed, the right to choose, and the right to be heard.

consumerism
Movement that pressures businesses to consider consumer needs and interests

The Right to Buy Safe Products

As mentioned previously, doing no harm is one of the foundations of corporate social responsibility. The United States and many other countries go to considerable lengths to ensure the safety of the products sold within their borders. The U.S. government imposes many safety standards that are enforced by the Consumer Product Safety Commission (CPSC), as well as by other federal and state agencies. Theoretically, companies that don't comply with these rules are forced to take corrective action. Moreover, the threat of product-liability suits and declining sales motivates companies to meet safety standards. After all, a poor safety record can quickly damage a hard-won reputation. However, unsafe goods and services remain a constant concern, given the ever-changing array of products available and the sheer magnitude of the monitoring effort.

Product safety concerns range from safe toys, food, and automobiles to less-tangible worries such as online privacy and **identity theft**, in which criminals steal personal information and use it to take out loans, request government documents, get expensive medical procedures, and commit other types of fraud. According to Federal Trade Commission estimates, some 9 million Americans are victims of identity theft every year.[37] Companies play a vital role in fighting this crime because they frequently collect

identity theft
Crimes in which thieves steal personal information and use it to take out loans and commit other types of fraud

EXHIBIT 4.7 Major Federal Consumer Legislation

Major federal legislation aimed at consumer protection has focused on food and drugs, false advertising, product safety, and credit protection.

LEGISLATION	MAJOR PROVISIONS
Food, Drug, and Cosmetic Act (1938)	Puts cosmetics, foods, drugs, and therapeutic products under Food and Drug Administration's jurisdiction; outlaws misleading labeling
Cigarette Labeling Act (1965)	Mandates warnings on cigarette packages and in ads
Fair Packaging and Labeling Act (1966, 1972)	Requires honest, informative package labeling; labels must show origin of product, quantity of contents, uses or applications
Truth-in-Lending Act (Consumer Protection Credit Act) (1968)	Requires creditors to disclose finance charge and annual percentage rate; limits cardholder liability for unauthorized use
Fair Credit Reporting Act (1970)	Requires credit-reporting agencies to set process for assuring accuracy; requires creditors to explain credit denials
Consumer Product Safety Act (1972)	Creates Consumer Product Safety Commission
Magnuson-Moss Warranty Act (1975)	Requires complete written warranties in ordinary language; requires warranties to be available before purchase
Alcohol Labeling Legislation (1988)	Requires warning labels on alcohol products, saying that alcohol impairs abilities and that women shouldn't drink when pregnant
Children's Online Privacy Protection Act (1988)	Gives parents control over the collection or use of information that websites can collect about children
Nutrition Education and Labeling Act (1990)	Requires specific, uniform product labels detailing nutritional information on every food regulated by the FDA
American Automobile Labeling Act (1992)	Requires carmakers to identify where cars are assembled and where their individual components are manufactured
Deceptive Mail Prevention and Enforcement Act (1999)	Establishes standards for sweepstakes mailings, skill contests, and facsimile checks to prevent fraud and exploitation
Controlling the Assault of Non-Solicited Pornography and Marketing Act (2003)	Known as CAN-SPAM, attempts to protect online consumers from unwanted and fraudulent e-mail
Consumer Product Safety Improvement Act (2008)	Strengthens standards for lead in children's products; mandates safety testing for imported children's products; creates a searchable database for reporting accidents, injuries, and illnesses related to consumer products

the information that identity thieves use to commit their fraud, including credit card and Social Security numbers. Any company that collects such information has a clear ethical obligation to keep it safe and secure.

The Right to Be Informed

Consumers have a right to know what they're buying, how to use it, and whether it presents any risks to them. They also have a right to know the true price of goods or services and the details of purchase contracts. Accordingly, numerous government regulations have been put in place to make sure buyers get the information they need to make informed choices. Of course, buyers share the responsibility here, at least morally if not always legally. Not bothering to read labels or contracts or not asking for help if you don't understand them is no excuse for not being informed.

Fortunately, both consumers and businesses can turn to a wide range of information sources to learn more about the goods and services they purchase. The spread of social media and their use in *social commerce* (see page 335), in which buyers help educate one another, has helped shift power from sellers to buyers. For just about every purchase you can envision these days, you can find more information about it before you choose.

The Right to Choose Which Products to Buy

Especially in the United States, the number of products available to consumers is truly amazing. But how far should the right to choose extend? Are we entitled to choose products that are potentially harmful, such as cigarettes, alcoholic beverages, guns, or even cars with low gas mileage? Should the government take measures to make such products illegal, or should consumers always be allowed to decide for themselves what to buy?

Consider cigarettes. Scientists determined long ago that the tar and nicotine in tobacco are harmful and addictive. In 1965, the Federal Cigarette Labeling and Advertising Act was passed, requiring all cigarette packs to carry the Surgeon General's warnings. Over the years, tobacco companies have spent billions of dollars to defend themselves in lawsuits brought by smokers suffering from cancer and respiratory diseases. Lawsuits and legislative activity surrounding tobacco products continue to this day—and are likely to continue for years. Meanwhile, consumers can still purchase cigarettes in the marketplace. As one tobacco company executive put it, "Behind all the allegations . . . is the simple truth that we sell a legal product."[38]

The Right to Be Heard

The final component of consumer rights is the right to be heard. As with the challenge of gathering information, social media give consumers numerous ways to ask questions, voice concerns, and provide feedback. Social media also let customers speak with a unified voice when they are unsatisfied. For instance, after a member of the blogging team at Southwest Airlines wrote what he thought was a routine post explaining something about the company's reservations policy, several hundred responses from frustrated customers—and former customers—told him the matter was anything but routine. In a follow-up post titled "I blogged. You flamed. We changed," he announced that after considering all the passenger feedback, Southwest was changing the policy.[39]

✓CHECKPOINT

LEARNING OBJECTIVE 5: Identify four fundamental consumer rights and business's responsibility to respect them.

Summary: Four fundamental consumer rights that form the basis of much of the consumer-related legislation in the United States are the right to safe products, the right to be informed, the right to choose, and the right to be heard. Many specific aspects of these rights are now embodied in government regulations, but others rely on business professionals to practice ethical and responsive decision making.

Critical thinking: (1) Is there a point at which responsibility for product safety shifts from the seller to the buyer? Explain your answer. (2) If providing full information about products raises prices, should businesses still be required to do so? Why or why not?

It's your business: (1) Do you rely on social media when making purchases? (2) Have you ever lodged a complaint with a business? What was the outcome?

Key terms to know: consumerism, identity theft

CSR: Employees

The past few decades have brought dramatic changes in the attitudes and composition of the global workforce. These changes have forced businesses to modify their recruiting, training, and promotion practices, as well as their overall corporate values and behaviors. This section discusses some key responsibilities that employers have regarding employees.

The Push for Equality in Employment

The United States has always stood for economic freedom and the individual's right to pursue opportunity. Unfortunately, in the past, many people were targets of economic **discrimination**, were relegated to low-paying, menial jobs, and were prevented from taking advantage of many opportunities solely on the basis of their race, gender, disability, or religion.

The Civil Rights Act of 1964 established the Equal Employment Opportunity Commission (EEOC), the regulatory agency that addresses job discrimination. The EEOC is responsible for monitoring the hiring practices of companies and for investigating complaints of job-related discrimination. It has the power to file legal charges against companies that discriminate and to force them to compensate individuals or groups who have been victimized by unfair practices. The Civil Rights Act of 1991 extended the original act by allowing workers to sue companies for discrimination and by granting women powerful legal tools against job bias.

discrimination
In a social and economic sense, denial of opportunities to individuals on the basis of some characteristic that has no bearing on their ability to perform in a job

Affirmative Action

In the 1960s, **affirmative action** programs were developed to encourage organizations to recruit and promote members of groups whose economic progress had been hindered through legal barriers or established practices. Affirmative action programs address a variety of situations, from college admissions to hiring to conducting business with government agencies (businesses that want to sell goods or services to the federal government are generally required to have an affirmative action program in place, for instance). Note that while affirmative action programs address a variety of population segments, from military veterans with disabilities to specific ethnic groups, in popular usage, "affirmative action" usually refers to programs based on race.

affirmative action
Activities undertaken by businesses to recruit and promote members of groups whose economic progress has been hindered through either legal barriers or established practices

Affirmative action remains one of the most controversial and politicized issues in business today, with opponents claiming it creates a double standard and can encourage reverse discrimination against white males, and proponents saying that it remains a crucial part of the effort to ensure equal opportunities for all. One of the key points of contention is whether affirmative action programs are still needed, given the various antidiscrimination laws now in place. Opponents assert that everyone has an equal shot at success now, so the programs are unnecessary and, if anything, should be based on income, not race; proponents argue that laws can't remove every institutionalized barrier and that discrimination going back decades has left many families and communities at a long-term disadvantage.[40]

Political debates aside, well-managed companies across the country are finding that embracing diversity in the richest sense is simply good business. You'll read more about *diversity initiatives* in Chapter 11.

People with Disabilities

In 1990, people with a wide range of physical and mental difficulties got a boost from the passage of the federal Americans with Disabilities Act (ADA), which guarantees equal opportunities in housing, transportation, education, employment, and other areas for the estimated 50 to 75 million people in the United States with disabilities. As defined by the 1990 law, *disability* is a broad term that protects not only those with physical handicaps but also those with cancer, heart disease, diabetes, epilepsy, HIV/AIDS, drug addiction, alcoholism, emotional illness, and other conditions. In most situations, employers cannot legally require job applicants to pass a physical examination as a condition of employment. Employers are also required to make reasonable accommodations to meet the needs of employees with disabilities, such as modifying work stations or schedules.[41]

Occupational Safety and Health

Every year more than 5,000 U.S. workers lose their lives on the job and thousands more are injured (see Exhibit 4.8).[42] During the 1960s, mounting concern about workplace hazards resulted in the passage of the Occupational Safety and Health Act of 1970, which set mandatory standards for safety and health and which established the Occupational Safety and Health Administration (OSHA) to enforce them. These standards govern everything from hazardous materials to *ergonomics*, the study of how people interact with machines. For instance, a major ergonomics issue in recent years has been the risk of repetitive stress injuries such as carpal tunnel syndrome, which can develop after prolonged use of computer keyboards and other devices that require repeated wrist action.

Concerns for employee safety can extend beyond a company's own workforce, and this concern is particularly acute for the many U.S. companies that contract out production to factories in Asia, Latin America, and parts of the United States to make products under their brand names. A number of these companies have been criticized for doing business with so-called *sweatshops*, a disparaging term applied to production facilities that treat workers poorly. Some of these factories have been accused of forcing employees to work 24 hours or more at a time, employing young children in unsafe conditions, or virtually imprisoning workers in conditions that have been compared to slavery.[43]

Mattel, Reebok, Patagonia, Liz Claiborne, Gap, and Nike are among the industry leaders that have responded to the poor working conditions in these factories.[44] Gap, which also owns Old Navy and Banana Republic, has a team of more than 80 inspectors who travel the globe to make sure contract manufacturers follow the company's *Code of Vendor Conduct*.[45] Nike, meanwhile, realized that setting standards and monitoring operations weren't improving conditions in its contract factories sufficiently and is now working closely with vendors to improve their operations and practices. As the company explains, "What we've learned, after nearly a decade, is that monitoring alone hasn't

Real-Time Updates

Learn More

Hiding the truth from U.S. companies

Learn how Chinese manufacturers hide abuses from the U.S. companies trying to monitor workers' rights. On mybizlab (www.mybizlab.com), you can access Real-Time Updates within each chapter or under Student Study Tools. Otherwise, go to http://real-timeupdates.com/bia5 and click on "Learn More."

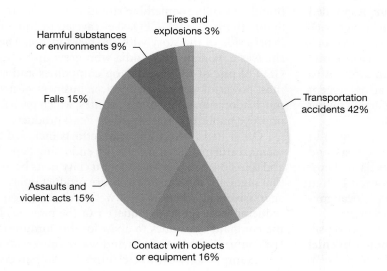

EXHIBIT 4.8

Workplace Killers

Every year, more than 5,000 American workers die on the job; transportation accidents are the leading cause of death in the workplace.

solved the problems. And many of the problems are recurring in the industry. Our focus now is getting to the root of the problems."[46]

Meanwhile, a number of groups, such as the Fair Labor Association (**www.fairlabor .org**), are also working to address these issues. American colleges have played an important role in this effort, by the way: More than 200 schools have joined the Fair Labor Association to ensure that school-logo products are manufactured in an ethical manner.[47]

✓ CHECKPOINT

LEARNING OBJECTIVE 6: Explain the responsibilities businesses have toward their employees.

Summary: Corporate social responsibility also applies internally, to the way employees are treated. Major issues include the push for equal opportunity, which includes affirmative action programs and regulations to protect the rights of people with disabilities, and occupational safety and health.

Critical thinking: (1) Does affirmative action seem like a fair approach? Why or why not? (2) Should employees automatically get paid more to work in hazardous jobs? Why or why not?

It's your business: (1) Have you ever experienced or observed discrimination on the job? If so, how did you handle the situation? (2) Has this chapter changed your perspective about the relationship between business and society? Why or why not?

Key terms to know: discrimination, affirmative action

Behind the Scenes

PepsiCo Responds to Protests over Water Usage and Product Safety

After India's Centre for Science and Environment (CSE) claimed that the beverages Pepsi manufactured and sold in India had unsafe levels of pesticides, the company responded in several ways, starting with a joint press conference with archrival Coke to dispute CSE's findings. Over the next couple of years, Pepsi executives met with CSE director Sunita Narain and Indian government officials in an attempt to iron out safety standards for beverages. Just as an agreement was about to be finalized, the government deferred, saying more research was required.

Narain angrily accused the government of caving in to corporate pressure. CSE then conducted more tests and released new data claiming that pesticide levels in Pepsi products were 30 times higher than the proposed Indian safety standards. Protests flared again, and some local governments once again banned Pepsi and Coke products.

Indra Nooyi, who had been playing a key role in Pepsi's efforts to counter CSE's campaign, was promoted to chief executive officer (CEO) of Pepsi shortly after. Her response to

CSE's new round of accusations was blunt: "For somebody to think that Pepsi would jeopardize its brand—its global brand—by doing something stupid in one country is crazy." Soon after becoming CEO, she traveled to India to discuss Pepsi's side of the story with the news media. The fact that she was a woman from India who grew up to become the CEO of one of the world's top companies and one of the most powerful women in American business garnered Nooyi much adoration in her home country, which probably helped improve public opinion regarding Pepsi products.

Other Pepsi communication efforts included advertisements featuring Indian celebrities endorsing Pepsi beverages and tours of the water treatment facility in its beverage plant that highlight steps taken to ensure product safety. Pepsi also aggressively attacked its own water consumption problem, reducing its usage to one quarter of the previous level. And the company continues to assist local communities around the country with new wells and water conservation efforts. For example, agriculture accounts for 80 percent of fresh water usage in India, and Pepsi is working with local farmers to adopt newer methods that use less water than traditional field flooding.

At least for the time being, the response seems to be working, halting the sales decline and quieting the critics. Pepsi continues to assert that the beverages it sells in India are safe and not only meet the Indian government requirements that were eventually finalized but are also on par with the most stringent food standards around the world.

Narain freely admits she chose Pepsi as a target partly because attacking a huge multinational corporation—particularly an American one—would draw attention to the problem of water shortages and pesticide contamination in India's water supply. Pepsi's water usage was certainly an issue, as the company itself admitted, but many pesticides come from the water supply, and Pepsi goes to extensive lengths to remove chemicals from that water. (You can watch a video of the water purification process at http://pepsiindia.co.in/video/pepsi.wmv.)

For her part, Nooyi also says she could've handled the situation better by traveling to India as soon as the controversy first erupted. She realizes that Pepsi must continue to educate consumers and the media about the company's products and its efforts to be a responsible corporate citizen. As water and other resources grow scarce in many regions and critics of globalization complain about "corporate colonialism" by multinational companies, executives will continue to face scrutiny. Despite the challenges, Nooyi is upbeat about Pepsi's future in India; the company recently announced it was going to invest a half-billion dollars on top of the billion it has already invested in the Indian market.[48]

Critical Thinking Questions

1. Pepsi asserts that its products meet all applicable government safety standards. From an ethical perspective, is this a sufficient response to concerns about consumer safety? Why or why not?

2. Was it ethical for Sunita Narain to single out Pepsi as a protest target, when the problems of industrial and agricultural water usage and groundwater contamination involve thousands of companies, farmers, and municipalities—and the presence of any pesticides in Pepsi beverages is a result of pesticides in the country's water supply and not a result of Pepsi's manufacturing processes? Why or why not?

3. Indra Nooyi stressed in an interview that bottled water and soda consume only 0.04 percent of the total water used by all industries throughout India. Explain whether or not you think this specific point is a valid response to the water-usage criticism.

LEARN MORE ONLINE

Visit the Pepsi India website at www.pepsiindia.co.in and read "Replenishing Water" in the "Performance with Purpose" section and the "Quality" section. Do you think the company does an effective job of responding to its critics? Does visiting the website confirm or change your opinion of the company? ∎

Key Terms

affirmative action (138)
cap and trade (134)
code of ethics (123)
conflicts of interest (125)
consumerism (135)
corporate social responsibility (CSR) (126)
discrimination (138)

ethical dilemma (124)
ethical lapse (124)
ethics (122)
identity theft (135)
insider trading (123)
nongovernmental organizations (NGOs) (130)
philanthropy (127)

strategic CSR (127)
sustainable development (134)
transparency (122)
whistleblowing (123)

Test Your Knowledge

Questions for Review

1. How do companies support ethical behavior?
2. How does ethics differ from corporate social responsibility?
3. What is a conflict of interest?
4. How are businesses responding to the environmental issues facing society?
5. What can a company do to assure customers that its products are safe?

Questions for Analysis

6. How do individuals employ philosophical principles in making ethical business decisions?

7. Why is it important for a company to balance its social responsibility efforts with its need to generate profits?

8. Why does a company need more than a code of ethics to be ethical?

9. Why can't legal considerations resolve every ethical question?

10. **Ethical Considerations.** Is it ethical for companies to benefit from their efforts to practice corporate social responsibility? Why or why not? How can anyone be sure that CSR efforts aren't just public relations ploys?

Questions for Application

11. Based on what you've learned about corporate social responsibility, what effect will CSR considerations have on your job search?

12. What steps could a bookstore take to engage in strategic CSR?

13. **Concept Integration.** Chapter 1 identified knowledge workers as a key economic resource of the 21st century. If an employee leaves a company to work for a competitor, what types of knowledge would be ethical for the employee to share with the new employer and what types would be unethical to share?

14. **Concept Integration.** Is it ethical for state and city governments to entice businesses to relocate their operations to that state or city by offering them special tax breaks that are not extended to other businesses operating in that area?

Practice Your Knowledge

Sharpening Your Communication Skills

Your employer makes a grand show of promoting strong ethics, with regular classes, posters in the hallways, a toll-free hotline, and more. However, as the economy has slowed down over the past few months, you've noticed that company managers aren't always practicing what they preach. They're cutting corners on product quality and squeezing suppliers by not paying bills on time. They even launched a frivolous lawsuit against an upstart competitor that will do little more than drain the new firm of funds and delay its entry into the market. This isn't the same company you were once so proud to work for. Write a brief e-mail message to your immediate supervisor, requesting a meeting to discuss your concerns.

Building Your Team Skills

All organizations can benefit from having a code of ethics to guide decision making. But whom should a code of ethics protect, and what should it cover? In this exercise, you and your team are going to draft a code of ethics for your college or university.

Start by thinking about who will be protected by this code of ethics. What stakeholders should the school consider when making decisions? What negative effects might decisions have on these stakeholders? Then think about the kinds of situations you want your school's code of ethics to cover. One example might be employment decisions; another might be disclosure of confidential student information.

Next, using Exhibit 4.1 as a model, draft your school's code of ethics (identify general principles and then provide specific guidelines). Write a general introduction explaining the purpose of the code and who is being protected. Next, write a positive statement to guide ethical decisions in each situation you identified earlier in this exercise. Your statement about promotion decisions, for example, might read: "School officials will encourage equal access to job promotions for all qualified candidates, with every applicant receiving fair consideration."

Compare your code of ethics with the codes drafted by your classmates. Did all the codes seek to protect the same stakeholders? What differences and similarities do you see in the statements guiding ethical decisions?

Expand Your Knowledge

Discovering Career Opportunities

Businesses, government agencies, and not-for-profit organizations offer numerous career opportunities related to ethics and social responsibility. How can you learn more about these careers?

1. Search the *Occupational Outlook Handbook* at **www.bls .gov/oco** for *occupational health and safety specialists and technicians*, jobs concerned with a company's responsibility toward its employees. What are the duties

and qualifications of the jobs you have identified? Are the salaries and future outlooks attractive for all of these jobs?

2. Select one job from the *Handbook* and search blogs, websites, and other sources to learn more about it. Try to find real-life information about the daily activities of people in this job. Can you find any information about ethical dilemmas or other conflicts in the duties of this position? What role do you think people in this position play within their respective organizations?

3. What skills, educational background, and work experience do you think employers are seeking in applicants for the specific job you are researching? What keywords do you think employers would search for when reviewing résumés submitted for this position?

Developing Your Research Skills

Articles on corporate ethics and social responsibility regularly appear in business journals and newspapers. Look in recent issues (print or online editions) to find one or more articles discussing one of the following ethics or social responsibility challenges faced by a business:

- Environmental issues, such as pollution, acid rain, and hazardous-waste disposal
- Employee or consumer safety measures
- Consumer information or education
- Employment discrimination or diversity initiatives
- Investment ethics
- Industrial spying and theft of trade secrets
- Fraud, bribery, and overcharging
- Company codes of ethics

1. What was the nature of the ethical challenge or social responsibility issue presented in the article? Does the article report any wrongdoing by a company or agency official? Was the action illegal, unethical, or questionable? What course of action would you recommend the company or agency take to correct or improve matters now?
2. What stakeholder group(s) is affected? What lasting effects will be felt by (a) the company and (b) this stakeholder group(s)?
3. Writing a letter to the editor is one way consumers can speak their mind. Review some of the letters to the editor in newspapers or journals. Why are letters to the editor an important feature for that publication?

Improve Your Tech Insights: Assistive Technologies

The term *assistive technologies* covers a broad range of devices and systems that help people with disabilities perform activities that might otherwise be difficult or impossible. These include technologies that help people communicate orally and visually, interact with computers and other equipment, and enjoy greater mobility, along with myriad other specific functions.

Assistive technologies create a vital link for thousands of employees with disabilities, giving them the opportunity to pursue a greater range of career paths and giving employers access to a broader base of talent. Plus, economy and society benefit when everyone who can make a contribution is able to, and assistive technologies will be an important part of the solution.

Research some of the technologies now on the market. AssistiveTech.net, www.assistivetech.net, is a great place to search for the many categories of assistive technologies now available; it also provides links to a variety of other sites. The Business Leadership Network, www.usbln.org, "recognizes and promotes best practices in hiring, retraining, and marketing to people with disabilities." For a look at the government's efforts to promote these technologies, visit the National Institute on Disability and Rehabilitation Research, www.ed.gov/about/offices/list/osers/nidrr. Also visit the Rehabilitation Engineering and Assistive Technology Society of North America, www.resna.org. Technology companies such as IBM (www.ibm.com/able) and Microsoft (www.microsoft.com/enable) also devote significant resources to developing assistive technologies and making information technology more accessible. Choose one assistive technology, and in a brief e-mail to your instructor, explain how this technology can help companies support employees or customers with disabilities.[49]

Video Discussion

Access the Chapter 4 video discussion in the End of Chapter Assignments section at www.mybizlab.com.

PEARSON
my*biz*lab

Log on to www.mybizlab.com to access the following study and assessment aids associated with this chapter:

- Interactive exercises
- Pre/post test
- Real-Time Updates
- Video application
- Customized study plans
- Biz Skills Simulations
- Quick Learning Guide

If you are not using mybizlab, you can access Real-Time Updates and Quick Learning Guides through http://realtimeupdates.com/bia5. The Quick Learning Guide (located under "Learn More" on the website) provides all six Checkpoints in a handy two-page format to help you study for exams or review important concepts whenever you need a quick refresher.

CHAPTER 5
Forms of Ownership

LEARNING OBJECTIVES

After studying this chapter, you will be able to

1 Define *sole proprietorship* and explain the six advantages and six disadvantages of this ownership model

2 Define *partnership* and explain the six advantages and three disadvantages of this ownership model

3 Define *corporation* and explain the four advantages and six disadvantages of this ownership model

4 Explain the concept of *corporate governance* and identify the three groups responsible for ensuring good governance

5 Identify the potential advantages of pursuing mergers and acquisitions as a growth strategy, along with the potential difficulties and risks

6 Define *strategic alliances* and *joint ventures* and explain why a company would choose these options over a merger or acquisition

Behind the Scenes

Scanning the Skies for Help at Sirius Satellite Radio

www.siriusxm.com

From the beginning, business has been up in the air—literally and figuratively—for Sirius and XM. Both companies use satellites to broadcast multiple radio channels, and both companies have struggled financially. Satellites are about the most expensive pieces of business equipment imaginable, costing more than $300 million each to build and launch. Sirius has three in the sky, XM has four, and both companies keep a spare on the ground, so satellite costs alone are pushing $3 billion. And the technology to transmit signals is only part of the cost. The companies spend millions more to snag high-profile personalities and popular sporting events, from Oprah Winfrey to the National Football League. Shock jock Howard Stern alone costs Sirius $100 million every year.

With costs like these, a company obviously needs a mammoth revenue stream to have any hope of turning a profit. However, that side of the equation isn't any easier. Accessing satellite radio requires a special receiver

Faced with mounting competition and a tough financial environment, Sirius CEO Mel Karmazin began exploring ways to join forces with rival satellite radio service XM Radio.

and a monthly subscription fee, which puts the service at a disadvantage when consumers compare it to free *terrestrial* radio (the regular old kind of radio). Sirius and XM counter that satellite is not only commercial-free and uncensored, but it offers content not available anywhere else. However, with the U.S. economy in the worst shape it has been in for decades, millions of consumers are cutting back on discretionary purchases such as entertainment.

If you were Mel Karmazin, CEO of Sirius, how would you address this challenge? Keeping costs under control as much as possible and aggressive marketing are obvious options, but is it time to rethink things from the ground up? Can the relatively small satellite radio market even support two independent providers, both of whom struggle with high costs? Would it make more sense to join forces with XM? If so, what would be the best approach—merge the two firms? Attempt to buy XM outright? Cooperate as two independent companies?[1] ∎

Introduction

One of the most fundamental decisions you must make when starting a business is selecting a form of business ownership. This decision can be complex and have far-reaching consequences for owners, employees, and customers. Picking the right ownership structure involves knowing your long-term goals and how you plan to achieve them. Your choice also depends on your desire for control and your tolerance for risk. Then as your business grows, you may need to modify the original structure, as Mel Karmazin of Sirius contemplated in the chapter-opening Behind the Scenes.

The three most common forms of business ownership are sole proprietorship, partnership, and corporation. Each form has its own characteristic internal structure, legal status, size, and fields to which it is best suited. Each has key advantages and disadvantages for the owners (see Exhibit 5.1 on the next page).

Sole Proprietorships

A **sole proprietorship** is a business owned by one person (although it may have many employees). Many farms, retail establishments, and small service businesses are sole proprietorships, as are many home-based businesses such as caterers, consultants, and

sole proprietorship
Business owned by a single person

EXHIBIT 5.1 Forms of Business Ownership

Each of the major forms of business ownership has distinct advantages and disadvantages

STRUCTURE	CONTROL	PROFITS AND TAXATION	LIABILITY EXPOSURE	EASE OF ESTABLISHMENT
Sole proprietorship	One owner has complete control	Profits and losses flow directly to the owners and are taxed at individual rates	Owner has unlimited personal liability for the business's financial obligations	Easy to set up; typically requires just a business license and a form to register the company name
General partnership	Two or more owners; each partner is entitled to equal control unless agreement specifies otherwise	Profits and losses flow directly to the partners and are taxed at individual rates; partners share income and losses equally unless the partnership agreement specifies otherwise	All partners have unlimited liability, meaning their personal assets are at risk to mistakes made by others partners	Easy to set up; partnership agreement not required but strongly recommended
Limited partnership	Two or more owners; one or more general partners manage the business; limited partners don't participate in the management	Same as for general partnership	Limited partners have limited liability (making them liable only for the amount of their investment); general partners have unlimited liability	Same as for general partnership
Corporation	Unlimited number of shareholders; no limits on stock classes or voting arrangements; ownership and management of the business are separate (shareholders in public corporations are not involved in management decisions; in private or closely held corporations, owners are more likely to participate in managing the business)	Profits are taxed at corporate rates; profits are taxed again at individual rates when (or if) they are distributed to investors as dividends	Investor's liability is limited to the amount of his or her investment	More complicated and expensive to establish than a sole proprietorship; requirements vary from state to state

freelance writers. Many of the local businesses you frequent around your college campus are likely to be sole proprietorships. You may be a sole proprietor yourself: If you are paid for performing any kind of service, from babysitting to website design, without being on a company's payroll, you are legally classified as a sole proprietor.[2]

Advantages of Sole Proprietorships

Operating as a sole proprietorship offers six key advantages:

■ **Simplicity.** A sole proprietorship is easy to establish and requires far less paperwork than other structures. About the only legal requirement for establishing a sole proprietorship is obtaining the necessary business licenses and permits required by the city, county, and state. Otherwise, by going into business without creating a partnership or a corporation, you legally establish yourself as a sole proprietor.[3]

- **Single layer of taxation.** Income tax is a straightforward matter for sole proprietorships. The federal government doesn't recognize the company as a taxable entity; all profit "flows through" to the owner, where it is treated as personal income and taxed accordingly.

- **Privacy.** Corporations are legally required to provide extensive public financial reports (including itemizing how much top managers are paid), and partners must share information with each other as well. However, beyond filing tax returns and certain other government reports that may apply to specific businesses, sole proprietors generally aren't required to report anything to anyone. Your business is your business. Of course, if you apply for a loan or solicit investors, you will need to provide detailed financial information to these parties.

- **Flexibility and control.** As a sole proprietor, you aren't required to get approval from a business partner, your boss, or a board of directors to change any aspect of your business strategy or tactics. As a sole proprietor, you can make your own decisions, from setting your own hours to deciding how much of the work you'll do yourself and how much you'll assign to employees. It's all up to you (within the limits of whatever contractual obligations you might have, of course, such as a franchising agreement— see page 183). Also, as the sole owner, whatever financial value exists in the business is yours. You can keep the business, sell it, give it away, or bequeath it to your children.

- **Fewer limitations on personal income.** As a partner in a partnership or an employee in a corporation, your income is established by various agreements and compensation policies. As a sole proprietor, you keep all the after-tax profits the business generates; if the business does extremely well, then you do extremely well. Of course, if the business doesn't generate any income, you don't get a paycheck.

- **Personal satisfaction.** For many sole proprietors, the main advantage is the satisfaction of working for themselves—of taking the risks and enjoying the rewards. If you work hard, make smart decisions, and have a little bit of luck, you get to see and enjoy the fruits of your labor. In contrast, when you are a small part of a large organization, your individual effort can have limited impact on the company's overall success or your personal income.

Disadvantages of Sole Proprietorships

For all its advantages, sole proprietorship also has six significant disadvantages:

- **Financial liability.** In a sole proprietorship, the owner and the business are legally inseparable, which gives the proprietor **unlimited liability**—any legal damages or debts incurred by the business are the owner's personal responsibility. If you aren't covered by appropriate insurance and run into serious financial or legal difficulty, such as getting sued for an accident that happened on your premises, you could lose not only the business but everything you own, including your house, your car, and your personal investments.

unlimited liability
Legal condition under which any damages or debts incurred by the business are the owner's personal responsibility

- **Demands on the owner.** Beware the old joke that working for yourself means you get to set your own hours—you can work whichever 80 hours a week you want. In addition to long hours, you often have the stress of making all the major decisions, solving all the major problems, and being tied so closely to the company that taking time off is sometimes impossible. Plus, business owners can feel isolated and unable to discuss problems with anyone.[4]

- **Limited managerial perspective.** Running even a simple business can be a complicated effort that requires expertise in accounting, marketing, information technology, business law, and many other fields. Few sole owners possess all the skills and experience to make consistently good decisions. Gauri Nanda (**www.nandahome.com**), who invented a robotic alarm clock that runs away from people who try to hit the snooze button too many times, says that her biggest regret is trying to do it all herself. "I would try to get more good help from the beginning."[5] To get broader input for important decisions, small business owners can also join networks or support groups where proprietors can turn to each other for advice.[6]

■ **Resource limitations.** Because they depend on a single owner, sole proprietorships usually have fewer financial resources and fewer ways to get additional funds from lenders or investors. This lack of capital can hamper a small business in many ways, limiting its ability to expand, to hire the best employees, and to survive rough economic periods.

■ **No employee benefits for the owner.** Moving from a corporate job to sole proprietorship can be a shock for employees accustomed to paid vacation time, sick leave, health insurance, and other benefits that many employers offer. Sole proprietors get none of these perks without paying for them out of their own pockets.

■ **Finite life span.** Although some sole proprietors pass their businesses on to their heirs, the owner's death may mean the demise of the business. And even if the business does transfer to an heir, the founder's unique skills may have been crucial to its successful operation.

✓CHECKPOINT

LEARNING OBJECTIVE 1: Define _sole proprietorship,_ and explain the six advantages and six disadvantages of this ownership model.

Summary: A sole proprietorship is a business owned by a single individual and legally inseparable from that person. The six advantages of this structure are simplicity, a single layer of taxation, privacy, flexibility and control, fewer limitations on personal income, and personal satisfaction. The six disadvantages are unlimited financial liability, demands on the owner, limited managerial perspective, resource limitations, no employee benefits for the owner, and finite life span.

Critical thinking: (1) How many sole proprietors do you know? Do they seem satisfied with the choice of working for themselves? Why or why not? (2) Would you ever consider going into business as a sole proprietor? Why or why not?

It's your business: (1) In your everyday consumer interactions, would you rather do business with a sole proprietorship or a corporation? Why? (2) What would be the potential advantages and disadvantages from a consumer's point of view?

Key terms to know: sole proprietorship, unlimited liability

Partnerships

partnership
An unincorporated company owned by two or more people

If going it alone isn't for you, you can team up with others by forming a **partnership**—a company that is owned by two or more people but is not a corporation. Roughly speaking, the partnership structure is appropriate for firms that need more resources and leadership talent than the sole proprietorship but don't need the fundraising capabilities or other advantages of a corporation. Many partnerships are small, with just a handful of owners. A few are very large, however; the accounting firm PricewaterhouseCoopers has more than 8,000 partners.[7] (Note that many companies refer to their employees as "partners," but that isn't the same thing as legal business partners.)

general partnership
Partnership in which all partners have joint authority to make decisions for the firm and joint liability for the firm's financial obligations

Partnerships come in two basic flavors. In a **general partnership**, all partners have _joint authority_ to make decisions for the firm and _joint liability_ for the firm's financial obligations.[8] If the partnership gets sued or goes bankrupt, all the partners have to dig into their own pockets to pay the bills, just as sole proprietors must.

To minimize personal liability exposure, some organizations opt instead for a **limited partnership**. Under this type of partnership, one or more persons act as *general partners* who run the business and have the same unlimited liability as sole proprietors. The remaining owners are *limited partners* who do not participate in running the business and who have **limited liability**—the maximum amount they are liable for is whatever amount each invested in the business.

Real-Time Updates

Learn More

Partner up with Nolo before you partner up for real

Learn more about the advantages and disadvantages of the partnership model and find out what you need to cover in the all-important partnership agreement. On mybizlab (**www.mybizlab.com**), you can access Real-Time Updates within each chapter or under Student Study Tools. Otherwise, go to **http://real-timeupdates.com/bia5** and click on "Learn More."

Two additional types of partnerships have been created in recent years to accommodate the needs of particular industries or professions. The **master limited partnership (MLP)** is allowed to raise money by selling *units* of ownership to the general public, in the same way corporations sell shares of stock to the public. This gives MLPs the fundraising capabilities of corporations without the double-taxation disadvantage (see "Disadvantages of Corporations"). Strict rules limit the types of companies that qualify for MLP status; most are in the energy industry.[9]

The **limited liability partnership (LLP)** was created to help protect individual partners in certain professions from major mistakes (such as errors that trigger malpractice lawsuits) by other partners in the firm. In an LLP, each partner has unlimited liability only for his or her own actions and at least some degree of limited liability for the partnership as a whole. Restrictions on who can form an LLP—and how much liability protection is offered under this structure—vary from state to state. In California, for example, only public accountants, lawyers, and architects are allowed to form LLPs.[10]

Advantages of Partnerships

Partnerships offer two of the same advantages as sole proprietorship plus four more that overcome some important disadvantages of being a sole owner:

- **Simplicity.** Strictly speaking, establishing a partnership is almost as simple as establishing a sole proprietorship; you and your partners just say you're in business together, apply for the necessary business licenses, and get to work. However, while this approach is legal, it is not safe or sensible. Partners need to protect themselves and the company with a partnership agreement (see "Keeping It Together: The Partnership Agreement" on the next page).

- **Single layer of taxation.** Income tax is also straightforward for partnerships. Profit is split between or among the owners based on whatever percentages they have agreed upon. Each owner then treats his or her share as personal income.

- **More resources.** One of the key reasons to partner up with one or more co-owners is to increase the amount of money you have to launch, operate, and grow the business. In addition to the money that owners invest themselves, a partnership can potentially raise more money because partners' personal assets support a larger borrowing capacity.

- **Cost sharing.** An important financial advantage in many partnerships is the opportunity to share costs. For example, a group of lawyers or doctors can share the cost of facilities and support staff while continuing to work more or less independently.

- **Broader skill and experience base.** Pooling the skills and experience of two or more professionals can overcome one of the major shortcomings of the sole proprietorship. If your goal is to build a business that can grow significantly over

limited partnership
Partnership in which one or more persons act as *general partners* who run the business and have the same unlimited liability as sole proprietors

limited liability
Legal condition in which the maximum amount each owner is liable for is equal to whatever amount each invested in the business

master limited partnership (MLP)
Partnership that is allowed to raise money by selling units of ownership to the general public

limited liability partnership (LLP)
Partnership in which each partner has unlimited liability only for his or her own actions and at least some degree of limited liability for the partnership as a whole

Partnerships can bring together business professionals with diverse skill sets and interests

time, a partnership can be much more effective than trying to build it up as a sole owner.[11]

■ **Longevity.** By forming a partnership, you increase the chances that the organization will endure, because new partners can be drawn into the business to replace those who die or retire. For example, even though the original partners in the several accounting firms that eventually became PricewaterhouseCoopers (the roots of which stretch back to 1849) died many years ago, the company continues.[12]

Disadvantages of Partnerships

Anyone considering the partnership structure needs to be aware of three potentially significant disadvantages:

■ **Unlimited liability.** All owners in a general partnership and the general partners in a limited partnership face the same unlimited liability as sole proprietors. However, the risk of financial wipeout can be even greater because a partnership has more people making decisions that could end in catastrophe (unless the company is formed as an LLP).

■ **Potential for conflict.** More bosses equals more chances for disagreement and conflict. Partners can disagree over business strategy, the division of profits (or the liability for losses), hiring and firing of employees, and other significant matters. Even simple interpersonal conflict between partners can hinder the company's ability to succeed. Given the potential for conflict, some experts recommend against equal ownership splits where everyone has an equal vote in how things are run.[13]

■ **Expansion, succession, and termination issues.** Partnerships need to consider how they will handle such issues as expanding by bringing in an additional partner, replacing a partner who wants to sell out or retire, and terminating a partner who is unable or unwilling to meet the expectations of his or her role in the organization. Such issues can destroy partnerships if the owners don't have clear plans and expectations for addressing them.

Keeping It Together: The Partnership Agreement

A carefully written *partnership agreement* can maximize the advantages of the partnership structure and minimize the potential disadvantages. Although state laws (everywhere except Louisiana) specify some basic agreements about business partnerships, these laws are generic and therefore not ideal for many partnerships.[14] At a minimum, the agreement should address investment percentages, profit sharing percentages, management responsibilities and other expectations of each owner, decision-making strategies, succession and exit strategies (if an owner wants to leave the partnership), criteria for admitting new partners, and dispute resolution procedures (including dealing with owners who aren't meeting their responsibilities).[15]

A clear and complete agreement is important for every partnership, but it can be particularly important when you are going into business with a friend, a spouse, or anyone else with whom you have a personal relationship. While you might have a great personal partnership, the dynamics of that relationship could get in the way of a successful business partnership. For instance, a couple that is accustomed to sharing decisions and responsibilities equally in their personal relationship could struggle in a business relationship in which one of them is the clear leader of the company. In addition, stresses and strains in the business relationship can filter into the personal relationship. To protect both the personal and professional partnerships, make sure you start with a clear understanding of what the business relationship will be.

√CHECKPOINT

LEARNING OBJECTIVE 2: Define *partnership*, **and explain the six advantages and three disadvantages of this ownership model.**

Summary: Partnership is a form of business structure in which two or more individuals share ownership of the firm. The two basic forms of partnership are *general partnership*, in which all owners play an active role and have unlimited liability, and the *limited partnership*, in which only the general partner or partners have active management roles and unlimited liability. Six key advantages of partnership are simplicity, a single layer of taxation, more resources, cost sharing, broader skill and experience base, and longevity. Three potential disadvantages are unlimited liability for general partners; potential for conflict; and expansion, succession, and termination issues.

Critical thinking: (1) Would you prefer going into a business with a seasoned professional you don't know well or someone you know, like, and trust but who doesn't have a lot of business experience? Why? (2) What are the three most important qualifications you would look for in a potential business partner?

It's your business: (1) Would you consider entering into a business partnership with your best friend? Why or why not? (2) Now turn the question around: Would your best friend consider having *you* as a business partner?

Key terms to know: partnership, general partnership, limited partnership, limited liability, master limited partnership (MLP), limited liability partnership (LLP)

Corporations

A **corporation** is a legal entity, distinct from any individual persons, with the power to own property and conduct business. It is owned by **shareholders**, investors who purchase shares of stock. The stock of a **private corporation**, also known as a *closely held* corporation, is owned by only a few individuals or companies and is not made available for purchase by the public. In contrast, the stock of a **public corporation** is sold to anyone who has the means to buy it—individuals, investment companies such as mutual funds, not-for-profit organizations, and other companies. These companies are said to be *publicly held* or *publicly traded*.

With their unique ability to pool money from outside investors, corporations can grow to enormous size. The annual revenues of the world's largest corporations, such as Wal-Mart, Exxon Mobil, and Royal Dutch Shell, are bigger than the entire economies of many countries.[16] However, many small firms and even individuals also take advantage of the unique benefits of corporate organization.

Corporations have played an essential role in the growth of the United States and many other countries. For example, the transportation options made possible by railways, commercial airplanes, and mass-produced cars and trucks were created by corporations. As Chapter 4 discusses, corporations have been accused, often rightly so, of causing or contributing to some of society's ills. However, many of the benefits of contemporary life, from life-saving medical treatments to the ability to visit loved ones thousands of miles away in a matter of hours, might not exist without the advances made by corporations.

Advantages of Corporations

Corporations have become such a major economic force because this structure offers four major advantages over sole proprietorships and partnerships:

- **Ability to raise capital.** The ability to pool money by selling shares of stock to outside investors is the reason corporations first came into existence, and this remains one of the key advantages of this structure. (As Chapter 18 explains, corporations can also raise money by selling *bonds*.) A number of firms have raised a billion

corporation
A legal entity, distinct from any individual persons, with the power to own property and conduct business

shareholders
Investors who purchase shares of stock in a corporation

private corporation
Corporation in which all the stock is owned by only a few individuals or companies and is not made available for purchase by the public

public corporation
Corporation in which stock is sold to anyone who has the means to buy it

dollars or more by selling stock to the public for the first time.[17] When India's Reliance Power went public in 2008, it raised $3 billion in a single minute.[18] The potential for raising vast amounts gives corporations an unmatched ability to invest in research, marketing, facilities, acquisitions, and other growth strategies.

liquidity
A measure of how easily and quickly an asset such as corporate stock can be converted into cash by selling it

- **Liquidity.** The stock of publicly traded companies has a high degree of **liquidity**, which means that investors can easily and quickly convert their stock into cash by selling it on the open market. In contrast, *liquidating* (selling) the assets of a sole proprietorship or a partnership can be slow and difficult. The liquidity helps make corporate stocks an attractive investment, which increases the number of people and institutions willing to invest in such companies. In addition, because shares have value established in the open market, a corporation can use shares of its own stock to acquire other companies.

- **Longevity.** Liquidity also helps give corporations a long life span; when shareholders sell or bequeath their shares, ownership simply passes to a new generation, so to speak. Finding willing buyers for a corporation's stock is generally much easier than finding willing buyers for a sole proprietorship or stakes in a partnership.

- **Limited liability.** The corporation itself has unlimited liability, but the various shareholders who own the corporation face only limited liability—their maximum potential loss is only as great as the amount they've invested in the company. Like liquidity, the protection offered by limited liability helps make corporate stocks an attractive investment.

Disadvantages of Corporations

The advantages of the corporate structure are compelling, but six significant disadvantages must be considered carefully:

- **Cost and complexity.** Starting a corporation is more expensive and more complicated than starting a sole proprietorship or a partnership, and "taking a company public" (selling shares to the public) can be extremely expensive for the firm and time-consuming for upper managers. For a large firm, the process can cost many hundreds of thousands of dollars and consume months of executive time.

- **Reporting requirements.** To help investors make informed decisions about stocks, government agencies require publicly traded companies to publish extensive and detailed financial reports. Particularly after the passage of the Sarbanes-Oxley Act, which you'll read about in Chapter 17, these reports can eat up a lot of staff and management time. Moreover, they can expose strategic information that might benefit competitors or discourage investors unwilling to wait for long-term results.

- **Managerial demands.** Top executives must devote considerable time and energy to meeting with shareholders, financial analysts, and the news media. By one estimate, CEOs of large publicly held corporations can spend as much as 40 percent of their time on these externally focused activities.[19]

- **Possible loss of control.** Outside investors who acquire enough of a company's stock can gain seats on the board of directors and therefore begin exerting their influence on company management. In extreme cases, outsiders can take complete control and even boot out the company founders if they believe a change in leadership is needed.

- **Double taxation.** Corporations must pay federal and state corporate income tax on the company's profits, and individual shareholders must pay income taxes on their share of the company's profits received as *dividends* (periodic payments that some corporations opt to make to shareholders.

- **Short-term orientation of the stock market.** Publicly held corporations release their financial results once every quarter, and this seemingly simple fact of life can have a damaging impact on the way companies are managed. The problem is that executives feel the pressure to constantly show earnings growth from quarter to quarter so that the stock price keeps increasing—even if there are smart, strategic reasons to sacrifice earnings in the short term, such as investing in new product development or retaining talented employees instead of laying them off during slow periods. Managers sometimes wind up zigzagging from one short-term fix to the next, trying to prop up the stock price for investors who don't have the patience for strategic, long-term plans to bear fruit. When executive compensation is closely tied to stock prices, managers may have even more incentive to compromise the long-term health of the company in order to meet quarterly expectations.[20] To escape this pressure, corporate leaders sometimes choose to take their companies private, meaning they buy all the shares held by the public and convert to privately held status.

Special Types of Corporations

As with the partnership structure, special types of corporations have been created to aid companies in particular situations. An **S corporation**, or *subchapter S corporation*, combines the capital-raising options and limited liability of a corporation with the federal taxation advantages of a partnership (although a few states tax S corporations like regular corporations).[21] Corporations seeking "S" status must meet certain criteria, including a maximum of 100 investors, all of whom must be U.S. residents.[22]

As its name suggests, the **limited liability company (LLC)** structure also offers the advantages of limited liability, along with the pass-through taxation benefits of a partnership. Furthermore, LLCs are not restricted in the number of shareholders they can have, and members' participation in management is not restricted as it is in limited partnerships. Given these advantages, the LLC structure is recommended for most small companies that aren't sole proprietorships.[23] Although LLCs are favored by many small companies, they are by no means limited to small firms. Some large and well-known firms have gone the LLC route, including BMW of North America, the Albertsons's grocery store chain, and GMAC, a $2 billion finance company.[24]

The labels applied to various types of corporations can be a bit confusing. The most important points to remember are the difference between privately and publically held corporations and the basic features of S corporations and LLCs. Exhibit 5.2 summarizes these features, along with some other terms you may run across in the business media.

S corporation
Type of corporation that combines the capital-raising options and limited liability of a corporation with the federal taxation advantages of a partnership

limited liability company (LLC)
Structure that combines limited liability with the pass-through taxation benefits of a partnership; the number of shareholders is not restricted, nor is members' participation in management

✓CHECKPOINT

LEARNING OBJECTIVE 3: Define *corporation,* **and explain the four advantages and six disadvantages of this ownership model.**

Summary: A corporation is a legal entity with the power to own property and conduct business. The four primary advantages of this structure are the ability to raise capital by selling shares of ownership, liquidity (meaning it is easy to convert shares of ownership to cash), longevity, and limited liability for owners. Six disadvantages are startup costs and complexity, ongoing reporting requirements, extra demands on top managers, potential loss of control, double taxation, and the short-term orientation of the stock market.

Critical thinking: (1) Why is the LLC structure recommended for most small companies that aren't sole proprietorships? (2) How can the demands of the stock market affect managerial decision making?

It's your business: Assume you own stock in a large, publicly traded corporation that is hiring a new CEO. All other things being equal, who would be a better choice: a brilliant strategic thinker who is a weak communicator with poor "people skills," or a gifted public speaker and motivator who is competent but perhaps not brilliant when it comes to strategy? Explain your answer.

Key terms to know: corporation, shareholders, private corporation, public corporation, liquidity, S corporation, limited liability company (LLC)

EXHIBIT 5.2 **Corporate Structures**

Different types of corporate structures serve different purposes for their owners. The first four terms are the most important to remember.

STRUCTURE	CHARACTERISTICS
Public corporation (also known as *publicly held* or *publicly traded*)	Corporation whose stock is sold to the general public
Private corporation (also known as *closely held*)	Corporation whose stock is held by a small number of owners and is not available for sale to the public
S corporation (also known as *subchapter S corporation*)	Corporation allowed to sell stock to a limited number of investors while enjoying the pass-through taxation of a partnership
Limited liability company (LLC)	Corporate structure with benefits similar to those of an S corporation, without the limitation on the number of investors
Subsidiary	Corporation primarily or wholly owned by another company
Parent company	Corporation that owns one or more subsidiaries
Holding company	Special type of parent company that owns other companies for investment reasons and usually exercises little operating control over those subsidiaries
Alien corporation	Corporation that operates in the United States but is incorporated in another country
Foreign corporation (sometimes called an *out-of-state corporation*)	Company that is incorporated in one state (frequently the state of Delaware, where incorporation laws are more lenient) but that does business in several other states where it is registered
Domestic corporation	Corporation that does business only in the state where it is chartered (incorporated)

Corporate Governance

board of directors
Group of professionals elected by shareholders as their representatives, with responsibility for the overall direction of the company and the selection of top executives

corporate governance
In a broad sense, describes all the policies, procedures, relationships, and systems in place to oversee the successful and legal operation of the enterprise; in a narrow sense, refers to the responsibilities and performance of the board of directors specifically

Although a corporation's shareholders own the business, few of them are typically involved in managing it, particularly if the corporation is publicly traded. Instead, shareholders who own *common stock* (see page 482) elect a **board of directors** to represent them, and the directors, in turn, select the corporation's top officers, who actually run the company (see Exhibit 5.3). The term **corporate governance** can be used in a broad sense

EXHIBIT 5.3 **Corporate Governance**

Shareholders of a corporation own the business, but their elected representatives on the board of directors hire the corporate officers who run the company and hire other employees to perform the day-to-day work. (Note that corporate officers are also employees.)

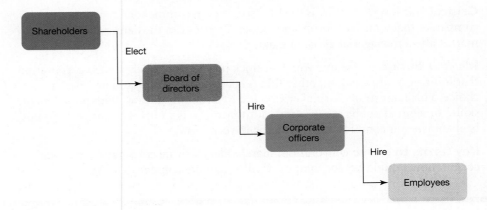

to describe all the policies, procedures, relationships, and systems in place to oversee the successful and legal operation of the enterprise. However, media coverage and public discussion tend to define governance in a more narrow sense, as the responsibilities and performance of the board of directors specifically.

Real-Time Updates

Learn More
Discover the challenges facing today's boards

Corporate governance expert Catherine Bromilow offers an update on the performance of corporate boards and the challenges they face in today's tough business environment. On mybizlab (www.mybizlab.com), you can access Real-Time Updates within each chapter or under Student Study Tools. Otherwise, go to http://real-timeupdates.com/bia5 and click on "Learn More."

Because serious corporate blunders can wreak havoc on the economy, effective corporate governance has become a vital concern for society as a whole, not just for the individual companies. For example, catastrophic mistakes made by one small division of the insurance giant American International Group (AIG) nearly destroyed the entire company, significantly contributed to the global economic collapse that began in 2008, and forced the U.S. government to pump at least $160 billion of taxpayers' money into the company to keep it afloat in an effort to contain the widespread damage.[25]

Shareholders

Shareholders, particularly those who own significant portions of a company's stock, play a key role in corporate governance. All shareholders who own common stock are invited to an annual meeting where top executives present the previous year's results and plans for the coming year and shareholders vote on various resolutions that may be before the board. Those who cannot attend the annual meeting in person can vote by **proxy**, signing and returning a slip of paper that authorizes management to vote on their behalf.

Because shareholders elect the directors, in theory they are the ultimate governing body of the corporation. However, a large corporation may have thousands or even millions of shareholders, so individual shareholders usually have little influence. A notable exception is *institutional investors*, such as pension funds, insurance companies, mutual funds, religious organizations, and college endowment funds. Those with large holdings of stock can have considerable influence over management. For example, the 275 institutions that make up the Interfaith Center on Corporate Responsibility (ICCR) collectively control $100 billion in corporate stock, giving them a powerful voice.[26]

Shareholder activism, in which shareholders press management on matters ranging from executive pay to many of the corporate social responsibility issues discussed in Chapter 4, has become an increasingly visible factor in corporate governance. Activist shareholders are becoming better organized and more sophisticated in proposals they present, forcing boards to pay more attention to the concerns they raise.[27] At the same time, more boards seem to recognize the benefits to be gained by engaging activists and listening to their concerns.[28] However, not everyone is happy with this development. Those who lean toward the minimalist view of CSR (see page 129), worry that such activism is beginning to undermine the ability of corporate boards to do their work effectively.[29]

Board of Directors

As the representatives of the shareholders, the board of directors is responsible for selecting corporate officers, guiding corporate affairs, reviewing long-term plans, making major strategic decisions, and overseeing financial performance. Depending on the size of the company, the board might have anywhere from 3 to 35 directors, although 15 to 25 is the typical range for traditional corporations and perhaps 5 to 10 for smaller or newer corporations. Boards are typically composed of major shareholders (both individuals and representatives of institutional investors), philanthropists, and executives from other corporations. Directors are usually paid a combination of an annual fee and *stock options*, the right to buy company shares at an advantageous price.

Much of the attention focused on corporate reform in recent years has zeroed in on boards, with various boards being accused of not paying close enough attention to what

proxy
Document authorizing another person to vote on behalf of a shareholder in a corporation

shareholder activism
Activities taken by shareholders (individually or in groups) to influence executive decision making in areas ranging from strategic planning to social responsibility

their companies were doing, approving management proposals without analyzing them carefully, being allied too closely with management to serve as the independent representatives of shareholders, or simply failing to add enough value to strategy planning. In response to both outside pressure and management's recognition of how important an effective board is, corporations are wrestling with a variety of board-related issues:

- **Composition.** Identifying the type of people who should be on the board can be a major challenge. The ideal board is a balanced group of seasoned executives, each of whom can "bring something to the table" that helps the corporation, such as extensive contacts in the industry, manufacturing experience, or insight into global issues, and so on. The ratio of insiders (company executives) to outsiders (independent directors) is another hot topic. Federal law now requires that the majority of directors be independent, but to be effective, these outsiders must also have enough knowledge about the inner workings of the organization to make informed decisions. Diversity is also important, to ensure that adequate attention is paid to issues that affect stakeholders who have been historically underrepresented on corporate boards. Women hold only 12 percent of all the seats on U.S. corporate boards, and members of ethnic minorities hold only 10 percent.[30]

- **Education.** Overseeing the modern corporation is an almost unimaginably complex task. Board members are expected to understand everything from government regulations to financial management to executive compensation strategies—in addition to the inner workings of the corporation itself. A key area of concern is the number of directors who aren't well versed enough in finance to understand their company's financial statements; this problem has led a number of companies to start educational programs for directors.[31]

- **Liability.** One of the more controversial reform issues has been the potential for directors to be held legally and financially liable for misdeeds of the companies they oversee. In a few extreme cases, directors have even been forced to pay fines out of their own pockets, although this is quite rare.[32]

- **Independent board chairs.** *The board chair* (or *chairman* as many companies refer to the position) oversees the board of directors—who are supposed to oversee the corporate officers who make up the top management team, while the CEO oversees the top management team. However, in many corporations, one person fills both roles, leading critics to ask how effectively such boards can oversee top management. The majority of large European companies now divide these responsibilities between two people, but that trend has not yet caught on widely in the United States. An emerging alternative is a *lead director*, an independent board member who guides the operation of the board and helps maintain its role as an independent voice in governance.[33]

- **Recruiting challenges.** Being an effective director in today's business environment is a tough job—so tough that good candidates may start to think twice about accepting directorships. Well-chosen board members are more vital than ever, though, so corporate and government leaders have no choice but to solve these challenges.

Corporate Officers

corporate officers
The top executives who run a corporation

The third and final group that plays a key role in governance are the **corporate officers**, the top executives who run the company. Because they implement major board decisions, make numerous other business decisions, ensure compliance with a dizzying range of government regulations, and perform other essential tasks, the executive team is the major influence on a company's performance and financial health. The highest ranking officer is the **chief executive officer (CEO)**, and that person is aided by a team of other "C-level" executives, such as the chief financial officer (CFO), chief information officer (CIO), chief technology officer (CTO), and the chief operating officer (COO)—titles vary from one corporation to the next.

chief executive officer (CEO)
The highest-ranking corporate officer

Corporate officers are hired by the board and generally have legal authority to conduct the company's business, in everything from hiring the rest of the employees to launching new products. The actions of these executives can make or break the company, so it is obviously in the board's interest to hire the best talent available, help them succeed in every way possible—and pay attention to what these managers are doing.

✓CHECKPOINT

LEARNING OBJECTIVE 4: Explain the concept of *corporate governance*, and identify the three groups responsible for ensuring good governance.

Summary: Corporate governance involves all the policies, procedures, relationships, and systems in place to oversee the successful and legal operation of the enterprise. More narrowly, it refers specifically to the responsibilities and performance of the board of directors. The three groups responsible for good governance are (1) the shareholders, who elect (2) the board of directors, who approve overall strategy and hire (3) the corporate officers who run the company.

Critical thinking: (1) Why are some shareholder activists pressuring corporations to increase the number of board seats held by women and minorities? (2) Why do so many European corporations now divide board chair and CEO responsibilities between two people?

It's your business: Should the qualifications of the board of directors play a role in your decision of whether to buy the stock of a particular corporation? Why or why not?

Key terms to know: board of directors, corporate governance, proxy, shareholder activism, corporate officers, chief executive officer (CEO)

Mergers and Acquisitions

If a company determines that it doesn't have the right mix of resources and capabilities to achieve its goals and doesn't want to develop them internally, it can purchase or partner with a firm that has what it needs. Businesses can combine permanently through either *mergers* or *acquisitions.* The two terms are often discussed together, usually with the shorthand phrase "M&A," or used interchangeably (although they are technically different, and the legal and tax ramifications can be quite different, depending on the details of the transaction).

In a **merger**, two companies join to form a single entity. Companies can merge either by pooling their resources or by one company purchasing the assets of the other.[34] Although not strictly a merger, a *consolidation*, in which two companies create a new, third entity that then purchases the two original companies, is often lumped together with the other two merger approaches.[35] (Adding to the confusion, businesspeople and the media often use the term consolidation in two general senses: to describe any combination of two companies, merger or acquisition, and to describe situations in which a wave of mergers and acquisitions sweeps across an entire industry, reducing the number of competitors.)

In an **acquisition**, one company simply buys a controlling interest in the voting stock of another company. In most acquisitions, the selling parties agree to be purchased; management is in favor of the deal and encourages shareholders to vote in favor of it as well. Since buyers frequently offer shareholders more than their shares are currently worth, sellers often have a motivation to sell. However, in some situations, a buyer attempts to acquire a company against the wishes of management. In such a **hostile takeover**, the buyer tries to convince enough shareholders to go against management and vote to sell.

To finance an acquisition, buyers can offer sellers cash, stock in the acquiring company, or a combination of the two. Another option involves debt. A **leveraged buyout (LBO)** occurs when someone purchases a company's publicly traded stock primarily by using borrowed funds. The debt is expected to be repaid with funds generated by the company's operations and, often, by the sale of some of its assets. LBOs can fail if the buyer must make huge interest and principle payments on the debt, which then depletes the amount of cash the company has for operations and growth.

merger
Action taken by two companies to combine as a single entity

acquisition
Action taken by one company to buy a controlling interest in the voting stock of another company

hostile takeover
Acquisition of another company against the wishes of management

leveraged buyout (LBO)
Acquisition of a company's publicly traded stock using funds that are primarily borrowed, usually with the intent of using some of the acquired assets to pay back the loans used to acquire the company

Advantages of Mergers and Acquisitions

Companies pursue mergers and acquisitions for a variety of reasons: They might hope to increase their buying power as a result of their larger size, increase revenue by cross-selling products to each other's customers, increase market share by combining product lines to provide more comprehensive offerings, or gain access to new expertise, systems, and teams of employees who already know how to work together. Or their primary interest could be in reducing overlapping investments and capacities in order to reduce ongoing costs, which is the main reason Sirius's Mel Karmazin contemplated a merger with rival XM Satellite Radio (see Behind the Scenes on page 162). Exhibit 5.4 identifies the most common types of mergers. Bringing a company under new ownership can also be an opportunity to replace or improve inept management and thereby help a company improve its performance.[36]

For many firms, a merger or acquisition is a rare event, but some other companies use acquisitions as a strategic tool to expand year after year. Microsoft, for example, has acquired more than 130 companies since 1987.[37]

Disadvantages of Mergers and Acquisitions

While the advantages can be compelling, joining two companies is a complex process because it involves virtually every aspect of both organizations. Here are just some of the daunting challenges that must be overcome:

- Executives have to agree on how the merger will be financed—and then come up with the money to make it happen.
- Managers need to decide who will be in charge after they join forces.
- Marketing departments need to figure out how to blend product lines, branding strategies, and advertising and sales efforts.
- Incompatible information systems (including everything from e-mail to websites to accounting software) may need to be rebuilt or replaced in order to operate together seamlessly.
- Companies must often deal with layoffs, transfers, and changes in job titles and work assignments.

EXHIBIT 5.4

Types of Mergers

A *vertical merger* occurs when a company purchases a complementary company at a different stage or level in an industry, such as a furniture maker buying a lumber supplier. A *horizontal merger* involves two similar companies at the same level; companies can merge to expand their product offerings or their geographic market coverage. In a conglomerate merger, a parent company buys companies in unrelated industries, often to diversify its assets to protect against downturns in specific industries.

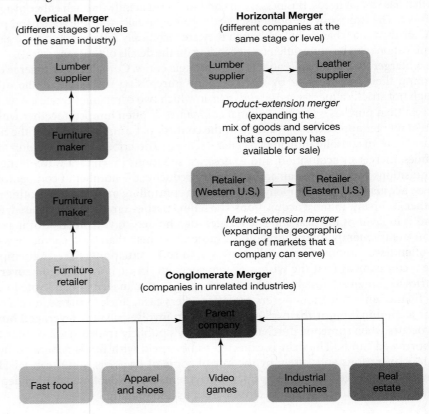

■ The *organizational cultures* (see page 202) of the two firms must be harmonized somehow, which can result in clashes between different values, management styles, communication practices, and other aspects of life on the job. An acquiring company that simply tries to impose its culture on the acquired firm can experience significant resistance and even widespread employee defections.

Moreover, while managers and employees are wrestling with all these challenges, they need to keep manufacturing products, satisfying customers, and tending to all the other daily details of business. Mergers can drive customers away if they feel neglected while the two companies are busy with all the internal chores of stitching themselves together.

Because of these risks and difficulties, two-thirds of mergers fail to meet their stated goals.[38] The worst deals can waste millions or billions of dollars and destroy massive amounts of *market valuation* (the total value of a company's stock). For example, Sprint acquired Nextel several years ago in the hope that combining these two wireless phone networks would create a more competitive alternative to AT&T and Verizon Wireless. However, problems such as incompatible technologies and conflicting cultures probably doomed the combination from the start, and only three years later, Sprint *wrote off* (essentially declaring as lost) most of the $35 billion it spent on the deal.[39]

Even with the risks and long odds, managers continue to pursue mergers and acquisitions, and some companies have become quite proficient at the process. IBM, for instance, has developed a comprehensive process for evaluating and implementing acquisitions. According to the company, its average acquisition doubles its revenue within two years. Toro, a maker of lawn care equipment, acknowledges the risks involved in deal making. One of its strategies is a "contra team" of senior executives, tasked with looking for weaknesses in any deal the company is considering. Such safeguards can help companies from getting caught up in the sense of urgency and enthusiasm that often accompanies deal making.[40]

Merger and Acquisition Defenses

Every corporation that sells stock to the general public is potentially vulnerable to takeover by any individual or company that buys enough shares to gain a controlling interest, although as mentioned earlier, most takeovers are friendly acquisitions welcomed by the acquired company. A hostile takeover can be launched in one of two ways: by tender offer or by proxy fight. In a *tender offer,* the buyer, or *raider,* as this party is sometimes called, offers to buy a certain number of shares of stock in the corporation at a specific price. The price offered is generally more, sometimes considerably more, than the current stock price so that shareholders are motivated to sell. The raider hopes to get enough shares to take control of the corporation and to replace the existing board of directors and management. In a *proxy fight,* the raider launches a public relations battle for shareholder votes, hoping to enlist enough votes to oust the board and management. Corporate boards and executives have devised a number of schemes to defend themselves against unwanted takeovers:

■ *The poison pill.* This plan, triggered by a takeover attempt, makes the company less valuable in some way to the potential raider, with the hope of discouraging the takeover. A common technique is to sell newly issued stock to current stockholders at prices below the market value of the company's existing stock, thereby instantly increasing the number of shares the raider has to buy.

■ *The shark repellent.* This tactic involves a requirement that stockholders representing a large majority of shares approve of any takeover attempt. Such a plan is viable only if the management team has the support of the majority of shareholders.

■ *The white knight.* A white night is a third company invited in to acquire a company that is in danger of being swallowed up in a hostile takeover.

Some critics believe that poison pills and other defenses are bad for shareholders because they can entrench weak management and discourage takeover attempts that would improve company value. For example, Yahoo, which has been struggling in recent years and has become vulnerable to takeover, tried to enact a provision that would give employees such generous severance packages in the event of a takeover that buying the company would become prohibitively expensive. After shareholders sued, a judge forced Yahoo to change the policy.[41]

✓CHECKPOINT

LEARNING OBJECTIVE 5: Identify the potential advantages of pursuing mergers and acquisitions as a growth strategy, along with the potential difficulties and risks.

Summary: Mergers and acquisitions can help companies reduce costs by eliminating redundancies and increasing buying power, increase revenue by cross-selling goods and services to each other's customers or expanding into new markets, and compete more effectively by adding new technologies or talented employees. However, the difficulties and risks are considerable: coming up with the money, deciding which managers will be in charge, merging marketing and sales efforts, reconciling information systems, dealing with redundant employees, and meshing different corporate cultures.

Critical thinking: (1) If you were on the board of directors at a company and the CEO proposed a merger with a top competitor, what types of questions would you want answered before you gave your approval? (2) If a CEO has the opportunity to merge with or acquire another company and is reasonably certain that the transaction will benefit shareholders, is the CEO obligated to pursue the deal? Why or why not?

It's your business: (1) Have you (or someone you know) ever experienced a merger or acquisition as an employee? Was your job affected? (2) Have you ever experienced a merger or acquisition as a customer? Did customer service suffer during the transition of ownership?

Key terms to know: merger, acquisition, hostile takeover, leverage buyout (LBO)

Strategic Alliances and Joint Ventures

Chapter 3 discusses strategic alliances and joint ventures from the perspective of international expansion, defining a **strategic alliance** as a long-term partnership between companies to jointly develop, produce, or sell products and a **joint venture** as a separate legal entity established by the strategic partners. Both of these options can be more attractive than a merger or acquisition in certain situations.

strategic alliance
A long-term partnership between companies to jointly develop, produce, or sell products

joint venture
A separate legal entity established by two or more companies to pursue shared business objectives

Strategic Alliances

Strategic alliances can accomplish many of the same goals as a merger or acquisition with less risk and work than permanently integrating two companies.[42] They can help a company gain credibility in a new field, expand its market presence, gain access to technology, diversify offerings, and share best practices without forcing the partners to become permanently entangled.

For example, Cisco Systems's core business is networking technologies that allow people to share information of all types over the Internet. Because a complete information system usually requires more than just networking, Cisco has formed a number of strategic alliances with companies that specialize in computers, mobile phones, software, business consulting, and other products and services. These relationships let Cisco focus on its core strengths while offering customers complete solutions.[43]

Strategic alliances aren't restricted to just two partners. To help electric companies and other utilities deliver energy more efficiently, Cisco teamed up with a half-dozen other large companies to form the Smart Energy Alliance.[44] A merger on this scale would've been unimaginably complex, but this strategic partnership allows the companies to collaborate without formally combining.

Joint Ventures

While strategic alliances avoid much of the work and risk of formal mergers, they don't create a unified entity that functions with a single management structure, information system, and other organizational elements. A joint venture lets companies create an operation that is more tightly integrated than a strategic alliance but without disrupting the original companies to the extent that a merger or acquisition does. In fact, after the spotty record of mergers and acquisitions in recent years, more companies are now considering joint ventures as a more attractive way to collaborate.[45]

The recent joint venture created by music retailer HMV and concert venue operator Mama Group is a great example of the synergies that a joint venture can create. HMV, one of the leading music retailers in the United Kingdom, was looking for opportunities to diversify beyond recorded music products, and Mama Group was looking for ways to expand ticket sales for its concert halls and clubs around the United Kingdom. The two firms created a company called Mean Fiddler Group Limited that now owns the venues; Mama Group operates them while HMV continues to focus on retail. The opportunities for synergy flow in both directions: HMV is opening retail stores at some of the venues, and Mean Fiddler promotes concert tickets to HMV's tremendous customer base.[46]

Exhibit 5.5 offers a quick graphical summary of the major ways businesses can join forces. For the latest information on company structure, corporate governance, and related issues, visit **http://real-timeupdates.com/bia5** and click on Chapter 5.

EXHIBIT 5.5 Options for Joining Forces

Companies can choose from a variety of ways to combine resources and capabilities.

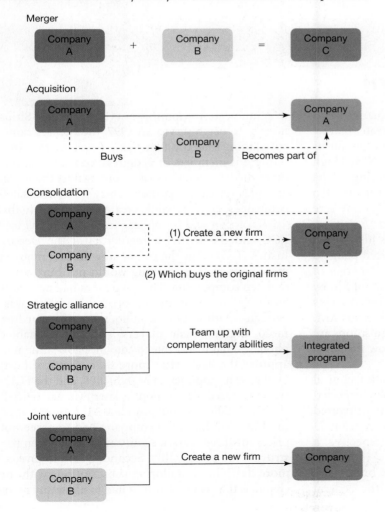

✓CHECKPOINT

LEARNING OBJECTIVE 6: Define *strategic alliances* and *joint ventures*, and explain why companies would choose these options over a merger or acquisition.

Summary: Strategic alliances can accomplish many of the same goals as a merger or acquisition with less risk and work than permanently integrating two companies. A joint venture lets companies create an operation that is more tightly integrated than a strategic alliance but without disrupting the original companies to the extent that a merger or acquisition does.

Critical thinking: Why are an increasing number of companies now considering joint ventures rather than mergers and acquisitions?

It's your business: Assume you've worked for years to build up a strong and independent company; would you be comfortable sharing power with another company in a strategic alliance or joint venture? Why or why not?

Key terms to know: strategic alliance, joint venture

Behind the Scenes

Teaming up for Survival at Sirius XM

Mergers and acquisitions can be exciting opportunities to expand by adding new product capabilities or greater market coverage. Unfortunately, such was not the case when Sirius CEO Mel Karmazin and his counterpart at XM, Hugh Panero, pondered the difficulties they were facing in the satellite radio business. Neither company had ever turned a profit, both were deeply in debt, costs were going nowhere but up, and the U.S. economy was slowing down.

Karmazin and Panero needed to join forces just to survive, and in early 2007, the companies announced plans to merge. (Although the deal was announced as a "merger of equals," it certainly looked more like an acquisition of XM by Sirius. Karmazin became the CEO of the combined Sirius XM, XM Satellite Radio became a subsidiary of Sirius XM, and Panero left the company later that year. Acquisitions are often presented to the public as mergers to allow the company being acquired to save a little face.)

By combining their competing efforts in both technical development and marketing, Karmazin and Panero expected to save $400 million in the first year. Outside analysts figured the two companies could eventually save anywhere from $3 billion to $7 billion overall. From a cost perspective, a merger clearly seemed to make sense.

A merger might've been the best choice, but it certainly wasn't an easy one. For starters, when the Federal

Communications Commission (FCC) granted Sirius and XM licenses to begin service in 1997, the licenses came with the stipulation that the two firms never merge. In addition, numerous members of Congress, consumer advocates, and other media companies came out against the merger on the grounds that allowing the country's only two satellite radio companies to merge would create a monopoly in that market.

Karmazin and his colleagues had to convince both the FCC and the antitrust regulators at the Department of Justice (DOJ) that the public now had so many entertainment choices that merging would not hurt consumers or dampen competition. The good news/bad news situation for Sirius XM was that the competitive landscape was crowded enough—with terrestrial radio, inexpensive or free Internet radio, digital music players, and music-enabled smartphones—that it was able to convince government officials to approve the deal. After more than a year of hearings, the DOJ gave its approval in March 2008, and the FCC commissioners cleared it four months later by a narrow 3–2 vote.

The DOJ didn't put any conditions on the approval, but the FCC did. First, the company had to agree not to raise prices for three years, a significant matter given the ongoing struggle for profitability. Second, it had to give consumers more flexibility in tailoring subscriptions with the specific channels they want. Third, it had to allow any manufacturer to produce and sell radios capable of receiving Sirius XM signals, a move designed to broaden consumer options and lower equipment prices. Fourth, the company had to increase educational programming and make 24 of its satellite channels available for lease by minority- and women-owned media providers.

The newly christened Sirius XM made it over all the regulatory hurdles, but life didn't get any easier. In fact, it got a lot worse almost immediately. The company relied on new car sales for a significant portion of its new subscribers; many new cars come with satellite radios as a standard or optional feature, and buyers often get free satellite service for a few months, after which the company hopes they've enjoyed it enough to become paying subscribers. Unfortunately, when the economy fell off the cliff in late 2008, new car sales went with it, squeezing the major source of new customers. To its great credit, the company did manage to keep adding new subscribers in this tough market, but not nearly enough to become profitable.

As if that weren't enough, the collapse of the global credit market in 2008 also threw a serious wrench into the company's financial management model. To finance those expensive satellites and on-air personalities, the company had been relying on a rolling series of short-term loans. However, as thousands of companies around the world discovered, all those credit faucets dried up practically overnight.

By early 2009 Sirius XM was perilously close to bankruptcy—and vulnerable to a hostile takeover by Dish Network, one of the two major satellite television services. With disaster looming, Karmazin found help in the form of a massive infusion of cash from Liberty Media, which—not coincidentally—controls DirecTV, Dish Network's major competitor in satellite television.

Liberty's money (partly a loan and partly an investment that gave Liberty a 40-percent share of ownership) gave Sirius XM a second chance at life, but the company's long-range future is anything but secure. The loan from Liberty has an eye-popping 15% interest rate, and it's only a short-term solution. Sirius XM needs to decrease its dependence on new-car sales and find more attractive long-term financing. Even that might not be enough. The deal with Liberty gives it an ownership stake in Sirius XM, and it could eventually seek a controlling interest and merge Sirius XM with its existing television and Internet services. In other words, Karmazin might have saved his company with one acquisition only to become the target of another himself.[47]

Critical Thinking Questions

1. Other than for purely financial reasons (interest on the loan and potential gains from its investment), why might Liberty Media want to help Sirius XM?
2. If Liberty Media eventually acquires Sirius XM, does that mean the Sirius-XM merger was a failure? Why or why not?
3. Sirius XM also makes its content available to subscribers online and is rumored to be working on a deal with Apple to make its content available on the iPhone and iPod products. Since these other media platforms compete with satellite services, why would the company expand its operations into these media?

LEARN MORE ONLINE

How has Sirius XM fared since its merger and the assistance from Liberty Media? Get the latest financial information from the company's website at www.siriusxm.com (look under "Investor Relations"). What is the business news media saying about the company's prospects? ■

Key Terms

acquisition (157)
board of directors (154)
chief executive officer (CEO) (156)
corporate governance (154)
corporate officers (156)
corporation (151)
general partnership (148)
hostile takeover (157)
joint venture (160)

leveraged buyout (LBO) (157)
limited liability (149)
limited liability company (LLC) (153)
limited liability partnership (LLP) (149)
limited partnership (149)
liquidity (152)
master limited partnership (MLP) (149)
merger (157)
partnership (148)

private corporation (151)
proxy (155)
public corporation (151)
S corporation (153)
shareholder activism (155)
shareholders (151)
sole proprietorship (145)
strategic alliance (160)
unlimited liability (147)

Test Your Knowledge

Questions for Review

1. What are the three basic forms of business ownership?
2. What is the difference between a general and a limited partnership?

3. What is a closely held corporation, and why do some companies choose this form of ownership?
4. How does unlimited liability put a business owner at risk?
5. What is the role of a company's board of directors?

Questions for Analysis

6. Why is it advisable for partners to enter into a formal partnership agreement?

7. Why might two companies choose to form a strategic alliance rather than pursuing a merger or acquisition?

8. To what extent do shareholders control the activities of a corporation?

9. How might a company benefit from having a diverse board of directors that includes representatives of several industries, countries, and cultures?

10. Ethical Considerations. Are poison pill defenses ethical? If a potential acquirer buys company stock legally, thereby becoming a part-owner of the company, should management be allowed to entrench itself against the wishes of this owner? Explain your answer.

Questions for Application

11. Do you own or have you ever considered owning stock? If so, what steps have you taken to ensure that company management has shareholder interests in mind?

12. Suppose you and some friends want to start a business to take tourists on wilderness backpacking expeditions. None of you has much extra money, so your plan is to start small. However, if you are successful, you would like to expand into other types of outdoor tours and perhaps even open up branches in other locations. What form of ownership should your new enterprise take, and why?

13. Visit Liberty Media's website www.libertymedia.com and find the company's corporate governance guidelines. Assume you're going to start a company that you plan to incorporate. Identify at least five principles of good governance from Liberty's website that you will use to guide the board of your new corporation.

14. Concept Integration. You've developed considerable expertise in setting up new manufacturing plants, and now you'd like to strike out on your own as a consultant who advises other companies. However, you recognize that manufacturing activity tends to expand and contract at various times during the business cycle (see Chapter 2). Do you think a single-consultant sole proprietorship or a small corporation with a half dozen or more consultants would be better able to ride out tough times at the bottom of a business cycle?

Practice Your Knowledge

Sharpening Your Communication Skills

You have just been informed that your employer is going to merge with a firm in Germany. Using online or library resources, find information on German business culture and customs and prepare a short report.

Building Your Team Skills

Imagine that the president of your college or university has just announced plans to retire. Your team, playing the role of the school's board of directors, must decide how to choose a new president to fill this vacancy next semester.

First, generate a list of the qualities and qualifications you think the school should seek in a new president. What background and experience would prepare someone for this key position? What personal characteristics should the new president have? What questions would you ask to find out how each candidate measures up against the list of credentials you have prepared?

Now list all the stakeholders that your team, as directors, must consider before deciding on a replacement for the retiring president. Of these stakeholders, whose opinions do you think are most important? Whose are least important? Who will be directly and indirectly affected by the choice of a new president? Of these stakeholders, which should be represented as participants in the decision-making process?

Select a spokesperson to deliver a brief presentation to the class summarizing your team's ideas and the reasoning behind your suggestions. After all the teams have completed their presentations, discuss the differences and similarities among credentials proposed by all the teams for evaluating candidates for the presidency. Then compare the teams' conclusions about stakeholders. Do all teams agree on the stakeholders who should participate in the decision-making process? Lead a classroom discussion on a board's responsibility to its stakeholders.

Expand Your Knowledge

Discovering Career Opportunities

Are you best suited to working as a sole proprietor, as a partner in a business, or as an employee or manager in a corporation? For this exercise, select three businesses with which you are familiar: one run by a single person, such as a dentist's practice or a local landscaping firm; one run by two or three partners, such as a small accounting firm; and one that operates as a corporation, such as Target or Wal-Mart.

1. Write down what you think you would like about being the sole proprietor, one of the partners, and the corporate manager or an employee in the businesses you have selected. For example, would you like having full responsibility for the sole proprietorship? Would you like being able to consult with other partners in the partnership before making decisions? Would you like having limited responsibility when you work for other people in the corporation?

2. Now write down what you might dislike about each form of business. For example, would you dislike the risk of bearing all legal responsibility in a sole proprietorship? Would you dislike having to talk with your partners before spending the partnership's money? Would you dislike having to write reports for top managers and shareholders of the corporation?

3. Weigh the pluses and minuses you have identified in this exercise. In comparison, which form of business most appeals to you?

Developing Your Research Skills

Review recent issues of business newspapers or periodicals (print or online editions) to find an article or series of articles illustrating one of the following business developments: merger, acquisition, hostile takeover, or leveraged buyout.

1. Explain in your own words what steps or events led to this development.

2. What results do you expect this development to have on (a) the company, (b) consumers, and (c) the industry the company is part of? Write down and date your answers.

3. Follow your story in the business news over the next month (or longer, as your instructor requests). What problems, opportunities, or other results are reported? Were these developments anticipated at the time of the initial story, or did they seem to catch industry analysts by surprise? How well did your answers to question 2 predict the results?

Improving Your Tech Insights: Groupware

Groupware, software that lets people communicate, share files, present materials, and work on documents simultaneously, is changing the way employees interact—and even the way businesses work together. For example, *shared workspaces* are "virtual offices" that give everyone on a team access to the same set of resources and information: databases, calendars, project plans, archived instant messages and e-mails, reference materials, and team documents. These workspaces (which are typically accessed through a web browser) make it easy for geographically dispersed team members to access shared files anytime, anywhere. Employees no longer need to be in the same office or even in the same time zone. They don't even need to be employees. Groupware makes it easy for companies to pull together partners and temporary contractors on a project-by-project basis. Groupware is often integrated with *web-based meeting* systems that combine instant messaging, shared workspaces, videoconferencing, and other tools.

Conduct research to identify a currently available groupware system. (Groupware systems aren't always identified as such, so you might want to search for "project collaboration systems" or similar terms.) Pick a company you might like to work for someday, and in a brief e-mail message to your instructor, explain how this particular groupware system could help the employees and managers in this company be more productive.[48]

Video Discussion

Access the Chapter 5 video discussion in the End of Chapter Assignments section at www.mybizlab.com.

PEARSON mybizlab

Log on to www.mybizlab.com to access the following study and assessment aids associated with this chapter:

- Interactive exercises
- Pre/post test
- Real-Time Updates
- Video application
- Customized study plans
- Biz Skills Simulations
- Quick Learning Guide

If you are not using mybizlab, you can access Real-Time Updates and Quick Learning Guides through http://realtimeupdates.com/bia5. The Quick Learning Guide (located under "Learn More" on the website) provides all six Checkpoints in a handy two-page format to help you study for exams or review important concepts whenever you need a quick refresher.

CHAPTER 6
Entrepreneurship and Small-Business Ownership

Behind the
Behind the Scenes

Bringing Traditional Healing Wisdom to Modern Consumers at Sister Sky

www.sistersky.com

For entrepreneurial inspiration, Monica Simeon didn't have to look very far. She learned how to run a business helping her father operate one of the first Native American casinos. She got the inspiration for her business while preparing batches of skin lotions based on traditional herbal remedies after commercial products didn't help with her son's severe eczema. And the opportunity to form a business partnership was as close as her sister, Marina TurningRobe.

Thus was born Sister Sky, which makes natural bath and body products based on recipes and natural plant knowledge handed down from generation to generation. The company is based on the Spokane Indian Reservation in northeast Washington state, where the sisters grew up—and grew into their entrepreneurial lifestyle.

Like many entrepreneurs, the sisters' vision is much broader than simply earning a living. They emphasize purity and authenticity in their products, whether it's using more expensive distilled water to avoid risks

Monica Simeon and Marina TurningRobe, the sisters behind Sister Sky bath and body products, have turned their business dreams into reality but still face some important challenges as they continue to grow.

of contamination, shunning the cheaper petroleum-based ingredients used in many mass-produced bath and body products, or staying true to the wisdom they have inherited from their ancestors. In addition, the sisters believe they have a duty to "promote cultural sharing in a positive way by educating consumers about the indigenous essence and spirit of the plant botanicals contained in our products." Finally, Simeon says, "One of our main goals is to improve the tribal economy by expanding opportunities for jobs beyond the casino."

If you were Simeon or TurningRobe, what steps would you take to make sure your young business made it through the launch stage and onto a path of sustainable growth and profitability? Where might you turn for advice and support if you needed it? How would you stay true to your vision of authentic and purposeful products while pursuing the goal of providing job opportunities—while meeting the unrelenting demands of managing a business in a highly competitive industry?[1] ∎

Introduction

Since you're studying business, chances are you've already had an idea or two for a new business. Are you ready to commit yourself fully to a business idea, as Monica Simeon and Marina TurningRobe (profiled in the chapter-opening Behind the Scenes) have done? Are you ready to make sacrifices and do whatever it takes to get your company off the ground? Should you start something from scratch or buy an existing business? Being an entrepreneur is one of the most exciting and important roles in business, but it requires high energy and some tough decision making, as you'll read in this chapter.

The Big World of Small Business

Many businesses start out the way Sister Sky did: with an entrepreneur (or two, in this case), a compelling idea, and the drive to succeed. Small-business ownership gives people like Monica Simeon and Marina TurningRobe the opportunity to pursue their dreams while making lasting and important contributions to their communities. Entrepreneurship also provides the platform for launching companies that grow to be quite large, too. With the exception of large operations spun off from existing companies, even the biggest corporations begin life as small businesses. The importance of small businesses in the U.S. economy is reflected in their sheer number: While there are roughly 17,000 large companies in the United States, there are more than 27 million small companies.[2]

Defining just what constitutes a small business is surprisingly tricky, but it is vitally important because billions of dollars are at stake when it comes to such things as employment regulations—from which the smallest companies are often exempt—and government contracts reserved for small businesses.[3] The U.S. Small Business Administration (SBA) starts by defining a **small business** as "one that is independently owned and operated and which is not dominant in its field of operation." Beyond that general starting point, the SBA defines the maximum size of "small" through either annual revenue or number of employees, and the limits vary by industry. For instance, in many agricultural categories, a company can make up to $750,000 and still be considered small, but Internet service providers can make up to $23 million a year and still be considered small. Similarly, in some industries, 100 employees is the limit; in others, it's 500, 750, 1,000, or even 1,500 people.[4]

small business
Company that is independently owned and operated, is not dominant in its field, and meets certain criteria for the number of employees or annual sales revenue

Economic Roles of Small Businesses

From employing millions of people to creating essential products, small businesses play a vital role in the U.S. economy. Here are some of major contributions small firms make:

- **They provide jobs.** Small businesses employ about half of the private-sector workforce in this country and create somewhere between two-thirds and three-fourths of new jobs. However, it's important to recognize that most of this job growth comes from that subset of small businesses whose goal is to grow into midsize or large businesses; the overwhelming majority of small businesses have no employees at all.[5]

- **They introduce new products.** The freedom to innovate that is characteristic of many small firms continues to yield countless advances in both technologies and marketable goods and services. Among all firms that apply for patents on new inventions, small businesses receive 13 times more patents per employee than larger firms.[6]

- **They supply the needs of larger organizations.** Many small businesses act as distributors, servicing agents, and suppliers to large corporations. In addition, government agencies often reserve a certain percentage of their purchasing contracts for small businesses.

- **They inject a considerable amount of money into the economy.** Small businesses pay nearly half the private-sector payroll in the United States and produce half the country's gross domestic product.[7]

- **They take risks that larger companies sometimes avoid.** Entrepreneurs play a significant role in the economy as risk takers, the people willing to try new and unproven ideas.

- **They provide specialized goods and services.** Small businesses frequently spring up to fill niches that aren't being served by existing companies.

Wayne Erbsen turned his passion for preserving and performing traditional music into a business that reaches customers all over the world from his home in Asheville, North Carolina. Native Ground Books & Music (www.nativeground.com) offers books and recordings of songs and folklore from the Civil War, the Old West, Appalachia, railroading, gospel, and many other elements of America's heritage.

Characteristics of Small Businesses

The majority of small businesses are modest operations with little growth potential, although some have attractive income potential for the solo businessperson. The self-employed consultant, the corner florist, the family-owned neighborhood pizza parlor, and small e-commerce ventures are sometimes called *lifestyle businesses* because they are built around the personal and financial needs of an individual or a family. In contrast, other firms are small simply because they are young, but they have ambitious plans to grow. These *high-growth ventures* are usually run by a team rather than by one individual, and they expand rapidly by obtaining a sizable supply of investment capital and by introducing new products or services to a large market.

Regardless of their primary objectives, small companies tend to differ from large enterprises in a variety of important ways. First, most small firms have a narrow focus, offering fewer goods and services to fewer market segments. Second, unless they are launched with generous financial backing, which is rare, small businesses have to get by with limited resources. Third, smaller businesses often have more freedom to innovate and move quickly. As they grow larger, companies tend to get slower and more bureaucratic. In contrast, entrepreneurial firms usually find it easier to operate "on the fly," making decisions quickly and reacting to changes in the marketplace.

Factors Contributing to the Increase in the Number of Small Businesses

Three factors are contributing to the increase in the number of small businesses today: e-commerce and other technological advances, the growing diversity in entrepreneurship, and corporate downsizing and outsourcing.

E-Commerce and Other Technologies

E-commerce and other technologies have spawned thousands of new business ventures in recent years—from firms that create the technology to firms that use it. The online auction site eBay is a great example. The company itself began as an entrepreneurial venture in 1995, when Pierre Omidyar created (on his home computer) an auction website that offered an alternative to flea markets and newspaper classifieds. Millions of users now conduct billions of dollars worth of transactions on the site, and many of them are "eBay entrepreneurs" whose entire businesses are based on using the site.[8]

The creative cycle hasn't stopped there, either. Some eBay users aren't happy about the company's business arrangements with larger retailers such as Buy.com, for example, so other online marketplaces such as Wigix (www.wigix.com) have sprung up to give people alternatives to eBay.[9]

Growing Diversity in Entrepreneurship

Small-business growth is also being fueled by women, minorities, immigrants, and young people who want alternatives to traditional employment. For instance, women now own more than 10 million U.S. businesses.[10] Minority business ownership is also on the rise across the United States. Minorities now own 15 percent of all U.S. businesses.[11] Part of this growth is attributed to firms that do a better job of marketing to specific segments of the population.

Real-Time Updates

Learn More

Do today's young entrepreneurs face the same challenges as those who came before?

Successful entrepreneur Jade Bourelle, who now mentors young entrepreneurs, discusses what motivates young people to go into business for themselves and the challenges they face. On mybizlab (**www.mybizlab .com**), you can access Real-Time Updates within each chapter or under Student Study Tools. Otherwise, go to **http://real-timeupdates.com/bia5** and click on "Learn More."

EXHIBIT 6.1 A New Generation of Collegiate Entrepreneurs

Following in the footsteps of Michael Dell (Dell), Larry Page and Sergey Brin (Google), and Mark Zuckerberg (Facebook), these college students didn't wait to graduate before taking the entrepreneurial plunge.

ENTREPRENEUR(S)	COLLEGE	COMPANY	PRODUCT(S)	URL
Brad Hargreaves, Matthew Brimer, Sean Mehra, Jeffrey Reitman	Yale	GXStudios	PickTeams online social game playing platform	http://pickteams.com
Zac Workman	Indiana University	ZW Enterprises	Punch Energy Drink, an all-natural energy drink	www.punchenergy.com
Arielle Patrice Scott, Jessica Mah, Andy Su	University of California, Berkeley	internshipIN	Website that connects start-up companies with internship candidates	www.internshipin.com
David Wachtel	University of Southern California	College Weekenders	Discounted travel packages for students to attend college sporting events	www.collegeweekenders.com
Scot Frank, Chris Varenhorst	Massachusetts Institute of Technology	Lingt Language	Online language-learning tools	http://lingtlanguage.com
Danny Klam	University of Houston	Simply Splendid Donuts and Ice Cream	Chain of donut and ice cream shops	www.ssdonuts.com

In addition, young people are one of the strongest forces in entrepreneurship today and launch the majority of all new businesses.[12] It's never too early to start. Facebook, Google, and Dell are just a few of the significant companies started by college students (see Exhibit 6.1). In the words of Joseph Keeley, who formed College Nannies and Tutors (www.collegenannies.com) when he was a freshman at the University of St. Thomas, "As a young entrepreneur, the risk is relatively low. If you have a well-thought-out plan, don't be afraid to execute it. The risk only gets higher as you get older." Keeley's initiative has paid off; his company now has franchise operations across the country and was recently recognized by *Entrepreneur* magazine as one of the top home-based franchise opportunities in the nation.[13] If you'd like to network with other aspiring entrepreneurs, check into such groups as the College Entrepreneurs Organization (www.c-e-o.org).

Downsizing and Outsourcing

Business start-ups often soar when the economy sours. During hard times, many companies downsize or lay off talented employees, who then have little to lose by pursuing self-employment. In fact, several well-known companies were started during recessions. Tech titans William Hewlett and David Packard joined forces in Silicon Valley in 1938 during the Great Depression. Bill Gates started Microsoft during the 1975 recession. And the founders of Sun Microsystems, Compaq Computer (now part of HP), Adobe Systems, and Lotus Development (now part of IBM) started their companies in 1982— in the midst of a recession and high unemployment.[14] During the worldwide recession that began in 2007 and showed few signs of abating well into 2009, another wave of entrepreneurs took their turn. "If there is a silver lining, the large-scale downsizing from major companies will release a lot of new entrepreneurial talent and ideas—scientists, engineers, business folks now looking to do other things," said Mark Cannice, who runs the entrepreneurship program at the University of San Francisco.[15]

Outsourcing, the practice of engaging outside firms to handle either individual projects or entire business functions (page 244) also creates numerous opportunities for small businesses and entrepreneurs. Some companies subcontract special projects and secondary business functions to experts outside the organization, while others turn to outsourcing as a way to permanently eliminate entire departments, and some laid-off employees even become entrepreneurs and sell services to their former employers.

For the latest information on entrepreneurship and small-business ownership, visit http://real-timeupdates.com/bia5 and click on Chapter 6.

✓CHECKPOINT

LEARNING OBJECTIVE 1: Highlight the contributions small businesses make to the U.S. economy.

Summary: Small businesses provide jobs, employing about half the private-sector workforce. They introduce new and innovative products, they supply many of the needs of larger organizations, they inject considerable amounts of money into the economy, they often take risks that larger organizations avoid, and they provide many specialized goods and services.

Critical thinking: (1) Why do you think many companies grow more risk-averse as they grow larger? (2) Could large businesses take the place of small businesses if they wanted to? For instance, could someone build a nationwide landscaping company? Why or why not?

It's your business: If you can't land the right job soon after graduation, would you consider starting a business? Why or why not?

Key terms to know: small business

The Entrepreneurial Spirit

To some people, working for themselves or starting a company seems a perfectly natural way to earn a living. To others, the thought of working outside the structure of a regular company might never occur to them or might seem too scary to even contemplate. However, every professional should understand the **entrepreneurial spirit**—the positive, forward-thinking desire to create profitable, sustainable business enterprises—and the role it can play in *every* company, not just small or new firms. The entrepreneurial spirit is vital to the health of the economy and to everyone's standard of living, and as you'll read in a moment, it can help even the largest and oldest companies become profitable and competitive.

entrepreneurial spirit
The positive, forward-thinking desire to create profitable, sustainable business enterprises

Why People Start Their Own Companies

Starting a company is nearly always a difficult, risky, exhausting endeavor that requires significant sacrifice. Why do people do it? Some want more control over their futures; others are simply tired of working for someone else. Some, such as Monica Simeon and Marina TurningRobe of Sister Sky, have new product ideas that they believe in with such passion that they're willing to risk everything on a start-up enterprise. Some start companies to pursue business goals that are important to them on a personal level. Jennie Baird, co-founder of Generation Grownup (www.generationgrownup.com), which publishes parenting-related websites, had two important reasons: "I wanted to take the opportunity

Frustrated in a tough job market, Alex Andon used his expertise in biology and aquarium design to launch Jellyfish Art (www .jellyfishart.com). The company specializes in the unique and demanding field of aquariums for jellyfish.

to be the one in control of innovation and work on something that I believe in."[16]

Another reason, one that becomes more common during tough job markets, is the inability to find attractive employment anywhere else. Alex Andon searched for months after being laid off from his job in the biotech industry. Out of frustration as much as anything ("I hate looking for work," he explains), he became an entrepreneur, putting his biology background to work launching Jellyfish Art (www.jellyfishart.com) to create and sell jellyfish aquariums.[17]

Qualities of Successful Entrepreneurs

While it's impossible to lump millions of people into a single category, successful entrepreneurs tend to share a number of characteristics:[18]

■ They love what they do and are driven by a passion to succeed—but they often don't measure success in strictly financial terms.

■ They are highly disciplined and willing to work long hours and make other significant sacrifices to achieve their goals.

■ They have a high degree of confidence and optimism, even in the face of failures and setbacks. Amazon.com founder Jeff Bezos worked tirelessly for years, in the face of frequent skepticism—including "expert" predictions that he would fail—before his company finally turned a profit. It is now a profitable retail giant that sells more than $20 billion worth of products every year.[19]

■ They like to control their destiny—and believe they have control over their destiny.

■ They relate well to others and have a talent for inspiring others in pursuit of a common goal.

■ They are curious and eager to learn whatever is necessary to reach their goals.

■ They learn from their mistakes and view failures and setbacks as opportunities to understand and improve.

■ They are highly adaptable; they stay tuned into their markets and change direction when needed to pursue new opportunities.

■ Contrary to popular stereotype, they are not compulsive gamblers who thrive on high-risk situations; rather, they embrace moderate risk when it is coupled with the potential for significant rewards.

If you share most or all of these traits, successful entrepreneurship could be in your future, too—if you're not already a hard-working entrepreneur.

Real-Time Updates

Learn More

Wondering if you're ready to start a business?

Take this online quiz to see if you're ready—and find out how to get ready if you're not quite there yet. On mybizlab (www.mybizlab.com), you can access Real-Time Updates within each chapter or under Student Study Tools. Otherwise, go to http://real-timeupdates.com/bia5 and click on "Learn More."

Innovating Without Leaving: Intrapreneurship

The entrepreneur's innovative spirit is so compelling, in fact, that many large companies and individuals within companies now try to express it through *intrapreneurship*, a term coined by business consultant Gifford Pinchot (www.intrapreneur.com) to designate entrepreneurial efforts within a larger organization.[20]

However, innovating within a larger organization is often much easier said than done because companies tend to become more analytical, more deliberate, more structured, and more careful as they mature. Mechanisms put in place to prevent mistakes can also hamper innovative thinking by restricting people to tried-and-true methods. Organizations can develop habits based on behaviors and decisions that made sense in the past but that no longer make sense as the business environment changes. Injecting the entrepreneurial spirit sometimes means going against the accepted wisdom.[21] In other words, it can be risky behavior that may or may not be rewarded.

To encourage the entrepreneurial spirit, companies such as Google and W.L. Gore (known most for its Gore-Tex waterproof fabric) take care to minimize the barriers that sap entrepreneurial energy and get in the way of creative thinking. At Gore, for example, employees have the freedom to define and initiate new projects, much as they would if they were independent entrepreneurs. The best project ideas attract additional team members and the necessary resources to succeed.[22]

✓CHECKPOINT

LEARNING OBJECTIVE 2: Identify the common traits of successful entrepreneurs.

Summary: The entrepreneurial spirit, the positive, forward-thinking desire to create profitable, sustainable business enterprises, is a good way to summarize the entrepreneurial personality. Specifically, successful entrepreneurs tend to love what they do and are driven by a passion to succeed at it, they are disciplined and willing to work hard, they are confident and optimistic, and they like to control their own destiny. Moreover, they relate well to others and have the ability to inspire others, they are curious, they learn from their mistakes without letting failure drag them down, they are adaptable and tuned into their environments, and they are moderate but careful risk takers.

Critical thinking: (1) Would someone who excels at independent entrepreneurship automatically excel at an intrapreneurial effort? Why or why not? (2) Does the inability or unwillingness to work within the constraints of a typical corporation mean someone is naturally suited to entrepreneurship? Why or why not?

It's your business: If you had to start a business right now and generate profit as quickly as possible, what kind of business would you start? Explain your answer.

Key terms to know: entrepreneurial spirit

The Start-Up Phase: Planning and Launching a New Business

The start-up phase is an exciting—and exhausting—time in a business owner's life. It's exciting because entrepreneurs and small-business owners love to roll up their sleeves and get to work, to make things happen, to create something out of nothing. It's exhausting because the list of tasks that must be accomplished can seem never-ending. Focusing that start-up energy and making sure the essential start-up tasks get done in the right order calls for some careful decision making and planning, starting with choosing the best ownership option and creating an effective business plan.

Small-Business Ownership Options

People with the entrepreneurial urge sometimes jump to the conclusion that starting a new company is the best choice, but it's definitely not the only choice—and not always the right choice. Before you decide, consider all three options: creating a new business, buying an

EXHIBIT 6.2

Weighing the Advantages and Disadvantages of Starting a New Business

Owning a business has many advantages, but you must also consider the potential drawbacks.

Advantages	Disadvantages
+ Control over your own destiny	− Uncertainty of income
+ Ability to reach your full potential	− Risk of losing your entire investment
+ Unlimited profits	− Long hours and hard work
+ Recognition for your efforts	− Complete responsibility
+ Doing what you enjoy	− High levels of stress
+ Opportunity to make a difference	− Lifestyle sacrifices during start-up

existing business, or obtaining a franchise. Creating a new business has many advantages and disadvantages (see Exhibit 6.2); in many cases, it can be the most difficult option.

If starting a company from scratch isn't the right choice for you, consider buying an existing business instead. This approach tends to reduce the risks—provided, of course, that you check out the company carefully. When you buy a healthy business, you generally purchase an established customer base, functioning business systems, a proven product or service, and a known location. You don't have to go through the challenging period of building a reputation, establishing a clientele, finding suppliers, and hiring and training employees. In addition, financing an existing business is often much easier than financing a new one; lenders are reassured by the company's history and existing assets and customer base. With these major details already settled, you can concentrate on making improvements.

Still, buying an existing business is not without disadvantages and risks. For starters, you may need a considerable amount of financing to buy a fully functioning company. You also inherit any problems the company has, from unhappy employees to obsolete equipment to customers with overdue accounts, and you may not discover some of these problems until you've signed the deal. Thorough research is a must.[23]

The third option, buying a franchise, combines many of the benefits of independent business ownership with the support that comes with being part of a larger organization. You can read more about franchising on page 183.

Blueprint for an Effective Business Plan

Although many successful entrepreneurs claim to have done little formal planning, they all have at least *some* intuitive idea of what they're trying to accomplish and how they hope to do it. In other words, even if they haven't produced a formal printed document, chances are they've thought through the big questions, which is just as important. As FedEx founder Fred Smith put it, "Being entrepreneurial doesn't mean [you] jump off a ledge and figure out how to make a parachute on the way down."[24]

business plan
Document that summarizes a proposed business venture, goals, and plans for achieving those goals

A **business plan** summarizes a proposed business venture, communicates the company's goals, highlights how management intends to achieve those goals, and shows how customers will benefit from the company's goods or services. Preparing a business plan serves three important functions. First, it guides the company operations and outlines a strategy for turning an idea into reality. Second, it helps persuade lenders and investors to finance your business if outside money is required. Third, it can provide a reality check in case an idea just isn't feasible.

If you are starting out on a small scale and using your own money, your business plan may be relatively informal. But at a minimum, you should describe the basic concept of the business and outline its specific goals, objectives, and resource requirements. A formal plan, suitable for presentation to outside lenders or investors, should cover these points:

- **Summary.** In one or two pages, summarize your business concept. Clearly articulate your business model and strategy for success—astute investors know what makes a business work, and they want to know that you do, too. Describe your product's market potential. Highlight some things about your company and its owners that will distinguish your firm from the competition. Summarize your financial projections and the amount of money investors can expect to make on their investment. Be sure to indicate how much money you will need and for what purpose.

- **Mission and objectives.** Explain the purpose of your business and what you hope to accomplish.

- **Company overview.** Give full background information on the origins and structure of your venture.

- **Management.** Summarize the background and qualifications of any key management personnel in your company.

- **Target market.** Provide data that will persuade an investor that you understand your target market. Be sure to identify the strengths and weaknesses of your competitors.

- **Marketing strategy.** Explain how you can profitably meet the needs of your target market; identify the goods or services you will provide, including their unique and compelling attributes; and explain your pricing, distribution, and promotion strategies.

- **Design and development plans.** If your products require design or development, describe the nature and extent of what needs to be done, including costs and possible problems.

- **Operations plan.** Provide information on the facilities, equipment, and labor needed.

- **Start-up schedule.** Forecast development of the company in terms of completion dates for major aspects of the business plan.

- **Major risk factors.** Identify all potentially negative factors and discuss them honestly.

- **Financial projections and requirements.** Include a detailed budget of start-up and operating costs, as well as projections for income, expenses, and cash flow for the first three years of business. Identify the company's financing needs and potential sources.

- **Exit strategy.** Explain how investors will be able to cash out or sell their investment, such as through a public stock offering, sale of the company, or a buyback of the investors' interest.

When covering these points, keep in mind that your audience wants short, concise information with realistic cost and revenue projections. Pay attention to quality, too; if your business plan is sloppy and unprofessional, readers will think you are too.

As important as planning is, it's equally important to monitor the market and be ready to adjust once you start moving. You don't want to be so locked into your plan that you refuse to adapt if things aren't working or if you fail to see changes in the market or new opportunities along the way.

Real-Time Updates

Learn More

Creating a winning business plan

Follow this detailed advice to create a thorough and compelling business plan. On mybizlab (**www.mybizlab.com**), you can access Real-Time Updates within each chapter or under Student Study Tools. Otherwise, go to **http://real-timeupdates.com/bia5** and click on "Learn More."

CHECKPOINT

LEARNING OBJECTIVE 3: Explain the importance of planning a new business, and outline the key elements in a business plan.

Summary: Planning is essential because it forces you to consider the best ownership strategy for your needs and circumstances (creating a new company, buying an existing company, or buying a franchise), and it forces you to think through the factors that will lead to success. An effective business plan should include your mission and objectives, company overview, management, target market, marketing strategy, design and development plans, operations plan, start-up schedule, major risk factors, and financial projections and requirements.

Critical thinking: (1) Why is it important to identify critical risks and problems in a business plan? (2) Many experts suggest that you write the business plan yourself, rather than hiring a consultant to write it for you. Why is this a good idea?

It's your business: (1) Think of several of the most innovative or unusual products you currently own or have recently used (don't forget about services as well). Were these products created by small companies or large ones? (2) Optimism and perseverance are two of the most important qualities for entrepreneurs. On a scale of 1 (lowest) to 10 (highest), how would you rate yourself on these two qualities? How would your best friend rate you?

Key terms to know: business plan

The Growth Phase: Nurturing and Sustaining a Young Business

So far, so good. You've done your planning and launched your new enterprise. Now the challenge is to keep going and keep growing toward your goals. To ensure a long and healthy life for your business, start by understanding the reasons new businesses can fail.

New Business Failure Rates

You may have heard some frightening "statistics" about the failure rate of new businesses, with various sources saying that 70, 80, or even 90 percent of new business ventures fail within 10 years. Unfortunately, there is a great deal of misinformation and misunderstood information out there about business failure rates. Many new businesses do indeed fail, and it's essential to understand why, but they don't fail at nearly the rates claimed in some of these gloom-and-doom reports.

Based on a comprehensive analysis using data from the U.S. Census Bureau, 50 percent of all employer firms (those that hire employees) were still in business after four years. Another 17 percent were no longer in operation but had closed "successfully," meaning the owner retired, sold the company, or otherwise ended on a positive note. In other words, averaged across all industries, only 33 percent actually "failed."[25]

Although the statistics aren't as gloomy as many people think, a 33-percent failure rate is still a figure that demands the entrepreneur's attention. To help make sure you end up among the 67 percent who are successful, start by understanding why businesses fail (see Exhibit 6.3). Poor management skills, inexperience in the chosen market sector, and insufficient financing are among the top 10 reasons for failure. And although it sounds counterintuitive, growing *too* quickly is also a significant source of business failures, for several reasons. Growth puts tremendous pressure on companies, in every area from finding enough qualified employees to financing new equipment or facilities. Plus, the entrepreneurial skills needed to get a business off the ground are not the same skills required to

- Managerial incompetence
- Lack of relevant experience
- Inadequate financing
- Poor cash management
- Lack of strategic planning
- Ineffective marketing
- Uncontrolled growth
- Poor location
- Poor inventory control
- Inability to make the transition from corporate employee to entrepreneur

EXHIBIT 6.3

Why New Businesses Fail

Experts have identified these 10 reasons as the most likely causes of new business failure.

transform a hot start-up into a stable business organization. In some cases, entrepreneurs have been able to reinvent themselves along the way and become successful executives. In others, they recognize their limitations and hire seasoned executives to take over, as eBay founder Pierre Omidyar did when he replaced himself with Meg Whitman—who has since led the company to dominance in its market.[26]

Perhaps one of the most important reasons companies fail is something that doesn't always show up in surveys. It's a simple matter of "motivational collapse," when the would-be entrepreneur encounters one too many setbacks and simply doesn't have the drive to keep going.[27] The truly committed entrepreneur, in contrast, keeps pushing onward, experimenting, making adjustments, and keeping his or her enthusiasm level high until things start to click. For example, one retailer might conclude that he or she chose a poor location and close the business in frustration. But another might work to understand why the location was poor—and then move the business to a better location and keep working and adjusting strategy until it succeeds.

Advice and Support for Business Owners

Keeping a business going is no simple task, to be sure. Fortunately, entrepreneurs can get advice and support from a wide variety of sources.

Government Agencies and Not-for-Profit Organizations

A number of city, state, and federal government agencies offer business owners advice, assistance, and even financing in some cases. For instance, many cities and states have an office of economic development (or similarly named agency) chartered with helping companies prosper so that they might contribute to the local or regional economy. At the federal level, small businesses can apply for loans backed by the Small Business Administration (www.sba.gov) and learn more about selling to the federal government—including bidding on the many contracts reserved for small or minority-owned companies—at www.business.gov. Many state government agencies also have special offices (check their websites) to help small firms compete.

Some of the best advice available to small businesses is delivered by thousands of volunteers from the Service Corps of Retired Executives (SCORE), a resource partner of the Small Business Administration. Through nearly 400 local chapters around the country and via e-mail, these experienced business professionals offer free advice and one-to-one counseling sessions on topics such as developing a business plan, securing financing, and managing business

 Real-Time Updates

Learn More
Increase your chances of success by learning from other entrepreneurs

SCORE advisor Lou Davenport shares the wisdom he has gained from helping struggling entrepreneurs. On mybizlab (www.mybizlab.com), you can access Real-Time Updates within each chapter or under Student Study Tools. Otherwise, go to http://real-timeupdates.com/bia5 and click on "Learn More."

growth. You can contact a local SCORE counselor or learn more about available programs at www.score.org.

Many colleges and universities also offer entrepreneurship and small-business programs. Check with your college's business school to see if resources are available to help you launch or expand a company. The U.S. Chamber of Commerce (www.chamberofcommerce.com) and its many local chambers offer advice and special programs for small business as well.

Business Partners

The companies you do business with can also be a source of advice and support. For example, Bank of America's (www.bankofamerica.com) Small Business Online Community offers a variety of articles, online tutorials, and forums where business owners can post questions.[28] Similarly, Microsoft's Small Business Center (www.microsoft.com/smallbusiness) provides free seminars, articles, and webcasts.[29] As you might expect, the free resources from these companies are part of their marketing strategies and so include a certain amount of self-promotion, but don't let that stop you from taking advantage of all the free advice you can get.

advisory board
A team of people with subject-area expertise or vital contacts who help a business owner review plans and decisions

EXHIBIT 6.4 **Social Networking for Entrepreneurs**

Here are just a few of the many online networks that provide advice and vital connections for entrepreneurs.

Mentors and Advisory Boards

Many entrepreneurs and business owners take advantage of individual mentors and advisory boards. Mentoring can happen through both formal programs such as SCORE and informal relationships developed in person or online (see Exhibit 6.4) for a list of top social networks for entrepreneurs). In either case, the advice of a mentor who has been down the road before can be priceless.

An **advisory board** is a form of "group mentoring" in which you assemble of team of people with subject-area expertise or vital contacts to help review plans and decisions. Unlike a corporate board of directors, an advisory board does not have legal responsibilities,

NETWORK	SPECIAL FEATURES	URL
Entrepreneur Connect	Social network created by *Entrepreneur* magazine	http://econnect.entrepreneur.com
PartnerUp	Helps entrepreneurs looking for people and resources	www.partnerup.com
StartupNation	Provides articles, forums, blogs, seminars, and podcasts	www.startupnation.com
LinkedIn	Not specifically for entrepreneurs, but so many business professionals are members of this popular network that most entrepreneurs should have a presence as well	http://linkedin.com
Biznik	Social network focused on collaboration, with entrepreneurs and small-business owners helping one another	http://biznik.com
Perfect Business	Resource-rich site that can help with all phases of starting a business	www.perfectbusiness.com
Go BIG Network	Bills itself as the world's biggest community of start-up companies	www.gobignetwork.com
Cofoundr	Private members-only network (you can't view other profiles without joining) for programmers, designers, investors, and others in the entrepreneurial community	http://cofoundr.com
The Funded	Lets entrepreneurs share information on venture capitalists and angel investors, including the amounts and terms they've been offered	http://thefunded.com
Young Entrepreneur	Popular site for active entrepreneurs and those considering entrepreneurship	www.youngentrepreneur.com

and you don't have to incorporate to establish an advisory board. In some cases, advisors will agree to help for no financial compensation. In other cases, particularly for growth companies that want high-profile experts, advisors agree to serve in exchange for either a fee or a small portion of the company's stock (up to 3 percent is standard).[30]

Print and Online Media

Your local library and the Internet offer information to help any small-business owner face just about every challenge imaginable. For instance, blogs written by business owners, investors, and functional specialists such as marketing consultants can offer valuable insights. Websites such as www.entrepreneurship.org provide free advice on every aspect of managing an entrepreneurial organization. Also, the websites affiliated with these well-known business magazines should be on every small-business owner's regular reading list:

- *Inc.* (www.inc.com). Be sure to check out the many "Resource Centers," addressing such topics as women in business, finance and capital, marketing, and law and taxation.
- *Business 2.0* (http://money.cnn.com/magazines/business2). Focused on technology-oriented businesses, this site offers lots of real-life success stories that profile entrepreneurs in action.
- *BusinessWeek* (www.businessweek.com/smallbiz). The small-business section of this widely read business magazine's website offers advice on every aspect of running a business.
- *Fortune Small Business* (http://money.cnn.com/magazines/fsb). Similar to *BusinessWeek*'s small-business coverage, this publication is affiliated with the highly regarded *Fortune* magazine.

Networks and Support Groups

No matter what industry you're in or what stage your business is in, you can probably find a local or online network of people with similar interests. Many cities across the country have local networks; search online for "entrepreneur network." Some entrepreneurs meet regularly in small groups to analyze each other's progress month by month. Being forced to articulate your plans and decisions to peers—and to be held accountable for results—can be an invaluable reality check. Some groups focus on helping entrepreneurs hone their presentations to potential investors. Ultra Light Startups, an organization in New York City, gives entrepreneurs the opportunity to practice their "pitches," compelling summaries of their business ventures.[31] In addition to local in-person groups, social networking technology gives entrepreneurs an endless array of opportunities to connect online (see Exhibit 6.4).

Business Incubators

Business incubators are centers that provide "newborn" businesses with just about everything a company needs to get started, from office space to information technology to management coaching, usually at sharply reduced costs. Most incubators are not-for-profit organizations affiliated with the economic development agencies of local or state governments or universities, although a number of for-profit incubators now exist as well, and some companies have internal incubators to nurture new ventures. Incubators have spread rapidly in the past two decades; there are about 1,000 in North America and another 6,000 around the world.[32] To learn more about incubators or to find one in your area, visit the National Business Incubation Association website at www.nbia.org.

    The surgical device maker Stereotaxis is a good example of the incubation concept in action. The company progressed through its early stages with the help of the Center for Emerging Technologies (CET), a not-for-profit incubator in St. Louis, Missouri, funded by such organizations as the University of Missouri–St. Louis and the Missouri Department of Economic Development. Stereotaxis operated out of CET's facilities for seven years, during which time it went public and continued to develop its technologies and expand its business operations. The company is now "out on its own" and continues to grow.[33]

business incubators
Facilities that house small businesses and provide support services during the company's early growth phases

✓CHECKPOINT

LEARNING OBJECTIVE 4: Identify the major causes of business failures, and identify sources of advice and support for struggling business owners.

Summary: Ten common reasons for failure are managerial incompetence, inexperience, inadequate financing, poor cash management, lack of strategy planning, ineffective marketing, uncontrolled growth, poor location, poor inventory control, and the inability to make the transition from corporate employee to independent entrepreneur. Another factor that can contribute to any of these explicit reasons is motivational collapse, when the entrepreneur simply gives up. For help and advice, business owners can turn to a variety of government agencies, not-for-profit organizations, business partners, mentors and advisory boards, print and online media, networks and support groups, and business incubators.

Critical thinking: (1) Why would a state or local government invest taxpayer dollars in a business incubator? (2) Can you think of any risks of getting advice from other entrepreneurs?

It's your business: (1) Have you ever shopped at a store or eaten in a restaurant and said to yourself, "This place isn't going to make it"? What factors caused you to reach that conclusion? (2) Does your college have an entrepreneur program or participate in a business incubator? If you wanted to start a business, how might these services help you?

Key terms to know: advisory board, business incubators

Financing Options for Small Businesses

As noted earlier, inadequate financing is one of the leading causes of new business failure. Entrepreneurs can underestimate how much they'll need by underestimating how long it will take to start making sales, overestimating their overall sales revenue, overestimating how quickly they'll actually get paid after making a sale (corporate customers often take 30 to 60 days or longer to pay, for instance), and underestimating expenses (things *always* go wrong and things *always* cost more than you expect). Entrepreneurs are optimists by nature, but experts strongly recommend against using best-case scenarios when estimating your financing needs. Lower your sales expectations, raise your expense estimates, and run your numbers past an experienced professional (such as a SCORE advisor) to make sure you've identified all the potential costs.

Figuring out *how much* you'll need requires good insights into the particular industry you plan to enter. Figuring out *where* to get the money is a creative challenge no matter which industry you're in. Financing a business enterprise is a complex undertaking, and chances are you'll need to piece together funds from multiple sources, possibly using a combination of *equity* (in which you give investors a share of the business in exchange for their money) and *debt* (in which you borrow money that must be repaid). You'll read more about equity and debt financing in Chapter 18. Again, use the resources available today for advice; they can point you in the right direction for seeking both *private financing* and *public financing*.

Seeking Private Financing

Private financing covers every source of funding except selling stock to the public via a stock market. Virtually every company starts with private financing, even companies that eventually go public. The range of private financing options is diverse, from personal savings to investment funds set up by large corporations looking for entrepreneurial innovations. Many firms get **seed money**, their very first infusion of capital, through family loans. If you

seed money
The first infusion of capital used to get a business started

go this route, be sure to make the process as formal as a bank loan would be, complete with a specified repayment plan. Otherwise, problems with the loan can cause problems in the family.[34] Four common categories of private financing are banks and microlenders, venture capitalists, angel investors, and personal credit cards and lines of credit.

Banks and Microlenders

Bank loans are one of the most important sources of financing for small business—but there's an important catch: In most cases, banks won't lend money to a start-up that hasn't established a successful track record.[35] As your company grows, a bank will nearly always be a good long-term partner, helping you finance expansions and other major expenses. However, about your only chance of getting a bank loan is by putting up marketable collateral, such as buildings or equipment, to back the loan.[36]

In response to the needs of entrepreneurs who don't qualify for standard bank loans or who don't need the amount of a regular loan, a number of organizations now serve as **microlenders**, offering loans up to $35,000 or so. Nearly 500 microlenders in the United States are members of the Association for Enterprise Opportunity (www.microenterpriseworks.org), which promotes entrepreneurship through both microloans and support services such as training and technical assistance.[37] The role of microlenders tends to grow when the economy is shrinking and conventional bank loans become harder to get. When global credit markets were stalled in 2008 and 2009, for example, even some larger, established companies turned to microlenders for help.[38]

microlenders
Organizations, often not-for-profit, that lend smaller amounts of money to business owners who might not qualify for conventional bank loans

Venture Capitalists

At the other end of the funding scale are **venture capitalists (VCs)**, investment specialists who raise pools of capital from large private and institutional sources (such as pension funds) to finance ventures that have high growth potential and a need for large amounts of capital. VC funding often makes the headlines in the business media, such as when a high-flying start-up gets an injection of $10 million or $20 million. However, VCs are extremely selective; they invest in only a few thousand companies in the United States every year.[39]

Given the amounts of money involved and the expectations of sizable returns, VCs usually invest in high-potential areas such as information technology, energy, biotechnology, and digital media. Unlike banks or most other financing sources, VCs do more than simply provide money. They also provide management expertise in return for a sizable ownership interest in the business. Once the business becomes profitable, VCs reap the reward by selling their interest to long-term investors, usually after the company goes public.

venture capitalists (VCs)
Investors who provide money to finance new businesses or turnarounds in exchange for a portion of ownership, with the objective of reselling the business at a profit

Angel Investors

Start-up companies that can't attract VC investment often look for **angel investors**, private individuals who put their own money into start-ups with the goal of eventually selling their interest for a large profit. These individuals are willing to invest smaller amounts than VCs and to stay involved with the company for a longer period of time. Many of these investors join *angel networks* or *angel groups* that invest together in chosen companies. Angel investing tends to have a more local focus than venture capitalism, so you can search for angels through local business contacts and organizations. You can also find many angel networks through *Inc.* magazine's Angel Investor Directory at www.inc.com or the Angel Capital Association at www.angelcapitalassociation.org.[40]

angel investors
Private individuals who invest money in start-ups, usually earlier in a business's life and in smaller amounts than VCs are willing to invest or banks are willing to lend

Credit Cards and Personal Lines of Credit

Up until the 2008 credit crunch, at least, credit cards and personal lines of credit were easy to come by; all that most people had to do was open their mail.

 Real-Time Updates

Learn More
Learn how to talk to an angel

Successful entrepreneur and angel investor David Rose offers advice on making your pitch to angle capitalists. On mybizlab (www.mybizlab.com), you can access Real-Time Updates within each chapter or under Student Study Tools. Otherwise, go to http://real-timeupdates.com/bia5 and click on "Learn More."

Given the easy access to this form of financing, it's no surprise that credit cards are a common source of capital for small businesses. Half of all entrepreneurs and small business owners use their cards to get cash for start-up or ongoing expenses.[41]

Funding a business with credit cards might be the only option many people have, but it is extremely risky. Unfortunately, there is no simple answer about using credit cards; some entrepreneurs have used them to launch successful, multimillion-dollar businesses, while others have destroyed their credit ratings and racked up debts that will take years to pay off.

Small Business Administration Assistance

The U.S. Small Business Administration (SBA) offers a number of financing options for small businesses. To get an SBA-backed loan, you apply to a regular bank, which actually provides the money; the SBA guarantees to repay between 50 and 85 percent of the loan (depending on the program) if you fail to do so. The upper limit on SBA-backed loans is currently $2 million. In addition to operating its primary loan guarantee program, the SBA also manages a microloan program in conjunction with nonprofit, community-based lenders. The limit on these loans is currently $35,000. The American Recovery and Reinvestment Act of 2009 allocated additional funds to the SBA to help small businesses struggling with a tight economy and reduced access to credit.[42]

Another option for raising money is one of the investment firms created by the SBA. These Small Business Investment Companies (SBICs) offer loans, venture capital, and management assistance, although they tend to make smaller investments and are willing to consider businesses that VCs or angel investors may not want to finance. The SBIC program has helped fund some of the best-known companies in the United States, including Apple, FedEx, Jenny Craig, and Outback Steakhouse.[43]

Going Public

initial public offering (IPO)
A corporation's first offering of shares to the public

Companies with solid growth potential may also seek funding from the public at large, although only a small fraction of the companies in the United States are publicly traded. Whenever a corporation offers its shares of ownership to the public for the first time, the company is said to be *going public*. The initial shares offered for sale are the company's **initial public offering (IPO)**. Going public is an effective method of raising needed capital, but it can be an expensive and time-consuming process with no guarantee you'll get the amount of money you need. Public companies must meet a variety of regulatory requirements, as you'll explore in more detail in Chapter 18.

✓CHECKPOINT

LEARNING OBJECTIVE 5: Discuss the principal sources of small-business private financing.

Summary: Sources of *private financing* for small businesses include banks and microlenders, venture capitalists, angel investors, credit cards and personal lines of credit, and loan programs from the Small Business Administration. Companies that reach sufficient size with continued growth potential have the additional option of seeking *public financing* by selling shares.

Critical thinking: (1) Would a profitable small business with only moderate growth potential be a good candidate for venture capitalist funding? Why or why not? (2) Why would angel investors help finance companies privately, rather than buying shares of publicly traded companies?

It's your business: Would you be willing to take on credit card debt in order to start a company? Why or why not?

Key terms to know: seed money, microlenders, venture capitalists (VCs), angel investors, initial public offering (IPO)

The Franchise Alternative

An alternative to buying an existing business is to buy a **franchise** in somebody else's business. This approach enables the buyer to use a larger company's trade name and sell its goods or services in a specific territory. In exchange for this right, the **franchisee** (the small-business owner who contracts to sell the goods or services) pays the **franchisor** (the supplier) an initial start-up fee, then monthly royalties based on sales volume. Franchises are a large and growing presence in the U.S. economy, with roughly 3,000 franchisor systems and a million individual franchised establishments.[44]

Types of Franchises

Franchises are of three basic types. A *product franchise* gives you the right to sell trademarked goods, which are purchased from the franchisor and resold. Car dealers and gasoline stations fall into this category. A *manufacturing franchise,* such as a soft-drink bottling plant, gives you the right to produce and distribute the manufacturer's products, using supplies purchased from the franchisor. A *business-format franchise* gives you the right to open a business using a franchisor's name and format for doing business. This format includes many well-known chains, including Taco Bell, Pizza Hut, UPS Stores, and Curves fitness centers.

Advantages of Franchising

Franchising is a popular option for many people because it combines at least some of the freedom of working for yourself with many of the advantages of being part of a larger, established organization. You can be your own boss, hire your own employees, and benefit directly from your hard work. If you invest in a successful franchise, you know you are getting a viable business model, one that has worked many times before. If the franchise system is well managed, you get the added benefit of instant name recognition, national advertising programs, standardized quality of goods and services, and a proven formula for success. Buying a franchise also gives you access to a support network and in many cases a ready-made blueprint for building a business. For an initial investment, you get services such as site-location studies, market research, training, and technical assistance, as well as assistance with building or leasing your structure, decorating the building, purchasing supplies, and operating the business during your initial ownership phase. Some franchisors also assist franchisees in financing the initial investment.

Disadvantages of Franchising

Although franchising offers many advantages, it is not the ideal vehicle for everyone. The biggest disadvantage is the lack of control relative to other ownership options. This lack of control can affect a franchise at multiple levels. First, when you buy into a franchise system, you agree to follow the business format, and franchisors can prescribe virtually every aspect of the business, from the color of the walls to the products you can carry. In fact, if your primary purpose in owning a business is the freedom to be your own boss, franchising probably isn't the best choice because you don't have a great deal of freedom in many systems. Second, as a franchisee, you usually have little control over decisions the franchisor makes that affect the entire system. Disagreements and even lawsuits have erupted in recent years over actions taken by franchisers regarding product supplies, advertising, and pricing.[45] Third, if the fundamental business model of the franchise system no longer works—or never worked in the first place—or if customer demand for the goods and services you sell declines, you don't have the option of changing your business in response.

franchise
Business arrangement in which one company (the franchisee) obtains the rights to sell the products and use various elements of a business system of another company (the franchisor)

franchisee
Business owner who pays for the rights to sell the products and use the business system of a franchisor

franchisor
Company that licenses elements of its business system to other companies (franchisees)

In addition, buying a franchise involves both initial costs associated with buying into a franchise system and regular payments after that, based on a percentage of sales revenue. These costs vary widely, based on the complexity and popularity of the franchise. A few thousand dollars can get you a simple franchise, but many run in the $10,000 to $50,000 range, and a franchise from a major system such as McDonald's or Subway typically costs several hundred thousand dollars.[46]

How to Evaluate a Franchising Opportunity

How do you protect yourself from a poor franchise investment? The best way is to study the opportunity carefully before you commit. Since 1978, the Federal Trade Commission (FTC) has required franchisors to disclose information about their operations to prospective franchisees. By studying this information, you can determine the financial condition of the franchisor and ascertain whether the company has been involved in lawsuits with franchisees.

Before signing a franchise agreement, it's also wise to consult an attorney. Buying a franchise is much like buying any other business: It requires analyzing the market, finding capital, choosing a site, hiring employees, buying equipment—and most important of all, evaluating the franchisor. One key tip: If the initial franchise fee is extremely high, this could be a sign that the franchisor makes most of its money from selling franchises, rather than sharing in the ongoing profits from those franchises.[47] In addition to the questions in Exhibit 6.5, consult *Buying a Franchise: A Consumer Guide*, a free publication from the FTC (www.ftc.gov).

EXHIBIT 6.5

Twelve Questions to Ask Before Signing a Franchise Agreement

A franchise agreement is a legally binding contract that defines the relationship between the franchisee and the franchisor. Before signing the franchise agreement, be sure to read the franchise disclosure document and consult an attorney.

1. What are the total start-up costs? What does the initial franchise fee cover? Does it include a starting inventory of supplies and products?

2. Who pays for employee training?

3. How are the periodic royalties calculated, and when are they paid?

4. Are all trademarks and names legally protected?

5. Who provides and pays for advertising and promotional items?

6. Who selects the location of the business?

7. Is the franchise assigned an exclusive territory?

8. If the territory is not exclusive, does the franchisee have the right of first refusal on additional franchises established in nearby locations?

9. Is the franchisee required to purchase equipment and supplies from the franchisor or other suppliers?

10. Under what conditions can the franchisor and/or the franchisee terminate the franchise agreement?

11. What restrictions are placed on the franchisee (in terms of selecting goods and services for sale, selling online, etc.)?

12. Can the franchise be assigned to heirs?

✓CHECKPOINT

LEARNING OBJECTIVE 6: Explain the advantages and disadvantages of franchising.

Summary: Franchising appeals to many because it combines some of the advantages of independent business ownership with the resources and support of a larger organization. It can also be less risky than starting or buying an independent business because you have some evidence that the business model works. The primary disadvantages are the lack of control and the costs, both the initial start-up costs and the monthly payments based on a percentage of sales.

Critical thinking: (1) Why might a business owner with a successful concept decide to sell franchises rather than expanding the company under his or her own control? (2) Why might someone with strong entrepreneurial spirit be dissatisfied with franchise ownership?

It's your business: (1) Are you a good candidate for owning and operating a franchise? Why or not? (2) Think about a small-business idea you've had or one of the small businesses you patronize frequently. Could this business be expanded into a national or international chain? Why or why not?

Key terms to know: franchise, franchisee, franchisor

Behind the Scenes

Building an Authentic and Purposeful Business at Sister Sky

Sisters Monica Simeon and Marina TurningRobe have committed themselves to making products that are both authentic and purposeful and in doing so have created a company that shares those same attributes. Of course, like just about every small business, Sister Sky has required intense dedication and many, many long days.

After Simeon and TurningRobe decided to turn their first homemade lotions into a real business, they started in a leased manufacturing space in Spokane, Washington. Both of their families would pitch in for 12-hour days, seven days a week—mixing, bottling, and boxing. When sales began to take off, they built their own manufacturing facility on the Spokane Indian Reservation as part of their commitment to help reservation economies diversify beyond gaming. Putting their houses up for collateral, they installed a $100,000 automated manufacturing system to replace much of the manual labor and expand their production volume. Beyond employing and mentoring fellow tribal members, the sisters also made a point of buying goods and services from other Native American–owned companies and served as entrepreneurial role models in Native American communities.

In addition to scaling up manufacturing, Simeon and TurningRobe had to adjust their original marketing strategy. They initially focused on the general gift market but found they were a tiny player in a vast market. Realizing that the cultural heritage of their product line gave them a unique advantage, they refocused on Native American hotels and resorts, particularly those with luxury spa services. They also now offer spa consulting services, helping property owners create culturally authentic environments and experiences for their guests.

To work toward fulfilling another of their goals, educating consumers and sharing their rich cultural heritage, the sisters also publish two blogs. Native Wisdom, www.native-wisdom.blogspot.com, shares "indigenous inspiration for wellness, harmony, and balance," while Sister Stories, www.sister-sky.blogspot.com, focuses on "improving the quality of our lives, reducing stress, and aging gracefully."

As is often the case, the challenges don't stop as a business grows, and Simeon and TurningRobe now face several classic small-business dilemmas. They've already begun to outgrow their new production facility and are planning an even larger one. However, the question remains as to whether they should continue to make their own products. They could outsource manufacturing to lower costs and stabilize inventory, as is often done in the industry, but doing so would run counter to their goal of expanding local employment opportunities.

They also face a classic time-management dilemma. Simeon's husband recently joined the company as production manager, which frees up the sisters' time for selling, but as Simeon now says, "We're so busy selling, we have no time to step back and strategize." A consultant who worked with them during a "business makeover" sponsored by *Fortune Small Business* magazine stressed that they really have no choice on this: They simply have to make time for strategizing, forcing themselves to step away from marketing and sales activities every quarter to review and adjust their business plan.

One of the key strategic decisions they must make is where to expand next. They've already moved beyond spa sales to high-end boutiques and gift shops, where their unique product concept appeals to consumers looking for something out of the ordinary. Also, having recently received Minority Business Enterprise (MBE) certification from the National Minority Supplier Development Council, the company is now approaching major hotel and resort chains such as Hilton and Starwood. Sister Sky's MBE status will help these large customers meet supplier diversity goals.

The next major decision is whether to open their own stores. TurningRobe is confident the opportunity is there.

"We know the opportunity exists—and we want to jump on it now!"[48]

Critical Thinking Questions

1. Which of the qualities of successful entrepreneurs have Simeon and TurningRobe demonstrated?
2. Should Simeon and TurningRobe consider lowering their ingredient costs by switching to petroleum-based ingredients or stopping their use of pure distilled water? Why or why not?
3. Would opening their own retail stores be a risky decision for Sister Sky? How would this change the company's business model?

LEARN MORE ONLINE

Go to http://real-timeupdates.com/bia5, click on "Learn More," and then select "Chapter 6. Sister Sky video." Would this video appeal to potential customers of Sister Sky products? What about potential investors? Why or why not? ■

Key Terms

advisory board (178)
angel investors (181)
business incubators (179)
business plan (174)
entrepreneurial spirit (171)

franchise (183)
franchisee (183)
franchisor (183)
initial public offering (IPO) (182)
microlenders (181)

seed money (180)
small business (168)
venture capitalists (VCs) (181)

Test Your Knowledge

Questions for Review

1. What are three essential functions of a business plan?
2. What is a business incubator?
3. What are the key reasons for most small-business failures?
4. What are the advantages of buying a business rather than starting one from scratch?
5. What are the advantages and disadvantages of owning a franchise?

Questions for Analysis

6. Do you expect that the number of entrepreneurs in the United States will grow in the next 10 years? Why or why not?
7. Why is the entrepreneurial spirit vital to the health of the nation's economy?
8. What factors should you consider before selecting financing alternatives for a new business?
9. What factors should you consider when evaluating a franchise agreement?

10. **Ethical Considerations.** You're thinking about starting your own hot dog and burger stand. You've got the perfect site in mind, and you've analyzed the industry and all the important statistics. You have financial backing, and you really understand the fast-food market. In fact, you've become a regular at a competitor's operation (down the road) for over a month. The owner thinks you're his best customer. He even wants to name a sandwich creation after you. But you're not there because you love the food. No, you're actually spying. You're learning everything you can about the competition so you can outsmart them. Is this behavior ethical? Explain your answer.

Questions for Application

11. Based on your total life experience up to this point—as a student, consumer, employee, parent, and any other role you might've played—what sort of business would you be best at running? Why?
12. Briefly describe an incident in your life in which you failed to achieve a goal you set for yourself. What did

you learn from this experience? How could you apply this lesson to a future experience as an entrepreneur?

13. **Concept Integration.** Entrepreneurs are one of the five factors of production as discussed in Chapter 2 (page 77). Review that material and explain why entrepreneurs are an important factor for economic success.

14. **Concept Integration.** Pick a local small business or franchise that you visit frequently and discuss whether that business competes on price, speed, innovation, convenience, quality, or any combination of those factors. Be sure to provide some examples.

Practice Your Knowledge

Sharpening Your Communication Skills

Effective communication begins with identifying your primary audience and adapting your message to your audience's needs. This is particularly true for business plans. One of the primary reasons for writing a business plan is to obtain financing. With that in mind, what do you think are the most important things investors will want to know? How can you convince them that the information you are providing is accurate? What should you assume investors know about your specific business or industry?

Building Your Team Skills

The questions shown in Exhibit 6.5 cover major legal issues you should explore before plunking down money for a franchise. In addition, however, there are many more questions you should ask in the process of deciding whether to buy a particular franchise.

With your team, think about how to investigate the possibility of buying a Papa John's franchise (go to www .papajohns.com, click on "Company Info," and then click "Franchise"). First, brainstorm with your team to draw up a list of sources (such as printed sources, Internet sources, and any other suitable sources) where you can locate basic background information about the franchisor. Also list at least two sources you might consult for detailed information about buying and operating a Papa John's franchise. Next, generate a list of at least 10 questions any interested buyer should ask about this potential business opportunity.

Choose a spokesperson to present your team's ideas to the class. After all the teams have reported, hold a class discussion to analyze the lists of questions generated by all the teams. Which questions were on most teams' lists? Why do you think those questions are so important? Can your class think of any additional questions that were not on any team's list but seem important?

Expand Your Knowledge

Discovering Career Opportunities

Would you like to own and operate your own business? Whether you plan to start a new business from scratch or buy an existing business or a franchise, you will need certain qualities to be successful. Start your journey to entrepreneurship by reviewing this chapter's section on entrepreneurs.

1. Which of the entrepreneurial characteristics mentioned in the chapter describe you? Which of those characteristics can you develop more fully in advance of running your own business?

2. Visit www.sba.gov, click on "Small Business Planner," and read the two documents "Is Entrepreneurship for You?" and "Do You Have What It Takes?" Does this information give you any important insights into whether you want to become an entrepreneur (or continuing as an entrepreneur if you already run a business)?

3. Study all the questions and points made in the two documents mentioned in the previous step. Which points

seem the most critical for entrepreneurial success? Which characteristics do you believe you already have? Before you go into business for yourself, which characteristics will you need to work on?

Developing Your Research Skills

Scan issues of print or online editions of business journals or newspapers for articles describing problems or opportunities faced by small businesses in the United States. Clip or copy three or more articles that interest you and then answer the following questions.

1. What problem or opportunity does each article present? Is it an issue faced by many businesses, or is it specific to one industry or region?

2. What could a potential small-business owner learn about the risks and rewards of business ownership from reading these articles?

3. How might these articles affect someone who is thinking about starting a small business?

Improving Your Tech Insights: Social Networking Technology

If you've used Friendster, Facebook, or MySpace, you're already familiar with social networking. Business versions of this technology are changing the way many professionals communicate. Social network applications, which can be either stand-alone software products or websites, help identify potential business connections by indexing e-mail and instant messaging address books, calendars, and message archives.

One of the biggest challenges small-business owners face is finding the right people and making those connections, whether you're looking for a new employee, an investor, a potential customer, or anyone else who might be important to the future of your business. With social network applications, businesspeople can reach more people than they could ever hope to reach via traditional, in-person networking. Visit several of the websites listed in Exhibit 6.4 and read about the benefits of joining these networks. In a brief e-mail to your instructor, describe how you could use these networks to locate potential candidates to serve on the advisory board of your small business (make up any details you need about your company).

Video Discussion

Access the Chapter 6 video discussion in the End of Chapter Assignments section at www.mybizlab.com.

---

mybizlab

Log on to www.mybizlab.com to access the following study and assessment aids associated with this chapter:

- Interactive exercises
- Pre/post test
- Real-Time Updates
- Video application
- Customized study plans
- Biz Skills Simulations
- Quick Learning Guide

If you are not using mybizlab, you can access Real-Time Updates and Quick Learning Guides through http://real-timeupdates.com/bia5. The Quick Learning Guide (located under "Learn More" on the website) provides all six Checkpoints in a handy two-page format to help you study for exams or review important concepts whenever you need a quick refresher.

CHAPTER 7

Management Roles, Functions, and Skills

LEARNING OBJECTIVES

After studying this chapter, you will be able to

1 Explain the importance of management and identify the three vital management roles

2 Describe the planning function and outline the strategic planning process

3 Describe the organizing function and differentiate among top, middle, and first-line management

4 Describe the leading function, leadership style, and organizational culture

5 Describe the controlling function and explain the four steps in the control cycle

6 Identify and explain four important types of managerial skills

Behind the Scenes

Wegmans Satisfies Customers by Putting Employees First

www.wegmans.com

Thousands of companies say "the customer is king" or use similar slogans, proclaiming in various ways that customers are their number one priority. Not Wegmans, a regional grocery store based in Rochester, New York. Wegmans makes a clear statement of its priorities: employees first, customers second.

What do customers think about this, you ask? They love it. Customers routinely drive miles out of their way, past other grocery stores, to shop at Wegmans. The company receives thousands of letters of praise every year from current customers—and several thousand more letters from consumers in cities where it doesn't have stores, begging the chain to open a Wegmans nearby.

Such enthusiasm has helped the company post a solid record of success since its founding back in 1915. As a private company, Wegmans isn't required to report its financial results to the public, but the numbers that are available are impressive. Its operating margin (a measure of profitability) is twice as high as that of national chains such as Safeway and Kroger. Sales per square foot, a key measure of selling efficiency, are estimated to be 50 percent higher than the industry average.

Wegmans CEO Danny Wegman carries on the family tradition of satisfying customers by paying attention to employees and their needs.

The *Wall Street Journal* once called Wegmans the "best chain in the country, maybe in the world."

Such results would be impressive in any industry, but they're almost unfathomable in the grocery retailing business, one of the toughest industries on earth. Most grocery retailers struggle with constant price wars that guarantee paper-thin profit margins (making one or two cents on every dollar of revenue is typical), frequent labor troubles, high employee turnover, and a customer base that views most grocery stores as virtually indistinguishable. And as if those problems aren't enough, grocers face the steamrolling cost efficiencies of Walmart and other discount mass merchandisers, which have already captured a third of the grocery business in the United States.

If you were Danny Wegman, the company's third-generation CEO, how would you sustain the Wegmans way of doing business in the face of relentless competitive pressures? How would you hold your own against the giant discounters that have rampaged through the grocery industry? How would you make sure that Wegmans attracts the best employees in the business and keeps them satisfied and productive?[1] ■

Introduction

management
Process of planning, organizing, leading, and controlling to meet organizational goals

Whether they are front-line supervisors or top executives such as Danny Wegman (profiled in the chapter-opening Behind the Scenes), managers have tremendous influence over the success or failure of the companies they lead. Leading seems to come naturally to Wegman, but he would probably be the first to tell you that **management**, the interrelated tasks of planning, organizing, leading, and controlling in pursuit of organizational goals,[2] is no easy job. In fact, according to one survey, more than a third of the people who take on new managerial positions fail within the first 18 months.[3] Even those who eventually succeed can struggle with the transition from individual contributor to manager. If you aspire to become a manager, you can improve your chances of success by gaining a thorough understanding of what being a manager really entails. This chapter explores the *roles* that managers play, the *functions* they perform, and essential *skills* they need.

The Roles of Management

Danny Wegman doesn't buy the merchandise from wholesalers, stock the shelves, or operate the cash registers, but the decisions he makes, the organizational framework he establishes, the expectations he sets, the managers he hires to oversee employees, and the culture he establishes as a role model all have enormous impact on the company's success. Likewise, the managers who report to Wegman, including his daughter, company president Colleen Wegman, aren't directly engaged in the tasks of buying and selling groceries. However, within the scope of his or her own responsibilities, each of these managers also has significant influence on the company's fortunes. While managers usually don't do the hands-on work in an organization, they create the environment and provide the resources that give employees the opportunities to excel in their work.

In addition, given the effect that managerial decisions and behaviors have on employees, customers, investors, and other stakeholders, it's no exaggeration to say that management is one of the most vital professions in the contemporary economy. Managers who guide their companies effectively and ethically contribute greatly to our standard of living and our economic security. By the same measure, managers who fail, through poor planning, misguided decisions, or questionable ethics, can create havoc that extends far beyond the walls of their own companies. In other words, the art and science of management is one of the most important functions in society, not just within the sphere of business.

All the **managerial roles** that leaders must play can be grouped into three main categories: interpersonal, informational, and decisional.

managerial roles
Behavioral patterns and activities involved in carrying out the functions of management; includes interpersonal, informational, and decisional roles

Interpersonal Roles

Management is largely a question of getting work accomplished through the efforts of other people, so managers must play a number of interpersonal roles, including providing leadership to employees, building relationships, and acting as a liaison between groups and individuals both inside and outside the company (such as suppliers, government agencies, consumers, labor unions, and community leaders). Effective managers tend to excel at networking, fostering relationships with many people within their own companies and within the industries and communities where their companies do business. In fact, the number of "connections" one has becomes an increasingly important asset the higher one rises in an organization. Social network technologies such as Facebook have been a huge boon to managerial networking, but building interpersonal relationships via "face time" is as important as ever, too.

Informational Roles

Managers spend a fair amount of time gathering information from sources both inside and outside the organization. The higher up they are, the more they rely on subordinates to collect, analyze, and summarize information—and the greater the risk that managers will fall out of touch with what is happening down on "the front lines" where the essential day-to-day work of the organization is performed. Today's companies have devised powerful and clever ways to collect and process information for managers. A good example is the *executive dashboard*, which, just like the dashboard in a car, provides quick-read summaries of vital performance variables (see Exhibit 7.1 on the next page).

The dashboard analogy is also a good way to think about the information challenges that managers face. As

Real-Time Updates

Learn More

How to be an inspiring leader

Communication coach Carmine Gallo explains how leaders can use communication techniques to inspire employees. On mybizlab (www .mybizlab.com), you can access Real-Time Updates within each chapter or under Student Study Tools. Otherwise, go to http://real-timeupdates .com/bia5 and click on "Learn More."

EXHIBIT 7.1

Executive Dashboards

To help managers avoid information overload, many companies now use executive dashboards to present carefully filtered highlights of key performance parameters. The latest generation of software makes it easy to customize screens to show each manager the specific summaries he or she needs to see.

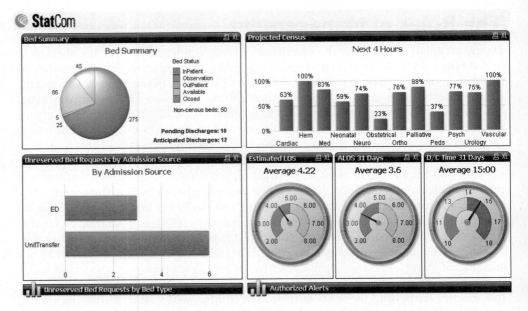

you're driving, making split-second decisions while keeping your eyes on the road, you don't need to know how full the water reservoir is or how fast the water pump is turning. Such details would overwhelm your decision making and serve no immediate purpose. However, if your engine is in danger of overheating because the water pump is failing, you need enough advance warning to take corrective action before it's too late, so your dashboard provides a quick summary through a temperature gauge or warning light. Similarly, managers must figure out what they need to know and when they need to know it. Generally speaking, as you progress higher up the organization, you need to monitor more information sources but see fewer details from each one.

Managers also communicate information to employees, other managers, and other stakeholders. This communication involves virtually every form of information, from technical and administrative information to motivational pep talks to strategic planning sessions. And it involves every form of media, from private conversations to videoconferences that connect managers with employees across the country or around the world.

The increasing use of social media such as blogs and wikis for both internal and external communication is changing the nature of the manager's informational role in many companies. In the past, communication was often concentrated in formal channels that tended to flow in only one direction at a time, such as from a manager down to his or her subordinates or from "the company" to customers. With social media, a more conversational model is emerging, in which more people can participate and communication is more immediate and less formal. For example, on Southwest Airlines's Nuts About Southwest blog (**www.blogsouthwest.com**), a team of employee and manager bloggers from around the company conduct what amounts to multiple ongoing conversations with thousands of Southwest customers. The smart use of social media is helping managers learn more from employees and customers and communicate back to these and other stakeholder groups more effectively.

Decisional Roles

From deciding how to respond to a customer complaint to deciding whether to acquire another company or develop a new product line, managers up and down the organizational ladder face an endless stream of decisions. Many of these decisions are fairly routine, such as choosing which of several job candidates to hire or setting the prices of new products. Other decisions, however, might occur only once or twice in a manager's career, such as responding to a product-tampering crisis or the threat of a hostile takeover. Some decisions are made after extensive information gathering and analysis; others have to be made on the spot, with little but judgment and intuition to guide the manager's choice. One of the most significant changes occurring in business management in recent years is the effort to push decision making as far down the organizational pyramid as possible, giving whichever employees face a particular situation the authority to make decisions about it. This approach not only accelerates and improves work flow and customer service but also frees up higher-level managers to work on more strategic matters.

Being able to move among these roles comfortably while performing the four basic management functions is just one of the many skills that managers must have. The following sections provide a closer look.

 **CHECKPOINT**

LEARNING OBJECTIVE 1: Explain the importance of management, and identify the three vital management roles.

Summary: While managers usually don't do the hands-on work in an organization, they create the environment and provide the resources that give employees the opportunities to excel in their work. Managerial responsibilities include creating the organizational framework, fostering a positive culture, setting expectations, and providing resources. The three vital managerial roles are interpersonal (interacting with others), informational (receiving and sharing information), and decisional (making decisions).

Critical thinking: (1) How are social media changing the nature of the manager's information role? (2) Would managers get more respect from employees if they "rolled up their sleeves" and pitched in with the daily work more often? Why or why not?

It's your business: (1) Review the process you went through to choose the college you are currently attending. What lessons from your experience could someone apply to managerial decision making? (2) Do you believe you have the right personality for management? If not, what areas would you work on?

Key terms to know: management, managerial roles

The Planning Function

Managers engage in **planning** when they develop strategies, establish goals and objectives for the organization, and translate those strategies and goals into action plans. **Strategic plans** outline the firm's long-range (often two to five years) organizational goals and set a course of action the firm will pursue to reach its goals. The *strategic planning process* consists of six interrelated steps: defining the organization's mission, vision, and values; performing a SWOT analysis; developing forecasts; analyzing the competition; establishing goals and objectives; and developing action plans (see Exhibit 7.2).

Define the Mission, Vision, and Values

To achieve any level of strategic clarity, planners first need to agree on the basic principles that define the organization, and such agreement can be articulated in three interrelated statements. First, a **mission statement** is a brief expression of *why* the company exists.[4] For example, the medical device manufacturer Welch Allyn defines its mission as giving "frontline care providers the ability to assess, diagnose, treat, and manage a wide variety of illnesses and diseases, focus on more patients, perform more procedures, and provide better on-site care."[5] This statement clearly defines the scope of the company's activities and its priorities in serving its target customers. Just as important, it eliminates activities the company could pursue, such as consumer products, but chooses not to.

Second, a **vision statement** is a brief expression of *what* the company aspires to be. The defense contractor Northrop Grumman puts it this way: "Our vision is to be the most trusted provider of systems and technologies that ensure the security and freedom of our

planning
Establishing objectives and goals for an organization and determining the best ways to accomplish them

strategic plans
Plans that establish the actions and the resource allocation required to accomplish strategic goals; they're usually defined for periods of two to five years and developed by top managers

mission statement
A brief statement of why an organization exists; in other words, what it aims to accomplish for customers, investors, and other stakeholders

vision statement
A brief and inspirational expression of what a company aspires to be

EXHIBIT 7.2

The Strategic Planning Process

Specific firms have their own variations of the strategic planning process, but these six steps offer a good general model. The circular arrangement is no coincidence, by the way. Strategic planning should be a never-ending process, as you establish strategies, measure outcomes, monitor changes in the business environment, and make adjustments as needed.

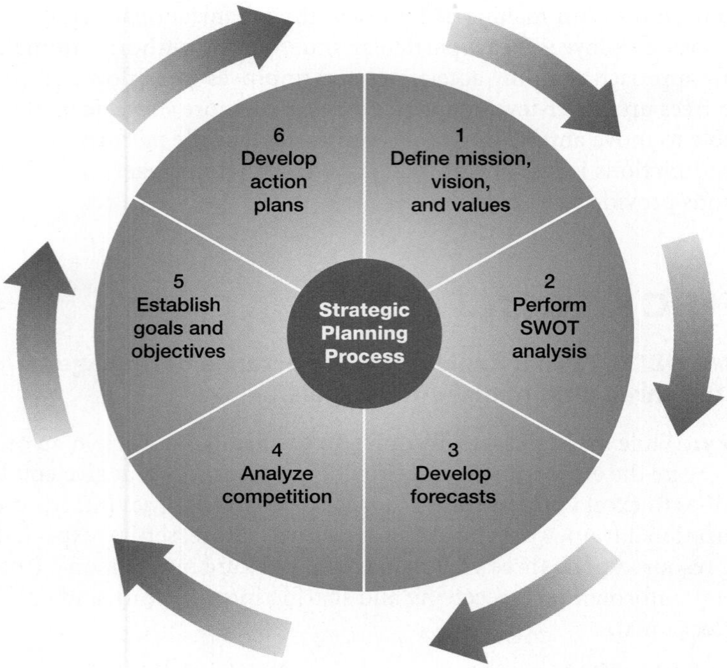

Strategic Planning Process

1 Define mission, vision, and values
2 Perform SWOT analysis
3 Develop forecasts
4 Analyze competition
5 Establish goals and objectives
6 Develop action plans

values statement
Brief articulation of the principles that guide a company's decisions and behaviors

nation and its allies."[6] Notice how this statement differs in both content and tone from the mission statement above. It provides some focus (for example, saying the company wants to be the *most trusted* provider, not necessarily the largest or the most technologically advanced) without getting into the specifics of a mission statement. It also inspires employees with a clear sense of purpose. (Note that these definitions of *mission* and *vision* are not universally agreed upon, and some companies use them interchangeably.)

Third, a **values statement** identifies the principles that guide the company's decisions and behaviors and establish expectations for everyone in the organization. For instance, in addition to such attributes as honesty, service, and inclusiveness, Enterprise Rent-a-Car identifies hard work as one of its values: "Learning how to run a successful business from the ground up and delivering our high standard of service is hard work. It's work that demands a deep personal commitment from each employee." In return, the company offers unusual opportunities to learn entrepreneurship and business management early in one's career.[7]

Mission, vision, and values statements are sometimes dismissed as vague "happy talk" that companies spend a lot of time creating but never look at again, and this criticism is sometimes deserved. However, if the statements are (1) crafted with the purpose of truly defining what the company stands for and (2) used in both strategic planning and the ongoing evaluation of the company's performance, they become essential parts of the company's "DNA." At Wegmans, for example, managers don't agonize over decisions about taking care of their employees; they simply do what is best for their employees because that is one of the company's fundamental values.

Assess the Company's Strengths, Weaknesses, Opportunities, and Threats

Before establishing long-term goals, a company needs to have a clear assessment of its strengths and weaknesses compared with the opportunities and threats it faces. Such analysis is commonly referred to as *SWOT*, which stands for strengths, weaknesses, opportunities, and threats (see Exhibit 7.3).

Strengths are positive internal factors that contribute to a company's success, which can be anything from a team of expert employees to financial resources to unique technologies. For instance, Cabot Corporation (www.cabot-corp.com) is a large manufacturer of

	POSITIVE, HELPFUL	NEGATIVE, HARMFUL
Internal	**Strengths** Examples: ■ Respected brand name ■ Financial resources ■ Strong management ■ Design patents	**Weaknesses** Examples: ■ Heavy debt ■ Poor credit rating ■ Aging products ■ Talent shortages
External (in some cases, threats can also come from internal sources)	**Opportunities** Examples: ■ Growing demand ■ Changing regulations ■ Easier access to capital ■ Weak competitors	**Threats** Examples: ■ Lawsuits ■ New regulations ■ Shrinking demand ■ Growing competition

EXHIBIT 7.3

SWOT Analysis

Identifying a firm's strengths, weaknesses, opportunities, and threats is a common strategic planning technique.

specialty chemicals and materials based in Boston. Two of its key strengths are its leading market position and its global operations.[8] *Weaknesses* are negative internal factors that inhibit the company's success, such as obsolete facilities, inadequate financial resources to fund the company's growth, or lack of managerial depth and talent. Two of Cabot's weaknesses are heavy reliance on major customers in some product lines and a continuing decline in its profits.[9] Identifying a firm's internal strengths and weaknesses helps management understand its current abilities so it can set proper goals.

After taking an inventory of the company's internal strengths and weaknesses, the next step is to identify the external opportunities and threats that might significantly affect the firm's ability to attain desired goals. *Opportunities* are positive situations that represent the possibility of generating new revenue. Cabot, for example, has new opportunities in Dubai and China after recently expanding its operations in those regions.[10] Shrewd managers and entrepreneurs recognize opportunities before others do, then promptly act on their ideas. Some opportunities are found in existing markets, going against established competitors by offering more attractive products.

Threats are negative forces that could inhibit a firm's ability to achieve its objectives, including such factors as new competitors, new government regulations, economic recession, changes in interest rates, disruptions in supply, technological advances that render products obsolete, theft of intellectual property, product liability lawsuits, and even the weather. Depending on the company and the industry, it can also be helpful to consider internal threats if they have the potential to disrupt business. For instance, among the threats Cabot faces in its business are health and safety risks associated with manufacturing and transporting hazardous chemicals. Externally, the company is also threatened by the global economic downturn and increased regulatory restrictions.[11]

Develop Forecasts

By its very nature, planning requires managers to make predictions about the future. Forecasting is a notoriously difficult and error-prone part of strategic planning. Managers need to predict not only *what* will (or will not) occur, but *when* it will occur and *how* it will affect their business. Forecasting is crucial to every company's success because it influences the decisions managers make regarding virtually every business activity. As Bernardo Huberman, a manager at HP who is involved in the company's efforts to improve forecasting, puts it, "A company that can predict the future is a company that is going to win."[12]

Managerial forecasts fall under two broad categories: *quantitative forecasts,* which are typically based on historical data or tests and often involve complex statistical computations, and *qualitative forecasts,* which are based more on intuitive judgments. Neither method is foolproof, but both are valuable tools and often used together to help managers to fill in the unknown variables that inevitably crop up in the planning process. For example, managers can make statistical projections of next year's sales based on data from previous years while factoring in their judgment about the impact of new competitors, changing regulations, or other external forces.

Analyze the Competition

The competitive context in which a company operates needs to be thoroughly understood and factored into the strategic planning process. Performing a SWOT analysis on each of your major competitors is a good first step. Identifying their strengths and weaknesses helps pinpoint your opportunities and threats. For instance, if you discover that the customer service of one of your competitors has been slipping lately, that could be a sign of financial difficulties or other weaknesses that could be opportunities for you to capture additional market share. Similarly, identifying your competitors' opportunities and threats can give you insight into what they might do next, and you can then plan accordingly.

Competitive analysis should always keep the customer's perspective in mind. You may believe you have the best product, the best reputation, and the best customer service, but the only beliefs that matter are the target customer's. Conversely, you might believe that a competitor's less-expensive products are inferior, but the products might well be good enough to meet customers' needs—meaning that the higher cost of your higher-quality products puts you at a disadvantage.

Establish Goals and Objectives

goal
Broad, long-range target or aim

objective
Specific, short-range target or aim

Although these terms are often used interchangeably, it helps to think of a **goal** as a broad, long-range accomplishment that the organization wants to attain in typically five or more years and to think of an **objective** as a specific, short-range target designed to help reach that goal. For Wegmans, a *goal* might be to capture 15 percent of the grocery market in the mid-Atlantic region over the next five years, and an *objective* might be to open four new stores in Virginia in the next two years.

To be effective, organizational goals and objectives should be SMART: *specific, measurable, attainable, relevant,* and *time limited.* (You may encounter other variations of the SMART acronym, but they all have the same general meaning.) For example, "substantially increase our sales" is a poorly worded statement because it doesn't define what *substantial* means or when it should be measured. For more on the benefits and risks of goal setting, see page 269.

Setting appropriate goals has many benefits: It increases employee motivation, establishes standards for measuring individual and group performance, guides employee activity, and clarifies management's expectations.

Develop Action Plans

tactical plans
Plans that define the actions and the resource allocation necessary to achieve tactical objectives and to support strategic plans

operational plans
Plans that lay out the actions and the resource allocation needed to achieve operational objectives and to support tactical plans

With strategic goals and objectives in place, the next step is to develop a plan to reach those goals and objectives. **Tactical plans** lay out the actions and the allocation of resources necessary to achieve specific, short-term objectives that support the company's broader strategic plan. Tactical plans typically focus on departmental goals and cover a period of one to three years. Their limited scope permits them to be changed more easily than strategic plans. **Operational plans** designate the actions and resources required to achieve the objectives of tactical plans. Operational plans usually define actions for less than one year and focus on accomplishing specific objectives, such as securing additional financing or opening a new retail channel.

Keep in mind that coming up with a brilliant strategy is only a small part of the equation of success; nothing matters without execution. Wegmans's strategy of supporting its employees and delighting its customers is easy to observe but difficult to copy day in and day out.

✓CHECKPOINT

LEARNING OBJECTIVE 2: Describe the planning function, and outline the strategic planning process.

Summary: Planning is the process of developing strategies, establishing goals and objectives for the organization, and translating those strategies and goals into action plans. Plans vary in their time frame and scope, from high-level, long-range strategic plans to lower-level, short-term operational plans. The strategic planning process consists of six interrelated steps: defining the organization's mission, vision, and values; performing a SWOT analysis; developing forecasts; analyzing the competition; establishing goals and objectives; and developing action plans.

Critical thinking: (1) Would Boeing and Old Navy develop strategic plans over the same time horizon? Why or why not? (2) How does the vision statement guide the planning process?

It's your business: (1) What is your personal vision statement for your career and your life? Have you ever thought about your future in this way? (2) Consider a career path that you might pursue upon graduation, and perform a quick SWOT analysis. What are some of your internal strengths and weaknesses and external opportunities and threats?

Key terms to know: planning, strategic plans, mission statement, vision statement, values statement, goal, objective, tactical plans, operational plans

The Organizing Function

Organizing, the process of arranging resources to carry out the organization's plans, is the second major function of managers. During the organizing stage, managers think through all the activities that employees perform, as well as all the facilities and equipment employees need in order to complete those activities. Managers also give people the ability to work toward organizational goals by determining who will have the authority to make decisions, to perform or supervise activities, and to distribute resources. Chapter 8 discusses the organizing function in more detail; for now, it's sufficient to recognize the three levels of management in a typical corporate hierarchy—top, middle, bottom—commonly known as the **management pyramid** (see Exhibit 7.4). Each level presents unique challenges for managers.

organizing
Process of arranging resources to carry out the organization's plans

management pyramid
Organizational structure divided into top, middle, and first-line management

EXHIBIT 7.4

The Management Pyramid

Here are some of the typical jobs in the three basic levels of management.

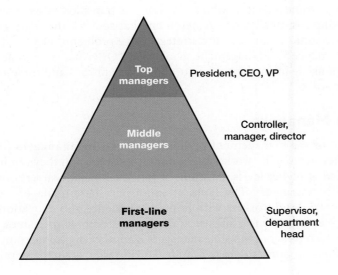

| Top managers | President, CEO, VP |

| Middle managers | Controller, manager, director |

| First-line managers | Supervisor, department head |

Top Management

top managers
Those at the highest level of the organization's management hierarchy; they are responsible for setting strategic goals, and they have the most power and responsibility in the organization

Top managers are the upper-level managers such as Danny Wegman who have the most power and who take overall responsibility for the organization. This tier includes corporate officers (see page 156) and usually the next layer or two of management beneath them, depending on the size and structure of the company. The term *executive* applies to top managers. Typical job titles include the "C" level positions (such as chief marketing officer and chief financial officer) and vice presidents (the largest corporations may have dozens of vice presidents overseeing various divisions or functions).

Top managers establish the structure for the organization as a whole, and they select the people who fill the upper-level positions. Top managers also make long-range plans, establish major policies, and often represent the company to the media, the community, and other stakeholders.

Two significant ways in which top management differs from lower management tiers are the long time frames with which executives must work and the magnitude of the decisions they need to make. For instance, building a new facility to expand production levels can take years, requiring executives to look far into the future to predict the types and quantities of products that customers will want to buy. Plus, the decision has dramatic implications for the company's success or failure. Building the wrong kind of facility or putting it in the wrong place or at the wrong time can damage or even destroy a company. Given the importance of these strategic decisions, the ability to make tough judgment calls is highly valued in top executives.

Middle Managers

middle managers
Those in the middle of the management hierarchy; they develop plans to implement the goals of top managers and coordinate the work of first-line managers

Middle managers have similar responsibilities but on a smaller scale, such as for an individual division or facility. The term *middle management* is somewhat vague, but in general, managers at this level report upward to top executives, while first-line managers report to them. In other words, they usually manage other managers, not workers. A smaller company might have a single layer of middle management (or none at all, in many cases), whereas a large corporation could have as a half dozen or more layers of middle managers.

The term "middle management" is sometimes used disparagingly, giving the impression that middle managers are "bureaucrats" who clog up the works without adding much value. Some highly regarded opinion leaders have gone so far as to blame them for much that ails the modern corporation.[13] Many companies have also *flattened* their organizational structures by removing one or more layers of middle management.

In a smartly organized and well-run company, however, middle managers play the essential role of translating strategic goals and objectives into the actions that allow the company to meet those targets. While they may not do the actual day-to-day work, middle managers are the ones who put the systems and resources in place so that front-line teams can work efficiently and with coordinated purpose. They also provide vital coaching and mentoring for first-line managers who are making the transition into management.

As leadership consultant Steve Arneson emphasizes, "It's the leaders in the middle who must communicate and execute strategy, solve problems, create efficiencies, and manage performance."[14] Management scholar Paul Osterman adds that middle managers "are responsible for making many of the judgment calls and trade-offs that shape the firm's success."

First-Line Managers

first-line managers
Those at the lowest level of the management hierarchy; they supervise the operating employees and implement the plans set at the higher management levels

At the bottom of the management pyramid are **first-line managers** (or *supervisory managers*). They oversee the work of operating employees, and they put into action the plans developed at higher levels. Positions at this level include supervisor, department head, and office manager.[15] The types of employees these managers supervise vary widely, from entry-level workers with limited experience and education to advanced experts in engineering, science, finance, and other professional specialties.

Reducing the number of first-line managers is another step some companies are taking to flatten their organizational pyramids. For instance, a company might remove a department supervisor and have the employees manage themselves as a team or may have the employees report up to someone who was previously considered a middle manager.

Like managers at the levels above them, first-line managers face challenges unique to their position in the hierarchy. As the direct interface between "management" and the employees, they have the most immediate responsibility for ensuring that necessary work is done according to agreed-upon performance standards. They must also deal with whatever friction might exist between employees and management. Supervisors are also usually quite involved in recruiting, hiring, and training of employees. In this role, they perform the vital task of making sure employees acquire the skills they need and adapt to the organization's culture.

✓CHECKPOINT

LEARNING OBJECTIVE 3: Describe the organizing function, and differentiate among top, middle, and first-line management.

Summary: The organizing function is the process of arranging the organization's resources in the best way possible to help reach goals and objectives. Top managers grapple with long-range, strategic issues and often must make decisions about events and conditions several years into the future. They also have important communication roles, representing the company to external stakeholders. Middle managers usually have responsibility over individual divisions or facilities and are charged with translating strategic plans into the tactical plans that will allow the company to reach its goals and objectives. First-line managers supervise nonmanagement employees; they have the shortest time horizons and greatest tactical perspective.

Critical thinking: (1) Why might a manager need to de-emphasize skills honed in previous positions as he or she rises through the organizational hierarchy? (2) Would top managers or first-line managers typically have more or less of the information they'd like to have for the decisions they need to make? Why?

It's your business: (1) Have you ever supervised others on the job or in volunteer work? If so, how would you rate your performance as a manager? (2) If you were suddenly promoted to manage the department you've been working in, would you change your "work" personality? Why or why not?

Key terms to know: organizing, management pyramid, top managers, middle managers, first-line managers

The Leading Function

Leading is the process of influencing and motivating people to work willingly and effectively toward common goals. Managers with good leadership skills have greater success in influencing the attitudes and actions of others and motivating employees to put forth their best performance.

All managers have to be effective leaders to be successful, but management and leadership are not the same thing. The easiest way to distinguish between the two is to view management as the rational, intellectual, and practical side of guiding an organization and to view leadership as the inspirational, visionary,

leading
Process of guiding and motivating people to work toward organizational goals

Real-Time Updates

Learn More
Do you have what it takes to be a successful leader?

Rate yourself on 10 essential attributes of leadership. On mybizlab (www .mybizlab.com), you can access Real-Time Updates within each chapter or under Student Study Tools. Otherwise, go to http://real-timeupdates .com/bia5 and click on "Learn More."

Real-Time Updates

Learn More
Find out why great leaders are made, not born
Explore the factors that produce great leaders and get advice on how to become one yourself. On mybizlab (**www.mybizlab.com**), you can access Real-Time Updates within each chapter or under Student Study Tools. Otherwise, go to **http://real-timeupdates.com/bia5** and click on "Learn More."

and emotional side. Both management and leadership involve the use of power, but management involves *position power* (so called since it stems from the individual's position in the organization), whereas leadership involves *personal power* (which stems from a person's own unique attributes, such as expertise or charisma).[16]

Successful leaders tend to share many of the same traits, but no magic set of personal qualities automatically destines someone for leadership. Nevertheless, in general, good leaders possess a balance of several types of intelligence:

- *Cognitive intelligence* involves reasoning, problem solving, memorization, and other rational skills. Obviously, leaders need a sufficient degree of cognitive intelligence to understand and process the information required for planning and decision making in the jobs.

- *Emotional intelligence* is a measure of a person's awareness of and ability to manage his or her own emotions. People with high emotional intelligence recognize their own emotional states and the effect those emotions have on others, they are able to regulate their emotional responses in order to control or reduce disruptive impulses and moods, and they have a high degree of empathy (the ability to understand others' feelings).[17]

- *Social intelligence* involves looking outward to understand the dynamics of social situations and the emotions of other people, in addition to your own.[18] Socially adept managers have a knack for finding and building common ground with people of all kinds. Moreover, leaders, in a sense, "infect" their organizations with their own emotions, positive or negative.[19]

All three types of intelligence are essential to building the competencies that lead to success. In fact, various studies suggest that in both leadership and life in general, emotional and social intelligence play a far greater role in success than purely cognitive intelligence.[20]

Developing an Effective Leadership Style

Leadership style can be viewed as finding the right balance between *what* the leader focuses on and *how* he or she makes things happen in the organization (see Exhibit 7.5). Every manager has a definite style, although good leaders usually adapt their approach to match the requirements of the particular situation.[21] Using the terminology from Exhibit 7.5, for instance, an executive who normally maintains a strategic outlook and enables others to make decisions might adopt a forceful operational focus to guide the company out of an emergency situation.

Across the range of leadership styles, you can find three basic types. **Autocratic leaders** control the decision-making process in their organizations, often restricting the decision-making freedom of subordinates. Autocratic leadership has a bad reputation, and when it's overused or used inappropriately, it can certainly produce bad results or stunt an organization's growth. However, companies can find themselves in situations where autocratic leadership is needed to guide the firm through challenging situations or to bring uncooperative units in line.

Democratic leaders, in contrast, delegate authority and involve employees in decision making. Even though their approach can lead to slower decisions, soliciting input from people familiar with particular situations or issues can result in better decisions. Meg Whitman, CEO of eBay, is a great example of a democratic leader. Even though she is considered one of the most influential executives in business today, she is well known

autocratic leaders
Leaders who do not involve others in decision making

democratic leaders
Leaders who delegate authority and involve employees in decision making

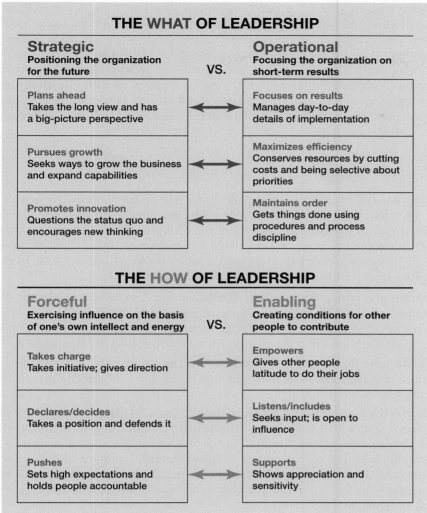

THE WHAT OF LEADERSHIP

Strategic
Positioning the organization
for the future

VS.

Operational
Focusing the organization on
short-term results

Plans ahead Takes the long view and has a big-picture perspective	←→	Focuses on results Manages day-to-day details of implementation
Pursues growth Seeks ways to grow the business and expand capabilities	←→	Maximizes efficiency Conserves resources by cutting costs and being selective about priorities
Promotes innovation Questions the status quo and encourages new thinking	←→	Maintains order Gets things done using procedures and process discipline

THE HOW OF LEADERSHIP

Forceful
Exercising influence on the basis
of one's own intellect and energy

VS.

Enabling
Creating conditions for other
people to contribute

Takes charge Takes initiative; gives direction	←→	Empowers Gives other people latitude to do their jobs
Declares/decides Takes a position and defends it	←→	Listens/includes Seeks input; is open to influence
Pushes Sets high expectations and holds people accountable	←→	Supports Shows appreciation and sensitivity

EXHIBIT 7.5

Leadership Style: A Question of Balance

Leadership style can be viewed as striking a balance between (a) a low-level operational outlook and a high-level strategic outlook and between (b) enabling others to make decisions and forcefully taking charge.

for delegating decision-making authority and claims that she doesn't consider herself to be powerful.[22] By spreading power around, Whitman is also practicing **participative management.**

The third leadership style takes its name from the French term *laissez-faire*, which can be translated roughly as "hands off." **Laissez-faire leaders** such as Danny Wegman take the role of supporters and consultants, encouraging employees' ideas and offering insights or opinions when asked. They emphasize **employee empowerment**—giving employees the power to make decisions that apply to their specific aspects of work. As Wegman puts it, "Once you share a common set of values, you can go and be yourself."[23]

Coaching and Mentoring

Leadership also carries an important responsibility for education and encouragement, resulting in the roles of coaching and mentoring. **Coaching** involves taking the time to meet with employees, discussing any problems that may hinder their ability to work effectively, and offering suggestions and encouragement to help them find their own solutions to work-related challenges. (Note that the term *executive coaching* usually refers to hiring an outside management expert to help senior managers.)

participative management
Philosophy of allowing employees to take part in planning and decision making

laissez-faire leaders
Leaders who leave most instances of decision making up to employees, particularly concerning day-to-day matters

employee empowerment
Granting decision-making and problem-solving authorities to employees so they can act without getting approval from management

coaching
Helping employees reach their highest potential by meeting with them, discussing problems that hinder their ability to work effectively, and offering suggestions and encouragement to overcome these problems

mentoring
Experienced managers guiding less-experienced colleagues in nuances of office politics, serving as a role model for appropriate business behavior, and helping to negotiate the corporate structure

Mentoring is similar to coaching but is based on long-term relationships between senior and junior members of an organization. The mentor is usually an experienced manager or employee who can help guide other managers and employees through the corporate maze. Mentors have a deep knowledge of the business and can explain office politics, serve as role models for appropriate business behavior, and provide valuable advice about how to succeed within the organization. Mentoring programs are used in a variety of ways, such as helping newly promoted managers make the transition to leadership roles and helping women and minorities prepare for advancement.

Managing Change

Change presents a major leadership challenge for one simple reason: Many people don't like it. They may fear the unknown, they may be unwilling to give up current habits or benefits, they may not trust the motives of the people advocating change, or they may simply have experienced too many change initiatives that didn't yield the promised results.[24] To improve the chances of success when the organization needs to change, managers can follow these steps:[25]

1. **Identify everything that needs to change.** Changes can involve the structure of the organization, technologies and systems, or people's attitudes, beliefs, skills, or behaviors.[26] One particular challenge for managers advocating change is understanding the ripple effect the change will have throughout the organization.[27]

2. **Identify the forces acting for and against the change.** By understanding these forces, managers can work to amplify the forces that will facilitate the change and remove or diminish the negative forces.

3. **Choose the approach best suited to the situation.** Managers can institute change through a variety of techniques, including communication, education, participation in decision making, negotiation, visible support from top managers or other opinion leaders, or coercive use of authority (usually recommended only for crisis situations). If you engage people in the change, asking for their input and advice so they can help design the changes, they'll be much more likely to embrace the new way of doing things.[28]

4. **Reinforce changed behavior and monitor continued progress.** Once the change has been made, managers need to reinforce new behaviors and make sure old behaviors don't creep back in.

Building a Positive Organizational Culture

organizational culture
A set of shared values and norms that support the management system and that guide management and employee behavior

Strong leadership is a key element in establishing a productive **organizational culture** (sometimes known as *corporate culture*)—the set of underlying values, norms, and practices shared by members of an organization (see Exhibit 7.6). When you visit an organization, observe how the employees work, dress, communicate, address each other, and conduct business. Culture can be a negative or a positive force in an organization, and managers set the tone by establishing expectations, defining rules and policies that shape behavior, and acting as role models. When Wegmans's employees see Danny Wegman enthusiastically embrace the challenges of the day and treat customers and colleagues with respect, that positive energy radiates throughout the culture. As employee Elaine Danar puts it, "I have an incredible sense of pride to represent this company."[29]

Positive cultures create an environment that encourages employees to make smart decisions for the good of the company and its customers. At companies with legendary corporate cultures, such as Wegmans, Nordstrom, and Southwest Airlines, employees routinely go the extra mile to make sure customers are treated well. In contrast, negative, dysfunctional cultures can lead employees to make decisions that are bad for customers and bad for the company.

Company Values

- Have you articulated a compelling vision for the company?
- Have you defined a mission statement, based on that vision?
- Do employees know how their work relates to this vision?
- Is there a common set of values that binds the organization together?
- Do you and other executives or owners demonstrate these values day in and day out?

People

- How are people treated?
- Do you foster an atmosphere of civility and respect?
- Do you value and encourage teamwork, with all ideas welcomed?
- Do you acknowledge, encourage, and act upon helpful ideas from employees?
- Do you give employees credit for their ideas?
- Have you shown a positive commitment to a balance between work and life?

Community

- Have you clarified how the company views its relationship with the community?
- Do your actions support that commitment to community?

Communication

- Do you practice and encourage open communication?
- Do you share operating information throughout the company?
- Do you survey employees on workplace issues and ask for their input on solutions?
- Is there an open-door policy for access to management?

Employee Performance

- Do you handle personnel issues with fairness and respect?
- Do employees receive feedback regularly?
- Are employee evaluations based on agreed-upon objectives?

EXHIBIT 7.6

Creating the Ideal Culture in Your Company

You can't create a culture directly, but you can establish the behaviors and values that in turn do create a culture. Use this list of questions to explore the many ways you can foster a positive culture—and avoid the growth of a negative culture.

CHECKPOINT

LEARNING OBJECTIVE 4: Describe the leading function, leadership style, and organizational culture.

Summary: Leading is the art and science of influencing and motivating people to work toward common goals. Leaders can exhibit a range of styles in what they choose to focus on (strategic versus operational matters) and how they make things happen (forcing versus enabling). Three specific leadership styles are autocratic, democratic, and laissez-faire. Organizational culture is the set of underlying values, norms, and practices shared by members of an organization.

Critical thinking: (1) Are management and leadership the same thing? If not, why not? (2) Can a single individual be an autocratic, a democratic, *and* a laissez-faire leader? Why or why not?

It's your business: (1) Regarding the three basic leadership styles—autocratic, democratic, and laissez-faire—what is your natural inclination? Think about times in school, at work, or in social situations in which you played a leadership role. How did you lead? (2) Does leadership experience in school activities such as student government and athletics help prepare you for business leadership? Why or why not?

Key terms to know: leading, autocratic leaders, democratic leaders, participative management, laissez-faire leaders, employee empowerment, coaching, mentoring, organizational culture

The Controlling Function

controlling
Process of measuring progress against goals and objectives and correcting deviations if results are not as expected

Controlling is the management function of keeping the company's activities on track toward previously established goals. The nature of control varies widely, from making direct intervention in a process to modifying policies or systems in a way that enables employees to reach their objectives.

The Control Cycle

A good way to understand managerial control is to envision the *control cycle*, a four-step process of (1) establishing performance standards based on the strategic plan, (2) measuring performance, (3) comparing performance to standards, and (4) responding as needed (see Exhibit 7.7). Of course, the specific steps taken in any situation depend on the industry, the company, the functional area within the company, and the manager's leadership style. In some cases, the control cycle is a formal process with explicit measurements, reports, and other tools. In others, control is subtle.

Establishing Performance Standards

standards
Criteria against which performance is measured

In the first step of the control cycle, managers set **standards**, the criteria against which performance will be measured. Top managers set standards for the organization as a whole, such as revenue and profitability targets. Then for their individual areas of responsibility, middle and first-line managers set standards based on the overall organizational standards of performance.

Knowing which variables to use as standards and the values to set as performance targets can require a lot of experience and experimentation. Each division or department needs to understand how its performance contributes to the company's overall performance and how it affects other *internal customers*, other parts of the company that receive or are affected by its output. For example, assume a group responsible for online advertising sends the leads it collects (the names of potential buyers) to the sales department, which is then responsible for closing as many sales as possible. A critical step in this process is *qualifying* the leads, determining whether each lead is truly interested and

EXHIBIT 7.7

The Control Cycle

The control cycle has four basic steps: (1) On the basis of strategic goals, top managers set the standards by which the organization's overall performance will be measured. (2) Managers at all levels measure performance. (3) Actual performance is compared with the standards. (4) Appropriate corrective action is taken (if performance meets standards, nothing other than encouragement is needed; if performance falls below standards, corrective action may include improving performance, establishing new standards, changing plans, reorganizing, or redirecting efforts).

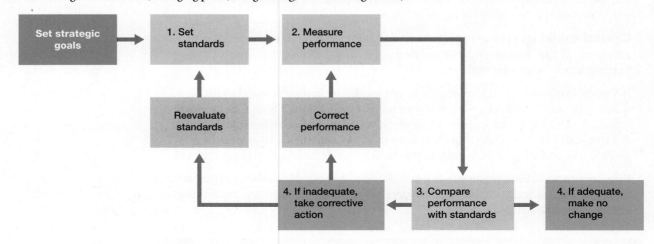

ready to make a purchase. The advertising group could *raise* its apparent performance by doing nothing to filter the leads it sends to sales, sending both qualified and unqualified leads, which the sales department would then have to spend time filtering to see which leads are worth pursuing—thereby lowering its performance and the performance of the company overall. A key responsibility for managers who oversee multiple departments is to make sure the various internal customers support each other in ways that are best for the company.

A common approach to setting standards is **benchmarking**, or collecting and comparing data on business practices in other companies and other industries. The variables that companies benchmark range from information systems and knowledge managing to human resource practices and financial returns.[30] HP, the computer and printer giant, benchmarks itself against competitors in multiple ways. "We want to be the best in class" in every business function says an executive.[31]

One of the most important performance variables that fall under managerial control is **quality**—a measure of how closely goods or services conform to predetermined standards and customer expectations. You'll learn more about quality in such areas as product and process quality in manufacturing and operations management (see page 255) and quality of hire in human resources (see page 291).

benchmarking
Collecting and comparing process and performance data from other companies

quality
A measure of how closely a product conforms to predetermined standards and customer expectations

Measuring Performance and Responding as Needed

In the second step of the control cycle, managers assess performance, using both quantitative (specific, numerical) and qualitative (subjective) performance measures. For example, many companies now use a **balanced scorecard**, which monitors performance from four perspectives: finances, operations, customer relationships, and the growth and development of employees and intellectual property.[32]

In the third step, managers compare performance with the established standards and search for the cause of any discrepancies. If the performance falls short of standards, the fourth step is to take corrective action. If performance meets or exceeds standards, no corrective action is taken. If results are below expectations, controls help managers take any necessary action, which can range from a minor adjustment in the recipe on a food production line to a complete strategic shift.

balanced scorecard
Method of monitoring the performance from four perspectives: finances, operations, customer relationships, and the growth and development of employees and intellectual property

Crisis Management: Maintaining Control in Extraordinary Circumstances

No matter how well a company plans for its future, mistakes and catastrophes happen. And although not every specific crisis can be envisioned, managers can plan how the company should respond to each type of possible event. **Crisis management** involves the decisions and actions needed to keep the company functioning smoothly and to tend to stakeholder needs both during and after an emergency.

When U.S. Airways Flight 1549 made a spectacularly successful emergency landing on New York's Hudson River in January 2009, the company stepped into action with a response that has been called a new role model for crisis management. As soon as passengers were

crisis management
Procedures and systems for minimizing the harm that might result from some unusually threatening situations

rescued, the airline immediately provided dry clothes, prepaid mobile phones, hot food, and hotel rooms. Employees were ready with emergency cash and credit cards to help passengers with personal expenses. The company provided rental cars or train tickets to those who weren't comfortable flying again, even arranging with executives at Hertz to make sure people who had lost their driver's licenses could still rent cars. By tending to seemingly every detail with speed and care, the

 Real-Time Updates

Learn More
Crisis management in a social media landscape
Social media are changing every aspect of business communication, including crisis management; learn how the rules are changing. On mybizlab (www.mybizlab.com), you can access Real-Time Updates within each chapter or under Student Study Tools. Otherwise, go to http://real-timeupdates.com/bia5 and click on "Learn More."

company not only took care of its customers but took care of its reputation as well. "I felt completely comfortable in their hands," said one passenger.[33]

Successful crisis management requires clear thinking and quick action while a crisis is unfolding, but smart companies don't wait until a crisis hits. A *crisis management* plan needs to contain both *contingency plans* to help managers make important decisions in a limited time frame and *communication plans* to reach affected parties quickly and forestall rumors and false information.

U.S. Airways's rapid, well-coordinated response was the outcome of careful planning and rehearsal. The company practices its emergency responses at least three times a year at every airport where it operates, and teams of employees are ready to travel to emergency locations at a moment's notice to provide whatever help is needed.[34] Not every company faces crises of this magnitude, of course, but every company does need to anticipate crises and have plans in place to protect customers, other stakeholders, and the company itself.

√CHECKPOINT

LEARNING OBJECTIVE 5: Describe the controlling function, and explain the four steps in the control cycle.

Summary: The controlling function consists of the activities and decisions involved in keeping the company's activities on track toward previously established goals. The four steps in the control cycle are establishing performance standards based on the strategic plan, measuring performance, comparing performance to standards, and responding as needed.

Critical thinking: (1) Why is it important to meet the needs of internal customers? (2) Is lowering performance standards in response to a failure to meet those standards necessarily a sign of "giving up"? Why or why not?

It's your business: (1) Do you benchmark your performance in any aspect of your personal or academic life? If yes, does it help you improve? If no, would it help you improve if you tried it? (2) Think back over any crises you've faced in your life. How well did you respond? What would you do differently in a future crisis?

Key terms to know: controlling, standards, benchmarking, quality, balanced scorecard, crisis management

Essential Management Skills

Managers rely on a number of skills to perform their functions and maintain a high level of quality in their organizations. These skills can be classified into four basic categories: *interpersonal, technical, conceptual,* and *decision-making*. As managers rise through the organization's hierarchy, they may need to strengthen their abilities in one or more of these skills. Such managers may also need to de-emphasize skills that helped them in lower-level jobs and develop different skills. For instance, staying closely involved with project details is often a plus for first-line supervisors, but it can lead to serious performance issues for higher-level managers who should be spending time on more strategic issues.[35]

Interpersonal Skills

interpersonal skills
Skills required to understand other people and to interact effectively with them

The various skills required to communicate with other people, work effectively with them, motivate them, and lead them are **interpersonal skills**. Because managers mainly get things done through people at all levels of the organization, they need good interpersonal skills in countless situations. Encouraging employees to work together toward common goals, interacting with employees and other managers, negotiating with partners and suppliers, developing employee trust and loyalty, and fostering innovation are all activities that require interpersonal skills.

Communication, or exchanging information, is the most important and pervasive interpersonal skill that managers use. Effective communication not only increases the manager's and the organization's productivity but also shapes the impressions made on colleagues, employees, supervisors, investors, and customers. In your role as a manager, communication allows you to perceive the needs of these stakeholders (your first step toward satisfying them), and it helps you respond to those needs.[36] Moreover, as the workforce becomes more diverse—and as more companies recognize the value of embracing diversity in their workforces—managers need to adjust their interactions with others, communicating in a way that considers the different needs, backgrounds, experiences, and expectations of their workforces.

Technical Skills

A person who knows how to operate a machine, prepare a financial statement, program a computer, or pass a football has **technical skills**; that is, the individual has the knowledge and ability to perform the mechanics of a particular job. Technical skills are most important at lower organizational levels because managers at these levels work directly with employees who are using the tools and techniques of a particular specialty, such as automotive assembly or computer programming.

However, in today's increasingly technology-driven business environment, managers often need to have a solid understanding of the processes they oversee. One obvious reason is that they need to grasp the technical matters if they are to make smart decisions regarding planning, organizing, leading, and controlling. Another key reason for understanding technical matters is that demonstrating a level of technical aptitude gives managers credibility in the eyes of their employees. Maria Azua, vice president of technology and innovation at IBM, says her experience as a programmer earlier in her career helped her earn respect from the people she now leads. "They don't see me as a stodgy executive who doesn't understand, because I've done the same work they do."[37]

Managers at all levels use **administrative skills**, which are the technical skills necessary to manage an organization, including scheduling, researching, analyzing data, and managing projects. Managers must know how to start a project or work assignment from scratch, map out each step in the process to its successful completion, develop project costs and timelines, and establish checkpoints at key project intervals.

technical skills
Ability and knowledge to perform the mechanics of a particular job

administrative skills
Technical skills in information gathering, data analysis, planning, organizing, and other aspects of managerial work

Conceptual Skills

Managers need **conceptual skills** to visualize organizations, systems, markets, and solutions—both as complete entities on their own and as interrelated pieces of a whole. For example, the most visible part of a company's accounting system is probably its accounting software, but the entire system also includes procedures, policies, and the people who process and use financial information. At the same time, the accounting system is also part of an overall business system and needs to integrate seamlessly with sales, purchasing, production, and other functions.

Conceptual skills are especially important to top managers, because they are the strategists who develop the plans that guide the organization toward its goals. Managers use their conceptual skills to acquire and analyze information, identify both problems and opportunities, understand the competitive environment in which their companies operate, and develop strategies and plans. The ability to conceptualize solutions that don't yet exist, to see things as they could be rather than simply as how they are, is a vital skill for executives.

conceptual skills
Ability to understand the relationship of parts to the whole

Decision-Making Skills

decision-making skills
Ability to identify a decision situation, analyze the problem, weigh the alternatives, choose an alternative, implement it, and evaluate the results

Decision-making skills involve the ability to define problems and opportunities and select the best course of action. To ensure thoughtful decision making, managers can follow a formal process such as the six steps highlighted in Exhibit 7.8:

1. **Recognize and define the problem or opportunity.** Most companies look for problems or opportunities by gathering customer feedback, conducting studies, or monitoring such warning signals as declining sales or profits, excess inventory buildup, or high customer turnover.

2. **Identify and develop options.** The goal of this step is to develop a list of alternative courses of action. A problem that is easy to identify, such as a steady decline in sales revenue, might not have any easy answers. This step requires solid conceptual skills. Managers may need to break old thinking habits and throw away long-held assumptions in order to find promising solutions to tough problems.

3. **Analyze the options.** Once the ideas have been generated, most companies develop a list of decision-making criteria, such as cost, feasibility, availability of existing resources, market acceptance, potential for revenue generation, and compatibility with the company's mission and vision, to evaluate the options. Some decisions present a simple yes/no choice, but others present multiple options that must be compared.

4. **Select the best option.** After all options have been analyzed, management selects the best one. For some decisions, quantitative analysis can identify a clear choice from among the available options. For other decisions, however, managers might have to rely on intuition and experience to point the way.

5. **Implement the decision.** After one option has been selected, it's time to implement the decision.

6. **Monitor the results.** Finally, managers monitor the results of decisions over time to see whether the chosen alternative works, whether any new problems or opportunities arise because of the decision, and whether the decision should be modified to meet changing circumstances.

Although this list presents a logical and comprehensive method for decision making, it's important to realize that managers frequently must make decisions with incomplete or imperfect information. In other words, you may not have all the information you need, and you may not have as much time as you'd like to take. In fact, in today's fast-moving markets, the ability to make good decisions with incomplete information has become a highly valued management skill.[38]

For the latest information on managerial skills, visit **http://real-timeupdates.com/bia5** and click on Chapter 7.

EXHIBIT 7.8

Steps in the Decision-Making Process

Following these six steps will help you make better decisions.

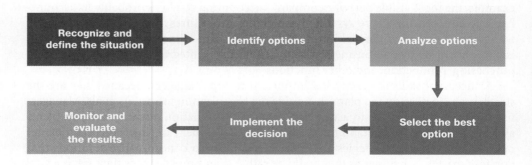

✓CHECKPOINT

LEARNING OBJECTIVE 6: Identify and explain four important types of managerial skills.

Summary: Interpersonal skills are the abilities to communicate with, motivate, and lead others. Technical skills involve the "mechanics" of a particular job, including the administrative skills of project management. Conceptual skills are the abilities to visualize organizations, systems, markets, and solutions—even when they may not exist yet. Decision-making skills include defining problems and opportunities and selecting the best course of action to take in each case.

Critical thinking: (1) Why is trust a vital aspect of a manager's interpersonal skills? (2) What are the risks of defining problems or opportunities poorly prior to making decisions?

It's your business: (1) Would you succeed as a manager if you started a company right out of college, without having gained any experience as an employee in another company? Why or why not? (2) How would you rate your conceptual skills? Does "seeing the big picture" come easily to you? If not, how might you improve in this area?

Key terms to know: interpersonal skills, technical skills, administrative skills, conceptual skills, decision-making skills

Behind the Scenes

Customers Believe in Wegmans Because Wegmans Believes in Its Employees

The conventional response to all challenges in the retail grocery industry is to just keep squeezing everything—customer service, wages, employee benefits, training, and anything else—to keep prices low and still eke out a profit. However, CEO Danny Wegman and his colleagues are adamant that joining the discounters in a never-ending race to cut, cut, cut is not the Wegmans way. Instead, the company defines its mission as being "the very best at serving the needs of our customers." In pursuit of that mission, the company makes employees its number-one priority and counts on employees to then meet the needs of customers.

To compete successfully against both traditional grocers and Walmart, Wegmans's strategy emphasizes a huge selection of products and employees who know food and love serving customers. The cheese department is a good example. Unlike the typical selection of two or three dozen varieties at most, Wegmans shoppers find four or five *hundred* varieties—and a knowledgeable staff that can help them select and serve the perfect cheese. In fact, chances are the department manager has been on a research tour of cheese-producing areas in

Europe to gain firsthand knowledge of the tastes and traditions of each region.

Such training is expensive, to be sure. Add in higher-than-average wages and employee benefits, and Wegmans's labor costs are higher than those of its competitors. Moreover, Wegmans managers exhibit a degree of personal concern for employees not often found in the hectic retail industry. As an example, when one manager whose job required frequent out-of-town travel learned that her mother had been diagnosed with cancer, Wegmans executives modified her responsibilities so that she could stay in town to care for her mother—before she even asked.

This investment in employees pays off in important ways. For starters, customers buy more when they understand how to use various products and are successful and satisfied with them. These positive experiences with Wegmans employees also help shoppers build emotional bonds with the store, further increasing customer loyalty. And employees who enjoy their work and feel they are treated with respect are more productive and less likely to leave in search of other jobs. Employee turnover (the percentage of the workforce that leaves and must be replaced every year) is a major expense for retailers, but turnover at Wegmans is a fraction of the industry average. As just one measure of the positive organizational culture at Wegmans, the company has made *Fortune* magazine's list of the *100 Best Companies to Work For* every year since the survey began—and is usually at or near the top of that list.

The mission to be the best at serving consumers extends to the company's decision-making style as well. For day-to-day decisions, laissez-faire management is widespread; executives want front-line employees to make whatever choices are needed to keep customers happy. Employees have the authority to make whatever choices are needed to satisfy customers. As one Wegmans executive joked, "We're a $3 billion company run by 16-year-old cashiers."[39]

Critical Thinking Questions

1. Wegmans has always been managed by members of the Wegman family. Do you think the company could continue its winning ways if the next generation doesn't want to take over, forcing the company to hire someone from outside the family as CEO? Explain your answer.
2. Would the Wegmans approach work for a car dealer? A bookstore? A manufacturer of industrial goods? Explain you answers.
3. How does low employee turnover contribute to Wegmans's distinct and positive corporate culture?

LEARN MORE ONLINE

Visit the Wegmans website at www.wegmans.com and click on "Careers." Read the information and watch the videos to learn more about working at Wegmans. Imagine yourself as someone who wants to join the company. Does the information on this website increase your interest in the company? Could you see yourself launching a career at Wegmans?

Key Terms

administrative skills (207)
autocratic leaders (200)
balanced scorecard (205)
benchmarking (205)
coaching (201)
conceptual skills (207)
controlling (204)
crisis management (205)
decision-making skills (208)
democratic leaders (200)
employee empowerment (201)
first-line managers (198)

goal (196)
interpersonal skills (206)
laissez-faire leaders (201)
leading (199)
management (190)
management pyramid (197)
managerial roles (191)
mentoring (202)
middle managers (198)
mission statement (193)
objective (196)
operational plans (196)

organizational culture (202)
organizing (197)
participative management (201)
planning (193)
quality (205)
standards (204)
strategic plans (193)
tactical plans (196)
technical skills (207)
top managers (198)
values statement (194)
vision statement (193)

Test Your Knowledge

Questions for Review

1. What is management? Why is it so important?
2. Why are interpersonal skills important to managers at all levels?
3. How does leadership differ from management?
4. What is forecasting, and how is it related to the planning function?
5. What is the goal of crisis management?

Questions for Analysis

6. How do the three levels of management differ?
7. How do autocratic, democratic, and laissez-faire leadership styles differ?

8. Why is cognitive intelligence alone insufficient for effective leadership?
9. Why are coaching and mentoring effective leadership techniques?
10. **Ethical Considerations.** When an organization learns about a threat that could place the safety of its workers or its customers at risk, is management obligated to immediately inform these parties of the threat? Explain your answer.

Questions for Application

11. Explain how you could apply the control cycle to both your college education and your career.

12. What are your long-term goals? Develop a set of long-term career goals for yourself and several short-term objectives that will help you reach those goals. Make sure your goals are SMART (see page 196).
13. **Concept Integration.** Using Welch Allyn's mission statement on page 193 as a model and the material you learned in Chapter 4, develop a mission statement that balances the pursuit of profit with responsibility to employees and community. Choose either a manufacturer of musical instruments or a retailer of children's clothing as the company.
14. **Concept Integration.** What is the principal difference between a business plan (as discussed in Chapter 6) and a strategic plan?

Practice Your Knowledge

Sharpen Your Communication Skills

Potential customers frequently visit your production facility before making purchase decisions. You and the people who report to you in the sales department have received extensive training in etiquette issues because you deal with high-profile clients. However, the rest of the workforce has not received such training, and you worry that someone might inadvertently say or do something that would offend one of these potential customers. In a two-paragraph e-mail, explain to the general manager why you think anyone who might come in contact with customers should receive basic etiquette training.

Building Your Team Skills

With a team of fellow students, perform a SWOT analysis for your college or university from the perspective of recruiting new students. Identify as many significant strengths and weaknesses as you can think of, being as objective as possible. Next, identify any important opportunities and threats you can find, such as demographic shifts or changes in government funding. Summarize your findings in a chart. Finally, evaluate your college's website and other promotional materials if available according to how well they present the school's strengths to prospective students.

Expand Your Knowledge

Discovering Career Opportunities

If you become a manager, how much of your day will be spent performing each of the four basic functions of management? This is your opportunity to find out. Arrange to shadow a manager (such as a department head, a store manager, or a shift supervisor) for a few hours. As you observe, categorize the manager's activities in terms of the four management functions and note how much time each activity takes. If observation is not possible, interview a manager in order to complete this exercise.

1. How much of the manager's time is spent on each of the four management functions? Is this the allocation you expected?
2. Ask whether this is a typical workday for this manager. If it isn't, what does the manager usually do differently? During a typical day, does this manager tend to spend most of the time on one particular function?
3. Of the four management functions, which does the manager believe is most important for good organizational performance? Do you agree?

Developing Your Research Skills

Find two articles in business journals or newspapers (print or online editions) that profile two senior managers who lead a business organization.

1. What experience, skills, and business background do the two leaders have? Do you see any striking similarities or differences in their backgrounds?

2. What kinds of business challenges have these two leaders faced? What actions did they take to deal with those challenges? Did they establish any long-term goals or objectives for their company? Did the articles mention a new change initiative?
3. Describe the leadership strengths of each person as they are presented in the articles you selected. Is either leader known as a team builder? Long-term strategist? Shrewd negotiator? What are each leader's greatest areas of strength?

Improving Your Tech Insights: Business Intelligence Systems

One of the maddening ironies of contemporary business is that many decision makers are awash in data but starved for true information and insights. *Business intelligence* (BI) systems aim to harness all that data and turn it into the information and insights that managers need.

Explore the products offered by several of the leading vendors, including Actuate (www.actuate.com), Cognos (www.cognos.com), SAP Business Objects (www.sap.com/solutions/sapbusinessobjects/index.epx), Information Builders (www.informationbuilders.com), Microsoft (www.microsoft.com/bi), Oracle (www.oracle.com), and SAS (www.sas.com). Research a BI system offered by one of these vendors, and in a brief e-mail to your instructor, summarize in your own words the system's benefits for managerial decision makers. (Business intelligence is a broad term that describes a variety of approaches, technologies, and specific products, so the field can be a bit confusing. Try several websites if needed to find a BI system that you can summarize briefly.)

Video Discussion

Access the Chapter 7 video discussion in the End of Chapter Assignments section at www.mybizlab.com.

PEARSON mybizlab

Log on to www.mybizlab.com to access the following study and assessment aids associated with this chapter:

- Interactive exercises
- Pre/post test
- Real-Time Updates
- Video application
- Customized study plans
- Biz Skills Simulations
- Quick Learning Guide

If you are not using mybizlab, you can access Real-Time Updates and Quick Learning Guides through http://real-timeupdates.com/bia5. The Quick Learning Guide (located under "Learn More" on the website) provides all six Checkpoints in a handy two-page format to help you study for exams or review important concepts whenever you need a quick refresher.

CHAPTER 8

Organization and Teamwork

LEARNING OBJECTIVES

After studying this chapter, you will be able to

1 Explain the major decisions needed to design an organization structure

2 Define four major types of organization structure

3 Explain how a team differs from a group and describe the six most common forms of teams

4 Highlight the advantages and disadvantages of working in teams and list the characteristics of effective teams

5 Review the five stages of team development and explain why conflict can arise in team settings

6 Identify helpful techniques for improving meeting productivity

Reinventing the Retail Experience at The Container Store

www.containerstore.com

Let's face it: Frontline jobs in retail don't have the greatest reputation. From an employee's perspective, these sales positions often combine low pay with high stress, leading to rapid burnout and frequent turnover. From a customer's perspective, frontline retail employees in some stores seem to fall into two categories: poorly trained, poorly motivated rookies or aggressive staffers who seem more intent on getting their commissions than helping customers.

What if you wanted to put a new face on retailing?

Effective team communication behind the scenes is key to creating positive customer experiences at The Container Score.

country, carries a staggering array of products that help customers organize their lives. The Container Store has storage solutions for every room in the house, from the kitchen to the garage to the home office. Employees are expected to help customers solve every storage problem imaginable, from sweaters to DVDs to rubber stamps to tax records, with a variety of boxes, baskets, hangers, hooks, closet organizers, and more.

If you were in Boone's and Tindell's shoes, what steps would you take to break out of the retail rut

What if you wanted shopping to be a pleasant, welcome experience for both employees and customers? Too much to ask for, perhaps?

This is the challenge Garrett Boone and Kip Tindell set for themselves when they opened the first The Container Store in Dallas, Texas. The chain, which has now expanded to several dozen locations across the

and create a company that is satisfying for both customers and employees? How would you attract the best and the brightest employees and pull off a minor miracle in retailing—hanging on to them year after year? How would you organize the staffs in your stores? How much information would you share with them, and how would you communicate it?[1] ■

Introduction

Organization might not seem like the most exciting topic in the business world, but as Garrett Boone and Kip Tindell (profiled in the chapter-opening Behind the Scenes) would no doubt tell you, it is one of the most important. This chapter discusses the most important issues to consider in designing an organization structure, explores ways to ensure productive teamwork, and concludes with some good advice on conducting effective meetings—a crucial skill for every manager.

Designing an Effective Organization Structure

organization structure
Framework enabling managers to divide responsibilities, ensure employee accountability, and distribute decision-making authority

A company's **organization structure** has a dramatic influence on the way employees and managers make decisions, communicate, and accomplish important tasks. This structure helps the company achieve its goals by providing a framework for managers to divide responsibilities, effectively distribute the authority to make decisions, coordinate and control the organization's work, and hold employees accountable for their work. In contrast, a poorly designed structure can create enormous waste, confusion, and frustration for employees, suppliers, and customers.

When managers design the organization's structure, they use an **organization chart** to provide a visual representation of how employees and tasks are grouped and how the lines of communication and authority flow (see Exhibit 8.1). An organization chart depicts the official design for accomplishing tasks that lead to achieving the organization's goals, a framework known as the *formal organization*. Every company also has an *informal organization*—the network of interactions that develop on a personal level among workers. Sometimes the interactions among people in the informal organization parallel their relationships in the formal organization, but often interactions transcend formal boundaries, such as when employees from various parts of the company participate in sports, social, or charitable activities together or use social media such as blogs to reach across organizational barriers.

In the past, organizations were usually designed around management's desire to control workers, with everything set up in a hierarchy. Today, however, the goal of many companies is an **agile organization** that allows employees to respond quickly to customer needs and changes in the business environment and to bring the best mix of talents and resources to every challenge.

To identify the best structure for their organizations, managers need to identify the organization's core competencies, clarify job responsibilities, define the chain of command, and organize the workforce in a way that maximizes effectiveness and efficiency.

organization chart
Diagram showing how employees and tasks are grouped and where the lines of communication and authority flow

agile organization
Company whose structure, policies, and capabilities allow employees to respond quickly to customer needs and changes in the business environment

EXHIBIT 8.1 Simplified Organization Chart

Organization charts portray the division of activities and responsibilities across the company.

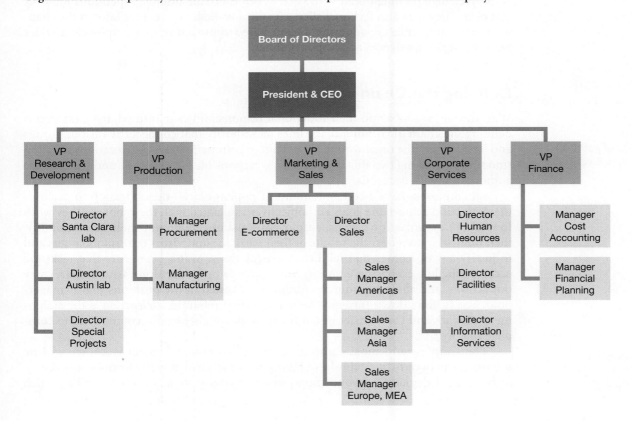

Identifying Core Competencies

Before they can decide how to organize, companies need to identify which business functions they should focus on themselves and which they should *outsource* (see page 244) to other companies. For instance, many companies outsource the payroll function because it doesn't make sense for them to invest the time needed to stay on top of frequent changes in income and related financial matters.[2]

core competencies
Activities that a company considers central and vital to its business

Core competencies are those activities in which a company excels and has the potential to create competitive advantages. For example, Disney is known the world over for its storytelling and entertainment prowess, having created a stable of characters that are practically family members to millions of children. This is one of its core competencies. When it wanted to expand into consumer electronics, with such products as a Mickey Mouse–inspired cordless phone, it teamed up with Motorola for the electronics and Frog Design for the product look and feel.[3] Rather than create a new electronic engineering division, Disney stuck to its core competencies and partnered with other firms to take advantage of their core competencies.

Identifying Job Responsibilities

Once the company knows what it wants to focus on, it can design each job that is necessary to deliver those competencies. A key decision here is finding the optimal level of **work specialization**, sometimes referred to as the *division of labor*—the degree to which organizational tasks are broken down into separate jobs.[4] Work specialization can improve organizational efficiency by enabling each worker to perform tasks that are well defined and that require specific skills. When employees concentrate on the same specialized tasks, they can perfect their skills and perform their tasks more quickly. In addition to aligning skills with job tasks, specialization prevents overlapping responsibilities and communication breakdowns.

work specialization
Specialization in or responsibility for some portion of an organization's overall work tasks; also called division of labor

However, organizations can overdo specialization. If a task is defined too narrowly, employees may become bored with performing the same limited, repetitive job over and over. They may also feel unchallenged and alienated. As you'll see later in the chapter, many companies are adopting a team-based approach to give employees a wider range of work experiences and responsibilities.

Defining the Chain of Command

With the various jobs and their individual responsibilities identified, the next step is defining the **chain of command**, the lines of authority that connect the various groups and levels within the organization. The chain of command helps organizations function smoothly by making two things clear: who is responsible for each task, and who has the authority to make decisions.

chain of command
Pathway for the flow of authority from one management level to the next

All employees have a certain amount of *responsibility*—the obligation to perform the duties and achieve the goals and objectives associated with their jobs. As they work toward the organization's goals, employees must also maintain their *accountability*, their obligation to report the results of their work to supervisors or team members and to justify any outcomes that fall below expectations. Managers ensure that tasks are accomplished by exercising *authority*, the power to make decisions, issue orders, carry out actions, and allocate resources. Authority is vested in the positions that managers hold, and it flows down through the management pyramid. *Delegation* is the assignment of work and the transfer of authority, responsibility, and accountability to complete that work.[5]

line organization
Chain-of-command system that establishes a clear line of authority flowing from the top down

The simplest and most common chain-of-command system is known as **line organization** because it establishes a clear line of authority flowing from the top down, as Exhibit 8.1 depicts. Everyone knows who is accountable to whom, as well as which

EXHIBIT 8.2 Simplified Line-and-Staff Structure

A line-and-staff organization divides employees into those who are in the direct line of command and those who provide staff (support) services to line managers at various levels. In this simplified example, the Government Affairs and Legal departments report to the CEO but would provide support to any department in the company as needed.

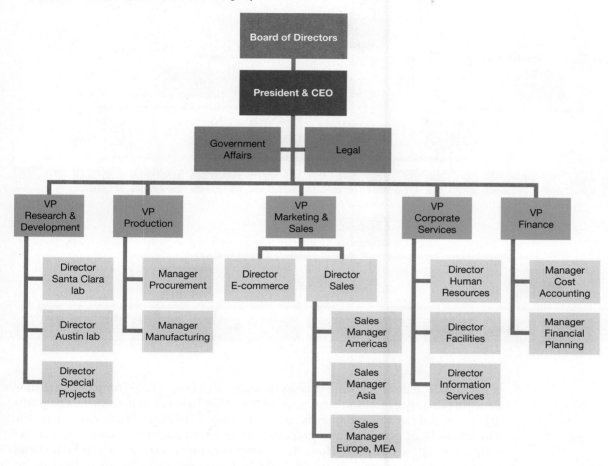

tasks and decisions each is responsible for. However, line organization sometimes falls short because the technical complexity of a firm's activities may require specialized knowledge that individual managers don't have and can't easily acquire. A more elaborate system called **line-and-staff organization** was developed out of the need to combine specialization with management control. In such an organization, managers in the chain of command are supplemented by functional groupings of people known as *staff*, who provide advice and specialized services but who are not in the line organization's overall chain of command (see Exhibit 8.2).

line-and-staff organization
Organization system that has a clear chain of command but that also includes functional groups of people who provide advice and specialized services

Span of Management

The number of people a manager directly supervises is called the **span of management**, or *span of control*. When a large number of people report directly to one person, that person has a wide span of management. This situation is common in *flat organizations* with relatively few levels in the management hierarchy. In contrast, *tall organizations* have many hierarchical levels, typically with fewer people reporting to each manager than is the case in a flat organization. In these organizations, the span of management

span of management
Number of people under one manager's control; also known as span of control

EXHIBIT 8.3 Flattening an Organization

In this simplified example, a layer of management (the business units) was removed to flatten the organization. In theory, this move reduces costs and speeds communication and decision making. One obvious downside is that the group managers now have to oversee six divisions.

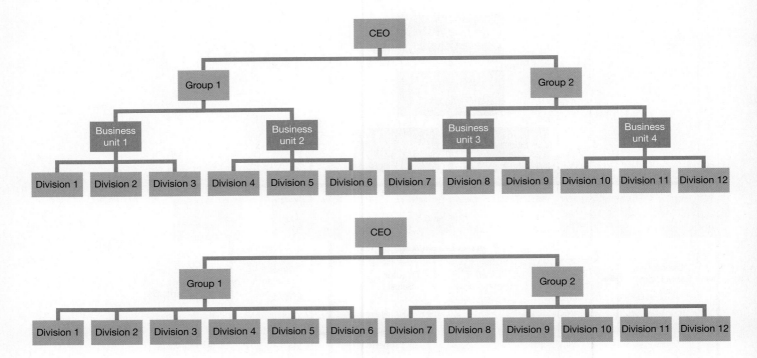

is narrow. To reduce the time it takes to make decisions, many companies are now flattening their organization structures by removing layers of management and pushing responsibilities and authority to lower levels (see Exhibit 8.3). Such moves have the added benefit of putting senior executives in closer contact with customers and the daily action of the business.[6] However, a flatter structure is not necessarily better in all respects. It increases the demand on individual managers and gives them less time to spend with each employee.

Centralization Versus Decentralization

centralization
Concentration of decision-making authority at the top of the organization

decentralization
Delegation of decision-making authority to employees in lower-level positions

Organizations that focus decision-making authority near the top of the chain of command are said to be centralized. **Centralization** can benefit a company by utilizing top management's experience and broad view of organizational goals. In addition, it can help companies coordinate large undertakings more efficiently, accelerate decisions that might otherwise get bogged down in discussions and disagreements, and reduce the number of overlapping capabilities.

In contrast, **decentralization** pushes decision-making authority down to lower organizational levels—such as department heads—while control over essential companywide matters remains with top management. Implemented properly, decentralization can stimulate responsiveness because decisions don't have to be referred up the hierarchy.[7] However, decentralization does not work in every situation or in every company. At times, strong authority from the top of the chain of command may be needed to keep the organization focused on immediate goals. In other cases, a company may need strong central decision making to coordinate efforts on complex projects or to present a unified image to customers. Managers should select the level of decision making that will most effectively serve the organization's needs given the individual circumstances.[8]

✓CHECKPOINT

LEARNING OBJECTIVE 1: Explain the major decisions needed to design an organization structure.

Summary: The first major decision is identifying core competencies, those functions where the company excels and wants to focus. From there, managers can identify job responsibilities (who does what and how much work specialization is optimum), the chain of command, the span of management for each manager, and the degree of centralization or decentralization of decision-making authority.

Critical thinking: (1) What are the risks of a poorly designed organization structure? (2) How does a flat structure change the responsibilities of individual managers?

It's your business: (1) What would you say are your two or three core competencies at this point in your career? (2) Would you function better in a highly centralized or highly decentralized organization? Why?

Key terms to know: organization structure, organization chart, agile organization, core competencies, work specialization, chain of command, line organization, line-and-staff organization, span of management, centralization, decentralization

Organizing the Workforce

The decisions regarding job responsibilities, span of management, and centralization versus decentralization provide the insights managers need in order to choose the best organization structure. The arrangement of activities into logical groups that are then clustered into larger departments and units to form the total organization is known as **departmentalization**.[9] The choice must involve both the *vertical structure*—how many layers the chain of command is divided into from the top of the company to the bottom—and the *horizontal structure*—how the various business functions and work specialties are divided across the company.

Variations in the vertical and horizontal designs of the organization can produce an almost endless array of structures—some flat, some wide; some simple and clear; others convoluted and complex. Within this endless variety of structure possibilities, most designs fall into one of four types: functional, divisional, matrix, and network. Companies can also combine two or more of these types in *hybrid structures*.

departmentalization
Grouping people within an organization according to function, division, matrix, or network

Functional Structures

The **functional structure** groups employees according to their skills, resource use, and job requirements. Common functional subgroups include research and development (R&D), production or manufacturing, marketing and sales, and human resources.

Splitting the organization into separate functional departments offers several advantages: (1) Grouping employees by specialization allows for the efficient use of resources and encourages the development of in-depth skills, (2) centralized decision making enables unified direction by top management, and (3) centralized operations enhance communication and the coordination of activities within departments. Despite these advantages, functional departmentalization can create problems with communication, coordination, and control, particularly as companies grow and become more complicated and geographically dispersed.[10] Moreover, employees may become too narrowly focused on departmental goals and lose sight of larger company goals. Firms that use functional structures often try to counter these weaknesses by using *cross-functional teams* to coordinate efforts across functional boundaries, as you'll see later in the chapter.

functional structure
Grouping workers according to their similar skills, resource use, and expertise

EXHIBIT 8.4

Customer Division Structure

Focusing each division on a single type of customer can help a company market its products more efficiently and serve customers more responsively.

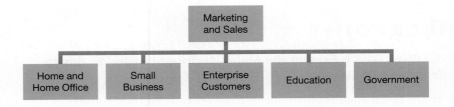

divisional structure
Grouping departments according to similarities in product, process, customer, or geography

Divisional Structures

The **divisional structure** establishes self-contained sub-organizations that encompass all the major functional resources required to achieve their goals—such as research and design, manufacturing, finance, and marketing.[11] In some companies, these divisions operate with great autonomy; such divisions are often called *business units*.

Many organizations use a structure based on *product divisions*—grouping around each of the company's products or family of products. In contrast, *process divisions* are based on the major steps of a production process. For example, Chevron has divisions for such process steps as exploration, refining, shipping, and marketing.[12] The third approach, *customer divisions*, concentrates activities on satisfying specific groups of customers (see Exhibit 8.4). Finally, geographic *divisions* help companies respond more easily to local customs, styles, and product preferences.

Divisional structures offer both advantages and disadvantages. First, because divisions are self-contained, they can react quickly to change, making the organization more flexible. In addition, because each division focuses on a limited number of products, processes, customers, or locations, divisions can often provide better service to customers.

However, divisional departmentalization can also increase costs through duplication (if every product division has its own human resources department, for example). Furthermore, poor coordination between divisions may cause them to focus too narrowly on divisional goals and neglect the organization's overall goals. Finally, divisions may compete with one another for resources and customers, causing rivalries that hurt the organization as a whole.[13]

Matrix Structures

matrix structure
Structure in which employees are assigned to both a functional group and a project team (thus using functional and divisional patterns simultaneously)

A **matrix structure** is an organizational design in which employees from functional departments form teams to combine their specialized skills (see Exhibit 8.5). This structure allows the company to pool and share resources across divisions and functional groups. The matrix may be a permanent feature of the organization's design, or it may be established to complete a specific project.

EXHIBIT 8.5

Matrix Structure

In a matrix structure, each employee is assigned to both a functional group (with a defined set of basic functions, such as production management) and a project team (which consists of members of various functional groups working together on a project, such as bringing out a new consumer product).

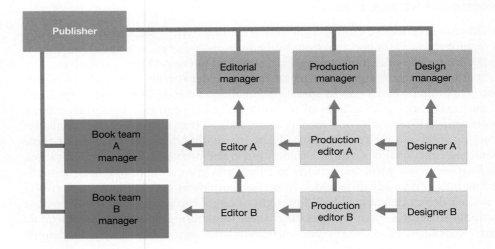

The matrix structure can help big companies function like smaller ones by allowing teams to devote their attention to specific projects or customers without permanently reorganizing the company's structure. A matrix can also make it easier to deploy limited resources where they're needed the most and to bring a mix of skills to bear on important tasks. On the downside, people in a matrix structure have to get used to reporting to two bosses, more communication and coordination is usually required, and struggles over resources can foster unhealthy competition between the two sides of the matrix.[14] Yahoo! relied on matrix organization for years, but when Carol Bartz took over as CEO in 2009, she dumped it in favor of a more centralized structure in order to simplify and accelerate decision making.[15]

Network Structures

A **network structure** stretches beyond the boundaries of the company to connect a variety of partners and suppliers that perform selected tasks for a headquarters organization. Also called a *virtual organization,* the network organization can outsource engineering, marketing, research, accounting, production, distribution, or other functions. The design of a network structure stems from decisions about core competencies, with executives deciding which functions to focus on internally and which to outsource.

The network structure presents an intriguing blend of benefits and risks. A virtual structure can lower costs and increase flexibility, allowing a company to react more quickly to market demands. It can also boost competitiveness by taking advantage of specific skills and technologies available in other companies. On the other hand, relying too heavily on outsiders can render the company vulnerable to events beyond its control, such as key suppliers going out of business, offering the same goods and services to its competitors, or going into direct competition with the company. Moreover, outsourcing too many fundamental tasks such as product design can leave a company without any real competitive distinctions to speak of.[16]

network structure
Structure in which individual companies are connected electronically to perform selected tasks for a small headquarters organization

CHECKPOINT

LEARNING OBJECTIVE 2: Define four major types of organization structure.

Summary: Companies can organize in four primary ways: by function, which groups employees according to their skills, resource use, and expertise; by division, which establishes self-contained departments formed according to similarities in product, process, customer, or geography; by matrix, which assigns employees from functional departments to interdisciplinary project teams and requires them to report to both a department head and a team leader; and by network, which connects separate companies that perform selected tasks for a headquarters organization.

Critical thinking: (1) Should The Container Store use the same organization structure in each of its stores around the country? Why or why not? (2) Why does a matrix structure create potential problems in the chain of command?

It's your business: (1) Do you think you would function well in a matrix structure, where you would need to report to two bosses simultaneously? Why or why not? (2) What about as a manager—could you share control with another manager?

Key terms to know: departmentalization, functional structure, divisional structure, matrix structure, network structure

Organizing in Teams

While the vertical chain of command is a tried-and-true method of organizing for business, it is limited by the fact that decision-making authority is often located high up the management hierarchy while real-world feedback from customers is usually located at or near the bottom of the hierarchy. Companies that organize vertically may become slow to react to change, and high-level managers may overlook many great ideas for improvement that originate in the lower levels of the organization. In addition, many business tasks and challenges demand the expertise of people who work in many parts of the company, isolated by the formal chain of command. To combat these issues, organizations such as The Container Store work to involve employees from all levels and functions of the organization in the decision-making process, using a variety of team formats in day-to-day operations.

Even though the team approach has many advantages, shifting to a team structure often requires a fundamental shift in the organization's culture. Teams must also have clear goals that are tied to the company's strategic goals, and their outcomes need to be measured and compared with benchmarks. Moreover, employees must be motivated to work together in teams.

What Is a Team?

team
A unit of two or more people who share a mission and collective responsibility as they work together to achieve a goal

A **team** is a unit of two or more people who work together to achieve a shared goal. Teams differ from work groups in that work groups interact primarily to share information and to make decisions to help one another perform within each member's area of responsibility. In other words, the performance of a work group is merely the summation of all group members' individual contributions.[17] In contrast, the members of a team have a shared mission and are collectively responsible for their work. By coordinating their individual efforts, the members of successful teams accomplish more together than they could individually, a result known as *synergy*.[18]

Although the team's goals may be set by either the team itself or someone in the formal chain of command, it is the job of the team leader to make sure the team stays on track to achieve those goals. Team leaders are often appointed by senior managers, but sometimes they emerge naturally as the team develops. Some teams complete their work and disband in a matter of weeks or months, while those working on complex projects can stay together for years.

Types of Teams

The type, structure, and composition of individual teams within an organization depend on the organization's strategic goals and the objective for forming the team. The six most common forms of teams are *problem-solving teams, self-managed teams, functional teams, cross-functional teams, virtual teams*, and *social networks and communities of practice*. Such classifications are not exclusive, of course. A problem-solving team may also be self-managed and cross-functional.

Problem-Solving Teams

problem-solving team
Team that meets to find ways of improving quality, efficiency, and the work environment

A **problem-solving team** is assembled to find ways of improving quality, efficiency, or other performance issues. In some cases, a team attacks a single, specific problem and disbands after presenting or implementing the solution. In other cases, the team continues to meet over time, evaluating trends and fixing new problems as they crop up. At the Massachusetts Eye & Ear Infirmary, for example, a team charged with addressing insurance claim denials meets regularly to solve individual cases and to investigate systematic issues that might be causing problems with multiple patient cases.[19]

Self-Managed Teams

self-managed team
Team in which members are responsible for an entire process or operation

As the name implies, a **self-managed team** manages its own activities and requires minimum supervision. Typically, these teams control the pace of work and determination of work assignments. Fully self-managed teams select their own members.

Self-managed teams represent a significant change for organizations and managers accustomed to rigid command-and-control structures. However, the potential advantages include lower costs, faster decision making, greater flexibility and innovation, and improved quality (stemming from the increased pride of ownership that the independent team feels in its work).[20]

Functional Teams

A **functional team**, or *command team*, is organized along the lines of the organization's vertical structure and thus may be referred to as a *vertical team*. Such teams are composed of managers and employees within a single functional department, and the structure of a vertical team typically follows the formal chain of command. In some cases, the team may include several levels of the organizational hierarchy within the same functional department.[21]

functional team
Team whose members come from a single functional department and that is based on the organization's vertical structure

Cross-Functional Teams

In contrast to functional teams, a **cross-functional team**, or *horizontal team*, draws together employees from various functional areas and expertise. Cross-functional teams can facilitate information exchange, help coordinate multiple organizational units, encourage new solutions for organizational problems, and aid the development of new organizational policies and procedures.[22] However, collaborating across organizational boundaries can be a challenge, particularly if participation on a cross-functional team conflicts with an individual's regular departmental workload or performance incentives.[23]

A cross-functional team can take on a number of formats. A **task force** is formed to work on a specific activity with a completion point. Several departments are usually involved so that all parties who have a stake in the outcome of the task are able to provide input. In contrast a **committee** usually has a long life span and may become a permanent part of the organization structure. Committees typically deal with regularly recurring tasks, such as addressing employee grievances.

cross-functional team
Team that draws together employees from different functional areas

task force
Team of people from several departments who are temporarily brought together to address a specific issue

committee
Team that may become a permanent part of the organization and is designed to deal with regularly recurring tasks

Virtual Teams

A **virtual team** is composed of members at two or more geographic locations. Research indicates that virtual teams can be as effective as face-to-face teams, as long as they take steps to overcome the disadvantages of not being able to communicate face to face.[24] For instance, some virtual teams meet in person at least once to allow the members to get to know one another before diving into their work.

To be successful, virtual teams should follow three basic rules. First, take full advantage of the diverse viewpoints, experiences, and skills of the various team members. One of the major benefits of virtual teams, in fact, is the opportunity to assemble teams of experts wherever they may be, rather than rely on the people who happen to work in a given geographic location. Second, use technology to replicate resources that in-person teams rely on. *Shared online workspaces* are one of the most popular tools for virtual teams because they give everyone access to information and documents the team uses. E-mail and instant messaging (IM) can be effective for occasional communication, but many teams discover that some people are either left out of important message exchanges—or everybody is deluged with every message. Blogs and wikis can cut down on the message overload and keep everyone in the loop. Third, take extra care to keep the team functioning effectively. Without the *nonverbal cues*, such as facial expressions and body language, that people rely on heavily when communicating in person, virtual communication is even more challenging. Teleconferencing and videoconferencing can help in this regard.[25]

virtual team
Team that uses communication technology to bring geographically distant employees together to achieve goals

Social Networks and Virtual Communities

Social networking technologies are redefining teamwork and team communication by helping erase the constraints of geographic and organization boundaries. In addition to enabling and enhancing teamwork, social networks have numerous other business

EXHIBIT 8.6 **Business Uses of Social Networking Technology**

Social networking has emerged as a powerful technology for enabling teamwork and enhancing collaboration in a variety of ways.

BUSINESS CHALLENGE	EXAMPLE OF SOCIAL NETWORKING IN ACTION
Assembling teams	Identifying the best people, both inside the company and in other companies, to collaborate on projects
Fostering the growth of communities	Helping people with similar—or complementary—interests and skills find each other in order to provide mutual assistance and development
Accelerating the evolution of teams	Accelerating the sometimes slow process of getting to know one another and identifying individual areas of expertise
Maintaining business relationships	Giving people an easy way to stay in contact after meetings and conferences
Supporting customers	Allowing customers to develop close relationships with product experts within the company
Integrating new employees	Helping new employees navigate their way through the organization, finding experts, mentors, and other important contacts
Easing the transition after reorganizations and mergers	Helping employees connect and bond after internal staff reorganizations or mergers with other organizations
Overcoming structural barriers in communication channels	Bypassing the formal communication system in order to deliver information where it is needed in a timely fashion
Solving problems	Finding "pockets of knowledge" within the organization—the expertise and experience of individual employees
Preparing for major meetings and events	Giving participants a way to meet before an event takes place, helping to ensure that the meeting or event becomes more productive more quickly
Sharing and distributing information	Making it easy for employees to share information with people who may need it—and for people who need information to find employees who might have it
Finding potential customers, business partners, and employees	Identifying strong candidates by matching user profiles with current business needs and linking from existing member profiles

applications and benefits (see Exhibit 8.6). While they are not always teams in the traditional sense, social networks and virtual communities often function as teams, helping people coordinate their efforts in pursuit of a shared goal.

The two fundamental elements of social networking technology are *profiles* (the information stored about each member of the network) and *connections* (mechanisms for finding and communicating with other members).[26] If you're familiar with MySpace or Facebook, you have a basic idea of how social networks function. Business-oriented networks such as LinkedIn (www.linkedin.com) function in much the same way, and they also have the potential to become vital elements of an organization's structure and communication channels. For example, some companies use social networking technologies to form *virtual communities* or *communities of practice* that link employees with similar professional interests throughout the company and sometimes with customers and suppliers as well.

The heavy-equipment manufacturer Caterpillar has more than 2,700 virtual teams or communities that discuss problems and share insights into improving quality and productivity. In Caterpillar's case, the communities are part of what the company describes as a "sharing culture," in which employees place a high value on helping one another, even when doing so brings no immediate benefit to the people offering the help.[27]

CHECKPOINT

LEARNING OBJECTIVE 3: Explain how a team differs from a group, and describe the six most common forms of teams.

Summary: The primary difference between a team and a work group is that the members of team work toward a shared goal, whereas members of a work group work toward individual goals. The six most common forms of teams are (1) problem-solving teams, which seek ways to improve a situation and then submit their recommendations; (2) self-managed teams, which manage their own activities and seldom require supervision; (3) functional teams, which are composed of employees within a single functional department; (4) cross-functional teams, which draw together employees from various departments and expertise in a number of formats such as task forces and committees; (5) virtual teams, which bring together employees from distant locations; and (6) social networks and communities of practice, which are typically less structured than teams but nonetheless share many aspects of teamwork and promote shared goals.

Critical thinking: (1) How might the work of a task force or committee disrupt the normal chain of command in an organization? (2) Should new hires with no business experience be assigned to virtual teams? Why or why not?

It's your business: (1) Would you function well in a virtual team setting that offered little or no chance for face-to-face contact with your colleagues? Why or why not? (2) If you had two similar job offers, one with a company that stresses teamwork and another with a company that stresses independent accomplishment, which would you choose? Why?

Key terms to know: team, problem-solving team, self-managed team, functional team, cross-functional team, task force, committee, virtual team

Ensuring Team Productivity

Even though teams can play a vital role in helping an organization reach its goals, they are not appropriate for every situation, nor do they automatically ensure higher performance. Understanding the advantages and disadvantages of working in teams and recognizing the characteristics of effective teams are essential steps in ensuring productive teamwork.

Advantages and Disadvantages of Working in Teams

Managers must weigh the pros and cons of teams when deciding whether and how to use them. A well-run team can deliver a variety of advantages:[28]

- **Higher-quality decisions.** Many business challenges require the input of people with diverse experiences and insights, and teams can be an effective way to bring these multiple perspectives together. Working in teams can unleash new levels of creativity and energy in workers who share a sense of purpose and mutual accountability. Effective teams can be better than top-performing individuals at solving complex problems.[29]

- **Increased commitment to solutions and changes.** Employees who feel they've had an active role in making a decision are more likely to support the decision and encourage others to accept it.

Real-Time Updates

Learn More
Taking teams to the top
Listen to these hands-on techniques for developing, launching, leading, and evaluating world-class teams. On mybizlab (www.mybizlab.com), you can access Real-Time Updates within each chapter or under Student Study Tools. Otherwise, go to http://real-timeupdates.com/bia5 and click on "Learn More."

- **Lower levels of stress and destructive internal competition.** When people work together toward a common goal, rather than competing for individual recognition, their efforts and energies tend to focus on the common good. The sense of belonging to a group and being involved in a collective effort can also be a source of job satisfaction for most people.
- **Improved flexibility and responsiveness.** Because they don't have the same degree of permanence as formal departments and other structural elements, teams are easier to reformulate to respond to changing business needs.

Furthermore, teams fill an individual worker's need to belong to a group, reduce employee boredom, increase feelings of dignity and self-worth, and reduce stress and tension between workers. While the advantages of teamwork help explain the widespread popularity of teams in today's business environment, teams also present a number of potential disadvantages, particularly if they are poorly structured or poorly managed:[30]

- **Inefficiency.** Even successful teams need to be on constant watch for inefficiency—spending more time than is necessary on their decisions and activities. Potential sources of inefficiency include internal politics, too much emphasis on consensus, and excessive socialization among team members.
- **Groupthink.** Like all social structures, business teams can generate tremendous pressures to conform with accepted norms of behavior. **Groupthink** occurs when these peer pressures cause individual team members to withhold contrary or unpopular opinions. The result can be decisions that are worse than the team members might've made individually.

groupthink
Uniformity of thought that occurs when peer pressures cause individual team members to withhold contrary or unpopular opinions

- **Diminished individual motivation.** Balancing the need for team harmony with individual motivation is a constant issue with teams. Without the promise of individual recognition and reward, high-performance individuals may feel less incentive to keep working at such high levels.
- **Structural disruption.** Teams can become so influential within an organization that they compete with the formal chain of command, in effect superimposing a matrix on the existing structure.
- **Excessive workloads.** The time and energy required to work on teams isn't free, and when team responsibilities are layered on top of individuals' regular job responsibilities, the result can be overload.

Characteristics of Effective Teams

To be successful, teams need to be designed as carefully as any other part of the organization structure. Establishing the size of the team is one of the most important decisions; the optimal size for teams is generally thought to be between 5 and 12 members. Teams with fewer members may lack the necessary range of skills, while larger teams may make it difficult for group members to bond properly and communicate efficiently. However, managers sometimes have no choice; complex challenges such as integrating two companies or designing complicated products can require very large teams, up to 100 people or more.[31]

EXHIBIT 8.7 Team Member Roles

Team members assume one of these four roles. Members who assume a dual role often make effective team leaders.

The types of individuals on the team is also vital. People who assume the *task-specialist role* focus on helping the team reach its goals. In contrast, members who take on the *socioemotional role* focus on supporting the team's emotional needs and strengthening the team's social unity. Some team members are able to assume dual roles, contributing to the task and still meeting members' emotional needs. These members often make effective team leaders. At the other end of the spectrum are members who are *nonparticpators* who contribute little to reaching the team's goals or to meeting members' socioemotional needs. Obviously, a team staffed with too many inactive members isn't going to accomplish much of anything. Exhibit 8.7 outlines the behavior patterns associated with each of these roles.

Beyond the right number of the right sort of people, effective teams share a number of other characteristics:[32]

- **Clear sense of purpose.** Team members clearly understand the task at hand, what is expected of them, and their respective roles on the team.

- **Open and honest communication.** The team culture encourages discussion and debate. Team members speak openly and honestly, without the threat of anger, resentment, or retribution. They listen to and value feedback from others. As a result, all team members participate. Conversely, members who either don't share valuable information because they don't understand that it's valuable—or worse, withhold information as a way to maintain personal power—can undermine the team's efforts.[33]

- **Creative thinking.** Effective teams encourage original thinking, considering options beyond the usual.

- **Accountability.** Team members commit to being accountable to each other.

- **Focus.** Team members get to the core issues of the problem and stay focused on key issues.

- **Decision by consensus.** All decisions are arrived at by consensus. But this point comes with a warning: Teams that worry too much about consensus can take forever to make decisions. In many cases, team members need to commit to the group's decision even though they may not all support it 100 percent.

For a brief review of characteristics of effective teams, see Exhibit 8.8 on the next page.

EXHIBIT 8.8

Characteristics of Effective Teams

Effective teams practice these good habits.

Make Effective Teamwork a Top Management Priority
■ Recognize and reward group performance where appropriate ■ Provide ample training opportunities for employees to develop team skills
Select Team Members Wisely
■ Involve key stakeholders and decision makers ■ Limit team size to the minimum number of people needed to achieve team goals ■ Select members with a diversity of views ■ Select creative thinkers
Build a Sense of Fairness in Decision Making
■ Encourage debate and disagreement without fear of reprisal ■ Allow members to communicate openly and honestly ■ Consider all proposals ■ Build consensus by allowing team members to examine, compare, and reconcile differences—but don't let a desire for 100 percent consensus bog the team down ■ Avoid quick votes ■ Keep everyone informed ■ Present all the facts
Manage Conflict Constructively
■ Share leadership ■ Encourage equal participation ■ Discuss disagreements openly and calmly ■ Focus on the issues, not the people ■ Don't let minor disagreements boil over into major conflicts
Stay on Track
■ Make sure everyone understands the team's purpose ■ Communicate what is expected of team members ■ Stay focused on the core assignment ■ Develop and adhere to a schedule ■ Develop rules and obey norms

✓CHECKPOINT

LEARNING OBJECTIVE 4: Highlight the advantages and disadvantages of working in teams, and list the characteristics of effective teams.

Summary: Teamwork has the potential to produce higher-quality decisions, increase commitment to solutions and changes, lower stress and destructive internal competition, and improve flexibility and responsiveness. The potential disadvantages include inefficiency, groupthink, diminished individual motivation, structural disruption, and excessive workloads. Effective teams have a clear sense of purpose, communicate openly and honestly, build a sense of fairness in decision making, think creatively, maintain accountability, stay focused on key issues, and emphasize consensus (while balancing the need for quick decision making).

Critical thinking: (1) Is groupthink similar to peer pressure? Why or why not? (2) Is supporting a group decision you don't completely agree with always a case of groupthink? Explain your answer.

It's your business: (1) How would you characterize the experience you've had working in teams throughout your high school and college years? (2) How can you apply experience gained on athletic teams and other collaborative activities to the business world?

Key terms to know: groupthink

Fostering Teamwork

Because teams are composed of unique individuals with different perspectives, the interpersonal relationships among team members require careful consideration. Two particularly important issues are team development and team conflict.

Team Development

Like the members who form them, teams grow and change over time. By anticipating these changes, team leaders can help groups reach their potential as quickly as possible. Several models of team development have been proposed over the years. One well-known model defined by researcher Bruce Tuckman identifies five stages of development, nicknamed *forming, storming, norming, performing,* and *adjourning*.[34]

- **Forming.** The forming stage is a period of orientation and ice-breaking. Members get to know each other, determine what types of behaviors are appropriate within the group, identify what is expected of them, and become acquainted with each other's task orientation.

- **Storming.** In the storming stage, members show more of their personalities and become more assertive in establishing their roles. Conflict and disagreement often arise during the storming stage as members jockey for position or form coalitions to promote their own perceptions of the team's mission. While it is necessary for this storming to occur, team members need to make sure the team doesn't tear itself apart before it has the chance to resolve these emerging conflicts.

- **Norming.** During the norming stage, these conflicts are resolved, and team harmony develops. Members come to understand and accept one another, reach a consensus on who the leader is (if that hasn't already been established formally), and reach agreement on member roles.

- **Performing.** In the performing stage, members are really committed to the team's goals. Problems are solved, and disagreements are handled with maturity in the interest of task accomplishment.

- **Adjourning.** Finally, if the team has a specific task to perform, it goes through the adjourning stage after the task has been completed. In this stage, issues are wrapped up, and the team is dissolved.

As the team moves through these various stages of development, two important developments occur. First, the team develops a certain level of **cohesiveness**, a measure of how committed the members are to the team's goals. The team's cohesiveness is reflected in meeting attendance, team interaction, work quality, and goal achievement. Cohesiveness is influenced by many factors, particularly competition and evaluation. If a team is in competition with other teams, cohesiveness increases as the team strives to excel. In addition, if a team's efforts and accomplishments are recognized by the organization, members tend to be more committed to the team's goals. Strong team cohesiveness generally results in high morale. Moreover, when cohesiveness is coupled with strong management support for team objectives, teams tend to be more productive.

cohesiveness
A measure of how committed the team members are to their team's goals

The second development is the emergence of **norms**, informal but often powerful standards of conduct that members share and use to guide their behavior. Norms define acceptable behavior by setting limits, identifying values, and clarifying expectations. By encouraging consistent behavior, norms boost efficiency and help ensure the group's survival. Individuals who deviate from these norms can find themselves ridiculed, isolated, or even removed from the group entirely (this fear is the leading cause of groupthink, by the way). Norms can be established in various ways: from early behaviors that set precedents for future actions, from significant events in the team's history, from behaviors that come to the team through outside influences, and from a leader's or member's explicit statements that have an impact on other members.[35]

norms
Informal standards of conduct that guide team behavior

Team Conflict

As teams mature and go about their work, conflicts can arise. Although the term *conflict* sounds negative, conflict isn't necessarily bad. Conflict can be *constructive* if it forces important issues into the open, increases the involvement of team members, and generates creative ideas for solving a problem. Teamwork isn't necessarily about happiness and harmony; even teams that have some interpersonal friction can excel if they have effective leadership and team players committed to strong results. As teamwork experts Andy Boynton and Bill Fischer put it, "Virtuoso teams are not about getting polite results."[36]

In contrast, conflict is *destructive* if it diverts energy from more important issues, destroys the morale of teams or individual team members, or polarizes or divides the team.[37] Destructive conflict can lead to *win-lose* or *lose-lose* outcomes, in which one or both sides lose, to the detriment of the entire team. If you approach conflict with the idea that both sides can satisfy their goals to at least some extent (a *win-win strategy*), you can minimize losses for everyone. For a win-win strategy to work, everybody must believe that (1) it's possible to find a solution that both parties can accept, (2) cooperation is better for the organization than competition, (3) the other party can be trusted, and (4) greater power or status doesn't entitle one party to impose a solution.

Causes of Team Conflict

Team conflicts can arise for a number of reasons. First, individuals may feel they are in competition for scarce or declining resources, such as money, information, and supplies. Second, team members may disagree over responsibilities. Third, poor communication can lead to misunderstandings and misperceptions. In addition, withholding information can undermine trust among members. Fourth, basic differences in values, attitudes, and personalities may lead to clashes. Fifth, power struggles may result when one party questions the authority of another or when people or teams with limited authority attempt to increase their power or exert more influence. Sixth, conflicts can arise because individual team members are pursuing different goals.[38]

Solutions to Team Conflict

As with any human relationship, the way a team approaches conflict depends to a large degree on how well the team was functioning in the first place. A strong, healthy team is more likely to view a conflict as simply another challenge to overcome—and can emerge from the conflict even stronger than before. In contrast, a generally dysfunctional team can disintegrate even further when faced with a new source of conflict.

The following seven measures can help team members successfully resolve conflict:

- **Proaction.** Deal with minor conflict before it becomes major conflict.
- **Communication.** Get those directly involved in a conflict to participate in resolving it.
- **Openness.** Get feelings out in the open before dealing with the main issues.
- **Research.** Seek factual reasons for a problem before seeking solutions.
- **Flexibility.** Don't let anyone lock into a position before considering other solutions.
- **Fair play.** Insist on fair outcomes and don't let anyone avoid a fair solution by hiding behind the rules.
- **Alliance.** Get opponents to fight together against an "outside force" instead of against each other.

Team members and team leaders can also take several steps to prevent conflicts. First, by establishing clear goals that require the efforts of every member, the team reduces the chance that members will battle over their objectives or roles. Second, by developing well-defined tasks for each member, the team leader ensures that all parties are aware of their responsibilities and the limits of their authority. And finally, by facilitating open communication, the team leader can ensure that all members understand their own tasks and objectives as well as those of their teammates. Communication builds respect and tolerance, and it provides a forum for bringing misunderstandings into the open before they turn into full-blown conflicts.

CHECKPOINT

LEARNING OBJECTIVE 5: Review the five stages of team development, and explain why conflict can arise in team settings.

Summary: Several models have been proposed to describe the stages of team development; the well-known model defined by researcher Bruce Tuckman identifies the stages as *forming, storming, norming, performing,* and *adjourning.* In the forming stage, team members become acquainted with each other and with the group's purpose. In the storming stage, conflict often arises as coalitions and power struggles develop. In the norming stage, conflicts are resolved and harmony develops. In the performing stage, members focus on achieving the team's goals. In the adjourning stage, the team dissolves upon completion of its task. Conflict can arise from competition for scarce resources; confusion over task responsibility; poor communication and misinformation; differences in values, attitudes, and personalities; power struggles; and incompatible goals.

Critical thinking: (1) How can a team leader know when to step in when conflict arises and when to step back and let the issue work itself out? (2) What are the risks of not giving new teams the time and opportunity to "storm" and "norm" before tackling the work they've been assigned?

It's your business: (1) Have you ever had to be teammates (in any activity) with someone you simply couldn't stand on a personal level? If so, how did this affect your performance as a team member? (2) Have you ever had to adapt your regular personality in order to succeed on a particular team? Was this a positive or negative experience?

Key terms to know: cohesiveness, norms

Improving Meeting Productivity

Well-run meetings can help you solve problems, develop ideas, and identify opportunities. Much of your workplace communication is likely to occur in small-group meetings; therefore, your ability to contribute to the company and to be recognized for those contributions will depend on your meeting skills.

Unfortunately, many meetings are unproductive. In one study, senior and middle managers reported that only 56 percent of their meetings were actually productive and that 25 percent of them could have been replaced by a phone call or a memo.[39] After confirming that a meeting is truly necessary, you can help ensure a productive meeting by preparing carefully, conducting the meeting efficiently, and using meeting technologies wisely.

Preparing for Meetings

Careful preparation helps you avoid the two biggest meeting mistakes: (1) holding a meeting when a blog posting or some other message would do the job and (2) holding a meeting without a specific goal in mind. Before you even begin preparing for a meeting, make sure holding a meeting is truly necessary. Once you're sure, proceed with four preparation tasks:

■ **Identify your purpose.** Whatever your purpose, identify what the best possible result of the meeting would be (such as "we carefully evaluated all three product ideas and decided which one to invest in"). Use this hoped-for result to shape the direction and content of the meeting.[40]

■ **Select participants for the meeting.** Be sure to invite everyone who needs to participate—but don't invite anyone who doesn't need to be there. Meetings with more than 10 or 12 people can become unmanageable if everyone is expected to participate in the discussion and decision making.

■ **Choose the time and prepare the facility.** Morning meetings can be more productive than afternoon sessions because people are fresher and not yet involved in the various problems and concerns of their working days. After selecting the time, plan the facility and layout carefully. For instance, if you want to encourage interaction, arranging chairs in a circle or U shape is more effective than seating in rows. Plus, give some attention to details such as room temperature, lighting, ventilation, acoustics, and refreshments; any of these details can make or break a meeting. If the meeting will take place online, make sure all participants have access to the necessary software before the meeting is set to begin.

agenda
List of topics to be addressed in a meeting, the person(s) responsible for each topic, and the time allotted to each topic

■ **Set the agenda.** The success of a meeting depends on the preparation of the participants. Distribute a carefully written **agenda**, a list of the topics to be addressed, the person(s) responsible for each topic, and the time allotted to each topic (see Exhibit 8.9). Be sure to send the agenda early enough to give participants enough

EXHIBIT 8.9 **Typical Meeting Agenda**

Agenda formats vary widely, depending on the complexity of the meeting and the presentation technologies that will be used. For an online meeting, for instance, a good approach is to first send a detailed planning agenda in advance of the meeting so that presenters know what they need to prepare. You can then create a simpler display agenda similar to this one to guide the progress of the meeting.

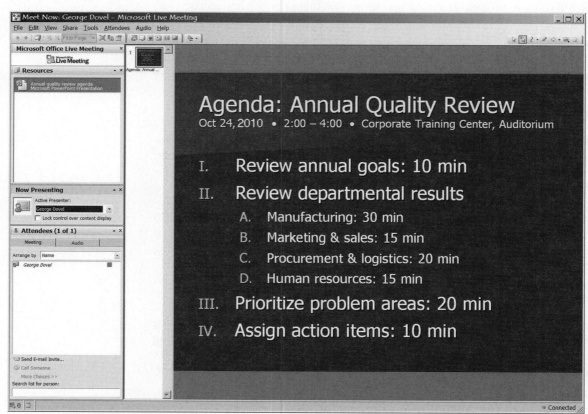

time to prepare. A productive agenda answers three key questions: (1) What do we need to do in this meeting to accomplish our goals? (2) What issues will be of greatest importance to all participants? (3) What information must be available in order to discuss these issues?[41]

Conducting Efficient Meetings

Everyone in a meeting shares the responsibility for making the meeting productive. If you're the designated leader of a meeting, however, you have an extra degree of responsibility and accountability. To ensure productive meetings, be sure to do the following:

- **Keep the discussion on track.** A good meeting leader draws out the best ideas the group has to offer and resolves differences of opinions while maintaining progress toward achieving the meeting's purpose and staying on schedule.

- **Follow agreed-upon rules.** The larger the meeting, the more formal you need to be to maintain order. Formal meetings use *parliamentary procedure*, a time-tested method for planning and running effective meetings.

- **Encourage participation.** Draw out quiet participants by asking for their input on issues that pertain to them.

- **Participate actively.** If you're a meeting participant, try to contribute to both the subject of the meeting and the smooth interaction of the group.

- **Close effectively.** At the conclusion of the meeting, verify that the objectives have been met or arrange for follow-up work, if needed. Summarize either the general conclusion of the discussion or the actions to be taken. Make sure all participants have a chance to clear up any misunderstandings.

minutes
Summary of the important information presented and the decisions made during a meeting

For formal meetings, it's good practice to appoint one person to record the **minutes**, a summary of the important information presented and the decisions made during a meeting. In smaller or informal meetings, attendees often make their own notes on their copies of the agenda. In either case, a clear record of the decisions made and the people responsible for follow-up action is essential.

Using Meeting Technologies

You can expect to use a variety of meeting-related technologies throughout your career, particularly for meetings among people in two or more locations. The simplest of the long-distance meeting tools provide communication through a single medium, such as audio teleconferencing, in which three or more people are connected by phone simultaneously. Instant messaging chat sessions can also serve as virtual meetings, with people participating by typing instead of talking.

Videoconferencing combines audio communication with live video, letting team members see each other, demonstrate

How many people are in this conference room in Chicago? Only the two people in the foreground; the other six are in Atlanta and London. Virtual meeting technologies such as this telepresence system connect people spread across the country or around the world.

products, and transmit other visual information. The most advanced systems feature *telepresence*, in which the interaction feels so lifelike that participants can forget that the person "sitting" on the other side of the table is actually in another city.[42]

Web-based meeting systems combine the best of instant messaging, shared work-spaces, and videoconferencing with other tools such as *virtual whiteboards* that let teams collaborate in real time. Using such systems, attendees can log on from a desktop or lap-top PC, a PDA, or even a web-enabled mobile phone from almost anywhere in the world.

Technology continues to create intriguing opportunities for online interaction. For instance, one of the newest virtual tools is *online brainstorming*, in which companies conduct "idea campaigns" to generate new ideas from people across the organization. These range from small team meetings to huge events such as IBM's giant InnovationJam, in which 100,000 IBM employees, family members, and customers from 160 countries were invited to brainstorm online for three days. In fact, online brainstorming has proven so successful that IBM now offers its Jam services to other companies.[43]

Companies are also beginning to experiment with virtual meetings and other com-munication activities in *virtual worlds*, most notably Second Life (**www.secondlife.com**). In much the same way that gamers can create and control characters (often known as *avatars*) in a multiplayer video game, professionals can create online versions of them-selves to participate in meetings, training sessions, sales presentations, and other activi-ties (see Exhibit 8.10).

For the latest information on organization and teamwork, visit **http://real-timeupdates .com/bia5** and click on Chapter 8.

✓CHECKPOINT

LEARNING OBJECTIVE 6: Identify helpful techniques for improving meeting productivity.

Summary: The three essential steps for improving meeting productivity are preparing carefully, conducting the meeting efficiently, and using meeting tech-nologies wisely. To prepare, first make sure you really need to have a meeting, then identify your purpose, select participants, choose the time, prepare the facility, and set and distribute the agenda. To conduct a meeting efficiently, be sure to keep discussions on track, follow agreed-upon rules, encourage participation (and participate actively yourself), and close effectively so that everyone knows what will happen next. Used wisely, meeting technologies can enhance collaboration, particularly with far-flung virtual teams.

Critical thinking: (1) Should meetings always follow a strict agenda? Why or why not? (2) Do virtual reality systems such as Second Life have the potential to be mainstream business tools? Why or why not?

It's your business: (1) Have you used any meeting technologies to work on school projects? (2) Have you played any multiplayer video games that require skills in collaboration? If so, how might you apply these skills to business meetings?

Key terms to know: agenda, minutes

EXHIBIT 8.10

Virtual Meetings in a Virtual World

Cranial Tap, whose online headquarters is shown here, is one of a growing number of firms that use Second Life as a virtual meeting place.

Behind the Scenes

Teaming Up for Success at The Container Store

The Container Store was not started with a modest goal. Founders Garrett Boone and Kip Tindell set out to become the "best retail store in the United States." Judging by feedback from customers and employees, they just might have succeeded.

As millions of frustrated consumers know all too well, though, delivering great customer service in retail environments isn't easy. The Container Store does it with strong company values, respect for employees, and a structure that promotes teamwork over individual competition. The company's values flow from the idea that people are its greatest asset because they are the key to exceptional service. The notion that "people are our greatest asset" is repeated often in the business world and often without substance to back it up, but The Container Store goes to extraordinary lengths to practice what it preaches.

When selecting new employees, for instance, the company engages in a comprehensive interviewing and selection process to find the perfect person for each position, driven by the belief that "one great person equals three good people in terms of business productivity." Most employees are college educated, almost half come from employee referrals, and most have been customers of the store. They are also self-motivated, team oriented, and passionate about customer service.

Those traits are enhanced by extensive employee development: New full-time employees receive over 200 hours of training in their first year and nearly that much every year thereafter. In comparison, most retailers give new workers less than 10 hours of training per year. As a result, The Container Store employees feel extremely confident in their ability to help customers, and positive feedback from customers continues to build that confidence.

The Container Store also pays three to four times the minimum wage, offering wages as much as 50 to 100 percent above those of other retailers. The financial security builds loyalty and helps keep annual turnover around 20 percent, a fraction of the typical turnover rates in the industry. What's more, salespeople are not paid commissions, unlike retail staffs in many other companies. Without the constant pressure to "make the numbers," it's easier for employees to take their time with customers, using their creative instincts and extensive training to design complete solutions to customers' storage problems. By not paying commissions, The Container Store also helps employees sense that they're all part of a team, rather than being in competition with one another.

That emphasis on teamwork is reinforced twice a day, before opening and after closing, through a meeting called "the huddle." Similar to a huddle in football, it helps give everyone a common purpose: set goals, share information, boost morale, and bond as a team. Morning sessions feature spirited discussions of sales goals and product applications and may include a chorus of "Happy Birthday" for celebrating team members. Evening huddles include more team building and friendly competitions such as guessing the daily sales figures. Tindell believes that full, open communication with employees takes courage but says, "The only way that people feel really, really a part of something is if they know everything."

The Container Store also differs dramatically from many retail establishments in the way it embraces part-time employees. These workers are essential at the busiest times, such as evenings and holiday seasons, but they are treated as second-class citizens in some companies. Not at The Container Store. To begin with, the company refers to them as "prime-time" employees, not part-time, since these staffers are most valuable in those prime-time rush periods. And these people also receive extensive training and are treated as equal members of the team at each store. As one prime-timer in Houston puts it, "Everyone is treated as an important human being. I don't feel like a part-time employee at all—I feel like a professional. They make belonging easy and a source of pride."

By aligning its corporate values with its management practices and its organization structure, The Container Store paves the way for its employees to deliver great customer service. And by frequently astonishing its employees with enlightened leadership, the company sets a strong example for the people in blue aprons who are expected to astonish customers every day.

People outside the company are starting to notice, too. The Container Store has become a consistent winner in such nationwide forums as the annual Performance Through People Award, presented by Northwestern University, and *Fortune* magazine's annual list of "The 100 Best Companies to Work For."[44]

Critical Thinking Questions

1. Based on what you're learned about the way employees at The Container Store interact with customers, do you think that the company emphasizes centralized or decentralized decision making? Explain your answer.

2. How might the company's emphasis on teamwork affect accountability and authority?

3. What effect might a change to commission-based compensation have on the team structure at The Container Store?

LEARN MORE ONLINE

Visit The Container Store's website at www.containerstore.com and read about the company's history, its culture, and the benefits it offers employees. What do you think of the company's belief that one great person equals three good people? What kinds of jobs are available in stores, the home office, and the distribution center? ▪

Key Terms

agenda (232)
agile organization (215)
centralization (218)
chain of command (216)
cohesiveness (229)
committee (223)
core competencies (216)
cross-functional team (223)
decentralization (218)
departmentalization (219)

divisional structure (220)
functional structure (219)
functional team (223)
groupthink (226)
line organization (216)
line-and-staff organization (217)
matrix structure (220)
minutes (233)
network structure (221)
norms (229)

organization chart (215)
organization structure (214)
problem-solving team (222)
self-managed team (222)
span of management (217)
task force (223)
team (222)
virtual team (223)
work specialization (216)

Test Your Knowledge

Questions for Review

1. What are the advantages and disadvantages of work specialization?

2. What are the advantages and disadvantages of functional departmentalization?

3. What are the advantages and disadvantages of working in teams?

4. What are the characteristics of tall organizations and flat organizations?

5. What is an agile organization?

Questions for Analysis

6. Why is it important for companies to decide on their core competencies before choosing an organization structure?

7. What can managers do to help teams work more effectively?

8. How can a virtual organization reduce costs?

9. How can companies benefit from using virtual teams?

10. **Ethical Considerations.** You were honored to be selected to serve on the salary committee of the employee negotiations task force. As a member of that committee, you reviewed confidential company documents listing the salaries of all department managers. You discovered that managers at your level are earning $25,000 more than you, even though you've been at the company the same amount of time. You feel that a raise is justified on the basis of this confidential information. How will you handle this situation?

Questions for Application

11. You've recently accepted a job as the U.S. sales manager for a German manufacturing company. One of your first assignments is serving on a virtual problem-solving team with colleagues from Germany, France, Japan, and South Korea. Budgets are tight, so you won't have the opportunity to meet with your teammates in person to get to know one another. What steps can you take to help the team develop into a cohesive and efficient unit?

12. You are the leader of a cross-functional work team whose goal is to find ways of lowering production costs. Your team of eight employees has become mired in the storming stage. They disagree on how to approach the task, and they are starting to splinter into factions. What can you do to help the team move forward?

13. **Concept Integration.** One of your competitors has approached you with an intriguing proposition. The company would like to merge with your company. The economies of scale are terrific. So are the growth possibilities. There's just one issue to be resolved. Your competitor is organized under a flat structure and uses lots of cross-functional teams. Your company is organized under a traditional tall structure that is departmentalized by function. Using your knowledge about culture clash (see page 159), what are the likely issues you will encounter if these two organizations are merged?

14. **Concept Integration.** Chapter 7 discussed several styles of leadership: autocratic, democratic, and laissez-faire. Using your knowledge about the differences in these leadership styles, which style would you expect to find under the following organization structures: (a) tall organization—departmentalization by function; (b) tall organization—departmentalization by matrix; (c) flat organization; and (d) self-directed teams?

Practice Your Knowledge

Sharpening Your Communication Skills

In group meetings, some of your colleagues have a habit of interrupting and arguing with the speaker, taking credit for ideas that aren't theirs, and shooting down ideas they don't agree with. You're the newest person in the group and not sure if this is accepted behavior in this company, but it concerns you both personally and professionally. Should you go with the flow and adopt their behavior or stick with your own communication style, even though you might get lost in the noise? In two paragraphs, explain the pros and cons of both approaches.

Building Your Team Skills

What's the most effective organization structure for your college or university? With your team, obtain a copy of your school's organization chart. If this chart is not readily available, gather information by talking with people in administration, and then draw your own chart of the organization structure.

Analyze the chart in terms of span of management. Is your school a flat or a tall organization? Is this organization structure appropriate for your school? Does decision making tend to be centralized or decentralized in your school? Do you agree with this approach to decision making?

Finally, investigate the use of formal and informal teams in your school. Are there any problem-solving teams, task forces, or committees at work in your school? Are any teams self-directed or virtual? How much authority do these teams have to make decisions? What is the purpose of teamwork in your school? What kinds of goals do these teams have?

Share your team's findings during a brief classroom presentation, and then compare the findings of all teams. Is there agreement on the appropriate organization structure for your school?

Expand Your Knowledge

Discovering Career Opportunities

Whether you're a top manager, first-line manager (supervisor), or middle manager, your efforts will affect the success of your organization. To get a closer look at what the responsibilities of a manager are, log on to the Prentice Hall Student Success SuperSite at www.prenhall.com/success. Click on Majors Exploration, and select "management" in the drop-down box. Then scroll down and read about careers in management.

1. What can you do with a degree in management?
2. What is the future outlook for careers in management?
3. Follow the link to the American Management Association website, and click on Research. Then scroll down and click on Administrative Professionals Current Concerns Survey. According to the survey, what has affected administrative professionals most recently? On which five tasks do managers spend most of their time?

Developing Your Research Skills

Although teamwork can benefit many organizations, introducing and managing team structures can be a real challenge. Search past issues of business journals or newspapers (print or online editions) to locate articles about how an organization has overcome problems with teams.

1. Why did the organization originally introduce teams? What types of teams are being used?

2. What problems did each organization encounter in trying to implement teams? How did the organization deal with these problems?
3. Have the teams been successful from management's perspective? From the employees' perspective? What effect has teamwork had on the company, its customers, and its products?

Improving Your Tech Insights: Wireless Networking

Wireless networking gives businesses two major benefits. The first is making information available where and when it can be most useful. The second major benefit is simplifying the connection between people and computers. This can help in a variety of ways, from making it easier to add networking to an older building that doesn't have wires running through the walls to enabling business teams to move around large corporate campuses (to attend team meetings, for example) without losing their connections to the company network. Research the ways businesses are using wireless networking to overcome organizational boundaries, enhance teamwork, or improve meetings. Identify three examples in a brief e-mail to your instructor.

Video Discussion

Access the Chapter 8 video discussion in the End of Chapter Assignments section at www.mybizlab.com.

PEARSON my**biz**lab

Log on to www.mybizlab.com to access the following study and assessment aids associated with this chapter:

- Interactive exercises
- Pre/post test
- Real-Time Updates
- Video application
- Customized study plans
- Biz Skills Simulations
- Quick Learning Guide

If you are not using mybizlab, you can access Real-Time Updates and Quick Learning Guides through http://realtimeupdates.com/bia5. The Quick Learning Guide (located under "Learn More" on the website) provides all six Checkpoints in a handy two-page format to help you study for exams or review important concepts whenever you need a quick refresher.

LEARNING OBJECTIVES

After studying this chapter, you will be able to

1 Explain the systems perspective and identify seven principles of systems thinking that can improve your skills as a manager

2 Describe the *value chain* and *value web* concepts and discuss the controversy over offshoring

3 Define *supply chain management* and explain its strategic importance

4 Identify the major planning decisions in production and operations management

5 Explain the unique challenges of service delivery

6 Highlight the differences between *quality control* and *quality assurance*

Customizing Dreams at Carvin Guitars

www.carvin.com

After beginning guitarists have mastered the nuances of "Mary Had a Little Lamb" and set their sights on making serious music, they often encounter a serious equipment dilemma. Low-cost, beginner guitars lack the materials and workmanship needed to produce top-quality sounds. Some are difficult to keep in tune, and some cannot produce true notes all the way up and down the neck. Plus, they just aren't very cool. Nobody wants to jump on stage in front of 50,000 adoring fans with a guitar purchased at the local discount store.

Carvin offers personalized guitars at affordable prices through a combination of sophisticated production systems and old-world handicraft.

And so the shopping begins, as the aspiring guitarist looks to find a better "axe." As with just about every product category these days, the array of choices is dizzying. For a few hundred dollars, budding musicians can choose from several imports that offer improved quality. Jumping up toward a thousand to two thousand dollars, they can enter the world of such classic American brands as Fender, Gibson, and Martin—a world that reaches up to $10,000 and beyond for limited-edition models. Musicians with that much to spend and several months to wait can also hire skilled instrument builders known as *luthiers* to create custom guitars that reflect their individual personalities and playing styles. Luthiers can custom-craft just about any attribute a guitarist might want, from the types of wood used in the body to the radius of the fingerboard.

But what if our superstar-in-training wants it all: world-class quality, the personalized touch of a custom guitar, and a mid-range price tag, without the long delays associated with handcrafted instruments?

That "sweet spot" in the guitar market is the territory staked out by Carvin, a San Diego company that has been in the instrument business for over 60 years. How could Carvin profitably do business in this seemingly impossible market segment? How could they quickly customize guitars and sell them in the $750 to $1,500 range without compromising quality?[1] ■

Introduction

Carvin (profiled in the chapter-opening Behind the Scenes) faced a classic systems challenge: how to design and operate business processes that would enable the company to deliver its unique value to customers. This chapter starts with an overview of systems concepts that every manager can use in any functional area; it then explores systems-related issues in the production function, including value chains and value webs, supply chain management, production and operations management, services delivery, and product and process quality.

The Systems View of Business

system
An interconnected and coordinated set of *elements* and *processes* that converts *inputs* to desired *outputs*

One of the most important skills you can develop as a manager is the ability to view business from a systems perspective. A **system** is an interconnected and coordinated set of *elements* and *processes* that converts *inputs* into desired *outputs*. A company is made up of numerous individual systems in the various functional areas, not only in manufacturing or operation but also in engineering, marketing, accounting, and other areas that together constitute the overall system that is the company itself. Each of these individual systems can also be thought of as a *subsystem* of the overall business.

Thinking in Systems

To grasp the power of systems thinking, consider a point, a line, and a circle (see Exhibit 9.1). If you poked your head into a nearby office building, what would this snapshot tell you? You could see only one part of the entire operation—and only at this one point in time. You might see people in the advertising department working on plans for a new ad campaign or people in the accounting department juggling numbers in spreadsheets, but neither view would tell you much about what it takes to complete these tasks or how that department interacts with the rest of the company.

If you stood and observed for several days, though, you could start to get a sense of how people do their jobs in this department. In the advertising department, for instance, you could watch as the staff transforms ideas, information, and goals into a plan that leads to the creation of a new online advertising campaign. Your "point" view would thereby extend into a "line" view, with multiple points connected in sequence. However, you still wouldn't have a complete picture of the entire process in action. Was the campaign successful? Did it generate enough revenue to finance another campaign? What did the marketing department learn from the campaign that could help it do even better next time? To see the process operate over and over, you need to connect the end of the line (the completion of this ad campaign) back to the beginning of the line (the start of the next ad campaign) to create a circle. Now you're beginning to form a systems view of what this department does and how its performance can be improved.

This circular view helps you understand the advertising system better, but it still isn't complete, because it doesn't show you how the advertising system affects the rest of the company, and vice versa. For instance, did the finance department provide enough money to run the ad campaign? Was the information technology group prepared to handle the surge in website traffic? Was the manufacturing department ready with enough materials to build the product after customers started placing orders? Were the sales and

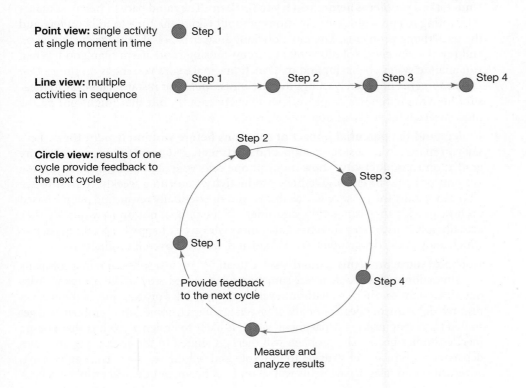

Point view: single activity at single moment in time — Step 1

Line view: multiple activities in sequence — Step 1 → Step 2 → Step 3 → Step 4

Circle view: results of one cycle provide feedback to the next cycle — Step 1, Step 2, Step 3, Step 4, Measure and analyze results, Provide feedback to the next cycle

EXHIBIT 9.1

From Point to Line to Circle: The Systems View

The systems view considers all the steps in a process and "closes the loop" by providing feedback from the output of one cycle back to the input of the next cycle.

customer service departments ready to handle the increase in their workloads? Each of these departments has its own system (its own "circle"), and all the subsystems connect to form the overall business system. Only by looking at the interconnected business system can you judge whether the ad campaign was a success for the company as a whole.

Managing Systems for Peak Performance

Professionals who specialize in systems analysis use a special language, complete with symbols that represent various elements and processes within a system. By simulating systems on computers, they can also predict the impact of business decisions before making any resource decisions (see Exhibit 9.2). These computer simulations, the basis of the related field of *systems dynamics*, allow decision makers to evaluate scenarios far more complicated than the human mind can grasp by looking at diagrams on paper.[2] However, even without learning the formal terminology, you can benefit from systems thinking by keeping these basic principles in mind:[3]

- **Help everyone see the big picture.** It's only human nature for individual employees and departments to focus on their own goals and lose sight of what the company as a whole is trying to accomplish. Showing people how they contribute to the overall goal—and rewarding them for doing so—helps ensure that the entire system works efficiently.

- **Understand how individual systems really work and how they interact.** Let's say you've just been put in charge of setting prices for a company that sells complex products to other companies. This industry has a long tradition in which suppliers set prices high but customers then negotiate down before purchasing. You conclude that all this negotiating is a waste of time since the prices usually end up at a lower level anyway. To make things efficient, you decide to lower the price to begin with and tell customers these new low prices aren't negotiable. Your prices are effectively the same as before, but sales drop off quickly. Why? You failed to realize that with the long history of price negotiations in this industry, purchasing agents in the customer organizations are rewarded for negotiating steep discounts. Buying from you makes the purchasing agents look bad because they can no longer negotiate big discounts. In other words, the change you made to your system made it incompatible with their systems.

- **Understand problems before you try to fix them.** The rapid pace of business makes it tempting to apply quick-fix solutions without taking the time to fully understand the underlying problems. The most obvious answer is not always the right answer, and poorly conceived solutions often end up causing more harm than good. When you analyze system behavior and malfunctions, make sure you focus on things that are *meaningful*, not merely things that are *measurable*. For instance, it's easy to measure how many reports employees write every month, but that might not be the most meaningful gauge of how well a process is working.

- **Understand the potential impact of solutions before you implement them.** Let's say you manage the customer support department, and one of the factors you are graded on is productivity—how many phone calls your staff can handle in a given amount of time. To encourage high productivity, you run a weekly contest to see who can handle the most calls. Trouble is, you're essentially rewarding people based on how quickly they can get the customer off the phone, not on how quickly they actually solve customer problems. Customers who aren't happy keep calling back—which adds to the department's workload and *decreases* overall productivity.

- **Don't just move problems around—solve them.** When one subsystem in a company is malfunctioning, its problems are sometimes just moved around the company, from one subsystem to the next, without ever getting solved. For example, if the market research department does a poor job of understanding customers, this problem will get shifted to the engineering department, which is likely to design a product that doesn't meet customer needs. The problem will then get shifted to the advertising and sales departments, which will struggle to promote and sell the product. The engineering, advertising, and sales departments will all underperform, but the real problem is back

EXHIBIT 9.2 **System Diagram and Simulation**

This example of a formal systems diagram models the flow of people at a ski resort, from arriving at the chairlift to taking the lift up to skiing down the hill, then returning to the lift line. The resort is anticipating a boom in business and needs to figure out how to handle the additional skiers. By mathematically modeling the number of skiers at each point in the system, the resort can simulate several options: doing nothing, getting a faster chairlift, switching to triple chairs, or switching to quadruple chairs. Doing nothing would result in a long line waiting to get on the lift, while getting a faster lift (shown in the graph) would solve that problem but result in overcrowding on the slope. The optimum solution turned out to be switching to quad chairs.

Ski Resort Dynamics
Core Model Structure

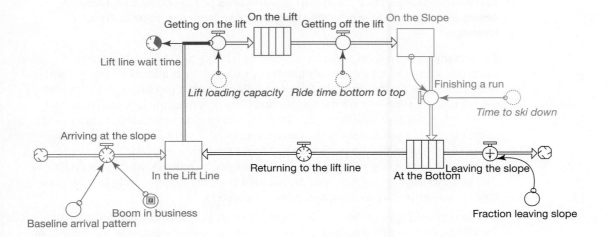

Ski Resort Dynamics
Simulate

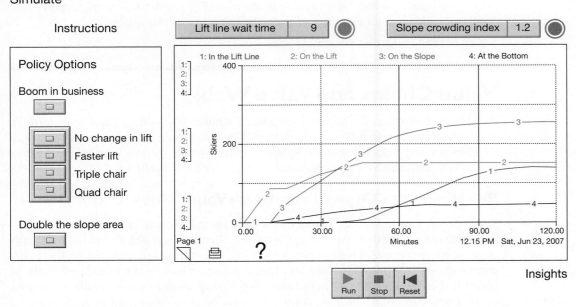

in the market research department. Market research in this case is a *leverage point*, where a relatively small correction could make the entire company perform better.

■ **Understand how feedback works in the system.** Systems respond to *feedback*, which is information from the output applied back to the input. In the case of an ad campaign, the response from target customers is a form of feedback that helps the department understand whether the campaign is working. Feedback can work in unanticipated ways, too. A good example is when managers send mixed signals to their employees, such as telling them that customer satisfaction is the top priority but then criticizing anyone who spends too much time helping customers. Employees will respond to this feedback by spending less time with customers, leading to a decline in customer satisfaction.

■ **Use mistakes as opportunities to learn and improve.** When mistakes occur, resist the temptation to just criticize or complain and then move on. Pull the team together and find out why the mistake occurred, and then identify ways to fix the system to eliminate mistakes in the future.

✓ CHECKPOINT

LEARNING OBJECTIVE 1: Explain the systems perspective, and identify seven principles of systems thinking that can improve your skills as a manager.

Summary: The systems perspective involves looking at business as a series of interconnected and interdependent systems, rather than as a lot of individual activities and events. Seven principles of systems thinking that can help every manager are (1) helping everyone see the big picture, (2) understanding how individual systems really work and how they interact, (3) understanding problems before you try to fix them, (4) understanding the potential impact of solutions before you implement, (5) avoiding the temptation to just move problems from one subsystem to the next without fixing them, (6) understanding how feedback works in a system so that you can improve each process by learning from experience, and (7) using mistakes as opportunities to learn and improve a system.

Critical thinking: (1) Why are leverage points in a system so critical to understand? (2) Why should a manager in marketing care about systems in the finance or manufacturing departments?

It's your business: (1) How could a systems approach to thinking help you get up to speed quickly in your first job after graduation? (2) Think back to your experience of registering for this class. How might you improve this system?

Key terms to know: system

Value Chains and Value Webs

value chain
All the elements and processes that add value as raw materials are transformed into the final products made available to the ultimate customer

As Chapter 1 explains, the essential purpose of a business is adding value, transforming lower-value inputs into higher-value outputs. The **value chain** is a helpful way to view all the elements and processes that add value as input materials are transformed into the final products made available to the ultimate customer (see Exhibit 9.3).[4]

Redefining the Organization with Value Webs

outsourcing
Contracting out certain business functions or operations to other companies

In the decades since Michael Porter introduced the value chain concept, many companies have come to realize that doing everything themselves is not always the most efficient or most successful way to run a business. Many now opt to focus on their core competencies (see page 216) and let other companies handle the remaining business functions—a strategy known as **outsourcing**. Hiring other firms to handle some tasks is not a new concept, to be sure; companies have been relying on other companies for specific services for as long as organized business has been around. For instance, advertising, public relations, accounting, and transportation are services that have a long history of being handled by outside firms. The term *outsourcing* is usually applied when a firm decides to move a significant function that was previously done in house, such as information technology or manufacturing, to an outside vendor.

EXHIBIT 9.3   **Input-Transformation-Output Relationships for Typical Production Services**

Both goods and services undergo a conversion process, but the components of the process vary to accommodate the differences between tangible and intangible outputs.

SYSTEM	REPRESENTATIVE INPUTS	TRANSFORMATION COMPONENTS	TRANSFORMATION FUNCTION	TYPICAL DESIRED OUTPUT
Restaurant	Hungry customers, food	Chef, wait staff, environment	Prepare and serve food	Satisfied customers
Automobile factory	Sheet steel, engine parts	Tools, equipment, workers	Fabricate and assemble cars	High-quality cars
Department store	Shoppers, stock of goods	Displays, salesclerks	Attract shoppers, promote products	Sales to satisfied customers
Online business information service	Company reports, interviews, research services	Researchers, writers, web producers, website servers	Research, analyze write content, produce web pages	Helpful web content for paid subscribers

The combination of extensive globalization in many industries and the development of electronic networking has made it easy for companies to connect with partners around the world. Instead of the linear value chain, some businesses now think in terms of **value webs**, multidimensional networks of suppliers and outsourcing partners.[5] Value webs enable the virtual or network organization structures discussed in Chapter 8.

The outsourced, value-web approach has several key advantages, including speed, flexibility, and the opportunity to access a wide range of talents and technologies that might be expensive or impossible to acquire otherwise. Established companies can narrow their focus to excel at their core competencies; entrepreneurs with product ideas can quickly assemble a team of designers, manufacturing plants, and distributors in far less time than it would take to build an entire company from scratch. When Jim Van Dine wanted to launch a sports shoe company to go up against the likes of Nike, Trek, and other established brands, he and his partners created a value web of freelance product designers, manufacturing consultants, and other independent specialists. Shoe companies normally take 10 months or more to design new models and get samples ready for retailers. Using a web of partners, Van Dine's team had 16 new shoe models ready in only two months. Their company, Keen Footwear (www.keenfootwear.com), took off like a rocket, registering $30 million in sales the first year. By comparison, Teva, another casual footwear maker, needed three years to hit $1 million in sales.[6]

For all its potential advantages, outsourcing does carry some risks, particularly in terms of control. For example, to get its new 787 Dreamliner to market as quickly as possible, Boeing outsourced the manufacturing of many parts of the new airliner to other manufacturers. Boeing managers initially decided not to impose the "Boeing way" on these suppliers, so it took a hands-off approach. However, the lack of control came to haunt the company. Many suppliers missed target dates, throwing the Dreamliner off schedule and costing Boeing billions of dollars in canceled sales and delivery penalties.[7]

value webs
Multidimensional networks of suppliers and outsourcing partners

The Offshoring Controversy

When companies outsource any function in the value chain, they usually eliminate many of the jobs associated

Real-Time Updates

Learn More

See global outsourcing in action

This interactive animation shows the true complexity of the outsourcing involved in Boeing's new 787 Dreamliner. On mybizlab (www.mybizlab .com), you can access Real-Time Updates within each chapter or under Student Study Tools. Otherwise, go to http://real-timeupdates.com/ bia5 and click on "Learn More."

offshoring
Transferring part or all of a business function to a facility (a different part of the company or another company entirely) in another country

with that function as well. And, increasingly, those jobs aren't going across the street to another local company but rather around the world in pursuit of lower costs, a variation on outsourcing known as **offshoring**. (Offshoring can shift jobs to another company or to an overseas division of the same company.)

Offshoring has been going on for decades, but it began to be a major issue for U.S. manufacturing in the 1980s and then for information technology in the 1990s. Today, offshoring is affecting jobs in science, engineering, law, finance, banking, and other professional areas. For example, Dell, HP, IBM, Microsoft, and Accenture are among the many U.S. technology firms that have already moved thousands of jobs to India, which has a large pool of educated workers willing to work for far less than U.S. technology workers. IBM now employs nearly as many workers in India as it does in the United States.[8]

The offshoring debate is a great example of conflicting priorities in the stakeholder model (see page 128), as the arguments for and against offshoring demonstrate.

The following points are frequently made in support of offshoring by U.S. companies:

- **Responsibility to shareholder interests.** Companies that engage in offshoring say they have a duty to manage shareholder investments for maximum gain, so it would be irresponsible not to explore cost-saving opportunities such as offshoring.

- **U.S. competitiveness.** Proponents say that offshoring is crucial to the survival of many U.S. companies and that it saves other U.S. jobs by making U.S. companies more competitive in the global marketplace.

- **Support for local customers around the world.** Some companies say that as they expand into other countries, they have no choice but to hire overseas in order to support local customers.

Those who question the wisdom of offshoring, in terms of either business strategy or national interests, raise a number of compelling issues as well:

- **What jobs will be left?** Opponents of offshoring say that companies are selling out the U.S. middle class in pursuit of profits and starting a trend that can only harm the country. Supporters counter that year after year, the U.S. economy has a remarkable record of creating challenging, high-paying jobs and that no correlation can yet be found between offshoring and U.S. unemployment rates.[9]

- **Hidden costs and risks.** Some company insiders and independent analysts say the real savings from offshoring are often not as significant as proponents have been claiming or not as great as they were in previous years. As a result, says J. Paul Dittman of the University of Tennessee, "Many firms are rethinking the mad rush to outsource outside the United States. The long supply lines, incredibly volatile fuel costs, exchange rates, the geopolitical risks have all come home to roost."[10] One response is *nearshoring*, moving to cheaper labor and materials markets that are closer to home to minimize transportation and management costs.[11] Even in pure service businesses where the physical movement of goods and materials isn't an issue, companies have to address training, communication challenges, management oversight, and the travel time and costs associated with on-site interaction. Offshoring can also involve significant transition costs and difficulties that aren't always considered.[12]

- **Responsiveness.** When companies rely on operations halfway around the world, they can become less responsive to marketplace trends and customer service matters.

- **Knowledge transfer and theft.** By hiring or paying other companies to perform technical and professional services, U.S. companies transfer important knowledge to these other countries—making them more competitive and potentially depleting the pools of expertise in this country.[13] In addition, offshoring can increase the risks of product piracy and the theft of intellectual property.[14]

- **National security concerns.** The weapons and systems used in national defense require lots of steel, semiconductors, and other manufactured materials. What if the United

States comes to rely heavily on other countries for things it needs to protect itself?[15] In the broader sense of economic security, offshoring can also inflict long-term damage on an industry's ability to compete by wiping out local infrastructure and technical skills.[16]

- **Health and safety issues.** Moving operations beyond U.S. borders raises concerns about the ability of regulators to oversee vital health and safety issues. For instance, as U.S. airlines struggle mightily to control costs, half of all the "heavy" maintenance performed on U.S. commercial aircraft is now offshored to places such as Hong Kong and El Salvador. In addition to the challenge of getting enough government inspectors abroad to check on all these facilities, employees in these overseas firms are not subjected to criminal background checks and drug testing as U.S. mechanics are.[17]

Measuring the impact of offshoring on the U.S. economy is difficult. For example, economists often struggle to identify the specific reasons one country gains jobs or another loses them. The emergence of new technology, phasing out of old technology, shifts in consumer tastes, changes in business strategies, and other factors can all create and destroy jobs.

One point just about everyone agrees on is that offshoring is not going away, so it's in everyone's best interest to make it work as well as possible. For example, how should companies be taxed when they have operations all over the world? Also, should unions and regulatory agencies make it more difficult for companies to move jobs overseas, or would it be more beneficial in the long run to let companies compete as vigorously as possible and focus on retraining American workers for new jobs here?

Based on recent trends, it seems likely that offshoring of tangible goods production could slow down, but offshoring of services is likely to speed up. The issues are not simple, however, and you can expect this debate to rage on for years.

✓CHECKPOINT

LEARNING OBJECTIVE 2: Describe the *value chain* and *value web* concepts, and discuss the controversy over offshoring.

Summary: The *value chain* includes all the elements and processes that add value as input materials are transformed into the final products made available to the ultimate customer. The *value web* concept expands this linear model to a multidimensional network of suppliers and outsourcing partners. In the complex argument over *offshoring*, the transfer of business functions to entities in other countries in pursuit of lower costs, proponents claim that (a) companies have a responsibility to shareholder interests to pursue the lowest cost of production, (b) offshoring helps U.S. companies be more competitive, and (c) some companies need to offshore in order to support local customers around the world. Those who question the value or wisdom of offshoring raise points about (a) the future of good jobs in the United States, (b), hidden costs and risks, (c) diminished responsiveness, (d) knowledge transfer and theft issues, (e) national security concerns, (f) and health and safety issues.

Critical thinking: (1) Do U.S. companies have an obligation to keep jobs in the United States? Why or why not? (2) Will global labor markets eventually balance out, with workers in comparable positions all over the world making roughly the same wages? Explain your answer.

It's your business: (1) In your own long-term career planning, have you taken "offshorability" of your target profession into account? (2) Should such concerns affect your career planning?

Key terms to know: value chain, outsourcing, value webs, offshoring

Supply Chain Management

supply chain
A set of connected systems that coordinates the flow of goods and materials from suppliers all the way through to final customers

supply chain management (SCM)
The business procedures, policies, and computer systems that integrate the various elements of the supply chain into a cohesive system

Regardless of how and where it is structured, the lifeblood of every production operation is the **supply chain**, a set of connected systems that coordinates the flow of goods and materials from suppliers all the way through to final customers. Companies with multiple customer bases can also develop a distinct supply chain to serve each segment.[18]

Supply chain management (SCM) combines business procedures and policies with information systems that integrate the various elements of the supply chain into a cohesive system. As companies rely more on outsourcing partners, SCM has grown far beyond the simple procurement of supplies to become a strategic management function that means the difference between success and failure. Successful implementation of SCM can have a profound strategic impact on companies, in three important ways:[19]

- **Managing risks.** SCM can help companies manage the complex risks involved in a supply chain, risks that include everything from cost and availability to health and safety issues.

- **Managing relationships.** SCM can also coordinate the numerous relationships in the supply chain and help managers focus their attention on the most important company-to-company relationships.

- **Managing trade-offs.** Finally, SCM helps managers address the many trade-offs in the supply chain. These trade-offs can be a source of conflict within the company, and SCM helps balance the competing interests of the various functional areas. This holistic view helps managers balance both capacity and capability along the entire chain.

The best supply chains function as true partnerships, with buyers and sellers coordinating their efforts in a win-win approach. For instance, both Toyota and Honda have developed close, cooperative relationships with U.S. parts suppliers as these Japanese firms have expanded their manufacturing presence in North America (60 percent of all Toyotas and 80 percent of all Hondas sold in North America are built in North America). In the Japanese tradition of *keiretsu*, the two companies have spent years "growing" a close-knit supply network that meets their needs and helps their suppliers run their businesses more successfully as well. By developing their supplier network, Toyota and Honda have been able to design new cars in half the time it takes Ford, GM, and Chrysler—all of which have a reputation for more adversarial relationships with their suppliers.[20]

Supply Chains Versus Value Chains

The terms *supply chain* and *value chain* are sometimes used interchangeably, and the distinction between them isn't always clear in everyday usage. One helpful way to distinguish between the two is to view the supply chain as the part of the overall value chain that acquires and manages the goods and services needed to produce whatever it is the company produces and then deliver it to the final customer. Everyone in the company is part of the value chain, but not everyone is involved in the supply chain.[21] Another way to distinguish the two is that the supply chain focuses on the "upstream" part of the process, collecting the necessary materials and supplies with an emphasis on reducing waste and inefficiency. The value chain focuses on the "downstream" part of the process and on adding value in the eyes of customers.[22] Because of the overlap between the two ideas, both conceptually and in terms of the processes and systems used, it's possible that they will increasingly merge in the coming years.

inventory
Goods and materials kept in stock for production or sale

Today's supply chains often span the globe, pulling in parts and materials from multiple countries.

Supply Chain Systems and Techniques

SCM is all about getting the right materials at the right price in the right place at the right time for successful production. Unfortunately, you can't just pile up huge quantities of everything you might eventually need, because **inventory**, the goods and materials kept in stock for production or sale, costs money to purchase and store. On the other hand, not having an adequate supply of inventory can result in expensive delays. This balancing act is the job of **inventory control**, which tries to determine the right quantities of supplies and products to have on hand and then tracks where those items are. One of the most important technologies to emerge in inventory control in recent years is *radio frequency identification (RFID)*.

Real-Time Updates

Learn More

Supply chain management is driving the new Ford

Ford Motor Company knows it needs to redefine how it does business; see how SCM plays a key role in this transformation. On mybizlab (www .mybizlab.com), you can access Real-Time Updates within each chapter or under Student Study Tools. Otherwise, go to http://real-timeupdates .com/bia5 and click on "Learn More."

RFID uses small antenna tags attached to products or shipping containers; special sensors detect the presence of the tags and can track the flow of goods through the supply chain.

Procurement, or *purchasing*, is the acquisition of the raw materials, parts, components, supplies, and finished products required to produce goods and services. The goal of purchasing is to make sure that the company has all the materials it needs, when it needs them, at the lowest possible cost. A company must always have enough supplies on hand to cover a product's *lead time*—the period that elapses between placing the supply order and receiving materials.

To accomplish these goals, operations specialists have developed a variety of systems and techniques over the years:

- **Material requirements planning (MRP)** helps a manufacturer get the correct materials where they are needed, when they are needed, without unnecessary stockpiling. Managers use MRP software to calculate when certain materials will be required, when they should be ordered, and when they should be delivered so that storage costs will be minimal. These systems are so effective at reducing inventory levels that they are used almost universally in both large and small manufacturing firms.

- **Manufacturing resource planning (MRP II)** expands the MRP with links to the company's financial systems and other processes. For instance, in addition to managing inventory levels successfully, an MRP II system can help ensure that material costs adhere to target budgets.[23] Because it draws together all departments, an MRP II system produces a companywide game plan that allows everyone to work with the same numbers. Moreover, the system can track each step of production, allowing managers throughout the company to consult other managers' inventories, schedules, and plans.

- **Enterprise resource planning (ERP)** extends the scope of resource planning and management even further to encompass the entire organization. ERP software programs are typically made up of modules that address the needs of the various functional areas, from manufacturing to sales to human resources. Some companies deploy ERP on a global scale, with a single centralized system connecting all their operations worldwide.[24]

inventory control
Determining the right quantities of supplies and products to have on hand and tracking where those items are

procurement
The acquisition of the raw materials, parts, components, supplies, and finished products required to produce goods and services

✓CHECKPOINT

LEARNING OBJECTIVE 3: Define *supply chain management*, and explain its strategic importance.

Summary: Supply chain management (SCM) combines business procedures and policies with information systems that integrate the various elements of the supply chain into a cohesive system. SCM helps companies manage risks, relationships, and trade-offs throughout their supply chains, building partnerships that help everyone in the supply chain succeed.

Critical thinking: (1) Why can't companies just stockpile huge inventories of all the parts and materials they need, rather than carefully managing supply from one day to the next? (2) Why would a company invest time and money in helping its suppliers improve their business practices? Why not just dump underperformers and get better suppliers?

It's your business: (1) In any current or previous job, what steps have supervisors taken to help you understand your role in the supply chain? (2) Is it dehumanizing to your colleagues and business partners to be participants in a supply chain? Why or why not?

Key terms to know: supply chain, supply chain management (SCM), inventory, inventory control, procurement

Production and Operations Management

The term *production* suggests factories, machines, and assembly lines staffed with employees making automobiles, computers, furniture, motorcycles, or other tangible goods. With the growth in the number of service-based businesses and their increasing importance to the economy, however, the term *production* is now used to describe the transformation of resources into both goods and services. The broader term **production and operations management**, or simply *operations management*, refers to overseeing all the activities involved in producing goods and services. Operations managers are responsible for a wide range of strategies and decisions, from locating production facilities to managing the supply chain.

production and operations management
Overseeing all the activities involved in producing goods and services

Facilities Location and Design

Choosing the location of production facilities is a complex decision that must consider such factors as land, construction, availability of talent, taxes, energy, living standards, transportation, and proximity to customers and business partners. Support from local communities and governments often plays a key role in location decisions as well. To provide jobs and expand their income and sales tax bases, local, state, and national governments often compete to attract companies by offering generous financial incentives such as tax reductions.

After a site has been selected, managers turn their attention to *facility layout,* the arrangement of production work centers and other elements (such as materials, equipment, and support departments) needed to process goods and services. Layout planning includes such decisions as how many steps are needed in the process, the amount and type of equipment and workers needed for each step, how each step should be configured, and where the steps should be located relative to one another.[25]

Well-designed facilities help companies operate more productively by reducing wasted time and wasted materials, but that is far from the only benefit. Smart layouts support close communication and collaboration among employees and help ensure their safety, both of which are important for employee satisfaction and motivation. In the delivery of services, facility layout can be a major influence on customer satisfaction because it affects the overall service experience.[26]

Forecasting and Capacity Planning

Using customer feedback, sales orders, market research, past sales figures, industry analyses, and educated guesses about the future behavior of customers and competitors, operations managers prepare *production forecasts*—estimates of future demand for the company's products. After product demand has been estimated, management must balance that with the company's capacity to produce the goods or services. The term *capacity* refers to the volume of manufacturing or service capability that an organization can handle. **Capacity planning** is the collection of long-term strategic decisions that establish the overall level of resources needed to meet customer demand. When managers at Boeing plan for the production of an airliner, they have to consider not only the staffing of thousands of people but also massive factory spaces, material flows from

capacity planning
Establishing the overall level of resources needed to meet customer demand

EXHIBIT 9.4 A Gantt Chart

A chart like this one enables a production manager to immediately see the dates on which production steps must be started and completed if goods are to be delivered on schedule. Some steps may overlap to save time. For instance, after three weeks of cutting table legs, cutting tabletops begins. This overlap ensures that the necessary legs and tops are completed at the same time and can move on together to the next stage in the manufacturing process.

ID	Task Name	Start Date	End Date	Duration	2010 August	September
1	Make legs	8/1/2010	8/28/2010	20d	▆▆▆▆▆	
2	Cut tops	8/22/2010	8/28/2010	5d	▆	
3	Drill	8/29/2010	9/4/2010	5d	▆	
4	Sand	9/5/2010	9/11/2010	5d		▆
5	Assemble	9/12/2010	9/25/2010	10d		▆▆
6	Paint	9/19/2010	9/25/2010	5d		▆

hundreds of suppliers around the world, internal deliveries, cash flow, tools and equipment, and dozens of other factors. Because of the potential impact on finances, customers, and employees—and the difficulty of reversing major decisions—capacity choices are among the most important decisions that top-level managers make.[27]

Scheduling

In any production process, managers must do *scheduling*—determining how long each operation takes and deciding which tasks are done in which order. Manufacturing facilities often use a *master production schedule (MPS)* to coordinate production of all the goods the company makes. Service businesses use a variety of scheduling techniques as well, from simple appointment calendars for a small business to the comprehensive online systems that airlines and other large service providers use.

To plan and track projects, managers throughout the company can use a *Gantt chart*, a special type of bar chart that shows the progress of all the tasks needed to complete a project (see Exhibit 9.4). For more complex projects, the *program evaluation and review technique (PERT)* is helpful. PERT helps managers identify the optimal sequencing of activities, the

EXHIBIT 9.5 Simplified PERT Diagram for Store Opening

This PERT diagram shows a subset of the many tasks involved in opening a new retail store. The tasks involved in staffing are on the critical path because they take the longest time to complete (51 days), whereas the promotion tasks can be completed in 38 days, and the merchandise tasks can be completed in 39 days. In other words, some delay can be tolerated in the promotion or merchandise tasks, but any delay in any of the staffing tasks will delay the store's opening day.

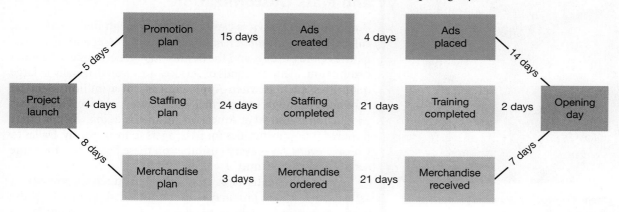

Real-Time Updates

Learn More

Lean manufacturing in action at Toyota Kentucky

See a Toyota progress from a roll of sheet steel to a complete car in only 20 hours. On mybizlab (www.mybizlab.com), you can access Real-Time Updates within each chapter or under Student Study Tools. Otherwise, go to http://real-timeupdates.com/bia5 and click on "Learn More."

critical path
In a PERT network diagram, the sequence of operations that requires the longest time to complete

productivity
The efficiency with which an organization can convert inputs to outputs

lean systems
Manufacturing systems that maximize productivity by reducing waste and delays

just-in-time (JIT)
Inventory management in which goods and materials are delivered throughout the production process right before they are needed

mass production
The creation of identical goods or services, usually in large quantities

customized production
The creation of a unique good or service for each customer

expected time for project completion, and the best use of resources. To use PERT, managers map out all the activities in a network diagram (see Exhibit 9.5). The longest path through the network is known as the **critical path** because it represents the minimum amount of time needed to complete the project. Tasks in the critical path usually receive special attention because they determine when the project can be completed.[28] (If anyone ever says that *you* are in the critical path, make sure you stay on schedule!)

Lean Systems

Throughout all the activities in the production process, operations managers pay close attention to **productivity**, or the efficiency with which they can convert inputs to outputs. (Put another way, productivity is equal to the value of the outputs divided by the value of the inputs.) Productivity is one of the most vital responsibilities in operations management because it is a key factor in determining the company's competitiveness and profitability. Companies that can produce similar goods or services with fewer resources have a distinct advantage over their competitors.

Lean systems, which maximize productivity by reducing waste and delays, are at the heart of many productivity improvement efforts. Many lean systems borrow techniques from Toyota; the *Toyota Production System* is world-renowned for its ability to continually improve both productivity and quality.[29] Central to the notion of lean systems is **just-in-time (JIT)** inventory management, in which goods and materials are delivered throughout the production process right before they are needed, rather than being stockpiled in inventories. Reducing stocks to immediate needs reduces waste and forces factories to keep production flowing smoothly.

The productivity and cost improvements from lean approaches can be dramatic. For example, Conmed, a maker of surgical devices based in Utica, New York, recently redesigned one of its assembly lines using lean concepts. The results were impressive: the same production in 80 percent less floor space with the cost of parts inventory dropping by more than 90 percent and worker productivity climbing by 21 percent. As more U.S. companies "go lean," the country's manufacturing sector stands a much better chance of competing with manufacturers in China and other locations with lower labor costs.[30]

Achieving such benefits requires constant attention to quality and teamwork, because with no spare inventory there is no room for delays or errors.[31] Without stockpiles of extra parts and materials, each stage in the production process goes idle if the stages before it have not delivered on time.

Mass Production, Customized Production, and Mass Customization

Both goods and services can be created through *mass production*, *customized production*, or *mass customization*, depending on the nature of the product and the desires of target customers. In **mass production**, identical goods or services are created, usually in large quantities, such as when Apple churns out a million identical iPhones. Although not normally associated with services, mass production is also what American Airlines is doing when it offers hundreds of opportunities for passengers to fly from, say, Dallas to Chicago every day—every customer on these flights gets the same service at the same time.

At the other extreme is **customized production**, sometimes called *batch-of-one production* in manufacturing, in which the producer creates a unique good or service for each customer. If you

Individual craftspeople often engage in customized production, creating a unique product for each customer.

order a piece of furniture from a local craftsperson, for instance, you can specify everything from the size and shape to the types of wood and fabric used. Or you can hire a charter pilot to fly you wherever you want, whenever you want. Both products are customized to your unique requirements.

Mass production has the advantage of economies of scale, but it can't deliver many of the unique goods and services that today's customers demand. On the other hand, fully customized production can offer uniqueness but usually at a much higher price. An attractive compromise in many cases is **mass customization**, in which part of the product is mass produced and then the remaining features are customized for each buyer. With design and production technologies getting ever more flexible, the opportunities for customization continue to grow. For instance, the Italian motorcycle maker Ducati can now scan a customer's body shape and create the perfect seat to fit.[32] And as you'll read at the end of the chapter, this is the approach Carvin took: Customers get the same basic guitar bodies but their own individual combinations of woods, fingerboard styles, finishes, and electronic components.

mass customization
Manufacturing approach in which part of the product is mass produced and the remaining features are customized for each buyer

✓CHECKPOINT

LEARNING OBJECTIVE 4: Identify the major planning decisions in production and operations management.

Summary: The major decisions in operations management include (1) facilities location and design; (2) forecasting and capacity planning to match resources with demand; (3) scheduling; (4) lean system design to reduce waste and delays; and (5) the choice of mass production, customized production, or mass customization.

Critical thinking: (1) Why is it essential to identify tasks in the critical path of a project? (2) How does mass customization help a company balance productivity and customer satisfaction?

It's your business: (1) The phrase "lean and mean" is sometimes used to describe lean systems. What are the risks of using such language? (2) Is this course an example of mass production, customization, or mass customization? Explain.

Key terms to know: production and operations management, capacity planning, critical path, productivity, lean systems, just-in-time (JIT), mass production, customized production, mass customization

The Unique Challenges of Service Delivery

The intangibility of services creates a number of unique challenges that can affect virtually every aspect of the business. With the majority of workers in the United States now involved in the service sector, managers in thousands of companies need to pay close attention to the unique challenges of delivering services: perishability, location constraints, scalability challenges, performance variability and perceptions of quality, and customer involvement and service provider interaction.

Perishability

Services are *perishable*, meaning they are consumed at the same time they are produced and cannot exist before or after that time. For example, if a 200-seat airliner takes off half empty, those 100 sales opportunities are lost forever. The airline can't create these products ahead of time and store them in inventory until somebody is ready to buy. Similarly, restaurants can seat only so many people every night, so empty tables represent revenue lost forever. This perishability can have a profound impact on the way service businesses are managed, from staffing (making sure enough people are on hand to help with peak demands) to pricing (using discounts to encourage people to buy services when they are available).

Location Constraints

Perishability also means that for many services, customers and providers need to be in the same place at the same time. The equipment and food ingredients used in a restaurant can be produced just about anywhere, but the restaurant itself needs to be located close to customers and be open when customers want to eat. One of the most significant commercial advantages of the Internet is the way it has enabled many service businesses to get around this constraint. Online retailers, information providers, and other e-businesses can locate virtually anywhere on the planet.

Scalability Challenges and Opportunities

scalability
The potential to increase production by expanding or replicating its initial production capacity

Any business that wants to grow must consider the issue of **scalability**, the potential to increase production by expanding or replicating its initial production capacity. Scaling up always creates some challenges, but service businesses that depend on the skills of specific professionals can be particularly difficult to scale. Examples range from chefs and interior designers to business consultants and graphic designers, particularly when the business is built around the reputation of a single person.

Of course, many goods businesses also rely on highly skilled production workers, but the potential to mechanize goods production can make it easier to scale up manufacturing in some cases. For example, by using computer-controlled routers to carve the bodies of its guitars, Carvin (page 258) frees itself from the constraint of hiring enough skilled carvers to do it all by hand.

Performance Variability and Perceptions of Quality

For many types of services, the quality of the service performance can vary from one instance to the next—and that quality is in the eye of the beholder and often can't be judged until after the service has been performed. If you manufacture scissors, you can specify a certain grade of steel from your suppliers and use automated machinery to produce thousands of identical scissors of identical quality. Many key attributes such as the size and strength of the scissors are *objective* and measurable, and customers can experience the *subjective* variables such as the feel and action before they buy. In other words, there is little mystery and little room for surprise in the purchase.

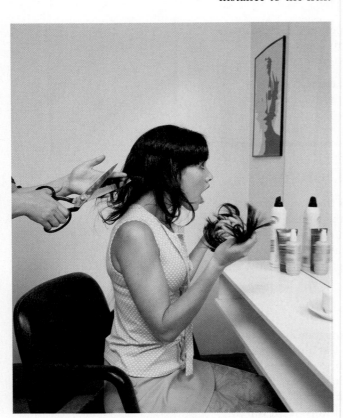

One of the many challenges of providing services is that the evaluation of quality is often subjective.

However, if you create a haircut using a pair of those scissors, perceptions of quality become almost entirely subjective *and* impossible to judge until after the service is complete. Plus, hair styling is a good example of a service in which *quality of experience* is an important part of customer perceptions as well, which is why, for instance, most salons pay a lot of attention to architecture, interior design, lighting, music, and other amenities that have nothing to do with the actual haircut itself.

Customer Involvement and Provider Interaction

One of the biggest differences between goods and services production is the fact that customers are often involved in—and thereby can affect the quality of—the service delivery. For instance, personal trainers can instruct clients in the proper way to exercise, but if the clients don't follow directions, the result will be unsatisfactory. Similarly, a business consultant relies on accurate information from managers in a client organization; lacking that, he or she will be unable to craft the most effective advice.

When customers and service providers interact, the quality of the interpersonal experience also affects customer perceptions of quality. In this sense, service delivery is something of a performance that needs to instill confidence in the client. Weak communication skills or poor etiquette can create dissatisfaction with a service experience that is satisfactory or even exceptional in all other respects.

For the latest information on production systems, visit http://real-timeupdates .com/bia5 and click on Chapter 9.

√ CHECKPOINT

LEARNING OBJECTIVE 5: Explain the unique challenges of service delivery.

Summary: The delivery of services presents a number of unique challenges, including (1) perishability, which means that services are consumed at the same time they are produced; (2) location constraints, which often require that customers and service providers be in the same place at the same time; (3) scalability challenges, which can make some types of service businesses more difficult to expand; (4) performance variability and perceptions of quality, which heighten the challenge of delivering consistent quality and increase the subjectivity of the customer experience; and (5) customer involvement and service provider interaction, which can put some of the responsibility for service quality on the customer's shoulders and increase the importance of the good interpersonal skills.

Critical thinking: (1) How can technology help some service businesses address the challenge of scalability? (2) If customers are paying for a service, why should they ever have to share in the responsibility of ensuring quality results?

It's your business: (1) Do you think you have a natural personality for working in a service business? Why or why not? (2) If you're not a "natural," what steps could you take to succeed in a service job anyway?

Key terms to know: scalability

Product and Process Quality

Whether dealing with goods or services, quality has become a global imperative in practically every industry. To survive, companies today must produce high-quality goods and services as efficiently as possible. In some industries, quality is literally a matter of life and death. Nearly 100,000 deaths in the United States every year are attributed to medical errors; in Canada, a quarter of all patients who seek medical care wind up getting another illness as a result of medical mistakes.[33] Even in less dramatic settings, quality problems waste time and money, frustrate customers, and erode confidence in companies and their products.

The traditional means of maintaining quality is called **quality control**—measuring quality against established standards after the good or service has been produced and weeding out any defects. A more comprehensive approach is **quality assurance**, a holistic system of integrated policies, practices, and procedures designed to ensure that every product meets preset quality standards. Quality assurance includes quality control as well as doing the job right the first time by designing tools and machinery properly, demanding quality parts from suppliers, encouraging customer feedback, training employees, empowering them, and encouraging them to take pride in their work.

Statistical Process Control and Continuous Improvement

Quality assurance often includes the use of **statistical process control (SPC)**, which involves taking samples from the process periodically and plotting observations of the

quality control
Measuring quality against established standards after the good or service has been produced and weeding out any defective products

quality assurance
A more comprehensive approach of companywide policies, practices, and procedures to ensure that every product meets quality standards

statistical process control (SPC)
Use of random sampling and control charts to monitor the production process

samples on a *control chart*. A large enough sample provides a reasonable estimate of the entire process. By observing the random fluctuations graphed on the chart, managers can identify whether such changes are normal or whether they indicate that some corrective action is required in the process.[34]

In addition to using SPC, companies can empower each employee to continuously improve the quality of goods production or service delivery. The Japanese word for continuous improvement is *kaizen*. Japanese manufacturers learned long before many U.S. manufacturers that continuous improvement is not something that can be delegated to one or a few people. Instead, it requires the full participation of every employee. This approach means encouraging all workers to spot quality problems, halt production when necessary, generate ideas for improvement, and adjust work routines as needed.[35]

Sometimes, however, the sure and steady pace of kaizen isn't fast enough to respond to problems or react to changes in the marketplace.[36] Toyota president Katsuaki Watanabe now encourages his employees to explore *kakushin*, meaning revolutionary change. Toyota's newest facility in Takaoka, Japan, represents such a radical departure. Rather than just being lean, the manufacturing process is "simple, slim, and speedy." By reducing complexity, Toyota hopes to dramatically reduce mistakes. For instance, one goal is to physically move parts as little as possible, since every move is an opportunity for a part to be damaged.[37]

Total Quality Management and Six Sigma

total quality management (TQM)
A management philosophy and strategic management process that focuses on delivering the optimal level of quality to customers by building quality into every organizational activity

One of the most comprehensive approaches to quality is known as **total quality management (TQM)**, which is both a management philosophy and a strategic management process that focuses on delivering the optimal level of quality to customers by building quality into every organizational activity. Implementing TQM requires six elements:[38]

- Management commitment to supporting TQM at every level in the organization
- Clear focus on customers and their needs
- Employee involvement throughout the organization
- Commitment to continuous improvement
- Willingness to treat suppliers as partners
- Meaningful performance measurements

TQM was one of the hot management topics in the 1980s and 1990s, and some businesses that tried to establish TQM failed at the effort, for reasons ranging from an inability to change the corporate culture to ineffective measurement techniques.[39] TQM doesn't receive the attention that it once did in the business media, either, and some observers now dismiss it as another management fad that came and went. However, the principles of TQM infuse much of today's managerial practice, even if managers don't always use the TQM label.[40]

Six Sigma
A rigorous quality management program that strives to eliminate deviations between the actual and desired performance of a business system

An alternative approach to focusing an organization on quality processes and products is **Six Sigma**, a "fully integrated management system" that "aligns business strategy with improvement efforts," in the words of Motorola, which pioneered the concept and has realized more than $17 billion in productivity savings from it since the late 1980s. (*Six sigma* is a statistical term that indicates 3.4 defects per million opportunities—near perfection, in other words.) Six Sigma is a highly disciplined, systematic approach to reducing the deviation from desired goals in virtually any business process, whether it's eliminating defects in the creation of a product or improving a company's cash flow.[41] Six Sigma efforts typically follow a five-step approach, known as DMAIC for short:[42]

1. **D**efine the problem that needs to solved
2. **M**easure current performance to see how far it deviates from desired performance

3. Analyze the root causes of this deviation from the ideal

4. Improve the process by brainstorming, selecting, and implementing changes

5. Control the process long-term to make sure performance continues to meet expectations

Real-Time Updates

Learn More
Explore the power of Six Sigma

This quick tour of Six Sigma concepts will help you understand why this is such a powerful approach to solving productivity and quality problems. On mybizlab (www.mybizlab.com), you can access Real-Time Updates within each chapter or under Student Study Tools. Otherwise, go to http://real-timeupdates.com/bia5 and click on "Learn More."

Six Sigma shares the same focus on the customer and emphasis on employee involvement as TQM but provides a simpler and widely accepted set of methods for business teams to follow. More than 80 percent of the largest companies in the United States now have Six Sigma programs, but like TQM, Six Sigma doesn't work when it is applied poorly or applied to the wrong problem. For instance, some experts argue that the rigid DMAIC framework can hamper the open-ended creative thinking that is required for new product design.[43]

Global Quality Standards

In addition to meeting the quality expectations of their customers, many companies now face the need to meet international quality standards as well. For instance, many companies in Europe require that suppliers comply with standards set by the International Organization for Standardization (ISO), a global network of performance standards bodies based in Geneva, Switzerland. The ISO oversees a vast array of product standards, but the two of most general concern to businesses are the *ISO 9000* family, which concerns quality and customer satisfaction, and *ISO 14000*, which concerns environmental issues. Hundreds of thousands of organizations around the world have implemented ISO standards, making it a universally recognized indicator of compliance. The ISO 9000 and ISO 14000 families both focus on management systems, the processes and policies that companies use to create their goods and services, rather than on the goods and services themselves. Achieving ISO certification sends a reassuring signal to other companies that your internal processes meet these widely accepted international standards.[44]

CHECKPOINT

LEARNING OBJECTIVE 6: Highlight the differences between *quality control* **and** *quality assurance.*

Summary: The two fundamental differences between quality control and quality assurance are timing and intent. Roughly speaking, quality control steps in at the end of a process to see whether anything went wrong, whereas quality assurance works right from the very beginning of the process to make sure everything goes right. With these two differences, you can see how a quality assurance approach is better for improving both product and process quality over time.

Critical thinking: (1) Why is quality control an essential part of quality assurance? (2) How can process simplicity contribute to quality?

It's your business: (1) Are the grades you get in your various classes an example of quality control or quality assurance? Explain your answer. (2) Have you ever tried anything like the Six Sigma DMAIC process in your own life, even partially or informally?

Key terms to know: quality control, quality assurance, statistical process control (SPC), total quality management (TQM), Six Sigma

Behind the Scenes

Carvin's Production System Satisfies Demanding Guitarists

Carvin has made a name for itself among serious guitarists by filling the gap between mass-produced and fully custom guitars. The company's secret has been perfecting the art and science of *mass customization*, the ability to adapt standardized products to the tastes of individual customers. In two to six weeks, and for roughly $700 to $1,500, Carvin can customize one of several dozen models of guitars and basses. All are available in a wide variety of woods, paints, stains, finishes, electronics, and even the slight curvature in the fingerboard; there are so many choices that the discussion boards on Carvin's website buzz with debates about which combinations are "best" for specific styles of music.

Carvin's factory combines old-world craftsmanship with new-world technologies. Because the custom guitars are built on a standard set of body shapes and styles, Carvin can use computer-controlled cutting and milling machines that cut and shape the bodies and necks quickly and precisely. A diamond-surface finishing machine mills fingerboards to tolerances of a thousandth of an inch. A dehumidification chamber removes internal stresses from the wood used in the guitar necks to minimize the chance of warping years down the road. Experienced craftspeople with sensitive eyes and ears take over from there, performing such tasks as matching veneer pieces on guitar tops (veneers are thin sheets of wood, usually exotic or expensive species), adjusting the action (the feel of the strings against the frets), and listening to the tone quality of finished instruments.

As with any customized offering, the buyer's involvement in the production process is a vital step in ensuring customer satisfaction. Carvin has several retail stores, but all are located in California, so most buyers interact with the company online. The company's website presents each guitar on a page that lists standard features, provides an interactive list of customization options, and computes the total price for the desired configuration. A pop-up window called the "virtual custom shop" lets online shoppers preview the many woods, paints, and stains. Buyers can quickly see what their dream instruments would look like in every shade from natural maple to translucent blue.

With this blend of automation and human touch, Carvin produces over 1,000 instruments a year that win rave reviews from appreciative customers. "Nothing can touch it in terms of sound quality and workmanship" and "I haven't seen anything close to this price that can outperform it" are typical of the comments that Carvin customers post online. Upon hearing a salesperson in another music store speak disparagingly of the brand, one indignant Carvin owner retrieved his guitar from his car and put on an impromptu concert for the store's sales staff to demonstrate just how good the Carvin product sounded. With a proven manufacturing approach and customer loyalty like that, Carvin will be fulfilling the musical dreams of guitarists for years to come.[45]

Critical Thinking Questions

1. If Carvin experienced an increase in orders from its website over a period of two weeks, should it expand its production capacity to make sure it can handle increased demand in the future? Why or why not?
2. Take the virtual tour of Carvin's factory at www .carvinguitars.com/factorytour. How does this information help convince potential buyers to consider Carvin?
3. Wooden musical instruments have been carved by hand for hundreds of years. Why wouldn't Carvin want to continue this tradition?

LEARN MORE ONLINE

Visit the Carvin website at www.carvin.com. How does the company promote its customized products? Step through the process of customizing a guitar or bass; would you feel comfortable purchasing a musical instrument in this manner? Take the virtual factory tour to see computer-controlled machinery and guitar builders in action. Visit the blog and online forums discussion boards; what are Carvin employees and customers talking about these days? ■

Key Terms

capacity planning (250)	inventory control (249)	mass production (252)
critical path (252)	just-in-time (JIT) (252)	offshoring (246)
customized production (252)	lean systems (252)	outsourcing (244)
inventory (248)	mass customization (253)	procurement (249)

production and operations
  management (250)
productivity (252)
quality assurance (255)
quality control (255)

scalability (254)
Six Sigma (256)
statistical process control (SPC) (255)
supply chain (248)
supply chain management (SCM) (248)

system (240)
total quality management
  (TQM) (256)
value chain (244)
value webs (245)

Test Your Knowledge

Questions for Review

1. What role does feedback play in a system?
2. What is a lean system?
3. What is scalability in terms of managing a service business?
4. What is mass customization?
5. Why is offshoring controversial?

Questions for Analysis

6. Why do some firms now think in terms of value webs instead of value chains?
7. How can supply chain management (SCM) help a company establish a competitive advantage?
8. How does perishability affect the delivery of services?
9. Why is it important to monitor performance variables that are the most meaningful, not those that are the most easily measurable?
10. **Ethical Considerations.** How does society's concern for the environment affect a company's decisions about facility location and layout?

Questions for Application

11. If 30 percent of the patrons eating at your restaurant say they won't eat there again, what steps would you take to define the problem(s) that needs to be solved, measure the relevant performance variables, and then analyze the root cause of the problems(s)?
12. You've developed a reputation as an outstanding math tutor, and you want to turn your talent into a full-time business after graduation. How will you address the challenge of scalability in your new venture?
13. Business is booming. Sales last month were 50 percent higher than the month before, and so far, this month is looking even better than last month. Should you hire more people to accommodate the increase? Explain your answer.
14. **Concept Integration.** How might quality standards affect the efforts of a company that wants to begin expanding internationally?

Practice Your Knowledge

Sharpening Your Communication Skills

As the newly hired manager of Campus Athletics, a shop featuring athletic wear bearing logos of colleges and universities, you are responsible for selecting the store's suppliers. Demand for merchandise with team logos and brands can be quite volatile. When a college team is hot, you've got to have merchandise. You know that selecting the right supplier is a task that requires careful consideration, so you have decided to host a series of selection interviews. Think about all the qualities you would want in a supplier, and develop a list of interview questions that will help you assess whether that supplier possesses those qualities.

Building Your Team Skills

Identify a company that has recently decided to offshore some part of its operations (search online news sources for "offshore outsourcing" or similar terms). With your team, analyze the potential impact of this decision on each of the groups identified in the stakeholder model in Exhibit 4.3 on page 128. Weighing the impact on all the stakeholders, vote on whether this was a wise decision for the company. Be prepared to present your conclusions to the class.

Expand Your Knowledge

Discovering Career Opportunities

Visit the *Occupational Outlook Handbook* at www.bls.gov/oco and locate "Industrial production managers" in the "Management" section.

1. What is the nature of the work? Does the combination of people management and technical problem solving appeal to you?

2. What is the outlook for careers in this profession? If you were interested in this field, would you consider it, given the job outlook?

3. If you decide you want to work in a production-related job, what additional classes should you consider taking before you graduate?

Developing Your Research Skills

Seeking increased efficiency and productivity, a growing number of producers of goods and services are applying technology to improve the production process. Find an article in a business journal or newspaper that discusses how one company used computer-aided design (CAD), computer-aided engineering (CAE), computer-integrated manufacturing (CIM), robots, or other technological innovations to refit or reorganize its production operations.

1. What problems led the company to rethink its production process? What kind of technology did it choose to address these problems? What goals did the company set for applying technology in this way?

2. Before adding the new technology, what did the company do to analyze its existing production process? What changes, if any, were made as a result of this analysis?

3. How did technology-enhanced production help the company achieve its goals for financial performance? For customer service? For growth or expansion?

Improving Your Tech Insights: Nanotechnology

Think small. Really small. Think about manufacturing products a molecule or even a single atom at a time. That's the scale of nanotechnology, a rather vague term that covers research and engineering done at nanoscale, or roughly 1/100,000 the width of a human hair.

The potential uses of nanotechnology range from the practical—smart materials that can change shape and heal themselves, more efficient energy generation and transmission, superstrong and superlight materials for airplanes, better cosmetics, smart medical implants, and ultrasmall computers—to the somewhat wilder—food-growing machines and microscopic robots that could travel through your body to cure diseases and fix injuries. (Like any new technology with lots of promise, nanotechnology also suffers from lots of hype.)

Nanotechnology products have begun to hit the market in a number of industries, from automotive materials to medicine to consumer products. According to the Project on Emerging Nanotechnologies, the most common nanotech consumer products are cosmetics and clothing.

Also, although they're slightly larger than the generally accepted scale of nanotechnology, *microelectromechanical systems (MEMS)* are already having a major impact in some industries. These tiny machines (pumps, valves, and so on), some no bigger than a grain of pollen, are used in the nozzles of ink-jet printers, air bag sensors, and ultraprecise miniature laboratory devices.

Conduct research to identify a product currently on the market that uses nanotechnology in some fashion. In an e-mail message to your instructor, describe the product, its target market, the role nanotechnology plays in the product's design, and any known safety concerns regarding the use of nanotechnology in this or similar products.[46]

Video Discussion

Access the Chapter 9 video discussion in the End of Chapter Assignments section at www.mybizlab.com.

PEARSON **my*biz*lab**

Log on to www.mybizlab.com to access the following study and assessment aids associated with this chapter:

- Interactive exercises
- Pre/post test
- Real-Time Updates
- Video application
- Customized study plans
- Biz Skills Simulations
- Quick Learning Guide

If you are not using mybizlab, you can access Real-Time Updates and Quick Learning Guides through http://realtimeupdates.com/bia5. The Quick Learning Guide (located under "Learn More" on the website) provides all six Checkpoints in a handy two-page format to help you study for exams or review important concepts whenever you need a quick refresher.

Employee Motivation

After studying this chapter, you will be able to

1 Define *motivation* and identify the classical motivation theories

2 Explain why *expectancy theory* is considered by many to be the best current explanation of employee motivation

3 Identify the strengths and weaknesses of *goal-setting theory*

4 Describe the *job characteristics model* and explain how it helps predict motivation and performance

5 Define *reinforcement theory* and differentiate between positive and negative reinforcement

6 List five managerial strategies that are vital to maintaining a motivated workforce

Behind the Scenes

Taking a Second Look at the Career Ladder

www.deloitte.com

The notion of a business career being a straight vertical ascent from the bottom to the top is so embedded in our thinking that it has its own well-used metaphor: *climbing the corporate ladder.* The basic idea is that you join the workforce after college, work hard for 30, 40, or 50 years, and are rewarded along the way with positions of increasing responsibility and reward.

There's just one small problem with this whole ladder idea—it has never been true for millions of business professionals, and it often doesn't work out even for those who believe in the promise of continuous career progress. Simple arithmetic will tell you that the continuous climb simply can't work for most people—there just aren't enough high-level jobs, and the number shrinks dramatically with each step up the ladder. Take the technology giant Intel, for example, which has roughly 150 vice presidents, 7 senior VPs, 4 executive VPs, and 1 CEO. That's about 160 slots at the top of the ladder. This might sound like a lot of opportunities—until you consider that Intel has 84,000 employees. Even if only 10 percent of these employees (8,400) aspire for the top rung, 8,240 of them aren't going to make it.

Having followed an unconventional career path herself, Cathy Benko helped redefine career options for Deloitte's employees.

The numbers don't tell the whole story, either. Many employees have other priorities and demands in life, from raising families and dealing with health issues to continuing their education and exploring different career specialties along the way. In other words, millions of employees are unwilling or unable to maintain a straight climb up the ladder, and reward systems built on a steady climb aren't going to do much to motivate these people. As consultant Bruce Tulgan puts it, "Paying your dues, moving up slowly and getting the corner office—that's going away. In 10 years, it will be gone."

Cathy Benko is one of many executives who have been pondering this dilemma. As vice chairman and chief talent officer for Deloitte & Touche USA LLP, a diversified accounting, consulting, and financial advisory firm, Benko guides company strategy for attracting, developing, and motivating a highly skilled workforce. She realizes that the ladder metaphor has never quite fit many employees—and that recent trends make it even less applicable to an ever-growing segment of the workforce. She knows the workplace needs to change to give employees a more satisfying, energizing, and motivating career path.

If you were Cathy Benko, what steps would you take to align the workplace with the changing workforce and make sure that every employee, on any career path, has a shot at success?[1] ∎

Introduction

Deloitte's Cathy Benko (profiled in the chapter-opening Behind the Scenes) knows that a one-size-fits-all approach to managing and motivating employees has never been effective—and it is growing less effective every year as the workplace and the workforce continue to change. She could also tell you that while motivation is a critical topic to study, it is also a challenging one to study because no single theory or model can explain every motivational situation; the forces that affect motivation can vary widely from person to person and situation to situation, and some managers and researchers continue to "rely on obsolete and discredited theories."[2] The various theories and models in this chapter each provide some insight into the complicated question of employee motivation. You'll notice a fair amount of overlap among some of the theories, but taken as a whole, they provide an overall picture of the challenges and rewards of motivating employees to higher performance.

What Motivates Employees to Peak Performance?

In your years as a student, you've surely experienced a few assignments that you just couldn't get excited about, for whatever reason. Without a strong intellectual or emotional connection to the work, chances are you didn't expend much more than the minimum amount of effort required. Conversely, let's hope you've also had assignments in which the opposite was true: You poured your heart and soul into these projects because you made a commitment to excel, and at some level, you even enjoyed what you were doing. In other words, you were *engaged* with the work and *motivated* to do your best.

Making sure employees are engaged and motivated is one of the most important challenges every manager faces. No matter how skillful employees may be and how supportive the work environment is, without the motivation to excel, they won't perform at a high level. This section digs into the meaning of motivation and then explores some of the early attempts to provide practical models for motivating employees.

What Is Motivation?

Motivation is a complex subject that defies easy explanation, and some of the brightest minds in the field of management have been working for decades to understand this mysterious force. For one example, things that motivate you might have no effect on other people—or even *demotivate* them. For another, some of the forces that motivate your behavior stem from deep within your subconscious mind, which means you might be driven by forces that you don't understand and can't even identify.

Starting with a basic definition, **motivation** is the combination of forces that prompt individuals to take certain actions and avoid others in pursuit of individual objectives. Pay close attention to *drive* and *actions* in this definition; they are key to understanding motivation.

In a workplace setting, motivation can be assessed by measuring four indicators: engagement, satisfaction, commitment, and intention to quit.[3] First, **engagement** reflects the degree of energy, enthusiasm, and effort each employee brings to his or her work. If you're "just not into it," chances are you won't perform at your best. Second, *satisfaction* indicates how happy employees are with the experience of work and the way they are treated. Third, *commitment* suggests the degree to which employees support the company and its mission. Fourth, *intention to quit* predicts the likelihood that employees will leave their jobs. A person who is engaged, satisfied, and committed and who has no intention of quitting can be safely said to be *motivated.*

These four indicators can identify who is motivated and who isn't, but they don't explain why. For that, it's necessary to dig deeper, looking into what drives people to choose certain actions and avoid others. Contemporary research suggests that motivation stems from four fundamental needs:[4]

- **The drive to acquire.** This includes the need not only for physical goods such as food and clothing but for enjoyable experiences and "psychological goods" such as prestige. Importantly, this drive is relative: Individuals want to know how well they're doing compared to others around them.

motivation
The combination of forces that moves individuals to take certain actions and avoid other actions

engagement
An employee's rational and emotional commitment to his or her work

Satisfied, motivated employees tend to be more productive and more effective, leading to higher rates of customer satisfaction and repeat business.

Real-Time Updates

Learn More

Satisfying the four fundamental drives of employee behavior

Identify techniques that help satisfy the four fundamental drives in any workplace. On mybizlab (www.mybizlab.com), you can access Real-Time Updates within each chapter or under Student Study Tools. Otherwise, go to http://real-timeupdates.com/bia5 and click on "Learn More."

- **The drive to bond.** Humans are social creatures, and the need to feel a part of something larger is a vital aspect of employee motivation. This drive can be helpful, such as when it inspires employees to contribute to the common good, but it can also be harmful, such as when it pits groups of employees against one another in an "us versus them" mentality.

- **The drive to comprehend.** Learning, growing, meeting tough challenges, making sense of things—these are satisfying outcomes based on the drive to understand the world around us.

- **The drive to defend.** An instinct to protect and a sense of justice can lead human beings to vigorously defend the people, ideas, and organizations they hold dear. This drive is beneficial when it motivates people to fight for what is right, but it can be harmful as well, such as when it motivates people to resist change.

According to Harvard professor Nitin Nohria and his colleagues, who helped identify and explain these four drives, satisfying all four needs is essential to being motivated. When a need goes unsatisfied—or even worse, is betrayed, such as when employees believe an organization they've supported and defended no longer cares about them—poor motivation is the result.[5]

Classical Theories of Motivation

The quest to understand employee motivation has occupied researchers for more than a century. This section offers a brief overview of five early theories that helped shape ideas about motivation. Although subsequent research has identified shortcomings in all these theories, each contributed to our current understanding of motivation, and each continues to influence managerial practice.

Taylor's Scientific Management

scientific management
Management approach designed to improve employees' efficiency by scientifically studying their work

One of the earliest motivational researchers, Frederick W. Taylor, a machinist and engineer from Philadelphia, studied employee efficiency and motivation in the late 19th and early 20th centuries. He is credited with developing **scientific management**, an approach that sought to improve employee efficiency through the scientific study of work. In addition to analyzing work and business processes in order to develop better methods, Taylor also popularized compensation schemes that emphasized financial incentives for good performance. His work truly revolutionized business and had a direct influence on the rise of the United States as a global industrial power in the first half of the 20th century.[6]

Although money proved to be a significant motivator for workers, scientific management didn't consider other motivational elements, such as opportunities for personal satisfaction. For instance, scientific management can't explain why someone still wants to work even though that person's spouse already makes a good living or why a successful executive will take a hefty pay cut to serve in government. Therefore, other researchers have looked beyond money to discover what else motivates people.

Maslow's Hierarchy of Needs

Maslow's hierarchy
Model in which a person's needs are arranged in a hierarchy, with the most basic needs at the bottom and the more advanced needs toward the top

In 1943 psychologist Abraham Maslow proposed a hypothesis that behavior is determined by a variety of needs, which he organized into categories arranged in a hierarchy. As Exhibit 10.1 shows, the most basic needs are at the bottom of this hierarchy and the more advanced needs are toward the top. In **Maslow's hierarchy**, all of the requirements for basic survival—food, clothing, shelter, and the like—fall into the category of *physiological needs*. These basic needs must be satisfied before the person can consider

EXHIBIT 10.1

Maslow's Hierarchy of Needs

According to Maslow, needs on the lower levels of the hierarchy must be satisfied before higher-level needs can be addressed (examples are shown to the right). This model offers a convenient way to categorize needs, but it lacks empirical validation.

higher-level needs such as *safety needs, social needs* (the need to give and receive love and to feel a sense of belonging), and *esteem needs* (the need for a sense of self-worth and integrity).[7]

At the top of Maslow's hierarchy is *self-actualization*—the need to become everything one can be. This need is also the most difficult to fulfill—and even to identify in many cases. Employees who reach this point work not just because they want to make money or impress others but because they feel their work is worthwhile and satisfying in itself. Self-actualization needs partially explain why some people make radical career changes or strike out on their own as entrepreneurs. Conversely, when faced with tough or unstable economic conditions, employees may temporarily downplay higher-order needs and focus on the physiological and safety needs—choosing a steady paycheck as more important than personal fulfillment.

Maslow's hierarchy is a convenient and logical way to classify human needs, and many people continue to use it to explain behavior. However, other researchers have not been able to experimentally verify that this is how motivation actually works.[8]

Theory X, Theory Y, and Theory Z

In the 1960s psychologist Douglas McGregor proposed two radically different sets of assumptions that underlie most management thinking, which he classified as *Theory X* and *Theory Y*. According to McGregor, **Theory X**–oriented managers believe that employees dislike work and can be motivated only by the fear of losing their jobs or by *extrinsic rewards*—those given by other people, such as money, promotions, and tenure. In contrast, **Theory Y**–oriented managers believe that employees like work and can be motivated by working for goals that promote creativity or for causes they believe in. Consequently, Theory Y–oriented managers seek to motivate employees through *intrinsic rewards*—which employees essentially give themselves.[9] As with Maslow's hierarchy, "Theory X" and "Theory Y" seem to have a permanent place in the management vocabulary, but they suffer from the same lack of empirical evidence.[10] (However, the distinction between intrinsic and extrinsic rewards remains a valid and essential aspect of many theories of motivation.)

In the 1980s, when U.S. businesses began to feel a strong competitive threat from Japanese companies, William Ouchi proposed another approach to motivation based on his comparative study of Japanese and U.S. management practices. His *Theory Z* merged the best of both systems, as expressed in seven principles: long-term employment, consensus-based decision making, individual responsibility, slow evaluation and promotion, informal control with formal measurements, a moderate degree of career specialization, and a holistic concern for the individual.[11] Although the phrase "Theory Z" isn't used much these days, many of the principles embodied in Theory Z have been widely embraced by contemporary managers.

Theory X
Managerial assumption that employees are irresponsible, are unambitious, and dislike work and that managers must use force, control, or threats to motivate them

Theory Y
Managerial assumption that employees enjoy meaningful work, are naturally committed to certain goals, are capable of creativity, and seek out responsibility under the right conditions

EXHIBIT 10.2

Two-Factor Theory

Hygiene factors such as working conditions and company policies can influence employee dissatisfaction. On the other hand, motivators such as opportunities for achievement and recognition can influence employee satisfaction.

Highly satisfied

Neither satisfied nor dissatisfied

Highly dissatisfied

Area of satisfaction

Motivators

Achievement
Recognition
Responsibility
Work itself
Personal growth

Motivators influence level of satisfaction

Area of dissatisfaction

Hygiene factors

Working conditions
Pay and security
Company policies
Supervisors
Interpersonal relationships

Hygiene factors influence level of dissatisfaction

Herzberg's Two Factors

In the 1960s Frederick Herzberg and his associates explored the aspects of jobs that make employees feel satisfied or dissatisfied. The researchers found that two entirely different sets of factors were associated with dissatisfying and satisfying work experiences. In **Herzberg's two-factor theory** (see Exhibit 10.2), so-called *hygiene factors* are associated with dissatisfying experiences, and *motivators* are associated with satisfying experiences. Hygiene factors are mostly extrinsic and include working conditions, company policies, pay, and job security. Motivators tend to be intrinsic and include achievement, recognition, responsibility, and other personally rewarding factors.[12] According to Herzberg's model, managers need to remove dissatisfying elements (such as unpleasant working conditions or low pay) *and* add satisfying elements (such as interesting work and professional recognition)—doing one or the other is not enough.[13]

Like Maslow's hierarchy and Theory X/Theory Y, the two-factor theory feels logical and helps explain part of the motivation puzzle. However, it has been criticized for the methodology used in the original research and the inability of subsequent research to validate the model. Also, while there is a strong causal link between customer satisfaction and profitability, it is far less clear whether satisfied *employees* automatically lead to satisfied *customers*.[14]

McClelland's Three Needs

The last of the classical theories to consider is the **three-needs theory** developed by David McClelland. McClelland's model highlights the *need for power* (having—and demonstrating—control over others), the *need for affiliation* (being accepted by others and having opportunities for social interaction), and the *need for achievement* (attaining personally meaningful goals).[15] Unlike the other classical theories, there is a lot of research to validate McClelland's ideas and to explain particular outcomes in the workplace. For example, those with a high need for achievement tend to make successful entrepreneurs or intrapreneurs, since they are driven by the need to accomplish goals that mean a lot to them personally. Note that this focus on personal achievement can actually get in the way of managerial effectiveness, which relies on the ability to influence others toward shared goals.[16]

Herzberg's two-factor theory
Model that divides motivational forces into satisfiers ("motivators") and dissatisfiers ("hygiene factors")

three-needs theory
David McClelland's model of motivation that highlights needs for power, affiliation, and achievement

Conversely, managers who are most successful in a conventional organizational structure tend to have a higher need for power and relatively little need for affiliation. They are less concerned with achieving personal goals or being well liked than they are with building up the influence needed to get things done through other people.[17]

While it helps explain motivation in various contexts, the biggest drawback to McClelland's approach is its limited practicality in terms of identifying needs and crafting motivational programs to harness them in beneficial directions. The three needs are subconscious, according to McClelland, and trained experts are required to help identify them in each individual.[18]

CHECKPOINT

LEARNING OBJECTIVE 1: Define *motivation*, and identify the classical motivation theories.

Summary: Motivation is the combination of forces that prompt individuals to take certain actions and avoid others in pursuit of individual objectives. Research suggests that four drives underlie all motivation: the drive to acquire tangible and intangible rewards, the drive to bond with others, the drive to comprehend, and the drive to defend. The classical motivation theories that helped shape today's thinking include Taylor's scientific management, Maslow's hierarchy of needs, McGregor's Theory X and Theory Y (and Ouchi's Theory Z), Herzberg's two factors, and McClelland's three needs.

Critical thinking: (1) How could a manager tap into the drive to defend to help rally employees? (2) Could Herzberg's hygiene factors help explain the significant problem of employee theft and embezzlement? Why or why not?

It's your business: (1) If you are a typical college student who doesn't have much financial security at the moment but you're simultaneously trying to fulfill higher-order needs such as social interaction and self-actualization through education, would it make more sense, according to Maslow, to drop out of college and work seven days a week so you could help ensure that your physiological and safety needs are met? (2) Do you think today's college students more closely match the descriptions of Theory X employees or Theory Y employees? What evidence can you provide to support your conclusion?

Key terms to know: motivation, engagement, scientific management, Maslow's hierarchy, Theory X, Theory Y, Herzberg's two-factor theory, three-needs theory

Explaining Employee Choices

The classical theories of motivation contributed in important ways to both managerial practices and the ongoing research into employee motivation, but each has been found wanting in some way or another. Starting with more contemporary theories, two models known as expectancy and equity help explain the choices that employees make.

Expectancy Theory

Expectancy theory, considered by some experts to offer the best available explanation of employee motivation, links an employee's efforts with the outcome he or she expects from that effort. Expectancy theory focuses less on the specific forces that motivate employees and more on the process they follow to seek satisfaction in their jobs. As shown in the diagram in Exhibit 10.3 on the next page, the effort employees will put forth depends on (1) their expectations regarding the level of performance they will be able to achieve, (2) their

expectancy theory
The idea that the effort employees put into their work depends on expectations about their own ability to perform, expectations about likely rewards, and the attractiveness of those rewards

EXHIBIT 10.3

Expectancy Theory

Expectancy theory suggests that employees base their efforts on expectations of their own performance, expectations of rewards for that performance, and the value of those rewards.

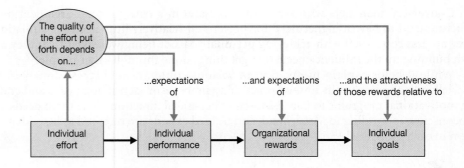

beliefs regarding the rewards that the organization will give in response to that performance, and (3) the attractiveness of those rewards relative to their individual goals.[19]

Exploring these linkages from both an employee's and a manager's perspective will give you an idea of how the expectancy model can explain employee behavior and prescribe managerial tactics to help motivate employees. First, as an employee, if you don't believe that the amount of effort you are willing or able to apply to a task will result in an acceptable level of performance, a natural response will be to say, "Well, why bother?" This uncertainty could come from many sources, such as doubts about your skills, confusion about the task, or a belief that "the system" is so broken that no matter how hard you try you can't succeed. Belief in your ability to complete a task is known as *self-efficacy*, and it can be increased by gaining experience, mimicking successful role models, getting encouragement from others, and sometimes even "psyching yourself up."[20] As a manager, your challenges would be to ensure that employees have the skills and confidence they need, that tasks are clearly defined, and that company policies and processes are functional.

Second, if you are confident that you can complete the task successfully, your next question is whether the organization will recognize and reward your performance. Will anybody care? Knowing you've done great work is its own reward, of course, but for many employees, this isn't enough. As a manager, your challenges include both establishing reward systems and expectations to minimize employee uncertainty and taking time from the daily chaos to acknowledge the efforts your employees make.

Third, if you're confident in your performance and the organization's response, the final question is whether the promised reward is something you value. What if you suspect that all you will get is some "certificate of appreciation" that the company hands out by the dozens? What if you might get a raise but what you really want is for your boss to acknowledge how important your contributions have been to the company? What if you might get a raise or public recognition, but what you really want is the chance to tackle some tough, high-visibility problems? As a manager, aligning rewards with employee priorities is an ongoing challenge; see "Reinforcing High-Performance Behavior" on page 275.

Equity Theory

Simply getting rewards, even if they are valuable and personally meaningful, isn't always enough to ensure satisfaction and motivation. Comparing our rewards to what others get seems to be a basic element of human nature. **Equity theory** addresses this issue by suggesting that employee satisfaction depends on the perceived ratio of inputs to outputs. If you work side by side with someone, doing the same job and giving the same amount of effort, only to learn that your colleague earns more money, would you be satisfied in your work and motivated to continue working hard? Chances are you will perceive a state of *inequity*, and you probably won't be happy with the situation. To remedy this perception of inequity, you might ask for a raise, decide not to work as hard, try to change perceptions of your efforts or their outcomes, or simply quit and find a new job. Any one of these steps has the potential to bring your perceived input/output ratio back into balance.[21] Some of the choices employees can make to address perceived inequity are obviously not desirable from an employer's point of view, so it's important to understand why employees might feel they aren't getting a fair shake.

equity theory
The idea that employees base their level of satisfaction on the ratio of their inputs to the job and the outputs or rewards they receive from it

Equity issues can show up in a number of areas. For example, in the aftermath of large-scale layoffs in many sectors of the economy in the past few years, many of the employees left behind feel a sense of inequity in being asked to shoulder the work of those who left, without getting paid more for the extra effort.[22] (There's even a name for this extra workload—*ghost work.*) Equity also plays a central role in complaints about gender pay fairness and executive compensation (see page 299) and in many unionizing efforts, whenever employees feel they aren't getting a fair share of corporate profits or are being asked to shoulder more than their fair share of hardships.

Research into equity theory has led to thinking about the broader concept of *organizational justice*, or perceptions of fairness in the workplace. These perceptions relate to outcomes, the processes used to generate those outcomes, and the way employees are treated during the process.[23] No reasonable employee expects to make as much as the CEO, for example, but as long as the process seems fair (both the employee's and the CEO's pay are related to performance, for example), most employees will be satisfied and the disparity won't affect their motivation. In fact, perceptions of fairness can have as much impact on overall employee satisfaction as satisfaction with pay itself.[24]

✓CHECKPOINT

LEARNING OBJECTIVE 2: Explain why *expectancy theory* is considered by many to be the best current explanation of employee motivation.

Summary: Expectancy theory suggests that the effort employees put into their work depends on expectations about their own ability to perform, expectations about the rewards the organization will give in response to that performance, and the attractiveness of those rewards relative to their individual goals. This theory is considered a good model because it considers the linkages between effort and outcome. For instance, if employees think a linkage is "broken," such as having doubts that their efforts will yield acceptable performance or worries that they will perform well but no one will notice, they're likely to put less effort into their work.

Critical thinking: (1) What steps could managers take to alleviate the self-doubt employees often feel when they join a company or move into a new position? (2) If you were a human resources manager in a large corporation, how might you respond to employees who complain that the CEO makes two or three hundred times more than they make?

It's your business: (1) Have you ever given less than your best effort in a college course because you didn't believe you were capable of excelling in the course? (2) Was the outcome satisfying? Would you handle a similar situation the same way in the future?

Key terms to know: expectancy theory, equity theory

Motivating with Challenging Goals

With the expectancy and equity theories offering some insight into why employees make the choices they make, the next step in understanding motivation is to explore specific leadership strategies that motivate employees. **Goal-setting theory**, the idea that carefully designed goals can motivate employees to higher performance, is one of the most important contemporary theories of motivation. It is both widely used and strongly supported by experimental research.[25] (However, as "Risks and Limitations of Goal-Setting Theory" on page 270 explains, some researchers assert that the benefits of goal setting have been overstated and the risks have been understated, partly as a result of research studies that fail to measure the full consequences of goal-driven behaviors.)

goal-setting theory
Motivational theory suggesting that setting goals can be an effective way to motivate employees

For goals to function as effective motivators, a number of criteria need to be met. These criteria include[26]

- Goals that are specific enough to give employees clarity and focus
- Goals that are difficult enough to inspire energetic and committed effort
- Clear "ownership" of goals so that accountability can be established
- Timely feedback that lets people know if they're progressing toward their goals and, if not, how to change course
- Individuals' belief in their ability to meet their goals
- Cultural support for the individual achievement and independence needed to reach the goals

As today's companies face the twin challenges of increasing global competition and a slow economy, goal setting could play an even more important role than it already does. In one recent survey, nearly half of professionals and managers said they weren't being challenged enough in their jobs.[27] In other words, without adding more staff or investing in new technologies, many companies already have a valuable resource that they could be making much better use of—if they can find strategically appropriate ways to challenge their current employees.

Management by Objectives

Goal-setting theory is frequently implemented through a technique known as **management by objectives (MBO)**, a companywide process that empowers employees and involves them in goal setting and decision making. This process consists of four steps: setting goals, planning actions, implementing plans, and reviewing performance (see Exhibit 10.4). Because employees at all levels are involved in all four steps, they learn more about company objectives and feel that they are an important part of the companywide team. Furthermore, they understand how their individual job functions contribute to the organization's long-term success.

One of the key elements of MBO is a collaborative goal-setting process. Together, a manager and employee define the employee's goals, the responsibilities for achieving those goals, and the means of evaluating individual and group performance so that the employee's activities are directly linked to achieving the organization's long-term goals. Jointly setting clear and challenging but achievable goals can encourage employees to reach higher levels of performance, although participation alone is no guarantee of higher performance.[28]

Risks and Limitations of Goal-Setting Theory

As powerful as goal setting can be, it is not a simple or risk-free management tool. Researchers Lisa Ordóñez, Maurice Schweitzer, Adam Galinsky, and Max Bazerman have documented a wide variety of ways in which goal setting can misfire, with results ranging from employee frustration to systematic underperformance to serious ethical and legal problems:[29]

- **Overly narrow goals.** Employees tend to broaden or narrow their view of a challenge based on how broadly or narrowly their goals have been defined. When goals are too narrow, people can miss vital aspects of the bigger picture. For instance, if salespeople are measured only on the number of sales made or total sales revenue, they might close sales in ways that help them "make their numbers" but ultimately harm the company—such as offering huge discounts or extending credit to customers who can't pay their bills.
- **Overly challenging goals.** Setting goals that are challenging but not too challenging to be reached can be something of an art form—with damaging consequences for misjudgments. Lofty goals can inspire great performance, but they can also lead to risky behavior, belligerent negotiating tactics, and ethical lapses as employees cut corners to reach targets.

EXHIBIT 10.4 Management by Objectives

The MBO process has four steps. This cycle is refined and repeated as managers and employees at all levels work toward establishing goals and objectives, thereby accomplishing the organization's strategic goals.

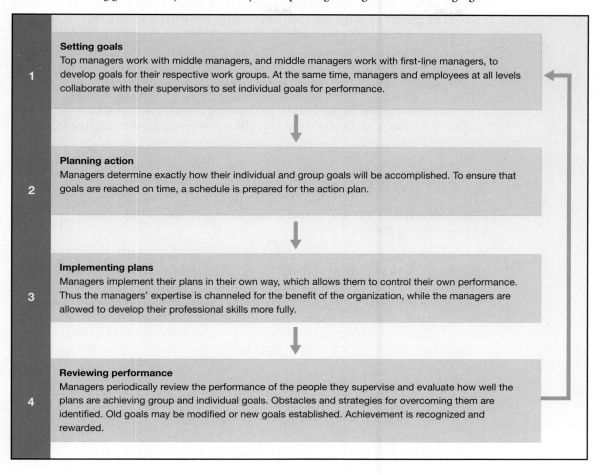

1

Setting goals
Top managers work with middle managers, and middle managers work with first-line managers, to develop goals for their respective work groups. At the same time, managers and employees at all levels collaborate with their supervisors to set individual goals for performance.

2

Planning action
Managers determine exactly how their individual and group goals will be accomplished. To ensure that goals are reached on time, a schedule is prepared for the action plan.

3

Implementing plans
Managers implement their plans in their own way, which allows them to control their own performance. Thus the managers' expertise is channeled for the benefit of the organization, while the managers are allowed to develop their professional skills more fully.

4

Reviewing performance
Managers periodically review the performance of the people they supervise and evaluate how well the plans are achieving group and individual goals. Obstacles and strategies for overcoming them are identified. Old goals may be modified or new goals established. Achievement is recognized and rewarded.

- **Inappropriate time horizons.** Too much emphasis on short-term performance can degrade long-term performance. A widespread and much-lamented example of this is the unhealthy focus that many publically traded companies place on quarterly performance in order to meet the stock market's expectations. This distorted focus can lead a firm to make decisions such as downsizing or cutting back on research that might help the bottom line in the short term but ultimately limit the company's ability to compete and grow.

- **Unintentional performance limitations.** Ironically, goals can limit performance potential when employees reach a goal and then stop trying, even though they could go beyond that level if reaching the goal didn't signal that it was acceptable to stop there. According to Ordóñez and her colleagues, sometimes telling employees to just "do your best" can result in higher performance than giving employees a specific performance target.

- **Missed learning opportunities.** Employees can get so focused on meeting deadlines and other goals that they overlook opportunities to learn, whether to improve their own skills, fix process problems, or adapt to changes in the business environment— all of which could benefit the company more than meeting the original goal.[30] You'll recall from Chapter 9's discussion of systems management that it is important to focus on performance variables that are the most *meaningful*, not just those that are the most easily *measurable*.

- **Unhealthy internal competition.** Goals can pit groups within a company against each other, which can be beneficial if the competition is healthy but ultimately harmful if it is not. For example, if a company's sales regions across the United States compete to see who can generate the most business during the year, the result could be greater sales for the company overall. But what if several regions refuse to cooperate to help land a big national client?

- **Decreased intrinsic motivation.** Relying too heavily on public goals and their extrinsic rewards can eventually dull the intrinsic motivation to do well for the sake of the work itself—one of the most powerful and sustainable motivators.

As you ponder these limitations of goal-setting theory, you can start to sense how important it is to set goals carefully and only after considering the potential consequences.

√CHECKPOINT

LEARNING OBJECTIVE 3: Identify the strengths and weaknesses of *goal-setting theory.*

Summary: Setting challenging goals has proven to be a dependable way to inspire employees to high levels of performance; goal setting is the foundation of a popular management system known as management by objectives (MBO). In addition to being widely used, goal-setting theory is strongly supported by experimental research. The weaknesses of goal setting generally lie in ways that the pursuit of goals can distort behavior. Potential problems include overly narrow or overly challenging goals, inappropriate time horizons, unintentional performance limitations, missed learning opportunities, unhealthy internal competition, and decreased intrinsic motivation.

Critical thinking: (1) Why is collaboration between employee and manager essential to goal setting in management by objectives? (2) How can overly narrow goals and overly challenging goals contribute to ethical lapses?

It's your business: (1) Do goals motivate you? Why or why not? Does it depend on whether the goals are your own or imposed by someone else?

Key terms to know: goal-setting theory, management by objectives (MBO)

Redesigning Jobs to Stimulate Performance

Along with setting challenging goals, many companies are exploring various ways to redesign the work itself to improve employee satisfaction and motivation.

The Job Characteristics Model

job characteristics model
Suggests that five core job dimensions influence three critical psychological states that determine motivation, performance, and other outcomes

The **job characteristics model** proposed by Richard Hackman and Greg Oldman (see Exhibit 10.5) has proven to be a reliable way to predict the effects of five *core job dimensions* on employee motivation and other positive outcomes.[31] Starting from the left side of the model, here are the job dimensions identified by Hackman and Oldman:

- **Skill variety**—the range of skills and talents needed to accomplish the responsibilities associated with the job. The broader the range of skills required, the more meaningful the work is likely to be to the employee.

- **Task identity**—the degree to which the employee has responsibility for completing an entire task, as opposed to being a "cog in a wheel," doing a small piece of a larger task. Greater task identity contributes to the sense of meaning in work.

EXHIBIT 10.5

Job Characteristics Model

Hackman and Oldman's job characteristics model shows the effect of core job dimensions on critical psychological states, which in turn determine motivation and other outcomes.

Core Job Dimensions
- Skill variety
- Task identity
- Task significance
- Autonomy
- Feedback

Critical Psychological States
- Experienced meaningfulness of work
- Experienced responsibility for results
- Knowledge of actual results

Personal and Work Outcomes
- Higher motivation
- Improved performance
- Greater job satisfaction
- Lower absenteeism and turnover

- **Task significance**—the employee's perception of the impact the job has on the lives of other people. Not surprisingly, jobs perceived to be more significant tend to feel more meaningful to employees.

- **Autonomy**—the degree of independence the employee has in carrying out the job.

- **Feedback**—timely information that tells employees how well they're doing in their jobs.

You can see that some of these dimensions relate to the nature of the work itself and others relate more to management decisions and leadership styles. Moving to the center of the diagram, these job dimensions contribute to three *critical psychological states:*

- **Experienced meaningfulness of the work**—a measure of how much employees care about the jobs they are doing.

- **Experienced responsibility for results**—the sense each employee has that his or her efforts contribute to the outcome.

- **Knowledge of actual results**—employees' awareness of the real-life results of their efforts.

Move to the right side of the diagram in Exhibit 10.5, and you'll see that increasing degrees of intensity in these psychological states lead to improvements in motivation, performance, job satisfaction, absenteeism (the amount of time employees miss work), and turnover (the rate at which employees leave their jobs). In other words, if employees believe their work is meaningful, believe their individual efforts are responsible at least in large part for the outcome of that work, and can see evidence of the results of their efforts, they are likely to be more motivated than they would otherwise. It's not hard to see how the reverse is true also. Employees who believe their work is meaningless, who don't feel much responsibility for the outcome, or who never get to see the results of their efforts aren't likely to be terribly motivated or satisfied.

One final aspect of job characteristics research explores how various types of employees respond to changes in the core job dimensions. Employees with strong *growth needs*, meaning they feel a strong need to increase self-esteem and self-actualization, respond more dramatically to improvements in job dimensions—and improvements in the critical psychological states will lead to greater increases in their motivation and the other positive outcomes.[32] Conversely, employees who feel little intrinsic need to grow can be among the most difficult to motivate, no matter what steps managers take.

The job characteristics model continues to offer helpful guidance as companies grapple with the challenges in today's work environment. For instance, as more companies increasingly rely on temporary workers to control costs or acquire skills that are needed only for specific projects, managers need to think carefully about the ways they supervise permanent versus temporary employees. As two examples, temporary workers may need to be assigned more discrete tasks that have enough task identity and autonomy to provide a sense of ownership and control, and managers need to make sure they don't take permanent employees for granted and fail to give them adequate feedback about their efforts.[33]

Approaches to Modifying Core Job Dimensions

The job characteristics model identifies the generic aspects of a job that can be adjusted to improve motivation, but it's up to individual companies and departments to identify and make the specific changes that are relevant to each job in the organization. Naturally, managers have only so much flexibility in making these adjustments—work is still work, and that work still needs to get done, one way or another. However, with some creative thinking and enlightened leadership, companies can make the overall work experience more meaningful and rewarding and therefore increase motivation, employee satisfaction, and overall productivity. Three popular approaches are job enrichment, job enlargement, and cross-training (note that these methods can address not only the issues in the job characteristics model but also matters related to *work-life balance* and other job satisfaction questions).

job enrichment
Making jobs more challenging and interesting by expanding the range of skills required

- **Job enrichment.** The strategy behind **job enrichment** is to make jobs more challenging and interesting by expanding the range of skills required—typically by expanding upward, giving employees some of the responsibilities previously held by their managers.[34] For example, an employee who had been preparing presentations for his or her boss to give to customers could be asked to give the presentations as well. Job enrichment needs to be approached carefully, however; some employees respond well, but for others, the increased responsibility is more a source of stress than inspiration.[35]

- **Job enlargement.** Whereas job enrichment expands vertically, *job enlargement* is more of a horizontal expansion, adding tasks that aren't necessarily any more challenging. If it simply gives workers more to do, job enlargement won't do much to motivate and will more likely demotivate. However, if jobs are enlarged in ways that increase worker knowledge, expansion can improve job satisfaction.[36]

cross-training
Training workers to perform multiple jobs and rotating them through these various jobs to combat boredom or burnout

- **Cross-training.** Job enrichment and job enlargement expand the scope of an individual job, whereas **cross-training** or *job rotation* involves training workers to perform multiple jobs and rotating them through these various jobs to combat boredom or burnout. Cross-training is also valuable in lean manufacturing (see page 252) because it lets companies keep staffs as small as possible and assign people wherever they are needed to handle fluctuations in workflow. And in a tight economy, cross-training helps companies address task needs without adding new staff.[37]

As noted earlier, some of the steps companies can take to improve motivation involve restructuring jobs, providing additional training, or making other explicit changes. However, in other instances, improvements can be made by changes in management attitudes and practices, such as giving employees more control over their work and providing timely feedback. The best solution is usually a combination of changes that accommodate the nature of the work and the abilities and interests of individual employees and managers.

 **CHECKPOINT**

LEARNING OBJECTIVE 4: Describe the *job characteristics model*, and explain how it helps predict motivation and performance.

Summary: The job characteristics model identifies five core job dimensions (skill variety, task identity, task significance, autonomy, and feedback) that create three critical psychological states (experienced meaningfulness of the work, experienced responsibility for results, and knowledge of actual results). Achieving these three states leads to improvements in motivation, job satisfaction, performance, absenteeism, and turnover.

Critical thinking: (1) Can the job characteristics model be used to motivate employees in such positions as janitors or security guards in a factory? How? (2) Is modifying the five core job dimensions likely to motivate employees who have low growth needs? Why or why not?

It's your business: (1) Has the requirement of working in teams ever lowered your motivation or satisfaction on a school project? If so, how does the job characteristics model explain this? (2) How does taking elective courses improve your experience of meaningfulness in your college "work"?

Key terms to know: job characteristics model, job enrichment, cross-training

Reinforcing High-Performance Behavior

Challenging goals and creative job designs can motivate employees to higher levels of performance, but managers also need to make sure that performance can be sustained over time. Employees in the workplace, like people in all aspects of life, tend to repeat behaviors that create positive outcomes for themselves and avoid or abandon behaviors that bring negative outcomes. **Reinforcement theory** suggests that managers can motivate employees by shaping their actions through *behavior modification*. Using reinforcement theory, managers try to systematically encourage those actions considered beneficial to the company. Reinforcement is a valuable motivational tool, but it has broad application whenever managers want to shape employee behavior.

Types of Reinforcement

Positive reinforcement offers pleasant consequences (such as a bonus, a raise, a promotion, or recognition) for completing or repeating a desired action. For example, specific praise from a manager, offered immediately after employees exhibit desired behaviors, is one of the most powerful motivators. Even a simple but sincere "thank you" provides emotional reward and encourages employees to repeat whatever behavior elicited the praise.[38] Positive reinforcement can also have a multiplier effect in which employees who receive positive reinforcement for one type of behavior are motivated to perform positively in other areas, an effect known as *chaining*.[39]

Many companies use some form of **incentives**, either monetary payments or other rewards of value, as positive reinforcement to motivate employees to achieve specific performance targets. Like praise and public recognition, incentive programs can become particularly important during economic slowdowns, when many employers can't afford to give big salary increases and companies aren't growing fast enough to create opportunities for career advancement.[40]

By contrast, **negative reinforcement** allows people to avoid unpleasant consequences by behaving in a particular way. "Negative reinforcement" is a confusing term because it sounds like punishment, and the terms are sometimes used interchangeably in casual speech. However, in psychological terminology, they have different meanings. Negative reinforcement encourages behavior through the removal or absence of an unpleasant outcome. While punishment *decreases* the likelihood that a particular behavior will be repeated (because something unpleasant—punishment—happens when that behavior is exhibited), negative reinforcement *increases* the likelihood that a behavior will be repeated (because an unpleasant outcome is avoided when that behavior is exhibited).[41]

Say you have been given a performance target of at least 50 sales calls every week. If you work diligently to make 52 calls this week and receive a $100 incentive bonus for doing so, the

reinforcement theory
A motivational approach based on the idea that managers can motivate employees by influencing their behaviors with positive and negative reinforcement

positive reinforcement
Encouraging desired behaviors by offering pleasant consequences for completing or repeating those behaviors

incentives
Monetary payments and other rewards of value used for positive reinforcement

negative reinforcement
Encouraging the repetition of a particular behavior (desirable or not) by not offering unpleasant consequences for the behavior

Recognition and reward programs can be powerful means for reinforcing desirable behaviors.

positive reinforcement (the addition of a pleasant outcome—the bonus) will encourage you to repeat this behavior. If you make 52 calls and don't get a bonus but you also don't get fired, the *negative reinforcement* (the avoidance of an unpleasant outcome—not getting fired) will also encourage you to repeat this behavior. If you slack off and make only 38 calls and your boss subtracts $100 from your paycheck, this *punishment* will discourage you from slacking off next week.

Of these three possibilities, you can see how positive reinforcement is the only one that injects positive energy into the situation. Fear can certainly be a powerful motivator, but it also adds stress and anxiety that can eventually lead to burnout and attrition as employees decide they don't want to deal with the constant pressure. And although punishment can be effective as a way to discourage particular behaviors, the effect isn't always permanent, and it can create serious morale problems.[42]

Unintended Consequences of Reinforcement

Reinforcement sounds like a simple enough concept, but the mechanisms of reinforcement can be subtle and the effects unexpected. Managers must be on constant alert for unintended consequences of incentives and other reinforcement efforts. For example, because they often focus on a single variable, incentive programs can distort performance by encouraging employees to focus on that variable to the detriment of other responsibilities.[43] If your salespeople get a bonus every time they land a new client but receive no penalties whenever an unhappy client leaves for a competitor, sales staffers will naturally tend to focus more effort on acquiring new clients than on making sure existing clients are satisfied.

Reinforcement doesn't have to involve explicit monetary incentives to distort behavior, either. For instance, imagine a manager who offers enthusiastic praise whenever employees suggest new ideas during meetings but never follows up to see if those employees actually do any work to implement their great ideas. He or she can be encouraging empty "happy talk" through both positive reinforcement (there are pleasant consequence for spouting out ideas during meetings) *and* negative reinforcement (there are no unpleasant consequences for not doing any of the work, so employees will continue to not do it).

✓CHECKPOINT

LEARNING OBJECTIVE 5: Define *reinforcement theory*, and differentiate between positive and negative reinforcement.

Summary: Reinforcement theory suggests that managers can motivate employees by systematically encouraging those actions that are beneficial to the company. Positive and negative reinforcement both tend to increase the specific behavior in question, but positive reinforcement does so by the experience of pleasant consequences by engaging in the behavior, while negative reinforcement does so by the avoidance of unpleasant consequences by engaging in the behavior. The term *negative reinforcement* is sometimes used in casual speech when people are really talking about *punishment*, which is discouraging a particular behavior by offering unpleasant consequences for it.

Critical thinking: (1) Is demoting an employee for failing to finish a project an attempt at negative reinforcement or punishment? Why? (2) In what ways is reinforcement theory similar to goal-setting theory?

It's your business: (1) How does your instructor in this course use positive reinforcement to motivate students to higher levels of performance? (2) If you study diligently to avoid being embarrassed when a professor calls on you in class, is this positive or negative reinforcement in action? Why?

Key terms to know: reinforcement theory, positive reinforcement, incentives, negative reinforcement

Motivational Strategies

Real-Time Updates

Learn More
Explore the elemental forces that create motivation

Take a closer look at causes, beliefs, emotions, and other forces that influence actions and decisions. On mybizlab (**www.mybizlab.com**), you can access Real-Time Updates within each chapter or under Student Study Tools. Otherwise, go to http://real-timeupdates.com/bia5 and click on "Learn More."

Regardless of the specific motivational theories that a company chooses to implement in its management policies and reward systems, managers can improve their ability to motivate employees by providing timely and frequent feedback, personalizing motivational efforts, adapting to circumstances and special needs, tackling workplace problems before they have a chance to destroy morale, and being inspirational leaders.

Provide Timely and Frequent Feedback

Imagine how you'd feel if you worked for weeks on a complex project for one of your classes, turned it in on time, and then heard . . . nothing. As days passed with no feedback, doubts would begin to creep in. Was your work so good that your professor is passing it around to other faculty members in sheer astonishment? Was it so bad that your professor is still searching for the words to describe it? Was your project simply lost in the shuffle and no one cares enough to find it?

No matter which theory of motivation an organization or manager subscribes to, providing timely and frequent feedback is essential. From the perspective of reinforcement theory, for example, feedback is the mechanism that shapes employee behavior. Without it, opportunities for positive reinforcement will be missed, and the effort put forth by employees will eventually wane because they'll see little reason to continue.

Feedback "closes the loop" in two important ways: It give employees the information they need to assess their own performance and make improvements if necessary, and it serves the emotional purpose of reassuring employees that someone is paying attention. Even if the feedback is constructive criticism, it lets employees know that what they do is important enough to be done correctly.

Make It Personal

A recurring theme in just about every attempt to explain motivation is that motivation is a very personal phenomenon. Rewards and feedback that stimulate one employee to higher achievement can have no effect on a second employee and demotivate a third. As you'll see in Behind the Scenes at the end of the chapter, customizing career paths is an essential aspect of how Cathy Benko and her colleagues at Deloitte help to personalize motivation and rewards.

In an ideal world, managers would be able to personalize motivational efforts completely, giving each employee the rewards and feedback that spur him or her to peak achievement. However, the need for fairness and the demands on a manager's time place practical limits on the degree to which motivational efforts can be individualized. For example, just because an employee might view time off as a more significant motivator than bonuses or recognition, you can't just give this person extra vacation days as a reward for top performance without offering the same reward possibilities to all employees. In addition, arranging or negotiating rewards on a case-by-case basis would consume too much of a manager's time.

The situation calls for a three-pronged approach. First, establish systems and policies that are as equitable and as automatic as possible, and explain to employees why they are fair. Second, build in as much flexibility as you can, such as offering employees the cash equivalent of paid time off if they prefer money over time. Third, get to know employees as individuals in order to understand what is important to each person. For example, research suggests that younger employees are more likely to be demotivated by uninteresting work than their older counterparts.[44] (Another possible explanation is that older workers have learned to accept the fact that work can't always be exciting and are more willing to do whatever needs to be done.) If one person craves intellectual challenges, give him or her the tough problems to solve. If another thrives on recognition, give that employee the chance to give presentations to upper management.

Of course, you need to give everyone an equal shot at opportunities, but as much as possible, let employees choose which opportunities and rewards they want to pursue. Employees understand that their managers can't always change "the system," but they do expect their managers to exercise some individual control over how policies are implemented and rewards are given.[45]

Adapt to Circumstances and Special Needs

Just as the dynamics of motivation vary from person to person, they can vary from one situation to the next. For example, a slow economy and rising unemployment introduce a number of stresses into the workplace that need to be considered from a motivational perspective. Employers have less to spend on factors that can help avert employee dissatisfaction (salary, for example) or that can spur motivation (such as bonuses and other incentives). As a result, satisfaction and motivation are in danger of slipping, but employees have fewer options for finding new jobs if they aren't happy. The big exceptions are a company's top performers. When unemployment is rising and money is tight, high performers in any industry can often find new opportunities where average performers cannot. In other words, when companies are struggling, their best employees—the ones they need the most—are the ones most likely to leave. Consequently, managers need to work extra hard to keep these top performers happy and motivated.[46]

The threat of layoffs can motivate some employees but demoralize others. Some will work harder in the hopes of minimizing their chances of being let go. Others, however, will wonder if there's any point in working hard if the economy is going to wipe out their jobs anyway. If layoffs are already starting to hit, survivors can be demoralized even further if they think the company is treating laid-off employees disrespectfully or unfairly.[47] Clearly, tough economic times put a huge motivational burden on managers, but those who treat employees with honesty and compassion stand the best chance of retaining the best people and keeping them motivated.

When the economy heats up again and unemployment drops, the balance of power shifts back toward workers. Employers who may have counted on job-loss fear as a motivator during the touch times will need to adjust strategies when employees have more options.[48]

Don't Let Problems Fester

An upbeat, supportive work environment can have a tremendous effect on employees, spurring them to greater individual performance and a richer sense of team spirit with their colleagues. Unfortunately, the opposite is just as true—a negative work environment can destroy motivation and productivity.

No workplace is immune from problems and conflicts, but negativity is an emotional "virus" that can infect an entire organization. Just as with physical health, managers must address workplace problems and conflicts quickly, before they multiply and erode employee morale. Left to fester long enough, these problems can destroy the sense of community in a company and leave employees feeling hopeless about the future.[49] Jumping on a problem quickly can have a double positive impact: It solves the problem, and it demonstrates to everyone that management cares about the emotional health of the workforce.

Be an Inspiring Leader

Theories and systems aside, inspired motivation in a business enterprise requires inspired leadership. To a large degree, good employees are already motivated—that's part of what makes them good employees. One of your jobs as a manager is to make sure you don't *demotivate* them. For example, in one recent survey of U.S. workers, more than a third said their supervisors' habits of **micromanaging**—overseeing every small detail of employees' work and refusing to give them freedom or autonomy—was destroying their initiative.[50] Managers with low emotional intelligence (see page 200) can create toxic work environments that demotivate even the most driven employees, so it is essential for managers to understand the effect that their behaviors and attitudes have on employees.

Real-Time Updates

Learn More

20 tips to keep yourself motivated

Whether it's losing 10 pounds or changing the world, these tips can get you started and keep you going. On mybizlab (**www.mybizlab.com**), you can access Real-Time Updates within each chapter or under Student Study Tools. Otherwise, go to **http://real-timeupdates.com/bia5** and click on "Learn More."

Motivate Yourself

This chapter has focused on systems that organizations can put in place and various steps managers can take to motivate employees. However, this emphasis shouldn't obscure the role and responsibility of employees themselves. Every employee has an ethical obligation to find the motivation to accomplish the tasks for which he or she is getting paid. Managers can foster motivation (and they can certainly diminish it through clumsy leadership), but the motivation has to originate from within each employee.

For the latest information on motivation, visit **http://real-timeupdates.com/bia5** and click on Chapter 10.

micromanaging
Overseeing every small detail of employees' work and refusing to give them freedom or autonomy

CHECKPOINT

LEARNING OBJECTIVE 6: List five managerial strategies that are vital to maintaining a motivated workforce.

Summary: No matter which motivational theories a company chooses to implement in its management policies and reward systems, managers can motivate employees more effectively by (1) providing timely and frequent feedback, (2) personalizing motivational efforts as much as possible while still being fair to all employees, (3) adapting motivational tactics to circumstances and special needs, (4) addressing workplace negativity before it has a chance to destroy morale, and (5) being inspirational leaders.

Critical thinking: (1) Referring to the job characteristics model, how does micromanaging destroy motivation?
(2) Annual performance reviews are common in many companies; how might this tactic fail to motivate employees?

It's your business: (1) If you are motivated more by the love of learning than the promised rewards of a grade, how can you motivate yourself when grades play a key role in your success as others perceive it? (2) Have you ever worked with someone (in a job or in school) whose negativity was contagious? How did you keep from letting that negativity drag down your own performance?

Key terms to know: micromanaging

Behind the Scenes

Motivating Individuals by Personalizing Careers at Deloitte

As the chief talent officer for a company brimming with talent, Deloitte's Cathy Benko knows how challenging it can be to create stimulating environments and opportunities to motivate a diverse workforce. And having traveled an unconventional path herself ("lots of zigs and zags" is how she describes it), she knows that a relentless 40-year climb up the corporate ladder is not for everyone.

The conventional ladder concept has never been right for many employees, and it is less appealing to a growing portion of the population. Benko explains that in the time span of just two generations, society and the workforce have been transformed to such an extent that the old ways of work don't work anymore. In studying this lack of fit between workplace and workforce, Benko and her colleagues identified five key issues:

- *A looming talent shortage.* Talk of not enough people to fill jobs might be difficult to fathom in the midst of a deep recession and high unemployment, but the long-term trend is unmistakable. By 2025, the shortage of knowledge workers could be as high as 35 million people.

- *A vastly different society.* The corporate ladder—and with it the idea of devoting one's working life to a single company in order to climb one's way to the top—was conceived back in a time when two-thirds of U.S. households consisted of married couples in which one spouse (usually the husband) went to work and the other (usually the wife) stayed home. In a sense, this family structure helped support the corporate ladder by "freeing" the husband to devote himself to his company and career. Today, however, only about 15 percent of households fit that mold, and the old workplace ideals clearly don't fit them.

- *Expanded professional roles for women.* After years of gender imbalance in the workplace, women now hold more than half of all management jobs (although the ratio at the top of the ladder is still biased strongly toward men). Plus, women now earn nearly 60 percent of bachelor's and master's degrees, so the presence of women in professional positions is only going to expand.

- *Different desires and expectations from men.* Meanwhile, a growing number of men are ready to explore a more balanced life with more flexibility and personal time than the constant ladder climb typically offers.

- *A dramatic shift in generational attitudes.* To a large degree, the Baby Boom generation (those born between 1946 and 1964) defined itself by work, and the more of it the better, it seemed for many. However, the two generations that came after, Generation X and Generation Y, have different outlooks, with a much stronger desire to adapt their work to their lives, rather than the other way around.

After pondering these tectonic shifts across the social landscape, Benko and Deloitte chose a new metaphor. Instead of a ladder, with its implication of a single path from bottom to top, they now speak in terms of a *lattice*, a cross-hatch of horizontal and vertical lines. Just as a rosebush on a garden lattice can grow sideways and even downward for a while if upward isn't the best choice at the moment, a career lattice offers employees much the same flexibility.

Deloitte calls the model "mass career customization," and it mimics the idea of mass customized production described in Chapter 9 (page 252). Employees define where they've been, where they are, and where they'd like to go next based on four variables: *pace* (from decelerated to accelerated), *workload* (reduced to full), *location/schedule* (restricted to not restricted), and *role* (individual contributor to leader). For example, to take time to have children or go back to college, a manager could step into a nonmanagerial individual contributor role with a reduced workload and less travel. "Our goal is to offer people options to keep their work and personal lives in sync," Benko explains, "and to give employers the loyalty of their best and brightest people. It ends up being a perfect fit."

Critical Thinking Questions

1. How might Deloitte's lattice approach help motivate employees and improve job satisfaction and performance?
2. How can managers determine whether a Deloitte employee is working at a decelerated pace in the career customization model or simply isn't working very hard?
3. What are the potential disadvantages from the company's point of view of giving employees this much flexibility?

LEARN MORE ONLINE

Visit the "Mass Career Customization" website at www.masscareercustomization.com, which offers more information about the Deloitte lattice model. Read "About MCC" and then try the "Interactive Exercise," where you can chart your own career (real or imaginary). You can also download a brief version of the book Benko co-authored with another Deloitte executive, Anne Weisberg. Does the lattice model sound appealing to you? ■

Key Terms

cross-training (274)
engagement (263)
equity theory (268)
expectancy theory (267)
goal-setting theory (269)
Herzberg's two-factor theory (266)
incentives (275)

job characteristics model (272)
job enrichment (274)
management by objectives
  (MBO) (270)
Maslow's hierarchy (264)
micromanaging (279)
motivation (263)

negative reinforcement (275)
positive reinforcement (275)
reinforcement theory (275)
scientific management (264)
Theory X (265)
Theory Y (265)
three-needs theory (266)

Test Your Knowledge

Questions for Review

1. What is motivation?
2. What is negative reinforcement?
3. What is management by objectives?
4. What is the expectancy theory?
5. What are the core job dimensions in the job characteristics model?

Questions for Analysis

6. How does the expectancy theory explain the effect of self-doubt on employee motivation?
7. What effect will job enhancement likely have on someone with low growth needs? Why?
8. How might a deadline that is too easy to meet cause someone to work more slowly than he or she might otherwise?
9. Why do managers often find it difficult to motivate employees who remain after downsizing?
10. **Ethical Considerations.** Motivational strategies that reward employees for meeting specific performance targets can encourage them to work hard—sometimes too hard. Overwork can contribute to mental and physical health problems as well as interfere with other aspects of employees' lives. As a manager, how do you determine how much work is too much for your employees?

Questions for Application

11. How do you motivate yourself when faced with school assignments or projects that are difficult or tedious? Do you ever try to relate these tasks to your overall career goals? Are you more motivated by doing your personal best or by outperforming other students?
12. You manage the customer service department for an online clothing retailer. Customers tend to call or e-mail with the same types of complaints and problems, day after day, and your employees are getting bored and listless. Some are starting to miss more days of work than usual, and several have quit recently. A few customers have called you directly to complain about poor treatment from your staff. Use the job characteristics model to identify several ways you could improve motivation, job satisfaction, and performance.
13. Imagine yourself in one of the jobs you would like to land after graduation. Thinking about the importance of personalizing motivational tactics whenever possible, identify several steps your manager could take to make sure you stay motivated. Would these steps be fair to other employees as well?
14. **Concept Integration.** Chapter 7 discusses several styles of leadership, including autocratic, democratic, and laissez-faire. How do each of these styles relate to Theory X and Theory Y assumptions about workers?

Practice Your Knowledge

Sharpening Your Communication Skills

Choose one of the major motivation theories discussed in this chapter: expectancy, goal-setting, job characteristics, or reinforcement. Create a brief electronic presentation (3–5 slides) using PowerPoint, Keynote, Google Docs, or a similar tool explaining the theory and identifying its strengths and weaknesses as a practical management approach.

Building Your Team Skills

With your teammates, explore the careers sections of the websites of six companies in different industries. Look for descriptions of the work environment, incentive

plans, career paths, and other information about how the company develops, motivates, and supports its employees. After you've compiled notes about each company, vote on the most appealing company to work for. Next, review the notes for this company and identify all the theories of motivation described in this chapter that the company appears to be using, based on the information on its website.

Expand Your Knowledge

Discovering Career Opportunities

Whether you're a top manager, first-line manager (supervisor), or middle manager, your efforts will affect the success of your organization. To get a closer look at the responsibilities of a manager, log on to the Prentice Hall Student Success SuperSite at www.prenhall.com/success. Click on "Majors Exploration" and then select "Business" and "Management" in the drop-down boxes. Then scroll down and read about careers in management. What can you do with a degree in management? What is the future outlook for careers in management? Follow the link to the American Management Association website, and click on "Research." Then scroll down and click on "Administrative Professionals Current Concerns Survey." According to the survey, what has affected administrative professionals most recently? On which five tasks do managers spend most of their time?

Developing Your Research Skills

Various periodicals and websites feature "best companies to work for" lists. Locate one of these lists and find a company that does a great job of attracting and motivating high performers. Learn as much as you can about the company's management philosophies. Which of the motivation theories does the company appear to be using? Summarize your findings in a brief e-mail message to your instructor.

Improving Your Tech Insights: Blogging and Microblogging

Blogging (and microblogging, of which Twitter is the best-known example) has revolutionized business communication in recent years. Far more than just another communication medium, blogging changes the relationship between companies and their stakeholders by transforming communication from a formal "we talk, you listen" mindset to an informal and interactive conversational mindset.

Identify a company in which one or more managers are regular bloggers or Twitter users. In a brief e-mail to your instructor, explain how the company uses blogging to build relationships with customers and potential customers, employees and potential employees, and other stakeholder groups.

Video Discussion

Access the Chapter 10 video discussion in the End of Chapter Assignments section at www.mybizlab.com.

Log on to www.mybizlab.com to access the following study and assessment aids associated with this chapter:

- Interactive exercises
- Pre/post test
- Real-Time Updates
- Video application
- Customized study plans
- Biz Skills Simulations
- Quick Learning Guide

If you are not using mybizlab, you can access Real-Time Updates and Quick Learning Guides through http://real-timeupdates.com/bia5. The Quick Learning Guide (located under "Learn More" on the website) provides all six Checkpoints in a handy two-page format to help you study for exams or review important concepts whenever you need a quick refresher.

CHAPTER 11

Employee Development and Support

After studying this chapter, you will be able to

1 Identify four contemporary staffing challenges and explain the process of planning for a company's staffing needs

2 Discuss the challenges and advantages of a diverse workforce and identify five major dimensions of workforce diversity

3 Describe the three phases involved in managing the employment lifecycle

4 Explain the steps used to develop and evaluate employees

5 Describe the major elements of employee compensation

6 Identify the most significant categories of employee benefits and services

Searching for the Perfect Blend of Employee Benefits at Starbucks

www.starbucks.com

Hiring, training, and compensating a diverse, global workforce is a difficult task for any company. But it is an especially daunting challenge in an industry whose annual employee turnover rate runs as high 300 percent or more. It can be even more of a challenge for a company that is striving to open a new store every day, despite an uncertain global economy and increasingly intense competition.

This was the high-pressure situation facing Starbucks as the company set out to spread its gourmet coffee across the world. Already, the rich aroma of fresh-brewed espresso was wafting through neighborhoods all over North America, with new stores planned for the United Kingdom, Japan, China, and many other countries. But company chairman Howard Schultz and his management team knew that good locations and top-quality coffee were just part of the company's formula for success.

To keep up with this ambitious schedule of new store openings, Starbucks had to find, recruit, and train

By offering benefits to all employees (including part-timers), Starbucks attracts and keeps quality employees.

hundreds of new employees every month, no easy feat "when there is a shortage of labor and few people want to work behind a retail counter," as Schultz noted. Moreover, Starbucks's employees (known internally as *partners*) had to deliver consistently superior customer service in every store and every market. In other words, Starbucks's employees had to do more than simply pour coffee—they had to believe passionately in the product and pay attention to all the details that can make or break the retail experience for the chain's millions of customers.

Schultz knew it would take more than good pay and company benefits to motivate and inspire employees. But what? If you were a member of Schultz's management team, how would you attract, train, and compensate a diverse workforce? What human resources policies and practices would you implement to motivate employees to give topnotch service?[1] ∎

Introduction

Howard Schultz (profiled in the chapter-opening Behind the Scenes) knows that hiring the right people to help a company reach its goals and then overseeing their training and development, motivation, evaluation, and compensation are critical to a company's success. This chapter explores the many steps companies take to build productive workforces, including solving staffing challenges, addressing workforce diversity, managing the employment lifecycle, developing employees, and providing compensation and benefits.

Keeping Pace with Today's Workforce

human resources (HR) management
Specialized function of planning how to obtain employees, oversee their training, evaluate them, and compensate them

The field of **human resources (HR) management** encompasses all the tasks involved in attracting, developing, and supporting an organization's staff, as well as maintaining a safe working environment that meets legal requirements and ethical expectations.[2] You may not pursue a career in HR specifically, but understanding the challenges and responsibilities of the HR function will make you a more successful manager.

Contemporary Staffing Challenges

Managers in every organization face an ongoing array of staffing challenges, including aligning the workforce with organizational needs, fostering employee loyalty, adjusting workloads and monitoring for employee burnout, and helping employees balance their work and personal lives:

Real-Time Updates

Learn More
Work-life balance at Microsoft

Listen as five Microsoft employees discuss how they balance personal interest with work demands and what they do to unwind from high-pressure jobs. On mybizlab (www.mybizlab.com), you can access Real-Time Updates within each chapter or under Student Study Tools. Otherwise, go to http://real-timeupdates.com/bia5 and click on "Learn More."

- **Aligning the workforce.** Matching the right employees to the right jobs at the right time can be a constant challenge. Externally, changes in market needs, competitive moves, advances in technology, and new regulations can all affect the ideal size and composition of the workforce. Internally, shifts in strategy, technological changes, and growing or declining product sales can force managers to realign their workforces.

- **Fostering employee loyalty.** Most companies can't guarantee long-term employment, but they want employees to commit themselves to the company. As the number of temporary employees and independent contractors increases, this challenge will only grow.

- **Monitoring workloads and avoiding employee burnout.** As companies try to beat competitors and keep workforce costs to a minimum, managers need to be on guard for *employee burnout*, a state of physical and emotional exhaustion that can result from constant exposure to stress over a long period of time. One of the potential downsides of ubiquitous connectivity is that many employees struggle to separate work life from personal life, which can create a feeling that work never ends.

- **Managing work-life balance.** The concern over workloads is one of the factors behind the growing interest in **work-life balance**, the idea that employees, managers, and entrepreneurs need to balance the competing demands of their professional and personal lives. Many companies are trying to make it easier for employees to juggle multiple responsibilities with on-site day-care facilities, flexible work schedules, and other options designed to improve **quality of work life (QWL)**.

work-life balance
Efforts to help employees balance the competing demands of their personal and professional lives

quality of work life (QWL)
Overall environment that results from job and work conditions

Planning for a Company's Staffing Needs

Planning for a company's staffing needs is a delicate balancing act. Hire too few employees and you can't keep pace with the competition or satisfy customers. Hire too many and you raise fixed costs above a level that revenues can sustain. To avoid either problem, HR managers work carefully to evaluate the requirements of every job in the company and to forecast the supply and demand for all types of talent (see Exhibit 11.1).

EXHIBIT 11.1 Steps in Human Resources Planning

Careful attention to each phase of this sequence helps ensure that a company will have the right human resources when it needs them.

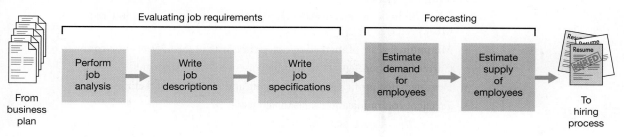

job description
Statement of the tasks involved in a given job and the conditions under which the holder of the job will work

job specification
Statement describing the kind of person who would be best for a given job—including the skills, education, and previous experience that the job requires

Evaluating Job Requirements

Through the process of *job analysis*, employers try to identify both the nature and demands of each position within the firm and the optimal employee profile to fill each position.[3] Once job analysis has been completed, the HR staff develops a **job description**, a formal statement summarizing the tasks involved in the job and the conditions under which the employee will work. In most cases, the staff will also develop a **job specification**, which identifies the type of personnel a job requires, including the skills, education, experience, and personal attributes that candidates need to possess[4] (see Exhibit 11.2).

EXHIBIT 11.2 Job Description and Specification

A well-written job description and specification tells potential applicants what to expect from the job and what employers will expect from them.

Job Title
Director of E-Marketing

Location
Denver, CO

Reports to
Vice President of Marketing

Job Detail

Soccer Scope is a leading retailer of soccer equipment, apparel, and accessories based in Denver, Colorado, with retail locations in 23 states. We seek to expand our online presence under the guidance of a director of e-marketing, a new managerial position to be based in our Denver headquarters.

The candidate who fills this position will be responsible for all nonstore aspects of our retailing efforts, including Soccer Scope's primary U.S. website and our country and region websites around the world, search-related advertising strategies, search engine optimization strategies, e-mail marketing campaigns, clicks-and-bricks integration strategy, affiliate marketing campaigns, customer retention efforts, and all aspects of online marketing research. The director of e-marketing will also work closely with the director of information technology to ensure the successful deployment of e-marketing platforms and with the director of retail operations to ensure a smooth clicks-and-bricks integration of offline and online retailing operations.

In addition to developing e-marketing strategies and directing e-marketing operations, the director is also responsible for leading a team of marketing and technical specialists who will implement and manage various programs.

Responsibilities
- Develop e-marketing strategies and plans consistent with Soccer Scope's overall business strategy and brand imperatives
- Establish and achieve aggressive customer acquisition and retention goals
- Coordinate efforts with technology and retailing counterparts to ensure successfully integrated online and offline marketing operations
- Assemble, lead, and develop an effective team of e-marketing professionals

Skills and Experience
- BA or BS in business, advertising, marketing, or related discipline required; MBA preferred
- Minimum 8 years of marketing experience, with at least 3 years in e-commerce
- Current and thorough understanding of e-marketing strategies
- Demonstrated proficiency in developing and executing marketing strategies
- Excellent communication skills in all media

Forecasting Supply and Demand

To forecast demand for the numbers and types of employees who will be needed at various times, HR managers weigh (1) forecasted sales revenues; (2) the expected **turnover rate**, the percentage of the workforce that leaves every year; (3) the current workforce's skill level, relative to the company's future needs; (4) impending strategic decisions; (5) changes in technology or other business factors that could affect the number and type of workers needed; and (6) the company's current and projected financial status.[5]

In addition to overall workforce levels, every company has a number of employees and managers who are considered so critical to the company's ongoing operations that HR managers work with top executives to identify potential replacements in the event of the loss of any of these people, a process known as **succession planning**.[6] A *replacement chart* identifies these key employees and lists potential replacements.

With some idea of future workforce demands, the HR staff then tries to estimate the *supply* of available employees. To ensure a steady supply of experienced employees for new opportunities and to maintain existing operations, successful companies focus heavily on **employee retention**.

If existing employees cannot be tapped for new positions, the HR team looks outside the company for people to join as either permanent employees or **contingent employees** who fulfill many of the responsibilities of regular employees but on a temporary basis. Already, such independent contractors make up 25 percent of the U.S. workforce, and that portion is expected to rise to 40 percent by 2019.[7]

turnover rate
Percentage of the workforce that leaves every year

succession planning
Workforce planning efforts that identify possible replacements for specific employees, usually senior executives

employee retention
Efforts to keep current employees

contingent employees
Nonpermanent employees, including temporary workers, independent contractors, and full-time employees hired on a probationary basis

Alternative Work Arrangements

To meet today's staffing and demographic challenges, many companies are adopting alternative work arrangements to better accommodate the needs of employees—and to reduce costs in many cases. Four of the most popular arrangements are flextime, telecommuting, job sharing, and flexible career paths:

- An increasingly important alternative work arrangement, *flextime* is a scheduling system that allows employees to choose their own hours, within certain limits. Of course, the feasibility of flextime differs from industry to industry and from position to position within individual companies. For instance, jobs that involve customer contact can require fixed working hours.

- *Telecommuting,* working from home or another location using computers and telecommunications equipment to stay in touch with colleagues, suppliers, and customers, helps employees balance their professional and personal commitments by spending less time in transit between home and work. Telecommuting also plays an important role in efforts to reduce energy usage. More than 10 percent of U.S. employees now telecommute some of the time, and at some companies, the majority of workers have access to this option. At the insurance firm MetLife, for example, nearly 70 percent of the workforce telecommutes.[8]

- *Job sharing,* which lets two employees share a single full-time job and split the salary and benefits, can be an attractive alternative for people who want part-time hours in situations normally reserved for full-time employees. After the British drugstore chain Boots implemented job sharing, the percentage of women who returned to the company after maternity leave jumped from 7 to 77 percent.[9]

- Perhaps the most challenging of all alternative work arrangements are situations in which employees want to limit their work time or leave the workforce entirely for an extended period to raise children, attend school, volunteer, or pursue other personal interests. Programs such as Deloitte's mass career customization (see page 280) give employees more freedom in designing their own career paths.

LEARNING OBJECTIVE 1: Identify four contemporary staffing challenges, and explain the process of planning for a company's staffing needs.

Summary: Four challenges that every HR department wrestles with are aligning the workforce with changing job requirements, fostering employee loyalty, monitoring workloads and avoiding employee burnout, and managing work-life balance. The process of planning for a company's staffing needs includes evaluating job requirements to develop *job descriptions* and *job specifications* and then forecasting the supply of and demand for various types of talent to ensure that the company has the right people in the right positions.

Critical thinking: (1) How can alternative work arrangements also help companies reduce costs and their impact on the environment? (2) How can electronic communication technologies contribute to employee burnout?

It's your business: (1) Would you prefer to work as an independent contractor or a permanent employee? What do you see as the advantages and disadvantages of each mode of work? (2) Would you function well as a full-time telecommuter? Why or why not?

Key terms to know: human resources (HR) management, work-life balance, quality of work life (QWL), job description, job specification, turnover rate, succession planning, employee retention, contingent employees

Managing a Diverse Workforce

The workforce is always in a state of change, whether from a shift in global immigration patterns or from the changing balance of age groups within a country's population. The companies that are most successful at managing and motivating their employees take great care to understand the diversity of their workforces and establish programs and policies that both embrace that diversity and take full advantage of diversity's benefits.

Dimensions of Workforce Diversity

Today's workforce is diverse in race, gender, age, culture, family structures, religion, sexual orientation, mental and physical ability, socioeconomic background, and education. Over the past few decades, many innovative companies have changed the way they approach workforce diversity, from seeing it as a legal matter to seeing it as a strategic opportunity to connect with customers and take advantage of the broadest possible pool of talent.[10] Smart business leaders such as Ron Glover, IBM's vice president of global workforce diversity, recognize the competitive advantages of a diverse workforce that offers a broader spectrum of viewpoints and ideas, helps companies understand and identify with diverse markets, and enables companies to benefit from a wider range of employee talents. According to Glover, more diverse teams tend to be more innovative over the long term than more homogeneous teams.[11]

Differences in everything from religion to ethnic heritage to military experience enrich the workplace, but all can create managerial challenges. A diverse workforce brings with it a wide range of skills, traditions, backgrounds, experiences, outlooks, and attitudes toward work—all of which can affect employee behavior on the job. Supervisors face the challenge of communicating with these diverse employees, motivating them, and fostering cooperation and harmony among them. Teams face the challenge of working together closely, and companies are challenged to coexist peacefully with business partners and with the community as a whole. Some of the most important diversity issues today include age, gender, race, religion, and ability.

Age

In U.S. culture, youth is associated with strength, energy, possibilities, and freedom. In contrast, age is often associated with declining powers and a loss of respect and authority. However, older workers can offer broader experience, the benefits of important business relationships nurtured over many years, and high degrees of "practical intelligence"—the ability to solve complex, poorly defined problems.[12]

In contrast, in cultures that value age and seniority, longevity earns respect and increasing power and freedom. For instance, in many Asian societies, the oldest employees hold the most powerful jobs, the most impressive titles, and the greatest degrees of freedom and decision-making authority. If a younger employee disagrees with one of these senior executives, the discussion is never conducted in public. The notion of "saving face"—of avoiding public embarrassment—is too strong. Instead, if a senior person seems to be in error about something, other employees will find a quiet, private way to communicate whatever information they feel is necessary.[13]

In addition to cultural values associated with various life stages, the multiple generations within a culture present another dimension of diversity. Today's workplaces can have as many as four distinct generations working side by side: *traditionalists* (those born before 1946), *baby boomers* (born between 1946 and 1964), *generation X* (born between 1965 and 1980), and *generation Y* (born after 1980).[14] Each of these generations has been shaped by dramatically different world events and social trends, so it is not surprising that they often have different values, expectations, and communication habits. As with all other cultural matters, success in building bridges starts with understanding the gaps between the two sides.

The number of U.S. workers over 65 has been growing in recent years, creating both opportunities and challenges for managers.

Gender

The statistical picture of men and women in the workforce is complex, and various parties have sliced and diced the data in order to promote a variety of conclusions. For years, many professions and the upper management ranks in virtually all industries were dominated by men. The Equal Pay Act of 1963 mandated equal pay for comparable work, and the Civil Rights Act of 1964 made it illegal for employers to practice **sexism**, or discrimination on the basis of gender. The United States has made important strides toward gender equity since then, but significant issues remain. For example, the Equal Employment Opportunity Commission (EEOC) still fields between 20,000 and 30,000 complaints a year regarding gender discrimination.[15] The goal of closing the *gender pay gap* to ensure comparable pay for comparable work is nearer but has not been achieved. Overall, woman currently earn 80 percent of what men earn, but the gap is greater for older workers and smaller for younger workers.[16]

Another significant issue is access to opportunities. Although women now hold half of all managerial positions, that ratio shrinks dramatically the higher you look in the organization. For example, among the thousand largest U.S. corporations, fewer than 3 percent have women as CEOs.[17] A lack of opportunities to advance into the top ranks is often referred to as the **glass ceiling**, implying that one can see the top but can't get there. The glass ceiling is an important issue for both women and minorities.

With laws against employment discrimination, a society that is now more supportive of women in professional roles, and strong evidence that companies in which women are given opportunities to lead outperform companies that don't, why do these gaps still exist? In addition to instances of simple discrimination, analysts suggest a variety of reasons, including women's lower levels

sexism
Discrimination on the basis of gender

glass ceiling
Invisible barrier attributable to subtle discrimination that keeps women and minorities out of the top positions in business

 Real-Time Updates

Learn More
Workforce diversity: a view from the top
Sara Lee CEO Brenda Barnes offers her take on the importance of giving all employees the opportunity to contribute their best. On mybizlab (**www.mybizlab.com**), you can access Real-Time Updates within each chapter or under Student Study Tools. Otherwise, go to **http://real-timeupdates.com/bia5** and click on "Learn More."

Managers have the responsibility to educate their employees on the definition and consequences of sexual harassment.

sexual harassment
Unwelcome sexual advance, request for sexual favors, or other verbal or physical conduct of a sexual nature within the workplace

of education and job training, different occupational choices, the need to juggle the heavy demands of both career and parenthood, and the career hit that women often take when they step out of the workforce for extended periods—since more women than men choose to be stay-at-home parents.[18]

Beyond pay and promotional opportunities, many working women also have to deal with **sexual harassment**, defined as either an obvious request for sexual favors with an implicit reward or punishment related to work, or the more subtle creation of a sexist environment in which employees are made to feel uncomfortable by lewd jokes, remarks, or gestures. Even though male employees may also be targets of sexual harassment and both male and female employees may experience same-sex harassment, sexual harassment of female employees by male colleagues continues to make up the majority of reported cases.[19] Most corporations now publish strict policies prohibiting harassment, both to protect their employees and to protect themselves from lawsuits.[20]

Race

In many respects, the element of race in the diversity picture presents the same concerns as gender: equal pay for equal work, access to promotional opportunities, and ways to break through the glass ceiling. And as with gender, the EEOC still receives thousands of complaints every year about racial discrimination.[21] However, while the ratio of men and women in the workforce remains fairly stable year to year, the ethnic composition of the United States has been on a long-term trend of greater and greater diversity. Even the term *minority*, as it applies to nonwhite residents, makes less and less sense every year because in many locations Caucasian Americans no longer constitute a majority. Unfortunately, as with average wages between women and men, disparity still exists along racial lines. Averaging across the entire workforce, Asian Americans earn the most, followed by Caucasian Americans, African Americans, and Hispanic Americans.[22]

Religion

The effort to accommodate employees' life interests on a broader scale has led a number of companies to address the issue of religion in the workplace. As one of the most personal aspects of life, of course, religion does bring potential for controversy in a work setting. On the one hand, some employees feel they should be able to express their beliefs in the workplace and not be forced to "check their faith at the door" when they come to work. On the other hand, companies want to avoid situations in which openly expressed religious differences might cause friction between employees or distract employees from their responsibilities.

Religion in the workplace is a complex and contentious issue—and it's getting more so every year, at least as measured by a significant rise in the number of religious discrimination lawsuits.[23] Beyond accommodating individual beliefs to a reasonable degree, as required by U.S. law, companies occasionally need to resolve situations that pit one group of employees against another or against the company's policies.[24] As more companies work to establish inclusive workplaces, and as more employees seek to integrate religious convictions into their daily work, you can expect to see this issue being discussed at many companies in the coming years.

Ability

People whose hearing, vision, cognitive ability, or physical ability to operate equipment is impaired can be at a significant disadvantage in the workplace. As with other elements of diversity, success starts with respect for individuals and sensitivity to differences. Employers can also invest in a variety of *assistive technologies* (see page 143 for more information) that help people with disabilities perform activities that might otherwise be difficult or impossible. These technologies include devices and systems that help people communicate orally and visually, interact with computers and other equipment, and enjoy greater mobility in the workplace. For example, designers can emphasize *web accessibility*, taking steps to make websites more accessible to people whose vision is limited. Assistive technologies create a vital link for employees with disabilities, giving them opportunities to pursue a greater range of career paths and giving employers access to a broader base of talent.

Diversity Initiatives

To respond to these many challenges—and to capitalize on the business opportunities offered by both diverse marketplaces and diverse workforces—companies across the country are finding that embracing diversity in the richest sense is simply good business. In response, thousands of U.S. companies have established **diversity initiatives**, which can include such steps as contracting with more suppliers owned by women and minorities, targeting a more diverse customer base, and supporting the needs and interests of a diverse workforce. For example, IBM established executive-led task forces to represent women, Asian Americans, African Americans, Hispanic Americans, Native Americans, people with disabilities, and individuals who are gay, lesbian, bisexual, and transgender. As the company puts it, "Our diversity is a competitive advantage and consciously building diverse teams helps us drive the best results for our clients." For instance, women and minorities are a significant presence in the small-business marketplace, and having women and minorities on product development and marketing teams helps IBM understand the needs of these customers.[25]

diversity initiatives
Programs and policies that help companies support diverse workforces and markets

CHECKPOINT

LEARNING OBJECTIVE 2: Discuss the challenges and advantages of a diverse workforce, and identify five major dimensions of workforce diversity.

Summary: Differences in everything from religion to ethnic heritage to military experience enrich the workplace and give employers a competitive advantage by offering better insights into a diverse marketplace. A diverse workforce brings with it a wide range of skills, traditions, backgrounds, experiences, outlooks, and attitudes toward work—all of which can affect employee behaviors, relationships, and communication habits. Five major dimensions of workforce diversity addressed in this chapter are age, gender, race, religion, and ability.

Critical thinking: (1) How could it benefit a company to invest in assistive technologies for its workers? (2) How might socioeconomic diversity in a company's workforce create both challenges and opportunities for the company?

It's your business: (1) What general opinions do you have of the generation that is older than you and the generation that is younger than you? What experiences and observations shaped these opinions? (2) Do you believe that any aspect of your background or heritage has held you back in any way in college or at work? Why?

Key terms to know: sexism, glass ceiling, sexual harassment, diversity initiatives

Managing the Employment Lifecycle

HR managers oversee employment-related activities from recruiting and hiring through termination and retirement.

Hiring Employees

The employment lifecycle starts with **recruiting**, the process of attracting suitable candidates for an organization's jobs. The recruiting function is often judged by a combination of criteria known as *quality of hire*, which measures how closely incoming employees meet

recruiting
Process of attracting appropriate applicants for an organization's jobs

Real-Time Updates

Learn More

An inside look at improving quality of hire

See how careful talent assessment helps companies find the right people for every position. On mybizlab (www.mybizlab.com), you can access Real-Time Updates within each chapter or under Student Study Tools. Otherwise, go to http://real-timeupdates.com/bia5 and click on "Learn More."

the company's needs.[26] Recruiters use a variety of resources, including internal searches, advertising, union hiring halls, college campuses and career offices, trade shows, *headhunters* (outside agencies that specialize in finding and placing employees), and social networking technologies Employers typically try to hire from within whenever possible or to invite outside candidates who are recommended by employees. Consequently, many job openings are never advertised to the public.

Most companies go through six steps to hire new employees:

1. Recruiters select a small number of qualified candidates from all of the applications and résumés received. Many organizations now use computer-based *applicant tracking systems* to manage the hiring process and identify the most attractive candidates for each job.

2. Recruiters then screen the candidates, typically through phone interviews, online tests, or on-campus interviews. Interviews at this stage are usually fairly structured, with applicants asked the same questions so that recruiters can easily compare responses.

3. Candidates who make it through screening are then invited to visit the company for another round of interviews. This process usually involves several interviews with a variety of colleagues, managers, and someone from the HR department, but the number and format of the interviews vary widely depending on the company and the job in question.

4. The interview team compares notes and assesses the remaining candidates. Team members sometimes lobby for or against individual candidates based on what they've seen and heard during interviews.

5. Recruiting specialists check references, research the backgrounds of the top few candidates, and in many cases subject applicants to a variety of preemployment tests. Given the financial and even legal risks associated with bad hiring decisions and, unfortunately, widespread dishonesty on résumés and job applications, most employers now research candidates carefully and thoroughly.

6. With all this information in hand, the hiring manager selects the most suitable person for the job and tenders a job offer.

Federal and state laws and regulations govern many aspects of the hiring process (see Exhibit 11.3 for a list of some of the most important employment-related laws). In particular, employers must respect the privacy of applicants and avoid discrimination. For instance, any form or testing that can be construed as a preemployment medical examination is prohibited by the Americans with Disabilities Act.[27]

Terminating Employees

termination
Process of getting rid of an employee through layoff or firing

HR managers have the unpleasant responsibility of **termination**—permanently laying off employees because of cutbacks or firing employees for poor performance or other

EXHIBIT 11.3 Major Employment Legislation

Here are some of the most significant sets of laws that affect employer-employee relations in the United States.

CATEGORY	LEGISLATION	HIGHLIGHTS
Labor and unionization	National Labor Relations Act, also known as the Wagner Act	Establishes the right of employees to form, join, and assist unions and the right to strike; prohibits employers from interfering in union activities
	Labor-Management Relations Act, also known as the Taft-Hartley Act	Expands union member rights; gives employers free speech rights to oppose unions; restricts union's strike options; gives the president the authority to impose injunctions against strikes
	Labor-Management Reporting and Disclosure Act, also known as the Landrum-Griffin Act	Gives union members the right to nominate and vote for union leadership candidates; combats financial fraud within unions
	State right-to-work laws	Gives individual employees the right to choose not to join a union
	Fair Labor Standards Act	Establishes minimum wage and overtime pay for nonexempt workers; sets strict guidelines for child labor
	Immigration Reform and Control Act	Prohibits employers from hiring illegal immigrants
Workplace safety	State workers' compensation acts	Require employers (in most states) to carry either private or government-sponsored insurance that provides income to injured workers
	Occupational Health and Safety Act	Empowers the Occupational Safety and Health Administration (OSHA) to set and enforce standards for workplace safety
Compensation and benefits	Employee Retirement Income Security Act	Governs the establishment and operation of private pension programs
	Consolidated Omnibus Budget Reconciliation Act (usually known by the acronym COBRA)	Requires employers to let employees or their beneficiaries buy continued health insurance coverage after employment ends
	Federal Unemployment Tax Act and similar state laws	Requires employers to fund programs that provide income for qualified unemployed persons
	Social Security Act	Provides a level of retirement, disability, and medical coverage for employees and their dependents; jointly funded by employers and employees
	Lilly Ledbetter Fair Pay Act	Amends and modifies several pieces of earlier legislation to make it easier for employees to file lawsuits over pay and benefit discrimination
Discrimination and accommodation	Civil Rights Act	Prohibits discrimination based on race, religion, national origin, or gender and requires employers to make reasonable accommodation for employees' religious practices
	Americans with Disabilities Act	Prohibits discrimination against employees with disabilities and requires employers to make reasonable accommodations for employees with disabilities
	Genetic Information Nondiscrimination Act	Prohibits employment discrimination on the basis of genetic information

layoffs
Termination of employees for economic or business reasons

reasons. **Layoffs** are the termination of employees for economic or business reasons unrelated to employee performance. As Michael Dell, founder and CEO of Dell, puts it, making cuts "is one of the hardest, most gut-wrenching decisions you can make as a leader." Layoffs are "an admission that we screwed up" by overhiring.[28] *Rightsizing* is a term used to imply that the organization is making changes in the workforce to match its business needs more precisely. Although rightsizing usually involves *downsizing* the workforce, companies sometimes add workers in some areas even while they eliminate jobs in others.

To help ease the pain of layoffs, many companies provide laid-off employees with job-hunting assistance. *Outplacement* services such as résumé-writing courses, career counseling, office space, and secretarial help are offered to laid-off executives and blue-collar employees alike. Large-scale outplacement efforts are often outsourced to specialist firms such as Challenger, Gray & Christmas (**www.challengergray.com**), which can help laid-off employees find jobs in much less time than they can usually do on their own.[29]

With many companies trimming workforces during a recession, managers need to take care not to discriminate against any segment of the workforce. Older workers appear to be a particularly vulnerable group because they usually have higher salaries and more expensive benefits, making them a more inviting target for cost cutting. Age-discrimination complaints related to layoffs are now at an all-time high.[30]

Terminating employment by firing is a complex subject with many legal ramifications, and the line between a layoff and a firing can be blurry. For instance, every state except Montana supports the concept of *at-will employment,* meaning that companies are free to fire nearly anyone they choose. Exceptions to this principle vary from state to state, but in general, employers cannot discriminate in firing, nor can they fire employees for whistle-blowing, filing a worker's compensation claim, or testifying against the employer in harassment or discrimination lawsuits.[31] If a terminated employee believes any of these principles have been violated, he or she can file a *wrongful discharge* lawsuit against the employer. In addition, employers must abide by the terms of an employment contract, if one has been entered into with the employee (these are much more common for executives than for lower-level employees). Some employers offer written assurances that they will terminate employees only *for cause,* which usually includes such actions as committing crimes or violating company policy.

Retiring Employees

Companies can face two dramatically different challenges regarding retiring employees. For companies that are short-handed, the challenge is to persuade older employees to delay retirement. Facing a shortage of chemical engineers, Dow Chemical had to persuade some of its 20,000 employees who are scheduled to retire by 2012 to continue working. The firm introduced a variety of programs, including three-day weeks, to entice older employees to stay.[32]

Conversely, companies with too many employees may induce employees to depart ahead of scheduled retirement days by offering them *early retirement,* using financial incentives known as **worker buyouts.** In recent years, companies in the U.S. auto industry have offered buyouts to thousands of workers as they attempt to align their workforces with declining revenues.[33]

In the past, **mandatory retirement** policies forced people to quit working as soon as they turned a certain age. However, the Age Discrimination in Employment Act now outlaws mandatory retirement based on age alone, unless an employer can demonstrate that age is a valid qualification for "normal operation of the particular business."[34]

worker buyouts
Distributions of financial incentives to employees who voluntarily depart; usually undertaken in order to reduce the payroll

mandatory retirement
Required dismissal of an employee who reaches a certain age

✓CHECKPOINT

LEARNING OBJECTIVE 3: Describe the three phases involved in managing the employment lifecycle.

Summary: The three phases of managing the employment lifecycle are hiring, termination, and retirement. The hiring phase typically involves six steps of selecting a small number of qualified candidates from all of the applications received, screening those candidates to identify the most attractive prospects, interviewing those prospects in depth to learn more about them and their potential to contribute to the company, evaluating and comparing interview results, conducting background checks and preemployment tests, and then selecting the best candidate for each position and making job offers. Termination can involve firing employees for poor performance or other reasons or laying off employees for financial reasons. Retirement offers a variety of challenges depending on the industry and the company's situation; overstaffed companies may induce some employees to retire early through buyouts, whereas others that face talent shortages may try to induce retirement-age employees to delay retirement.

Critical thinking: (1) Why would a company spend money on outplacement counseling and other services for laid-off employees? (2) Why would a company spend money to induce retirement-age employees to stay on board for a while, rather than simply hiring younger employees to take their place?

It's your business: (1) Has anything been posted online that might embarrass you during a background search? (2) Have you ever been interviewed over the phone or via computer? If so, did you feel you were able to present yourself effectively without face-to-face contact?

Key terms to know: recruiting, termination, layoffs, worker buyouts, mandatory retirement

Developing and Evaluating Employees

Another major contribution that HR makes is helping managers throughout the company align employee skill sets with the evolving requirements of each position. This effort includes appraising employee performance, managing training and development programs, and promoting and reassigning employees.

Appraising Employee Performance

How do employees (and their managers) know whether they are doing a good job? How can they improve their performance? What new skills should they learn? Managers attempt to answer these questions by developing **performance appraisals** to objectively evaluate employees according to set criteria. The ultimate goal of performance appraisals is not to judge employees but rather to improve their performance. Thus, experts recommend that performance reviews be an ongoing discipline—not just a once-a-year event linked to employee raises. As Chapter 10 points out, employees need regular feedback so that any deficiencies can be corrected quickly.

Most companies require regular written evaluations of each employee's work. To ensure objectivity and consistency, firms generally use a standard company performance appraisal form to evaluate employees. The evaluation criteria are in writing so that both employee and supervisor understand what is expected and are therefore able to determine whether the work is being done adequately (see Exhibit 11.4 on the next page).

performance appraisals
Evaluations of employees' work according to specific criteria

EXHIBIT 11.4 **Sample Performance Appraisal Form**

Many companies use forms like this (either printed or online) to ensure that performance appraisals are as objective as possible.

Name _____	Title _____ Service Date _____ Date _____
Location _____	Division _____ Department _____
Length of Time in Present Position	Period of Review Appraised by _____
_____	From: ___ To: ___ Title of Appraisor _____

Area of Performance	Comment	Rating
Job Knowledge and Skill Understands responsibilities and uses background for job. Adapts to new methods/techniques. Plans and organizes work. Recognizes errors and problems.		5 4 3 2 1
Volume of Work Amount of work output. Adherence to standards and schedules. Effective use of time.		5 4 3 2 1
Quality of Work Degree of accuracy—lack of errors. Thoroughness of work. Ability to exercise good judgment.		5 4 3 2 1
Initiative and Creativity Self-motivation in seeking responsibility and work that needs to be done. Ability to apply original ideas and concepts.		5 4 3 2 1
Communication Ability to exchange thoughts or information in a clear, concise manner. Ability to deal with different organizational levels of clientele.		5 4 3 2 1
Dependability Ability to follow instructions and directions correctly. Performs under pressure. Reliable work habits.		5 4 3 2 1
Leadership Ability/Potential Ability to guide others to the successful accomplishment of a given task. Potential for developing subordinate employees.		5 4 3 2 1

5. Outstanding	Employee who consistently exceeds established standards and expectations of the job.
4. Above Average	Employee who consistently meets established standards and expectations of the job. Often exceeds and rarely falls short of desired results.
3. Satisfactory	Generally qualified employee who meets job standards and expectations. Sometimes exceeds and may occasionally fall short of desired expectations. Performs duties in a normally expected manner.
2. Improvement Needed	Not quite meeting standards and expectations. An employee at this level of performance is not quite meeting all the standard job requirements.
1. Unsatisfactory	Employee who fails to meet the minimum standards and expectations of the job.

I have had the opportunity to read this performance appraisal.	How long has this employee been under your supervision?
Signature Date	Signature of Supervisor Date

Written evaluations also provide a record of the employee's performance, which may protect the company in cases of disputed terminations.[35]

The specific measures of employee performance vary widely by job, company, and industry. Most jobs are evaluated in several areas, including tasks specific to the position, contribution to the company's overall success, and interaction with colleagues and customers. For example, a production manager might be evaluated on the basis of communication skills, people management, leadership, teamwork, recruiting and employee development, delegation, financial management, planning, and organizational skills.[36]

Many performance appraisals require the employee to be rated by several people (including more than one supervisor and perhaps several co-workers). This practice further promotes fairness by correcting for possible biases. The ultimate in multidimensional reviews is the **360-degree review**, in which a person is given feedback from subordinates (if the employee has supervisory responsibility), peers, and superiors. The multiple viewpoints can uncover weaknesses that employees and even their direct managers might not be aware of, as well as contributions and achievements that might have been overlooked in normal reviews.[37] To ensure anonymity and to compile the multiple streams of information, 360-degree reviews are often conducted via computer. Experts also recommend that 360-degree reviews not be used to set salaries and that reviewers be thoroughly trained in the technique.[38]

360-degree review
Multidimensional review in which a person is given feedback from subordinates, peers, and superiors

Evaluating individual performance is a challenge in organizations where employees work in teams. Assessments by the team leader are important, of course, but they can't always sort out what each member contributed to the overall output, particularly in teams that operate with a great deal of autonomy. A good way to address this problem is to have each team member evaluate his or her own contribution and that of every other team member as well. A manager who oversees the team can then compare all the assessments (which are done anonymously) to look for patterns—who contributes the bulk of the new ideas, who's just along for the ride, and so on.[39]

In addition to formal, periodic performance evaluations, many companies evaluate some workers' performance continuously, using **electronic performance monitoring (EPM)**, sometimes called *computer activity monitoring*. For instance, customer service and telephone sales representatives are often evaluated by the number of calls they complete per hour and other variables. Newer software products extend this monitoring capability, from measuring data input accuracy to scanning for suspicious words in employee e-mails. As you can imagine, EPM efforts can generate controversy in the workplace, elevating employee stress levels and raising concerns about invasion of privacy.[40]

electronic performance monitoring (EPM)
Real-time, computer-based evaluation of employee performance

Training and Developing Employees

With the pace of change in everything from government regulations to consumer tastes to technology, employee knowledge and skills need to be constantly updated. Consequently, the most successful companies place a heavy emphasis on employee training and development efforts, for everyone from entry-level workers to the CEO. Overall, U.S. companies now spend more than $50 billion a year on training.[41]

Training usually begins with **orientation programs** designed to ease the new hire's transition into the company and to impart vital knowledge about the organization and its rules, procedures, and expectations. Effective orientation programs help employees become more productive in less time, help eliminate confusion and mistakes, and can significantly increase employee retention rates.[42]

orientation programs
Sessions or procedures for acclimating new employees to the organization

Training and other forms of employee development continue throughout the employee's career in most cases. Many HR departments maintain a **skills inventory**, which identifies both the current skill levels of all the employees and the skills the company needs in order to succeed. Depending on the industry, some of the most common subjects for ongoing training include problem solving, new products, sales, customer service, safety, sexual harassment, supervision, quality, strategic planning, communication, time management, and team building.[43]

skills inventory
A list of the skills a company needs from its workforce, along with the specific skills that individual employees currently possess

Promoting and Reassigning Employees

Most companies usually prefer to look within the organization to fill job vacancies. In part, this "promote from within" policy allows a company to benefit from the training and experience of its own workforce. This policy also rewards employees who have worked hard and demonstrated the ability to handle more challenging tasks. In addition, morale is usually better when a company promotes from within because employees see that they can advance. For example, Enterprise Rent-A-Car, one of the nation's largest employers of new college graduates, has used its strong tradition of promoting from within as a major selling point to potential employees.[44]

However, a possible pitfall of internal promotion is that a person may be given a job beyond his or her competence. The best salesperson in the company is not necessarily a good candidate for sales manager, because managing often requires a different set of skills. If the promotion is a mistake, the company not only loses its sales leader but also risks demoralizing the sales staff. Companies can reduce such risks through careful promotion policies and by providing support and training to help promoted employees perform well.

✓CHECKPOINT

LEARNING OBJECTIVE 4: Explain the steps used to develop and evaluate employees.

Summary: The effort to develop and evaluate employees includes appraising employee performance, managing training and development programs, and promoting and reassigning employees. Managers use performance appraisals to give employees feedback and develop plans to improve performance shortcomings. In a 360-degree review, an employee is evaluated by subordinates (if applicable), peers, and superiors. Training and development efforts begin with orientation for new hires and continue throughout a person's career in many cases. When employees have reached sufficient skill levels to take on new challenges, they may be considered for promotion into positions of more responsibility.

Critical thinking: (1) How can employers balance the need to provide objective appraisals that can be compared across the company's entire workforce with the desire to evaluate each employee on an individual basis? (2) Beyond increasing their skill and knowledge levels, how can training improve employees' motivation and job satisfaction? (Review Chapter 10 if you need to.)

It's your business: (1) Have you ever had a performance appraisal that you felt was inaccurate or unfair? How would you change the process as a result? (2) Do the methods your college or university uses to evaluate your performance as student accurately reflect your progress? What changes would you make to the evaluation process?

Key terms to know: performance appraisals, 360-degree review, electronic performance monitoring (EPM), orientation programs, skills inventory

Administering Employee Compensation

Pay and benefits are of vital interest to all employees, of course, and these subjects also consume considerable time and attention in HR departments. For many companies, payroll is the single biggest expense, and the cost of benefits, particularly health care, continues to climb. Consequently, **compensation**, the combination of direct payments such as wages or salary and indirect payments through employee benefits, is one of the HR manager's most significant responsibilities.

Salaries and Wages

Most employees receive the bulk of their compensation in the form of **salary**, if they receive a fixed amount per year, or **wages**, if they are paid by the unit of time (hourly, daily, or weekly) or by the unit of output (often called "getting paid by the piece" or "piecework"). The Fair Labor Standards Act, introduced in 1938 and amended many times since then, sets specific guidelines that employers must follow when administering salaries and wages,

compensation
Money, benefits, and services paid to employees for their work

salary
Fixed cash compensation for work, usually by yearly amount; independent of the number of hours worked

wages
Cash payment based on the number of hours the employee has worked or the number of units the employee has produced

including setting a minimum wage and paying overtime for time worked beyond 40 hours a week. However, most professional and managerial employees are considered exempt from these regulations, meaning, for instance, their employers don't have to pay them for overtime. The distinction between *exempt employees* and *nonexempt employees* is based on job responsibilities and pay level. In general, salaried employees are exempt, although there are many exceptions.[45]

Both wages and salaries are, in principle, based on the contribution of a particular job to the company. Thus, a sales manager, who is responsible for bringing in sales revenue, is paid more than a secretary, who handles administrative tasks but doesn't sell or supervise. However, pay often varies widely by position, industry, and location. Among the best-paid employees in the world are chief executive officers of large U.S. corporations.

Compensation has become a hot topic in recent years, at both ends of the pay scale. At the low end, for instance, many retail businesses, employees, and unions are wrestling with the downward pressure on wages and benefits exerted by Walmart's enormous presence in the economy. With more than a million employees, the company's cost-conscious strategy that benefits millions of consumers also indirectly affects thousands of people who've never worked there. As other stores try to compete with Walmart, many feel they have no choice but to pay their employees less and offer fewer benefits. Economists continue to study Walmart's impact on wages and benefits, but a definitive answer has yet to emerge.[46]

At the upper end of the pay scale, executive compensation, and the pay of CEOs in particular, has generated its own brand of controversy. CEOs typically receive complex compensation packages that include a base salary plus a wide range of benefits and bonuses, including *golden handshakes* when they join a company and *golden parachutes* when they leave. Annual CEO compensation packages of $10 million to $20 million or more are not uncommon these days. Thirty years ago, the average CEO of a public company made roughly 40 times more than the average hourly worker; today, it's well over 500 times more.[47]

Outrage over outsized compensation packages have spiked in recent years, particularly when it comes to CEOs who receive multimillion-dollar compensation while their companies—and their companies' stock prices—suffer mightily. A major concern in executive compensation is that many CEOs are paid based on what their peers make, rather than on meaningful long-term performance. Not only does this approach not tie pay to performance, but with so many CEOs serving on each other's boards, board members can indirectly influence their own salaries by paying other CEOs more. For example, even as General Motors's stock price plummeted as the company headed toward eventual bankruptcy, GM's board continued to pay former CEO Richard Wagoner hefty compensation based on what his peers at more successful companies were making.[48]

Incentive Programs

As Chapter 10 mentions, many companies provide managers and employees with **incentives** to encourage productivity, innovation, and commitment to work. Incentives are typically cash payments linked to specific goals for individual, group, or companywide performance. In other words, achievements, not just activities, are made the basis for payment. The success of these programs often depends on how closely incentives are linked to actions within the employee's control:

- For both salaried and wage-earning employees, one type of incentive compensation is the **bonus**, a payment in addition to the regular wage or salary. Performance-based

bonus
Cash payment, in addition to regular wage or salary, that serves as a reward for achievement

Sales professionals usually earn at least part of their income through commissions; the more they sell, the more they earn.

commissions
Employee compensation based on a percentage of sales made

profit sharing
The distribution of a portion of the company's profits to employees

gain sharing
Tying rewards to profits or cost savings achieved by meeting specific goals

pay for performance
Incentive program that rewards employees for meeting specific, individual goals

knowledge-based pay
Pay tied to an employee's acquisition of knowledge or skills; also called competency-based pay or skill-based pay

bonuses have become an increasingly popular approach to compensation as more companies shift away from automatic annual pay increases.[49]

- In contrast to bonuses, **commissions** are a form of compensation that pays employees in sales positions based on the level of sales made within a given time frame.

- Employees may be rewarded for staying with a company and encouraged to work harder through **profit sharing**, a system in which employees receive a portion of the company's profits.

- Similar to profit sharing, **gain sharing** ties rewards to profits (or cost savings) achieved by meeting specific goals such as quality and productivity improvement.

- A variation of gain sharing, **pay for performance** requires employees to accept a lower base pay but rewards them with bonuses, commissions, or stock options if they reach agreed-upon goals. To be successful, this method needs to be complemented with effective feedback systems that let employees know how they are performing throughout the year.[50]

- Another approach to compensation being explored by some companies is **knowledge-based pay**, also known as *competency-based pay* or *skill-based pay*, which is tied to employees' knowledge and abilities rather than to their job per se. More than half of all large U.S. companies now use some variation on this incentive.[51]

✓CHECKPOINT

LEARNING OBJECTIVE 5: Describe the major elements of employee compensation.

Summary: For most employees, the bulk of their compensation comes in the form of *salary*, if they receive a fixed amount per year, or *wages*, if they are paid by the unit of time or unit of output. In addition to their base salary or wages, some employees are eligible for a variety of incentive programs, including bonuses, commissions, profit sharing, and gain sharing. In some cases, employers offer pay for performance plans that have a lower base salary but allow employees to earn more by hitting specific performance goals. Some companies are also exploring knowledge-based pay, which rewards employees for acquiring information or developing skills related to their jobs.

Critical thinking: (1) What are some potential risks or limitations of performance-based pay systems? (2) How does equity theory (see Chapter 10) explain the anger some employees feel about the compensation packages their company CEOs receive?

It's your business: (1) If you worked for a large corporation, would a profit-sharing plan motivate you? Why or why not? (2) What questions would you ask before you accepted a sales position in which most of your compensation would be based on commissions, rather than base salary?

Key terms to know: compensation, salary, wages, bonus, commissions, profit sharing, gain sharing, pay for performance, knowledge-based pay

Employee Benefits and Services

Companies also regularly provide **employee benefits**—elements of compensation other than wages, salaries, and incentives. These benefits may be offered as either a preset package—that is, the employee gets whatever insurance, paid holidays, pension plan, and other benefits the company sets up—or as flexible plans, sometimes known as **cafeteria plans** (so called because of the similarity to choosing items from a menu). The benefits most commonly provided by employers are insurance, retirement benefits, employee stock-ownership plans, stock options, and family benefits. As you read the following sections, you'll begin to understand why the field of benefits has become such a complex area in business today, and why benefits often figure strongly in union contract negotiations, strategic planning decisions, and even national public policy debates.

employee benefits
Compensation other than wages, salaries, and incentive programs

cafeteria plans
Flexible benefit programs that let employees personalize their benefits packages

Insurance

Employers can offer a range of insurance plans to their employees, including life, health, dental, vision, disability, and long-term-care insurance. Although employers are under no general legal obligation to provide insurance coverage (except in union contracts, for instance), many companies view these benefits as a competitive necessity, to attract and retain good employees.

Perhaps no other issue illustrates the challenging economics of business today than health-care costs in general and health insurance in particular. With medical costs rising much faster than inflation in general, companies are taking a variety of steps to manage the financial impact, including forcing employees to pick up more of the cost, reducing or eliminating coverage for retired employees, auditing employees' health claims, monitoring employees' health and habits, dropping spouses from insurance plans, or even firing employees who are so sick or disabled that they are no longer able to work. The situation is particularly acute for small businesses, which don't have the purchasing power of large corporations.[52]

Health-care costs—including the question of how to insure the millions of U.S. residents without health insurance—will continue to be a major topic of discussion and reform efforts in the coming years. In aggregate, the United States spends enough to provide adequate care for everyone, but the system is plagued by waste, inefficiency, and imbalance. Per capita, the United States spends more on health care than any other country, but according to a number of key measures, the quality of care is lower than in many other countries.[53] In 2009, President Barack Obama called the health-care system a "ticking time bomb" that threatened to bankrupt the U.S. economy.[54]

In the true spirit of entrepreneurship, however, U.S. companies aren't just giving up in the face of rising costs. Exhibit 11.5 shows a sample of many creative ways employers, insurers, and public officials are trying to offer adequate coverage at manageable costs.

Retirement Benefits

Many employers offer **retirement plans**, which are designed to provide continuing income after the employee retires. Company-sponsored retirement plans can be categorized as either *defined benefit plans*, in which companies specify how much they will pay employees upon retirement, or *defined contribution plans*, in which companies specify how much they will put into the retirement fund (by matching employee contributions, for instance), without guaranteeing any specific payouts during retirement. Although both types are technically **pension plans**, when most people speak of pension plans, they are referring to traditional defined benefit plans.[55]

retirement plans
Company-sponsored programs for providing retirees with income

pension plans
Generally refers to traditional, defined benefit retirement plans

Defined benefit plans are far less common than they were in the past, and some of the remaining plans are in serious financial trouble. To meet their current and future obligations to employees, pension fund managers invest some of the company's cash and assume those investments will grow enough to cover future retirement needs. However,

EXHIBIT 11.5 Creative Approaches to Skyrocketing Health-Care Costs

For a variety of reasons—cost control, competitiveness, and concern for their employees—
U.S. companies are tackling high health-care costs in a variety of ways.

High-deductible insurance	One of the simplest changes is switching to high-deductible insurance, in which the employee must pay more of his or her medical expenses directly before insurance kicks in. This not only lowers insurance premiums, but advocates say it forces employees to use health-care services more carefully.
Health Savings Accounts (HSAs)	HSAs let employees sock away part of their salaries tax-free and use the money to pay for medical care or spend it on other things if they stay healthy.
In-house clinic	A few companies have saved by opening their own private clinics on site, giving them more control over costs and removing the insurance layer from the health-care model. However, this option is attractive only to companies with large, geographically concentrated workforces.
Health insurance buying groups	Smaller employers can band together to increase their purchasing power. After joining the employers' group Presidion, the Tampa, Florida, restaurant chain Ragin' Ribs cut its health-care costs by 25 percent. Similar organizations also exist to help independent contractors save on insurance.
Employer-driven quality improvements	An even more comprehensive cooperative effort is the Leapfrog Group, a nonprofit coalition representing a variety of employers and health-care plans; Leapfrog offers incentives to hospitals and health-care providers to reduce preventable medical errors, improve the quality of care, and in doing so, also cut costs dramatically.
Insurance for the uninsured	A coalition of large employers recently formed the Affordable Health Care Solution, a giant purchasing cooperative that lowers the cost of insurance for independent contractors, part-timers, and others who can't afford insurance.
Sliding-scale plans	With a sliding-scale program, employers charge for health insurance based on salary, making insurance more affordable for lower-wage workers.
Wellness programs	Many employers have discovered that a great way to cut health-care costs is to keep employees healthier in the first place; wellness programs can include everything from dietary advice to exercise facilities to smoking-cessation classes.

dramatic investment losses in recent years have left many plans underfunded, some by billions of dollars, forcing those companies to redirect cash from other purposes.[56]

Defined contribution plans are similar to savings plans; they provide a future benefit based on annual employer contributions, voluntary employee matching contributions, and accumulated investment earnings. Employers can choose from several types of defined contribution plans, the most common of which is known as a **401(k) plan**. In a 401(k) plan, employees contribute a percentage of their pretax income, and employers often match that amount or some portion of it.[57]

Some 10 million U.S. employees are now enrolled in a type of defined benefit plan known as an **employee stock-ownership plan (ESOP)**, in which a company places some or all of its stock in trust, with each eligible employee entitled to a certain portion. (Most ESOPs are in closely held corporations whose stock isn't available for sale to the public.) Many companies report that ESOPs help boost employee productivity because workers perceive a direct correlation between their efforts and the value of the company stock price.[58]

401(k) plan
A defined contribution retirement plan in which employers often match the amount employees invest

employee stock-ownership plan (ESOP)
Program enabling employees to become partial owners of a company

Stock Options

A related method for tying employee compensation to company performance is the stock option plan. **Stock options** grant employees the right to purchase a set number of shares of the employer's stock at a specific price, called the *grant* or *exercise price*, during a certain time period. Options typically *vest* over a number of years, meaning that employees can purchase a prorated portion of the shares every year until the vesting period is over (at which time they can purchase all the shares they are entitled to). The

stock options
Contract allowing the holder to purchase or sell a certain number of shares of a particular stock at a given price by a certain date

major attractions of stock options from an employer's point of view are that they provide a means of compensation that doesn't require any cash outlay and provide a means of motivating employees to work hard to make sure the stock price increases.

The popularity of stock options has waned somewhat in recent years, following a change in accounting rules that forced companies to account for the value of outstanding options in their annual financial reports. Before that change, investors and regulators argued that companies were hiding the true costs of options and thereby reporting inflated earnings.[59]

Stock options also figure in the controversy about executive compensation, for a couple of reasons. First, from the recipient's point of view, there is no real risk associated with stock options. Second, this lack of risk exposure can lead to riskier decision making. In fact, research suggests that CEOs who are compensated primarily through stock options tend to make poorer decisions regarding acquisitions, and their companies are more likely to experience accounting irregularities.[60]

Other Employee Benefits

Employers offer a variety of other benefits, some mandated by government regulation and some offered voluntarily to attract and support employees. Here are some of the more common benefits:

- **Paid vacations and sick leave.** Some companies offer separate vacation and sick days; others combine the paid time off in a single "bucket" and let employees choose how to use the time.

- **Family and medical leave.** The Family Medical and Leave Act (FMLA) of 1993 requires employers with 50 or more workers to provide up to 12 weeks of unpaid leave per year for childbirth, adoption, or the care of oneself, a child, a spouse, or a parent with serious illness.[61]

- **Child-care assistance.** Nearly half of all companies now offer some sort of child-care assistance, including discounted rates at nearby child-care centers or on-site day-care centers.[62]

- **Elder-care assistance.** Many employers now offer some form of elder-care assistance to help employees with the responsibility of caring for aging parents.

- **Tuition loans and reimbursements.** U.S. companies contribute roughly $10 billion every year to continuing education for their employees.[63]

- **Employee assistance programs.** One of the most cost-effective benefits employers can establish is an **employee assistance program (EAP)**, which offers private and confidential counseling to employees who need help with issues related to substance abuse, domestic violence, finances, stress, family issues, and other personal problems.[64]

For the latest information on employee benefits and other human resources topics, visit http://real-timeupdates.com/bia5 and click on Chapter 11.

employee assistance program (EAP)
Company-sponsored counseling or referral plan for employees with personal problems

Trust Insurance employee Kathy Hatfield gets to spend time with her daughters at the company's on-site day-care center. Such centers reduce costs and stress for employees with children.

✓CHECKPOINT

LEARNING OBJECTIVE 6: Identify the most significant categories of employee benefits and services.

Summary: The major types of employee benefits are insurance and retirement benefits. Companies can help employees with the cost of many types of insurance, including life, health, dental, vision, disability, and long-term care. Retirement programs fall into two basic categories: defined benefit programs, which promise a specific amount per month after retirement, and defined contribution programs, in which the company contributes a certain amount per month or year to an investment account but doesn't guarantee payment levels after retirement. Other important benefits are paid vacations and sick leave, family and medical leave, child- and elder-care assistance, tuition reimbursements or loans, and employee assistance programs that deal with personal matters such as substance abuse or domestic violence.

Critical thinking: (1) Why are stock options a controversial employee benefit, particularly for top executives? (2) What are the risks of investing in an ESOP?

It's your business: (1) Would you take stock options in lieu of a higher salary? Why or why not? (2) Would you be willing to forego health insurance or a retirement plan for higher salary or wages? Why or why not?

Key terms to know: employee benefits, cafeteria plans, retirement plans, pension plans, 401(k) plan, employee stock-ownership plan (ESOP), stock options, employee assistance program (EAP)

Behind the Scenes

Perking Up the Perfect Blend at Starbucks

On the fast track toward global growth, the Starbucks chain transformed the ordinary cup of coffee into a wide variety of taste choices for millions of coffee lovers. Along the way, the company's astonishing success encouraged competitors to join the fray. To stay on top, Starbucks managers had to ensure that their stores provided the best service along with the best coffee—which meant attracting, training, and compensating a diverse and dedicated workforce.

Guided by the company mission statement, Howard Schultz and his managers designed a variety of human resources programs to motivate Starbucks employees. First, they raised employees' base pay. Next, management bucked the trend in the industry by offering full medical, dental, life insurance, and disability insurance benefits to every employee who worked at least 20 hours per week. These employees were also eligible for paid vacation days and retirement savings plans, benefits not commonly available to part-time restaurant workers. Finally, Starbucks invested in its workforce by providing new hires with 24 hours of training

about the finer points of coffee brewing as well as the company's culture and values.

But the most innovative benefit brewed up by management was its Bean Stock, a program offering stock options not just to upper-echelon managers but to all partners who worked 20 or more hours per week. "We established Bean Stock in 1991 as a way of investing in our partners and creating ownership across the company," explained Bradley Honeycutt, vice president of human resource services. "It's been a key to retaining good people and building loyalty." For those who wanted to enlarge their financial stake in Starbucks, management devised a program that permitted employees to buy company stock at a discount. Owning a piece of the company motivated employees to take customer service to an even higher level of excellence. "We do everything we possibly can to get our customers to come back," says Schultz.

To help partners better balance their work and family obligations—another priority for Starbucks—the human resources department designed a comprehensive work-life program featuring flexible work schedules, access to employee assistance specialists, and referrals for child-care and elder-care support. The company also encouraged employees to become involved in their local communities, and it honored employees whose achievements exemplified the company's values. Finally, to encourage open communication and employee feedback, good or bad, management began holding a series of open forums in which company performance, results, and plans were openly discussed. Employees were encouraged to share ideas. "There is a tremendous amount of sharing in the company," notes Schultz. "It makes everybody think like an owner."

While most CEOs say that people are their most important asset, Starbucks lives that idea every day by giving people a stake in the outcome and treating them with respect and dignity. In all, putting employees first has helped Starbucks expand by attracting an energetic, committed workforce and keeping turnover to around 60 percent—one-fifth the industry average. With the workforce now around 175,000 employees and growth opportunities harder to come by, that care and attention will be more important than ever.[65]

Critical Thinking Questions

1. Why do Starbucks's human resources managers need to be kept informed about any changes in the number and timing of new store openings planned for the coming year?
2. Why does Starbucks offer benefits to its part-time labor force?
3. How does Starbucks's generous employee-benefits program motivate its employees?

LEARN MORE ONLINE

Visit the Starbucks website at **www.starbucks.com** and click on "Career Center." Explore how Starbucks presents its HR policies to potential employees. Browse the pages and videos that discuss working at Starbucks. Read about company culture, diversity, benefits, and learning and career development. Why would Starbucks post information about company culture in this section of the website? Why would job candidates be interested in learning about the culture as well as the employee benefits and training at Starbucks? ∎

Key Terms

360-degree review (297)
401(k) plan (302)
bonus (299)
cafeteria plans (301)
commissions (300)
compensation (298)
contingent employees (287)
diversity initiatives (291)
electronic performance monitoring (EPM) (297)
employee assistance program (EAP) (303)
employee benefits (301)
employee retention (287)
employee stock-ownership plan (ESOP) (302)

gain sharing (300)
glass ceiling (289)
human resources (HR) management (284)
job description (286)
job specification (286)
knowledge-based pay (300)
layoffs (294)
mandatory retirement (294)
orientation programs (297)
pay for performance (300)
pension plans (301)
performance appraisals (295)
profit sharing (300)
quality of work life (QWL) (285)
recruiting (291)

retirement plans (301)
salary (298)
sexism (289)
sexual harassment (290)
skills inventory (297)
stock options (303)
succession planning (287)
termination (293)
turnover rate (287)
wages (298)
worker buyouts (294)
work-life balance (285)

Test Your Knowledge

Questions for Review

1. What is the purpose of conducting a job analysis? What are some of the techniques used for gathering information?
2. What are some strategic staffing alternatives that organizations use to avoid overstaffing and understaffing?
3. Why do some companies use preemployment drug testing while others don't?
4. What do human resources managers do?
5. What is the glass ceiling?

Questions for Analysis

6. How do incentive programs encourage employees to be more productive, innovative, and committed to their work?
7. What are the advantages and disadvantages of 401(k) retirement plans?
8. Why do some employers offer comprehensive benefits even though the costs of doing so have risen significantly in recent years?

9. The 1986 Immigration Reform and Control Act forbids companies to hire illegal aliens but at the same time prohibits discrimination in hiring on the basis of national origin or citizenship status. How can companies satisfy both requirements of this law?

10. **Ethical Considerations.** Corporate headhunters have been known to raid other companies of their top talent to fill vacant or new positions for their clients. Is it ethical to contact the CEO of one company and lure him or her to join the management team of another company?

Questions for Application

11. Assume you are the manager of human resources at a manufacturing company that employs about 500 people. A recent cyclical downturn in your industry has led to financial losses, and top management is talking about laying off workers. Several supervisors have come to you with creative ways of keeping employees on the payroll, such as exchanging workers with other local companies. Why might you want to consider this option? What other options exist besides layoffs?

12. What steps could you take as the owner of a small software company to foster "temporary loyalty" from the independent programmers you frequently hire for short durations (one to six months)?

13. When you begin interviewing as you approach graduation, you will need to analyze job offers that include a number of financial and nonfinancial elements. Which of these aspects of employment are your top three priorities: a good base wage; bonus or commission opportunities; profit-sharing potential; rapid advancement opportunities; flexible work arrangements; good health-care insurance coverage; or a strong retirement program? Which of these elements would you be willing to forego in order to get your top three?

14. **Concept Integration.** Of the five levels in Maslow's hierarchy of needs, which is satisfied by offering salary? By offering health-care benefits? By offering training opportunities? By developing flexible job descriptions?

Practice Your Knowledge

Sharpening Your Communication Skills

A visit to CCH's SOHO Guide at www.toolkit.cch.com can help you reduce your legal liability whether you are laying off or firing a single employee or are contemplating a companywide reduction in your workforce. Visit the website and scroll down to the "Small Business Guide" and click on "People Who Work for You" followed by "Firing and Termination" to find out the safest way to fire someone from a legal standpoint before it's too late. Learn why it's important to document disciplinary actions. Then use the information at this website to write a short memo to your instructor summarizing how to set up a termination meeting and what you should say and do at the meeting when you fire an employee.

Building Your Team Skills

Team up with a classmate to practice your responses to interview questions. Use the list of common interview questions provided in the Prologue, and take turns posing and responding to those questions. Which questions did you find most difficult to answer? What insights did you gain about your strengths and weaknesses by answering those questions? Why is it a good idea to rehearse your answers before going to an interview?

Expand Your Knowledge

Discovering Career Opportunities

If you pursue a career in human resources, you'll be deeply involved in helping organizations find, select, train, evaluate, and retain employees. You have to like people and be a good communicator to succeed in HR. Is this field for you? Using your local Sunday newspaper, the *Wall Street Journal,* and online sources such as Monster (www.monster.com), find ads seeking applicants for positions in the field of human resources.

1. What educational qualifications, technical knowledge, or specialized skills are applicants for these jobs expected to have? How do these requirements fit with your background and educational plans?

2. Next, look at the duties mentioned in the ad for each job. What do you think you would be doing on an aver-

age day in these jobs? Does the work in each job sound interesting and challenging?

3. Now think about how you might fit into one of these positions. Do you prefer to work alone, or do you enjoy teamwork? How much paperwork are you willing to do? Do you communicate better in person, on paper, or by phone? Considering your answers to these questions, which of the HR jobs seems to be the closest match for your personal style?

Developing Your Research Skills

Locate one or more articles in business journals or newspapers (print or online editions) that illustrate how a company or industry is adapting to changes in its workforce. (Examples include retraining, literacy or basic-skills training, flexible benefits, and benefits aimed at working parents or people who care for aging relatives.)

1. What changes in the workforce or employee needs caused the company to adapt? What did the company do to respond to these changes? Was the company's response voluntary or legally mandated?

2. Is the company alone in facing these changes, or is the entire industry trying to adapt? What are other companies in the industry doing to adapt to the changes?

3. What other changes in the workforce or in employee needs do you think this company is likely to face in the next few years? Why?

Improving Your Tech Insights: Telecommuting Technologies

In simplest form, telecommuting doesn't require much more than a computer, a telephone, and access to the Internet. However, most corporate employees need a more comprehensive connection to their offices, with such features as secure access to confidential files, groupware, and web-based virtual meetings that let people communicate and share information over the Internet.

When they're used successfully, telecommuting technologies can reduce facility costs, put employees closer to customers, reduce traffic and air pollution in congested cities, give companies access to a wide range of independent talent, and let employees work in higher-salary jobs while living in lower-cost areas of the country. In the future, these technologies have the potential to change business so radically they could even influence the design of entire cities. With less need to pull millions of workers into central business districts, business executives, urban planners, and political leaders have the opportunity to explore such new ideas as *telecities*—virtual cities populated by people and organizations who are connected technologically, rather than physically.

Telecommuting offers compelling benefits, but it must be planned and managed carefully. Conduct some online research to find out what experts believe are the keys to success. Start with the Telework Coalition, www.telcoa .org. You can also find numerous articles in business publications (search for both "telecommuting" and "telework"). In a brief e-mail to your instructor, provide four or five important tips for ensuring successful telecommuting work arrangements.[66]

Video Discussion

Access the Chapter 11 video discussion in the End of Chapter Assignments section at www.mybizlab.com.

PEARSON mybiz**lab**

Log on to www.mybizlab.com to access the following study and assessment aids associated with this chapter:

- Interactive exercises
- Pre/post test
- Real-Time Updates
- Video application
- Customized study plans
- Biz Skills Simulations
- Quick Learning Guide

If you are not using mybizlab, you can access Real-Time Updates and Quick Learning Guides through http://real-timeupdates.com/bia5. The Quick Learning Guide (located under "Learn More" on the website) provides all six Checkpoints in a handy two-page format to help you study for exams or review important concepts whenever you need a quick refresher.

CHAPTER 12
Management-Workforce Relations

Behind the Scenes

An Epic Fight over Money at American Axle & Manufacturing

www.aam.com

In business and in life, studying the mistakes and misfortunes of others can be a great learning opportunity. And you'd have to search far and wide to find a situation with more learning opportunities than the bitter struggle between American Axle & Manufacturing (AAM) and the United Auto Workers (UAW). Bad luck, bad timing, bad decisions, bad blood—this story has it all.

AAM was created in 1994 when General Motors (GM) sold five aging manufacturing plants to a group of investors that included veteran auto executive Richard Dauch, who became CEO of the new company. With GM as its largest customer, AAM expanded to more than 30 plants around the world. Along the way, Dauch demonstrated the fierce determination that one might expect from a former Purdue University fullback. For instance, concerned about the dangerous effects of alcohol consumption on workplace safety, he secretly purchased several bars and liquor stores in the vicinity of AAM's plants in the Detroit area—and tore them all down.

By 2004, AAM had become one of the world's major auto suppliers, but Dauch wasn't happy with the cost structure at the five original factories in Michigan and New York, which had inherited generous labor contracts

The contentious relationship between the United Auto Workers and American Axle & Manufacturing reached a boiling point in 2008.

from their GM days. That year, a major competitor, Dana Corporation, won a concession from the UAW to begin offering new hires lower wages and fewer benefits. Dauch wanted the same deal, which would've meant cutting hourly wages in half. The union resisted, saying that unlike Dana, AAM was profitable. Dauch was also the highest paid executive in the auto industry, making his request for wage reductions even harder for the union to swallow.

With auto sales slowing over the next few years as the economy slid toward a deep recession, Dauch believed he was running out of options. By 2008 he had run out of patience. Explaining that the five plants in question hadn't been profitable for the past three years, he made the conflict even more personal by publicly criticizing the attitude and absenteeism rates of his Detroit area employees. "This isn't a North America problem, or a Michigan problem. It isn't a union problem. It's a Detroit problem. Detroit has an entitlement culture—'You owe me this job.'" Pointing out that in his entire career he had taken only three and a half sick days, he said, "I've got employees who miss two or three days a week."

The stage was set for a showdown. If you were Richard Dauch, how would you handle the situation? Or from the other side, if you were Ron Gettelfinger, president of the UAW, how would you react to AAM's demands?[1] ■

Introduction

At one level, the conflict between AAM and the UAW (profiled in the chapter-opening Behind the Scenes) is about money. But at a deeper level, the conflict is a fundamental disagreement about rights and responsibilities—about the very purpose of a business.[2] Is it to protect the interests of investors who provide the money to launch and expand a company? Or is the purpose of a company to protect the interests of the employees who get the work done? Balancing those competing ideals and demands is at the heart of labor relations, the subject of this chapter.

The Role of Labor Unions

labor relations
Relationship between organized labor and management (in their role as representative of business owners)

Perhaps nothing represents the potential for stress in the stakeholder model more than **labor relations**, the relationship between organized labor and business owners. Although they work toward common goals in most cases, managers and employees do face an inherent conflict over resources: Managers such as Richard Dauch want to minimize the costs of operating the business, whereas employees want to maximize salaries and ensure good benefits and safe, pleasant working conditions.

labor unions
Organizations that represent employees in negotiations with management

If employees believe they are not being treated fairly and can't get their needs met by negotiating individually with management, they may have the option of joining **labor unions**, organizations that seek to protect employee interests by negotiating with employers for better wages and benefits, improved working conditions, and increased job security. "The Organizing Process" starting on page 315 explains how a group of employees can elect to have a union represent them.

(A note on terminology: *Labor* can refer to either unions specifically or the workforce as a whole; you can tell by the context which definition is meant. *Organized labor* always refers to unions. And *management* in any discussion of union issues refers to managers in their role as representatives of company ownership.)

Unionization: The Employee's Perspective

The most fundamental appeal of unionization is strength in numbers, giving workers the opportunity to negotiate on a more equal footing with management (who represent company ownership). With this negotiating power, union members and supporters point to a number of ways workers benefit from union membership:[3]

- **Higher compensation.** According to the U.S. Bureau of Labor Statistics, union members currently earn about 20% more than nonunion workers, taken as an average across the entire workforce.[4] However, the trend of higher wages for union workers might be slowing down; in recent years, average union wages have not increased as much as nonunion wages.[5] (Note that this figure and all data related to organized labor in this chapter refer to the private sector only and do not reflect union membership in the public sector, including employees in government, public education, and services such as fire and police.)

- **Greater benefits.** As with compensation, union members receive greater benefits, on average, than nonunion employees. For instance, 51 percent of nonunion workers have retirement plans through their employer, compared to 86 percent of union workers. For health care benefits, the difference is about the same, 52 versus 79 percent.[6]

seniority
Length of time someone has worked for his or her current employer

- **Influence over hiring, promotions, and layoffs.** Union contracts usually have specific provisions about hiring, promotions, and layoffs, particularly with regard to **seniority**, the length of time someone has worked for his or her current employer. For example, when a company is laying off employees, union contracts often specify that those with lowest seniority are let go first, and when employees are rehired, those with the most seniority are hired first.

- **Working conditions and workplace safety.** Many unionization efforts focus on issues of workplace safety, breaks, training, and other aspects of life on the job.

- **Formal processes for employee grievances, discipline, and other matters.** Union contracts typically spell out formal procedures for such matters as disciplining employees. According to Mariah DeForest, a management consultant who specializes in manufacturing employment, "Unfair supervisory behavior is the most important reason that employees seek out a union."[7]

- **Solidarity and recognition.** Aside from tangible and measurable benefits, union membership can appeal to workers who feel unappreciated, humiliated, or let down by management.

Given the apparent advantages of belonging to a union, why don't all workers want to join? One possible explanation is the success of union efforts that led to such legislative victories as creating the standard 40-hour work week, setting the minimum wage, abolishing child labor, mandating equal pay for equal work, and prohibiting job discrimination. With these improvements already in place, many workers don't feel the need to join a union.[8] Other reasons employees might not want to join include being forced to pay union dues (which typically range from $25 to $50 per month[9]); being forced to help fund (through those monthly dues) political activities they may not support; being held back in their careers by union seniority rules; and being forced to accept the union as the sole intermediary with management, rather than negotiating raises, job assignments, and other matters on their own.

Unionization: Management's Perspective

Either as business owners themselves or as the representatives of owners, managers obviously have an interest in minimizing costs to maximize profits. Although this is sometimes portrayed as simple greed by union sympathizers, in general, management's top priority is making sure their firms can remain competitive. For example, by containing the ongoing costs of providing compensation and benefits, a firm is better able to invest in facilities, equipment, and new product development.[10]

In addition to direct costs, other management concerns regarding unions include flexibility and productivity. Union contracts often include **work rules** or *job rules* that specify such things as the tasks certain employees are required to do or are forbidden to do. For instance, management might want employees to be cross-trained on a variety of tasks and machines so that production supervisors have more flexibility in responding to changes in product demand. In a recent contract negotiation with the International Association of Machinists (IAM), for example, Boeing had to withdraw a proposed work rule change that would have required machinists to operate multiple machines.[11] In the auto industry, an analysis that compared Chrysler, Ford, and GM with Toyota concluded that union work rules forced the U.S. carmakers to create 8,200 more jobs than they would not have created otherwise.[12] Former General Electric CEO Jack Welch is blunt in his appraisal: "Work rules kill productivity. We've seen it in industry after industry."[13]

However, as with many issues in labor relations, the question of productivity is complex and not easily answered. To begin with, productivity in its full scope is difficult to measure. As just one example, a firm can reduce its spending on research and thereby make its overall productivity (as measured by dollars earned divided by dollars spent) look higher in the short term, but the long-term effect of less research could be less-competitive products or missed opportunities to improve manufacturing processes—both of which will hurt productivity eventually. Comparing one firm's productivity over time is also difficult because so many variables can change, as is comparing productivity between two firms.

The effect of unionization has been studied extensively over the years. In a review of 73 of these studies, professors Christos Doucouliagos and Patrice Laroche found 45 studies that showed a positive effect of unions on productivity and 28 studies that showed a negative effect. Their analysis of this research suggests that unions have had a net negative effect on productivity in the United Kingdom and Japan but a net positive effect on productivity in the United States. However, those productivity gains are offset by the higher average wages that unionized workers receive. "When the productivity and wage effects are combined, we can conclude that unions have a negative impact on profitability."[14]

Whether this is a negative or positive outcome depends on your perspective. It is clearly a negative outcome for shareholders and proprietors, but the higher wages are obviously a positive outcome for workers and, by extension, the communities in which those workers live—including the various businesses they patronize with their paychecks.

work rules
Common element of labor contracts specifying such things as the tasks certain employees are required to do or forbidden to do

✓CHECKPOINT

LEARNING OBJECTIVE 1: Explain the role of labor unions, and contrast the perspectives of employees and employers on the issue of unionization.

Summary: *Labor unions* are organizations that seek to protect employee interests by negotiating with employers for better wages and benefits, improved working conditions, and increased job security. The foundation of unionization is strength in numbers, giving workers the opportunity to negotiate on a more equal footing with company management. From an employee's perspective, unions offer the tangible benefits of greater compensation and benefits and the intangible benefits of solidarity and recognition. From an employer's perspective, unions can present a challenge in terms of costs and flexibility, ultimately creating concerns about a firm's ability to compete against companies with lower costs and greater agility.

Critical thinking: (1) Why is it so difficult to come up with a single conclusive answer about the effects of unionization on business productivity? (2) How do labor relations demonstrate the stresses inherent in the stakeholder model?

It's your business: (1) Union supporters often talk about the need for greater democracy in the workplace. Explain why you agree or disagree with this sentiment. (2) Would you rather be promoted on the basis of seniority or of merit? Why?

Key terms to know: labor relations, labor unions, seniority, work rules

Unionization in Historical Perspective

Any attempt to understand labor relations today needs to consider the long history of the labor-management relationship. Although money is usually the core issue at stake, the relationship is a lot more complicated than that. Disputes sometimes take on a pitched emotional tone as the two sides fight for respect, control, and political influence. The division runs deeper than matters of employment and business operations, too; supporters and opponents of unionism often have profoundly different beliefs about fundamental economic principles and the ideal nature of society itself. This section provides an overview of how the relationship between unions and company ownership has evolved over the years and where the union movement stands today.

Unions can trace their history back nearly a thousand years, to early guilds in Europe that gave craftspeople bargaining power over merchants. In the United States, the Industrial Revolution in the second half of the 1800s and the Great Depression of the 1930s were formative events in the history of unionization. Violent and even deadly behavior on both sides was not uncommon in these early years, with tumultuous riots, attacks by management security forces or government troops on union workers, attacks by union members on nonunion workers, and physical destruction of nonunion building projects, such as the dynamiting of the *Los Angeles Times* building in 1910.[15] After repeated strikes and protests over unsafe working conditions, abusive management practices, long hours, child labor, and other concerns, unions gradually found a sympathetic ear in Congress (see Exhibit 12.1). This section discusses three historically significant pieces of legislation. The Employee Free Choice Act (see page 325), currently under consideration, has the potential to be every bit as significant.

Power to the Unions: The Wagner Act of 1935

National Labor Relations Act
Legislation passed in 1935 that established labor relations policies and procedures for most sectors of private industry; commonly known as the Wagner Act

In 1935, Congress passed the **National Labor Relations Act**, also known as the Wagner Act. This landmark legislation established labor relations policies and procedures for most sectors of private industry (railroad and airline unions are addressed separately by the Railway Labor Act[16]), and its provisions remain a topic of ongoing controversy between labor and management. Key provisions of the Wagner Act include[17]

EXHIBIT 12.1 Major Pieces of Labor Relations Legislation

Most major labor legislation was enacted in the 1930s and 1940s. Subsequent legislation amends and clarifies earlier laws. The Employee Free Choice Act has not passed Congress as of late 2009.

LEGISLATION	KEY PROVISIONS
Norris-La Guardia Act of 1932	Limits companies' ability to obtain injunctions against union strikes, picketing, membership drives, and other activities.
National Labor Relations Act of 1935 (Wagner Act)	Gives employees the right to form, join, or assist labor organizations; the right to bargain collectively with employers through elected union representatives; and the right to engage in strikes, picketing, and boycotts. Prohibits certain unfair labor practices by the employer and union. Establishes the National Labor Relations Board to supervise union elections and to investigate charges of unfair labor practices by management.
Labor-Management Relations Act of 1947 (Taft-Hartley Act)	Amends Wagner Act to affirm employees' rights to not participate in union activities other than *union shop* provisions, identifies several unfair labor practices, restricts union's strike options, and prohibits strikes in the public sector. Gives states the freedom to pass right-to-work laws.
Labor-Management Reporting Act of 1959 (Landrum-Griffin Act)	Amends Taft-Hartley Act and Wagner Act to protect members' rights within the union and to control union corruption. Requires all unions to file annual financial reports with the U.S. Department of Labor, making union officials more personally responsible for the union's elections. Also establishes the right to sue unions and the right to attend and participate in union meetings.
Plant-Closing Notification Act of 1988	Requires employers to give employees and local elected officials 60 days advance notice of plant shutdowns or massive layoffs.
Employee Free Choice Act (pending)	Would make it easier for unions to organize workplaces by introducing a new card check–only option that would lead to union certification if more than 50 percent of employees sign authorization cards; would also allow either party to request mediation if a CBA cannot be finalized within 90 days of certification, and if the CBA isn't finalized within 120 days, the dispute would be sent to mandatory arbitration.

- Affirming and protecting the rights of employees to join and assist labor unions, to negotiate with employers through union representatives, and to strike
- Outlawing attempts by employers to interfere with employees' rights to organize, to discriminate against employees on the basis of their union activities or interests, or to interfere with union activities
- Requiring employers to bargain in good faith with unions
- Establishing the National Labor Relations Board (NLRB), www.nlrb.gov, responsible for preventing and remedying unfair labor practices and overseeing the elections that allow unions to represent particular groups of employees

The Wagner Act profoundly altered the balance of power in U.S. industry. Union membership grew dramatically in the decade that followed, to the point where unions could virtually shut down entire industries through strikes. Not surprisingly, business leaders were vigorously opposed to the Wagner Act and the growing power of unions. The opinion of automotive pioneer Henry Ford that "labor union organizations are the worst thing that ever struck the earth"[18] is probably an accurate reflection of the mindset of many company owners and managers at the time.

Power to the Owners: The Taft-Hartley Act of 1947

During and after World War II, public opinion began to turn against unions, partly in response to union workers striking during wartime. Business organizations—and even some union leaders who felt the law gave other unions unfair advantages—were furiously lobbying Congress to amend the Wagner Act.[19] Congress eventually passed the **Labor-Management Relations Act** of 1947, also known as the Taft-Hartley Act. This legislation addressed many concerns raised by business owners and shifted the balance of power again. Its key provisions include[20]

Labor-Management Relations Act Legislation passed in 1947 that addressed many concerns raised by business owners and shifted the balance of power again; commonly known as the Taft-Hartley Act

- Guaranteeing the right of employees not to join or support unions, except where required by a *union shop* agreement, and granting to each state the right to choose whether it would allow union shops (see "Union Security and Right-to-Work Laws" on the next page)
- Outlawing coercion of or discrimination against employees by unions
- Allowing employers more freedom of speech to dissuade workers from voting for unionization
- Requiring unions to bargain in good faith with employers
- Restricting or outlawing various strike activities by unions, including striking with the intent of forcing an employer to create new jobs for union workers
- Giving the president the authority to outlaw strikes that threaten national security

Unions widely referred to Taft-Hartley as a "slave-labor act," but they were unsuccessful at blocking or changing it.[21] To combat the enlarged power of employers, union leaders made more attempts to cooperate among themselves. This eventually led to the merger in 1955 of the two major U.S. labor federations, the American Federation of Labor (AFL) and a group that had splintered off from the AFL in the 1930s, the Congress of Industrial Organizations (CIO).

Power to Union Members: The Landrum-Griffith Act of 1959

Labor-Management Reporting and Disclosure Act
Legislation passed in 1959 designed to ensure democratic processes and financial accountability within unions; commonly known as the Landrum-Griffith Act

In the decade or so following Taft-Hartley, legislative attention shifted to the internal operation of the major unions. Two major concerns at the time were corruption and communism. New leadership in the AFL-CIO responded by expelling from the federation some unions accused of criminal activities or communist domination.[22] Congressional inquiries into financial fraud by union leaders, meanwhile, led to passage of the **Labor-Management Reporting and Disclosure Act** of 1959, commonly known as the Landrum-Griffith Act. The overall intent of this act is ensuring democratic processes and financial accountability within unions, including freedom of speech for union members, the right to secret ballot elections of union leadership, and financial transparency in the use of union funds.[23]

 **CHECKPOINT**

LEARNING OBJECTIVE 2: Identify the three most important pieces of labor relations legislation in the 20th century.

Summary: Three major pieces of legislation passed in the 20th century still define many aspects of labor relations and the management of labor unions themselves. The National Labor Relations Act of 1935, better known as the Wagner Act, gives employees the right to unionize and bargain collectively with employers and the right to strike, picket, and boycott. The Labor-Management Relations Act of 1947, better known as the Taft-Hartley Act, affirms employees' rights to not participate in union activities other than *union shop* provisions, identifies several unfair labor practices, restricts unions' strike options, prohibits strikes in the public sector, and gives states the freedom to pass right-to-work laws. The Labor-Management Reporting Act of 1959, better known as the Landrum-Griffin Act, protects members' rights within the union and limits the potential for corruption by union officials.

Critical thinking: (1) Why are disputes between labor and management often more complicated than just matters of money? (2) Would you agree that the struggle between labor and management has, to at least some degree, been a matter of legislative overcorrection? Why or why not?

It's your business: (1) Do you believe it is appropriate for unions to be involved in political activities? Why or why not? (2) Given the long and complex history of unionization, many people now have an emotional response to the word "union." Do you respond positively or negatively when you hear the word? Why?

Key terms to know: National Labor Relations Act, Labor-Management Relations Act, Labor-Management Reporting and Disclosure Act

The Organizing Process

A key element in most labor relations laws is the process of organizing union representation for a particular group of workers. This section looks at the union organizing process, starting with the concepts of union security and right to work, the two main types of unions, and the structure of union organizations.

Union Security and Right-to-Work Laws

When a union negotiates a contract, it usually tries to obtain some degree of **union security**, measures that protect the union's right to represent workers. The most extreme form is the *closed shop*, in which an employer is allowed to hire only union members; this was made illegal by Taft-Hartley. In a **union shop**, employees don't have to be members when they are hired, but they must join the union within a specified period of time. Any employee who doesn't join the union by that time or maintain union membership after that must be released by the employer. In an *agency shop*, employees aren't required to join the union but must pay the equivalent of union dues.[24] Interestingly, one nationwide survey indicates that most employees, even union members, don't support the concept of a union shop.[25]

One of the most important changes brought about by the Taft-Hartley Act was allowing individual states to pass laws prohibiting union and agency shops. In the 50-plus years following Taft-Hartley, 22 states have passed such **right-to-work laws** (see Exhibit 12.2 on the next page). These laws remain a strong point of contention between union supporters and opponents. As with many other issues in labor relations, the argument is complex. Businesses and other supporters of right-to-work laws say that compulsory union membership violates individual rights, removes a key reason for unions to stay responsive to member needs, and makes a state less attractive to business. Union leaders and their supporters claim that all workers benefit from union advocacy and so it is not unreasonable to require all workers to support those efforts through membership, and they point to studies showing that right-to-work states have lower average wages as well.[26]

Types of Unions

Unions are of two basic types, with different implications for organizing employees and interacting with management. *Craft unions* offer membership to workers with a specific craft or skill, such as carpentry, masonry, or electrical work. In some instances, craft unions negotiate contracts for certain categories of work at a single employer. In others, particularly in the building trades, these unions often negotiate with a number of employers in a given geographic area. As employees move from one project to another, they remain covered by the same contract.[27] A key feature of craft union membership is the *apprenticeship* model, in which beginners receive training under union auspices. The International Brotherhood of Electrical Workers is an example of a craft union.

In contrast to craft unions, *industrial unions* seek to represent all workers at a given employer or location, regardless of profession or skill level. Rather than belonging to a single union for their entire careers as with craft unions, workers usually join an industrial union because they are required to when going to work at a union shop and often leave the union if they leave a particular job.[28] The United Auto Workers (UAW) is an example of an industrial union.

union security
Measures that protect the union's right to represent workers

union shop
Unionized workplace in which employees are required to maintain union membership

right-to-work laws
State laws that prohibit union and agency shops

EXHIBIT 12.2 **Right-to-Work States**

Twenty-two states currently have some form of right-to-work laws.

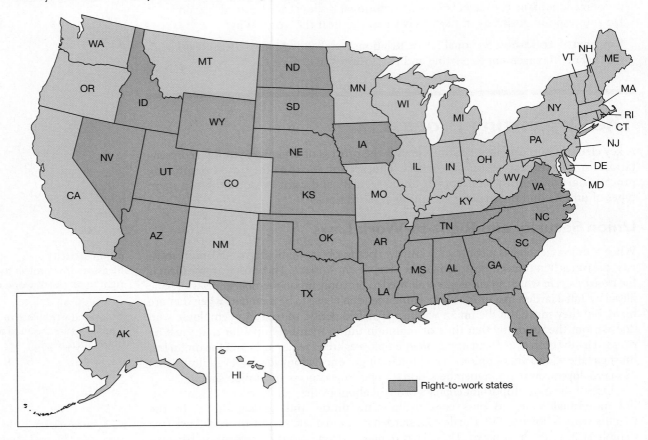

How Unions Are Structured

locals
Local unions that represent employees in a specific geographic area or facility

Many unions are organized at local, national, and international levels. **Locals**, or local unions, represent employees in a specific geographic area or facility. Members are informally known as the *rank-and-file*. Each department or facility also elects a *shop steward*, who works in the facility as a regular employee and serves as a liaison with supervisors whenever problems arise. In large locals and in locals that represent employees at several locations, an elected full-time *business agent* visits the various work sites to negotiate with management and enforce the union's agreements with those companies.

national union
Nationwide organization composed of many local unions that represent employees in specific locations

A **national union** is a nationwide organization composed of many local unions that represent employees in specific locations; examples include the UAW and the United Steelworkers of America. *International unions*, such as the Service Employees International Union (SEIU), have members in more than one country. A national union is responsible for such activities as organizing in new areas or industries, negotiating industrywide contracts, assisting locals with negotiations, administering benefits, lobbying Congress, and lending assistance in the event of a strike. Local unions send representatives to the national delegate convention, submit negotiated contracts to the national union for approval, and provide financial support in the form of dues. They have the power to negotiate with individual companies or plants and to undertake their own membership activities. Unions can also be members of a *labor federation* such as the AFL-CIO, giving them a larger, unified voice for political activities and membership drives.

Union Organizing Drives

Unions seek the legal authority to represent a group of workers through a process known as an *organizing drive* (see Exhibit 12.3). A drive starts when workers contact a

EXHIBIT 12.3 The Union Organizing Process

This diagram summarizes the steps a labor union takes when organizing a group of employees and becoming certified to represent them in negotiations with management. The certification election is necessary only if management is unwilling to recognize the union. Note that the Employee Free Choice Act would modify this process.

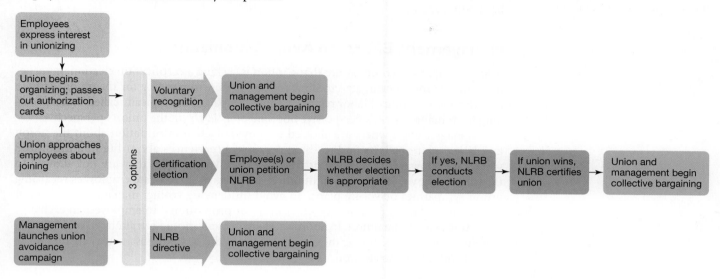

union expressing interest in joining or a union organizer contacts workers to promote the benefits of union membership. After this initial expression of interest, the union forms an organizing committee and launches its strategy for securing the right to represent those employees, employees who wish to have the union represent them sign **authorization cards**, and company management usually tries to persuade employees that unionization would not be in their best interest.

The next step can go in one of three directions. (Note that if some version of the Employee Free Choice Act described on page 325 is signed into law, the procedures described here will change.) First, the union and the interested employees can try to pressure the employer into voluntarily recognizing the union as the employees' representative. Boycotts, picketing, strikes, and publicity campaigns are common tactics for this approach.[29] Employers can agree to a "card check," which tallies the number of employees who have signed authorization cards; if more than 50 percent of the affected employees have signed, the company has to accept the union as the employees' representative. Second, if the employer doesn't voluntarily accept the union, employees or the union can petition the NLRB to conduct a secret-ballot **certification election**. The NLRB usually requires verification that at least 30 percent of the employees in an appropriate *bargaining unit* are interested in union membership before it will proceed with an election. (Unions typically don't request a vote until they have cards from 60 or 70 percent of the bargaining unit, however, because a significant number of employees who sign cards end up voting against the union.[30]) The NLRB has a number of guidelines for determining which employees are eligible to vote as part of the bargaining unit, but roughly speaking, it requires that employees share the same working conditions.[31] Third, in rare cases, the NRLB can unilaterally direct the employer to bargain with the union if the board determines that a fair election isn't possible.

If a majority of the affected employees vote to make the union their bargaining agent, the NRLB certifies the results and grants the union the authority to begin negotiating with the employer on the employees' behalf. In recent years, unions have won 55 to 60 percent of certification elections.[32] If the union is certified, the employer is then required to negotiate with the union for at least one year on the terms of the contract with employees (covering wages, benefits, work rules, and other factors). These first-time negotiations can be difficult, but they are concluded within the first year most of the time.[33]

authorization cards
Cards signed by employees to indicate interest in having a union represent them

certification election
Secret-ballot election overseen by the NLRB to determine whether a union gains the right to represent a group of employees

decertification
Employee vote to take away a
union's right to represent them

Even when a union wins a certification election, there's no guarantee that it will represent a particular group of employees forever. Sometimes employees become dissatisfied with their union and no longer wish to be represented by it. When this happens, the union members can take a **decertification** vote to take away the union's right to represent them. If the majority votes for decertification, the union is removed as the bargaining agent.

Management Efforts to Avoid Unionization

After a company becomes aware that a union is seeking a certification election, management may launch a campaign to dissuade employees from voting for the union. True to the adversarial nature of labor relations, these campaigns are typically called *union avoidance* from management's perspective but *union busting* from the union's perspective.

Managers and owners are allowed to provide factual information about the union and labor relations laws and to share personal experiences about life in a unionized workplace. However, under the provisions of the Wagner Act, they are not allowed to threaten employees for engaging in union activities or interrogate employees regarding union sympathies or voting plans. To avoid influencing voting, managers are also not allowed to make any promises (such as raises or promotions) to employees in exchange for voting against the union. In addition, management should refrain from offering new benefits to employees during the organizing drive; this can be construed as an attempt to unfairly influence the election.[34]

√CHECKPOINT

LEARNING OBJECTIVE 3: Explain how unions are structured, and describe the organizing process.

Summary: Unions can be structured at local, national, and international levels. A *local* represents employees in a specific area or facility. A union *organizing drive* starts when one or more employees contact a union and express interest in joining or a union organizer contacts employees and gets them to consider the benefits of joining. The organizer then asks employees to sign *authorization cards* to indicate their interest in having a union represent them. At that point, the employer asks for a *card check* count; if more than 50 percent of affected employees have signed, the employer must accept the union as a bargaining agent. If the employer doesn't voluntarily accept the union or agree to a card check, the union can petition the NLRB for a certification election if at least 30 percent of employees have signed. In rare cases, the NLRB can order the employer to bargain with the union if the board believes a fair election is not possible.

Critical thinking: (1) Why does the concept of an *agency shop* exist, since employees in such facilities aren't required to join the union? (2) Why do union organizers usually gather authorization cards from well over 50 percent of the employees in a bargaining unit before petitioning the NLRB for a certification election?

It's your business: (1) If you were an entrepreneur ready to start a new company, would state right-to-work laws affect your decision about choosing a location for your business? Why or why not? (2) Union supporters argue that all workers benefit from the improvements in working conditions that unionization has helped bring about over the years; do you agree that all workers are in unions' debt? Why or why not?

Key terms to know: union security, union shop, right-to-work laws, locals, national union, authorization cards, certification election, decertification

The Collective Bargaining Process

After a union has been recognized as the exclusive bargaining agent for a group of employees, its main job is to negotiate employment contracts with management. In a process known as **collective bargaining**, union and management negotiators work together to forge the human resources policies that will apply to all employees covered by the contract. **Collective bargaining agreements (CBAs)**, the contracts that result from this process, are always a compromise between the desires of union members and those of management. The union pushes for the best possible deal for its members, and management tries to negotiate agreements that are best for the company (and the shareholders, if a corporation is publicly held). Exhibit 12.4 illustrates the collective bargaining process. (*Labor contract* is often used as a synonym for a collective bargaining agreement. Individual employees, particularly in upper management positions, can also have *employment contracts* that aren't associated with union membership.)

Labor agreements usually cover a wide range of issues, often in considerable detail. The current CBA between the National Hockey League and the NHL Players' Association, for instance, is roughly the size of this textbook.[35] The details vary widely by industry and profession, naturally, but the most common issues addressed are compensation, benefits, working conditions, and job security and seniority.

collective bargaining
Negotiation between union and management negotiators to forge the human resources policies that will apply to all employees covered by a contract

collective bargaining agreements (CBAs)
Contracts that result from collective bargaining

Negotiating an Agreement

When the negotiating teams representing the union and management sit down together, they state their opening positions and each side discusses its position point by point. The National Labor Relations Act specifies certain topics that must be addressed in collective bargaining, including compensation, working hours, and conditions of employment.[36] Offers and counteroffers are made during *bargaining* as each side decides how far it is willing to compromise in order to reach agreement. In most cases, union representatives don't have the authority to agree to a contract during these negotiations. Instead, their members authorize them to secure the best offer they can and bring that back to the membership for a vote.[37]

In addition to the actual terms of the contract, an acrimonious long-term relationship between the two sides can sometimes complicate negotiations, creating a "win at all

EXHIBIT 12.4 The Collective Bargaining Process

Contract negotiations go through the four basic steps shown here. Note that the Employee Free Choice Act would modify this process.

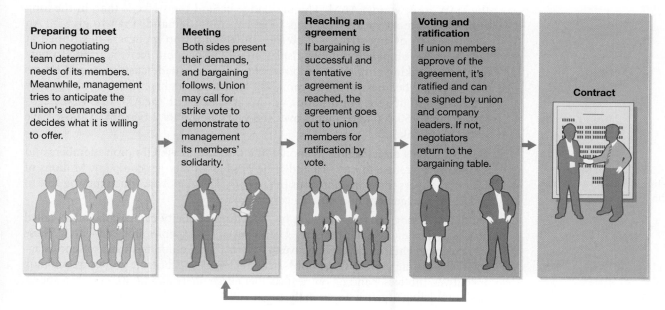

Preparing to meet
Union negotiating team determines needs of its members. Meanwhile, management tries to anticipate the union's demands and decides what it is willing to offer.

Meeting
Both sides present their demands, and bargaining follows. Union may call for strike vote to demonstrate to management its members' solidarity.

Reaching an agreement
If bargaining is successful and a tentative agreement is reached, the agreement goes out to union members for ratification by vote.

Voting and ratification
If union members approve of the agreement, it's ratified and can be signed by union and company leaders. If not, negotiators return to the bargaining table.

Contract

costs" competition or encouraging aggressive stances when sensible compromise would be better for everyone concerned.[38] If negotiations reach an impasse, outside help may be needed. The most common alternative is **mediation**—bringing in an impartial third party to study the situation, explore new options, improve communication, and make recommendations for resolution of the differences. The Taft-Hartley Act established the Federal Mediation and Conciliation Service (FMCS), www.fmcs.gov, to provide free mediation services during labor contract disputes. Federal mediators help resolve contract impasses roughly 85 percent of the time.[39] However, mediators can only offer suggestions, and their solutions are not binding.

When a legally binding settlement is needed, the negotiators may submit to **arbitration**—a process in which an impartial referee listens to both sides and then makes a judgment by accepting one side's view. In *compulsory arbitration*, the parties are required by a government agency to submit to arbitration; in *voluntary arbitration*, the parties agree on their own to use arbitration to settle their differences.

mediation
Use of an impartial third party to help resolve bargaining impasses

arbitration
Decision process in which an impartial referee listens to both sides and then makes a judgment by accepting one side's view

Exercising Options When Negotiations Break Down

The vast majority of management-union negotiations are settled without the need for either side to take further action. However, negotiations occasionally reach an impasse, and neither side is willing to compromise enough to reach an agreement. Both labor and management are able to draw on many powerful options when negotiations or mediation procedures break down.

Labor's Options

Strikes and picket lines are perhaps labor's best-known tactics, but other options are also used.

strike
Temporary work stoppage aimed at forcing management to accept union demands

- **Strike.** The most powerful weapon that organized labor can use is the **strike**, a temporary work stoppage aimed at forcing management to accept union demands. As you'll see in the Behind the Scenes at the end of the chapter, this is the option the UAW took against AAM. The basic idea behind the strike is that, in the long run, it costs more in lost earnings to resist union demands than to give in. An essential part of any strike is *picketing*, in which union members positioned at entrances to company premises display signs and pass out leaflets, trying to persuade nonstriking employees to join them and to persuade customers and others to stop doing business with the company. Strikes are high-profile events, but they are actually quite rare. For instance, unions affiliated with the AFL-CIO have negotiated some 150,000 agreements over the years, and only 2 percent of those have resulted in strikes.[40]

boycott
Pressure action by union members and sympathizers who refuse to buy or handle the product of a target company

- **Boycott.** A less direct union weapon is the **boycott**, in which union members and sympathizers refuse to buy or handle the product of a target company. Millions of union members form an enormous bloc of purchasing power, which may be able to pressure management into making concessions.

- **Publicity.** Labor can press its case by launching publicity campaigns, often called *corporate campaigns,* against the target company and companies affiliated with it. These campaigns might include sending investors alerts that question the firm's solvency, staging rallies during peak business hours, sending letters to charitable groups questioning executives' motives, handing out leaflets that allege safety and health-code violations, and stimulating negative stories in the press.

Labor's other options include *slowdowns,* in which employees continue to do their jobs but at a slow enough pace to disrupt operations, and *sickouts,* in which employees feign illness and stay home.

Management's Options

From its side, management can use a number of legal methods to pressure unions when negotiations stall:

- **Strikebreakers.** When union members walk off their jobs, management can legally replace them with **strikebreakers**, nonunion workers hired to do the jobs of striking workers. (Union members brand them as "scabs.")

When contract talks broke down between grocery workers and major grocery chains in Southern California, the result was a strike that lasted four and a half months.

- **Lockouts.** The U.S. Supreme Court has upheld the use of **lockouts**, in which management prevents union employees from entering the workplace, in order to pressure the union to accept a contract proposal. A lockout is management's counterpart to a strike. It is a preemptive measure designed to force a union to accede to management's demands. Lockouts are legal only if the union and management have come to an impasse in negotiations and the employer is defending a legitimate bargaining position. During a lockout, the company may hire temporary replacements as long as it has no anti-union motivation and negotiations have been amicable.[41]

- **Injunctions.** An **injunction** is a court order that requires one side in a dispute to refrain from or engage in a particular action. In the early days of unionism, companies typically sought injunctions to order striking employees back to work on the grounds that the strikers were interfering with business. Today, injunctions are legal only in certain cases. For example, the president of the United States has the right, under the Taft-Hartley Act, to obtain a temporary injunction to halt a strike deemed harmful to the national interest, such as a wide-scale transportation strike.

strikebreakers
Nonunion workers hired to do the jobs of striking workers

lockouts
Decision by management to prevent union employees from entering the workplace; used to pressure the union to accept a contract proposal

injunction
Court order that requires one side in a dispute to refrain from or engage in a particular action

✓CHECKPOINT

LEARNING OBJECTIVE 4: Describe the collective bargaining process.

Summary: In collective bargaining, union and management teams negotiate the human resources policies that will apply to all employees covered by the contract, which is known as a collective bargaining agreement (CBA). If the two sides cannot reach agreement, they can seek outside help through mediation or arbitration.

Critical thinking: (1) Given the history of union-management relations, why do you think mediation tends to be so successful at resolving bargaining impasses? (2) Why would an employer resort to a lockout?

It's your business: (1) Should U.S. consumers be pressured to buy products made in the United States? Why or why not? (2) Would you refuse to shop at a store that was being picketed by union members? Why or why not?

Key terms to know: collective bargaining, collective bargaining agreements (CBAs), mediation, arbitration, strike, boycott, strikebreakers, lockouts, injunction.

Grievance, Discipline, and Arbitration Procedures

A key element of labor legislation and labor contracts is providing the means to ensure compliance with laws and contract terms. The NLRB acts on complaints of unfair labor practices, and labor contracts contain provisions for handling employee grievances, disciplining employees, and resolving disputes through arbitration.

Unfair Labor Practices

During organizing campaigns and contract negotiations and through the duration of a completed CBA, unions and management are prohibited from engaging in unlawful acts known as **unfair labor practices**.[42] The NLRB lists the following as examples of unfair practices by employers:[43]

- Threatening employees with termination or cuts in benefits if they vote for union or engage in any other activity protected by the Wagner Act or other laws
- Threatening to close a facility if employees vote for union representation
- Interrogating employees about union sympathies or activities in ways that could "interfere with, restrain, or coerce" employees trying to exercise their legal rights
- Responding to organizing campaigns by offering wage or benefit improvements as a way to thwart unionization efforts
- Punishing employees for unionization activity by transferring them, giving them more difficult work assignments, or terminating them

The NLRB also responds to complaints about unfair labor practices on the part of unions. Examples of these include[44]

- Attempting to scare employees into supporting the union by telling them they will lose their jobs otherwise
- Refusing to process grievance claims made by employees who have criticized union officials
- Attempting to get an employee fired for not complying with a union shop agreement when the employee has paid or offered to pay an initiation fee and monthly dues
- Discriminating against employees or giving preferential treatment in union hiring halls (facilities where members of craft unions receive job assignments) because of race or union activities

Resolving Employee Grievances

If an employee or a union believes an employer is not abiding by the terms of a collective bargaining agreement, most agreements specify procedures for filing a **grievance**, a formal complaint against the employer. Grievances can range from the petty to the profound. In some cases, employees may file complaints simply to express frustration, and unions may file grievances as a way to show their power. More substantial reasons include clarifying details of the contract, addressing alleged contract violations by the employer, laying the groundwork for future contract negotiations, and contesting management decisions.[45]

For example, several Boston television stations recently decided to pool news gathering resources by sending out a single crew to news locations and sharing the video

unfair labor practices
Unlawful acts made by either unions or management

grievance
Formal complaint against an employer

footage. Station managers said the pooling effort frees up camera operators and technicians to work on other stories, but the International Brotherhood of Electrical Workers interpreted the move as a way to eventually eliminate jobs.[46]

Grievance procedures usually specify a multistep *escalation* process, which typically starts on a small scale with just the employee, his or her supervisor, and the union shop steward. If those parties are unable to resolve the situation, the process escalates, involving higher levels of management on both the employer and union sides. If the highest level of escalation fails to produce an agreeable solution, either party can then decide to submit the grievance to arbitration (see "Arbitrating Disputes" below).[47]

Disciplining Employees

Collective bargaining agreements also outline procedures for disciplining employees who violate either the terms of the agreement or company policies. For minor offenses, an escalating process known as **progressive discipline** usually starts with an oral warning for the first offense, followed by a written warning, then another written warning and suspension without pay, and then finally termination after the fourth offense. For serious offenses such as theft, unsafe behavior, or participation in unauthorized strikes, employees can be terminated immediately.[48]

progressive discipline
Escalating process of discipline that gives employees several opportunities to correct performance problems before being terminated

Arbitrating Disputes

In addition to being used to finalize the collective bargaining agreement, arbitration can also be used to interpret or apply the provisions of the agreement.[49] If employee grievances cannot be resolved through the agreed-upon grievance procedure or an employee or his or her union dispute disciplinary action taken by an employer, the next step is usually arbitration. The issues brought to arbitration cover a wide range, including disputes over wages, seniority, terminations, employee discipline, job posting, and the use of subcontractors.[50] (Note that arbitration is not limited to labor contracts. As a prominent form of *alternative dispute resolution*, arbitration is used throughout the business world to resolve consumer complaints, various commercial contracts, health care claims, and even international trade disputes.[51])

Most labor agreements include provisions for arbitrating disputes that cannot be resolved through normal grievance procedures. However, if one party refuses to submit to arbitration, the other party can either take the matter to court or ask an arbitrator to rule on it. Roughly 10 percent of labor contract cases brought to federal arbitrators involve the determination of *arbitrability*.[52] If the arbitrator determines that the labor contract addresses the issue at hand, he or she will deny the request for arbitration and direct the parties to use the grievance procedures in the contract.

One of the key differences between arbitration and the civil justice system is that in arbitration, the union and the employer get to select the arbitrator (they also share the cost of the service). Both the FMCS and organizations such as the American Arbitration Association maintain rosters of approved arbitrators, known in the profession as "neutrals," with experience in labor contract disputes. Most arbitrators are chosen on a case-by-case basis, but in some instances, a union and an employer agree to a permanent arbitrator to hear grievances throughout the life of the contract.[53]

✔CHECKPOINT

LEARNING OBJECTIVE 5: Explain the procedures for addressing employee grievances and arbitrating disputes.

Summary: The Wagner Act and subsequent legislation identify a number of unfair labor practices, and the NLRB can take action to remedy these whenever a union or an employer files a complaint. In addition, collective bargaining agreements typically include provisions for addressing employee grievances, for disciplining employees who violate the terms of their employment contracts or other workplace rules, and for arbitrating disputes over the interpretation or application of bargain agreements. Grievance procedures usually start on a small scale, involving the employee, the shop steward, and the supervisor. If that group is unable to resolve the complaint, the process escalates, involving higher levels of authority in both the union and the company. If the process is exhausted without resolution, the grievance can be submitted to arbitration, in which an impartial third party makes a decision in the matter.

Critical thinking: (1) Is it in a union's best interest for its members to comply with all the terms of a collective bargaining agreement? Why or why not? (2) What risks do unions and employers take in deciding to use arbitration?

It's your business: (1) Have you ever witnessed theft or other serious violations by employees in a workplace? What disciplinary measures were taken? (2) Do you believe that employees should be given multiple chances after committing minor offenses in the workplace, as progressive discipline procedures allow? Why or why not?

Key terms to know: unfair labor practices, grievance, progressive discipline

The Labor Movement Today

From any participant's perspective—employee, union leader, or company manager—the matter of unionization is clearly not a simple one. As unions move forward, they face three key challenges: conflict within the union movement, the quest to expand union membership, and the ongoing effort to secure passage of the Employee Free Choice Act.

Conflict Within the Union Movement

Most coverage of labor relations conflicts focuses on disagreements between unions and company management. However, leaders must also address the challenge of internal conflict, both inside individual unions or federations and between unions. For example, after criticizing the AFL-CIO for being too slow to adapt to the changing world of business, several major unions recently formed an alternative coalition known as Change to Win, whose member unions now represent some 6 million workers.[54] Another recurring issue is the attempt by some unions to "raid" other unions for members. For example, the Service Employees International Union and the new National Union of Healthcare Workers are locked in a bitter struggle for workers in the health-care industry. Ironically, the two unions accuse each other of some of the same improper behavior unions often accuse employers of during organizing elections.[55]

Union Membership

With their influence based on having a collective voice, unions place a high priority on recruiting and retaining members. Unfortunately for unions, the long-term trend has not been positive in this respect, at least in the private sector. From a peak of more than one-third of the workforce in the 1950s, union membership in the private sector is now less than 8 percent. As you can see in Exhibit 12.5, union membership varies widely by industry.[56]

True to the often combative nature of the relationship, each side blames organized labor's decline on the other. Some business leaders say unions don't

Real-Time Updates

Learn More

The EFCA: A union view

See what the AFL-CIO has to say about the Employee Free Choice Act. On mybizlab (www.mybizlab.com), you can access Real-Time Updates within each chapter or under Student Study Tools. Otherwise, go to http://real-timeupdates.com/bia5 and click on "Learn More."

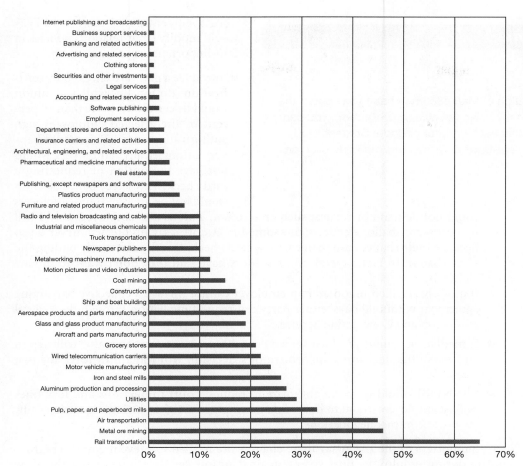

EXHIBIT 12.5

Union Membership in Selected Industries

Union membership varies widely by industry, as you can see from this selection of 40 industry sectors.

Percentage of private sector workforce in unions (2008 data)

have anything relevant to offer workers in today's environment of more enlightened and supportive management. Union leaders say managers use every tactic they can think of, both legal and illegal, to thwart unionization efforts, a situation they hope to remedy with the Employee Free Choice Act.

Do more U.S. workers *want* to be represented by unions? The answer to that question seems to depend on who is doing the asking and how the question is phrased. One 2005 survey said that 53 percent of nonunion workers "definitely or probably would vote in favor of union representation in their workplace."[57] However, other surveys produce different figures. For instance, another 2005 survey said that only 16 percent would "definitely" vote union and another 20 percent would "probably" vote for a union, for a total positive response of 36 percent.[58] In a 2009 survey that asked the simple yes or no question, "Would you like to belong to a labor union where you work?" only 9 percent said yes.[59] Clearly, some employees who are not now in unions would like to be, but just how many is not clear.

The Employee Free Choice Act

No labor relations issue in recent years has stirred as much controversy as the **Employee Free Choice Act (EFCA)**, legislation that would significantly alter the union election provisions of the Wagner Act. The EFCA was first introduced in Congress in 2003 and again several times since. As of late 2009, it had been passed by the House of Representatives but not by the Senate. Chances appear good that it will eventually pass in some form.

Employee Free Choice Act (EFCA) Pending legislation that would significantly alter the union election provisions of the Wagner Act, making it easier for unions to organize groups of workers

As currently written, the EFCA would modify labor relations policies in four important ways:[60]

- Introduce a new card check–only certification option in which a union would be certified if more than 50 percent of the affected employees sign authorization cards. This would happen automatically; employers would not have the option of requesting a card check. The secret-ballot election would not be required, and employers could not demand or request such an election. Unions and employees could still request secret-ballot elections, but some EFCA critics say unions will never do so because their chances are better with a card check, thereby effectively ending the secret ballot. In fact, several union leaders have said they don't want to pursue elections.[61]

- If a newly certified union and an employer cannot finalize a collective bargaining agreement within 90 days, either party can request mediation through the Federal Mediation and Conciliation Service.

- If mediation cannot produce agreement within 30 days, an arbitrator will step in and make the decision. The arbitrator's decision will remain in force for two years.

- The NLRB would have the authority to request court injunctions and levy fines against employers found to have violated employees' rights during organizing campaigns or contract negotiations.

Supporters of the EFCA say these changes are needed to prevent employers from intimidating employees into voting against union certification during the time between the 30-percent authorization-card trigger and the secret ballot.[62] This new version of the card check procedure would allow them to quietly recruit employees without spurring an anti-union campaign from management.[63] They also assert that many collective bargaining agreements take so long to be finalized that many employees who vote for a union still don't have a contract after a year or more. The EFCA would force a time limit.[64]

Some of the opposition to the EFCA has not been subtle, to put it mildly. Bernie Marcus, co-founder and former CEO of The Home Depot, calls the EFCA "the demise of a civilization."[65] Opponents of the EFCA are most vocal in their criticism of the first and third changes, the loss of the secret ballot elections and the imposition of mandatory arbitration. EFCA opponents worry that union organizers will pressure employees into signing authorization cards because unlike secret ballot voting, knowledge of who did and didn't sign an authorization card is not a secret. As the process now stands, even if employees sign authorization cards, they don't have to vote for the union in the certification election—a key protection that lets them make their final choices in private.[66] Former U.S. Senator George McGovern, who describes himself as a "longtime friend of labor unions," advocated against the EFCA partly because of how it makes workers vulnerable to pressure from union organizers.[67]

The other major objection to the EFCA is mandatory arbitration, particularly the ideas that both sides will lose the freedom to negotiate and that an arbitrator could decide wages, benefits, work rules, and other essential aspects of operating a business, even though that person may have little or no experience in that industry. As the U.S. Chamber of Commerce puts it, as an employer, "you could be stuck with a contract that is completely incompatible with your cost structure and your business model—and you would have to live with that contract for two years."[68]

For the latest information on the EFCA and other labor relations topics, visit http://real-timeupdates.com/bia5 and click on Chapter 12.

✓CHECKPOINT

LEARNING OBJECTIVE 6: List the major challenges facing unions today, and explain the potential impact of the Employee Free Choice Act.

Summary: Unions currently face three key challenges. The first is conflict within the union movement, in terms of both disagreements over how to lead the union movement forward and competition between unions to organize some of the same groups of employees. Second, unions face the need to rebuild membership rolls; union participation has been generally on the decline since the 1950s. Third, unions have been lobbying vigorously for several years to secure passage of the Employee Free Choice Act. This legislation would make it easier for unions to organize employees by limiting the options available to employers and forcing the resolution of bargaining efforts through the use of mandatory arbitration.

Critical thinking: (1) What evidence would you need to reach a solid conclusion about why union membership has declined in the private sector over the past 50 years? (2) Why do you suppose different surveys generate such wildly varying responses to questions about whether nonunion employees would like to join a union?

It's your business: (1) With everything you've learned about labor relations so far, would you describe yourself as more pro-union or more anti-union? Why? (2) How would you respond to your workplace becoming unionized through a card check, rather than a secret-ballot election?

Key terms to know: Employee Free Choice Act (EFCA)

Behind the Scenes

Labor Conflict Comes to a Head at AAM

The standoff between AAM and the UAW is emblematic of the seismic changes shaking up the U.S. automotive industry and much of the manufacturing sector in general. Labor agreements from years past left companies at a competitive disadvantage in an increasingly global economy where workers in many other countries made far less than U.S. workers. In addition to this structural change in the labor market, the deteriorating U.S. economy was putting a traumatic squeeze on auto sales.

AAM hoped to address the situation by convincing the UAW to agree to lower salaries for new hires and to a buyout program for existing workers, with the idea that the company could pay some current employees to leave and then hire new employees at half the old wages. Unwilling to make the compromises AAM demanded, the 3,650 UAW workers at five AAM plants in Michigan and New York went on strike against the company in late February 2008.

Within a week, the shutdown at AAM began to affect production at GM because AAM was the sole supplier of axles for GM's light trucks and sport utility vehicles made in North America. Before long, more than 42,000 GM employees were idle, and the strike eventually cost GM nearly $2 billion at a time the giant automaker was itself struggling to survive. The slowdown also rippled back to other GM suppliers, who had to reduce production as well.

The UAW had reached historic agreements with the three major automakers the year before, and union-management relations in the industry had been on a relatively positive trend as a result. The situation was far different in the negotiations to end the strike at AAM. Dauch threatened to close the five plants if the union wouldn't budge. "We have the flexibility to source all of our business to other locations around the world, and we have the right to do so. We will not be forced into bankruptcy in order to reach a market-competitive cost structure in the United States. If we cannot compete for new contracts in the U.S., there will be no work in the original plants." With manufacturing plants in Mexico, Brazil, England, Scotland, Poland, and China, and plans to add facilities in Thailand and India, AAM certainly had other options and opportunities to pursue.

UAW president Ron Gettelfinger accused the company of trying to dictate terms rather than negotiating and said that AAM "wants to take us to the cleaners." He added, "A line has been drawn in the sand, and that is where we are." In the midst of the wrangling, the union filed an unfair labor practices complaint, accusing AAM of withholding information. Then AAM began advertising for new workers, claiming it wanted to be ready to bring on new employees in case existing employees would agree to buyouts and early retirement packages. The union responded to the ads by accusing the company of trying to hire scabs to replace strikers. Further rubbing salt into union wounds, a month into the strike, AAM gave Dauch a 9.6 percent raise and $4 million worth of stock and stock options.

After nearly three months, negotiations finally produced an agreement the rank and file were willing to vote for. AAM got the lower wages it wanted, but victory came with a cost. To reduce headcount, the firm offered the choice of a $140,000 severance payment to leave outright or $55,000 to retire early. For those who stayed, it agreed to "buydowns" that give employees close to $100,000 each over a three-year period to help them adjust to lower wages. The concessions will cost the company $400 to $450 million—but allow it to save $300 million in wage and benefit costs every year going forward. GM played a key role in the process, chipping in $215 million to help fund the payments to AAM employees.

The agreement ended the strike, but it didn't end the challenges. As the automotive market continued to crumble through 2008 and 2009, AAM's financial picture worsened, leading some to speculate it might have to declare bankruptcy at some point. The relationship of the UAW and AAM is also far from certain. As one seasoned industry observer put it, "What's unknown is whether they can, or want to, work together for the long term."[69]

Critical Thinking Questions

1. If you were a procurement manager at GM, how might the strike at AAM affect your long-term thinking?
2. What effect did Richard Dauch's public statements and actions likely have on negotiations?
3. Can wages in the U.S. auto industry ever return to their historical highs? Why or why not?

LEARN MORE ONLINE

Visit the AAM website at www.aam.com, click on "Media," and then read some of the recent news releases. Was the company profitable in the most recent quarter? Has there been any news about labor relations issues at AAM? Click over to the "Investors" section and look at the stock information. AAM shares were selling for as low as $0.26 at one point; where is the share price today? ∎

Key Terms

arbitration (320)
authorization cards (317)
boycott (320)
certification election (317)
collective bargaining (319)
collective bargaining agreements (CBAs) (319)
decertification (318)
Employee Free Choice Act (EFCA) (325)
grievance (322)

injunction (321)
Labor-Management Relations Act (313)
Labor-Management Reporting and Disclosure Act (315)
labor relations (310)
labor unions (310)
locals (316)
lockouts (321)
mediation (320)
National Labor Relations Act (312)

national union (316)
progressive discipline (323)
right-to-work laws (315)
seniority (310)
strike (320)
strikebreakers (321)
unfair labor practices (322)
union security (315)
union shop (315)
work rules (311)

Test Your Knowledge

Questions for Review

1. How did the Wagner Act affect the balance of power between unions and employers?
2. From an employee's perspective, what are the potential benefits of unionization?
3. How does mediation differ from arbitration?
4. What is a right-to-work law?
5. What is a collective bargaining agreement?

Questions for Analysis

6. What are some of the explanations for the decline in labor union membership in the past 50 years?
7. How does the long history of labor-management relations affect labor relations in today's economy?
8. How does the relationship between labor and management reflect the potential for conflict in the stakeholder model?
9. Why are many employers not in favor of the Employee Free Choice Act?
10. **Ethical Considerations.** Is it wrong for employees to try to convince each other to vote for or against unionization?

How much pressure should employees be allowed to exert on each other during union organizing campaigns?

Questions for Application

11. What advice would you give the founders of a new company who want to avoid unionization efforts among their workforce as the company grows?
12. You work as an organizer for a union that is trying to persuade workers in the banking industry to unionize. You've collected authorization cards from 52 percent of the workers at a particular company. Should you file a petition with the NLRB for a secret-ballot election? Why or why not? (Assume the Employee Free Choice Act has not yet become law.)
13. A co-worker is arguing that the president should not have the authority to issue an injunction to stop a strike because doing so violates the legal rights of workers. How would you respond?
14. **Concept Integration.** Which motivation theory or theories discussed in Chapter 10 help explain the sometimes contentious nature of labor relations?

Practice Your Knowledge

Sharpening Your Communication Skills

Identify a recent situation in which a labor union went on strike in an attempt to force an employer to drop plans to reduce wages, benefits, or job security. Choose either the union's position or the company's position, and do the research necessary to write a compelling one-page argument for your side.

Building Your Team Skills

Form a team with several students who have chosen the same side in the dispute from "Sharpening Your Communication Skills." In a debate against another team that has taken the other side in the dispute, try to convince the rest of the class that your side is justified in taking the stance it took. Be prepared to address points likely to be raised by your opponents.

Expand Your Knowledge

Discovering Career Opportunities

Mediation and arbitration are forms of *alternative dispute resolution (ADR)*, so named because they offer alternatives to resolving disputes through lawsuits. Mediate.com (www.mediate.com/about) offers extensive information about mediation, and the American Arbitration Association (www.adr.org) offers information about arbitration. The "Judges, Magistrates, and Other Judicial Workers" section of the Occupational Outlook Handbook (www.bls.gov/oco/ocos272.htm) also provides information on careers in arbitration. Visit these sites and explore the world of ADR. Is this a career you might want to pursue? What additional education would you need?

Developing Your Research Skills

Conduct research to determine the current status of the Employee Free Choice Act. Has it been passed by the Congress and enacted into law? If it is now federal law, what has the response been from unions, employees, and employers? Have any legal challenges been mounted against it? What effect has it had on unionization and the economy?

Improving Your Tech Insights: Employee Monitoring Software

Is Big Brother watching while you work? Chances are extremely good that at least one form of electronic activity will be monitored in whatever workplace you join after graduation. The costs of inappropriate behavior can be so high that the majority of employers now monitor or control access to the Internet, telephone conversations (although employers are not allowed to record personal calls), voice mail, e-mail, instant messaging (but not text messaging, generally speaking), and other electronic media. Many employers also use keystroke monitoring or screen image recording software to keep track of what employees are doing at their computers. Many businesses also use video monitors throughout company facilities.

Employers have a number of concerns, including lost productivity, release of company secrets or confidential customer records, the viewing and sending of inappropriate material, and illegal activities by employees. Privacy advocates may not like all the monitoring, but current laws provide little protection for employee privacy, and courts have ruled that employers have the right to control the use of company-owned systems and to protect confidential information. In a brief e-mail message to your instructor, summarize this dilemma and its possible effects on employee-management relations.[70]

Video Discussion

Access the Chapter 12 video discussion in the End of Chapter Assignments section at www.mybizlab.com.

PEARSON mybizlab

Log on to www.mybizlab.com to access the following study and assessment aids associated with this chapter:

- Interactive exercises
- Pre/post test
- Real-Time Updates
- Video application
- Customized study plans
- Biz Skills Simulations
- Quick Learning Guide

If you are not using mybizlab, you can access Real-Time Updates and Quick Learning Guides through http://realtimeupdates.com/bia5. The Quick Learning Guide (located under "Learn More" on the website) provides all six Checkpoints in a handy two-page format to help you study for exams or review important concepts whenever you need a quick refresher.

CHAPTER 13

The Art and Science of Marketing

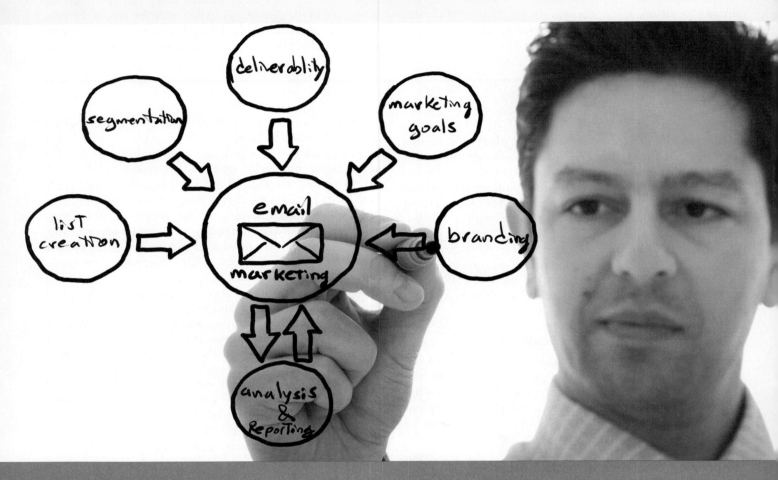

After studying this chapter, you will be able to

1 Define *marketing* and explain its role in society

2 Identify three trends that help define contemporary marketing

3 Differentiate *consumer buying behavior* and *organizational buying behavior*

4 Define *strategic marketing planning* and identify the four basic options for pursuing new marketing opportunities

5 Identify the four steps needed to craft a marketing strategy

6 Describe the four main components of the marketing mix

Behind the Scenes

Toyota Scion: Connecting with a New Generation of Car Buyers

www.scion.com

If you are in your twenties and in the market for your first new car, are you likely to rush out and buy the same car your parents have? You know—that sensible, conventional car such as the Toyota they drive to the grocery store and to your little sister's soccer practice?

Toyota's marketing experts know you probably won't, and they know this because they have already tried selling conventional cars to younger buyers using conventional advertising messages. Over the past few decades, Toyota has grown to a position of prominence in the United States by offering your parents refreshing alternatives to the cars that *their* parents drove; now the company wants to continue that cycle of success with the next generation of drivers.

Scion Vice President Mark Templin and his colleagues knew the conventional Toyota approach wouldn't work with this new audience, but what approach would? The search for an answer started with research, research, and more research. And that approach to research had to be unconventional—for example, hiring 50 young Californians to record video diaries with their friends. The company even went so far as to learn how core groups of trendsetters discover new ideas and products before spreading them through the larger population. The research yielded a wide range of insights, including

Scion Vice President Mark Templin, shown here at the Chicago Auto Show, helps shape Scion as a unique brand in the automotive marketplace.

the fact that Japan has emerged as a new center of cool and the realizations that young adults strongly resist being sold to and put a high priority on individualism, self-expression, and authenticity.

The research results helped Toyota create a new line of cars called Scion, the most unconventional of which is the aggressively boxy xB model. The cars benefit from the Toyota heritage of top-notch quality at low prices, and Toyota and after-market suppliers created a wide range of accessories to let buyers personalize their cars—from illuminated cup holders to colored steering wheels. A small number of "Release Series" limited-edition vehicles help create buzz each year, too.

If you had Mark Templin's assignment to market an entirely new line of cars to a generation of drivers who are skeptical about advertising and leery of buying products that "old people" buy, what kind of marketing strategy would you put in place? How would you shape the design of the products to make sure they're different enough to attract the target audience but not so different as to become oddities that no one would buy? What steps would you take to make Scion part of the cultural landscape? How would you get the Scion message out to an audience that doesn't like to be advertised to or sold to?[1] ■

Introduction

Toyota's experience in introducing the Scion brand (profiled in the chapter-opening Behind the Scenes) illustrates the complex challenge of fashioning an appealing blend of products, prices, distribution methods, and customer communication efforts—the essential elements of marketing. This chapter introduces the basic concepts of marketing; products and pricing are addressed in Chapter 14, distribution and marketing logistics in Chapter 15, and customer communication in Chapter 16.

Avon has made breast cancer awareness and research funding a focus of its cause-related marketing.

Marketing in a Changing World

Marketing a product line such as the Toyota Scion requires a wide range of skills, from research and analysis to strategic planning to persuasive communication. On the job and in the media, you will encounter many uses of the term *marketing*, from the broad and strategic to the narrow and tactical. However, noted marketing professors Philip Kotler and Gary Armstrong offer a definition that does a great job of highlighting the contemporary flavor of customer-focused marketing: **Marketing** is "the process by which companies create value for customers and build strong customer relationships in order to capture value from customers in return."[2] The ideas of *value*, the *exchange* of value, and lasting *relationships* are essential elements of successful marketing.

In addition to goods and services, marketing applies to not-for-profit organizations, people, places, and causes. Politicians and celebrities constantly market themselves. So do places that want to attract residents, tourists, and business investments. **Place marketing** describes efforts to market geographic areas ranging from neighborhoods to entire countries. **Cause-related marketing** promotes a cause or a social issue—such as physical fitness, cancer awareness, environmental sustainability—while also promoting a company and its products.

The Role of Marketing in Society

Marketing plays an important role in society by helping people satisfy their needs and wants and by helping organizations determine what to produce.

Needs and Wants

Individuals and organizations have a wide variety of needs, from food and water necessary for survival to transaction processing systems that make sure a retail store gets paid for all the credit card purchases it records. As a consumer, you experience a **need** anytime a difference or a gap exists between your actual state and your ideal state. You're hungry and you don't want to be hungry: You need to eat. Needs create the motivation to buy products and are, therefore, at the core of any discussion of marketing.

Your **wants** are based on your needs but are more specific. Producers do not create needs, but they do try to shape your wants by exposing you to attractive choices. For instance, when you *need* some food, you may *want* a Snickers bar, an orange, or a seven-course dinner at the swankiest restaurant in town. If you have the means, or *buying power*, to then purchase the product you want, you create *demand* for that product.[3]

Exchanges and Transactions

When you participate in the **exchange process**, you trade something of value (usually money) for something else of value. When you make a purchase, you encourage the producer of that item to create or supply more of it. In this way, supply and demand tend toward balance, and society obtains the goods and services that are most satisfying. When the exchange actually occurs, it takes the form of a **transaction**. Party A gives Party B $1.29 and gets a medium Coke in return. A trade of values takes place.

Most transactions in today's society involve money, but money is not necessarily required. Bartering or trading, which predates the use of cash, is making a big comeback thanks to the Internet. Hundreds of online barter exchanges are now in operation in the United States alone. Intermediaries such as BizXchange (**www.bizx.com**) facilitate cashless trading among multiple members through a system of credits and debits.

marketing
The process of creating value for customers and building relationships with those customers in order to capture value back from them

place marketing
Marketing efforts to attract people and organizations to a particular geographic area

cause-related marketing
Identification and marketing of a social issue, cause, or idea to selected target markets

need
Difference between a person's actual state and his or her ideal state; provides the basic motivation to make a purchase

wants
Specific goods, services, experiences, or other entities that are desirable in light of a person's experiences, culture, and personality

exchange process
Act of obtaining a desired object or service from another party by offering something of value in return

transaction
Exchange of value between parties

For instance, an advertising agency might trade services to a dairy farm, which then trades products to a catering company, which then trades services to the advertising agency. By eliminating the need for trading partners to have exactly complimentary needs at exactly the same time, these exchanges make it easy for companies to buy and sell without using cash.[4]

The Four Utilities

To encourage the exchange process, marketers enhance the appeal of their goods and services by adding **utility**, which is any attribute that increases the value that customers place on the product (see Exhibit 13.1). When organizations change raw materials into finished goods, they are creating *form utility* desired by consumers. When supermarkets provide fresh, ready-to-eat dishes as an alternative to food ingredients, they are creating form utility. In other cases, marketers try to make their products available when and where customers want to buy them, creating *time utility* and *place utility*. Overnight couriers such as FedEx create time utility, whereas coffee carts in office buildings and ATMs in shopping malls create place utility. Services such as Apple's iTunes create both time and place utility: you can purchase music almost instantly, without leaving your computer. The final form of utility is *possession utility*—the satisfaction that buyers get when they actually possess a product, both legally and physically. Mortgage companies, for example, create possession utility by offering loans that allow people to buy homes they could otherwise not afford.

utility
Power of a good or service to satisfy a human need

The Marketing Concept

Business's view of the marketing function has evolved rather dramatically over the decades. In years past, many companies pursued what was known as the *product concept*, which was essentially to focus on the production of goods and count on customers to figure out which products they need and take the steps to find and purchase them. In other words, the product concept views the primary purpose of a business as making things, not satisfying customers. As markets evolved and competition heated up, the *sales concept* began to take over, which emphasizes building a business by generating as many sales transactions as possible. The customer features more prominently in the sale concept, but only as a target to be sold to, not as a partner in a mutually satisfying relationship.

In contrast, today's most successful companies tend to embrace the **marketing concept**, the idea that companies should respond to customers' needs and wants while seeking long-term profitability and coordinating their own marketing efforts to achieve

marketing concept
Approach to business management that stresses customer needs and wants, seeks long-term profitability, and integrates marketing with other functional units within the organization

EXHIBIT 13.1 Examples of the Four Utilities

The utility of a good or service has four aspects, each of which enhances the product's value to the consumer.

UTILITY	EXAMPLE
Form utility	Kettle Valley's Fruit Snack (www.kettlevalley.net) bars provide the nutritional value of real fruit in a form that offers greater convenience and longer storage life.
Time utility	LensCrafters (www.lenscrafters.com) has captured a big chunk of the market for eyeglasses by providing on-the-spot, one-hour service.
Place utility	By offering convenient home delivery of the latest fashion apparel and accessories, dELiA*s (www.delias.com) catalog and website have become favorites of teenage girls.
Possession utility	RealNetworks's Rhapsody music streaming service (www.rhapsody.com) gives customers the option of buying individual songs.

EXHIBIT 13.2

The Selling Concept Versus the Marketing Concept

Firms that practice the selling concept sell what they make rather than make what the market wants. In contrast, firms that practice the marketing concept determine the needs and wants of a market and deliver the desired product or service more effectively and efficiently than competitors do.

Starting point	Focus	Means	Ends
Factory	Existing products	Selling and promoting	Profits through sales volume

The Selling Concept

Market	Customer needs	Customer communication	Profits through customer satisfaction

The Marketing Concept

relationship marketing
A focus on developing and maintaining long-term relationships with customers, suppliers, and distribution partners for mutual benefit

customer loyalty
Degree to which customers continue to buy from a particular retailer or buy the products of a particular manufacturer or service provider

the company's long-term goals (see Exhibit 13.2). These *customer-focused* companies build their marketing strategies around the goal of long-term relationships with satisfied customers.[5] The term **relationship marketing** is often applied to these efforts to distinguish them from efforts that emphasize production or sales transactions. One of the most significant goals of relationship marketing is **customer loyalty**, the degree to which customers continue to buy from a particular retailer or buy the products offered by a particular manufacturer. The payoff from becoming customer-focused can be considerable, but the process of transforming a product- or sales-driven company into one that embraces the marketing concept can take years and involve changes to major systems and processes throughout the company, as well as the basic culture of the company itself.[6]

Why all the emphasis on customer service and customer satisfaction in the marketing concept, by the way? It's not just about being nice and helpful; satisfying customers is simply smart business. For one thing, keeping your existing customers is usually much cheaper and easier than finding new customers. For another, satisfied customers are the best promotion a company can hope for, particularly given the power of social media and social commerce (see the next page).

✓ CHECKPOINT

LEARNING OBJECTIVE 1: Define *marketing*, and explain its role in society.

Summary: Marketing can be defined as "the process by which companies create value for customers and build strong customer relationships in order to capture value from customers in return." The marketing function guides a company in selecting which products to offer, how much to charge for them, how to distribute them to customers, and how to promote them to potential buyers. Marketing plays an important role in society by helping people satisfy their needs and wants and by helping organizations determine what to produce.

Critical thinking: (1) Should every company see long-term relationships with customers to the same degree? Why or why not? (2) Would a company that already dominates its markets ever care about the marketing concept? Why or why not?

It's your business: (1) What is your reaction when you feel as though you're being "sold to" by a company that is clearly more interested in selling products than in meeting your needs as an individual consumer? (2) Do you want to have a "relationship" with any of the companies that you currently patronize as a customer? Why or why not?

Key terms to know: marketing, place marketing, cause-related marketing, need, wants, exchange process, transaction, utility, marketing concept, relationship marketing, customer loyalty

Challenges in Contemporary Marketing

As business has progressed from the product concept to the sales concept to the marketing concept, the role of marketing has become increasingly complicated. You'll read about some specific challenges in this and the next three chapters, but here are three general issues that many marketing organizations are wrestling with today: involving the customer in the marketing process, making data-driven decisions, and conducting marketing activities with greater concern for ethics and etiquette.

Involving the Customer in the Marketing Process

A central element in the marketing concept is involving the customer as a partner in a mutually beneficial relationship, rather than treating the customer as a passive recipient of products and promotional messages. Involving the customer has always been relatively easy for small, local companies and for large companies with their major customers. For instance, a neighborhood bistro or coffee shop can prepare foods and drinks just the way their regular customers want, and satisfied customers are happy to tell friends and family about their favorite places to eat and drink. At the other extreme, a maker of jet engines such Pratt & Whitney or Rolls-Royce works closely with its airplane manufacturing customers to create exactly the products those customers want.

The challenge has been to replicate this level of intimacy on a broader scale, when a company has thousands of customers spread across the country or around the world. Two sets of technologies have helped foster communication and collaboration between companies and their customers. The first is **customer relationship management (CRM)** systems, which capture, organize, and capitalize on all the interactions that a company has with its customers, from marketing surveys and advertising through sales orders and customer support. A CRM system functions like an institutional memory for the company, allowing it to record and act on the information that is pertinent to each customer relationship.

CRM can be a powerful means to foster relationships, but to a certain degree, conventional CRM simply computerizes an existing way of doing business. A more dramatic step is enabling **social commerce** using blogs, wikis, *user-generated content* such as online videos or customer-created advertising, and other technologies that usually fall under the banner of *Web 2.0*. These communication tools let customers communicate with companies, with each other, and with influences in the marketplace such as prominent bloggers and journalists. For example, social networks such as Facebook have the potential to redefine advertising because consumers tend to view friends and peers as more reliable sources of product information than advertising.[7] As Chapter 16 explains, advertisers are learning to enable and participate in these online conversations, rather than blasting out messages to passive audiences as they did in the past. Another valuable use of social media is listening to feedback from customers.[8] Innovative companies are beginning to integrate these two relationship technologies, combining the data capture and retrieval of CRM with the interactivity of social media.[9]

customer relationship management (CRM)
Type of information system that captures, organizes, and capitalizes on all the interactions that a company has with its customers

social commerce
The creation and sharing of product-related information among customers and potential customers

Making Data-Driven Marketing Decisions

Learning more about customers is one aspect of the larger challenge of collecting, analyzing, and using data to make marketing decisions. Marketers in every industry would like to have better insights for making decisions and better ways of measuring the results of every marketing initiative. Pioneering retailer John Wannamaker said a hundred years ago that "Half the money I spend on advertising is wasted. The trouble is, I don't know which half."[10] Actually, Wannamaker was probably overly optimistic. In one extensive study, advertising was found to increase revenue for just over half of new products but for only one-third of existing products.[11] In other words, according to this research, the advertising campaigns for two-thirds of established products in the marketplace don't bring in more revenue.

Understandably, top executives are demanding that marketing departments do a better job of justifying their budgets and finding the most effective ways of meeting marketing objectives. However, this accountability challenge is not a simple one, and the problem

Real-Time Updates

Learn More
Marketing research tutorial

This three-part series offers a great overview of research strategies and techniques. On mybizlab (www.mybizlab.com), you can access Real-Time Updates within each chapter or under Student Study Tools. Otherwise, go to http://real-timeupdates.com/bia5 and click on "Learn More."

may never be completely solvable for many companies. With so many sources of information in the marketplace, for example, identifying which sources influence buyer behavior can be difficult.

In the early days of Internet commerce, hope ran high that the ability to track users as they surfed the web would make it easier to track responses to advertising. Tracking individual aspects of marketing effectiveness, such as click-through rates for an online ad, can produce useful data. Ironically, though, there is now such a blizzard of online data that "we've created a quagmire of data that obscures the bigger picture more effectively than it paints it."[12] Plus, over the long term, so many things contribute to or detract from a firm's ability to meet its marketing objectives that isolating the effects of individual tactics can be quite difficult. However, a number of firms, including Procter & Gamble, Kraft Foods, Coca-Cola, and Wachovia (now part of Wells Fargo), have developed sophisticated tracking systems that show managers how various marketing investments contribute to overall company goals.[13]

marketing research
The collection and analysis of information for making marketing decisions

The process of gathering and analyzing *market intelligence* about customers, competitors, and related marketing issues is known as **marketing research**. As markets grow increasingly dynamic and open to competition from all corners of the globe, today's companies realize that information is the key to successful action. Without it, they're forced to use guesswork, analogies from other markets that may or may not apply, or experience from the past that may not correspond to the future.[14]

At the same time, however, marketing research can't provide the answer to every strategic or tactical question. As a manager or entrepreneur, you'll find yourself in situations that require creative thinking and careful judgment to make the leap beyond what the data alone can tell you. Research techniques range from the basic to the exotic, from simple surveys to advanced statistical techniques to neurological scanning that tries to discover how and why customers' brains respond to visual and verbal cues about products. You can see a sample of techniques in Exhibit 13.3.

Marketing with Greater Concern for Ethics and Etiquette

Under pressure to reach and persuade buyers in a business environment that gets more fragmented and noisy all the time, marketers occasionally step over the line and engage in practices that are rude, manipulative, or even downright deceptive. The result is an increasing degree of skepticism of and hostility toward advertising and other marketing activities.[15]

permission-based marketing
Marketing approach in which firms first ask permission to deliver messages to an audience and then promise to restrict their communication efforts to those subject areas in which audience members have expressed interest

To avoid intensifying the vicious circle in which marketers keep doing the same old things, only louder and longer—leading customers to get more angry and more defensive—some marketers are looking for a better way. Social commerce shows a lot of promise for redefining marketing communication from one-way promotion to two-way conversation. Another hopeful sign is **permission-based marketing**, in which marketers invite potential or current customers to receive information in areas that genuinely interest them. Many websites now take this approach, letting visitors sign up for specific content streams with the promise that they won't be bombarded with information they don't care about.

stealth marketing
The delivery of marketing messages to people who are not aware that they are being marketed to; these messages can be delivered by either acquaintances or strangers, depending on the technique

At the same time, the emergence of **stealth marketing**, in which customers don't know they're being marketed to, has raised an entirely new set of concerns about ethics and intrusion. One stealth marketing technique is sending people into public places to use particular products in a conspicuous manner and then discuss them with strangers—as though they were just regular people on the street, when in fact they are employed by a marketing firm. Another is to pay consumers (or reward them with

EXHIBIT 13.3 Marketing Research Techniques

Marketers can use a wide variety of techniques to learn more about customers, competitors, and threats and opportunities in the marketplace.

TECHNIQUE	EXAMPLES
Observation	Any in-person, mechanical, or electronic technique that monitors and records behavior, including website usage tracking and monitoring of blogs and social networking websites.
Surveys	Data collection efforts that measure responses from a representative subset of a larger group of people; can be conducted in person (when people with clipboards stop you in a mall, that's called a *mall intercept*), over the phone, by mail or e-mail, or online. Designing and conducting a meaningful survey requires thorough knowledge of statistical techniques such as *sampling* to ensure valid results that truly represent the larger group. For this reason, many of the simple surveys that you see online these days do not produce statistically valid results.
Interviews and focus groups	One-on-one or group discussions that try to probe deeper into issues than a survey typically does. *Focus groups* involve a small number of people guided by a facilitator while being observed or recorded by researchers. Unlike surveys, interviews and focus groups are not designed to collect statistics that represent a larger group; their real value is in uncovering issues that might require further study.
Process data collection	Any method of collecting data during the course of other business tasks, including warranty registration cards, sales transaction records, gift and loyalty program card usage, and customer service interactions.
Experiments	Controlled scenarios in which researchers adjust one or more variables to measure the effect these changes have on customer behavior. For instance, separate groups of consumers can be exposed to different ads to see which ad is most effective. *Test marketing*, the launch of a product under real-world conditions but on a limited scale (such as in a single city), is a form of experimental research.
Ethnographic research	A branch of anthropology, ethnography studies people in their daily lives to learn about their needs, wants, and behaviors in real-life settings.
Neuromarketing studies	Neuromarketing research measures brain activity while customers are viewing or interacting with products and brands.

insider information and other perks) to promote products to their friends without telling them it's a form of advertising. Critics complain that such techniques are deceptive because they don't give their targets the opportunity to raise their instinctive defenses against the persuasive powers of marketing messages. Consequently, stealth campaigns can be viewed as both deceptive and exploitative, particularly when children are either used as agents in these campaigns or selected as targets.[16]

 **CHECKPOINT**

LEARNING OBJECTIVE 2: Identify three trends that help define contemporary marketing.

Summary: Three general issues that many marketing organizations are wrestling with today are involving the customer in the marketing process, making data-driven decisions, and conducting marketing with greater concern for ethics and etiquette. Allowing customers greater involvement is essential to relationship marketing and the marketing concept, and it is being driven today by *social commerce*—customers using Web 2.0 communication tools to converse with companies and each other. Data-driven decision making is a top priority as many companies struggle to justify and optimize marketing expenditures. Public opinion of business in general and marketing in particular is at a low point these days, prompting many professionals to take a closer look at their business practices and relationships with customers.

Critical thinking: (1) How can technology help companies replicate the community feel of a small neighborhood business on a global scale? (2) Why is stealth marketing considered unethical by some critics?

It's your business: (1) Are you so loyal to any brands or companies that you refuse to accept substitutes—so much so that if you can't have your favorite product, you'll do without? What is it about these products that earns your continued loyalty? (2) Have you ever been a target of stealth marketing? If so, how did you feel about the company after you learned you had been marketed to without your knowledge?

Key terms to know: customer relationship management (CRM), social commerce, marketing research, permission-based marketing, stealth marketing

Understanding Today's Customers

To implement the marketing concept, companies must have good information about what customers want. This is a challenge because today's customers, both individual consumers and organizational buyers, are a diverse and demanding group, with little patience for marketers who do not understand them or will not adapt business practices to meet their needs. For instance, consumers faced with complex purchase decisions such as cars can now find extensive information online about products, prices, competitors, customer service rankings, safety issues, and other factors. They no longer have to put their fate entirely in the hands of companies that once had the upper hand by hoarding all the information.

The first step toward understanding customers is recognizing the different purchase and ownership habits of the **consumer market**, made up of individuals and families who buy for personal or household use, and the **organizational market**, composed of both companies and a variety of noncommercial institutions, from local school districts to the federal government.

The Consumer Decision Process

Think about several purchase decisions you've made recently. Classical economics suggests that your **customer buying behavior** would follow the rational process in Exhibit 13.4, first recognizing a need, gathering information, identifying alternative solutions, then making your choice from those alternatives. But how often do you really make decisions like that? Researchers now understand that consumer behavior tends to

consumer market
Individuals or households that buy goods and services for personal use

organizational market
Businesses, nonprofit organizations, and government agencies that purchase goods and services for use in their operations

customer buying behavior
Behavior exhibited by buyers as they consider, select, and purchase goods and services

EXHIBIT 13.4 The Rational Model of Buyer Decisions

In the classic, rational model of buyer behavior, customers work through several steps in logical order before making a purchase decision. However, newer research shows that most consumer decisions are less rational and more subconscious than the classical model suggests.

1. Need recognition
2. Information search
3. Evaluation of alternatives
4. Purchase
5. Postpurchase evaluation

be far less logical and far more complicated—and more interesting—than this model suggests. In fact, some research suggests that as much as 95 percent of the decision-making process is subconscious and that sensory cues can play a much larger role than objective information.[17] The emerging field of *behavioral economics* is starting to offer better insights into consumer behavior by incorporating a broader (and somewhat less-flattering) view of the way people really make decisions.[18]

Even in situations in which consumers gather lots of information and appear to be making a well-thought-out, rational decision, they often are acting more on gut feelings and emotional responses. For instance, you might see one of the latest Scion models drive past on the street, and in that split second—before you even start "thinking" about it—you've already decided to buy one just like it. Sure, you'll gather brochures, do research on the Internet, test-drive other models, and so on, but chances are you're not really evaluating alternatives. Instead, your rational, conscious brain is just looking for evidence to support the decision that your emotional, semi-conscious brain has already made.

Moreover, we consumers make all kinds of decisions that are hard to explain by any rational means. We might spend two weeks gathering data on $200 music players and then choose a college with a $20,000 annual tuition simply because our best friend is going there. Sometimes we buy things for no apparent reason other than the fact that we have money in our pockets. As a result, at one time or another, all consumers suffer from **cognitive dissonance**, which occurs when our beliefs and behaviors don't match. A common form of this situation is *buyer's remorse*, when we make a purchase and then regret doing so—sometimes immediately after the purchase.

You can start to understand why so many decisions seem mysterious from a rational point of view if you consider all the influences that affect purchases:

cognitive dissonance
Tension that exists when a person's beliefs don't match his or her behaviors; a common example is *buyer's remorse*, when someone regrets a purchase immediately after making it

- **Culture.** The cultures (and subgroups within cultures) that people belong to shape their values, attitudes, and beliefs and influence the way they respond to the world around them.

- **Socioeconomic level.** In addition to being members of a particular culture, people also perceive themselves as members of a certain social class—be it upper, middle, lower, or somewhere in between. In general, members of various classes pursue different activities, buy different goods, shop in different places, and react to different media—or at least like to believe they do.

- **Reference groups.** Consumers are also influenced by *reference groups* that provide information about product choices and establish values that individual consumers perceive as important. Reference groups can be either *membership* or *aspirational*. As the name suggests, membership groups are those to which consumers actually belong; families, networks of friends, clubs, and work groups are common examples. In contrast, consumers don't belong to aspirational reference groups but use them as role models for style, speech, opinions, and various other behaviors.[19] For instance, millions of consumers buy products that help them identify with popular musicians or professional athletes.

- **Situational factors.** These factors include events or circumstances in people's lives that are more circumstantial but that can influence buying patterns. Such factors can range from having a coupon to celebrating a holiday to being in a bad mood. If you've ever indulged in "retail therapy" to cheer yourself up, you know all about situational factors—and the buyer's remorse that often comes with it.

Real-Time Updates

Learn More
Take a closer look at consumer buying behavior

This tutorial dives into the "why" and "how" of consumer choices. On mybizlab (**www.mybizlab.com**), you can access Real-Time Updates within each chapter or under Student Study Tools. Otherwise, go to **http://real-timeupdates.com/bia5** and click on "Learn More."

■ **Self-image.** Many consumers tend to believe that "you are what you buy," so they make or avoid choices that support their desired self-images. Marketers capitalize on people's need to express their identity through their purchases by emphasizing the image value of goods and services.

The Organizational Customer Decision Process

The purchasing behavior of organizations is easier to understand because it's more clearly driven by economics and influenced less by subconscious and emotional factors. Here are some of the significant ways in which organizational purchasing differs from consumer purchasing:[20]

■ **An emphasis on economic payback and other rational factors.** Much more so than with consumer purchases, organizational purchases are carefully evaluated for financial impact, reliability, and other objective factors. Organizations don't always make the best choices, of course, but their choices are usually based on a more rational analysis of needs and alternatives. This isn't to say that emotions play little or no role in the purchase decision, however; organizations don't make decisions, people do. Fear of change, fear of failure, excitement over new technologies, and the pride of being associated with world-class suppliers are just a few of the emotions that can influence organizational purchases.

■ **A formal buying process.** From office supplies to new factories, most organizational purchases follow a formal buying process, particularly in mid- to large-size companies. In fact, the model in Exhibit 13.4 is a better representation of organizational purchasing than it is of consumer purchasing, although organizational purchasing often includes additional steps such as establishing budgets, analyzing potential suppliers, and requesting proposals.

■ **Greater complexity in product usage.** The Apple iPhone is a great example of how consumer and organizational markets differ. While the iPhone was instantly popular with vast numbers of consumers, breaking into the corporate market is a much greater challenge because these buyers need to address such issues as compatibility with corporate communication systems and legal requirements of data retention and security.[21] In addition, the *network effect*, in which the value of a product increases with the number of customers who use it, can be a key decision driver.[22] A major reason that other software providers have so much trouble putting a dent in Microsoft's dominance of the corporate market is that business users need compatibility, so it is simpler to select the tools that more people already use. Also, organizations sometimes continue to use products long after better substitutes become available if the costs and complexity of updating outweigh the advantages of the newer solutions.

■ **The participation and influence of multiple people.** Except in the very smallest businesses, the purchase process usually involves a group of people. This team can include end users, technical experts, the manager with ultimate purchasing authority, and a professional purchasing agent whose job includes researching suppliers, negotiating prices, and evaluating supplier performance. Multiple family members play a part in many consumer purchases, of course, but not with the formality apparent in organizational markets.

■ **Close relationships between buyers and sellers.** Close relationships between buyers and sellers are common in organizational purchasing. In some cases, employees from the seller even have offices inside the buyer's facility to promote close interaction.

Real-Time Updates

Learn More

Take a closer look at organizational buying behavior

Learn more about how businesses make purchasing decisions. On mybizlab (www.mybizlab.com), you can access Real-Time Updates within each chapter or under Student Study Tools. Otherwise, go to http://real-timeupdates.com/bia5 and click on "Learn More."

CHECKPOINT

LEARNING OBJECTIVE 3: Differentiate *consumer buying behavior* **and** *organizational buying behavior.*

Summary: Classical economic theory suggests that consumers follow a largely rational process of recognizing a need, searching for information, evaluating alternatives, making a purchase, and evaluating the product after use or consumption. However, recent research into behavioral economics and consumer psychology suggests that many consumer purchases are far less rational. Much of this decision making happens subconsciously and is driven to a large degree by emotion, culture, and situational factors. Organizational buying behavior comes much closer to the rational model of classical economics because these purchases are usually judged by their economic value to the organization. The most significant ways in which organizational purchasing differs from consumer purchasing are an emphasis on economic payback, a formal buying process, greater complexity in product usage, purchasing groups, and close relationships between buyers and sellers.

Critical thinking: (1) Can business-to-business marketers take advantage of new insights into consumer buying behavior? Why or why not? (2) How could families and individual consumers benefit from adopting some elements of organizational buying behavior?

It's your business: (1) Do you read product reviews online before making important purchases? Why or why not? Have you ever contributed to social commerce by posting your own reviews or product advice? (2) Why did you buy the clothes you are wearing at this very moment?

Key terms to know: consumer market, organizational market, customer buying behavior, cognitive dissonance

Identifying Market Opportunities

With insights into your customers' needs and behaviors, you're ready to begin planning your marketing strategies. **Strategic marketing planning** is a process that involves three steps: (1) examining your current marketing situation, (2) assessing your opportunities and setting your objectives, and (3) developing a marketing strategy to reach those objectives (see Exhibit 13.5 on the next page). Companies often record the results of their planning efforts in a formal *marketing plan.*

A solid marketing strategy both flows from and supports the overall business strategy; it is also closely coordinated with other functional strategies. For instance, to reach out to younger drivers with the high-quality, low-cost Scion, Toyota needs not only an effective marketing strategy but a manufacturing strategy that can create the necessary products, a financial strategy that supports the price levels required by the marketing strategy, a human resource strategy that makes sure the right workers are in place across all the functions, and so on. The process starts with examining the current marketing situation.

strategic marketing planning The process of examining an organization's current marketing situation, assessing opportunities and setting objectives, and then developing a marketing strategy to reach those objectives

Examining the Current Marketing Situation

Examining your current marketing situation includes reviewing your past performance (how well each product is doing in each market where you sell it), evaluating your competition, examining your internal strengths and weaknesses, and analyzing the external environment.

EXHIBIT 13.5 The Strategic Marketing Planning Process

Strategic marketing planning comprises three steps: (1) examining your current marketing situation, (2) assessing your opportunities and setting objectives, and (3) developing your marketing strategy.

Examine Current Marketing Situation

✓ Review past/current performance

✓ Evaluate competition

✓ Examine internal strengths and weaknesses

✓ Analyze external environment

Assess Opportunities and Set Objectives

✓ Assess product and market opportunities

✓ Set specific and measurable objectives

Develop Marketing Strategy

✓ Segment market

✓ Choose target market

✓ Position product

✓ Develop marketing mix

Reviewing Performance

Unless you're starting a new business, your company has a history of marketing performance. Maybe sales have slowed in the past year, maybe you've had to cut prices so much that you're barely earning a profit, or maybe sales have been strong and you have money to invest in new marketing activities. Reviewing where you are and how you got there is critical, because you will want to learn from your mistakes and repeat your successes—without getting trapped in mindsets and practices that need to change for the future, even if they were successful in the past.

Evaluating Competition

In addition to reviewing past performance, you must also evaluate your competition. If you own a Burger King franchise, for example, you need to watch what McDonald's and Wendy's are doing. You also have to keep an eye on Taco Bell, KFC, Pizza Hut, and other restaurants in addition to paying attention to any number of other ways your customers might satisfy their hunger—including fixing a sandwich at home. Furthermore, you need to watch the horizon for trends that could affect your business, such as consumer interest in organic foods or locally produced ingredients.

When economic conditions in the housing market deteriorated in recent years, many homes were resold through large auctions, such as this event in New York City.

Examining Internal Strengths and Weaknesses

Successful marketers try to identify sources of competitive advantage and areas that need improvement. They look at such factors as financial resources, production capabilities, distribution networks, brand awareness, business partnerships, managerial expertise, and promotional capabilities. This step is important because you can't develop a successful marketing strategy if you don't know your strengths as well as your limitations. On the basis of your internal analysis, you will be able to decide whether your business should (1) limit itself to those opportunities for which it possesses the required strengths or (2) challenge itself to reach higher goals by acquiring and developing new strengths.

Analyzing the External Environment

Marketers must also analyze a number of external environment factors when planning their marketing strategies. These factors include:

Real-Time Updates

Learn More

Will it last? Separating trends from fads

Trend analyst Henrik Vejlgaard offers advice on distinguishing short-term fads from long-term trends. On mybizlab (**www.mybizlab.com**), you can access Real-Time Updates within each chapter or under Student Study Tools. Otherwise, go to **http://real-timeupdates.com/bia5** and click on "Learn More."

- **Economic conditions.** Marketing activities are greatly affected by trends in interest rates, inflation, unemployment, personal income, and savings rates. During recessions, consumers still aspire to enjoy the good life, but they are forced by circumstances to alter their spending patterns.[23] "Affordable luxuries" become particularly appealing during these times, for example. Recessions also create opportunities for agile and aggressive companies to take business away from companies weakened by poor sales and deteriorating finances.[24]

- **Natural environment.** Changes in the natural environment can affect marketers, both positively and negatively. Interruptions in the supply of raw materials can upset even the most carefully conceived marketing plans. Floods, droughts, and cold weather can affect the price and availability of many products as well as the behavior of target customers.

- **Social and cultural trends.** Planners also need to study the social and cultural environment to determine shifts in customer needs, values, and behaviors. With more buyers conscious of the environmental impact of consumption, for example, more companies are tapping into the "greening" trend with eco-friendly products and messages.

- **Laws and regulations.** Like every other function in business, marketing is controlled by laws at the local, state, national, and international levels. From product design to pricing to advertising, virtually every task you'll encounter in marketing is affected by laws and regulations.

- **Technology.** When technology changes, so must your marketing approaches. Technological innovations can help a company in some instances and hurt it in others. For example, online retailing has helped numerous companies reach customers around the world, but it has exposed them to competition from around the world, too. *Disruptive technologies*, those that fundamentally change the nature of an industry, can be powerful enough to create or destroy entire companies.

Assessing Opportunities and Setting Objectives

After you've examined the current marketing situation, you're ready to assess your marketing opportunities and set your objectives. Successful companies are always on the lookout for new marketing opportunities, which can be classified into four options.[25] **Market penetration** involves selling more of your existing products into the markets you already serve. **Product development** is creating new products for those current markets, while **market development** is selling your existing products to new markets. Finally, **diversification** involves creating new products for new markets.

These four options are listed in order of increasing risk. Market penetration can be the least risky because your products already exist, and the market has already demonstrated some level of demand for your products. At the other extreme, creating new products for new markets is usually the riskiest choice of all because you encounter uncertainties in both dimensions (you may fail to create the product you need, and the market might not be interested in it).

market penetration
Selling more of a firm's existing products into the markets it already serves

product development
Creating new products for a firm's current markets

market development
Selling existing products to new markets

diversification
Creating new products for new markets

market share
A firm's portion of the total sales in a market

After you've framed the opportunity you want to pursue, you are ready to set your marketing objectives. A common marketing objective is to achieve a certain level of **market share**, which is a firm's portion of the total sales within a market (market share can be defined by either number of units sold or by sales revenue).

CHECKPOINT

LEARNING OBJECTIVE 4: Define *strategic marketing planning*, and identify the four basic options for pursuing new marketing opportunities.

Summary: Strategic marketing planning involves the three steps of (1) examining the current marketing situation (including past performance, competition, internal strengths and weaknesses, and the external environment); (2) assessing market opportunities and setting marketing objectives; and (3) developing a marketing strategy to reach those objectives. The four basic options for pursuing market opportunities are *market penetration* (selling more existing products into the current markets), *product development* (creating new products for current markets), *market development* (selling existing products to new markets), and *diversification* (creating new products for new markets).

Critical thinking: (1) Why is it important to analyze past performance before assessing market opportunities and setting objectives? (2) Why is diversification considered riskier than market penetration, product development, and market development strategies?

It's your business: (1) Do you see yourself as a trendsetter in any aspect of your life? (2) How could the four options for pursing market opportunities be applied to your career planning at various stages in your career? (Think of your skills as the products you have to offer.)

Key terms to know: strategic marketing planning, market penetration, product development, market development, diversification, market share

Crafting a Marketing Strategy

Using the current marketing situation and your objectives as your guide, you're ready to develop a **marketing strategy**, which consists of dividing your market into *segments*, choosing your *target markets* and the *position* you'd like to establish in those markets, and then developing a *marketing mix* to help you get there.

marketing strategy
Overall plan for marketing a product; includes the identification of target market segments, a positioning strategy, and a marketing mix

market
A group of customers who need or want a particular product and have the money to buy it

market segmentation
Division of a diverse market into smaller, relatively homogeneous groups with similar needs, wants, and purchase behaviors

Dividing Markets into Segments

A **market** contains all the customers who might be interested in a product and can pay for it. However, most markets contain subgroups of potential customers with different interests, values, and behaviors. To maximize their effectiveness in reaching these subgroups, many companies subdivide the total market through **market segmentation**, grouping customers with similar characteristics, behaviors, and needs. Each of these market segments can then be approached by offering products that are priced, distributed, and promoted in a unique way that is most likely to appeal to that segment. The overall goal of market segmentation is to understand why and how certain customers buy what they buy so that you use your finite resources to create and market products in the most efficient manner possible.[26]

Four fundamental factors marketers use to identify market segments are demographics, psychographics, geography, and behavior:

- **Demographics.** When you segment a market using **demographics**, the statistical analysis of a population, you subdivide your customers according to characteristics such as age, gender, income, race, occupation, and ethnic group.

- **Psychographics.** Whereas demographic segmentation is the study of people from the outside, **psychographics** is the analysis of people from the inside, focusing on their psychological makeup, including attitudes, interests, opinions, and lifestyles. Psychographic analysis focuses on why people behave the way they do by examining such issues as brand preferences, media preferences, values, self-concept, and behavior.

- **Geography.** When differences in buying behavior are influenced by where people live, it makes sense to use **geographic segmentation**. Segmenting the market into different geographic units such as regions, cities, counties, or neighborhoods allows companies to customize and sell products that meet the needs of specific markets and to organize their operations as needed.

- **Behavior. Behavioral segmentation** groups customers according to their relationship with products or response to product characteristics. To identify behavioral segments, marketers study such factors as the occasions that prompt people to buy certain products, the particular benefits they seek from a product, habits and frequency of product usage, and the degree of loyalty they show toward a brand.[27]

demographics
Study of statistical characteristics of a population

psychographics
Classification of customers on the basis of their psychological makeup, interests, and lifestyles

geographic segmentation
Categorization of customers according to their geographic location

behavioral segmentation
Categorization of customers according to their relationship with products or response to product characteristics

Starting with these variables, researchers can also combine different types of data to identify target segments with even greater precision. One of the better known of these approaches is the PRIZM system developed by Claritas Corporation (**www.claritas.com**). Using geographic, demographic, and behavioral data, PRIZM divides the U.S. consumer market into dozens of "neighborhood" types such as "Bright Lites Li'l City" (childless professional couples living in upscale communities near big cities) and "Young Digerati" (ethnically diverse and technically sophisticated young urbanites).[28] Ace Hardware, for example, used PRIZM to relocate 30 stores to neighborhoods with higher concentrations of target customers, and many Ace stores use the system to select the optimum mix of products to offer based on neighborhood profiles.[29]

Choosing Your Target Markets

After you have segmented your market, the next step is to find appropriate target segments, or **target markets**, on which to focus your efforts. Marketers use a variety of criteria to narrow their focus to a few suitable market segments, including the magnitude of potential sales within each segment, the cost of reaching those customers, fit with a firm's core competencies, and any risks in the business environment.

Exhibit 13.6 on the next page diagrams four strategies for reaching target markets. Companies that practice *undifferentiated marketing* (also known as *mass marketing*) ignore differences among buyers and offer only one product or product line and present it with the same communication, pricing, and distribution strategies to all potential buyers. Undifferentiated marketing has the advantages of simplicity and economies of scale, but it can be less-effective at reaching some portions of the market.

By contrast, companies that manufacture or sell a variety of products to several target customer groups practice *differentiated marketing*. This is Toyota's approach, with the Scion brand aimed at young buyers, the Toyota brand for its core audience, and the Lexus brand for those wanting a luxury car. Differentiated marketing is a popular strategy, but it requires substantial resources because the company has to tailor products, prices, promotional efforts, and distribution arrangements for each customer group. The differentiation should be based on meaningful differences that don't alienate any audiences, too. When Dell launched its Della website to promote the company's Netbook line of computers to

target markets
Specific customer groups or segments to whom a company wants to sell a particular product

EXHIBIT 13.6

Market-Coverage Strategies

Four alternative market-coverage strategies are undifferentiated marketing, differentiated marketing, concentrated marketing, and micromarketing.

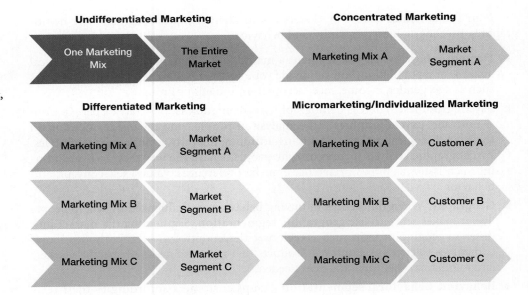

Undifferentiated Marketing

One Marketing Mix → The Entire Market

Concentrated Marketing

Marketing Mix A → Market Segment A

Differentiated Marketing

Marketing Mix A → Market Segment A

Marketing Mix B → Market Segment B

Marketing Mix C → Market Segment C

Micromarketing/Individualized Marketing

Marketing Mix A → Customer A

Marketing Mix B → Customer B

Marketing Mix C → Customer C

women without extensive computer backgrounds, the attempt was widely criticized by journalists and bloggers. Dell used "all the ridiculous 'women's advertising' clichés you could imagine," in the words of *Advertising Age* columnist Teressa Iezzi, including emphasizing the use of computers for shoe shopping and finding recipes.[30]

Concentrated marketing focuses on only a single market segment. With this approach, you acknowledge that various other market segments may exist but you choose to target just one. The biggest advantage of concentrated marketing is that it allows you to focus all your time and resources on a single type of customer (which is why this approach is usually the best option for start-up companies, by the way). The strategy can be risky, however, because you've staked your fortunes on just one segment.

Micromarketing, or *individualized marketing*, is the narrowest strategy of all, in which firms target a single location or even a single customer.[31] This can range from customizable products to *major accounts* sales teams that craft entire marketing programs for each of their largest customers.

Achieving success in any market segment can take time and significant investment, so embracing market segments for the long term is essential. For example, Procter & Gamble, the company behind the Pampers brand of disposable diapers, targets women before their babies are born and maintains a relationship with them for years afterward.[32] In fact, many companies now think in terms of *customer lifetime value*, the total potential revenue from each customer over a certain time span minus the cost of attracting and keeping that customer. This approach lets companies focus on their most valuable customers while deciding what to do with their less-profitable customers (such as abandoning these customers or changing marketing strategies to make pursuing them more profitable).[33]

Staking out a Position in Your Target Markets

After you have decided which segments of the market to enter, your next step is to decide what *position* you want to occupy in those segments. **Positioning** is the process of designing a company's offerings, messages, and operating policies so that both the company and its products occupy distinct and desirable competitive positions in your target customers' minds. For instance, for every product category that you care about as a consumer, you have some ranking of desirability in your mind—you believe that certain colleges are more prestigious than others, that certain brands of shoes are more fashionable than others, that one video game system is better than the others, and so on. Successful marketers are careful to choose the position they'd like to occupy in buyers' minds. One of Toyota's original goals in positioning the Scion brand was to make sure buyers *didn't* think it was a Toyota, and therefore, the parent company name is rarely seen in Scion promotions.

positioning
Managing a business in a way designed to occupy a particular place in the minds of target customers

A vital and often overlooked aspect of positioning is that although marketers take all kinds of steps to position their products, it is *customers* who ultimately decide on the positioning—they're the ones who interpret the many messages they encounter in the marketplace and decide what they think and feel about each product. For example, you can advertise that you have a luxury product, but if consumers aren't convinced, it's not really positioned as a luxury product. The only result that matters is what the customer believes. Scion's Mark Templin puts it this way: "Everyone works so hard to control and define what their brand stands for, when they ought to just let the consumer do it."[34]

In their attempts to secure favorable positions, marketers can emphasize such variables as product attributes, customer service, brand image (such as reliability or sophistication), price (such as low cost or premium), or category leadership (such as the leading online bookseller). For example, BMW and Porsche work to associate their products with performance, Mercedes Benz with luxury, and Volvo with safety.

✓ CHECKPOINT

LEARNING OBJECTIVE 5: Identify the four steps needed to craft a marketing strategy.

Summary: Crafting a marketing strategy involves dividing your market into *segments*, choosing your *target markets* and the *position* you'd like to establish in those markets, and then developing a *marketing mix* to help you get there. Segmentation (using demographics, psychographics, geography, and behavior) allows a company to select parts of the market most likely to respond to specific marketing programs. Companies can use one of four approaches to selecting target markets: undifferentiated (mass) marketing, differentiated marketing (with a different marketing mix for each segment), concentrated marketing (focusing on a single market segment), and micromarketing or individualized marketing. A *position* refers to the position a company or brand occupies in the mind of the target market segments. In creating a *marketing mix*, companies define the products they will offer, the prices they will charge, distribution methods, and customer communication efforts.

Critical thinking: (1) Would two companies interested in the same group of customers automatically use the same target market approach (such as differentiated or concentrated)? Why or why not? (2) Why aren't marketers ultimately in control of the positions their products achieve in the marketplace?

It's your business: (1) Think of three car brands or specific models. How are these products positioned in your mind? What terms do you use to describe them? (2) Given your transportation needs in the near future (assuming you will need a car), which model is the most desirable? The least desirable?

Key terms to know: marketing strategy, market, market segmentation, demographics, psychographics, geographic segmentation, behavioral segmentation, target markets, positioning

The Marketing Mix

After you've segmented your market, selected your target market, and taken steps to position your product, your next task is to develop a marketing mix. A firm's **marketing mix** consists of product, price, distribution, and customer communication (see Exhibit 13.7 on the next page). (You might also hear references to "the four Ps" of the marketing mix,

marketing mix
The four key elements of marketing strategy: product, price, distribution, and customer communication

EXHIBIT 13.7 The Marketing Mix

Whether it's Dutch Boy offering a more convenient package for paint or the fast-food chain Taco Bell expanding into retail grocery products, marketing professionals constantly look for new opportunities to improve the strength of their marketing mixes.

which is short for products, pricing, place or physical distribution, and promotion. However, with the advent of digital goods and services, distribution is no longer exclusively a physical concern. And many companies now view customer communication as a broader and more interactive activity than the functions implied by *promotion*.)

Products

In common usage, *product* usually refers to a tangible good, and a *service* refers to an intangible performance. However, for the purposes of studying marketing, it is helpful to define **product** as the bundle of value offered for the purpose of satisfying a want or a need in a marketing exchange. In this expanded definition, both tangible goods and intangible services are considered products. The reason for taking this broader view of *product* is that it encourages a more holistic look at the entire offering, which can include the brand name, design, packaging, support services, warranty, the ownership experience, and other attributes.

product
Bundle of value that satisfies a customer need or want

For example, if you buy a pair of $200 Dolce & Gabbana sunglasses with the brand's prominent "DG" initials on the side, you are buying much more than a device that holds a couple of protective lenses in front of your eyes. You are buying a shopping and ownership experience that is distinctly different from buying a pair of $5 sunglasses from a discount drugstore. You are buying the opportunity to feel a particular way about yourself and to present a particular image to the world around you. You are buying the right to brand yourself with the Dolce & Gabbana brand and everything that brand means to you. All these elements constitute the Dolce & Gabbana product. You'll explore products in more detail in Chapter 14.

Pricing

Price, the amount of money customers pay for the product (including any discounts), is the second major component of a firm's marketing mix. Looking back at Kotler and Armstrong's definition of marketing, price is the *value captured* from customers in exchange for the value offered in the product. Setting and managing a product's price is one of the most critical decisions a company must make, because price is the only element in a company's marketing mix that produces revenue—all other elements represent costs. Moreover, setting a product's price not only determines income but also can differentiate a product from the competition. Determining the right price is not an easy task, and marketers constantly worry whether they've turned away profitable customers by charging too much or "left money on the table" by charging too little.

price
The amount of money charged for a product or service

A number of factors influence pricing decisions, including marketing objectives, government regulations, production costs, customer perceptions, competition, and customer demand. A company's costs establish the minimum amount it can charge, and the various external forces establish the maximum. Somewhere in between those two extremes lies an optimum price point. Products also exhibit different levels of *price elasticity*, which is a measure of how sensitive customers are to changes in price. If you don't have a smartphone yet, and the price of these products drops by 25 percent, you might well be tempted to buy one. In contrast, if the price of broccoli drops by 25 percent, chances are you won't eat more veggies as a result. You can read more about pricing in Chapter 14.

Distribution

Distribution is the third marketing-mix element. It covers the organized network of firms and systems that move goods and services from the producer to the customer. This network is also known as *marketing channels*, *marketing intermediaries*, or **distribution channels**. As you can imagine, channel decisions are interdependent with virtually everything else in the marketing mix. Key factors in distribution planning include customer needs and expectations, product support requirements, market coverage, distribution costs, competition, and positioning. For example, to lower the risk for dealers with the new Scion brand, Toyota allows existing Toyota dealers to co-locate Scion's retail facilities on the same sites where they sell the Toyota brand. However, to protect the exclusive image of its Lexus brand, the company requires any dealer that wants to carry Lexus to build and staff an entirely separate dealership that carries only Lexus.[35]

distribution channels
Systems for moving goods and services from producers to customers; also known as marketing channels

Marketing intermediaries perform a variety of essential marketing functions, including providing information to customers, providing feedback to manufacturers, providing sales support, gathering assortments of goods from multiple producers to make shopping easier for customers, and transporting and storing goods. These intermediaries fall into two general categories: *wholesalers* and *retailers*. The basic distinction between them is that wholesalers sell to other companies whereas retailers sell to individual consumers. Across industries, you can find tremendous variety in the types of wholesalers and retailers, from independent representatives who sell products from several manufacturers to huge distribution companies with national or international scope to purely digital retailers such as Apple's iTunes service. You can read more about distribution in Chapter 15.

Customer Communication

promotion
Wide variety of persuasive techniques used by companies to communicate with their target markets and the general public

In traditional marketing thought, the fourth element of the marketing mix is **promotion**, all the activities a firm undertakes to promote its products to target customers. The goals of promotion include *informing*, *persuading*, and *reminding*. Among these activities are advertising in a variety of media, personal selling, public relations, and sales promotion. Promotion may take the form of direct, face-to-face communication or indirect communication through such media as television, radio, magazines, newspapers, direct mail, billboards, transit ads, social media, and other channels.

However, as "Involving the Customer in the Marketing Process" on page 335 points out, today's leading companies have moved beyond the unidirectional approach of promotion to interactive customer communication. By talking *with* their customers instead of *at* their customers, marketers get immediate feedback on everything from customer service problems to new product ideas. Promotion is still a vital part of customer communication, but by encouraging two-way conversations, whether it's two people talking across a desk or an online network spread across the globe, marketers can also learn while they are informing, persuading, and reminding. Moreover, by replacing "sales pitches" with conversations and giving customers some control over the dialog, marketers can also help break down some of the walls and filters that audiences have erected after years of conventional marketing promotion.[36] Chapter 16 offers a closer look at customer communication.

For the latest information on marketing principles, visit **http://real-timeupdates .com/bia5** and click on Chapter 13.

✓CHECKPOINT

LEARNING OBJECTIVE 6: Describe the four main components of the marketing mix.

Summary: The four elements of the marketing mix are product, price, distribution, and customer communication. Products are goods, services, persons, places, ideas, organizations, or anything else offered for the purpose of satisfying a want or need in a marketing exchange. Price is the amount of money customers pay for the product. Distribution is the organized network of firms that move the goods and services from the producer to the customer. Customer communication involves the activities used to communicate with and promote products to target markets.

Critical thinking: (1) Why is price sometimes referred to as captured value? (2) Why do companies that embrace relationship marketing focus on "customer communication" rather than "promotion"?

It's your business: (1) If you could buy a product from a website or a store right down the street and the cost was the same, where would you make your purchase? Why? (2) When buying products, do you tend to seek out products with visible logos (such as the Nike swoosh or the Dolce & Gabbana initials) or do you ignore such products? Or do you not care one way or the other? Why?

Key terms to know: marketing mix, product, price, distribution channels, promotion

Behind the Scenes

Scion's New-Generation Marketing Strategy Pays Off

Toyota's research discoveries have shaped virtually every aspect of its efforts in marketing the Scion line. The company downplays the Toyota name, even though it has a worldwide reputation for value and quality, and shuns most traditional mass-market advertising. Instead it favors small-scale, neighborhood-centered promotions that allow trendsetters to "discover" the Scion product line and share the word with other young adults (for example, putting posters near popular hangouts, bearing phrases such as "Ban Normality" and "No Clone Zone").

Whereas the Toyota brand might be the very definition of automotive conformity these days, the Scion brand emphasizes individuality at every turn. Under the theme "United by Individuality," the company sponsors gatherings where owners can show off their customized Scions. To reach an even wider audience, the "Tweaks" section of the Scion website displays photos from owners who have personalized their Scions with custom paint, lighting packages, and other personal touches.

As part of the quest to reach younger buyers, Toyota even started a music label, Scion A/V, to help promote musical groups and to work with a variety of DJs in cities around the country whose Scion-sponsored concerts, in turn, present Scion as a cutting-edge brand for a new generation. Scion marketers also work with emerging fashion designers and artists to further align the brand with cultural forces that shape the buying influences of younger drivers. Scion owners can show off their cars at Scion VIP nights, gatherings designed, of course, to attract even more potential owners.

By virtue of these media and event choices, much of Scion marketing is hidden from older buyers, although that hasn't stopped many of them from buying. In fact, the number of buyers in their 50s and 60s has pushed the average age of Scion owners to 39 years—although that is the lowest among all auto brands and significantly below Toyota's average age of 54.

By combining an appealing product, competitive pricing, and promotional efforts that tell the world Scion is not your average automobile, the Scion launch exceeded Toyota's expectations, even during a time when the economy was still sputtering and most of the automotive world's attention was focused on SUVs and pickups. The company continues to add to a loyal base of customers who are happy to buy a Toyota product even though buying a "Toyota" might be about the last thing they'd like to do with their hard-earned money.

With Scion, Toyota has also accomplished a financial feat of some note. Unlike Saturn, for example, General Motors's initiative to create a separate car brand, Scion is already profitable. In fact, even though Scions cost about $10,000 less than the average passenger vehicle now on the market, each one generates as much profit as the average Toyota model.

Success invites competition, naturally. Korean automaker Kia is now trying to out-Scion Scion with its own offbeat model, the Soul. Like Toyota, the average Kia owner is 50-something, but the company is targeting younger buyers. Tom Loveless, who heads Kia sales in North America, expresses a hope that sounds like it's right out of the Scion playbook, too: "It might actually become cool to drive a Kia."[37]

Critical Thinking Questions

1. What other product categories would you apply the Scion marketing approach to?
2. Why would younger buyers possibly shun a brand that their parents remain loyal to?
3. As Scion sales grow, the newness wears off, and more owners come to grips with the fact that they're really driving Toyotas, do you think the allure of the Scion brand will diminish?

LEARN MORE ONLINE

Visit the Scion website at www.scion.com. What is your first impression of Scion's online presence? How is the presentation of cars balanced with information about culture and community? What do you think of the ability to customize a Scion product online? Do you find any discussion of price? How authentic does the "Scion culture" message seem to you? Overall, does Scion's marketing mix make you intrigued enough to learn more about the cars? ■

Key Terms

behavioral segmentation (345)
cause-related marketing (332)
cognitive dissonance (339)
consumer market (338)
customer buying behavior (338)
customer loyalty (334)

customer relationship management (CRM) (335)
demographics (345)
distribution channels (349)
diversification (343)
exchange process (332)

geographic segmentation (345)
market (344)
market development (343)
market penetration (343)
market segmentation (344)
market share (344)

marketing (332)
marketing concept (333)
marketing mix (347)
marketing research (336)
marketing strategy (344)
need (332)
organizational market (338)
permission-based marketing (338)

place marketing (332)
positioning (346)
price (349)
product (348)
product development (343)
promotion (350)
psychographics (345)
relationship marketing (334)

social commerce (335)
stealth marketing (338)
strategic marketing planning (341)
target markets (345)
transaction (332)
utility (333)
wants (332)

Test Your Knowledge

Questions for Review

1. What is strategic marketing planning, and what is its purpose?
2. Why are top executives pushing for more accountability from the marketing function?
3. What external environmental factors affect strategic marketing decisions?
4. What are the four basic components of the marketing mix?
5. How does the organizational market differ from the consumer market?

Questions for Analysis

6. How can marketing research help companies improve their marketing efforts?
7. Why do companies segment markets?
8. Why does a company need to consider its current marketing situation, including competitive trends, when setting objectives for market share?
9. Why would consumers knowingly buy counterfeit luxury brands?

10. **Ethical Considerations.** Is it ethical to observe shoppers for the purposes of marketing research without their knowledge and permission? Why or why not?

Questions for Application

11. Think of a product you recently purchased and review your decision process. Why did you need or want that product? How did the product's marketing influence your purchase decision? How did you investigate the product before making your purchase decision? Did you experience cognitive dissonance after your decision?
12. How might a retailer use relationship marketing to improve customer loyalty?
13. If you were launching a new manufacturing company, would you draft your marketing plan or design your production processes first? Why?
14. **Concept Integration.** How might the key economic indicators discussed in Chapter 2, including consumer price index, inflation, and unemployment, affect a company's marketing decisions?

Practice Your Knowledge

Sharpening Your Communication Skills

In small groups as assigned by your instructor, take turns interviewing each person in the group about a product that each person absolutely loves or detests. Try to probe for the real reasons behind the emotions, touching on all the issues you read about in this chapter, from self-image to reference groups. Do you see any trends in the group's collective answers? Do people learn anything about themselves when answering the group's questions? Does anyone get defensive about his or her reasons for loving or hating a product? Be prepared to share with the class at least two marketing insights you learned through this exercise.

Building Your Team Skills

In the course of planning a marketing strategy, marketers need to analyze the external environment to consider how forces outside the firm may create new opportunities and challenges. One important environmental factor for merchandise buyers at Sears is weather conditions. For example, when merchandise buyers for lawn and garden products think about the assortment and number of products to purchase for the chain's stores, they don't place any orders without first poring over long-range weather forecasts for each market. In particular, temperature and precipitation predictions for the coming 12 months are critical to the company's marketing plan, because they offer clues to consumer demand for barbecues, lawn furniture, gardening tools, and other merchandise.

What other products would benefit from examining weather forecasts? With your team, brainstorm to identify at least three types of products (in addition to lawn and garden items) for which Sears should examine the weather as part of its analysis of the external environment. Share your recommendations with the entire class. How many teams identified the same products your team did?

Expand Your Knowledge

Discovering Career Opportunities

Jobs in marketing cover a wide range of activities, including a variety of jobs such as personal selling, advertising, marketing research, product management, and public relations. You can get more information about various marketing positions by consulting the *Occupational Outlook Handbook* (www.bls.gov/oco), job-search websites such as Career Builder (www.careerbuilder.com) and Monster (www.monster.com), and other online resources.

1. Select a specific marketing job that interests you, and use the sites mentioned above to find out more about this career path. What specific duties and responsibilities do people in this position typically handle?

2. Search through help-wanted ads in newspapers, specialized magazines, or websites to find two openings in the field you are researching. What educational background and work experience are employers seeking in candidates for this position? What kind of work assignments are mentioned in these ads?

3. Now think about your talents, interests, and goals. How do your strengths fit with the requirements, duties, and responsibilities of this job? Do you think you would find this field enjoyable and rewarding? Why?

Developing Your Research Skills

From recent issues of business journals and newspapers (print or online editions), select an article that describes in some detail a particular company's attempt to build relationships with its customers (either in general or for a particular product or product line).

1. Describe the company's market. What geographic, demographic, behavioral, or psychographic segments of the market is the company targeting?

2. How does the company communicate with and learn about its customers?

3. According to the article, how successful has the company been in understanding its customers?

Improving Your Tech Insights: Search Engines

As almost every web user knows, search engines identify individual webpages that contain specific words or phrases you've asked for. Search engines have the advantage of scanning millions or billions of individual webpages, and the best engines use powerful ranking algorithms to present the pages that are probably the most relevant to your search request. In addition, search engines such as Google Book Search now allow you to search through scanned copies of printed books.

For all their ease and power, search engines have three main disadvantages you should be aware of: (1) No human editors are involved in evaluating the quality of the content you find on these pages; (2) various engines use different search techniques, so one engine might miss a site or page that another one finds; and (3) search engines can't reach all the content on many websites.

The realm of out-of-reach pages is sometimes called the *hidden Internet* or the *deep web* because conventional search techniques can't access them. Fortunately, new search tools continue to reach more and more of this content. To explore some of these, visit http://real-timeupdates.com/bia5, click on "Learn More," and then "Chapter 13. See your way into the invisible Internet."

To see how search engines can return markedly different results, search on the phrase "Apple computer market share" in Google (www.google.com), Bing (www.bing.com), and SurfWax (www.surfwax.com). In a brief e-mail message to your instructor, describe the differences and similarities among the three search results. Which search engine gave you the best results? How many of the search results were more than a year out of date? How might the differences among the search engines affect the work of a businessperson preparing a report on Apple's share of the personal computer market?

Video Discussion

Access the Chapter 13 video discussion in the End of Chapter Assignments section at www.mybizlab.com.

PEARSON mybizlab

Log on to www.mybizlab.com to access the following study and assessment aids associated with this chapter:

- Interactive exercises
- Pre/post test
- Real-Time Updates
- Video application
- Customized study plans
- Biz Skills Simulations
- Quick Learning Guide

If you are not using mybizlab, you can access Real-Time Updates and Quick Learning Guides through http://real-timeupdates.com/bia5. The Quick Learning Guide (located under "Learn More" on the website) provides all six Checkpoints in a handy two-page format to help you study for exams or review important concepts whenever you need a quick refresher.

CHAPTER 14

Product and Pricing Strategies

LEARNING OBJECTIVES

After studying this chapter, you will be able to

1 Identify the main types of consumer and organizational products and describe the four stages in the life cycle of a product

2 Describe six stages in the product development process

3 Define brand and explain the concepts of brand equity and brand loyalty

4 Identify four ways of expanding a product line and discuss two risks that product-line extensions pose

5 List the factors that influence pricing decisions and explain break-even analysis

6 Identify nine common pricing methods

Transforming a World-Class Athlete into a World-Class Brand

www.annikasorenstam.com

Start reading a list of Annika Sorenstam's accomplishments on the golf course, and you might have to stop halfway through and take a nap. Here's the short version: 89 tournament wins worldwide, including 10 major championships, and more than $20 million in prize winnings, with many millions more in product endorsements. Before she stepped away from competitive golf in late 2008, she dominated the woman's professional circuit the same way her contemporary Tiger Woods dominated the men's. And like Woods, she rose high enough to achieve that ultimate badge of celebrity: one-name status. Millions of golf fans don't need to hear a last name; for them, she is simply Annika.

Her career on the course has clearly been a resounding success. But having achieved more before age 40 than most people could hope to achieve in several lifetimes, Sorenstam isn't ready to stop. In fact, she's starting all over again, this time in a multifaceted business career.

Sorenstam likes to measure herself against the best of the best. In fact, after dominating women's golf, she was

Professional golfer Annika Sorenstam is building a brand image to power her postgolf business career.

the first woman to play in a professional men's tournament in more than 50 years. She did so not to make any kind of grand statement but simply to see how her skills compared to those of her male counterparts.

In her new career, Sorenstam is once again measuring herself against top performers, including such figures as basketball star Michael Jordan and golfers Arnold Palmer and Jack Nicklaus. Palmer and Nicklaus are particularly apt role models, both having built golf-centric business empires and remained vibrant public figures in the game years after hitting their last competitive shots.

Sorenstam believes it's high time a woman joined their ranks. "Ask a person on the street to name five male athletes who have made a name for themselves outside their sport—no problem," she says. "Ask the same question about women athletes? They can't name one." She plans to be the first. What advice would you give her to make the transition from golf star to business star, from Annika the Athlete to Annika the Brand?[1] ∎

Introduction

This chapter explores two of the four elements in the marketing mix, product and price. Annika Sorenstam's challenge in defining the Annika brand (profiled in the chapter-opening Behind the Scenes) is an essential part of product strategy. She also faces another challenge that you'll read more about in this chapter: assembling the right mix of goods and services as part of a firm's overall product mix. Finally, as in every business, Sorenstam has to engage in careful financial analysis and make shrewd pricing decisions to stay both competitive and profitable.

Characteristics of Products

As the central element in every company's exchanges with its customers, products naturally command considerable attention from managers planning new offerings and coordinating the marketing mixes for their existing offerings. To understand the nature of

EXHIBIT 14.1

The Product Continuum

Products contain both tangible and intangible components; predominantly tangible products are categorized as goods, whereas predominantly intangible products are categorized as services.

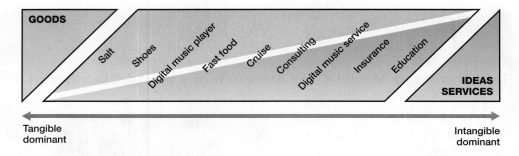

these decisions, it's important to recognize the various types of products and the stages that products go through during their "lifetime" in the marketplace.

Types of Products

Think about Doritos tortilla chips, Intel semiconductors, and your favorite musical artist. You wouldn't market all these products in the same way because buyer behavior, product characteristics, market expectations, competition, and other elements of the equation are entirely different.

Classifying products on the basis of tangibility and application can provide useful insights into the best ways to market them. Some products are predominantly tangible; others are mostly intangible. Most products, however, fall somewhere between those two extremes. The *product continuum* indicates the relative amounts of tangible and intangible components in a product (see Exhibit 14.1). Education is a product at the intangible extreme, whereas salt and shoes are at the tangible extreme.

To provide a more complete solution to customer needs, many companies find success by *augmenting* a core product with accessories, services, and other elements (see Exhibit 14.2). For example, when GlaxoSmithKline introduced its Alli weight-loss pill, the company augmented Alli with a weight-loss program that included counseling,

EXHIBIT 14.2

Augmenting the Basic Product

Product decisions also involve how much or how little to augment the core product with additional goods and services.

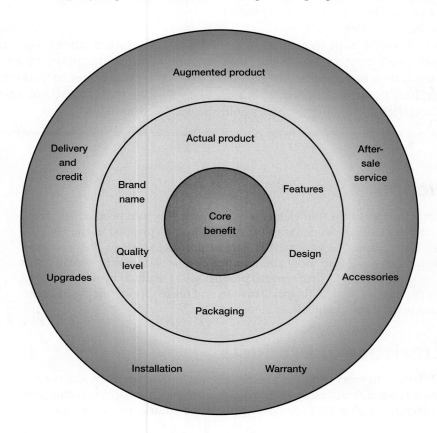

online networking, and other tools to help people use the product successfully.[2] In some cases, these enhancements are included in the price of the product, but product augmentation can also be a way to increase revenue, by offering new services and accessories or by charging for enhancements that were previously included at no charge.[3]

 Real-Time Updates

Learn More

Benefits and brands: key product decisions

Explore the wide range of decisions that go into product planning. On mybizlab (**www.mybizlab.com**), you can access Real-Time Updates within each chapter or under Student Study Tools. Otherwise, go to **http://real-timeupdates.com/bia5** and click on "Learn More."

Consumer Products

Organizations and consumers use many of the same products, but they can use them for different reasons and in different ways. Individual consumers or households generally purchase smaller quantities of goods and services for personal use. Products that are primarily sold to individuals for personal consumption are known as *consumer products*. Consumer products can be classified into four subgroups, depending on how people shop for them:

- Everyday goods and services that people buy frequently, usually without much conscious planning, are known as **convenience products**.

- **Shopping products** are fairly important goods and services that people buy less frequently, such as computers and college educations. Because the stakes are higher and the decisions more complex, such products require more thought and comparison shopping.

- **Specialty products** are particular brands that the buyer especially wants and will seek out, regardless of location or price, such as Suzuki violin lessons or Bang & Olufsen home entertainment gear.

- In some instances, including life insurance, cemetery plots, and products that are new to the marketplace, consumers aren't looking for the product in question. The marketing challenges for these *unsought products* include making consumers aware of their existence and convincing people to consider them.

convenience products
Everyday goods and services that people buy frequently, usually without much conscious planning

shopping products
Fairly important goods and services that people buy less frequently with more planning and comparison

specialty products
Particular brands that the buyer especially wants and will seek out, regardless of location or price

Industrial and Commercial Products

Organizational products, or *industrial and commercial products*, are generally purchased by organizations in large quantities and used to create other products or operate the organization. **Expense items** are relatively inexpensive goods that organizations generally use within a year of purchase, such as printer cartridges and paper. **Capital items** are more expensive products with a longer useful life. Examples include computers, vehicles, production machinery, and even entire factories. Businesses and other organizations also buy a wide variety of services, from facilities maintenance all the way up to temporary executives.

Aside from dividing products into expense and capital items, industrial buyers and sellers often classify products according to their intended use:

- *Raw materials* such as iron ore, crude petroleum, lumber, and chemicals are used in the production of final products.

- *Components* such as semiconductors and fasteners also become part of the manufacturers' final products.

- *Supplies* such as pencils, nails, and lightbulbs that are used in a firm's daily operations are considered expense items.

- *Installations* such as factories, power plants, and airports are major capital projects.

- *Equipment* includes items such as desks, computers, and factory robots.

- *Business services* range from landscaping and cleaning to complex services such as management consulting and auditing.

expense items
Inexpensive products that organizations generally use within a year of purchase

capital items
More expensive organizational products with a longer useful life, ranging from office and plant equipment to entire factories

The Product Life Cycle

product life cycle
Four stages through which a product progresses: introduction, growth, maturity, and decline

Most products undergo a **product life cycle**, passing through four distinct stages in sales and profits: introduction, growth, maturity, and decline (see Exhibit 14.3). The marketing challenge changes from stage to stage, sometimes dramatically.

The product life cycle can describe a product class (gasoline-powered automobiles), a product form (sport utility vehicles), or a brand or model (Ford Explorer). Product classes and forms tend to have the longest life cycles, whereas specific brands tend to have shorter life cycles. The amount of time that a product remains in any one stage depends on customer needs and preferences, economic conditions, the nature of the product, and the marketer's strategy. Still, the proliferation of new products, changing technology, globalization, and the ability to quickly imitate competitors is hurtling many product forms and brands through their life cycles much faster today than in the past.

Introduction

The first stage in the product life cycle is the *introductory stage*, which extends from the research-and-development (R&D) phase through the product's first commercial availability. The introductory stage is a crucial phase that requires careful planning and often considerable investment. Marketing staffs often work long hours for weeks or months before a product launch, preparing promotional materials, training sales staff, completing packaging, finalizing the price, and wrapping up countless other tasks. Some markets offer the luxury of building demand over time if the introduction isn't a blockbuster, but in others, a weak introduction can doom a product. The opening weekend for a movie, for instance, often determines its success or failure—a tremendously stressful scenario for people who have invested months or years and many millions of dollars making the film.

Growth

After the introductory stage comes the *growth stage*, marked by a rapid jump in sales—assuming the product is successful—and, usually, an increase in the number of competitors and distribution outlets. As competition increases, so does the struggle for market share. This situation creates pressure to introduce new product features and to maintain large promotional budgets and competitive prices. With enough growth, however, a firm may be able to reach economies of scale that allow it to create and deliver its products less expensively than in the introduction phase. Thus, the growth stage can reap handsome profits for those who survive.

EXHIBIT 14.3

The Product Life Cycle

Most products and product categories move through a life cycle similar to the one represented by the curve in this diagram. However, the duration of each stage varies widely from product to product. Automobiles have been in the maturity stage for decades, but faxing services barely made it into the introduction stage before being knocked out of the market by low-cost fax machines that every business and home office could afford.

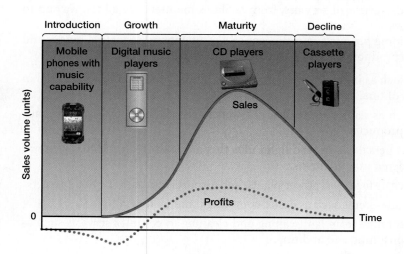

Maturity

During the *maturity stage*, usually the longest in the product life cycle, sales begin to level off. Markets tend to get saturated with all the supply that buyers demand, so the only way a firm can expand its sales in this phase is to win sales away from other suppliers. Because the costs of introduction and growth have diminished in this stage, most companies try to keep mature products alive so they can use the resulting profits to fund the development of new products (often referred to as "milking a cash cow").

Decline

Although maturity can be extended for many years, most products eventually enter the *decline stage*, when sales and profits slip and then fade away. Declines occur for several reasons: changing demographics, shifts in popular taste, overwhelming competition, and advances in technology. For instance, as smartphones such as the iPhone and Blackberry add more and more capabilities, they are pushing other product categories into decline, including personal digital assistants (PDAs), handheld GPS navigation devices, music players, digital cameras, and portable gaming devices.[4]

When a product begins to decline, the company must decide whether to reduce the product's costs to compensate for declining sales or to discontinue it altogether and focus on developing newer products. Of course, companies can try to make their products more compelling and competitive at any stage. From subtle refinements to complete makeovers, product improvements can sometimes be a way to maintain competitiveness and maximize the returns on the money and effort invested in a product.

CHECKPOINT

LEARNING OBJECTIVE 1: Identify the main types of consumer and organizational products, and describe the four stages in the life cycle of a product.

Summary: Consumer products can be identified as *convenience, shopping, specialty,* or *unsought* products, distinguished primarily by the amount of thought and effort that goes into buying them. Organizational products are divided into *expense items,* less-expensive goods used in production or operations; *capital items,* more expensive goods and facilities with useful lives longer than a year; and *business services.* The product life cycle consists of (1) the introductory stage, during which marketers focus on stimulating demand for the new product; (2) the growth stage, when marketers focus on increasing the product's market share; (3) the maturity stage, during which marketers try to extend the life of the product by highlighting improvements or by repackaging the product in different sizes; and (4) the decline stage, when firms must decide whether to reduce the product's costs to compensate for declining sales or to discontinue it.

Critical thinking: (1) Do manufacturers have a responsibility to create safe products even if customers don't care and don't want to pay for safety features? Why or why not? (2) Do automobiles ever enter the decline stage of the product life cycle? Explain your answer.

It's your business: (1) Have you ever had the urge to be "the first one on the block" to buy a new product, try a new fashion, or discover a new musical artist? (2) If so, were you pleased or displeased when "the masses" began to imitate your choice? What does your reaction say about you as a consumer?

Key terms to know: convenience products, shopping products, specialty products, expense items, capital items, product life cycle

Real-Time Updates

Learn More
Managing the product portfolio

Explore the choices that product and brand managers make as they try to maintain competitive product portfolios. On mybizlab (www.mybizlab.com), you can access Real-Time Updates within each chapter or under Student Study Tools. Otherwise, go to http://real-timeupdates.com/bia5 and click on "Learn More."

The New-Product Development Process

Mad scientists and basement inventors still create new products, but many of today's products appear on the market as a result of a rigorous, formal **product development process**—a method of generating, selecting, developing, and commercializing product ideas (see Exhibit 14.4).

product development process
A formal process of generating, selecting, developing, and commercializing product ideas

Idea Generation

The first step is to come up with some ideas that will satisfy unmet needs. Customers, competitors, and employees are often the best source of new-product ideas. Companies can also hire *trend watchers*, monitor social media to spot shifts in consumer tastes, or use *crowdsourcing* to invite the public to submit ideas or product designs. Some ideas are more or less sheer luck: The microwave oven was invented after a Raytheon engineer in the 1940s noticed that a chocolate bar in his pocket melted when he stood close to a radar component known as a magnetron.[5] The popular photo-sharing website Flickr (www.flickr.com) started as a feature in a massively multiplayer online game; developers soon realized the photo-sharing tool was a better business opportunity than the game they were creating.[6] Of course, many "new" product ideas are simply improvements to or variations on existing products, but even those slight alterations can generate big revenues.

Idea Screening

From all the ideas under consideration, the company selects a few that appear to be worthy of further development, applying broad criteria such as whether the product can use existing production facilities and how much technical and marketing risk is involved. Research suggests that sharply narrowing the possibilities at this stage is better than keeping a large number of ideas alive, since each idea competes for attention or resources until it is abandoned or implemented as a real product.[7] In the case of industrial or technical products, this phase is often referred to as a *feasibility study*, in which the product's features are defined and its workability is tested. In the case of consumer products, marketing consultants and advertising agencies are often called in to help evaluate new ideas. In some cases, potential customers are asked what they think of a new product idea—a process known as *concept testing*. Some companies involve customers early in the design process to make sure new products truly meet customer needs instead of the design team's perception of customer needs. Xerox's Chief Technology Officer Sophie Vandebroek refers to her company's approach as "customer-led innovation" and says that "dreaming with the customer" is essential to creating the right products.[8]

Business Analysis

A product idea that survives the screening stage is subjected to a business analysis. During this stage, the company reviews the sales, costs, and profit projections to

EXHIBIT 14.4

The Product Development Process

The product development process is designed to identify the product ideas most likely to succeed in the marketplace.

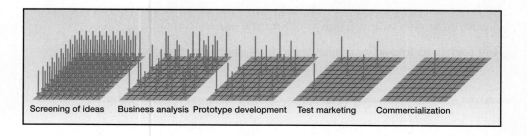

Screening of ideas   Business analysis   Prototype development   Test marketing   Commercialization

determine whether they meet the company's objectives. To do so, the company forecasts the probable sales of the product, assuming various pricing strategies. In addition, it estimates the costs associated with various levels of production. Given these projections, analysts calculate the potential profit that will be achieved if the product is introduced. If the product meets the company's objectives, it can then move to the product development stage.

Prototype Development

At this stage, the firm actually develops the product concept into a physical product. The firm creates and tests a few samples, or **prototypes**, of the product, including its packaging. These units are rigorously analyzed for durability, manufacturability, customer appeal, and other vital criteria. In addition, the company begins to plan for large-scale production and identifies the resources required to bring the product to market.

prototypes
Preproduction samples of products used for testing and evaluation

Test Marketing

During **test marketing**, the firm introduces the product in selected markets and monitors consumer reactions. Test marketing gives the marketer experience with marketing the product before going to the expense of a full introduction. For instance, producers of television programs can test shows in local or regional markets to gauge viewer appeal before going nationwide. Playwright and actor Tyler Perry launched two new national shows after regional tests indicated strong market appeal, for example.[9] Companies can also release products early to get feedback from potential customers before finalizing features and functions. Software developers frequently do this through *beta* versions. Test marketing can be expensive and time-consuming, however, so not all companies choose to take this step with every new product.

test marketing
Product development stage in which a product is sold on a limited basis to gauge its market appeal

Commercialization

The final stage of development is **commercialization**, the large-scale production and distribution of products that have survived the testing process. This phase (also referred to as a *product launch*) requires the coordination of many activities—manufacturing, packaging, distribution, pricing, and promotion. Some companies roll out their new products gradually, going from one geographic area to the next. This plan enables them to spread the costs of launching the product over a longer period and to refine their strategy as the rollout proceeds.

commercialization
Large-scale production and distribution of a product

√CHECKPOINT

LEARNING OBJECTIVE 2: Describe six stages in the product development process.

Summary: The first two stages of product development involve generating and screening ideas to isolate those with the most potential. In the third stage, promising ideas are analyzed to determine their likely profitability. Those that appear worthwhile enter the fourth stage, the prototype development stage, in which a limited number of the products are created. In the fifth stage, the product is test marketed to determine buyer response. Products that survive the testing process are then commercialized, the final stage.

Critical thinking: (1) Apple claims to never do any marketing research for new product ideas but instead creates products that Apple employees themselves would be excited to have. What are the risks of this approach? Would it work for all consumer and organizational markets? (2) Consumers and government regulators sometimes complain about identical products being sold at different prices to different customers as part of test marketing efforts. Are such tests ethical? Why or why not?

It's your business: (1) What currently unavailable services can you think of that could be offered on mobile phones? (2) In addition to the mobile phone itself, what other product elements (such as a website or phone accessories) would be required to launch such a service?

Key terms to know: product development process, prototypes, test marketing, commercialization

Product Identities

Creating an identity for products is one of the most important decisions marketers make. That identity is encompassed in the **brand**, which can have meaning at three levels: (1) a unique name, symbol, or design that sets the product apart from those offered by competitors; (2) the legal protections afforded by a trademark and any relevant intellectual property; and (3) the overall company or organizational brand.[10] For instance, the Nike "swoosh" symbol is a unique identifier on every Nike product, a legally protected piece of intellectual property, and a symbol that represents the entire company.

Branding helps a product in many ways. It gives customers a way of recognizing and specifying a particular product so that they can choose it again or recommend it to others. It provides consumers with information about the product. It facilitates the marketing of the product. And it creates value for the product. This notion of the value of a brand is also called **brand equity**. In fact, a brand name can be an organization's most valuable asset. According to Interbrand, a leading global branding consultancy, the world's most valuable brands—including Coca-Cola, Microsoft, IBM, and General Electric—are each worth more than $50 billion—and that's just the intangible value of the brand name.[11] Strong brands simplify marketing efforts because the target audience tends to associate positive qualities with any product that carries a respected brand name—and vice versa. For instance, the quality of most cars from General Motors, Ford, and Chrysler is now comparable to cars from Toyota and Honda, but the U.S. automakers are still fighting a "reputational deficit" created by mediocre products from years past.[12]

Customers who buy the same brand again and again are evidence of the strength of **brand loyalty**, or commitment to a particular brand. Brand loyalty can be measured in degrees. The first level is *brand awareness*, which means that people are likely to buy a product because they are familiar with it. The next level is *brand preference*, which means people will purchase the product if it is available, although they may still be willing to experiment with alternatives if they cannot find the preferred brand. The third and ultimate level of brand loyalty is *brand insistence*, the stage at which buyers will accept no substitute. Some brands, such as Harley-Davidson motorcycles and American Girl dolls, can acquire such a deep level of meaning to loyal consumers that the brands become intertwined with the narratives of the consumers' life stories.[13]

Brand Name Selection

Jeep, Levi's 501, and iPod are **brand names**, the portion of a brand that can be spoken, including letters, words, or numbers. Annika Sorenstam (see page 375) uses her first name in all capital letters as her brand name. McDonald's golden arches and the Nike "swoosh" symbol are examples of a **brand mark**, the portion of a brand that cannot be expressed verbally. A **logo** is a concise graphical and/or textual representation of the brand name. The choice of a brand name and any associated brand marks can be a critical success factor.

brand
A name, term, sign, symbol, design, or combination of those used to identify the products of a firm and to differentiate them from competing products

brand equity
The value that a company has built up in a brand

brand loyalty
The degree to which customers continue to purchase a specific brand

brand names
Portion of a brand that can be expressed orally, including letters, words, or numbers

brand mark
Portion of a brand that cannot be expressed verbally

logo
A concise graphical and/or textual representation of a brand name

Brands help consumers make confident choices from the thousands of products available in today's supermarkets.

Brand names and brand symbols may be registered with the Patent and Trademark Office as **trademarks**, brands that have been given legal protection so that their owners have exclusive rights to their use. The Lanham Trademark Act, a federal law, prohibits the unauthorized use of a trademark on goods or services when the use would likely confuse consumers as to the origin of those goods and services. For trademark infringement, the evidence must show that an appreciable number of ordinary prudent purchasers are likely to be confused as to the source, sponsorship, affiliation, or connection of the goods or services.[14] Companies zealously protect their brand names because if a name becomes too widely used in a general sense, it no longer qualifies for protection under trademark laws. Cellophane, kerosene, linoleum, escalator, zipper, shredded wheat, and raisin bran are just a few of the many brand names that have passed into public domain, much to their creators' dismay.

Brand Sponsorship

Brand names may be associated with a manufacturer, a retailer, a wholesaler, or a combination of business types. Brands offered and promoted by a national manufacturer, such as Procter & Gamble's Tide detergent and Pampers disposable diapers, are called **national brands**. **Private brands** are not linked to a manufacturer but instead carry a wholesaler's or a retailer's brand. DieHard batteries and Kenmore appliances are private brands sold by Sears. As an alternative to branded products, some retailers also offer **generic products**, which are packaged in plain containers that bear only the name of the product. Note that "generics" is also a term used in the pharmaceutical industry to describe products that are copies of an original drug (other companies are allowed to make these copies after the patent on the original drug expires).

Co-branding occurs when two or more companies team up to closely link their names in a single product. For example, Lenovo sells laptop computers co-branded with Disney's Power Rangers brand. The co-branding arrangement is aimed at families in which young children can influence the PC purchase decision.[15] Companies can also **license**, or offer to sell, the rights to well-known brand names and symbols. Movies, particularly those aimed at children, often hit the market with an array of licensing deals with fast-food chains and other consumer products companies.

Packaging

Most tangible products need some form of packaging to protect them from damage or tampering, but packaging can also play an important role in a product's marketing strategy. Packaging makes products easier to display, facilitates the sale of smaller products, serves as a means of product differentiation, and enhances the product's overall appeal and convenience. Packaging can significantly influence buyer perceptions, too, sometimes in surprising ways. For instance, packages with simple geometric lines (such as cylinders or rectangles) are perceived as being larger than geometrically complex packages of the same volume. Package designers can use these perceptual effects to create particular images for their products.[16]

Packaging can also involve decisions over assortment and quantity, about which items to include as the product offering and in what quantities. For example, recorded music has gone through several packaging incarnations over the decades with *singles* (vinyl "45s" and individual digital downloads), *albums* (vinyl "LPs," several kinds of tape, compact discs [CDs], and box sets), and *EPs* (originally "extended play" vinyl but now refers to any physical or digital package that falls between singles and albums in terms of song quantity).

In the retailing environment, packaging plays a key role in reducing

trademarks
Brands that have been given legal protection so that their owners have exclusive rights to their use

national brands
Brands owned by the manufacturers and distributed nationally

private brands
Brands that carry the label of a retailer or a wholesaler rather than a manufacturer

generic products
Products characterized by a plain label, with no advertising and no brand name

co-branding
Partnership between two or more companies to closely link their brand names together for a single product

license
Agreement to produce and market another company's product in exchange for a royalty or fee

---

🎺 **Real-Time Updates**

Learn More
The incredible shrinking package

Food companies hit by higher costs are responding with smaller packages. On mybizlab (www.mybizlab.com), you can access Real-Time Updates within each chapter or under Student Study Tools. Otherwise, go to http://real-timeupdates.com/bia5 and click on "Learn More."

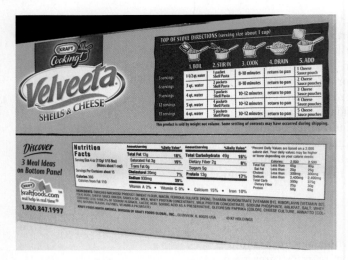

Product packaging usually has a number of functions, from promoting and protecting the product to displaying legally required health and safety information to providing instructions for use.

shoplifting; retailers have put a lot of pressure on manufacturers to adopt packages that are difficult to conceal or to open in the store. Those stiff plastic packages known as "clamshells" that consumers love to hate—and that account for hundreds of injuries every year as people attempt to slice them open—are one such response to shoplifting. Many manufacturers know that consumers despise the clamshell concept (some even refer to it privately as "rage wrap"), so package designers are working on alternatives.[17] Packaging is also a major environmental concern, in both the resources used and waste generated, so expect innovations and new regulations in this area in the coming years.

Labeling

Labeling is an integral part of packaging. Whether the label is a separate element attached to the package or a printed part of the container, it serves to identify a brand and communicate multiple types of information, from promotional messages to legally required safety or nutritional data. The labeling of foods, drugs, cosmetics, and many health products is regulated under various federal laws, which often require disclosures about potential dangers, benefits, and other issues consumers need to consider when making a buying decision.

√ CHECKPOINT

LEARNING OBJECTIVE 3: Define brand, and explain the concepts of brand equity and brand loyalty.

Summary: *Brand* encompasses the various elements of product identity and meaning. *Brand equity* reflects the value of a brand name based on its strength and appeal in the marketplace and its power as a communication vehicle. *Brand loyalty* can be defined at three levels: brand awareness, in which the buyer is familiar with the product; brand preference, in which the buyer will select the product if it is available; and brand insistence, in which the buyer will accept no substitute.

Critical thinking: (1) Can a brand with a bad reputation be rescued? Would a company be wiser to just drop a "bad brand" and start fresh with something new? (2) Is staying with the same product only a case of brand "loyalty"? Could other factors be in play that lead consumers or organizations not to switch brands? Explain your answer.

It's your business: (1) How many visible brand marks are you currently wearing? Are these common brands? (2) What do you think these brands say about you?

Key terms to know: brand, brand equity, brand loyalty, brand names, brand mark, logo, trademarks, national brands, private brands, generic products, co-branding, license

Product-Line and Product-Mix Strategies

In addition to developing product identities, a company must continually evaluate what kinds of products it will offer. To stay competitive, most companies continually add and drop products to ensure that declining items will be replaced by growth products.

Companies that offer more than one product also need to pay close attention to how those products are positioned in the marketplace relative to one another. The responsibility for managing individual products, product lines, and product mixes is usually assigned to one or more managers in the marketing department. In a smaller company, the *marketing manager* tackles this effort; in larger companies with more products to manage, individual products or groups of products are usually assigned to **brand managers**, known in some companies as *product managers* or *product line managers*.

brand managers
Managers who develop and implement the marketing strategies and programs for a specific product or brand

Product Lines

A **product line** is a group of products from a single manufacturer that are similar in terms of use or characteristics. The General Mills (**www.generalmills.com**) snack-food product line, for example, includes Bugles, Fruit Roll-Ups, and Nature Valley Granola Bars. Within each product line, a company confronts decisions about the number of goods and services to offer. On the one hand, offering additional products can help a manufacturer boost revenues and increase its visibility in retail stores. On the other hand, creating too many products and product variations can be expensive for everyone in the supply chain and confusing to buyers.

product line
A series of related products offered by a firm

Product Mix

An organization with several product lines has a **product mix**—a collection of diverse goods or services offered for sale. The General Mills product mix includes cereals, baking products, desserts, snack foods, and entrees (see Exhibit 14.5). Three important dimensions of a company's product mix are *width*, *length*, and *depth*, and each dimension presents its own set of challenges and opportunities. A product mix is *wide* if it has several different product lines. General Mills's product mix, for instance, is fairly wide, with roughly a dozen separate product lines. A company's product mix is *long* if it carries several items in its product lines, as General Mills does. For instance, General Mills produces multiple cereal brands within the ready-to-eat cereal line. A product mix is *deep* if it has a number of versions of *each* product in a product line. The Cheerios brand, for example, currently has more than a dozen different varieties.[18]

product mix
Complete list of all products that a company offers for sale

When deciding on the dimensions of a product mix, a company must weigh the risks and rewards associated with various approaches. Some companies limit the number of product offerings and focus on selling a few items in higher quantities. Doing so can keep production and marketing costs lower through economies of scale. However, counting too heavily on a narrow group of products leaves a company vulnerable to competitive threats and market shifts. Other companies diversify their product offerings as a protection against shifts in consumer tastes, economic conditions, and technology, or as a way to build marketing synergy by offering complementary products. For example, Apple was strictly a computer manufacturer for many years, but the addition of the iPod and then iPhone product lines not only gave the company major new revenue streams but also helped turn around its declining computer sales by boosting the Apple brand name and retail presence.[19]

Retailers often have considerable influence in manufacturers' product line decisions as well, particularly in the store-based retail channel. In general, the more revenue a manufacturer represents, the better chance it has of getting all-important shelf space. Consequently, retail store aisles tend to be dominated by a few large brands, and manufacturers look for ways to build portfolios of best sellers that can command attention at the retail level.

In contrast to store-based retailing and its frequent focus on a small number of best sellers, online retailing presents much better opportunities for large numbers of specialized and low-volume products. Without the physical limitations of a "bricks and mortar" facility, online retailers can offer a much greater variety of products. For example, the average physical bookstore might offer 40,000 volumes, whereas the major online book retailers offer several million.[20] While these products may individually sell at lower volumes, collectively they represent a substantial business opportunity that has been

EXHIBIT 14.5

The Product Mix at General Mills (selected products)

These selected products from General Mills illustrate the various dimensions of its product mix. The mix is *wide* because it contains multiple product lines (cereals, fruit snacks, pasta, soup, yogurt, and more). The cereal product line is *long* because it contains many individual brands (only four of which are shown here). And these four cereal brands show different depths. The Trix brand is a shallow line, whereas the Cheerios brand is *deep*.

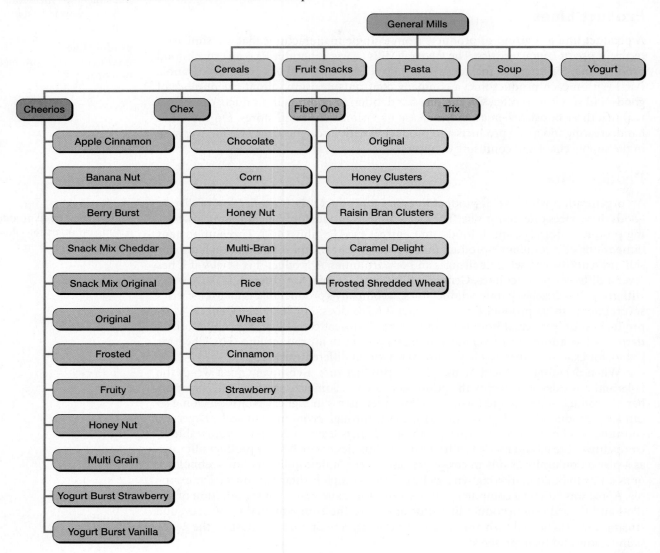

termed the *long tail* (referring to a sales volume graph in which a vast number of low-volume products stretches out toward infinity).[21]

Product Expansion Strategies

As Exhibit 14.6 shows, you can expand your product line and mix in a number of ways. One approach is to introduce additional items in a given product category under the same brand name—such as new flavors, forms, colors, ingredients, or package sizes. Another approach is to expand a product line to add new and similar products with the same product name—a strategy known as **family branding**. For instance, the ESPN family includes not only the original ESPN cable sports channel, but also the ESPN2,

family branding
Using a brand name on a variety of related products

EXHIBIT 14.6 **Expanding the Product Line**

Companies use one or more of these product-line expansion methods to pursue new opportunities.

METHOD OF EXPANSION	OBJECTIVE	EXAMPLE
Line filling	Developing items to fill gaps in the market that have been overlooked by competitors or have emerged as consumer tastes and needs shift	Taylor Guitars's new 200 Series, priced between the 100 Series entry-level models and the company's professional series
Line extension	Creating a variation of an existing product	Crest Pro-Health Enamel Shield Toothpaste
Brand extension	Using the brand of existing products on products in a different new category	Iams pet insurance (Iams is a brand of pet food)
Line stretching	Adding items with price points above or below the current product line	Volkswagen Passat CC (priced above the regular Passat models)

ESPN Classics, and ESPN Deportes TV channels, as well as ESPN Radio, *ESPN the Magazine*, ESPN Zone restaurants, and a variety of other product lines.[22]

Conversely, in a **brand extension**, a company applies a successful brand name to a new product category in the hopes that the recognition and reputation of the brand will give it a head start in the new category. Building on the name recognition of an existing brand cuts the costs and risks of introducing new products. However, product-line extensions present two important risks that marketers need to consider carefully. First, stretching a brand to cover too many categories or types of products can dilute the brand's meaning in the minds of target customers. For instance, if ESPN were to branch out into business and financial news, its original sports audience might wonder whether the company was still committed to being a leader in sports journalism, and the business news audience might wonder what value a sports media company could bring to financial news. Second, additional products do not automatically guarantee increased sales revenue. Marketers need to make sure that new products don't simply *cannibalize*, or take sales away from, their existing products.

brand extension
Applying a successful brand name to a new product category

Product Strategies for International Markets

As Chapter 3 notes, product adaptation is one of the key changes that companies need to consider when moving into other countries. First, managers must decide on which products and services to introduce in which countries. When selecting a country, they must take into consideration the type of government, market-entry requirements, tariffs and other trade barriers, cultural and language differences, consumer preferences, foreign-exchange rates, and differing business customs. Then, they must decide whether to standardize the product, selling the same product everywhere, or to customize the product to accommodate the lifestyles and habits of local target markets. A company may change only the product's name or packaging, or it can modify the product's components, size, and functions.

For example, the social network site hi5 (www.hi5.com) has become one of the world's most popular websites through extensive adaption, including localization in more than 60 languages around the world.[23] Similarly, French consumers have been eating at McDonald's (www.mcdonalds.fr) since the company first arrived in 1972, but the burger giant has a unique look in that country. To accommodate a culture known for its cuisine and dining experience, many McDonald's outlets in France have

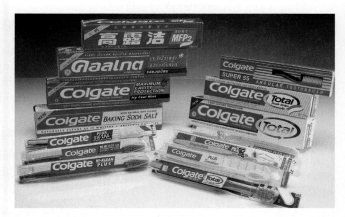

Notice how these localized versions of a Colgate toothpaste package maintain key brand identifiers such as color and type style.

upgraded their decor to a level that would make them almost unrecognizable in the United States. The restaurants have hardwood floors, brick architecture, armchairs, and extras such as free wireless that entice customers to linger over their meals. And while the basic burger offerings remain roughly the same, menus include local cheeses, brioche (a soft bread common in France), and *croques monsieurs* (a traditional grilled ham and cheese sandwich).[24]

For the latest information on product and branding strategies, visit http://real-timeupdates.com/bia5 and click on Chapter 14.

✓CHECKPOINT

LEARNING OBJECTIVE 4: Identify four ways of expanding a product line, and discuss two risks that product-line extensions pose.

Summary: A product line can be expanded by filling gaps in the market, extending the line to include new varieties of existing products, extending the brand to new product categories, and stretching the line to include lower- or higher-priced items. Two of the biggest risks with product-line extensions are losing brand identity and coherence (weakening of the brand's meaning) and cannibalizing of sales of other products in the product line.

Critical thinking: (1) If McDonald's had been relatively unknown to French diners when the company entered that market in 1972, would it have made more sense to use a different and more "French-sounding" brand name? Why or why not? (2) Would a consumer-products manufacturer ever want to create more product extensions and variations than it could explain in terms of pure market appeal? Why or why not?

It's your business: (1) Citing specific examples, how has branding helped you as a consumer? Think about the assurance you have buying a known and trusted brand, for example. (2) Think about some of the consumer products you buy frequently, such as cereal, painkillers, or snack foods. Do you appreciate the range of choices available to you when you shop for these items, or do you wish that companies would narrow the options to a handful in each category? Why?

Key terms to know: brand managers, product line, product mix, family branding, brand extension

Pricing Strategies

The second key element in the marketing mix is pricing. Recall from the definition in Chapter 13 that pricing involves *capturing value* back from the customer in exchange for the value provided in the product. Setting and managing prices is a combination of strategic considerations and careful financial analysis.

Strategic Considerations in Pricing

Managers must consider a variety of internal and external factors when establishing prices, including the firm's marketing objectives, government regulations, customer perceptions, market demand, and competition:

■ **Marketing objectives.** The first step in setting a price is to match it to the objectives set in the strategic marketing plan. Is the goal to increase market share, increase sales, improve profits, project a particular image, or combat competition? As you can see in the following section on pricing methods, price is a flexible tool that can help a firm achieve a wide variety of marketing objectives.

- **Government regulations.** Government plays a big role in pricing in many industries. To protect consumers and encourage fair competition, governments around the world have enacted various price-related laws over the years. These regulations are particularly important in three areas of prohibited behavior: (1) *price fixing*—an agreement among two or more companies supplying the same type of products as to the prices they will charge, (2) *price discrimination*—the practice of unfairly offering attractive discounts to some customers but not to others, and (3) *deceptive pricing*—pricing schemes that are considered misleading. For instance, comparing a discounted sale price to a "regular price" that has never actually been charged is considered deceptive.[25]

- **Customer perceptions.** Another consideration is the perception of quality that your price will elicit from your customers. When people shop, they usually have a rough price range in mind. An unexpectedly low price triggers fear that the item is of low quality. On the other hand, an unexpectedly high price makes buyers question whether the product is worth the money. Of course, in some consumer markets, high price is part of the appeal because it connotes quality and even exclusivity. Specific numbers can have perceptual effect as well, such as the well-known "9 effect." You've probably noticed that many prices end in a 9, such as $9.99 or $5,999. Your conscious mind says, "Gimme a break; we all know that's really $10 or $6,000." However, research suggests that our minds equate that 9 with a bargain— even when it isn't. In one experiment, for example, a dress sold more when priced at $39 than when it was priced at $34.[26]

- **Market demand.** The discussion of supply and demand in Chapter 2 points out that market demand usually fluctuates as prices fluctuate. Theoretically, if the price for an item is too high, demand falls and the producers reduce their prices to stimulate demand. Conversely, if the price for an item is too low, demand increases and the producers are motivated to raise prices. As prices climb and profits improve, producers boost their output until supply and demand are in balance and prices stabilize. Nonetheless, the relationship between price and demand isn't always this perfect. Some goods and services are relatively insensitive to changes in price; others are highly sensitive. Buyers can also exhibit different levels of price sensitivity. For instance, brand-loyal customers tend to be less sensitive to price, meaning they will stick with a brand even as the price increases, whereas other buyers will begin switching to cheaper alternatives.[27] Marketers refer to this sensitivity as **price elasticity**—how responsive demand will be to a change in price.

- **Competition.** Competitive prices are obviously a major consideration whenever a firm is establishing or changing its prices. The easier it is for buyers to compare prices, for instance, the more important competitive prices become, particularly when buyers don't perceive much difference among the available products. Many drivers don't perceive much difference in the quality of gasoline and therefore shop by convenience and price. With services such as GasBuddy (www.gasbuddy.com) and GPS-enabled smartphone software such as WHERE, drivers can easily get directions to the cheapest gas in the neighborhood.[28] Such technologies make price comparison almost effortless in many instances, so companies that can't establish perceptions of meaningful competitive differentiation don't have much hope of commanding higher prices than the competition.

Cost Structure and Break-Even Analysis

Every company has a particular *cost structure* that determines how much it must spend to create and market its products. Some of these costs remain the same regardless of production and sales volume. Such **fixed costs** include rent or

price elasticity
A measure of the sensitivity of demand to changes in price

fixed costs
Business costs that remain constant regardless of the number of units produced

Buyers often believe that prices ending in "9" are a bargain, which is why these fast-food products are priced at 99 cents and not an even dollar amount.

variable costs
Business costs that increase with the number of units produced

break-even analysis
Method of calculating the minimum volume of sales needed at a given price to cover all costs

break-even point
Sales volume at a given price that will cover all of a company's costs

mortgage payments, insurance premiums, real estate taxes, and salaries. These are costs incurred just to "keep the doors open," without creating or selling anything. In contrast, **variable costs**, including raw materials, supplies consumed during production, shipping, and sales commissions, do vary with changes in production and sales volume. Obviously, the more a company can lower its cost structure, the more flexibility it has in setting prices and ensuring desirable levels of profit.

The cost to create and sell each product is a combination of fixed and variable costs. A critical calculation in setting prices is **break-even analysis**, determining the number of units a firm must sell at a given price to recoup both fixed and variable costs—to "break even," in other words. The **break-even point** is the minimum sales volume the company must achieve to avoid losing money. Sales volume beyond the break-even point will generate profits; sales volume below the break-even amount will result in losses.

You can determine the break-even point in number of units with this simple calculation:

$$\text{Break-even point} = \frac{\text{Fixed costs}}{\text{Selling price} - \text{Variable costs per unit}}$$

For example, if you wanted to price haircuts at $20 and you had fixed costs of $60,000 and variable costs per haircut of $5, you would need to sell 4,000 haircuts to break even:

$$\text{Break-even point} = \frac{\$60,000}{\$20 - \$5} = 4,000 \text{ units}$$

Of course, $20 isn't your only pricing option. Why not charge $30 instead? When you charge the higher price, you need to give only 2,400 haircuts to break even (see Exhibit 14.7). However, before you raise your haircut prices to $30, bear in mind that a lower price may attract more customers and enable you to make more money in the long run.

✓ CHECKPOINT

LEARNING OBJECTIVE 5: List the factors that influence pricing decisions, and explain break-even analysis.

Summary: Strategic considerations in pricing include marketing objectives, government regulations, customer perceptions, market demand, and competition. *Break-even analysis* is a way to determine how many units (the *break-even point*) a firm needs to produce in order to begin turning a profit by covering its fixed and variable costs. The break-even point is calculated by dividing fixed costs by the difference between the selling price and the variable costs per unit.

Critical thinking: (1) Why wouldn't a firm just drop any product that isn't selling in high enough volume to reach its break-even point? (2) Is "9" style pricing ethical? Why or why not?

It's your business: (1) Do you factor in the value of your time when you price-comparison shop? Why or why not? (2) As a consumer taking charge of your own financial future, what lessons could you take from the business concepts of fixed and variable costs?

Key terms to know: price elasticity, fixed costs, variable costs, break-even analysis, break-even point

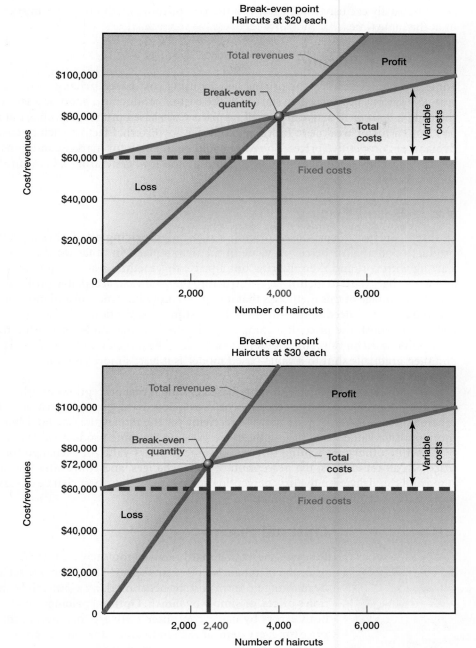

Break-even point
Haircuts at $20 each

Break-even point
Haircuts at $30 each

EXHIBIT 14.7

Break-Even Analysis

The break-even point is the point at which revenues just cover costs. After fixed costs and variable costs have been met, any additional income represents profit. The graphs show that at $20 per haircut, the break-even point is 4,000 haircuts; charging $30 yields a break-even point at only 2,400 haircuts.

Note that break-even analysis doesn't dictate what price you *should* charge; rather, it provides some insight into the price you *can* charge and begin to generate profit. With the break-even point in hand, you can then factor in the various strategic considerations to determine price using one of the methods discussed in the next section.

Pricing Methods

Break-even analysis and the various strategic considerations help managers establish an overall framework of pricing possibilities. You can think of costs as establishing the pricing "floor," whereas demand, competition, and other factors establish the "ceiling." Somewhere between those two limits lies the ideal price for each product. Managers can apply a variety of methods to pinpoint specific prices. Note that some of these methods aren't mutually exclusive; managers can use two or more methods, either in succession or at the same time.

Cost-Based Pricing

cost-based pricing
Method of setting prices based on production and marketing costs, rather than conditions in the marketplace

Some companies simplify the pricing task by using **cost-based pricing**, also known as *cost-plus pricing*, in which they start with the cost of producing a good or a service and then add a *markup* to arrive at the selling price. Cost-based pricing is simple, but it suffers from a major weakness: It doesn't consider any external factors such as customer demand or competitive prices. The price could be too high for market conditions, leaving the company uncompetitive, or it could be too low, generating less profit than it could otherwise.

Value-Based Pricing

value-based pricing
Method of setting prices based on customer perceptions of value

In sharp contrast to cost-based pricing, **value-based pricing** establishes a price on a product's potential or perceived value in the marketplace. In other words, rather than starting with cost and then figuring out a price, this method starts with a target price and works backward to identify a cost structure that will yield acceptable profit margins. The disadvantage of this method is that it requires more information and more analysis, because managers need to measure or at least estimate perceptions of customer value in order to establish the price. If a company lacks the information to establish a realistic price point based on value, one option is to introduce the product using cost-based pricing and then gradually shift to a value-based model as it learns more about how customers perceive the product.[29]

An additional challenge with value-based pricing is that perceptions of value change over time. For example, in a recession or depression, hard-pressed consumers take a much harder look at the value they are receiving for the money they spend. Many want more product value while paying the same price or the same product value at a lower price, while others are willing to give up some product value in exchange for lower prices. In all these cases, the perception of value changes, and companies that understand and can deliver on the new perceptions of value stand the best chance of surviving or even thriving during tough times.[30]

optimal pricing
Computer-based pricing method that creates a demand curve for every product to help managers select a price that meets specific marketing objectives

Optimal Pricing

Research shows that many retailers routinely underprice or overprice the merchandise on their shelves. They generally set a price by marking up from cost, by benchmarking against the competition's prices, or simply by hunch. **Optimal pricing** can minimize both errors by using computer software to generate the ideal price for every item, at each individual store, at any given time.

A price-optimization program feeds reams of data from checkout scanners, seasonal sales figures, competitors, and other sources into probability algorithms to come up with an individual demand curve for each product in each store. From that, retailers can identify which products are the most price sensitive. Then they can adjust prices up or down according to each store's priorities—profit, revenue, or market share. Some systems also let store managers conduct "what if" analyses based on past sales data, helping them see the potential effect of proposed price changes.[31]

Customers who need to have the latest and greatest products are often willing to pay higher prices than those who wait until later in the product life cycle.

Skim Pricing

During the introductory phase of the product life cycle, a company may opt to take advantage of strong demand from *early adopters* before competitors can enter the market and exert downward pressure on prices. To achieve this goal, the company can charge a high initial price—a practice known as **skim pricing**—with the intention of dropping the price later. *Early adopters*, those customers who tend to jump on new products quickly, are often willing to pay a premium to get their hands on the new products as soon as possible. In consumer markets, some people simply want to have the latest and greatest before anyone else; in organizational markets, new types of equipment can give companies a short-term competitive advantage.

skim pricing
Charging a high price for a new product during the introductory stage and lowering the price later

Penetration Pricing

Skim prices are set high with the understanding that many customers won't be willing to pay them. In contrast, companies use **penetration pricing** to build sales volume by charging a low initial price. This approach has the added advantage of discouraging competition, because the low price—which competitors would be pressured to match—limits the profit potential for everyone. (If the intent of penetration is to drive competitors out of business, though, companies open themselves up to charges of illegal *predatory pricing*.)

penetration pricing
Introducing a new product at a low price in hopes of building sales volume quickly

However, penetration pricing doesn't work if the company can't sustain the low price levels profitably, if prices for a particular product are inelastic, or if customers weigh other factors more heavily than price. Moreover, as mentioned earlier, prices that are far below the market's expectations can raise concerns about quality, reliability, and safety. Everyone would like to pay less for medical care, but few people would be willing to go to cut-rate clinics if they thought their health might be jeopardized.

Loss-Leader Pricing

As part of a larger marketing plan, some companies occasionally resort to **loss-leader pricing**, setting a price on one product so low that they lose money on every sale (or earn very little profit in some cases) but recoup that loss by enticing customers to try a new product or buy other products. For instance, grocery stores can use milk and other staples as loss leaders to encourage shoppers to visit.

loss-leader pricing
Selling one product at a loss as a way to entice customers to consider other products

Auction Pricing

In an *auction*, the seller doesn't set a firm price but allows buyers to competitively bid on the products being sold. Auctions used to be confined to a few market sectors such as fine art, agricultural products, and government bonds, but that all changed when eBay turned selling and buying via auctions into a new national pastime. Many companies now use eBay and other auction sites to sell everything from modular buildings to tractors to industrial equipment. In *procurement auctions* or *reverse auctions*, potential buyers identify the goods or services they need and the prices they're willing to pay, then suppliers respond with offers at the prices they're willing to charge. The travel website Priceline.com, for example, lets buyers enter a price they're willing to pay and then see whether airlines, hotels, and other providers are willing to sell at that price.[32]

participative pricing
Allowing customers to pay the amount they think a product is worth

Participative Pricing

One of the most unusual pricing strategies is **participative pricing**, sometimes known as "pay what you want," in which customers literally get to pay as much as they think a product is worth. While it might sound like a strategy for financial disaster, with participative pricing, buyers sometimes pay *more* than the company would normally charge.[33] When

 Real-Time Updates

Learn More
Stop discounting to sell more
Danny Wegman (profiled in Chapter 7) explains how moving away from temporary discounts led to higher overall sales. On mybizlab (www .mybizlab.com), you can access Real-Time Updates within each chapter or under Student Study Tools. Otherwise, go to http://real-timeupdates .com/bia5 and click on "Learn More."

the band Radiohead let buyers name their own price for a recent downloadable album, the band made more money from that album than from downloads on all their other studio albums combined.[34]

Free Pricing

Even more radical than participative pricing is no price at all. However, giving goods and services away can make a lot of sense in the right situation, such as when a new company is trying to make a name for itself in the marketplace.[35] Another use of free pricing is when some customers are charged enough to provide free goods and services for other customers.[36] A common strategy involves giving some level of service away for free to everyone but charging others for certain services. For example, by offering free tools for buyers and sellers, the real-estate valuation website Zillow (**www.zillow.com**) has built up an audience of millions of monthly visitors. This audience is the key selling feature used to entice advertisers, who are the company's paying customers.[37] Giving away some products while maintaining full prices for others (the common "buy one, get one free" approach) is also a way to effectively offer discounted pricing without the risk of creating expectations of lower prices.[38]

Price Adjustment Tactics

discounts
Temporary price reductions to stimulate sales or lower prices to encourage certain behaviors such as paying with cash

After they've established initial price points, many companies stay on the lookout for potential advantages that can be gained by adjusting prices up or down over time. Companies can offer a variety of **discounts**, such as temporary price reductions to stimulate sales, price reductions for paying early or paying in cash, or *volume discounts* for buying in bulk.

Although discounts are a popular way to boost sales of a product, the down side is that they can touch off *price wars* between competitors. Price wars can occur whenever (a) one supplier believes that underpricing the competition is the best way—or perhaps the only way—for it to increase sales volume and (b) customers believe that price is the only meaningful differentiator among the various suppliers. This situation occurs frequently in the air travel industry, which is why it has been wracked with price wars ever since it was deregulated years ago. Price wars present two significant dangers: that customers will begin to believe that price is the only factor to care about in the market and that desperate competitors will cut prices so far that they'll damage their finances—perhaps beyond repair.

bundling
Offering several products for a single price that is presumably lower than the total of the products' individual prices

Sometimes sellers combine several of their products and sell them at one reduced price. This practice, called **bundling**, can also promote sales of products consumers might not otherwise buy—especially when the combined price is low enough to entice them to purchase the bundle. Examples of bundled products are season tickets, vacation packages, computer software with hardware, and wrapped packages of shampoo and conditioner.

dynamic pricing
Continually adjusting prices to reflect changes in supply and demand

Finally, companies can constantly reprice their products in response to supply and demand fluctuations, a tactic known as **dynamic pricing**. Dynamic pricing not only enables companies to move slow-selling merchandise instantly but also allows companies to experiment with different pricing levels. Because price changes are immediately distributed via computer networks, customers always have the most current price information. Airlines and hotels have used this type of continually adjusted pricing for years, a technique often known as *yield management*. However, companies need to be careful not to alienate customers by creating so much pricing uncertainty that purchasing becomes a frustrating cat-and-mouse game. In fact, noted brand strategist Al Ries calls dynamic pricing the "ultimate brand destruction machine" because it rewards buyers for price shopping rather than being loyal to a single brand.[39]

For the latest information on pricing strategies and tactics, visit **http://realtimeupdates.com/bia5** and click on Chapter 14.

√CHECKPOINT

LEARNING OBJECTIVE 6: Identify nine common pricing methods.

Summary: (1) *Cost-based* or *cost-plus pricing* takes the cost of producing and marketing a product and adds a markup to arrive at the selling price. (2) *Value-based pricing* seeks to establish the perceived value of the product in the eyes of target customers and sets a price based on that. (3) *Optimal pricing* is a computer-based method that uses sales data to create a demand curve for every product, allowing managers to select prices based on specific marketing objectives. (4) *Skim pricing* is setting an initial price that is relatively high in order to capitalize on pent-up demand or the lack of direct competition for a new product. (5) *Penetration pricing* is setting a price low enough to achieve targeted sales volumes. (6) *Loss-leader pricing* is setting the price artificially low on one product in order to attract buyers for other products. (7) *Auction pricing* is letting buyers determine the selling price by bidding against one another; in a reverse auction, buyers state a price they are willing to pay and sellers choose whether to match it. (8) *Participative pricing* lets buyers pay whatever they think a product is worth. (9) *Free pricing* involves giving away products to some customers (as a means of attracting paying customers, for example) or giving away some products but charging for others.

Critical thinking: (1) What steps could a company take to determine the perceived value of its products in its target markets? (2) How can patterns of temporary price discounts "train" consumers to stop buying at full price?

It's your business: (1) Have you ever bid on anything on eBay, another online auction site, or an in-person auction? If so, how did you decide how much to bid? Did you set a maximum price you'd allow yourself to spend? Did you get caught up in the competitive emotions of bidding against someone else? (2) Have you ever purchased a hot new product as soon as it hit the market, only to see the price drop a few months later? If so, did you resolve never to buy so quickly again?

Key terms to know: cost-based pricing, value-based pricing, optimal pricing, skim pricing, penetration pricing, loss-leader pricing, participative pricing, discounts, bundling, dynamic pricing

Behind the Scenes

Building the Annika Brand

Annika Sorenstam is approaching her second career the same way she approached her first. In golf, she reached the top of her sport by learning from the best, surrounding herself with a supportive team, setting ambitious goals, and working as hard as it takes to reach those goals.

A central element in her business plan is the role she herself plays as the core of the "Annika" brand. As a young player in her native Sweden, she was so reluctant to step into the limelight

that she would falter toward the end of tournaments to avoid winning and facing the media attention that came with it. She clearly fixed that problem, transforming herself into a quietly confident but ferocious competitor who often left other players in the dust as she went on to win nearly 90 times worldwide.

However, as she was nearing retirement from golf and ramping up her business activities, she realized that the persona she had become known for on the course didn't lend itself to her ambitions for the Annika brand. Research by branding consultant Duane Knapp showed that people respected Sorenstam's competitive drive but really had no sense of who she was as a person. Even her own husband says she was viewed by the public as "the stoic Swede who will step on your throat" on the way to victory and not the "humble, pretty, and hilarious" woman he knew off the course.

Transforming Annika the feared competitor into Annika the warm and welcoming brand icon was a top priority. A good example of this effort is her blog (www.annikablog .com), which gives visitors the chance to know her as she lives off the course, including her love of gourmet cooking, her passion for skiing, and her new role as a first-time mother. Her Twitter updates also help build a relationship with fans as she discusses doing the everyday things everyday people do.

Along with crafting an inviting brand image that more accurately reflects her true personality, Sorenstam is busy expanding the Annika product line. She continues to endorse many of the same goods and services she promoted as an active player, including Callaway Golf, Lexus, and Rolex. Other business partnerships include an Annika-branded clothing line with Cutter & Buck, Annika wine, and Annika perfume.

A central element in her product portfolio is the Annika Academy, a golf instruction facility in Reunion, Florida, that offers lessons, corporate outings, golf vacations, and the opportunity to train with the same advisors and coaches who work with Sorenstam. For the ultimate golf experience, a lucky few visitors every year can buy the three-day, $12,000 "Soren-Slam" package, which includes nine holes of golf with Sorenstam herself.

Following another path blazed by her golf-business mentors, Sorenstam also launched a golf course design business, with courses so far in Canada, China, Malaysia, South Africa, and the United States. Having had the opportunity to play some of the finest and most historic golf courses in the world, she combines that experience with her insights as a professional to create challenging but playable courses. Her designs also aim to right an aesthetic wrong shared by too many golf courses: The best views of both the playing area and the surrounding landscape are found on the men's tee boxes. (Golf courses have different sets of tee boxes to reflect the different hitting lengths of average male and female players.) On her courses, women will enjoy the same quality of experience as the men.

Sorenstam had an interest in finance from any early age, and that passion is reflected in yet another part of the product mix, the Annika Financial Group. This small advisory firm helps other professional athletes manage their money and achieve financial security in their postathletic lives.

With a recrafted brand image and a growing product portfolio, Sorenstam is off to a hot start in her quest to be the first woman to join the exclusive club of former athletes who have truly made it big in business. Michael Jordan is "Air Jordan," Arnold Palmer is the "The King," Jack Nicklaus is "The Golden Bear," and Greg Norman, another golf empire builder, is "The Shark." Who knows—perhaps Annika "The Avenger"?[40]

Critical Thinking Questions

1. Golfers who take lessons and purchase other services from the Annika Academy presumably share at least some of Sorenstam's passion for winning. Would toning down the competitive aspect of Sorenstam's public persona negatively affect the Annika brand in the eyes of Academy customers? Explain your answer.

2. Sorenstam's charitable efforts include the Annika Foundation, which you can read about on her website. How does her work with the Make-A-Wish Foundation and other activities contribute to her brand equity?

3. Explain how the brand extension efforts in wine, perfume, and financial advice can reasonably fit under the umbrella of the Annika brand.

LEARN MORE ONLINE

Visit Sorenstam's main website at www.annikasorenstam .com, her blog at www.annikablog.com, and the Annika Academy website at www.annikaacademy.com. What is your overall impression of Sorenstam as a businessperson and of the Annika brand as a product identifier? Do these communication efforts help in the effort to shift her public image away from that of the fierce competitor? ■

Key Terms

brand (362)
brand equity (362)
brand extension (367)
brand loyalty (362)
brand managers (365)
brand mark (362)
brand names (362)
break-even analysis (370)
break-even point (370)

bundling (374)
capital items (357)
co-branding (363)
commercialization (362)
convenience products (357)
cost-based pricing (372)
discounts (374)
dynamic pricing (374)
expense items (357)

family branding (366)
fixed costs (369)
generic products (363)
license (363)
logo (362)
loss-leader pricing (373)
national brands (363)
optimal pricing (372)
participative pricing (373)

Test Your Knowledge

Questions for Review

1. What is test marketing?
2. What are the four main subgroups of consumer products?
3. How does cost-based pricing differ from value-based pricing?
4. What are the functions of packaging?
5. How many books will a publisher have to sell to break even if fixed costs are $100,000, the selling price per book is $60, and the variable costs per book are $40?

Questions for Analysis

6. Why is cost-based pricing risky?
7. Why is it important to review the objectives of a strategic marketing plan before setting a product's price?
8. Why do businesses continually introduce new products, given the high costs of the introduction stage of the product life cycle?
9. Why are some well-established brands worth millions or even billions of dollars?
10. **Ethical Considerations.** If your college neighborhood is typical, many companies in the area adorn themselves in your school colors and otherwise seek to identify their names with your school name and thereby encourage business from students. Some of these firms probably have brand licensing agreements with your college or are involved in sponsoring various groups on campus. However, chances are some of them are using school colors and other branding elements without having any formal arrangement with the college. In other words, they may be getting commercial benefit from the association without paying for it.[41] Is this ethical? Why or why not?

Questions for Application

11. Do you consider yourself an *early adopter* when it comes to trying out new products or new fashions, or do you tend to take a wait-and-see attitude? How does your attitude toward new products and new ideas influence your decision making as a consumer?
12. In what ways might Mattel modify its pricing strategies during the life cycle of a toy product?
13. **Concept Integration.** Review the theory of supply and demand in Chapter 2 (see pages 81–83). How do skimming and penetration pricing strategies influence a product's supply and demand?
14. **Concept Integration.** Review the discussion of cultural differences in international business in Chapter 3 (see pages 108–109). Which cultural differences do you think Disney had to consider when planning its product strategies for Disneyland Paris? Originally the company offered a standardized product but was later forced to customize many of the park's operations. What might have been some of the cultural challenges Disney experienced under a standardized product strategy?

Practice Your Knowledge

Sharpening Your Communication Skills

Now's your chance to play the role of a marketing specialist trying to convince a group of customers that your product concept is better than the competition's. You're going to wade into the industry battle over digital photo printing. Choose a side: either the photo printer manufacturers, who want consumers to buy printers to print their own digital photos (visit HP at www.hp.com for a good overview of photo-quality printers), or the service providers, who claim their way is better (visit one of the many retailers that offer a service-based approach, such as www.cvs.com or www.walmart.com). Prepare a short presentation on why the approach you've chosen is better for consumers. Feel free to segment the consumer market and choose a particular target segment if that bolsters your argument.

Building Your Team Skills

Select a high-profile product with which you and your teammates are familiar. Do some online research to learn more about that brand. Then answer these questions and prepare a short group presentation to your classmates summarizing your findings.

- Is the product a consumer product, an organizational product, or both?
- At what stage in its life cycle is this product?
- Is the product a national brand or a private brand?
- How do the product's packaging and labeling help boost consumer appeal?
- How is this product promoted?

- Is the product mix to which this product belongs wide? Long? Deep?

- Is the product sold in international markets? If so, does the company use a standardized or a customized strategy?

- How is the product priced in relation to competing products?

Expand Your Knowledge

Discovering Career Opportunities

Being a marketing manager is a big responsibility, but it can be a lot of fun at the same time. Read what the U.S. Department of Labor has to say about the nature of the work, working conditions, qualifications, and job outlook for marketing managers by accessing the Bureau of Labor Statistics's *Occupational Outlook Handbook* at www.bls.gov/oco.

1. What does a marketing manager do?
2. What are some key questions you might want to ask when interviewing for a job in marketing?
3. What training and qualifications should a marketing manager have?

Developing Your Research Skills

Scan recent business journals and newspapers (print or online editions) for an article related to one of the following:

- New-product development
- The product life cycle
- Brand extensions
- Pricing strategies
- Packaging

1. Does this article report on a development in a particular company, several companies, or an entire industry? Which companies or industries are specifically mentioned?
2. If you were a marketing manager in this industry, what concerns would you have as a result of reading the article? What questions do you think companies in this industry (or related ones) should be asking? What would you want to know?
3. In what ways do you think this industry, other industries, or the public might be affected by this trend or development in the next five years? Why?

Improving Your Tech Insights: Location and Tracking Technologies

Location and tracking technologies cover a wide range of capabilities. Radio frequency identification (RFID) technology uses small scannable tags attached to products or even people and pets. RFID is being implemented extensively in retail and wholesale distribution systems to enhance inventory management. Parents and caregivers can also use RFID to check on elderly relatives, pets, or children. The Great America amusement park in Santa Clara, California, offers RFID bracelets for $5 so parents and children can reconnect if they get separated in the crowds. The Food and Drug Administration (FDA) has approved an implantable device that stores medical information that emergency personnel could retrieve with a quick scan, even if the patient is unconscious.

The Global Positioning System (GPS) can pinpoint any location on Earth using a network of satellites and small transceivers. Trucking fleets use GPS to keep track of all their vehicles to optimize scheduling and make sure drivers stay on assigned routes. Some rental car companies use GPS to see whether drivers break the speed limit or venture outside of permitted rental territories. *Enhanced 911*, or *E911*, uses either GPS or cell phone towers to let emergency personnel pinpoint the location of people calling on cell phones. GPS-enabled smartphones are creating a dizzying array of new location-based services, from "friend finders" such as Loopt to shopping and dining guides to wireless payment systems.

Using online research tools, identify at least one emerging business opportunity that could take advantage of location and tracking technologies. In an e-mail message to your instructor, describe the opportunity and briefly explain how the technology would be used.[42]

Video Discussion

Access the Chapter 14 video discussion in the End of Chapter Assignments section at www.mybizlab.com.

Log on to www.mybizlab.com to access the following study and assessment aids associated with this chapter:

- Interactive exercises
- Pre/post test
- Real-Time Updates
- Video application
- Customized study plans
- Biz Skills Simulations
- Quick Learning Guide

If you are not using mybizlab, you can access Real-Time Updates and Quick Learning Guides through http://realtimeupdates.com/bia5. The Quick Learning Guide (located under "Learn More" on the website) provides all six Checkpoints in a handy two-page format to help you study for exams or review important concepts whenever you need a quick refresher.

Distribution and Marketing Logistics

Behind the Scenes

Costco Makes the Good Life More Affordable

www.costco.com

With an unusual mix of low prices and quality goods, Costco Wholesale has become the country's largest and most profitable warehouse club chain. The company knows that low prices on high-quality, high-end merchandise can transcend the common notion of "discount." And, in what amounts to a treasure hunt played out along Costco's cement-floor aisles, the high/ low shopping experience is a powerful elixir for middle-class shoppers.

Once new members get the hang of the treasure hunt mentality, they get hooked on Costco because even though they don't know what will be on display, they're sure it will be something at a price that will make the good life more affordable. Like other warehouse clubs, Costco Wholesale sells a mix of everything from giant boxes of cereal to

Costco shoppers have learned to look for great buys on both everyday items and on an ever-changing mix of luxury and specialty goods.

patio furniture. In fact, Costco often asks vendors to change their factory runs to produce specially built packages that are bigger and cheaper. Unlike with other warehouse clubs, Costco shoppers can occasionally find $10,000 diamond rings and grand pianos along with mouthwash and laundry detergent. Costco also entices shoppers with in-store bakeries and ready-to-eat dishes, as well as optical departments, insurance, and other services that reflect the same high-quality, low-price model as the packaged merchandise.

If you were Costco president and CEO Jim Sinegal, how would you keep Costco on the leading edge of retailing? How would you integrate your physical retail stores with your online e-commerce operation? What can you do to keep your bargain-conscious but demanding customers coming back for more?[1] ■

Introduction

Marketing intermediaries such as Costco (profiled in the chapter-opening Behind the Scenes) play an essential role in marketing products created by other companies. This chapter explores the many contributions these intermediaries make, both at the retailing stage that is visible to all consumers and the less visible but no less important wholesaling stage. Manufacturers and other producers need to understand the distribution process in order to select the right intermediaries and work with them effectively. And, of course, wholesalers and retailers are business entities themselves, with their own strategic questions and operating challenges.

The Role of Marketing Intermediaries

As Chapter 13 points out, a *distribution channel*, or *marketing channel*, is an organized network of firms that work together to get goods and services from producer to customer. Whether you're selling digital music files or scrap iron stripped out of old ships, your **distribution strategy**, or overall plan for moving products to buyers, will play a major role in your success.

Think of all the products you buy: food, cosmetics, clothing, sports equipment, train tickets, gasoline, stationery, appliances, music, books, and all the rest. How many of these products do you buy directly from the producer? For most people, the answer is not many. Most companies that create products do not sell these goods directly to the final users. Instead, producers in many industries work with **marketing intermediaries** to bring their products to market. Even some service companies rely on other firms to perform services on their behalf.

Wholesaling Versus Retailing

Intermediaries can be grouped into two general types: wholesalers and retailers. **Wholesalers** sell to organizational customers, including other wholesalers, companies, government agencies, and educational institutions. In turn, the customers of wholesalers either resell the products or use them to make products of their own.

Unlike wholesalers, **retailers** primarily sell products to consumers for personal use. Retailers can operate out of a physical facility (department store, gas station, kiosk), through vending equipment (soft drink machine, newspaper box, automated teller), or from a virtual store (via telephone, catalog, website).

Terminology in the distribution field can get a bit confusing, starting with the multiple uses of the term "wholesale." For instance, even though Costco and other warehouse-type stores often use the "wholesale" label to describe themselves, they function as both wholesalers and retailers simultaneously. Small-business owners, for instance, are enthusiastic Costco shoppers because the store is a low-cost place to buy supplies and equipment. In these cases, Costco is functioning as a wholesaler. However, when selling to consumers, Costco is technically operating as a retailer, not a wholesaler. The distinction is important because business strategies for wholesaling and retailing are dramatically different in many ways. As just one example, you'll recall from Chapter 13 that even when they buy the same products, consumers and organizations usually make purchases for different reasons. Because their motivations and expectations are different, consumers (reached by retailers) and organizations (reached by wholesalers) don't respond to marketing programs the same way.

Contributions of Marketing Intermediaries

Wholesalers and retailers are instrumental in creating three of the four forms of utility mentioned in Chapter 13: They provide the items customers need in a convenient location (place utility), they save customers the time of having to contact each manufacturer to purchase a good (time utility), and they provide an efficient process for transferring products from the producer to the customer (possession utility). In addition to creating utility, wholesalers and retailers perform the following distribution functions:

- **Matching buyers and sellers.** By making sellers' products available to multiple buyers, intermediaries such as Costco reduce the number of transactions between producers and customers. In the business-to-business market, the industrial distributor Grainger (www.grainger.com) is a good example of the enormous scale that can be achieved in bringing buyers and sellers together. Boasting a portfolio of more than 870,000 products, Grainger connects more than 3,000 suppliers with 1,800,000 organizational customers.[2] These customers are saved the time and trouble of working with multiple suppliers, and the product suppliers get access to more customers than all but the very largest of them could ever hope to reach on their own. Although "cutting out the middleman" is sometimes used as a promotional slogan, intermediaries such as Grainger can actually make commerce more efficient by reducing the number of contact points between buyers and sellers (see Exhibit 15.1 on the next page).

distribution strategy
Firm's overall plan for moving products to intermediaries and final customers

marketing intermediaries
Businesspeople and organizations that assist in moving and marketing goods and services between producers and consumers

wholesalers
Intermediaries that sell products to other intermediaries for resale or to organizations for internal use

retailers
Intermediaries that sell goods and services to individuals for their own personal use

EXHIBIT 15.1

How Intermediaries Simplify Commerce

Intermediaries actually reduce the price customers pay for many goods and services, because they reduce the number of contacts between producers and consumers that would otherwise be necessary. They also create place, time, and possession utility.

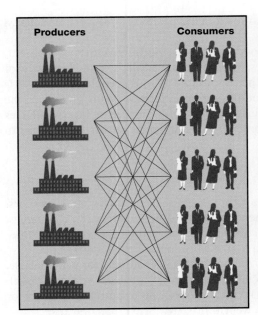

Number of transactions required when consumers buy directly from manufacturers

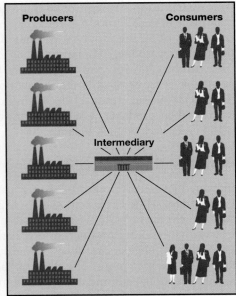

Number of transactions required when buying is conducted via intermediary

- **Providing market information.** Retail intermediaries, such as Amazon and Macy's, collect valuable data about customer purchases: who buys, how often, and how much. For example, e-commerce records and data from "frequent shopper" cards help retailers spot buying patterns, providing vital market information they can then share with producers to optimize product mixes and promotional efforts.

- **Providing promotional and sales support.** Many intermediaries assist with advertising, in-store displays, and other promotional efforts for some or all of the products they sell. Some also employ sales representatives who can perform a number of selling and customer relationship functions.

- **Gathering assortments of goods.** Nordstrom, Staples, and other intermediaries receive bulk shipments from producers and break them into more convenient units (known as *breaking bulk*) by sorting, standardizing, and dividing bulk quantities into smaller packages.

- **Transporting and storing products.** Many intermediaries maintain inventories of merchandise that they acquire from producers so they can quickly fill customers' orders. In many cases retailers purchase this merchandise from wholesalers who, in addition to breaking bulk, may also transport the goods from the producer to the retail outlets.

- **Assuming risks.** When intermediaries accept goods from manufacturers, they usually take on the risks associated with damage, theft, product perishability (in the sense of tangible goods that are vulnerable to rotting, for instance), and obsolescence. For example, if products stocked or displayed at Costco are stolen, Costco assumes responsibility for the loss.

- **Providing financing.** Large intermediaries sometimes provide loans to smaller producers.

- **Completing product solutions.** In some industries, producers rely on a class of intermediaries often called *value-added resellers (VARs)* or *system integrators* to complete or customize solutions for customers. For instance, IrisInk (**www.irisink .com**) is a "Pro-Video VAR" for Apple, meaning it can combine Apple computers with other hardware and software elements to create professional video production facilities for its clients.[3] By partnering with companies such as IrisInk, Apple is able to reach a wider range of customers without the need to develop specialized expertise in multiple industries.

- **Facilitating transactions and supporting customers.** Intermediaries can perform a variety of other functions that help with the selection, purchase, and use of products. Commercial real estate brokers, for example, can negotiate prices and contract terms on behalf of buyers and sellers. In a variety of industries, intermediaries help customers select the products that fit their needs and then provide customer support and technical assistance after the sale.

✓CHECKPOINT

LEARNING OBJECTIVE 1: Explain the role of marketing intermediaries in contemporary business, and list the eight primary functions that intermediaries can perform.

Summary: Intermediaries can be responsible for any and all aspects of distribution, one of the key elements in any firm's marketing mix. The two major categories are *wholesalers*, which buy from producers and sell to retailers, to other wholesalers, and to organizational customers such as businesses, government agencies, and institutions; and *retailers*, which buy from producers or wholesalers and sell the products to the final consumers. These marketing intermediaries bring products to market and help ensure that the goods and services are available in the right time, place, and amount. Depending on their position in the channel, intermediaries can perform the eight key functions of matching buyers and sellers; providing market information; providing promotional and sales support; sorting, standardizing, and dividing merchandise; transporting and storing products; assuming risks; providing financing; and completing production solutions.

Critical thinking: (1) Why wouldn't Apple develop the expertise to create professional video studios and other solutions that its channel partners now develop? (2) How can Costco be both a wholesaler and a retailer at the same time?

It's your business: (1) If you had the choice of buying a product directly from the manufacturer or from a local retailer, which would you choose? Why? (2) Have you ever had to work with more than one retailer to get a complete product solution (such as getting car parts or home improvement supplies from multiple stores)? Was the experience satisfactory?

Key terms to know: distribution strategy, marketing intermediaries, wholesalers, retailers

Wholesaling and Industrial Distribution

Although largely unseen by consumers, wholesaling is a huge presence in the economy, with over $5 trillion in sales every year in the United States alone.[4] By connecting producers with retailers and organizational customers, wholesalers play a vital role in nearly every industry in the world.

Major Types of Wholesalers

Most wholesalers are independent companies that can be classified as *merchant wholesalers*, *agents*, or *brokers*. Beyond this simple distinction, the terminology surrounding wholesaling can be rather confusing. For instance, "agents" and "brokers" are also

Real-Time Updates

Learn More

An inside look at contemporary distribution

See how electronics distributor Avnet adds value in the distribution channel. On mybizlab (www.mybizlab.com), you can access Real-Time Updates within each chapter or under Student Study Tools. Otherwise, go to http://real-timeupdates.com/bia5 and click on "Learn More."

common in services retailing (including real estate agents and stockbrokers). Likewise, as mentioned earlier, many retail firms use "warehouse" or "wholesale" in their company or store names to convey low prices to consumers. Just remember the simple rule: When a marketing intermediary is selling to individual consumers, it's functioning as a retailer; when an intermediary sells to any type of organization, from a mom-and-pop store to the Pentagon, it's functioning as a wholesaler.

merchant wholesalers
Independent wholesalers that take legal title to goods they distribute

The majority of wholesalers are **merchant wholesalers**, independently owned businesses that buy from producers, take legal title to the goods, and then resell them to retailers or to organizational buyers. The field of merchant wholesaling includes a handful of multibillion-dollar firms such as Grainger in industrial supplies, Avnet (www.avnet.com) in electronic components, McKesson (www.mckesson.com) in health care, and Supervalu (www.supervalu.com) in groceries. However, most of the nation's 250,000 merchant wholesalers are small companies—in fact, roughly two-thirds have fewer than five employees.[5]

full-service merchant wholesalers
Merchant wholesalers that provide a wide variety of services to their customers, such as storage, delivery, and marketing support

Full-service merchant wholesalers provide a wide variety of services, such as storage, selling, order processing, delivery, and promotional support. *Rack jobbers*, for example, are full-service merchant wholesalers that set up displays in retail outlets, stock inventory, and perform other services such as marking prices on merchandise displayed in a particular section of a store. *Limited-service merchant wholesalers*, on the other hand, provide fewer services. Natural resources such as lumber, grain, and coal are usually marketed through a class of limited-service wholesalers called *drop shippers*, which take ownership but not physical possession of the goods they handle.

distributors
Merchant wholesalers that sell products to organizational customers for internal operations or the production of other goods, rather than to retailers for resale

Merchant wholesalers can also be distinguished by their customers. Supervalu and others that sell primarily to other intermediaries are usually known in the trade simply as *wholesalers*. In contrast, Avnet and others that sell goods to companies for use in their own products and operations are usually called **distributors**.

agents and brokers
Independent wholesalers that do not take title to the goods they distribute but may or may not take possession of those goods

Unlike merchant wholesalers, **agents and brokers** never actually own the products they handle, and they perform fewer services. Their primary role is to bring buyers and sellers together; they are generally paid a commission (a percentage of the money received) for arranging sales. Producers of industrial parts often sell to business customers through brokers. *Manufacturers' representatives*, another type of agent, sell various noncompeting products to customers in a specific region. By representing several manufacturers' products, these reps achieve enough volume to justify the cost of a direct sales call.

The Outlook for Wholesaling

"Changes and challenges" would be a good way to sum up the outlook for wholesalers. While financial performance for the sector as a whole has been at least as robust as the economy overall,[6] the business of wholesaling is changing in ways that are helping some wholesalers and threatening others. Four trends in particular are likely to reshape the wholesaling business in the coming years:

- **Integrated logistics management.** The outsourcing trend discussed in Chapter 9 is definitely having an impact in the wholesaling sector as *third-party logistics* firms continue to take over a wide range of tasks in supply chain management, including not only traditional wholesaling activities but also order fulfillment, product repair, customer service, and other functions. These "3PL" firms have been growing much faster than conventional wholesalers in recent years, reflecting the desire by many manufacturers to focus on core production activities.[7] The emergence of

3PL is coming from two directions, as transportation companies such as UPS and FedEx and wholesalers such as Supervalu and McKesson expand the scope of their services. In fact, you'd be hard pressed from McKesson's description of itself to recognize that the company is in fact a major wholesaler: "McKesson is a health care services company dedicated to helping its customers deliver high-quality health care by reducing costs, streamlining processes, and improving the quality of care and patient safety."[8]

- **Threat of disintermediation.** For many years, and particularly since the advent of the Internet and the growth of e-commerce, various observers have predicted the widespread **disintermediation** of wholesalers, meaning their role would be taken over by manufacturers on the upstream end or by customers (retailers and other organizational buyers) on the downstream end. While this has certainly happened in specific instances in various industries, and the share of wholesaling activity performed by independent wholesalers appears to be shrinking somewhat, wholesalers as a group have not disappeared to the extent that some predicted.[9] The concurrent trend toward outsourcing may be countering the predicted trend toward disintermediation. In other words, the fact that more suppliers and customers *can* perform many wholesaling functions doesn't mean they necessarily *should*. The bottom line is that intermediaries, in whatever form, will continue to play an integral role in the distribution process as long as they can add value and perform essential services more effectively and more efficiently than either manufacturers or customers.[10]

  disintermediation
  The replacement of intermediaries by producers, customers, or other intermediaries when those other parties can perform channel functions more effectively or efficiently

- **Unbundling of services.** The conventional way that merchant wholesalers generate revenue and earn profits is by purchasing products from manufacturers at a discount and reselling them to retailers or organizational buyers at a markup. Whatever services a wholesaler provides are covered by that markup. However, a growing number of wholesaling customers would like to see these services "unbundled" so they can pay for specific distribution services individually.[11] If this trend catches on, it could change the business model for many wholesalers.

- **Industry consolidation.** With all the forces at play in the marketplace, consolidation seems likely as large firms with economies of scale buy up or drive out smaller, less-competitive firms. In addition, a growing number of customers are pursuing *strategic sourcing*, in which they forge closer relationships with a smaller number of strategic distribution partners.[12]

✓CHECKPOINT

LEARNING OBJECTIVE 2: Identify the major types of wholesalers, and summarize four trends shaping the future of wholesaling.

Summary: Most wholesalers can be classified as *merchant wholesalers, agents,* or *brokers.* Merchant wholesalers are independently owned businesses that buy from producers, take legal title to the goods, and then resell them to retailers or to organizational buyers. Merchant wholesalers can be distinguished by level of service (*full-service* versus *limited-service*) and target customers (*wholesalers* that sell goods to retailers for the purpose of then reselling them to consumers and *distributors* that sell goods to organizations for internal operation use or to make other products). In contrast to merchant wholesalers, agents and brokers do not assume ownership but focus on bringing buyers and sellers together. Four trends shaping wholesaling are integrated logistics management, the threat of disintermediation, the unbundling of services, and industry consolidation.

Critical thinking: (1) Why does McKesson promote itself as a health care services company, rather than as a logistics company? (2) Why might a manufacturer choose to hire a third-party logistics firm rather than a conventional wholesaler or distributor?

It's your business: (1) Considering the forces shaping wholesaling, would you consider a career in this sector? Why or why not? (2) If your family ran a small industrial products wholesaler that was facing the threat of disintermediation, how would you respond?

Key terms to know: merchant wholesalers, full-service merchant wholesalers, distributors, agents and brokers, disintermediation

Retailing

In contrast to wholesalers, retailers are a highly visible element in the distribution chain. In addition to providing convenient access to products and supporting consumers with a variety of presale and postsale services, retailers play a major role in the buying process because many consumer buying decisions are made in the retail setting. Consequently, retailing involves a blend of the distribution and customer communication elements of the marketing mix. The term *shopper marketing*, or *in-store marketing*, refers to communication efforts directed at consumers while they are in the retail setting.[13] To be sure, the degree to which decision making occurs in the store varies across product categories, consumers, and purchasing situations. For example, consumers engaged in home remodeling projects typically have a clear idea of what they want to buy before they get to the store, so the in-store decisions relate more to specific colors and textures than to broad product categories.[14] In other instances, in-store signs, product labels, and other factors can influence the types of products and specific brands that consumers choose.

Given the importance of the shopping environment, it comes as no surprise that retailers spend considerable time and money crafting physical spaces and shopping experiences that are intended to shape consumer behavior, addressing everything from lighting and color palettes to music and employee attire. No detail seems to be too small. For instance, the attractiveness of employees and even other shoppers can influence consumer choices. Although consumers are generally put off by the realization that other shoppers have touched the products on display in a store, if they see an *attractive* person touch a product, people tend to think more highly of that product.[15]

Retailing Formats

With so much effort directed toward influencing buying decisions across so many categories of products and diverse segments in the consumer market, the retail sector has evolved into a dizzying array of store types and formats. Much of this evolution can be explained by a concept called the **wheel of retailing**. In this model, an innovative retailer with low operating costs attracts a following by offering low prices and limited service. As this store adds more services to broaden its appeal, its prices creep upward, opening the door for a new generation of lower-priced competitors. Eventually, these competitors also upgrade their operations and are replaced by still other lower-priced stores that later follow the same upward pattern. For instance, Walmart reshaped retailing with low prices enabled by the company's extraordinary abilities at cost control and efficiency but now finds itself facing new low-price competition from the likes of Family Dollar Stores and Dollar General. For instance, during the recent recession, Family Dollar was one of the rare success stories in all of retailing, gaining market share as more shoppers turned to it for food and household essentials.[16]

Regardless of product offerings or target markets, all retailing efforts can be divided into *store* formats—based in physical store locations—and *nonstore* formats—which take place anywhere and everywhere outside of physical stores. Exhibit 15.2 summarizes the most important store formats. **Department stores** are the classic major retailers in the United States, with the likes of Bloomingdale's, Macy's, Nordstrom, Dillard's, and Kohl's generally offering a range of clothing, accessories, bedding, and other products for the

wheel of retailing
Evolutionary process by which stores that feature low prices gradually upgrade until they no longer appeal to price-sensitive shoppers and are replaced by a new generation of leaner, low-price competitors

department stores
Large stores that carry a variety of products in multiple categories, such as clothing, housewares, gifts, bedding, and furniture

EXHIBIT 15.2 Retail Store Formats

The term *retailer* covers many types of outlets. This table shows some of the most common types.

RETAIL FORMAT	KEY FEATURES	EXAMPLES
Department store	Offers a wide variety of merchandise under one roof in departmentalized sections and many customer services	Dillard's, J. C. Penney, Nordstrom
Specialty store	Offers a complete selection in a narrow range of merchandise, often with extensive customer services	Payless Shoes, R.E.I.
Category killer	Type of specialty store focusing on specific products on a massive scale and dominating retail sales in respective products categories	Office Depot; Bed, Bath & Beyond; Lowe's
Discount store	Offers a wide variety of merchandise at low prices with relatively fewer services	Dollar General, Target, Walmart
Off-price store	Offers designer and brand-name merchandise at low prices and with relatively fewer services	T.J. Maxx, Marshall's
Convenience store	Offers limited range of convenience goods, long service hours, and quick checkouts	7-Eleven, AM-PM
Factory/retail outlet	Large outlet store selling discontinued items, overruns, and factory seconds	Nordstrom Rack, Nike outlet store
Supermarket	Large, self-service store offering a wide selection of food and nonfood merchandise	Kroger, Safeway
Hypermarket	Giant store offering both food and general merchandise at discount prices	Walmart Super Centers, Carrefour
Warehouse club	Large, warehouse-style store that sells food and general merchandise at discount prices; some require club membership	Sam's Club, Costco
Online retailer	Web-based store offering anything from a single product line to comprehensive selections in multiple product areas; can be web-only (e.g., Amazon.com) or integrated with physical stores (e.g., REI.com)	Amazon.com, REI.com

home. **Specialty stores** such as jewelers and bicycle shops offer a limited number of product lines but an extensive selection of brands, styles, sizes, models, colors, materials, and prices within each line. Huge specialty stores such as The Home Depot and Bed, Bath and Beyond that tend to dominate those sectors of retail are known as *category killers.*

Retailers can also be distinguished by their pricing strategies. Family Dollar Stores and Walmart, for example, are **discount stores**, which feature a wide variety of aggressively priced everyday merchandise. **Off-price retailers** such as Filene's Basement and T.J. Maxx take a slightly different approach, offering more limited selections of higher-end products such as designer label clothing at steeply discounted prices.[17]

In the nonstore arena, **online retailers** can be either Internet-only operations such as fashion retailer Bluefly (www.bluefly.com) or online extensions of store-based operations, such as the sites run by J. C. Penney (www.jcpenney.com) and other department stores. Online stores still account for less than 10 percent of U.S. retail sales overall, but they have a become major force in some product categories—such as books, for example, where online sales now outpace store sales.[18] Electronic commerce, or **e-commerce**, is not limited to retailing, to be sure. Companies ranging from small specialty wholesalers to the world's largest distribution firms rely on the Internet as well.

specialty stores
Stores that carries only a particular type of goods, often with deep selection in those specific categories

discount stores
Retailers that sell a variety of everyday goods below the market price by keeping their overhead low

off-price retailers
Stores that sell designer labels and other fashionable products at steep discounts

online retailers
Companies that use e-commerce technologies to sell over the Internet; includes Internet-only retailers and the online arm of store-based retailers

Real-Time Updates

Learn More
The 10-second website test

See how Red Oxx uses its e-commerce presence to build a retail brand. On mybizlab (www.mybizlab.com), you can access Real-Time Updates within each chapter or under Student Study Tools. Otherwise, go to http://real-timeupdates.com/bia5 and click on "Learn More."

e-commerce
The application of Internet technologies to wholesaling and retailing

Meanwhile, the mail-order firms that inspired e-commerce are still going strong in many industries. Attractive catalogs are a powerful marketing tool, but printing and mailing them is expensive, so many mail-order firms are working to integrate their catalog efforts with e-commerce to maximize sales. Vending machines and interactive kiosks are an important format for many food and convenience goods as well. One interesting new entry in this category is Coinstar's Redbox movie rental machines, which started as an experiment in McDonald's restaurants but became so popular that they are now starting to worry online rental leader Netflix.[19]

The Outlook for Retailing

Retailing has always been a challenging field, and it's not getting any easier for many companies in the sector. Of course, disruption for some can mean opportunities for others. Retailers that survive and succeed over the long term tend to do the same things well: (1) maintaining a clear sense of purpose in the minds of target customers, (2) crafting an overall shopping experience that complements the purchases customers are making, (3) protecting the credibility of the retail brand, and (4) adapting to consumer trends without overreacting to short-term fads.[20]

Here are six major forces shaping the future of retailing:

■ **Overcapacity.** In too many categories, there are simply too many stores to support current levels of business activity. Shopping malls in particular, those icons of contemporary consumer life, have become a symbol for much of what ails retailing. A furious spate of mall building in the past couple of decades left the country with hundreds more malls than the economy could really support, even as the rise of online retailing and the growth of standalone discounters were drawing shoppers away from malls. In fact, a hundred or so malls across the country are now considered "dead" because they have such low revenues and high vacancy rates.[21]

■ **Continued growth in online retailing.** The growth rate of online retailing has outpaced store-based retailing in recent years, and that trend is likely to continue. Not only are more consumers buying online, but many store-based retailers are trying to reduce their fixed costs by shifting more activity to the Internet.[22] The companies most likely to succeed online are store-based retailers with strong reputations and loyal customers, Internet-only retailers such as Amazon (www.amazon.com) and the jewelry store Blue Nile (www.bluenile.com) that have achieved the economies of scale necessary to be profitable, and niche players that can combine unusual products and great customer service.[23]

■ **Growth of multichannel retailing.** The growth in online retailing also reflects the fact that today's consumers increasingly combine online and offline shopping, such as researching products online and then making the purchase in a physical store or the other way around.[24] To stay in contact with consumers as they move from one retail channel to the next, more companies now emphasize **multichannel retailing**, a term for any

Pop-up stores can function as promotional events to help create buzz in the marketplace, or they can function as temporary outlets for seasonal merchandise.

coordinated effort to reach customers through more than one retail channel.[25]

- **Format innovations.** As companies endlessly search for that magic formula to attract customers and generate profitable sales, they continue to experiment with retailing formats. Recent innovations include *hybrid stores* that combine different types of retailers or different retail companies in the same facility and *pop-up stores* that exist for only a short time and are designed more as attention-getting events than as ongoing retail operations.[26]

- **Retail theater.** Increasingly, retail stores aren't just places to buy things; they're becoming places to research new technologies, learn about cooking, socialize, or simply be entertained for a few minutes while going through the drudgery of picking out the week's groceries—a tactic known as **retail theater**. Many of Apple's retail outlets look more like art galleries than stores, and they offer a multifaceted shopping and learning experience for both kids and adults.[27] CVS's new Beauty 360 shops, which feel more like theater stages than traditional drug stores, give customers greater opportunities to learn about and experiment with various cosmetics.[28]

- **Threat of disintermediation.** Like wholesalers, retailers face the threat of disintermediation if suppliers or customers don't think they add sufficient value or if other types of retailers can do the job better. For instance, with its vast product selection and flexible rental terms, Netflix used its online/mail approach to displace many store-based DVD movie rental outlets. However, as noted earlier, Netflix is now under attack from Redbox's self-service kiosk approach. At the same time, digital-only downloads for both portable devices and full-sized TVs are starting to replace DVD sales and rentals.[29]

No, this isn't some trendy new restaurant—it's a grocery store. Whole Foods Markets aims to make food shopping more enjoyable by making the retail environment more interesting and more pleasant.

multichannel retailing
Coordinated efforts to reach consumers through more than one retail channel

retail theater
The addition of entertainment or education aspects to the retail experience

✓CHECKPOINT

LEARNING OBJECTIVE 3: Identify the major retailing formats, and summarize six trends shaping the future of retailing.

Summary: Retailers come in many shapes and sizes, but the significant store formats include department stores, specialty stores, category killers, discount stores, and off-price retailers. The two most widely known nonstore retailers are online retailers and mail-order firms. The future of retailing is being shaped by such forces as overcapacity, continued growth in online retailing, the growth of multichannel retailing, format innovations such as hybrid stores, the use of retail theater, and the threat of intermediation.

Critical thinking: (1) Would it ever make sense for Amazon to open retail stores? Why or why not? (2) Moving into the future, what effect is online retailing likely to have on the oversupply of retail store space in the United States?

It's your business: (1) How have your shopping patterns changed in the past five years, in terms of how you research purchases and where you make those purchases? (2) Roughly what percentage of all your purchases do you make online? What could store-based retailers do to attract a greater portion of your business?

Key terms to know: wheel of retailing, department stores, specialty stores, discount stores, off-price retailers, online retailers, e-commerce, multichannel retailing, retail theater

Distribution Strategies

Manufacturers and other producers face some critical decisions when selecting marketing channels for their product. Should we sell directly to end users or rely on intermediaries? Which intermediaries should we choose? Should we try to sell our products in every available outlet or limit distribution to a few exclusive outlets? Should we use more than one channel?

Building an effective channel system can take years and, as with all marketing relationships, requires commitment. Successful *trading partners*, a general term for any group of companies involved in a distribution network, work to establish relationships that are mutually beneficial and built on trust.

distribution mix
Combination of intermediaries and channels a producer uses to reach target customers

The ideal **distribution mix**—number and type of intermediaries—varies widely from industry to industry and even from company to company within the same industry. For example, Black & Decker (**www.blackanddecker.com**) distributes its power tools through hundreds of hardware stores and home centers such as Lowe's and The Home Depot along with a wide range of online retailers, including Amazon.com.[30] Black & Decker sells to both consumers and professionals; it wants to reach a broad audience, and its products don't require extensive support from retailers, so these mass market intermediaries make perfect sense. In contrast, Felder (**http://usa.felder-gruppe.at**), an Austrian company that manufacturers top-of-the line woodworking machines for professional use, makes it products available through only three company-owned stores in the entire United States.[31]

Customer Needs and Expectations

The primary function of distribution channels is delivering value to customers, so channel strategy decisions should start with customer needs and expectations.[32] For instance, how do customers want and expect to purchase your product? If you have a food product, for example, are customers willing to drive to specialty stores to buy it, or does it need to be available in their regular grocery stores if you're to have any hope of selling it? Do customers expect to sample or try on products before they buy? Do they need help from trained product experts? What other goods and services do customers expect to be able to purchase at the same time or at least from the same supplier? By understanding these needs and expectations, producers can "work backward," so to speak, from their final customers back to their production facilities, to determine the right mix of channel features and functions.

Product Support Requirements

Products vary widely in the amount of skilled support they may require before and after the sale. Consider a mass spectrometer, the laboratory instrument you see being used in TV shows such as *CSI* to identify unknown substances found at crime scenes. In real life, these complex machines require significant technical skills to sell and to support after the sale, which is why companies that make them, such as Agilent Technologies (**www.agilent.com**) generally sell them through their own salesforces.

Real-Time Updates

Learn More
Distribution decisions: choosing and using channels

Explore the decisions marketing managers face when they choose and manage distribution channels. On mybizlab (**www.mybizlab.com**), you can access Real-Time Updates within each chapter or under Student Study Tools. Otherwise, go to **http://real-timeupdates.com/bia5** and click on "Learn More."

Segmentation, Targeting, and Positioning

Just as producers segment markets, choose target segments, and try to position their products within those segments, marketing intermediaries make strategic marketing decisions regarding their own businesses. For instance, Super Jock'n Jill (**www.superjocknjill.com**) an athletic shoe retailer in Seattle, focuses on quality shoes and clothing for people who are serious about physical fitness. The store offers clinics on nutrition and injury prevention, sponsors races and running clubs, posts race results on its website, and takes other steps to support local walkers and runners.[33]

Tellingly, Super Jock'n Jill doesn't sell shoes from its website, probably because the company emphasizes individualized analysis and fitting by knowledgeable sales staff—and it offers the almost unheard of option of letting shoppers lace on shoes and go for a run to test comfort and performance under real-life conditions. In other words, if you produce mass-market sneakers that are more about fashion than performance, this store won't help you reach your target audience.

Competitors' Distribution Channels

Marketing managers must consider the distribution decisions that competitors have already made or are likely to make in the future. For instance, if you are a new producer trying to break into a particular market, you need to encourage buyers to consider your goods along with the products they already know about, so putting your products side-by-side with the competition in retail outlets is probably the right choice. In other cases, you might want to distance yourself from competitors, either to make direct comparisons more difficult or to avoid being associated with competitive products.

Of course, marketing intermediaries have their own decisions to make about which products to carry and how to allocate their finite "bandwidth," whether it's the number of sales representatives or physical shelf space in a retail store. Because of these capacity limitations in the channel, producers often compete for the attention and resources of intermediaries. In some industries, channel capacity is at such a premium that retailers can demand payments from producers in exchange for carrying their products for an agreed-upon length of time. These *slotting allowances* are now common in the grocery business, for example, particularly for new products. Retailers are naturally reluctant to give up shelf space to unproven products, so slotting allowances help offset the financial risk of bringing in new products. Slotting allowances have grown common enough, in fact, that economic policymakers have begun to investigate their potential impact on competition and consumer prices.[34]

Competition in the channel is not limited to physical stores, of course. With tens of thousands of programs listed in the Apple iTunes "app store" (www.apple.com/iphone/apps-for-iphone), for example, software developers are eager to get the greatest exposure possible. The key to success appears to be creating apps that get users excited, and when large numbers of users download an app, that gets the attention of Apple staff, who can then bestow the coveted and highly visible "Feature App" or "Staff Pick" status on a product.[35]

Established Industry Patterns and Requirements

Over the years, all industries develop certain patterns of distribution. If you try to "buck the system," you might uncover a profitable new opportunity—or you might fail to reach your target customers entirely. Specific industries have other considerations as well, such as the need to get perishable food items to retail locations quickly or government regulations that dictate how and where certain products (hazardous chemicals and pharmaceuticals, for example) can be sold.

Distribution patterns can vary dramatically from country to country, too. Whereas consumers in the United States do a lot of their food shopping at a relatively small number of "big box" retailers, in developing countries most consumers do most of their food shopping at tiny "mom-and-pop" stores and street vendors. In Peru, for instance, with a population less than one-tenth that of the United States, Coca-Cola's retail channel includes 240,000 individual mom-and-pop outlets. From technology investments to support services, working with such a high number of low-volume retailers presents Coke with a very different distribution challenge than it has in the United States.[36]

✓CHECKPOINT

LEARNING OBJECTIVE 4: Explain the strategic decisions that manufacturers must make when choosing distribution channels.

Summary: Defining a distribution strategy requires consideration of such issues as customer needs and expectations; product support requirements; segmentation, targeting, and positioning objectives; competitors' distribution channels; and established distribution patterns and requirements.

Critical thinking: (1) Would two manufactures trying to reach the same customer segment with similar products use identical distribution mixes? Why or why not? (2) Is channel conflict necessarily always bad for everyone involved? Explain your answer.

It's your business: (1) You've probably seen television commercials advertising products that are "not available in stores." How does that lack of availability in stores affect your perception of those products? (2) Would knowing that a manufacturer had to pay a retailer to gain shelf space for a particular product change your perception of that product? Why or why not?

Key terms to know: distribution mix

Considerations in Channel Design and Management

In addition to these strategic considerations, marketing managers need to consider five attributes that help define the function and effectiveness of any distribution channel: *channel length, market coverage, distribution costs, channel conflict,* and *channel organization and control.*

Channel Length

As you no doubt sense by now, distribution channels come in all shapes and sizes. Some channels are short and simple; others are long and complex. Many businesses purchase goods they use in their operations directly from producers, so those distribution channels are short. Boeing, for example, purchases many of the parts and supplies it needs to build airplanes directly from over 10,000 companies.[37] In contrast, the channels for consumer goods are usually longer and more complex (see Exhibit 15.3).

The four primary channels for consumer goods are

- **Producer to consumer.** Producers that sell directly to consumers through catalogs, telemarketing, infomercials, and the Internet are using the shortest, simplest distribution channel. Dell is an excellent example of a company using a producer-to-consumer channel. By selling directly to consumers, Dell gains more control over pricing, promotion, service, and delivery. Although this approach eliminates

EXHIBIT 15.3 Common Distribution Channel Models

Producers can choose from a variety of distribution channel configurations. Channels in consumer markets tend to be longer (with more participants) than channels in organizational markets.

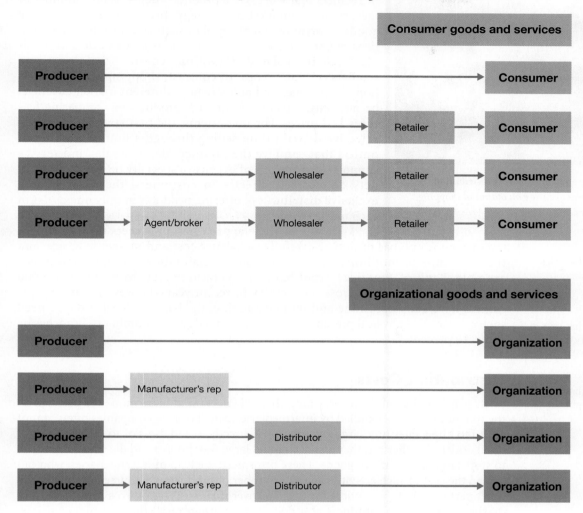

payments to channel members, it also forces producers to handle distribution functions such as storing inventory and delivering products.

- **Producer to retailer to consumer.** Many producers create longer channels by selling their products to retailers, who then resell them to consumers. Weber grills, Benjamin Moore paint, and GE light bulbs are typical of the many products distributed in this way.

- **Producer to wholesaler to retailer to consumer.** Most manufacturers of supermarket and pharmaceutical items rely on longer channels when selling to such retailers as Albertsons, Safeway, and Walgreens. They sell their products to wholesalers such as Supervalu, which in turn sell to the retailers. This approach works particularly well for small producers that lack the resources to sell or deliver merchandise to individual retail sites. It is also beneficial to retailers that lack the space to store container-size shipments of each product they sell.

- **Producer to agent/broker to wholesaler to retailer to consumer.** Additional channel levels are common in certain industries, such as agriculture, where specialists are required to negotiate transactions or to perform interim functions such as sorting, grading, or subdividing the goods.

Marketers of luxury products often use exclusive distribution through carefully selected stores to ensure an optimum shopping experience for their customers.

intensive distribution
Market coverage strategy that tries to place a product in as many outlets as possible

selective distribution
Market coverage strategy that uses a limited number of carefully chosen outlets to distribute products

exclusive distribution
Market coverage strategy that gives intermediaries exclusive rights to sell a product in a specific geographic area

channel conflict
Disagreement or tension between two or more members in a distribution channel, such as competition between channel partners trying to reach the same group of customers

Market Coverage

The appropriate market coverage—the number of wholesalers or retailers that will carry a product—depends on a number of factors in the marketing strategy. Inexpensive convenience goods or organizational supplies such as computer paper and pens sell best if they are available in as many outlets as possible. Such **intensive distribution** requires wholesalers and retailers of many types. In contrast, shopping goods such as home appliances and autos require different market coverage, because customers shop for such products by comparing features and prices. For these items, the best strategy is usually **selective distribution**, selling through a limited number of outlets that can give the product adequate sales and service support. If producers of expensive specialty or technical products do not sell directly to customers, they may choose **exclusive distribution**, offering products in only one outlet in each market area.

With any of these approaches, producers need to choose the optimum number of outlets carefully to balance cost and market coverage, and then continue to monitor market conditions to maintain a healthy balance. For example, Bank of America's retail banking operations grew to more than 6,000 branches as it expanded across the country in recent years. However, as more consumers have adopted online and mobile banking, the bank realized it didn't need such an extensive physical presence and decided to reduce the number of branches by about 10 percent.[38]

Distribution Costs

Costs play a major role in determining channel selection. It takes money to perform all the functions that are handled by intermediaries. Small or new companies often cannot afford to hire a salesforce large enough to sell directly to end users or to call on a host of retail outlets. Neither can they afford to build large warehouses and distribution centers to store large shipments of goods. These firms need the help of intermediaries, who can spread the cost of such activities across a number of products. Of course, intermediaries don't perform all these services for free. To cover their costs and turn a profit, intermediaries generally buy products at a discount and then resell them at higher prices, although as noted earlier, some wholesaling customers are starting to push for per-item cost structures.

Channel Conflict

Individual channel members naturally focus on running their own businesses as profitably as possible, which can lead to **channel conflict**, or disagreement over rights and responsibilities of the organizations in a distribution channel. Channel conflict may arise for a number of reasons, such as when producers provide inadequate support to their channel partners, when markets are oversaturated with intermediaries, when producers try to expand sales by adding additional channels, either on their own or through new intermediaries, or when some intermediaries bear the cost of developing new markets or promoting products only to see the sales revenue go to other intermediaries. For example, conflict between full-service and discount or online retailers continues to be an issue because shoppers can often take advantage of the opportunity to visit full-service retailers to examine products and get information from product experts—and they buy at lower prices from discounters or online stores. The full-service retailers not only lose the sale but end up helplessly helping their competitors make those sales.

Channel Organization and Control

To minimize costs and the potential for channel conflict, channel partners can take steps to work out issues of organization and control. Without some degree of coordination, the various companies involved will pursue their own economic interests, often to the detriment of the channel as a whole.

Producers and intermediaries can achieve this coordination through **marketing systems**, in which the channel participants agree to operate as a cohesive system under the leadership of one of the participants.[39] The agreement can be brought about through *ownership* (when the production and distribution firms are owned by a single company), *contracts* (when the participants have formal agreements that specify their rights and responsibilities, such as the franchising agreements discussed in Chapter 6), and *economic power* (when one player is so big that its economic presence is enough to encourage or even force cooperation from the other participants in the channel).[40] For example, one of the fundamentals of Costco's success is that it sells products in such high volume that many producers can't afford *not* to accommodate Costco's demands for specific price points and packaging configurations. If they don't play by Costco's rules, so to speak, they risk missing out on a major source of distribution for their products.

Exhibit 15.4 offers of a summary of the major factors to consider regarding distribution channels.

marketing systems
Arrangements by which channel partners coordinate their activities under the leadership of one of the partners

EXHIBIT 15.4 Factors That Influence Distribution Channel Choices

Designing a distribution mix is rarely a simple task; here are some of the most important factors to consider.

FACTOR	ISSUES TO CONSIDER
Customer needs and expectations	Where are customers likely to look for your products? How much customer service do they expect from the channel? Can you make your offering more attractive by choosing an unconventional channel?
Product support requirements	How much training do salespeople need to present your products successfully? How much after-sale support is required? Who will answer questions when things go wrong?
Segmentation, targeting, and positioning	Which intermediaries can present your products to target customers while maintaining your positioning strategy?
Competitors' distribution channels	Which channels do your competitors use? Do you need to use the same channels in order to reach your target customers, or can you use different channels to distinguish yourself?
Established industry patterns and requirements	Which intermediaries are already in place? Can you take advantage of them, or do you need to find or create alternatives? Will retailers demand that you use specific wholesalers or distributors?
Channel length	Do you want to deal directly with customers? *Can* you? Do you need to engage other intermediaries to perform vital functions?
Market coverage	Are you going for intensive, selective, or exclusive distribution? Are the right intermediaries available in your target markets? Can they handle the volumes at which you hope to sell?
Distribution costs	How much will intermediaries add to the price that final customers will eventually pay? Put another way, how much of a discount from the retail price will intermediaries expect from you?
Channel conflict	What are the potential sources of channel conflict, both now and in the future? If such conflict can't be avoided, how will you minimize its effect?
Channel organization and control	How much control do you need to maintain as products move through the channel—and how much can you expect to maintain with each potential intermediary? What happens if you lose control? Who leads the channel?

CHECKPOINT

LEARNING OBJECTIVE 5: Identify five key attributes of distribution channel design and management.

Summary: Five key attributes of channel design and management are channel length (the number of layers between producers and target customers), market coverage needs (intense, selective, or exclusive distribution), distribution costs (all the costs involved in using a particular channel), channel conflict (disagreement and tension between channel partners), and channel organization and control (attempts to coordinate the activities of a channel into a cohesive marketing system).

Critical thinking: (1) Does exclusive distribution limit the potential size of a manufacturer's market? Why or why not? (2) Is it ethical for one participant in a channel to have power over the marketing system through sheer economic power alone? Why or why not?

It's your business: (1) Does knowing that a product is available only in selected retail outlets affect your assessment of its quality? (2) Have you ever been skeptical of "shipping and handling" charges added to products you've ordered? Did these charges affect your buying decisions?

Key terms to know: intensive distribution, selective distribution, exclusive distribution, channel conflict, marketing systems

Physical Distribution and Logistics

In addition to assembling and managing the organizations and systems that make up a distribution channel, any firm that deals in physical goods needs to figure out the best way to move those products so they are available to customers at the right place, at the right time, and in the right amount. **Physical distribution** encompasses all the activities required to move finished products from the producer to the consumer, including forecasting, order processing, inventory control, warehousing, materials handling, and transportation (see Exhibit 15.5).

Physical distribution may not be the most glamorous aspect of business, but it is one of the most critical. Behind every luxury storefront or cutting-edge e-commerce website is a vast network of facilities, vehicles, and information systems that make sure products arrive at their destinations. The secret to making it all happen on time is **logistics**, the planning and movement of goods and information throughout the supply chain. As managers try to squeeze cost efficiencies and competitive advantages everywhere they can, logistics has taken on key strategic importance for many companies.

Success in physical distribution requires achieving a competitive level of customer service at the lowest total cost. Doing so requires trade-offs because as the level of service improves, the cost of distribution usually increases. For instance, if you reduce the level of inventory to cut your storage costs, you run the risk of being unable to fill orders in a timely fashion. Or, if you use slower forms of transportation, you can reduce your shipping costs, but you might aggravate customers. The trick is to optimize the total cost of achieving the desired level of service. This optimization requires a careful analysis of each step in the distribution process in relation to every other step in the physical distribution process. Of course, when companies reduce mistakes and

physical distribution
All the activities required to move finished products from the producer to the consumer

logistics
The planning, movement, and flow of goods and related information throughout the supply chain

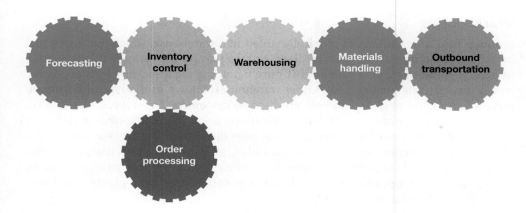

EXHIBIT 15.5

Steps in the Physical Distribution Process

The phases of a distribution system should mesh as smoothly as the cogs in a machine. The objective of the process is to provide a target level of customer service at the lowest overall cost.

eliminate inefficiencies, they can lower costs *and* improve service, which is the goal of every logistics manager.

In-House Operations

The components of the distribution process can be divided into in-house operations and outbound transportation. The in-house steps include forecasting, order processing, inventory control, warehousing, and materials handling.

Forecasting

To control the flow of products through the distribution system, a firm must have an accurate estimate of demand. To some degree, historical data can be used to project future sales, but despite heavy investments in information technology, forecasting remains a major logistical challenge for many companies. The situation can be made even murkier when economic conditions change, such as when consumer purchasing stalled in many categories during the recession that began in December 2007. As one analyst put it, "The fundamental premise that retailers can look at historical sales data and expect there to continue to be a year-over-year increase in consumer spending no longer holds true."[41]

Order Processing

Order processing involves preparing orders for shipment and receiving orders when shipments arrive. It includes a number of activities, such as checking the customer's credit, recording the sale, making the appropriate accounting entries, arranging for the item to be shipped, adjusting the inventory records, and billing the customer. Because order processing involves direct interaction with the customer, it affects a company's reputation for customer service. To keep buyers happy, companies should establish ambitious standards for accuracy and timeliness in order fulfillment.

order processing
Functions involved in receiving and filling customers' orders

Inventory Control

As Chapter 9's discussion of just-in-time systems points out, in an ideal world, a company would always have just the right amount of goods on hand to fill the orders it receives. In reality, however, inventory and sales are seldom in perfect balance. For instance, many firms like to keep a ready supply of finished goods on hand so that they can fill orders as soon as they arrive. But how much inventory is enough? If your inventory is too large, you incur extra expenses for storage space, handling, insurance, and taxes; you also run the risk of product obsolescence. On the other hand, if your inventory is too low, you may lose sales when the product is not in stock. The objective of inventory control is to resolve these issues. Inventory managers decide how much product to keep on hand and when to replenish the supply of goods in inventory. They also decide how to allocate products to customers if orders exceed supply.

Warehousing

warehouse
Facility for storing inventory

distribution centers
Advanced warehouse facilities that specialize in collecting and shipping merchandise

Products held in inventory are physically stored in a **warehouse**, which may be owned by the manufacturer, by an intermediary, or by a private company that leases space to others. Some warehouses are almost purely holding facilities, in which goods are stored for relatively long periods. Other warehouses, known as **distribution centers**, serve as command posts for moving products to customers. In a typical distribution center, goods produced at a variety of locations are collected, sorted, coded, and redistributed to fill customer orders. Leading-edge distribution centers use some of the most advanced technologies in business today, including satellite navigation and communication, voice-activated computers, wireless data services, machine vision, robots, radio frequency identification (RFID) tags and scanners, and planning software that relies on artificial intelligence.

Materials Handling

materials handling
Movement of goods within a firm's warehouse terminal, factory, or store

An important part of warehousing activities is **materials handling**, the movement of goods within and between physical distribution facilities. One main area of concern is storage method—whether to keep supplies and finished goods in individual packages, in large boxes, or in sealed shipping containers. The choice of storage method depends on how the product is shipped, in what quantities, and to which locations. For example, a company that typically sends small quantities of goods to widely scattered customers wouldn't want to use large containers. Materials handling also involves keeping track of inventory so that the company knows where in the distribution process its goods are located and when they need to be moved.

Transportation

For any business, the cost of transportation is normally the largest single item in the overall cost of physical distribution. When choosing a mode of transportation, managers must also evaluate other marketing issues, including storage, financing, sales, inventory size, speed, product perishability, dependability, flexibility, and convenience. Each of the six major modes of transportation has distinct advantages and disadvantages:

- **Rail.** Railroads can carry heavier and more diverse cargo and a larger volume of goods than any other mode of transportation. The obvious disadvantage of trains is that they are constrained to tracks, so they can rarely deliver goods directly to customers.

- **Trucks.** Trucks offer the convenience of door-to-door delivery and the ease and efficiency of travel on public highways. However, large, heavy loads are often better handled by water or rail, and some perishable loads may need to travel by air for the shortest possible delivery time over long distances.

- **Ships and barges.** The cheapest method of transportation is via water, and this is the preferred method for such low-cost bulk items as oil, coal, ore, cotton, and lumber. Water transport is slow, however, and like rail, must be combined with another mode of delivery for most shipments.

- **Air.** Air transport offers the primary advantage of speed over long distances, but it imposes limitations on the size, shape, and weight of shipments. It also tends to be the most expensive form of transportation; however, when speed is a priority, air is usually the only way to go.

- **Pipelines.** For products such as gasoline, natural gas, and coal or wood chips (suspended in liquid), pipelines are an effective mode of transportation. The major downsides are slow speeds and inflexible routes.

Moving goods quickly, accurately, and safely is a strategic priority for every company that depends on physical distribution.

■ **Digital networks.** Any product that exists in or can be converted to digital format, from books and movies to software to product design files, can be transported over the Internet and other digital networks. The range of digital products is fairly limited, of course, but the Internet has certainly revolutionized industries such as entertainment and publishing.

Shippers can also combine the benefits of multiple modes by using **intermodal transportation**. With *containerized shipping*, for instance, standard-size freight containers can be moved from trucks to railroads to ships for maximum flexibility.

For the latest information on wholesaling, retailing, and marketing logistics, visit http://real-timeupdates.com/bia5 and click on Chapter 15.

intermodal transportation
The coordinated use of multiple modes of transportation, particularly with containers that can be shipped by truck, rail, and sea

CHECKPOINT

LEARNING OBJECTIVE 6: Highlight the major components of physical distribution and logistics.

Summary: The major components of a firm's distribution process are order processing, inventory control, warehousing, materials handling, and outbound transportation. When choosing the best method of outbound transportation, such as truck, rail, ship, airplane, and pipeline, you should consider cost, storage, sales, inventory size, speed, product perishability, dependability, flexibility, and convenience.

Critical thinking: (1) Given the huge volume of small packages that Amazon ships every year, should it consider starting its own transportation company instead of giving all that business to FedEx and other shippers? Why or why not? (2) If another high-tech company approached Dell with a partnership proposal to build and operate several distribution centers that would ship both companies' products to customers, what would you advise Dell to do? Why?

It's your business: (1) Online retailers sometimes use free shipping as a promotional appeal. Do you think most consumers really believe the shipping is "free" and not just factored into the product's price? (2) Have you ever paid extra for expedited shipping for an order placed on a website? Was it worth the extra expense?

Key terms to know: physical distribution, logistics, order processing, warehouse, distribution centers, materials handling, intermodal transportation

Behind the
Scenes

Costco Pushes Its Supply Chain to Satisfy Customers

The merchandise sold at Costco may be similar to that of its two main competitors—Sam's Club and BJ's—but Costco aims to be a cut above by offering many unique or unusual items. Its stores also look slightly more upscale than other club stores, the brands it carries have more cachet, and the products are often a bit more expensive, but they still offer extremely good value. And unlike some discounters, Costco does not have everything under the sun.

The stores carry only about 4,000 products, which is a small fraction of the more than 100,000 items stocked by other warehouse clubs and conventional discounters such as Target and Walmart. About 3,000 of Costco's products are a consistent array of carefully chosen basics, from canned tuna to laundry detergent to printer cartridges. The other 1,000 items are a fast-moving assortment of goods such as designer-label clothing, watches, and premium wines. These items change week to week, reinforcing the idea of buying something when you see it because it'll probably be gone next week.

Costco prefers to offer name-brand products and has successfully introduced some branded luxury items such as Kate Spade and Coach purses. However, high-end suppliers such as Cartier and Cannondale flinch at the idea of their goods being sold in a warehouse setting, so carrying those brands isn't always possible. Some suppliers, hoping to protect their higher-end retail customers, have been known to spurn Costco's offers "officially," only to call back later to quietly cut a deal. In other cases, Costco goes on its own treasure hunts, using third-party distributors to track down hot products, even though these "gray market" channels can be unpredictable. And if that doesn't work, Costco can commission another manufacturer to create a lookalike product—leather handbags are one example—with its own Kirkland Signatures label.

To give its millions of members the best prices on everything, Costco negotiates directly—and fiercely—with suppliers. Aiming to be known as the toughest negotiators in the business, Costco's buyers won't let up until they get their target price on the merchandise. Often, the "right" price is determined by how much cheaper Costco can make a product itself. Using this approach, the company has managed to drive down price points in several categories, such as over-the-counter drugs. Costco then passes on the savings to customers, who never pay more than 15 percent above Costco's cost. CEO Jim Sinegal is determined not to let the wheel of retailing take Costco for a spin, either. "When I started, Sears, Roebuck was the Costco of the country, but they allowed someone else to come in under them. We don't want to be one of the casualties. We don't want to turn around and say, 'We got so fancy we've raised our prices,' and all of a sudden a new competitor comes in and beats our prices."

Inventory turnover rate is also key to Costco's financial success. By focusing on fast-selling items, the company moves its merchandise significantly faster than competitors—so quickly, in fact, that it often sells products to shoppers before it has to pay its suppliers.

Costco is rolling through its third decade with strong financial health, a dominant market position, and millions of consumers and business customers that rely on Costco bargains. Online sales continue to expand, with $2 billion of 2008's $72 billion in sales coming through the company's website. International expansion is another item on Costco's strategic menu for the next few years, although the company will maintain a sensible pace of adding only a few new international stores per year, including additional stores in Asia and expansion into Australia and across Europe. For instance, the company thinks Taiwan could support 20 Costco stores and Japan could support 50, but finding enough land for the giant footprint of a warehouse store—typically 15 acres—that is near population centers but not in areas with zoning regulations that prohibit big-box retailers is a particular challenge in some of these countries.[42]

Critical Thinking Questions

1. If customers repeatedly ask Costco to carry certain items that the company thinks are outside its price/quality "comfort zone" (because they're too expensive or not of high enough quality), should it give in and carry the items? Why or why not?

2. Most of the items on Costco's website are available only through Costco; should it expand its online product selection to include more commonly available products, since an online store doesn't have the physical constraints of a brick-and-mortar location? Why or why not?

3. If Costco can't find enough land in, say, Japan, to build its usual store format, should it leverage the Costco brand name anyway and build something such as conventional department stores or grocery stores in these areas? Why or why not?

LEARN MORE ONLINE

Explore the Costco website at www.costco.com. What evidence do you see of "clicks-and-bricks" integration with the physical stores? Are sales promoted online? How much product information is available? Are nonmembers allowed to make purchases online? How does the online experience at Costco compare to another discounter such as Walmart (www.walmart.com) or to a specialty retailer such as Bluefly (www.bluefly.com)? ■

Key Terms

agents and brokers (384)
channel conflict (394)
department stores (386)
discount stores (387)
disintermediation (385)
distribution centers (398)
distribution mix (390)

distribution strategy (381)
distributors (384)
e-commerce (388)
exclusive distribution (394)
full-service merchant wholesalers (384)
intensive distribution (394)

intermodal transportation (399)
logistics (396)
marketing intermediaries (381)
marketing systems (395)
materials handling (398)
merchant wholesalers (384)
multichannel retailing (389)

off-price retailers (387)
online retailers (387)
order processing (397)
physical distribution (396)

retail theater (389)
retailers (381)
selective distribution (394)
specialty stores (387)

warehouse (398)
wheel of retailing (386)
wholesalers (381)

Test Your Knowledge

Questions for Review

1. What is a distribution channel?
2. What are the two main types of intermediaries and how do they differ?
3. What forms of utility do intermediaries create?
4. How does a specialty store differ from a category killer and a discount store?
5. What are some of the main causes of channel conflict?

Questions for Analysis

6. How might a once-valued intermediary find itself threatened with disintermediation?
7. How do marketing systems help avert channel conflict?
8. What are some of the challenges facing retailers and wholesalers today?
9. How could strategic planning help a discount retailer avoid the pitfalls of the wheel of retailing?
10. **Ethical Considerations.** Manufacturers that have been selling to wholesalers and other intermediaries occasionally decide to start selling directly to end customers, which of course puts them in competition with the channel partners that have been selling for them. Even if this is legal, do you think such moves are ethical? Why or why not?

Questions for Application

11. Compare the prices of three products offered at a retail outlet with the prices charged if you purchase those products by mail order (catalog or phone) or over the Internet. Be sure to include extra costs such as handling and delivery charges. Which purchasing format offers the lowest price for each of your products?
12. Imagine that you own a small specialty store selling handcrafted clothing and jewelry. What are some of the nonstore retail options you might explore to increase sales? What are the advantages and disadvantages of each option?
13. **Concept Integration.** Chapter 9 discussed the fact that supply chain management integrates all the activities involved in the production of goods and services from suppliers to customers. What are the benefits of involving wholesalers and retailers in the design, manufacturing, or sale of a company's products?
14. **Concept Integration.** Which of the four basic functions of management discussed in Chapter 7 would be involved in decisions that establish or change a company's channels of distribution? Explain your answer.

Practice Your Knowledge

Sharpening Your Communication Skills

Sales of your DJ equipment (turntables, amplifiers, speakers, mixers, and related accessories) have been falling for months, even as more and more music fans around the world try their hand at being DJs. Magazine reviews and professional DJs give your equipment high marks, your prices are competitive, and your advertising presence is strong. Suspecting that the trouble is in the distribution channel, you and a half dozen fellow executives go on an undercover shopping mission at retail stores that carry your products—and you're quickly appalled by what you see. The salespeople in these stores clearly don't understand your products, so they either give potential customers bad information about your products or steer them to products from your competitors. No wonder sales are falling off a cliff.

The executive team is split over the best way to solve this dilemma; you convince them that retraining your existing channel partners would be less expensive and less disruptive than replacing them. Now you have to convince store managers to let you pull their staffs off the sales floor for a half day so you can train them. Each store will lose a half day's revenue, and each sales rep will lose commissions for that time as well. Draft a short e-mail for the store managers, explaining why the training would be well worth their time. Make up any details you need to complete the message.

Building Your Team Skills

Complicated or confusing shopping experiences are one of the biggest challenges for online retailing. Customers who can't find what they're looking for or who get lost filling out order forms, for instance, often just click away and leave their virtual shopping carts. Unfortunately, consumers don't always perceive the shopping experience the same way, so it's not always easy for website developers to craft the ideal e-retail experience.

Your team's task is to analyze the shopping experience on three competitive e-tail sites and from that analysis decide how a new competitor in the market could create a better customer experience. First, choose a product that everyone in the group finds interesting but that none of you have purchased online before. Then identify three websites that are likely to offer the product; sites such as www.shopzilla.com, www.shopping.com, and www.pricegrabber.com can help with this step if you're not sure where to look. Next, individually (so you can't guide each other), each person in the group should then shop the three sites for your chosen product (if you can't find the exact model, choose something similar). Answer the following questions about each site:

1. Did you have any trouble finding the right website?
2. How difficult was it to find the product you wanted?

3. How much information was available? Complete product details or just a few highlights? A static photo or a three-dimensional (3D) virtual experience that let you explore the product from all angles?
4. How easy was it to compare this product to similar products?
5. Could you find the store's privacy and return policies? Were they acceptable to you?
6. How long did it take to get from the site's homepage to the point at which you could place an order for the specific product?
7. What forms of help were available in case you had questions or concerns?
8. Go ahead and place your item in the shopping cart to simulate placing an order (don't actually buy the product, of course!).

Summarize your impression of each of the three sites, and then compare notes with your teammates. Based on the strengths and weaknesses of each site, identify four pieces of advice for a company that wants to compete against these sites.

Expand Your Knowledge

Discovering Career Opportunities

Retailing is a dynamic, fast-paced field with many career opportunities in both store and nonstore settings. In addition to hiring full-time employees when needed, retailers of all types often hire extra employees on a temporary basis for peak selling periods, such as the year-end holidays. You can find out about seasonal and year-round job openings by checking newspaper classified ads, looking for signs in store windows, browsing the websites of online retailers, and checking Craigslist (www.craigslist.org) and other sites.

1. Select a major retailer, such as a chain store in your area or a retailer on the Internet. Is this a specialty store, discount store, department store, or another type of retailer?
2. Visit the website of the retailer you selected. Does the site discuss the company's hiring procedures? If so, what are they? What qualifications are required for a position with the company?
3. Research your chosen retailer using library sources or online resources. Is this retailer expanding? Is it profitable? Has it recently acquired or been acquired by another firm? What are the implications of this acquisition for job opportunities?

Developing Your Research Skills

Find an article in a business journal or newspaper (online or print editions) discussing changes a company is making to its distribution strategy or channels. For example, is a manufacturer selling products directly to consumers? Is a physical retailer offering goods via a company website? Is a company eliminating an intermediary? Has a nonstore retailer decided to open a physical store? Is a category killer opening smaller stores? Has a major retail tenant closed its store in a mall?

1. What changes in the company's distribution structure or strategy have taken place? What additional changes, if any, are planned?
2. What were the reasons for the changes? What role, if any, did e-commerce play in the changes?
3. If you were a stockholder in this company, would you view these changes as positive or negative? What, if anything, might you do differently?

Improving Your Tech Insights: Supply Chain Integration Standards

How do Amazon's computers know which book to reorder from its suppliers when you order one from Amazon's website? Who makes sure RFID readers know how to detect RFID tags accurately and make sure databases know what to do with the data? How does every one of the billions of barcodes now in use get the right combination of black and white stripes? All these decisions are guided by industry groups that define the standards and technologies that make sure supply chains work together, from producers to wholesalers to retailers.

Supply chain standardization might not be the most pulse-pounding technology from a consumer's point of view, but global business simply wouldn't work without it—and consumers benefit from the lower prices and better service that standards enable. Moving forward, advances in supply-chain integration promise to remove billions of dollars of errors and inefficiencies from supply chains in many industries.

Visit the website of GS1 (www.gs1.org), a global, not-for-profit organization that develops and oversees a number of supply chain standards. The brochure "What Is GS1?," available on the About Us page, explains the importance of global business standards and describes bar codes, RFID tagging, the Global Data Synchronization Network, and other efforts. In a brief e-mail to your instructor, describe one of the GS1 standards and explain how it helps businesses operate more efficiently and serve customers more effectively.

Video Discussion

Access the Chapter 15 video discussion in the End of Chapter Assignments section at www.mybizlab.com.

PEARSON my*biz*lab

Log on to www.mybizlab.com to access the following study and assessment aids associated with this chapter:

- Interactive exercises
- Pre/post test
- Real-Time Updates
- Video application
- Customized study plans
- Biz Skills Simulations
- Quick Learning Guide

If you are not using mybizlab, you can access Real-Time Updates and Quick Learning Guides through http://real-timeupdates.com/bia5. The Quick Learning Guide (located under "Learn More" on the website) provides all six Checkpoints in a handy two-page format to help you study for exams or review important concepts whenever you need a quick refresher.

CHAPTER 16
Customer Communication

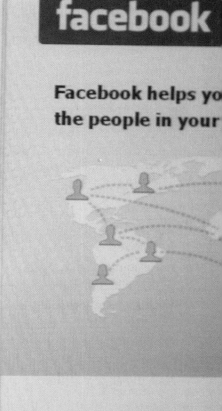

Behind the Scenes

Pulling in the Crowds at SeaWorld San Antonio

www.seaworldsanantonio
.com

Theme parks offer plenty of ways for visitors to find a few hours of fun in the sun, enjoy some entertainment, and maybe give themselves a good scare on the roller coaster. From a marketing point of view, however, there is the never-ending challenge of creating new reasons to visit. Consumers who've "been there, done that" at a particular theme park are understandably tempted to take their entertainment dollars somewhere else unless the park can offer fresh attractions to lure them back.

To quickly build interest in the new Journey to Atlantis water ride, SeaWorld San Antonio turned to a new generation of customer communication tools.

One of three SeaWorld parks run by Busch Entertainment Corporation (the other two are in San Diego and Orlando), the 250-acre SeaWorld San Antonio, is the world's largest marine life theme park. In addition to numerous marine life exhibits, shows, and other attractions, the park offers several hair-raising rides, including the eight-story-high Great White roller coaster and the 65-mile-per-hour Steel Eel "hypercoaster." Both are exciting rides, but coaster enthusiasts who've already ridden them might not feel any immediate urge to revisit SeaWorld.

But they certainly would be interested in a new ride, and SeaWorld was ready to offer one with Journey to Atlantis, a combination roller coaster/water ride. Although not a thrill ride in the sense of pushing the limits of speed and performing gravity-defying stunts, Journey to Atlantis does offer great views of San Antonio at the top and a grand splashdown into a lake awaiting riders at the bottom—a perfect way to cool off on a hot Texas afternoon.

With Journey to Atlantis nearing completion ahead of schedule, the customer communication team needed to get the word out quickly about this new ride. If you were public relations specialist Kami Huyse, how would you identify the right audience and reach out to them with information about the new ride? How would you develop relationships with coaster enthusiasts—people who don't hesitate to travel just about anywhere to try a new ride—and encourage them to add Journey to Atlantis to their must-try lists? And how would you build excitement and energy around a product that really needs to be experienced to be fully appreciated?[1] ∎

Introduction

When SeaWorld San Antonio (profiled in the chapter-opening Behind the Scenes) needed to generate awareness for its new Journey to Atlantis ride, the company and its communication team had a dizzying array of choices for reaching out to potential park visitors. This chapter, our final discussion of the marketing function, explains how marketers set communication goals, define messages, and choose from the ever-growing array of media options to reach target audiences.

Customer Communication: Challenges, Strategies, and Issues

Not long ago, marketing communication was largely about companies broadcasting carefully scripted messages to a mass audience that often had few, if any, ways to respond. Moreover, customers and other interested parties had few ways to connect with one another to ask questions about products, influence company decisions, or offer each other support.

However, a variety of technologies have enabled and inspired a new approach to customer communication. In contrast to the "we talk, you listen" mindset of the past, this new **social communication model** is *interactive* and *conversational*. As corporate communication specialist Caroline Kealey puts it, traditional practices of "issuing messages through static,

social communication model
Approach to communication based on interactive social media and conversational communication styles

hierarchical, and largely one-way channels are fading into obsolescence."[2] Today's audiences are no longer passive recipients of messages but demand to be active participants in a meaningful conversation. On the surface, this approach might look like it has just added a few new electronic media tools to the traditional arsenal of television, radio, newspapers, and magazines. However, as Exhibit 16.1 shows, the changes are much deeper and more profound. "Social Media in the Marketing Process" on page 422 discusses this new model in more detail.

In this new world of interactive communication, it's more vital than ever to have a strategy that (1) establishes *clear communication goals*, (2) defines *compelling messages* to help achieve those goals, and (3) outlines a *cost-effective media mix* to engage target audiences.

Establishing Communication Goals

Communication activities can meet a wide range of marketing goals, but only if these activities are crafted with clear goals based on where the target audience is in the purchasing cycle.[3]

- **Generating awareness.** People obviously can't buy things they don't know about, so *awareness advertising* and similar efforts seek to introduce new companies or new products.

- **Providing information and creating positive emotional connections.** The next step is to build logical and emotional acceptance for the company and its products. For example, most consumers know about Walmart's low prices, but in recent years, the retailer's image had grown stale and uninspiring in the minds of many shoppers. A new ad campaign that reminded shoppers they could save money *and* live better created a positive emotional bond that helped Walmart turn sales around in a tough economy.[4]

EXHIBIT 16.1

The Social Model of Customer Communication

The new social model of customer communication differs from the conventional promotion model in a number of significant ways.

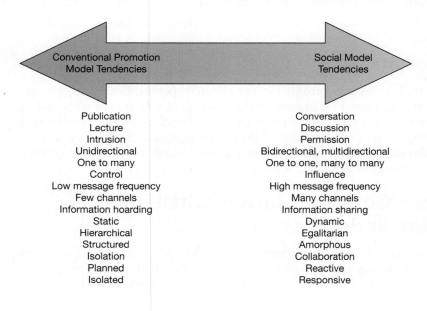

Conventional Promotion Model Tendencies	Social Model Tendencies
Publication	Conversation
Lecture	Discussion
Intrusion	Permission
Unidirectional	Bidirectional, multidirectional
One to many	One to one, many to many
Control	Influence
Low message frequency	High message frequency
Few channels	Many channels
Information hoarding	Information sharing
Static	Dynamic
Hierarchical	Egalitarian
Structured	Amorphous
Isolation	Collaboration
Planned	Reactive
Isolated	Responsive

- **Building preference.** If buyers accept a product as a potential solution to their needs, the next step is to encourage them to prefer it over all other products they may be considering.

- **Stimulating action.** Now comes the most critical step—convincing the consumer or organization to act on that product preference to make a purchase, using a compelling *call to action.*

- **Reminding past customers.** Past customers are often the best prospects for future sales, so *reminder advertising* tells these buyers that a product is still available or a company is ready to serve their needs.

The nature of these goals varies by market segment and product category. Generally speaking, the more complicated and important the purchase is, the more comprehensive the communication effort needs to be. Shopping and specialty products, for instance, require providing more information, often spread out over several communication activities—such as a television commercial that introduces a product and encourages consumers to visit a website to learn more and from there to visit a retail store to talk with a sales representative.

Defining Customer Messages

After establishing communication goals, the marketer's next step is to define the **core message.** This is the single most important idea the company hopes to convey to the target audience about a product. Ideally, the message can be expressed in a single sentence, such as "The Caterpillar 385C Ultra High Demolition Excavator can increase productivity at every stage of the most demanding demolition projects."[5] Notice how this statement highlights a key customer benefit (productivity) and identifies the target audience (companies that demolish buildings).

Of course, no one is going to shell out a million dollars for a 100-ton piece of equipment based on a single sentence. Think of the core message as the foundation on which the marketing team can build successive layers of detail and explanation, with each communication effort expanding on the core message. For instance, advertisements try to communicate a few key points quickly, without going into great detail. A sales presentation could go into more detail, and a technical brochure or a website can provide extensive information.

As Exhibit 16.1 notes, one of the most significant changes that the social communication model has brought to marketing is that companies now have far less control of their messages. After a message is released into the wild, so to speak, bloggers, reporters, industry analysts, and other parties will begin to repeat it, enhance it, change it, or even refute it. Starting with a clear and compelling core message increases the chances that the message will reach its target audience intact. If the core message is not clear or not credible, it will surely be altered or refuted as it passes from one outside commentator to the next.

core message
The single most important idea an advertiser hopes to convey to the target audience about its products or the company

Assembling the Communication Mix

With clear goals and a compelling message, the next step is to share that message using a **communication mix**, also known as a *media mix* or *promotional mix*, through some combination of advertising, direct marketing, personal selling, sales promotion, social media, and public relations. Crafting the optimal mix is one of the toughest decisions marketing managers face and requires constant monitoring as markets change. For example, Reckitt Benckiser, a leading maker of consumer packaged goods, recently shifted $20 million from its television (TV) advertising budget to online video in order to reach the expanding online audience.[6]

To assemble the best mix, companies have to consider a range of product, market, and distribution channel factors. Product factors include the type of product, its price range, and its stage in the product life cycle (see page 358). For example, an innovative technical product may require intensive educational efforts in the introduction and growth stages to help customers understand and appreciate its value. Market factors include the type of intended customers (consumers versus organizations), the nature of the competition, and the size and geographic spread of the target market.

communication mix
Blend of communication vehicles—advertising, direct marketing, personal selling, sales promotion, social media, and public relations—that a company uses to reach current and potential customers

push strategy
Promotional strategy that focuses on intermediaries, motivating them to promote or *push* products toward end users

pull strategy
Promotional strategy that stimulates consumer demand via advertising and other communication efforts, thereby creating a *pull* effect through the channel

integrated marketing communications (IMC)
Strategy of coordinating and integrating communication and promotion efforts with customers to ensure greater efficiency and effectiveness

Channel factors include the need for intermediaries, the type of intermediaries available, and the ability of those companies to help with communication. A key decision is whether to focus communication efforts on the intermediaries or on final customers. With a **push strategy**, a producer focuses on intermediaries, trying to persuade wholesalers or retailers to carry its products and promote those products to *their* customers. Conversely, with a **pull strategy**, the producer appeals directly to end customers. Customers learn of the product through these communication efforts and request it from retailers (in the case of consumers) or wholesalers (in the case of business customers). For example, if a television commercial encourages you to "ask your pharmacist" about a specific product, the company is using a pull strategy. Many companies use both push and pull strategies to increase the impact of their promotional efforts.

With the number of communication vehicles continuing to expand, the need for companies to "speak with one voice" becomes even greater. **Integrated marketing communications (IMC)** is a strategy of coordinating and integrating all communication and promotional efforts to ensure clarity, consistency, and maximum communications impact.[7] However, companies obviously can't control all the messages their target audiences receive, particularly now that customers are empowered through social media. While the company is working to integrate its outgoing communication efforts, the customer is also integrating all the incoming messages he or she is receiving (see Exhibit 16.2).

Communication Laws and Ethics

As marketing and selling grow increasingly complex, so do the legal ramifications of marketing communication. In the United States, the Federal Trade Commission (FTC) has the authority to impose penalties against advertisers who violate federal standards for truthful advertising. Other federal agencies have authority over advertising in specific industries, such as transportation and financial services. Individual states have additional laws that apply. The legal aspects of promotional communication can be quite complex and vary from state to state and from country to country, but if you are involved in customer communication in any form you need to pay close attention to the following legal aspects:[8]

- **Marketing and sales messages must be truthful and nondeceptive.** The FTC considers messages to be deceptive if they include statements that are likely to mislead reasonable customers and the statements are an important part of the purchasing decision. Failing to include important information is also considered deceptive. The FTC also looks at *implied claims*—claims you don't explicitly make but that can be inferred from what you do or don't say.

- **You must back up your claims with evidence.** Offering a money-back guarantee or providing letters from satisfied customers is not enough, for instance; you must still be able to support your claims with objective evidence such as a survey or scientific study.

EXHIBIT 16.2

Message Integration in Customer Communication

To maximize efficiency and consistency, companies need to integrate their customer communication efforts. However, customers also integrate messages on the receiving end—including messages that might contradict messages from the company.

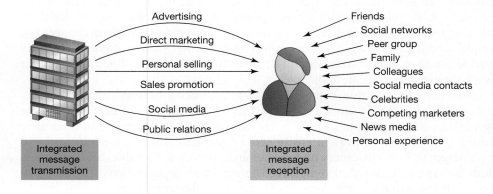

■ **Marketing and sales messages are considered binding contracts in many states.** If you imply or make an offer and then can't fulfill your end of the bargain, you can be sued for breach of contract.

■ **In most cases, you can't use a person's name, photograph, or other identity without permission.** You can use images of people considered to be public figures as long as you don't unfairly imply that they endorse your message.

Consumer privacy provides a great example of the legal and ethical complexities in contemporary marketing communication. Technology keeps enabling new ways to peer into people's lives, including *behavioral targeting*, in which companies serve up online ads based on a person's web surfing behavior; the capture and analysis of information that people divulge on Facebook, Twitter, and other social media; and the creation of detailed personal profiles by pulling together everything from credit histories to mobile phone calling and data retrieval patterns.[9] Expect privacy to remain a hot topic in coming years as society continually tries to identify the "shifting boundaries between public and private spaces and purposes," in the words of *Harvard Business Review* senior editor Lew McCreary.[10]

Regarding privacy and other aspects of communication, responsible companies recognize the vital importance of ethical standards. Professional associations such as the American Association of Advertising Agencies (www.aaaa.org), the Direct Marketing Association (www.the-dma.org), and the American Marketing Association (www.marketingpower.com) devote considerable time and energy to ethical issues in marketing, including ongoing education for practitioners and self-regulation efforts aimed at avoiding or correcting ethical lapses. For instance, the National Advertising Review Council (www.narcpartners.org), whose members include advertisers, agencies, and the general public, works with the Better Business Bureau to investigate and resolve complaints of deceptive advertising in order to foster public trust.[11]

✓CHECKPOINT

LEARNING OBJECTIVE 1: Describe the three major tasks in crafting a communication strategy, and identify four important legal aspects of marketing communication.

Summary: The three major tasks in developing a communication strategy are establishing clear communication goals, defining compelling messages to help achieve those goals, and outlining a cost-effective media mix to engage target audiences. Four important issues in communications law are making sure advertising claims are truthful and nondeceptive, supporting claims with real evidence, recognizing that marketing and sales messages are contractual obligations in many cases, and avoiding the unauthorized use of a person's name or image.

Critical thinking: (1) Why do credit card companies target students even though most have little or no income? (2) Would it be wise for a manufacturer that is new to a particular industry (and unknown within it) to invest most of its promotional resources in a pull strategy? Why or why not?

It's your business: (1) What is your "core message" as a future business professional? How would you summarize, in one sentence, what you can offer a company? (2) Does knowing that advertisers are trying to track your online behavior in order to target you with personalized ads make you want to limit or change your web surfing? Do you think advertisers have the right to do this? Why or why not?

Key terms to know: social communication model, core message, communication mix, push strategy, pull strategy, integrated marketing communications (IMC)

Advertising

Advertising can be defined as the "placement of announcements and persuasive messages in time or space purchased in any of the mass media."[12] In other words, advertisers buy time on radio or television and space in print and online media. Two key points here are that advertising is paid for and it is carried by someone else's medium. (Companies sometimes own the media in which they advertise, but this is not the usual case.) This section offers a quick overview of the various types of advertising, the appeals most commonly used in advertising, and the advantages and disadvantages of major advertising media.

Types of Advertising

Companies can use advertising for a variety of purposes. The most common type, **product advertising**, promotes the features and benefits of specific products. The term **comparative advertising** is applied to ads that specifically highlight how one product is better than its competitors. Strong comparative messages can boost sales, but the approach is risky. Competitors are likely to sue if they believe their products have been portrayed unfairly, and sometimes *attack ads* can decrease sales for an entire product category by emphasizing the negative aspects of the products in question.[13]

In some countries, comparative ads are tightly regulated and sometimes banned, but that is clearly not the case in the United States. Indeed, the FTC encourages advertisers to use direct product comparisons with the intent of better informing customers. Comparative advertising is frequently used by competitors vying with the market leader, but it is useful whenever a company believes it has some specific product strengths that are important to customers. However, given the damage that unfair comparative advertising can cause, both federal regulations and industry guidelines established by the American Association of Advertising Agencies address the issues of fairness and accuracy in comparative advertising.[14]

Institutional advertising is designed to create goodwill and build a desired image for a company rather than to promote specific products. For example, a firm might promote its commitment to sustainable business practices or workforce diversity. Institutional ads that address public issues are called **advocacy advertising**. With recent efforts to overhaul health insurance in the United States, for instance, many companies with a financial stake in the outcome have been using advertising to present their points of view.[15]

Advertising can also be classified according to the sponsor. *National advertising* is sponsored by companies that sell products on a nationwide basis. The biggest national advertisers spend a *lot* on advertising, with companies such as Verizon and AT&T spending over a billion dollars a year.[16] In contrast, *local advertising* is sponsored by a local merchant; grocery store ads are a good example. *Cooperative advertising* involves a financial arrangement in which companies with products sold nationally share the costs of local advertising with local marketing intermediaries.

Advertising Appeals

A key decision in planning a promotional campaign is choosing the **advertising appeal**, the creative tactic designed to capture the audience's attention and promote preference for the product or company being advertised. Marketers can choose from seven basic appeals (note that these appeals are not limited to advertising; they are used in other types of persuasive communication as well):[17]

- **Logic.** The basic approach with a logical appeal is to make a claim based on a rational argument supported by solid evidence. Not surprisingly, business-to-business advertising relies heavily on logical appeals, because businesses have logical concerns—profitability, process improvements, quality, and other financial and technical concerns. However, marketers should not ignore the emotional aspects of business purchasing. Managers put their reputations and sometimes their careers on the line when they make major purchase decisions, so advertisers need to consider these emotional elements. Logical appeals are also used in consumer advertising whenever the purchase decision has a rational component and logic might help persuade buyers to consider or prefer a particular product.

- **Emotion.** An emotional appeal calls on audience feelings and sympathies rather than facts, figures, and rational arguments (see Exhibit 16.3 on the next page). Emotional appeals range from sentimental to terrifying. On the lighter side, flowers, greeting cards, and gifts are among the products usually sold with a positive emotional appeal. Other companies appeal to a broad range of fears: personal and family safety, financial security, social acceptance, and business success or failure. To be effective, appeals to fear must be managed carefully. Laying it on too thick can anger the audience or even cause them to block out the message entirely.

- **Humor.** In a world cluttered with advertising, humor is frequently used to capture people's attention. However, humor can be tricky; sometimes it can offend audiences, tainting the brand, or the humor can be so memorable that audiences remember the joke but not the product being advertised.[18]

- **Celebrity.** The thinking behind celebrity involvement in advertising is that people will be more inclined to use products endorsed by a celebrity because they will identify with and want to be like this person (no matter how far-fetched such aspirations might be at a purely logical level). Celebrities can also bring new excitement, humor, energy, and even perceived value to a product. In addition to being expensive, however, celebrity endorsements can be risky because the brand's image becomes linked to the celebrity's image, including whatever behavioral missteps and other image problems the celebrity experiences in his or her personal life.[19]

- **Sex.** Sex-oriented appeals are the most controversial type of advertising, in terms of both social reaction and promotional effectiveness. Although the phrase "sex sells" is often repeated, it isn't always true. Sexual appeals can definitely be effective, but the degree of effectiveness varies by product, audience, and the role of the sexual imagery or narrative in the advertising. For example, sexual appeals have been shown to be more effective with audiences who have a low level of emotional or intellectual engagement with the purchase than with audiences who are more involved.[20]

- **Music.** With its ability to create emotional bonds and "embed" itself in listeners' memories, music can be a powerful aspect of advertising. Marketers can take several approaches to integrating music into radio, television, or online advertising, including composing *jingles* specifically for commercials, licensing popular songs for use in commercials (although these fees can run into the millions of dollars for hit songs), or working with emerging artists to write songs specifically with advertising use in mind.[21]

- **Scarcity.** If a product is in limited supply or available only for a limited time, advertisers can use this scarcity to encourage consumer responses.

Note that these appeals are not mutually exclusive. For example, ads can use humor to catch an audience's attention and then use emotion to strengthen the bond with the brand or logic to show the superiority of a product.

Real-Time Updates

Learn More
Super Bowl commercials: relive the best of the best

See why the Super Bowl has become an annual showcase of television advertising. On mybizlab (www.mybizlab.com), you can access Real-Time Updates within each chapter or under Student Study Tools. Otherwise, go to http://real-timeupdates.com/bia5 and click on "Learn More."

EXHIBIT 16.3 **Emotional and Logical Appeals in Marketing Messages**

Both these websites promote materials used in homes, but their respective messages use different blends of logical and emotional appeals. Premier Building Systems relies primarily on logical appeals in its messages to architects and home builders. In contrast, in its messages to homeowners, Gladiator GarageWorks balances logical and emotional appeals in describing its garage organizers.

To help convince home builders to use its innovative panel system instead of traditional frame construction, Premier Building Systems focuses on logical factors such as cost, efficiency, and quality.

Gladiator® GarageWorks uses a combination of logical and emotional appeals by promising to make your garage "a place to work, entertain and show off to your friends and neighbors."

Gladiator® GarageWorks website photograph used with permission of Whirlpool Corporation

Advertising Media

Advertising appeals have remained fairly consistent over the years, but **advertising media**, or channels of communication, have been in a state of almost-constant change for the past several decades. For example, it wasn't too long ago that advertisers could rely on three national television networks and a handful of popular magazines to quickly reach the majority of consumers in the United States. Today, these established media are fighting for a declining share of advertisers' budgets as other media options seem to pop up every week. The proliferation of media has created two significant challenges: the *fragmentation* of audiences into larger numbers of smaller groups and the growing *clutter* of advertising messages. Much of the work advertising teams engage in focuses on meeting these two challenges.

advertising media
Communications channels, such as newspapers, radio, television, and the World Wide Web

Choosing the right media can be as important as selecting the type of advertising and the advertising appeal. A *media plan* outlines the advertising budget, the schedule of when ads will appear, and a discussion of the **media mix**—the combination of print, broadcast, online, and other media to be used in the campaign. To create the media mix, advertising experts factor in the characteristics of the target audience, the types of media that will reach the largest audience in the most cost-effective way, and the strengths and weaknesses of the various media as they relate to the product and its marketing message (see Exhibit 16.4 on the next page).

media mix
Combination of print, broadcast, online, and other media used for an advertising campaign

The next several years should be an interesting time for advertisers as they sort through the ever-expanding range of media options. For instance, as more companies gain experience with online advertising and as consumers spend more time online, the various forms of online media will continue to capture a larger share of media budgets. Like its competitor Reckitt Benckiser mentioned earlier in the chapter, consumer goods giant Procter & Gamble is shifting more of its huge advertising budget online because that's where the audience is. "Our media strategy is pretty simple: Follow the consumer," says global marketing officer Marc Pritchard. "And the consumer is becoming more and more engaged in the digital world."[22] At the same time, a number of companies that were launched in the online environment, including Amazon.com (mixed merchandise), Hulu (TV and movies), Zappos (shoes and accessories), and Kayak (travel), have used television and other offline media as a way to expand sales.[23]

Two particular trends are likely to shape advertising media in the coming years. First, the lines between advertising, entertainment, and *value-added content* (such as informative articles and how-to videos) will continue to blur. For example, more advertisers are borrowing storytelling techniques and other methods from the entertainment industry to make their TV commercials, online videos, and other ads more entertaining and thus more likely to be watched.[24] **Product placement**, in which companies pay to have their products displayed or used in television shows, movies, and video games, is already a multibillion-dollar business and is sure to grow as advertisers respond to the increasing number of ways consumers have to ignore, skip, or block ads—and as content producers look for new cash flow opportunities. Product placement ranges from subtle brand displays in the background of a scene to active engagement with a product, such as when talk show host Bonnie Hunt got a makeover in a Walgreens drug store.[25]

product placement
The paid display or use of products in television shows, movies, and video games

Second, technical innovations will continue to create new advertising tools and techniques, including the behavioral targeting methods described on page 428 and more sophisticated tracking and pricing models that tie advertising costs to measurable results.[26] To counter the low response rates of conventional banner ads on websites, for instance, marketers are trying new ways

 Real-Time Updates

Learn More
Inventing new ways to engage the audience

See how prominent television advertisers are responding to the changing world of media. On mybizlab (**www.mybizlab.com**), you can access Real-Time Updates within each chapter or under Student Study Tools. Otherwise, go to **http://real-timeupdates.com/bia5** and click on "Learn More."

EXHIBIT 16.4 Advantages and Disadvantages of Major Advertising Media

Each medium has strengths and weaknesses; companies often combine two or more media in an advertising campaign to maximize their promotional effectiveness.

MEDIUM	ADVANTAGES	DISADVANTAGES
Newspapers	Extensive market coverage; low cost; short lead time for placing ads; good local market coverage; geographic selectivity; credibility	Poor graphic quality; short life span; cluttered pages; visual competition from other ads; printed papers have rapidly declining readership in many cities
Television	Great impact; broad reach; appealing to senses of sight, sound, and motion; creative opportunities for demonstration; high attention; entertainment carryover	High cost for production and air time; less audience selectivity; long preparation time; commercial clutter; short life for message; vulnerability to being skipped or muted; losing ground to new media options
Radio	Low cost; high frequency; immediacy; highly portable; high geographic and demographic selectivity	No visual possibilities; short life for message; commercial clutter; lower attention than television; declining audience share; low level of engagement
Magazines	Good production quality; long life; local and regional market selectivity; authority and credibility; multiple readers extend reach of each issue; close bond with readers	Limited demonstration possibilities; long lead time between placing and publishing ads; lots of ad clutter; high cost; declining readership for many titles
Product placement	Offers a way to get around viewers' advertising filters; chance for high visibility in the right program, movie, or game	Limited choice of vehicles; unpredictable; effectiveness is linked to the popularity of the programming; risk of overuse could reduce effectiveness over time
Fixed web (from stationary computers)	Rich media options and interactivity can make ads more compelling and more effective; changes and additions can be made quickly and easily in most cases; webpages can provide an almost unlimited amount of information; can be measured and personalized through tracking and targeting capabilities; instant links to online retailing and influence on store-based retail sales; growing audiences for Internet radio and video	Extreme degree of audience fragmentation (millions of websites); increasing clutter (such as pop-up ads); technical glitches can interrupt ad display; not as portable as magazines, newspapers, or mobile web; ad-blocking software can prevent ads from being displayed
Mobile web (from mobile phones and other handheld devices)	In addition to almost every advantage of the fixed web other than display size: highly portable; constant, "always-on" presence (most people have their phones with them much of the time); opportunity for location-based advertising; possibilities for narrow targeting	Many users won't tolerate advertising intrusions via mobile phone; small screen size limits display possibilities

of integrating advertising with site content.[27] The number of *hybrid media* will grow, such as interactive purchasing systems that combine product placement with direct-response retailing so that consumers can use their TV remotes to buy products shown in a program.[28] As online video expands, so too will connections with advertising and retailing, including software that turns images of people and products in a video into clickable hyperlinks—so that a viewer can instantly order the same clothes an actor or host is wearing, for example.[29]

√CHECKPOINT

LEARNING OBJECTIVE 2: Identify the major types of advertising, the most common advertising appeals, and the most important advertising media.

Summary: The major types of advertising based on the type of message are *product* advertising (promotes the benefits of a product), *comparative* advertising (compares a product to competitors' products), *institutional* advertising (promotes a company or other organization), and *advocacy* advertising (conveys information and opinions about public issues). Advertising can also be categorized by sponsor, including *national, local,* and *cooperative* advertising. The most common advertising appeals are logic, emotion, humor, celebrity, sex, music, and scarcity. Major advertising media include newspapers, television, radio, magazines, product placement, fixed web (from computers), and mobile web (from mobile phones and other handheld devices).

Critical thinking: (1) Do fragmented media make it easier or harder for marketers to engage in segmented or concentrated marketing? Explain your answer. (2) Why would a company such as McDonald's, which is already well known to virtually all consumers in the United States, continue to spend heavily on advertising?

It's your business: (1) Have you ever believed that you could create better advertising for a product than the company behind the product created? If so, explain the type of appeal you would've used and why. (2) Do you find that you tend to watch and listen to most television commercials, or do you mute or channel surf during commercials? If you pay attention to commercials, what is it that captures your interest?

Key terms to know: advertising, product advertising, comparative advertising, institutional advertising, advocacy advertising, advertising appeal, advertising media, media mix, product placement

Direct Marketing

Although it is similar to advertising in many respects, **direct marketing**, defined as direct communication other than personal sales contacts, differs in three important ways. First, it uses *personally addressable* media such as letters and e-mail messages to deliver targeted messages to individual consumers or organizational purchasers. Second, direct marketing doesn't involve the purchase of time or space in other media; the advertiser controls the delivery mechanism and decides when, where, and how the message is delivered. Third, direct marketing has a *direct response* aspect that often isn't present in advertising. While effective direct marketing works to build lasting relationships with customers, its primary emphasis is generating sales *now*. In fact, according to the Direct Marketing Association (www.the-dma.org), a trade group of advertisers and marketing agencies, direct marketing efforts on average yield twice the return on investment of other marketing efforts.[30]

direct marketing
Direct communication other than personal sales contacts designed to stimulate a measurable response

Direct Marketing Techniques

Direct marketing has evolved dramatically from its early days, when pioneering promotional efforts such as the Sears catalog in the late 1800s helped establish *mail order* on a massive scale.[31] Direct marketing is now a computer-intensive multimedia effort that includes mail, telephone, and online media. The heart of any direct marketing effort is a **customer database** that contains contact histories, purchase records, and profiles of each buyer or potential buyer. (Direct marketing is sometimes referred to as *database marketing*.) The data can range from basic demographic information to records of all customer contacts to detailed purchasing records and other behavioral data. These databases also play a vital role in relationship marketing because they enable a company to personalize its interaction with every customer.

customer database
Computer file that contains contact histories, purchase records, and profiles of each buyer or potential buyer

The *measurability* of direct marketing is one of its greatest appeals. If you mail a promotional flyer to 1,000 people and 36 of them call to place an order, you know the campaign had a 3.6 percent response rate. Because direct responses are directly measurable (unlike many advertising efforts), direct marketing lends itself to constant experimentation and improvement. This is particularly true with online direct marketing efforts, where changes can be made cheaply and quickly.

Just as many retailers now reach out to customers in multiple ways through multichannel retailing (see page 388), many companies now integrate direct marketing with other communication efforts in *multichannel marketing campaigns*. For instance, customer databases are now expanding to include everything from widget usage on social networks to mobile web and phone usage.[32]

Direct Marketing Media

The catalogs that helped launch direct marketing over a hundred years ago are still a force today, as a look inside any mailbox in the country will confirm. Here is a brief look at the major media used in direct marketing:

direct mail
Printed materials addressed to individual consumers, households, or business contacts

- **Mail.** The largest category of direct media is **direct mail**, printed material addressed to an individual or a household.[33] Direct mail has the key advantage of being able to put promotional materials, ranging from simple letters and glossy catalogs to DVDs and product samples, directly into the hands of a target audience. Direct mail also plays an important role in driving shoppers to e-commerce websites.

- **E-mail.** The ability to send millions of messages in a matter of minutes at almost no cost made e-mail a hit with direct marketers—and practically destroyed e-mail as a viable communication medium in the minds of some users tired of the deluge of unwanted "spam." The spam problem notwithstanding, e-mail marketing remains the fastest-growing direct marketing medium.[34] To minimize the level of annoyance and to help potential customers get the information they really do want, many companies now emphasize permission-based e-mail marketing, usually by asking customers or website visitors to *opt-in* to mailing lists.

- **Direct response online.** The interactive, adaptable nature of websites allows them to go far beyond static advertising media to become direct, personalized communication channels. As Amazon.com founder Jeff Bezos explains, referring to the fact that every returning customer is greeted with a customized storefront based on his or her shopping patterns, "If we have 72 million customers, we should have 72 million stores."[35]

search engine marketing
Automated presentation of ads that are related to either the results of an online search or the content being displayed on other webpages

- **Search engine marketing.** With millions of web users relying on search engines such as Google and Bing every day, **search engine marketing**, or *search advertising*, has become an important marketing medium (see Exhibit 16.5). Although it doesn't quite fit the traditional categories of either advertising or direct marketing, search engine marketing comes closer to being a direct medium because it is individualized to each web user. Search advertising works in two basic ways. First, advertisers can pay to display small ads whenever the keywords they select are used in a search. These are the "sponsored results" that can appear above and to the right of the actual search results. In Google's model, for example, advertisers bid on keywords through an online auction; the more an advertiser is willing to pay for particular keywords, the more prominently its ad is displayed. Second, these ads can also appear on the many websites that are in the search engine's *advertising exchange* or *advertising network*, a collection of websites that sell space on their pages for such ads.[36] These ads are triggered by content on a webpage and can appear anywhere on the page, even inserted between sections of an online article.

- **Telephone.** The telephone is a major promotional tool in both consumer and organizational markets and for both *inbound* (when buyers call in to place orders) and *outbound* (when sellers contact potential buyers with sales offers) marketing. After rising complaints from consumers about telemarketers interrupting them at home, Congress created the National Do Not Call Registry, which gives individuals the opportunity to have their numbers removed from telemarketers' lists. However,

EXHIBIT 16.5 Search Engine Marketing

Sponsored search results display ads based on the terms entered into a search engine.

Search-related advertising features also appear in other tools, depending on the particular search engine

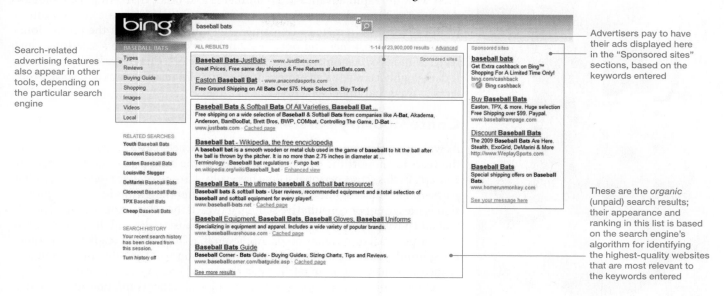

Advertisers pay to have their ads displayed here in the "Sponsored sites" sections, based on the keywords entered

These are the *organic* (unpaid) search results; their appearance and ranking in this list is based on the search engine's algorithm for identifying the highest-quality websites that are most relevant to the keywords entered

marketers can still call businesses as well as consumers who have purchased from them in the past.

■ **Direct response television.** Once limited to *infomercials,* sometimes with dodgy-looking offers, **direct response television** is now used by many well-known and respected companies. A major advantage of the longer infomercial format and full-time shopping channels is the opportunity to demonstrate products and engage viewers in a way that isn't possible with 30- or 60-second commercials.

direct response television
The use of television commercials and longer-format infomercials that are designed to stimulate an immediate purchase response from viewers

 **CHECKPOINT**

LEARNING OBJECTIVE 3: Explain how direct marketing differs from advertising, and identify the major forms of direct media.

Summary: Direct marketing differs from advertising in three important ways: (1) it uses *personally addressable* media such as letters and e-mail messages to deliver targeted messages to individual consumers or organizational purchasers, (2) it doesn't involve the purchase of time or space in other media, and (3) it has a *direct response* aspect that often isn't present in advertising. The major categories of direct marketing media are mail (including catalogs), e-mail, search engine marketing, telephone, and direct response television.

Critical thinking: (1) Would an iPhone app that streams QVC or another shopping channel to mobile phones be an effective direct-marketing medium? Why or why not? (2) If direct marketing has a better return on investment than other forms of promotion, why do companies bother with anything but direct marketing?

It's your business: (1) As a rough guess, what percentage of the direct marketing messages you receive in a given week are effectively targeted to your needs as a consumer? Identify a recent example that was well targeted and one that was not. (2) Have you ever responded to the offer in a "spam" e-mail message? If so, what enticed you to do so?

Key terms to know: direct marketing, customer database, direct mail, search engine marketing, direct response television

Personal Selling

Even with the rapid advance of e-commerce and other marketing technologies, **personal selling**, the one-on-one interaction between a salesperson and a prospective buyer, remains a fundamentally important part of the promotional mix in many consumer and organizational markets. Although a salesforce can't reach millions of customers at once like a website or a direct marketing program, today's highly trained sales professionals can build relationships and solve problems in ways that impersonal media can't match.

Contemporary Personal Selling

As with other elements of the communication mix, personal selling has evolved over the years to support the contemporary idea of the customer-oriented marketing concept. In this sense, personal selling has evolved from *peddling products* to *creating partnerships* with customers.[37] One of the most important shifts in the sales profession is the advent of **consultative selling**, in which the salesperson acts as a consultant and advisor who helps current and potential customers find the best solutions to their personal or business needs. And even if a shopper isn't ready to buy something immediately, a good consultative salesperson will view the interaction as a chance to build a long-term relationship that could lead to sales in the future.[38]

Opportunities to integrate personal selling with other communication and distribution efforts continue to grow. For example, online agents can use instant messaging chat capability to answer questions and help shoppers find the right products for their needs. Using systems such as Livehelper (www.livehelper.com), sales and customer service representatives can spot returning customers and engage them with conversations using information based on past purchases and chat sessions.[39]

The Personal-Selling Process

Personal selling varies widely from industry to industry, with some sales being completed in a matter of minutes and others taking weeks or months. Time is often the salesperson's most valuable asset, so it must be spent wisely—focusing on the most valuable prospects who are most likely to purchase. The following steps can be adapted to almost any sales situation (see Exhibit 16.6):

■ **Step 1: Prospecting.** The process of finding and qualifying potential customers is known as **prospecting**. This step usually involves three activities: (1) *generating sales leads*—names of individuals and organizations that might be likely prospects for the company's product; (2) *identifying prospects*—potential customers who indicate a need or a desire for the seller's product; and (3) *qualifying prospects*—the process of figuring out which prospects have both the authority and the available money to buy. Companies with advanced databases can have a big advantage at this stage by making it easier to identify the best prospects.

■ **Step 2: Preparing.** With a list of strong prospects in hand, the salesperson's next step is to prepare for the *sales call* (in person, over the phone, or online via videoconferencing or other methods). Preparation starts with creating a prospect profile, which includes the names of key people, their role in the decision-making process, and other relevant information, such as the prospect's buying needs, motive for buying, and names of

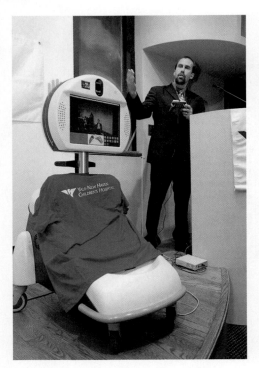

Personal selling is an important promotional element for many business-to-business marketers.

personal selling
One-on-one interaction between a salesperson and a prospective buyer

consultative selling
Approach in which the salesperson acts as a consultant and advisor to help customers find the best solutions to their personal or business needs

prospecting
Process of finding and qualifying potential customers

EXHIBIT 16.6

The Personal-Selling Process

The personal-selling process can involve up to seven steps, starting with prospecting for sales leads and ending with following up after the sale has been closed.

1	2	3	4	5	6	7
Prospecting →	Preparing →	Approaching →	Uncovering needs and presenting solutions →	Handling objections →	Closing →	Following up

current suppliers. The salesperson then establishes specific objectives to achieve during the sales call, which vary depending on where the buyer is in the decision cycle. Finally, the salesperson prepares a presentation, which can be as basic as a list of points to discuss or as elaborate as a product demonstration or multimedia presentation.

■ **Step 3: Approaching the prospect.** First impressions can make or break a sale, so knowledgeable salespeople take care to (1) craft the appropriate appearance, both for themselves and everything that represents them, from business cards to websites; (2) maintain behaviors and attitudes that are professional, courteous, and confident without being arrogant; and (3) prepare opening lines that include a brief greeting and introduction, followed by a few carefully chosen words that establish a good rapport with the potential customer.

■ **Step 4: Uncovering needs and presenting solutions.** After the conversation has been initiated, the next step is understanding the customer's specific needs. The biggest mistake a salesperson can make at this stage is talking instead of listening. The most extreme form of this is the *canned sales pitch*, in which the salesperson recites or even reads a stock message with no regard for the customer's unique circumstances. In contrast, today's enlightened sales professionals focus on questioning and listening before offering a solution that meets each prospect's unique needs.

■ **Step 5: Handling objections.** Potential customers can express a variety of objections to the products they are considering, and salespeople need to be ready with answers and alternatives. In fact, many successful salespeople look at objections as a sign of the prospect's interest and as an opportunity to develop new ideas that will strengthen future presentations.

■ **Step 6: Closing.** Bringing the sales process to a successful conclusion by asking for and receiving an affirmative purchase decision is known as **closing**. Closing can be a difficult step for beginning salespeople or those who lack confidence in what they are selling. However, experienced professionals know to look for signs that the prospect is ready to make a decision and use a variety of techniques such as offering to write up an order to promote a definitive answer.[40]

closing
Point at which a sale is completed

■ **Step 7: Following up.** Most companies depend on repeat sales and referrals from satisfied customers, so it's important that salespeople follow up after the sale to make sure customers are satisfied with their purchases. Staying in touch gives a company the opportunity to answer questions, address areas of confusion or dissatisfaction with a purchase, and show customers it is a reliable partner for the long haul.

✓CHECKPOINT

LEARNING OBJECTIVE 4: Describe *consultative selling*, and explain the personal-selling process.

Summary: Consultative selling is a combination of persuasion and advice, in which the salesperson acts as a consultant and advisor who helps current and potential customers find the best solutions to their personal or business needs. The seven general steps in personal selling are (1) *prospecting*, finding prospects and qualifying them; (2) *preparing*, creating a prospect profile, setting objectives for the call, and preparing a presentation; (3) *approaching* the prospect, with the goal of making a positive first impression; (4) *uncovering* the customer's needs and *presenting* appropriate solutions; (5) *handling objections*, using audience comments as an opportunity to strengthen the presentation; (6) *closing*, focusing on completing the sale; and (7) *following up* after the sale to make sure the buyer is satisfied.

Critical thinking: (1) Why is the canned approach inadequate for many selling situations? (2) Why should a salesperson take the time to qualify sales leads?

Sales Promotion

sales promotion
Wide range of events and activities designed to promote a brand or stimulate interest in a product

Sales promotion consists of short-term incentives to build the reputation of a brand, encourage the purchase of a product, or simply enhance relationships with current and potential customers. Sales promotion consists of two basic categories: consumer promotion and trade promotion.

Consumer Promotions

Companies use a variety of consumer promotional tools and incentives to stimulate repeat purchases and to entice new users:

- **Contests and other audience involvement tactics.** Giving consumers the opportunity to participate in contests, games, sweepstakes, surveys, and other activities, particularly if there is a chance for consumers to demonstrate cleverness or creativity, is a great way to build energy around a brand (see Exhibit 16.7).

coupons
Certificates that offer discounts on particular items and are redeemed at the time of purchase

- **Coupons.** The biggest category of consumer promotion is **coupons**, certificates that spur sales by giving buyers a discount when they purchase specified products. Couponing is an inefficient technique, however—consumers redeem only 1 percent

EXHIBIT 16.7 Consumer Promotions Using Social Media

Amy Reed, owner of Pittsburgh's Chickdowntown clothing store, makes extensive use of social media for consumer promotions.

Describes a contest conducted on her Twitter account

Posts comments from some of her Twitter followers, which helps to build the sense of community among her fans

Uses consumer promotion techniques to build an audience on various social media sites

Offers discounts to readers of her blog, which adds financial value to the sense of being part of her community

of the 300 billion paper coupons distributed every year in the United States.[41] Moreover, many of the purchases made with coupons would've been made anyway, only serving to lower the seller's income. The most intriguing recent development in couponing is the *mobile coupon*, an electronic coupon sent to a consumer's mobile phone, often in conjunction with GPS mapping capabilities. For instance, systems are now appearing that offer coupons to shops or restaurants within driving or walking distance of a person's current location.[42]

- **Rebates.** With **rebates** companies offer partial reimbursement of the price as a purchase incentive. Rebates can be an effective way to boost sales, but they obviously cut into per-unit profits—and the effect can be more or less permanent when frequent rebates in an industry encourage buyers to delay purchases until a rebate program is available. For example, a majority of new cars sold in the United States involve rebate programs, so many consumers expect car prices to be discounted through rebates.[43]

- **Point-of-purchase.** The **point-of-purchase (POP) display** is an in-store presentation designed to stimulate immediate sales. POP displays are a vital element in the marketing effort for many products sold at retail stores. Not only do they represent the manufacturer's last chance to communicate with the consumer, but they help capture *impulse purchases*—unplanned purchases that can make up as much as 50 percent of sales in mass merchandise stores and supermarkets.[44] POP displays are going digital, too, offering such capabilities as free ringtones to shoppers with Bluetooth-enabled phones.[45]

- **Samples and trial-use versions.** Samples are an effective way to introduce a new product, encourage nonusers to try an existing product, encourage current buyers to use the product in a new way, or expand distribution into new areas. Many software products are also offered as trial versions to let customers try before buying.

- **Special-event sponsorship.** Sponsoring special events has become one of the most popular sales promotion tactics, with thousands of companies spending billions of dollars to sponsor events ranging from golf to opera.

- **Other promotions.** Other popular consumer sales promotion techniques include in-store demonstrations, loyalty and frequency programs such as frequent-flyer miles, and **premiums**, which are free or bargain-priced items offered to encourage the consumer to buy a product. **Specialty advertising** (on pens, calendars, T-shirts, mouse pads, and other items) helps keep a company's name in front of customers for a long period of time.

Trade Promotions

Although shoppers are more aware of consumer promotions, **trade promotions** aimed at inducing wholesalers or retailers to sell a company's products actually account for the larger share of promotional spending and can be the single largest item in a manufacturer's marketing budget.[46] The most popular trade promotions are **trade allowances**, which involve discounts on product prices, free merchandise, or other payments such as the retail slotting fees mentioned in Chapter 15. The intermediary can either pocket the savings to increase profits or pass the savings on to the consumer to generate additional sales. Trade allowances are commonly used when adopting a push marketing strategy because they encourage the intermediaries to carry new products or to sell higher volumes of current products.

The chief downside of trade allowances is that they can create the controversial practice of *forward buying*, in which a customer loads up on merchandise while the price is low. For example, if the producer of Bumble Bee tuna offers retailers a 20 percent discount for a period of 6 weeks, a retailer might choose to buy enough tuna to last 8 or 10 weeks. Purchasing this excessive amount at the lower price increases the retailer's profit, but at the expense of the producer's profit.

Point-of-purchase displays, such as this Duracell battery display by the checkout stand at a Staples store in Miami, are a widely used sales promotion tactic.

rebates
Partial reimbursement of price, offered as a purchase incentive

point-of-purchase (POP) display
Advertising or other display materials set up at retail locations to promote products to potential customers as they are making their purchase decisions

premiums
Free or bargain-priced items offered to encourage consumers to buy a product

specialty advertising
Advertising that appears on various items such as coffee mugs, pens, and calendars, designed to help keep a company's name in front of customers

trade promotions
Sales-promotion efforts aimed at inducing distributors or retailers to push a producer's products

trade allowances
Discounts or other financial considerations offered by producers to wholesalers and retailers

Besides trade allowances, other popular trade promotions are dealer contests and bonus programs designed to motivate distributors or retailers to push particular merchandise. Product samples are also common in many business marketing efforts. For instance, semiconductor manufacturers often provide samples of electronic components to engineers who are designing new products, knowing that if the prototype is successful, it could lead to full-scale production—and orders for thousands or millions of components.

✓CHECKPOINT

LEARNING OBJECTIVE 5: Define sales promotion, and identify the major categories of consumer and trade promotions.

Summary: The two main types of sales promotion are consumer promotion and trade promotion. Consumer promotions are intended to motivate the final consumer to try new products or to experiment with the company's brands. Examples include contests, coupons, rebates, point-of-purchase displays, samples, special-event sponsorship, premiums, and specialty advertising. Trade promotions are designed to induce wholesalers and retailers to promote a producer's products. Common trade promotions include trade allowances, dealer contests, bonus programs, and samples.

Critical thinking: (1) If 99 percent of coupons are never used, why do companies keep printing so many? (2) If wholesalers and retailers can make money selling a manufacturer's product, why would the manufacturer need to offer incentives such as sales contests?

It's your business: (1) How can sales promotions reduce the reluctance that buyers might feel about trying an unfamiliar product? (2) Have you ever participated in a sales promotion without really realizing you were doing so? For example, have you ever entered a sweepstakes sponsored by a company without thinking that you were getting on the company's mailing list or otherwise participating in a marketing activity?

Key terms to know: sales promotion, coupons, rebates, point-of-purchase (POP) display, premiums, specialty advertising, trade promotions, trade allowances

social media
Communication vehicles such as blogs, user-contributed content sites, and social booking sites, in which customers and other members of the public can participate

Social Media and Public Relations

All the communication methods discussed so far in this chapter involve activities by companies themselves to transmit carefully crafted and controlled messages to target audiences. The final two methods, social media and public relations, differ in two respects: They rely on others to forward or create promotional messages, and they don't provide anywhere near the level of control over those messages that conventional marketing methods offer.

Real-Time Updates

Learn More
Using social media to build your business and your brand

These six steps can help any novice make the most of social media as a business tool. On mybizlab (www.mybizlab.com), you can access Real-Time Updates within each chapter or under Student Study Tools. Otherwise, go to http://real-timeupdates.com/bia5 and click on "Learn More."

Social Media in the Marketing Process

Social media include any communication vehicles in which customers and other members of the public can participate, including social networks, blogs, microblogs such as Twitter, wikis, *user-contributed content* websites such as YouTube, and *social bookmarking* sites such as Digg and Delicious. Nicholas Kinports of the product design and marketing firm Maddock Douglas (www.maddockdouglas.com) offers a good summary of the role social media play in buyer decision making:[47]

> The modern consumer is savvy, aware, and fully able to make informed decisions, thanks to a wealth of information freely available on the Internet. The consumer of the near future will make purchase decisions based on information gleaned from unbiased peers and influencers. Social media is the latest tool through which these interactions occur.

Social media activities combine the newest communication technologies with the oldest form of marketing communication in the world, **word of mouth**—customers and other parties transmitting information about companies and products through personal conversations. The term *viral marketing* describes the effect of people spreading marketing messages, mimicking the spread of biological viruses from person to person.

Although promotional communication efforts can use social media, such as through *buzz marketing* tactics that try to generate "buzz" among consumers so they'll be motivated to learn more about a particular product, these techniques are probably better for customer service, rumor control, research, and relationship building than for blatant product promotion.[48] To use social media for promotion, marketers should focus on providing value-added information, such as better ways to use their products.

An intriguing new research application involving social media is *sentiment analysis*, tracking social media with automated language-analysis software that tries to take the pulse of public opinion and identify influential opinion makers. Social media can be "an incredibly rich vein of market intelligence," says Margaret Francis of San Francisco's Scout Labs (www.scoutlabs.com).[49]

The "social" label notwithstanding, the social communication model is by no means limited to the consumer sector. Technical professionals were using the Internet for communication years before the World Wide Web was invented, and now businesspeople in just about every industry use social media to share ideas, ask questions, and compare products. In fact, many businesspeople are far more active in social media than the average consumer.[50]

word of mouth
Communication among customers and other parties, transmitting information about companies and products through personal conversations

Communication Strategies for Social Media

Audiences in the social media environment are not willing to be passive recipients in a structured, one-way information delivery process—or to rely solely on promotional messages from marketers. This notion of interactive participation is the driving force behind **conversation marketing**, in which companies *initiate* and *facilitate* conversations in a networked community of customers, journalists, bloggers, Twitter users, and other interested parties. Social media can be a powerful communication channel, but companies should follow these guidelines in order to meet audience expectations:[51]

- **Join existing conversations.** Search for online conversations that are already taking place. Answer questions, solve problems, and respond to rumors and misinformation.
- **Facilitate community building.** Make sure customers and other audiences can connect with the company and with each other.
- **Initiate and respond to conversations within the community.** Through website content, blog postings, RSS newsfeeds, newsletters, and other tools, marketers can start conversations by providing useful information to current and potential customers. As you can see in the Behind the Scenes wrap-up at the end of the chapter, this effort was key to SeaWorld's success in launching its new water coaster ride.

conversation marketing
Approach to customer communication in which companies initiate and facilitate conversations in a networked community of potential buyers and other interested parties

■ **Identify and support champions.** In marketing, *champions* are enthusiastic fans of a company and its products—so enthusiastic that they help spread the company's message, defend it against detractors, and help other customers use its products.

■ **Restrict conventional promotional efforts to the right time and right place.** Persuasive communication efforts are still valid for specific communication tasks, such as regular advertising and the product information pages on a website, but efforts to inject "salespeak" into social media conversations will be rejected by the audience.

Brand Communities

brand communities
Formal or informal groups of people united by their interest in and ownership of particular products

Another major impact of social media has been the rapid spread of **brand communities**, people united by their interest in and ownership of particular products. These communities can be formal membership organizations, such as the longstanding Harley Owners Group (HOG), or informal networks of people with similar interests. They can be fairly independent from the company behind the brand or can have the active support and involvement of company management, as is the case of Harley-Davidson's support of the motorcycle enthusiasts who are members of HOG (*hog* is an affectionate nickname for a Harley).[52]

Social media are natural communication vehicles for brand communities because these tools let people bond and share information on their own terms. And because a strong majority of consumers now trust their peers more than any other source of product information—including conventional advertising techniques—formal and informal brand communities are becoming an essential information source in consumer buying behavior.[53]

Public Relations

public relations
Nonsales communication that businesses have with their various audiences (includes both communication with the general public and press relations)

Public relations encompasses a wide variety of nonsales communications that businesses have with their many stakeholders, including communities, investors, industry analysts, government agencies, and activists. Companies rely on public relations to build a favorable corporate image and foster positive relations with all these groups.

Public relations efforts often involve the news media, with companies offering information to print, broadcast, and online journalists in the hope that these intermediaries will pass the message along to their audiences. If the information is likely to interest their audiences, journalists will help "spread the word," in the best cases generating high levels of public awareness at much lower cost than a company could achieve on its own through paid advertising.[54]

press release
Brief statement or video program released to the press announcing new products, management changes, sales performance, and other potential news items; also called a *news release*

press conference
In-person or online gathering of media representatives at which companies announce new information; also called a *news conference*

Two standard tools for communicating with the media are the press release and the press conference. A traditional **press release** is a short message sent to the media covering topics that are of potential news interest; a *video news release* is a brief video clip sent to television stations. Companies use news releases in the hopes of getting favorable news coverage about themselves and their products. When a business has significant news to announce, it will often arrange a **press conference** at which reporters can listen to company representatives and ask questions.

Until recently, press releases were intended only for members of the news media and were crafted in a way to provide information to reporters who would then write their own articles. Thanks to the Internet, however, the nature of the press release is changing. Many companies now view it as a general-purpose tool for communicating directly with customers and other audiences, writing *direct-to-consumer press releases*. As news media expert David Meerman Scott puts it, "Millions of people read press releases directly, unfiltered by the media. You need to be speaking directly to them."[55] Similarly, the traditional press conference is being replaced in many cases with *webcasts*, online presentations that can reach thousands of viewers at once and be archived for later retrieval.

For the latest information on customer communication strategies, techniques, and tools, visit http://real-timeupdates.com/bia5 and click on Chapter 16.

✓CHECKPOINT

LEARNING OBJECTIVE 6: Explain the uses of social media in customer communication and the role of public relations.

Summary: Social media have several potential uses in customer communication, including customer service, rumor control, research, and relationship building. They can also be used for promotion, but that should be done in an indirect, customer-focused manner. Because consumers and investors support companies with good reputations, smart companies use public relations to build and protect their image. They communicate with consumers, investors, industry analysts, and government officials through the media. They pursue and maintain press relations with representatives of newspapers, television, and other broadcast media so that they can provide effective news releases (also known as press releases) and hold effective news conferences.

Critical thinking: (1) If marketers are advised against blatant product promotion in social media, why should they bother using these media at all? (2) Why are press relations so critical to the launch of many new products?

It's your business: (1) Have you ever used social media to ask questions about a product or to criticize or compliment a company? Did anyone from the company respond? (2) Do you consider yourself a member of any brand communities (formal or informal)? What effect do these groups have on your purchasing behavior?

Key terms to know: social media, word of mouth, conversation marketing, brand communities, public relations, press release, press conference

Behind the Scenes

SeaWorld San Antonio Gets Social to Build Interest in New Ride

When SeaWorld San Antonio needed to get the word out quickly about its new Journey to Atlantis water coaster ride, public relations specialist Kami Huyse of My PR Pro (http://myprpro.com) worked with SeaWorld's Director of Communications Fran Stephenson to survey their options. The team had three objectives: (1) build relationships with the community of coaster enthusiasts, (2) create awareness of the new ride, and (3) increase visitor traffic. You can see that these goals stretch across three time frames: long-term relationship building, mid-term awareness, and short-term sales. It's a lot to ask of any communication campaign—and particularly a campaign with the time and budget limits that Huyse and Stephenson faced.

Hard-core roller coaster enthusiasts are *really* enthusiastic about their coasters. They like to learn about new rides, compare their impressions of rides they've been on, organize trips to visit rides around the country, and even work to preserve some of the classic old roller coasters that dot the American landscape. Dozens of websites, forums, blogs, and coaster groups share information, including the 7,000-member American Coaster Enthusiasts (www.aceonline.org). With

Huyse's expertise in social media, she recognized an opportunity when she saw one: They would connect with the "thrill ride" community online.

Their research identified 22 blogs and forums that were particularly active and influential in the enthusiast community. "The primary strategy was to treat coaster bloggers as a VIP audience and to create content to suit their needs," she explains. These bloggers were also invited to attend a special prelaunch media day to test-drive Journey to Atlantis.

As part of this effort to provide opinion influencers and the general public with enticing content about the new ride, SeaWorld's in-house communication staff created 11 videos and a 45-image photo collection that were made available for public use through YouTube, Flickr, and Veoh. The staff also created a content-rich website with social media functionality to add to SeaWorld's existing web presence to serve as the "hub" of the launch campaign.

The results? One of the knocks against social media as a business communication platform is that its effects can be difficult or impossible to measure. While that is true in many cases, Huyse and her colleagues were able to make three specific measurements that highlight the success of SeaWorld's social media effort. First, of the 22 targeted VIP enthusiast groups, more than half covered the opening in their blogs or forums, including the influential Theme Park Insider website. Second, more than 50 other websites created links to the Journey to Atlantis campaign website, and 30 of those were from coaster enthusiast websites. These numbers might sound small, but remember that social media is a game of multiplication: Small numbers of people spreading a message can quickly turn into large numbers.

The third and ultimately most important measurement is the impact on SeaWorld's business. Fortunately for Huyse's team, a measuring device was already in place: the exit surveys that SeaWorld routinely conducts, asking park visitors about their experiences and decisions to visit. Using data from this survey, the team could identify which media efforts drove visitors to the park most effectively and then calculate the cost-effectiveness of each method to see how the social media campaign compared to SeaWorld's other, ongoing promotional efforts. While television was almost as effective as online efforts at driving traffic through the front gate, the net cost to get one visitor through the front gate was nearly five times higher for television. And in terms of actual sales, based on SeaWorld's average per capita revenue figure, the social media campaign generated more than $2.6 million in revenue—for only $44,000 in total costs. From a marketing point of view, that's even more thrilling than a ride on the latest roller coaster.

Critical Thinking Questions

1. With social media proving to be a cost-effective way to attract park visitors, should SeaWorld abandon its other promotional efforts and focus everything on social media? Why or why not?
2. What steps can SeaWorld take to maintain a relationship with coaster enthusiasts, now that the excitement surrounding the new ride has faded?
3. Do coaster fans such as members of American Coaster Enthusiasts constitute a brand community as described in the chapter? Why or why not?

LEARN MORE ONLINE

Search online for commentary and media materials relating to the Journey to Atlantis ride at SeaWorld San Antonio. (Be aware that different rides with the same name exist at the other SeaWorld parks.) Imagine that you're a coaster enthusiast. Based on what you see online, would you consider visiting San Antonio to ride Journey to Atlantis? Why or why not? ■

Key Terms

advertising (410)
advertising appeal (410)
advertising media (413)
advocacy advertising (410)
brand communities (424)
closing (419)
communication mix (407)
comparative advertising (410)
consultative selling (418)
conversation marketing (423)
core message (407)
coupons (420)
customer database (415)
direct mail (416)

direct marketing (415)
direct response television (417)
institutional advertising (410)
integrated marketing communications (IMC) (408)
media mix (413)
personal selling (418)
point-of-purchase (POP) display (421)
premiums (421)
press conference (424)
press release (424)
product advertising (410)
product placement (413)

prospecting (418)
public relations (424)
pull strategy (408)
push strategy (408)
rebates (421)
sales promotion (420)
search engine marketing (416)
social communication model (406)
social media (422)
specialty advertising (421)
trade allowances (421)
trade promotions (421)
word of mouth (423)

Test Your Knowledge

Questions for Review

1. What is an advertising appeal?
2. What are some common types of consumer promotion?
3. What are two key ways in which the social communication model differs from conventional promotional communication?
4. What is the difference between using a push strategy and using a pull strategy to promote products?

5. What are the advantages of personal selling over other forms of customer communication?

Questions for Analysis

6. Why is it important for sales professionals to qualify prospects?
7. Do marketers have any control over social media? Why or why not?

8. Why do some companies avoid e-mail marketing, particularly to noncustomers?

9. What are the potential disadvantages of using celebrity appeals in advertising?

10. **Ethical Considerations.** Is your privacy being violated when a website you visit displays ads that are personalized in any way, even if it's just geographically targeted to the local area (based on your computer's Internet address)? Why or why not?

Questions for Application

11. If you were a real estate agent, how would you determine whether it's worth investing a significant amount of time in a particular prospect?

12. Would it be a good idea to "repurpose" conventional press releases as posts on your company blog? Why or why not?

13. Think about an advertisement (in any medium) that had either a strongly positive or strongly negative effect on your attitude toward the product being advertised or the advertiser itself. Why did the ad have this effect? If you responded positively to the ad, do you think you were being manipulated in any way? If you responded negatively—and you are a potential buyer of the product that was advertised—what changes would you make to the ad to make it more successful?

14. **Concept Integration.** Should companies involve their marketing channels in the design of their customer communication programs? What are the advantages and disadvantages of doing so?

Practice Your Knowledge

Sharpening Your Communication Skills

The good news: The current events blog you started as a hobby has become quite popular. The bad news: The blog now takes up so much of your time that you've had to quit a part-time job you were using to supplement your regular income. After some discussions with other bloggers, you decide to join Google's AdSense program (www.google.com/adsense) to help pay for the costs of operating your blog. With this program, small ads triggered by keywords in the content you publish will appear on your site. However, you're worried that your audience will think you've "sold out" because you're now generating revenue from your blog. Write a short message that could be posted on your blog, explaining why you consider it necessary to run ads and assuring your readers of your continued objectivity, even if that means criticizing organizations whose ads might appear on your blog.

Building Your Team Skills

In small groups, discuss three or four recent ads or consumer promotions (in any media) that you think were particularly effective. Using the knowledge you've gained from this chapter, try to come to agreement on which attributes contributed to the success of each ad or promotion. For instance: Was it persuasive? Informative? Competitive? Creative? Did it have logical or emotional appeal? Did it stimulate you to buy the product? Why? Compare your results with those of other teams. Did you mention the same ads? Did you list the same attributes?

Expand Your Knowledge

Discovering Career Opportunities

Jobs in customer communication—advertising, direct marketing, personal selling, sales promotion, social media, and public relations—are among the most exciting and challenging in all of marketing. Choose a particular job in one of these areas. Using personal contacts, local directories of businesses or business professionals, or online resources such as company websites or search engines (including Twitter and blog search tools), arrange a brief phone, e-mail, or personal interview with a professional working in your chosen marketing field.

1. What are the daily activities of this professional? What tools and resources does this person use most often on the job? What does this professional like most and least about the job?

2. What talents and educational background does this professional bring to the job? How are the person's skills and knowledge applied to handle the job's daily activities?

3. What advice does the person you are interviewing have for newcomers entering this field? What can you do now to get yourself started on a career path toward this position?

Developing Your Research Skills

Choose an article from recent issues of business journals or newspapers (print or online editions) that describes the advertising or promotion efforts of a particular company or trade association.

1. Who is the company or trade association targeting?

2. What specific marketing objectives is the organization trying to accomplish?

3. What role does advertising play in the promotion strategy? What other promotion techniques does the article mention? Are any of them unusual or noteworthy? Why?

Improving Your Tech Insights: Individualized Advertising

Don't be surprised if you look out the window one morning to see clouds in the sky arranged in letters that spell out your name and invite you to try a refreshing bottle of Coke or remind you to get your oil changed at Jiffy Lube.

Maybe it won't get quite that far, but advertisers are perfecting a variety of technologies that allow them to pinpoint individual audience members with customized messages. One interesting effect of this is that some advertising media or retailing formats are starting to look more like direct marketing media. As the chapter notes, Amazon.com has already personalized a store front for every one of its 72 million customers. Here are a few other examples: personalized magazine covers (including one that showed an aerial photograph of each subscriber's neighborhood with his or her home or office circled in red); commercials on digital cable systems that can be targeted to viewers in an individual neighborhood or even an individual household (with messages shaped by the demographics of the residents of the house); narrowly focused audio messages that can be aimed at a single shopper in a retail store; Google's Gmail e-mail service, which serves up ads based on specific words in your e-mail messages; and Google's new behavioral targeting technology, which it calls "interest-based advertising," which displays ads based on your web surfing patterns.

Identify one form of individualized advertising now in use (you can search for "individualized advertising," "personalized advertising," "behavioral targeting," or "interest-based advertising"). In a brief e-mail to your instructor, describe the technology, explain how it helps businesses reach customers more effectively, and identify any privacy concerns connected to the medium.[56]

Video Discussion

Access the Chapter 16 video discussion in the End of Chapter Assignments section at www.mybizlab.com.

PEARSON mybizlab

Log on to www.mybizlab.com to access the following study and assessment aids associated with this chapter:

- Interactive exercises
- Pre/post test
- Real-Time Updates
- Video application
- Customized study plans
- Biz Skills Simulations
- Quick Learning Guide

If you are not using mybizlab, you can access Real-Time Updates and Quick Learning Guides through http://real-timeupdates.com/bia5. The Quick Learning Guide (located under "Learn More" on the website) provides all six Checkpoints in a handy two-page format to help you study for exams or review important concepts whenever you need a quick refresher.

CHAPTER 17

Financial Information and Accounting Concepts

LEARNING OBJECTIVES

After studying this chapter, you will be able to

1 Define *accounting* and describe the roles of private and public accountants

2 Explain the impact of accounting standards such as **GAAP** and the Sarbanes-Oxley Act on corporate accounting

3 Describe the *accounting equation* and explain the purpose of *double-entry bookkeeping* and the *matching principle*

4 Identify the major financial statements and explain how to read a balance sheet

5 Explain the purpose of the income statement and statement of cash flows

6 Explain the purpose of ratio analysis and list the four main categories of financial ratios

Behind the Scenes

Reality Comes Knocking at the Googleplex

www.google.com

You may have received some nice employee benefits somewhere along the line, but did an armored truck ever back up to the front door to hand out a thousand dollars to every employee at Christmastime?

As Google's dominance of the profitable search engine market grew in recent years and its stock price soared, the company looked like it just might end up with all the cash in the world. To create one of the world's best places to work, the

When expenses began to grow faster than revenues, Google CEO Eric Schmidt began a systematic evaluation of how the company was spending its cash.

Mountain View, California, Internet giant sometimes spent money as if it had unlimited cash, too. Employee perks ranged from a companywide ski trip and an annual cash bonus—which really was delivered by armored truck—to free meals cooked by gourmet chefs and on-site massages, doctors, and car service.

Beyond these mere amenities, Google created one of the most interesting and stimulating workplaces imaginable. Engineers were allowed to spend up to 20 percent of their time exploring whatever fascinated them, even if those adventures weren't directly related to the company's current business efforts. Those explorations often did lead to new products and features, though, as Google's product line expanded far beyond its original search engine.

As it launched new projects and business initiatives right and left, Google kept hiring the best and the brightest and by 2008 had 20,000 employees and another 10,000

contractors. It had also acquired more than 50 other companies, paying from a few million dollars to get small niche companies on up to $1.65 billion to buy YouTube and $3.1 billion to buy the online advertising company DoubleClick.

Cash was flowing in, cash was flowing out, and all was good in the Googleplex, as the company's headquarters complex is known. But reality has a way of catching up to even the highest flying companies, and Google would prove no exception. Internally, after a decade of rampant growth, expenses were eating up an ever-larger share of revenue. Externally, the global economy was cooling off quickly in late 2007 and into 2008, and one company after another began trimming advertising budgets. In spite of its many product innovations and explorations, Google still depended on search engine advertising for nearly all its revenue. Online advertising wasn't getting chopped quite as severely as ads for television and other traditional media, but the spending reductions were serious enough to slow Google's sales growth. With expenses growing faster than revenue, something had to give.

If you were CEO Eric Schmidt, how would you bring spending under control without alienating a workforce that has come to expect a certain level of pampering—and without stifling innovation, the engine behind the company's spectacular growth?[1] ∎

Introduction

With years of experience managing complex business operations, Google's Eric Schmidt (profiled in the chapter-opening Behind the Scenes) could tell you how vital it is to have accurate, up-to-date accounting information. After an introduction to what accountants do and the rules they are expected to follow, this chapter explains the fundamental concepts of the accounting equation and double-entry bookkeeping. It then explores the primary "report cards" used in accounting: the balance sheet, income statement, and statement of cash flows. The chapter wraps up with a look at trend analysis and ratio analysis, the tools that managers, lenders, and investors use to predict a company's ongoing health.

Understanding Accounting

Accounting is the system a business uses to identify, measure, and communicate financial information to others, inside and outside the organization. Financial information is important to businesses such as Google for two reasons: First, it helps managers and owners plan and control a company's operations and make informed business decisions. Second, it helps outsiders evaluate a business. Suppliers, banks, and other lenders want to know whether a business is creditworthy; investors and shareholders are concerned with its profit potential; government agencies are interested in its tax accounting.

Because outsiders and insiders use accounting information for different purposes, accounting has two distinct facets. **Financial accounting** is concerned with preparing financial statements and other information for outsiders such as stockholders and *creditors* (people or organizations that have lent a company money or have extended it credit); **management accounting** is concerned with preparing cost analyses, profitability reports, budgets, and other information for insiders such as management and other company decision makers. To be useful, all accounting information must be accurate, objective, consistent over time, and comparable to information supplied by other companies.

accounting
Measuring, interpreting, and communicating financial information to support internal and external decision making

financial accounting
Area of accounting concerned with preparing financial information for users outside the organization

management accounting
Area of accounting concerned with preparing data for use by managers within the organization

What Accountants Do

Some people confuse the work accountants do with **bookkeeping**, which is the clerical function of recording the economic activities of a business. Although some accountants do perform bookkeeping functions, their work generally goes well beyond the scope of this activity. Accountants prepare financial statements, analyze and interpret financial information, prepare financial forecasts and budgets, and prepare tax returns. Some accountants specialize in certain areas of accounting, such as *cost accounting* (computing and analyzing production and operating costs), *tax accounting* (preparing tax returns and interpreting tax law), financial analysis (evaluating a company's performance and the financial implications of strategic decisions such as product pricing, employee benefits, and business acquisitions), or *forensic accounting* (combining accounting and investigating skills to assist in legal and criminal matters).

In addition to traditional accounting work, accountants may also help clients improve business processes, plan for the future, evaluate product performance, analyze profitability by customer and product groups, design and install new computer systems, assist companies with decision making, and provide a variety of other management consulting services. Performing these functions requires a strong business background and a variety of business skills beyond accounting.

bookkeeping
Recordkeeping; the clerical aspect of accounting

private accountants
In-house accountants employed by organizations and businesses other than a public accounting firm; also called *corporate accountants*

Private Accountants

Private accountants work for corporations, government agencies, and not-for-profit organizations. Their titles vary by function and include *corporate accountant, managerial accountant,* or

Real-Time Updates

Learn More
Considering a career in accounting?
This comprehensive directory can help you explore the profession and find potential employers. On mybizlab (**www.mybizlab.com**), you can access Real-Time Updates within each chapter or under Student Study Tools. Otherwise, go to **http://real-timeupdates.com/bia5** and click on "Learn More."

EXHIBIT 17.1 Typical Finance Department

Here is a typical finance department of a large company. In smaller companies, the controller may
be the highest-ranking accountant and report directly to the president. The top executive in
charge of finance is often called the chief financial officer (CFO).

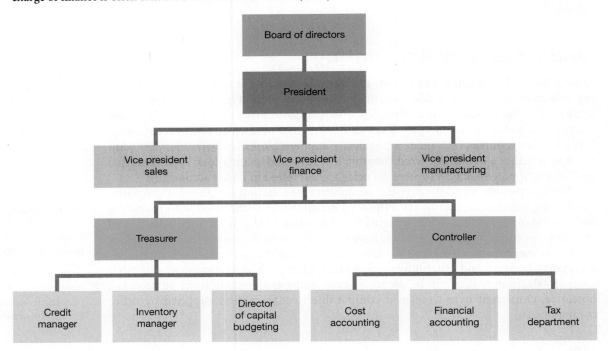

controller
Highest-ranking accountant in a
company, responsible for overseeing
all accounting functions

cost accountant.[2] Private accountants generally work together as a team under the supervision of the organization's **controller**, who reports to the vice president of finance or
the chief financial officer (CFO). Exhibit 17.1 shows the typical finance department of a
large company. In smaller organizations, the controller may be in charge of the company's entire finance operation and report directly to the president.

**certified public accountants
(CPAs)**
Professionally licensed accountants
who meet certain requirements for
education and experience and who
pass a comprehensive examination

Although certification is not required of private accountants, many are licensed
certified public accountants (CPAs). Specific requirements vary by state, but to receive
a CPA license, an individual must complete a certain number of hours of college-level
coursework, have a minimum number of years of work experience in the accounting
field, and pass the Uniform CPA Exam.[3] A growing number of private accountants are
becoming *certified management accountants (CMAs)*; to do so they must pass an intensive exam sponsored by the Institute of Management Accountants.[4]

Public Accountants

public accountants
Professionals who provide
accounting services to other
businesses and individuals for a fee

In contrast to private accountants, **public accountants** are independent of the businesses,
organizations, and individuals they serve. Most public accountants are employed by public accounting firms that provide a variety of accounting and consulting services to their
clients. The largest of these, four international networks known as the "Big Four," are
Deloitte Touche Tohmatsu (www.deloitte.com), Ernst & Young (www.ey.com), KPMG
(www.kpmg.com), and PricewaterhouseCoopers (www.pwcglobal.com). Whether they
belong to one of these giant networks (each of whom employs over 100,000 people) or to
a smaller independent firm, public accountants generally are CPAs and must obtain CPA
and state licensing certifications before they are eligible to conduct an **audit**—a formal
evaluation of a company's accounting records and processes to ensure the integrity and
reliability of a company's financial statements.

audit
Formal evaluation of the fairness
and reliability of a client's financial
statements

By the way, if you've shied away from accounting as a career choice because of popular stereotypes about it being a dull job fit only for "bean counters," it's time to take another look. Partly as a consequence of financial scandals in recent years and the growing complexity of accounting regulations, accounting specialists are now in demand in many industries. Employment is growing faster than average for all accounting occupations, while salaries and benefits are increasing as everybody from the Big Four to the FBI to corporations both large and small actively recruit accountants to help navigate the challenging landscape of contemporary business finance.[5]

✓CHECKPOINT

LEARNING OBJECTIVE 1: Define *accounting,* **and describe the roles of private and public accountants.**

Summary: Accounting is the system a business uses to identify, measure, and communicate financial information to others, inside and outside the organization. Accountants perform a wide variety of tasks, including preparing financial statements, analyzing and interpreting financial information, preparing financial forecasts and budgets, preparing tax returns, interpreting tax law, computing and analyzing production costs, evaluating a company's performance, and analyzing the financial implications of business decisions. Private accountants work for corporations, government agencies, and not-for-profit organizations, performing various accounting functions for their employers. Public accountants, in contrast, sell their services to individuals and organizations. One of the most important functions of public accountants is performing audits, a formal evaluation of a company's accounting records and processes.

Critical thinking: (1) Why would a private accountant bother with becoming a CPA? (2) What effect can unreliable or uncertain accounting have on the economy?

It's your business: (1) How rigorous are your personal bookkeeping and accounting efforts? Do you keep accurate records, analyze spending, and set budgets? (2) If you don't really account for your personal finances, how might doing so help you, now and in the future?

Key terms to know: accounting, financial accounting, management accounting, bookkeeping, private accountants, controller, certified public accountants (CPAs), public accountants, audit

The Rules of Accounting

In order to make informed decisions, investors, bankers, suppliers, and other parties need some means to verify the quality of the financial information that companies release to the public. They also need some way to compare information from one company to the next. To accommodate these needs, financial accountants are expected to follow a number of rules, some of which are voluntary and some of which are required by law.

Accounting Standards: GAAP and IFRS

Accounting is based on numbers, so it might seem a fairly straightforward task to tally up a company's revenues and costs to determine its net profits. However, accounting is often anything but simple. For instance, *revenue recognition,* how and when a company records incoming revenue, is a particularly complex topic.[6] As just one example, should a company record revenue (a) when it ships products to customers, (b) when it bills customers, (c) when customers actually pay, or (d) after everyone has paid and any products that are going to be returned for refunds have been returned (since refunds reduce revenue)? If customers are in financial trouble and taking a long time to pay or are not paying at all, or if a poorly designed product is generating a lot of returns, the differences can be substantial.

Standardizing Through GAAP

generally accepted accounting principles (GAAP)
U.S. standards and practices used by accountants in the preparation of financial statements

To help ensure consistent financial reporting, a series of basic accounting standards and procedures have been agreed on over the years by regulators, auditors, and company representatives. The **generally accepted accounting principles (GAAP)** aim to give a fair and true picture of a company's financial position and enable outsiders to make confident analyses and comparisons. GAAP can't prevent every reporting abuse, but it does make distorting financial results in order to fool outsiders more difficult.[7] Companies can still provide "non-GAAP" financial results to investors—as Google does, for example—but they must label these figures as non-GAAP data.

external auditors
Independent accounting firms that provide auditing services for public companies

As Chapter 18 notes, companies whose stock is publicly traded in the United States are required to file audited financial statements with the Securities and Exchange Commission (SEC). During an audit, CPAs who work for an independent accounting firm, also known as **external auditors**, review a client's financial records to determine whether the statements that summarize these records have been prepared in accordance with GAAP. Then auditors summarize their findings in a report attached to the client's published financial statements. Sometimes these reports disclose information that might materially affect the client's financial position, such as the bankruptcy of a major supplier, a large obsolete inventory, costly environmental problems, or questionable accounting practices. Most companies, however, receive a clean audit report, which means that to the best of the auditors' knowledge the company's financial statements are accurate.

To assist with the auditing process, many large organizations use internal auditors—employees who investigate and evaluate the organization's internal operations and data to determine whether they are accurate and whether they comply with GAAP, federal laws, and industry regulations. Although this self-checking process is vital to an organization's financial health, an internal audit is not a substitute for having an independent auditor look things over and render an unbiased opinion.

The Shift Toward International Standards

GAAP has helped standardize accounting for companies in the United States, but the situation is more complicated at the international level because GAAP is not used in other countries. The lack of global standardization creates extra work for U.S. multinationals, essentially forcing them to keep two sets of books. As Richard Fearon, CFO of Eaton Corporation, which has operations in 30 countries, puts it, "It's really not cost efficient to maintain two sets of books on different standards."[8] It has also been a sticking point for non-U.S. companies that have wanted to sell shares on U.S. stock exchanges. In fact, up until 2007, the SEC required non-U.S. companies wanting to sell stock on U.S. exchanges to reconcile their financial reports with GAAP standards.

international financial reporting standards (IFRS)
Accounting standards and practices used in many countries outside the United States

A movement is underway to bring U.S. accounting practices more in line with international standards by merging GAAP with the **international financial reporting standards (IFRS)** overseen by the London-based International Accounting Standards Board.

When and how the transformation will occur is still being hammered out, but the change seems inevitable. "We do have the best reporting system," says Robert Herz, chairman of the U.S. Financial Accounting Standards Board, the agency in charge of GAAP, "but the rest of the world will not accept it. It's too detailed for them."[9]

PDF

Real-Time Updates

Learn More
Implications of going international: GAAP vs. IFRS

Get a high-level view of the challenges and benefits of transitioning from GAAP to IFRS. On mybizlab (**www.mybizlab.com**), you can access Real-Time Updates within each chapter or under Student Study Tools. Otherwise, go to **http://real-timeupdates.com/bia5** and click on "Learn More."

Just how complex and expensive it will be for various companies to shift from GAAP to IFRS isn't clear yet either. In general, the shift could take several years of work and will require a comprehensive reevaluation of a company's finances. The implications could be significant. For example, corporate income tends to come out higher under IFRS than it does under GAAP, which could conceivably increase companies' tax obligations.[10]

Changing to IFRS should help investors who want to purchase stocks of companies based in other countries, help U.S. stock exchanges by making them more competitive in world capital markets, help foreign companies that want to sell stock in the United States, and help multinational companies by letting them settle on a single set of accounting standards. On the other hand, the cost of conversion might not yield many benefits for smaller U.S. companies with no foreign operations.[11]

Sarbanes-Oxley

The need for and complexity of financial reporting standards is highlighted in the controversial story of **Sarbanes-Oxley**, the informal name of the Public Company Accounting Reform and Investor Protection Act. (You'll hear it referred to as "Sox" or "Sarbox" as well.) Passed in the wake of several cases of massive accounting fraud, most notably involving the energy company Enron and the telecom company WorldCom, Sarbanes-Oxley changed public company accounting in a number of important ways. Its major provisions include[12]

Sarbanes-Oxley
Informal name of comprehensive legislation designed to improve integrity and accountability of financial information

- Outlawing most loans by corporations to their own directors and executives
- Creating the Public Company Accounting Oversight Board (PCAOB) to oversee external auditors
- Requiring corporate lawyers to report evidence of financial wrongdoing
- Prohibiting external auditors from providing certain nonaudit services
- Requiring that audit committees on the board of directors have at least one financial expert and that the majority of board members be independent (not employed by the company in an executive position)
- Prohibiting investment bankers from influencing stock analysts
- Requiring CEOs and CFOs to sign statements attesting to the accuracy of their financial statements
- Requiring companies to document and test their internal financial controls and processes

The last item in particular, the result of the brief "Section 404" of the legislation, generated considerable controversy. Representative Michael Oxley, co-sponsor of the legislation, says that "99.9 percent of the complaints you hear are about 404." Oxley adds that it's not the two paragraphs in this section of the legislation that caused so much grief but rather the several hundred pages of regulations the PCAOB generated to enforce it.[13] As one financial writer put it, the requirements were so sweeping that they left financial executives "awash in a vast sea of details, with little ability to set priorities about what to focus on in their compliance efforts."[14]

After a lot of initial criticism about the costs of compliance and a shift in the PCAOB's stance to let companies focus on monitoring the riskiest financial decisions instead of every mundane transaction, complaints about Sarbox have leveled off in recent years.[15] However, as business and political leaders continue to grapple with the fallout of the banking crisis that threw the world economy into a traumatic tailspin in 2008 and 2009, Sarbox could serve as an instructive lesson in how—or how not—to respond to a financial panic.

✓CHECKPOINT

LEARNING OBJECTIVE 2: Explain the impact of accounting standards such as GAAP and the Sarbanes-Oxley Act on corporate accounting.

Summary: Accounting standards such as GAAP help ensure consistent financial reporting, which is essential for regulators and investors to make informed decisions. To ensure consistency on a global scale, GAAP is likely to be merged with the international financial reports standards (IFRS) in the coming years. Sarbanes-Oxley introduced a number of rules covering the way publicly traded companies manage and report their finances, including restricting loans to directors and executives, creating a new board to oversee public auditors, requiring corporate lawyers to report financial wrongdoing, requiring CEOs and CFOs to sign financial statements under oath, and requiring companies to document their financial systems.

Critical thinking: (1) Should U.S. public companies with no significant overseas business activity be forced to follow international accounting standards? Why or why not? (2) How does requiring CEOs to personally attest to the accuracy of financial statements eliminate errors and misrepresentations?

It's your business: (1) How might the convergence of GAAP and IFRS in the coming years affect you as an investor? (2) If you were considering buying stock in a company, would you support rigorous and detailed financial accountability such as that called for by Section 404 of Sarbanes-Oxley? Why or why not?

Key terms to know: generally accepted accounting principles (GAAP), external auditors, international financial reporting standards (IFRS), Sarbanes-Oxley

Fundamental Accounting Concepts

In their work with financial data, accountants are guided by three basic concepts: the *fundamental accounting equation*, *double-entry bookkeeping*, and the *matching principle*. Here is a closer look at each of these essential ideas.

The Accounting Equation

assets
Any things of value owned or leased by a business

liabilities
Claims against a firm's assets by creditors

owners' equity
Portion of a company's assets that belongs to the owners after obligations to all creditors have been met

For thousands of years, businesses and governments have kept records of their **assets**—valuable items they own or lease, such as equipment, cash, land, buildings, inventory, and investments. Claims against those assets are **liabilities**, or what the business owes to its creditors—such as lenders and suppliers. For example, when a company borrows money to purchase a building, the lender has a claim against the company's assets. What remains after liabilities have been deducted from assets is **owners' equity**:

$$\text{Assets} - \text{Liabilities} = \text{Owners' equity}$$

As a simple example, if your company has $1,000,000 in assets and $800,000 in liabilities, your equity would be $200,000:

$$\$1,000,000 - \$800,000 = \$200,000$$

Using the principles of algebra, this equation can be restated in a variety of formats. The most common is the simple **accounting equation**, which serves as the framework for the entire accounting process:

$$\text{Assets} = \text{Liabilities} + \text{Owners' equity}$$
$$\$1,000,000 = \$800,000 + \$200,000$$

accounting equation
Basic accounting equation stating that assets equal liabilities plus owners' equity

This equation suggests that either creditors or owners provide all the assets in a corporation. Think of it this way: If you were starting a new business, you could contribute cash to the company to buy the assets you needed to run your business or you could borrow money from a bank (the creditor) or you could do both. The company's liabilities are placed before owners' equity in the accounting equation because creditors get paid first. After liabilities have been paid, anything left over belongs to the owners. As a business engages in economic activity, the dollar amounts and composition of its assets, liabilities, and owners' equity change. However, the equation must always be in balance; in other words, one side of the equation must always equal the other side.

For example, if Google purchases $1,000,000 worth of computers on credit, assets would increase by $1,000,000 (the cost of the computers) and liabilities would also increase by $1,000,000 (the amount the company owes the computer vendor), keeping the accounting equation in balance. But if Google paid cash outright for the equipment (instead of arranging for credit), the company's total assets and total liabilities would not change, because the $1,000,000 increase in equipment would be offset by an equal $1,000,000 reduction in cash. In fact, the company would just be switching assets—cash for equipment.

Double-Entry Bookkeeping and the Matching Principle

To keep the accounting equation in balance, most companies use a **double-entry bookkeeping** system that records every transaction affecting assets, liabilities, or owners' equity. Each transaction is entered twice, as a pair of offsetting entries, to ensure that the equation stays in balance. (The double-entry method predates computers by hundreds of years and was originally created to minimize errors caused by entering and adding figures by hand.)

The **matching principle** requires that expenses incurred in producing revenues be deducted from the revenue they generated during the same accounting period. This matching of expenses and revenue is necessary for the company's financial statements to present an accurate picture of the profitability of a business. Accountants match revenue to expenses by adopting the **accrual basis** of accounting, which states that revenue is recognized when you make a sale or provide a service, not when you get paid. Similarly, your expenses are recorded when you receive the benefit of a service or when you use an asset to produce revenue—not when you pay for it. Accrual accounting focuses on the economic substance of the event instead of on the movement of cash. It's a way of recognizing that revenue can be earned either before or after cash is received and that expenses can be incurred when you receive a benefit (such as a shipment of supplies) whether before or after you pay for it.

double-entry bookkeeping
Method of recording financial transactions requiring two offsetting entries for every transaction to ensure that the accounting equation is always kept in balance

matching principle
Fundamental principle requiring that expenses incurred in producing revenue be deducted from the revenues they generate during an accounting period

accrual basis
Accounting method in which revenue is recorded when a sale is made and expense is recorded when it is incurred

Real-Time Updates

Learn More
Explore the accounting equation

Get a better feel for the accounting equation with these practical examples. On mybizlab (**www.mybizlab.com**), you can access Real-Time Updates within each chapter or under Student Study Tools. Otherwise, go to **http://real-timeupdates.com/bia5** and click on "Learn More."

cash basis
Accounting method in which revenue is recorded when payment is received and expense is recorded when cash is paid

If a business runs on a **cash basis**, the company records revenue only when money from the sale is actually received. Your checking account is a simple cash-based accounting system: You record checks, debit card charges, and ATM withdrawals at the time of purchase and record deposits at the time of receipt. Cash-based accounting is simple, but it can be misleading. It's easy to inflate income, for example, by delaying the payment of bills. For that reason, public companies are required to keep their books on an accrual basis.

depreciation
Accounting procedure for systematically spreading the cost of a tangible asset over its estimated useful life

Depreciation, or the allocation of the cost of a tangible long-term asset over a period of time, is another way that companies match expenses with revenue. During the normal course of business, a company enters into many transactions that benefit more than one accounting period—such as the purchase of buildings, inventory, and equipment. When Google buys a piece of real estate, for example, instead of deducting the entire cost of the item at the time of purchase, the company *depreciates* it, or spreads its cost over a certain number of years (as specified by tax regulations) because the asset will likely generate income for many years. If the company were to expense long-term assets at the time of purchase, its apparent financial performance would be distorted negatively in the year of purchase and positively in all future years when these assets generate revenue.

✓ CHECKPOINT

LEARNING OBJECTIVE 3: Describe the *accounting equation*, and explain the purpose of *double-entry bookkeeping* and the *matching principle*.

Summary: The basic accounting equation is Assets = Liabilities + Owners' equity. Double-entry bookkeeping is a system of recording every financial transaction twice in order to keep the accounting equation in balance. The matching principle makes sure that expenses incurred in producing revenues are deducted from the revenue they generated during the same accounting period.

Critical thinking: (1) How does double-entry bookkeeping help eliminate errors? (2) Why is accrual-based accounting considered more fraud-proof than cash-based accounting?

It's your business: (1) Does looking at the accounting equation make you reconsider your personal spending habits? (Think about taking on liabilities that don't create any long-term assets, for example.) (2) How would accrual basis accounting give you better insights into your personal finances?

Key terms to know: assets, liabilities, owners' equity, accounting equation, double-entry bookkeeping, matching principle, accrual basis, cash basis, depreciation

Using Financial Statements: The Balance Sheet

As a company conducts business day after day, sales, purchases, and other transactions are recorded and classified into individual accounts. After these individual transactions are recorded and then summarized, accountants must review the resulting transaction summaries and adjust or correct all errors or discrepancies before **closing the books**, or transferring net revenue and expense items to *retained earnings*. In a way, this is what you do every month when you get your bank statement. You might think you have $50 left in your account but then see your statement and realize with delight that you forgot

closing the books
Transferring net revenue and expense account balances to retained earnings for the period

EXHIBIT 17.2 The Accounting Process

The accounting process involves numerous steps between recording the sales and other transactions to the internal and external reporting of summarized financial results. (The paper forms illustrated here are classic accounting forms; today, nearly all companies record this information on computers.)

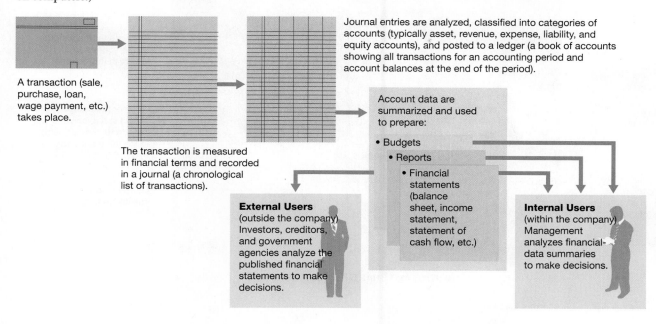

A transaction (sale, purchase, loan, wage payment, etc.) takes place.

The transaction is measured in financial terms and recorded in a journal (a chronological list of transactions).

Journal entries are analyzed, classified into categories of accounts (typically asset, revenue, expense, liability, and equity accounts), and posted to a ledger (a book of accounts showing all transactions for an accounting period and account balances at the end of the period).

Account data are summarized and used to prepare:

- Budgets
  - Reports
    - Financial statements (balance sheet, income statement, statement of cash flow, etc.)

External Users
(outside the company)
Investors, creditors, and government agencies analyze the published financial statements to make decisions.

Internal Users
(within the company)
Management analyzes financial-data summaries to make decisions.

to record the $100 check your dear, sweet grandmother sent you (and your true balance is $150)—or realize with dismay that you forgot to record the $300 ATM withdrawal you made on spring break (and your true balance is negative $250).

Exhibit 17.2 presents the process for putting all of a company's financial data into standardized formats that can be used for decision making, analysis, and planning. To make sense of these individual transactions, accountants summarize them by preparing financial statements.

Understanding Financial Statements

Financial statements consist of three separate but interrelated reports: the *balance sheet*, the *income statement*, and the *statement of cash flows*. These statements are required by law for all publicly traded companies, but they are vital management tools for every company, no matter how large or small. Together these statements provide information about an organization's financial strength and ability to meet current obligations, the effectiveness of its sales and collection efforts, and its effectiveness in managing its assets. Organizations and individuals use financial statements to spot opportunities and problems, to make business decisions, and to evaluate a company's past performance, present condition, and future prospects. Whether the company is a one-person consulting firm or a multinational firm with a hundred thousand employees, financial statements are a vital tool.

The following sections examine the financial statements of Computer Central Services, a hypothetical company engaged in direct sales and distribution of personal computers and accessories. In the past year, the company shipped over 2.3 million orders, amounting to more than $1.7 billion in sales—a 35 percent increase in sales over the prior year. The company's daily sales volume has grown considerably over the last decade—from $232,000 to $6.8 million. Because of this tremendous growth and the increasing demand for new computer products, the company recently purchased a 276,000-square-foot building.

EXHIBIT 17.3 Balance Sheet for Computer Central Services

The categories used on Computer Central Services's year-end balance sheet are typical.

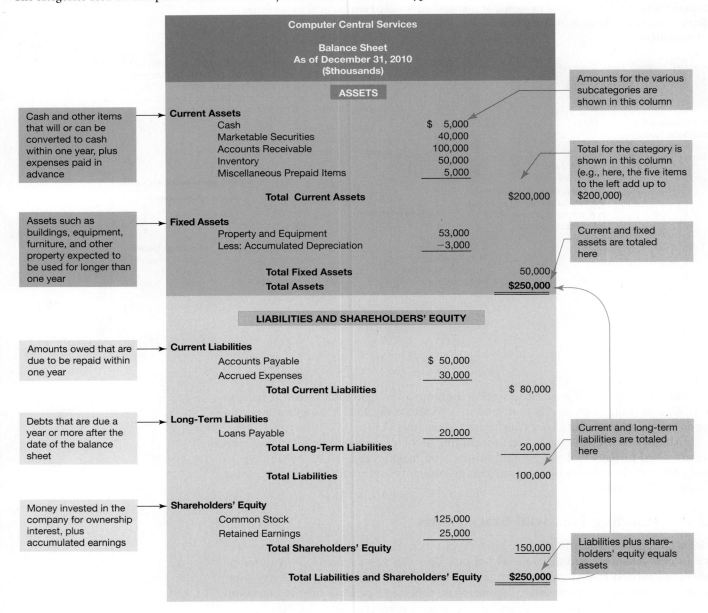

Cash and other items that will or can be converted to cash within one year, plus expenses paid in advance

Assets such as buildings, equipment, furniture, and other property expected to be used for longer than one year

Amounts owed that are due to be repaid within one year

Debts that are due a year or more after the date of the balance sheet

Money invested in the company for ownership interest, plus accumulated earnings

Amounts for the various subcategories are shown in this column

Total for the category is shown in this column (e.g., here, the five items to the left add up to $200,000)

Current and fixed assets are totaled here

Current and long-term liabilities are totaled here

Liabilities plus shareholders' equity equals assets

Computer Central Services

Balance Sheet
As of December 31, 2010
($thousands)

ASSETS

Current Assets		
Cash	$ 5,000	
Marketable Securities	40,000	
Accounts Receivable	100,000	
Inventory	50,000	
Miscellaneous Prepaid Items	5,000	
Total Current Assets		$200,000
Fixed Assets		
Property and Equipment	53,000	
Less: Accumulated Depreciation	−3,000	
Total Fixed Assets		50,000
Total Assets		**$250,000**

LIABILITIES AND SHAREHOLDERS' EQUITY

Current Liabilities		
Accounts Payable	$ 50,000	
Accrued Expenses	30,000	
Total Current Liabilities		$ 80,000
Long-Term Liabilities		
Loans Payable	20,000	
Total Long-Term Liabilities		20,000
Total Liabilities		100,000
Shareholders' Equity		
Common Stock	125,000	
Retained Earnings	25,000	
Total Shareholders' Equity		150,000
Total Liabilities and Shareholders' Equity		**$250,000**

Balance Sheet

balance sheet
Statement of a firm's financial position on a particular date; also known as a *statement of financial position*

calendar year
Twelve-month accounting period that begins on January 1 and ends on December 31

fiscal year
Any 12 consecutive months used as an accounting period

The **balance sheet**, also known as the *statement of financial position*, is a snapshot of a company's financial position on a particular date (see Exhibit 17.3). In effect, it freezes all business actions and provides a baseline from which a company can measure change. This statement is called a balance sheet because it includes all elements in the accounting equation and shows the balance between assets on one side of the equation and liabilities and owners' equity on the other side. In other words, as in the accounting equation, a change on one side of the balance sheet means changes elsewhere.

Every company prepares a balance sheet at least once a year, most often at the end of the **calendar year**, covering from January 1 to December 31. However, many business and government bodies use a **fiscal year**, which may be any 12 consecutive months. For example, a company may use a fiscal year of June 1 to May 31 because its peak selling season ends in May. Its fiscal year would then correspond to its full annual cycle of manufacturing and selling. Some companies prepare a balance sheet more often than once a year, perhaps at the end of each month or quarter. Thus, every balance sheet is dated to show the exact date when the financial snapshot was taken.

By reading a company's balance sheet you should be able to determine the size of the company, the major assets owned, any asset changes that occurred in recent periods, how the company's assets are financed, and any major changes that have occurred in the company's debt and equity in recent periods. Most companies classify assets, liabilities, and owners' equity into categories such as those shown in the Computer Central Services balance sheet.

Assets

As discussed earlier in this chapter, an asset is something owned by a company with the intent to generate income. Assets can be *tangible* or *intangible*. Tangible assets include land, buildings, and equipment. Intangible asset include intellectual property (such as patents and business methods), *goodwill* (which includes company reputation), brand awareness and recognition, workforce skills, management talent, and even customer relationships.[16]

As you might expect, assigning value to intangible assets is not an easy task, but these assets make up an increasingly important part of the value of many contemporary companies.[17] For instance, much of the real value of a company such as Google is not in its tangible assets, but in its search engine algorithms, software designs, brand awareness, and the brainpower of its workforce. The company's 2008 balance sheet, for example, listed nearly $6 billion in goodwill and other intangibles.[18]

Most often, the asset section of the balance sheet is divided into *current assets* and *fixed assets*. **Current assets** include cash and other items that will or can become cash within the following year. **Fixed assets** (sometimes referred to as *property, plant,* and *equipment*) are long-term investments in buildings, equipment, furniture and fixtures, transportation equipment, land, and other tangible property used in running the business. Fixed assets have a useful life of more than one year. For example, Computer Central Services's fixed assets include the company's warehouse and office facilities.

Assets are listed in descending order by *liquidity*, or the ease with which they can be converted into cash. Thus, current assets are listed before fixed assets. The balance sheet gives a subtotal for each type of asset and then a grand total for all assets. Computer Central Services's current assets consist primarily of cash, investments in short-term marketable securities such as money-market funds, *accounts receivable* (amounts due from customers), and inventory (such as computers, software, and other items the company sells to customers).

current assets
Cash and items that can be turned into cash within one year

fixed assets
Assets retained for long-term use, such as land, buildings, machinery, and equipment; also referred to as *property, plant, and equipment*

Liabilities

Liabilities may be current or long-term, and they are listed in the order in which they will come due. The balance sheet gives subtotals for **current liabilities** (obligations that will have to be met within one year of the date of the balance sheet) and **long-term liabilities** (obligations that are due one year or more after the date of the balance sheet), and then it gives a grand total for all liabilities.

Current liabilities include accounts payable, short-term financing, and accrued expenses. *Accounts payable* includes the money the company owes its suppliers as well as money it owes vendors for miscellaneous services (such as electricity and telephone charges). *Short-term financing* consists of trade credit—the amount owed to suppliers for products purchased but not yet paid for—and commercial paper—short-term promissory notes. *Accrued expenses* are expenses that have been incurred but for which bills have not yet been received. For example, because

current liabilities
Obligations that must be met within a year

long-term liabilities
Obligations that fall due more than a year from the date of the balance sheet

 Real-Time Updates

Learn More
Balance sheets made easy

Get comfortable with balances sheets with this two-part series. On mybizlab (**www.mybizlab.com**), you can access Real-Time Updates within each chapter or under Student Study Tools. Otherwise, go to **http://real-timeupdates.com/bia5** and click on "Learn More."

Computer Central Services's salespeople earn commissions, the company has a liability to those employees after the sale is made—regardless of when a check is issued to the employee. Thus, the company must record this liability because it represents a claim against company assets. If such expenses and their associated liabilities were not recorded, the company's financial statements would be misleading and would violate the matching principle (because the commission expenses that were earned at the time of sale would not be matched to the revenue generated from the sale).

Long-term liabilities include loans, leases, and bonds. A borrower makes principal and interest payments to the lender over the term of the loan, and its obligation is limited to these payments (see the "Debt versus Equity Financing" discussion in Chapter 18 on page 463). Rather than borrowing money to make purchases, a firm may enter into a *lease*, under which the owner of an item allows another party to use it in exchange for regular payments. Bonds are certificates that obligate the company to repay a certain sum, plus interest, to the bondholder on a specific date. Bonds are traded on organized securities exchanges and are discussed in detail in Chapter 19.

Owners' Equity

retained earnings
The portion of shareholders' equity earned by the company but not distributed to its owners in the form of dividends

The owners' investment in a business is listed on the balance sheet under owners' equity (or *shareholders'* or *stockholders' equity* for corporations). Sole proprietorships list owner's equity under the owner's name with the amount (assets minus liabilities). Small partnerships list each partner's share of the business separately, and large partnerships list the total of all partners' shares. In a corporation, the shareholders' total investment value is the sum of two amounts: the total value of the all the shares currently held, plus **retained earnings**—cash that is kept by the company rather than distributed to shareholders in the form of dividends. As Exhibit 17.3 shows, Computer Central Services had retained earnings amounting to $25 million. The company doesn't pay dividends—many small and growing corporations don't—but rather builds its cash reserves to fund expansion in the future. (Shareholders' equity can be slightly more complicated than this, depending on how the company's shares were first created, but this gives you the basic idea of how the assets portion of the balance sheet works.)

 **CHECKPOINT**

LEARNING OBJECTIVE 4: Identify the major financial statements, and explain how to read a balance sheet.

Summary: The three major financial statements are the balance sheet, the income statement, and the statement of cash flows. The balance sheet provides a snapshot of the business at a particular point in time. It shows the size of the company, the major assets owned, the ways the assets are financed, and the amount of owners' investment in the business. Its three main sections are assets, liabilities, and owners' equity.

Critical thinking: (1) Why do analysts need to consider different factors when evaluating a company's ability to repay short-term versus long-term debt? (2) Would the current amount of the owners' equity be a reasonable price to pay for a company? Why or why not?

It's your business: (1) What are your current and long-term financial liabilities? Are these liabilities restricting your flexibility as a student or consumer? (2) As a potential employee, what intangible assets can you offer a company?

Key terms to know: closing the books, balance sheet, calendar year, fiscal year, current assets, fixed assets, current liabilities, long-term liabilities, retained earnings

Using Financial Statements: Income and Cash Flow Statements

In addition to the balance sheet, the two other fundamentally important financial statements are the income statement and the statement of cash flows.

Income Statement

If the balance sheet is a snapshot, the income statement is a movie. The **income statement**, or *profit-and-loss statement* or simply "P&L," shows an organization's profit performance over a period of time, typically one year. It summarizes revenue from all sources as well as all **expenses**, the costs that have arisen in generating revenues. Expenses and income taxes are then subtracted from revenues to show the actual profit or loss of a company, a figure known as **net income**—also called profit or, informally, the *bottom line*. By briefly reviewing a company's income statements, you should have a general sense of the company's size, its trend in sales, its major expenses, and the resulting net income or loss. Owners, creditors, and investors can evaluate the company's past performance and future prospects by comparing net income for one year with net income for previous years. Exhibit 17.4 shows the income statement for Computer Central Services.

income statement
Financial record of a company's revenues, expenses, and profits over a given period of time; also known as *profit-and-loss statement*

expenses
Costs created in the process of generating revenues

net income
Profit earned or loss incurred by a firm, determined by subtracting expenses from revenues; casually referred to as the *bottom line*

EXHIBIT 17.4 **Income Statement for Computer Central Services**

An income statement summarizes the company's financial operations over a particular accounting period, usually a year.

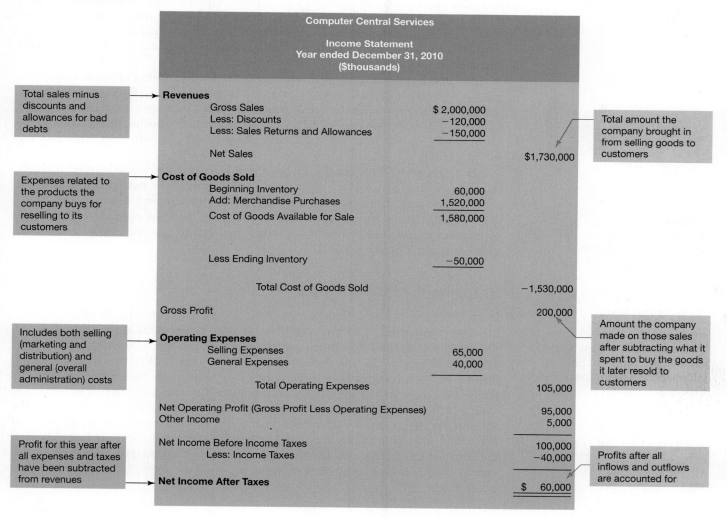

Computer Central Services	
Income Statement	
Year ended December 31, 2010	
($thousands)	

Revenues		
Gross Sales	$ 2,000,000	
Less: Discounts	−120,000	
Less: Sales Returns and Allowances	−150,000	
Net Sales		$1,730,000
Cost of Goods Sold		
Beginning Inventory	60,000	
Add: Merchandise Purchases	1,520,000	
Cost of Goods Available for Sale	1,580,000	
Less Ending Inventory	−50,000	
Total Cost of Goods Sold		−1,530,000
Gross Profit		200,000
Operating Expenses		
Selling Expenses	65,000	
General Expenses	40,000	
Total Operating Expenses		105,000
Net Operating Profit (Gross Profit Less Operating Expenses)		95,000
Other Income		5,000
Net Income Before Income Taxes		100,000
Less: Income Taxes		−40,000
Net Income After Taxes		$ 60,000

Total sales minus discounts and allowances for bad debts

Total amount the company brought in from selling goods to customers

Expenses related to the products the company buys for reselling to its customers

Includes both selling (marketing and distribution) and general (overall administration) costs

Amount the company made on those sales after subtracting what it spent to buy the goods it later resold to customers

Profit for this year after all expenses and taxes have been subtracted from revenues

Profits after all inflows and outflows are accounted for

cost of goods sold
Cost of producing or acquiring a company's products for sale during a given period

Expenses include both the direct costs associated with creating or purchasing products for sale and the indirect costs associated with operating the business. If a company manufactures or purchases inventory, the cost of storing the product for sale (such as heating the warehouse, paying the rent, and buying insurance on the storage facility) is added to the difference between the cost of the beginning inventory and the cost of the ending inventory in order to compute the actual cost of items that were sold during a period—or the **cost of goods sold**. The computation can be summarized as follows:

Cost of goods sold = Beginning inventory + Net purchases − Ending inventory

gross profit
Amount remaining when the cost of goods sold is deducted from net sales; also known as *gross margin*

operating expenses
All costs of operation that are not included under cost of goods sold

As shown in Exhibit 17.4, cost of goods sold is deducted from sales to obtain a company's **gross profit**—a key figure used in financial statement analysis. In addition to the costs directly associated with producing goods, companies deduct **operating expenses**, which include both *selling expenses* and *general expenses*, to compute a firm's *net operating income*. Net operating income is often a better indicator of financial health because it gives an idea of how much cash the company is able to generate. For instance, a company with a sizable gross profit level can actually be losing money if its operating expenses are out of control—and if it doesn't have enough cash on hand to cover the shortfall, it could soon find itself bankrupt.[19] *Selling expenses* are operating expenses incurred through marketing and distributing the product (such as wages or salaries of salespeople, advertising, supplies, insurance for the sales operation, depreciation for the store and sales equipment, and other sales department expenses such as telephone charges). *General expenses* are operating expenses incurred in the overall administration of a business. They include such items as professional services (such as accounting and legal fees), office salaries, depreciation of office equipment, insurance for office operations, and supplies.

A firm's net operating income is then adjusted by the amount of any nonoperating income or expense items such as the gain or loss on the sale of a building. The result is the firm's net income or loss before income taxes (losses are shown in parentheses), a key figure used in budgeting, cash-flow analysis, and a variety of other financial computations. Finally, income taxes are deducted to compute the company's net income or loss for the period.

In recent years, many companies have been using another measure of profitability, particularly when they solicit money from outside investors or put the company up for sale. Venture capitalists and other investors often view *earnings before interest, taxes, depreciation, and amortization*, or **EBITDA**, as a "purer" measure of profitability because it provides a clear look at revenue minus expenses and ignores various accounting moves that can affect net income.[20]

EBITDA
Earnings before interest, taxes, depreciation, and amortization; a simpler and more direct measure of income

Statement of Cash Flows

statement of cash flows
Statement of a firm's cash receipts and cash payments that presents information on its sources and uses of cash

In addition to preparing a balance sheet and an income statement, all public companies and many privately owned companies prepare a **statement of cash flows**, or *cash flow statement*, to show how much cash the company generated over time and where it went (see Exhibit 17.5). The statement of cash flows tracks the cash coming into and flowing out of a company's bank accounts. It reveals the increase or decrease in the company's cash for the period and summarizes (by category) the sources of that change. From a brief review of this statement you should have a general sense of the amount of cash created or consumed by daily operations, the amount of cash invested in fixed or other assets, the amount of debt borrowed or repaid, and the proceeds from the sale of stock or payments for dividends. In addition, an analysis of cash flows provides a good idea of a company's ability to pay its short-term obligations when they become due.

EXHIBIT 17.5 Statement of Cash Flows for Computer Central Services

A statement of cash flows shows a firm's cash receipts and cash payments as a result of three main activities—operating, investing, and financing—for an identified period of time (such as the year indicated here).

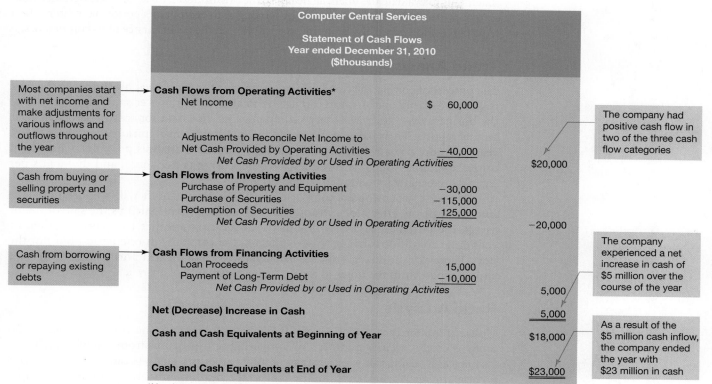

Most companies start with net income and make adjustments for various inflows and outflows throughout the year

Cash from buying or selling property and securities

Cash from borrowing or repaying existing debts

The company had positive cash flow in two of the three cash flow categories

The company experienced a net increase in cash of $5 million over the course of the year

As a result of the $5 million cash inflow, the company ended the year with $23 million in cash

Computer Central Services

Statement of Cash Flows
Year ended December 31, 2010
($thousands)

Cash Flows from Operating Activities*		
Net Income		$ 60,000
Adjustments to Reconcile Net Income to Net Cash Provided by Operating Activities	−40,000	
Net Cash Provided by or Used in Operating Activities		$20,000
Cash Flows from Investing Activities		
Purchase of Property and Equipment	−30,000	
Purchase of Securities	−115,000	
Redemption of Securities	125,000	
Net Cash Provided by or Used in Operating Activities		−20,000
Cash Flows from Financing Activities		
Loan Proceeds	15,000	
Payment of Long-Term Debt	−10,000	
Net Cash Provided by or Used in Operating Activites		5,000
Net (Decrease) Increase in Cash		5,000
Cash and Cash Equivalents at Beginning of Year		$18,000
Cash and Cash Equivalents at End of Year		$23,000

*Numbers preceded by minus sign indicate cash outflows

✓CHECKPOINT

LEARNING OBJECTIVE 5: Explain the purpose of the income statement and statement of cash flows.

Summary: The income statement, also known as the profit and loss statement, reflects the results of operations over a period of time. It gives a general sense of a company's size and performance. The statement of cash flows shows how a company's cash was received and spent in three areas: operations, investments, and financing. It gives a general sense of the amount of cash created or consumed by daily operations, fixed assets, investments, and debt over a period of time.

Critical thinking: (1) How could two companies with similar gross profit figures end up with dramatically different net operating income? (2) How might a statement of cash flows help a turnaround expert decide how to rescue a struggling company?

It's your business: (1) What would your personal income statement look like today? Are you operating "at a profit" or "at a loss"? (2) What steps could you take to reduce your "operating expenses"?

Key terms to know: income statement, expenses, net income, cost of goods sold, gross profit, operating expenses, EBITDA, statement of cash flows

Analyzing Financial Statements

After financial statements have been prepared, managers, investors, and lenders use these statements to evaluate the financial health of the organization, make business decisions, and spot opportunities for improvements by looking at the company's performance in relation to its past performance, the economy as a whole, and the performance of its competitors.

Trend Analysis

The process of comparing financial data from year to year to see how they have changed is known as *trend analysis*. You can use trend analysis to uncover shifts in the nature of the business over time. Most large companies provide data for trend analysis in their annual reports. Their balance sheets and income statements typically show three to five years or more of data (making comparative statement analysis possible). Changes in other key items—such as revenues, income, earnings per share, and dividends per share—are usually presented in tables and graphs.

Of course, when you are comparing one period with another, it's important to take into account the effects of extraordinary or unusual items such as the sale of major assets, the purchase of a new line of products from another company, weather, or economic conditions that may have affected the company in one period but not the next. These extraordinary items are usually disclosed in the text portion of a company's annual report or in the notes to the financial statements.

Ratio Analysis

Unlike trend analysis, which tracks *absolute* numbers from one year to the next, ratio analysis creates *relative* numbers by comparing sets of figures from a single year's performance. By using ratios rather than absolute amounts, analysts can more easily assess a company's performance from one year to the next or compare it with other companies. A variety of commonly used ratios help companies understand their current operations and answer some key questions: Is inventory too large? Are credit customers paying too slowly? Can the company pay its bills? Ratios also set standards and benchmarks for gauging future business by comparing a company's scores with industry averages that show the performance of competition. Every industry tends to have its own "normal" ratios, which act as yardsticks for individual companies.

Types of Financial Ratios

Financial ratios can be organized into the following groups, as Exhibit 17.6 shows: profitability, liquidity, activity, and leverage (or debt).

Profitability Ratios

You can analyze how well a company is conducting its ongoing operations by computing *profitability ratios*, which show the state of the company's financial performance or how well it's generating profits. Three of the most common profitability ratios are **return on sales**, or *profit margin* (the net income a business makes per unit of sales); **return on equity** (net income divided by owners' equity); and **earnings per share** (the profit earned for each share of stock outstanding). Exhibit 17.6 shows how to compute these profitability ratios by using the financial information from Computer Central Services.

Liquidity Ratios

Liquidity ratios measure a firm's ability to pay its short-term obligations. As you might expect, lenders and creditors are keenly interested in liquidity measures. A company's **working capital** (current assets minus current liabilities) is an indicator of liquidity because it represents current assets remaining after the payment of all current liabilities. The dollar amount of working capital can be misleading, however. For example, it may

---

return on sales
Ratio between net income after taxes and net sales; also known as *profit margin*

return on equity
Ratio between net income after taxes and total owners' equity

earnings per share
Measure of a firm's profitability for each share of outstanding stock, calculated by dividing net income after taxes by the average number of shares of common stock outstanding

working capital
Current assets minus current liabilities

EXHIBIT 17.6 How Well Does This Company Stack Up?

Financial ratios are a quick and convenient way to evaluate how well a company is performing in relation to prior performance, the economy as a whole, and the company's competitors.

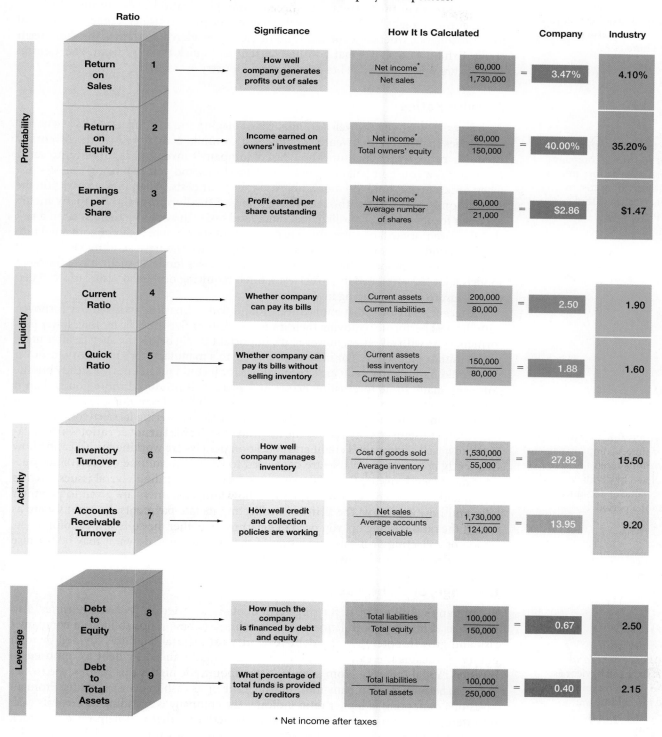

* Net income after taxes

include the value of slow-moving inventory items that cannot be used to help pay a company's short-term debts.

A different picture of the company's liquidity is provided by the **current ratio**—current assets divided by current liabilities. This figure compares the current debt owed

current ratio
Measure of a firm's short-term liquidity, calculated by dividing current assets by current liabilities

quick ratio
Measure of a firm's short-term liquidity, calculated by adding cash, marketable securities, and receivables, then dividing that sum by current liabilities; also known as the *acid-test ratio*

with the current assets available to pay that debt. The **quick ratio**, also called the *acid-test ratio*, is computed by subtracting inventory from current assets and then dividing the result by current liabilities. This ratio is often a better indicator of a firm's ability to pay creditors than the current ratio because the quick ratio leaves out inventories—which at times might be difficult to sell. Analysts generally consider a quick ratio of 1.0 to be reasonable, whereas a current ratio of 2.0 is considered a safe risk for short-term credit. Exhibit 17.6 shows that both the current and quick ratios of Computer Central Services are well above these benchmarks and industry averages.

Activity Ratios

inventory turnover ratio
Measure of the time a company takes to turn its inventory into sales, calculated by dividing cost of goods sold by the average value of inventory for a period

Activity ratios analyze how well a company is managing and making use of its assets. For companies that maintain inventories, the most common activity ratio is the **inventory turnover ratio**, which measures how fast a company's inventory is turned into sales. Inventory is a constant balancing act—hold too little, and you risk being out of stock when orders arrive; hold too much, and you raise your costs. When inventory sits on the shelf, money is tied up without earning interest; furthermore, the company incurs expenses for its storage, handling, insurance, and taxes. In addition, there is often a risk that the inventory will become obsolete or go out of style before it can be converted into finished goods and sold. Car dealers, for example, face the never-ending challenge of selling this year's models before next year's arrive. Newer models usually make the older models a lot less attractive in buyers' eyes, often requiring dealers to resort to steep discounts just to get rid of aging inventory.[21]

A recent study of U.S. manufacturers found wide disparities in inventory turnover, with the best performers moving their inventory four or five times faster than lower performers.[22] As with all ratios, however, it's important to dig below the surface after making an initial comparison. For instance, a decline in a manufacturer's inventory turnover ratio could indicate that sales are slowing down, or it could mean sales are steady but the company made some forecasting errors and as a result produced more goods than it needed. Conversely, a company with a high ratio could be discounting heavily and not making as much money as it could by raising prices and lowering its sales volume.

accounts receivable turnover ratio
Measure of time a company takes to turn its accounts receivable into cash, calculated by dividing sales by the average value of accounts receivable for a period

Another useful activity ratio is the **accounts receivable turnover ratio**, which measures how well a company's credit and collection policies are working by indicating how frequently accounts receivable are converted to cash. The volume of receivables outstanding depends on the financial manager's decisions regarding several issues, such as who qualifies for credit and who does not, how long customers are given to pay their bills, and how aggressive the firm is in collecting its late payments. Be careful here as well. If the ratio is going up, you need to determine whether the company is doing a better job of collecting or if sales are rising. If the ratio is going down, it may be because sales are decreasing or because collection efforts are lagging.

Leverage, or Debt, Ratios

debt-to-equity ratio
Measure of the extent to which a business is financed by debt as opposed to invested capital, calculated by dividing the company's total liabilities by owners' equity

A company's ability to pay its long-term debts is reflected in its *leverage ratios*, also known as *debt ratios*. Both lenders and investors use these ratios to judge a company's risk and growth potential. The **debt-to-equity ratio** (total liabilities divided by total equity) indicates the extent to which a business is financed by debt as opposed to invested capital (equity). From a lender's standpoint, the higher this ratio is, the riskier the loan, because the company must devote more of its cash to debt payments. From an investor's standpoint, a higher ratio indicates the company is spending more of its cash on interest payments rather than investing in activities that will help raise the stock price.[23] Chapter 18 compares the advantages and disadvantages of debt and equity financing.

debt-to-assets ratio
Measure of a firm's ability to carry long-term debt, calculated by dividing total liabilities by total assets

The **debt-to-assets ratio** (total liabilities divided by total assets) indicates how much of the company's assets are financed by creditors. As with debt-to-equity, the higher this ratio gets, the riskier the company looks to a lender. From an investor's perspective, though, a high level of debt relative to assets could indicate that a company is making aggressive moves to grow without diluting the value of existing shares by offering more shares for sale.[24] However, having a high level of debt to assets, or being *highly leveraged*, puts a company at risk. Those assets may not be able to generate enough cash to pay back the debt, or lenders and suppliers might cut off the company's credit.

Again, with every ratio, use the ratio as a helpful initial indicator but then dig below the surface to see what the numbers really mean.

For the latest information on accounting practices and financial reporting, visit http://real-timeupdates.com/bia5 and click on Chapter 17.

✓CHECKPOINT

LEARNING OBJECTIVE 6: Explain the purpose of ratio analysis, and list the four main categories of financial ratios.

Summary: Financial ratios provide information for analyzing the health and future prospects of a business. Ratios facilitate financial comparisons among different-size companies and between a company and industry averages. Most of the important ratios fall into one of four categories: profitability ratios, which show how well the company generates profits; liquidity ratios, which measure the company's ability to pay its short-term obligations; activity ratios, which analyze how well a company is managing its assets; and debt ratios, which measure a company's ability to pay its long-term debt.

Critical thinking: (1) Why is it so important to be aware of extraordinary items when analyzing a company's finances? (2) Why is the quick ratio frequently a better indicator than the current ratio of a firm's ability to pay its bills?

It's your business: (1) Assume you are about to make a significant consumer purchase, and the product is available at two local stores, one with high inventory turnover and one with low. Which store would you choose based on this information? Why? (2) If you were applying for a home mortgage loan today, would a lender view your debt-to-assets ratio favorably? Why or why not?

Key terms to know: return on sales, return on equity, earnings per share, working capital, current ratio, quick ratio, inventory turnover ratio, accounts receivable turnover ratio, debt-to-equity ratio, debt-to-assets ratio

Behind the
Scenes

Google This: "Cost Control"

By just about any measure you can think of, Google is one of the most spectacular success stories in the history of business. However, even a company as wealthy as Google has to control spending.

Google's case is unusual in the sense of its sheer scale, but the story is not unique. When a young company is growing quickly and money is pouring in from sales or from investors, there is a natural tendency to focus on building the business and capturing market opportunities. The less exciting—but ultimately no less important—task of creating a sustainable cost structure with rigorous expense management often doesn't get as much attention in the early years.

In some companies, rapid growth in a hot economy can mask serious underlying problems that threaten the long-term viability of the enterprise. In the dot-com boom of the late

1990s, for instance, more than a few high-flying companies fell to earth when investors who had enjoyed a rocket ride in the stock market realized the companies didn't have workable business models.

Google's revenue had been increasing at a spectacular pace, from $10.6 billion in 2006, to $16.6 billion in 2007, to $21.8 billion in 2008. However, expenses were growing at an even faster rate. As a result, the company's profit margin dropped from 29 percent in 2006 to around 20 percent in 2008 (still 5 percentage points better than the industry average); 2008 ended with the first-ever drop in quarterly profits in the company's history.

The cooling economy and slowing profits didn't expose any fatal flaws in the Google business model, but the drop certainly was a wakeup call that emphasized the need to transition to the next stage of organizational development. It was time for the accounting and financial management functions to play a more prominent role and to transform a wild and wooly entrepreneurial success story into a major corporation with stable finances.

Back in 2001, Google co-founders Larry Page and Sergey Brin brought in Eric Schmidt, a seasoned technology industry executive, to guide the company's growth beyond its initial start-up stage. Under Schmidt's leadership, Google expanded from 200 employees to more than 20,000 and secured its place as one of the world's most influential companies. In 2008, facing the need for a more methodical approach to accounting and financial management, Schmidt brought in another executive with a proven track record in corporate leadership. Patrick Pichette made his name helping Bell Canada reduce operating expenses by $2 billion, and his proven ability to bring expenses in line with revenue was just what Google needed. Plus, his experience with the Six Sigma process and quality control (see page 256) should be an interesting element to blend into Google's freewheeling culture.

Pichette and other executives are tackling expenses at three levels: employee perks, staffing, and project investment. It's safe to say the employee perks are still better than you'll find just about anywhere, but they have been trimmed back to save money. The company no longer pays for the annual trip, and the $1,000 annual cash bonus was replaced with a $400 G1 smartphone. The 50 percent discount on Google-branded clothes and other products was reduced to 20 percent, and the subsidy on hybrid vehicles was trimmed as well. On the plus side, employees still get free gourmet meals and subsidized concierge services to take some of the hassle out of handling life's little chores.

At the staffing level, Google is taking a much harder look at hiring practices to better align staffing with project needs. Tellingly, the first layoffs in the company's history, in January 2009, involved 100 recruiters whose services were no longer needed because Google's hiring rate had slowed so dramatically. Thousands of contract workers have been let go as well. The vaunted "20 percent time" was reevaluated, too, with the company deciding to focus engineers' time more directly on core projects.

At the project and program level, Google is scrutinizing its investments more carefully and pulling the plug on less-promising activities. For instance, it stopped developing Lively, a virtual world that would've competed with SecondLife, and it shut down dMarc Broadcasting, a radio advertising company it had acquired in 2006.

While continuing to manage costs more carefully, the company is also stepping up its efforts to generate more revenue. Key areas of focus include expanding its activities in mobile phone advertising and display advertising (graphical ads as opposed to the text-only ads that now appear next to Google searches), as well as growing its software revenues. Figuring out a way to turn YouTube into a profitable business will be a top priority as well.

So far the results look promising. Expenses are down, and free cash flow is up dramatically. And even after that rough patch when the economy slowed ad sales, Google still ended 2008 with over $20 billion in current assets. It might not have an infinite supply of money, but with a new focus on careful accounting, Google will have plenty of cash to keep its innovation engine churning out new ideas for years to come.[25]

Critical Thinking Questions

1. Given the eventual need for rigorous financial management, should every company have extensive cost controls in place from the first moment of operation? Explain your answer.
2. Halfway through its 2009 fiscal year, Google had a debt-to-equity ratio of 0.04. Microsoft, one of its key competitors, had a debt-to-equity ratio of 0.15. From a bank's point of view, which of the two companies is a more attractive loan candidate, based on this ratio? Why?
3. At the end of 2008, Google's current ratio was 8.77. Midway through 2009, the current ratio was up to 11.91. Does this make Google more or less of a credit risk in the eyes of potential lenders? Why?

LEARN MORE ONLINE

Visit Google's "Investor Relations" section at http://investor.google.com. Peruse "What's New?" to see the latest financial news. How does the company's financial health look at present? What do the trends for revenue, expenses, and income look like? Does the company report both GAAP and non-GAAP financial results? Why does it report non-GAAP figures? ∎

Key Terms

accounting (431)
accounting equation (437)
accounts receivable turnover
      ratio (448)
accrual basis (437)
assets (436)
audit (432)
balance sheet (440)
bookkeeping (431)
calendar year (440)
cash basis (438)
certified public accountants
      (CPAs) (432)
closing the books (438)
controller (432)
cost of goods sold (444)
current assets (441)
current liabilities (441)
current ratio (447)

debt-to-assets ratio (448)
debt-to-equity ratio (448)
depreciation (438)
double-entry
      bookkeeping (437)
earnings per share (446)
EBITDA (444)
expenses (443)
external auditors (434)
financial accounting (431)
fiscal year (440)
fixed assets (441)
generally accepted accounting
      principles (GAAP) (434)
gross profit (444)
income statement (443)
international financial reporting
      standards (IFRS) (434)
inventory turnover ratio (448)

liabilities (436)
long-term liabilities (441)
management
      accounting (431)
matching principle (437)
net income (443)
operating expenses (444)
owners' equity (436)
private accountants (431)
public accountants (432)
quick ratio (448)
retained earnings (442)
return on equity (446)
return on sales (446)
Sarbanes-Oxley (435)
statement of
      cash flows (444)
working capital (446)

Test Your Knowledge

Questions for Review

1. What is GAAP?
2. What is the value of an income statement?
3. What are the three main profitability ratios, and how is each calculated?
4. What is an audit, and why is it performed?
5. What is the matching principle?

Questions for Analysis

6. Why would a company bother with double-entry book-keeping?
7. Why would a bank lending officer be interested in the cash flow statement of a company that is applying for a loan?
8. Why are the costs of fixed assets depreciated?
9. Why are the GAAP and IFRS standards being converged?
10. **Ethical Considerations.** In the process of closing the company books, you encounter a problematic transaction. One of the company's customers was invoiced twice for the same project materials, resulting in a $1,000 overcharge. You immediately notify the controller, whose response is, "Let it go, it happens often." What should you do now?

Questions for Application

11. If you were asked to lend money to your cousin's clothing store to help her through a slow sales period, would you be more interested in looking at the current ratio or the quick ratio as a measure of liquidity? Why?
12. The senior partner of an accounting firm is looking for ways to increase the firm's business. What other services besides traditional accounting can the firm offer to its clients? What new challenges might this additional work create?
13. Visit the websites of Google and Microsoft and retrieve their annual reports. Using these financials, compute the working capital, current ratio, and quick ratio for each company. Does one company appear to be more liquid than the other? Why?
14. **Concept Integration.** Your appliance manufacturing company recently implemented a just-in-time inventory system (see Chapter 9) for all parts used in the manufacturing process. How might you expect this move to affect the company's inventory turnover rate, current ratio, and quick ratio?

Practice Your Knowledge

Sharpening Your Communication Skills

Obtain a copy of the annual report of a business and examine what the report shows about finances and current operations.

- Consider the statements made by the CEO regarding the past year: Did the company do well, or are changes in operations necessary to its future well-being? What are the projections for future growth in sales and profits?

- Examine the financial summaries for information about the fiscal condition of the company: Did the company show a profit?

- If possible, obtain a copy of the company's annual report from the previous year, and compare it with the current report to determine whether past projections were accurate.

- Prepare a brief written summary of your conclusions.

Building Your Team Skills

Divide into small groups and compute the following financial ratios for Alpine Manufacturing using the company's balance sheet and income statement. Compare your answers to those of your classmates:

- Profitability ratios: return on sales; return on equity; earnings per share
- Liquidity ratios: current ratio; quick ratio
- Activity ratios: inventory turnover; accounts receivable turnover
- Leverage ratios: debt to equity; debt to total assets

ALPINE MANUFACTURING INCOME STATEMENT YEAR ENDED DECEMBER 31, 2010	
Sales	$1,800
Less: Cost of Goods Sold	1,000
Gross Profit	$800
Less: Total Operating Expenses	450
Net Operating Income Before Income Taxes	350
Less: Income Taxes	50
Net Income after Income Taxes	$300

ALPINE MANUFACTURING BALANCE SHEET DECEMBER 31, 2010		
ASSETS		
Cash	$100	
Accounts Receivable (beginning balance $350)	300	
Inventory (beginning balance $250)	300	
Current Assets	700	
Fixed Assets	2,300	
Total Assets		$3,000
LIABILITIES AND SHAREHOLDERS' EQUITY		
Current Liabilities (beginning balance $300)	$400	
Long-Term Debts	1,600	
Shareholders' Equity (100 common shares outstanding valued at $12 each)	1,000	
Total Liabilities and Shareholders' Equity		$3,000

Expand Your Knowledge

Discovering Career Opportunities

People interested in entering the field of accounting can choose among a wide variety of careers with diverse responsibilities and challenges. Visit the "Accountants and Auditors" page at www.bls.gov/oco/ocos001.htm to read more about career opportunities in accounting.

1. What are the day-to-day duties of this occupation? How would these duties contribute to the financial success of a company?
2. What skills and educational qualifications would you need to enter this occupation? How do these qualifications fit with your current plans, skills, and interests?

3. What kinds of employers hire people for this position? According to your research, does the number of employers seem to be increasing or decreasing? How do you think this trend will affect your employment possibilities if you choose this career?

Developing Your Research Skills

Select an article from a business journal or newspaper (print or online editions) that discusses the quarterly or year-end performance of a company that industry analysts consider notable for either positive or negative reasons.

1. Did the company report a profit or a loss for this accounting period? What other performance indicators were reported? Is the company's performance improving or declining?

2. Did the company's performance match industry analysts' expectations, or was it a surprise? How did analysts or other experts respond to the firm's actual quarterly or year-end results?

3. What reasons were given for the company's improvement or decline in performance?

Improving Your Tech Insights: GRC Software

The Sarbanes-Oxley Act's requirement that publicly traded companies regularly verify their internal accounting controls spurred the development of software tools to help companies flag and fix problems in their financial systems. In the past few years, a number of software vendors have gone beyond Sarbox compliance to integrate the monitoring of a wide range of legal and financial issues that require management attention. This new category of software is generally known as *governance, risk, and compliance (GRC) software*. GRC capabilities can either be built into other software packages (such as accounting and finance software, process management software, or business intelligence software) or offered as standalone compliance programs. Vendors that offer GRC capabilities include Oracle (www.oracle.com), SAP (www.sap.com), and OpenPages (www.openpages.com), among many others.

Explore one GRC software solution, and in a brief e-mail message to your instructor, describe the benefits of using this particular software package.[26]

Video Discussion

Access the Chapter 17 video discussion in the End of Chapter Assignments section at www.mybizlab.com.

Log on to www.mybizlab.com to access the following study and assessment aids associated with this chapter:

- Interactive exercises
- Pre/post test
- Real-Time Updates
- Video application
- Customized study plans
- Biz Skills Simulations
- Quick Learning Guide

If you are not using mybizlab, you can access Real-Time Updates and Quick Learning Guides through http://real-timeupdates.com/bia5. The Quick Learning Guide (located under "Learn More" on the website) provides all six Checkpoints in a handy two-page format to help you study for exams or review important concepts whenever you need a quick refresher.

Behind the Scenes

Charging Ahead: Visa Searches for Funds

www.visa.com

The story of Visa, Inc., is a story of big numbers. As the world's largest processor of credit and debit card transactions, Visa provides essential services to more than 16,000 financial institutions, which have issued 1.7 billion Visa-branded cards. The 28 million merchants that accept Visa ring up nearly 60 billion transactions a year.

Visa's history began in 1958 when Bank of America premiered the BankAmericard in Fresno, California, just as the concept of general-purpose credit cards was taking hold across the Unites States. (*Charge cards* issued and accepted by a single company, such as a gas station or hotel chain, had been around for several decades by then.) These new *revolving* credit accounts, which let consumers charge purchases and pay them off over time, revolutionized consumer and business purchasing and changed the way consumers and companies manage their finances.

Over the next 50 years, the business venture that began as BankAmericard grew and transformed into the Visa International Service Association, a global payments processing system jointly owned by thousands of member banks and other financial institutions. The BankAmericard became the Visa card, and Visa became one of the world's best-known and most valuable brands.

With growth and change came challenges, and by 2007 Visa had more than a few challenges on its hands.

Visa faced the challenge of going public during the worst economic conditions in recent memory. The executive team is shown here at the New York Stock Exchange on the day the company went public.

While Visa remained a privately held joint venture, archrival MasterCard had become a public company in 2006, raising $2.4 billion with its initial stock offering. MasterCard's stock price continued to climb, giving an already strong competitor more financial power and flexibility, including the ability to attract and motivate top employees with stock options. As competition—and opportunities—grew, Visa needed cash to keep investing in payment processing technologies, including smart cards with embedded computer chips and phone-based mobile commerce payments. At the same time, Visa was also facing several billion dollars in liabilities from lawsuits filed by merchants and rival card companies American Express and Discover. To top it off, the six major banks that were Visa's primary owners were facing a massive liquidity crisis after the subprime mortgage crisis and the global credit freeze that followed. They needed cash by the bucketful.

Selling stock for the first time through an initial public offering (IPO) of its own seemed like the obvious answer to Visa's funding challenges. However, did an IPO make sense when the global economy was in the process of falling off a cliff? Did Visa choose the right financing option and the right time to execute it? Would the IPO be another big number in a company history of big numbers, or would it be a big-time failure?[1] ∎

Introduction

From the coffee shop down the street to the world's largest corporations, every business enterprise needs cash, although not always the billions of dollars that Visa needed. In this chapter, you'll learn more about the major financial decisions companies make, starting with the process of developing a financial plan, creating and maintaining budgets, and then comparing ways to finance both ongoing operations and growth opportunities.

The Role of Financial Management

financial management
Planning for a firm's money needs and managing the allocation and spending of funds

Planning for a firm's money needs and managing the allocation and spending of funds are the foundations of **financial management**, or *finance*. In most smaller companies, the owner is responsible for the firm's financial decisions, whereas in larger operations, financial management is the responsibility of the finance department. This department, which includes the accounting function, reports to a vice president of finance or a chief financial officer (CFO).

No matter what size the company, decisions regarding company finances must consider three fundamental concepts. First, every company has to balance short-term and long-term financial demands. Companies have to meet payroll, pay bills, and make regular tax payments, for example, so there is a constant need for ready cash—and it's up to the finance manager to make sure that money is available. At the same time, executives need to think about the future. If the firm spends too much money meeting short-term demands, it won't have enough money to make strategic investments for the future, such as building new facilities or conducting research and development for the next generation of products. This is one of the reasons you sometimes hear about companies laying off employees even when they have millions of dollars in the bank. Conversely, if the firm spends too little in the short term, it can lose key employees to better-paying competitors, compromise product quality or customer service, or create other problems with long-term consequences. Put another way, a company that mismanages its short-term finances won't have a long term to worry about.

risk-return trade-off
The balance of potential risks against potential rewards

Second, most financial decisions involve balancing potential risks against potential rewards, known as a **risk-return trade-off**. Generally speaking, the higher the perceived risk, the higher the potential reward, and vice versa. However, this rule doesn't always hold true. For example, a company with free cash could (A) invest it in the stock market, which offers potentially high returns but at moderate to high risk; (B) put the money in a bank account, which has little to no risk but very low return; or (C) invest in a new facility or a new product, which could yield high returns, moderate returns, or no returns at all. Whether it's an entrepreneur putting everything she owns on the line to launch a new venture or a team of corporate executives making multimillion-dollar strategic investments, financial managers often face high-stress decisions that can make or break their companies. To make things even more stressful, the *safest* choice isn't always the *best* choice. For instance, if you're hording cash while competitors are investing in new products or new stores, you could be setting yourself up for a big decline in revenue.

Third, financial choices can have a tremendous impact on a company's flexibility and resiliency. For example, companies that are *highly leveraged* (carrying a lot of debt, in other words) are forced to devote more of their cash flow to debt service and therefore can't spend that money on advertising, staffing, or product development. Heavy debt loads and low cash flow make a company more vulnerable to economic downturns, too. In contrast, companies with lots of cash on hand can weather tough times and make strategic moves their debt-constrained competitors can't make. In fact, well-funded companies often view recessions as opportunities to take market share from weaker competitors or simply to buy them outright.[2] The semiconductor giant Intel uses downturns to invest in major facility upgrades, enabling it to respond more aggressively when the economy turns around and demand picks up.[3]

Financial management involves making decisions about alternative sources and uses of funds, with the goal of maximizing a company's value. To achieve this goal, financial managers

Real-Time Updates

Learn More
Seven who made it big

See how seven determined entrepreneurs financed the growth of their business empires. On mybizlab (www.mybizlab.com), you can access Real-Time Updates within each chapter or under Student Study Tools. Otherwise, go to http://real-timeupdates.com/bia5 and click on "Learn More."

develop and implement a firm's financial plan, monitor cash flow and decide how to manage excess funds, and budget for expenditures and improvements. In addition, these managers raise capital as needed and oversee the firm's relationships with banks and other financial institutions.

Developing a Financial Plan

Successful financial management starts with a **financial plan**, a document that outlines the funds a firm will need for a certain period of time, along with the sources and intended uses of those funds. The financial plan takes its input from three information sources:

financial plan
A document that outlines the funds needed for a certain period of time, along with the sources and intended uses of those funds

- The strategic plan, which establishes the company's overall direction and identifies the need for major investments, expanded staffing, and other activities that will require funds
- The company's financial statements, including the income statement and the statement of cash flows, which tell the finance manager how much cash the company has now and how much it is likely to generate in the near future
- The external financial environment, including interest rates and the overall health of the economy

By considering information from these three sources, managers can identify how much money the company will need and how much it will have to rely on external resources to complement its internal resources over the span of time covered by the financial plan (see Exhibit 18.1).

EXHIBIT 18.1 Financial Management

Financial management involves finding suitable sources of funds and deciding on the most appropriate uses for those funds.

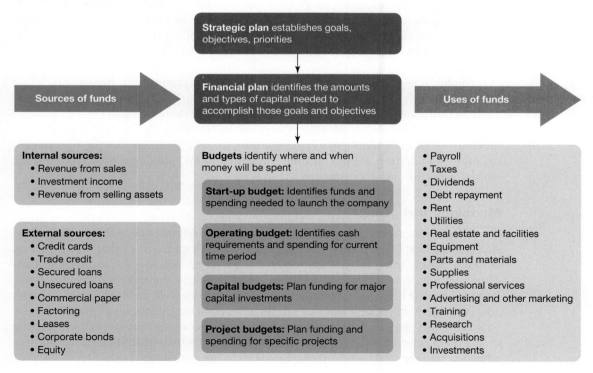

Strategic plan establishes goals, objectives, priorities

Sources of funds

Financial plan identifies the amounts and types of capital needed to accomplish those goals and objectives

Uses of funds

Internal sources:
- Revenue from sales
- Investment income
- Revenue from selling assets

External sources:
- Credit cards
- Trade credit
- Secured loans
- Unsecured loans
- Commercial paper
- Factoring
- Leases
- Corporate bonds
- Equity

Budgets identify where and when money will be spent

Start-up budget: Identifies funds and spending needed to launch the company

Operating budget: Identifies cash requirements and spending for current time period

Capital budgets: Plan funding for major capital investments

Project budgets: Plan funding and spending for specific projects

- Payroll
- Taxes
- Dividends
- Debt repayment
- Rent
- Utilities
- Real estate and facilities
- Equipment
- Parts and materials
- Supplies
- Professional services
- Advertising and other marketing
- Training
- Research
- Acquisitions
- Investments

Real-Time Updates

Learn More

A great role model in a world of big spenders

Hot Studio's Maria Guidice explains the design firm's frugal approach to finance. On mybizlab (**www.mybizlab.com**), you can access Real-Time Updates within each chapter or under Student Study Tools. Otherwise, go to **http://real-timeupdates.com/bia5** and click on "Learn More."

Monitoring Cash Flow

Overall income as identified in the income statement is important, of course, but knowing precisely how much cash is flowing into and out of the company—and when—is critical, since cash is necessary to purchase the assets and supplies a company needs to operate and to pay dividends to shareholders, for those corporations that pay dividends. Cash flow is generally related to net income; that is, companies with relatively high accounting profits generally have relatively high cash flow, but the relationship is not precise.

Companies that don't keep a close eye on cash flow can find themselves facing a *liquidity crisis*, having insufficient cash to meet their short-term needs. When the recession that began in December 2007 collided with the credit crisis of 2008, many firms found themselves in a liquidity crisis that hit from two directions at once: sales revenue plunged, taking cash flow with it, and the banks many companies had relied on for short-term credit to even out dips in their cash flow ran into their *own* liquidity crises and severely curtailed lending. Caught with no money and no way to borrow, many cash-strapped companies had no choice but to reduce their workforces in order to survive. Whenever economic storm clouds are gathering, financial managers need to jump into action to strengthen balance sheets and do whatever they can to ensure positive cash flow as conditions deteriorate.[4]

A vital step in maintaining positive cash flow is monitoring *working capital accounts:* accounts receivable, accounts payable, inventory, and cash.

Managing Accounts Receivable and Accounts Payable

accounts receivable
Amounts that are currently owed to a firm

Keeping an eye on **accounts receivable**—the money owed to the firm by its customers—is one way to manage cash flow effectively. The volume of receivables depends on the financial manager's decisions regarding several issues: who qualifies for credit and who does not, how long customers are given to pay their bills, and how aggressive the firm is in collecting its debts. In addition to setting guidelines and policies for handling these issues, the financial manager analyzes the firm's outstanding receivables to identify patterns that might indicate problems and establishes procedures for collecting overdue accounts.

accounts payable
Amounts that a firm currently owes to other parties

The flip side of managing receivables is managing **accounts payable**—the bills that the company owes to its suppliers, lenders, and other parties. Here the objective is generally to postpone paying bills until the last moment, because doing so obviously allows the firm to hold on to its cash as long as possible. However, the financial manager also needs to weigh the advantages of paying promptly if doing so entitles the firm to cash discounts. In addition, paying on time is essential to maintaining a good credit rating, which lowers the cost of borrowing.

Managing Inventory

Inventory is another area in which financial managers can fine-tune the firm's cash flow. As Chapter 9 explains, inventory sitting on the shelf represents capital that is tied up without earning interest. Furthermore, the firm incurs expenses for storage and handling, insurance, and taxes. In addition, there is always the risk that inventory will become obsolete before it can be converted into finished goods and sold. Thus, the firm's goal is to maintain enough inventory to fill orders in a timely fashion at the lowest cost. To achieve this goal, financial managers work with operations managers and marketing managers to determine the *economic order quantity (EOQ)*, or quantity of materials that, when ordered regularly, results in the lowest ordering and storage costs.

Managing Cash Reserves

Financial managers also serve as guardians of the company's cash reserves, whether that cash is from investors that have funded a start-up venture or from profitable product sales in an established company. The nature of this challenge varies widely, depending on the nature of the business, the firm's overall financial health, and management's predictions for the economy. For instance, start-ups usually have a finite pool of cash from their investors and need to manage that cash wisely so they don't run out of funds before the new business can start to generate cash on its own. At the other extreme, an established company with many successful and profitable products can generate more cash than it needs for both ongoing operations and "rainy day" emergency funds. In other cases, firms with seasonal business patterns, such as sports teams, retailers that depend heavily on holiday spending, and agricultural operations, generate temporary cash reserves that need to fund operations for the entire year.

Regardless of where the cash comes from or how it will eventually be spent, financial managers need to figure out what to do with it until the company needs to spend it. Chapter 19 describes many of the investment opportunities that companies have for cash that isn't currently needed.

✓CHECKPOINT

LEARNING OBJECTIVE 1: Identify three fundamental concepts that affect financial decisions, and identify the primary responsibilities of a financial manager.

Summary: Decisions regarding company finances must take into account three fundamental concepts. First, every company has to balance short-term and long-term financial demands. Failure to do so can lead to serious cash flow problems and even bankruptcy. Second, most financial decisions involve a *risk-return trade-off* in which, generally speaking, the higher the perceived risk, the higher the potential reward, and vice versa. Third, financial choices can have a tremendous impact on a company's flexibility and resiliency. Overburdening a company with debt limits its strategic options and makes it vulnerable to economic slowdowns. Financial managers are responsible for developing and implementing a firm's financial plan, monitoring cash flow and managing excess funds, and budgeting for expenditures and improvements. In addition, these managers raise capital as needed and oversee the firm's relationships with banks and other financial institutions.

Critical thinking: (1) What role does the company's strategic plan play in the process of financial management? (2) Does it ever make sense for a profitable company with positive cash flow to seek external financing? Why or why not?

It's your business: (1) Do you have a financial plan for getting through college? If not, how would such a plan help you? (2) Do you maintain a budget for your personal finances? If not, how do you monitor cash flow to make sure you don't run out of money each month?

Key terms to know: financial management, risk-return trade-off, financial plan, accounts receivable, accounts payable

The Budgeting Process

In addition to developing a financial plan and monitoring cash flow, financial managers are responsible for developing a **budget**, a financial guide for a given period, usually the company's fiscal year, or for the duration of a particular project. Like a good personal or

budget
Planning and control tool that reflects expected revenues, operating expenses, and cash receipts and outlays

household budget, a company budget identifies where and when money will be spent throughout the year. Particularly in larger organizations, budgeting is often a combination of *top-down*, in which top executives specify the amount of money each functional area can have based on the company's total available budget for the year, and *bottom-up*, in which individual supervisors and managers add up the amounts they need based on number of employees, project expenses, supplies, and other costs. For example, for Microsoft's 2009 and 2010 fiscal years, CEO Steven Ballmer specified that the company would spend $27.5 billion on operating expenses, with roughly half of that amount going to sales and marketing, about a third to research and development, and the rest to general and administrative costs.[5]

Finalizing the budget is usually a matter of negotiation and compromise in which financial managers try to reconcile the top-down and bottom-up numbers. After a budget has been developed, the finance manager compares actual results with projections to discover variances and recommends corrective action, a process known as **financial control**.

financial control
The process of analyzing and adjusting the basic financial plan to correct for deviations from forecasted events

Budgeting Challenges

The budgeting process might sound fairly straightforward, but in practice, it can turn into an exhausting, time-consuming chore that everyone dreads and few managers find satisfactory. Budgeting is a challenge for several reasons. First, a company always has a finite amount of money available to spend each year, and every group in the company is fighting for a share of it. Consequently, individual department managers can spend a considerable amount of time making a case for their budgetary needs, and top executives frequently need to make tough choices that won't please everybody. A constant struggle in this respect is to allocate budgets in ways that are best for the company as a whole, even if that means giving some divisions or departments less than they believe they need.

Second, managers often can't predict with complete accuracy how much revenue will come in or how much the various items covered by the budget will cost during the time frame covered by the budget. For instance, some expenses are routine and predictable, but others are variable and some can be almost impossible to predict. Fixed salaries are easy to predict month to month, but energy costs fluctuate—sometimes wildly so. In some cases, companies can protect themselves against future price increases by **hedging**, arranging contracts that allow them to buy supplies in the future at designated prices. During a 10-year span when most airlines struggled mightily with rising fuel costs, for example, Southwest Airlines saved several billion dollars through farsighted fuel hedging.[6] The obvious risk of hedging against rising prices is that prices could instead drop over the duration of the contract, leaving a company paying more than it would have to otherwise. Chapter 19 addresses hedging in more detail.

hedging
Protecting against cost increases with contracts that allow a company to buy supplies in the future at designated prices

Another alternative is *rolling forecasts*, in which the company starts the year with a budget based on revenue and cost assumptions made at that point but then reviews economic performance every month or every quarter to see whether the budget needs to be modified as the year progresses.[7] For example, at the San Francisco company CaseCentral, which provides information systems to law firms, managers review the budget every month and create a new forecast for the next three months. If results don't align with expectations at any point, managers reset the budget.[8]

Another effective tool in volatile situations is *scenario planning*, in which managers identify two or more possible ways that events could unfold—different scenarios, that is—and have a budgetary response ready for each one. For instance, if an economic slowdown in the coming year is possible but not certain, managers could plan one budget that reflects current revenue trends and one budget that reflects a decline in sales. The firm could start the year with the more optimistic forecast, but then if the more pessimistic scenario unfolds, the second budget kicks in and all departments then reduce spending accordingly. Scenario planning is particularly valuable for long-range planning, because the longer the time frame, the harder it is to pin down revenues and costs with any degree of accuracy.

Third, even if they can predict how much revenue will come in or how much various things will cost, managers can't always be sure how much they *should* spend in each part of the budget. A common practice is to take the amounts spent the previous year and increment them (if the company is growing) or decrement them (if the company is shrinking) to arrive at this year's budget. However, this practice is a bit like cost-

Real-Time Updates

Learn More

Small business budgeting: how to make it work

Follow these six steps to create a better budget for your small business. On mybizlab (**www.mybizlab.com**), you can access Real-Time Updates within each chapter or under Student Study Tools. Otherwise, go to **http://real-timeupdates.com/bia5** and click on "Learn More."

plus pricing (see page 372) in that it is simple to do but can produce seriously flawed numbers by ignoring real-world inputs. For instance, the amount a given department spent last year might've been too high or too low to begin with—and it could bear no relation to what it should spend to meet challenges and opportunities in the coming year. This practice also encourages a "use it or lose it" mentality, where at the end of the year managers hurriedly spend any remaining money in their budgets, even if doing so doesn't make financial sense, because they know if they don't spend it all, their budgets will be reduced for the next year.

A more responsive—but more difficult and time-consuming—approach is **zero-based budgeting**, in which each department starts from zero every year and must justify every item in the budget.[9] This approach forces each department to show how the money it wants to spend will support the overall strategic plan. The downside to zero-based budgeting is the amount of time it takes. One practical alternative is a hybrid approach in which zero-basing is reserved for those areas of the budget with the greatest flexibility, such as advertising and various development projects.[10]

zero-based budgeting
Budgeting approach in which each department starts from zero every year and must justify every item in the budget, rather than simply adjusting the previous year's budget amounts

Types of Budgets

A company can have up to four types of budgets, depending on the nature and age of its business:

- Before a new company starts business, the entrepreneurial team assembles a **start-up budget** or *launch budget* that identifies all the money it will need to spend to "get off the ground." A major concern at this stage is the *burn rate*, the rate at which the company is using up the funds from its initial investors. If the burn rate is too high, the firm risks running out of money before it can start generating sustainable sales revenues and become self-funding. Start-up budgets can be the most difficult of all because the company doesn't have any operating history to use as a baseline. Feedback from other entrepreneurs, experienced early-stage investors, and advisors such as SCORE executives or business incubators (see page 179) can be invaluable.

- After a company gets through the start-up phase, the financial manager's attention turns to the **operating budget**, sometimes known as the *master budget*, which identifies all sources of revenue and coordinates the spending of those funds throughout the coming year. Operating budgets help financial managers estimate the flow of money into and out of the business by structuring financial plans within a framework of estimated revenues, expenses, and cash flows. The operating budget incorporates any special budgets, such as *capital* and *project budgets*.

- A **capital budget** outlines expenditures for real estate, new facilities, major equipment, and other **capital investments**. For smaller capital purchases, a company might designate a certain percentage of its annual operating budget for capital items every year. Significant capital investments might require planning over the course of multiple years as the company assembles the necessary funds and makes payments on the purchases while maintaining its ongoing operating budget.

start-up budget
Budget that identifies the money a new company will need to spend to launch operations

operating budget
Also known as the *master budget*, budget that identifies all sources of revenue and coordinates the spending of those funds throughout the coming year

capital budget
Budget that outlines expenditures for real estate, new facilities, major equipment, and other capital investments

capital investments
Money paid to acquire something of permanent value in a business

project budget
Budget that identifies the costs needed to accomplish a particular project

■ Another special type of budget that has to be coordinated with the operating budget is the **project budget**, which identifies the costs needed to accomplish a particular project, such as conducting the research and development of a new product or moving a company to a new office building. Project managers typically request funding based on their estimates of the cost to complete the project and its value to the company. They then have the responsibility of making sure the project is completed on budget.

✓CHECKPOINT

LEARNING OBJECTIVE 2: Describe the budgeting process, three major budgeting challenges, and the four major types of budgets.

Summary: A budget is a financial guide for a given time period or project, indentifying how much money will be needed and where and when it will be spent. Budgeting often combines top-down mandates, whereby company executives identify how much money each functional area will have to spend, and bottom-up requests, whereby individual division or department managers add up the funding they'll need to meet their respective goals. Three major budgeting challenges are (1) reconciling the competing demands on the finite amount of money the company has to spend, (2) trying to predict future costs, and (3) deciding how much to spend in each area of the budget. Four major types of budgets are the *start-up budget*, which guides companies during the launch phase of a new company; the *operating* or *master budget*, which outlines all spending during a given time period (typically a year) and incorporates various special budgets; *capital budgets*, which plan expenditures on major capital purchases; and *project budgets*, which guide spending on projects such as new product launches.

Critical thinking: (1) What are some of the risks of failing to create and manage budgets? (2) How does zero-based budgeting help a company spend its cash in the most effective ways possible?

It's your business: (1) What steps would you take to identify the costs of a two-week trip to Scotland next summer? (2) Assume you need to raise $3,000 between now and graduation for a down payment on a car. How would budgeting and financial control help you meet this objective?

Key terms to know: budget, financial control, hedging, zero-based budgeting, start-up budget, operating budget, capital budget, capital investments, project budget

Financing Alternatives: Factors to Consider

Whether it is an entrepreneurial venture hunting for start-up capital to develop products and hire staff or an established corporation looking for short-term funds to help pay the bills during a slow selling season, companies often find themselves in need of additional cash. Every firm's need for cash and its ability to get money from various external sources is unique, and it's up to financial executives to find the right source or combination of sources. The credit crunch that rippled through the economy beginning in 2008 made many funding sources more expensive and more difficult to get, further complicating the financial manager's job. In the words of Jim Ziozis, president of the Mineola, New York, furniture supplier Linon Home Décor, "The days of cheap, free-flowing money are gone."[11]

This section explores the factors that finance managers consider when they are looking for outside funds, and the next three sections cover the three major categories of financing: short-term debt, long-term debt, and equity.

Debt Versus Equity Financing

The most fundamental decision a company faces regarding financing is whether it will obtain funds by **debt financing**, borrowing money, or by **equity financing**, selling ownership shares in the company. To meet their changing needs over time, many firms use a combination of debt and equity financing, and many use several kinds of debt financing at the same time for different purposes.

Note that business debt usually doesn't have the same negative connotations as consumer debt. Whereas consumers are advised to avoid most kinds of debt if at all possible, and being in debt is often a sign of financial trouble or financial mismanagement, robust and well-run businesses of all shapes and sizes use debt as a routine element of financial management. The key difference is that—unlike nearly all consumer debt other than loans for education—businesses can make money by borrowing money. Of course, companies can get into debt trouble through bad choices and bad luck, just as consumers can, and it's up to financial managers to make smart borrowing choices.

When choosing between debt and equity financing, companies consider a variety of issues, including the prevailing interest rates, maturity, the claim on income, the claim on assets, and the desire for ownership control. Exhibit 18.2 summarizes these considerations.

debt financing
Arranging funding by borrowing money

equity financing
Arranging funding by selling ownership shares in the company, publicly or privately

EXHIBIT 18.2 Debt Versus Equity Financing

When choosing between debt and equity financing, companies evaluate the characteristics of both types of funding.

CHARACTERISTIC	DEBT	EQUITY
Maturity	**Specific:** In most cases, specifies a date by which debt must be repaid.	**N/A:** Equity funding does not need to be repaid.
Claim on income	**Nondiscretionary, usually a recurring cost and usually fixed:** Debt obligations must be repaid, regardless of whether the company is profitable; payments can be regular (e.g., monthly), balloon (repaid all at once), or a combination.	**Discretionary cost:** At management's discretion and if company is profitable, shareholders may receive dividends after creditors have been paid; however, company is not required to pay dividends.
Claim on assets	**Priority:** Lenders have prior claims on assets.	**Residual:** Shareholders have claims only after the firm satisfies claims of lenders.
Influence over management	**Usually little:** Lenders usually have no influence over management unless debit vehicles come with conditions or management fails to make payments on time.	**Varies:** As owners of the company, shareholders can vote on some aspects of corporate operations, although in practice only large shareholders have much influence. Private equity holders (such as venture capitalists) can have considerable influence.
Tax consequences	**Deductible:** Debt payments reduce taxable income, lowering tax obligations.	**Not deductible:** Dividend payments are not tax deductible.
Employee benefit potential	**N/A:** Does not create any opportunities for compensation alternatives such as stock options.	**Stock options:** Issuing company shares creates the opportunity to use stock options as a motivational tool.

Of course, not every firm has access to every financing option, and sometimes companies have to take whatever they can get. For instance, only companies that are already public or are prepared to go public (see "Public Stock Offerings" on page 473) can raise funds by selling shares on the open market. Similarly, as you'll read in the sections on debt financing, some debt options are not available to small companies.

Length of Term

short-term financing
Financing used to cover current expenses (generally repaid within a year)

long-term financing
Financing used to cover long-term expenses such as assets (generally repaid over a period of more than one year)

Financing can be either short term or long term. **Short-term financing** is any financing that will be repaid within one year, whereas **long-term financing** is any financing that will be repaid in a period longer than one year. The primary purpose of short-term financing is to ensure that a company maintains its liquidity, or its ability to meet financial obligations (such as inventory payments) as they become due. By contrast, long-term financing is used to acquire long-term assets such as buildings and equipment or to fund expansion via any number of growth options.

Cost of Capital

cost of capital
Average rate of interest a firm pays on its combination of debt and equity financing

In general, a company wants to obtain money at the lowest cost and least amount of risk. However, lenders and investors want to receive the highest possible return on their investment, also at the lowest risk. A company's **cost of capital** is the average rate of interest it must pay on its debt and equity financing. For any form of financing to make economic sense, the expected returns must exceed the cost of capital. Consequently, financial managers study capital costs carefully in relation to the intended uses of those funds. At the same time, the potential sources of external funds, from banks to stock market investors to suppliers who sell on credit, also analyze a company's plans and prospects to figure out if helping the company is a safe and sensible use of their capital.

During the recent credit crisis, when sources of available credit shrunk dramatically and the limited credit that was available became quite expensive, companies were forced to rethink their approaches to financing.

Cost of capital depends on three main factors: the risk associated with the company, the prevailing level of interest rates, and management's selection of funding vehicles.

Risk

Lenders that provide money to businesses expect their returns to be in proportion to the two types of risk they face: the quality and length of time of the venture. Obviously, the more financially solid a company is, the less risk investors face and the less money they will demand in compensation. Just as in consumer credit, where protecting your *credit score* is vital to securing credit at reasonable rates, companies must also guard their reputations as being good credit and investment risks.

prime interest rate
Lowest rate of interest charged by banks for short-term loans to their most creditworthy customers

In addition to perceived risk, time also plays a vital role. Because a dollar will be worth less tomorrow than it is today, lenders need to be compensated for waiting to be repaid. As a result, for a given type of debt, long-term financing generally costs a company more than short-term financing.

Interest Rates

Regardless of how financially solid a company is, the cost of money will vary over time because interest rates fluctuate. The **prime interest rate** (often called simply the *prime*) is the lowest

Real-Time Updates

Learn More
Getting your credit report is essential—and free

You need to know what credit rating agencies know—or think they know—about you. On mybizlab (www.mybizlab.com), you can access Real-Time Updates within each chapter or under Student Study Tools. Otherwise, go to http://real-timeupdates.com/bia5 and click on "Learn More."

interest rate offered on short-term bank loans to preferred borrowers. The prime changes irregularly and, at times, quite frequently. Sometimes it changes because of supply and demand; at other times it changes because the prime rate is closely tied to the *discount rate*, the interest rate that the Federal Reserve charges on loans to commercial banks and other depository institutions (see page 508).

Companies must take such interest rate fluctuations into account when making financing decisions. For instance, a company planning to finance a short-term project when the prime rate is 3 percent would want to reevaluate the project if the prime rose to 6 percent a few months later. Even though companies try to time their borrowing to take advantage of drops in interest rates, this option is not always possible. A firm's need for money doesn't always coincide with a period of favorable rates. At times, a company may be forced to borrow when rates are high and then renegotiate the loan when rates drop. Sometimes projects must be put on hold until interest rates become more affordable.

Opportunity Cost

Using a company's own cash to finance its growth has one chief attraction: No interest payments are required. Nevertheless, such internal financing is not free; using money for any particular purpose has an *opportunity cost*, defined in Chapter 2 as value of the most appealing alternative from all those that weren't chosen. For instance, a company might be better off investing its excess cash in external opportunities, such as stocks of other companies, and borrowing money to finance its own growth. Doing so makes sense as long as the company can earn a greater *rate of return* (the percentage increase in the value of an investment) on those investments than the rate of interest paid on borrowed money.

This concept is called **leverage** because the loan acts like a lever: It magnifies the power of the borrower to generate profits (see Exhibit 18.3). However, leverage works both ways: Borrowing may magnify your losses as well as your gains. Because most companies require some degree of external financing from time to time, the issue is not so much whether to use outside money; rather, it's a question of how much should be raised, by what means, and when. The answers to such questions determine the firm's **capital structure**, the total mix of debt and equity financing it uses to meet its short- and long-term needs.

leverage
Technique of increasing the rate of return on an investment by financing it with borrowed funds

capital structure
A firm's mix of debt and equity financing

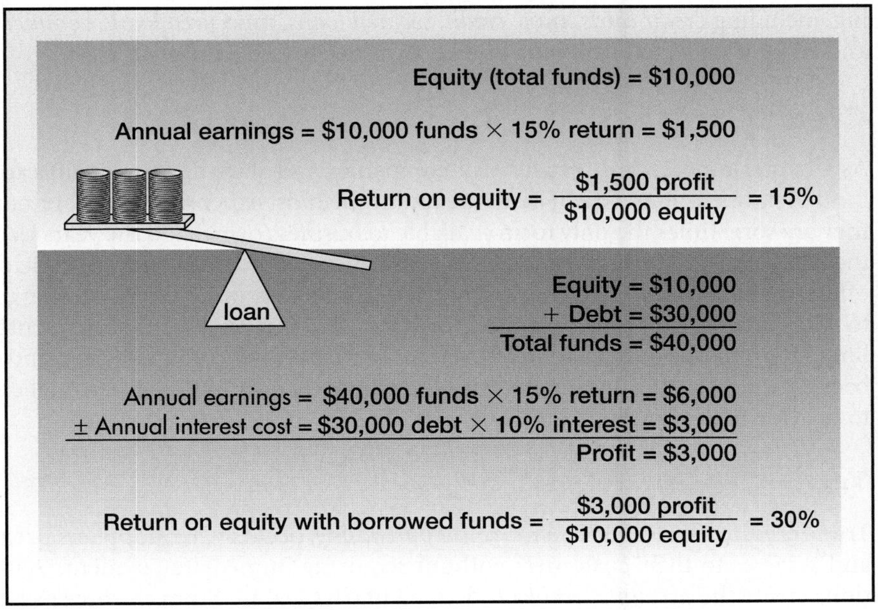

EXHIBIT 18.3

Financial Leverage

If you invest $10,000 of your own money in a business venture and it yields 15 percent (or $1,500), your return on equity is 15 percent. However, if you borrow an additional $30,000 at 10 percent interest and invest a total of $40,000 with the same 15 percent yield, the ultimate return on your $10,000 equity is 30 percent (or $3,000). The key to using leverage successfully is to try to make sure that your profit on the total funds is greater than the interest you must pay on the portion of it that is borrowed.

Equity (total funds) = $10,000

Annual earnings = $10,000 funds × 15% return = $1,500

Return on equity = $\dfrac{\$1,500 \text{ profit}}{\$10,000 \text{ equity}}$ = 15%

loan

Equity = $10,000
+ Debt = $30,000
Total funds = $40,000

Annual earnings = $40,000 funds × 15% return = $6,000
± Annual interest cost = $30,000 debt × 10% interest = $3,000
Profit = $3,000

Return on equity with borrowed funds = $\dfrac{\$3,000 \text{ profit}}{\$10,000 \text{ equity}}$ = 30%

✔CHECKPOINT

LEARNING OBJECTIVE 3: Compare the advantages and disadvantages of debt and equity financing, and explain the two major considerations in choosing from financing alternatives.

Summary: Debt financing offers a variety of funding alternatives and is available to a wider range of companies than equity financing. It also doesn't subject management to outside influence the way equity financing does, and debt payments reduce a company's tax obligations. On the downside, except for trade credit, debt financing always puts a demand on cash flow, so finance managers need to consider whether a company can handle debt payments. The major advantages of equity financing are the fact that the money doesn't have to be paid back and the resulting discretionary drain on cash flow (publicly held companies don't have to pay regular dividends if they choose not to). The major disadvantages are the dilution of management control and the fact that equity financing, public equity financing in particular, is not available to many firms. The two major considerations in choosing financing alternatives are *length of term*, the duration of the financing, and *cost of capital*, the average cost to a company of all its debt and equity financing.

Critical thinking: (1) What factors might lead a company to gain additional funds through debt financing rather than through equity financing? (2) Why does consumer debt have a more negative connotation than business debt?

It's your business: (1) Do you know your credit score, or have you ever looked at your credit report? To learn more about free credit reports, visit **www.ftc.gov/freereports**. (2) How should the cost of capital figure into your decisions about attending college, buying cars, and buying housing?

Key terms to know: debt financing, equity financing, short-term financing, long-term financing, cost of capital, prime interest rate, leverage, capital structure

Financing Alternatives: Short-Term Debt

Financial managers have a number of options when it comes to short-term debt financing, including *credit cards, trade credit, secured loans, unsecured loans, commercial paper*, and an alternative to borrowing known as *factoring* (see Exhibit 18.4).

Credit Cards

As Chapter 6 notes, half of all small companies and start-ups use credit cards to help fund their operations. Credit cards are one of the most expensive forms of financing, but they are sometimes the only form available to business owners. In the years leading up to the 2008 credit crunch, anyone with a pulse and mailbox could get multiple credit card offers, making cards a tempting way to get cash to start or expand a business, or simply to stay afloat during rough patches. However, card issuers recently began cutting credit limits for millions of card holders, even those with strong credit histories, and these cutbacks are affecting many small businesses whose owners use their personal credit cards to provide funds for their companies.[12]

Trade Credit

trade credit
Credit obtained by the purchaser directly from the supplier

Trade credit, often called *open-account purchasing*, occurs when suppliers provide goods and services to their customers without requiring immediate payment. Such transactions create the *accounts receivable* defined in Chapter 17. From the buyer's perspective,

EXHIBIT 18.4 Sources of Short-Term Debt Financing

Businesses have a variety of short-term debt financing options, each with its own advantages and disadvantages.

SOURCE	FUNDING MECHANISM	LENGTH OF TERM	ADVANTAGES	DISADVANTAGES AND LIMITATIONS
Credit cards	Essentially creates a short-term loan every time cardholder makes purchases or gets a cash advance	Revolving (no fixed repayment date)	Widely available; convenient; no external scrutiny of individual purchases	High interest rates; availability decreasing after the credit crunch; ease of use and lack of external scrutiny can lead to overuse
Trade credit	Allows buyer to make purchases without immediately paying for them	Typically 30 to 90 days	Usually free (no interest) as long as payment is made by due date; enables purchaser to manage cash flow more easily; consolidates multiple purchases into a single payment	Buyer often needs to establish a payment history with seller before credit will be extended; availability and terms vary from seller to seller; some sellers may require promissory note and charge interest
Secured loans	Lender provides cash using borrower's assets (such as inventory or equipment) as collateral; also known as *asset-based loans*	Up to 1 year (for short-term loans)	Can provide financing for companies that don't qualify for unsecured loans or other alternatives	More expensive than some other options
Unsecured loans	Lender provides lump sum of cash via a promissory note or on-demand access to cash via a credit line	Up to 1 year (for short-term loans)	Provides cash or access to cash without requiring borrower to pledge assets as collateral	Cost varies according to borrower's credit rating; often not available to customers with unproven or poor credit history
Commercial paper	Participating in the global *money market*, large institutional investors provide unsecured, short-term loans to corporations	Up to 270 days (longer in special cases)	Less expensive and less trouble to get than conventional loans; can generate very large amounts of cash fairly quickly, from $100,000 to many millions	Available only to large corporations with strong credit ratings; proceeds can only be used to purchase current assets, not fixed assets
Factoring	Company sells its accounts receivable to an intermediary that collects from the customer	N/A	Frees up working capital; makes cash flow more predictable; can provide some protection from bad debts and customer bankruptcies; often can be arranged more quickly than a loan	Expensive (annualized costs can be 30–40 percent)

trade credit allows the company to get the goods and services it needs without immediately disrupting its cash flow. Trade credit can also lower transaction costs for buyers (as well as sellers) by consolidating multiple purchases into a single payment. In many cases, credit is extended at no interest for a short period (typically 30 days).

From the seller's perspective, offering credit terms is often a competitive necessity, and doing so can allow a supplier to sell more to each customer because purchase levels aren't constrained to buyers' immediate cash balances. However, like all other forms of credit, trade credit involves costs and risks. Allowing customers to delay payments affects the seller's cash flow and exposes it to the risk that some customers won't be able to pay when their bills come due. Extending trade credit can also reduce the company's own credit worthiness because lenders will look at how quickly it is closing its accounts receivable. Companies that offer trade credit should be sure to check the credit worthiness of all buyers, keep credit limits low for new customers until they establish a reliable payment history, and keep a close eye on every customer's payment status.[13]

Secured Loans

secured loans
Loans backed up with assets that the lender can claim in case of default, such as a piece of property

Secured loans are those backed by something of value, known as **collateral**, that may be seized by the lender in the event that the borrower fails to repay the loan. Common types of collateral include property, equipment, accounts receivable, inventories, and securities.

collateral
Tangible asset a lender can claim if a borrower defaults on a loan

Unsecured Loans

unsecured loans
Loans requiring no collateral but a good credit rating

Unsecured loans are ones that require no collateral. Instead, the lender relies on the general credit record and the earning power of the borrower. To increase the returns on such loans and to obtain some protection in case of default, most lenders insist that the borrower maintain some minimum amount of money on deposit at the bank—a **compensating balance**—while the loan is outstanding.

compensating balance
Portion of an unsecured loan that is kept on deposit at the lending institution to protect the lender and increase the lender's return

A common example of an unsecured loan is a **line of credit**, which is an agreed-on maximum amount of money a bank is willing to lend a business. Once a line of credit has been established, the business may obtain unsecured loans for any amount up to that limit. The key advantage of a line of credit over a regular loan is that interest is usually not charged on the untapped amount (although a type of credit line that guarantees access up to a specified amount usually has a modest interest rate on the untapped amount). For example, say a small company has a $100,000 line of credit. If it has accessed $40,000 of that limit, it will pay interest on just the $40,000 but still have access to the remaining $60,000 if it needs more funds.

line of credit
Arrangement in which the financial institution makes money available for use at any time after the loan has been approved

In the recent credit crunch, line-of-credit financing became a source of shock and anxiety for many companies that had relied on credit lines to even out dips in their cash flow or simply to have as a backup in case their finances floundered. When bankers began to have liquidity troubles themselves, many lowered their borrowers' credit lines or canceled them entirely, removing a cushion that these firms had been counting on. At same time, other companies with lines of credit that didn't need cash tapped their lines anyway just in case they lost access to these funds. In other words, they borrowed money they didn't need just to make sure they had it in hand in case they did need it in the future.[14]

Commercial Paper

commercial paper
Short-term *promissory notes,* or contractual agreements, to repay a borrowed amount by a specified time with a specified interest rate

When businesses need a sizable amount of money for a short period of time, they can issue **commercial paper**—short-term *promissory notes,* or contractual agreements, to repay a borrowed amount by a specified time with a specified interest rate. Commercial paper is usually sold only by major corporations with strong credit ratings, in denominations of $100,000 or more and with maturities of up to 270 days (the maximum allowed by the Securities and Exchange Commission [SEC] without a formal registration process). Commercial paper is normally issued to secure funds for such short-term needs as buying supplies and paying rent, rather than financing major expansion projects. Because the amounts are generally so large, these notes are usually purchased by various investment funds and not by individual investors. The volume of commercial paper has been shrinking in recent years but still accounts for more than $1 trillion in active promissory notes at any given time.[15]

Factoring and Receivables Auctions

Businesses with slow-paying trade credit customers—some organizational customers can take months to pay their bills—and tight cash flow have the option of selling their accounts receivable, a method known as **factoring**. Although it's not really a form of borrowing in the conventional sense, factoring is an alternative to short-term debt financing.

Factoring involves several steps. First, a *factor* or *factoring agent* purchases a company's receivables, paying the company a percentage of the total outstanding amount, typically 70 to 90 percent. Second, the factoring agent then collects the amounts owed, freeing the company from the administrative tasks of collection. Third, after a customer pays the factor, the factor then makes a second payment to the company, keeping a percentage as a fee for its services. Some factors assume the risk that customers won't ever pay (and their fees are naturally higher), while others don't, in which case the company has to refund the initial payment it received from the factor.[16]

The use of factoring has increased in recent years, particularly as banks and other lenders have reduced the level of credit that many businesses rely on to manage cash flow. Because it is a comparatively expensive method, factoring is generally best suited for profitable, growing companies with pressing cash flow needs and large, creditworthy customers (businesses or government agencies, not consumers) who are likely to pay their bills but are just slow in doing so.[17] Particularly for companies that sell to retailers, factoring is sometimes a necessity because they have contracts that require them to keep retailers supplied with inventory on a regular schedule and need the cash flow to do so.[18]

An innovative twist on factoring is the *receivables auction*, pioneered by The Receivables Exchange (www.receivablesxchange.com). Using an online format somewhat like eBay and other auction sites, companies post their receivables for investors to bid on. Those who offer the best combination funding amount and fees win the business.[19]

factoring
Obtaining funding by selling accounts receivable

✓ CHECKPOINT

LEARNING OBJECTIVE 4: Identify the major categories of short-term debt financing.

Summary: The major categories of short-term debt financing are *credit cards*, *trade credit* (the option to delay paying for purchases for 30 to 60 days or more), *secured loans* (loans backed by sellable assets such as land, equipment, or inventory), *unsecured loans* (loans and lines of credit extended solely on the borrower's creditworthiness), *commercial paper* (short-term promissory notes issued by major corporations), and *factoring* (selling a firm's accounts payable to a third-party financer; strictly speaking, not a form of debt financing).

Critical thinking: (1) How does getting a secured loan using accounts receivable as collateral differ from factoring? (2) Why would any seller offer trade financing, since it ties up working capital without generating any income through interest payments?

It's your business: (1) Would you launch a new company if the only way to finance it was through the use of your personal credit cards? Why or why not? (2) Which of the short-term debt alternatives identified in this section are available to you as a consumer?

Key terms to know: trade credit, secured loans, collateral, unsecured loans, compensating balance, line of credit, commercial paper, factoring

Financing Alternatives: Long-Term Debt

In addition to the various short-term debt alternatives, a number of long-term debt financing options are available as well. Although some of these are similar in concept to short-term debt, the longer time spans create a different set of decisions for both borrowers and lenders. The most common long-term debt alternatives include *long-term loans*, *leases*, and *corporate bonds* (see Exhibit 18.5).

Long-Term Loans

Long-term loans, sometimes called *term loans*, can have maturities between 1 and 25 years or so, depending on the lender and the purpose of the loan. (Some lenders designate loans with maturities between one and three years as *intermediate-term loans*.[20]) Common reasons for taking out long-term loans are to buy real estate, to build or expand facilities, to acquire other companies, to purchase equipment or inventory, to refinance existing debt at lower interest rates, or to provide working capital.[21] Long-term loans on real estate are called *mortgages*.

EXHIBIT 18.5 **Sources of Long-Term Debt Financing**

Long-term debt financing can provide funds for major asset purchases and other investments needed to help companies grow.

SOURCE	FUNDING MECHANISM	LENGTH OF TERM	ADVANTAGES	DISADVANTAGES AND LIMITATIONS
Long-term loans	Bank or other lender provides cash; borrower agrees to repay according to specific terms	From 1 to 25 years	Can provide substantial sums of money without diluting ownership through sale of equity; allows company to make major purchases of inventory, equipment, and other vital assets	Not all companies can qualify for loans and acceptable terms; payments tie up part of cash flow for the duration of the loan; purchases made via loans require substantial down payments
Leases	Company earns the right to use an asset in exchange for regular payments; arrangement can be directly between lessor and lessee or can involve a third party such as a bank	Typically several years for equipment and vehicles; longer for real estate	Usually require lower down payments than loans; can provide access to essential assets for companies that don't qualify for loans; let company avoid buying assets that are likely to decline in value or become obsolete; often free company from maintenance and other recurring costs	Can restrict how assets can be used; company doesn't gain any equity in return for lease payments, except in the case of lease-to-own arrangements; can be more expensive than borrowing to buy
Corporate bond	Company sells bonds to investors with the promise to pay interest and repay the principle according to a set schedule	Typically from 10 to 30 years	Can generate more cash with longer repayment terms than are possible with loans	Available only to large companies with strong credit ratings

Long-term loans can be an attractive option for borrowers because they can provide substantial capital without the need to sell equity in the company. However, because these loans tie up a lender's capital for a long period of time and usually involve large sums of money, lending standards tend to be fairly stringent and not all companies can qualify. Lenders usually look at "the five Cs" when considering applications for these loans:[22]

- **Character.** Includes not only the personal and professional character of the company owners but also their experience and qualifications to run the type of business for which they plan to use the loan proceeds.

- **Capacity.** To judge the company's capacity or ability to repay the loan, lenders scrutinize debt ratios, liquidity ratios, and other measures of financial health. For small businesses, the owners' personal finances are also evaluated.

- **Capital.** Lenders want to know how well *capitalized* the company is, whether it has enough capital to succeed. For small business loans in particular, they also want to know how much money the owners themselves have already invested in the business.

- **Conditions.** Lenders look at the overall condition of the economy as well as conditions within the applicant's specific industry to determine whether they are comfortable with the business's plans and capabilities.

- **Collateral.** Long-term loans are usually secured through collateral of some kind. Lenders expect to be repaid from the borrower's cash flow, but in case that is inadequate, they look for assets that could be used to repay the loan, such as real estate or equipment.

An old joke about applying for bank loans suggests that the only way to qualify for a loan is to prove you don't need the money. This is an exaggeration, of course, but it is grounded in fact. Before they will part with their capital, particularly in tough economic conditions, lenders want a high degree of assurance that they'll get their money back.

Leases

Rather than borrowing money to purchase an asset, a firm may enter into a **lease**, under which the owner of an asset (the *lessor*) allows another party (the *lessee*) to use it in exchange for regular payments. (Leasing is similar to renting; a key difference is that leases fix the terms of the agreement for a specific amount of time.) Leases are commonly used for real estate, major equipment, and vehicles. In some cases, the lease arrangement is made directly between the asset owner and the lessee. In other cases, a bank or other financial firm provides leasing services to its clients and takes care of payments to the lessor.

Leasing may be a good alternative for a company that has difficulty obtaining a loan because of a poor credit rating or that is unwilling or unable to use its working capital for a down payment on a loan. Creditors are more willing to provide a lease than a loan because, should the company fail, the lessor need not worry about a default on loan payments; it can simply repossess the asset it legally owns. Some firms use leases to finance significant portions of their assets, particularly in industries such as airlines, where assets are mostly large, expensive pieces of equipment. Leasing can also provide more flexibility than purchasing through a loan. For instance, a growing company with expanding office space requirements can lease additional space when needed without the cost and delay of buying and selling real estate.

lease
Agreement to use an asset in exchange for regular payment; similar to renting

Corporate Bonds

When a company needs to borrow a large sum of money, it may not be able to get the entire amount from a single source. Under such circumstances, it may try to borrow from many individual investors by issuing **bonds**—certificates that obligate the company to repay a certain sum, plus interest, to the bondholder on a specific date. (Note that although bondholders buy bonds, they are acting as lenders.)

bonds
Method of funding in which the issuer borrows from an investor and provides a written promise to make regular interest payments and repay the borrowed amount in the future

secured bonds
Bonds backed by specific assets that will be given to bondholders if the borrowed amount is not repaid

debentures
Corporate bonds backed only by the reputation of the issuer

convertible bonds
Corporate bonds that can be exchanged at the owner's discretion into common stock of the issuing company

sinking fund
Account into which a company makes annual payments for use in redeeming its bonds in the future

Companies issue a variety of corporate bonds. **Secured bonds**, like secured loans, are backed by company-owned property (such as airplanes or plant equipment) that passes to the bondholders if the issuer does not repay the amount borrowed. *Mortgage bonds*, one type of secured bond, are backed by real property owned by the issuing corporation. **Debentures** are unsecured bonds, backed only by the corporation's promise to pay. Because debentures are riskier than other types of bonds, the companies that issue them must pay higher interest rates to attract buyers. **Convertible bonds** can be exchanged at the investor's option for a certain number of shares of the corporation's common stock. Because of this feature, convertible bonds generally pay lower interest rates.

Of course, organizations that issue bonds must eventually repay the borrowed amount to the bondholders. Normally, this repayment is done when the bonds mature, but the cost of retiring the debt can be staggering, because bonds are generally issued in quantity—perhaps thousands of individual bonds in a single issue. To ease the cash flow burden of redeeming its bonds all at once, a company can issue *serial bonds*, which mature at various times, as opposed to *term bonds*, which mature all at the same time.

Another way of relieving the financial strain of retiring many bonds all at once is to set up a **sinking fund**. When a corporation issues a bond payable by a sinking fund, it must set aside a certain sum of money each year to pay the debt. This money may be used to retire a few bonds each year, or it may be set aside to accumulate until the issue matures.

With most bond issues, a corporation retains the right to pay off the bonds before maturity. Bonds containing this provision are known as *callable bonds*, or *redeemable bonds*. If a company issues bonds when interest rates are high and then rates fall later on, it may want to pay off its high-interest bonds and sell a new issue at a lower rate. However, this feature carries a price tag: Investors must be offered a higher interest rate to encourage them to buy callable bonds.

Corporate bonds, as well as bonds issued by various government bodies, are discussed from an investor's perspective in Chapter 19.

✓ CHECKPOINT

LEARNING OBJECTIVE 5: Identify the major categories of long-term debt financing.

Summary: The three major categories of long-term debt financing are *long-term loans* (substantial amounts of capital for major purchases or other needs, on terms up to 25 years, usually secured by assets), *leases* (similar to renting, conferring the rights to use an asset in exchange for regular payments), and *bonds* (certificates that obligate the company to repay a specified sum, plus interest, to the bondholder on a specific date).

Critical thinking: (1) How could rates of technological change affect a company's decision about whether to buy or lease equipment, vehicles, and other assets? (2) Why would lenders want to see that a business already has some level of capitalization before giving it access to more capital by means of a loan?

It's your business: (1) Have you ever signed a lease on an apartment or rental housing? Did you understand the difference between leasing and renting at that point? (2) Have you ever leased a car? If so, did you compare the total costs of leasing versus the cost of buying? Why did you decide to lease rather than buy?

Key terms to know: lease, bonds, secured bonds, debentures, convertible bonds, sinking fund

Financing Alternatives: Equity

The most far-reaching alternative for securing funds is to sell shares of ownership in the company. Even the most thorough loan application reviews and strict repayment terms can't match the degree to which selling equity changes the way a company is managed. In the most extreme cases, selling equity can lead to the founders of a firm being ousted from the company. Even when owners retain control, equity financing can complicate operations by adding new layers of public scrutiny and accountability. Finally, the process of obtaining equity financing is expensive and time-consuming, so even those companies that could obtain it don't always choose to do so—and some that have sold equity to the public choose to reverse the decision by buying it back.

With all these caveats, why would any company bother with equity financing? The answer is the tremendous upside potential for the company as a whole and for any individual or organization that owns shares. Equity financing has fueled the growth of most of the major corporations in the world, and it has contributed to the financial security of millions of employees (and made millionaires out of thousands of employees, too). Plus, unlike debt financing, selling stock can continue to generate money for years if share prices continue to increase.

Although this option is available to only a small fraction of companies, it is one of the most powerful forms of financing. Moreover, it directly and indirectly plays a huge role in the economy by giving both individual and institutional investors the opportunity to increase their own capital by investing in company shares. This section takes a quick look at the private and public varieties of equity financing, and Chapter 19 discusses equities from an investor's point of view.

Venture Capital and Other Private Equity

As Chapter 6 points out, venture capitalists (VCs), as well as angel investors for companies that aren't yet ready for VC funding, are a key source of equity financing for a certain class of start-up companies. In exchange for a share of ownership, VCs can invest millions of dollars in companies long before those firms can qualify for most other forms of financing, so they represent an essential form of funding for high-growth ventures. VCs also provide managerial expertise and industry connections that can be crucial to new companies.

However, VCs are one of the most specialized and least widely available forms of funding, and most firms have no chance of getting venture capital. VCs typically look for privately held firms that are already well established enough to be able to use a significant amount of money and are positioned to grow aggressively enough to give the VCs a good shot at eventually selling their interests at a handsome profit. Not all VC-backed firms grow enough to pay back their investors, so VCs count on getting very high returns from a handful of winners.

Venture capital is a specialized form of funding known as **private equity** (ownership assets that aren't publicly traded), and other forms of private equity can provide funding for companies that are beyond the start-up stage. For instance, the leveraged buyouts discussed in Chapter 5 are usually done with private equity funds. Other uses of private equity are taking companies private by buying up all publicly held shares and rescuing companies that are on the verge of bankruptcy.

private equity
Ownership assets that aren't publicly traded; includes venture capital

Public Stock Offerings

Going public, offering shares of stock to the public through a stock market such as the New York Stock Exchange, can generate millions or even billions of dollars in funding. As you can read in the Behind the Scenes wrap-up starting on page 475, this is the financing path Visa chose, and its initial public offering (IPO) raised a record $19.6 billion.[23]

However, going public is not for the faint of heart. The process takes months of management time and attention, can cost several million dollars, and exposes the company to

Real-Time Updates

Learn More
Get the inside scoop on IPO activity

Renaissance Capital is the go-to source for information on IPOs. On mybizlab (www.mybizlab.com), you can access Real-Time Updates within each chapter or under Student Study Tools. Otherwise, go to http://real-timeupdates.com/bia5 and click on "Learn More."

rigorous scrutiny (which isn't necessarily a bad thing, of course). Complaining that the process had become too difficult in the wake of some high-profile accounting scandals that tightened oversight of public companies, former PayPal CEO Peter Thiel remarked several years ago that "Going public today is a process I wouldn't wish upon my worst enemy."[24] Moreover, companies have no assurance that efforts to go public will pay off. Some offerings fail to sell at the hoped-for share price, and some offerings are withdrawn before going public because their backers don't think the market conditions are strong enough. Like the economy as a whole, the market for IPOs runs in cycles, and timing the IPO is one of the key factors for success (see Exhibit 18.6).

Despite the costs and risks, the potential rewards are so high that every year thousands of companies around the world make the attempt to go public. The legal, financial, and promotional steps in the process can be grouped into three phases:[25]

- **Preparing the IPO.** Preparing the offering involves assembling a team of advisors that includes legal experts, a public accounting firm to serve as auditor, and an **underwriter**, a specialized type of bank known as an *investment bank* that buys the shares from the company and sells them to investors. (To spread the risk, a lead underwriter usually assembles a syndicate of other underwriters.) Working with company management, this team prepares required financial statements, organizes a board of directors, hires a public relations firm to begin promoting the upcoming offering, and engages in *due diligence* to make sure the company's financial policies and systems meet the expectations and legal requirements of public ownership.

- **Registering the IPO.** Before a company can sell shares to the public in the United States, it must first register with the SEC. This process includes submitting the **prospectus**, which discloses required information about the company, its finances, and its plans for using the money it hopes to raise. The SEC reviews the information and typically requests modifications and additional information to make the filing conform with all applicable regulations.

- **Selling the IPO.** In advance of the stock being officially offered for sale, the company and its team promote the offering privately to institutional investors through a

underwriter
A specialized type of bank that buys the shares from the company preparing an IPO and sells them to investors

prospectus
SEC-required document that discloses required information about the company, its finances, and its plans for using the money it hopes to raise

EXHIBIT 18.6

Global IPO Activity

The number of initial public offerings (IPOs) tends to track the stock market's ups and downs. This graph compares global IPO activity with the year-end level of the S&P 500 Index, a common composite measure of stock market values.

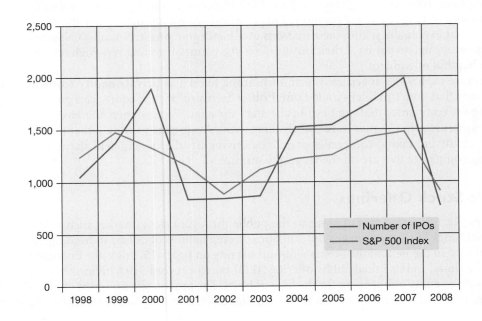

series of meetings call the *road show*. Although the IPO is the first "public" offering, shares are usually offered only to institutional investors or selected individual investors before the IPO date. Based on the demand they perceive during the road show, the company and the underwriter decide how to price the IPO shares. After the SEC approves the registration, the stock begins trading on a designated stock exchange, and the company is now officially public.

As with corporate bonds, this chapter's coverage of stocks is from the stock issuer's perspective; Chapter 19 addresses stocks from the investor's perspective.

For the latest information on financial management and funding alternatives, visit http://real-timeupdates.com/bia5 and click on Chapter 18.

✓CHECKPOINT

LEARNING OBJECTIVE 6: Describe the two options for equity financing, and explain how companies prepare an initial public offering.

Summary: Equity financing can be accomplished through *private equity* (ownership assets that aren't publicly traded the way shares of company stock are) or the issuance of public stock. Private equity investments such as venture capital are often used at specific points in a company's growth history, such as to get the company off the ground or to perform a leveraged buyout. Preparing for an initial public offering (IPO) involves a number of financial, legal, and promotional activities that fall into three stages: (1) preparing the IPO by assembling a team that includes a public auditor and an underwriter, preparing required financial statements, and making sure the company's financial statements and systems are up to public company standards; (2) registering the IPO with the SEC and responding to any demands for additional information from the SEC; and (3) selling the IPO, primarily through a *road show*, a series of presentations to institutional investors aimed at getting them interested in buying blocks of the soon-to-be released stock.

Critical thinking: (1) High-technology firms tend to dominate IPO filings year after year; why do you suppose this is? (2) Why does the volume of IPOs tend to track the ups and downs of the stock market?

It's your business: (1) Have you or has anyone you know ever been employed with a pre-IPO stage company? Did the company make it to the IPO stage successfully? (2) Choose any business that you might like to start as an entrepreneur. How would you make a compelling pitch to private equity investors to encourage them to invest in your company?

Key terms to know: private equity, underwriter, prospectus

Behind the Scenes

Visa Funds Its Future with Record-Setting IPO

If ever a company needed a few billion dollars, it was Visa in late 2007. Still operating as a privately held joint venture owned by its member banks, Visa didn't have access to the stock market as a fundraising mechanism. Archrival MasterCard was reaping the benefits of its recent IPO, generating several billion dollars in fresh capital and creating the opportunity to use stock options to recruit and reward employees. Moreover, after settling lawsuits brought against it by merchants and two credit card companies, Visa had rung up more than $4 billion in legal liabilities. Plus, the six large banks that made up the primary ownership group within the Visa association were desperately in need of cash to help ride out the recession and the credit crunch. On top of these challenges, Visa had to keep investing in new payment processing systems and technologies as consumers around the world continued to increase their use of conventional credit and debit cards and as promising new opportunities such as mobile commerce were coming up to speed.

An IPO could help solve all these funding dilemmas, but it would prove to be much more complicated than a normal IPO. One of the essential steps was creating a company that could actually go public. In late 2007, Visa Inc., was spun off from the Visa association as a wholly owned subsidiary. This new firm is the company that actually filed the IPO—with the U.S. economy in the depths of the worst downturn since the Great Depression of the 1930s and the financial services industry in turmoil. One could hardly have picked a worse time to go public, as evidenced by how the normal annual flow of IPOs had slowed to a trickle.

However, Visa had several factors working in its favor. First, with one of the world's best-known brand names and a half century of growth behind it, Visa didn't need to introduce itself to investors the way most companies do when pitching an IPO. Second, in investor-speak, Visa had a wide "economic moat," meaning its revenue-generating capacity was safeguarded by barriers to entry—including a powerful brand, established relationships with millions of companies worldwide, and a global transaction-processing network—that new market entrants would find hard to overcome. Third, and most important from the timing perspective, Visa isn't really a financial services company in the sense of lending money or issuing credit cards, so it wasn't exposed to the credit meltdown the way banks and credit card companies were. Although it is intertwined with the financial sector, Visa is actually more of a data processing company than a finance company.

In its prospectus, Visa indicated that it expected to net $16 or $17 billion from the IPO and intended to distribute $10 billion of that to its member institutions, use another $3 billion toward its legal liabilities, and reserve the remaining few billion for general corporate purposes. It was a staggering amount of money to generate in an IPO during the best of times and an almost unimaginable amount to generate during the worst of times.

But that is exactly what Visa did. It went public on March 19, 2008, and broke the record for the largest IPO ever by a U.S. company—over $19 billion after some optional shares were redeemed by the two lead underwriters on the giant deal, Goldman Sachs and JPMorgan Chase. As both an underwriter earning fees on the IPO and one of the cash-hungry member banks of the Visa association benefiting from the stock sale, JPMorgan Chase made over $1 billion on the deal.

In the year and a half following the IPO, Visa's new stock fared well, rising roughly 8 to 10 percent during a time when MasterCard's stock dropped by the same amount and the stock market overall dropped by 25 percent. The company's growth in the coming years could be hampered by any protracted slowdown in consumer spending, because fewer purchases mean fewer transactions for Visa to process. However, with more transactions shifting from cash to cards and credit card use only just beginning to ramp up in many areas around the world, the company's long-term growth looks positive. As a "new" 50-year-old company, Visa is in solid shape as it moves into the future.

Critical Thinking Questions

1. How might Visa executives use scenario planning in the budgeting process?
2. Could Visa have accomplished its funding goals through short-term or long-term debt financing instead? Why or why not?
3. As Visa continues to explore growth opportunities, should it consider becoming a lender by issuing cards itself or lending money to banks that issue cards? Why or why not?

LEARN MORE ONLINE

Visit Visa's website at www.visa.com and locate the investors section. Has the company reported any significant financial news in the past year? Has it resolved its outstanding legal issues? What were its net income and earnings per share for the more recent fiscal year? Has company management expressed any concerns about ongoing cash flow issues? ■

Key Terms

accounts payable (458)	capital structure (465)	debentures (472)
accounts receivable (458)	collateral (468)	debt financing (463)
bonds (471)	commercial paper (468)	equity financing (463)
budget (459)	compensating balance (468)	factoring (469)
capital budget (461)	convertible bonds (472)	financial control (460)
capital investments (461)	cost of capital (464)	financial management (456)

financial plan (457)
hedging (460)
lease (471)
leverage (465)
line of credit (468)
long-term financing (464)
operating budget (461)

prime interest rate (464)
private equity (473)
project budget (462)
prospectus (474)
risk-return trade-off (456)
secured bonds (472)
secured loans (468)

short-term financing (464)
sinking fund (472)
start-up budget (461)
trade credit (466)
underwriter (474)
unsecured loans (468)
zero-based budgeting (461)

Test Your Knowledge

Questions for Review

1. What is the difference between a secured and an unsecured loan?
2. What is the primary goal of financial management?
3. What types of investments and expenditures are typically considered in the capital budgeting process?
4. How can factoring help a company manage its cash flow?
5. What does it mean when someone refers to a company's capital structure?

Questions for Analysis

6. How does factoring differ from short-term debt?
7. Why do lenders often refuse to finance 100 percent of the cost of a purchase, requiring borrowers to make a down payment that covers a portion (typically from 10 to 25 percent) of the purchase price? After all, a lender could potentially earn more by financing the entire purchase amount.
8. Why is careful management of accounts receivable and accounts payable so essential to ensuring positive cash flow?
9. Would it be wise for a young company that is growing quickly but still hasn't achieved profitability to attempt to issue bonds as a way to expand its working capital? Why or why not?
10. **Ethical Considerations.** Budget projections always involve a degree of judgment because managers can never predict the future with total accuracy. For instance, one manager with an optimistic view and another manager with a pessimistic view could look at the same set of facts and arrive at distinctly different conclusions about the company's financial prospects. When budgets will influence decisions made by investors or lenders, how should the people who prepare the budgets deal with the variance between optimistic and pessimistic viewpoints? On the one hand, being too pessimistic could result in lower levels of funding, which could be detrimental to employees, existing investors, existing creditors, and other financial stakeholders. On the other hand, being too optimistic could be detrimental to prospective investors or creditors. How do you find the right balance?

Questions for Application

11. You're getting ready to expand your woodworking hobby into a full-time business of building custom kitchen cabinets. To create top-quality cabinets, you know you'll need to upgrade from the consumer-grade machinery you have now to industrial-grade equipment. The new equipment will be much more expensive but, if properly cared for, should last for decades, and you hope to be in business for at least 20 years. If the overall costs of leasing this equipment or borrowing money to buy it are roughly the same, which financing method would you choose? Why?
12. The company you co-founded last year is growing rapidly and has strong prospects for an IPO in the next year or two. The additional capital that an IPO could raise would let you hire the brightest people in the industry and continue to innovate with new product research. There is one potential glitch: You and the rest of the executive team have been so focused on launching the business that you haven't paid much attention to financial control. You've had plenty of funds from venture capitalists and early sales, so working capital hasn't been a problem, but an experienced CEO in your industry recently told you that you'll never have a successful IPO unless you clean up the financial side of the house. Your cofounders say they are too busy chasing great opportunities right now, and they want to wait until right before the IPO to hire a seasoned financial executive to put things in order. What should you do and why?
13. Why might a company's board of directors decide to lease office space even though it would be more economical to purchase the property and finance it with a long-term loan?
14. **Concept Integration.** Review the definitions of current and fixed assets in Chapter 17 (see page 441). Why would a potential lender be interested in these two classes of assets when reviewing the balance sheet of a company applying for a long-term loan?

Practice Your Knowledge

Sharpening Your Communication Skills

You've just been hired as the CFO of a start-up company that is just a few months away from launching its first products. Unfortunately, the company is running short of cash and doesn't have enough to pay for initial manufacturing costs. Your boss, Connie Washington, is getting frantic. She has worked for several years to get to this point, and she doesn't want the company to collapse before it even starts selling products. She comes to you asking for ideas to generate some funds—immediately, if not sooner. Several investors have expressed interest in helping with financing, but Connie doesn't want to surrender any control by using equity financing. She wants to start applying for loans, even stacks of credit cards if that's what it takes.

However, you don't think piling on debt is such a wise idea at this point. The company doesn't have any revenue yet, and there's no guarantee that the new products will be successful. You'd rather share the risk with some equity investors, even if that means that Connie will have to give up some of her managerial authority. Draft a short memo to Connie explaining why you think equity financing is a better option at this stage (make up any details you need).

Building Your Team Skills

You and your team are going to build an operating expense budget worksheet for a neighborhood Domino's pizza franchise. Begin by brainstorming a list of expenses that are typical of a franchise delivery restaurant. One way to do so is to think about the company's process—from making the pizza to delivering it. List the types of expenses and then group your list into categories such as delivery, marketing, manufacturing, financing, and so on. Leave the budget dollar amounts blank. Finally, develop a list of capital investments your company will make over the next three to five years. Compare your budget worksheets to those of the other teams in your class. Which operating and capital expenses did other teams have that your team did not? Which expenses did your team have that other teams omitted? Did all the teams categorize the expenses in a similar manner?

Expand Your Knowledge

Discovering Career Opportunities

People interested in entering the field of financial management can choose among a wide variety of careers with diverse responsibilities and challenges. Visit the "Financial Managers" page at www.bls.gov/oco/ocos010.htm to read more about career opportunities in financial management.

1. What are the day-to-day duties of this occupation? How would these duties contribute to the financial success of a company?
2. What skills and educational qualifications would you need to enter this occupation? How do these qualifications fit with your current plans, skills, and interests?
3. What kinds of employers hire people for this position? According to your research, does the number of employers seem to be increasing or decreasing? How do you think this trend will affect your employment possibilities if you choose this career?

Developing Your Research Skills

Choose a recent article from a business journal or newspaper (print or online editions) that discusses the financing arrangements or strategies of a particular company.

1. What form of financing did the company choose? Did the article indicate why the company selected this form of financing?
2. Who provided the financing for the company? Was this arrangement considered unusual, or was it routine?
3. What does the company intend to do with the arranged financing—purchase equipment or other assets, finance a construction project, finance growth and expansion, or do something else?

Developing Your Tech Insights: Credit Scoring Software

Credit scoring software is a type of business intelligence software that measures the credit worthiness of applications for credit cards, mortgages, business loans, and other forms of credit. It has the dual objective of filtering out applications that don't meet a lender's criteria while speeding up the process for applications that do meet the criteria.

Using sophisticated mathematical models based on historical records, credit scoring software helps lenders decide which applicants to accept and how much credit to extend to each one. In addition, software with *predictive modeling* or *predictive analytics* helps predict which applicants will make the best customers (lowest risk and highest profit potential) for a given lender. Explore the credit scoring and risk assessment products offered by Fair Isaac (www.fico.com), Equifax (www.equifax.com/commercial/risk/en_us), or another company in this industry. Choose one product, and in a brief e-mail message to your instructor, explain how this tool can help lenders make better decisions.

Video Discussion

Access the Chapter 18 video discussion in the End of Chapter Assignments section at www.mybizlab.com.

PEARSON
my*biz*lab

Log on to www.mybizlab.com to access the following study and assessment aids associated with this chapter:

- Interactive exercises
- Pre/post test
- Real-Time Updates
- Video application
- Customized study plans
- Biz Skills Simulations
- Quick Learning Guide

If you are not using mybizlab, you can access Real-Time Updates and Quick Learning Guides through http://real-timeupdates.com/bia5. The Quick Learning Guide (located under "Learn More" on the website) provides all six Checkpoints in a handy two-page format to help you study for exams or review important concepts whenever you need a quick refresher.

CHAPTER 19

Financial Markets and Investment Strategies

Behind the
Scenes

Chesapeake Energy Searches for Stability in a Volatile World

www.chk.com

Imagine trying to run a company when the prices you can charge are subject to wild swings beyond your control and you have no idea in advance how much you'll get for the product you sell. It goes for around $3 for several years, then suddenly jumps to $10, then immediately collapses back to $3, shoots up to $14, bounces around $8 for a couple of years, spikes at $12, then plunges to $3 again. The price triples—then collapses, then quadruples—then collapses, and then 15 years later, it is right back where it started.

Chesapeake Energy's financial managers are responsible for making sure the company has the funds it needs to invest in capital projects and sustain ongoing operations (such as this drilling platform in Fort Worth, Texas).

Meanwhile, your business involves massive capital investments, occasional joint ventures and acquisitions, and high ongoing operating costs. You need a constant stream of cash to run the business, but you can't plan cash flows because you don't know how much revenue you'll receive from one year to the next.

Welcome to the wild world of the natural gas business. Those are actual prices that gas producers received from 1995 through 2009 for the standard unit of natural gas, a thousand cubic feet. (Prices were even more volatile than these selected price points indicate, in fact.)

Now imagine you're Elliot Chambers, corporate finance manager of Oklahoma City–based Chesapeake Energy, one of the nation's leading gas producers. Your job is to make sure the company has the funds it needs to pay drilling-rights leases on millions of acres of land, develop new exploration technologies, drill and operate new wells, and support more than 7,000 employees. And you have to do it while your incoming revenue is jumping around like a grasshopper in a frying pan. How can you plan for the long term when income is so volatile? What financial tools can you use to stabilize cash flow and protect the company from price collapses?[1] ∎

Introduction

Whether you're a corporate financial manager like Chesapeake Energy's Elliot Chambers (profiled in the chapter-opening Behind the Scenes) or an individual investor taking charge of your financial future, you'll need to understand securities markets and investment strategies. This chapter starts by describing the most common types of securities investments—stocks, bonds, and mutual funds—followed by the more advanced tools that professionals such as Chambers use. The final two sections describe the markets where financial investments are bought and sold and provide an overview of investing strategies.

Stocks

Stock refers to ownership of or equity in a company, and a *share* of stock represents a specific portion of ownership. Stocks are part of a class of investments known as **securities**, along with bonds, mutual funds, and several others discussed in this chapter.

stock
Ownership of or equity in a company; a *share* of stock represents a specific portion of ownership

securities
Investments such as stocks, bonds, options, futures, and commodities

Chapters 5 and 18 discuss the perspective of corporations selling stock; this section looks at the perspective of investors buying and owning stock.

Types of Stock

common stock
Shares of ownership that include voting rights

capital gains
Increases in the value of a stock or other asset

Companies can issue two major forms of stock, *common stock* and *preferred stock*. **Common stock** is the type people are usually referring to when they talk about stocks. Common stock ownership has three potential benefits. The first is the opportunity to realize significant **capital gains**, or increases in the value of the stock, over time. The second potential advantage is receiving regular income in the form of dividends. However, not all stocks pay dividends, and for those that do, management is under no legal obligation to keep paying dividends. The third benefit of common stock ownership is the right to vote on certain major corporate decisions, including electing the board of directors. (In practice, however, only the very largest stockholders have much influence in the voting.)

The two major disadvantages of owning common stock are risk and volatility. Although stocks have historically outperformed most other investments, it must be emphasized that capital gains are in no way guaranteed. Individual stocks can lose value if the company doesn't meet investor expectations—and even become worthless if the company declares bankruptcy. And the stock market as a whole can tank, dramatically pulling down the value of shares across the board, irrespective of the performance of individual companies. For instance, over the span of just four weeks in the fall of 2008, the U.S. stock market lost a third of its value.[2] Even when a stock does appreciate in value over the long term, its price will show some degree of *volatility*, or uncertainty, over the short term. For example, even while generally trending upward, the price may drop and stay down for months or years at a stretch.

preferred stock
Shares of ownership without voting rights but with defined dividends

The second major category of stock is **preferred stock**, which can be thought of as a hybrid that combines attributes of common stock and corporate bonds. Preferred stock can be issued in several types with different rights and obligations for the buyer and seller. But generally speaking, like common stock, preferred stock represents equity in the company. Preferred stock is usually less volatile than common stock, which makes it attractive to risk-averse investors, but it also doesn't appreciate to the degree that common stock does. Unlike common stock, preferred stock does not come with any voting rights, and it can be *called*, or repurchased on demand, by the issuing company.

Preferred stocks resemble bonds in the sense that they pay fixed dividends—and at higher rates than either common stocks or bonds. Preferred shareholders also have a greater claim to assets than common shareholders, meaning they get paid first in the event of cash flow problems or bankruptcy. Finally, owning preferred stock has significant tax advantages for U.S. corporations, making it a common investment vehicle for corporate financial managers.[3]

In addition to the legally defined categories of common and preferred, investors also informally divide stock into a variety of categories based on their investment potential (see Exhibit 19.1).

Stock Valuation

Determining the value of a stock is obviously important for both sellers and buyers, but it is not a simple matter. At any point in time, each stock has several different values. One of the more confusing is *par value*, which is the value assigned to each share when the stock is first issued. For common stock, par typically doesn't have much meaning. However, par value is quite important for preferred stock, because it is the value on which dividend percentages are based.

book value
Difference between the assets and liabilities as listed on the balance sheet

For common stock, you'll hear several terms used to describe its value. **Book value** per share is the difference between the assets and liabilities as listed on the balance sheet, divided by the number of shares in circulation. In theory, this is how much you would get for each share you hold if the company were shut down and sold off tomorrow. As a

EXHIBIT 19.1 Investment Categories of Common Stock

The investing community categorizes stocks according to their particular investment potential. These aren't official definitions, and no central authority decides which stocks fall in which category, but these labels are an effective way to view potential investments. Of course, a stock can change categories if its appeal to investors changes.

STOCK CATEGORY	CHARACTERISTICS
Blue chip	Stocks of major, well-established corporations with demonstrated ability to manage their way through every kind of economic condition; such stocks are usually considered safe, if not necessarily thrilling, choices
Income	Stocks purchased primarily for dividend payouts, rather than capital gains potential; companies tend to be older, stable firms with fairly predictable profits but lower prospects for growth
Growth	Stocks from rapidly growing companies that usually reinvest profits (to keep growing) rather than paying dividends; investors buy these stocks for potential capital gains, not income; companies tend to be smaller and younger, and many are in the technology sector
Cyclical	Stocks from companies whose earnings tend to track the ups and downs of the economy in a predictable pattern—in other words, their revenue and profits grow as the economy grows and shrink as the economy shrinks; many of these companies are in basic industries such as housing and transportation
Defensive or counter-cyclical	In contrast to companies with cyclical stocks, these companies tend to fare better when the economy is doing worse, and vice versa; for example, new car sales decline in a falling economy but car repair businesses usually increase revenue as people try to hang onto their automobiles longer
Large cap, mid cap, small cap	General designations for the size of a company's *market capitalization* (the market value of its stock multiplied by the number of shares in circulation); small caps tend to be higher-risk, higher-reward than large caps, with mid caps somewhere in between—but these are averages over time, not predictions for specific stocks
Penny stock	Stocks that sell for less than one dollar per share or, more generally, stocks that are highly speculative (risky, but with upside potential, in other words); tend to be from newer companies or established companies whose stock has plummeted for some reason

measure of stock value, book value has two shortcomings. First, the assets or liabilities—particularly intangibles—might not be valued accurately on the balance sheet. In fact, some investors ignore intangibles entirely when computing book value. Second, book value looks backward (at what the company has already done) rather than forward (at what it could do in the future).[4]

In contrast, the **market value**, or *market price*, is the price at which the stock is actually selling in the stock market. Market value is forward looking in that it incorporates investor expectations about future earnings. Critically, market value also reflects, particularly in the short term, the emotional reactions of buyers and sellers. This *market sentiment* can range from irrational optimism to irrational pessimism at the extremes, and it can push prices higher or lower than objective financial analysis would indicate. Whether or not the market over time puts an accurate price on stocks (the *efficient market* theory) is a subject of ongoing debate.

market value
The price at which the stock is actually selling in the stock market

Book value is what the balance sheet says the company is worth, and market value is what the stock market says the company is worth, but **intrinsic value** is an attempt to establish what the company is *really* worth. Investors have come up with various ways to estimate intrinsic value by including both quantitative financial factors and such qualitative factors as intangible assets, management capability, and the company's competitive strengths within its industry. Obviously, intrinsic value is not a precise number because it relies in part on subjective assessments, and different analysts can arrive at different values for the same stock.[5]

intrinsic value
An estimate of what a company is actually worth, independent of book and market values

price-earnings ratio
Market value per share divided by the earnings per share

Much of the analysis of stock investing involves deciding whether the current market value is *overpriced* or *underpriced* relative to intrinsic value and other factors. Exhibit 19.2 shows the key variables that investors use to track stocks, including **price-earnings ratio**, or *p/e ratio*, defined as the market value per share divided by the earnings per share. The p/e ratio is often used to assess how a stock is priced, based on company earnings for the previous year (or anticipated earnings for the coming year, in which case it is known as *forward p/e*). A higher than average p/e suggests that investors expect the company to grow vigorously, but a p/e that is too high can mean the stock is overpriced and vulnerable to a decline. A lower than average p/e might suggest an overlooked stock with upside potential—or a troubled company in which investors have lost confidence. In other words, like every financial ratio, the p/e should be the beginning of an investigation, not the end.

EXHIBIT 19.2 How to Read a Stock Quotation

Whether you get quotes from a newspaper or website, you'll usually see some combination of the variables listed here. In addition, financial websites usually let you click through to additional data, such as charts of the stock's price going back several months or years. What can you surmise about these four stocks based on these data points? (On this particular day, stocks were down across the U.S. market, which is why all four dropped.)

(1)	(2)	(3) 52-WEEK HIGH	52-WEEK LOW	(4) DIV	(5) YLD %	(6) PE	(7) VOL	(8) HI	LOW	(9) CLOSE	(10) NET CHG
STOCK	SYM										
Apple	AAPL	148.92	62.58	–	–	38.55	24,230,234	135.95	131.50	131.85	−3.40%
Nordstrom	JWN	59.70	33.06	$0.54	1.12%	18.02	3,155,658	48.21	46.07	46.07	−4.36%
Starbucks	SBUX	40.01	25.22	–	–	32.22	16,806,057	26.95	26.30	26.31	−2.27%
Disney	DIS	36.09	27.99	$0.31	0.90%	15.96	12,642,400	34.62	33.84	33.90	−1.34%

1. **Stock:** The company's name may be abbreviated in newspaper listings.

2. **Symbol:** Symbol under which this stock is traded on stock exchanges.

3. **52-week high/low:** Indicates the highest and lowest trading price of the stock in the past 52 weeks plus the most recent week but not the most recent trading day (adjusted for splits). Stocks are quoted in dollars and cents. In most newspapers, bold-faced entries indicate stocks whose price changed by at least 4% but only if the change was at least $0.75 a share.

4. **Dividend:** Dividends are usually annual payments based on the last quarterly or semiannual declaration, although not all stocks pay dividends. Special or extra dividends or payments are identified in footnotes.

5. **Yield:** The percentage yield shows dividends as a percentage of the share price.

6. **PE:** Price-earnings ratio, calculated by dividing the stock's closing price by the earnings per share for the latest four quarters.

7. **Volume:** Daily total of shares traded. The format of the numbers varies by source; some show exact numbers (as above), but others show hundreds of shares.

8. **High/low:** The stock's highest and lowest price for that day.

9. **Close:** Closing price of the stock that day.

10. **Net change:** Change in share price from the close of the previous trading day.

Typical common stock footnotes: d—new 52-week low; n—new; pf—preferred; s—stock split or stock dividend of 25 percent or more in previous 52 weeks; u—new 52-week high; v—trading halted on primary market; vi—in bankruptcy; x—ex dividend (the buyer won't receive a recently declared dividend, but the seller will)

If a company's management team believes that the firm's shares are undervalued, it can opt to repurchase some of the shares through a *stock buyback*, thereby reducing the number of shares outstanding. This move can be a good sign for investors because it usually indicates that management believes strongly in the company's prospects, and it tends to drive the share price up by lowering the supply of the stock and improving the p/e ratio. Buybacks are also done to counter the *dilution* effects of employee stock options; when employees exercise stock options, they increase the number of shares outstanding, which can tend to drive market value down.[6]

In other instances, a board may decide that a stock's price has risen so high that it has become prohibitive for many investors to purchase or simply gotten out of line with similar stocks. In such cases, the company may announce a **stock split**, in which it divides each share into two or more new shares, and the market value is then reduced by the same ratio. Although a stock split doesn't create more wealth for shareholders, it does give them more shares to take advantage of future price increases.

stock split
Act of dividing a share into two or more new shares and reducing the market value by the same ratio

CHECKPOINT

LEARNING OBJECTIVE 1: Distinguish between common and preferred stock, and explain the difference between market value and intrinsic value.

Summary: Common stock is the type most people are referring to when they speak of stock. It offers the opportunity for significant capital gains, many (but by no means all) common stocks pay dividends, and holders of common stock vote on certain company decisions such as electing directors. The major downsides of common stock are risk and volatility. Preferred stock has some of the attributes of common stock and some attributes of corporate bonds. On the plus side, it pays dividends, is less volatile than common stock, and has tax advantages for corporate investors. On the minus side, it doesn't appreciate as quickly as common stock, it doesn't confer voting rights, and it can be called (repurchased) by the company at any time. Market value is the price at which a stock is currently trading. Intrinsic value is a judgment of how much the company (and therefore its stock) is really worth.

Critical thinking: (1) Assuming both can be calculated with reasonable accuracy, does book value or intrinsic value give a more accurate assessment of a company's value? Why? (2) If the average p/e in a particular industry is 16, and you've identified a stock in that industry with a p/e of only 9, does this automatically mean it is a good buy? Why or why not?

It's your business: (1) As an investor, how well do you think you could handle the volatility of the stock market, knowing the value of your investments could drop dramatically from time to time? (2) How could you apply your experiences as an employee and as a consumer to determine the intrinsic value of a stock?

Key terms to know: stock, securities, common stock, capital gains, preferred stock, book value, market value, intrinsic value, price-earnings ratio, stock split

Bonds

Bonds are the second major category of securities investments. Chapter 18 discusses bonds as a fund-raising mechanism for corporations; bonds are also issued by various government bodies, from local governments up to the U.S. Treasury. Every bond is characterized by three key variables:

- The **face value**, also called *par value* or *denomination*, is the amount of money, or *principal*, the bond buyer is lending to the bond issuer. Bonds are usually issued in

face value
Amount of money, or *principal*, a bond buyer lends to a bond issuer; also known as *par value* or *denomination*

multiples of $1,000, such as $5,000, $10,000, and $50,000. After a bond is in circulation, its *market value* fluctuates over time, primarily as a function of prevailing interest rates and the company's financial performance and its perceived ability to repay the bond. For instance, if prevailing interest rates drop after a bond is issued, that bond's market value will increase because it pays higher interest than newer bonds are paying.

maturity date
Date on which the principal of a bond will be repaid in full

- The **maturity date** is the date on which the principal will be repaid in full. Corporate bonds typically mature in three to seven years, whereas government bonds mature in anywhere from 30 days to 30 years. Note that bondholders aren't required to keep bonds until maturity; bonds are bought and sold on the open market in much the same way that stocks are.

yield
Interest income a purchaser receives from the bond

- The **yield** on a bond is the interest income a purchaser receives from the bond. Yield can get a little confusing, but here are the basics. When a bond is first sold, the issuer offers a specific annual interest rate, known as the *coupon*. A $1,000 bond with an 8 percent coupon, for example, pays $80 a year in interest. If the market value of the bond never fluctuated, the investor's yield would always be equal to this initial coupon rate. However, because market values do in fact fluctuate, the *current yield* also fluctuates over time. Current yield is equal to the coupon divided by the current market value; when the market value goes down, the yield goes up, and vice versa. If that $1,000 bond is currently selling for $800, the $80 in interest it continues to pay every year now reflects a current yield of 10 percent. Moreover, to choose between bonds with different coupons and maturities, investors can compare their *yield-to-maturity*, which is the yield each bond will generate from a specific point in time until its maturity date.

Bond quotation tables (see Exhibit 19.3) list the key variables to watch when monitoring bonds. When reading these tables, remember that the price is quoted as a percentage of the bond's value. For example, a $1,000 bond shown closing at 65 actually sold at $650.

EXHIBIT 19.3 How to Read a Bond Quotation

Bond quotations usually show some combination of these variables. Newspaper quotations typically show the company name, coupon, and maturity date in abbreviated form. For instance, the Time Warner bond would be listed as TimeWar 9 1/8 13 (where 9 1/8 is the coupon and 13 represents the year 2013). Some listings also provide such variables as daily volume, change in price from the previous day, and the months in which the bond pays out dividends.

(1) ISSUER	(2) COUPON	(3) MATURITY	(4) CUR YLD	(5) RATINGS	(6) CLOSE	(7) CUSIP
Avnet	6.000	09-01-2015	6.071	Ba1/BBB-	98.836	053807AM5
General Electric	5.000	20-01-2013	4.981	Aaa/AAA	100.390	369604AY9
Morgan Stanley	4.000	01-15-2010	4.078	Aa3/AA-	98.082	61746SBC2
Time Warner	9.125	01-15-2013	7.850	Baa2/BBB+	116.239	887315AK5

1. **Issuer:** Name of company or organization that issued the bond.

2. **Coupon:** The rate of interest that the issuer promises to pay, expressed as an annual percentage of the bond's face value.

3. **Maturity:** Date on which the principle is due and payable to the bondholder.

4. **Current yield:** Annual interest divided by the closing price.

5. **Ratings:** Moody's and S&P ratings for each bond (ratings are provided on some websites).

6. **Close:** Price of the bond at the close of the last day's business; the value shown represents the price per $1,000 expressed in hundreds. The Morgan Stanley bond, for instance, has a price of $980.82 per $1,000.

7. **CUSIP:** A unique identifier for municipal, U.S. government, and corporate bonds assigned by the Committee on Uniform Security Identification Procedures (CUSIP).

Advantages and Disadvantages of Bonds

Bonds offer three key advantages to investors. First, most bonds are less risky than stocks and many other investments. Particularly with government bonds, there is less chance that one's investment will decline in value or, in the worst-case scenario, be wiped out entirely. Second, bonds offer lower volatility than stocks, which makes them a good choice for investors who need to be able to count on earning a predictable interest rate and receiving their loaned principle back at a specific date. For instance, people saving for college educations or retirement often rely on bonds because they can be reasonably sure the money will be there when they need it. Third, corporate bonds with twice-yearly interest payments can provide a regular source of income. Not all bonds offer regular payments, however. With a *zero-coupon bond*, for example, the purchaser buys the bond at a discount from the face value and then at maturity is repaid the full face value; the difference is the interest earned.[7]

In keeping with the concept of risk-reward trade-off, however, bonds compensate for the safety and predictability with lower average returns, over time, than stocks.[8] The interest rate for each bond reflects its *duration* (how long until it matures, in other words) and its *credit quality*. Bonds with longer maturities offer higher interest rates than bonds with shorter maturities, and bonds with lower credit ratings offer higher rates than bonds with higher credit ratings.

The perceived credit quality of a bond is closely tied to the financial stability of the issuing company. *Credit rating agencies* such as Standard & Poor's (S&P) and Moody's

Real-Time Updates

Learn More

Learn the basics of successful bond investing

Explore the possibilities of corporate, government, municipal, and other types of bonds. On mybizlab (www.mybizlab.com), you can access Real-Time Updates within each chapter or under Student Study Tools. Otherwise, go to http://real-timeupdates.com/bia5 and click on "Learn More."

EXHIBIT 19.4 Corporate Bond Ratings

Standard & Poor's (S&P) and Moody's Investors Service are the two dominate firms that rate the safety of corporate bonds. Low-rated bonds, often known as *high-yield* or informally as *junk bonds*, pay higher interest rates to compensate investors for the higher risk.

	S&P	INTERPRETATION	MOODY'S	INTERPRETATION
Investment grade	AAA	Highest rating	Aaa	Prime quality
	AA	Very strong capacity to pay	Aa	High grade
	A	Strong capacity to pay; somewhat susceptible to changing business conditions	A	Upper-medium grade
	BBB	More susceptible than A-rated bonds	Baa	Medium grade
Not investment grade	BB	Somewhat speculative	Ba	Somewhat speculative
	B	Speculative	B	Speculative
	CCC	Vulnerable to nonpayment in default	Caa	Poor standing; may be in default
	CC	Highly vulnerable to nonpayment	Ca	Highly speculative; often in default
	C	Bankruptcy petition filed or similar action taken	C	Lowest rated; extremely poor chance of ever attaining real investment standing
	D	In default		

rate bonds on the basis of the issuer's financial strength. Exhibit 19.4 on the previous page shows that the safest corporate bonds are rated AAA (S&P) and Aaa (Moody's). (As you can read in Chapter 20, these rating agencies also played a controversial role in the subprime mortgage meltdown that triggered the recent global recession.) During economic turmoil, a bond can be *downgraded* if the rating agencies determine that the issuer's finances are deteriorating. *Defaults*, when companies cannot pay back bondholders at maturity, also increase during economic slowdowns, particularly among riskier *high-yield bonds*, often referred to as *junk bonds*.[9]

Another disadvantage with some bonds is a *call provision*, meaning (as with preferred stocks) that the issuer has the right to call, or repurchase the bond before maturity.[10] Issuers of such bonds may opt to call them in if interest rates drop after the bonds are issued. This is good news for the issuer (who no longer has to pay at the original rate) but bad news for the bondholder (who no longer receives the anticipated interest income). Callable bonds compensate for this potential loss of income for the bondholder with higher interest rates.

Types of Bonds

Chapter 18 described the three major types of corporate bonds: *secured bonds* backed by company assets, *debentures* backed only by the corporation's promise to pay, and *convertible bonds* that can be exchanged at the investor's option for a certain number of shares of the corporation's common stock. These bonds have varying degrees of risk and so offer varying levels of interest in compensation.

Unlike stocks, where corporations are the only issuers, the bond market also includes a wide range of bonds from federal, state, and local governments and agencies. To generate funds to operate the federal government, the U.S. Treasury Department offers several types of bonds, primarily classified by maturity. **Treasury bills** (often referred to informally as *T-bills*) are short-term U.S. government bonds that are repaid in less than one year. Like zero-coupon corporate bonds, Treasury bills are sold at a discount and redeemed at face value. The difference between the purchase price and the redemption price is the interest earned for the time period. **Treasury notes** are intermediate-term U.S. government bonds with maturities of 1 to 10 years. **Treasury bonds** are long-term U.S. government bonds with maturities of more than 10 years. With a newer alternative, **Treasury inflation-protected securities (TIPS)**, the principal amount is tied to the Consumer Price Index to protect against the erosion of buying power over time.[11] In addition to these Treasury issues, the federal government also sells a variety of *savings bonds* aimed at individual investors.

In general, U.S. government securities pay lower interest than corporate bonds because they are considered safer. They also have tax advantages in that investors pay no state or local income tax on interest earned on these bonds.

Municipal bonds (often informally called *munis*) are issued by states, cities, and various government agencies to raise money for public projects such as building schools, highways, and airports. A *general obligation bond* is a municipal bond backed by the taxing power of the issuing government. When interest payments come due, the issuer makes payments out of its tax receipts. In contrast, a *revenue bond* is a municipal bond backed by the money to be generated by the project being financed. For example, revenue bonds issued by a city airport are paid from revenues raised by the airport's operation.

The appeal of municipal bonds is usually a combination of yield, the potential for tax-exempt income, and relatively low risk. Municipal bonds are generally considered to be safe investments, second only to U.S. Treasury issues.[12] However, defaults have occurred. In fact, during the recession in 2008, more than four times as many municipal bonds as corporate bonds defaulted, although the total dollar amount of the municipal defaults was a small fraction of the corporate defaults.[13]

Treasury bills
Short-term debt securities issued by the federal government; also referred to as *T-bills*

Treasury notes
Debt securities issues by the federal government that are repaid within 1 to 10 years after issuance

Treasury bonds
Debt securities issued by the federal government that are repaid more than 10 years after issuance

Treasury inflation-protected securities (TIPS)
Treasury issues in which the principal amount is tied to the Consumer Price Index to protect the buyer against the effects of inflation

municipal bonds
Bonds issued by states, cities, and various government agencies to fund public projects

✓CHECKPOINT

LEARNING OBJECTIVE 2: Explain the three key variables that distinguish bonds, compare the advantages and disadvantages of owning bonds, and list the major types of bonds.

Summary: The three key variables that distinguish bonds are *face value* (the amount the buyer is lending to the issuer), *maturity date* (the date on which the principle will be repaid in full), and *yield* (the interest a bond issuer pays to the buyer). Bonds have three advantages: lower risks than stocks, less volatility, and regular income (with many corporate bonds). The major types of bonds are corporate bonds, U.S. Treasury issues (including Treasury bills, Treasury notes, Treasury bonds, and TIPS), and municipal bonds.

Critical thinking: (1) Why do bonds offer lower average rates of return than stocks? (2) If a company's newest product flops in the marketplace, what effect is that likely to have on the current yield of the company's bonds?

It's your business: (1) If you were approaching retirement age, would you have a higher percentage of bonds or stocks in your portfolio? Why? (2) Would you ever consider investing in high-yield ("junk") bonds? Why or why not?

Key terms to know: face value, maturity date, yield, Treasury bills, Treasury notes, Treasury bonds, Treasury inflation-protected securities (TIPS), municipal bonds

Mutual Funds

As beneficial as they can be, stocks and bonds present three major challenges for individual investors. First, researching, selecting, and monitoring the stocks and bonds in an investment portfolio can be a full-time job. Second, even if they have time, many individuals don't have the expertise needed to fully evaluate many investment alternatives. Third, most individuals don't have enough investment funds to achieve a safe level of **portfolio diversification**—spreading their investment across enough different vehicles to protect against significant declines in any one vehicle. For instance, if you had $1,000 to invest, you might be able to buy a single small bond, *or* a couple of shares of Google, *or* a half dozen shares of Apple, *or* a dozen shares of Visa. If the one investment you chose underperformed, you'd be out of luck. Even with $10,000 or $100,000, it's still hard to achieve significant diversification.

The financial industry's response to these three challenges is **mutual funds**, financial instruments that pool money from many investors to buy a diversified mix of stocks, bonds, or other securities. By buying shares of a single mutual fund, you can indirectly invest in dozens of securities, depending on the fund's investment profile.

portfolio diversification
Spreading investments across enough different vehicles to protect against significant declines in any one vehicle

mutual funds
Financial instruments that pool money from many investors to buy a diversified mix of stocks, bonds, or other securities

Advantages and Disadvantages of Mutual Funds

Mutual funds offer three primary advantages. First, by pooling money from thousands of clients, a mutual fund can spread its investments across a variety of securities. Doing so decreases the odds of a few poor performers pulling down results—and increases the odds of "catching fire" with a few hot performers. For example, American Century Capital Growth is a fund that invests in the stocks of large companies that have strong prospects for growth. With over $30 million to invest, the fund can diversify across a wide range of industries and companies. Its largest industry sector, health care, represents only 17 percent of the fund's holdings, and none of the roughly 100 stocks in the fund represents more than 4 percent of its holdings.[14] The average individual investor would never be able to achieve this level of diversification. (Note that not all mutual funds are broadly diversified; some specialized funds invest in a single industry or geographic region, for instance.)

The second advantage of mutual funds is professional management. Mutual funds are managed by experienced investors or teams of investors. The manager of the American Century Capital Growth fund, for example, is a chartered financial analyst with years of experience in equities markets.[15]

The third advantage of funds is simplifying decision making for individual investors, who don't have to dig into the financial details of various securities. Ironically, though, mutual funds have to some degree been a victim of their own success in this regard. So many funds are now available that selecting the right one can seem as complicated as selecting individual stocks and bonds. In fact, Morningstar (**www.morningstar.com**), a popular research service for investors, tracks nearly twice as many mutual funds (13,000) as individual stocks (7,000).[16]

The primary disadvantage of mutual funds is cost. Mutual funds charge an annual management fee, typically ranging from 1 to 1.5 percent of the amount invested. This might not sound like much, but it can definitely eat into your gains (or add to your losses) over time. More-expensive funds don't necessarily generate better returns than less-expensive funds, so be sure to check the total annual **expense ratio** or *management expense ratio* when comparing funds. In addition to annual expenses, funds can charge a variety of "shareholder fees," including a sales commission known as a **load** when a fund is bought or sold. As their name indicates, **no-load funds** do not charge these loads, although they can charge other fees and still call themselves no-load funds.[17] Unless you can find convincing evidence that a load fund will perform better than a similar no-load fund, the no-load choice is probably the better choice.

Another potential disadvantage of mutual funds is their performance relative to the stock market as a whole. Even with full-time professional management, many mutual funds do not perform as well as the overall markets in which they invest. In fact, many investors and securities experts believe it is impossible to consistently "beat the market."[18] This sentiment has fueled the growth of **index funds**, mutual funds that mirror the composition of a particular **index**, a statistical indicator of the prices of a representative group of securities. For example, the Vanguard 500 fund mirrors the composition of the Standard & Poor's 500, an index based on the stock of 500 large U.S. companies that is frequently used as an indicator of the stock market's overall performance.[19] The Vanguard 500 fund will never outperform the S&P 500, but it will never underperform it, either. The key advantage of index funds is lower cost; with no *active management*, the cost of running an index fund is lower, and those savings are passed on in the form of lower expense ratios. Indexing is also commonly used by **exchange traded funds (ETFs)**, funds that are traded on public exchanges in the same way as stocks. (Conventional mutual funds are not traded on exchanges.) Index ETFs combine the advantages of indexing with the flexibility of buying and selling stocks.

Choosing Mutual Funds

As noted earlier, with thousands of funds now on the market, choosing the right fund or combination of funds takes some research. The first step is to understand the various types of funds and their investment priorities and strategies. The major categories include

- *Money-market funds*, which invest in high-quality, short-term debt issues from governments and corporations
- *Growth funds*, which invest in stocks of rapidly growing companies
- *Value funds*, which invest in stocks considered to be selling below their true value
- *Income funds*, which invest in securities that pay high dividends and interest

expense ratio
Annual cost of owning a mutual fund, expressed as a percentage

load
Sales commission charged when buying or selling a mutual fund

no-load funds
Mutual funds that do not charge loads

index funds
Mutual funds that mirror the composition of a particular market or index

index
Statistical indicator of the rise and fall of a representative group of securities

exchange traded funds (ETFs)
Mutual funds whose shares are traded on public exchanges in the same way as stocks

Real-Time Updates

Learn More
How much does that fund really cost?
These handy calculators let you compare the real costs of mutual funds. On mybizlab (**www.mybizlab.com**), you can access Real-Time Updates within each chapter or under Student Study Tools. Otherwise, go to **http://real-timeupdates.com/bia5** and click on "Learn More."

- *Balanced funds*, which invest in a combination of stocks and bonds
- *Sector funds*, also known as *specialty* or *industry funds*, which invest in companies within a particular industry, such as technology or health care
- *Target-date funds*, which attempt to maintain a desirable balance of risk and growth potential based on a target retirement date
- *Global funds*, which invest in foreign and U.S. securities
- *International funds*, which invest strictly in foreign securities
- *Socially responsible funds*, which make investment choices based on criteria related to corporate social responsibility

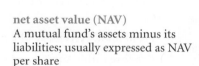

Real-Time Updates

Learn More

Find the funds that are right for you

Mutual fund screeners such as this help you filter out the worst and find the best funds for your portfolio. On mybizlab (**www.mybizlab.com**), you can access Real-Time Updates within each chapter or under Student Study Tools. Otherwise, go to **http://real-timeupdates.com/bia5** and click on "Learn More."

Within these categories, you can also find subcategories based on company size, such as a large company value fund or a small company growth fund. A key decision when selecting the type of funds is to understand your *risk tolerance* because various funds have more aggressive or more cautious approaches.

After you have an idea of the fund categories that meet your needs, you can use a *fund screener* (see the Real-Time Updates item on this page, for example) to select attractive candidates based on performance, expense ratio, minimum investment, and other criteria.

Unlike stocks, where you purchase a specific number of shares at a certain price, when you buy a mutual fund, the sum of money you invest is divided into a number of shares based on the fund's **net asset value (NAV)**—the fund's assets minus its liabilities. For instance, if you invest $1,000 in a no-load fund whose NAV per share that day is $47.93, you will receive 20.86 shares ($1,000 divided by $47.93). You can find the current NAV per share and other key variables in a mutual fund quotation (see Exhibit 19.5).

net asset value (NAV)
A mutual fund's assets minus its liabilities; usually expressed as NAV per share

✓CHECKPOINT

LEARNING OBJECTIVE 3: Define *mutual fund*, and explain the advantages and disadvantages of this popular investment vehicle.

Summary: A *mutual fund* is an investment vehicle that pools money from many investors to purchase a diversified mix of securities. The three primary advantages of mutual funds are portfolio diversification, professional management, and relative simplicity. The primary disadvantage is cost, along with the fact that many funds don't perform as well as the market overall, despite professional management.

Critical thinking: (1) How might the constant scrutiny and demand for consistent results affect the long-term performance of a mutual fund? (2) If many funds don't outperform the market, why would anybody bother to invest in mutual funds, particularly in perennial laggards?

It's your business: (1) Would your inclination be to invest in mutual funds or to do the research yourself and invest in individual stocks and bonds? Why? (2) Would investing in socially responsible funds that share your personal values be an effective way to support causes you believe in? Why or why not?

Key terms to know: portfolio diversification, mutual funds, expense ratio, load, no-load funds, index funds, index, exchange traded funds (ETFs), net asset value (NAV)

EXHIBIT 19.5 How to Read a Mutual Fund Quotation

Mutual fund quotations typically show such variables as the *net asset value* (NAV) of one share, the change in NAV from the previous day, expense ratio, and returns over various time spans. Some listings (particularly those offered online) also show fund objective or investing style, asset allocation, minimum investment amount, and risk/reward assessments.

(1) FUND NAME	(2) SYMBOL	(3) NAV	(4) CHANGE	(5) YTD	3 YR	5 YR	(6) FRONT LOAD	(7) EXPENSE RATIO	(8) YIELD
Lord Abbett CA Tax-Free Income	LCFIX	$10.62	−$0.03	−0.51	3.92	3.76	3.25	0.93	4.00
FBR Small Cap	FBRVX	$55.38	−$0.86	2.84	18.00	25.39	None	1.38	–
Janus Contrarian	JSVAX	$19.00	−$0.29	12.89	26.32	24.65	None	1.69	–
Vanguard Mid Cap Index	VIMSX	$20.60	−$0.59	4.17	17.39	17.49	None	0.22	–

1. **Fund name:** Name of mutual fund.

2. **Symbol:** Fund's symbol.

3. **NAV:** Net asset value, the per-share value of the fund.

4. **Change:** Decrease or increase in NAV from previous day.

5. **YTD, 3 yr, 5 yr:** Performance year-to-date, over the past 3 years, over the past 5 years (expressed as a percentage increase or decrease).

6. **Front load:** Percentage of a new investment charged as a sales fee; no-load funds do not charge a front load.

7. **Expense ratio:** Annual cost of owning the mutual fund.

8. **Yield:** Annual yield of income-producing funds, expressed as a percentage.

Derivatives

derivatives
Contracts whose value is derived from some other entity (usually an asset of some kind, but not necessarily); used to hedge against or speculate on risk

Most individuals don't venture too far beyond stocks, bonds, and mutual funds, but businesses and other organizations use a wide range of other financial vehicles to meet specific needs. While you may never be personally involved with any of the financial instruments in this section, it's important to recognize what they are, given their importance to many businesses and their role in the economy.

Derivatives are contracts whose value is derived from some other entity, which is usually an asset of some kind, but not necessarily.[20] Derivatives can be based on stocks, bonds, pools of debt, agriculture products, interest rates, life insurance policies, and even the weather, to name just a few.[21] The basic premise of a derivative is transferring risk from a party that wants to *decrease* its risk exposure to a party willing to *increase* its risk exposure in exchange for the opportunity to pursue higher profits. In other words, derivatives can be used defensively, to protect profits by *hedging* a position to guard against the risk of a sudden loss, or offensively, to seek profits by *speculating* on future price changes.

For example, a bank with many home mortgage loans might want to pay someone to shoulder the risk of those loans defaulting, or during the growing season a grain producer might want to protect itself from a possible drop in grain prices at harvest time. In both cases, a derivative is a tool to accomplish this exchange. An essential point here is that derivatives don't eliminate or even reduce the risk; they simply transfer it from one party to another.[22]

The ability to buy and sell risk is an important part of today's global economy—estimates put the total value of derivative contracts worldwide at $700 trillion—and derivatives are used by a wide variety of corporations, banks, governments, not-for-profit organizations, and institutional investors.[23] However, mistakes with derivatives can be quite costly and can magnify financial calamities such as the subprime mortgage crisis (see Chapter 20) when the parties involved don't understand the risks, don't manage the risks responsibly, or make decisions based on faulty predictions.

Another potential worry with derivatives occurs when *both* parties in a contract are speculating, rather than one party hedging and the other speculating. This can happen when a party that doesn't own an asset (such as a portfolio of home loans or a field full of grain, from the earlier examples) initiates a derivative on it, purely for the purpose of speculation. When the auto parts maker Delphi defaulted on $2 billion worth of bonds, it was discovered that derivatives equalling more than 10 times that amount had been contracted by multiple speculators.[24]

The field of derivatives is immensely complex, with many types of derivatives across a variety of industries, but the following discussions offer a quick tour of the major types.

Options and Financial Futures

An **option** is the purchased right—but not the obligation—to buy or sell a specified number of shares of a stock or other security at a predetermined price during a specified period. Investors who trade options are betting that the price of the stock will either rise or decline. All options fall into two broad categories: *puts* and *calls*; Exhibit 19.6 explains the rights acquired with each type. Like all derivatives, options can be used offensively by speculators hoping to profit from future price changes or defensively by hedgers to protect their existing positions against future losses. In addition to individual stocks, options can also be created using an index of stocks, interest rates, and other financial variables.

An important note here on terminology: *Hedge funds* started in the 1950s as a defensive investment strategy, but the term is now applied to a wide variety of private investment funds—many of which use aggressive and often risky strategies that have nothing to do with hedging.[25] Some of the biggest financial catastrophes in recent years have involved hedge funds whose risky speculation backfired on them.

Financial futures are similar to options, but they are legally binding contracts to buy or sell a financial instrument (such as stocks, Treasury bonds, and foreign currencies) for a set price at a future date. Options and futures—like all derivatives—are riskier than conventional securities, so they should be considered only by knowledgeable investors who are using capital they can afford to lose. Futures often involve a high degree of leverage, in the sense that you can buy a very large futures contract with a very small "down payment." This leverage can greatly magnify both gains and losses, depending on how prices change over time.

option
The purchased right—but not the obligation—to buy or sell a specified number of shares of a stock at a predetermined price during a specified period

financial futures
Contracts to buy or sell a financial instrument (such as stocks, Treasury bonds, and foreign currencies) for a set price at a future date

EXHIBIT 19.6 Types of Options

All stock options fall into two broad categories: puts and calls.

TYPE	OPTION HOLDER'S RIGHT	BUYER'S BELIEF	SELLER'S BELIEF
Call	The right to buy the stock at a fixed price until the expiration date	Buyer believes price of underlying stock will increase. Buyer can buy stock at a set price and sell it at a higher price for a capital gain.	Seller believes price of underlying stock will decline and that the option will not be exercised. Seller earns a premium.
Put	The right to sell the stock at a fixed price until the expiration date	Buyer believes price of underlying stock will decline and wants to lock in a fixed profit. Buyer usually already owns shares of underlying stock.	Seller believes price of underlying stock will rise and that the option will not be exercised. Seller earns a premium.

Real-Time Updates

Learn More
The next bubble?

George Soros worries that investors pulling out of currency markets are creating a new bubble in commodities. On mybizlab (**www.mybizlab .com**), you can access Real-Time Updates within each chapter or under Student Study Tools. Otherwise, go to **http://real-timeupdates.com/bia5** and click on "Learn More."

commodities futures
Contracts to buy or sell specific amounts of commodities for a set price at a future date

currency futures
Contracts to buy or sell amounts of specified currency at some future date

credit derivatives
Derivatives used to reduce a lender's exposure to credit risk

Commodities Futures

Commodities—agricultural products, petroleum, metals, and other basic goods—are frequently bought and sold through futures contracts as well. **Commodities futures** are an essential hedging tool for many agricultural, industrial, or commercial buyers and sellers of commodities. Buyers of commodities (those companies that actually use the commodities, in other words) use futures contracts to protect against future price increases, and suppliers use these contracts to protect themselves from future price decreases. As you can read in the Behind the Scenes wrap-up at the end of the chapter, this hedging technique is how Chesapeake Energy tries to safeguard its revenue stream from unpredictable price drops. In addition to parties that actually produce or use the commodities, financial speculators who aren't involved with the actual commodities themselves also buy and sell commodities futures in the attempt to profit from price changes.

Commodities futures are an important financial management tool for companies such as Chesapeake, whose cash flows and incomes are closely linked to the prices of commodity goods. However, like options and financial futures, commodities can be a risky investment for speculators trying to predict future price changes. Speculators have lost millions of dollars in commodities futures—and a few years ago, a hedge fund manager speculating on natural gas futures singlehandedly lost 6 *billion* dollars.[26]

Currency Futures

For companies that conduct business in multiple currencies around the world, variations in exchange rates between two currencies can affect profitability. To hedge against exchange rate shifts that will affect them negatively, these firms can use **currency futures**, contracts to buy or sell amounts of specified currency at some future date. As with other types of futures contracts, the flip side of hedging is speculating, and speculation in the *foreign exchange market*, commonly known as *forex*, is a booming worldwide industry. Currency trading takes place 24 hours a day during the week, with an average daily volume of several trillion dollars.[27]

Credit Derivatives

Credit derivatives are used to reduce a lender's exposure to credit risk. The most notable—and notorious—type is the *credit default swap*, which was at the center of the recent meltdown in the credit markets. A credit default swap works much like an insurance policy. For example, a lender can transfer the risk of a loan portfolio (without actually transferring the loans themselves) in exchange for periodic payments. If the loans go bad, the party that now owns the risk is on the hook for it. These swaps are a useful concept, but things got messy in recent years because the contracts themselves can be bought and sold—and buyers sometimes didn't understand what they were buying or didn't have the capital needed to meet the financial obligations they were taking over.[28] Unlike stocks, for example, which have to meet certain financial criteria before they can be listed on a stock exchange, credit derivatives are sold entirely *over the counter*, with no exchange mechanisms or regulatory oversight to help ensure that the deals are financially sound.

These instruments have been criticized in recent years for being extremely complex, largely unregulated, and hidden from public scrutiny—despite being capable of triggering chain reactions across the economy. In 2009, President Barack Obama proposed broad changes to the regulation of derivatives, including requiring that many credit derivatives be traded in a central clearinghouse with government oversight.[29]

✓CHECKPOINT

LEARNING OBJECTIVE 4: Define *derivative*, **and identify the major types of derivatives.**

Summary: A derivative is a contract whose value is based on some underlying asset or other entity. Except for when they are used purely for speculative purposes, the intent of derivatives is to transfer risk from a party that wants to decrease its risk exposure to a party willing to increase its risk exposure in exchange for the opportunity to generate profits. The major types of derivatives are options, financial futures, commodities futures, currency futures, and credit derivatives.

Critical thinking: (1) What is the perceived danger in over-the-counter derivatives? (2) Would options and futures be a wise investment for someone getting close to retirement who wants to create a final boost to his or her nest egg before retiring? Why or why not?

It's your business: (1) Over-the-counter credit derivatives are private contracts between two companies; is it appropriate for the government to force them to be sold on regulated exchanges as commodities are? Why or why not? (2) Should speculating via derivatives be outlawed in the United States, as it is in some countries? Why or why not?

Key terms to know: derivatives, option, financial futures, commodities futures, currency futures, credit derivatives

Financial Markets

Market is one of those potentially confusing financial terms that is used in a variety of ways in different contexts. For example, when you hear commentators refer to "the market," with no qualifiers, they are probably referring to the stock market and specifically to one or more stock market indexes. Also, a market can be a specific group of organizations or a looser conglomeration of trading activity. (Speaking of "trading," be aware that this usually means buying and selling, not bartering or exchanging without the use of money.) Finally, securities markets can be divided into *primary markets*, which handle the initial issues of stocks (initial public offerings [IPOs], in other words) and bonds, and *secondary markets*, which handle all the public buying and selling after that.

stock exchanges
Organizations that facilitate the buying and selling of stock

NYSE
The New York Stock Exchange, one of the oldest and most widely recognized exchanges in the world

The Stock Market

Organizations that facilitate the buying and selling of stock are known as **stock exchanges.** Some of these are actual physical facilities, whereas others are primarily computer networks. The most famous of the physical variety is the New York Stock Exchange (**NYSE**), one of several exchanges owned by NYSE Euronext (www.euronext.com). The NYSE, often referred to as the "Big Board," is located just off Wall Street

 Real-Time Updates

Learn More
Practice your investment skills

Use this portfolio simulator to learn how to buy and sell stocks without risking any money. On mybizlab (www.mybizlab.com), you can access Real-Time Updates within each chapter or under Student Study Tools. Otherwise, go to http://real-timeupdates.com/bia5 and click on "Learn More."

in New York City (leading to the frequent use of "Wall Street" as a metaphor for either the stock market or the larger community of financial companies in the immediate area). Tokyo, London, Frankfurt, Paris, Toronto, and Montreal also have stock exchanges with national or international importance, and smaller regional exchanges play an important role in buying and selling many lesser-known stocks.

NASDAQ
An electronic stock exchange that competes with the NYSE

The NYSE's major competitor is the **NASDAQ** (pronounced "nazzdack"), a computerized stock exchange originated by the National Association of Securities Dealers and now owned by NASDAQ OMX Group (**www.nasdaq.com**). Home to such high-profile stocks as Amazon.com, Apple, eBay, Intel, and Microsoft, NASDAQ is the country's largest stock exchange in terms of the number of companies listed and average daily trading volume.[30]

Stocks that don't meet the listing requirements of an exchange can be sold over the counter (OTC). Together, the various stock exchanges around the world and the OTC market make up the overall "stock market."

The Bond Market

bond market
The collective buying and selling of bonds; most bond trading is done over the counter, rather than in organized exchanges

Unlike the stock market, in which most buying and selling is coordinated by organizations such as the NYSE and NASDAQ, most trading in the **bond market** is over the counter, taking place outside of an organized exchange. Consequently, the bond market is much more diffuse and decentralized than the stock market, and the processes for buying and selling depends on the type of bond. In the primary market, new issues of Treasury bonds, for example, can be purchased directly from the Treasury Department (**www.treasurydirect.gov**). In the secondary market, bonds are traded through a wide variety of brokers and agents (who buy and sell on behalf of customers) and dealers (who buy bonds and then resell them from their own inventories).[31]

The Money Market

money market
Over-the-counter marketplace for short-term debt instruments such as Treasury bills and commercial paper

The **money market** is an over-the-counter marketplace for short-term debt instruments such as Treasury bills and commercial paper. Its purpose is to help corporations and government agencies meet short-term liquidity needs. Unlike stocks and many bonds, the amounts traded in the money market are far beyond the reach of individual investors, so the money market is used by corporations, governments, banks, and other financial institutions. However, individuals can invest indirectly by purchasing *money market mutual funds*. These funds offer relatively low returns, but they are considered a relatively safe place to keep money that might be needed on short notice.[32]

The Derivatives Market

derivatives market
Includes exchange trading (for futures and some options) and OTC trading (for all other derivatives, at least currently)

The **derivatives market** is as diverse as the field of derivatives themselves and includes both exchange-traded and OTC derivatives. Futures and some options are traded on organized exchanges with time-tested financial controls and government regulation. All other derivatives, including the credit default swaps that made headlines in recent years, are traded over the counter.[33] However, as noted earlier, an effort is underway to require many OTC derivatives to be traded on exchanges as a way to improve oversight and to make sure the parties to these contracts understand what they're getting into before they sign.

√CHECKPOINT

LEARNING OBJECTIVE 5: Describe the four major types of financial markets.

Summary: The *stock market* is a collection of individual stock exchanges (such as the NYSE and NASDAQ) and the over-the-counter market that facilitate the buying and trading of company stocks. In contrast to the stock market, nearly all trading in the *bond market* is over the counter. The *money market* is where short-term debt instruments such as corporate paper are issued and traded; this is also an over-the-counter market. The derivatives market is a diverse collection of both exchanges (for some options and all futures) and over-the-counter trading (for all other types—although this may change in the coming years).

Critical thinking: (1) What is the difference between the primary market and the secondary market? (2) Why do individual investors participate in the stock and bond markets but not in the money market?

It's your business: (1) What is your emotional reaction to the term "Wall Street"? Explain your answer. (2) Given all the calamity in the financial markets in recent years, are you now more or less inclined to pursue a career in financial services? Why?

Key terms to know: stock exchanges, NYSE, NASDAQ, bond market, money market, derivatives market

Investment Strategies and Techniques

Learning how to make smart investment choices should be high on your life-skills to-do list. With many employers cutting back or eliminating retirement plans and with Social Security facing an uncertain future, you need to take charge of your financial future. This section offers a basic framework for beginning your education as an investor, whether you're investing for yourself and your family or for your company. Be sure to check out Appendix D (available online at www.mybizlab.com) as well, which offers a broader view of personal financial planning.

Establishing Investment Objectives

A common mistake in investing is chasing after promising investments without having any long-range goals in mind. Ask yourself the following questions before you invest:

- **Why do you want to get more money?** Simply piling up cash is not a terribly useful goal because it won't help you make the choices and trade-offs you'll need to make.

- **How much will you need—and when?** Identify how much money you'll need for significant events, from major purchases to college educations to retirement.

- **How much can you invest?** Make a realistic assessment of how much you can invest now and then every month thereafter. You can get started in some mutual funds with as little as $100, so don't let limited cash hold you back.

- **How much risk are you willing to accept?** Identify your tolerance for risk, based on your personality, financial circumstances, and stage in life. As with most everything in finance, risk is inversely related to potential **rate of return**, the gain (or loss) of an investment over time.

rate of return
Gain (or loss) of an investment over time, expressed as a percentage

- **How much liquidity do you need?** Money that you may need in the short term should not be tied up in long-term investments.

- **What are the tax consequences?** Various investments have different tax ramifications, and some are designed specifically to minimize taxes.

By answering these questions, you'll be able to establish realistic investment objectives that are right for you and your family.

Learning to Analyze Financial News

Knowing how to analyze financial news is essential to making good investment choices. Investors have access to more information than ever before, and much of this information is free (and chances are your college or community library has subscriptions to many of the sources that aren't free). You can quickly uncover basic information about a company on its website or a directory such as Hoover's (www.hoovers.com), scan its "financials" on Google Finance (www.google.com/finance) or Yahoo! Finance (http://finance.yahoo.com), read in-depth articles from numerous business periodicals online, judge customer sentiment by reading comments on social commerce sites, catch late-breaking news on 24-hour cable TV channels, and monitor the company and its industry using a variety of newsfeeds and social media.

Unfortunately, so much information is available that to avoid being overwhelmed, you almost need to take a defensive posture, filtering out information that is irrelevant and keeping a sharp eye for information that is biased or unreliable. This information overload carries the additional risk of prompting investors to make snap decisions based on something they heard on CNBC or something that just popped up on Twitter.

Fortunately, the vast majority of the information out there won't apply to you and your investments. Much of it is detailed material aimed at financial specialists, and much of it is short-term "noise" that probably won't affect you in the long term. To make the best use of all this information without getting overwhelmed or sidetracked, start on a small scale. Learn the basic language of investing on a site such as Investopedia (www.investopedia.com), a free website owned by *Forbes* magazine with extensive content written by investment professionals.

You'll gradually pick up on the terminology and start to identify the themes you need to care about and which of the many arcane topics you can leave to the specialists. For instance, you'll soon get familiar with the general conditions of the stock market and learn the terms that define its ups and downs (see Exhibit 19.7). If stock prices have been rising over a long period, for instance, the industry and the media will often describe this situation as a **bull market**. The reverse is a **bear market**, one characterized by a long-term trend of falling prices.

Finally, one more bit of good news: Virtually everything you learn in this course and in other business courses will help you analyze business and financial news and become a more successful investor. When you know what makes companies successful, you can apply this insight to choosing investments with solid growth potential.

Creating an Investment Portfolio

No single investment provides an ideal combination of income, growth potential, safety, liquidity, and tax consequences. For this reason, investors build **investment portfolios**, or collections of various types of investments. Managing a portfolio to balance potential returns with an acceptable level of risk is known as **asset allocation**, dividing investments among *cash instruments* such as money-market mutual funds, *income instruments* such as government and corporate bonds, and equities (mainly common stock). In general, younger investors want to focus on *building* capital through equity investments, whereas older investors want to focus on *protecting* capital through income and cash instruments, so they rebalance their portfolios over time.

bull market
Market situation in which most stocks are increasing in value

bear market
Market situation in which most stocks are decreasing in value

investment portfolios
Collections of various types of investments

asset allocation
Managing a portfolio to balance potential returns with an acceptable level of risk

EXHIBIT 19.7 The Stock Market's Ups and Downs

The peaks and valleys on this chart represent swings in the Dow Jones Industrial Average (DJIA), a widely used index of U.S. stock prices.

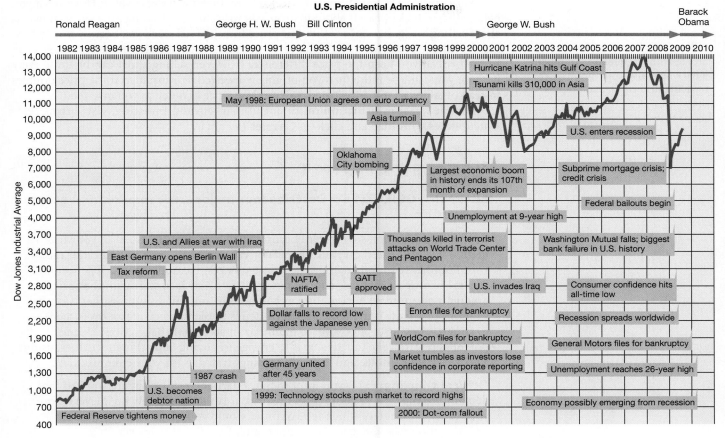

Buying and Selling Securities

In most cases, buying and selling securities requires a **broker**, an expert who has passed a series of formal examinations and is legally registered to buy and sell securities on behalf of individual and institutional investors. You pay *transaction costs* for every order, and these fees vary by the level of service you get. A *full-service broker* advises you on selecting investments, for example, whereas a *discount broker* provides fewer services and generally charges lower commissions as a result.

When you buy or sell a stock, you can use a variety of order types to accomplish different goals. The simplest is a **market order**, which tells the broker to buy or sell at the best price that can be negotiated at the moment. Because you can't be sure where prices will finalize with market orders, you can use a **limit order** to specify the highest price you are willing to pay when buying or the lowest price at which you are willing to sell. If you're worried about price declines on a stock you own, you can set a **stop order** that tells the broker to sell if the price drops to a certain level.

More experienced investors can use a number of buying and selling strategies beyond simple cash purchases of stock. With **margin trading**, investors buy stock using a combination of their own cash and money borrowed from their brokers. The appeal of margin trading is leverage, amplifying potential gains by using someone else's money in addition to your own. Margin trading is risky, however, because it also amplifies losses. In fact, with leverage, you can lose more money than you originally invested. And if prices are dropping and you want to hang on until they climb back up, you might not be allowed to. If the stock price drops so low that it violates the maximum leverage allowed

broker
Certified expert who is legally registered to buy and sell securities on behalf of individual and institutional investors

market order
Type of securities order that instructs the broker to buy or sell at the best price that can be negotiated at the moment

limit order
Order that stipulates the highest or lowest price at which the customer is willing to trade securities

stop order
Order to sell a stock when its price falls to a particular point to limit an investor's losses

margin trading
Borrowing money from brokers to buy stock, paying interest on the borrowed money, and leaving the stock with the broker as collateral

in your account, you can be forced to sell immediately. When the stock market plunged in late 2008, Elliot Chambers's boss at Chesapeake Energy, CEO Aubrey McLendon, was forced to sell nearly all of his Chesapeake stock at a loss because of such *margin calls*.[34]

Most investors buy stock with the anticipation that it will rise in value. However, if you believe that a stock's price is about to drop, you may choose a trading procedure known as **short selling**, or "going short." With this procedure, you sell stock you borrow from a broker in the hope of buying it back later at a lower price. After you return the borrowed stock to the broker, you keep the price difference. However, selling short can be quite risky because you can lose more than you originally invested. For instance, if the price doubles instead of falling as you anticipated, you can lose twice as much as you invested.

For the latest information on financial markets and investing, visit **http://real-timeupdates.com/bia5** and click on Chapter 19.

short selling
Selling stock borrowed from a broker with the intention of buying it back later at a lower price, repaying the broker, and keeping the profit

✓CHECKPOINT

LEARNING OBJECTIVE 6: Describe four major steps required to become an investor.

Summary: The first step toward becoming an investor is to establish your investment objectives, based on your financial needs and goals, your tolerance for risk, your liquidity requirements, and tax consequences that apply to you. The second step is learning to analyze financial news; the best way is to start with the basics, gradually accumulate information as you need it, and filter out news that is irrelevant or potentially unreliable. The third step is to plan and create an investment portfolio, using asset allocation to maintain an acceptable balance of risk and potential reward. The fourth step is to engage in buying and selling securities, using a broker of your choice and the right trading strategies for your circumstances.

Critical thinking: (1) If you want to buy a particular stock but are worried that demand from investors could push the price to an unreasonably high level before your order is executed, which type of order would you specify? Why? (2) Does a low p/e ratio mean that a stock is a good buy? Explain your answer.

It's your business: (1) Do you think you currently have the discipline needed to control your spending in order to free up cash for regular investing? If not, what changes could you make? (2) Do you own any stocks, mutual funds, or other financial investments? What steps did you take to research these investments before you made them?

Key terms to know: rate of return, bull market, bear market, investment portfolios, asset allocation, broker, market order, limit order, stop order, margin trading, short selling

Behind the Scenes

Chesapeake Energy Hedges Its Way to the Future

In many industries, prices tend to follow reasonably predictable patterns over time, such as rising in line with inflation or declining as a result of new technologies and greater production efficiencies. Commodities such as natural gas are a different beast altogether, with wide and often unpredictable swings. However, producers can't always adjust their ongoing operating expenses to match revenue, at least not with anywhere near the same rapidity at which prices fluctuate. For example, gas companies can spend millions or billions of dollars in exploration and leasing costs (to secure drilling rights from property owners) before production can even begin. If they then decide to limit output because prices are dropping, they can be left with an expensive asset that's generating little or no revenue.

Because operating costs can't be cranked up or down to match revenues, an increasingly common financial strategy for producers is to even out the revenue stream through the use of commodities futures. By locking in prices months in advance to increase the predictability of their cash flows, companies are better able to manage major capital budgets and their overall operating budgets. At Oklahoma City's Chesapeake Energy, the nation's largest independent producer of natural gas, futures contracts are an integral part of the company's financial strategy.

Of course, Chesapeake's corporate finance manager Elliot Chambers would probably be the first to tell you that even though hedging can reduce a company's risk exposure, it is not without risks of its own. Companies that guess incorrectly about future price shifts can pay dearly. For instance, in the second quarter of 2008, Chesapeake had *paper losses* of $3.4 billion on its hedging contracts because market prices had risen higher than the prices it had previously locked in in those contracts.

Such losses are known as paper losses, or *unrealized losses*, because they happen only "on paper" until the futures contract actually comes due. Let's say that in January, Chesapeake signs a futures contract to sell gas at $6 per thousand cubic feet in October. However, if market prices rise to $8 in June, the company has a paper loss at that point of $2 per unit. It hasn't *actually* lost the $2 in June because it doesn't have to settle the contract until October, so the loss is considered to have happened only "on paper."

Interim paper losses might sound like they're not a problem because no money changes hands. After all, the market price in this example could settle back to $6 by October, in which case Chesapeake would essentially break even—or make money if the market price drops below $6 by October. However, the reason paper losses matter is that accounting regulations require companies to treat these losses as real in their ongoing financial statements. In other words, when Chesapeake had paper losses of $3.4 billion on its hedging contracts in the second quarter of 2008, that loss showed up in the quarterly income statement. And since the stock market pays very close attention to quarterly income statements, a company's stock can get hammered even though such losses are (as yet) still on paper.

True to the wild nature of the natural gas market, halfway through the third quarter of 2008, Chesapeake's futures contracts had swung around in the positive direction, giving it a paper *gain* at one point of $4.7 billion. Like a paper loss, this paper gain doesn't involve any money changing hands, but it must be accounted for in the financial statements.

When the contracts come due, losses or gains become quite real. If market prices at that point are higher than the price in the contract, Chesapeake suffers because it is forced to sell product at less than it could've gotten otherwise. Conversely, if market prices are lower than the contract

price, the other party loses and Chesapeake wins because the other party has to pay more than the market price.

Clearly, hedging is not an exact science or a perfect remedy, but it does bring predictability to a company's cash flow and thereby allow it to plan the massive capital projects needed to bring new production online. Moreover, if a company does well over time, hedging can be a source of revenue. In its 2008 annual report, for instance, Chesapeake said hedging had increased its revenues by more than $2.4 billion over the previous three years. Because the uncertainties of hedging are lower than the uncertainties of *not* hedging, the company plans to keep using these contracts as a central component of its financial plan.

By the way, anyone following the use of commodities futures in the natural gas market must wonder *why* gas prices swing up and down so unpredictably—and in ways that aren't always related to supply and demand. After watching the gyrations in energy prices over the last few years and the destruction that derivatives recently caused in the banking industry, government regulators now worry that the very same financial tools that producers use to protect themselves from violent price swings could be contributing to those swings in the first place. The federal Commodity Futures Trading Commission contends that in the hands of speculators, commodities futures contracts are disrupting prices in ways that harm consumers and industrial energy users. The commission is considering placing restrictions on speculators who trade commodities futures with no intent of buying or selling the actual commodities themselves.

In response, hedgers such as Chesapeake say they can't run their businesses without the participation of speculators because they provide the financial predictability necessary to plan budgets in an inherently unstable industry. For instance, Chambers told the commission that without speculators, Chesapeake would never have been able to invest the $3.75 billion it took to discover and develop a major new source of natural gas in Louisiana in 2008.

With the United States looking for ways to reduce its dependence on imported oil, the plentiful supply of domestic natural gas is playing an increasingly important role in national policy discussions. It could come down to a tug-of-war between the need to develop more domestic sources in the long term and the need to bring stability to end-user energy prices in the short term.[35]

Critical Thinking Questions

1. If speculators are barred from investing in futures contracts, how will that change Chesapeake's approach to financial management? (Assume that natural gas distributors and other major customers would still be able to engage in futures contracts from a commodity buyer's perspective.)

2. Why do you suppose accounting regulations require companies to report paper losses or gains from futures contracts in their financial statements?

3. Should the government continue to allow speculation in natural gas futures as a way to keep developing domestic

energy sources, even if it can be proven that speculation contributes to price volatility for producers and customers? Why or why not?

LEARN MORE ONLINE

Visit Chesapeake's "Investors" section at www.chk.com/investors. Click on "News Summary" to see the latest financial news from the company. How does Chesapeake's financial health look at present? What do the trends for revenue, expenses, and income look like? Read the "Letter to Shareholders." Does it mention hedging? If so, have the company's hedging activities been beneficial in the most recent year? ■

Key Terms

asset allocation (498)
bear market (498)
bond market (496)
book value (482)
broker (499)
bull market (498)
capital gains (482)
commodities futures (494)
common stock (482)
credit derivatives (494)
currency futures (494)
derivatives (492)
derivatives market (496)
exchange traded funds (ETFs) (490)
expense ratio (490)
face value (485)
financial futures (493)

index (490)
index funds (490)
intrinsic value (483)
investment portfolios (498)
limit order (499)
load (490)
margin trading (499)
market order (499)
market value (483)
maturity date (486)
money market (496)
municipal bonds (488)
mutual funds (489)
NASDAQ (496)
net asset value (NAV) (491)
no-load funds (490)
NYSE (495)

option (493)
portfolio diversification (489)
preferred stock (482)
price-earnings ratio (484)
rate of return (497)
securities (481)
short selling (500)
stock (481)
stock exchanges (495)
stock split (485)
stop order (499)
Treasury bills (488)
Treasury bonds (488)
Treasury inflation-protected securities (TIPS) (488)
Treasury notes (488)
yield (486)

Test Your Knowledge

Questions for Review

1. What is the money market?
2. How does a commodities future differ from buying a commodity outright?
3. What are the main differences between common and preferred stock?
4. What happens during a 2-for-1 stock split?
5. What is a p/e ratio, and what does it signify to an investor?

Questions for Analysis

6. How can asset allocation be used to diversify against risk?
7. If an investor had enough money to diversify adequately through buying individual securities, why might he or she still consider buying mutual funds instead?
8. When might an investor sell a stock short? What risks are involved in selling short?
9. Why are debentures considered riskier than other types of bonds?
10. Ethical Considerations. Would it be ethical for you to write in your personal blog about the positive outlook on a stock that you own, without telling readers that you own the stock? Why or why not?

Questions for Application

11. If you are worried that a frenzied market will drive the price of a particular stock too high before your broker can execute a buy order, which type of order would you use?
12. If investors want a steady, predictable flow of cash, what types of investments should they seek and why?
13. If your bank specializes in lending money to home builders and the forecast for new home sales is predicting a decline in the coming months, what type of financial instrument could you use to protect against builders defaulting on loans because they are unable to sell the houses they've built?
14. Concept Integration. Review the discussion of mission statements on page 193 in Chapter 7. Suppose you were thinking about purchasing 100 shares of common stock in General Electric. Why might you want to first review the company's mission statement? What would you be looking for in the company's mission statement that could help you decide whether or not to invest?

Practice Your Knowledge

Sharpening Your Communication Skills

Interviewing a full-service broker is one of the most important steps you can take before hiring that broker to execute your trades or manage your funds and investment portfolio. Practice your communication skills by developing two sets of questions:

1. Questions you might ask a stockbroker to help you decide whether you would use his or her services.

2. Questions you might pose to that broker to help you evaluate the merits of purchasing a specific security.

Building Your Team Skills

You and your team are going to pool your money and invest $5,000. Before you plunge into any investments, how can you prepare yourselves to be good investors? First, consider your group's goals. What will you and your teammates do with any profits generated by your investments? Once you have agreed on a goal for your team's

profits, think about how much money you will need to achieve this goal and how soon you want to achieve it.

Next, think about how much risk you personally are willing to take to achieve the goal. Bear in mind that safer investments generally offer lower returns than riskier investments—and certain investments, such as stocks, can lose money. Now hold a group discussion to find a level of risk that feels comfortable for everyone on your team.

After your team has decided how much risk to take, consider which investments are best suited to your group's goals and chosen risk level. Will you choose stocks, bonds, a combination of both, or other securities? What are the advantages and disadvantages of each type of investment for your team's situation? Then come to a decision about specific investment opportunities—particular stocks, for example—that your group would like to investigate further.

Compare your group's goal, risk level, and investment possibilities with those of the other teams in your class and discuss the differences and similarities you see.

Expand Your Knowledge

Discovering Career Opportunities

Think you might be interested in a job in the securities and commodities industry? This industry has one of the most highly educated and skilled workforces of any industry. View the "Securities, Commodities, and Financial Services Sales Agents" page at www.bls.gov/oco/ocos122.htm to read more about these professions.

1. What are the licensing and continuing education requirements for securities brokers?

2. What is the typical starting position for many people in the securities industry?

3. What factors are expected to contribute to the projected long-term growth of this industry?

Developing Your Research Skills

Stock market analysts advise investors (both individuals and institutions) on which stocks to buy, sell, or hold. Changes in their opinions are called *upgrades* or *downgrades*, depending on the direction of their outlook. Changing a "hold" recommendation to a "buy" recommendation is an upgrade, for example. Find a stock that has been recently upgraded or downgraded (you can use New Ratings, www.newratings.com, or a similar source), and then perform some research on that company so you can answer the following questions:

1. Why did the analysts change their rating on this stock? Was it in response to something the company said or

did? Is the company performing better or worse than its competitors? Do you think the rating change is fair to the company?

2. How did the rating change affect the company's stock price?

3. How has the company's stock been performing relative to the Dow Jones Industrial Average (DJIA) and S&P 500 indexes?

Improving Your Tech Insights: Online Investing Tools

The Internet has been a boon for individual investors, helping to level the playing field with professional and institutional investors by making in-depth information easily accessible. In addition to information, a number of websites now offer handy interactive tools for investors. Find an online tool that could help you as an investor, anything from a stock screener to an investing tutorial to a portfolio simulator. In a brief e-mail message to your instructor, describe the benefits—and any risks—of using this tool.

Video Discussion

Access the Chapter 19 video discussion in the End of Chapter Assignments section at www.mybizlab.com.

PEARSON
my*biz*lab

Log on to www.mybizlab.com to access the following study and assessment aids associated with this chapter:

- Interactive exercises
- Pre/post test
- Real-Time Updates
- Video application
- Customized study plans
- Biz Skills Simulations
- Quick Learning Guide

If you are not using mybizlab, you can access Real-Time Updates and Quick Learning Guides through http://real-timeupdates.com/bia5. The Quick Learning Guide (located under "Learn More" on the website) provides all six Checkpoints in a handy two-page format to help you study for exams or review important concepts whenever you need a quick refresher.

The Money Supply and Banking Systems

Behind the Scenes

JPMorgan Chase's Jamie Dimon Sees Warning Signs in the Subprime Market

www.jpmorganchase.com
Few companies in the United States can match the long and storied history of the banking conglomerate JPMorgan Chase. After 200 years of mergers and acquisitions, the current firm is built on the foundation of more than 1,000 banking companies whose roots stretch all the way back to 1799—companies that helped finance the construction of the Erie Canal and the Brooklyn Bridge, the growth of the railroad and steel industries, and the country's westward expansion in the 19th and 20th centuries. Before the founding of the Federal Reserve System in 1913, J. Pierpont Morgan, one of the firm's namesakes, more or less acted as the country's central bank, working to stabilize the economy and to rescue troubled banks—and New York City itself on one occasion.

JPMorgan Chase CEO Jamie Dimon knew how lucrative the subprime mortgage market could be, but he couldn't ignore the danger signs.

The executives who have led JPMorgan Chase and its predecessor firms over the past two centuries, including current CEO Jamie Dimon, have seen good times, bad times, and everything in between. For example, the U.S. economy was struggling after the collapse of the dot-com stock market bubble in 2000 and the terrorist attacks in September 2001, but things began to pick up in 2002 when home prices across the country started to soar. The housing boom was fueled by a combination of low interest rates and plentiful credit that made buying a home easier, driving up demand. Subprime mortgages—homes loans for people with low credit ratings who would've had difficulty getting financing in the past—became much more common. Before long, making money in real estate almost became a national obsession—and lots of people were making money, including JPMorgan Chase's investment banking arm.

This part of the company created investment securities for hedge funds and institutional investors by pooling lots of individual mortgages. JPMorgan Chase was a major player in this *debt securitization* market, but it hadn't jumped into the subprime market with the wild abandon that some of its Wall Street competitors had shown. Those investment banks were raking in billions of dollars of fees from this business, and some managers inside JPMorgan Chase were pushing the company to get more involved in subprimes. However, the research-obsessed Dimon was piecing together some disturbing information that made him wary about the risks in the subprime market.

Fortune magazine recently described Dimon as "the most watched, most discussed, most loved, and most feared banker in the world today." You might not be the most loved or most feared banker in the world, but if you were in Jamie Dimon's shoes, what would you do? Would you expand a line of business that was generating cash by the bucketful, or would you trust your instincts and get out while it was still safe?[1] ∎

Introduction

JPMorgan Chase's Jamie Dimon, profiled in the chapter-opening Behind the Scenes, was one of many banking executives who had to confront one of the biggest financial disasters in recent history. As you'll read in this chapter and in the Behind the Scenes wrap-up at the end of the chapter, some managers made better decisions than others, and failure came with a very high price.

This chapter takes a different approach than the other 19 chapters. Part 1, "Business as Usual," offers a quick overview of the money supply and the major participants in the banking system. Part 2, "System in Crisis," then shifts gears and tells the story of the housing bubble and the subprime mortgage crisis that by 2008 had created one of the most severe financial collapses in U.S. history. You and your family may well have suffered during the crisis, from loss of employment, declines in investments, or difficulties in getting student loans or other forms of financing. Although the peak of this crisis has passed, the damage left behind is still affecting virtually every student, taxpayer, parent, and business professional in the entire country. There is little doubt that as a taxpayer you will help pay for cleaning up this mess for years to come.

In a sense, this story is a fitting conclusion to a business textbook, because it highlights the tremendous benefits that capitalism can bring to a society—and the tremendous dangers of capitalism when it is practiced without ethical principles or sensible controls. A single chapter can't hope to convey the complexity of this story, and some aspects are necessarily simplified. However, this condensed version of the tale will help you understand what happened, why it happened, and what can be done to prevent it from happening again. It's a complicated story, but it offers perhaps the most important lesson to be learned in this entire course.

Part 1: Business as Usual

Most every aspect of business you've studied in this course—from understanding the basic economics of supply and demand to paying employees, pricing products, and buying advertising—involves money. Now it's time to explore money itself, along with the organizations that influence how much money is available in the economy, how much it costs to borrow it, and what services these organizations provide to consumers and business customers.

The Money Supply and the Federal Reserve System

The $10 bill you're carrying around in your pocket and the billions of dollars that a company such as JPMorgan Chase moves around the world are all part of a vast collection known as the *money supply*. The nature of this supply affects virtually every aspect of your financial life, from how big your car payments will be to how soon you'll be able to retire.

The Many Faces of Money

Money, defined as anything generally accepted as a means of paying for goods and services, performs four financial functions. First, it serves as a *medium of exchange*, a tool for simplifying transactions between buyers and sellers. Second, it serves as a *unit of accounting*—a measure of value, in other words—so that buyers and sellers don't have to negotiate the relative worth of dissimilar items with every transaction. Third, money serves as a temporary *store of value*—a way of accumulating wealth until it is needed. Fourth, money serves as a standard of *deferred payment*, meaning it can be used to represent debt obligations.[2]

Every economy has a certain amount of money in circulation at any given point in time, a quantity known as the **money supply**. The money supply is a closely watched economic variable because it affects interest rates, inflation, and other vital aspects of the economy's health.[3] The money supply can be measured in several ways; economists focus on two quantities known as *M1* and *M2*. M1 consists primarily of currency (paper money) held by the public and *demand deposits*, money held in checking accounts and other accounts that allow accountholders to withdraw funds immediately, on demand. M2 is a broader measure, incorporating M1 plus savings accounts, balances in retail

money
Anything generally accepted as a means of paying for goods and services; serves as a medium of exchange, a unit of accounting, a store of value, and a standard of deferred value

money supply
The amount of money in circulation at any given point in time

Federal Reserve System
The central banking system of the United States; responsible for regulating banks and implementing monetary policy

money market mutual funds, and *time deposits*—money held in interest-paying accounts that may restrict the owner's right to withdraw funds on short notice (including savings accounts and certificates of deposit).[4]

The Federal Reserve System

In response to repeated financial panics in the late 19th and early 20th centuries, Congress created a national central bank, the **Federal Reserve System**, in 1913 to help stabilize the U.S. banking industry. The "Fed," as the system is commonly known, has two main components: a network of 12 regional banks that oversee the nation's banks and a board of governors that determine policy. In addition, about a third of the commercial banks in the United States are members of the Fed system, making them eligible to borrow money from the Fed to fund their operations.[5]

The Fed has a pervasive role in the U.S. economy, with four primary responsibilities:[6]

- Conducting *monetary policy*—managing the money supply, essentially—with the objectives of maximizing employment, controlling inflation, and ensuring moderate long-term interest rates
- Supervising and regulating financial institutions
- Maintaining the overall stability of the economy
- Providing a variety of transactional services, including facilitating payments between banks and processing checks

Managing the money supply is a delicate balancing act. If the supply grows too quickly, the economy can "overheat" and lead to runaway inflation. If the money supply shrinks too quickly, the economy can stall, with less money and credit available for businesses to expand and for consumers to make purchases.

federal funds rate
Interest rate that member banks charge each other to borrow money overnight from the funds they keep in the Federal Reserve accounts

The Fed's task is made even more difficult by the fact that there is no single, simple way to control the money supply and thereby guide the economy. Much of the Fed's influence is exerted through two interest rates. The **federal funds rate** is the rate that member banks charge each other to borrow money overnight from the funds they keep in the Federal Reserve accounts. (You'll often hear this rate referred to as the *overnight rate*.) The Fed doesn't set this rate directly. Instead, it sets a target rate and then works toward that rate by buying and selling Treasury bonds, bills, and notes to increase or decrease the money supply, which in turn decreases or increases the funds rate. Roughly speaking:

Fed buys Treasuries ⟶ increases money supply ⟶ decreases federal funds rate
Fed sells Treasuries ⟶ decreases money supply ⟶ increases federal funds rate

Because these transactions take place on the open market, they are known as *open-market operations*.[7]

discount rate
Interest rate that member banks pay when they borrow funds from the Fed

The Fed's other key interest rate (which it does set directly) is the **discount rate**, the rate that member banks pay when they borrow funds from the Fed. When the Fed changes the discount rate, each member bank generally changes its *prime rate*, which is the rate a bank charges its best loan customers. (Many other interest rates are also based on the prime rate.) Raising the discount rate discourages loans and therefore tightens the money supply; lowering it encourages lending and expands the money supply.

reserves
Sums of money, equal to a certain percentage of their deposits, that banks are legally required to keep on hand

In addition to these two interest rates, the Fed has two other main tools for managing the money supply. First, all financial institutions must set aside **reserves**, sums of money equal to a certain percentage of their deposits. The Fed can change the *reserve requirement*, the percentage of deposits that banks must set aside, to influence

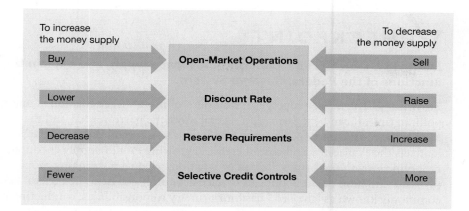

EXHIBIT 20.1

Influencing the Money Supply

The Federal Reserve uses four tools to influence the money supply as it attempts to stimulate economic growth while keeping inflation and interest rates at acceptable levels.

the money supply. Raising the reserve requirement slows down the economy because banks have less money to lend; lowering it boosts the economy. However, the Fed rarely uses this technique because it is costly to implement, and a small change can have a drastic effect.[8] Second, the Fed can also use *selective credit controls* to set the terms of credit for various kinds of loans. This tool includes the power to set margin requirements, the percentage of the purchase price that an investor must pay in cash when purchasing a stock or a bond on margin (see page 499). By altering margin requirements, the Fed is able to influence how much cash is tied up in stock market transactions.

Exhibit 20.1 summarizes the effects of the tools the Fed has at its disposal.

Other Government Banking Agencies and Institutions

The Fed shares responsibility for banking oversight and financial activities with a number of other agencies and semi-independent institutions. The most significant at the federal level include

- **FDIC.** After thousands of banks failed in the United States during the Great Depression, the government established the **Federal Deposit Insurance Corporation (FDIC)**, www.fdic.gov, to protect money in customer accounts and to manage the transition of assets whenever a bank fails. Banks pay a fee to join the FDIC network, and in turn, the FDIC guarantees to cover any losses from bank failure up to a maximum of $100,000 per account (temporarily raised to $250,000 through 2013).[9]

- **Fannie Mae.** To spur homeownership after the Depression, Congress established the Federal National Mortgage Association (FNMA), now officially known as **Fannie Mae**. Through its mandate to help low- to middle-income home buyers by guaranteeing and buying mortgages originated by banks and other lenders, Fannie Mae essentially created the **secondary mortgage market**. This "behind the scenes" market provides much of the funds that are loaned to home buyers. Fannie Mae was spun off as a quasi-independent corporation in 1968 and remains a dominant force in the mortgage business.[10] The company invested heavily in subprime mortgages and had to be rescued by the federal government in 2008 (see page 522).

- **Freddie Mac.** Another major player in the secondary market is **Freddie Mac**, created in 1970 as the Federal Home Loan Mortgage Corporation. Like Fannie Mae, Freddie Mac is a quasi-independent corporation—and it also had to be rescued in 2008 after overloading with poor-quality mortgage debt.

Federal Deposit Insurance Corporation (FDIC)
Federal agency responsible for protecting money in customer accounts and managing the transition of assets whenever a bank fails

Fannie Mae
Government-sponsored enterprise responsible for guaranteeing and funding home mortgages

secondary mortgage market
Financial market in which mortgages are bought and sold, providing much of the funds that are loaned to home buyers

Freddie Mac
Secondary mortgage institution similar to Fannie Mae

✓CHECKPOINT

LEARNING OBJECTIVE 1: Describe the *money supply*, and explain the functions of the Federal Reserve System.

Summary: The money supply is the amount of money in circulation at any given point in time. It can be measured in several ways; the narrower M1 and the broader M2 are the most common. The money supply is a vital economic variable because it affects the availability and cost of credit. A growing money supply encourages economic growth but brings the risk of inflation, whereas a shrinking money supply keeps inflation in check but can squelch economic activity. The Federal Reserve, commonly known as "the Fed," has four primary responsibilities: conducting monetary policy (primarily by adjusting interest rates, either directly or by shrinking or expanding the money supply), supervising and regulating financial institutions, maintaining the overall stability of the economy, and providing a variety of services to financial firms and government bodies (such as facilitating payments between banks and processing checks).

Critical thinking: (1) Why does the Fed want to avoid an "overheating" economy? (2) Why can't the Fed just control inflation directly?

It's your business: (1) In general terms, how might Fed decisions over the next several years affect your life? (2) If you are hoping to get a loan to expand your business, will you welcome the news that the money supply is expanding? Why or why not?

Key terms to know: money, money supply, Federal Reserve System, federal funds rate, discount rate, reserves, Federal Deposit Insurance Corporation (FDIC), Fannie Mae, secondary mortgage market, Freddie Mac

The Financial Services Industry

A wide range of companies help consumers and businesses with every aspect of banking and financial management. These services can be divided into commercial banking, investment banking, and other financial services.

Commercial Banking

commercial banks
Financial institutions that accept deposits, offer various types of checking and savings accounts, and provide loans

Commercial banks are financial institutions that, generally speaking, accept deposits, offer various types of checking and savings accounts, and provide loans. The terminology can be confusing because some of these institutions don't call themselves banks, and some people use *commercial bank* to refer to banks that serve businesses only, not consumers. However, "commercial banking" is a good way to distinguish this class of services from investment banking as well as nonbanking financial services. A wide range of services fall under this umbrella, and many banking companies offer multiple services; here are the major types:

retail banks
Banks that provide financial services to consumers

- **Retail banks** service consumers with checking and savings accounts, debit and credit cards, and loans for homes, cars, and other major purchases.

merchant banks
Banks that provide financial services to businesses; can also refer to private equity management

- **Merchant banks** offer financial services to businesses, particularly in the area of international finance. *Merchant banking* is sometimes more narrowly defined as managing private equity investments, making it more akin to investment banking.[11]

thrift banks
Banking institutions that offer deposit accounts and focus on offering home mortgage loans; also called *thrifts* or *savings and loan associations*

- **Thrift banks**, also called *thrifts* or *savings and loan associations*, offer deposit accounts and focus on offering home mortgage loans.

- **Credit unions** are not-for-profit, member-owned cooperatives that offer deposit accounts and lending services to consumers and small businesses. Note that thrifts and credit unions do not refer to themselves as banks, but the broad definition of banking works for the purpose of distinguishing them from investment banks.

- **Private banking** is a range of banking services for high net-worth (as in, wealthy) individuals and families, such as managing real estate and other investments, setting up trust funds, and planning philanthropic giving.[12]

The range of services that banks and other financial firms are legally allowed to offer has changed over time, and some of these changes have been controversial. For example, risky investment activity by commercial banks (using depositors' funds in some cases) was blamed by some experts for the stock market crash that triggered the Great Depression. In response, the Glass-Steagall Act of 1933 (which also established the FDIC) aimed to restore confidence in U.S. financial houses by restricting investment banks and commercial banks from crossing into each others' businesses and potentially abusing their fiduciary duties at the expense of customers. Another key objective of Glass-Steagall was ensuring that a catastrophic failure in one part of the finance industry would not invade every other part, as it did in 1929.[13]

Beginning in 1980, several waves of deregulation dramatically reshaped the banking and financial services industries—and in the eyes of some observers, helped create or worsen the meltdown you'll read about in Part 2 of this chapter. After several decades of lobbying by the banking industry, piecemeal exemptions to the law, and regulatory changes that chipped away at the wall between commercial and investment banking, the Financial Services Modernization Act of 1999 repealed Glass-Steagall.[14] As a result of this legislation and several other regulatory changes over the past 30 years, many of the barriers that once separated various kinds of banking, investing, and insurance services are now gone, paving the way for colossal, multifaceted firms such as JPMorgan Chase and Bank of America.

Investment Banking

Investment banks offer a variety of services related to initial public stock offerings, mergers and acquisitions, and other investment matters. For example, the *underwriting* function when a company goes public that you read about in Chapter 18 is performed by investment banks. Investment banks are typically active investors of their own funds as well.

For decades, investment banks were the giants of Wall Street, and the names of five in particular dominated the history of high finance in the United States: Bear Stearns (founded in 1923), Goldman Sachs (1869), Lehman Brothers (1850), Merrill Lynch (1915), and Morgan Stanley (1935). All five were caught up in the subprime mortgage mess, and with a rapidity that shocked the financial world, all five ceased to exist as independent investment banks by the end of 2008. On the brink of collapse, Bear Stearns was rescued in a last-second deal by JPMorgan Chase. Merrill Lynch was rescued by another huge commercial bank, Bank of America. Goldman Sachs and Morgan Stanley converted themselves to bank holding companies, giving them access to government assistance available only to commercial banks. And Lehman Brothers collapsed in the largest bankruptcy in U.S. history.[15] The functions of investment banking continue, to be sure, but the industry itself will never be the same.

Other Financial Services

In addition to commercial banks of all shapes and sizes, a variety of other types of firms provide essential financial services to consumers and businesses. Some complement services offered by commercial banks; others compete with commercial banks in one or more areas. For example, in addition to commercial banks and thrifts, mortgages (real-estate loans) can be originated by **independent mortgage companies**, which use their own funds, and **mortgage brokers**, which initiate loans on behalf of a mortgage lender in exchange for a fee.

---

credit unions
Not-for-profit, member-owned cooperatives that offer deposit accounts and lending services to consumers and small businesses

private banking
Banking services for wealthy individuals and families

investment banks
Firms that offer a variety of services related to initial public stock offerings, mergers and acquisitions, and other investment matters

independent mortgage companies
Nonbank companies that use their own funds to offer mortgages

mortgage brokers
Nonbank companies that initiate loans on behalf of a mortgage lender in exchange for a fee

finance companies
Nonbank institutions that lend money to consumers and businesses for cars and other vehicles, home improvements, expansion, purchases, and other purposes

credit rating agencies
Companies that offer opinions about the creditworthiness of borrowers and of specific investments

A variety of nonbank institutions lend money to consumers and businesses for vehicles, home improvements, expansion, purchases, and other purposes. Some of these **finance companies** are independent; others are affiliated with retailers or manufacturers. For example, Toyota Financial Services, a wholly owned subsidiary of Toyota Motor Corporation, offers car loans to drivers buying Toyota vehicles.[16] Credit cards are another major category of lending; some cards are issued by banks, whereas others are issued by retailers and credit card companies such as American Express.

Credit rating agencies offer opinions about the creditworthiness of borrowers and of specific investments, such as the corporate bonds discussed in Chapter 18. Moody's, Standard & Poor's, and Fitch are the major rating agencies of businesses and securities; Equifax, Experian, and TransUnion are the major agencies that rate consumer creditworthiness. Before any bank or finance company will give you a loan, it will check your *credit rating* to judge the level of risk you represent as a borrower.

✓CHECKPOINT

LEARNING OBJECTIVE 2: Identify the most common types of commercial banking institutions, and distinguish commercial banking from investment banking.

Summary: Commercial banks are financial institutions that, generally speaking, accept deposits, offer various types of checking and savings accounts, and provide loans. Using this definition, the sphere of commercial banking includes retail banks, merchant banks (but not the merchant banking that refers to private equity investing), thrift banks (also known as savings and loans), credit unions, and private banking. Note that the term "commercial bank" is sometimes used to refer to banks that serve businesses only, not consumers. Investment banking differs from commercial banking in that it is not involved with accepting deposits and making loans but rather in helping businesses with major financial events such as initial public offerings and mergers and acquisitions, as well as managing investments for corporate clients.

Critical thinking: (1) Why might credit unions want to promote themselves as not being banks in the popular usage of the term? (2) With the demise or transformation of the great investment banks of Wall Street, has the need for investment banking disappeared? Explain your answer.

It's your business: (1) Do you know your credit rating? You can get free credit reports through www.ftc.gov/freereports. (2) Does the not-for-profit, member-ownership aspect of credit unions appeal to you? Why or why not?

Key terms to know: commercial banks, retail banks, merchant banks, thrift banks, credit unions, private banking, investment banks, independent mortgage companies, mortgage brokers, finance companies, credit rating agencies

Part 2: System in Crisis

Banks and other financial companies provide vital services for consumers, businesses, and governments. From getting loans for cars, homes, and college educations to having convenient access to cash stored safely in bank accounts, the quality of contemporary life would not be possible without these services. At the same time, banking and financial services have such a pervasive presence that problems in the financial sector can spread across the economy, creating widespread havoc.

This part of the chapter switches gears to tell the recent story of how an interconnected series of bad decisions, bad luck, fraud, regulatory failures, recklessness, and the unintended consequences of good intentions led to a global economic meltdown in September 2008 that very nearly pushed the United States into a second Great Depression.[17]

Trouble on Main Street: The Housing Bubble

The year 2001 was a bleak time for the U.S. economy. The stock market had tumbled after the burst of the *dot-com bubble* of the late 1990s, in which waves of Internet companies rushed to go public to take advantage of the growing investor interest in Internet-related stocks. These stocks fed a classic **bubble**, when frenzied demand for an asset (such as stocks or real estate) pushes the price of that asset far beyond its true economic value. When the overhyped, overpriced dot-com stocks eventually fell to earth, they triggered an economic slowdown that got even worse after the terrorist attacks of September 11, 2001.

bubble
Market situation in which frenzied demand for an asset pushes the price of that asset far beyond its true economic value

Recovering from the Dot-Com Bubble

To stimulate the economy, the Fed worked to reduce the federal funds rate, which had been as high as 6.5 percent the previous year, to as low as 1 percent.[18] It was an effective stimulant, and the economy began growing again. However, the low rates had two unintended consequences: they helped fuel a new bubble in housing (lower interest rates made home mortgages more attractive), and they prompted a vast pool of institutional investment funds to start looking for something more rewarding than Treasury issues (lower interest rates made these debt instruments less attractive). What made this new bubble particularly huge and ultimately so destructive was that these two economic forces, Main Street and Wall Street, began feeding off each other, pumping up the bubble from both ends.

Lower interest rates can heat up the housing market in several ways. First, lower rates mean lower monthly payments for a given loan amount, so more people can afford houses. Second, for the same monthly payment, people can afford bigger mortgages, which can spur them to move up to more expensive homes. And third, lower rates coupled with overheated demand and easier access to credit helped transform the humble home from simply a place to live into a way to make money. All these factors drove prices way out of line with actual value in dozens of cities across the country.

Creating a New Bubble in Housing

Before long, houses became the new dot-com stocks. Demand was so intense in some cities that buyers bidding against each other would drive prices tens of thousands of dollars above what sellers originally asked. Home prices surged every year from 2002 through 2006 (see Exhibit 20.2 on the next page).[19] *Flipping*—buying a house, making some quick fixes to raise its value or simply waiting for prices to rise, and reselling it for a big profit—became so popular that there were even television shows devoted to this new get-rich-quick scheme. To meet the demand for new homes, builders cranked out houses and condos as fast as they could, sometimes selling them before they even broke ground for construction.

Real-Time Updates

Learn More

The supply/demand puzzle in the housing boom

See why classical supply and demand dynamics struggle to explain the housing bubble. On mybizlab (**www.mybizlab.com**), you can access Real-Time Updates within each chapter or under Student Study Tools. Otherwise, go to **http://real-timeupdates.com/bia5** and click on "Learn More."

EXHIBIT 20.2

The Housing Bubble

Using 2000 as the base year (index = 100), this graph shows how rapidly home prices grew in the years that followed—far out of line with fundamental economic value.

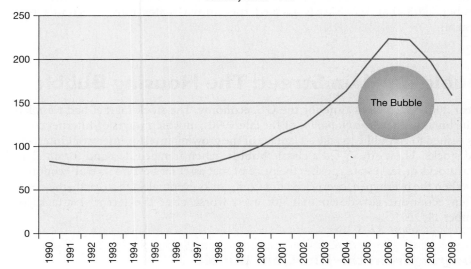

U.S. Home Prices
10-city composite index
January 2000=100

The Bubble

loan-to-value (LTV)
The percentage of an asset's market value that a lender is willing to finance when offering a loan; the rest of the purchase price has to be paid by the buyer as a down payment

The feeling was widespread that if you weren't making money in real estate, you were missing out. The real estate industry certainly wasn't shy about promoting this belief, either. David Lereah, chief economist of the National Association of Realtors, published a book titled *Are You Missing the Real Estate Boom?* in which he stated that "I believe that in years to come, historians will see the beginning of the 21st century as the 'golden age' of real estate."[20] Lereah would later earn the distinction of being named by *Time* magazine as one of its "25 People to Blame for the Financial Crisis."[21]

Old-School Mortgage Lending

While the housing bubble was growing, the business of lending money to home buyers was changing dramatically. In a fashion somewhat similar to corporate bonds, mortgages come in several categories that can be distinguished by risk. This risk is a matter of (a) the borrower's income, assets, and credit history; (b) the amount of the loan and the percentage of the house's value that this amount represents; and (c) the nature of the repayment plan.

Up through the 1980s, home mortgages were not particularly easy to get. First, borrowers had to have written proof of sufficient income to make the payments, assets to serve as collateral, and a history of responsible credit use. Second, the maximum **loan-to-value (LTV)**, the amount of the loan relative to a house's assessed value, was usually 75 to 80 percent, meaning banks wouldn't lend more than 75 to 80 percent of market value. Borrowers had to come up with a 20- to 25-percent down payment, which for many people required years of saving. Third, most mortgages had a fixed and therefore predictable interest rate for the life of the loan, and monthly payments were high enough to pay down part of the principal every month in addition to paying interest.

To give more people access to homeownership—and, not coincidentally, increase the available market for lenders—all three sets of criteria began to be modified over time. In the early days of the bubble, the negative effect of this decline in lending standards was masked by a robust economy. However, when the economy began to sputter in 2005, the full impact of these lower standards started to become painfully clear.[22]

✓CHECKPOINT

LEARNING OBJECTIVE 3: Explain the meaning of an economic *bubble*, and describe the forces behind the housing bubble of 2002–2006.

Summary: A *bubble* occurs when frenzied demand for an asset (such as stocks or real estate) pushes the price of that asset far beyond its true economic value. The 2002–2006 housing bubble was inflated by several forces, including low interest rates set by the Fed in an attempt to reinvigorate the economy after the collapse of the dot-com bubble a few years prior (which made credit cheaper and more widely available and prompted institutional investors to search for more profitable investments than Treasury securities), the widespread—and widely promoted—belief that consumers were missing out if they didn't invest in real estate even as prices were climbing, and a decline in lending standards.

Critical thinking: (1) Can bubbles be avoided? After all, they involve lots of human emotion triumphing over logic. Explain your answer. (2) Should the federal government take steps to promote and enable homeownership, as it has done a number of times since the Great Depression, or leave the ability to buy up to the resources and efforts of individuals? Why or why not?

It's your business: (1) Would you purchase a house if you couldn't afford a down payment but a lender was willing to finance the deal at 100 percent LTV? Why or why not? (2) Did you or your family get caught up in the real estate bubble, either on the positive upswing or the negative deflation of the bubble? What effect did the bubble have on your family?

Key terms to know: bubble, loan-to-value (LTV)

More Trouble on Main Street: Subprime Lending

The overheated housing market might have just been an "ordinary" bubble that eventually burst and burned the latecomers who got in the game after all the profits had already been taken out (which happens with every bubble). However, this bubble contained a special poison: millions of *adjustable rate* and *subprime mortgages*.

Adjustable Rate Mortgages

An **adjustable rate mortgage (ARM)** features variable interest rates over the life of the loan. ARMs appeal to lenders because they offer some protection against interest rate hikes that increase the lenders' cost of funds. ARMs appeal to home buyers because of *teaser rates*, low introductory rates that, in addition to saving money on interest, can make it possible for some people to buy more house than they can really afford. Repayment details vary from ARM to ARM, but in general, borrowers can get lower payments based on a fixed interest rate for a few years, at which point the interest resets to a variable rate that tracks some agreed-upon index. The risk for borrowers here is obvious: If interest rates skyrocket, so do monthly payments, a phenomenon known as *payment shock*.[23]

In the early 1980s, a California bank began selling the **option ARM**, an ARM that let borrowers choose from several repayment options, including making monthly payments that didn't even cover the accruing interest on their mortgages.[24] In these

adjustable rate mortgage (ARM) Mortgage that features variable interest rates over the life of the loan

option ARM Type of ARM that lets borrowers choose from several repayment options

negative amortization
Payment situation in which the balance owed on a loan increases over time rather than decreases

cases, borrowers experienced **negative amortization**, meaning the balances they owed on their loans *increased* over time rather than decreased. Option ARMs let borrowers underpay in the early years but required them to overpay in later years to compensate, often with much higher monthly payments than borrowers could afford—when you read page 519, see what hedge fund manager John Devaney had to say about these loans. However, the instant gratification aspect of option ARMs made them a hit with home buyers, and despite the risks, lenders across the country jumped on the bandwagon and wrote $700 billion worth of option ARMs between 2004 and 2007.[25]

No-Documentation Loans and High LTVs

This time period also saw an increase in *low-documentation* and even *no-documentation* loans, in which borrowers didn't have to provide some or all of the usual written proof of income and assets. At Wachovia, a once-major bank that eventually went bankrupt as the crisis unfolded, 85 percent of the option ARMs it made lacked any proof of income or assets.[26] In the words of *Washington Post* economics writer Frank Ahrens, before long "loans were given to people with no income, no jobs, and no assets."[27]

Loan-to-value was another long-held lending practice that slipped during the housing boom. Many new loans were written with 90, 95, 100—even as high as 125 percent LTVs.[28] In other words, some borrowers were loaned more money than their houses were worth, a practice justified by the belief that prices were climbing so quickly that market prices would soon reach and surpass the loan amount. However, if prices didn't climb—or worse yet, fell—borrowers with high LTVs could find themselves owing more on their houses than the houses are worth.

Subprime Mortgages

prime mortgages
Home loans offered to the most creditworthy customers

subprime mortgages
Home loans for borrowers with low credit scores

In addition to creating new types of loans to sell, the mortgage industry also began lowering lending standards. After years of a robust economy, by the late 1990s most people who could qualify for **prime mortgages**—meaning they had reliable incomes, sufficient assets, and good credit histories—already owned homes. To sign up more borrowers, mortgage originators began to offer more **subprime mortgages**, home loans for borrowers with low credit scores. Subprime mortgages had been in limited use for decades as a means to accommodate borrowers with blemished credit histories, but when the housing boom took off, so did subprime lending. At its peak in 2006, more than 20 percent of all new mortgages were subprime—and half of all subprimes were ARMs, meaning borrowers with already-shaky finances were particularly vulnerable to payment shock when low initial rates expired (see Exhibit 20.3).[29]

default
Situation in which borrowers stop making payments on a loan

At this point, you're no doubt wondering why lenders were making loans that were extremely likely to **default** (meaning borrowers stop making payments) and consumers were signing up for loans they couldn't possibly afford. In the old days, whenever a bank lent a homeowner money, the bank usually kept the loan on its books and therefore kept the risk that the homeowner might not pay the money back. Because they kept the risk, banks were careful about lending. However, with the growth of the *secondary mortgage market* (see page 509), many mortgage lenders no longer carry the risk of borrower default. Instead, they sell the loan to investors, thereby passing the risk on to somebody else.

For their part, consumers kept doing it because they let themselves get talked into the notion that home prices would keep rising forever—it was a housing boom, after all. Rising prices would boost the equity in their homes to the point where, if they needed to, they could refinance on more sensible terms. Borrowers didn't dream up this scheme all on their own, to be sure; it was pitched relentlessly by mortgage originators, real estate agents, and home builders.

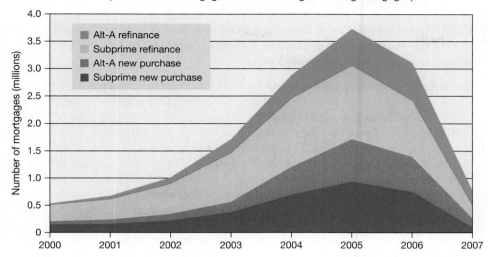

Nonprime Mortgages
(Includes new mortgages and refinancing of existing mortgages)

Legend:
- Alt-A refinance
- Subprime refinance
- Alt-A new purchase
- Subprime new purchase

Y-axis: Number of mortgages (millions)

EXHIBIT 20.3

Nonprime Lending

This graph shows the number of *nonprime* home loans created between 2000 and 2007. (Nonprime includes subprime loans and the "Alt-A" category between prime and subprime, which is where many no-documentation loans are categorized.) The graph includes new lending and refinancing, when a homeowner replaces an existing loan with a new loan. Notice the correlation between this graph and the inflation of the housing bubble in Exhibit 20.2.

Any analysis of the subprime situation needs to address the controversy surrounding the role played by the Community Reinvestment Act (CRA). This 1977 legislation was intended to make sure that federally chartered financial institutions meet the needs of their local communities and particularly that they don't discriminate against creditworthy customers in low-income and minority neighborhoods.[30] Some critics contend that the CRA, specifically a 1995 revision, played a major role in or even caused the subprime crisis by forcing banks to make too many low-quality loans in order to meet CRA guidelines.[31]

However, a CRA link is not apparent for the vast majority of subprime loans. In a joint statement, the presidents of the Federal Reserve Banks of Boston and San Francisco asserted that "There is no empirical evidence to support the claim that the CRA is responsible for the crisis."[32] For example, during the peak subprime lending period from 2005 through 2006, only 6 percent of new subprime loans were made by institutions covered by the CRA lending to borrowers in areas used to evaluate CRA performance.[33] Moreover, the biggest surge in subprime lending didn't happen until 10 years after the 1995 revision of the CRA.

Mortgage Fraud

All this risky behavior was bad enough, but sadly there is more to this story. Without strict standards of proof or close oversight, mortgage application abuse was probably inevitable. It's not hard to see why no-documentation mortgages soon became known as "liar loans," with some borrowers or mortgage originators simply making up numbers for borrowers' income and assets. Under pressure from unscrupulous lenders and builders, some *appraisers*, professionals hired to give an independent assessment of a home's value, contributed to the problem by inflating the appraisal value of homes so that buyers could quality for larger loans.

After the FBI began investigating subprime loans, assistant director Chris Swecker observed that fraud was so pervasive that it "has the potential to be an epidemic."[34] In an interview after the bubble collapsed, Richard Bitner, who built a business buying subprime loans to resell to investors, said, "by the time we hit 2004, I estimated that three out of every four deals we were looking at were somehow deceptive, fraudulent, or manipulated. There was a huge breakdown. We truly felt like we couldn't trust anybody."[35]

✓CHECKPOINT

LEARNING OBJECTIVE 4: Describe the innovations and evolutions in mortgage lending that expanded homeownership but ultimately triggered the subprime meltdown.

Summary: These innovations started with the adjustable rate mortgage (ARM), which was created to protect lenders from interest range changes over the life of the loan but which also appealed to homebuyers because of the frequent use of teaser rates that reduced monthly payments in the early years of the loan. A subsequent innovation, the option ARM, let borrowers choose from several repayment options, including making monthly payments that didn't even cover the accruing interest on their mortgages. Lending standards were also lowered in several respects, including reducing or even eliminating the requirement to document a borrower's income or assets; raising loan-to-value (LTV) percentages from the longstanding 80 percent up to 90, 95, or 100 percent, or even higher; and expanding the use of subprime lending, granting loans to people whose credit scores prevent them from getting prime-rate loans. These changes to lending practices, together with widespread fraud in mortgage origination, set the stage for a spectacular market failure as soon as home prices stopped their upward surge.

Critical thinking: (1) Governments frequently enact laws and regulations that prevent people from making decisions and behaving in ways that could harm them. Should the government outlaw option ARMs that allow negative amortization to occur? Why or why not? (2) Why do you think mortgage fraud was able to increase so rapidly during this time period?

It's your business: (1) Would you agree to an ARM with low teaser rates if you weren't positive you would be able to afford the higher monthly payments that would kick in after the teaser rate resets to the permanent fixed rate? Why or why not? (2) How would you respond if a mortgage lender offered a way to get you into a more expensive home than you know you can afford?

Key terms to know: adjustable rate mortgage (ARM), option ARM, negative amortization, prime mortgages, subprime mortgages, default

Trouble on Wall Street: Mortgage-Backed Securities

Meanwhile, far at the other end of the financial galaxy, a large and mostly invisible force from Wall Street had been encouraging the lenders on Main Street to make as many loans as they could—prime, subprime, fixed rate, option ARM, whatever. Thanks in large part to the low rates offered on Treasury issues, institutional investors and hedge funds were looking for opportunities with higher returns, and they found what they were seeking in *mortgage-backed securities*.

Securitization of Debt

For all types of lenders, a vital source of funds is the *secondary mortgage market*, in which mortgage originators sell their loans to investors. The system has been in place since Fannie Mae's creation in the 1930s, and it has become an essential part of home-ownership in the United States. Although selling loans might sound like an odd concept, every loan represents a stream of future cash flow (the sum of all the payments due from the borrower) and therefore has an identifiable value and can be sold as an asset. Selling loans also transfers the risk associated with these loans—a useful economic function but one that got out of hand during the housing bubble and helped bring down the economy.

In the secondary market, individual loans are often pooled together and transformed into investments through the process of **securitization**, which allows investors to buy shares of a given pool. **Asset-backed securities (ABSs)** are securities based on auto loans, credit card debts, and other loan assets; **mortgage-backed securities (MBSs)** are specifically based on home mortgages.[36] Over half of all mortgages in the United States now end up in MBSs.[37] By pooling many individual mortgages, an MBS issuer can create a series of bonds that pay out based on the incoming monthly payments from all those homeowners. MBSs have been around for several decades, but they mushroomed during the housing boom.[38]

Oversimplifying somewhat, you can think of an MBS as a container that holds a collection of mortgage contracts. Money flows into the container when borrowers make their monthly mortgage payments, some of which goes to paying off those debts and some of which flows back out of the container in the form of regular payments to investors. Of course, not all investors want the same balance of risk and reward. Some want more reward (higher interest) and are willing to shoulder more risk, while others want just the opposite. To offer a range of bonds to satisfy these various needs, MBS issuers can slice, or *tranch*, the MBS into multiple layers, each offering bonds of different credit ratings and interest rates.

All tranches might contain risky debt, including option ARMs, no-documentation loans, and subprimes. However, the tranches at the top of the "container" are the first to receive cash as monthly mortgage payments come in. Because these tranches are paid first, the risk of them defaulting is lower, and therefore, credit rating agencies give these tranches their highest quality ratings. Some risky mortgages will surely default, but the thinking is that there will always be enough money to at least pay off the mortgages in the upper tranches, hence the high credit rating the bonds at this level received.

Investors in the lower tranches get paid only after the upper tranches have been funded and interest payments have been made to those investors. Because they would be the first to default if enough borrowers stopped making their mortgage payments, the lowest tranches in an MBS are considered highly speculative (the equivalent of junk bonds), and they pay higher interest to compensate for the higher risk.

Securitization doesn't stop with MBSs, however. Investments such as *collateralized debt obligations (CDOs)* can be created using bonds from multiple MBSs and other debt pools. During the subprime heyday, CDO creators were some of the biggest buyers of the middle and lower tranches of MBSs. The CDOs were also tranched, generating layers of bonds with different credit ratings. A crucial aspect here is that the top tranches of these investments were *also* given the highest credit ratings, even though they were built out of medium- and low-quality tranches of MBSs (see Exhibit 20.4 on the next page). Debate continues as to whether rating agencies assigned these high ratings because they didn't understand what they were rating, were pressured into it by their customers (the CDO creators), or simply didn't believe that massive mortgage defaults were possible. Whatever the case, this proved to be one of the most fundamental mistakes in the entire mess.

Securitized debts with a range of risk/reward offerings were a hit with investors such as pension plans, mutual fund companies, and hedge funds, who could choose how much risk they were willing to accept and get an interest rate to match. Referring to option ARMs, in which his company invested heavily through CDOs, hedge fund manager John Devaney said, "The consumer has to be an idiot to take on one of those loans, but it has been one of our best-performing investments."[39] Hedge funds typically went after the highest paying and therefore riskiest tranches—and magnified the payments and risks with extensive leveraging, too.

securitization
Process in which debts such as mortgages are pooled together and transformed into investments

asset-backed securities (ABSs)
Credit derivatives based on auto loans, credit card debts, and other loan assets

mortgage-backed securities (MBSs)
Credit derivatives based on home mortgages

EXHIBIT 20.4 Debt Securitization

This simplified view of debt securitization shows that mortgage-backed securities (MBSs) are built from multiple mortgages, and collateralized debt obligations are then built from multiple MBSs (many using the middle and lower tranches of the MBSs). When mortgage defaults began to rise, the lower tranches in many MBSs ran dry of funds, which meant that many CDOs based on those tranches didn't get funded at all.

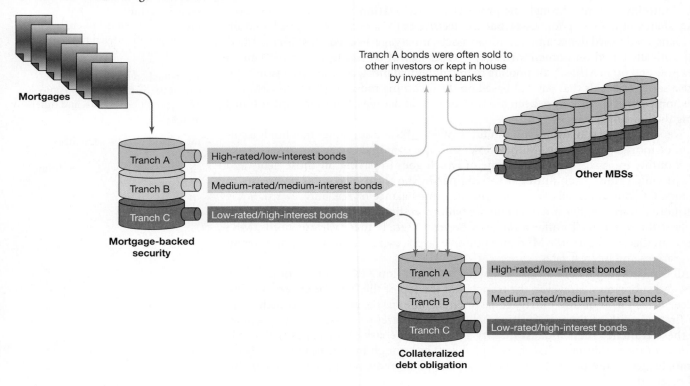

Shock to the System

Remember the whole scheme of homeowners being able to replace risky, expensive option ARMs and subprime loans with more sensible financing after the value of their homes rose high enough? Unfortunately, exactly the opposite happened. In 2006, the four-year run-up in housing prices came to a screeching halt, and to the surprise of everyone who thought home prices could never fall, they did just that. Meanwhile, interest rates had been climbing, shocking ARM borrowers when monthly payments climbed higher than many could handle. And as home prices tumbled, many homeowners lost whatever slim equity they might've had. Thousands upon thousands couldn't make their payments, couldn't refinance to get lower payments, and couldn't sell as housing demand shriveled. Defaults and **foreclosures**, when lenders take possession of homes after borrowers default on their payments, began to climb.[40]

foreclosures
Lenders taking possession of homes after borrowers default on their payments

Before long, the problem spread to CDOs that had loaded up on subprime and option ARM mortgages. The first major shock came in July 2007, when surging defaults led to the collapse of two hedge funds owned by Bear Stearns, wiping out the $1.6 billion investors had sunk into them. Although the funds had some insurance through credit default swaps (see page 494 in Chapter 19), it wasn't nearly enough to protect Bear Stearns from the combination of massive leverage and widespread defaults.[41]

Not long after, American Home Mortgage, one of the largest mortgage companies in the country, filed for bankruptcy when it could no longer get funds to make new loans. Several dozen lenders had failed by that point, but American Home Mortgage got everybody's attention because it had done almost no subprime lending. The company failed because so many buyers were fleeing the secondary mortgage market after getting burned by subprime failures, leaving the firm without access to cash.[42] As Frank Ahrens of the *Washington Post* later put it, "The cascade of failure had begun."[43]

✓ CHECKPOINT

LEARNING OBJECTIVE 5: Explain how debt securitization increased the funds available for home lending but also helped inflate the housing bubble.

Summary: Debt securitization allows frontline lenders to sell their loans to investors and use the proceeds to issue new loans. To accommodate investors with different levels of risk tolerance, these securities were often tranched, or sliced, into different levels of interest payment and default risks, and then additional investments were created out of middle and lower tranches. Securitization helped fuel the housing bubble by making more money available for lending in general and by expanding the secondary market for subprime loans in particular.

Critical thinking: (1) Is tranching of pooled-debt securities necessarily a bad idea? Why or why not? (2) Would the housing bubble have grown as big and collapsed so destructively if there had been no secondary mortgage market? Explain your answer.

It's your business: (1) What is your reaction to John Devaney's statement that "The consumer has to be an idiot to take on" an option ARM? (2) What would you do if you needed a new residence during a housing bubble, knowing that prices were inflated and likely to fall at some point? Explain your answer.

Key terms to know: securitization, asset-backed securities (ABSs), mortgage-backed securities (MBSs), foreclosures

It All Comes Undone: The Meltdown of 2008

In one respect, "bubble" is an unfortunate name to describe overheated markets that grow out of control, because the word conjures up images of something soft and harmless. When they burst—and they always do—economic bubbles unleash waves of destruction that harm not only those people whose behavior helped pump the bubble up but millions of innocent bystanders as well. Replace the image of an innocent bubble with the image of an out-of-control firestorm, and you'll have a more accurate idea of what happens when a bubble pops.

The Bubble Bursts

Through the fall of 2007, the unstable housing market remained a primary concern for business and political leaders alike. In September, the Fed pushed its funds rate down to 4.75 percent, the first decrease in more than four years, hoping to ease the pressure on mortgages and reinvigorate the economy. However, property values and home sales continued to plummet as the country fell into a recession so deep that many began to worry about a second Great Depression. In January 2008, Bank of America bought out Countrywide Financial, rescuing the nation's largest mortgage company—and one of the most aggressive forces behind the subprime boom. By May, Bear Stearns's subprime woes had pushed it to the edge of bankruptcy; it was rescued by JPMorgan Chase with financial help from the Treasury Department.

In June, the FBI announced the arrest of more than 400 mortgage brokers, appraisers, and builders for fraudulent mortgage schemes. A month later, federal banking regulators shut down IndyMac Bank after customers, worried about the bank's collapse, withdrew more than a billion dollars in a matter of days. IndyMac was then the second-largest bank failure in U.S. history, but it would soon be pushed down to third place by a new all-time champion of banking failure.[44] The housing bubble had burst, but the destruction was only just beginning.

Real-Time Updates

Learn More
How the dream machine collapsed

This two-part series offers a simple overview of how the great money-making scheme in the mortgage business fell apart. On mybizlab (www.mybizlab.com), you can access Real-Time Updates within each chapter or under Student Study Tools. Otherwise, go to http://real-timeupdates.com/bia5 and click on "Learn More."

September 2008: Giants Fall and Markets Freeze

Over the span of a couple of weeks in September 2008, the financial sector saw so many changes that one stunning headline barely made it onto the front page before it was pushed off by yet another staggering revelation. By month's end, some of the biggest names in the banking industry had fallen, the stock market was tumbling, the investment bank as a unique financial institution had essentially disappeared, and the worldwide banking system had very nearly ground to a halt.

The first to fall that month were Fannie Mae and Freddie Mac. The pair had been late to join the subprime stampede, and like all latecomers to a bubble, they paid dearly. The federal government seized both institutions and began injecting billions of dollars into each in the hope of propping up the housing market by ensuring the continued supply of new loans.[45]

A week later, under pressure from the federal government, Bank of America bought the struggling Merrill Lynch, the giant brokerage house and investment bank.[46] On the following day came what was perhaps the single biggest psychological blow of the entire crisis: Lehman Brothers, one of the last remaining icons of the Wall Street investment bank establishment, filed for bankruptcy—the largest bankruptcy in U.S. history. Lehman's collapse helped crush investor confidence in financial stocks, triggering a stock market plunge that vaporized trillions of dollars of net worth in a matter of weeks.[47]

The day after Lehman's filing brought the unexpected—and for many people, extremely confusing—announcement that the government was spending $85 billion (an amount that would soon double) to take over the insurance company American International Group (AIG). Banks failing because of bad loans made sense, but what on earth was an insurance company doing in the middle of this mess? The answer was derivatives, derivatives, and more derivatives. AIG had been investing in subprime mortgages itself *and* insuring other subprime investors against losses via credit default swaps. Through these swaps, AIG wound up being responsible for much of the subprime risk across the entire mortgage industry, although few people outside of AIG (and few on the inside, as it turned out) realized just how much risk the firm had taken on. As defaults spread, AIG couldn't come up with the cash it needed to cover its own losses or to fulfill its obligations on all those swaps. Fearing that an AIG bankruptcy would bring down the entire banking system, the government felt it had no choice but to bail the company out.[48]

The carnage continued the following week when Washington Mutual, another aggressive subprime lender, was shut down by federal regulators after loan failures and massive withdrawals by nervous customers drained the bank's cash. Washington Mutual's collapse was the biggest bank failure in U.S. history, and history was made again four days later when the Dow Jones suffered its largest one-day point drop ever.[49] The only good news was that September 2008 was finally over.

Unfortunately, the bad news wasn't. As one bank after another scrambled for cash to stay open, a **liquidity crisis** rippled through the economy. One hedge fund manager compared it to "an underwater earthquake" as the $4 trillion money market stopped buying the commercial paper on which corporations rely heavily for short-term financing.[50] Before long, businesses of every size found themselves caught in a **credit freeze**, with lines of credit and other sources of funding shrinking or disappearing without warning. After years of dishing out cash to anyone with a pulse, lenders suddenly got careful, cutting off credit to all but the most gold-plated customers. The Fed eventually lowered the federal funds rate to essentially zero percent, pushing monetary policy as

liquidity crisis
Severe shortage of liquidity throughout a sector of the economy or the entire economy, during which companies can't get enough cash to meet their operating needs

credit freeze
Situation in which credit has become so scarce that it is virtually unavailable, at any cost, to most potential borrowers

far as it could be pushed, but credit remained tight.[51] Companies that had nothing to do with mortgages or derivatives suffered, and unemployment continued to rise. Cautious businesses and fearful consumers cut back on spending, which reduced business revenues and tax receipts for strained local and state governments even as more people needed government assistance.

Real-Time Updates

Learn More
Crisis? What crisis?

See how big banks are taking advantage of the troubled economy by buying up smaller banks. On mybizlab (www.mybizlab.com), you can access Real-Time Updates within each chapter or under Student Study Tools. Otherwise, go to http://real-timeupdates.com/bia5 and click on "Learn More."

The long Wall Street reign of the independent investment bank came to an end when the only two major players still standing, Goldman Sachs and Morgan Stanley, were allowed to become commercial bank holding companies in order to take advantage of borrowing and government assistance options available to commercial banks.[52]

After two years of unprecedented government intervention, the economy began to show faint signs of pulling out of the recession by the fall of 2009, although there was no relief yet for the U.S. workforce as unemployment hit a 26-year high. Moreover, thousands of risky ARMs created during the subprime boom have yet to reset, meaning more homeowners will be facing payment shock in the next few years. The federal government was still propping up the housing market with its various investments in financial firms, and some economists said that support would be essential for several more years at least.[53]

Lessons Learned?

Didn't anybody see this coming? Absolutely. Worries about the housing bubble, risky lending, and unregulated mortgage derivatives began appearing several years before it all collapsed.[54] As you can read in the Behind the Scenes wrap-up on page 525, JPMorgan Chase's Jamie Dimon was so worried about a subprime meltdown that he ordered his firm to get out of that market when it was the hottest and most lucrative thing on Wall Street. After earlier encouraging the use of ARMs because they can save buyers thousands of dollars in interest, in 2005 then-chairman of the Federal Reserve Alan Greenspan began warning bankers about the increasing use of "exotic" forms of ARMs.[55] However, these voices of caution were often lost in the roar of money making or simply dismissed as too pessimistic. When economist Nouriel Roubini warned that "the risk of a U.S. recession turning into a systemic financial meltdown cannot be ruled out," he was nicknamed "Dr. Doom."[56] Too many people were making too much money to pay attention to economic fundamentals.

A year after the September 2008 meltdown, bank analyst Chris Whalen said the fact that anyone was surprised by Lehman's fall just shows how naïve people had become. Particularly in the financial profession, he says, people were "convinced that there is no risk. From the collapse of the private mortgage firms in '07, all the way through '08, we were still sleepwalking our way through the crisis . . . it was fantasyland."[57]

Fantasyland turned out to be an expensive place to live. Through 2008, the 10 largest banks in North America collectively lost nearly a half trillion dollars in the crisis.[58] Hundreds of banks are still teetering on the edge of solvency and could fail in the coming years.[59] Far removed from the poor decision making at the center of the crisis, careers were derailed, families were disrupted, and communities were devastated. People who had carefully saved and invested for years saw their retirement accounts cut in half, delaying their retirements—and keeping them in positions that would've otherwise opened up for younger workers and managers. Whatever stage of life you are in now—student, part-time worker, full-time worker, business owner, parent, renter, homeowner, whatever—the subprime meltdown has affected you directly or indirectly and will continue to do so for years to come.

Exhibit 20.5 on the next page summarizes the key lessons that should be learned from this catastrophe. Whether they will be learned is up to the consumers, business

EXHIBIT 20.5 Lessons to Learn from the Subprime Meltdown

The subprime meltdown offers many lessons for consumers, investors, bankers, and regulators. Whether these lessons get learned and stay learned is another thing entirely.

LESSON	COMMENTS
Transferring risk does not reduce or eliminate the risk—and sometimes it can even increase risk.	The risk of subprime defaults moved all the way through the system, from lenders to investment banks to hedge funds and institutional investors, without ever being diminished or successfully managed. Moreover, credit default swaps not only didn't protect investors from subprime defaults in many cases but may have actually increased total risk by making more companies dependent on one another's decision making and financial solvency.
Decoupling risk from responsibility leads to risky and irresponsible behavior.	If people begin to believe there will be no serious consequences for risky, unethical, or even illegal behavior—a condition known as *moral hazard*—they will be more likely to engage in those behaviors. If mortgage brokers can make foolish or fraudulent loans and immediately pass the risk of default to someone else, or if big banks believe the government will bail them out next time they gamble and lose, what's to stop them from behaving that way?
Individual short-term incentives can overpower logic and collective long-term consequences.	The probability of specific, immediate rewards is always going to win out over the possibility of vague, long-term risks. Within companies and across industries, business and political leaders need to understand how reward systems motivate behavior—and fix reward systems that tolerate or encourage foolish behavior.
Unregulated private contracts can have damaging public consequences.	The proper degree of economic regulation is an ongoing philosophical debate, but few rational people would argue that if private business dealings (such as CDOs and credit default swaps) carry significant public risks, then regulators should at least pay attention. The unregulated financial derivatives market created a *shadow banking system* that performed some of the same functions as the real banking system but without the essential checks and balances that keep a banking system from spinning out of control.
If something seems too good to be true, it is.	This lesson has been learned, unlearned, and relearned countless times over the years but never seems to stick. There is no magic in the financial markets.
Innovation can be dangerous if it outpaces our ability to understand it or control it.	This danger will always be with us because regulation and other controls always lag innovation. However, leaders need to remember that innovation often creates new and unforeseen risks, so they need to proceed with caution and be ready to react quickly.
Leverage can be dangerous, and massive leverage can be deadly.	Borrowing money to make money is not an inherently bad thing; banks, hedge funds, and individual investors do it all the time and live to tell about it. However, the more you leverage, the more vulnerable you are to declines in the value of the investment. With massive leverage (20 to 1, 30 to 1, and so on), the tiniest blip in asset value can wipe you out.
The past is not always a reliable guide to the future.	The belief that home prices never fall was the delusion at the core of this entire mess. However, bubble-inflated prices *always* fall, which is the historical precedent people should have been using instead. The difference between *unlikely* and *impossible* is huge.
Computer models and quantitative analysis must *support* experience and common sense, not *replace* them.	Quantitative analysis is a powerful tool for solving problems—but only those problems that can be accurately quantified. Ignoring experience and common sense in favor of models—and worse yet, distorting your view of reality so that it fits the model's mechanical view of the world—is a recipe for disaster.
Investors must understand the quality of the information they use to make investment decisions.	Many investors in CDOs and other complex financial products relied on flawed information from credit rating agencies—information that was based on faulty assumptions or perhaps even deliberately skewed in some cases.

managers, financial professionals, investors, regulators, and political leaders who control or participate in the banking system. Clay Ewing, an executive with German American Bancorp in Jaspar, Indiana, might've summed up the lessons to be learned most succinctly when he observed, "Banking should not be exciting. If banking gets exciting, there is something wrong with it."[60]

For the latest information on the banking industry, visit http://real-timeupdates .com/bia5 and click on Chapter 20.

√CHECKPOINT

LEARNING OBJECTIVE 6: Describe how the banking industry was restructured as a result of the subprime crisis.

Summary: The two biggest structural changes in the banking industry were consolidation and the disappearance or transformation of the five iconic Wall Street investment banks. First, as relatively healthier banks such as JPMorgan Chase and Bank of America took over ailing banks and mortgage companies, the banking industry consolidated around a smaller number of bigger players. Second, five investment banks that had largely defined Wall Street for many decades—Bear Stearns, Goldman Sachs, Lehman Brothers, Merrill Lynch, and Morgan Stanley—ceased to operate as independent investment banks. They either were purchased by commercial banks (Bear Stearns and Merrill Lynch), transformed themselves into commercial bank holding companies (Goldman Sachs and Morgan Stanley), or disappeared entirely (Lehman Brothers).

Critical thinking: (1) Should the government limit any company's ability to grow to the point that its failure could seriously damage the overall economy? Why or why not? (2) Do you think everyone in the financial services industry "learned their lessons" and won't repeat the mistakes that led to the 2008 meltdown? Why or why not?

It's your business: (1) Were you or your family affected by the credit freeze that spread after the 2008 subprime meltdown? Did it affect your college plans? (2) What impact might the meltdown have on your career? Explain your answer.

Key terms to know: liquidity crisis, credit freeze

Behind the Scenes

JPMorgan Chase Says Thanks but No Thanks to the Subprime Bubble

By 2006, JPMorgan Chase's mortgage securitization business was booming, and the company had begun to ramp up its activities in the subprime market, as both a mortgage originator and packager of mortgage-based assets. JPMorgan Chase was a major player in other types of debt securitization, so growing its presence in the subprime market, where other Wall Street giants were raking in billions in fees, seemed to make sense. "It would have been a natural for us," said Bill Winters, who was co-CEO of the investment banking unit at the time.

However, JPMorgan Chase is famous on Wall Street for its rigorous risk-management system and a culture of careful analysis and thoughtful strategizing. For example, managers are expected to compile and understand highly detailed reports on their areas of responsibility so that Dimon and the executive team can clearly see the costs, profits, and risks involved in every line of business.

In late 2006, Dimon and his top managers saw a crucial warning sign: late payments on competitors' subprime mortgages were rising. The subprime loans JPMorgan Chase had written itself continued to perform reasonably well, but Dimon concluded that lending standards were "deteriorating across the industry." Even though its own mortgage origination business was maintaining its usual standards, by pooling subprime loans from multiple sources, its mortgage securitization business exposed the company to the risky practices of other lenders.

The firm considered using credit default swaps to hedge against the risk of widespread loan defaults in its securities portfolios. However, the cost of credit default swaps was rising as well, reflecting the growing default rates, to the point that paying to hedge its positions in subprimes would've cost the company as much as it could earn. "We saw no profit, and lots of risk, in holding subprime paper on our balance sheet," Winters later explained.

By reviewing market conditions across all of JPMorgan Chase's lines of business, Dimon was one of the first to recognize that the subprime market was about to transform from a cash-generating dream machine into an economy-destroying nightmare. Ironically, in light of the criticism that repealing Glass-Steagall and letting companies combine commercial and investment banking contributed to the economic meltdown, it was the ability to see both ends of the subprime bubble at once—the individual loans on Main Street and the securitization business on Wall Street—that alerted Dimon to the danger. "We have a gold mine of knowledge," he explains.

Armed with this information, Dimon moved quickly. He telephoned the executive in charge of securitized products, who was on vacation in Rwanda, and instructed him to start moving JPMorgan Chase out of the subprime market. Dimon was blunt: "This stuff could go up in smoke!" Managers across the bank responded, selling $12 billion worth of the company's own subprime mortgages, curtailing its securitization business in subprimes, and advising private banking clients to sell the subprime securities they held. It meant walking away from a business that was still generating mountains of money and even losing key employees to banks that stayed in the business, but as Dimon explained later, "Everyone was trying to grow in products we didn't want to grow in, so we let them have it." At that point, for example, Bear Stearns and Merrill Lynch each held roughly $40 billion of subprime debt.

JPMorgan Chase didn't escape the meltdown unscathed, to be sure. Its vast exposure to mortgages, credit card debt, and auto loans led to some losses as the economy crumbled, and its large stock holdings in Fannie Mae and Freddie Mac were all but wiped out. However, during a time when losing less was considered winning, JPMorgan Chase was definitely one of Wall Street's winners. Its subprime losses were "only" $5 billion, compared to the $26 billion lost by Merrill Lynch and the $33 billion lost by Citigroup, and it remained healthy enough to acquire Bear Stearns and the assets of Washington Mutual when those two giants fell on their faces. Dimon and company also helped refute the notion that giant banking companies are a risk to the economy by virtue of being "too big to fail." It was JPMorgan Chase's vast scope that helped Dimon recognize a complex, interconnected problem that was about to sink the entire economy.[61]

Critical Thinking Questions

1. How might the pressures of being public corporations have affected the decision making of JPMorgan Chase's competitors?
2. What might've happened if JPMorgan Chase's competitors had tried to bail out of the subprime market at the same time as Dimon was directing his company to do so?
3. Did the executives at companies that chose to stay in the subprime market behave unethically by not bailing out when JPMorgan Chase did? Why or why not?

LEARN MORE ONLINE

Visit the JPMorgan Chase website at www.jpmorganchase.com and explore the company's three major banking brands. Read "Our Business Principles," available in the "About Us" section. What does the company say about managing risk in financial markets? Read the latest annual "Corporate Responsibility Report," available in the "Corporate Responsibility" section. What does the company say about its financial responsibility to investors and customers? ∎

Key Terms

adjustable rate mortgage (ARM) (515)
asset-backed securities (ABSs) (519)
bubble (513)
commercial banks (510)
credit freeze (522)
credit rating agencies (512)
credit unions (511)

default (516)
discount rate (508)
Fannie Mae (509)
Federal Deposit Insurance
   Corporation (FDIC) (509)
federal funds rate (508)
Federal Reserve System (508)

finance companies (512)
foreclosures (520)
Freddie Mac (509)
independent mortgage companies
   (511)
investment banks (511)
liquidity crisis (522)

loan-to-value (LTV) (514)
merchant banks (510)
money (507)
money supply (507)
mortgage-backed securities
　(MBSs) (519)

mortgage brokers (511)
negative amortization (516)
option ARM (515)
prime mortgages (516)
private banking (511)
reserves (508)

retail banks (510)
secondary mortgage market (509)
securitization (519)
subprime mortgages (516)
thrift banks (510)

Test Your Knowledge

Questions for Review

1. How do commercial banks differ from investment banks?
2. What does securitization of debt mean?
3. What is a bubble?
4. What is a subprime mortgage?
5. What are the primary responsibilities of the Federal Reserve System?

Questions for Analysis

6. How did the decline in lending standards contribute to the financial meltdown of 2008?
7. How did low interest rates contribute to the housing bubble and the subsequent financial crisis?
8. How does the money supply affect the cost and availability of credit?
9. Generally speaking, what effect did the repeal of the Glass-Steagall Act have on the banking industry?

10. **Ethical Considerations.** How did the decoupling of risk and reward contribute to the problems in the subprime mortgage industry?

Questions for Application

11. If a consumer with a relatively low credit score applied for a loan from your bank, what other criteria might you consider before deciding to grant a loan?
12. As a corporate financial manager, what steps could you take to protect your company from a liquidity crisis?
13. If you were in charge of monetary policy and wanted to lower the federal funds rate, would you buy or sell Treasury securities on the open market? Why?
14. **Concept Integration.** It what ways did the housing bubble and subprime crisis violate the responsibilities suggested by the stakeholder model (see page 128)?

Practice Your Knowledge

Sharpening Your Communication Skills

As a loan officer at Long Isle Community Bank, your responsibilities include the unpleasant task of informing some applicants that their loans have not been approved. Today you need to write a letter to Geoff Winders, a customer who applied for a home mortgage but was turned down by the bank's loan committee because his credit score was too low. You can temper the bad news with the suggestion that Mr. Winders attend the free credit repair seminar, Back on Track, that Long Isle offers every Saturday afternoon from 1:00 to 3:00. Write a brief letter that opens by thanking Mr. Winders for being a customer of the bank and for considering the bank for his home mortgage needs. Explain the reason his application was rejected and extend the offer of attending the free seminar.

Building Your Team Skills

With teammates as assigned by your instructor, choose a type of business that you would like to own and manage. Next, identify three institutions in your town or city that could provide the banking services your company would need, based on your growth plans for the first five years (make up any details you need). Choose a branch of a national bank, a smaller community bank, and a credit union. Research the services and capabilities of each and decide which one is the right choice for your company. Present your results using presentation slides, a wiki, or whatever media option your instructor indicates.

Expand Your Knowledge

Discovering Career Opportunities

Is a career in community banking for you? Bankers in smaller banks deal with a wide variety of customers, products, transactions, and inquiries every working day. To get a better idea of what community bankers do,

explore the Independent Community Bankers of America website at www.icba.org and visit a local independent bank branch.

1. Talk with a customer service representative or an officer about the kinds of customers this bank serves.

Does it handle a high volume of business banking transactions, or is it more geared to consumer banking needs? How does the mix of consumer and business customers affect the branch's staffing and working hours?

2. What banking services are offered by this bank? Does the bank have specialized experts on staff to service these customers? What kind of skills, experience, education, and licenses must these experts have?

3. What kinds of entry-level jobs in this bank are appropriate for your background? What are the advancement opportunities within the bank and within the bank organization? Now that you have a better idea of what community banking is, how does this career fit with your interests and goals?

Developing Your Research Skills

Many observers criticized the role played by the credit rating agencies Moody's, Standard & Poor's, and Fitch in the subprime crisis. Two particular criticisms are that bond rating agencies are paid by bond issuers, which could lead them to issue biased ratings, and that the agencies gave their top ratings to mortgage-backed securities that contained low-quality debts. Do the research necessary to find answers to the following questions:

1. Have any major changes in the debt rating process been proposed or enacted, such as having a not-for-profit organization provide impartial ratings instead of or in addition to the commercial agencies?

2. Have any investors or other parties successfully sued a rating agency for providing misleading information?

3. Has Congress or any federal agency taken any steps to change the laws and regulations that affect the operation of credit rating agencies?

Improving Your Tech Insights: Identity Theft Detection Systems

Identity theft, which Chapter 4 defines as the theft and fraudulent use of personal information, is a huge problem for consumers and the banks, financial services companies, and retailers that handle their confidential personal information. To help combat the problem, the Fair and Accurate Credit Transactions Act (FACTA) requires financial institutions, retailers, and service providers such as mobile phone companies to have procedures in place to catch suspicious activities. These "Red Flags Rules" are designed to identify suspicious transactions, documents, and other events or elements that could signal a case of identity theft.

Given the millions of consumer transactions that occur every day, singling out suspicious behavior is no small task. To help companies implement the FACTA Red Flags Rules, a variety of software companies offer automated monitoring, verification, and authentication tools. Research one of these software solutions, such as that offered by RSA (www.rsa.com). In a brief e-mail message to your instructor, explain how it helps banks and other firms meet the Red Flags Rules.[62] You can also read more about the rules at www.ftc.gov/redflagsrule.

Video Discussion

Access the Chapter 20 video discussion in the End of Chapter Assignments section at www.mybizlab.com.

PEARSON **my*biz*lab**

Log on to www.mybizlab.com to access the following study and assessment aids associated with this chapter:

- Interactive exercises
- Pre/post test
- Real-Time Updates
- Video application
- Customized study plans
- Biz Skills Simulations
- Quick Learning Guide

If you are not using mybizlab, you can access Real-Time Updates and Quick Learning Guides through http://realtimeupdates.com/bia5. The Quick Learning Guide (located under "Learn More" on the website) provides all six Checkpoints in a handy two-page format to help you study for exams or review important concepts whenever you need a quick refresher.

Notes

Prologue

1. Jeffrey R. Young, "'E-Portfolios' Could Give Students a New Sense of Their Accomplishments," *Chronicle of Higher Education*, 8 March 2002, A31.

2. Brian Carcione, e-portfolio [accessed 20 December 2006] http://eportfolio .psu.edu.

3. Nancy M. Somerick, "Managing a Communication Internship Program," *Bulletin of the Association for Business Communication* 56, no. 3 (1993): 10–20.

4. Fellowforce website [accessed 8 August 2009] www.fellowforce.com.

5. Bureau of Labor Statistics, *2006–2007 Occupational Outlook Handbook* [accessed 16 August 2007] www.bls .gov/oco.

6. Anne Fisher, "How to Get Hired by a 'Best' Company," *Fortune*, 4 February 2008, 96.

7. Anne Fisher, "Greener Pastures in a New Field," *Fortune*, 26 January 2004, 48.

8. Liz Ryan, "Etiquette for Online Outreach," Yahoo! Hotjobs website [accessed 26 March 2008] http:// hotjobs.yahoo.com.

9. Career and Employment Services, Danville Area Community College website [accessed 23 March 2008] www .dacc.edu/career; Career Counseling, Sarah Lawrence College website [accessed 23 March 2008] www.slc.edu/ occ/index.php; Cheryl L. Noll, "Collaborating with the Career Planning and Placement Center in the Job-Search Project," *Business Communication Quarterly* 58, no. 3 (1995): 53–55.

10. Rockport Institute, "How to Write a Masterpiece of a Résumé" [accessed 16 October 1998] www.rockportinstitute .com/résumés.html.

11. "How to Ferret Out Instances of Résumé Padding and Fraud," *Compensation & Benefits for Law Offices*, June 2006, 1+.

12. "Resume Fraud Gets Slicker and Easier," CNN.com [accessed 11 March 2004] www.cnn.com.

13. Lisa Takeuchi Cullen, "Getting Wise to Lies," *Time*, 1 May 2006, 59; "Resume Fraud Gets Slicker and Easier;" Employment Research Services website [accessed 18 March 2004] www .erscheck.com.

14. "How to Ferret Out Instances of Résumé Padding and Fraud."

15. Jacqueline Durett, "Redoing Your Résumé? Leave Off the Lies," *Training*, December 2006, 9; "Employers Turn Their Fire on Untruthful CVs," *Supply Management*, 23 June 2005, 13.

16. Cynthia E. Conn, "Integrating Writing Skills and Ethics Training in Business Communication Pedagogy: A Résumé Case Study Exemplar," *Business Communication Quarterly*, June 2008, 138–151; Marilyn Moats Kennedy, "Don't Get Burned by Résumé Inflation," *Marketing News*, 15 April 2007, 37–38.

17. Pam Stanley-Weigand, "Organizing the Writing of Your Resume," *Bulletin of the Association for Business Communication* 54, no. 3 (September 1991): 11–12.

18. Susan Vaughn, "Answer the Hard Questions Before Asked," *Los Angeles Times*, 29 July 2001, W1–W2.

19. John Steven Niznik, "Landing a Job with a Criminal Record," About.com [accessed 12 December 2006] http:// jobsearchtech.about.com.

20. Richard H. Beatty and Nicholas C. Burkholder, *The Executive Career Guide for MBAs* (New York: Wiley, 1996), 133.

21. Adapted from Burdette E. Bostwick, *How to Find the Job You've Always Wanted* (New York: Wiley, 1982), 69–70.

22. Norma Mushkat Gaffin, "Recruiters' Top 10 Resume Pet Peeves," Monster.com [accessed 19 February 2004] www.monster.com; Beatty and Burkholder, *The Executive Career Guide for MBAs*, 151.

23. Rockport Institute, "How to Write a Masterpiece of a Résumé."

24. Beverly Culwell-Block and Jean Anna Sellers, "Résumé Content and Format—Do the Authorities Agree?" *Bulletin of the Association for Business Communication* 57, no. 4 (1994): 27–30.

25. Ed Tazzia, "Wanted: A Résumé That Really Works," *Brandweek*, 15 May 2006, 26.

26. John Sullivan, "Résumés: Paper, Please," *Workforce Management*, 22 October 2007, 50; "Video Résumés Offer Both Pros and Cons During Recruiting," *HR Focus*, July 2007, 8.

27. Ellen Joe Pollock, "Sir: Your Application for a Job Is Rejected; Sincerely, Hal 9000," *Wall Street Journal*, 30 July 1998, A1, A12.

28. "Scannable Resume Design," ResumeEdge.com [accessed 19 February 2004] www.resumeedge .com.

29. Kim Isaacs, "Tips for Creating a Scannable Résumé," Monster.com [accessed 19 February 2004] www .monster.com.

30. Christian Anderson, "New Year's Resolutions—Jobster Style," Jobster blog, 21 December 2007 [accessed 28 March 2008] www.jobster.blogs .com.

31. Sarah E. Needleman, "Why Sneaky Tactics May Not Help Resume; Recruiters Use New Search Technologies to Ferret Out Bogus Keywords," *Wall Street Journal*, 6 March 2007, B8.

32. "The Writer Approach," *Los Angeles Times*, 17 November 2002, W1.

33. Fisher, "How to Get Hired by a 'Best' Company."

34. Sarah E. Needleman, "Speed Interviewing Grows as Skills Shortage Looms; Strategy May Help Lock in Top Picks; Some Drawbacks," *Wall Street Journal*, 6 November 2007, B15.

35. Scott Beagrie, "How to Handle a Telephone Job Interview," *Personnel Today*, 26 June 2007, 29.

36. "Hiring Process," Google website [accessed 2 January 2009] www.google .com.

37. Fisher, "How to Get Hired by a 'Best' Company."

38. "What's a Group Interview," About.com Tech Careers [accessed 5 April 2008] http://jobsearchtech .about.com.

39. Fisher, "How to Get Hired by a 'Best' Company."

40. Chris Pentilla, "Testing the Waters," *Entrepreneur*, January 2004 [accessed 27 May 2006] www .entrepreneur.com; Terry McKenna, "Behavior-Based Interviewing," *National Petroleum News*, January 2004, 16; Nancy K. Austin, "Goodbye Gimmicks," *Incentive*, May 1996, 241.

41. Robert Gifford, Cheuk Fan Ng, and Margaret Wilkinson, "Nonverbal Cues in the Employment Interview: Links Between Applicant Qualities and Interviewer Judgments," *Journal of Applied Psychology* 70, no. 4 (1985): 729.

42. Robin White Goode, "International and Foreign Language Skills Have an Edge," *Black Enterprise*, May 1995, 53.

43. Joan Lloyd, "Changing Workplace Requires You to Alter Your Career Outlook," *Milwaukee Journal Sentinel*, 4 July 1999, 1; Camille DeBell, "Ninety Years in the World of Work in America," *Career Development Quarterly* 50, no. 1 (September 2001): 77–88.

Chapter 1

1. Adapted from Bill Palladino, "Music Business Economics 101," Claudia Schmidt website [accessed 10 May 2009] www.claudiaschmidt.com; Enter the Haggis website [accessed 5 May 2009] www.enterthehaggis.com; Brian Buchanan, "21st Century Rockstardom," blog post, 7 April 2008 [accessed 5 May 2009] www.enterthehaggis.com; Christopher Knab, "Oh, How the Music Business Keeps Changing," Music Biz Academy.com, January 2009 [accessed 5 May 2009] www.musicbizacademy.com; Ethan Smith, "Can He Save Rock 'n' Roll?," *Wall Street Journal*, 21 February 2009 [accessed 30 April 2009] http://online.wsj.com.

2. "Gross-Domestic-Product-by-Industry Accounts," U.S. Bureau of Economic Analysis website, 28 April 2009 [accessed 2 May 2009] www.bea.gov.

3. "The 2008 Fortune 500," *Fortune*, 4 May 2009 [accessed 2 May 2009] www.fortune.com.

4. "IBM 2008 Annual Report" [accessed 1 May 2009] www.ibm.com.

5. "SOI Tax Stats–Integrated Business Data," IRS website [accessed 29 April 2009] www.irs.gov.

6. "SOI Tax Stats–Integrated Business Data."

7. Cheryl Winokur Munk, "4 Generations," *Community Banker*, January 2009, 30–33.

8. "iTunes Store Top Music Retailer in the US," Apple press release, 3 April 2008 [accessed 6 May 2009] www.apple.com.

9. "Hey Big (R&D) Spenders," *Industry Week*, December 2008, 63.

10. "2008 R&D Spending by U.S. Biopharmaceuticals at Record Levels," *Biotech Financial Reports*, April 2009, 1–3.

11. Career profiles in this section adapted from U.S. Bureau of Labor Statistics, *Occupational Outlook Handbook, 2008–2009 Edition* [accessed 27 April 2009] www.bls.gov/oco.

12. Kris Dunn, "The Five Sweetest Jobs in HR and Talent Management," *Workforce*, July 2008 [accessed 27 April 2009] www.workforce.com.

13. Meredith Levinson, "Should You Get an MBA?" *CIO*, 5 July 2007 [accessed 28 April 2009] www.cio.com.

14. Adapted from Desktop Factory website [accessed 9 May 2009] www.desktopfactory.com; Dimension 3D Printing website [accessed 9 May 2009] www.dimensionprinting.com; Stratasys website [accessed 9 May 2009] www.stratasys.com; Z Corporation [accessed 9 May 2009] www.zcorp.com.

Chapter 2

1. Suntech Power website [accessed 14 May 2009] www.suntech-power.com; Bill Powell, "China's New King of Solar," *FSB: Fortune Small Business*, 11 February 2009, 68–71; Nick Hodge, "Grid Parity: Renewables vs. Coal," *Wealth Daily*, 28 November 2007 [accessed 14 May 2009] www.wealthdaily.com; Solar Energy Initiative, U.S. Department of Energy website [accessed 14 May 2009] www.eere.energy.gov; "Frost & Sullivan 2008 Global Solar Energy Development Company of the Year Award," Suntech Power website [accessed 15 May 2009] www.suntech-power.com; John Kell, "Earnings Preview: Solar Cos Focus on Financing, Margins," *Wall Street Journal*, 16 April 2009 [accessed 15 May 2009] http://online.wsj.com; Jennifer Kho, "Solar Prices Drop, Deeper Discounts Expected," Earth2tech, 23 February 2009 [accessed 15 May 2009] www.earth2tech.com; Kate Galbraith, "Europe's Way of Encouraging Solar Power Arrives in the U.S.," *New York Times*, 12 March 2006 [accessed 16 May 2009] www.nytimes.com; Jack Yetiv, "When Will Solar Achieve Grid Parity? We're Already There!" Seeking Alpha blog, 21 April 2008 [accessed 16 May 2009] www.seekingalpha.com; Kevin Kelleher, "Report: First Solar Reaches Grid Parity," Earth2tech, 21 December 2008 [accessed 15 May 2009] www.earth2tech.com; Josie Garthwaite, "Solar Shakeout Under Way, Serious Oversupply to Come, Report Says," Earth2tech, 18 February 2009 [accessed 15 May 2009] www.earth2tech.com.

2. Roger LeRoy Miller, *Economics Today*, 15th ed. (Boston: Addison Wesley, 2010), 28.

3. Miller, *Economics Today*, 31.

4. Ronald M. Ayers and Robert A. Collinge, *Economics: Explore and Apply* (Upper Saddle River, N.J.: Pearson Prentice Hall, 2005), 97–103.

5. Landon Thomas, Jr., "Thriving Norway Provides an Economics Lesson," *New York Times*, 13 May 2009 [accessed 16 May 2009] www.nytimes.com.

6. Emily Thornton, "Roads to Riches," *BusinessWeek*, 7 May 2007 [accessed 5 June 2007] www.businessweek.com; Palash R. Ghosh, "Private Prisons Have a Lock on Growth," *BusinessWeek*, 6 July 2006 [accessed 5 June 2007] www.businessweek.com.

7. Peter Gumbel, "Saving Britain's Broken Bank," *Fortune*, 29 April 2009 [accessed 16 May 2009] http://money.cnn.com.

8. Colin Barr, "What Is Nationalization?" *Fortune*, 20 February 2009 [accessed 16 May 2009] http://money.cnn.com.

9. Tom Raum, "GM, Under U.S. Control, Braces for Smaller Future," *Philadelphia Inquirer*, 3 June 2009 [accessed 10 June 2009] www.philly.com.

10. "Frost & Sullivan 2008 Global Solar Energy Development Company of the Year Award."

11. Chris Isidore, "It's Official: Recession Since Dec. '07," CNNMoney.com, 1 December 2008 [accessed 17 May 2009] http://money.cnn.com; Greg Burns, "Is Recession's End Here? Economist Sticks with May 15 as Bottom of the Bust," *Chicago Tribune*, 17 May 2009 [accessed 17 May 2009] www.chicagotribune.com.

12. Jonathan Rauch, "Capitalism's Fault Lines," *New York Times*, 14 May 2009 [accessed 20 May 2009] www.nytimes.com.

13. Miller, *Economics Today*, 174.

14. Miller, *Economics Today*, 160.

15. Miller, *Economics Today*, 160.

16. Miller, *Economics Today*, 164–165.

17. Penelope Wang, "What's Really Driving Skyrocketing Prices," *Money*, 13 April 2009 [accessed 17 May 2009] http://money.cnn.com.

18. Henry Cheeseman, *Business Law*, 7th ed. (Upper Saddle River, N.J.: Pearson Prentice Hall, 2010), 725–726.

19. James Kanter, "Europe Fines Intel $1.45 Billion in Antitrust Case," *New York Times*, 13 May 2009 [accessed 18 May 2009] www.nytimes.com.

20. Hilary Lewis, "DOJ's Antitrust Crackdown Could Scuttle Live Nation-Ticketmaster Merger (LYV, TKTM)," *The Business Insider*, 11 May 2009 [accessed 18 May 2009] www.businessinsider.com; Jim DeRogatis, "Recapping the Ticketmaster/Live Nation Hearing on Capitol Hill," *Chicago Sun-Times*, 24 February 2009 [accessed 18 May 2009] http://blogs.suntimes.com.

21. Broome County Empire Zone website [accessed 18 May 2009] www.broomezone.com.

22. Miller, *Economics Today*, 169.

23. "Consumer Price Index," U.S. Bureau of Labor Statistics website [accessed 18 May 2009] www.bls.gov; Jyoti Thottam, "Why Aren't Your Prices Falling?" *Time*, 26 May 2003, 53.

24. U.S. Bureau of Labor Statistics website [accessed 18 May 2009] www.bls.gov; Jon E. Hilsenrath, "Producer-Price

Drop Signals Change in Inflation Dynamics," *Wall Street Journal*, 13 September 2004, A2.

25. Adapted from Stephen Baker, "How Much Is That Worker Worth?" *BusinessWeek*, 23 March 2009, 46–48; Doug Henschen, "IDC Reports on BI Sales: Which Vendors Are Hot?" *Intelligent Enterprise*, 1 July 2007 [accessed 6 August 2007] www .intelligententerprise.com; Angoss website [accessed 21 May 2009] www .angoss.com.

Chapter 3

1. Ed Waller, "African Adventures for MTV Networks," C21 Media.net, 9 April 2009 [accessed 22 May 2009] www.c21media.net; MTV Base website [accessed 22 May 2009] www.mtvbase .com; MTV website [accessed 22 May 2009] www.mtv.com; Quentin Hardy, "Hope & Profit in Africa," *Forbes*, 18 June 2007, 92–117; Diane Coetzer, "Smith, Ludacris Help Launch African MTV Channel," Billboard.com, 21 April 2005 [accessed 16 June 2007] www .billboard.com; Damien Rafferty, "MTV Base (UK): Championing African Music," Fly Global Music Culture website, 31 May 2007 [accessed 16 June 2007] www.fly.co.uk; "MTV Base Africa on MTV Base UK," Africa on Your Street, BBC website [accessed 16 June 2007] www.bbc.co.uk; "The Road from Soldier back to Child," *Africa Recovery*, October 2001, 10+; "Africa Gets Own MTV Channel Today," Afrol News, 22 February 2005 [accessed 16 June 2007] www.afrol.com; "MTV Music Channels Top Cool Survey Again," BizCommunity.com, 30 May 2007 [accessed 16 June 2007] www.bizcommunity.com.
2. Ricky W. Griffin and Michael W. Pustay, *International Business*, 6th ed. (Upper Saddle River, N.J.: Pearson Prentice Hall, 2010), 6.
3. Griffin and Pustay, *International Business*, 12.
4. Holley H. Ulbrich and Mellie L. Warner, *Managerial Economics* (New York: Barron's Educational Series, 1990), 190.
5. Griffin and Pustay, *International Business*, 13.
6. Griffin and Pustay, *International Business*, 14.
7. "President Bush's Statement on Open Economies," FDCH Regulatory Intelligence Database, 10 May 2007 [accessed 29 June 2007] www.ebsco .com; Vladimir Masch, "A Radical Plan to Manage Globalization," *BusinessWeek*, 24 February 2007, 11; Philip Levy, "Trade Truths for Turbulent Times," *BusinessWeek*, 24 February 2007, 9.

8. "Twelve Myths About Hunger," Institute for Food and Development Policy website [accessed 27 January 2005] www.foodfirst.com.
9. Peter Davis, "Investment and the Development Theory Myth," *Ethical Corporation*, October 2006, 29–30.
10. Moisés Naim, "Globalization," *Foreign Policy*, March–April 2009, 28–34.
11. Steve Stecklow and Erin White, "At Some Retailers, 'Fair Trade' Carries a Very High Cost," *Wall Street Journal*, 8 June 2004, A1, A10.
12. Fair Trade Federation website [accessed 24 May 2009] www.fairtradefederation .org; TransFair USA website [accessed 24 May 2009] www.transfairusa.org.
13. "Protectionism Fades, So EU Carmakers Must Fight," *Automotive News Europe*, 11 June 2007, 10.
14. John D. Daniels, Lee H. Radebaugh, and Daniel P. Sullivan, *International Business*, 10th ed. (Upper Saddle River, N.J.: Pearson Prentice Hall, 2004), 182.
15. "Principles of the Trading System," World Trade Organization website [accessed 22 May 2009] www.wto.org.
16. "10 Common Misunderstandings About the WTO," World Trade Organization website [accessed 22 May 2009] www.wto.org.
17. Joe Chidley, "The WTO at the Brink," *Canadian Business*, 10 April 2009, 35–39.
18. International Monetary Fund website [accessed 22 May 2009] www.imf.org.
19. Griffin and Pustay, *International Business*, 189–190; "IMF Conditionality," International Monetary Fund website [accessed 22 May 2009] www.imf.org.
20. World Bank Group website [accessed 22 May 2009] www.worldbank.org.
21. "North American Free Trade Agreement (NAFTA)," USDA Foreign Agricultural Service website [accessed 29 June 2007] www.fas.usda.gov.
22. Griffin and Pustay, *International Business*, 288.
23. "Fool Me Twice? Chamber of Commerce Distorts NAFTA Record, Hides CAFTA Costs," Public Citizen, March 2005 [accessed 23 May 2009] www.citizen.org; "North American Free Trade Agreement (NAFTA)," Public Citizen website [accessed 28 January 2005] www.publiccitizen.org; Debra Beachy, "A Decade of NAFTA," *Hispanic Business*, July/August 2004, 24–25; Geri Smith and Cristina Lindblad, "Mexico: Was NAFTA Worth It?" *BusinessWeek*, 22 December 2003, 66–72; Charles J. Walen, "NAFTA's Scorecard: So Far, So Good," *BusinessWeek*, 9 July 2001, 54–56.
24. "NAFTA Facts," Office of the United States Trade Representative website,

March 2008 [accessed 23 May 2009] www.ustr.gov.
25. Europa (EU gateway site) [accessed 23 May 2009] http://europa.eu.
26. "How the Euro Benefits Us All," European Community website [accessed 23 May 2009] http://europa.eu.
27. "About APEC," APEC website [accessed 23 May 2009] www.apec.org.
28. Linda Beamer and Iris Varner, *Intercultural Communication in the Workplace*, 2nd ed. (New York: McGraw-Hill Irwin, 2001), 3.
29. Daniels, et al., *International Business*, 335.
30. Russell Mokhiber, "Paying for Pay-Offs," *Multinational Monitor*, January–February 2009, 52; Griffin and Pustay, *International Business*, 129–130.
31. "FAQs for Journalists; Facts and Figures on Corruption," Transparency International [accessed 23 May 2009] www.transparency.org.
32. "FAQs for Journalists; Facts and Figures on Corruption."
33. Dionne Searcey, "U.S. Cracks Down on Corporate Bribes," *Wall Street Journal*, 26 May 2009 [accessed 26 May 2009] http://online.wsj.com.
34. Organisation for Economic Co-Operation and Development website [accessed 29 June 2007] www.oecd.org.
35. Tobias Webb and John Russell, "Stop Paying and They Stop Asking," *Ethical Corporation*, September 2006, 42–43; Zara Maung, "Cross-Continental Road to Honesty," *Ethical Corporation*, October 2006, 14–15.
36. James Wilfong and Toni Seger, *Taking Your Business Global* (Franklin Lakes, N.J.: Career Press, 1997), 289.
37. Export.gov [accessed 23 May 2009] www.export.gov.
38. "Partnering for Success," Boehringer Ingelheim [accessed 23 May 2009] www.boehringer-ingelheim.com.
39. Hoovers website [accessed 23 May 2009] www.hoovers.com.
40. Geoffrey A. Fowler, "Viacom, Boosting China Toehold, Enter Beijing Television Venture," *Wall Street Journal*, 24 September 2004, B4.
41. Janet Ong, "Amazon to Boost Spending on China Unit," *Seattle Times*, 5 June 2007 [accessed 5 June 2007] http:// seattletimes.nwsource.com.
42. Griffin and Pustay, *International Business*, 168.
43. Griffin and Pustay, *International Business*, 170.
44. Griffin and Pustay, *International Business*, 310–311.
45. Leighann C. Neilson and Megha Chadha, "International Marketing Strategy in the Retail Banking Industry: The Case of ICICI Bank in Canada," *Journal of Financial Services Marketing*, December 2008, 204–220.

46. Elizabeth Esfahni, "Thinking Locally, Succeeding Globally," *Business 2.0*, December 2005, 96–98.

47. Erin White and Jeffrey A. Trachtenberg, "'One Size Doesn't Fit All': At WPP, Sir Martin Sorrell Sees Limits to Globalization," *Wall Street Journal*, 1 October 2003, B1, B2.

48. Om Malik, "The New Land of Opportunity," *Business 2.0*, July 2004, 72–79.

49. Griffin and Pustay, *International Business*, 555.

50. Griffin and Pustay, *International Business*, 559.

51. See note 1.

52. Adapted from Beth Murtagh, "U.S. Steel Files Trade Complaint Against China for Steel Dumping," *Pittsburgh Business Times*, 11 May 2009 [accessed 23 May 2009] www.bizjournals.com.

53. Adapted from Steve Lohr, "As Travel Costs Rise, More Meetings Go Virtual," *New York Times*, 22 July 2008 [accessed 23 July 2008] www.nytimes.com.

54. Adapted from "Overview," Telepresence World website [accessed 29 June 2007] www.telepresenceworld. com; Rick Whiting, "Innovation: Videoconferencing's Virtual Room," *InformationWeek*, 1 April 2002, 14; Teliris website [accessed 29 June 2007] www.teliris.com.

55. Adapted from "USAJobs: International Trade Specialist," USA Jobs website [accessed 23 May 2009] http:// jobsearch.usajobs.gov.

Chapter 4

1. "PepsiCo Lines up $500m for India, Undeterred by Singur," *The Statesman* (Kolkata, India), 22 September 2008, 10; "Environmental Sustainability," PepsiCo website [accessed 3 June 2009] www.pepsico.com; Diane Brady, "Pepsi: Repairing a Poisoned Reputation in India," *BusinessWeek*, 11 June 2007, 46–54; PepsiCo website [accessed 9 June 2007] ww.pepsico.com; Diane Brady, "Pepsi's Troubled Water in India" multimedia presentation [accessed 9 June 2007] www.businessweek .com; "PepsiCo's Products Are Safe," press release, 12 August 2006 [accessed 9 June 2007] www.pepsiindia .co.in; Annette Farr, "View from a Farr—Coke and Pepsi See Green," Just-Drinks.com, 15 May 2007 [accessed 9 June 2007] www.just-drinks.com; "'Pepsi-Coke: Quit India Campaign' Coke and Pepsi vs. People of India," Navdanya website, 19 September 2004 [accessed 9 June 2007] www.navdanya .org; Miranda Kennedy, "Coke, Pepsi Fizzling in India?" Marketplace, 14 August 2006 [accessed 9 June 2007]

http://marketplace.publicradio.org; Centre for Science and Environment, "CSE Dares Cola Companies to Come Clean," press release, 7 August 2006 [accessed 9 June 2007] www.cseindia .org.

2. Lydia Saad, "Nurses Shine, Bankers Slump in Ethics Ratings," Gallup, 24 November 2008 [accessed 29 May 2009] www.gallup.com.

3. Ken Schachter, "MySpace, States Agree on Predator Shields," *Red Herring*, 14 January 2008, 5; Rakesh Khurana, "The Future of Business School," *BusinessWeek*, 26 May 2009 [accessed 29 May 2009] www.businessweek.com.

4. James O'Toole and Warren Bennis, "What's Needed Next: A Culture of Candor," *Harvard Business Review*, June 2009, 54–61.

5. Paula Lehman, "The Marshall of MySpace," *BusinessWeek*, 23 April 2007, 85–88.

6. O'Toole and Bennis, "What's Needed Next: A Culture of Candor," 59.

7. "Personal Leadership in Business Ethics," United Technologies website [accessed 10 June 2007] www.utc .com.

8. United Technologies, *2008 Annual Report*, 28.

9. Ben Levisohn, "Getting More Workers to Whistle," *BusinessWeek*, 28 January 2008, 18.

10. "Less Than Half of Privately Held Businesses Support Whistleblowing," Grant Thornton website [accessed 13 October 2008] www.internationalbusinessreport.com.

11. Mahzarin R. Banaji, Max H. Bazerman, and Dolly Chugh, "How (Un)Ethical Are You?" *Harvard Business Review*, December 2003, 56–64.

12. Michael Porter and Mark Kramer, "Strategy & Society: The Link Between Competitive Advantage and Corporate Social Responsibility," *Harvard Business Review*, December 2006, 78–92.

13. Ian Wilhelm, "A Surge in Corporate Giving," *Chronicle of Philanthropy*, 17 August 2006 [accessed 19 June 2007] http://find.galegroup.com.

14. David Grayson and Adrian Hodges, "Forget Responsibility, Think Opportunities," *The Observer*, 4 June 2004 [accessed 19 June 2007] http:// observer.guardian.co.uk.

15. Porter and Kramer, "Strategy & Society: The Link Between Competitive Advantage and Corporate Social Responsibility."

16. Porter and Kramer, "Strategy & Society: The Link Between Competitive Advantage and Corporate Social Responsibility."

17. "New Initiative Creates Partnerships on Water Projects Across Africa,"

Greenbiz.com, 7 June 2004 [accessed 18 June 2007] www.greenbiz.com.

18. Timothy M. Devinney, "Is the Socially Responsible Corporation a Myth? The Good, the Bad, and the Ugly of Corporate Social Responsibility," *Academy of Management Perspectives*, May 2009, 44–56.

19. Milton Friedman "The Social Responsibility of Business Is to Increase Its Profits," *New York Times Magazine*, 13 September 1970 [accessed 15 June 2007] www.umich.edu/~thecore.

20. "Social Responsibility: 'Fundamentally Subversive'?" Interview with Milton Friedman, *BusinessWeek*, 15 August 2005 [accessed 14 June 2007] www .businessweek.com.

21. Henry G. Manne, "Milton Friedman Was Right," *WSJ OpinionJournal*, 24 November 2006 [accessed 15 June 2007] www.opinionjournal.com.

22. Alexei M. Marcoux, "Business Ethics Gone Wrong," *Cato Policy Report*, May/June 2000 [accessed 14 June 2007] www.cato.org.

23. Milton Friedman, John Mackey, and T. J. Rodgers, "Rethinking the Social Responsibility of Business," *Reason Online*, October 2005 [accessed 23 September 2009] www.reason.com.

24. "Electric Power Annual," U.S. Department of Energy website [accessed 20 June 2007] www .energy.gov.

25. Kas Thomas, "Google Uses More Electricity Than Most Countries on Earth," assertTrue() blog, 9 March 2009 [accessed 1 June 2009] http:// asserttrue.blogspot.com; Rich Miller, "Google Data Center FAQ," Data Center Knowledge website, 26 August 2008 [accessed 1 June 2009] www .datacenterknowledge.com.

26. Urs Hölzle, "Energy and the Internet," The Official Google Blog, 11 May 2009 [accessed 1 June 2009] http:// googleblog.blogspot.com.

27. eSolar website [accessed 1 June 2009] www.esolar.com.

28. "Step 5: An Efficient and Clean Energy Future," Google website [accessed 1 June 2009] www.google.com.

29. "Reducing Our Footprint," Google website [accessed 1 June 2009] www .google.com.

30. Cap and Trade 101, U.S. Environmental Protection Agency website [accessed 1 June 2009] www.epa.gov.

31. John M. Broder, "From a Theory to a Consensus on Emissions," *New York Times*, 16 May 2009 [accessed 1 June 2009] www.nytimes.com.

32. John Carey, "Obama's Cap-and-Trade Plan," *BusinessWeek*, 5 March 2009 [accessed 1 June 2009] www .businessweek.com.

33. "Report of the World Commission on Environment and Development," United Nations General Assembly, 96th Plenary Meeting, 11 December 1987 [accessed 20 June 2007] www.un.org.

34. Ursula M. Burns, "Is the Green Movement a Passing Fancy?" *BusinessWeek*, 27 January 2009 [accessed 31 May 2009] www.businessweek.com.

35. Pete Engardio, "Beyond the Green Corporation," *BusinessWeek*, 29 January 2007 [accessed 20 June 2007] www.businessweek.com.

36. Engardio, "Beyond the Green Corporation."

37. "About Identity Theft," Federal Trade Commission website [accessed 30 May 2009] www.ftc.gov.

38. Action on Smoking and Health website [accessed 15 March 2005] www.ash.org; Chris Burritt, "Fallout from the Tobacco Settlement," *Atlanta Journal and Constitution*, 22 June 1997, A14; Jolie Solomon, "Smoke Signals," *Newsweek*, 28 April 1997, 50–51; Marilyn Elias, "Mortality Rate Rose Through '80s," *USA Today*, 17 April 1997, B3; Mike France, Monica Larner, and Dave Lindorff, "The World War on Tobacco," *BusinessWeek*, 11 November 1996; Richard Lacayo, "Put Out the Butt, Junior," *Time*, 2 September 1996, 51; Elizabeth Gleick, "Smoking Guns," *Time*, 1 April 1996, 50.

39. Courtland L. Bovée and John V. Thill, *Business Communication Today*, 10th ed. (Upper Saddle River, N.J.: Pearson Prentice Hall, 2010), 176–177.

40. Lorraine Woellert, "Anger on the Right, Opportunity for Bush," *BusinessWeek*, 7 July 2003 [accessed 24 January 2005] www.businessweek.com; Roger O. Crockett, "The Great Race Divide," *BusinessWeek*, 14 July 2003 [accessed 24 January 2005] www.businessweek.com; Earl Graves, "Celebrating the Best and the Brightest," *Black Enterprise*, February 2005, 16.

41. "Disability Discrimination," Equal Employment Opportunity Commission website [accessed 12 June 2007] www.eeoc.gov.

42. "Injuries, Illnesses, and Fatalities," Bureau of Labor Statistics [accessed 31 May 2009] www.bls.gov/iif.

43. Abigail Goldman, "Sweat, Fear, and Resignation amid All the Toys," *Los Angeles Times*, 26 November 2004, A1, A30–A32.

44. Edward Iwata, "How Barbie Is Making Business a Little Better," *USA Today*, 27 March 2006, B1–B2.

45. "Improving Factory Conditions," Gap website [accessed 2 June 2009] www.gap.com.

46. "Workers & Factories: Improving Conditions in Our Contract Factories," Nike website [accessed 2 June 2009] www.nike.com.

47. Fair Labor Association website [accessed 2 June 2009] www.fairlabor.org.

48. See note 1.

49. Adapted from IBM Human Ability and Accessibility Center [accessed 31 May 2009] www-3.ibm.com/able; AssistiveTech.net [accessed 31 May 2009] www.assistivetech.net; Business Leadership Network website [accessed 31 May 2009] www.usbln.org; National Institute on Disability and Rehabilitation Research website [accessed 31 May 2009] www.ed.gov; Rehabilitation Engineering and Assistive Technology Society of North America website [accessed 31 May 2009] www.resna.org.

Chapter 5

1. Adapted from Olga Kharif, "Serious Threats to Sirius Radio," *BusinessWeek*, 30 March 2009 [accessed September 23, 2009] www.businessweek.com; Greg Avery, "Malone's Liberty Media Invests $530M in Sirius XM Radio," *Denver Business Journal*, 17 February 2009 [accessed 27 March 2009] www.bizjournals.com; Ronald Grover, "John Malone: King of Satellite?" *BusinessWeek*, 18 February 2009 [accessed 27 March 2009] www.businessweek.com; David Goldman, "XM–Sirius Merger Approved by DOJ," CNN.com, 24 March 2008 [accessed 27 March 2009] http://money.cnn.com; Olga Kharif, "More Static for Sirius–XM Deal, *BusinessWeek*, 8 May 2008 [accessed 27 March 2009] www.businessweek.com; Jeffrey H. Birnbaum, "Radio Merger Under Fire from Black Lawmakers," *Washington Post*, 17 June 2008 [accessed 27 March 2009] www.washingtonpost.com; Kim Hart, "Satellite Radio Merger Approved," *Washington Post*, 26 July 2008 [accessed 27 March 2009] www.washingtonpost.com; "Sirius Completes Acquisition of XM Satellite," Reuters, 29 July 2008 [accessed 27 March 2009] www.reuters.com; Olga Kharif, "Sirius XM Is in a Serious Bind," *BusinessWeek*, 17 September 2008 [accessed 27 March 2009] www.businessweek.com; Olga Kharif, "Sirius-XM: A Long, Challenging Road Ahead," *BusinessWeek*, 11 November 2008 [accessed 27 March 2009] www.businessweek.com; Andrew Ross Sorkin and Zachery Kouwe, "Sirius XM Prepares for Possible Bankruptcy," *New York Times*, 11 February 2009 [accessed 27 March 2009] www.nytimes.com; "Sirius Satellite Radio: Corporate Overview," Sirius XM website [accessed 27 March 2009] www.sirius.com.

2. "Sole Proprietorship Basics," Nolo [accessed 10 March 2009] www.nolo.com.

3. "Sole Proprietorship FAQ," Nolo [accessed 10 March 2009] www.nolo.com.

4. William Atkinson, "Emotional Exhaustion: When You Have No Energy Left to Give," *LP/Gas*, June 2005, 17–20.

5. "6 CEOs Share Their Biggest Regrets," *Inc.* [accessed 11 March 2009] www.inc.com.

6. "Join the Club," *Entrepreneur*, December 2008, 89.

7. "Facts and Figures," PriceWaterhouseCoopers [accessed 10 March 2009] www.pwc.com.

8. "Partnership Basics," Nolo [accessed 10 March 2009] www.nolo.com.

9. Michael Cumming, "What Is a Master Limited Partnership?" Morningstar, 9 August 2007 [accessed 12 March 2009] www.morningstar.com.

10. "Limited Liability Partnerships," California Business Portal [accessed 12 March 2009] www.sos.ca.gov.

11. Kelly K. Spors, "So, You Want to Be an Entrepreneur," *Wall Street Journal*, 23 February 2009 [accessed 31 March 2009] http://online.wsj.com.

12. "Facts and Figures," PriceWaterhouseCoopers.

13. Stephanie Clifford, "10 Questions to Ask Your Partner (Before You Sign an Agreement)," *Inc.*, November 2006 [accessed 11 March 2009] www.inc.com.

14. "Creating a Partnership Agreement," Nolo [accessed 11 March 2009] www.nolo.com.

15. "Creating a Partnership Agreement."

16. "2008 Fortune Global 500," *Fortune* [accessed 12 March 2009] www.fortune.com; "The World Factbook," Central Intelligence Agency [accessed 12 March 2009] www.cia.gov.

17. "Largest US IPOs," Renaissance Capital IPO Home [accessed 12 March 2009] www.ipohome.com.

18. "India's Biggest IPO Raises $3 Billion in a Minute for Reliance Power," *International Herald Tribune*, 15 January 2008 [accessed 12 March 2009] www.iht.com.

19. Geoffrey Colvin and Ram Charan, "Private Lives," *Fortune*, 27 November 2006, 190–198.

20. Sanford M. Jacoby and Sally Kohn, "Japan's Management Approaches Offer Lessons for U.S. Corporations," *Seattle Times*, 27 March 2009 [accessed 29 March 2009] www.seattletimes.com.

21. "S Corporation Facts," Nolo [accessed 13 March 2009] www.nolo.com.

22. "Business Subchapter S Corporation," Lawfirms.com [accessed 13 March 2009] www.lawfirms.com.

23. "How to Choose the Right Legal Structure," *Inc.*, January–February 2009 [accessed 10 March 2009] www.inc.com.

24. Hoovers [accessed 13 March 2009] www.hoovers.com.

25. Vidya Ram, "AIG Blames Its London Office," *Forbes*, 3 March 2009 [accessed 13 March 2009] www.forbes.com.

26. "About ICCR: FAQ," Interfaith Center on Corporate Responsibility [accessed 13 March 2009] www.iccr.org; William J. Holstein, "Unlikely Allies," *Directorship*, 3 October 2006 [accessed 1 July 2007] www.forbes.com.

27. Jena McGregor, "Activist Investors Get More Respect," *BusinessWeek*, 11 June 2007, 34–35.

28. "Posner and Sherman on the Transformation of the Activist Investor," The Deal.com, 11 November 2008 [accessed 13 March 2009] www.thedeal.com.

29. Martin Lipton, "Shareholder Activism and the 'Eclipse of the Public Corporation,'" *The Corporate Board*, May/June 2007, 1–5.

30. Carol Bowie, "Independent Board Chairs: A Trend Picks Up Speed," *The Corporate Governance Advisor*, March–April 2009, 14–16; Cora Daniels, "Finally in the Director's Chair," *Fortune*, 4 October 2004, 42–44; David A. Nadler, "Building Better Boards," *Harvard Business Review*, May 2004, 102–111; Judy B. Rosener, "Women on Corporate Boards Make Good Business Sense," *Directorship*, May 2003 [accessed 18 February 2005] www.womensmedia.com.

31. Joann S. Lublin, "Back to School," *Wall Street Journal*, 21 June 2004, R3.

32. Joann S. Lublin, Theo Francis, and Jonathan Weil, "Directors Are Getting the Jitters," *Wall Street Journal*, 13 January 2005, B1, G6; Jack Milligan, "Targeting the Board," *Bank Director*, 4th Quarter 2003 [accessed 18 February 2005] www.bankdirector.com.

33. Jeffrey M. Stein and Parth S. Munshi, "The Changing Role of the Lead Director," *The Corporate Governance Advisor*, November–December 2008, 11–18.

34. "Mergers & Acquisitions Explained," Thomson Investors Network [accessed 8 April 2004] www.thomsoninvest.net.

35. *The PSI Opportunity* (online newsletter), PSI website [accessed 8 April 2004] www.psiusa.com.

36. "Spring Merger Fever," *Wall Street Journal*, 22 May 2007, A14.

37. "Microsoft Corporation M&A Summary," The Alacra Store [accessed 13 March 2009] www.alacrastore.com.

38. "The Contra Team," *Business 2.0*, April 2006, 83.

39. "Sprint-Nextel Joins the 'Worst Mergers in History' Club," Portfolio.com, 28 February 2008 [accessed 14 March 2009] www.portfolio.com.

40. "IBM Acquisition Performance—On Track," IBM website [accessed 1 July 2007] www.ibm.com; "Spring Merger Fever," *Wall Street Journal*, 22 May 2007, A14; "The Contra Team," *Business 2.0*, April 2006, 83; Larry Selden and Geoffrey Colvin, "M&A Needn't Be a Loser's Game," *Harvard Business Review*, June 2003, 70–79.

41. Nancy Gohring, "Judge OKs Settlement in Yahoo 'Poison Pill' Shareholder Suit," *Computerworld*, 9 March 2009 [accessed 14 March 2009] www.computerworld.com.

42. Michael Hickins, "Searching for Allies," *Management Review*, January 2000, 54–58.

43. "Strategic Alliances," Cisco Systems [accessed 14 March 2009] www.cisco.com.

44. Smart Energy Alliance website [accessed 14 March 2009] www.smart-energy-alliance.com.

45. "Joint Ventures Overtake M&A," PricewaterhouseCoopers 12th Annual Global CEO Survey [accessed 14 March 2009] www.pwc.com.

46. "Mama Thinks Big in Live Tie-in with HMV," *Music Week*, 24 January, 1.

47. See note 1.

48. Adapted from 37Signals website [accessed 2 July 2007] www.37signals.com; Tony Kontzer, "Learning To Share," *InformationWeek*, 5 May 2003, 28; Jon Udell, "Uniting Under Groove," *InfoWorld*, 17 February 2003 [accessed 9 September 2003] www.elibrary.com; Alison Overholt, "Virtually There?" *Fast Company*, 14 February 2002, 108.

Chapter 6

1. Adapted from Patricia Gray, "Conditioning a Firm for Growth," *Fortune Small Business*, 3 December 2007; Sister Sky website [accessed 29 March 2009] www.sistersky.com; "Necessity Inspires This Mother's Invention: New Body Lotion Is Nature-based Eczema Treatment," press release, 2 July 2007 [accessed 29 March 2009] www.theproductrocket.com; A.J. Naff, "Sister Sky: A Perfect Blend of Entrepreneurship and Native Wisdom," *Indian Gaming*, June 2008, 32–33.

2. "Advocacy Small Business Statistics and Research," U.S. Small Business Administration [accessed 30 March 2009] www.sba.gov.

3. Bernard Stamler, "Redefinition of Small Leads to a Huge Brawl," *New York Times*, 21 September 2004, G8.

4. "Table of Small Business Size Standards Matched to North American Industry Classification System Codes," U.S. Small Business Administration [accessed 30 March 2009] www.sba.gov.

5. "How Important Are Small Businesses to the U.S. Economy?" U.S. Small Business Administration [accessed 30 March 2009] www.sba.gov; Malik Singleton, "Same Markets, New Marketplaces," *Black Enterprise*, September 2004, 34; Edmund L. Andrews, "Where Do the Jobs Come From?" *New York Times*, 21 September 2004, E1, E11.

6. "How Important Are Small Businesses to the U.S. Economy?"

7. "How Important Are Small Businesses to the U.S. Economy?"

8. "eBay Inc.: A Short History," eBay [accessed 31 March 2009] www.ebay.com; Karen E. Klein, "Tough Times for eBay Entrepreneurs," *BusinessWeek*, 23 July 2008 [accessed 30 March 2009] www.businessweek.com.

9. Wigix [accessed 30 March 2009] www.wigix.com; "Tough Times for eBay Entrepreneurs."

10. National Association of Women Business Owners [accessed 30 March 2009] www.nawbo.com.

11. "Advocacy Small Business Statistics and Research," U.S. Small Business Administration [accessed 30 March 2009] www.sba.gov.

12. Norman Scarborough and Thomas Zimmerer, *Effective Small Business Management* (Upper Saddle River, N.J.: Pearson Prentice Hall, 2002), 16.

13. College Nannies & Tutors [accessed 30 March 2007] www.collegenannies.com; Stacy Perman, "The Startup Bug Strikes Earlier," *BusinessWeek*, 31 October 2005 [accessed 3 July 2007] www.businessweek.com.

14. Jim Hopkins, "Bad Times Spawn Great Start-Ups," *USA Today*, 18 December 2001, 1B; Alan Cohen, "Your Next Business," *FSB*, February 2002, 33–40.

15. Matt Richtel and Jenna Wortham, "Weary of Looking for Work, Some Create Their Own," *New York Times*, 13 March 2009 [accessed 30 March 2009] www.nytimes.com.

16. Heather Green, "Self-Help for Startups," *BusinessWeek*, 5 February 2009 [accessed 31 March 2009] www.businessweek.com.

17. Richtel and Wortham, "Weary of Looking for Work, Some Create Their Own."

18. Kelly K. Spors, "So, You Want to Be an Entrepreneur," *Wall Street Journal*, 23

February 2009 [accessed 1 April 2009] http://online.wsj.com; Marshall Goldsmith, "Demonstrating the Entrepreneurial Spirit," *BusinessWeek*, 26 August 2008 [accessed 30 March 2009] www.businessweek.com; Sarah Pierce, "Spirit of the Entrepreneur," *Entrepreneur*, 28 February 2008 [accessed 30 March 2009] www.entrepreneur.com; "Are You Ready? U.S. Small Business Administration website [accessed 21 February 2005] www.sba.gov; "Entrepreneurial Test," SBA Online Women's Business Center, U.S. Small Business Administration website [accessed 21 February 2005] www.sba.gov; Scarborough and Zimmerer, *Effective Small Business Management*, 4.

19. "Amazon.com," Hoover's [accessed 30 March 2009] www.hoovers.com; Pierce, "Spirit of the Entrepreneur."

20. Intrapreneur [accessed 31 March 2009] www.intrapreneur.com.

21. Jeffrey Bussgang, "Think Like a VC, Act Like an Entrepreneur," *BusinessWeek*, 14 August 2008 [accessed 31 March 2009] www.businessweek.com.

22. "A Team-Based, Flat Lattice Organization," W. L. Gore website [accessed 31 March 2009] www.gore.com.

23. "Buy a Business," U.S. Small Business Administration [accessed 3 July 2007] www.sba.gov.

24. Joshua Hyatt, "The Real Secrets of Entrepreneurs," *Fortune*, 15 November 2004, 185–202.

25. Brian Headd, "Redefining Business Success: Distinguishing Between Closure and Failure," *Small Business Economics* 21, 51–61, 2003.

26. Hyatt, "The Real Secrets of Entrepreneurs."

27. Joel Spolsky, "Start-up Static," *Inc.*, March 2009, 33–34.

28. Bank of America website [accessed 1 April 2009] http://smallbusinessonlinecommunity.bankofamerica.com.

29. Microsoft Small Business Center [accessed 1 April 2009] www.microsoft.com/smallbusiness.

30. Christine Comaford-Lynch, "Don't Go It Alone: Create an Advisory Board," *BusinessWeek*, 1 February 2007 [accessed 4 July 2007] www.businessweek.com.

31. Green, "Self-Help for Startups."

32. National Business Incubation Association website [accessed 1 April 2009] www.nbia.com.

33. National Business Incubation Association website [accessed 1 April 2009] www.nbia.com; Center for Emerging Technologies website [accessed 1 April 2009] www.emergingtech.org; Stererotaxis website [accessed 1 April 2009] www.stereotaxis.com.

34. Paulette Thomas, "It's All Relative," *Wall Street Journal*, 29 November 2004, R4, R8.

35. Reed Albergotti, "Long Shot," *Wall Street Journal*, 29 November 2004, R4; Scarborough and Zimmerer, *Effective Small Business Management*, 439.

36. Bob Zider, "How Venture Capital Works," *Harvard Business Review*, November/December 1998, 131–139.

37. Association for Enterprise Opportunity website [accessed 1 April 2009] www.microenterpriseworks.org.

38. Anjali Cordeiro, "Microlenders Widen Their Client Base," *Wall Street Journal*, 31 March 2009 [accessed 1 April 2009] http://online.wsj.com.

39. National Venture Capital Association website [accessed 1 April 2009] www.nvca.org.

40. "Angel Investor Directory," *Inc.*, [accessed 1 April 2009] www.inc.com; William Payne, "What to Expect from Angel Networks," *American Venture*, September/October 2004, 38–39; Kaufman Foundation, "Business Angel Investing Groups Growing in North America," October 2002 [accessed 21 February 2005] www.angelcapitalassociation.org.

41. David Port, "APR Hikes Ambush Biz Owners," *Entrepreneur*, 16 March 2009 [accessed 1 April 2009] www.entrepreneur.com; Bobbie Gossage, "Charging Ahead," *Inc.*, January 2004 [accessed 1 April 2009] www.inc.com.

42. U.S. Small Business Administration website [accessed 1 April 2009] www.sba.gov.

43. U.S. Small Business Administration website [accessed 1 April 2009] www.sba.gov.

44. Eddy Goldberg, "The Basics of Franchising," Franchising.com [accessed 1 April 2009] www.franchising.com; Sarah Max, "The Franchising Way to Grow," *BusinessWeek*, 5 December 2008 [accessed 1 April 2009] www.businessweek.com.

45. Douglas MacMillan, "Franchise Owners Go to Court," *BusinessWeek*, 29 January 2007 [accessed 4 July 2007] www.businessweek.com; Jill Lerner, "UPS Store Dispute Escalating," *Atlanta Business Chronicle*, 24 February 2006 [accessed 4 July 2007] www.bizjournals.com.

46. Franchising.com [accessed 1 April 2009] www.franchising.com; "Frequently Asked Questions–Qualifications," McDonald's website [accessed 1 April 2009] www.aboutmcdonalds.com.

47. Amey Stone, "Before You Ink That Contract . . ." *BusinessWeek*, 14 April 2005 [accessed 3 July 2007] www.businessweek.com.

48. See note 1.

Chapter 7

1. Adapted from Wegmans website [accessed 3 April 2009] www.wegmans.com; "100 Best Companies to Work For," *Fortune* [accessed 3 April 2009] http://money.cnn.com/magazines/fortune; Matthew Boyle, "The Wegmans Way," *Fortune*, 24 January 2005 [accessed 11 August 2007] www.fortune.com; William Conroy, "Rochester, N.Y.-Based Grocer Tops Magazine's Best Employer Rankings," *Asbury Park* (NJ) *Press*, 11 January 2005 [accessed 8 March 2005] www.ebsco.com; Matthew Boyle, "The Wegmans Way," *Fortune*, 24 January 2005, 62–68; "UCCNet Designated as U.S. Data Pool of Choice by Leading Retailers," UCCNet website [accessed 8 March 2005] www.uccnet.org; Joy Davis, "Caring for Employees Is Wegmans' Best Selling Point," *Democrat and Chronicle* (Rochester, NY), 6 February 2005 [accessed 8 March 2005] www.democratandchronicle.com; Michael A. Prospero, "Employee Innovator: Wegmans," *Fast Company*, October 2004, 88; Matt Glynn, "Employees of Rochester, N.Y.-Based Grocer Celebrate Firm's Top Ranking," *Buffalo* (NY) *News*, 11 January 2005 [accessed 8 March 2005] www.ebsco.com.

2. Richard L. Daft, *Management,* 6th ed. (Mason, Ohio: Thompson South-Western, 2003), 5.

3. Anne Fisher, "Starting a New Job? Don't Blow It," *Fortune*, 24 February 2005 [accessed 26 February 2005] www.fortune.com.

4. Daniel S. Cochran, Fred R. David, and C. Kendrick Gibson, "A Framework for Developing an Effective Mission Statement," *Journal of Business Strategies*, Fall 2008, 27–39.

5. Welch Allyn website [accessed 4 April 2009] www.welchallyn.com.

6. Northrop Grumman website [accessed 4 April 2009] www.northropgrumman.com.

7. Enterprise Rent-A-Car Careers website [accessed 4 April 2009] www.erac.com.

8. Datamonitor, "Cabot Corporation SWOT Analysis" [accessed 3 April 2009] www.ebsco.com.

9. "Cabot Corporation SWOT Analysis."

10. "Cabot Corporation SWOT Analysis."

11. "Cabot Corporation SWOT Analysis."

12. Barbara Kiviat, "The End of Management?" *Time Bonus Section: Inside Business*, August 2004.

13. Dean Foust, "Speaking up for the Organization Man," *BusinessWeek*, 9 March 2009, 78.

14. Steve Arneson, "Lead from the Middle," *Leadership Excellence*, March 2008, 19.

15. Daft, *Management*, 13.

16. Daft, *Management*, 514–515.

17. "Sometimes, EQ Is More Important Than IQ," CNN.com, 14 January 2005 [accessed 14 January 2005] www.cnn.com; Daniel Goleman, "What Makes a Leader?" *Harvard Business Review*, November–December 1998, 92–102; Shari Caudron, "The Hard Case for Soft Skills," *Workforce*, July 1999, 60–66.

18. James G. Clawson, *Level Three Leadership: Getting Below the Surface*, 2nd ed. (Upper Saddle River, N.J.: Prentice Hall, 2003), 116.

19. Cary Cherniss, "Emotional Intelligence: What It Is and Why It Matters," Consortium for Research on Emotional Intelligence in Organizations website [accessed 4 April 2009] www.eiconsortium.com.

20. Cherniss, "Emotional Intelligence: What It Is and Why It Matters."

21. Daniel Goleman, "Leadership That Gets Results," *Harvard Business Review*, March–April 2000, 78–90.

22. Patricia Sellers, "eBay's Secret," *Fortune*, 18 October 2004, 161–178; Nick Wingfield, "Auctioneer to the World," *Wall Street Journal*, 5 August 2004, B1, B6.

23. Wegmans website [accessed 3 April 2009] www.wegmans.com.

24. Jeffrey D. Ford and Laurie W. Ford, "Decoding Resistance to Change," *Harvard Business Review*, April 2009, 99–103; Daft, *Management*, 382; Stephen Robbins and David DeCenzo, *Fundamentals of Management*, 4th ed. (Upper Saddle River, N.J.: Prentice Hall, 2003), 209.

25. Robbins and DeCenzo, *Fundamentals of Management*, 211; Daft, *Management*, 384, 396.

26. Robbins and DeCenzo, *Fundamentals of Management*, 210–211.

27. Ford and Ford, "Decoding Resistance to Change."

28. Paul Hebert, "People Don't Hate Change—They Hate You Trying to Change Them," Fistful of Talent blog, 6 April 2009 [accessed 7 April 2009] www.fistfuloftalent.com.

29. "High Standards," video, Wegmans website [accessed 3 April 2009] www.wegmans.com.

30. The Benchmarking Exchange website [accessed 9 August 2007] www.benchnet.com.

31. "Extreme Benchmarking," *Business 2.0*, April 2006, 81.

32. Kevin J. Gregson, "Converting Strategy to Results," *American Venture*, September/October 2004, 16–18.

33. Dean Foust, "US Airways: After the 'Miracle on the Hudson,'" *BusinessWeek*, 2 March 2009, 31.

34. Foust, "US Airways: After the 'Miracle on the Hudson.'"

35. Robert E. Kaplan and Robert B. Kaiser, "Developing Versatile Leadership," *MIT Sloan Management Review*, Summer 2003, 19–26.

36. Courtland L. Bovée and John V. Thill, *Business Communication Today*, 9th ed. (Upper Saddle River, N.J.: Pearson Prentice Hall, 2008), 4.

37. Holly Ocasio Rizzo, "Patently Successful," *Hispanic Business*, April 2007, 34–36.

38. Geoff Gloeckler, "The Case Against Case Studies," *BusinessWeek*, 4 February 2008, 66–67.

39. See note 1.

Chapter 8

1. The Container Store website [accessed 14 April 2009] www.containerstore.com; "100 Best Companies to Work For," *Fortune* [accessed 14 April 2009] www.fortune.com; Bob Nelson, "Can't Contain Excitement at The Container Store," BizJournals.com [accessed 11 March 2005] www.bizjournals.com; Mike Duff, "Top-Shelf Employees Keep Container Store on Track," *DSN Retailing Today*, 8 March 2004, 7, 49; Bob Nelson, "The Buzz at The Container Store," *Corporate Meetings & Incentives*, June 2003, 32; Jennifer Saba, "Balancing Act," *Potentials*, 1 October 2003 [accessed 15 April 2004] www.highbeam.com; Peter S. Cohan, "Corporate Heroes," *Financial Executive*, 1 March 2003 [accessed 15 April 2004] www.highbeam.com; Margaret Steen, "Container Store's Focus on Training a Strong Appeal to Employees," *Mercury News* (San Jose, Calif.), 6 November 2003 [accessed 15 April 2004] www.highbeam.com; Holly Hayes, "Container Store Brings Clutter Control to San Jose, Calif.," *Mercury News* (San Jose, Calif.), 17 October 2003, 1F; "Performance Through People Award," press release, 10 September 2003; David Lipke, "Container Store's CEO: People Are Most Valued Asset," *HFN*, 13 January 2003 [accessed 9 March 2003] www.highbeam.com; Lorrie Grant, "Container Store's Workers Huddle Up to Help You Out," 30 April 2002, *USA Today*, B1.

2. "Benefits of Outsourcing Payroll," *Practical Accountant*, November 2008, SR9.

3. "Disney Consumer Electronics," case study, Frog Design [accessed 8 April 2009] www.frogdesign.com.

4. Stephen P. Robbins and David A. DeCenzo, *Management*, 4th ed. (Upper Saddle River, N.J.: Pearson Prentice Hall, 2004), 142–143.

5. Charles R. Greer and W. Richard Plunkett, *Supervision: Diversity and Teams in the Workplace*, 10th ed. (Upper Saddle River, N.J.: Prentice Hall, 2003), 77.

6. Caroline Ellis, "The Flattening Corporation," *MIT Sloan Management Review*, Summer 2003, 5.

7. Gareth R. Jones, *Organizational Theory, Design, and Change*, 4th ed. (Upper Saddle River, N.J.: Pearson Prentice Hall, 2004), 109.

8. Jones, *Organizational Theory, Design, and Change*, 109–111.

9. Richard L. Daft, *Management*, 6th ed. (Mason, Ohio: Thompson South-Western, 2003), 320.

10. Jones, *Organizational Theory, Design, and Change*, 163.

11. Jones, *Organizational Theory, Design, and Change*, 167.

12. "Our Businesses," Chevron website [accessed 8 April 2009] www.chevron.com.

13. Daft, *Management*, 324–327.

14. Jerald Greenberg and Robert A. Baron, *Behavior in Organizations*, 8th ed. (Upper Saddle River, N.J.: Prentice Hall, 2003), 558–560; Daft, *Management*, 329.

15. Robert D. Hof, "Yahoo's Bartz Shows Who's Boss," *BusinessWeek*, 2 March 2009 [accessed 8 April 2009] www.businessweek.com.

16. Pete Engardio and Bruce Einhorn, "Outsourcing Innovation," *BusinessWeek*, 21 March 2005, 84–94.

17. Stephen P. Robbins, *Essentials of Organizational Behavior*, 6th ed. (Upper Saddle River, N.J.: Prentice Hall, 2000), 105.

18. Greer and Plunkett, *Supervision*, 293.

19. "Attacking Claim Denials," *Receivables Report for America's Health Care Financial Managers*, October 2007, 1–6.

20. Steven A. Frankforter and Sandra L. Christensen, "Finding Competitive Advantage in Self-Managed Work Teams," *Business Forum* 27, no. 1 (2005): 20–24.

21. Daft, *Management*, 594; Robbins and DeCenzo, *Fundamentals of Management*, 336.

22. Daft, *Management*, 618; Robbins and DeCenzo, *Fundamentals of Management*, 262.

23. Morten T. Hansen, "When Internal Collaboration Is Bad for Your Company," *Harvard Business Review*, April 2009, 82–88.

24. Jerry Fjermestad, "Virtual Leadership for a Virtual Workforce," *Chief Learning Officer*, March 2009, 36–39.

25. Jenny Goodbody, "Critical Success Factors for Global Virtual Teams," *Strategic Communication Management*, February/March 2005, 18–21; Ann Majchrzak, Arvind Malhotra, Jeffrey Stamps, and Jessica Lipnack, "Can Absence Make a Team Grow Stronger?" *Harvard Business Review*, May 2004, 131–137.

26. Christopher Carfi and Leif Chastaine, "Social Networking for Businesses & Organizations," white paper, Cerado website [accessed 13 August 2008] www.cerado.com.

27. "Caterpillar—Collaboration Through Communities of Practice," video, Community Intelligence [accessed 8 April 2009] www.community-intelligence.com; David Pescovitz, "Technology of the Year: Social Network Applications," *Business 2.0*, November 2003, 113–114.

28. Robbins and DeCenzo, *Fundamentals of Management*, 257–258; Daft, *Management*, 634–636.

29. "Groups Best at Complex Problems," *Industrial Engineer*, June 2006, 14.

30. Robert Kreitner, *Management*, 9th ed. (Boston: Houghton Mifflin, 2004), 475–481; Daft, *Management*, 635–636.

31. Lynda Gratton and Tamara J. Erickson, "8 Ways to Build Collaborative Teams," *Harvard Business Review*, November 2007, 100–109.

32. Jon R. Katzenbach and Douglas K. Smith, "The Discipline of Teams," *Harvard Business Review*, July/August 2005, 162–171; Laird Mealiea and Ramon Baltazar, "A Strategic Guide for Building Effective Teams," *Public Personnel Management*, Summer 2005, 141–160; Larry Cole and Michael Cole, "Why Is the Teamwork Buzz Word Not Working?" *Communication World*, February/March 1999, 29; Patricia Buhler, "Managing in the 90s: Creating Flexibility in Today's Workplace," *Supervision*, January 1997, 24+; Allison W. Amason, Allen C. Hochwarter, Wayne A. Thompson, and Kenneth R. Harrison, "Conflict: An Important Dimension in Successful Management Teams," *Organizational Dynamics*, Autumn 1995, 20+.

33. Jared Sandberg, "Some Ideas Are So Bad That Only a Team Effort Can Account for Them," *Wall Street Journal*, 29 September 2004, B1.

34. Mark K. Smith, "Bruce W. Tuckman—Forming, Storming, Norming, and Performing in Groups," Infed.org [accessed 5 July 2005] www.infed.org; Robbins and DeCenzo, *Fundamentals of Management*, 258–259; Daft, *Management*, 625–627.

35. Jones, *Organizational Theory, Design, and Change*, 112–113; Greenberg and Baron, *Behavior in Organizations*, 280–281; Daft, *Management*, 629–631.

36. Andy Boynton and Bill Fischer, *Virtuoso Teams: Lessons from Teams That Changed Their Worlds* (Harrow, UK: FT Prentice Hall, 2005), 10.

37. Thomas K. Capozzoli, "Conflict Resolution—A Key Ingredient in Successful Teams," *Supervision*, November 1999, 14–16.

38. Daft, *Management*, 631–632.

39. "Better Meetings Benefit Everyone: How to Make Yours More Productive," *Working Communicator Bonus Report*, July 1998, 1.

40. Cyrus Farivar, "How to Run an Effective Meeting," BNET website [accessed 12 August 2008] www.bnet.com.

41. "Better Meetings Benefit Everyone."

42. Steve Lohr, "As Travel Costs Rise, More Meetings Go Virtual," *New York Times*, 22 July 2008 [accessed 23 July 2008] www.nytimes.com.

43. IBM Jam program website [accessed 7 April 2009] www.collaborationjam.com; "Big Blue Brainstorm," *BusinessWeek*, 7 August 2006 [accessed 15 August 2006] www.businessweek.com; Roger O. Crockett, "The 21st Century Meeting," *BusinessWeek*, 26 February 2007, 72–79.

44. See note 1.

Chapter 9

1. Carvin website [accessed 4 June 2009] www.carvin.com; Carvin MySpace page [accessed 4 June 2009] www.myspace.com/officialcarvin; "Carvin AW175" (product reviews), Harmony Central website [accessed 18 March 2005] www.harmonycentral.com; "Carvin CT6M California Carved Top," *Guitar Player*, December 2004 [accessed 18 March 2005] www.guitarplayer.com; Rich Krechel, "Some Custom-made Guitars Can Cost $4,000 to $8,000," *St. Louis Post Dispatch*, 27 September 2001, 16.

2. Lawrence M. Fisher, "The Prophet of Unintended Consequences," *Strategy+Business*, Fall 2005, 78–89.

3. Adapted in part from Russell L. Ackoff, "Why Few Organizations Adopt Systems Thinking," Ackoff Center Weblog, 7 March 2007 [accessed 23 June 2007] http://ackoffcenter.blogs.com; Daniel Aronson, "Introduction to Systems Thinking," The Thinking Page website [accessed 21 June 2007] www.thinking.net; "What Is Systems Thinking?" The Systems Thinker website [accessed 21 June 2007] www.thesystemsthinker.com; Peter Senge, *The Fifth Discipline: The Art and Practice of the Learning Organization* (New York: Doubleday, 1994), 57–67.

4. Stephen P. Robbins and David A. DeCenzo, *Fundamentals of Management*, 4th ed. (Upper Saddle River, N.J.: Pearson Prentice Hall, 2004), 405.

5. Peter Fingar and Ronald Aronica, "Value Chain Optimization: The New Way of Competing," *Supply Chain Management Review*, September–October 2001, 82–85.

6. Michael V. Copeland and Andrew Tilin, "The Instant Company," *Business 2.0*, June 2005, 82–94.

7. Jeffrey Rothfeder, "Bumpy Ride," *Portfolio*, May 2009 [accessed 23 June 2009] www.portfolio.com.

8. Alan S. Brown, "A Shift in Engineering Offshore," *Mechanical Engineering*, March 2009, 24–29.

9. William T. Dickens and Stephen J. Rose, "Blinder Baloney," *The International Economy*, Fall 2007, 18+.

10. "Supply Chain News: The Seven Timeless Challenges of Supply Chain Management," *SupplyChainDigest*, 2 June 2009 [accessed 6 June 2009] www.scdigest.com.

11. Phil Fersht, Dana Stiffler, and Kevin O'Marah, "The Ins and Outs of Offshoring," *Supply Chain Management Review*, March 2009, 10–11.

12. Ajay K. Goel, Nazgol Moussavi, and Vats N. Srivatsan, "Time to Rethink Offshoring?" *McKinsey Quarterly*, 2008 Issue 4, 108–111; Anita Hawser, "Offshoring Industry Faces New Opponent: Its Clients," *Global Finance*, November 2007, 6; Brown, "A Shift in Engineering Offshore."

13. Brown, "A Shift in Engineering Offshore."

14. John Ferreira and Len Prokopets, "Does Offshoring Still Make Sense?" *Supply Chain Management Review*, January/February 2009, 20–27.

15. Dan Gilmore, "Can—and Should—Western Manufacturing Be Saved?" *SupplyChainDigest*, 28 May 2009 [accessed 5 June 2009] www.scdigest.com.

16. Ferreira and Prokopets, "Does Offshoring Still Make Sense?"

17. Geri Smith and Justin Bachman, "The Offshoring of Airplane Care," *BusinessWeek*, 10 April 2008 [accessed 5 June 2009] www.businessweek.com; Susan Carey and Alex Frangos, "Airlines, Facing Cost Pressure, Outsource Crucial Safety Tasks," *Wall Street Journal*, 21 January 2005, A1, A5.

18. Bruce Constantine, Brian Ruwadi, and Josh Wine, "Management Practices That Drive Supply Chain Success," *McKinsey Quarterly*, 2009 Issue 2, 24–26.

19. Tim Laseter and Keith Oliver, "When Will Supply Chain Management Grow Up?" *Strategy+Business*, Fall 2003,

32–36; Robert J. Trent, "What Everyone Needs to Know About SCM," *Supply Chain Management Review*, 1 March 2004 [accessed 16 April 2004] www.manufacturing.net.

20. Joann Muller, "A Savior from the East," *Forbes*, 4 June 2007, 112–113; Jeffrey K. Liker and Thomas Y. Choi, "Building Deeper Supplier Relationships," *Harvard Business Review*, December 2004, 104–113.

21. Trent, "What Everyone Needs to Know About SCM."

22. Andrew Feller, Dan Shunk, and Tom Callarman, "Value Chains Versus Supply Chains," *BPTrends*, March 2006 [accessed 24 June 2007] www.bptrends.com.

23. Lee J. Krajewski and Larry P. Ritzman, *Operations Management: Processes and Value Chains*, 7th ed. (Upper Saddle River, N.J.: Pearson Prentice Hall, 2005), 744.

24. Malcolm Wheatley and Kevin Parker, "Rise in Global Enterprise Deployments Seen as Response to Far-Flung Supply Networks," *Manufacturing Business Technology*, May 2007, 26–27.

25. Krajewski and Ritzman, *Operations Management: Processes and Value Chains*, 299–300.

26. Russell and Taylor, *Operations Management: Focusing on Quality and Competitiveness*, 161.

27. Krajewski and Ritzman, *Operations Management: Processes and Value Chains*, 244–245.

28. Robert Kreitner, *Management*, 9th ed. (Boston: Houghton Mifflin, 2004), 202–203.

29. Krajewski and Ritzman, *Operations Management: Processes and Value Chains*, 482–483.

30. Pete Engardio and Jean McGregor, "Lean and Mean Gets Extreme," *BusinessWeek*, 23 March 2009, 60–62.

31. Russell and Taylor, *Operations Management: Focusing on Quality and Competitiveness*, 511.

32. Kenneth Korane, "Mass Production òut, Mass Customization in," *Machine Design*, 21 August 2009, S2–S4.

33. "To Err Is Human—To Delay Is Deadly," *Consumers Union*, May 2009 [accessed 6 June 2009] www.safepatientproject.org; Alan Young, "Healing Corrupted by Practices of Big Pharma," *Toronto Star*, 11 April 2004 [accessed 17 April 2004] www.highbeam.com; Kathleen Longcore, "Group Aims to Fix Medical Mistakes, Shorten Recovery with Technology," *Grand Rapids Press* (Grand Rapids, MI), 3 April 2004 [accessed 17 April 2004] www.highbeam.com.

34. Mark Davis, Nicholas Aquilano, and Richard Chase, *Fundamentals of Operations Management*, 4th ed. (Burr Ridge, Ill.: McGraw Hill/Irwin, 2003), 177–179; Russell and Taylor, *Operations Management*, 131.

35. Russell and Taylor, *Operations Management*, 131.

36. "Idea: Kaizen," *Economist*, 14 April 2009 [accessed 6 June 2009] www.economist.com.

37. Thomas A. Stewart and Anand P. Ramand, "Lessons from Toyota's Long Drive," *Harvard Business Review*, July–August 2007, 74–83.

38. Dale H. Besterfield, Carol Besterfield-Michna, Glen H. Besterfield, and Mary Besterfield-Sacre, *Total Quality Management*, 3rd ed. (Upper Saddle River, N.J.: Pearson Prentice Hall, 2003), 2–3.

39. Leland Teschler, "TQM Comes Down to Earth," *Machine Design*, 14 September 2006, 8; Besterfield, et al., *Total Quality Management*, 10–13.

40. John McQuaig, "Whatever Happened to TQM?" *Wenatchee Business Journal*, October 2004, C8.

41. Steven Minter, "Six Sigma's Growing Pains," *IndustryWeek*, May 2009, 34–36; Tom McCarty, "Six Sigma at Motorola," *EuropeanCEO*, September–October 2004 [accessed 21 March 2005] www.motorola.com.

42. McCarty, "Six Sigma at Motorola"; General Electric, "What Is Six Sigma?" GE website [accessed 21 March 2005] www.ge.com.

43. Timothy Stansfield and Ronda Massey, "A Remedy to Fad Fatigue," *Industrial Management*, March 2007, 26–30; Brian Hindo, "Six Sigma: So Yesterday?" *BusinessWeek*, 11 June 2007 [accessed 26 June 2007] www.businessweek.com.

44. International Organization for Standardization website [accessed 6 June 2009] www.iso.org.

45. See note 1.

46. Adapted from National Nanotechnology Initiative website [accessed 28 June 2007] www.nano.gov; Project on Emerging Nanotechnologies website [accessed 28 June 2007] www.nanotechproject.org; Barnaby J. Feder, "Technology: Bashful vs. Brash in the New Field of Nanotech," *New York Times*, 15 March 2004 [accessed 16 April 2004] www.nytimes.com; "Nanotechnology Basics," Nanotechnology Now website [accessed 16 April 2004] www.nanotech-now.com; Center for Responsible Nanotechnology website [accessed 16 April 2004] www.crnano.org; Gary Stix, "Little Big Science," *Scientific American*, 16 September 2001 [accessed 16 April 2004] www.sciam.com; Tim Harper, "Small Wonders," *Business 2.0*, July 2002 [accessed 16 April 2004] www.business2.com; Erick Schonfeld, "A Peek at IBM's Nanotech Research," *Business 2.0*, 5 December 2003 [accessed 16 April 2004] www.business2.com; David Pescovitz, "The Best New Technologies of 2003," *Business 2.0*, November 2003, 109–116.

Chapter 10

1. Cathy Benko, "Up the Ladder? How Dated, How Linear," *New York Times*, 9 November 2008 [accessed 18 June 2009] www.deloitteandtouche.org; Mass Career Customization website [accessed 17 June 2009] www.masscareercustomization.com; Anne Fisher, "When Gen X Runs the Show," *Time*, 25 May 2009, 48–49; Lisa Takeuchi Cullen, "Flex Work Is Not the Answer," Work in Progress blog, 10 October 2007 [accessed 17 June 2009] http://workinprogress.blogs.time.com; Laura Fitzpatrick, "We're Getting off the Ladder," *Time*, 5 May 2009, 45; "Customizing Your Career," Deloitte website [accessed 17 June 2009] http://careers.deloitte.com; "Mass Career Customization," PBWC Connections website [accessed 17 June 2009] www.pbwcconnections.com; Intel Corporation website [accessed 17 June 2009] www.intel.com; "Intel Corporation," Hoovers [accessed 17 June 2009] www.hoovers.com.

2. Piers Steel and Cornelius J. König, "Integrating Theories of Motivation," *Academy of Management Review* 31, no. 4 (2006): 889–913.

3. Nitin Nohria, Boris Groysberg, and Linda-Eling Lee, "Employee Motivation: A Powerful New Model," *Harvard Business Review*, July–August 2008, 78–84.

4. Nohria, Groysberg, and Lee, "Employee Motivation: A Powerful New Model."

5. Nohria, Groysberg, and Lee, "Employee Motivation: A Powerful New Model."

6. Robbins and DeCenzo, *Fundamentals of Management*, 27–29.

7. Andrew J. DuBrin, *Applying Psychology: Individual & Organizational Effectiveness*, 6th ed. (Upper Saddle River, N.J.: Pearson Prentice Hall, 2004), 122–124.

8. Stephen P. Robbins and Mary Coulter, *Management*, 10th ed. (Upper Saddle River, N.J.: Pearson Prentice Hall, 2009), 342.

9. Richard L. Daft, *Management*, 6th ed. (Mason, Ohio: Thomson South-Western, 2003), 547; Robbins and DeCenzo, *Fundamentals of Management*, 283–284; DuBrin, *Applying Psychology: Individual & Organizational Effectiveness*, 15–16.

10. Stephen P. Robbins and Timothy A. Judge, *Essentials of Organizational Behavior*, 10th ed. (Upper Saddle River, N.J.: Pearson Prentice Hall, 2010), 64.

11. Richard L. Daft, "Theory Z: Opening the Corporate Door for Participative Management," *Academy of Management Executive*, November 2004, 117–121.

12. Daft, *Management*, 552–553.

13. Robbins and Judge, *Essentials of Organizational Behavior*, 66.

14. Rosa Chun and Gary Davies, "Employee Happiness Isn't Enough to Satisfy Customers," *Harvard Business Review*, April 2009, 19; Robbins and Judge, *Essentials of Organizational Behavior*, 66.

15. Saundra K. Ciccarelli and Glenn E. Meyer, *Psychology* (Upper Saddle River, N.J.: Prentice Hall, 2006), 339–340.

16. "Seeking to Hire Strong Leaders? Buyer Beware!" *Compensation & Benefits for Law Offices*, September 2006, 1+.

17. David C. McClelland and David H. Burnham, "Power Is the Great Motivator," *Harvard Business Review*, January 2003, 117–126; Robbins and Judge, *Essentials of Organizational Behavior*, 66–67.

18. Robbins and Judge, *Essentials of Organizational Behavior*, 67.

19. Robbins and DeCenzo, *Fundamentals of Management*, 289.

20. Robbins and Judge, *Essentials of Organizational Behavior*, 72.

21. Daft, *Management*, 554–555.

22. Eryn Brown, "How to Get Paid What You're Worth," *Business 2.0*, May 2004, 102–110.

23. Robbins and Judge, *Essentials of Organizational Behavior*, 75.

24. Deborah Archambeault, Christopher M. Burgess, and Stan Davis, "Is Something Missing from Your Company's Satisfaction Package?" *CMA Management*, May 2009, 20–23.

25. Robbins and Coulter, *Management*, 346.

26. Bill Lycette and John Herniman, "New Goal-Setting Theory," *Industrial Management*, September 2008, 25–30; Robbins and Coulter, *Management*, 346–347.

27. Patricia O'Connel, "Companies' Secret Weapon: Underutilized Executives," *BusinessWeek*, 2 March 2009, 14.

28. Robbins and Coulter, *Management*, 346.

29. Lisa Ordóñez, Maurice Schweitzer, Adam Galinsky, and Max Bazerman, "Goals Gone Wild: The Systematic Side Effects of Overprescribing Goal Setting," *Academy of Management Perspectives*, February 2009, 6–16.

30. Robert D. Ramsey, "Why Deadlines and Quotas Don't Always Work," *Supervision*, October 2008, 3–5.

31. Richard J. Hackman and Greg R. Oldman, "Motivation Through the Design of Work: Test of a Theory,"

Organizational Behavior & Human Performance, August 1976, 250–279; Robbins and Judge, *Essentials of Organizational Behavior*, 81–82; Jed DeVaro, Robert Li, and Dana Brookshire, "Analysing the Job Characteristics Model: New Support from a Cross-Section of Establishments," *International Journal of Human Resource Management*, June 2007, 986–1003.

32. Robbins and Judge, *Essentials of Organizational Behavior*, 82.

33. Stuart D. Galup, Gary Klein, and James J. Jiang, "The Impacts of Job Characteristics on IS Employee Satisfaction: A Comparison Between Permanent and Temporary Employees," *Journal of Computer Information Systems*, Summer 2008, 58–68.

34. Robbins and Coulter, *Management*, 348.

35. Scott Lazenby, "How to Motivate Employees: What Research Is Telling Us," *Public Management*, September 2008, 22–25.

36. Robbins and Coulter, *Management*, 348.

37. "Caution Urged in Expanding Cross-Training of CU Staff," *Credit Union Journal*, 5 January 2009, 18.

38. Debi O'Donovan, "Motivation Is Key in a Crisis and Words Can Be the Best Reward," *Employee Benefits*, April 2009, 5.

39. Timothy R. Hinkin and Chester A. Schriesheim, "Performance Incentives for Tough Times," *Harvard Business Review*, March 2009, 26.

40. Tom Washington, "Incentives Play Big Part in Motivation During Recession," *Employee Benefits*, April 2009, 14.

41. Ciccarelli and Meyer, *Psychology*, 179.

42. Robbins and Coulter, *Management*, 348.

43. Dan Heath and Chip Heath, "The Curse of Incentives," *Fast Company*, February 2009, 48–49.

44. "Tailor Motivation Techniques to the Worker," *Teller Vision*, March 2009, 5–6.

45. Nohria, Groysberg, and Lee, "Employee Motivation: A Powerful New Model."

46. Edward E. Lawler III, "Value-Based Motivation," *BusinessWeek*, 27 April 2009, 22.

47. Joan Lloyd, "Threat of Layoffs Demoralizes Employees," *Receivables Report for America's Health Care Financial Managers*, May 2009, 10–11.

48. Lawler, "Value-Based Motivation."

49. Betty MacLaughlin Frandsen, "Overcoming Workplace Negativity," *Long-Term Living: For the Continuing Care Professional*, March 2009, 26–27.

50. "Don't Be a Drag," *CA Magazine*, January–February 2009, 9.

Chapter 11

1. Adapted from "Starbucks Company Fact Sheet," Starbucks website [accessed 23 June 2009] www

.starbucks.com; "Starbucks Corporation," Hoovers [accessed 23 June 2009] www .hoovers.com; "Mr. Coffee," *Context*, August–September 2001, 20–25; Jennifer Ordonez, "Starbucks' Schultz to Leave Top Post, Lead Global Effort," *Wall Street Journal*, 7 April 2000, B3; Karyn Strauss, "Howard Schultz: Starbucks' CEO Serves a Blend of Community, Employee Commitment," *Nation's Restaurant News*, January 2000, 162–163; Carla Joinson, "The Cost of Doing Business?" *HR Magazine*, December 1999, 86–92; "Interview with Howard Schultz: Sharing Success," *Executive Excellence*, November 1999, 16–17; Kelly Barron, "The Cappuccino Conundrum," *Forbes*, 22 February 1999, 54–55; Naomi Weiss, "How Starbucks Impassions Workers to Drive Growth," *Workforce*, August 1998, 60–64; Scott S. Smith, "Grounds for Success," *Entrepreneur*, May 1998, 120–126; "Face Value: Perky People," *The Economist*, 30 May 1998, 66; Howard Schultz and Dori Jones Yang, "Starbucks: Making Values Pay," *Fortune*, 29 September 1997, 261–272.

2. Gary Dessler, *A Framework for Human Resource Management*, 3rd ed. (Upper Saddle River, N.J.: Pearson Prentice Hall, 2004), 2.

3. Dessler, *A Framework for Human Resource Management*, 66.

4. Dessler, *A Framework for Human Resource Management*, 72.

5. Dessler, *A Framework for Human Resource Management*, 74–75.

6. Shari Randall, "Succession Planning Is More Than a Game of Chance," *Workforce Management* [accessed 1 May 2004] www.workforce.com.

7. Anne Fisher, "When Gen X Runs the Show," *Time*, 25 May 2009, 48–49.

8. "More Than One in 10 Employees Do Some Telecommuting," *HR Focus*, June 2009, 9; "2008 100 Best Companies," *Working Mother* [accessed 20 June 2009] www.workingmother.com.

9. Clare Brennan, "What Is Job-Sharing?" iVillage [accessed 31 March 2005] www .ivillage.co.uk.

10. Nancy R. Lockwood, "Workplace Diversity: Leveraging the Power of Difference for Competitive Advantage," *HR Magazine*, June 2005, special section 1–10.

11. Podcast interview with Ron Glover, IBM website [accessed 17 August 2008] www.ibm.com.

12. Peter Coy, "Old. Smart. Productive." *BusinessWeek*, 27 June 2005 [accessed 24 August 2006] www.businessweek .com; Iris Beamer and Linda Varner, *Intercultural Communication in the Global Workplace*, 3rd ed. (Columbus, Ohio: McGraw-Hill/Irwin, 2004), 107–108.

13. Beamer and Varner, *Intercultural Communication in the Global Workplace*, 107–108.

14. Nancy Sutton Bell and Marvin Narz, "Meeting the Challenges of Age Diversity in the Workplace," *The CPA Journal*, February 2007 [accessed 17 August 2008] www.nysscpa.org.

15. "Sex-Based Charges: FY 1997–FY 2008," EEOC website [accessed 21 June 2009] www.eeoc.gov.

16. "Highlights of Women's Earnings in 2007," October 2008, U.S. Bureau of Labor Statistics, 1.

17. "Women CEOs of the Fortune 1000," June 2009, Catalyst website [accessed 21 June 2009] www.catalyst.org.

18. Gretchen Morgenson, "Working Girls," *New Republic*, 19 March 2007, 56–59; Francine D. Blau and Lawrence M. Kahn, "The Gender Pay Gap: Have Women Gone as Far as They Can?" *Academy of Management Perspectives*, February 2007, 7–23.

19. "Sexual Harassment Charges: EEOC & FEPAs Combined: FY 1997–FY 2006," EEOC website [accessed 13 August 2007] www.eeoc.gov.

20. Robert Kreitner, *Management*, 9th ed. (Boston: Houghton Mifflin, 2004), 375–377; "One-Fifth of Women Are Harassed Sexually," *HR Focus*, April 2002, 2.

21. "Race-Based Charges: FY 1997–FY 2008," EEOC website [accessed 21 June 2009] www.eeoc.gov.

22. "Usual Weekly Earnings of Wage and Salary Workers: First Quarter 2009," U.S. Bureau of Labor Statistics, 16 April 2009 [accessed 21 June 2009] www.bls.gov.

23. Mark D. Downey, "Keeping the Faith," *HR Magazine*, January 2008, 85–88.

24. Vadim Liberman, "What Happens When an Employee's Freedom of Religion Crosses Paths with a Company's Interests?" *Conference Board Review*, September/October 2007, 42–48.

25. "Diversity 3.0," IBM website [accessed 21 June 2009] www.ibm.com; Wendy Harris, "Out of the Corporate Closet," *Black Enterprise* [accessed 13 August 2007] http://integrate.factivia.com; David A. Thomas, "Diversity as Strategy," *Harvard Business Review*, September 2004, 98–108; Joe Mullich, "Hiring Without Limits," *Workforce Management*, June 2004, 53–58; Mike France and William G. Symonds, "Diversity Is About to Get More Elusive, Not Less," *BusinessWeek*, 7 July 2003 [accessed 24 January 2005] www.businessweek.com; Anne Papmehl, "Diversity in Workforce Paying Off, IBM Finds," *Toronto Star*, 7 October 2002 [accessed 4 November 2003] www.elibrary.com.

26. Samuel Greengard, "Quality of Hire: How Companies Are Crunching the Numbers," *Workforce Management*, July 2004 [accessed 8 July 200] www.workforce.com.

27. Steven Mitchell Sack, "The Working Woman's Legal Survival Guide: Testing," FindLaw.com [accessed 22 February 2004] www.findlaw.com; David W. Arnold and John W. Jones, "Who the Devil's Applying Now?" *Security Management*, March 2002, 85–88.

28. Adam Cohen and Cathy Booth Thomas, "Inside a Layoff," *Time*, 16 April 2001, 38–40.

29. Challenger, Gray & Christmas website [accessed 18 August 2007] www.challengergray.com.

30. Russ Banham, "Age Bias Claims Rise," *Treasury & Risk*, May 2009, 14–15.

31. John Jude Moran, *Employment Law: New Challenges in the Business Environment*, 2nd ed. (Upper Saddle River, N.J.: Pearson Prentice Hall, 2002), 127; Dan Seligman, "The Right to Fire," *Forbes*, 10 November 2003, 126–128.

32. Pete Engardio, "Managing the New Workforce," *BusinessWeek*, 20 & 27 August 2007, 48–51.

33. Chris Isidore, "GM Offers Workers up to $140K to Leave," CNNMoney.com, 22 March 2006 [accessed 18 August 2007] http://money.cnn.com.

34. "The Age Discrimination in Employment Act of 1967," U.S. Equal Employment Opportunity Commission website [accessed 10 July 2009] www.eeoc.gov; Henry R. Cheeseman, *Contemporary Business and E-Commerce Law*, 7th ed. (Upper Saddle River, N.J.: Pearson Prentice Hall, 2010), 522–523.

35. Dessler, *A Framework for Human Resource Management*, 198.

36. PerformanceNow.com website [accessed 2 May 2004] www.performancenow.com; Dessler, *A Framework for Human Resource Management*, 199.

37. Tracy Gallagher, "360-Degree Performance Reviews Offer Valuable Perspectives," *Financial Executive*, December 2008, 61.

38. Dessler, *A Framework for Human Resource Management*, 198–199.

39. Andrew E. Jackson, "Recognizing the 'I' in Team," *Industrial Engineer*, March 2005, 38–42.

40. Jeff St. John, "Kennewick, Wash., 'Snoop' Software Maker Also Protects Privacy," *Tri-City Herald* (Kennewick, Wash.), 17 April 2004 [accessed 2 May 2004] www.highbeam.com; Dessler, *A Framework for Human Resource Management*, 204–205.

41. Margery Weinstein, "Learning Dollars," *Training*, April 2007, 6.

42. Carol A. Hacker, "New Employee Orientation: Make It Pay Dividends for Years to Come," *Information Systems Management*, Winter 2004, 89–92.

43. T. Galvin, "2003 Industry Report," *Training*, October 2003, 30–31.

44. Alison Stein Wellner, "The Pickup Artists," *Workforce Management*, July 2004 [accessed 6 April 2005] www.workforce.com.

45. Dessler, *A Framework for Human Resource Management*, 223–225.

46. Maria Panaritis, "Acme and Its Union Are Nearing a Showdown," *Philadelphia Inquirer*, 24 June 2009 [accessed 25 June 2009] www.philly.com; Michael J. Hicks, "Estimating Wal-Mart's Impacts in Maryland: A Test of Identification Strategies and Endogeneity Tests," *Eastern Economic Journal* 34, no. 1 (Winter 2008): 56–73.

47. Christopher Farrell, "Stock Options for All!" *BusinessWeek*, 20 September 2002 [accessed 18 August 2007] www.businessweek.com; Gary Strauss and Barbara Hansen, "CEO Pay Packages 'Business as Usual,'" *USA Today*, 31 March 2005, B2.

48. Emily Lambert, "The Right Way to Pay," *Forbes*, 11 May 2009, 78–80.

49. Jeff D. Opdyke, "Getting a Bonus Instead of a Raise," *Wall Street Journal*, 29 December 2004, D1–D2.

50. Paul Loucks, "Creating a Performance-Based Culture," *Benefits & Compensation Digest*, July 2007, 36–39.

51. Dessler, *A Framework for Human Resource Management*, 231–232.

52. Gregory Lopes, "Firms Dock Pay of Obese, Smokers," *Washington Times*, 13 August 2007 [accessed 14 August 2007] www.washingtontimes.com; Joseph Weber, "Health Insurance: Small Biz Is in a Bind," *BusinessWeek*, 27 September 2004, 47–48; Joseph Pereira, "Parting Shot: To Save on Health-Care Costs, Firms Fire Disabled Workers," *Wall Street Journal*, 14 July 2003, A1, A7; Timothy Aeppel, "Ill Will: Skyrocketing Health Costs Start to Pit Worker vs. Worker," *Wall Street Journal*, 17 July 2003, A1, A6; Vanessa Furhmans, "To Stem Abuses, Employers Audit Workers' Health Claims," *Wall Street Journal*, 31 March 2004, B1, B7; Milt Freudenheim, "Employees Paying Ever-Bigger Share for Health Care," *New York Times*, A1, C2; Julie Appleby, "Employers Get Nosy About Workers' Health," *USA Today*, 6 March 2003, B1–B2; Ellen E. Schultz and Theo Francis, "Employers' Caps Raise Retirees' Health-Care Costs," *Wall Street Journal*, 25 November 2003, B1,

B11; Vanessa Fuhrmans, "Company Health Plans Try to Drop Spouses," *Wall Street Journal*, 9 September 2003, D1, D2.

53. Victoria Colliver, "We Spend More, but U.S. Health Care Quality Falls Behind," *San Francisco Chronicle*, 10 July 2007 [accessed 14 August 2007] www.scrippsnews.com; Steve Lohr, "The Disparate Consensus on Health Care for All," *New York Times*, 6 December 2004, C16; Sara Schaefer and Laurie McGinley, "Census Sees a Surge in Americans Without Insurance," *Wall Street Journal*, 30 September 2003, B1, B6; "Half of Health Care Spending Is Wasted, Study Finds," *Detroit News*, 10 February 2005 [accessed 5 April 2005] www.detnews.com.

54. Charles Babington, "Health Care 'Ticking Time Bomb'" *Seattle Times*, 16 June 2009 [accessed 22 June 2009] www.seattletimes.com.

55. James H. Dulebohn, Brian Murray, and Minghe Sun, "Selection Among Employer-Sponsored Pension Plans: The Role of Individual Differences," *Personal Psychology*, Summer 2000, 405–432.

56. Carroll Lachnit, "The Drowning Pool," *Workforce Management*, October 2004, 12; Keith Naughton, "Business's Killer I.O.U.," *Newsweek*, 6 October 2003, 42–44; Christine Dugas, "Companies Consider Pension Freezes," *USA Today*, 7 January 2004, B1.

57. George Van Dyke, "Examining Your 401k," *Business Credit*, January 2000, 59.

58. The ESOP Association website [accessed 22 June 2009] www.esopassociation.org; Dessler, *A Framework for Human Resource Management*, 282.

59. Michelle Kessler, "Fears Subside over Accounting for Stock Options," *USA Today*, 1 January 2006 [accessed 18 August 2007] www.usatoday.com; Robert A. Guth and Joann S. Lublin, "Tarnished Gold: Microsoft Users Out Era of Options," *Wall Street Journal*, 9 July 2003, A1, A9; John Markoff and David Leonhardt, "Microsoft Will Award Stock, Not Options, to Employees," *New York Times*, 9 July 2003, A1, C4.

60. Sydney Finkelstein, "Rethinking CEO Stock Options," *BusinessWeek*, 20 April 2009, 23.

61. Cheeseman, *Contemporary Business and E-Commerce Law*, 626.

62. Patrick J. Kiger, "Child-Care Models," *Workforce Management*, April 2004, 38.

63. Andy Meisler, "A Matter of Degrees," *Workforce Management*, May 2004, 32–38; Stephanie Armour, "More Firms Help Workers Find Home Sweet Home," *USA Today*, 30 August 2004, C1–C2.

64. Atkinson, "Wellness, Employee Assistance Programs"; Kevin Dobbs, Jack Gordon, and David Stamps, "EAPs Cheap but Popular Perk," *Training*, February 2000, 26.

65. See note 1.

66. Adapted from "Benchmarking Study Finds 'Telework' Has Evolved into a Mainstream Way of Working; Now, 'It's Just Work,'" press release, Telework Coalition, 9 March 2006 [accessed 11 August 2007] www.telcoa.org; Rich Karlgaard, "Outsource Yourself," *Forbes*, 19 April 2004 [accessed 24 April 2004] www.highbeam.com; David Kirkpatrick, "Big-League R&D Gets Its Own eBay," *Fortune*, 3 May 2004 [accessed 24 April 2004] www.highbeam.com; Joseph N. Pelton, "The Rise of Telecities: Decentralizing the Global Society," *The Futurist*, 1 January 2004 [accessed 24 April 2004] www.highbeam.com.

Chapter 12

1. Nolan Finley, "Detroit's Entitlement Culture Withers a Bright, Blue Dream," *Detroit News*, 30 April 2009 [accessed 11 July 2009] www.detroitnews.com; Geoffrey Rogow, "American Axle Declines 13% on Bankruptcy Worry," *Wall Street Journal*, 7 July 2009 [accessed 10 July 2009] http://online.wsj.com; Jeff Bennett, "American Axle Lifts Pay of Top Executive by 9.6%," *Wall Street Journal*, 25 March 2008 [accessed 10 July 2009] http://online.wsj.com; Jeff Bennett, "GM Is Hit Hard by Parts Strike," *Wall Street Journal*, 29 March 2008 [accessed 10 July 2009] http://online.wsj.com; John D. Stoll, "Corporate News: American Axle, UAW Harden Positions; Parties May Want GM to Boost Offer to Help End Strike," *Wall Street Journal*, 12 May 2008 [accessed 10 July 2009] http://online.wsj.com; Kris Maher, "Corporate News: Unions Find the Economy Is Tough on Bargaining; Conditions Make for Tough Talks," *Wall Street Journal*, 4 April 2008 [accessed 10 July 2009] http://online.wsj.com; Terry Kosdrosky and Bhattiprolu Murti, "Corporate News: GM Offers $200 Million to End Supplier Strike," *Wall Street Journal*, 9 May 2008 [accessed 10 July 2009] http://online.wsj.com; Terry Kosdrosky and Jeff Bennett, "Strike Idles American Axle Factories; UAW Resists Cost Cuts Sought by Big Supplier for GM and Chrysler," *Wall Street Journal*, 27 February 2008 [accessed 10 July 2009] http://online.wsj.com; Terry Kosdrosky and John D. Stoll, "Corporate News: End to Axle Strike Will Let GM Ramp Up Production," *Wall Street Journal*, 19 May 2008 [accessed 10 July 2009] http://online.wsj.com; Terry Kosdrosky and Neal E. Boudette, "American Axle Strike Tests UAW; Union Won't Readily Accept Terms Offered by Profitable Supplier," *Wall Street Journal*, 12 March 2008 [accessed 10 July 2009] http://online.wsj.com; Terry Kosdrosky, "GM Halts Work at More Plants Due to Strike at Parts Supplier," *Wall Street Journal*, 1 March 2008 [accessed 10 July 2009] http://online.wsj.com; Terry Kosdrosky, "Impact of American Axle Strike on GM Keeps Growing," *Wall Street Journal*, 10 March 2008 [accessed 10 July 2009] http://online.wsj.com; Robert E. Brooks, "All or Nothing, Sooner or Later," *Forging*, March/April 2008, 4; "American Axle Resumes Operations, but Will Close Two Forge Shops," *Forging*, May/June 2008, 6; "Dauch Sends Wrong Signals as Axle Strike Drags," *Automotive News*, 31 March 2008, 12; David Barkholz and Robert Sherefkin, "Dick Dauch's Labor Journey: Hero to Demon," *Automotive News*, 7 April 2008, 3–4; David Welch, "GM's Broken Axle," *BusinessWeek*, 31 March 2008, 10; "UAW Strikes American Axle in Wage Stare-Down," *Forging*, March/April 2008, 6.

2. Robert Brooks, "The Meaning of It All," *Foundry Management & Technology*, March 2008, 4.

3. Adapted in part from Michael R. Carrell and Christina Heavrin, *Labor Relations and Collective Bargaining: Cases, Practice, and Law*, 9th ed. (Upper Saddle River, N.J.: Pearson Prentice Hall, 2010), 76–81.

4. "Employer Costs for Employee Compensation—March 2009," U.S. Bureau of Labor Statistics news release, 20 June 2009 [accessed 25 June 2009] www.bls.gov.

5. "Corporate News: Unions Find the Economy Is Tough on Bargaining; Conditions Make for Tough Talks; A Fear of Striking."

6. "The Union Advantage in Pay and Benefits," United Auto Workers website [accessed 25 June 2009] www.uaw.org.

7. Mariah DeForest, "Will Your Employees Go Union?" *Foundry Management & Technology*, September 2008, 36–39.

8. Carrell and Heavrin, *Labor Relations and Collective Bargaining*, 79.

9. "Average Dues and Due Growth," data from Labor Management Reporting and Disclosure Act, quoted in Mark Brenner, "Give Your Union a Dues Checkup," Labor Notes [accessed 25 June 2009] www.labornotes.org.

10. Carrell and Heavrin, *Labor Relations and Collective Bargaining*, 316–317.

11. Stanley Holmes, "Boeing: An End to Strike Turbulence," *BusinessWeek*, 25

September 2005 [accessed 26 June 2009] www.businessweek.com.

12. Michelle Krebs, "Study: Union Work Rules Cost Big Three," Edmunds AutoObserver, 20 June 2007 [accessed 26 June 2009] www.autoobserver.com.

13. Jack Welch and Suzy Welch, "A Week of Blows to Business," *BusinessWeek*, 18 May 2009 [accessed 26 June 2009] www.businessweek.com.

14. Christos Doucouliagos and Patrice Laroche, "What Do Unions Do to Productivity: A Meta-analysis," *Industrial Relations*, October 2003, 650–691.

15. Philip Taft, "Workers of a New Century," U.S. Department of Labor website [accessed 30 June 2009] www.dol.gov.

16. Carrell and Heavrin, *Labor Relations and Collective Bargaining*, 26–27.

17. Carrell and Heavrin, *Labor Relations and Collective Bargaining*, 29; "Overview," U.S. National Labor Relations Board website [accessed 30 June 2009] www.nlrb.gov; Henry R. Cheeseman, *Contemporary Business and E-Commerce Law*, 7th ed. (Upper Saddle River, N.J.: Pearson Prentice Hall, 2010), 501.

18. Irving Bernstein, "Americans in Depression and War," U.S. Department of Labor website [accessed 30 June 2009] www.dol.gov.

19. Jack Barbash, "Unions and Rights in the Space Age," U.S. Department of Labor website [accessed 30 June 2009] www.dol.gov.

20. Barbash, "Unions and Rights in the Space Age"; Carrell and Heavrin, *Labor Relations and Collective Bargaining*, 33.

21. Barbash, "Unions and Rights in the Space Age."

22. Barbash, "Unions and Rights in the Space Age."

23. "Landrum-Griffin Act," *West's Encyclopedia of American Law*, 2nd ed., Jeffrey Lehman and Shirelle Phelps, eds. (Detroit: Gale, 2005), 200–201.

24. Cheeseman, *Contemporary Business and E-Commerce Law*, 522–523; Carrell and Heavrin, *Labor Relations and Collective Bargaining*, 145–149.

25. Zogby International, "The Attitudes and Opinions of Unionized and Non-Unionized Workers Employed in Various Sectors of the Economy Toward Organized Labor."

26. Carrell and Heavrin, *Labor Relations and Collective Bargaining*, 149–151.

27. Carrell and Heavrin, *Labor Relations and Collective Bargaining*, 122–123.

28. Carrell and Heavrin, *Labor Relations and Collective Bargaining*, 123–124.

29. Carrell and Heavrin, *Labor Relations and Collective Bargaining*, 138.

30. James Sherk, "Employee Free Choice Act Effectively Eliminates Secret Ballot Organizing Elections," Heritage Foundation, 27 August 2008 [accessed 3 July 2009] www.heritage.org.

31. "Procedures Guide," U.S. National Labor Relations Board website [accessed 28 June 2009] www.nlrb.gov.

32. DeForest, "Will Your Employees Go Union?"

33. Carrell and Heavrin, *Labor Relations and Collective Bargaining*, 138.

34. "National Labor Relations Act," U.S. National Labor Relations Board website [accessed 28 June 2009] www.nlrb.gov; John Horowitz, "Employee Free Choice Act—Things to Avoid During Union Organizing Campaign," Employee Free Choice Act blog, 4 November 2008 [accessed 28 June 2009] http:// employeefreechoiceact.foxrothschild. com; Carrell and Heavrin, *Labor Relations and Collective Bargaining*, 170–171; Cheeseman, *Contemporary Business and E-Commerce Law*, 502–503.

35. "Collective Bargaining Agreement Between National Hockey League and National Hockey League Players' Association, July 22, 2005–September 15, 2011," NHL website [accessed 29 June 2009] www.nhl.com.

36. "National Labor Relations Act," U.S. National Labor Relations Board website [accessed 28 June 2009] www.nlrb.gov.

37. Carrell and Heavrin, *Labor Relations and Collective Bargaining*, 201–202.

38. "The Strike Zone: How to Defuse Protracted Labor Conflicts," *Negotiation*, March 2008, 6–7.

39. U.S. Federal Mediation and Conciliation Service website [accessed 28 June 2009] www.fmcs.gov.

40. Carrell and Heavrin, *Labor Relations and Collective Bargaining*, 107.

41. Paul D. Staudohar, "Labor Relations in Basketball: The Lockout of 1998–99," *Monthly Labor Review*, April 1999, 3–9; E. Edward Herman, *Collective Bargaining and Labor Relations*, 4th ed. (Upper Saddle River, N.J.: Prentice Hall, 1998), 61; "NLRB Permits Replacements During Legal Lockout," *Personnel Journal*, January 1987, 14–15.

42. "Fact Sheet," U.S. National Labor Relations Board website [accessed 7 July 2009] www.nlrb.gov.

43. "The National Labor Relations Board and You: Unfair Labor Practices," U.S. National Labor Relations Board website [accessed 7 July 2009] www.nlrb.gov.

44. "The National Labor Relations Board and You: Unfair Labor Practices."

45. Carrell and Heavrin, *Labor Relations and Collective Bargaining*, 483.

46. Michael Grotticelli, "Union Members Challenge Shared News Coverage," *Broadcast Engineering*, 8 June 2009

[accessed 28 June 2009] http:// broadcastengineering.com.

47. "Grievance Handling," United Electrical, Radio and Machine Workers of America website [accessed 28 June 2009] www.rankfile-ue.org; Carrell and Heavrin, *Labor Relations and Collective Bargaining*, 481–486.

48. Carrell and Heavrin, *Labor Relations and Collective Bargaining*, 487–491.

49. Carrell and Heavrin, *Labor Relations and Collective Bargaining*, 510.

50. "Federal Mediation and Conciliation Service, 2008 Annual Report," U.S. Federal Mediation and Conciliation Service website [accessed 29 June 2009] www.fmcs.gov.

51. American Arbitration Association website [accessed 29 June 2009] www .adr.org.

52. "Federal Mediation and Conciliation Service, 2008 Annual Report."

53. Carrell and Heavrin, *Labor Relations and Collective Bargaining*, 513.

54. Change to Win website [accessed 26 June 2009] www.changetowin.org.

55. Paul Pringle, SEIU Borrows Business' Anti-Union Tactics to Fend Off a Rival," *Los Angeles Times*, 30 June 2009 [accessed 1 July 2009] www.latimes .com.

56. "Union Members Summary," U.S. Bureau of Labor Statistics website, 28 January 2009 [accessed 29 June 2009] www.bls.gov.

57. Ian Robinson, "What Explains Unorganized Workers' Growing Demand for Unions?" *Labor Studies Journal* 33, no. 3 (September 2008): 235–242.

58. Zogby International, "The Attitudes and Opinions of Unionized and Non-Unionized Workers Employed in Various Sectors of the Economy Toward Organized Labor," August 2005, Public Service Research Council website [accessed 30 June 2009] www .psrconline.org.

59. Rasmussen Reports, "Toplines—Unions I—March 13–14, 2009," Rasmussen Reports website [accessed 30 June 2009] www.rasmussenreports.com.

60. Richard B. Hankins and Seth H. Borden, "The Employee Free Choice Act," Kilpatrick Stockton LLP white paper [accessed 3 July 2009] www .kilpatrickstockton.com; Liz Wolgemuth, "5 Things to Know About the Employee Free Choice Act," *U.S. News and World Report*, 24 June 2009 [accessed 3 July 2009] www.usnews.com.

61. Sherk, "Employee Free Choice Act Effectively Eliminates Secret Ballot Organizing Elections."

62. Kate Bronfenbrenner, "A War Against Organizing," *Washington Post*, 3 June 2009 [accessed 3 July 2009] www .washingtonpost.com.

63. Steven Greenhouse, "Bill Easing Unionizing Is Under Heavy Attack," *New York Times*, 8 January 2009 [accessed 3 July 2009] www.nytimes .com.

64. Wolgemuth, "5 Things to Know About the Employee Free Choice Act."

65. Thomas Frank, "It's Time to Give Voters the Liberalism They Want," *Wall Street Journal*, 19 November 2008 [accessed 30 June 2009] http://online.wsj.com.

66. George McGovern, "My Party Should Respect Secret Union Ballots," *Wall Street Journal*, 8 August 2008 [accessed 3 July 2009] http://online.wsj.com.

67. McGovern, "My Party Should Respect Secret Union Ballots."

68. George McGovern, "The 'Free Choice' Act Is Anything But," *Wall Street Journal*, 7 May 2009 [accessed 30 June 2009] http://online.wsj.com; Wolgemuth, "5 Things to Know About the Employee Free Choice Act."

69. See note 1.

70. "Electronic Monitoring in the Workplace: Common Law & Federal Statutory Protection," The National Workrights Institute [accessed 9 July 2009] www.workrights.org; "Employee Monitoring: Is There Privacy in the Workplace?" Privacy Rights Clearinghouse [accessed 9 July 2009] www.privacyrights.org; Brittany Petersen, "Employee Monitoring: It's Not Paranoia—You Really Are Being Watched!" *PC Magazine*, 26 May 2008 [accessed 9 July 2009] www.pcmag.com.

Chapter 13

1. Kathy Jackson, "Kia Is Hoping to Sell Its Soul to Young Folks," *Automotive News*, 30 March 2009, 18; Scion website [accessed 15 July 2009] www.scion .com; "Scion History," Edmunds.com [accessed 15 July 2009] www.edmunds .com; Alan Ohnsman and Jeff Bennett, "Toyota Puts Hipness Ahead of Sales for New Scion Cars," Bloomberg.com, 8 February 2007 [accessed 5 August 2007] www.bloomberg.com; Mark Rechtin, "Scion's Dilemma," *AutoWeek*, 23 May 2006 [accessed 5 August 2007] www .autoweek.com; Michael Paoletta, "Toyota's Scion Starts Label," *Billboard*, 26 March 2005, 8+; "2005 Scion tC," Edmunds.com [accessed 12 April 2005] www.edmunds.com; "10 Hottest Cars and Trucks in 2004," *Advertising Age*, 20 December, 28; David Welch, "Not Your Father's . . . Whatever," *BusinessWeek*, 15 March 2004, 82–84; Daren Fonda, "Scion Grows Up," *Time (Canada)*, 16 August 2004, 61; Katherine Zachery, "The Makings of a Hit," *Ward's Auto World*, June 2004, 42; Christopher Palmeri, "Toyota's Youth Models Are Having Growing Pains," *BusinessWeek*, 31 May 2004, 32; Steven Kichen, "Scion's Smart Moves," *Forbes*, 12 October 2004 [accessed 12 April 2005] www.forbes.com; Norihiko Shirouzu, "Scion Plays Hip-Hop Impresario to Impress Young Drivers," *Wall Street Journal*, 5 October 2004, B1+; Phil Patton, "As Authentic as 'The Matrix' or Menudo," *New York Times*, 25 July 2004, sec. 12, 1+; Dan Lienert, "What's New? With Toyota's Scion, Youth Must Be Served," *New York Times*, 19 October 2003 [accessed 12 November 2003] www.nytimes.com; Fara Warner, "Learning How to Speak to Gen Y," *Fast Company*, July 2003, 36; Darren Fonda, "Baby, You Can Drive My Car," *Time*, 30 June 2003, 46; Christopher Palmeri, Ben Elgin, and Kathleen Kerwin, "Toyota's Scion: Dude, Here's Your Car," *BusinessWeek*, 9 June 2003, 44; Jonathan Fahey, "For the Discriminating Body Piercer," *Forbes*, 12 May 2003, 136; George Raine, "Courting Generation Y," *San Francisco Chronicle*, 11 May 2003, I3.

2. Philip Kotler and Gary Armstrong, *Principles of Marketing*, 13th ed. (Upper Saddle River, N.J.: Pearson Prentice Hall, 2010), 5.

3. Kotler and Armstrong, *Principles of Marketing*, 6.

4. BizXchange website [accessed 13 July 2009] www.bizx.com.

5. June Lee Risser, "Customers Come First," *Marketing Management*, November/December 2003, 22–26.

6. Ranjay Gulati and James B. Oldroyd, "The Quest for Customer Focus," *Harvard Business Review*, April 2005, 92–101.

7. Jonathan L. Yarmis, "How Facebook Will Upend Advertising," *BusinessWeek*, 28 May 2008 [accessed 13 July 2009] www.businessweek.com.

8. Paul Gunning, "Social Media Reality Check," *Adweek*, 8 June 2008, 18.

9. Jeremiah Owyang, "When Social Media Marries CRM Systems," Web Strategy blog, 3 June 2008 [accessed 13 July 2009] www.web-strategist.com.

10. "Sorry, John," *Adweek*, 22 June 2009, 9.

11. Dominique M. Hanssens, Daniel Thorpe, and Carl Finkbeiner, "Marketing When Customer Equity Matters," *Harvard Business Review*, May 2008, 117–123.

12. "Sorry, John."

13. Hanssens, et al., "Marketing When Customer Equity Matters."

14. Eric Almquist, Martin Kon, and Wolfgang Bock, "The Science of Demand," *Marketing Management*, March/April 2004, 20–26; David C. Swaddling and Charles Miller, "From Understanding to Action," *Marketing Management*, July/August 2004, 31–35.

15. "Marketing Under Fire," *Marketing Management*, July/August 2004, 5.

16. Kelly D. Martin and N. Craig Smith, "Commercializing Social Interaction: The Ethics of Stealth Marketing," *Journal of Public Policy & Marketing*, Spring 2008, 45–56; Robert Berner, "I Sold It Through the Grapevine," *BusinessWeek*, 29 May 2006, 32; "Undercover Marketing Uncovered," CBSnews.com, 25 July 2004 [accessed 11 April 2005] www.cbsnews.com; Stephanie Dunnewind, "Teen Recruits Create Word-of Mouth 'Buzz' to Hook Peers on Products," *Seattle Times*, 20 November 2004 [accessed 11 April 2005] www.seattletimes.com.

17. Dan Hill, "Why They Buy," *Across the Board*, November–December 2003, 27–32; Eric Roston, "The Why of Buy," *Time*, April 2004.

18. Dan Ariely, "The End of Rational Economics," *Harvard Business Review*, July/August 2009, 78–84.

19. Michael R. Solomon, *Consumer Behavior*, 6th ed. (Upper Saddle River, N.J.: Pearson Prentice Hall, 2004), 366–372.

20. Based in part on James C. Anderson and James A. Narus, *Business Market Management: Understanding, Creating, and Delivering Value*, 2nd ed. (Upper Saddle River, N.J.: Pearson Prentice Hall, 2004), 114–116.

21. Daniel Lyons, "Tough Customers," *Forbes Asia*, 7 April 2008, 69.

22. Gerard J. Tellis, Eden Yin, and Rakesh Niraj, "Does Quality Win? Network Effects Versus Quality in High-Tech Markets," *Journal of Marketing Research*, May 2009, 135–149.

23. Eric Beinhocker, Ian Davis, and Lenny Mendonca, "The 10 Trends You Have to Watch," *Harvard Business Review*, July/August 2009, 55–60.

24. Beinhocker, et al., "The 10 Trends You Have to Watch."

25. Kotler and Armstrong, *Principles of Marketing*, 43–46.

26. Gordon A. Wyner, "Pulling the Right Levers," *Marketing Management*, July/August 2004, 8–9.

27. Kotler and Armstrong, *Principles of Marketing*, 196–197.

28. Claritas Corporation website [accessed 14 July 2009] www.claritas.com; Haya El Nassar and Paul Overberg, "Old Labels Just Don't Stick in 21st Century," *USA Today*, 17 December 2003; Michael J. Weiss, *The Clustering of America* (New York: Harper & Row, 1988), 41.

29. Ace Hardware case study, Claritas website [accessed 14 July 2009] www .claritas.com.

30. Teressa Iezzi, "Dell's Della Debacle an Example of Wrong Way to Target

Women," *Advertising Age*, 25 May 2009, 13; Matt Hickey, "Dell's Della Site for Gals Causes Facepalmage," Crave blog, 14 May 2005 [accessed 15 July 2009] http://news.cnet.com.

31. Kotler and Armstrong, *Principles of Marketing*, 205–207.

32. Jeneanne Rae, "New Thinking About Consumer Marketing," *BusinessWeek*, 30 June 2009, 16.

33. Detlef Schoder, "The Flaw in Customer Lifetime Value," *Harvard Business Review*, December 2007, 26.

34. Rechtin, "Scion's Dilemma."

35. Kichen, "Scion's Smart Moves."

36. Paul Gillin, *The New Influencers: A Marketer's Guide to the New Social Media* (Sanger, Calif.: Quill Driver Books, 2007), xi.

37. See note 1.

Chapter 14

1. Annika Sorenstam website [accessed 28 July 2009] www.annikasorenstam.com; Annika Academy website [accessed 28 July 2009] www.theannikaacademy.com; Jeff Chu, "A New Course for Sörenstam," *Time South Pacific* (Australia/New Zealand edition), 12 January 2009, 46–47; Brian McCallen, "Annika on Course," *Forbes*, 8 October 2007, 68–69; Eben Harrell, "Calling Time," *Time South Pacific* (Australia/New Zealand edition), 26 May 2008, 5; Edward Schmidt, Jr., "Fierce Competition," *Meeting News*, 8 October 2007, 60; Barry Janoff, "Sorenstam Scores with Sponsors; Foul Called on NBA's Offseason," *Brandweek*, 1 October 2007, 12; Jessica Shambora, "Stroke of Genius," *Fortune*, 10 November 2008, 62–64.

2. Jeneanne Rae, "New Thinking About Consumer Marketing," *BusinessWeek*, 30 June 2009, 16.

3. Werner Reinartz and Wolfgang Ulaga, "How to Sell Services More Profitably," *Harvard Business Review*, May 2008, 90–96.

4. Jenna Wortham, "Sending GPS Devices the Way of the Tape Deck?" *New York Times*, 7 July 2009 [accessed 18 July 2009] www.nytimes.com.

5. David Armstrong, Monte Burke, Emily Lambert, Nathan Vardi, and Rob Wherry, "85 Innovations," *Forbes*, 23 December 2002, 122–202.

6. Michael V. Copeland and Om Malik, "How to Build a Bulletproof Startup," *Business 2.0*, June 2006 [accessed 7 August 2007] www.business2.com.

7. Nicolas Block, Kara Gruver, and David Cooper, "Slimming Innovation Pipelines to Fatten Their Returns," *Harvard Management Update*, August 2007, 3–5.

8. Nanette Byrnes, "Xerox' New Design Team: Customers," *BusinessWeek*, 7 May 2007, 72.

9. Andrew Krukowski, "Testing the Waters in Syndication," *Television Week*, 20 April 2009, 3+.

10. David Haigh and Jonathan Knowles, "How to Define Your Brand and Determine Its Value," *Marketing Management*, May/June 2004, 22–28.

11. David Kiley, "Best Global Brands," *BusinessWeek*, 6 August 2007, 56–64.

12. Jean Halliday, "Lutz: GM Product Is Better; Now It Must Erase 'Reputational Deficit,'" *Advertising Age*, 1 June 2009, 6.

13. Nina Diamond, John F. Sherry, Albert M. Muñiz, Mary Ann McGrath, Robert V. Kozinets, and Stefania Borghini, "American Girl and the Brand Gestalt: Closing the Loop on Sociocultural Branding Research," *Journal of Marketing*, May 2009, 118–134.

14. Janell M. Kurtz and Cynthia Mehoves, "Whose Name Is It Anyway?," *Marketing Management*, January/February 2002, 31–33.

15. "Lenovo to Sell Disney-Branded PCs," *Business Standard* (Mumbai), 7 August 2007 [accessed 7 August 2007] www.business-standard.com.

16. Lawrence L. Garber Jr., Eva M. Hyatt, and Ünal Ö. Boya, "The Effect of Package Shape on Apparent Volume: An Exploratory Study with Implications for Package Design," *Journal of Marketing Theory & Practice*, Summer 2009, 215–234.

17. Margaret Webb Pressler, "Do Not Pry Open Until Christmas: The Hard Truth About Hated 'Clamshell' Packaging," *Washington Post*, 30 November 2006 A1+; Jennifer Saranow, "The Puncture Wound I Got for Christmas," *Wall Street Journal*, 30 December 2004, D1+.

18. General Mills website [accessed 26 July 2009] www.generalmills.com.

19. Betsy Morris and Joan L. Levinstein, "What Makes Apple Golden," *Fortune*, 17 March 2008, 68–74; Bharat N. Anand, "The Value of a Broader Product Portfolio," *Harvard Business Review*, January 2008, 20–22.

20. Erik Brynjolfsson, Yu (Jeffrey) Hu, and Duncan Simester, "Goodbye Pareto Principle, Hello Long Tail: The Effects of Search Costs on the Concentration of Sales," research paper, February 2007 [accessed 7 August 2007] http://papers.ssrn.com.

21. Chris Anderson, "The Long Tail," *Wired*, October 2004 [accessed 7 August 2007] www.wired.com.

22. "About ESPN," ESPN website [accessed 26 July 2009] www.joinourteam.espn.com.

23. Jessi Hempel, "hi5 Guns for Facebook," *Fortune*, 27 October 2008, 14.

24. Andrew Shanahan, "Why Did France Fall in Love with McDonald's?" *The Guardian*, 24 July 2008 [accessed 26 July 2009] www.guardian.co.uk; Carol Matlack, "What's This? The French Love McDonald's?" *BusinessWeek*, 13 January 2003, 50; Shirley Leung, "Armchairs, TVs and Espresso—Is It McDonald's?" *Wall Street Journal*, 30 August 2002, A1, A6.

25. "Land of Leather Guilty of Misleading Customers," *Cabinet Maker*, 29 May 2009, 5.

26. Eric Anderson and Duncan Simester, "Mind Your Pricing Cues," *Harvard Business Review*, September 96–103.

27. Edward Ramirez and Ronald E. Goldsmith, "Some Antecedents of Price Sensitivity," *Journal of Marketing Theory & Practice*, Summer 2009, 199–213.

28. WHERE website [accessed 26 July 2009] http://where.com.

29. Elisabeth A. Sullivan, "Value Pricing: Smart Marketers Know Cost-Plus Can Be Costly," *Marketing News*, 15 January 2008, 8.

30. Peter J. Williamson and Ming Zeng, "Value-for-Money Strategies for Recessionary Times," *Harvard Business Review*, March 2009, 66–74.

31. Revionics website [accessed 27 July 2009] www.revionics.com; Amy Cortese, "The Power of Optimal Pricing," *Business 2.0*, September 2002, 68–70.

32. Priceline website [accessed 27 July 2009] www.priceline.com.

33. Ju-Young Kim, Martin Natter, and Martin Spann, "Pay What You Want: A New Participative Pricing Mechanism," *Journal of Marketing*, January 2009, 44–58.

34. John Varcoe, "Lunatics in Charge," *NZ Marketing Magazine*, June 2009, 10.

35. Don Moyer, "That's Going to Cost You," *Harvard Business Review*, May 2009, 132.

36. Sunil Gupta and Carl F. Mela, "What Is a Free Customer Worth?" *Harvard Business Review*, November 2008, 102–109.

37. "About Us," Zillow website [accessed 27 July 2009] www.zillow.com.

38. "How About Free? The Price Point That Is Turning Industries on Their Heads," Knowledge@Wharton, 4 March 2009 [accessed 27 July 2009] http://knowledge.wharton.upenn.edu.

39. Al Ries, "Variable Pricing Is Ultimate Brand-Destruction Machine," *Advertising Age*, 8 June 2009, 11.

40. See note 1.

41. Aubrey Kent and Richard M. Campbell, Jr., "An Introduction to Freeloading: Campus-Area Ambush Marketing," *Sport Marketing Quarterly* 16, no. 2 (2007): 118–122.

42. Adapted from Valerie Bennett and Andrew Capella, "Location-Based Services," IBM website [accessed 27 July 2009] www.ibm.com; David LaGress,

"They Know Where You Are," *U.S. News & World Report*, 8 September 2003, 32–38; Christopher Elliott, "Some Rental Cars Are Keeping Tabs on Drivers," *New York Times*, 13 January 2004, C6; Kristi Heim, "Microchips in People, Packaging and Pets Raise Privacy Questions," *Seattle Times*, 18 October 2004 [accessed 18 October 2004] www.seattletimes.com; Andrew Heining and Christa Case, "Are Book Tags a Threat?" *Christian Science Monitor*, 5 October 2004 [accessed 7 October 2004] www.csmonitor.com; Corie Lok, "Wrist Radio Tags," *Technology Review*, November 2004, 25; Brian Albright, "RFID Dominates Frontline's Supply Chain Week," *Frontline Solutions*, November 2003, 10–13.

Chapter 15

1. Datamonitor, "Costco Wholesale Corporation: Company Profile," 18 March 2009; Costco website [accessed 30 July 2009] www.costco.com; "Analyst Picks and Pans: MCD, COST, YUM, TSN," *BusinessWeek*, 21 May 2009 [accessed 31 July 2009] www.businessweek.com; Michelle V. Rafter, "Welcome to the Club," *Workforce Management*, April 2005, 41–46; David Meier, "It's the Employees, Stupid," MotleyFool.com, 17 September 2004 [accessed 7 October 2004] www.fool.com; Steven Greenhouse, "How Costco Became the Anti-Wal-Mart, *New York Times*, 17 July 2005 [accessed 1 August 2009] www.nytimes.com; Jeff Malester, "Costco Sales Rise 10%, Hit $12.4 Billion in Fis. Q2," *Twice*, 7 March 2005, 53; Ilana Polyak, "Warehouse Sale," *Kiplinger's Personal Finance*, May 2005, 67; Suzanne Wooley, "Costco? More Like Costgrow," *Money*, August 2002, 44–46; "Costco: A Cut Above," *Retail Merchandiser*, July 2002, 44; Pete Hisey, "Costco.com Means Business," *Retail Merchandiser*, October 2001, 36; Shelly Branch, "Inside the Cult of Costco," *Fortune*, 6 September 1999, 184–188.

2. "Grainger at a Glance," Grainger website [accessed 29 July 2009] www.grainger.com.

3. IrisInk website [accessed 30 July 2009] www.irisink.com.

4. "Estimated Sales and Inventories of U.S. Merchant Wholesalers: 2002 through 2007" and "Estimated Sales and Commissions of Electronic Markets, Agents, Brokers, and Commission Merchants for the United States: 2004 through 2007," U.S. Census Bureau website [accessed 30 July 2009] www.census.gov.

5. "Wholesale Trade," U.S. Bureau of Labor Statistics website [accessed 30 July 2009] www.bls.gov.

6. "State of the Wholesale Distribution Industry," National Association of Wholesaler-Distributors website [accessed 30 July 2009] www.naw.org.

7. Philip Kotler and Gary Armstrong, *Principles of Marketing*, 13th ed. (Upper Saddle River, N.J.: Pearson Prentice Hall, 2010), 362–363; Bert Rosenbloom, "The Wholesaler's Role in the Marketing Channel: Disintermediation Vs. Reintermediation," *International Review of Retail, Distribution & Consumer Research*, September 2007, 327–339.

8. McKesson website [accessed 30 July 2009] www.mckesson.com.

9. Rosenbloom, "The Wholesaler's Role in the Marketing Channel: Disintermediation Vs. Reintermediation."

10. Rosenbloom, "The Wholesaler's Role in the Marketing Channel: Disintermediation Vs. Reintermediation."

11. Rosenbloom, "The Wholesaler's Role in the Marketing Channel: Disintermediation Vs. Reintermediation."

12. "Wholesale Trade"; Rosenbloom, "The Wholesaler's Role in the Marketing Channel: Disintermediation Vs. Reintermediation."

13. Jack Neff, "Trouble in Store for Shopper Marketing?" *Advertising Age*, 2 March 2009, 3+.

14. Jeneanne Rae, "New Thinking About Consumer Marketing," *BusinessWeek*, 30 June 2009, 16.

15. Jennifer J. Argo, Darren W. Dahl, and Andrea C. Morales, "Positive Consumer Contagion: Responses to Attractive Others in a Retail Context," *Journal of Marketing Research*, December 2008, 690–701.

16. Kerry Grace Benn, "Family Dollar Earnings Jump 36%, Boosts Fiscal-Year View," *Wall Street Journal*, 8 July 2009 [accessed 31 July 2009] http://online.wsj.com.

17. Teri Agins, "What Is 'Off-Price'?" *Wall Street Journal*, 17 July 2009 [accessed 31 July 2009] http://online.wsj.com.

18. "Web to Become Top Sales Channel by 2012," *Bookseller*, 24 April 2009, 10; "Quarterly Retail E-Commerce Sales: 1st Quarter 2009," U.S. Census Bureau, 15 May 2009 [accessed 31 July 2009] www.census.gov.

19. Jessia Mintz, "Redbox Might Just Overtake Netflix," *Seattle Times*, 21 June 2009 [accessed 31 July 2009] www.seattletimes.com; Sarah McBride, "Sony Pictures, Redbox Sign Movie Agreement," *Wall Street Journal*, 21 July 2009 [accessed 31 July 2009] http://online.wsj.com.

20. "What the Leaders Do Right," *Chain Store Age*, February 2008, 7A.

21. Kris Hudson and Vanessa O'Connell, "Recession Turns Malls Into Ghost Towns," *Wall Street Journal*, 22 May 2009 [accessed 31 July 2009] http://online.wsj.com; Glen A. Bere, "Big Boxes Pop Up in Regional Malls, Altering Landscape for Chain Stores," *National Jeweler*, 16 May 2005, 1+; Bruce Horovitz and Lorrie Grant, "Changes in Store for Department Stores?" *USA Today*, 21 January 2005, B1–B2; Dean Starkman, "As Malls Multiply, Developers Fight Fiercely for Turf," *Wall Street Journal*, 19 April 2002, A1, A6; Robert Berner and Gerry Khermouch, "Retail Reckoning," *BusinessWeek*, 10 December 2001, 72–77.

22. Rick Braddock, "Lessons of Internet Marketing from FreshDirect," *Wall Street Journal*, 11 May 2009 [accessed 31 July 2009] http://online.wsj.com.

23. Cate T. Corcoran, "Delivering the Goods: E-Tailing Sales to Rise But Gains Seen Slowing," *Women's Wear Daily*, 5 May 2009, 1.

24. Jacques Bughin, Amy Guggenheim Shenkan, and Marc Singer, "How Poor Metrics Undermine Digital Marketing," *McKinsey Quarterly*, 2009 Issue 1, 106–107.

25. "Location-Free Shopping," *Chain Store Age*, February 2009, 13A.

26. Sharon Edelson, "Pop-Ups Offer Retailers Multiple Benefits," *Women's Wear Daily*, 19 May 2009, 12.

27. Jim Dalrymple, "Inside the Apple Stores," *Macworld*, June 2007, 16–17; Andy Serwer, "The iPod People Have Invaded Apple's Stores," *Fortune*, 13 December 2004, 79.

28. Rob Eder, "CVS Unveils High-End Beauty 360 Store," *Drug Store News*, 17 November 2008, 1+.

29. Mintz, "Redbox Might Just Overtake Netflix"; Marija Jaroslavskaja, "Cost of Market Domination," *Video Business*, 19 January 2009, 21.

30. Black & Decker website [accessed 29 July 2009] www.blackanddecker.com.

31. Felder website [accessed 29 July 2009] http://usa.felder-gruppe.at.

32. Kotler and Armstrong, *Principles of Marketing*, 349.

33. Super Jock'n Jill website [accessed 28 July 2009] www.superjocknjill.com.

34. Øystein Foros and Hans Jarle Kind, "Do Slotting Allowances Harm Retail Competition?" *Scandinavian Journal of Economics* 110, no. 2 (2008): 367–384; U.S. Federal Trade Commission, "Slotting Allowances in the Retail Grocery Industry: Selected Case Studies

in Five Product Categories," November 2003 [accessed 29 July 2009] www.ftc .gov.

35. Jeffrey M. O'Brien, "The Wizards of Apps," *Fortune*, 5 May 2009, 29–30.

36. Carlos Niezen and Julio Rodriguez, "Distribution Lessons from Mom and Pop," *Harvard Business Review*, April 2008, 23–24.

37. Tom Stundza, "Boeing Picks Top Nine Suppliers of the Year for 2008," *Purchasing*, 7 April 2009 [accessed 29 July 2009] www.purchasing.com.

38. Dan Fitzpatrick, "BofA Plans to Cut 10% of Branches," *Wall Street Journal*, 28 July 2009 [accessed 29 July 2009] http://online.wsj.com.

39. Kotler and Armstrong, *Principles of Marketing*, 344.

40. Adapted from Kotler and Armstrong, *Principles of Marketing*, 344–345.

41. Connie Robbins Gentry, "Lights, Cameras, Delayed Action," *Chain Store Age*, June 2009, 29.

42. See note 1.

Chapter 16

1. Kami Huyse, "Case Study: ROI of Social Media Campaign for SeaWorld San Antonio—A Year Later," Communication Overtones blog, 18 April 2008 [accessed 18 August 2009] http://overtonecomm. blogspot.com; SeaWorld San Antonio website [accessed 18 August 2009] www .seaworldsanantonio.com; Shel Israel, "GNTV: Making a Splash with Social Media Measurement," Global Neighbourhoods blog, 28 March 2008 [accessed 18 August 2009] http:// redcouch.typepad.com/weblog; American Coaster Enthusiasts website [accessed 18 August 2009] www .aceonline.org.

2. Caroline Kealey, "Web 2.0: The Medium Is the Message, but What's the Result?" *CW Bulletin*, October 2007 [accessed 24 July 2008] www.iabc.com.

3. Philip Kotler and Gary Armstrong, *Principles of Marketing*, 13th ed. (Upper Saddle River, N.J.: Pearson Prentice Hall, 2010), 409–140.

4. Suzanne Kapner, "Wal-Mart Enters the Ad Age," *Fortune*, 18 August 2008, 30.

5. Adapted from Caterpillar website [accessed 2 August 2009] www.cat.com.

6. Jack Neff, "Package-Goods Puzzle: A Tale of Two Brands," *Advertising Age*, 11 May 2009, 14.

7. Kotler and Armstrong, *Principles of Marketing*, 405.

8. "Frequently Asked Advertising Questions: A Guide for Small Business," U.S. Federal Trade Commission website [accessed 3 August 2009] www.ftc.gov.

9. Stephanie Clifford, "Ads Follow Web Users, and Get More Personal," *New York Times*, [accessed 3 August 2009] www.nytimes.com; Suzanne Kapner, "Facebook Tries to Sell Its Friends Again," *Fortune*, 16 February 2009, 24; Robert D. Hof, "Behavioral Targeting: Google Pulls Out the Stops," *BusinessWeek*, 12 March 2009, 2; Heather Green, "Spies in Your Mobile Phone," *BusinessWeek*, 14 January 2009, 10.

10. Lew McCreary, "What Was Privacy?" *Harvard Business Review*, October 2008, 123–131.

11. National Advertising Review Council website [accessed 3 August 2009] www .narcpartners.org.

12. American Marketing Association website [accessed 3 August 2009] www .marketingpower.com.

13. Emily Bryson York, "The Gloves Are Off: More Marketers Opt for Attack Ads," *Advertising Age*, 25 May 2009, 4.

14. William Wells, John Burnett, and Sandra Moriarty, *Advertising: Principles & Practice*, 6th ed. (Upper Saddle River, N.J.: Pearson Prentice Hall, 2003), 47–48.

15. Peter Overby, "Millions Spent on Ad War over Health Care Overhaul," National Public Radio website, 21 July 2009 [accessed 3 August 2009] www .npr.org.

16. Maureen Morrison, "Verizon Tops AT&T as Most-Advertised Brand," *Advertising Age*, 22 June 2009 [accessed 3 August 2009] http://adage.com.

17. Adapted from Kenneth E. Clow and Donald Baack, *Integrated Advertising, Promotion, and Marketing Communications*, 4th ed. (Upper Saddle River, N.J.: Pearson Prentice Hall, 2010), 153–167.

18. Clow and Baack, *Integrated Advertising, Promotion, and Marketing Communications*, 155–156.

19. Steve McKee, "The Trouble with Celebrity Endorsements," *BusinessWeek*, 17 November 2008, 10.

20. Sanjay Putrevu, "Consumer Responses Toward Sexual and Nonsexual Appeals," *Journal of Advertising*, Summer 2008, 57–69.

21. Clow and Baack, *Integrated Advertising, Promotion, and Marketing Communications*, 162–164.

22. Jack Neff, "'Passion for Digital' Pumps P&G's Spending," *Advertising Age*, 8 June 2009, 3, 18.

23. Andrew McMains and Brian Morrissey, "Online Brands Turn to Traditional Ads," *Adweek*, 22 June 2009, 7; Christopher Meyer, "The Year of Marketing Dangerously," *Harvard Business Review*, October 2008, 26–27.

24. Kotler and Armstrong, *Principles of Marketing*, 436–437.

25. Janet Stilson, "The Clutter Busters," *Adweek*, 2 March 2009, 7.

26. Ben Kunz, "A Pricing Revolution Looms in Online Advertising," *BusinessWeek*, 7 April 2009, 20.

27. Brian Morrissey, "Thinking Beyond the Banner," *Adweek*, 8 June 2009, 9.

28. Meyer, "The Year of Marketing Dangerously."

29. Douglas MacMillan, "What Works in Online Video Advertising?" *BusinessWeek*, 28 January 2009, 26.

30. "What Is the Direct Marketing Association?" Direct Marketing Association website [accessed 15 August 2009] www.the-dma.org.

31. "History of the Sears Catalog," Sears Archives [accessed 15 August 2009] www.searsarchives.com.

32. "Direct Marketing Association 2008 Annual Report," Direct Marketing Association website [accessed 15 August 2009] www.the-dma.org.

33. Carol Krol, "E-Mail, Fastest Growing Direct Marketing Segment, Expands Double Digits," *DMNews*, 4 August 2009 [accessed 16 August 2009] www .dmnews.com.

34. Krol, "E-Mail, Fastest Growing Direct Marketing Segment, Expands Double Digits."

35. Kotler and Armstrong, *Principles of Marketing*, 489.

36. "Google Adwords," Google website [accessed 18 August 2007] www.google .com; Danny Sullivan, "Major Search Engines and Directories," *Search Engine Watch*, 28 March 2007 [accessed 2 July 2007] http:// searchenginewatch.com; Thomas Claburn, "Google, Yahoo Gain Search Market Share; Microsoft, Time Warner Lose," *InformationWeek*, 21 November 2006 [accessed 2 July 2007] www .informationweek.com.

37. Gerald L. Manning and Barry L. Reece, *Selling Today*, 9th ed. (Upper Saddle River, N.J.: Pearson Prentice Hall, 2004), 7–8.

38. Howard Feiertag, "Build Your Group Sales by Consultative Selling," *Hotel & Motel Management*, 15 June 2009, 10.

39. Live Chat Support Software Review, TopTenReviews [accessed 15 August 2009] www.toptenreviewes.com.

40. Kotler and Armstrong, *Principles of Marketing*, 474–475.

41. Dan Balaban, "Will Tough Times Spell Greater Opportunity for Mobile Coupons?" *Cards & Payments*, March 2009, 14–17.

42. "SpotOn GPS Platform Enables LBS Ad Delivery," *GPS World*, July 2009, 28.

43. Clow and Baack, *Integrated Advertising, Promotion, and Marketing Communications*, 334.

44. Clow and Baack, *Integrated Advertising, Promotion, and Marketing Communications*, 284.
45. Patricia Moore, "The Power of POP," *AdMedia*, March 2008, 34–38.
46. Clow and Baack, *Integrated Advertising, Promotion, and Marketing Communications*, 340.
47. G. Michael Maddock and Raphael Louis Viton, "The Smart Way to Tap Social Media," *BusinessWeek*, 27 May 2009, 17.
48. Paul Gunning, "Social Media Reality Check," *Adweek*, 8 June 2009, 18; Gene Marks, "Beware Social Media Marketing Myths," *BusinessWeek*, 27 May 2009, 7.
49. Alex Wright, "Mining the Web for Feelings, Not Facts," *New York Times*, 23 August 2009 [accessed 9 September 2009] www.nytimes.com.
50. Josh Bernoff, "Why B-to-B Ought to Love Social Media," *Marketing News*, 15 April 2009, 20.
51. Josh Bernoff, "Social Strategy for Exciting (and Not So Exciting) Brands," *Marketing News*, 15 May 2009, 18; Larry Weber, *Marketing to the Social Web* (Hoboken, N.J.: Wiley, 2007), 12–14; David Meerman Scott, *The New Rules of Marketing and PR* (Hoboken, N.J.: Wiley, 2007), 62; Paul Gillin, *The New Influencers* (Sanger, Calif.: Quill Driver Books, 2007), 34–35; Jeremy Wright, *Blog Marketing: The Revolutionary Way to Increase Sales, Build Your Brand, and Get Exceptional Results* (New York: McGraw-Hill, 2006), 263–365.
52. Susan Fournier and Lara Lee, "Getting Brand Communities Right," *Harvard Business Review*, April 2009, 105–111.
53. Patrick Hanlon and Josh Hawkins, "Expand Your Brand Community Online," *Advertising Age*, 7 January 2008, 14–15.
54. Steve McKee, "Why PR Is the Prescription," *BusinessWeek*, 13 April 2009, 8.
55. David Meerman Scott, *The New Rules of Marketing and PR* (Hoboken, N.J.: Wiley, 2007), 62.
56. Adapted from Miguel Helft, "Google to Offer Ads Based on Interests," *New York Times*, 11 March 2009 [accessed 17 August 2009] www.nytimes.com; "Nick Gillespie Discusses the Personalized Cover of *Reason* Magazine and the Possibilities of Database Technology" (interview), Talk of the Nation, National Public Radio, 4 May 2003 [accessed 6 May 2004] www.highbeam.com; Kevin J. Delaney, "Will Users Care if Gmail Invades Privacy?" *Wall Street Journal*, 6 April 2004, B1, B3; Allison Fass, "Spot On," *Forbes*, 23 June 2003, 140; "Hey You! How About Lunch?" *Wall Street Journal*, 1 April 2004, B1, B5.

Chapter 17

1. Julianne Pepitone, "Google Beats Profit Estimates," CNNMoney.com, 16 April 2009 [accessed 23 August 2009] http://money.cnn.com; "Frugal Google," *Fortune*, 22 January 2009 [accessed 23 August 2009] http://money.cnn.com/magazines/fortune; Miguel Helft, "Google's Profit Surges in Quarter," *New York Times*, 16 July 2009 [accessed 23 August 2009] www.nytimes.com; Catherine Clifford, "Layoffs Hit Google: 200 Jobs Cut," CNNMoney.com, 26 March 2009 [accessed 23 August 2009] http://money.cnn.com; Adam Lashinsky, "Belt-Tightening at Google," *Fortune*, 22 January 2009 [accessed 23 August 2009] http://money.cnn.com/magazines/fortune; Adam Lashinsky, "The Axman Comes to Google," *Fortune*, 23 March 2009 [accessed 23 August 2009] http://money.cnn.com/magazines/fortune; Google website [accessed 23 August 2009] www.google.com; Jessica E. Vascellaro and Scott Morrison, "Google Gears Down for Tougher Times," *Wall Street Journal*, 3 December 2008 [accessed 23 August 2009] http://online.wsj.com; Abbey Klaassen, "A Maturing Google Buckles Down and Searches for Cost Savings," *Advertising Age*, 1 December 2008, 3, 29.
2. "Accountants and Auditors," *Occupational Outlook Handbook, 2008–09 Edition*, U.S. Bureau of Labor Statistics website [accessed 19 August 2009] www.bls.gov.
3. "Frequently Asked Questions," American Institute of Certified Public Accountants website [accessed 19 August 2009] www.aicpa.org.
4. "Certification," Institute of Management Accountants website [accessed 19 August 2009] www.imanet.org.
5. "Accountants and Auditors," *Occupational Outlook Handbook, 2008–09 Edition*; Nanette Byrnes, "Green Eyeshades Never Looked So Sexy," *BusinessWeek*, 10 January 2005, 44; "Rules Make Accountants Newly Hot Commodity," *Oregonian*, 13 April 2005 [accessed 24 April 2005] www.ebsco.com.
6. Sarah Johnson, "Goodbye GAAP," *CFO*, 1 April 2008 [accessed 19 August 2009] www.cfo.com.
7. "Detecting Two Tricks of the Trade," Investopedia.com [accessed 19 August 2009] www.investopedia.com.
8. Johnson, "Goodbye GAAP."
9. Johnson, "Goodbye GAAP."
10. Johnson, "Goodbye GAAP."
11. Johnson, "Goodbye GAAP."
12. "Summary of SEC Actions and SEC Related Provisions Pursuant to the Sarbanes-Oxley Act of 2002," SEC website [accessed 9 May 2004] www.sec.gov; "Sarbanes-Oxley Act's Progress," *USA Today*, 26 December 2002 [accessed 9 May 2004] www.highbeam.com.
13. Scott Leibs, "Five Years and Counting," *CFO*, 1 July 2007 [accessed 9 July 2007] www.cfo.com.
14. David M. Katz, "CFOs Seek Sarbox Triage," *CFO*, 9 February 2006 [accessed 19 August 2009] www.cfo.com.
15. Sarah Johnson, "PCAOB Chairman Mark Olson to Retire," *CFO*, 9 June 2009 [accessed 19 August 2009] www.cfo.com.
16. Thayne Forbes, "Valuing Customers," *Journal of Database Marketing & Customer Strategy Management*, October 2007, 4–10.
17. Baruch Lev, "Sharpening the Intangibles Edge," *Harvard Business Review*, June 2004, 109–116.
18. "Google Inc. Financials," Google Finance, [accessed 20 August 2009] www.google.com/finance.
19. "How to Spot Trouble in Your Financials," *Inc.*, October 2004, 96.
20. "Bobbie Gossage," Cranking Up the Earnings," *Inc.*, October 2004, 54; Rick Wayman, "EBITDA: The Good, the Bad, and the Ugly," Investopedia.com [accessed 25 April 2005] www.investopedia.com.
21. Amy Wilson, "Old Vehicles Clog Dealer Lots," *Automotive News*, 11 May 2009, 4.
22. "Inventory Turnover," *Controller's Report*, October 2008, 13–14.
23. Jeffery Slater, *College Accounting: A Practical Approach*, 11th ed. (Upper Saddle River N.J.: Pearson Prentice Hall, 2010), 741.
24. Slater, *College Accounting: A Practical Approach*, 735.
25. See note 1.
26. Adapted from Mary Hayes Weier, "Companies Look to Contain Risk with GRC Software," *InformationWeek*, 5 April 2008 [accessed 24 August 2009] www.informationweek.com; OpenPages website [accessed 24 August 2009] www.openpages.com; Oracle website [accessed 24 August 2009] www.oracle.com; GRC Software Seems to Be Rising," FierceComplianceIT, 12 March 2007 [accessed 24 August 2009] www.fiercecomplianceit.com; James Kobielus, "Compliance-Enabling Technologies via SOA on the Rise," ITWorldCanada, 8 March 20007 [accessed 24 August 2009] www.itworldcanada.com.

Chapter 18

1. *Visa Inc. Annual Report 2008*; "Visa Inc, Corporate Overview," Visa website [accessed 2 September 2009] www.visa

.com; Katie Benner, "Visa's Record IPO Rings up 28% Gain," *Fortune*, 19 March 2008 [accessed 2 September 2009] http://money.cnn.com; Tami Luhby, "JPMorgan Chase Makes $1B-plus on Visa IPO," CNNMoney.com, 21 March 2008 [accessed 2 September 2009] http://money.cnn.com; M.J. Stephey, "A Brief History of: Credit Cards," *Time*, 23 April 2009 [accessed 2 September 2009] www.time.com; "Form S-1 Registration Statement, Visa Inc." U.S. Securities and Exchange Commission website [accessed 2 September 2009] www.sec.gov; *Visa Inc*, Datamonitor, 9 March 2009.

2. Emily Thornton and Frederick Jespersen, "Corporate Cash: Big Stockpiles for Tough Times," *BusinessWeek*, 5 March 2009, 11.

3. David McCann, "For Intel, the Future Is Now," *CFO*, 25 August 2009 [accessed 25 August 2009] www.cfo.com.

4. Janice DiPietro, "Protecting Liquidity in Tough Times," *Financial Executive*, June 2009, 61.

5. Benjamin J. Romano, "Microsoft Strategic Update: Ballmer Tells Wall Street More Dramatic Cost Cutting Would Be 'Imprudent,'" *Seattle Times*, 24 February 2009 [accessed 28 August 2009] www.seattletimes.com.

6. "Smart Fuel Strategy Means Profit for Southwest," *News & Observer* (Raleigh, N.C.), 1 July 2008 [accessed 27 August 2009] www.newsobserver.com.

7. Mahmut Akten, Massimo Giordano, and Mari A. Scheiffele, "Just-in-Time Budgeting for a Volatile Economy," *McKinsey Quarterly*, 2009, Issue 3, 115–121.

8. Karen M. Kroll, "Staying on Course," *CFO*, June 2008, 75–77.

9. Martin Labbe, "Budgeting the Proper Way," *Fleet Owner*, December 2008, 39.

10. Akten, et al., "Just-in-Time Budgeting for a Volatile Economy."

11. John Daly, "The State of the Factoring Industry," *The Secured Lender*, November–December 2008, 36–40.

12. "Banks Cut Credit for 58M Card Holders in 1 Year," *New York Times*, 20 August 2009 [accessed 27 August 2009] www.nytimes.com.

13. "How to Create a Smart Credit Policy," *Inc.*, March 2009, 37–40.

14. Vincent Ryan, "Rethinking Capital," *CFO*, November 2008, 81–84.

15. Anusha Shrivastava, "Commercial Paper Falls to a Five-Year Low," *Wall Street Journal*, 15 May 2009 [accessed 27 August 2009] http://online.wsj.com.

16. "Turn Your Receivables into Quick Cash," CNNMoney.com, 21 November 2008 [accessed 28 August 2009] http://money.cnn.com/smallbusiness; David Worrell, "Taking the Sting out of Receivables," Investopedia.com [accessed 28 August 2009] www.investopedia.com

17. Maureen Farrell, "The Check Is in the Mail," *Forbes*, 11 May 2009, 56–57; "Invoice Factoring Basics," Invoice Factoring Group [accessed 28 August 2009] http://factoring.qlfs.com; "Turn Your Receivables into Quick Cash;" Worrell, "Taking the Sting out of Receivables."

18. "Demand for Factoring High," *The Secured Lender*, April 2009, 26–29.

19. "How It Works," The Receivables Exchange [accessed 31 August 2009] www.receivablesxchange.com.

20. "Bank-Term Loans," *Entrepreneur* [accessed 29 August 2009] www.entrepreneur.com.

21. "Small Business Administration (SBA) Loans," U.S. Bank website [accessed 29 August 2009] www.usbank.com.

22. "Bank-Term Loans"; "Financing for Your Future—The Five C's of Credit," PNC website [accessed 29 August 2009] www.pnc.com.

23. Ben Steverman, "IPOs: Back from the Dead?" *BusinessWeek*, 9 March 2008, 12.

24. Marguerite Rigoglioso, "The Risky Business of Going Public," *Stanford GSB News*, March 2003 [accessed 29 August 2009] www.gsb.stanford.edu.

25. "The Corporate Handbook Series: Going Public," U.S. Securities and Exchange Commission website [accessed 29 August 2009] www.sec.gov; Matt H. Evans, "Excellence in Financial Management: Course 13: Going Public," Excellence in Financial Management website [accessed 29 August 2009] www.exinfm.com.

Chapter 19

1. Adapted from Ann Davis, "Hedges Pay Off for Gas Producers," *Wall Street Journal*, 13 August 2009 [accessed 12 September 2009] http://online.wsj.com; Chesapeake Energy website [accessed 12 September 2009] www.chk.com; Peter Carbonara, "The Folly of Betting Where Oil Will Go," *BusinessWeek*, 6 October 2008, 47; Alan Brochstein, "Natural Gas: Extreme Contango Suggests Caution for E&P Companies," Seeking Alpha, 6 September 2009 [accessed 12 September 2009] http://seekingalpha.com; Christopher Helman, "Would BP Please Buy Chesapeake Energy?" *Forbes*, 29 April 2009 [accessed 12 September 2009] www.forbes.com; Jesse Bogan, "Terrible Twos Near for Natural Gas," *Forbes*, 8 August 2009 [accessed 12 September 2009] www.forbes.com; Jesse Bogan, "Too Much Gas," *Forbes*, 22 May 2009 [accessed 12 September 2009] www.forbes.com; Ben Casselman, "Energy Firms Hedge with an Edge," *Wall Street Journal*, 29 July 2009 [accessed 12 September 2009] http://online.wsj.com; Jack Money, "Chesapeake's Hedging Loss Is More Than Meets the Naked Eye," *The Oklahoman*, 2 August 2008 [accessed 13 September 2009] www.istockanalyst.com; Chesapeake Energy, "September 2009 Investor Presentation" [accessed 13 September 2009] www.chk.com.

2. Ben Steverman, "The Buffett Way: Time for a Rethink?" *BusinessWeek*, 31 March 2009, 27.

3. Tom Drinkard, "A Primer on Preferred Stock," Investopedia.com [accessed 5 September 2009] www.investopedia.com.

4. Arthur J. Keown, *Personal Finance: Turning Money into Wealth*, 3rd ed. (Upper Saddle River, N.J.: Pearson Prentice Hall, 2003), 420.

5. Robert G. Hagstrom, Jr., *The Warren Buffett Way* (New York: Wiley, 1995), 36.

6. Cory Janssen, "A Breakdown of Stock Buybacks," Investopedia.com [accessed 5 September 2009] www.investopedia.com.

7. Jack R. Kapoor, Les R. Dlabay, and Robert J. Hughes, *Personal Finance*, 7th ed. (Boston: McGraw-Hill Irwin, 2004), 500.

8. Keown, *Personal Finance: Turning Money into Wealth*, 417.

9. "U.S. Junk Bond Default Rate Rises to 10.2 pct—S&P," Reuters, 3 September 2009 [accessed 6 September 2009] www.reuters.com.

10. Keown, *Personal Finance: Turning Money into Wealth*, 449.

11. "Treasury Inflation-Protected Securities (TIPS)," U.S. Department of Treasury website [accessed 10 September 2009] www.treasurydirect.gov.

12. Kapoor, Dlabay, and Hughes, *Personal Finance*, 506.

13. Jack Colombo, "Muni Bond Default Parade Plays On," *Forbes*, 15 January 2009 [accessed 6 September 2009] www.forbes.com.

14. "American Century Capital Growth," Morningstar [accessed 7 September 2009] www.morningstar.com; data current as of 30 June 2009.

15. "American Century Capital Growth," Yahoo! Finance [accessed 7 September 2009] http://finance.yahoo.com.

16. Morningstar website [accessed 7 September 2009] www.morningstar.com.

17. "Invest Wisely: An Introduction to Mutual Funds," U.S. Securities and Exchange Commission website [accessed 7 September 2009] www.sec.gov.

18. Sam Mamudi, "Active Vs. Passive: Indexing Wins '09," *Wall Street Journal*,

5 March 2009 [accessed 8 September 2009] http://online.wsj.com.

19. Vanguard website [accessed 8 September 2009] http:// personal.vanguard.com.

20. Mayra Rodriquez Valladares, "Overview of Derivatives," archived presentation, CME Group website [accessed 10 September 2009] www.cmegroup.com.

21. Marcy Gordon, "Behind Obama's Plan to Rein in Derivatives," *BusinessWeek*, 13 August 2009, 12; "'Life Settlements' Bonds Could Be Wall Street's Next Big Act," *MarketWatch*, 6 September 2009 [accessed 6 September 2009] www .marketwatch.com.

22. Carol J. Loomis, "Derivatives: The Risk That Still Won't Go Away," *Fortune*, 24 June 2009 [accessed 8 September 2009] http://money.cnn.com.

23. Valladares, "Overview of Derivatives."

24. Valladares, "Overview of Derivatives."

25. Charles R. Morris, *The Two Trillion Dollar Meltdown* (New York: Public Affairs, 2008), 115.

26. Bethany McLean, "The Man Who Lost $6 Billion," *Fortune*, 21 July 2008, 134–144.

27. *Triennial Central Bank Survey: December 2007*, Bank for International Settlements website [accessed 8 September 2009] www.bis.org.

28. Wayne Pinsent, "Credit Default Swaps: An Introduction," Investopedia.com [accessed 8 September 2009] www .investopedia.com.

29. Marcy Gordon, "Behind Obama's Plan to Rein in Derivatives," *BusinessWeek*, 13 August 2009, 12; Colin Barr, "Geithner to Rein in Derivatives," *Fortune*, 13 May 2009 [accessed 8 September 2009] http://money.cnn.com.

30. Datamonitor, "NASDAQ OMX Group, Inc.: Company Profile," 16 July 2008, 19; NASDAQ website [accessed 10 September 2009] www.nasdaq.com.

31. Securities Industry and Financial Markets Association, "Buying and Selling Bonds," Investing in Bonds.com [accessed 10 September 2009] www .investinginbonds.com.

32. Andrew Beattie, "Money Market Vs. Savings Accounts," Investopedia.com [accessed 10 September 2009] www .investopedia.com.

33. Valladares, "Overview of Derivatives."

34. Ben Casselman, "Margin Calls Hitting More Executive Suites," *Wall Street Journal*, 13 October 2008 [accessed 12 September 2009] http://online.wsj.com.

35. See note 1.

Chapter 20

1. Adapted from Peter Eavis, "Jamie Dimon Heads Back to the Future," *Wall Street Journal*, 1 October 2009 [accessed 1 October 2009] http://online.wsj.com; JPMorgan Chase website [accessed 30 September 2009] www.jpmorganchase .com; "The History of JPMorgan Chase & Co.," JPMorgan Chase website [accessed 29 September 2009] www .jpmorganchase.com; Shawn Tully, "In This Corner! The Contender," *Fortune*, 29 March 2006 [accessed 29 September 2009] http://money.cnn.com; Shawn Tully, "Jamie Dimon's Swat Team," *Fortune*, 2 September 2008 [accessed 29 September 2009] http://money.cnn. com; David Ellis and Jeanne Sahadi, "JPMorgan Buys WaMu," CNNMoney.com, 26 September 2008 [accessed 30 September 2009] http:// money.cnn.com; "25 People to Blame for the Financial Crisis," *Time* [accessed 16 September 2009] www.time.com.

2. Roger LeRoy Miller, *Economics Today*, 15th ed. (Boston: Addison Wesley, 2010), 367–368.

3. Miller, *Economics Today*, 371.

4. *The Federal Reserve System: Purposes & Functions*, 9th ed. (Washington, D.C.: Board of Governors of the Federal Reserve System, 2005), 118–119.

5. *The Federal Reserve System: Purposes & Functions*, 60.

6. *The Federal Reserve System: Purposes & Functions*, 1.

7. *The Federal Reserve System: Purposes & Functions*, 36.

8. *The Federal Reserve System: Purposes & Functions*, 41.

9. FDIC website [accessed 27 September 2009] www.fdic.gov.

10. Fannie Mae website [accessed 27 September 2009] www.fanniemae .com.

11. Valentine V. Craig, "Merchant Banking: Past and Present," U.S. Federal Deposit Insurance Corporation website [accessed 27 September 2009] www .fdic.gov.

12. "Private Banking," J.P.Morgan website [accessed 27 September 2009] www .jpmorgan.com.

13. Stephan Labaton, "Accord Reached on Lifting Depression-Era Barriers Among Financial Industries," *New York Times*, 23 October 1999, A1, B4.

14. "The Long Demise of Glass-Steagall," PBS Frontline [accessed 27 September 2009] www.pbs.org.

15. Roddy Boyd, "The Last Days of Bear Stearns," *Fortune*, 31 March 2008 [accessed 27 September 2009] http:// money.cnn.com; "About Us," Goldman Sachs website [accessed 27 September 2009] www2.goldmansachs .com; "Factbox: A Brief History of Lehman Brothers," Reuters, 13 September 2008, [accessed 27 September 2009] www.reuters.com; "Our History," Merrill Lynch website [accessed 27 September 2009] www.ml .com; "Company History," Morgan Stanley website [accessed 27 September 2009] www.morganstanley.com; Sam Mamudi, "Lehman Folds with Record $613 Billion Debt," MarketWatch, 15 September 2008 [accessed 27 September 2009] www.marketwatch .com.

16. Toyota Financial Services website [accessed 28 September 2009] www .toyotafinancial.com.

17. In addition to the specific citations that follow, the material in the second half of the chapter was adapted from the following sources: Frank Ahrens, "Anatomy of a Crisis," webcast, *Washington Post* [accessed 13 September 2009] www.washingtonpost.com; Ryan Barnes, "The Fuel That Fed the Subprime Meltdown," Investopedia.com [accessed 15 September 2009] www .investopedia.com; "Economy in Turmoil," MSNBC.com [accessed 15 September 2009] www.msnbc.com; "25 People to Blame for the Financial Crisis."

18. "Historical Changes of the Target Federal Funds and Discount Rates," Federal Reserve Bank of New York [accessed 20 October 2009] www .newyorkfed.org.

19. Ahrens, "Anatomy of a Crisis."

20. "The Meltdown in Words," *Newsweek* [accessed 16 September 2009] www .newsweek.com.

21. "25 People to Blame for the Financial Crisis."

22. Dennis Capozza and Robert van Order, "Dissecting Defaults," *Mortgage Banker*, August 2009, 34–38.

23. "Consumer Handbook on Adjustable-Rate Mortgages," Federal Reserve Board [accessed 20 October 2009] www .federalreserve.gov.

24. "Consumer Handbook on Adjustable-Rate Mortgages"; "25 People to Blame for the Financial Crisis."

25. Colin Barr, "WaMu: The Forgotten Bank Failure," *Fortune*, 10 September 2009 [accessed 14 September 2009] http://money.cnn.com.

26. Barr, "WaMu: The Forgotten Bank Failure."

27. Ahrens, "Anatomy of a Crisis."

28. Barnes, "The Fuel That Fed the Subprime Meltdown."

29. Sumit Agarwal and Calvin T. Ho, "Comparing the Prime and Subprime Mortgage Markets," *Chicago Fed Letter*, August 2007, 1–4.

30. Kevin Kane and Lorraine Woos, "Is CRA Responsible for the Meltdown?" *Mortgage Banking*, May 2009, 32–41.

31. "25 People to Blame for the Financial Crisis."

32. Eric Rosengren and Janet Yellen, "Foreward," in *Revisiting the*

CRA: Perspectives on the Future of the Community Reinvestment Act (published by the Federal Reserve Banks of Boston and San Francisco, 2009), 1.

33. Randall Kroszner, "The Community Reinvestment Act and the Recent Mortgage Crisis," in Revisiting the CRA: Perspectives on the Future of the Community Reinvestment Act (published by the Federal Reserve Banks of Boston and San Francisco, 2009), 8–11.
34. "The Meltdown in Words."
35. Kirk Shinkle, "Inside the Subprime Debacle," U.S. News & World Report, 21 July 2008, 112.
36. "About MBS/ABS," Investinginbonds.com [accessed 19 September 2009] www.investinginbonds.com.
37. Richard J. Rosen, "The Role of Securitization in Mortgage Lending," Chicago Fed Letter, November 2007, 1–4.
38. "25 People to Blame for the Financial Crisis."
39. "25 People to Blame for the Financial Crisis."
40. "The Meltdown in Words."
41. "Dissecting the Bear Stearns Hedge Fund Collapse," Investopedia.com [accessed 14 October 2009] www.investopedia.com.
42. "American Home Mortgage Seeks Chapter 11 Bankruptcy Protection," New York Times, 7 August 2007 [accessed 22 September 2009] www.nytimes.com.
43. Ahrens, "Anatomy of a Crisis."
44. "Feds Take Over Mortgage Lender IndyMac," MSNBC.com, 12 July 2008 [accessed 22 September 2009] www.msnbc.com.
45. Bill Saporito, "Top 10 Financial Collapses," Time [accessed 23 September 2009] www.time.com.
46. Dan Fitzpatrick and Joann S. Lublin, "Bank of America Chief Resigns Under Fire," Wall Street Journal, 1 October 2009 [accessed 1 October 2009] http://online.wsj.com.
47. Andy Serwer, Nina Easton, and Allan Sloan, "Geithner: 'We Were Looking at the Abyss,'" Fortune, 10 September 2009 [accessed 23 September 2009] http://money.cnn.com; Saporito, "Top 10 Financial Collapses;" "Record Stock Market Falls in 2008," BBC News, 31 December 2008 [accessed 1 October 2009] http://news.bbc.co.uk.
48. Michael Lewis, "The Man Who Crashed the World," Vanity Fair, August 2009 [accessed 23 September 2009] www.vanityfair.com.
49. Binyamin Appelbaum, "U.S. Forces WaMu Sale as Bank Founders," Washington Post, 26 September 2008 [accessed 23 September 2009] www.washingtonpost.com.
50. Mohamed El-Erian, "When Wall Street Nearly Collapsed," Fortune [accessed 14 October 2009] http://money.cnn.com.
51. "Fed Overnight Rate at 0% for Most of Next Year, Predicts J.P. Morgan Securities," Financial Week, 1 December 2008 [accessed 25 September 2009] www.financialweek.com
52. Allan Sloan, "Lessons of the Crash of '08," Fortune, 14 September 2009 [accessed 23 September 2009] http://money.cnn.com.
53. Jon Hilsenrath and Deborah Solomon, "No Easy Exit for Government as Housing Market's Savior," Wall Street Journal, 15 September 2009 [accessed 15 September 2009] http://online.wsj.com.
54. Gretchen Morgenson, "Housing Bust: It Won't Be Pretty," New York Times, 25 July 2004 [accessed 12 January 2005] www.nytimes.com; Christopher Palmeri and Rich Miller, "ARMed and Dangerous?" BusinessWeek, 12 April 2004, 82–84.
55. Palmeri and Miller, "Armed and Dangerous?;" "Greenspan Sharpens Warning About 'Exotic' Mortgages," Mortgage Banking, November 2005, 10–11.
56. "The Meltdown in Words."
57. Mohamed El-Erian, "When Wall Street Nearly Collapsed."
58. "U.S. Banks Post Some of the Worst Losses of Banks Globally in 2008," Mortgage Banking, August 2008, 16.
59. Marcy Gordon, "FDIC Says Bank Failures to Cost Around $100B," Seattle Times, 29 September 2009 [accessed 29 September 2009] www.seattletimes.com.
60. David Segal, "We're Dull, Small Banks Say, and Have Profit to Show for It," New York Times, 11 May 2009 [accessed 29 September 2009] www.nytimes.com.
61. See note 1.
62. Adapted from "Meeting the FACTA Identity Theft 'Red Flag' Rules," RSA website [accessed 28 September 2009] www.rsa.com; "New 'Red Flag' Requirements for Financial Institutions and Creditors Will Help Fight Identity Theft," U.S. Federal Trade Commission website [accessed 28 September 2009] www.ftc.gov.

Appendix A

(appendixes available online at http://www.mybizlab.com)

1. Henry R. Cheeseman, Business Law, 7th ed. (Upper Saddle River, N.J.: Pearson Prentice Hall, 2010), 849.
2. Cheeseman, Business Law, 281.
3. George A. Steiner and John F. Steiner, Business, Government, and Society (New York: McGraw-Hill, 1991), 149.
4. Lee Applebaum, "The 'New' Business Courts," Business Law Today, March/April 2008 [accessed 10 October 2009] www.abanet.org.
5. Cheeseman, Business Law, 75.
6. Nancy K. Kubasek, Bartley A. Brennan, and M. Neil Browne, The Legal Environment of Business, 3rd ed. (Upper Saddle River, N.J.: Pearson Prentice Hall, 2003), 306.
7. Kubasek, Brennan, and Browne, The Legal Environment of Business, 184.
8. Cheeseman, Business Law, 89.
9. Mark A. Hofmann, "Tort Reform Backers Win Some Battles to Reduce Liability Risks," Business Insurance, 3 November 2008, 19–21.
10. Cheeseman, Business Law, 158–159.
11. Cheeseman, Business Law, 154.
12. Kubasek, Brennan, and Browne, The Legal Environment of Business, 128.
13. Samuel Maull, "Judge Rules No Damages to Rosie, Publisher," AP Online, 20 February 2004 [accessed 16 May 2004] www.highbeam.com.
14. Cheeseman, Business Law, 330.
15. Kubasek, Brennan, and Browne, The Legal Environment of Business, 160; Douglas Whitman and John William Gergacz, The Legal Environment of Business (New York: McGraw-Hill, 1990), 260.
16. Cheeseman, Business Law, 111.
17. Betsy D. Gelb and Partha Krishnamurthy, "Protect Your Product's Look and Feel from Imitators," Harvard Business Review, October 2008, 36.
18. Cheeseman, Business Law, 116.
19. Cheeseman, Business Law, 119.
20. Unintended Consequences: Ten Years under the DMCA, white paper, Electronic Frontier Foundation, October 2008, 1.
21. Cheeseman, Business Law, 341.
22. "Bankruptcy Basics," Administrative Offices of the U.S. Courts website [accessed 10 October 2009] www.uscourts.gov.

Appendix B

1. "Spotlight on Risk," Harvard Business Review, October 2009, 67.
2. Nassim N. Taleb, Daniel G. Goldstein, and Mark W. Spitznagel, "The Six Mistakes Executives Make in Risk Management," Harvard Business Review, October 2009, 78–81.
3. Mark S. Dorfman, Introduction to Risk Management and Insurance, 8th ed. (Upper Saddle River, N.J.: Pearson Prentice-Hall, 2005), 19–24.

4. Robert S. Kaplan, Anette Mikes, Robert Simons, Peter Tufano, and Michael Hofmann, "Managing Risk in the New World," *Harvard Business Review*, October 2009, 69–75.

5. Dorfman, *Introduction to Risk Management and Insurance*, 153.

6. Nick Whitfield, "Business Interruption May Cost More than Damage," *Business Insurance*, 4 August 2008, 17–19.

7. Roberto Ceniceros, "Studio Fire Sparks Business Interruption Losses," *Business Insurance*, 9 June 2008, 4.

8. "Understanding General Liability Insurance," Dun & Bradstreet website [accessed 13 October 2009] http://smallbusinessdnb.com.

9. Karen E. Klein, "Is Liability Insurance a Must to Go Global?" *BusinessWeek*, 18 June 2008 [accessed 13 October 2009] www.businessweek.com.

10. Dorfman, *Introduction to Risk Management and Insurance*, 391.

11. Dorfman, *Introduction to Risk Management and Insurance*, 394.

12. "Understanding General Liability Insurance."

13. "Key Person Insurance Can Help Companies Mourning an Owner or Executive," Insure.com, 28 May 2009 [accessed 13 October 2009] www.insure.com; Dorfman, *Introduction to Risk Management and Insurance*, 51.

14. Nancy L. Bolton, "Self-Insurance Survival: Creating a Health Plan in Unsuccessful Times," *Employee Benefit News*, July 2009, 14–16.

15. Zack Phillips, "In Tight Market Energy Firms Drop Cover, Cross Fingers," *Business Insurance*, 31 August 2009, 1+.

16. Joanne Wojcik, "Microsoft Relies on Self-Insurance for Most Exposures," *Business Insurance*, 20 April 2009, 34–37.

17. Blue Cross and Blue Shield Association website [accessed 13 October 2009] www.bcbs.com.

18. Dorfman, *Introduction to Risk Management and Insurance*, 73.

19. Dorfman, *Introduction to Risk Management and Insurance*, 74.

20. "CIGNA Preferred Provider Organization (PPO)," Cigna website [accessed 13 October 2009] www.cigna.com.

21. "Fact Sheet: Dramatic Growth of Health Savings Accounts (HSAs)," U.S. Department of the Treasury website [accessed 13 October 2009] www.ustreas.gov.

22. "Individual: The HSA for Life Health Savings Account," Bank of America website [accessed 13 October 2009] www.bankofamerica.com.

23. Stacey L. Bradford, "Do You Need Disability Insurance?" *SmartMoney*, 10 September 2008 [accessed 13 October 2009] www.smartmoney.com.

24. Dorfman, *Introduction to Risk Management and Insurance*, 461–468.

25. Jack Hough, "Should You Hurry to Buy Life Insurance?" *SmartMoney*, 18 September 2009 [accessed 13 October 2009] www.smartmoney.com; Miriam Gottfried, "Should You Buy Term Life Insurance?" *SmartMoney*, 10 September 2009 [accessed 13 October 2009] www.smartmoney.com; Dorfman, *Introduction to Risk Management and Insurance*, 256–260.

26. Ginger Applegarth, "Term or Permanent Life Insurance?" MSN Money, 21 July 2009 [accessed 13 October 2009] http://articles.moneycentral.msn.com.

27. Dorfman, *Introduction to Risk Management and Insurance*, 263–265.

Appendix C

1. Daniel Lyons, "Too Much Information," *Forbes*, 13 December 2004, 110–115.

2. Irma Becerra-Fernandez, Avelino Gonzalez, and Rajiv Sabherwal, *Knowledge Management* (Upper Saddle River, N.J.: Pearson Prentice Hall, 2004), 200.

3. Kenneth C. Laudon and Jane P. Laudon, *Management Information Systems*, 8th ed. (Upper Saddle River, N.J.: Pearson Prentice Hall, 2004), 325.

4. Victoria Murphy Barret, "Fight the Jerks," *Forbes*, 2 July 2007, 52–54.

5. "Cyber-Gloom on the Horizon," *Accountancy*, January 2009, 59; Spencer E. Ante and Brian Grow, "Meet the Hackers," *BusinessWeek*, 29 May 2006 [accessed 26 June 2007] www.businessweek.com.

6. Robert McMillan, "Data Scam Hits Grad Students," *Computerworld*, 9 June 2008, 6.

7. "Boom Time for Cybercrime," *Consumer Reports*, June 2009, 18–21; Sharon Gaudin, "The Move to Web 2.0 Increases Security Challenges," *InformationWeek*, 24 May 2007 [accessed 26 June 2007] www.informationweek.com.

8. "Employee Communication Is Cause for Concern," Duane Morris LLP website, 23 August 2006 [accessed 4 October 2006] www.duanemorris.com.

9. Greg Burns, "For Some, Benefits of E-Mail Not Worth Risk," *San Diego Union-Tribune*, 16 August 2005, A1, A8; Pui-Wing Tam, Erin White, Nick Wingfield, and Kris Maher, "Snooping E-Mail by Software Is Now a Workplace Norm," *Wall Street Journal*, 9 March 2005, B1+.

10. Jeffrey Gangemi, "Cybercriminals Target Small Biz," *BusinessWeek*, 11 December 2006 [accessed 26 June 2007] www.businessweek.com.

11. Al Senia, "High-Tech Handsets Are Hacker Bait," *BusinessWeek*, 10 January 2007 [accessed 26 June 2007] www.businessweek.com; Ken Belson, "Hackers Are Discovering a New Frontier: Internet Telephone Service," *New York Times*, 2 August 2004, C4; Yuki Noguchi, "Hold the Phone: Hackers Starting to Infect Our Cells," *Seattle Times*, 26 November 2004 [accessed 26 November 2004] www.seattletimes.com; Steven Ranger, "Mobile Virus Epidemic Heading This Way," *Test Bed Blog*, 10 February 2005 [accessed 10 February 2005] www.vnunet.com; Stephanie N. Mehta, "Wireless Scrambles to Batten Down the Hatches," *Fortune*, 18 October 2004, 275–280.

12. Sharon Gaudin, "Thumb Drives Replace Malware as Top Security Concern, Study Finds," *InformationWeek*, 7 May 2007 [accessed 26 June 2007] www.informationweek.com.

13. Tara Craig, "How to Avoid Information Overload," *Personnel Today*, 10 June 2008, 31; Jeff Davidson, "Fighting Information Overload," *Canadian Manager*, Spring 2005, 16+.

14. Edward Cone, "Dealing with Data Overload," *CIO Insight*, January/February 2009, 16–17.

15. Sushil K. Sharma and Jatinder N. D. Gupta, "Improving Workers' Productivity and Reducing Internet Abuse," *Journal of Computer Information Systems*, Winter 2003–2004, 74–78.

16. Jack Trout, "Beware of 'Infomania,'" *Forbes*, 11 August 2006 [accessed 5 October 2006] www.forbes.com.

17. Laudon and Laudon, *Management Information Systems*, 208.

18. Stuart Crainer and Des Dearlove, "Making Yourself Understood," *Across the Board*, May/June 2004, 23–27.

19. Steve Lohr, "As Travel Costs Rise, More Meetings Go Virtual," *New York Times*, 22 July 2008 [accessed 23 July 2008] www.nytimes.com.

Appendix D

1. Jack R. Kapoor, Les R. Dlabay, and Robert J. Hughes, *Personal Finance*, 7th ed. (New York: McGraw-Hill/Irwin, 2004), 18.

2. "Interview Tips," WiserAdvisor.com [accessed 14 October 2009] www.wiseradvisor.com.

3. Arthur J. Keown, *Personal Finance: Turning Money into Wealth*, 3rd ed. (Upper Saddle River, N.J.: Prentice Hall, 2003), 52–53.

4. Kapoor et al., *Personal Finance*, 11; Lawrence J. Gitman and Michael D. Joehnk, *Personal Financial Planning*,

10th ed. (Mason, Ohio: Thomson South-Western, 2005), 5.

5. Gitman and Joehnk, *Personal Financial Planning*, 15.

6. Deborah Fowles, "The Psychology of Spending Money," About.com [accessed 22 May 2004] www.about.com.

7. Gitman and Joehnk, *Personal Financial Planning*, 15.

8. Kathy Kristof, "Crushed by College," *Forbes*, 2 February 2009, 60–65.

9. Kristof, "Crushed by College."

10. Ben Elgin, "Study Now—and Pay and Pay and Pay Later," 21 May 2007, *BusinessWeek*, 66–67; Kristof, "Crushed by College."

11. Philip Reed, "Drive a (Nearly) New Car for (Almost) Nothing," Edmunds.com [accessed 22 May 2004] www.edmunds.com.

12. Chandler Phillips, "Confessions of a Car Salesman," Edmunds.com [accessed 22 May 2004] www.edmunds.com.

13. Eryn Brown, "How to Get Paid What You're Worth," *Business 2.0*, May 2004, 102–110, 134.

14. Keown, *Personal Finance: Turning Money into Wealth*, 143–148; Gitman and Joehnk, *Personal Financial Planning*, 140–147.

15. Kapoor et al., *Personal Finance*, 222.

16. "Ads Promising Debt Relief May Be Offering Bankruptcy," FTC Consumer Alert [accessed 23 May 2004] www.ftc.gov.

17. Christopher Conkey, "Bankruptcy Overall Means Tougher Choices," *Wall Street Journal*, 22 May 2005 [accessed 10 June 2005] www.wsj.com.

18. Kapoor et al., *Personal Finance*, 582.

Illustration and Text Credits

Prologue

1. Exhibit 3 - Source: The Riley Guide [accessed 5 August 2009] www.rileyguide.com; SimplyHired website [accessed 5 August 2009] www.simplyhired.com; Indeed website [accessed 5 August 2009] www.indeed.com; CollegeRecruiter.com [accessed 5 August 2009] www.collegerecruiter.com; Jobster website [accessed 30 March 2008] www.jobster.com; InternshipPrograms.com [accessed 30 March 2008] http://internshipprograms.com.

2. Exhibit 8 - Source: Adapted from Joe Conklin, "Turning the Tables: Six Questions to Ask Your Interviewer," *Quality Progress*, November 2007, 55;

Andrea N. Browne, "Keeping the Momentum at the Interview; Ask Questions, Do Your Research, and Be a Team Player," *Washington Post*, 29 July 2007, K1; Marilyn Sherman, "Questions R Us: What to Ask at a Job Interview," *Career World*, January 2004, 20; H. Lee Rust, *Job Search: The Complete Manual for Jobseekers* (New York: American Management Association, 1979), 56.

3. Exhibit 9 - Source: Adapted from InterviewUp website [accessed 6 April 2008] www.interviewup.com; "Interview Questions Asked by Recruiters," Northwestern University Career Services website [accessed 18 October 2009] www.northwestern.edu/careers.

Chapter 1

1. Exhibit 1.3 - Kurt Badenhausen, "The Best States for Business," *Forbes*, 31 July 2008 [accessed 6 May 2009] www.forbes.com.

2. Exhibit 1.5 - Adapted from Arlene Dohm and Lynn Schniper, "Occupational Employment Projections to 2016," *Monthly Labor Review*, November 2007, 86–125.

Chapter 2

1. Exhibit 2.4 - Roger LeRoy Miller, *Economics Today*, 15th ed. (Boston: Addison Wesley, 2010), 175.

Chapter 3

1. Exhibit 3.1 - Michael E. Porter and Klaus Schwab, *Global Competitiveness Report 2008–2009*, World Economic Forum website [accessed 27 May 2009] www.weforum.org.

2. Exhibit 3.2 - "U.S. International Trade in Goods and Services," U.S. Bureau of Economic Analysis website [accessed 24 May 2009] www.bea.gov.

3. Exhibit 3.3 - Adapted from "Strong Dollar, Weak Dollar: Foreign Exchange Rates and the U.S. Economy," Federal Reserve Bank of Chicago website [accessed 24 May 2009] www.chicagofed.org; Edmund L. Andrews, "Strong Dollar, Weak Dollar: Anyone Have a Scorecard?," *New York Times*, 24 September 2003 [accessed 11 December 2009] www.nytimes.com; Javier C. Hernandez, "October U.S. Trade Deficit Narrowed as Exports Rose," *New York Times*, 11 December 2009 [accessed 11 December 2009] www.nytimes.com.

4. Exhibit 3.5 - Courtland L. Bovée and John V. Thill, *Business Communication Today*, 10th ed. (Upper Saddle River, N.J.: Pearson Prentice Hall, 2010), 76.

Chapter 4

1. Exhibit 4.1 - Adapted from "AT&T Inc. Code Of Ethics," AT&T website [accessed 3 June 2009] www.att.com.

2. Exhibit 4.2 - Adapted from Manuel Velasquez, Claire Andre, Thomas Shanks, S.J., and Michael J. Meyer, "Thinking Ethically: A Framework for Moral Decision Making," Markkula Center for Applied Ethics, Santa Clara University [accessed 3 June 2009] www.scu.edu; Ben Rogers, "John Rawls," *The Guardian*, 27 November 2002 [accessed 3 June 2009] www.guardian.co.uk; Irene Van Staveren, "Beyond Utilitarianism and Deontology: Ethics in Economics," *Review of Political Economy*, January 2007, 21–35.

3. Exhibit 4.5 - "Energy in Brief," U.S. Energy Information Administration website [accessed 3 June 2009] www.eia.doe.gov.

4. Exhibit 4.6 - U.S. Environmental Protection Agency website [accessed 3 June 2009] www.epa.gov.

5. Exhibit 4.8 - "Census of Fatal Occupational Injuries," U.S. Bureau of Labor Statistics website [accessed 3 June 2009] www.bls.gov.

Chapter 6

1. Exhibit 6.1 - Adapted from "The Coolest College Start-ups," *Inc.* [accessed 2 April 2009] www.inc.com; Punch Energy website [accessed 2 April 2009] www.punchenergy.com; PickTeams website [accessed 2 April 2009] http://pickteams.com; internshipIN website [accessed 2 April 2009] www.internshipin.com; Simply Splendid Donuts & Ice Cream website [accessed 2 April 2009] www.ssdonuts.com.

2. Exhibit 6.2 - Adapted from Norman M. Scarborough and Thomas W. Zimmerer, *Effective Small Business Management*, 7th ed. (Upper Saddle River, N.J.: Prentice Hall, 2003), 9–14.

3. Exhibit 6.3 - Adapted from Norman M. Scarborough and Thomas W. Zimmerer, *Effective Small Business Management*, 7th ed. (Upper Saddle River, N.J.: Prentice Hall, 2003), 27–29.

4. Exhibit 6.4 - Adapted from Dan Schawbel, "Top 10 Social Networks for Entrepreneurs," Mashable 12 March 2009 [accessed 2 April 2009] http://mashable.com.

5. Exhibit 6.5 - Adapted from "Buying a Franchise: A Consumer Guide," U.S. Federal Trade Commission website [accessed 2 April 2009] www.ftc.gov.

Chapter 7

1. Exhibit 7.5 - Robert E. Kaplan and Robert B. Kaiser, "Stop Overdoing Your

Strengths," *Harvard Business Review*, February 2009, 100–103.

2. Exhibit 7.6 - Adapted from Andrew Bird, "Do You Know What Your Corporate Culture Is?" *CPA Insight*, February, March 1999, 25–26; Gail H. Vergara, "Finding a Compatible Corporate Culture," *Healthcare Executive*, January/February 1999, 46–47; Hal Lancaster, "To Avoid a Job Failure, Learn the Culture of a Company First," *Wall Street Journal*, 14 July 1998, B1.

Chapter 8

1. Exhibit 8.6 - Adapted from Christopher Carfi and Leif Chastaine, "Social Networking for Businesses & Organizations," white paper, Cerado website [accessed 13 August 2008] www.cerado.com; Anusorn Kansap, "Social Networking," PowerPoint presentation, Silpakorn University [accessed 14 August 2008] http://real-timeupdates.com; "Social Network Websites: Best Practices from Leading Services," white paper, 28 November 2007, FaberNovel Consulting [accessed 14 August 2008] www.fabernovel.com.

Chapter 9

1. Exhibit 9.2 - Used with permission from isee systems, Inc., www.iseesystems.com.

2. Exhibit 9.3 - Peter Fingar and Ronald Aronica, "Value Chain Optimization: The New Way of Competing," *Supply Chain Management Review*, September–October 2001, 82. Reprinted by permission of YGS Group.

Chapter 10

1. Exhibit 10.2 - *Management, Fourth Edition*, by Richard L. Daft copyright © 1997 by Harcourt Inc., reproduced by permission of the publisher.

2. Exhibit 10.3 - Adapted from Stephen P. Robbins and David A. DeCenzo, *Fundamentals of Management*, 4th ed. (Upper Saddle River, N.J.: Pearson Prentice Hall, 2004), 289.

3. Exhibit 10.5 - Adapted from Richard J. Hackman and Greg R. Oldman, "Motivation Through the Design of Work: Test of a Theory," *Organizational Behavior & Human Performance*, August 1976, 250–279.

Chapter 11

1. Figure 11.3 - Adapted from Richard Nelson Bolles, *What Color Is Your Parachute?* (Berkeley, Calif.: Ten Speed Press, 2009), www.tenspeed.com.

2. Figure 11.4 - Adapted from Henry R. Cheeseman, *Contemporary Business and E-Commerce Law*, 7th ed. (Upper Saddle River, N.J.: Pearson Prentice Hall, 2010), 487–495; "The Lilly Ledbetter Fair Pay Act of 2009," U.S. White House website [accessed 23 June 2009] www.whitehouse.gov.

3. Figure 11.6 - Adapted from Sarah Rubenstein, "Keeping Coverage," *Wall Street Journal*, 24 January 2005, R5; "Multiple Employer Initiatives: Working for Better Health Care," *HRFocus*, July 2004, 11–15; Traci Purdum, "Health Care for All," *IndustryWeek*, August 2004, 12; Milt Freudenheim, "60 Companies Plan to Sponsor Health Coverage for Uninsured," *New York Times*, 27 January 2005, C1, C17; Michelle Rafter, "The Insider: Health Care Benefits," *Workforce Management*, December 2004, 72; Maryann Hammers, "Sliding-Scale Plans Seeing a Renaissance," *Workforce Management*, January 2005, 22; Vanessa Furhmans, "One Cure for High Health Costs: In-House Clinics at Companies," *Wall Street Journal*, 11 February 2005, A1, A8; Charlotte Huff, "The Insider: Health Benefits," *Workforce Management*, November 2004, 69–70; Eve Tahmincioglu, "Tackling the High Cost of Health Benefits Takes Some Creativity," *New York Times*, 26 August 2004, C6; Carrie Coolidge, "Saving for Your Health," *Forbes*, 13 December 2004, 240–244; Sara Horowitz, "Ensure They're Insured," *Harvard Business Review*, December 2004, 24; Kris Maher, "Popular . . . but Cheap," *Wall Street Journal*, 24 January 2005, R4.

Chapter 12

1. Figure 12.2 - Based on "Table of State Right-to-Work Laws as of January 1, 2006," U.S. Department of Labor website [accessed 7 July 2009] www.dol.gov.

2. Figure 12.3 - Based on Michael R. Carrell and Christina Heavrin, *Labor Relations and Collective Bargaining: Cases, Practice, and Law*, 9th ed. (Upper Saddle River, N.J.: Pearson Prentice Hall, 2010), 129–134; "Procedures Guide," U.S. National Labor Relations Board website [accessed 28 June 2009] www.nlrb.gov.

3. Figure 12.5: Based on data from "Union Membership and Coverage Database from the CPS," Unionstats.com [accessed 10 July 2009] http://unionstats.gsu.edu.

Chapter 13

1. Figure 13.2 - Philip Kotler and Gary Armstrong, *Principles of Marketing*, 13th ed. (Upper Saddle River, N.J.: Pearson Prentice Hall, 2010), 10.

2. Figure 13.3 - Adapted from Ken Anderson, "Ethnographic Research: A Key to Strategy," *Harvard Business Review*, March 2009, 24; Emily R. Murphy, Judy Illes, and Peter B. Reiner, "Neuroethics of Neuromarketing," *Journal of Consumer Behaviour*, July–October 2008, 293–302; Dick Bucci, "Recording Systems Add More Depth when Capturing Answers," *Marketing News*, 1 March 2005, 50; Laurence Bernstein, "Enough Research Bashing!" *Marketing*, 24 January 2005, 10; Naresh K. Malhotra, *Basic Marketing Research* (Upper Saddle River, N.J.: Pearson Prentice Hall, 2002), 110–112, 208–212, 228–229.

3. Figure 13.6 - Adapted from Philip Kotler and Gary Armstrong, *Principles of Marketing*, 13th ed. (Upper Saddle River, N.J.: Pearson Prentice Hall, 2010), 201–207.

Chapter 14

1. Figure 14.2 - Adapted from Philip Kotler and Gary Armstrong, *Principles of Marketing*, 10th ed. (Upper Saddle River, N.J.: Pearson Prentice Hall, 2004), 279.

2. Figure 14.3 - Adapted from Philip Kotler and Gary Armstrong, *Principles of Marketing*, 10th ed. (Upper Saddle River, N.J.: Pearson Prentice Hall, 2004), 330.

3. Figure 14.5 - Based on General Mills website [accessed 27 July 2009] www.generalmills.com.

Chapter 15

1. Figure 15.1 - Adapted from Philip Kotler, *Marketing Management*, 10th ed. (Upper Saddle River, N.J.: Pearson Prentice Hall, 2000), 491.

Chapter 16

1. Figure 16.4 - Adapted from Jeffrey M. O'Brien, "The Wizards of Apps," *Fortune*, 5 May 2009, 29–30; Christopher Meyer, "The Year of Marketing Dangerously," *Harvard Business Review*, October 2008, 26–27; Magid Abraham, "The Off-Line Impact of Online Ads," *Harvard Business Review*, April 2008, 28; Michael A. Wiles and Anna Danielova, "The Worth of Product Placement in Successful Films: An Event Study Analysis," *Journal of Marketing*, July 2009, 44–63; Sarah Chung and Tina Hedges, "Is Your Digital Marketing a Turn-On?" *Global Cosmetic Industry*, July 2009, 22–24; Douglas MacMillan, "What Works in Online Video Advertising?" *BusinessWeek*, 28 January 2009, 26; Guy Yaniv, "Sold on Mobile Marketing:

Effective Wireless Carrier Mobile Advertising and How to Make It Even More So," *International Journal of Mobile Marketing*, December 2008, 86–91; Kenneth E. Clow and Donald Baack, *Integrated Advertising, Promotion, and Marketing Communications*, 4th ed. (Upper Saddle River, N.J.: Pearson Prentice Hall, 2010), 219–229.

Chapter 18

1. Exhibit 18.6 - IPO activity from *Shifting Landscape—Are You Ready? Global IPO Trends Report 2009*, Ernst & Young, 2009, 6; S&P 500 data from "S&P 500 Index," CNNMoney.com [accessed 31 August 2009] http://money.cnn.com.

Chapter 19

1. Exhibit 19.1 - Adapted from Arthur J. Keown, *Personal Finance: Turning Money into Wealth*, 3rd ed. (Upper Saddle River, N.J.: Pearson Prentice Hall, 2003), 424–425; Jack R. Kapoor, Les R. Dlabay, and Robert J. Hughes, *Personal Finance*, 7th ed. (Boston: McGraw-Hill Irwin, 2004), 460–461.

2. Exhibit 19.7 - DJIA month-end data retrieved from Dow Jones Averages [accessed 12 September 2009] www.djaverages.com

Chapter 20

1. Exhibit 20.2 - "S&PCase-Shiller Home Price Indices, September 29, 2009: Historical Values" [accessed 1 October 2009] www2.standardandpoors.com.

2. Exhibit 20.3 - William B. Shear, Director of Financial Markets and Community Investment, U.S. Government Accountability Office, "Characteristics and Performance of Nonprime Mortgages," 28 July 2009, memo to Representative Carolyn B. Maloney and Senator Charles R. Schumer.

3. Exhibit 20.5 - Adapted from Stephen Gandel, "Why Your Bank Is Broke," *Time*, 31 January 2009 [accessed 1 October 2009] www.time.com; Eric Gelman, "Fear of a Black Swan," *Fortune*, 3 April 2008 [accessed 1 October 2009] http://money.cnn.com; Frank Ahrens, "Anatomy of a Crisis," webcast, *Washington Post* [accessed 13 September 2009] www.washingtonpost.com; Ryan Barnes, "The Fuel That Fed the Subprime Meltdown," Investopedia.com [accessed 15 September 2009] www.investopedia.com; "Economy in Turmoil," MSNBC.com [accessed 15 September 2009] www.msnbc.com; "25

People to Blame for the Financial Crisis," *Time* [accessed 16 September 2009] www.time.com.

Appendix A

1. Exhibit A.1: Adapted from Bartley A. Brennan and Nancy Kubasek, *The Legal Environment of Business* (New York: Macmillan, 1988), 24; Douglas Whitman and John Gergacz, *The Legal Environment of Business*, 2nd ed. (New York: Random House, 1988), 22, 25.

2. Exhibit A.3: Adapted from Richard A. Brealely and Stewart C. Myers, *Principles of Corporate Finance*, 4th ed. (New York: McGraw-Hill, 1991), 761–765.

Appendix B

1. Exhibit B-4: Adapted from Mark S. Dorfman, *Introduction to Risk Management and Insurance*, 8th ed. (Upper Saddle River, N.J.: Pearson Prentice Hall, 2005), 296–301.

Appendix D

1. Exhibit D.5: Adapted from Lawrence J. Gitman and Michael D. Joehnk, *Personal Financial Planning*, 10th ed. (Mason, Ohio: Thomson South-Western, 2005), 139–143; Jack R. Kapoor, Les R. Dlabay, and Robert J. Hughes, *Personal Finance*, 7th ed. (New York: McGraw-Hill/Irwin, 2004), 141; Arthur J. Keown, *Personal Finance: Turning Money into Wealth*, 3rd ed. (Upper Saddle River, N.J.: Prentice Hall, 2003), 150.

Photo Credits

Prologue

36   Mark Richards/PhotoEdit Inc.
49   Jon Feingersh/zefa/Jon Feingersh

Chapter 1

51   Alamy Images Royalty Free
52   Enter the Haggis
55   Jim Bryant/Landov Media
71   Rob Lewine/CORBIS
72   Enter the Haggis

Chapter 2

75   Carlos Osorio/AP Wide World Photos
76   AP Wide World Photos
79   Eric Risberg/AP Wide World Photos

92   Getty Images, Inc.
93   AP Wide World Photos

Chapter 3

97   iStockphoto
98   MTV Networks Africa
106   Ramon Espinosa/AP Wide World Photos
113   Getty Images
116   MTV Networks Africa

Chapter 4

120   Getty Images
121   Frank May/AP Wide World Photos
132   Basel Action Network (www.ban.org)
140   Frank May/AP Wide World Photos

Chapter 5

144   Beth Hall/Bloomberg via Getty Images
145   Even Agostini/AP Wide World Photos
149   Alamy Images Royalty Free
162   Even Agostini/AP Wide World Photos

Chapter 6

166   iStockphoto
167   Sister Sky
168   Photo by Tim Barnwell
172   Jim Wilson/Redux Pictures
185   Sister Sky

Chapter 7

189   Ed Horowitz/Image Bank/Getty Images
190   Wegmans Food Markets, Inc.
209   Wegmans Food Markets, Inc.

Chapter 8

213   PhotoDisc/Getty Images
214   Stuart Bayer/The Journal News
233   Peter Wynn Thompson/The New York Times\Redux Pictures
235   Stuart Bayer/The Journal News

Chapter 9

239   Vasily Smirnov/Shutterstock
240   Carvin Customized Guitars/CARVIN Customized Guitars
248   Macduff Everton/CORBIS-NY

Glossary

360-degree review Multidimensional review in which a person is given feedback from subordinates, peers, and superiors

401(k) plan A defined contribution retirement plan in which employers often match the amount employees invest

accounting Measuring, interpreting, and communicating financial information to support internal and external decision making

accounting equation Basic accounting equation stating that assets equal liabilities plus owners' equity

accounts payable Amounts that a firm currently owes to other parties

accounts receivable Amounts that are currently owed to a firm

accounts receivable turnover ratio Measure of time a company takes to turn its accounts receivable into cash, calculated by dividing sales by the average value of accounts receivable for a period

accrual basis Accounting method in which revenue is recorded when a sale is made and expense is recorded when it is incurred

acquisition Action taken by one company to buy a controlling interest in the voting stock of another company

adjustable rate mortgage (ARM) Mortgage that features variable interest rates over the life of the loan

administrative skills Technical skills in information gathering, data analysis, planning, organizing, and other aspects of managerial work

advertising The delivery of announcements and promotional messages via time or space purchased in various media

advertising appeal Creative tactic designed to capture the audience's attention and promote preference for the product or company being advertised

advertising media Communications channels, such as newspapers, radio, television, and the World Wide Web

advisory board A team of people with subject-area expertise or vital contacts who help a business owner review plans and decisions

advocacy advertising Advertising that presents a company's opinions on public issues such as education or health care

affirmative action Activities undertaken by businesses to recruit and promote members of groups whose economic progress has been hindered through either legal barriers or established practices

agenda List of topics to be addressed in a meeting, the person(s) responsible for each topic, and the time allotted to each topic

agents and brokers Independent wholesalers that do not take title to the goods they distribute but may or may not take possession of those goods

agile organization Company whose structure, policies, and capabilities allow employees to respond quickly to customer needs and changes in the business environment

angel investors Private individuals who invest money in start-ups, usually earlier in a business's life and in smaller amounts than VCs are willing to invest or banks are willing to lend

arbitration Decision process in which an impartial referee listens to both sides and then makes a judgment by accepting one side's view

asset allocation Managing a portfolio to balance potential returns with an acceptable level of risk

asset-backed securities (ABSs) Credit derivatives based on auto loans, credit card debts, and other loan assets

assets Any things of value owned or leased by a business

audit Formal evaluation of the fairness and reliability of a client's financial statements

authorization cards Cards signed by employees to indicate interest in having a union represent them

autocratic leaders Leaders who do not involve others in decision making

balance of payments Sum of all payments one nation receives from other nations minus the sum of all payments it makes to other nations, over some specified period of time

balance of trade Total value of the products a nation exports minus the total value of the products it imports, over some period of time

balance sheet Statement of a firm's financial position on a particular date; also known as a statement of financial position

balanced scorecard Method of monitoring the performance from four perspectives: finances, operations, customer relationships, and the growth and development of employees and intellectual property

barrier to entry Any resource or capability a company must have before it can start competing in a given market

bear market Market situation in which most stocks are decreasing in value

behavioral segmentation Categorization of customers according to their relationship with products or response to product characteristics

benchmarking Collecting and comparing process and performance data from other companies

board of directors Group of professionals elected by shareholders as their representatives, with responsibility for the overall direction of the company and the selection of top executives

bond market The collective buying and selling of bonds; most bond trading is done over the counter, rather than in organized exchanges

bonds Method of funding in which the issuer borrows from an investor and provides a written promise to make regular interest payments and repay the borrowed amount in the future

bonus Cash payment, in addition to regular wage or salary, that serves as a reward for achievement

book value Difference between the assets and liabilities as listed on the balance sheet

bookkeeping Recordkeeping; the clerical aspect of accounting

boycott Pressure action by union members and sympathizers who refuse to buy or handle the product of a target company

brand A name, term, sign, symbol, design, or combination of those used to identify the products of a firm and to differentiate them from competing products

brand communities Formal or informal groups of people united by their interest in and ownership of particular products

brand equity The value that a company has built up in a brand

brand extension Applying a successful brand name to a new product category

brand loyalty The degree to which customers continue to purchase a specific brand

brand managers Managers who develop and implement the marketing strategies and programs for a specific product or brand

brand mark Portion of a brand that cannot be expressed verbally

brand names Portion of a brand that can be expressed orally, including letters, words, or numbers

break-even analysis Method of calculating the minimum volume of sales needed at a given price to cover all costs

break-even point Sales volume at a given price that will cover all of a company's costs

broker Certified expert who is legally registered to buy and sell securities on behalf of individual and institutional investors

bubble Market situation in which frenzied demand for an asset pushes the price of that asset far beyond its true economic value

budget Planning and control tool that reflects expected revenues, operating expenses, and cash receipts and outlays

bull market Market situation in which most stocks are increasing in value

bundling Offering several products for a single price that is presumably lower than the total of the products' individual prices

business Any profit-seeking organization that provides goods and services designed to satisfy customers' needs

business cycles Fluctuations in the rate of growth that an economy experiences over a period of several years

business incubators Facilities that house small businesses and provide support services during the company's early growth phases

business mindset A view of business that considers the myriad decisions that must be made and the many problems that must be overcome before companies can deliver the products that satisfy customer needs

business model A concise description of how a business intends to generate revenue

business plan Document that summarizes a proposed business venture, goals, and plans for achieving those goals

cafeteria plans Flexible benefit programs that let employees personalize their benefits packages

calendar year Twelve-month accounting period that begins on January 1 and ends on December 31

cap and trade Type of environmental policy that gives companies some degree of freedom in addressing the environmental impact of specified pollutants, either by reducing emissions to meet a designated allowance or buying allowances to offset any amount by which it is over its allowance

capital The physical, human-made elements used to produce goods and services, such as factories and computers; can also refer to the funds that finance the operations of a business

capacity planning Establishing the overall level of resources needed to meet customer demand

capital budget Budget that outlines expenditures for real estate, new facilities, major equipment, and other capital investments

capital gains Increases in the value of a stock or other asset

capital investments Money paid to acquire something of permanent value in a business

capital items More expensive organizational products with a longer

useful life, ranging from office and plant equipment to entire factories

capital structure A firm's mix of debt and equity financing

capitalism Economic system based on economic freedom and competition

cash basis Accounting method in which revenue is recorded when payment is received and expense is recorded when cash is paid

cause-related marketing Identification and marketing of a social issue, cause, or idea to selected target markets

centralization Concentration of decision-making authority at the top of the organization

certification election Secret-ballot election overseen by the NLRB to determine whether a union gains the right to represent a group of employees

certified public accountants (CPAs) Professionally licensed accountants who meet certain requirements for education and experience and who pass a comprehensive examination

chain of command Pathway for the flow of authority from one management level to the next

channel conflict Disagreement or tension between two or more members in a distribution channel, such as competition between channel partners trying to reach the same group of customers

chief executive officer (CEO) The highest-ranking corporate officer

closing Point at which a sale is completed

closing the books Transferring net revenue and expense account balances to retained earnings for the period

coaching Helping employees reach their highest potential by meeting with them, discussing problems that hinder their ability to work effectively, and offering suggestions and encouragement to overcome these problems

co-branding Partnership between two or more companies to closely link their brand names together for a single product

code of ethics Written statement setting forth the principles that guide an organization's decisions

cognitive dissonance Tension that exists when a person's beliefs don't match his or her behaviors; a common example is

buyer's remorse, when someone regrets a purchase immediately after making it

cohesiveness A measure of how committed the team members are to their team's goals

collateral Tangible asset a lender can claim if a borrower defaults on a loan

collective bargaining Negotiation between union and management negotiators to forge the human resources policies that will apply to all employees covered by a contract

collective bargaining agreements (CBAs) Contracts that result from collective bargaining

commercial banks Financial institutions that accept deposits, offer various types of checking and savings accounts, and provide loans

commercial paper Short-term promissory notes, or contractual agreements, to repay a borrowed amount by a specified time with a specified interest rate

commercialization Large-scale production and distribution of a product

commissions Employee compensation based on a percentage of sales made

committee Team that may become a permanent part of the organization and is designed to deal with regularly recurring tasks

commodities futures Contracts to buy or sell specific amounts of commodities for a set price at a future date

common stock Shares of ownership that include voting rights

communication mix Blend of communication vehicles—advertising, direct marketing, personal selling, sales promotion, social media, and public relations—that a company uses to reach current and potential customers

comparative advertising Advertising technique in which two or more products are explicitly compared

compensating balance Portion of an unsecured loan that is kept on deposit at the lending institution to protect the lender and increase the lender's return

compensation Money, benefits, and services paid to employees for their work

competition Rivalry among businesses for the same customers

competitive advantage Some aspect of a product or company that makes it more appealing to target customers

conceptual skills Ability to understand the relationship of parts to the whole

conflicts of interest Situations in which competing loyalties can lead to ethical lapses; in business, situations in which a business decision may be influenced by the potential for personal gain

consultative selling Approach in which the salesperson acts as a consultant and advisor to help customers find the best solutions to their personal or business needs

consumer market Individuals or households that buy goods and services for personal use

consumer price index (CPI) Monthly statistic that measures changes in the prices of a representative collective of consumer goods and services

consumerism Movement that pressures businesses to consider consumer needs and interests

contingent employees Nonpermanent employees, including temporary workers, independent contractors, and full-time employees hired on a probationary basis

controller Highest-ranking accountant in a company, responsible for overseeing all accounting functions

controlling Process of measuring progress against goals and objectives and correcting deviations if results are not as expected

convenience products Everyday goods and services that people buy frequently, usually without much conscious planning

conversation marketing Approach to customer communication in which companies initiate and facilitate conversations in a networked community of potential buyers and other interested parties

convertible bonds Corporate bonds that can be exchanged at the owner's discretion into common stock of the issuing company

core competencies Activities that a company considers central and vital to its business

core message The single most important idea an advertiser hopes to convey to the target audience about its products or the company

corporate governance In a broad sense, describes all the policies, procedures, relationships, and systems in place to oversee the successful and legal operation of the enterprise; in a narrow sense, refers to the responsibilities and performance of the board of directors

corporate officers The top executives who run a corporation

corporate social responsibility (CSR) The idea that business has obligations to society beyond the pursuit of profits

corporation A legal entity, distinct from any individual persons, with the power to own property and conduct business

cost of capital Average rate of interest a firm pays on its combination of debt and equity financing

cost of goods sold Cost of producing or acquiring a company's products for sale during a given period

cost-based pricing Method of setting prices based on production and marketing costs, rather than conditions in the marketplace

coupons Certificates that offer discounts on particular items and are redeemed at the time of purchase

credit derivatives Derivatives used to reduce a lender's exposure to credit risk

credit freeze Situation in which credit has become so scarce that it is virtually unavailable, at any cost, to most potential borrowers

credit rating agencies Companies that offer opinions about the creditworthiness of borrowers and of specific investments

credit unions Not-for-profit, member-owned cooperatives that offer deposit accounts and lending services to consumers and small businesses

crisis management Procedures and systems for minimizing the harm that might result from some unusually threatening situations

critical path In a PERT network diagram, the sequence of operations that requires the longest time to complete

cross-functional team Team that draws together employees from different functional areas

cross-training Training workers to perform multiple jobs and rotating them through these various jobs to combat boredom or burnout

culture A shared system of symbols, beliefs, attitudes, values, expectations, and norms for behavior

currency futures Contracts to buy or sell amounts of specified currency at some future date

current assets Cash and items that can be turned into cash within one year

current liabilities Obligations that must be met within a year

current ratio Measure of a firm's short-term liquidity, calculated by dividing current assets by current liabilities

customer buying behavior Behavior exhibited by buyers as they consider, select, and purchase goods and services

customer database Computer file that contains contact histories, purchase records, and profiles of each buyer or potential buyer

customer loyalty Degree to which customers continue to buy from a particular retailer or buy the products of a particular manufacturer or service provider

customer relationship management (CRM) Type of information system that captures, organizes, and capitalizes on all the interactions that a company has with its customers

customized production The creation of a unique good or service for each customer

debentures Corporate bonds backed only by the reputation of the issuer

debt financing Arranging funding by borrowing money

debt-to-assets ratio Measure of a firm's ability to carry long-term debt, calculated by dividing total liabilities by total assets

debt-to-equity ratio Measure of the extent to which a business is financed by debt as opposed to invested capital, calculated by dividing the company's total liabilities by owners' equity

decentralization Delegation of decision-making authority to employees in lower-level positions

decertification Employee vote to take away a union's right to represent them

decision-making skills Ability to identify a decision situation, analyze the problem, weigh the alternatives, choose an alternative, implement it, and evaluate the results

default Situation in which borrowers stop making payments on a loan

deflation Economic condition in which prices fall steadily throughout the economy

demand Buyers' willingness and ability to purchase products

demand curve Graph of the quantities of product that buyers will purchase at various prices

democratic leaders Leaders who delegate authority and involve employees in decision making

demographics Study of statistical characteristics of a population

department stores Large stores that carry a variety of products in multiple categories, such as clothing, housewares, gifts, bedding, and furniture

departmentalization Grouping people within an organization according to function, division, matrix, or network

depreciation Accounting procedure for systematically spreading the cost of a tangible asset over its estimated useful life

deregulation Relying on the market to prevent excesses and correct itself over time

derivatives Contracts whose value is derived from some other entity (usually an asset of some kind, but not necessarily); used to hedge against or speculate on risk

derivatives market Includes exchange trading (for futures and some options) and OTC trading (for all other derivatives, at least currently)

direct mail Printed materials addressed to individual consumers, households, or business contacts

direct marketing Direct communication other than personal sales contacts designed to stimulate a measurable response

direct response television The use of television commercials and longer-format infomercials that are designed to stimulate an immediate purchase response from viewers

discount rate Interest rate that member banks pay when they borrow funds from the Fed

discount stores Retailers that sell a variety of everyday goods below the market price by keeping their overhead low

discounts Temporary price reductions to stimulate sales or lower prices to encourage certain behaviors such as paying with cash

discrimination In a social and economic sense, denial of opportunities to individuals on the basis of some characteristic that has no bearing on their ability to perform in a job

disintermediation The replacement of intermediaries by producers, customers, or other intermediaries when those other parties can perform channel functions more effectively or efficiently

distribution centers Advanced warehouse facilities that specialize in collecting and shipping merchandise

distribution channels Systems for moving goods and services from producers to customers; also known as marketing channels

distribution mix Combination of intermediaries and channels a producer uses to reach target customers

distribution strategy Firm's overall plan for moving products to intermediaries and final customers

distributors Merchant wholesalers that sell products to organizational customers for internal operations or the production of other goods, rather than to retailers for resale

diversification Creating new products for new markets

diversity initiatives Programs and policies that help companies support diverse workforces and markets

divisional structure Grouping departments according to similarities in product, process, customer, or geography

double-entry bookkeeping Method of recording financial transactions requiring two offsetting entries for every transaction to ensure that the accounting equation is always kept in balance

dumping Charging less than the actual cost or less than the home-country price for goods sold in other countries

dynamic pricing Continually adjusting prices to reflect changes in supply and demand

earnings per share Measure of a firm's profitability for each share of outstanding stock, calculated by dividing net income after taxes by the average number of shares of common stock outstanding

EBITDA   Earnings before interest, taxes, depreciation, and amortization; a simpler and more direct measure of income

e-commerce   The application of Internet technologies to wholesaling and retailing

economic environment   The conditions and forces that affect the cost and availability of goods, services, and labor and thereby shape the behavior of buyers and sellers

economic globalization   The increasing integration and interdependence of national economies around the world

economic indicators   Statistics that measure the performance of the economy

economic system   Means by which a society distributes its resources to satisfy its people's needs

economics   The study of how society uses scarce resources to produce and distribute goods and services

economies of scale   Savings from buying parts and materials, manufacturing, or marketing in large quantities

economy   The sum total of all the economic activity within a given region

electronic performance monitoring (EPM)   Real-time, computer-based evaluation of employee performance

embargo   Total ban on trade with a particular nation (a sanction) or of a particular product

employee assistance program (EAP)   Company-sponsored counseling or referral plan for employees with personal problems

employee benefits   Compensation other than wages, salaries, and incentive programs

employee empowerment   Granting decision-making and problem-solving authorities to employees so they can act without getting approval from management

Employee Free Choice Act (EFCA)   Pending legislation that would significantly alter the union election provisions of the Wagner Act, making it easier for unions to organize groups of workers

employee retention   Efforts to keep current employees

employee stock-ownership plan (ESOP)   Program enabling employees to become partial owners of a company

engagement   An employee's rational and emotional commitment to his or her work

entrepreneurial spirit   The positive, forward-thinking desire to create profitable, sustainable business enterprises

entrepreneurship   The combination of innovation, initiative, and willingness to take the risks required to create and operate new businesses

equilibrium point   Point at which quantity supplied equals quantity demanded

equity financing   Arranging funding by selling ownership shares in the company, publicly or privately

equity theory   The idea that employees base their level of satisfaction on the ratio of their inputs to the job and the outputs or rewards they receive from it

ethical dilemma   Situation in which more than one side of an issue can be supported with valid arguments

ethical lapse   Situation in which an individual or group makes a decision that is morally wrong, illegal, or unethical

ethics   The rules or standards governing the conduct of a person or group

ethnocentrism   Judging all other groups according to the standards, behaviors, and customs of one's own group

etiquette   The expected norms of behavior in any particular situation

exchange process   Act of obtaining a desired object or service from another party by offering something of value in return

exchange rate   Rate at which the money of one country is traded for the money of another

exchange traded funds (ETFs)   Mutual funds whose shares are traded on public exchanges in the same way as stocks

exclusive distribution   Market coverage strategy that gives intermediaries exclusive rights to sell a product in a specific geographic area

expectancy theory   The idea that the effort employees put into their work depends on expectations about their own ability to perform, expectations about likely rewards, and the attractiveness of those rewards

expense items   Inexpensive products that organizations generally use within a year of purchase

expense ratio   Annual cost of owning a mutual fund, expressed as a percentage

expenses   Costs created in the process of generating revenues

export subsidies   A form of financial assistance in which producers receive enough money from the government to allow them to lower their prices in order to compete more effectively in the world market

exporting   Selling and shipping goods or services to another country

external auditors   Independent accounting firms that provide auditing services for public companies

face value   Amount of money, or principal, a bond buyer lends to a bond issuer; also known as par value or denomination

factoring   Obtaining funding by selling accounts receivable

fair trade   A voluntary approach to trading with artisans and farmers in developing countries, guaranteeing them above-market prices as a way to protect them from exploitation by larger, more powerful trading partners

family branding   Using a brand name on a variety of related products

Fannie Mae   Government-sponsored enterprise responsible for guaranteeing and funding home mortgages

Federal Deposit Insurance Corporation (FDIC)   Federal agency responsible for protecting money in customer accounts and managing the transition of assets whenever a bank fails

federal funds rate   Interest rate that member banks charge each other to borrow money overnight from the funds they keep in the Federal Reserve accounts

Federal Reserve System   The central banking system of the United States; responsible for regulating banks and implementing monetary policy

finance companies   Nonbank institutions that lend money to consumers and businesses for cars and other vehicles, home improvements, expansion, purchases, and other purposes

financial accounting   Area of accounting concerned with preparing financial information for users outside the organization

financial control The process of analyzing and adjusting the basic financial plan to correct for deviations from forecasted events

financial futures Contracts to buy or sell a financial instrument (such as stocks, Treasury bonds, and foreign currencies) for a set price at a future date

financial management Planning for a firm's money needs and managing the allocation and spending of funds

financial plan A document that outlines the funds needed for a certain period of time, along with the sources and intended uses of those funds

first-line managers Those at the lowest level of the management hierarchy; they supervise the operating employees and implement the plans set at the higher management levels

fiscal policy Use of government revenue collection and spending to influence the business cycle

fiscal year Any 12 consecutive months used as an accounting period

fixed assets Assets retained for long-term use, such as land, buildings, machinery, and equipment; also referred to as property, plant, and equipment

fixed costs Business costs that remain constant regardless of the number of units produced

foreclosures Lenders taking possession of homes after borrowers default on their payments

foreign direct investment (FDI) Investment of money by foreign companies in domestic business enterprises

franchise Business arrangement in which one company (the franchisee) obtains the rights to sell the products and use various elements of a business system of another company (the franchisor)

franchisee Business owner who pays for the rights to sell the products and use the business system of a franchisor

franchisor Company that licenses elements of its business system to other companies (franchisees)

Freddie Mac Secondary mortgage institution similar to Fannie Mae

free trade International trade unencumbered by restrictive measures

free-market system Economic system in which decisions about what to produce and in what quantities are decided by the market's buyers and sellers

full-service merchant wholesalers Merchant wholesalers that provide a wide variety of services to their customers, such as storage, delivery, and marketing support

functional structure Grouping workers according to their similar skills, resource use, and expertise

functional team Team whose members come from a single functional department and that is based on the organization's vertical structure

gain sharing Tying rewards to profits or cost savings achieved by meeting specific goals

general partnership Partnership in which all partners have joint authority to make decisions for the firm and joint liability for the firm's financial obligations

generally accepted accounting principles (GAAP) U.S. standards and practices used by accountants in the preparation of financial statements

generic products Products characterized by a plain label, with no advertising and no brand name

geographic segmentation Categorization of customers according to their geographic location

glass ceiling Invisible barrier attributable to subtle discrimination that keeps women and minorities out of the top positions in business

global strategy Highly centralized approach to international expansion, with headquarters in the home country making all major decisions

goal Broad, long-range target or aim

goal-setting theory Motivational theory suggesting that setting goals can be an effective way to motivate employees

goods-producing businesses Companies that create value by making "things," most of which are tangible (digital products such as software are a notable exception)

grievance Formal complaint against an employer

gross domestic product (GDP) Value of all the final goods and services produced by

businesses located within a nation's borders; excludes outputs from overseas operations of domestic companies

gross national product (GNP) Value of all the final goods and services produced by domestic businesses that includes receipts from overseas operations and excludes receipts from foreign-owned businesses within a nation's borders

gross profit Amount remaining when the cost of goods sold is deducted from net sales; also known as gross margin

groupthink Uniformity of thought that occurs when peer pressures cause individual team members to withhold contrary or unpopular opinions

hedging Protecting against cost increases with contracts that allow a company to buy supplies in the future at designated prices

Herzberg's two-factor theory Model that divides motivational forces into satisfiers ("motivators") and dissatisfiers ("hygiene factors")

hostile takeover Acquisition of another company against the wishes of management

human resources All the people who work for an organization

human resources (HR) management Specialized function of planning how to obtain employees, oversee their training, evaluate them, and compensate them

identity theft Crimes in which thieves steal personal information and use it to take out loans and commit other types of fraud

import quotas Limits placed on the quantity of imports a nation will allow for a specific product

importing Purchasing goods or services from another country and bringing them into one's own country

incentives Monetary payments and other rewards of value used for positive reinforcement

income statement Financial record of a company's revenues, expenses, and profits over a given period of time; also known as profit-and-loss statement

independent mortgage companies Nonbank companies that use their own funds to offer mortgages

index Statistical indicator of the rise and fall of a representative group of securities

index funds   Mutual funds that mirror the composition of a particular market or index

inflation   Economic condition in which prices rise steadily throughout the economy

information technology (IT)   Systems that promote communication and information usage through the company or allow companies to offer new services to their customers

initial public offering (IPO) A corporation's first offering of shares to the public

injunction   Court order that requires one side in a dispute to refrain from or engage in a particular action

insider trading   The use of unpublicized information that an individual gains from the course of his or her job to benefit from fluctuations in the stock market

institutional advertising   Advertising that seeks to create goodwill and to build a desired image for a company, rather than to promote specific products

integrated marketing communications (IMC)   Strategy of coordinating and integrating communication and promotion efforts with customers to ensure greater efficiency and effectiveness

intensive distribution   Market coverage strategy that tries to place a product in as many outlets as possible

intermodal transportation   The coordinated use of multiple modes of transportation, particularly with containers that can be shipped by truck, rail, and sea

international financial reporting standards (IFRS)   Accounting standards and practices used in many countries outside the United States

interpersonal skills   Skills required to understand other people and to interact effectively with them

intrinsic value   An estimate of what a company is actually worth, independent of book and market values

inventory   Goods and materials kept in stock for production or sale

inventory control   Determining the right quantities of supplies and products to have on hand and tracking where those items are

inventory turnover ratio   Measure of the time a company takes to turn its inventory into sales, calculated by dividing cost of goods sold by the average value of inventory for a period

investment banks   Firms that offer a variety of services related to initial public stock offerings, mergers and acquisitions, and other investment matters

investment portfolios   Collections of various types of investments

job characteristics model   Suggests that five core job dimensions influence three critical psychological states that determine motivation, performance, and other outcomes

job description   Statement of the tasks involved in a given job and the conditions under which the holder of the job will work

job enrichment   Making jobs more challenging and interesting by expanding the range of skills required

job specification   Statement describing the kind of person who would be best for a given job—including the skills, education, and previous experience that the job requires

joint venture   A separate legal entity established by two or more companies to pursue shared business objectives

just-in-time (JIT)   Inventory management in which goods and materials are delivered throughout the production process right before they are needed

knowledge   Expertise gained through experience or association

knowledge-based pay   Pay tied to an employee's acquisition of knowledge or skills; also called competency-based pay or skill-based pay

labor relations   Relationship between organized labor and management (in their role as representative of business owners)

labor unions   Organizations that represent employees in negotiations with management

Labor-Management Relations Act   Legislation passed in 1947 that addressed many concerns raised by business owners and shifted the balance of power again; commonly known as the Taft-Hartley Act

Labor-Management Reporting and Disclosure Act   Legislation passed in 1959 designed to ensure democratic processes and financial accountability within unions; commonly known as the Landrum-Griffith Act

laissez-faire leaders   Leaders who leave most instances of decision making up to employees, particularly concerning day-to-day matters

layoffs   Termination of employees for economic or business reasons

leading   Process of guiding and motivating people to work toward organizational goals

lean systems   Manufacturing systems that maximize productivity by reducing waste and delays

lease   Agreement to use an asset in exchange for regular payment; similar to renting

legal and regulatory environment   Laws and regulations at the local, state, national, and even international level

leverage   Technique of increasing the rate of return on an investment by financing it with borrowed funds

leveraged buyout (LBO)   Acquisition of a company's publicly traded stock using funds that are primarily borrowed, usually with the intent of using some of the acquired assets to pay back the loans used to acquire the company

liabilities   Claims against a firm's assets by creditors

license   Agreement to produce and market another company's product in exchange for a royalty or fee

licensing   Agreement to produce and market another company's product in exchange for a royalty or fee

limit order   Order that stipulates the highest or lowest price at which the customer is willing to trade securities

limited liability   Legal condition in which the maximum amount each owner is liable for is equal to whatever amount each invested in the business

limited liability company (LLC)   Structure that combines limited liability with the pass-through taxation benefits of a partnership; the number of shareholders is not restricted, nor is members' participation in management

limited liability partnership (LLP) Partnership in which each partner has unlimited liability only for his or her own actions and at least some degree of limited liability for the partnership as a whole

limited partnership Partnership in which one or more persons act as general partners who run the business and have the same unlimited liability as sole proprietors

line of credit Arrangement in which the financial institution makes money available for use at any time after the loan has been approved

line organization Chain-of-command system that establishes a clear line of authority flowing from the top down

line-and-staff organization Organization system that has a clear chain of command but that also includes functional groups of people who provide advice and specialized services

liquidity A measure of how easily and quickly an asset such as corporate stock can be converted into cash by selling it

liquidity crisis Severe shortage of liquidity throughout a sector of the economy or the entire economy, during which companies can't get enough cash to meet their operating needs

load Sales commission charged when buying or selling a mutual fund

loan-to-value (LTV) The percentage of an asset's market value that a lender is willing to finance when offering a loan; the rest of the purchase price has to be paid by the buyer as a down payment

locals Local unions that represent employees in a specific geographic area or facility

lockouts Decision by management to prevent union employees from entering the workplace; used to pressure the union to accept a contract proposal

logistics The planning, movement, and flow of goods and related information throughout the supply chain

logo A concise graphical and/or textual representation of a brand name

long-term financing Financing used to cover long-term expenses such as assets (generally repaid over a period of more than one year)

long-term liabilities Obligations that fall due more than a year from the date of the balance sheet

loss-leader pricing Selling one product at a loss as a way to entice customers to consider other products

macroeconomics The study of "big picture" issues in an economy, including competitive behavior among firms, the effect of government policies, and overall resource allocation issues

management Process of planning, organizing, leading, and controlling to meet organizational goals

management accounting Area of accounting concerned with preparing data for use by managers within the organization

management by objectives (MBO) A motivational approach in which managers and employees work together to structure personal goals and objectives for every individual, department, and project to mesh with the organization's goals

management pyramid Organizational structure divided into top, middle, and first-line management

managerial roles Behavioral patterns and activities involved in carrying out the functions of management; includes interpersonal, informational, and decisional roles

mandatory retirement Required dismissal of an employee who reaches a certain age

margin trading Borrowing money from brokers to buy stock, paying interest on the borrowed money, and leaving the stock with the broker as collateral

market A group of customers who need or want a particular product and have the money to buy it

market development Selling existing products to new markets

market environment A company's target customers, the buying influences that shape the behavior of those customers, and competitors that market similar products to those customers

market order Type of securities order that instructs the broker to buy or sell at the best price that can be negotiated at the moment

market penetration Selling more of a firm's existing products into the markets it already serves

market segmentation Division of a diverse market into smaller, relatively homogeneous groups with similar needs, wants, and purchase behaviors

market share A firm's portion of the total sales in a market

market value The price at which the stock is actually selling in the stock market

marketing The process of creating value for customers and building relationships with those customers in order to capture value back from them

marketing concept Approach to business management that stresses customer needs and wants, seeks long-term profitability, and integrates marketing with other functional units within the organization

marketing intermediaries Businesspeople and organizations that assist in moving and marketing goods and services between producers and consumers

marketing mix The four key elements of marketing strategy: product, price, distribution, and customer communication

marketing research The collection and analysis of information for making marketing decisions

marketing strategy Overall plan for marketing a product; includes the identification of target market segments, a positioning strategy, and a marketing mix

marketing systems Arrangements by which channel partners coordinate their activities under the leadership of one of the partners

Maslow's hierarchy Model in which a person's needs are arranged in a hierarchy, with the most basic needs at the bottom and the more advanced needs toward the top

mass customization Manufacturing approach in which part of the product is mass produced and the remaining features are customized for each buyer

mass production The creation of identical goods or services, usually in large quantities

master limited partnership (MLP) Partnership that is allowed to raise money by selling units of ownership to the general public

matching principle Fundamental principle requiring that expenses incurred in producing revenue be deducted from the revenues they generate during an accounting period

materials handling Movement of goods within a firm's warehouse terminal, factory, or store

matrix structure Structure in which employees are assigned to both a functional group and a project team (thus using functional and divisional patterns simultaneously)

maturity date Date on which the principal of a bond will be repaid in full

media mix Combination of print, broadcast, online, and other media used for an advertising campaign

mediation Use of an impartial third party to help resolve bargaining impasses

mentoring Experienced managers guiding less-experienced colleagues in nuances of office politics, serving as a role model for appropriate business behavior, and helping to negotiate the corporate structure

merchant banks Banks that provide financial services to businesses; can also refer to private equity management

merchant wholesalers Independent wholesalers that take legal title to goods they distribute

merger Action taken by two companies to combine as a single entity

microeconomics The study of how consumers, businesses, and industries collectively determine the quantity of goods and services demanded and supplied at different prices

microlenders Organizations, often not-for-profit, that lend smaller amounts of money to business owners who might not qualify for conventional bank loans

micromanaging Overseeing every small detail of employees' work and refusing to give them freedom or autonomy

middle managers Those in the middle of the management hierarchy; they develop plans to implement the goals of top managers and coordinate the work of first-line managers

minutes Summary of the important information presented and the decisions made during a meeting

mission statement A brief statement of why an organization exists; in other words, what it aims to accomplish for customers, investors, and other stakeholders

monetary policy Government policy and actions taken by the Federal Reserve Board to regulate the nation's money supply

money Anything generally accepted as a means of paying for goods and services; serves as a medium of exchange, a unit of accounting, a store of value, and a standard of deferred value

money market Over-the-counter marketplace for short-term debt instruments such as Treasury bills and commercial paper

money supply The amount of money in circulation at any given point in time

monopolistic competition Situation in which many sellers differentiate their products from those of competitors in at least some small way

monopoly Situation in which one company dominates a market to the degree that it can control prices

mortgage brokers Nonbank companies that initiate loans on behalf of a mortgage lender in exchange for a fee

mortgage-backed securities (MBSs) Credit derivatives based on home mortgages

motivation The combination of forces that moves individuals to take certain actions and avoid other actions

multichannel retailing Coordinated efforts to reach consumers through more than one retail channel

multidomestic strategy Decentralized approach to international expansion in which a company creates highly independent operating units in each new country

multinational corporations (MNCs) Companies with operations in more than one country

municipal bonds Bonds issued by states, cities, and various government agencies to fund public projects

mutual funds Financial instruments that pool money from many investors to buy a diversified mix of stocks, bonds, or other securities

NASDAQ An electronic stock exchange that competes with the NYSE

national brands Brands owned by the manufacturers and distributed nationally

National Labor Relations Act Legislation passed in 1935 that established labor relations policies and procedures for most sectors of private industry; commonly known as the Wagner Act

national union Nationwide organization composed of many local unions that represent employees in specific locations

nationalizing Government takeover of selected companies or industries

natural resources Land, forests, minerals, water, and other tangible assets usable in their natural state

need Difference between a person's actual state and his or her ideal state; provides the basic motivation to make a purchase

negative amortization Payment situation in which the balance owed on a loan increases over time rather than decreases

negative reinforcement Encouraging the repetition of a particular behavior (desirable or not) by not offering unpleasant consequences for the behavior

net asset value (NAV) A mutual fund's assets minus its liabilities; usually expressed as NAV per share

net income Profit earned or loss incurred by a firm, determined by subtracting expenses from revenues; casually referred to as the bottom line

network structure Structure in which individual companies are connected electronically to perform selected tasks for a small headquarters organization

no-load funds Mutual funds that do not charge loads

nongovernmental organizations (NGOs) Nonprofit groups that provide charitable services or promote social and environmental causes

norms Informal standards of conduct that guide team behavior

not-for-profit organizations Organizations that provide goods and services without having a profit motive; also called nonprofit organizations

NYSE The New York Stock Exchange, one of the oldest and most widely recognized exchanges in the world

objective Specific, short-range target or aim

off-price retailers Stores that sell designer labels and other fashionable products at steep discounts

offshoring Transferring part or all of a business function to a facility (a different part of the company or another company entirely) in another country

online retailers Companies that use e-commerce technologies to sell over the Internet; includes Internet-only retailers and the online arm of store-based retailers

operating budget Also known as the master budget, budget that identifies all sources of revenue and coordinates the spending of those funds throughout the coming year

operating expenses All costs of operation that are not included under cost of goods sold

operational plans Plans that lay out the actions and the resource allocation needed to achieve operational objectives and to support tactical plans

operations management Management of the people and processes involved in creating goods and services

opportunity cost The value of the most appealing alternative not chosen

optimal pricing Computer-based pricing method that creates a demand curve for every product to help managers select a price that meets specific marketing objectives

option The purchased right—but not the obligation—to buy or sell a specified number of shares of a stock at a predetermined price during a specified period

option ARM Type of ARM that lets borrowers choose from several repayment options

order processing Functions involved in receiving and filling customers' orders

organization chart Diagram showing how employees and tasks are grouped and where the lines of communication and authority flow

organization structure Framework enabling managers to divide responsibilities, ensure employee accountability, and distribute decision-making authority

organizational culture A set of shared values and norms that support the management system and that guide management and employee behavior

organizational market Businesses, nonprofit organizations, and government agencies that purchase goods and services for use in their operations

organizing Process of arranging resources to carry out the organization's plans

orientation programs Sessions or procedures for acclimating new employees to the organization

outsourcing Contracting out certain business functions or operations to other companies

owners' equity Portion of a company's assets that belongs to the owners after obligations to all creditors have been met

participative management Philosophy of allowing employees to take part in planning and decision making

participative pricing Allowing customers to pay the amount they think a product is worth

partnership An unincorporated company owned by two or more people

pay for performance Incentive program that rewards employees for meeting specific, individual goals

penetration pricing Introducing a new product at a low price in hopes of building sales volume quickly

pension plans Generally refers to traditional, defined benefit retirement plans

performance appraisals Evaluations of employees' work according to specific criteria

permission-based marketing Marketing approach in which firms first ask permission to deliver messages to an audience and then promise to restrict their communication efforts to those subject areas in which audience members have expressed interest

personal selling One-on-one interaction between a salesperson and a prospective buyer

philanthropy The donation of money, time, goods, or services to charitable, humanitarian, or educational institutions

physical distribution All the activities required to move finished products from the producer to the consumer

place marketing Marketing efforts to attract people and organizations to a particular geographic area

planned system Economic system in which the government controls most of the factors of production and regulates their allocation

planning Establishing objectives and goals for an organization and determining the best ways to accomplish them

point-of-purchase (POP) display Advertising or other display materials set up at retail locations to promote products to potential customers as they are making their purchase decisions

portfolio diversification Spreading investments across enough different vehicles to protect against significant declines in any one vehicle

positioning Managing a business in a way designed to occupy a particular place in the minds of target customers

positive reinforcement Encouraging desired behaviors by offering pleasant consequences for completing or repeating those behaviors

preferred stock Shares of ownership without voting rights but with defined dividends

premiums Free or bargain-priced items offered to encourage consumers to buy a product

press conference In-person or online gathering of media representatives at which companies announce new information; also called a news conference

press release Brief statement or video program released to the press announcing new products, management changes, sales performance, and other potential news items; also called a news release

price The amount of money charged for a product or service

price elasticity A measure of the sensitivity of demand to changes in price

price-earnings ratio Market value per share divided by the earnings per share

prime interest rate Lowest rate of interest charged by banks for short-term loans to their most creditworthy customers

prime mortgages Home loans offered to the most creditworthy customers

private accountants In-house accountants employed by organizations and businesses other than a public accounting firm; also called corporate accountants

private banking Banking services for wealthy individuals and families

private brands Brands that carry the label of a retailer or a wholesaler rather than a manufacturer

private corporation Corporation in which all the stock is owned by only a few individuals or companies and is not made available for purchase by the public

private equity   Ownership assets that aren't publicly traded; includes venture capital

privatizing   Turning over services once performed by the government by allowing private businesses to perform them instead

problem-solving team   Team that meets to find ways of improving quality, efficiency, and the work environment

procurement   The acquisition of the raw materials, parts, components, supplies, and finished products required to produce goods and services

producer price index (PPI)   A statistical measure of price trends at the producer and wholesaler levels

product   Bundle of value that satisfies a customer need or want

product advertising   Advertising that promotes specific goods and services

product development   Creating new products for a firm's current markets

product development process   A formal process of generating, selecting, developing, and commercializing product ideas

product life cycle   Four stages through which a product progresses: introduction, growth, maturity, and decline

product line   A series of related products offered by a firm

product mix   Complete list of all products that a company offers for sale

product placement   The paid display or use of products in television shows, movies, and video games

production and operations management   Overseeing all the activities involved in producing goods and services

productivity   The efficiency with which an organization can convert inputs to outputs

professionalism   The quality of performing at a high level and conducting oneself with purpose and pride

profit   Money left over after all the costs involved in doing business have been deducted from revenue

profit sharing   The distribution of a portion of the company's profits to employees

progressive discipline   Escalating process of discipline that gives employees several opportunities to correct performance problems before being terminated

project budget   Budget that identifies the costs needed to accomplish a particular project

promotion   Wide variety of persuasive techniques used by companies to communicate with their target markets and the general public

prospecting   Process of finding and qualifying potential customers

prospectus   SEC-required document that discloses required information about the company, its finances, and its plans for using the money it hopes to raise

protectionism   Government policies aimed at shielding a country's industries from foreign competition

prototypes   Preproduction samples of products used for testing and evaluation

proxy   Document authorizing another person to vote on behalf of a shareholder in a corporation

psychographics   Classification of customers on the basis of their psychological makeup, interests, and lifestyles

public accountants   Professionals who provide accounting services to other businesses and individuals for a fee

public corporation   Corporation in which stock is sold to anyone who has the means to buy it

public relations   Nonsales communication that businesses have with their various audiences (includes both communication with the general public and press relations)

pull strategy   Promotional strategy that stimulates consumer demand via advertising and other communication efforts, thereby creating a pull effect through the channel

pure competition   Situation in which so many buyers and sellers exist that no single buyer or seller can individually influence market prices

push strategy   Promotional strategy that focuses on intermediaries, motivating them to promote or push products toward end users

quality   A measure of how closely a product conforms to predetermined standards and customer expectations

quality assurance   A more comprehensive approach of companywide policies, practices, and procedures to ensure that every product meets quality standards

quality control   Measuring quality against established standards after the good or service has been produced and weeding out any defective products

quality of work life (QWL)   Overall environment that results from job and work conditions

quick ratio   Measure of a firm's short-term liquidity, calculated by adding cash, marketable securities, and receivables, then dividing that sum by current liabilities; also known as the acid-test ratio

rate of return   Gain (or loss) of an investment over time, expressed as a percentage

rebates   Partial reimbursement of price, offered as a purchase incentive

recession   Period during which national income, employment, and production all fall; defined as at least six months of decline in the GDP

recovery   Period during which income, employment, production, and spending rise

recruiting   Process of attracting appropriate applicants for an organization's jobs

regulation   Compared to deregulation, relying on laws and policies to govern economic activity

reinforcement theory   A motivational approach based on the idea that managers can motivate employees by influencing their behaviors with positive and negative reinforcement

relationship marketing   A focus on developing and maintaining long-term relationships with customers, suppliers, and distribution partners for mutual benefit

research and development (R&D)   Functional area responsible for conceiving and designing new products

reserves   Sums of money, equal to a certain percentage of their deposits, that banks are legally required to keep on hand

retail banks   Banks that provide financial services to consumers

retail theater   The addition of entertainment or education aspects to the retail experience

retailers Intermediaries that sell goods and services to individuals for their own personal use

retained earnings The portion of shareholders' equity earned by the company but not distributed to its owners in the form of dividends

retirement plans Company-sponsored programs for providing retirees with income

return on equity Ratio between net income after taxes and total owners' equity

return on sales Ratio between net income after taxes and net sales; also known as profit margin

revenue Money a company brings in through the sale of goods and services

right-to-work laws State laws that prohibit union and agency shops

risk-return trade-off The balance of potential risks against potential rewards

S corporation Type of corporation that combines the capital-raising options and limited liability of a corporation with the federal taxation advantages of a partnership

salary Fixed cash compensation for work, usually by yearly amount; independent of the number of hours worked

sales promotion Wide range of events and activities designed to promote a brand or stimulate interest in a product

Sarbanes-Oxley Informal name of comprehensive legislation designed to improve integrity and accountability of financial information

scalability The potential to increase production by expanding or replicating its initial production capacity

scientific management Management approach designed to improve employees' efficiency by scientifically studying their work

search engine marketing Automated presentation of ads that are related to either the results of an online search or the content being displayed on other webpages

secondary mortgage market Financial market in which mortgages are bought and sold, providing much of the funds that are loaned to home buyers

secured bonds Bonds backed by specific assets that will be given to bondholders if the borrowed amount is not repaid

secured loans Loans backed up with assets that the lender can claim in case of default, such as a piece of property

securities Investments such as stocks, bonds, options, futures, and commodities

securitization Process in which debts such as mortgages are pooled together and transformed into investments

seed money The first infusion of capital used to get a business started

selective distribution Market coverage strategy that uses a limited number of carefully chosen outlets to distribute products

self-managed team Team in which members are responsible for an entire process or operation

seniority Length of time someone has worked for his or her current employer

service businesses Companies that create value by performing activities that deliver some benefit to the customer

sexism Discrimination on the basis of gender

sexual harassment Unwelcome sexual advance, request for sexual favors, or other verbal or physical conduct of a sexual nature within the workplace

shareholder activism Activities taken by shareholders (individually or in groups) to influence executive decision making in areas ranging from strategic planning to social responsibility

shareholders Investors who purchase shares of stock in a corporation

shopping products Fairly important goods and services that people buy less frequently with more planning and comparison

short selling Selling stock borrowed from a broker with the intention of buying it back later at a lower price, repaying the broker, and keeping the profit

short-term financing Financing used to cover current expenses (generally repaid within a year)

sinking fund Account into which a company makes annual payments for use in redeeming its bonds in the future

Six Sigma A rigorous quality management program that strives to eliminate deviations between the actual and desired performance of a business system

skills inventory A list of the skills a company needs from its workforce, along with the specific skills that individual employees currently possess

skim pricing Charging a high price for a new product during the introductory stage and lowering the price later

small business Company that is independently owned and operated, is not dominant in its field, and meets certain criteria for the number of employees or annual sales revenue

social commerce The creation and sharing of product-related information among customers and potential customers

social communication model Approach to communication based on interactive social media and conversational communication styles

social environment Trends and forces in society at large

social media Communication vehicles such as blogs, user-contributed content sites, and social booking sites, in which customers and other members of the public can participate

socialism Economic system characterized by public ownership and operation of key industries combined with private ownership and operation of less-vital industries

sole proprietorship Business owned by a single person

span of management Number of people under one manager's control; also known as span of control

specialty advertising Advertising that appears on various items such as coffee mugs, pens, and calendars, designed to help keep a company's name in front of customers

specialty products Particular brands that the buyer especially wants and will seek out, regardless of location or price

specialty stores Stores that carries only a particular type of goods, often with deep selection in those specific categories

stakeholders Internal and external groups affected by a company's decisions and activities

standards Criteria against which performance is measured

start-up budget Budget that identifies the money a new company will need to spend to launch operations

statement of cash flows   Statement of a firm's cash receipts and cash payments that presents information on its sources and uses of cash

statistical process control (SPC)   Use of random sampling and control charts to monitor the production process

stealth marketing   The delivery of marketing messages to people who are not aware that they are being marketed to; these messages can be delivered by either acquaintances or strangers, depending on the technique

stereotyping   Assigning a wide range of generalized attributes, which are often superficial or even false, to an individual based on his or her membership in a particular culture or social group

stock   Ownership of or equity in a company; a share of stock represents a specific portion of ownership

stock exchanges   Organizations that facilitate the buying and selling of stock

stock options   Contract allowing the holder to purchase or sell a certain number of shares of a particular stock at a given price by a certain date

stock split   Act of dividing a share into two or more new shares and reducing the market value by the same ratio

stop order   Order to sell a stock when its price falls to a particular point to limit an investor's losses

strategic alliance   A long-term partnership between companies to jointly develop, produce, or sell products

strategic CSR   Social contributions that are directly aligned with a company's overall business strategy

strategic marketing planning   The process of examining an organization's current marketing situation, assessing opportunities and setting objectives, and then developing a marketing strategy to reach those objectives

strategic plans   Plans that establish the actions and the resource allocation required to accomplish strategic goals; they're usually defined for periods of two to five years and developed by top managers

strike   Temporary work stoppage aimed at forcing management to accept union demands

strikebreakers   Nonunion workers hired to do the jobs of striking workers

subprime mortgages   Home loans for borrowers with low credit scores

succession planning   Workforce planning efforts that identify possible replacements for specific employees, usually senior executives

supply   Specific quantity of a product that the seller is able and willing to provide

supply chain   A set of connected systems that coordinates the flow of goods and materials from suppliers all the way through to final customers

supply chain management (SCM)   The business procedures, policies, and computer systems that integrate the various elements of the supply chain into a cohesive system

supply curve   Graph of the quantities that sellers will offer for sale, regardless of demand, at various prices

sustainable development   Operating business in a manner that minimizes pollution and resource depletion, ensuring that future generations will have vital resources

system   An interconnected and coordinated set of elements and processes that converts inputs to desired outputs

tactical plans   Plans that define the actions and the resource allocation necessary to achieve tactical objectives and to support strategic plans

target markets   Specific customer groups or segments to whom a company wants to sell a particular product

tariffs   Taxes levied on imports

task force   Team of people from several departments who are temporarily brought together to address a specific issue

team   A unit of two or more people who share a mission and collective responsibility as they work together to achieve a goal

technical skills   Ability and knowledge to perform the mechanics of a particular job

technological environment   Forces resulting from the practical application of science to innovations, products, and processes

termination   Process of getting rid of an employee through layoff or firing

test marketing   Product development stage in which a product is sold on a limited basis to gauge its market appeal

Theory X   Managerial assumption that employees are irresponsible, are unambitious, and dislike work and that managers must use force, control, or threats to motivate them

Theory Y   Managerial assumption that employees enjoy meaningful work, are naturally committed to certain goals, are capable of creativity, and seek out responsibility under the right conditions

three-needs theory   David McClelland's model of motivation that highlights needs for power, affiliation, and achievement

thrift banks   Banking institutions that offer deposit accounts and focus on offering home mortgage loans; also called thrifts or savings and loan associations

top managers   Those at the highest level of the organization's management hierarchy; they are responsible for setting strategic goals, and they have the most power and responsibility in the organization

total quality management (TQM)   A management philosophy and strategic management process that focuses on delivering the optimal level of quality to customers by building quality into every organizational activity

trade allowances   Discounts or other financial considerations offered by producers to wholesalers and retailers

trade credit   Credit obtained by the purchaser directly from the supplier

trade deficit   Unfavorable trade balance created when a country imports more than it exports

trade promotions   Sales-promotion efforts aimed at inducing distributors or retailers to push a producer's products

trade surplus   Favorable trade balance created when a country exports more than it imports

trademarks   Brands that have been given legal protection so that their owners have exclusive rights to their use

trading blocs   Organizations of nations that remove barriers to trade among their members and that establish uniform barriers to trade with nonmember nations

transaction   Exchange of value between parties

transnational strategy   Hybrid approach that attempts to reap the benefits of international scale while being responsive to local market dynamics

transparency   The degree to which affected parties can observe relevant aspects of transactions or decisions

Treasury bills   Short-term debt securities issued by the federal government; also referred to as T-bills

Treasury bonds   Debt securities issued by the federal government that are repaid more than 10 years after issuance

Treasury inflation-protected securities (TIPS)   Treasury issues in which the principal amount is tied to the Consumer Price Index to protect the buyer against the effects of inflation

Treasury notes   Debt securities issues by the federal government that are repaid within 1 to 10 years after issuance

turnover rate   Percentage of the workforce that leaves every year

underwriter   A specialized type of bank that buys the shares from the company preparing an IPO and sells them to investors

unemployment rate   Portion of the labor force (everyone over 16 who has or is looking for a job) currently without a job

unfair labor practices   Unlawful acts made by either unions or management

union security   Measures that protect the union's right to represent workers

union shop   Unionized workplace in which employees are required to maintain union membership

unlimited liability   Legal condition under which any damages or debts incurred by the business are the owner's personal responsibility

unsecured loans   Loans requiring no collateral but a good credit rating

utility   Power of a good or service to satisfy a human need

value chain   All the elements and processes that add value as raw materials are transformed into the final products made available to the ultimate customer

value webs   Multidimensional networks of suppliers and outsourcing partners

value-based pricing   Method of setting prices based on customer perceptions of value

values statement   Brief articulation of the principles that guide a company's decisions and behaviors

variable costs   Business costs that increase with the number of units produced

venture capitalists (VCs)   Investors who provide money to finance new businesses or turnarounds in exchange for a portion of ownership, with the objective of reselling the business at a profit

virtual team   Team that uses communication technology to bring geographically distant employees together to achieve goals

vision statement   A brief and inspirational expression of what a company aspires to be

wages   Cash payment based on the number of hours the employee has worked or the number of units the employee has produced

wants   Specific goods, services, experiences, or other entities that are desirable in light of a person's experiences, culture, and personality

warehouse   Facility for storing inventory

wheel of retailing   Evolutionary process by which stores that feature low prices gradually upgrade until they no longer appeal to price-sensitive shoppers and are replaced by a new generation of leaner, low-price competitors

whistleblowing   The disclosure of information by a company insider that exposes illegal or unethical behavior by others within the organization

wholesalers   Intermediaries that sell products to other intermediaries for resale or to organizations for internal use

word of mouth   Communication among customers and other parties, transmitting information about companies and products through personal conversations

work rules   Common element of labor contracts specifying such things as the tasks certain employees are required to do or forbidden to do

work specialization   Specialization in or responsibility for some portion of an organization's overall work tasks; also called division of labor

worker buyouts   Distributions of financial incentives to employees who voluntarily depart; usually undertaken in order to reduce the payroll

working capital   Current assets minus current liabilities

work-life balance   Efforts to help employees balance the competing demands of their personal and professional lives

yield   Interest income a purchaser receives from the bond

zero-based budgeting   Budgeting approach in which each department starts from zero every year and must justify every item in the budget, rather than simply adjusting the previous year's budget amounts

Brand, Organization, Name, and Website Index

NOTE: Page numbers that start with A, B, C, or D refer to Appendix A, B, C, or D, which can be found online at www.mybizlab.com.

Subject Index

NOTE: Page numbers that start with A, B, C, or D refer to Appendix A, B, C, or D, which can be found online at www.mybizlab.com.

A

accountability, 69
  of employees, 216
  in teams, 227
accountants, 63, 64
  types of, 431–432
accounting, 431–449
  careers in, 67
  fraud in, 435
  principles of, 436–438
  rules of, 433–436
  types of, 431
accounting equation, 436–437
accounting firms, 432
accounting managers, 63
accounting process, 439
accounting standards, 435–436
accounts payable, 441, 458
accounts receivable, 441, 458, 466
  selling, 469
accounts receivable turnover ratio,
  447, 448
accrual basis bookkeeping, 438
accrued expenses, 441–442
achievement need, 266
acid-test ratio, 447, 448
acquisitions, 157–160, 161
  defenses against, 159–160
  government approval of, 89
action plans, 196–197
actively managed funds, 490
activists
  environmental, 130
  shareholder, 155
  social, 130
activity ratios, 447, 448
actuaries, B-3
additive fabrication, 74, 315
adjustable-rate mortgage (ARM),
  515–516
  see also option ARM mortgages
administrative law, A-1–A-2
administrative skills, 207
advantage, comparative, 99, 103
advertising, 349, 410–419
  appeals in, 410–412
  awareness, 406
  careers in, 66
  core message of, 407
  deceptive, 408–409
  ethics in, 337, 408–409

individualized, 428
media for, 413–414
online, 335, 413–414
in promotional mix, 410–419
reminder, 407
search engine, 416, 417
specialty, 421
types of, 410
unwanted, C-3
advertising exchange, 416
advertising network, 416
advisory boards, for small business,
  178–179
advocacy advertising, 410
adware, 151, C-3
affiliation need, 266
affirmative action, 138
Africa, 98, 116–117
African Americans, earnings of, 290
age composition, of workforce, 289
age discrimination, 289, 294
Age Discrimination in Employment
  Act, 294
agencies, 88
  administrative, A-1
  regulatory, 88
  for small business, 177–178
agency relationships, A-4
agency shops, 315
agenda, for meetings, 232
agents, 383, 384, 393
agile organization, 215
air pollution, 132
air transport, 398
air travel industry, 374
aircraft industry, 100
airplane emergency crash landing,
  205–206
Alcohol Labeling Legislation, 136
alien corporation, 154
alternative dispute resolution (ADR), 329
American Automobile Labeling Act, 136
American Recovery and Reinvestment
  Act of 2009, 182
Americans with Disabilities Act, 138, 293
amortization, negative, 516
Angel Investor Directory, 181
angel investors, 181
angel networks, 181
annual meeting, corporate, 155
annual reports, 446, 451

antitrust legislation, 89
appeals, logical vs. emotional, 410–412
appellate court, A-2
applicant tracking system, 292
appraisers, home, 517, 521
apprenticeship, 316
arbitrability, 323
arbitration, 320, 323, 326, 329, A-4
Are You Missing the Real Estate Boom?
  (Lereah), 514
artificial intelligence, 149, C-3
Asia-Pacific Economic Cooperation
  (APEC), 107, 108
Asian Americans, 290
aspirational reference groups, 339
asset allocation, 498
asset-backed securities (ABSs), 519
assets, 54
  in accounting equation, 436–437
  intellectual, 77
  liquid, D-10
  personal, D-3, D-4
  types of, 441
assistive technologies, 143, 290
Association of Southeast Asian Nations
  (ASEAN), 107
at-will employment, 294
athletes, as brands, 355, 375–376
attack ads, 410
attractiveness, products and, 386
auction pricing, 373
audience
  interactive communication
    with, 406
  fragmentation of, 413, 414
auditors, 67, 434, 435
  of IPOs, 474
audits, 432
augmenting, of products, 356–357
Australia, 108
authority, 216
  coercive use of, 202
  delegation of, 200
authorization cards, 317, 326
auto industry, 309, 311, 327–328, 331,
  350, 362
auto insurance, D-4
autocratic leaders, 200
automobile industry, 62
avatars, 234
awareness advertising, 406